HOLT McDOUGAL

Psychology
Principles in Practice

Spencer A. Rathus

HOLT McDOUGAL
a division of Houghton Mifflin Harcourt

Author

Spencer A. Rathus, Ph.D.

Dr. Spencer A. Rathus obtained his Ph.D. from the University of Albany. He has experience as a clinical psychologist, professor, researcher, and author. As a clinician, Rathus has worked at a community mental health center, in private practice, and with college students. He is currently on the faculty at The College of New Jersey. As a researcher, he has published some 30 articles in professional journals and authored the widely used Rathus Assertiveness Schedule.

Rathus has published numerous college textbooks in a number of areas, including child and adolescent development, lifespan development, abnormal psychology, and the psychology of adjustment. An introductory psychology textbook authored by Dr. Rathus, *Psychology: Concepts and Connections,* is now in its 10th edition.

Rathus is a member of the American Psychological Association, serves on the American Psychological Association Task Force on Diversity Issues at the Precollege and Undergraduate Levels of Education in Psychology, and speaks at a variety of professional functions.

ISBN 13: 978-0-55-400401-3

ISBN 10: 0-55-400401-1

8 9 10 11 12 0914 20 19 18 17 16 15 14 13 12
4500369651

Teacher Consultant

Jim Matiya
Carl Sandburg High School
Orland Park, IL

Teacher Reviewers

Lydia Fitzgerald
Faribault High School
Faribault, MN

Belinda G. Hutsenpiller
Frank W. Cox High School
Virginia Beach, VA

Dale Kinney
Ralston Senior High School
Ralston, NE

Jennifer Mamula
Seminole High School
Sanford, FL

Rachael Peterson
Martin High School
Arlington, TX

Kathleen Reuther
Marquette High School
Chesterfield, MO

January Rowe
Melissa High School
Melissa, TX

Linda Rubio
Homer Hanna High School
Brownsville, TX

Greg Talberg
Howell High School
Howell, MI

Academic Reviewers

Dr. Timothy Anderson
Vanderbilt University
Abnormal Psychology

Dr. Thomas Bradbury
University of California,
  Los Angeles
Developmental Psychology

Dr. David Cohen
University of Texas at Austin
Clinical Psychology

Dr. Terry Davidson
Purdue University
Behavioral Neuroscience

Dr. Jeremiah Faries
Northwestern University
Cognitive Psychology

Dr. Anne C. Fletcher
University of North Carolina
  at Greensboro
*Developmental Psychology,
Adolescence*

Dr. Michela Gallagher
University of North Carolina,
  Chapel Hill
*Experimental/Biological and
Cognitive Psychology*

Dr. Calvin P. Garbin
University of Nebraska
Quantitative and Research Methods

Dr. Carol Kozak Hawk
Austin Community College
University of Texas at Austin
Developmental Psychology

Dr. Julie Hubbard
University of Delaware
Child Clinical Psychology

Dr. Aida Hurtado
University of California, Santa Cruz
Social Psychology

Dr. Daniel N. McIntosh
University of Denver
Social Psychology

Dr. Bertram Malle
University of Oregon
Social Psychology

Dr. Nancy Russo
Arizona State University
Social Psychology, Gender

Dr. Arthur Staats
University of Hawaii
Cognitive Psychology, Intelligence

Dr. Keith D. White
University of Florida
Biological Psychology

Dr. Kevin Williams
State University of New York,
  Albany
Behavioral Psychology

Contents

UNIT 1 Introduction to Psychology

CHAPTER 2

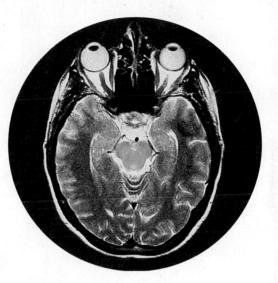
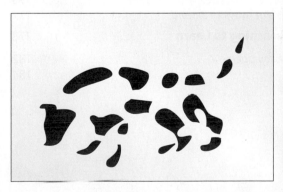

UNIT 3 Learning and Cognition 155

CHAPTER 6

UNIT 6 Health and Adjustment **469**

Features

Online Resources

Explore a whole new world of online learning. At thinkcentral.com *you will find all the components and resources for this book, along with additional content including interactive features, Webquests, videos, and more.*

INTERACTIVE FEATURES

Go online to extend your learning with interactive features that focus on key topics in psychology.

WEBQUEST

Go online to explore Webquests and extend your knowledge of psychology.

Watch the Video
Explore the world of psychology.

Watch chapter-based videos to see real-world examples and applications of psychology content.

PSYCHOLOGY IN TODAY'S WORLD

Apply psychological concepts to understand important issues in the world today.

CAREERS IN PSYCHOLOGY

Explore career possibilities in different fields of psychology.

Statistically Speaking...

Analyze the data that supports psychological concepts.

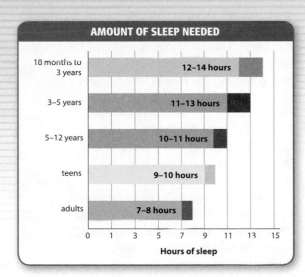

AMOUNT OF SLEEP NEEDED

Age	Hours of sleep
18 months to 3 years	12–14 hours
3–5 years	11–13 hours
5–12 years	10–11 hours
teens	9–10 hours
adults	7–8 hours

Hours of sleep

74% Percentage of Americans who do not get enough sleep

10–50% Percentage of children who have nightmares

10–30% Percentage of children who have sleepwalking episodes

Sources: National Sleep Foundation; Diagnostic and Statistical Manual of Mental Disorders

CHARTS, GRAPHS, AND DIAGRAMS

Analyze information presented visually to learn more about psychology.

Charts

Graphs

Diagrams

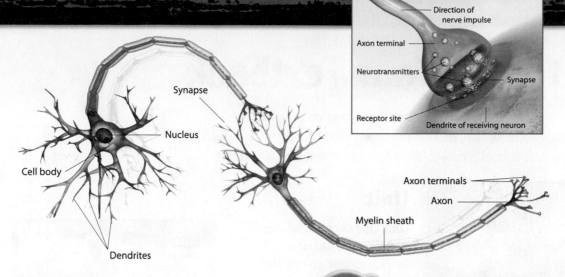

Direction of nerve impulse
Axon terminal
Neurotransmitters
Synapse
Receptor site
Dendrite of receiving neuron

Synapse
Nucleus
Cell body
Dendrites
Axon terminals
Axon
Myelin sheath

QUICK FACTS

Review key concepts with these summaries of important facts.

Perspectives on

Compare different views on aspects of psychology.

How to Use Your Textbook

Holt McDougal Psychology: Principles in Practice was created to make your study of psychology an enjoyable, meaningful experience. Take a few minutes to become familiar with the book's easy-to-use organization and special features.

Unit

Unit Openers list the chapter titles within each unit to preview the material you are about to explore.

Careers in Psychology

features appear at the end of each unit. Each one profiles a career area within psychology and includes a short activity on how to write using APA style the way psychologists do.

Chapter

Chapter Openers include a Case Study that deals with a real-world application or example of chapter content. Chapter openers also feature Chapter at a Glance, which summarizes the key points from each section.

Chapter Reviews provide a full array of assessments and direct you to online features.

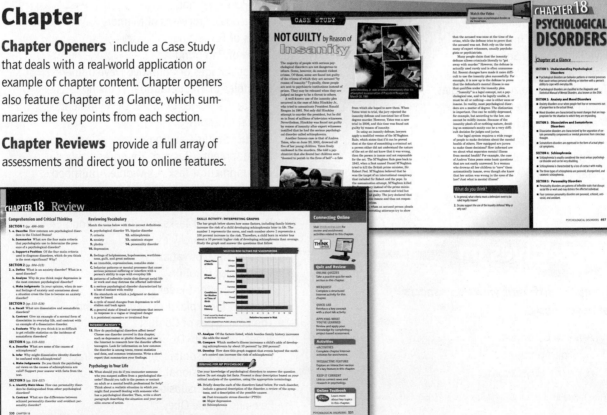

Section

Each section begins with a Main Idea statement, Reading Focus questions, and Vocabulary terms. In addition, each section includes the following special features:

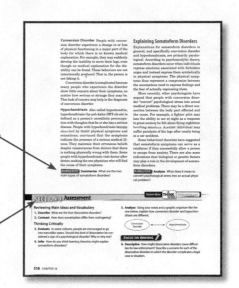

Taking Notes graphic organizers help you record key ideas as you read.

Psychology Close Up features begin each section with an engaging story, example, or anecdote.

Reading Check questions throughout each section provide frequent opportunities to review and assess your understanding of what you read.

Section Assessments help you demonstrate your understanding of main ideas and key content. There is also assessment practice online.

Hands-On Activities

Holt McDougal Psychology: Principles in Practice provides many opportunities for you to learn psychology content by completing individual and group activities.

Quick Labs in each chapter help you learn and apply chapter content by completing a short activity.

Webquests point you to engaging online activities linked to chapter content.

Applying What You've Learned features at the end of each chapter provide opportunities to complete individual and group labs, simulations, and experiments.

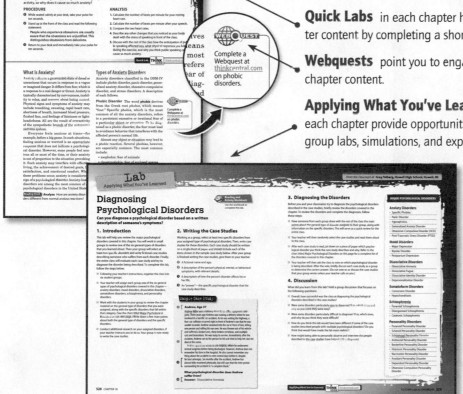

Time Line of Psychology

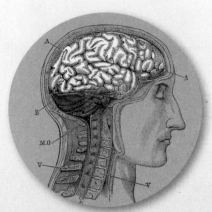

▲ **1890** William James publishes *Principles of Psychology.*

▲ **1926** Jean Piaget publishes his first studies of child development.

▲ **1861** Pierre-Paul Broca pioneers the discovery of specialized functions in different parts of the brain.

1878 G. Stanley Hall earns the first Ph.D. degree in a psychological field in the United States.

1900 Sigmund Freud publishes *The Interpretation of Dreams.*

1913 Carl Jung forms his school of analytical psychology.

1875   **1900**   **1925**

1920 John B. Watson and Rosalie Rayner use classical conditioning to teach Little Albert to fear what he had enjoyed before.

▼ **1905** Alfred Binet and Theodore Simon create the Binet-Simon scale.

▲ **1870** In Paris, neurologist Jean-Martin Charcot begins research into hysteria, now called conversion disorder, and hypnosis.

1896 The first psychological clinic opens at the University of Pennsylvania.

1963
Stanley Milgram addresses obedience to authority in the Milgram experiment.

▼ **1969** Harry Harlow publishes his experiment on affection development in monkeys.

▲ **1937** Anna Freud publishes *The Ego and the Mechanisms of Defense.*

2000 The *DSM-IV-TR*™ is published.

1943 Abraham Maslow describes his hierarchy of needs.

1950   1975   2000

1951 The Asch experiments demonstrate the power of conformity in groups.

▼ **1982** Carol Gilligan publishes *In a Different Voice,* bringing feminist psychology to the attention of the mental health profession.

▼ **1938** B. F. Skinner publishes *The Behavior of Organisms: An Experimental Analysis,* introducing behavior analysis.

1961 Albert Bandura studies behavioral patterns of aggression in the Bobo doll experiment.

1971 The Stanford prison experiment focuses on the human response to captivity.

SKILLS HANDBOOK

To maximize your study and understanding of psychology, use the Skills Handbook to review and practice a variety of key skills.

Critical Thinking Skills

Identifying Main Ideas and Details

Define the Skill

The **main idea** is the central thought in a passage. It is a general statement that conveys the key concept the author wants the reader to know. The main idea can come at the beginning, middle, or end of a passage, although it is most often found at the beginning. The main idea can be one or two sentences and can be implied or directly stated.

Details are statements that support or explain the main idea. Details are specific and provide additional information to the reader, such as the *who, what, when, where, why,* and *how* of the main idea. Details include statements, statistics, examples, explanations, and descriptions.

Learn the Skill

Read the passage below and note how the details support the main idea.

> Many children walk in their sleep. Sleepwalkers may roam about almost nightly during stages of deep sleep. They may respond to questions while they are up and about, but when they wake up they typically do not remember what they did or said. Contrary to myth, there is no evidence that sleepwalkers become violent or upset if they are awakened. However, because sleepwalkers are not fully conscious and thus may be prone to accidentally hurting themselves, they should be supervised if possible.

Main Idea
Many children walk in their sleep.

Details			
Detail 1	**Detail 2**	**Detail 3**	**Detail 4**
Sleepwalking may occur almost nightly.	Sleepwalkers do not remember what happened while they were up and about.	Sleepwalkers do not become violent or upset if awakened.	Sleepwalkers should be supervised if possible.

Apply the Skill

Turn to Section 2 of the chapter titled "Consciousness" and locate the "Narcolepsy" subhead. Use a graphic organizer like the one above to identify the main idea and details of the passage.

1. Identify the main idea in the passage. Restate it in your own words.

2. What details support the main idea?

3. Explain how the details add to the main idea.

Identifying Cause and Effect

Define the Skill

Identifying cause and effect can help you to become a critical thinker and to better understand what you read. A **cause** is something that brings about an action or condition. Often, a cause will be directly stated in the text, but sometimes it will be implied, or stated indirectly. An **effect** is an event that happens as the result of a cause. A cause may have more than one effect. Similarly, an effect may have several causes. By identifying causes and effects, you will be able to determine why certain events occurred, whether certain events are related, and what the relationship is between events.

Learn the Skill

Use the following strategies to identify cause and effect.

> **Could tinkering with the body's endocrine system <u>cause</u> a violent rampage?** The memorial in this photo is for professional wrestler Chris Benoit and his family, all of whom died in a double murder-suicide in 2007. Benoit had a prescription for anabolic steroids, synthetic hormones that build muscle and strength. Police speculated that Benoit killed his family <u>as a result of</u> steroid abuse. Steroids can have devastating side effects: irritability and uncontrolled anger, depression, and suicidal thoughts.
>
> Violence wasn't typical of Benoit's nature, <u>so</u> the wrestler's father agreed to have his son's brain analyzed. The <u>results</u> showed that Benoit's brain was similar to that of an 85-year-old Alzheimer's patient. Although repeated concussions from his wrestling bouts probably <u>caused</u> the damage, the steroids could have <u>contributed to</u> an agitated mental state and horrible acts of violence.

1 Identify the causes of events. Look for reasons that prompted a given event to occur. Words such as *since, cause, because, so, therefore,* and *due to* can signal a causal relationship among events.

2 Identify the effects of events. Look for phrases and clue words that indicate consequences, such as *thus, brought about, led to, consequently,* and *result.*

3 Connect causes and effects. Consider why certain causes led to an event and why the event turned out as it did. Remember that an event can be both a cause and an effect.

Apply the Skill

1. What was the cause of the events described in the passage?
2. List the various effects described in the passage.
3. What is the ultimate outcome described in the passage? Why might that outcome have resulted from the cause you identified?

Identifying Problems and Solutions

Define the Skill

Mental health professionals writing about people's problems often structure their writing by identifying a problem and then describing its actual or possible solutions. By **identifying problems and solutions,** you can better understand the challenges that people face and the means by which they resolve such difficulties.

Learn the Skill

Look for problems that are identified in the reading and then determine what solutions may be appropriate. Some problems have more than one solution.

People are often unaware of their false assumptions, <u>even though the assumptions influence their conscious thoughts and actions.</u> The role of the therapist in REBT is first to identify and then to challenge the false assumptions. To teach individuals to think more realistically, <u>REBT therapists use techniques such as role-playing and modeling.</u> Role-playing helps individuals see how their assumptions affect their relationships . . .

<u>Individuals in rational-emotive behavior therapy may also receive homework assignments.</u> For example, they may be asked to read relevant literature, listen to tapes of psychotherapy sessions, or carry out experiments designed to test their assumptions. The more faithfully patients complete their homework, the more likely it is that their therapy will succeed.

Problem
People often have false assumptions.

Solution 1
REBT therapists use role-playing and modeling to address those assumptions.

Solution 2
Individuals in REBT therapy also receive homework assignments.

Apply the Skill

Use a graphic organizer like the one above to identify the problems and solutions in the following passage.

An approach-approach conflict is the least stressful type of conflict because the choices are positive. In this situation, each of the goals is both desirable and within reach. For example, suppose you were accepted by several colleges. You would then be faced with an approach-approach conflict because you have to choose which college to attend. An approach-approach conflict is usually resolved by making a decision. However, after the decision is made, the person may still have persistent self-doubts about whether he or she has made the right decision.

1. What is an approach-approach conflict? What example is given?

2. What is usually the solution for an approach-approach conflict?

Drawing Conclusions

Define the Skill

Writing in the social sciences provides you with facts and information. But often you have to determine the meaning of information on your own. You need to combine the information with your prior knowledge to draw conclusions about the reading. In **drawing conclusions**, you analyze the reading and form opinions about its meaning.

Learn the Skill

To draw conclusions, combine the information you find in the reading with what you already know. Look for a common link or theme. Then put it all together.

> In some studies, animals or people have been deprived only of REM (rapid-eye-movement) sleep. People and animals deprived of REM sleep tend to show what psychologists call REM-rebound. They catch up on their REM sleep by having much more of it when they sleep later on. REM sleep seems to serve particular psychological functions. Animals and people who are deprived of REM sleep learn more slowly than usual. They also forget more rapidly what they have learned. Other research findings suggest that REM sleep may help brain development in infants and "exercise" brain cells in adults.

Information gathered from the passage you are reading		**What you already know about the topic**		**What all the information adds up to—your conclusion**
REM sleep is essential for optimal performance for people and animals.	**+**	You feel dull and listless if you don't get enough uninterrupted sleep.	**=**	For good mental health, one should get plenty of uninterrupted REM sleep.

Apply the Skill

Read the following sentences. Think about what you know about peer pressure today. Use the process above to draw conclusions about the passage.

> Parents often worry that their adolescent children's needs for peer approval will influence them to engage in risky or unacceptable behavior. However, the assumption that parents and peers often pull an adolescent in different directions does not seem to be borne out by reality.
>
> In fact, parental and peer influences often coincide to some degree. For example, research suggests that peers are more likely to urge adolescents to work for good grades and complete high school than they are to try to involve them in drug abuse, sexual activity, or delinquency.

1. How do parents sometime misjudge adolescent peer influence?

2. What can you conclude about how adolescents evaluate the influence of peers and parents?

Interpreting Line and Bar Graphs

Define the Skill

Graphs are diagrams that present statistical or numeric data. They can display amounts, trends, ratios, or changes over time. A **line graph** is a visual representation of data organized so that you can see a pattern of change over time. In most cases, the *vertical axis* of a line graph shows quantities while the *horizontal axis* shows time. A **bar graph** compares quantities. A single bar graph compares one set of data, while a double bar graph compares two sets of data. Knowing how to interpret line graphs and bar graphs can help you recognize trends and patterns.

Learn the Skill

Use the following strategies to interpret the line graph.

1 **Read the title of the graph.** The title tells you the subject or purpose of the graph.

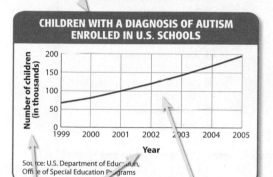

2 **Read the horizontal and vertical axis labels.** The labels explain what the graph measures and gives the units of measurement.

3 **Analyze the information on the graph.** Look at the slant of the line. The closer the line is to being parallel to the horizontal axis, the slower the change. The closer the line is to being perpendicular to the horizontal axis, the quicker the change.

Use the following strategies to interpret the bar graph.

1 **Read the title of the graph.** Read the title and the legend to determine the subject of the graph.

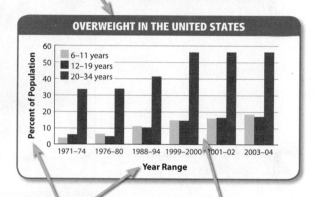

2 **Read the horizontal and vertical axis labels.** The labels tell what the bar graph measures and gives the units of measurement.

3 **Analyze the information on the graph.** Compare the amounts shown on the bar graph.

Apply the Skill

1. What information does the line graph compare?
2. What information does the bar graph compare?
3. What conclusion can you draw from the data in the bar graph?

Interpreting Pie Graphs

Define the Skill

A **pie graph** is a circular chart that shows how individual parts relate to the whole. The circle of the pie symbolizes the whole amount. The slices of the pie represent the individual parts of the whole. Knowing how to interpret pie graphs will allow you to better understand and evaluate data.

Learn the Skill

Use the following strategies to interpret the pie graph.

1 **Read the title of the graph.** The title tells you the subject or purpose of the graph.

2 **Read the percentages.** Compare the sizes of each piece within the graph.

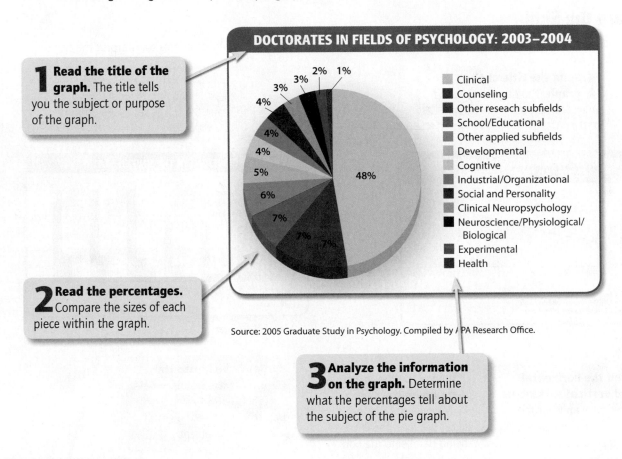

DOCTORATES IN FIELDS OF PSYCHOLOGY: 2003–2004

- Clinical
- Counseling
- Other reseach subfields
- School/Educational
- Other applied subfields
- Developmental
- Cognitive
- Industrial/Organizational
- Social and Personality
- Clinical Neuropsychology
- Neuroscience/Physiological/Biological
- Experimental
- Health

Source: 2005 Graduate Study in Psychology. Compiled by APA Research Office.

3 **Analyze the information on the graph.** Determine what the percentages tell about the subject of the pie graph.

Apply the Skill

1. What information does the pie graph compare?
2. In which field of psychology did the largest number of graduates earn doctoral degrees?
3. Which three fields had about the same number of doctoral graduates?

Interpreting Charts

Define the Skill

Charts are visual representations of information. Psychologists use charts to organize, condense, simplify, and summarize information in a convenient format. *Simple charts* combine or compare information. *Tables* classify information by groups. Numbers, percentages, dates, and other data can be classified in the columns and rows of a table for reference and comparison. *Diagrams* illustrate the steps involved in a process so that the information is easier to understand. Knowing how to read and use charts allows you to interpret, compare, analyze, and evaluate information.

Learn the Skill

Use the following strategies to interpret the chart.

1 **Read the title of the chart.** The title tells you the subject of the chart.

2 **Look at the way the information is organized.** Charts can be organized alphabetically, chronologically, or by topic.

3 **Analyze the information found in the chart.** Interpret, compare, and contrast the information in the chart to draw conclusions and make inferences or predictions.

PERSONALITY DISORDERS AND THEIR CHARACTERISTICS

Personality disorders are inflexible and lasting patterns of behavior that hamper social functioning. Listed here from the *DSM-IV-TR* are the 10 specific personality disorders and their main characteristics.

Personality Disorder	Main Characteristics
Paranoid	Suspiciousness and distrust about others' motives
Schizoid	Detachment from social relationships
Schizotypal	Acute discomfort in close relationships; eccentricities of behavior
Antisocial	Disregard for the rights of others
Borderline	Instability in interpersonal relationships and self-image
Histrionic	Excessive emotionality, need for attention
Narcissistic	Grandiosity, need for admiration, lack of empathy
Avoidant	Social inhibitions, feelings of inadequacy
Dependent	Submissive, clinging
Obsessive-Compulsive	Obsession with orderliness, perfectionism, and control

Apply the Skill

1. How is the information in the chart organized?
2. How does this chart help you remember the various personality disorders?

Interpreting Thematic Maps

Define the Skill

Thematic maps provide information in spatial terms. You can use thematic maps to compare how various phenomena are reflected in different places. Thematic maps can show information such as population density, economic activity, political and military alliances, and other similar topics.

Learn the Skill

Use the following strategies to interpret thematic maps.

1 **Read the title and legend.** The title will help you identify the subject and the purpose of the map. The legend explains the meaning of the colors on the map.

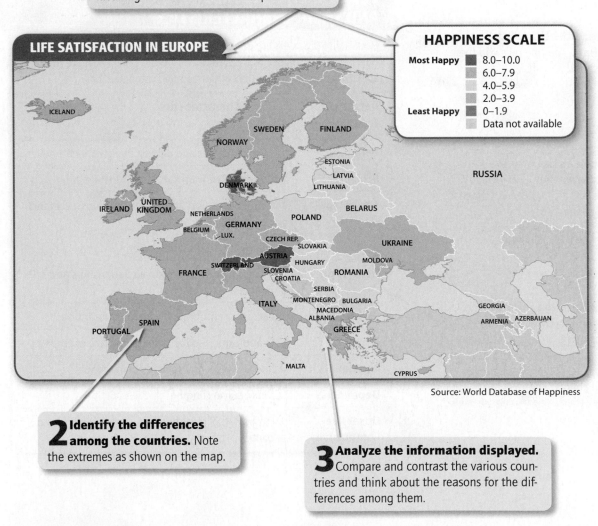

LIFE SATISFACTION IN EUROPE

HAPPINESS SCALE

Most Happy		8.0–10.0
		6.0–7.9
		4.0–5.9
		2.0–3.9
Least Happy		0–1.9
		Data not available

Source: World Database of Happiness

2 **Identify the differences among the countries.** Note the extremes as shown on the map.

3 **Analyze the information displayed.** Compare and contrast the various countries and think about the reasons for the differences among them.

Apply the Skill

1. What is the purpose of this thematic map?
2. Which large country scores the lowest on the "happiness scale"?

Analyzing Primary Sources

Define the Skill

A **primary source** is a document or other artifact created by people who are present at events either as witnesses or participants. Usually, you can identify a primary source by reading for first-person clues, such as *I*, *we*, and *our*. Primary sources are valuable tools because they give firsthand information about an event, situation, or time period.

Learn the Skill

Use the following strategies to analyze primary sources.

In 1903 W.E.B. Du Bois published a classic work titled The Souls of Black Folk. *The book is partly autobiographical, and in the following excerpt, Du Bois reveals how he felt when he first learned, as a schoolboy, that he was "different from the others" and "shut out from their world." The incident may seem trivial, but it had a profound effect on him for the rest of his life.*

1 **Identify the author or creator of the primary source and when the source was created.** The author and the date the primary source was created give you a context in which to place the document.

66It is in the early days of rollicking boyhood that the revelation first bursts upon one, all in a day, as it were. I remember well when the shadow swept across me. I was a little thing, away up in the hills of New England . . . In a wee wooden schoolhouse, something put it into the boys' and girls' heads to buy gorgeous visiting-cards—ten cents a package—and exchange. The exchange was merry, till one girl, a tall newcomer, refused my card . . . Then it dawned upon me with a certain suddenness that I was different from the others; or like, mayhap, in heart and life and longing, but shut out from their world by a vast veil. I had thereafter no desire to tear down that veil, to creep through; I held all beyond it in common contempt, and lived above it in a region of blue sky and great wandering shadows. That sky was bluest when I could beat my mates at examination-time, or beat them at a foot-race . . . 99

2 **Compare details in the primary source to what you know about the event, situation, or time period.** The time frame of the primary source allows you to make connections between your previous knowledge and the information the document provides.

3 **Determine why the author created the primary source.** Each document has a particular purpose and can be used by its author to inform, persuade, direct, or influence the audience.

Apply the Skill

1. Recall what you have learned in other social studies classes. What era or situation is Du Bois describing in this excerpt?
2. How does Du Bois's memoir affect your knowledge of that era or situation?

Analyzing Secondary Sources

Define the Skill

A **secondary source** is an account created by someone who was not present at the actual event about which he or she is writing. Or, the writer gathers data from various sources to report on a situation. Writers of secondary sources rely on primary sources in order to write their secondary source accounts. Secondary sources often contain summaries and analyses of events. Your textbook, for example, can be considered a secondary source. Before determining whether a document is a primary or secondary source, you must pay attention to how the document is presented.

Learn the Skill

Use the following strategies to analyze secondary sources.

1 Identify the source. Examine any source information to learn the origins of the document and its author.

Christopher Browning's book, *Ordinary Men: Reserve Police Battalion 101 and the Final Solution in Poland* describes the events and motives that caused 500 middle-class, middle-aged German men to terrorize Jews in Poland in July of 1942. It was easier for most of these policemen to join in the killing than to break ranks and refuse to participate. By November of 1943, these ordinary civilians had murdered at least 85,000 Jewish people.

Before the killing began the commanding officer, Major Trapp, explicitly offered to excuse any man who did not want to participate in the impending mass murder. Trapp's offer thrust responsibility onto each man individually. Still, between 80 to 90 percent of the men participated in the killing, finding it too difficult not to conform. Unlike soldiers, these policemen had the burden of choice. They were not "just following orders." Rather, the pressure to conform to their peers' expectations was paramount.

In his book, Browning notes that no member of Reserve Police Battalion 101 who refused to participate was physically harmed or punished. Instead, outright refusal to participate brought more subtle consequences, such as the threat of isolation from the group.

2 Analyze the summary of historical events provided by the source. The author of a secondary source usually offers a summary of events or of a time period.

3 Identify the author's purpose. Look for clues that indicate the intention of the author.

Apply the Skill

1. How do you know that this passage is not a primary source?

2. Why might this passage actually be called a tertiary source?

3. What is this writer's point of view? What can you conclude is Christopher Browning's point of view?

Interpreting Cartoons

Define the Skill

Although most **cartoons** are just meant to be funny, many of them can also shed light on social science concepts. Some cartoons, including political or editorial cartoons, express specific points of view. Cartoons that appear in popular magazines or newspapers may also present a certain viewpoint. Cartoons of this type often poke fun at the foibles of modern life. Artists may use exaggeration, either in the text or the drawing, to help make their point. Although some cartoons are not at all realistic, for the reader to understand them and the humor there must be some elements in the cartoon to which the reader can relate.

Learn the Skill

Use the acronym **BASIC** to analyze cartoons.

"Son, it's important to remember that it's O.K. to be depressed."

Background Knowledge Place the cartoon in its context. Use your prior knowledge of what is being depicted to analyze the cartoon's message about the particular issue, person, or event.

Argument Determine what message the artist is trying to convey. Analyze the message that the artist is sending to the audience.

Symbolism Analyze any symbols in the cartoon. Symbols can be used to represent large groups that cannot be depicted easily or to stand for a person or an event. Symbols can also be used to simplify the cartoon or make its message clearer to the audience.

Irony Examine any irony that is present in the cartoon. Irony is the use of words or images to express something other than, and often the opposite of, their literal meaning.

Caricature Caricature, or exaggeration, is often used in cartoons. Exaggerated facial features or figures are used to make a point. Analyze any caricature present in the cartoon and consider what the meaning of such exaggerations might be.

Apply the Skill

1. On what issue is the artist commenting?
2. What elements are exaggerated in the cartoon?
3. Why can you still understand the cartoon, although elements are exaggerated?

Determining Relevance

Define the Skill

When conducting research, you will likely be faced with a great variety of different sources. Identifying which sources will help you is an important task. One step in identifying your sources is to determine their relevance. **Determining relevance** means deciding if a piece of information is related to your topic. It also involves identifying *how* something is related to your topic.

Learn the Skill

Use the following strategies to determine the relevance of information.

1 **Identify the specific topic.** Determine what types of sources address your research topic. Define your specific task to narrow down what types of information you need. Write down any questions for which you need answers.

2 **Locate a variety of sources.** Use several resources to track down sources. Encyclopedias, periodicals, monographs, and electronic databases are just a few types of resources you can use.

New Search	Advanced Boolean ▾	Additional Search
amnesia	Search
Save Checked	Save All on Page

Num	Mark	Search Results	Type of Source	Year Published
1		*The Amnesias: A Clinical Textbook of Memory Disorders,* by Andrew C. Papanicolaou	Book	2005
2		*The Merck Manuals Online Medical Library: Dissociative Amnesia*	Web site	2005
3		"Patients with hippocampal amnesia cannot imagine new experiences," by Hassabis, Kumaran, Vann, and Maguire	Journal article	2007
4		*The Vintage Book of Amnesia: An Anthology of Writing on the Subject of Memory Loss,* by Jonathan Lethem (Editor)	Anthology of short stories and articles	2000
5		*Unknown White Male*	Documentary film	2005

3 **Examine the sources carefully.** Identify the purpose of the source and the information it provides.

4 **Determine what information is useful for your topic.** Decide if the information in the sources can help you answer the list of questions you created.

Apply the Skill

1. List several resources you might use to find information on the topic of amnesia.

2. How might you evaluate each of the sources listed above?

3. What sources from the list above would be relevant to your research? Explain.

Developing and Testing Hypotheses

Define the Skill

A **hypothesis** is a testable statement about the relationship between two or more factors. Hypotheses are possible explanations based on facts. Because they can be tested, hypotheses can be proved or disproved.

Learn the Skill

Use the following strategies to learn to develop and test hypotheses.

1 Identify the question. Examine the issue at hand to find the trend, relationship, or event that you want to explain.

2 Examine the facts. Identify all the facts surrounding the question. The facts may support several different conclusions.

3 Consider what you already know about the issue. Use your own prior knowledge to help you formulate a hypothesis.

4 Develop a hypothesis that addresses the question. Analyze the facts and your own knowledge to form a conclusion, explanation, or prediction.

Question: What has caused the drop in Millborough High School students' consumption of sugar-sweetened soft drinks?

FACTS:
- The soft drink machines were moved from the busiest hallway to an exterior patio.
- The Millborough Student Council sponsored a poster contest about the connection between sugar consumption and obesity.
- Three popular flavors were removed from the soft drink machines.
- The cost of soft drinks has risen, because of a rise in the price of sugar and other agricultural products.
- A local physician discussed soft drinks and early-onset diabetes at a parent-teacher association meeting.
- The cheerleaders and varsity football team all pledged to switch from soft drinks to unsweetened iced tea.

Hypothesis: Millborough High School students reduced their consumption of sugar-sweetened soft drinks because of the perceived health risks.

FACTS THAT SUPPORT HYPOTHESIS:
The student council publicized the connection between soft drinks and obesity.
Many students' parents were alerted to the diabetes risk presented by soft drinks.
Several prominent students switched from soft drinks to unsweetened iced tea.

FACTS THAT REFUTE HYPOTHESIS:
The soft drink machines were less conveniently located.
Three popular flavors were removed from the soft drink machines.
The cost of soft drinks has risen.

5 Test your hypothesis. Conduct research to test your hypothesis. Identify facts that support or refute your conclusion. Depending on your findings, you may need to modify your hypothesis.

Apply the Skill

1. Develop a list of facts and a hypothesis that might explain why diagnoses of bipolar disorder have increased in recent years.
2. Use a graphic organizer like the one above to test your hypothesis.

Evaluating Information on the Internet

Define the Skill

The **Internet** is an international computer network that connects schools, businesses, government agencies, and individuals. Every Web site on the Internet has its own address called a *URL*. Each URL has a domain. The *domain* tells you the type of Web site you are visiting. Common domains in the United States are .com, .net, .org, .edu, and .gov. A Web site with the domain .edu means that it is sponsored by an educational institution. A Web site with the domain .gov means that it is sponsored by a government institution. The collection of Web sites throughout the world is called the *World Wide Web.*

The Internet can be a valuable research tool. Evaluating the content found on the Internet will help you determine its accuracy and reliability.

Learn the Skill

Use the following strategies to evaluate information on the Internet.

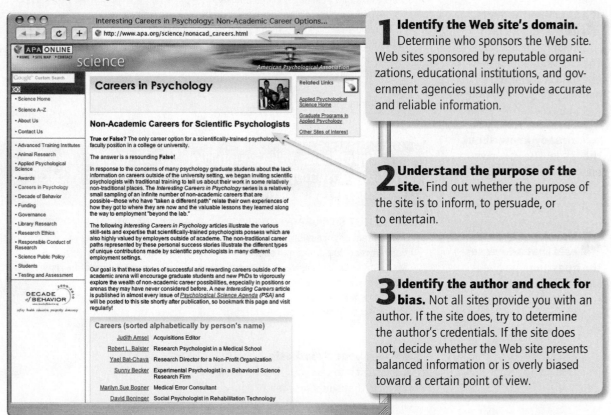

1 Identify the Web site's domain. Determine who sponsors the Web site. Web sites sponsored by reputable organizations, educational institutions, and government agencies usually provide accurate and reliable information.

2 Understand the purpose of the site. Find out whether the purpose of the site is to inform, to persuade, or to entertain.

3 Identify the author and check for bias. Not all sites provide you with an author. If the site does, try to determine the author's credentials. If the site does not, decide whether the Web site presents balanced information or is overly biased toward a certain point of view.

Apply the Skill

1. What is the domain of the Web site? Do you think the information on the Web site will be reliable? Why or why not?

2. What is the purpose of this Web site?

3. Do you think this Web site presents a balanced point of view or a biased point of view? Explain your response.

Synthesizing Information from Multiple Sources

Define the Skill

An important critical thinking skill is synthesizing information. **Synthesizing information** means combining information from different sources. Each source you use might provide different information on a particular topic or issue. Synthesizing the information from all of your sources will help you to produce a new idea, point of view, or interpretation.

Learn the Skill

Use the following strategies to practice synthesizing information from multiple sources.

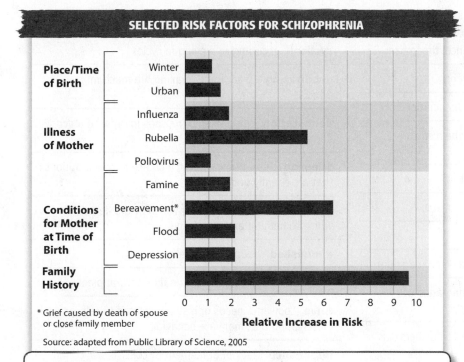

SELECTED RISK FACTORS FOR SCHIZOPHRENIA

Place/Time of Birth
- Winter
- Urban

Illness of Mother
- Influenza
- Rubella
- Poliovirus

Conditions for Mother at Time of Birth
- Famine
- Bereavement*
- Flood
- Depression

Family History

0 1 2 3 4 5 6 7 8 9 10
Relative Increase in Risk

* Grief caused by death of spouse or close family member

Source: adapted from Public Library of Science, 2005

1 Evaluate each source. Analyze each source to determine if the source is valid and reliable. Determine if the various sources are comparable.

2 Examine the information from each source. Identify the key facts presented in each source separately. Make a list of the information that each source provides.

3 Compare the information from your various sources. Identify similarities and differences between the sources and analyze relationships between the sources.

4 Synthesize the information from the sources. Draw conclusions based on the information from each of your sources. Use your conclusions to create your own interpretation, point of view, or idea on the topic.

from Chapter 18, Section 4

Explaining Schizophrenia . . . Problems in the central nervous system may involve neurotransmitters as well as brain structures, and research has focused on one particular neurotransmitter: dopamine. According to the dopamine theory of schizophrenia, people with schizophrenia use more dopamine than other people do, although they may not produce more of it. Why? They may have more dopamine receptors in the brain than other people, or their dopamine receptors may be hyperactive.

Apply the Skill

1. Are the sources above valid and reliable? How can you tell?
2. What similarities and differences exist between the two sources?
3. What conclusions can you draw based on the information in these two sources?

Building Your Vocabulary

Holt McDougal Psychology: Principles in Practice helps you build your vocabulary by focusing on two types of vocabulary words. Terms that are essential to your mastery of the course content are listed at the beginning of every section and are highlighted in yellow. You will find the definitions of these words as you read the section. The definitions are also in the Glossary. Academic Vocabulary words are words you need to know for other classes, too. They are underlined in the text and defined in the margins. Below is a list of these Academic Vocabulary words, along with their definitions.

Academic Vocabulary/Definition

abstract   not part of concrete existence; theoretical

acquisition   attainment or achievement

alienation   isolation, estrangement, dissociation

anabolic   a phase of metabolism in which substances are synthesized into living tissue

aptitude   an inherent ability; a talent

assess   to judge or determine

auditory   related to hearing

bias   a personal and sometimes unreasoned judgment

brittle   having little elasticity; easily damaged or cracked

chemotherapy   treatment of disease using chemicals to kill cells

circumstances   situations or conditions

colleagues   co-workers or associates

compliance   acting in accord with a wish, request, or demand

concur   to be of the same opinion; agree

consistent   in agreement with, compatible

coping skills   skills to contend with difficulties successfully

criteria   the standards on which a judgment or decision may be based

cyclical   recurring or moving in cycles

debilitating   weakening, making life much more difficult

deliberation   discussion of reasons in order to reach a decision

dilemma   situation requiring a choice between options that are equally undesirable

dimensions   the range over which or the degree to which something extends; scope

diminished   reduced or weakened

displace   move from an original or natural place

drive   powerful needs or instincts related to self-preservation that motivate behavior

dissonance   lack of agreement or consistence; conflict

eclectic   selecting elements from a variety of sources, systems, or styles

empathy   sympathy; understanding of others' feelings

ethnic group   a group of people who share a common culture, race, or national origin

eulogy   a speech praising a person who has just died

euphoria   a feeling of great happiness or well-being

exemplify   to show or illustrate by example

facility   ability or aptitude

Academic Vocabulary/Definition

foreboding   sense of impending evil or misfortune

fugue   disturbed state of consciousness in which someone performs acts in full awareness but later cannot remember

geriatrics   the branch of medicine that focuses on the diseases and problems of the elderly

interpersonal   relating to the interactions between individuals

interracial   involving or composed of different races

involuntary   acting or done without or against one's will

isolation   being alone or away from others

membrane   a thin layer of tissue that covers or lines an organ

morality   the concept of right or good conduct

mortality   inevitable death

mutation   a sudden and random change in the genetic material of a cell

neutral   not aligned with any position

ostracize   to reject or exclude

peers   people who have equal standing with one another in rank, class, or age

percentile   one of a set of points on a scale arrived at by dividing a group into parts in order of magnitude

peripheral   relating to the outer edge of the body

phenomenon   an observable event or occurrence

preconceptions   opinions formed in advance of adequate knowledge or experience

propitious   favorable, advantageous

questionnaire   a form containing a set of questions addressed to a statistically significant number of subjects

ratio   the relationship in quantity, amount, or size between two or more things

relaxation technique   any method or activity that helps a person to relax

repressed   excluded from the conscious mind

resilient   marked by the ability to recover quickly

respiratory system   the system of organs and passages involved in the intake and exchange of oxygen and carbon dioxide between a living organism and its environment

reticular   resembling a net in appearance or form

scales   standards of measurement or judgment; criteria

secrete   to release a liquid substance

socioeconomic   involving both social and economic factors

standardized   designed to be given under specified, standard conditions

static   having no motion

stimuli   outside facts that directly influence a person

stimulus   something that causes a response

stream of consciousness   thought regarded as a flowing series of images and ideas running through the mind

subjective   not objective, personal

sustain   to keep alive or to supply with nourishment

theorist   one who speculates, or formulates a theory

theorize   propose a theory about; speculate about

toxin   a poison produced by certain animals, plants, and bacteria

utopian   ideal

validation   the act of establishing the soundness of an idea or theory; corroboration

variable   subject to change

vicarious   experienced indirectly through the experience of another

Using Statistics

Analyzing Observations

Conducting a research study is actually only a small part of the research process. Imagine that you decide to conduct a survey about the amount of television teenagers watch daily. After you have conducted interviews and received dozens of completed questionnaires you would probably feel overwhelmed by the amount of data you had collected. What is the next step?

When faced with this situation, psychologists use mathematical procedures, involving statistics to organize, analyze, and interpret the data. Psychologists then use the statistical analyses to construct charts and graphs. In short, statistics help psychologists make sense of their research findings.

Understanding Frequency

One of the most common forms of statistical analysis researchers use to organize their data is the frequency distribution. A frequency distribution is a way of arranging data to determine how often a certain piece of data—such as a score, salary, or age—occurs. In setting up a frequency distribution, researchers arrange the data from highest to lowest, and enter a mark when a piece of data occurs. The sum of each group's marks determines the frequency.

If there are too many different pieces of data to list individually, as is sometimes true for class scores, a researcher may substitute specific numerical spans, called class intervals, for individual scores. Again, the data are arranged from highest to lowest. A frequency distribution would allow a teacher to see at a glance how well a group of students did on a test, for instance, but it does not provide any information about individual performance.

Understanding Bell Curves

A useful statistical concept for psychologists is the bell curve, or normal curve. The bell curve is an ideal, a hypothetical standard against which actual categories of people or things (such as scores) can be measured and compared. Usually, bell curves are used to categorize characteristics of people in large groups. The closer the group comes to the center of the curve, where the most "normal" traits congregate, the more validity the study appears to have.

For example, the bell curve, "Distribution of IQ Scores," shown on the following page, illustrates a hypothetical standard against which actual IQ scores can be compared. This bell curve is a model of an ideal. It shows what would happen if the largest number of scores fell exactly in the middle of a range of scores. A comparison of the actual scores against this bell curve tells a researcher how representative the IQ test really is.

Correlations represent the relationship between two variables. When two variables show a positive correlation, one rises as the other rises. If the two variables are negatively correlated, one of the variables rises as the other falls. A bell curve is a normal frequency distribution. This means that after counting the frequency of specific data, researchers can create an arrangement, or distribution, that is concentrated on or near the curve's center, which represents the norm. The fewest entries of data should appear at the far ends of the distribution—away from the highly concentrated norm.

It follows then that when the graphed results of an experiment come close to matching a bell curve, the results are assumed to be highly representative of that experiment. If most scores or data cluster towards the ends of the curve, however, the experiment or test is assumed to be unrepresentative of the group.

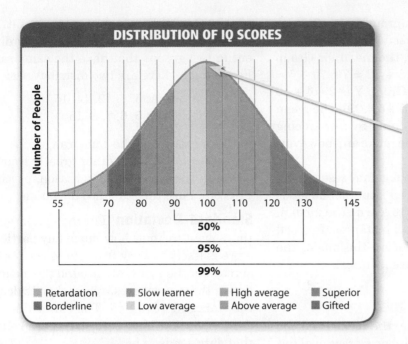

DISTRIBUTION OF IQ SCORES

Number of People

55   70 80 90 100 110 120 130   145

50%

95%

99%

■ Retardation   ■ Slow learner   ■ High average   ■ Superior
■ Borderline   ■ Low average   ■ Above average ■ Gifted

This bell curve is a model of an ideal. It shows what would happen if the largest number of scores fell exactly in the middle of a range of scores. A comparison of the actual scores against this bell curve tells a researcher how representative the IQ test really is.

Bell curves and frequency distributions seem very complicated. However, they are simply ways to condense information and put it in a visual form. Within moments of glancing at a real plotted curve and the bell curve beside it, researchers can judge approximately how far from the norm their experimental group was, and how closely their results conform to what is "perfectly" normal.

Mode, Mean, and Median: Measures of Central Tendency

Three other measures are used to compare data that fall within the central points of a distribution: the mode, the mean, and the median.

Mode Simply, the mode is the piece of data that occurs most often in a given set of numbers. To find the mode, examine any frequency distribution and choose the number that appears most often. The mode is of limited use to researchers because "occurring most often" in a distribution may mean, for example, that this number occurred only twice among fifty different test scores.

Mean The mean is an average. The mean is found by adding all the scores or data together and then dividing that sum by the number of scores. The formula for finding the mean is:

$$mean = \frac{sum\ of\ the\ scores}{number\ of\ scores}$$

A significant disadvantage of using the mean is that any extreme score, whether high or low, distorts a researcher's results. For instance, if five waiters earn $300, $350, $325, $390, and $600 per week respectively, the mean—or average—weekly salary for this group would be $393. Yet four of the five waiters earn less than the average amount. In this circumstance, using the mean would not necessarily be representative of the waiters' wages.

Median The median is the score or piece of data that falls precisely in the middle of all the scores when they are arranged in descending order. Exactly half of the students score above the median, and exactly half score below it. In the previous example of waiters' salaries, the median would be $350, because two waiters earned more and two earned less.

The median, unlike the mean, is usually an actual number or score. To find the median of an even number of scores, you would find the median of the two numbers that fall in the middle, and then take the mean of those two central numbers in the distribution.

One major advantage of the median is that extreme scores, high or low, will not affect it. For example, examine the following two distributions:

Group X: 4, 10, 16, 18, 22
Group Y: 4, 10, 16, 18, 97

The median for each group is 16, because that number falls precisely in the middle of all the scores. However, the mean for Group X is 14 (4 + 10 + 16 + 18 + 22 = 70; 70 ÷ 5 = 14), while the mean for Group Y is 29 (4 + 10 + 16 + 18 + 97 = 145; 145 ÷ 5 = 29). The mean changes dramatically simply by introducing one extreme score. The median, however, remains the same.

The kind of central point that researchers choose to use in any given situation depends on what they are trying to learn. The median is not the best choice in all instances. In a bell curve—the idealized norm—the mode, the mean, and the median are identical.

Variability

Knowing what the mode, the mean, and the median are tells a researcher a great deal but not everything about the data. Researchers also need to know how much variability there is among the scores in a group of numbers. That is, researchers must discover how far apart the numbers or scores are in relation to the mean. For this purpose, psychologists use two measures: the range and the standard deviation.

Range The range is the mathematical difference between the highest and lowest scores in a frequency distribution. If the highest grade in a class is 100 and the lowest is 60, the range is 40 (100 − 60 = 40). Two groups of numbers may have the same mean but different ranges. For example, consider the batting averages of two baseball teams:

> Team A: 210 250 285 300 340
> Team B: 270 270 275 285 285

The mean for each team is 277. However, the range for Team A is 130 points, whereas the range for Team B is 15 points. This would tell a researcher that Team B is more alike in its batting abilities than is Team A.

The range tells psychologists how similar the subjects in each group are to one another in terms of what is being measured. This information could not be obtained from the mode, mean, or median alone, since each is just one number and not a comparison.

The disadvantage of the range, though, is that it takes only the lowest and highest scores into account. The middle numbers may be substantially different in two groups that have the same range. For example, here are two distributions:

> Group A: 5, 8, 12, 14, 15
> Group B: 5, 6, 7, 8, 15

Each group has the same range of 10. But the scores in Group A differ greatly from the scores in Group B. For this reason, psychologists often use the standard deviation.

Standard Deviation Psychologists sometimes want to know how much any particular score is likely to vary from the mean, or how spread out the scores are around the mean. To derive these measures, researchers calculate the standard deviation. The closer the standard deviation is to zero, the more reliable that data tends to be.

Let's say that the standard deviation of Team A's batting average is about 44.2, and the standard deviation of Team B's batting average is 6.8. From this information we know that the typical score of Team A will fall within 44.2 points of the mean, and the typical score of Team B will be within 6.8 points of the mean. This tells us that the quality of batting is more consistent on Team B than on Team A.

Two bell curves can have the same mode, mean, and median, but different standard deviations. If you were plotting two bell curves on a line graph, and one curve had a much larger standard deviation than the other, the curve with the larger standard deviation would show a more pronounced bell shape on the graph.

Correlation Correlation is a measure of the relationship between two variables. A variable is any behavior or condition that can change in quantity or quality. Examples of variables that people frequently encounter are age, hair color, weight, and height. Correlation and causation are two types of relationships between variables that have great importance for psychologists.

When two variables are related, they are said to have a correlation. Changes in variables often occur together. Sometimes, an increase or decrease in one is accompanied by a corresponding increase or decrease in the other. For example, a decrease in someone's caloric intake is accompanied by a decrease in that person's weight. Such variables are said to be positively correlated. Sometimes, when one variable increases, the other decreases, or vice-versa. These variables are said to be negatively correlated.

Correlation Coefficient

The correlation coefficient describes the degree of relationship between variables. The concept of correlation allows researchers to predict the value of one variable if they know the value of the other and the way that the variables are correlated. A perfect positive correlation would have a coefficient of +1.00; a perfect negative correlation has a coefficient of −1.00. A correlation coefficient of zero indicates that there is no correlation between two variables.

Perfect positive correlations (+1.00 coefficient), when graphed, form a straight line that leans to the right; a perfect negative correlation (−1.00 coefficient), shown on a line graph, would form a straight line that leans to the left. In reality, few correlations are perfect. While one variable may increase or decrease in relation to the other, both variables probably will not change to the same degree.

Here is an example of a strong negative correlation with predictive potential: the more hours a person spends commuting to work, the less he or she enjoys driving. We can predict that if the person shortens the commute, his or her enjoyment of driving will increase.

Causation

Although correlation is an important concept in statistics, it does not explain everything about relationships between variables. For one thing, correlation does not speak to the concept of causation. No correlation, of any degree, in itself proves that one variable causes another.

It is sometimes difficult to determine whether one variable actually causes another. Researchers determine causal relationships scientifically rather than relying on the intuitive sense of causality that may be implied in a correlation. They compare the differences between an experimental group—the group that displays the condition that is being studied—and a control group, in which this condition is not present. The independent variable is the variable being manipulated.

If Group A is exposed to a virus and gets sick, and Group B is exposed to the same virus but has been vaccinated and does not become ill, there appears to be a causal relationship at work. It seems that the vaccine protected Group B from the virus, and therefore from illness. But researchers probably would want to examine how the vaccine actually worked—if it did. It may have been coincidental that Group B remained well.

POSITIVE AND NEGATIVE CORRELATIONS

Positive Correlation
Generally speaking, people who have a higher need for achievement achieve higher salaries.

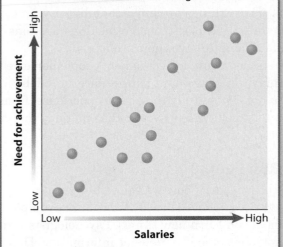

Negative Correlation
Generally speaking, the immune systems of people who are under high amounts of stress tend to function more poorly than the immune systems of people who are under less stress.

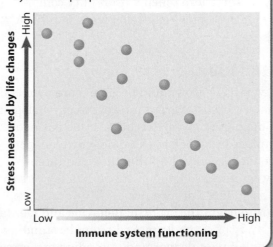

Why Psychology Matters

Have you ever wondered . . .
why people dream?
how stress could affect your health?
why some memories are more vivid than others?
how a baby perceives the world?

Psychology and Your World

When you think of psychology, what comes to mind? Perhaps you picture a person on a couch talking to a therapist. Maybe you picture a scientist in a laboratory carrying out experiments with rats. These things are important, but psychology includes much more. Psychology involves asking questions about people and trying to solve their problems.

Psychologists study every aspect of how people perceive the world. You may take a brilliant sunset for granted, but psychologists do not. They study the entire experience, from how colors stimulate cells in the eyes to the emotions that a beautiful sunset evokes.

Psychology and People

Psychologists study people—how we think, how we see ourselves, and why we behave the way we do. For example, every day at school you learn new things. Psychologists want to know how people learn and remember information. How much do you think your brain can remember? Believe it or not, psychologists report that there is no known limit to how much you can learn.

Psychologists are also interested in why things go wrong with people's minds. Why do some people become anxious or depressed? Why do some lose touch with reality completely? Professional psychologists try to develop ways to relieve problems like these.

Psychology and You

Over the years, you have grown and become more able and self-reliant. This process is of great interest to psychologists who study how life differs at various stages, such as adolescence. For example, psychologists examine why teenagers strive for independence, why they often have an intense need for privacy, and why so many teenagers take risks they would not take as children or as adults.

You are about to begin the study of behavior and mental processes—the study of psychology. And by understanding psychology, you will gain a deeper understanding of yourself and others.

UNIT 1 Introduction to Psychology

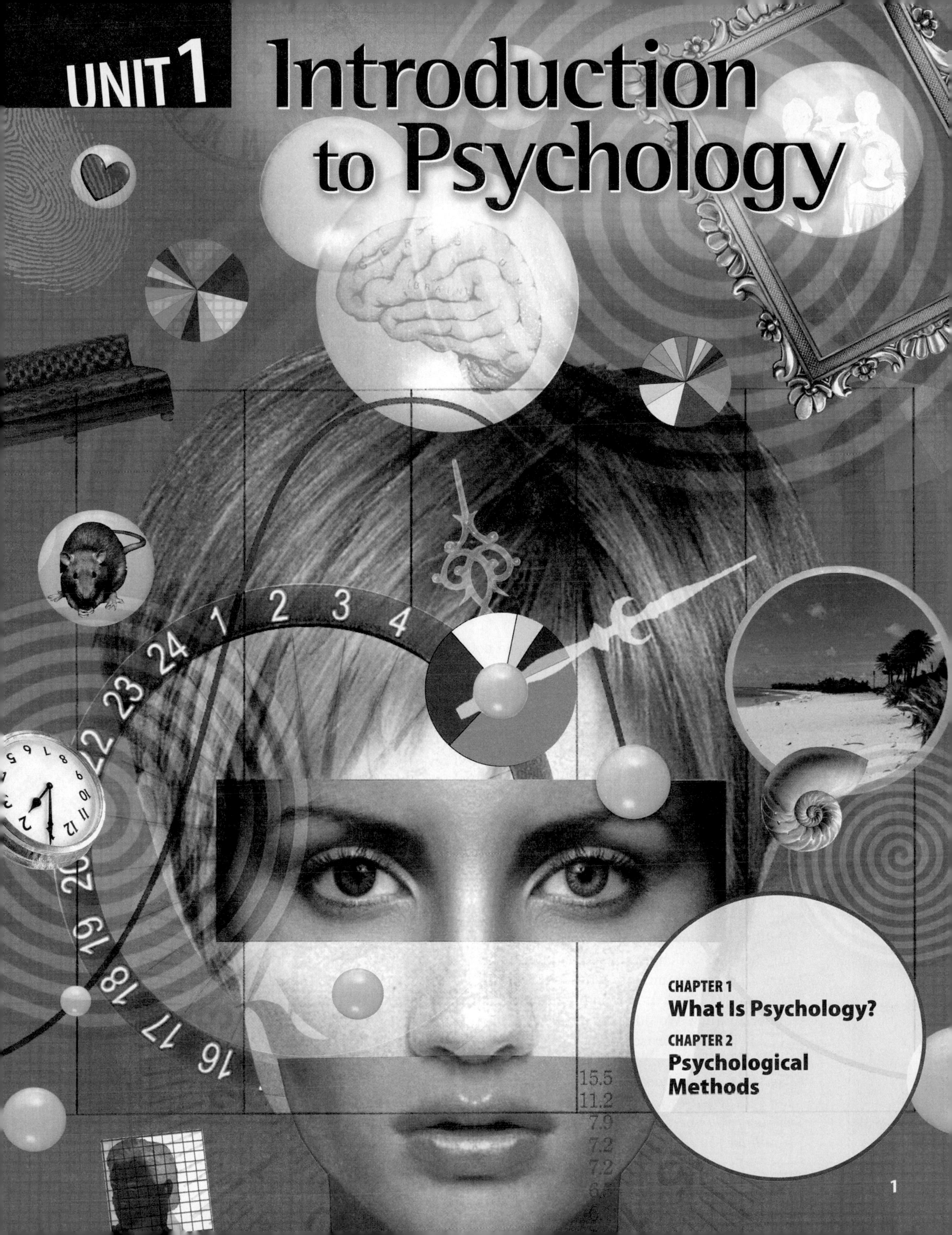

15.5
11.2
7.9
7.2
7.2
6.

1

A SOCIAL SCIENCE vs. a False SCIENCE

The false science of astrology uses the 12 signs of the zodiac to try to explain the past and predict the future.

This chapter explores the scientific approaches and methods of psychologists. Psychologists are critical thinkers, which means that they are skeptical. They insist on seeing the evidence before they will accept people's claims and arguments about what is truth and what is fiction. As scientists, psychologists know that beliefs about the behavior of cosmic rays, chemical compounds, cells, or people must be supported by evidence. Persuasive arguments and reference to authority figures do *not* constitute scientific evidence.

False sciences, on the other hand, do not rely on verifiable evidence. Even so, false science is widespread. Think of the claims made by tabloid newspapers—each week, they publish doomsday reports that foretell the end of the world and describe ten new encounters with extraterrestrials.

By examining one false science—that of astrology—we can learn why false science is unreliable. Astrology is based on the idea that the positions of the stars, moon, and planets can affect human personality and destiny. One can also supposedly foretell the future by studying the positions of these bodies. Astrologers prepare forecasts called horoscopes, which are based on people's birth dates and indicate what is safe for them to do. Read the following description of personality. Would it be on target if you read it in your horoscope?

You have the inner potential for change. You have unused potential that you have not yet turned to your advantage. There are parts of your personality known to you alone. You have the ability to handle conflicting demands. You also have a strong potential for improvement.

This horoscope would actually apply to many different kinds of people. The tendency to believe such a general personality report is called the Barnum effect, after circus promoter P. T. Barnum, who once said that a good circus had to "have something for everyone." General personality reports "have something for everyone," which allows palm readers and fortune-tellers to sound as if they are right on target.

Supporters of astrology might offer the following arguments:

- Astrology has been practiced for many centuries and is part of many cultures.
- Astrology seems to provide a path to meaning in life and, for a fortunate few, a road to riches.
- People in high positions have followed the advice of astrologers.
- If one heavenly body, the moon, is powerful enough to sway the tides of the seas, why should the pulls of the stars and planets not affect people's destinies?
- Astrology is a special art and not a science. Therefore, we should not subject astrology to scientific testing.

CHAPTER 1

WHAT IS PSYCHOLOGY?

Think critically about the claims of astrologers. For example, does the sole fact that astrology has a lengthy tradition mean that it is true? Are the tides similar to human personality and destiny?

Astrological predictions routinely fail. But does it matter? Will believers in astrology be persuaded by facts? Probably not. Even in our age of scientific enlightenment, millions of people will continue to consult their horoscopes.

Psychology, on the other hand, is grounded in facts. It is a true science. Psychological findings are of value because they are routinely subjected to careful scrutiny. Theories are tested according to the scientific method. If the evidence does not support a theory, it is discarded, and psychologists search for new answers. In this chapter and throughout this book, you will learn about the rigorous application of the science of psychology to questions that have concerned humankind for centuries.

Chapter at a Glance

SECTION 1: Why Study Psychology?

■ Psychology is the scientific study of human behavior and mental processes.

■ Psychologists seek to observe, describe, explain, predict, and modify behavior and mental processes.

■ Psychologists rely on research to learn whether certain methods will work before they use them to help people.

SECTION 2: What Psychologists Do

■ Major fields in psychology include clinical, developmental, and experimental psychology.

■ Psychologists also work in applied, or specialized fields, such as community, forensic, and health psychology.

SECTION 3: A History of Psychology

■ Psychology is as old as human history, with its roots going back to ancient Egypt and Greece.

■ The scientific approach, which began in the 1500s, led to the birth of modern psychology in the 1800s.

■ Modern psychologists continually propose new theories focused on behavioral and cognitive research.

SECTION 4: Contemporary Perspectives

■ Some contemporary psychologists focus on the role of biology or the role of the mind in seeking to understand behavior and mental processes.

■ Other psychologists study how our personal experience affects how we perceive the world.

■ Still other psychologists take a more holistic approach and study the interaction of biology, psychology, and social factors and their combined impact on people.

Psychologists carry out true scientific research and processes. Here, a psychologist uses a video of a healthy arm to help alleviate the "phantom pain" of a patient's amputated arm.

What do you think?

1. What is the basic way in which psychology differs from false sciences?

2. Why do you think false sciences are so widespread?

Why Study Psychology?

Before You Read

Main Idea
Psychology is a science. Like other scientists, psychologists seek to explain and control behavior and mental processes and test their ideas through research methods.

Reading Focus
1. How are behavior and mental processes different?
2. What are some basic goals of psychology?
3. How is psychology a science?

Vocabulary
psychology
behavior
cognitive activities
psychological constructs
theory
principle

TAKING NOTES Use a graphic organizer like this one to take notes on the goals of psychology.

SEARCHING the SELF-HELP AISLE

"I do want to solve all my problems, but I'll wait till it comes out in soft cover."

PSYCHOLOGY CLOSE UP

Are self-help books psychologically sound? You've seen them in bookstores—entire aisles filled with books promising to make us thin, rich, and happy. Yet psychologists say that some of these self-help books give bad advice, such as encouraging their readers to vent their anger. In fact, most psychologists maintain that venting anger just helps keep it alive. Some even claim that self-help books can distract and harm their readers. Those with severe depression, for instance, are unlikely to find answers to their very real problems in a book. Unchecked, the disease may spiral out of control.

Of course, some self-help books actually do get it right. They stress the importance of family, friends, and healthy relationships. But they also provide something that may be more important than advice: they give their readers hope. Still, hope alone cannot effect change. Only those books that do not offer simplistic solutions and instead provide a sound scientific basis for their advice are most valuable. In other words, people should seek support from a source that is well researched, well documented, and proven to be effective—support that is rooted in the science of psychology. ■

Behavior and Mental Processes

Psychology is the scientific study of human behavior and mental processes. **Behavior** is any action that people can observe or measure. Behavior includes activities such as walking and talking, pressing a switch, turning left or right, sleeping, eating, and drinking. Behavior also includes automatic body functions such as heart rate, blood pressure, digestion, and brain activity. Behavior can be measured by simple observation or by laboratory instruments. For example, brain activity can be measured by scientific instruments such as the electroencephalograph (EEG).

Cognitive activities are mental processes. These activities include dreams, perceptions, thoughts, and memories. Brain waves that indicate dreaming can be measured, but dreaming itself is a mental process—dreams are known only to the dreamer. In addition, activity of the cells in a person's eyes can be measured as they respond to color, but only you can see your own mental image of the world. Memories, too, are private mental processes that cannot be measured.

Psychologists are also interested in studying people's emotions, or feelings. Emotions can affect both behavior and mental processes. For example, you might experience anxiety when you think about presenting a report in front of your class. Your heart might even race a bit at the thought. Your heart activity is an example of behavior, but your thoughts about presenting the report are private mental processes. We would be unable to observe or measure your thoughts directly. In this situation, researchers might use **psychological constructs** to learn more about human behavior. These constructs are used to talk about something we cannot see, touch, or measure directly.

Reading Check **Summarize** What do psychologists study?

The Goals of Psychology

Scientists seek to observe, describe, explain, predict, and control the events they study. Similarly, psychologists observe and describe behavior and mental processes to better understand them. This process enables psychologists to explain, predict, and help clients control their behavior.

Explaining Behavior An example of how psychologists apply the goals of psychology can be seen in the case of Alex Rodriguez, third baseman for the New York Yankees. In 2000, Rodriguez became the highest-paid athlete in sports history. He won many awards for his hitting and fielding, including Player of the Year in 2000 and 2002. He even earned the distinction of becoming the youngest player in baseball to hit 500 home runs. However, in time Rodriguez gained notoriety for another kind of behavior: an inability to produce hits in the postseason. Most famously, he was criticized for his performance in the 2004 American League Championship Series against the Boston Red Sox. In game six of the series, Rodriguez hit a ground ball to the Red Sox pitcher for an easy out. He compounded his weak performance by swatting the ball out of the pitcher's glove just before he was tagged out—in clear violation of the rules. The umpires called Rodriguez out, and he left the field to the boos of the New York fans.

Losing one's "cool" and failing to perform effectively in a crucial situation—such as during an important game or while taking a major test—can be very hard on a person. This type of failure can hurt an individual's self-esteem and self-confidence.

Sports psychologists can help athletes such as Alex Rodriguez handle performance problems by applying the goals of psychology. First, they observe and describe the behavior. By measuring athletes' heart rates and other body processes, psychologists know that problems may occur when athletes are highly excited. Interviews with athletes reveal that they often feel anxious during big games. They may become distracted by the cheers or jeers of the crowd and lose their concentration. They cannot focus on the jobs they are supposed to be doing.

Psychologists then explain the behavior in terms of the feelings of anxiety and the distractions that hinder the athletes' performance. The relationship between anxiety and performance is somewhat complex. A little anxiety is often a good thing. It motivates us to practice for a game or to study for a test. It makes us alert and ready. On the other hand, too much anxiety is harmful. It may make us shaky and distract us from the task at hand.

Can You Change Your Behavior?

One reason to study psychology is to better understand why you act as you do. As a result, you might be able to figure out how to change the aspects of your behavior with which you are unhappy.

PROCEDURE

❶ Identify an activity that you enjoy doing. You might name a school activity, a hobby, or a sport you play.

❷ On a piece of notebook paper, write two reasons explaining why you enjoy the activity.

   a. _____

   b. _____

❸ Write two aspects of your performance that you would like to change.

   a. _____

   b. _____

ANALYSIS

1. Get together with a partner and share your notes.

2. Take turns explaining the behavior that you would like to change.

3. Take turns describing how you feel when the behavior occurs.

4. List the suggestions that you and your partner come up with to change or control your behavior.

   a. _____

   b. _____

Quick Lab THINK central thinkcentral.com

CASE STUDY
CONNECTION

A Social Science
Psychology is a social science, but it is rooted in the natural sciences.

Predicting and Controlling Psychologists predict that athletes will do best when anxiety is moderate. Consequently, they help athletes change and control their behavior and mental processes by teaching them ways of keeping their anxiety at a tolerable level. Psychologists also teach athletes how to filter out distracting noises and focus on the game.

One method that sports psychologists recommend to help athletes perform more effectively under pressure is called positive visualization. In this method, athletes imagine themselves in a critical game situation. For example, a basketball player might imagine taking a free throw during a close game. She sees herself raising the ball with one hand and guiding it with the other. She then imagines releasing the ball and watching it glide through the net.

The goal of "controlling" behavior and mental processes is often misunderstood. Some people mistakenly think that psychologists seek ways to make people behave as the psychologists want them to. This is not so. Psychologists know that people should be free to make their own decisions. Psychologists know much about the factors that influence human behavior, and they use this knowledge to help people accomplish their own goals.

Reading Check **Find the Main Idea** How do psychologists help change behavior?

Psychology as a Science

Although psychology is a social science, it has foundations in the natural sciences. The social sciences, which also include history, anthropology, economics, political science, and sociology, deal with the structure of human society and the nature and interactions of the individuals who make up society. These individuals and their behavior and mental processes are the focus of psychology.

The natural sciences, which include biology, chemistry, and physics, are concerned with the nature of the physical world. Some areas that psychologists study, such as the functioning of the brain, are closely related to the natural sciences, particularly biology. Like natural scientists, psychologists seek to answer questions by following the steps involved in scientific research. These steps include conducting surveys and experiments, collecting and analyzing data, and drawing logical conclusions.

Psychological Research As a science, psychology tests ideas through various research methods. Two widely used methods are surveys and experimentation. A survey is a method of collecting data that usually involves asking questions of people in a particular group. Experimentation usually involves either human participants or animals.

Although most psychologists are interested mainly in human behavior, some choose to focus on animal behavior, such as that of gorillas, rats, pigeons, and even sea snails. Some psychologists believe that research findings with certain animals can be applied to human beings. The biological functioning of these animals and even their psychological responses to some situations are often similar to those of people. Others, however, argue that humans are so distinct that we can only learn about them by studying people. The truth probably lies somewhere in between. For example, by studying the nerve cells of squid, psychologists have been able to learn about the workings of human nerve cells. However, only by studying people can psychologists learn about uniquely human qualities such as morality, values, and love.

Psychologists rely on research to learn whether certain methods will work before they use them with clients. Of course, when the research is conducted with human beings, psychologists make every effort to protect the research participants.

Psychological Theories Psychologists organize their research about behavior and mental processes into theories. A **theory** is a statement that attempts to explain why things are the way they are and why they happen the way they do. Psychological theories discuss principles that govern behavior and mental processes. A **principle** is a basic truth or law, such as the assumption that you will get better grades if you study more. Psychological theories may include statements about behavior (such as sleeping or aggression), mental processes (such as memories and mental images), and biological processes (such as the effect of chemicals in the brain).

A useful psychological theory allows psychologists to predict behavior and mental processes. For example, if a theory about fatigue is useful, psychologists can apply it to predict when people will or will not sleep. If a theory does not accurately predict behavior or mental processes, psychologists consider revising or replacing the theory.

In psychology, as in other sciences, many theories have been found inadequate for explaining or predicting the things with which they are concerned. As a result, these theories have been discarded or revised. For example, many psychologists once believed that stomach contractions were the cause of hunger. But then it was observed that many people feel hungry even when they do not have stomach contractions. As a result, psychologists now believe that stomach contractions are only one of many factors affecting appetite.

Reading Check **Compare** In what ways is psychology similar to other sciences?

SECTION 1 Assessment

Reviewing Main Ideas and Vocabulary

1. **Define** What does *theory* mean? What does *principle* mean?

2. **Summarize** Why do psychologists believe that a little anxiety can be a good thing?

Thinking Critically

3. **Define** What is a key difference between behavior and cognitive activities?

4. **Explain** What characteristics of psychology differentiate it from other related social sciences?

5. **Evaluate** Why is it important that psychologists allow their clients to make their own decisions?

6. **Make Judgments** Using your notes, make a judgment about the adequacy of each theory listed in the graphic organizer below.

Theory	Judgment
People function better with adequate sleep.	
You will lose weight if you exercise.	
Dreams reveal a great deal about our anxieties.	

FOCUS ON WRITING

7. **Persuasive** Write a paragraph in which you try to convince your parents why you should be allowed to take psychology rather than some other course.

Neuroimaging and Cognitive Research

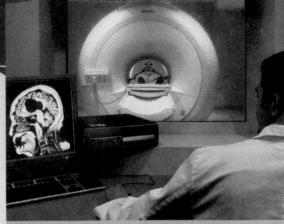

A patient undergoes 3D MRI brain scanning, which allows the examiner to view the brain from every angle.

Imagine being able to peer inside a living human brain and watch it light up as it works. Neuroimaging allows scientists to do just that. Using noninvasive techniques such as positron emission topography (PET) and magnetic resonance imaging (MRI), scientists can create images that show how the brain changes as it processes mental functions.

Neuroimaging has been particularly useful in cognitive research, the study of mental processes and mental disorders. For example, during REM sleep—the stage of sleep when dreams are most vivid—neuroscientists have found that the part of the brain involved in logical reasoning becomes relatively inactive, while those parts involved in visual perception and emotions become more stimulated. Neuroscientists have also discovered that they can identify and chart brain activity by detecting areas of increased or decreased blood flow. As neuroscientists trace the brain's functioning, they can literally watch it at work.

Psychologists hope that the pictures of the brain produced by neuroimaging will improve their ability to diagnose and cure mental disorders. Research in the field has been promising. In one study, scientists noted differences in the brains of people with social anxiety disorder during public speaking. PET scans revealed that blood flow increased in a part of the brain that generates the fear response. Conversely, blood flow in the brains of people without the disorder increased to an area linked with thinking skills (Tillfors et al., 2001). In a study on depression, researchers found that participants' brains registered sharp dips and spikes in activity as their moods changed under the influence of antidepressant drugs or placebos. The study helped the researchers locate a spot in the brain that may regulate neural activity during depression (Mayberg et al., 2005).

Neuroimaging has also been used in the study of Alzheimer's disease. Images of the brain have shown that the hippocampus, the part that plays a major role in short-term memory retention, shrinks in patients with Alzheimer's. Researchers hope that PET and MRI scans will help scientists measure this and other changes in the brain before patients show symptoms of the disease.

While neuroimaging has provided invaluable information about the brain, some psychologists remain skeptical. They claim that the neuroimages tell us much about how the brain behaves but little or nothing about how the mind, or conscious thought, works. Although the cognitive processes of the brain are related to its physical functioning, we don't really know how the two interact. In addition, many psychologists question neuroimaging research because they say that our brains are not all the same. In fact, they may differ as much as people's personalities. After all, the human brain is probably the most complex object in all of scientific study. It may be interesting and useful to see which part of the brain lights up on a particular scan. However, as one psychologist has said, "It's not at all easy to know what that activity might really mean."

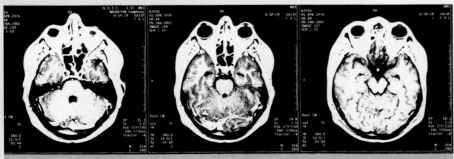

These three panels of an MRI brain scan show evidence of an abnormality.

Thinking Critically

1. **Analyze** Why might neuroimaging be an important aid in the treatment of mental disorders?

2. **Discuss** Do you think neuroimaging has much practical application in psychology? Why or why not?

Current Research **THINK** central thinkcentral.com

What Psychologists Do

Before You Read

Main Idea

Psychologists work in many different fields, but they all focus on studying and explaining behavior and mental processes.

Reading Focus

1. What are some of the major fields in psychology?

2. How do specialists in some applied fields of psychology serve people's needs?

Vocabulary

psychiatrist
basic research

TAKING NOTES Use a graphic organizer like this one to take notes on the major fields and specialties in psychology.

Field	Characteristics

Up Close and Personal

PSYCHOLOGY CLOSE UP

You mean I'm supposed to talk to them? You've exchanged your likes and dislikes in music. You've shared your thoughts on your favorite movies. You've even discovered that you both dream of becoming a doctor. You're best friends. Surely it's a minor detail that you've never met. With networking Web sites like Facebook and MySpace, people today can make dozens of new friends with a few mouse clicks. The trouble is that some of these people have forgotten—or have never learned—how to actually talk to someone face-to-face.

To help students with their interpersonal skills, New York University offered a seminar in 2007 to their incoming freshmen called "Facebook in the Flesh." The seminar provided an interactive workshop in which students paired off and talked for six minutes. To help them break the ice, the leader of the seminar provided a few sample questions, such as "What drew you to NYU?" and "What do you think of this workshop so far?" At the conclusion of the workshop, some of the students agreed that the encounter had been difficult; Facebook, they said, was easier. How, they asked, do you let someone know you want to talk? "Just smile," they were told.

As virtual communication becomes the principal means of connecting with others, more people may need seminars like this one. This may be a job for social psychologists. Helping people learn how to behave in social situations is one of the things they do. In this section, you will learn about social psychology as well as the work undertaken in many other fields. ◼

Major Fields in Psychology

Many psychologists share a keen interest in behavior, and all believe in the value of scientific research. They also share the belief that theories about behavior and mental processes should be supported by scientific evidence. They accept something as true only if the evidence shows it is so.

Some psychologists are interested mainly in research. They investigate the factors that give rise to behaviors and that explain certain mental processes. They form theories about why people and animals do the things they do. Then they test their theories by predicting when specific behaviors will occur.

Other psychologists consult. That means that they apply psychological knowledge in the form of therapy to help people change their behavior so that they can better meet their own goals. Still other psychologists teach, sharing their knowledge of psychology in classrooms and workshops.

Clinical Psychology Clinical psychologists make up the largest group of psychologists. Clinical psychologists are the people most of us think of when we hear the term "psychologist." Specialty areas within this field include child mental health, adult mental health, learning disabilities, geriatrics, and general health.

ACADEMIC VOCABULARY

geriatrics the branch of medicine that focuses on the diseases and problems of the elderly

The psychologists in this field help people with psychological problems, such as anxiety or depression, or severe psychological disorders, such as schizophrenia. Clinical psychologists help their clients overcome problems and adjust to the demands of their lives. They also help people who have problems with relationships, drug abuse, or weight control.

Clinical psychologists are trained to evaluate psychological problems through the use of interviews and psychological tests. Then these psychologists try to help clients understand and resolve their problems by changing ineffective or harmful behavior.

The work environment for clinical psychologists can include hospitals, prisons, university clinics, and private practices. Some clinical psychologists divide their time between clinical practice, teaching, and research.

These psychologists should not be confused with psychiatrists. A **psychiatrist** is a medical doctor who specializes in the treatment of psychological problems and who can prescribe medication for clients. Psychologists also specialize in the treatment of psychological problems, but because they are not medical doctors, they may not prescribe medication for their clients. However, clinical psychologists often work together with psychiatrists to consult and determine the best course of treatment for a complex patient problem.

INTERACTIVE ✳

Statistically Speaking...

Graduate Programs in Psychology

Universities typically offer graduate programs in many fields of psychology. As you can see from the pie graph, however, nearly half of all new doctoral graduates in psychology emerge from the clinical program.

Skills Focus INTERPRETING GRAPHS Which field is the second most popular? Which field is least popular?

Source: 2005 *Graduate Study in Psychology.*
Compiled by the APA Research Office.

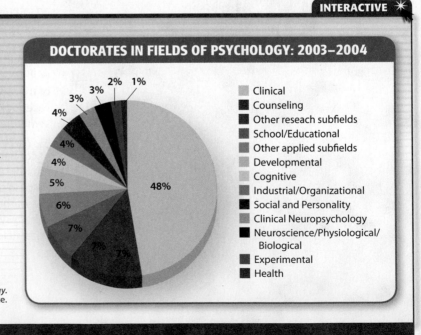

DOCTORATES IN FIELDS OF PSYCHOLOGY: 2003–2004

48%
7%
7%
6%
5%
4%
4%
4%
3%
3%
2%
1%

- Clinical
- Counseling
- Other reseach subfields
- School/Educational
- Other applied subfields
- Developmental
- Cognitive
- Industrial/Organizational
- Social and Personality
- Clinical Neuropsychology
- Neuroscience/Physiological/ Biological
- Experimental
- Health

Interactive Feature THINKcentral thinkcentral.com

Counseling Psychology Like clinical psychologists, counseling psychologists use interviews and tests to identify their clients' problems. Counseling psychologists typically treat people who have adjustment problems rather than serious psychological disorders. For example, a counseling psychologist's clients may have difficulty making decisions about their careers, or they may find it hard to make friends. They may be experiencing conflicts with family members, teachers, employers, or colleagues. Counseling psychologists help their clients clarify their goals, overcome their adjustment problems, and meet challenges. Counseling psychologists are often employed in businesses and in college and university counseling and testing centers.

School Psychology Your school district may employ one or more school psychologists. School psychologists identify and help students who have problems that interfere with learning. Typical problems that school psychologists deal with include peer group and family problems, and learning disorders, which are problems in learning to read, write, or do math.

School psychologists identify students with problems by talking with teachers, parents, and the students themselves. School psychologists may also administer tests, such as intelligence tests and achievement tests. These tests, which are usually given to large groups of students, help identify students with special abilities as well as students who need assistance. For example, a school psychologist might notice a student's exceptional results on the math section of an achievement test and recommend placing her in an advanced math class.

School psychologists also observe students in the classroom to see how they interact with their teachers and peers. After gathering the information they need, school psychologists advise teachers, school officials, and parents about how to help certain students reach their potential or overcome any learning difficulties they might have.

In addition, school psychologists make recommendations regarding the placement of students in special classes and programs. In some school districts, student placement is the major responsibility of the school psychologist.

Educational Psychology Like school psychologists, educational psychologists are concerned with helping students learn. But they generally focus on course planning and instructional methods for an entire school system rather than on designing a program of study for an individual student.

Educational psychologists are concerned with theoretical issues that relate to measurement of abilities, learning, and child and adolescent development. Their research interests include the ways in which learning is affected by the following:

- psychological factors, such as motivation, emotions, creativity, and intelligence
- cultural factors, such as religious beliefs and language
- economic factors, such as the level of income earned by a person's family
- instructional methods used in the classroom

Some educational psychologists help prepare standardized tests, such as the Scholastic Aptitude Test (SAT). They study various tests to determine the type of test that can most effectively predict success in college. They may also examine individual test items to determine whether these items adequately test critical thinking skills and make a useful contribution to the test as a whole.

Developmental Psychology Developmental psychologists study the changes that occur throughout a person's life span. These changes can be of the following types:

- physical (including changes in height and weight, adolescent growth, sexual maturity, and the physical aspects of aging)
- emotional (for example, development of self-concept and self-esteem)
- cognitive (such as changes from childhood to adulthood in mental images of the world outside or how children learn right from wrong)
- social (such as formation of bonds between parents and children, relationships with peers, or intimate relationships between adults)

Developmental psychologists also attempt to sort out the relative influences of heredity and the environment on development.

Some developmental psychologists are especially interested in the challenges of adolescence. For example, how do adolescents handle the often contradictory messages of peers (who pressure them to act in one way) and parents (who want them to act in another way)? How can psychologists help parents and school officials encourage adolescents to avoid activities that may be harmful to their physical and psychological well-being? What are the causes of depression and suicide among teens? How can people help prevent these painful situations from occurring?

Personality Psychology Personality psychologists identify human characteristics, or traits. Shyness and friendliness are examples of traits. Personality psychologists look for the many different traits people have and study the traits' development. Personality psychologists share with clinical psychologists an interest in the origins of psychological problems and disorders. These psychologists are also concerned with issues such as anxiety, aggression, and gender roles. Gender roles are the behavior patterns expected of women and men in a given culture.

Social Psychology Social psychologists are concerned with people's behavior in social situations. Whereas personality psychologists tend to look within people for explanations of behavior, social psychologists generally focus on external influences. Social psychologists study the following issues:

- the ways in which women and men typically behave in a given setting
- the physical and psychological factors that attract people to one another
- the reasons people tend to conform to group standards and expectations
- how people's behavior changes when they are members of a group
- the reasons for and the effects of prejudice and discrimination within various groups and from one group to another
- the situations in which people are hostile and those in which they help others

Experimental Psychology Psychologists in all specialties may conduct experimental research. However, experimental psychologists conduct research into basic processes

CAREERS IN PSYCHOLOGY

Specialized Fields

There is an astoundingly diverse range of specialized fields in psychology and a wide variety of settings in which psychologists work. Here are a few examples.

Environmental Psychology

Does crowding in cities make people irritable? Does smog have an effect on people's ability to learn? Environmental psychologists ask such questions. They focus on the ways in which people influence and are influenced by their physical environment. Environmental psychologists study whether buildings and cities serve human needs. They also investigate the psychological effects of extremes in temperature, noise, and lighting.

such as the functions of the nervous system. Other basic processes include sensation and perception, learning and memory, and thinking and motivation.

Experimental psychologists explore the biological and psychological reasons for cognitive behavior. Some combine the two and focus on the relationships between biological changes (such as the release of hormones into the bloodstream) and psychological events (such as feelings of anxiety). These psychologists are called biological psychologists.

Experimental psychologists are more likely than other psychologists to engage in basic research. **Basic research** is research that has no immediate application and is done for its own sake. The findings of experimental psychologists are often put into practice by other psychological specialists. For example, basic research into motivation has helped clinical and counseling psychologists develop ways of helping people control their eating habits. Basic research into learning and memory has helped educational psychologists enhance learning conditions in schools.

Reading Check **Infer** Which types of psychologists might treat patients with eating disorders?

Environmental psychologists study how light affects mood in patients with Seasonal Affective Disorder, also known as winter depression.

Comparative Psychology

What do bats have in common with dolphins? How does the prehistoric rhinoceros compare with the modern rhino? Comparative psychologists study animal behavior to try to answer such questions. They also compare the similarities and differences among different animals—modern and ancient—to gain an understanding of evolutionary relationships. The work of Charles Darwin inspired modern research on animal behavior. Today comparative psychology is a multidisciplinary field that includes the contributions of psychologists, biologists, anthropologists, ecologists, geneticists, and many others.

Consumer Psychology

Have you ever noticed that in many supermarkets, milk is shelved far away from the store entrance? Its placement results from the work of consumer psychologists, who study and predict the behavior of shoppers. Milk is placed at the rear of the store because it is an item that many people buy frequently. Its placement ensures that shoppers will pass—and perhaps buy—other items on the way to the milk shelf. Consumer psychologists also assist others in applying the findings of their studies. For instance, they work with advertisers to create effective newspaper ads and television commercials.

Applied Fields in Psychology

You have already read about sports psychologists and how they can help athletes. There are several other specialties in psychology.

Industrial and Organizational Psychology

Industrial psychologists focus on people and work. Organizational psychologists study the behavior of people in organizations, such as business firms. Industrial psychology and organizational psychology are closely related. Psychologists in these fields are often trained in both areas.

Industrial and organizational psychologists are employed by corporations to improve working conditions and increase worker output. They may assist in hiring, training, and promoting employees. They may also devise psychological tests for job applicants and conduct research into the factors that contribute to job satisfaction. In addition, some industrial and organizational psychologists help employees who have problems on the job.

Human Factors Psychology

Human factors psychology is somewhat related to industrial and organizational psychology. Psychologists in this field attempt to find the best ways to design products for people to use. These products include those that are used in schools, the workplace, and the home. Human factors psychologists consider the following when they become involved in the design of a product:

- how people will use a particular product
- how the product affects people in their daily lives
- the shape, look, and feel of the product
- how to engineer the product so that it is safe, comfortable to use, and durable

Community Psychology

Community psychologists study and help create social systems that promote and foster individual well-being. These social systems might include mental health centers, hospital programs, and school-based programs. Community psychologists focus on the following:

- promoting change in the social environment rather than in the individual
- helping relatively powerless social groups, such as children and the elderly, develop coping strategies
- preventing threats to mental health in the social environment

Forensic Psychology When an attorney wants an expert witness to testify whether a person accused of a crime is or is not competent to stand trial, the attorney might call on a forensic psychologist. These psychologists work within the criminal justice system. In addition to testifying about the psychological competence of defendants, they may explain how certain kinds of psychological problems give rise to criminal behavior. Police departments employ psychologists to do some of the following jobs:

- assist in the selection of police officers
- help police officers cope with job stress
- train police officers in the handling of dangerous situations they may encounter, such as suicide threats, hostage crises, and family violence

Health Psychology Health psychologists examine the ways in which behavior and mental processes are related to physical health. They often work with many different health care professionals, including physicians, nurses, dentists, and dieticians. Health psychologists study the effects of stress on health problems such as headaches and heart disease. Many also focus on prevention and reducing the risk of disease. For instance, they help people adopt healthful behaviors such as a balanced diet and exercising.

Rehabilitation Psychology Psychologists in this field work with patients who are struggling with the effects of a disability. A disability is a condition that limits physical, sensory, cognitive, or emotional functioning. Rehabilitation psychologists may work with patients who are dealing with the effects of stroke, brain disease, amputation, or vision impairment. People with disabilities may have difficulty working, taking care of themselves or their families, or engaging in normal activities. Rehabilitation psychologists help their patients develop strategies to compensate for the disability and live meaningful lives.

Cross-Cultural Psychology Traditionally, psychology studies have focused on people in industrialized nations. Cross-cultural psychologists, on the other hand, study behavior and mental processes under different cultural conditions. For instance, they examine such issues as depression and anxiety to gauge whether these concepts are perceived differently in different cultures.

Cross-cultural psychologists have been able to bring new insights to standard psychological theories. For example, they have discovered that visual perception develops differently in cultures as a result of the shapes and angles people are exposed to every day.

Reading Check **Summarize** What do forensic psychologists do?

Online Quiz **THINK** central · thinkcentral.com

SECTION 2 Assessment

Reviewing Main Ideas and Vocabulary

1. **Describe** What are some of the typical problems that a school psychologist might encounter?

2. **Recall** Which field of psychology focuses on the engineering and design of products used in everyday life?

Thinking Critically

3. **Compare and Contrast** In what way does the role of a psychiatrist and that of a psychologist differ?

4. **Draw Conclusions** Social psychologists study group dynamics. Why do you think people's behavior may change when they are part of a group?

5. **Evaluate** What are some of the difficulties that cross-cultural psychologists might encounter when they conduct their research?

6. **Categorize** Using your notes and a graphic organizer like the one below, identify the psychologists who might work in a school setting and explain what their role would be in that setting.

Psychologist	Role

FOCUS ON WRITING

7. **Expository** If you decided to become a psychologist, which field would you prefer? Explain your choice in a paragraph.

PSYCHOLOGY IN TODAY'S WORLD

Inside the Criminal Mind

A horrific crime is committed. Police detectives and forensic experts study the crime scene in minute detail. But in addition to the officers, a psychological profiler examines the evidence. After he inspects the body, evaluates the footprint on the dusty floor, and scrutinizes the cryptic message scrawled on the wall, the profiler declares that the suspect is a young, white male who lives with his parents and is uncomfortable around women. Is he right? Probably not.

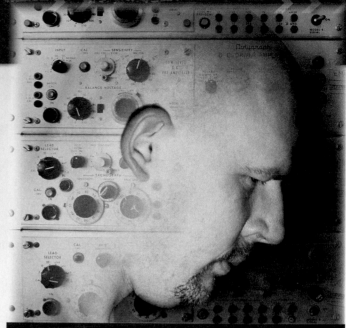

For years, science has tried to probe the workings of the mind.

Popularized in television shows and movies, the profiler is a celebrated figure in forensic psychology. Yet some have compared profilers to psychics or astrologers because they often give a broad description of a suspect that could fit just about anyone. In fact, even when the description almost completely misses the mark, investigators tend to remember the few details the profiler got right: He *was* wearing a double-breasted suit, and he *does* live with his mother. Unfortunately, the truly salient details about his age, ethnicity, and personality were completely wrong.

Perhaps people just want to believe that we possess the ability to see inside a criminal's mind. This

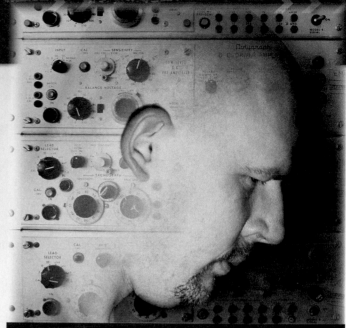

A polygraph measures such processes as blood pressure, respiration, and heart rate, but does it show when someone is lying?

might explain the fascination with lie-detector tests. Even though experts have concluded that the polygraph, which measures the physical changes that occur in reaction to questions, is unreliable, thousands of polygraph tests are conducted every year. Many who support the use of polygraphs claim that they are accurate 90 percent of the time. However, that also means that the polygraph fails one out of ten times—unacceptable odds for innocent suspects. Not surprisingly, the results of polygraph tests are not admissible in court.

Other methods for detecting lies have been devised. For instance, some psychologists claim that liars betray themselves by their behavior. Liars, they say, are likely to speak more slowly, shift in their chair, and nervously fuss with their hair. The trouble is, this profile could also describe the behavior of a person who is afraid of being disbelieved.

One of the latest developments in criminal mind-reading lies in the use of brain imaging. Scientists have used magnetic resonance imaging (MRI) scans for years to identify neurological disorders. Now some researchers believe that the scans can be used

to detect lies. MRI scans show the changes in blood flow when the brain performs mental processes. Since lying is believed to require more cognitive activity, the scans will reveal more blood flow when someone does not tell the truth. But many psychologists remain unconvinced. They question the assumption behind all lie-detector tests: that lying is in some way upsetting to the liar.

Unfortunately, criminals—like everyone else—are not so easily profiled. As much as we would like to believe that their actions will unmask them or that their hearts will race when they tell a lie, it doesn't usually work that way. In the meantime, psychologists will continue to explore the human mind, and maybe someday we'll be better able to tell who's lying and who's not.

Thinking Critically

1. **Infer** Why do people want to believe that a reliable lie-detector test can be developed?

2. **Discuss** Do you think a reasonable profile of a suspect can ever be deduced from crime scene evidence? Why or why not?

A History of Psychology

Before You Read

Main Idea

Since ancient times, philosophers and scientists have studied behavior and mental processes. Psychologists throughout history have continued to refine and develop these studies.

Reading Focus

1. What were some early views and beliefs about human behavior?
2. Who were some of the pioneers of psychology?
3. What modern developments in psychology have dominated much of the 20th century?

Vocabulary

introspection
associationism
structuralism
functionalism
psychoanalysis
psychodynamic thinking
behaviorism
Gestalt psychology

TAKING NOTES Use a graphic organizer like this one to take notes on the different schools of psychology.

School	Ideas

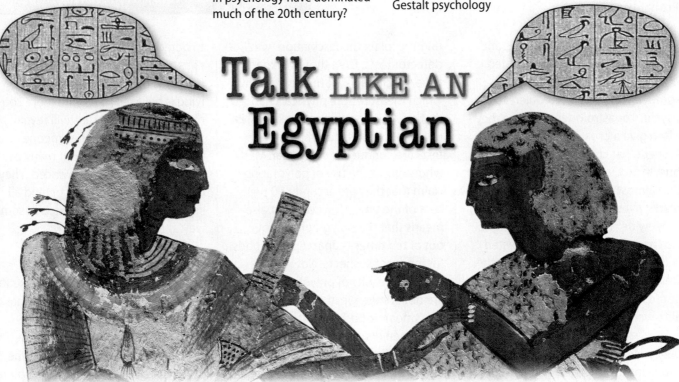

Talk LIKE AN Egyptian

PSYCHOLOGY CLOSE UP

What was the first psychological study? According to Greek historian Herodotus, the first recorded psychological study in history took place in Egypt in the latter half of the 600s B.C. Psamtik I, the king of Egypt at the time, wanted to prove that the Egyptian civilization was the oldest on earth. To test his hypothesis, Psamtik selected two babies from a lower-class family and gave them over to the care of a local shepherd. The shepherd was given strict instructions to treat the children well but to never speak a word to them. The king believed that, without any prompting, the children would naturally speak what he considered to be the original and most ancient language of humankind—Egyptian.

Unfortunately, Psamtik's hypothesis proved false. When the children were about two years old, the shepherd reported that they had uttered a word that sounded like *becos*. No doubt the children had just been babbling, but the king was greatly encouraged. It turned out, however, that *becos* was not an Egyptian word. It was Phrygian for *bread*. The heartbroken king came to the conclusion that the Phrygians were a more ancient people than the Egyptians.

Today, of course, we know that children who are not exposed to speech will not spontaneously speak any language at all, much less Egyptian. However, Psamtik did question how the mind works. That would be the focus of psychological studies for the next 2,600 years. ■

Early Views and Beliefs

We have always been interested in the behaviors of others. Thus psychology is as old as human history. Written accounts of the interest in people's actions, motives, and thoughts can be traced as far back as the philosophers and scientists of ancient times.

Ancient Greece More than 2,000 years ago, Plato (428–348 or 347 B.C.), a student of the philosopher Socrates in ancient Greece, recorded his teacher's advice: "Know thyself." This phrase has remained an important motto of psychological study ever since. Socrates suggested that we can learn much about ourselves by carefully examining our own thoughts and feelings. Psychologists call this method of learning **introspection,** which means "looking within."

One of Plato's students, Greek philosopher Aristotle (384–322 B.C.), raised many questions about human behavior that are still discussed. Aristotle outlined the laws of **associationism,** which are still at the heart of learning theory more than 2,000 years later. He showed how experiences often remind us of similar experiences in the past, how the face of a loved one makes us feel secure, and how thought leads to ideas as we dream and as we daydream. One of Aristotle's works is called *Peri Psyches,* which means "about the mind." Aristotle's approach was scientific. He argued that human behavior, like the movements of the stars and the seas, is subject to certain rules and laws. He believed one such universal law was that people are motivated to seek pleasure and to avoid pain—a view still found in some modern psychological theories. *Peri Psyches* also explores topics such as sensation and perception, thought, intelligence, needs and motives, feelings and emotions, and memory.

The ancient Greeks also theorized about various psychological problems, such as confusion and bizarre behavior. Throughout human history, many people have attributed such disorders to supernatural forces. The ancient Greeks generally believed that the gods punished people for wrongdoing by causing them confusion and madness. However, the Greek physician Hippocrates (c. 460–c. 377 B.C.) rejected these beliefs. He suggested that such problems are caused by

Early Psychologists In ancient cultures, a shaman was believed to cure what would be considered psychological disorders today by consulting the spirit world. Here, people honor a contemporary shaman in a traditional ceremony in Mongolia. *Why might people have looked to shamans and the spirit world for answers to their disorders?*

abnormalities in the brain and had a rational explanation. This idea that biological factors can affect our thoughts, feelings, and behavior influenced thinking about psychology for more than 2,000 years.

The Middle Ages Greek thinking about the human mind was lost during the Middle Ages. Most Europeans of this period believed that problems such as agitation and confusion were signs of possession by demons. A popular belief of the time was that possession was punishment for sins or the result of deals that those afflicted had made with the devil.

Certain "tests" were used to determine whether a person was possessed. One of the most infamous tests, the water-float test, was based on the principle that pure metals sink to the bottom during the smelting process whereas impure metals float to the surface. Individuals who were suspected of being possessed were thrown into deep water. Suspects who managed to keep their heads above water were assumed to be impure and in league with the devil. They were judged to be guilty and were then executed for associating with the devil. Those who sank to the bottom, on the other hand, were judged to be pure. Unfortunately, they met the same fate as the "guilty"—they died.

Reading Check **Summarize** What basic foundations of psychology did the ancient Greeks set forth?

Structuralism

Wilhelm Wundt

- Because Wundt established psychology as a field of study separate from philosophy and the natural sciences, Wundt is considered one of the founders of modern psychology.
- The lab Wundt set up in 1879 is still in operation today.
- He viewed mental processes as activities and classified feelings as pleasant or unpleasant, tense or relaxed, and excited or depressed.

Functionalism

William James

- In addition to being the father of American psychology, James is considered one of America's greatest philosophers.
- Trained in medicine, James commented that the first lecture on psychology he ever heard was the first one he presented as a new instructor at Harvard.
- He believed that since the truth of an idea can never be proved, we should focus instead on how practical or productive an idea is—its "cash value," as he called it.

Pioneers in Psychology

People of the 1500s, 1600s, and 1700s witnessed great scientific and intellectual advances. In the 1500s, for example, Polish astronomer Nicolaus Copernicus challenged the widely held view that the sun revolved around Earth, suggesting instead that Earth revolves around the sun. In the 1600s English scientist Sir Isaac Newton formulated the laws of gravity and motion. English philosopher John Locke, building on principles of associationism, theorized that knowledge is not inborn but is learned from experience. In the late 1700s French scientist Antoine Lavoisier founded the science of chemistry and explained how animals and plants use oxygen in respiration.

The scientific approach also led to the birth of modern psychology in the 1800s. Psychologists argued that ideas about human behavior and mental processes should be supported by evidence. In the late 1800s psychological laboratories were established in Europe and the United States. In these laboratories, psychologists studied behavior and mental processes using a series of experiments to test a single theory—methods similar to those Lavoisier had used to study chemistry. Most historians of psychology point to the year 1879 as the beginning of psychology as a modern laboratory science. In that year, German psychologist Wilhelm Wundt established his laboratory in Leipzig.

Wilhelm Wundt and Structuralism Wilhelm Wundt (1832–1920) and his students founded a field of psychology that came to be known as **structuralism.** Structuralists were concerned with discovering the basic elements of consciousness. Wundt broke down consciousness into objective sensations and subjective feelings. Objective sensations were assumed to accurately reflect the outside world. Subjective feelings were thought to include emotional responses and mental images.

Structuralists believed that the human mind functioned by combining these basic elements of experience. For example, a person can experience an apple objectively by observing its shape, color, texture, and taste. The person can also experience the apple subjectively by remembering how good it feels to bite into one. Using the method of introspection, Wundt and his students carefully examined and reported their experiences.

William James and Functionalism A decade after Wundt established his laboratory, Harvard University professor William James (1842–1910) asserted that conscious experience could not be broken down as structuralists believed. James maintained that experience is a continuous "stream of consciousness." He focused on the relationships between experience and behavior and described his views in *The Principles of Psychology*. Many consider this book, published in 1890, to be the first modern psychology textbook.

ACADEMIC VOCABULARY

stream of consciousness thought regarded as a flowing series of images and ideas running through the mind

Psychoanalysis

Sigmund Freud

- Freud's declaration that people essentially have little free will and are subject to the workings of the unconscious mind was highly revolutionary.

- He psychoanalyzed himself and extensively studied his own dreams, memories, and personality and concluded that he had many mental disorders and fears.

- Many psychologists were initially scandalized by Freud's emphasis on the sexual origins of psychological disorders.

Behaviorism

John B. Watson

- Watson's most famous experiment involved conditioning a small child to fear a white rat by associating the rat with a loud, frightening sound.

- He believed that people have three basic emotional reactions: fear, rage, and love.

B. F. Skinner

- In contrast with Watson, Skinner believed that behavior depended on what happened after a stimulus—an event or sensation—and not before. He called this "operant behavior."

James was one of the founders of the school of **functionalism.** Functionalists were concerned with how mental processes help organisms adapt to their environment. They stressed the application of their findings to everyday situations.

Functionalism differed from structuralism in several ways. Whereas structuralism relied only on introspection, the methods of functionalism included behavioral observation in the laboratory as well as introspection. The structuralists tended to ask: What are the elements (structures) of psychological processes? The functionalists, on the other hand, tended to ask: What are the purposes (functions) of behavior and mental processes? What do certain behaviors and mental processes accomplish for the person (or animal)?

Functionalists proposed that adaptive behavior patterns are learned and maintained because they are successful. Less-adaptive behavior patterns are dropped or are discontinued. Adaptive (successful) actions are repeated and eventually become habits. The formation of habits is seen in such acts as riding a bicycle. At first, this act requires our full attention. But through repetition—and success—it becomes automatic. The multiple tasks involved in learning to type on a keyboard or to write in longhand also become routine through successful repetition. Habit allows us to take the mechanics of typing or writing for granted and to concentrate instead on what we are typing or writing.

Sigmund Freud and Psychoanalysis

Sigmund Freud (1856–1939), a Viennese physician, was perhaps the most famous of the early psychologists. The school of thought that he founded, called **psychoanalysis**, emphasizes the importance of unconscious motives and internal conflicts in determining and understanding human behavior.

Freud's theory, more than the others, has become a part of popular culture. You may be familiar with several Freudian concepts. For example, have you ever tried to interpret a slip of the tongue, or have you ever tried to figure out the meaning of a dream you had? The ideas that people are driven by hidden impulses and that verbal slips and dreams represent unconscious wishes largely reflect Freud's influence on popular culture.

Structuralists and functionalists conducted their research in the laboratory. However, Freud gained his understanding of human behavior through consultations with patients. He encouraged them to talk through their problems, a method that came to be called a "talking cure." Freud was astounded at how little insight these patients had into their own ideas and feelings. The ultimate goal of his consultations was to release the powerful emotional energy that he believed was locked in the unconscious mind. He came to believe that unconscious processes, particularly sexual and aggressive urges, are more important than conscious experience in governing people's behavior and feelings.

Complete a Webquest at thinkcentral.com on Sigmund Freud and psychoanalysis.

Freud's theory, which is sometimes called **psychodynamic thinking,** assumed that most of what exists in an individual's mind is unconscious and consists of conflicting impulses, urges, and wishes. According to Freud's theories, human behavior is aimed at satisfying these desires, even though some of them seem socially inappropriate or even unacceptable. But at the same time, people want to see themselves as good and decent human beings. Freud attempted to help people gain insight into their unconscious conflicts and find socially acceptable ways of expressing their wishes and meeting their needs.

Reading Check **Find the Main Idea** According to Freud, what is the key to people's behavior?

Modern Developments in Psychology

As the 20th century progressed, new psychological theories were proposed. Like the earlier pioneers, modern psychologists focused on behavioral and cognitive approaches.

John B. Watson and Behaviorism Picture a hungry rat in a maze. It moves along until it reaches a place where it must turn left or right. If the rat is consistently rewarded with food for turning right at that place, it will learn to turn right when it arrives there the next time—at least, when it is hungry. But what does the rat *think* when it is learning to turn right at that place in the maze?

Does it seem absurd to try to place yourself in the mind of a rat? It did to John B. Watson (1878–1958) when he was asked by examiners to consider this question as a requirement for his doctoral degree in psychology.

The question was part of the exam because functionalism was the dominant school of psychology at the time. Watson agreed with the functionalist focus on the importance of learning, but he believed that it was unscientific to study a construct like consciousness—particularly the consciousness of animals. He saw consciousness as a private event that is known only to the individual. He asserted that if psychology was to be a natural science, like physics or chemistry, it must be limited to observable, measurable events—that is, to behavior. As the founder of the school of **behaviorism,** Watson defined psychology as the scientific study of observable behavior.

Watson once famously claimed that he could take a group of healthy children and train them to become doctors or lawyers or any other kind of specialist. With this claim, Watson laid the foundation for the classic behaviorist belief: Regardless of who we think we really are inside, we can be totally conditioned by external events. Our belief in individual choice is just an illusion.

GESTALT DRAWINGS

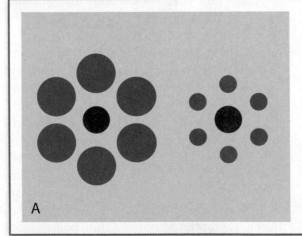

These drawings demonstrate the idea that the perception of something is affected by the context in which it occurs. Two images that are identical may appear to be different if their surroundings are different.

Skills Focus **INTERPRETING VISUALS**

In Drawing A, are the two dark blue circles the same size? In Drawing B, what is the second symbol in each row?

B. F. Skinner and Reinforcement Harvard University psychologist B. F. Skinner (1904–1990) added to the behaviorist tradition by introducing the concept of reinforcement. Skinner showed that when an animal is reinforced, or rewarded, for performing an action, it is more likely to perform that action again in the future. He demonstrated that laboratory animals, such as rats and pigeons, are capable of learning complex behavior patterns if they are reinforced in the right ways. Behaviorists have taught animals to push buttons, climb ladders, push toys across the floor, and even shoot baskets by rewarding the animals for performing the desired behavior.

According to Skinner, people learn in the same way animals do. Like animals, people learn to behave in certain ways because they have received the positive or negative reinforcement that guides their behavior.

Skinner scorned the efforts of other psychologists to try to understand the inner person. He believed that the effort to study personalities and feelings was unscientific. According to Skinner, all we can know are the external causes of behavior and what happens as a result of that behavior. "Thinking is behaving," he claimed. "The mistake is in allocating the behavior to the mind."

The Gestalt School **Gestalt psychology** developed as an alternative to behaviorism and structuralism. German psychologists Max Wertheimer, Kurt Koffka, and Wolfgang Köhler felt that behaviorism was only concerned with treating a specific problem outside of its larger context. These psychologists were fascinated by the ways in which context influences people's interpretation of information. They formed the core of the school of Gestalt psychology in the early 20th century. The psychology of *Gestalt,* which means "shape" or "form" in German, is based on the idea that our perceptions of objects are more than the sums of their parts. Rather, they are wholes that give shape, or meaning, to the parts. As such, Gestalt psychology rejects the structuralist idea that experience can be broken down into individual parts or elements.

This theory can be demonstrated with a few basic principles. One of the principles is similarity. According to this principle, when objects look similar, people tend to recognize a pattern and perceive them as a united whole. According to the principle of closure, people fill in the missing information when enough of the shape of an object is indicated.

Gestalt psychologists also reject the behaviorist notion that psychologists should concentrate only on observable behavior. In addition, Gestalt psychologists believe that learning is active and purposeful. They disagree with the behaviorist view that learning is mechanical.

Köhler and the other founders of Gestalt psychology demonstrated that much learning, particularly problem solving, is accomplished by insight, not by mechanical repetition. Insight is the reorganization of perceptions that enables an individual to solve a problem. In other words, insight is the sudden appearance of the Gestalt, or form, that enables the individual to see the solution.

Reading Check **Draw Conclusions** How do you think B. F. Skinner would view introspection?

Online Quiz **THINK** central thinkcentral.com

SECTION 3 Assessment

Reviewing Main Ideas and Vocabulary

1. **Recall** What are the laws of associationism?
2. **Identify** Who established the world's first psychology lab?

Thinking Critically

3. **Draw Conclusions** How did the scientific method, which began to be applied in the mid-1500s, influence the development of psychology?
4. **Interpret** According to Gestalt psychology, what is the relationship of something's parts to the whole?
5. **Support a Position** Do you agree with John B. Watson that a child can be trained to become a doctor, lawyer, or other specialist? Explain your answer.
6. **Compare and Contrast** Using your notes and a graphic organizer like the one below, describe the main differences between structuralism and functionalism and what they have in common.

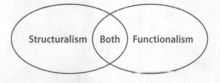

Structuralism | Both | Functionalism

FOCUS ON WRITING

7. **Descriptive** Describe a psychological problem that Sigmund Freud might find interesting.

Contemporary Perspectives

Before You Read

Main Idea

Contemporary psychologists have been influenced by the work of earlier pioneers. They have expanded traditional research to develop new and different approaches.

Reading Focus

1. What is the role of biology in behavior and survival?

2. What role does the mind play in determining behavior?

3. How does the role of experience affect behavior?

4. What factors influence the biopsychosocial perspective?

Vocabulary

biological perspective
evolutionary perspective
cognitive perspective
humanistic perspective
psychoanalytic
  perspective
learning perspective
social-learning theory
sociocultural perspective

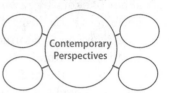

TAKING NOTES Use a graphic organizer like this one to take notes on contemporary perspectives on psychology.

Contemporary Perspectives

Can you tell what emotions this woman is expressing?

Another Kind of Smart

PSYCHOLOGY CLOSE UP

What's your EQ? By the 1990s, some psychologists had begun to claim that our EQ, or emotional quotient, is as important—if not more so—than our IQ, or intelligence quotient. Emotional intelligence refers to the ability to recognize and understand your own feelings as well as those of others. Psychologists first developed a technique for measuring emotional intelligence by testing how well subjects could identify emotions in other people's facial expressions.

Some researchers believe that emotional intelligence can be learned. They claim that people who learn how to understand and control their emotions can live more contented lives. Yet critics of emotional intelligence say that different emotions, like different types of intelligence, should be examined separately. Not everyone, after all, can master all emotions. Some people may be good at handling anger, for example, but not fear. The critics also claim that not every situation calls for the same emotion; a wide range of emotional responses may be appropriate.

Emotional intelligence is just one of the theories contemporary psychologists are studying. In this section, you will learn about other avenues of research in the ever-expanding science of psychology. ■

The Role of Biology

Today few psychologists describe themselves as structuralists or functionalists. Few would consider themselves Gestalt psychologists, although the school of Gestalt psychology has inspired current research in perception and problem solving. The numbers of traditional behaviorists and psychoanalysts also have been declining.

Nevertheless, the historical traditions of psychology find expression in contemporary perspectives on psychology. Each perspective emphasizes different topics of investigation and has different approaches. An important approach focuses on the role of biology.

The Biological Perspective The **biological perspective** of psychology emphasizes the influence of biology on our behavior. This perspective has roots in associationism. Psychologists assume that our mental processes—our thoughts, fantasies, and dreams—are made possible by the nervous system. They point particularly to its key component, the brain. Biologically oriented psychologists look for the connections between events in the brain, such as the activity of brain cells, and behavior and mental processes. They use several technologies, such as CAT scans and PET scans, to show which parts of the brain are involved in various mental processes. Biological psychology has shown that certain parts of the brain are highly active when we listen to music, other parts are active when we solve math problems, and still other parts are involved with certain psychological disorders. Biological psychologists have also learned that certain chemicals in the brain are connected with the storage of information—that is, the formation of memories.

Moreover, biological psychologists are interested in the influences of hormones and genes. Hormones are chemicals that glands release into the bloodstream to set in motion various body functions, such as growth or digestion. Genes are the basic units of heredity. Biological psychologists study the influences of genes on personality traits, psychological health, and various behavior patterns.

The Evolutionary Perspective Tied to biology, the **evolutionary perspective** focuses on the evolution of behavior and mental processes.

British scientist Charles Darwin theorized that in the struggle for survival, the most adaptive organisms have a greater chance of enduring. For example, people who are naturally resistant to certain diseases are more likely to transmit their genes to future generations. Evolutionary psychologists suggest that many kinds of behavior patterns, such as aggression, are examples of adaptive behavior. These psychologists believe that people learn to act in certain ways for their survival and then pass this behavior down.

Reading Check **Draw Conclusions** What role does biology play in our mental processes?

The Role of the Mind

For centuries, philosophers and scientists have been intrigued by the workings of the mind. It is not surprising, therefore, that many contemporary psychologists emphasize the role of cognition.

The Cognitive Perspective The **cognitive perspective** emphasizes the role that thoughts play in determining behavior. Cognitive psychologists study mental processes to understand human nature. They investigate the ways in which people perceive information and make mental images of the world, solve problems, and dream and daydream. Cognitive psychologists, in short, study what we refer to as the mind.

The cognitive tradition has roots in Socrates' maxim "Know thyself" and in his method of introspection for learning about the self. Cognitive psychology also has roots in structuralism, functionalism, and Gestalt psychology. Each of these schools of thought has addressed issues that are of interest to cognitive psychologists.

Another aspect of the cognitive perspective involves information processing. Many cognitive psychologists have been influenced by computer science. They see the computer as a metaphor for the brain. Computers process information to solve problems. Information is first fed into the computer. The information is then placed in the working memory while the computer processes it. After processing, the information is stored more or less permanently on the computer's hard drive, a compact disk, or another storage device.

Birth Order

According to some who follow the psychoanalytic perspective, the order in which one is born into a family can have a major impact on personality.

First-Born Children First-borns tend to be high-achievers, responsible, and conservative.

Middle Children Middle children tend to be even-tempered, loyal, and hard-working.

Last-Born Children Last-born children tend to be likeable, spontaneous, and persistent.

Only Children Only children tend to be confident, intelligent, and organized.

Many psychologists speak of people as having working memories and storage facilities (or long-term memories). If information has been placed in computer storage or in a person's long-term memory, it must first be retrieved before it can be worked on again. To retrieve information from computer storage, people must know the name of the data file and the process for retrieving data files. Similarly, cognitive psychologists believe people need certain cues to retrieve information from their long-term memories. Otherwise, it is lost to them.

Cognitive psychologists sometimes refer to our strategies for solving problems as our "software." In this computer metaphor, our brains are the "hardware" that runs our mental programs. In other words, our brains are our own *very* personal computers.

Cognitive psychologists believe that people's behavior is influenced by their values, their perceptions, and their choices. For example, an individual who interprets a casual remark as an insult may react with hostility. But the same remark directed at another person might be perceived very differently by that person and thus may meet with a completely different reaction.

The Humanistic Perspective The **humanistic perspective** stresses the human capacity for self-fulfillment and the importance of consciousness, self-awareness, and the capacity to make choices. Consciousness is seen by humanistic psychologists as the force that shapes human personality.

Humanistic psychology considers people's personal experiences to be the most important aspect of psychology. Humanistic psychologists believe that self-awareness, experience, and choice permit us to "invent ourselves." In other words, they enable us to fashion our growth and our ways of relating to the world as we go through life. Unlike the behaviorists, who assume that behavior is caused largely by the stimuli that act upon us, humanistic psychologists believe that we are free to choose our own behavior.

The humanistic perspective views people as basically good and desiring to be helpful to others. Humanistic psychologists help people explore their feelings, manage their negative impulses, and realize their potential.

Critics of the humanistic perspective, particularly behaviorists, insist that psychology should be scientific and address only observable events. They argue that people's inner experiences are unsuited to scientific observation and measurement. However, humanistic psychologists insist that inner experience is vital to the understanding of human nature.

The Psychoanalytic Perspective As you have learned, the **psychoanalytic perspective** stresses the influence of unconscious forces on human behavior. In the 1940s and 1950s, psychoanalytic theory dominated the practice of psychotherapy and greatly influenced psychology and the arts. Although psychoanalytic thought no longer dominates psychology, its influence continues to be felt. Psychologists who follow Sigmund Freud's approach today focus less on the roles of unconscious sexual and aggressive impulses and more on conscious choice.

Freud believed that aggressive impulses are common reactions to the frustrations of daily life and that we seek to vent these impulses on other people. Because we fear rejection or retaliation, we put most aggressive impulses out of our minds. But by holding aggression in, we set the stage for future explosions. Pent-up aggressive impulses demand outlets. Partial outlets can be provided by physical activity. Unfortunately, we may also direct hostile impulses toward strangers.

Reading Check **Compare and Contrast** How do humanistic and psychoanalytic psychologists differ in their views of what drives behavior?

The Role of Experience

Many psychologists study the impact of environment on behavior and mental processes. Environment includes all the ways in which someone experiences the world.

The Learning Perspective The **learning perspective** emphasizes the effects of experience on behavior. In the views of many psychologists, learning is the essential factor in observing, describing, explaining, predicting, and controlling behavior. However, the term *learning* can have different meanings in psychology. For example, behaviorists and social-learning theorists have different attitudes toward the role of consciousness in learning.

John B. Watson and other behaviorists found no role for consciousness. They believed that people act and react because of their learning histories and the influence of their situations, not because of conscious choice. Behaviorists emphasize the importance of environmental influences and focus on the learning of habits through repetition and reinforcement.

In contrast, **social-learning theory** suggests that people can change their environments or create new ones. Furthermore, social-learning theory holds that people can learn intentionally by observing others. However, people's expectations and values influence whether they *choose* to do what they have learned how to do.

Psychologists who take the learning perspective believe that behavior is learned either from direct experience or by observing other people. For example, people will behave a certain way when they expect to be rewarded for that behavior. Like cognitive theorists, social-learning theorists believe that people act in a particular way only when they recognize that the circumstances call for that behavior. For example, we act with friendliness when we are treated well.

Contemporary Psychological Perspectives

These eight broad perspectives are the most common ways that contemporary psychologists view behavior today.

Perspective	Subject Matter	Key Assumption	Influenced By
Biological	Nervous system, glands and hormones, genetic factors	Biological processes influence behavior and mental processes.	Associationism and neuroscience
Evolutionary	Physical traits, social behavior	Adaptive organisms survive and transmit their genes to future generations.	Charles Darwin and evolution
Cognitive	Interpretation of mental images, thinking, language	Perceptions and thoughts influence behavior.	Structuralism, functionalism, and Gestalt psychology
Humanistic	Self-concept	People make free and conscious choices based on their unique experiences.	Introspection and belief in free will
Psychoanalytic	Unconscious processes, early childhood experiences	Unconscious motives influence behavior.	Sigmund Freud
Learning	Environmental influences, learning, observational learning	Personal experiences and reinforcement guide individual development.	John B. Watson and behaviorism
Sociocultural	Ethnicity, gender, culture, religion, socio-economic status	Sociocultural, biological, and psychological factors create individual differences.	Social, environmental, and cross-cultural psychology
Biopsychosocial	Biology, psychology, social factors	Mental processes are influenced by the interaction of biological, psychological, and social factors.	Holistic health and social psychology

The Sociocultural Perspective Those psychologists who adhere to the **sociocultural perspective** study the influences of ethnicity, gender, culture, and socio-economic status on behavior and mental processes. By taking these factors into account, psychologists can better understand how people act and think.

One kind of diversity involves ethnicity. Members of an ethnic group are united by their cultural heritage, race, language, or common history. The sociocultural perspective helps people appreciate the cultural heritages and historical issues of various ethnic groups. Some of the psychological issues related to ethnicity are the following: the inclusion of people from various ethnic minority groups in psychological studies, bilingualism, ethnic differences in intelligence test scores, ethnic differences in vulnerability to health problems ranging from obesity to high blood pressure and cancer, and prejudice.

Sociocultural theorists also study gender, which is the state of being male or being female. Gender is not simply a matter of anatomy. It involves a complex web of cultural expectations and social roles that affect people's self-concepts and aspirations as well as their behavior.

Reading Check **Find the Main Idea** How can ethnicity and gender affect cultural expectations and social roles?

The Biopsychosocial Perspective

According to the biopsychosocial perspective, mental processes are influenced by the interaction of biological processes, psychological dispositions, and social factors. This holistic approach is actually very old, dating back to the time of the ancient Greeks.

The modern model for the approach was developed by American physician George Engel in relation to the treatment of heart disease. Engel suggested that the biological progress of heart disease should not be studied in isolation. The impact on the patient of cultural, social, and psychological factors also needs to be considered. Genetic predispositions to the disease, for instance, as well as the patient's diet, exercise, stress levels, and financial status should be taken into account. According to Engel, a physician's ability to treat the disease would be severely limited without an understanding of the psychosocial interactions with the cardiovascular system.

In recent years, biopsychosocial psychologists have taken the approach a step further. Some psychologists now claim that our social relationships from birth have a direct impact on our biological development.

Reading Check **Make Generalizations** What generalization can you make about the relation of the biopsychosocial approach to other psychological perspectives?

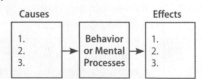
Online Quiz THINK central thinkcentral.com

SECTION 4 Assessment

Reviewing Main Ideas and Vocabulary

1. Identify What metaphor do cognitive psychologists use to describe the functioning of the brain?

2. Describe How do humanistic psychologists view people?

Thinking Critically

3. Explain According to the biological perspective, what occurs during our activities and mental processes?

4. Contrast How do learning theorists differ from social-learning theorists in their ideas on behavior?

5. Develop What are some questions that a psychologist who is following the biopsychosocial approach might ask of a new cancer patient?

6. Identify Cause and Effect Select one of the perspectives you have read about. Then, using your notes and a graphic organizer like the one below, list what the theorists of this perspective believe are the causes and effects of behavior or mental processes.

Causes		Effects
1. 2. 3.	Behavior or Mental Processes	1. 2. 3.

FOCUS ON WRITING

7. Persuasive Write an e-mail in which you encourage a friend to seek help from a psychologist who specializes in one of the approaches you have learned about in this section.

Bringing Diversity into Psychology

Like many other academic fields, psychology was dominated in the past by white men. Not only were the psychologists themselves mostly white men, but most of their research used white male participants and tended to explore issues that were relevant primarily to white men. In recent decades, however, that has changed.

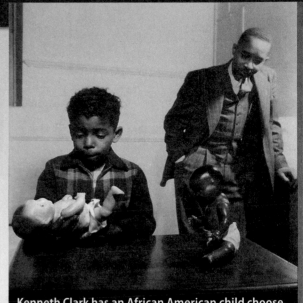

Kenneth Clark has an African American child choose the "nice" doll in his landmark study on the effects of segregation.

Many psychologists today are women and members of traditionally under-represented ethnic groups. In fact, white men now obtain fewer than half of the doctoral degrees in psychology. African Americans make up 6 percent to 7 percent of the first-year students in doctoral departments in psychology, and Hispanics make up 5 percent. Two thirds of the doctoral degrees in psychology are awarded to women.

Not only are psychologists as a group more diverse now than they used to be, so is their research. A great deal of current psychological research deals with questions of gender, culture, prejudice, and stereotypes. The work of African American psychologist Kenneth Bancroft Clark exemplifies such research.

Clark was born in the Panama Canal Zone in 1914, the son of West Indian parents. Miriam Clark, his mother, brought her children to the United States for their education. They settled in the Harlem section of New York City.

Although most African American children at the time were advised to attend vocational high schools, where they could learn specific job skills, Kenneth Clark attended an academic high school. He went on to Howard University in Washington, D.C., where he majored in psychology and married Mamie Phipps. The Clarks then attended Columbia University, where they both earned Ph.D. degrees in psychology.

In 1946 the Clarks founded the Northside Center for Child Development. Kenneth and Mamie Clark's clinical work led to several studies showing the negative effect of segregation on the self-esteem of African American children. In one well-known study from 1947, African American children were asked to choose between white and black dolls after being given instructions such as "Give me the pretty doll" or "Give me the doll that looks bad." The Clarks reported that most children preferred the white dolls over the black ones and concluded that the children were demonstrating their feelings that society as a whole pre-ferred white people.

In the early 1950s Kenneth Clark began working with the National Association for the Advancement of Colored People (NAACP) to end school segregation. In 1954, when the Supreme Court overturned the "separate but equal" doctrine, it cited Clark's ground-breaking work on the effects of discrimination on the personality development of both African American and white children. In his book, *Prejudice and Your Child*, published in 1955, Clark described the effects of segregation on white children as well as those on African American children.

Clark's later work examined the quality of education and the prob-lems of juvenile delinquency and crime. He was among the first experts to recommend preschool classes, after-school programs, and commu-nity participation. His efforts encour-aged society to re-evaluate and rede-fine racial identity in America.

Thinking Critically

1. **Elaborate** What do you think might have been the effects of segregation on white children?

2. **Discuss** Why is it important for psy-chologists of different genders and cultural backgrounds to carry out research on behavior and mental pro-cesses?

Public Perceptions of Psychology

What perceptions—and misperceptions—do people have about the field of psychology?

Reading and Activity Workbook

Use the workbook to complete this lab.

1. Introduction

As psychology continues to evolve and expand, many people have questions and misconceptions about what it really involves. This lab will help you understand how psychology, as a field of study, is perceived by the general public. You will conduct a survey, asking some basic questions about psychology. You and your classmates will have decided on the best answer for each question before you begin. Then, in a class discussion, you will compare your survey answers with those of your classmates. You will also compare the answers you receive from survey respondents with the answers your class compiles. In this lab, you will:

■ Select five people outside of your class to take the survey. Make sure the five participants you choose have not been selected by your classmates. (Each student in the class will be choosing five different participants.) You may ask your friends, but be sure to include at least two adults (perhaps a teacher, a parent or other older relative, a neighbor, a store clerk, or a close family friend).

■ Conduct the survey and record the responses. Note that "I don't know" is an acceptable response.

■ Compare your survey with those of your classmates and discuss the responses you receive.

■ Write what you have learned about psychology from conducting the survey.

When you are done with the lab, you may find that you have a greater appreciation for psychology—and even for your psychology class!

2. Conducting the Survey

As a class, discuss possible responses for the eight questions below. Use the chapter and your class notes during the discussion. Then come to a consensus on the best answer for each question. Appoint a recorder to write down the answers you agree upon. Here are the questions you will pose in your survey:

■ What is psychology?

■ What do psychologists do?

■ What are some of the fields in psychology?

■ Where do psychologists work?

■ How long has psychology been a recognized field of study?

■ Who is Sigmund Freud?

■ Who are some other well-known psychologists?

■ From what sources have you derived your information about psychology?

Before you conduct your survey, prepare your questionnaire. Write or type each question on a piece of paper, leaving plenty of room for each response. At the top of the page, write "Name" on one line and "Age" on the line below. This information will help you keep track of your participants. Finally, make four more copies of the questionnaire. You will use one copy for each participant.

When you conduct your survey, remember to maintain a courteous and professional manner—even with your friends. Keep in mind that a survey is a scientific method for collecting data. You will obtain serious responses—and thus useful and valid information—if you treat the exercise seriously.

3. Evaluating the Responses

Study the survey responses you received. Note any patterns in the survey. For example:

- Are there any questions that most of your participants got right or wrong?

- Are there some unusual answers?

- How many people out of the five you surveyed correctly identified Sigmund Freud?

- How many of your participants rely on television and movies for information about psychology?

Summarize your survey results. Be sure to record any unusual answers too. Then write a paragraph in which you reflect on what the results reveal about people's perceptions of psychology.

Successful survey takers engage their participants by asking follow-up questions that begin with "why" and "how."

4. Discussion and Writing

Now get together with a small group of classmates. Compare your survey answers with those of the group and with the agreed-upon answers. Discuss the surveys, focusing on the following questions:

- How do the answers from your participants compare with the answers your class compiled?

- Are people generally knowledgeable about psychology?

- Are there some common misconceptions or misunderstandings about psychology? Why do you believe this is the case?

- How did answers from adults compare with those of your peers?

- Where do people tend to get their information? Do you think these sources are useful or reliable?

- Did your participants tend to confuse the science of psychology with so-called popular psychology?

- Why is it important to study psychology scientifically?

Finally, write a paragraph in which you summarize your own views on some or all of the discussion questions. In addition, address the following: How do you think people can become better educated about the science of psychology? How might they benefit from a better understanding of the field?

When you are done writing, you might want to share your thoughts and ideas with your survey participants. That might be a good first step in clearing up their misconceptions and helping them learn what psychology really entails.

Comprehension and Critical Thinking

SECTION 1 (pp. 4–7)

1. a. Identify What are some examples of cognitive activities?

   b. Summarize How do psychologists help their patients control feelings of anxiety?

   c. Support a Position Do you think it is worthwhile for psychologists to conduct their research using animal subjects? Why or why not?

SECTION 2 (pp. 9–14)

2. a. Recall To which field of psychology does the largest number of psychologists belong?

   b. Draw Conclusions How does the work of experimental psychologists benefit psychologists in other fields?

   c. Evaluate Why do you think there are so many specialties in psychology?

SECTION 3 (pp. 16–21)

3. a. Identify Main Ideas What phrase, dating back to ancient Greece, has remained a motto of psychological study?

   b. Identify Cause and Effect According to psychologist B. F. Skinner, what happens as a result of positive reinforcement?

   c. Make Judgments Judge the impact of Freud on psychological study. Do you think he's had a largely positive impact or a negative one? Explain your ideas.

SECTION 4 (pp. 22–26)

4. a. Describe According to cognitive psychologists, what influences people's behavior?

   b. Compare In what way are the biological and the biopsychosocial perspectives alike?

   c. Support a Position Which perspective do you think reflects the most positive approach to human behavior? Which reflects the most negative approach? Explain your answers.

Reviewing Vocabulary

Match the terms below with their correct definitions.

5. psychology   **10.** psychoanalysis

6. cognitive activities   **11.** behaviorism

7. associationism   **12.** Gestalt psychology

8. structuralism   **13.** social-learning theory

9. functionalism   **14.** ethnic group

A. school of psychology concerned with how mental processes help organisms adapt to environments

B. the study of behavior and mental processes

C. school of psychology based on the idea that our perceptions of objects are more than the sums of their parts

D. mental processes

E. school of psychology concerned with discovering the basic elements of consciousness

F. the theory that people can change their environments or create new ones

G. a group of people who share a common culture, race, or national origin

H. school of psychology concerned with the scientific study of observable actions

I. the theory that experiences often remind us of similar experiences in the past

J. school of psychology that emphasizes the importance of unconscious motives in human behavior

INTERNET ACTIVITY ✳

15. Choose a field in psychology that interests you and research the following questions: What services do psychologists in this field provide? How much money do they make? What important studies are currently being conducted in this field? Present your findings in an oral report.

Psychology in Your Life

16. Watch one of your favorite programs on television—drama or situation comedy—and observe the characters' behaviors. Consider these questions as you watch: What behaviors do you observe? How are the characters' thoughts (or other cognitive activities) and emotions revealed? Choose the character that interests you the most. Then, in a paragraph or two, explain the character's behavior in terms of his or her emotions.

SKILLS ACTIVITY: INTERPRETING GRAPHS

Study the bar graph below. Then use the information to help you answer the questions that follow.

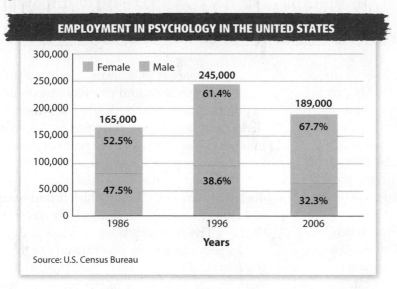

EMPLOYMENT IN PSYCHOLOGY IN THE UNITED STATES

Source: U.S. Census Bureau

17. Compare What percentage of employed psychologists in 2006 were female? How does that number compare with the percentage of male psychologists?

18. Analyze What trends does the graph show?

19. Make Judgments What factors may have encouraged more women to become psychologists in recent years?

WRITING FOR AP PSYCHOLOGY

Use your knowledge of psychology theorists to answer the question below. Do not simply list facts. Present a clear argument based on your critical analysis of the question, using the appropriate psychology terminology.

20. Briefly identify each psychology theorist below. For each one, provide a general description of the theoretical approach he developed and his impact on psychology.
- Sigmund Freud
- John B. Watson
- B. F. Skinner

Connecting Online

Visit thinkcentral.com for review and enrichment activities related to this chapter.

THINK central

Quiz and Review

ONLINE QUIZZES
Take a practice quiz for each section in this chapter.

WEBQUEST
Complete a structured Internet activity for this chapter.

QUICK LAB
Reinforce a key concept with a short lab activity.

APPLYING WHAT YOU'VE LEARNED
Review and apply your knowledge by completing a project-based assessment.

Activities

eACTIVITIES
Complete chapter Internet activities for enrichment.

INTERACTIVE FEATURE
Explore an interactive version of a key feature in this chapter.

KEEP IT CURRENT
Link to current news and research in psychology.

Online Textbook

Click for More

Learn more about key topics in this chapter.

Learning from a FLAWED EXPERIMENT

In 1927, researchers began a study in the Hawthorne plant of the Western Electric Company in Cicero, Illinois. They had been called in by the factory's managers to find out what conditions in the factory might be changed to boost productivity. The researchers designed a study to understand the effect of rest periods, workdays, and work weeks on productivity.

The researchers selected five women as participants in the study. The women were to work as a team in a room where they could be observed. The researchers introduced rest pauses of varying lengths throughout the workday. They observed the women to see how their productivity was affected. The researchers began to shorten the workday and the work week while they observed changes in productivity.

At first, the researchers observed that as they increased rest periods and shortened the workday and work week, the women's overall output increased. It appeared that, with more rest, workers returned to their jobs refreshed and therefore were able to produce more. To check their findings, the researchers slowly returned to the original schedule—with shorter rest periods, a longer workday, and a longer work week.

To the surprise of the researchers, productivity remained higher than it had been at the beginning of the study. How could that be? The research team concluded that the increase in output was caused not by the length of rest periods, workdays, and work weeks, but by the participants' awareness that they were being observed. They felt special because of the attention and they worked harder.

This phenomenon came to be known as the "Hawthorne effect." It was a valuable finding, and led to the theory that one effective way to increase worker productivity was simply to pay more attention to the workers. However, the finding was a result of a flawed study design.

Women factory workers such as these assembled electrical equipment at the Hawthorne plant.

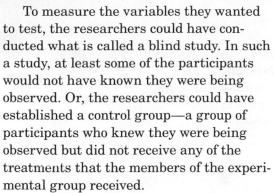

CHAPTER 2
PSYCHOLOGICAL METHODS

To measure the variables they wanted to test, the researchers could have conducted what is called a blind study. In such a study, at least some of the participants would not have known they were being observed. Or, the researchers could have established a control group—a group of participants who knew they were being observed but did not receive any of the treatments that the members of the experimental group received.

The design of the Hawthorne study had some other flaws as well. For one thing, the experimental group was very small. A sample size of five is not large enough for drawing conclusions about the larger population. Furthermore, the sample did not remain constant over the course of the whole experiment. Two of the women in the group were replaced in the middle of the study, for various reasons. Their removal may have biased the results.

Moreover, the researchers may have misinterpreted the results of the study. The conclusion that productivity remained high even after the women returned to the original schedule was not completely correct. Total output stayed about the same, but it was achieved in more hours. In other words, hourly productivity actually dropped. In addition, the researchers never considered that the longer one does a job, the more skilled one becomes. That in itself may increase productivity.

The flaws that were exposed in the Hawthorne plant study make a critical point about the methods of psychological research. Research methods must be sound if the results of the study are to be reliable.

What do you think?

1. What flaws did the Hawthorne study have, and how did these flaws affect the study's outcome?

2. What is the Hawthorne effect, and why do some people question its existence?

Chapter at a Glance

SECTION 1: Conducting Research

■ Scientific research consists of five basic steps: forming a research question, forming a hypothesis, testing the hypothesis, analyzing the results, and drawing conclusions.

■ After the five steps are completed, scientists attempt to replicate the results and often ask new questions based on those results.

SECTION 2: Surveys, Samples, and Populations

■ Scientists use the survey method by interviewing people or distributing questionnaires.

■ Scientists must carefully choose which groups of people they wish to study.

SECTION 3: Using Observation for Research

■ There are a number of other methods of observation besides the survey method: the testing method, the case-study method, the longitudinal and cross-sectional methods, the naturalistic-observation method, and the laboratory-observation method.

■ Correlation describes relationships but does not reveal cause and effect. In analyzing the results of observations, correlation is an important technique.

SECTION 4: Experimental and Ethical Issues

■ Researchers use experiments to answer questions about cause and effect. When conducting experiments, researchers must consider such things as independent and dependent variables, control groups, and the placebo effect.

■ Psychologists follow ethical practices and standards when working with people or animals.

Conducting Research

Before You Read

Main Idea

The steps that scientists follow in conducting research are fundamental to reaching reliable conclusions. Psychologists follow similar steps in conducting their research.

Reading Focus

1. What are the five basic steps in scientific research?
2. What are two further steps involved in scientific research?

Vocabulary

constructs
hypothesis
replicated

TAKING NOTES Use a graphic organizer like this one to record the steps of scientific research.

Steps of Scientific Research
1.
2.
3.
4.
5.

DESCARTES, MIND, AND MATTER

PSYCHOLOGY CLOSE UP

How can a scientific mistake lead to a scientific truth?

René Descartes, a French thinker of the 17th century, wrote a book titled *Meditations on First Philosophy* (1641). In it, he helped to develop the scientific method. For Descartes, the body was matter but the mind was spirit. The question was, how did the two interact? He argued that the mind and body influenced one another through the pineal gland, a small organ in the brain. Descartes thought that all sensations that needed to be combined to be processed—such as the separate images from each eye—come together in the pineal gland. Thus, the pineal gland was a kind of third eye in the brain.

Many years later, the very scientific method that Descartes helped to create provided the means to disprove his theory about the pineal gland. The steps that scientists follow in conducting research are fundamental in reaching solid conclusions. Those same steps are used in psychological research. So, in spite of his faulty pineal gland theory, Descartes can be credited with helping psychology become a real science. ■

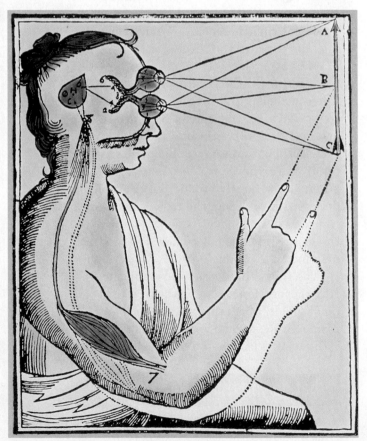

This illustration from a book by Descartes shows how an image is relayed from the eyes to the pineal gland.

The Steps of Scientific Research

Psychology, like chemistry and biology, is an experimental science. Therefore, assumptions (such as about the behavior of chemical compounds, cells, or people) must be supported by evidence. It is not enough to argue that something is true just because someone says it is. Psychologists and other scientists make it their business to be skeptical of claims that lack actual scientific evidence.

Psychologists use a variety of research methods to study behavior and mental processes. These methods differ, but psychologists tend to follow the same general procedure when conducting their research. This procedure consists of five steps: forming a research question, forming a hypothesis, testing the hypothesis, analyzing the results, and drawing conclusions.

Forming a Research Question Psychologists begin a study by forming a research question. Many research questions arise from daily experience. Aggressiveness, for example, or anxiety are experienced by everyone but they are psychological **constructs.** It can be assumed they are present, but they cannot be seen or measured directly. Therefore, research questions are best directed toward behavior.

Scientists, for example, might decide to observe the behavior of fighting fish in order to study aggression. By creating the right conditions, such scientists are able to observe fish and how they react to changes in their environment. Similarly, psychologists bring animals or people into laboratory environments where they can observe them under carefully controlled conditions. At other times, psychologists study the behavior of organisms in the field—that is, where the organisms live naturally. In addition, psychologists sometimes get information by conducting experiments.

Other questions arise out of psychological theory. According to social-learning theorists, for example, people learn by observing others. These theorists might ask, what effects does television violence have on viewers?

Forming a Hypothesis After psychologists ask a research question, they form a hypothesis about the answer. A **hypothesis** is an educated guess. The accuracy of a hypothesis can be tested by research.

Psychologists may word a hypothesis in the form of an if-then statement. If-then reasoning is an example of social scientific reasoning. For example, scientists who study fish would be engaging in if-then reasoning if they made the following statement: *If* Siamese fighting fish are put together, *then* they will attack one another. This is not only social scientific reasoning, but also an educated guess. The guess is based on the fact that the fish are nicknamed "fighting fish." Because it is only an educated guess, a hypothesis must be tested. That is what researchers and scientists do in their experiments.

Testing the Hypothesis Because psychology is a science, psychological knowledge rests on carefully examined human experience. No matter how good a hypothesis sounds and no matter how many people believe it, a hypothesis cannot be considered to be correct until it has been scientifically tested and proved to be right. Psychologists do not rely on people's opinions. Instead, they examine the evidence and draw their own conclusions based upon that evidence.

Psychologists, like the scientists who study fighting fish, answer research questions or test hypotheses through a variety of methods. For example, to test the hypothesis that two fighting fish would attack each other, the most efficient method would probably be to put two real fish in the same tank. A second method might be to use a mirror to create the illusion of another fighting fish. Scientists might hope that the fish would react to its reflection in the same way it would react to a real fish. In that way they would be able to find out whether it is true that fighting fish do attack each other. Thus, holding a mirror in front of the fish is another reasonable method to test the hypothesis that two fighting fish would attack each other.

Analyzing the Results After psychologists have tested their hypothesis, they analyze their results. In other words, they ask what their findings mean. If scientists saw a fighting fish fan out its fins and puff up its cheeks apparently in reaction to seeing the image of another fish, they would have to figure out how to interpret that reaction. Some might interpret the fish's actions as going into an attack position.

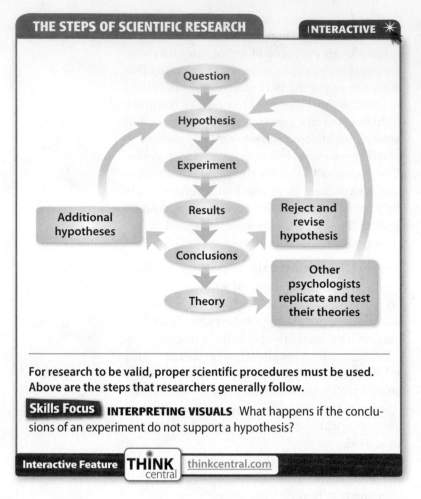

THE STEPS OF SCIENTIFIC RESEARCH

INTERACTIVE ✳

For research to be valid, proper scientific procedures must be used. Above are the steps that researchers generally follow.

Skills Focus INTERPRETING VISUALS What happens if the conclusions of an experiment do not support a hypothesis?

Interactive Feature THINK central thinkcentral.com

ACADEMIC VOCABULARY
validation the act of establishing the soundness of an idea or theory; corroboration

In most psychological studies, psychologists collect a great deal of information, or data. They might spend weeks, months, or even years in that step of the process. The more information collected, the more complex a task it is to analyze it.

Often, psychologists look for patterns and relationships in the data. They must decide which data support their hypothesis and which data do not.

Drawing Conclusions Once psychologists have analyzed their research observations, they draw conclusions about their questions and their hypotheses. These conclusions are useful in the development and <u>validation</u> of theories in psychology.

When their observations do not support their hypotheses, they often must change the theories or beliefs from which the hypotheses were derived. Therefore, psychologists need to keep open minds. They must be willing to adjust or modify their hypotheses if their findings make it necessary to do so.

In the fish example, once the scientists had seen how the fighting fish reacted to the image of another fish and had interpreted that reaction as an attack reaction, they might have concluded that, yes, fighting fish do fight each other. Then they would be satisfied that their hypothesis was correct.

If the fighting fish had not had such a reaction, they would not have been able to conclude that the hypothesis was correct. They would not necessarily have been able to prove that the hypothesis was incorrect, however. Maybe the fighting fish realized that it was only looking at a reflection and not at a real fish. Thus, the scientists would have had to do more research.

Reading Check **Find the Main Idea** Where does a hypothesis occur in the steps of research?

Further Steps in Scientific Research

The five steps in scientific research are not the end of the story, however. There are two additional steps that scientists must take, whether they are studying animals such as fish or people.

Replication Even when a study carefully follows proper procedures, its findings might just represent a random occurrence. Maybe the scientists just had a weird fish; maybe other fighting fish would react differently. For the findings of a study to be confirmed, the study must be **replicated.** That is, the study must be repeated—and it must produce the same results as before. If a study does not produce the same results more than once, the results may not have been accurate.

When scientists replicate a study but obtain different results than were obtained the first time, the findings of the first study are questioned. This is one reason that most psychologists do not believe that extrasensory perception (ESP) is a valid scientific phenomenon, even though some isolated studies have supported the existence of ESP. These studies have not yielded the same results when replicated.

Sometimes scientists repeat a study under different circumstances than those in the original study. In the fish example, to confirm the hypothesis that fighting fish attack each other, it would probably be most accurate to replicate the experiment by using two or more fish rather than one fish and its reflection.

Sometimes researchers repeat a study using a different set of participants. The scientists who study fish could have tried the same experiment with a few other fighting fish. If these fish acted differently than the first fish did, this would indicate that the first fish was somehow unusual. The scientists might even try the experiment with different *types* of fighting fish to see if all the fish have the same reaction. They might also try the experiment with both male and female fighting fish. In many animal species, males have different behavior patterns than females.

In a study in which people are the participants, researchers might want to replicate the study using participants who differ not only in gender but also in such characteristics as age, ethnicity, social and economic background, level of education, and also in geographic setting. For example, if a study was done for the first time only with teenagers, the researchers might include other age groups the next time. That way, the researchers could be sure that the findings were consistent among a variety of age groups.

New Questions Whether the findings of a research study support or contradict the hypothesis of that study, they are likely to lead to new research questions. For example, *why* do fighting fish attack each other? Does it have to do with mating, with territory, or with something else entirely? Is it a reaction they have at birth, or do they learn it as they mature? Are there any circumstances under which fighting fish do *not* attack each other? Do people ever act like that? These are some examples of new questions that can arise.

Once new questions have been asked, the process begins all over again. The researchers must propose a new hypothesis about the answer to the new question. And once again, the hypothesis must be tested.

The rest of this chapter explores the different types of research methods that psychologists use to test hypotheses. These methods include the survey method, various observational methods, and the experimental method.

Each of these methods has advantages and disadvantages, and some methods are better suited to certain kinds of research studies than are other methods of research. It would be convenient if there were one perfect method that could be used in all circumstances.

But human beings are complex, and the human experience has many dimensions. Thus, several different research methods are needed to study it.

Reading Check **Summarize** Why must a study be replicated? Give three reasons.

SECTION 1 Assessment

Reviewing Main Ideas and Vocabulary

1. **Summarize** What are the five steps of scientific research?
2. **Define** What does *replicated* mean?

Thinking Critically

3. **Explain** What two distinct paths can flow from the conclusions of scientific research?
4. **Infer** What do psychologists do once they have analyzed their research observations?
5. **Draw Conclusions** What happens when scientists get different results the second time they conduct a study?
6. **Infer** Why might it be important to have a variety of participants in a psychological study?

7. **Analyze** Using your notes and a graphic organizer like the one below, explain each of the five steps in scientific research.

1.	
2.	
3.	
4.	
5.	

FOCUS ON WRITING

8. **Expository** In a paragraph, explain some of the similarities between the ways in which scientists might study fish and psychologists might study people.

Surveys, Samples, and Populations

Before You Read

Main Idea

One way to gather information is by asking people directly. Psychologists use this method to study people's attitudes and behaviors.

Reading Focus

1. What is the survey method?
2. How do populations and samples affect research?
3. How do psychologists select samples?
4. Why must researchers be careful in generalizing results?
5. What is volunteer bias?

Vocabulary

survey
target population
sample
random sample
stratified sample
bias
volunteer bias

TAKING NOTES Use a graphic organizer like this one to take notes on surveys, samples, and populations.

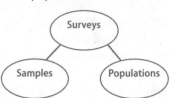

Watching WHAT You Watch

PSYCHOLOGY CLOSE UP

What happened to your favorite show? Do you know how your favorite shows are cancelled or renewed? Usually it's based on information gathered through samples taken by Nielsen Media Research, which provides the Nielsen ratings for television shows by sampling the U.S. population. The Nielsen Company samples television viewing in 25,000 homes. These households receive a fee for allowing their TV-watching to be monitored. A meter is attached to the television set. This meter records the channel being watched; the information is retrieved by a Nielsen computer. Each person in a household has an individual button to record which program he or she is watching. A rating of 15 means that 15 percent of U.S. homes with televisions watched a particular show. Television networks use the ratings to decide which programs to renew and which to cancel.

The Nielsen ratings also provide the networks and advertisers with demographic data about the viewing audience. This information is important to advertisers who hope to reach a particular demographic, such as young people or adult women. Networks typically cancel a show that receives low ratings and renew a show with high ratings. For these reasons, it is very important that the 25,000 households chosen for sampling accurately reflect the viewing habits of the entire country. Likewise, accurate sampling is important in psychology. ■

The Survey Method

When the scientists who study fish wanted to know what fighting fish would do to each other, it would have been convenient if they could have just asked the fish. But, of course, fish cannot talk. People, on the other hand, *can* talk. Thus, when psychologists want to find out about people's attitudes and behaviors, one possible way to gather information is to ask people directly.

Gathering information by asking people directly is usually accomplished by means of a survey. In a **survey,** people are asked to respond to a series of questions about a particular subject.

Psychologists D. L. DuBois and B. J. Hirsch, for example, used the survey method to examine mixed-race friendships among high school students. The survey asked high school students to identify the races of their friends. More than 80 percent of white and African American students reported having a friend of the other race in school. However, far fewer students reported seeing these friends outside of school. DuBois and Hirsch concluded that the reason may be that even though many of the respondents attended integrated schools, the neighborhoods they lived in may have been segregated.

Psychologists conduct surveys by asking people to fill out written questionnaires or by interviewing people orally. By distributing questionnaires or by conducting interviews over the telephone or in person, researchers can rapidly survey thousands of people. Computers often aid in the analysis of the information collected.

The findings of interviews and questionnaires may not be completely accurate. People may not be honest, for whatever reasons, about their attitudes or behavior. Some people may fear that their responses will not be kept confidential. Thus, they answer only what they are willing to reveal to the world at large. Other respondents may try to please the interviewers by saying what they think the interviewers want to hear.

The significant risk of obtaining inaccurate data through interviews and questionnaires became clear from the results of a 1960s survey about tooth-brushing habits. If people had brushed their teeth as often as they claimed, and used the amount of toothpaste they said they used, three times as much toothpaste would have been sold in the United States as was actually sold at that time. The survey respondents might not have wanted the interviewers to know that they did not brush their teeth as often as their dentists advised, and for this reason the survey did not accurately report reality.

Reading Check **Summarize** How do psychologists conduct surveys?

Populations and Samples

When researchers conduct any type of study, they must consider what group or groups of people they wish to examine and how respondents will be selected. This is particularly true with surveys.

Imagine that your town or city is about to hold a referendum on whether to institute a 10:00 P.M. curfew for people under the age of 18. How might you most accurately predict the outcome of the referendum? You might conduct a poll by asking people how they are planning to vote. But whom would you select to be in the poll?

Suppose you only polled the students in your psychology class. Do you think you would be able to make an accurate prediction? Probably not. Many of the people in your psychology class are probably under the age of 18 and thus might be particularly likely to oppose the curfew, because they believe it would restrict their freedom. However, these students are too young to vote. The voters in the actual referendum would all be at least 18. Since the curfew would not restrict them, they might be more inclined to vote for it. Thus, a poll of your psychology class would probably not be very useful for predicting the outcome of this particular referendum.

To accurately predict an outcome, it is necessary to study a group that represents the **target population.** A target population is the whole group you want to study or describe. In the curfew example, the target population consists of all possible voters on the referendum. It does not consist of nonvoters. The question is not whom the referendum will affect if passed, but whether the referendum will be passed or not. Thus, only voters are relevant to the survey.

ACADEMIC VOCABULARY

questionnaire a form containing a set of questions addressed to a statistically significant number of subjects

The Survey Method

In the survey method, people respond to questions about a particular subject. This enables the researcher to gather information about many people. For example, what are your classmates' favorite television shows? Use two survey methods to learn their favorite shows.

PROCEDURE

❶ Divide the class in half.

❷ Have three or four students interview half of the class. The surveyors should divide up this half so that each is interviewing a roughly equal number of students.

❸ Have the other half of the class write down their preferred television shows and submit them anonymously to the surveyors.

ANALYSIS

1. Compare the results about preferred shows between the two halves of the class.

2. Compile lists of the shows that people who were interviewed claimed to watch and another list of the shows that people who wrote their responses claimed to watch.

3. Are people more willing to admit watching certain shows if their responses are anonymous? Why might this be? Discuss the survey findings.

Quick Lab **THINK** central **thinkcentral.com**

It would be costly and difficult to interview or question every member of a target population (in this case, all voters in the area). Instead, researchers study a **sample,** which is only part of the target population.

Reading Check **Summarize** What is a target population?

Selecting Samples

Psychologists select samples scientifically to ensure that the samples accurately represent the populations they are supposed to represent. A sample should be as similar as possible to the target population. Otherwise, researchers will be unable to use the sample to make accurate predictions about the population from which the sample is drawn.

A high school class does not represent all the people in the town or city where a school is located, particularly in terms of opinions on an issue that pertains to age (such as a curfew for people under 18). Thus, the answers of people in a high school class might be biased (and of course most high school students are not old enough to vote). In this case, they would probably be biased against the curfew. On the other hand, researchers probably could predict the outcome of the referendum by interviewing as a sample a large number of people who represent all voters in the same town or city.

One way that scientists obtain a sample that they hope represents the target population is by using a **random sample.** In a random sample, individuals are selected by chance from the target population. Each member of the population has an equal chance of being chosen. If the random sample is big enough, chances are that it will accurately represent the whole population.

Researchers can also use a stratified sample. In a **stratified sample,** subgroups in the population are represented proportionally in the sample. For instance, about 12 percent of the American population is African American. A stratified sample of the population would thus be about 12 percent African American.

A large random sample is likely to be accurately stratified even if researchers take no special steps to ensure that it is. A random sample of 1,000 to 1,500 people will usually represent the general American population reasonably well. A sample of 5 million motorcycle owners, however, would not.

A large sample size by itself does not necessarily guarantee that a sample represents a target population, particularly if the sample is not a random sample. Motorcycle owners do not represent all people in the United States.

Reading Check **Summarize** What is the difference between random and stratified samples?

Generalizing Results

Sometimes, for one reason or another, researchers do not use a sample that represents an entire population. In some cases, the researchers want to know about only one group within the population. Therefore, they have no reason to study other groups. In other cases, it may be impractical or impossible to obtain a random or stratified sample; thus, they work with a sample that does not represent the whole population.

In such cases, researchers are cautious about generalizing their findings to groups other than those from which their samples were drawn. For example, some scientists study the ability of chimpanzees to use sign language. They work with a particular group of chimpanzees in their research. Some chimpanzees in the group are more adept than others at using sign language. But whatever results the scientists come up with in observing their group of chimpanzees, they could not know for sure if they would get the same results with other animals.

The same is true with people. Researchers cannot learn about the preferences of all people by studying only one group of people, such as men. In a study about car preferences, for example, psychologists would avoid generalizing from a sample that was made up only of men because men's preferences for cars might not be the same as women's. In other words, if researchers found that men prefer certain types of cars, the researchers could not conclude that women prefer those same types of cars if the study did not include women. The results of such a study on car preference might be used by researchers to choose car names that might appeal to a particular age and gender group within a population.

The gender of the individuals in the sample is not the only characteristic that researchers must take into account. For instance, researchers cannot learn about the attitudes of Americans in general if they limit their observations to people who live in one part of the country (for example, the Midwest) or to people from one socioeconomic background (for example, wealthy people).

Reading Check **Draw Conclusions** What are some limitations on generalizing results?

Volunteer Bias

Researchers often have little control over who responds to surveys. Although the researchers may choose to whom they give a questionnaire, they cannot force people to complete it. Another factor psychologists must take into account is **bias,** a predisposition to a certain point of view despite what the facts suggest.

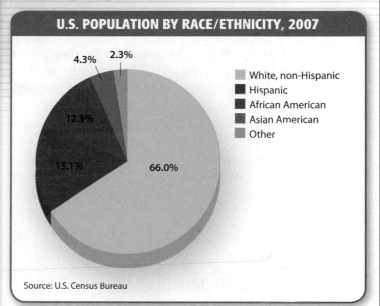

Statistically Speaking...

Ethnic Diversity in the United States
Figures show that Hispanics are the fastest-growing ethnic group in the United States. The pie graph below shows the U.S. population by race/ethnicity. The percentages below that show the percentage by which each group grew between 2000 and 2007.

U.S. POPULATION BY RACE/ETHNICITY, 2007

- White, non-Hispanic
- Hispanic
- African American
- Asian American
- Other

4.3% 2.3%
12.3%
15.1%
66.0%

Source: U.S. Census Bureau

27.6% Hispanic
25.1% Asian
17.0% Other
7.6% African American
1.7% White

Skills Focus INTERPRETING GRAPHS In a stratified sample consisting of 100 people, how many African Americans would you expect to find in the sample?

People who volunteer to participate in studies may bring with them a **volunteer bias**—that is, they may have a different outlook from people who do not volunteer for research studies. Volunteers are usually more willing than other people to disclose personal information. Volunteers may also be more interested in research than people who do not volunteer. Furthermore, they may have more spare time to participate in research studies than other people. Depending on what the study is about, any or all of these factors—as well as others—could skew the results. That is, these factors could slant the results in a particular direction.

Have you ever filled out and returned a questionnaire printed in a magazine? Popular magazines such as *Glamour, Seventeen,* and *Psychology Today* often survey readers' attitudes about various topics and behaviors in certain circumstances. Such a questionnaire might, for instance, ask readers how they like to spend their leisure time. Do they prefer to go to the movies, visit with friends, read magazines, listen to music, or play video games? Or the questionnaire might ask readers their opinions on politics, clothes, celebrities, and a number of other popular topics on which people tend to have a variety of opinions.

Thousands of readers complete these questionnaires and send them in. But do the respondents really represent the general population of the United States? Probably not. In a magazine survey, a disproportionate number of responses to the question about leisure time posed above would probably be "read magazines." After all, the questionnaire itself comes from a magazine. People who do not like to read magazines probably would not fill out the questionnaire. They would not have seen it in the first place. Also, readers who have enough time to fill out the questionnaire may have different leisure preferences from people who are too busy to fill out the questionnaire. Such magazine surveys are affected by volunteer bias. This volunteer bias might influence the research findings.

In addition, many magazines are so-called niche publications. That is, they are meant to appeal to a particular target demographic, whether it be homemakers, teenagers, young adult men, young adult women, middle-aged men, and so forth. In addition to target audiences based on age, there are also audiences that are targeted because of their specific interests, such as model railroads, interior design, baseball cards, racing cars, dolls, and so on. These are some of the reasons that researchers must be on guard against volunteer bias in analyzing their research.

Reading Check **Draw Conclusions** What is the basic problem with volunteer bias in terms of research results?

SECTION 2 Assessment

Reviewing Main Ideas and Vocabulary

1. **Summarize** What is the main reason that interviews and questionnaires are not completely accurate?

2. **Describe** What random sample size is likely to be accurately stratified even if the researcher takes no special steps to ensure that it is?

Thinking Critically

3. **Explain** What should a sample be similar to in order to ensure that it accurately represents the population that it is supposed to represent?

4. **Categorize** What are some of the factors that researchers must take into account in generalizing their findings?

5. **Analyze** Using your notes and a graphic organizer like the one below, explain the importance of surveys, populations, and samples in psychological research.

Importance in Psychological Research
Surveys:
Populations:
Samples:

FOCUS ON WRITING

6. **Expository** Review the information on questionnaires and interviews in the discussion of the survey method. Then choose a topic that you would like to investigate. Write a series of questions for your questionnaire or survey.

Diversity in Research

Most psychologists today appreciate the need to allow for the wider diversity of members of society in their research. This has not always been the case. For example, men have been included as research study participants more often than women. This led psychologists to mistakenly generalize their findings beyond men.

Diversity and Research Pools Many research participants were originally drawn from the armed services and universities (for example, in the 1940s during World War II). The majority of people in the armed services were male. And only in recent years has the number of women in colleges and universities grown equal to and exceeded that of men. Because of this, researchers tended to conclude that what was true for white men was true for all of society. When this sort of overgeneralization occurred, important distinctions between groups tended to be ignored.

Diversity and Health Health has been an area where cultural, ethnic, and gender differences have not always been taken into account. Some surprising results have been obtained as studies have broadened their scope beyond white men. For example, researchers have discovered significant differences between how men and women are affected by heart disease. Although women receive less treatment for heart disease than men, they are at greater risk of dying from the condition. Researchers are studying whether this increased risk exists because of differences in the treatment women receive from health care providers.

Diversity and Ethnic Differences Research results have also revealed differences among ethnic groups as the pool of study participants has broadened. Researchers have learned that African Americans of both genders are more likely to suffer from heart disease than white Americans. This higher risk arises, in part, from correspondingly higher rates of hypertension in the African American population.

Diversity and Domestic Violence This is another area of study that has benefited from studies with more diversified groups of participants. Much research has been performed on the prevalence of violence against women. But more recent research has revealed that men, too, are victims of domestic violence. Psychologists have also studied the effects that domestic violence has beyond the victim of the physical assault. Children in particular suffer emotionally in a household where violence occurs.

Diversity and Older Populations Recent research has also focused on issues significant to members of the older population. Studies have shed light on topics of concern to the elderly, such as the way older people cope with the changes in their health and in social relationships.

Diversity and the APA The American Psychological Association (APA) recommends that the write-up of a study's results include a clear description of the research sample in terms of ethnicity, gender, and any other potentially relevant characteristics. For example, if a sample uses only male participants, the report should include this information. When such descriptions are included, the reader is less likely to assume that a study's findings apply equally to all groups.

Thinking Critically

1. **Analyze** What might be some ways to increase the number of participants from traditionally underrepresented groups in psychological studies?

2. **Discuss** How might you and your classmates respond to a question about the effect of after-school jobs on your education? How might students respond differently in a school with a different ethnic make-up?

Using Observation for Research

Before You Read

Main Idea

Psychologists use many different methods of observation in conducting their research. Then they use correlation to analyze and interpret their results.

Reading Focus

1. What are some of the methods of observation in psychological research?

2. How do researchers analyze their observations?

Vocabulary

case study
longitudinal method
cross-sectional method
naturalistic observation
laboratory observation
correlation
positive correlation
negative correlation

TAKING NOTES Use a graphic organizer like this one to take notes on methods of observation.

Methods of Observation
1.
2.
3.
4.
5.
6.

THE BABY BOX

Parents check on their infant in a so-called "baby box" invented by the psychologist B. F. Skinner.

PSYCHOLOGY CLOSE UP

Would you put a baby in a "baby box"? B. F. Skinner was an important American psychologist. He became famous in the field of behavioral psychology for his study of the observable behavior of animals and humans. For the study of animals, he developed the "Skinner box," in which animals were kept under continuous observation. During World War II, he created the first "baby box," a controlled environmental chamber for infants. It was also called an "air

crib." His daughter Deborah spent part of her first two years in a baby box or air crib. The air crib was soundproof, germ-free, and air-conditioned. It was meant to work as a positive, ideal environment for the first two years of life.

Skinner boxes for the study of animals are examples of laboratories created for the purpose of observation. Laboratories allow psychologists to control the environment of a study. However, such controlled experiments call for great care in analyzing the results of the study. ■

Methods of Observation

Almost everyone, at one time or another, observes other people. We observe people as they talk, eat, work, play, and interact with others and with us. Based on our observations of other people (and also of ourselves), we tend to make generalizations about human behavior and human nature.

Our observations and generalizations usually serve us fairly well in our daily lives. But no matter how many experiences we have had, most of our personal observations are fleeting and haphazard. We sift through experience for things that interest us, but we often ignore the obvious because it does not fit our ideas about how things ought to be. Thus, we cannot draw scientific conclusions based only on our own unstructured observations.

Even the most respected psychologists may use their personal observations as a starting point for their research and as the basis for their hypotheses. Once they have begun their investigations, however, psychologists use more careful methods of observation. The survey method, discussed earlier, is one such method of observation. Other methods of observation include the testing, case-study, longitudinal, cross-sectional, naturalistic-observation, and laboratory-observation methods.

The Testing Method Psychologists sometimes use psychological tests to learn about human behavior. There are several types of psychological tests. Intelligence tests measure general learning ability. Aptitude tests measure specific abilities and special talents, such as musical ability and mechanical skills. Still other tests measure vocational interests.

Personality tests are another type of test psychologists use. Personality tests measure people's character traits and temperament. For example, personality tests might be used to assess whether people are socially outgoing or aggressive. Personality tests might also be used to diagnose such psychological problems as anxiety and depression.

The Case-Study Method Another research method psychologists use is the case-study method. A **case study** is an in-depth investigation of an individual or a small group. To learn about the people who are being studied, researchers may observe or speak with them,

interview others who know them, and find out more about their backgrounds and personal histories. Psychologists use what they learn in a case study to generalize broader principles that apply to the larger population.

Sigmund Freud developed psychoanalytic theory largely on the basis of case studies. Freud carefully studied the people who sought his help. He interviewed some of them for many years, developing as complete a record of their childhoods as he could. He also looked for the factors that seemed to contribute to their problems.

Some case studies focus on rare circumstances or events. One such case study involved a girl named Genie. When she was only 20 months old, her father locked her in a small room. She was kept there until she was rescued at the age of 13. Her social contacts were limited to her mother, who fed her, and her father, who often beat her. No one spoke to her. And in all those years, she herself did not say a word.

After her rescue, Genie's language acquisition followed the normal sequence of language development. Genie never learned to use language as well as most people, however. This case study suggests that there is a special period in early childhood when it is easiest for people to learn language.

Although case studies sometimes offer great insights, psychologists are cautious about generalizing from case studies. This is particularly true of case studies that cannot be replicated, such as Genie's. Because of the rarity and cruelty of Genie's experience, scientists would never repeat this study. Thus they cannot know for sure, on the basis of Genie's experience alone, whether the theory about a special language-learning period in childhood is correct. Perhaps other unknown factors were responsible for Genie's apparent inability to achieve full language competence.

Furthermore, case studies lend themselves to some of the same pitfalls that surveys do, particularly when the case studies are based on interviews with people about their past experiences. Most people's memories are filled with a great many gaps and inaccuracies. Some of these inaccuracies occur because people tend not to remember the details of events clearly. Some people even intentionally distort their pasts to impress the researcher.

And sometimes without meaning to, researchers encourage people to answer in certain ways to fulfill the researchers' expectations. For example, some psychoanalysts have been criticized for encouraging people to interpret their behavior according to Freud's psychoanalytic theory.

The Longitudinal Method Just as Freud studied some of his patients over a matter of years, so too do some psychological studies observe participants over a long period of time. Some research topics, such as those concerned with development during the life span, deal with how people change over time.

To study such topics, psychologists often use the **longitudinal method.** In this method, researchers select a group of participants and then observe those participants over a period of time, often years or even decades. By using this method, psychologists can observe the ways in which individuals change over time.

Usually the observations are conducted at intervals, perhaps once a year. For example, if psychologists wanted to find out more about how people learn language, they might select a group of six-month-olds who are not yet using language. Then once a month,

the researchers might observe the children to find out how their language skills are changing over time. By the time the children are three or four years old, they are no longer learning language at such a rapid pace. The psychologists might then observe them only once or twice a year.

Needless to say, longitudinal studies are extremely time-consuming. Imagine how much patience you would need knowing that even if you started a study right now, you would not get conclusive results for another 5, 10, or 15 years. Moreover, longitudinal studies tend to be expensive, and they are risky. There is often no guarantee that participants will remain available over the long time period that they are to be studied.

The Cross-Sectional Method To avoid some of the problems with longitudinal studies, psychologists may use the cross-sectional method to track changes over time. In the **cross-sectional method,** instead of following a set of individuals over a number of years, researchers select a sample that includes people of different ages. The researchers then compare the behavior of the participants in the different age groups. For example, in a

Six Methods of Observation

Testing Method

Description Several types of tests measure various elements of human behavior such as abilities, interests, and personality.

Advantages Convenient method for researchers to gain insight into certain aspects of an individual's abilities or behavior.

Disadvantages Does not always provide a complete representation of an individual's true abilities or personality.

Case-Study Method

Description Researchers conduct in-depth investigations of individuals or small groups.

Advantages Provides insight into specific cases.

Disadvantages May focus on isolated circumstances or events that cannot be replicated. People interviewed in case studies may distort their past experiences. Researchers may unintentionally encourage people to answer questions a certain way.

Longitudinal Method

Description A group of participants are observed at intervals over an extended period of time.

Advantages Enables researchers to see how individuals change over time.

Disadvantages Time-consuming and expensive. Participants may not be available for the duration of the study.

language-learning study, psychologists might select 12-month-olds, 14-month-olds, and 16-month-olds. They would then observe the language skills of members of each age group and compare the groups with one another in order to make generalizations about how children learn language over time.

Information gained in cross-sectional studies is less reliable than information from longitudinal studies. When psychologists study one individual over a period of time, as in a longitudinal study, they know that any changes they observe in that individual are due to her or his experiences or development. But when they compare groups of people of different ages at the same time, as in a cross-sectional study, psychologists cannot be certain what factors are responsible for differences among the participants. Perhaps the differences are due to developmental changes, but perhaps the participants were simply different from the beginning.

The Naturalistic-Observation Method One way that psychologists find out about children's language skills is to observe children as they use language naturally, such as while they interact with other children in play groups.

This method is called **naturalistic observation,** or field study. People often use naturalistic observation in their daily lives without even knowing it. That is, they observe other people or animals in the "field"—in their natural habitats. In the case of people, field settings include homes, schools, restaurants—any place where people spend time.

If scientists want to use naturalistic observation to observe chimpanzees, they have to go to a rain forest or jungle—someplace where chimpanzees exist naturally. But without realizing it, we use naturalistic observation all the time to watch people. For example, while working at a restaurant, a waiter can not avoid noticing the different ways that customers eat their food. Some people gobble down their meals quickly, almost without pausing. Others eat delicately, carefully chewing each bite. A waiter might wonder what accounts for these differences in eating habits among the customers.

Psychologists also wonder about such questions. They have used the naturalistic observation method to study how people eat. They have watched people in restaurants to learn, for example, whether slender people and heavy people eat their meals differently.

Cross-Sectional Method

Description Researchers compare differences and similarities among people in different age groups at a given time.

Advantages Less time-consuming than the longitudinal method for studying changes over time.

Disadvantages Differences between the members of the sample cannot necessarily be attributed to age or development.

Naturalistic-Observation Method

Description Researchers observe the behavior of people or animals in their natural habits.

Advantages Enables researchers to witness the behavior of people or animals in settings that are not artificial.

Disadvantages Researchers have no control over the setting or the events that occur.

Laboratory-Observation Method

Description Participants are observed in a laboratory setting.

Advantages Enables researchers to precisely control certain aspects of the study.

Disadvantages Laboratories cannot duplicate real-life environments.

Such field research has shown that heavy people tend to eat somewhat more rapidly than slender people. Heavy people also chew less often and leave less food on their plates.

This type of study has led to suggestions about how heavy people might diet more effectively. For example, they might take less food and eat more slowly so that when they clean their plates, they have eaten less.

In naturalistic observation, psychologists try not to interfere with the organisms they are observing. In the restaurant example, psychologists would not ask the diners questions or encourage them to eat a particular food. They would simply observe people eating.

The Laboratory-Observation Method Sometimes it is more useful for a psychologist to observe behavior in a laboratory rather than in the field. This method is called **laboratory observation.** Laboratories are not necessarily sterile rooms tended by people in white coats; a laboratory is any place that provides the opportunity for observation or experimentation. As such, many laboratories are quite informal. A workplace can be a laboratory for observing certain kinds of behavior.

For scientists who study chimpanzees, an enclosure that simulates their natural habitat is a type of laboratory. To make the environment suitable for the chimpanzees, scientists have to do many things, such as monitor the temperature and the food. Once they have set up the laboratory, they are able to observe the behavior of the chimps. They observe them run and climb, create and defend their territory, attract mates, and breed.

Psychologists often study animals by using the laboratory-observation method. B. F. Skinner created special enclosed environments, which became known as Skinner boxes, to study the behavior of animals such as rats. In one of these miniature laboratories, a food pellet drops into the box when the rat in the box presses a lever. Rats quickly learn to press the levers, especially when they are hungry. Other psychologists have built mazes to see how effectively rats learn routes through the mazes. Both the Skinner box and the maze are examples of laboratories.

Psychologists sometimes use a laboratory to control the environment of a study. For example, if they wanted to see whether the amount of light in a room affects how much people eat, they would need to be able to control the lighting in the room where people were eating. Similarly, a fish tank is a place where a scientist can observe the behavior of the fish while he or she controls what happens in the environment. The scientist could, for instance, observe how the fish respond if he or she changes the temperature of the water or the type of food he feeds them.

Reading Check **Describe** How does the cross-sectional method fix the longitudinal method?

Analyzing the Observations

Once psychologists have made their observations, they must analyze and interpret them. One method they use is **correlation,** which is a measure of how closely one thing is related to another. The stronger the correlation between two things, the more closely those two things are related. For example, there is a strong correlation between height and ability to reach items that are located on the top shelf of a cabinet. The taller the person, the greater that person's ability to reach the top shelf.

In psychology, researchers often look for correlations between various characteristics or traits. For instance, are people who feel a stronger need for achievement more likely to advance in their jobs? What is the relationship between stress and health? What is the connection between students' grades and extracurricular involvement?

Positive and Negative Correlation To determine whether there is a correlation between achievement and occupational success, a researcher might compare need for achievement as measured by a personality test with the salaries of the test takers. There is, in fact, a correlation between the need for achievement and salaries; it is a **positive correlation.** That is, as one goes up, so does the other. Generally speaking, people who feel a greater need to achieve earn more money.

There are, of course, some exceptions. Some people are highly motivated to achieve, but they do not have high-paying jobs. Others are average in their need for achievement but earn very high incomes. Therefore, factors other than a need for achievement also contribute to high salaries. One such factor is the type of job one has; people in some kinds of jobs earn more than people in other kinds of jobs. In addition, for people to succeed, they also have to know how to interact with others, how to manage people, and how to manage multiple tasks at one time. Thus, there is a positive correlation between success and a variety of factors.

In contrast, there is a **negative correlation** between stress and health. As one goes up, the other goes down. As the amount of stress on people increases, their immune systems become less capable of fighting off illness—thus, the greater the stress, the poorer the health. This is why students under stress are more likely than other students to get colds.

Limits of Correlation Correlation describes relationships. It does not, however, reveal cause and effect. Just because two things are related does not necessarily mean that one causes the other.

For example, suppose you were conducting a study in your school and discovered a positive correlation between students' grades and their level of involvement in extracurricular activities. In other words, you found that students who earn high grades in their classes also participate heavily in extracurricular activities. Does this mean that earning high grades *causes* students to become involved in extracurricular activities or that involve-

Cause and Effect or Correlation?
Suppose that of all the students in the school band, only the tuba players get good grades. *Did they get good grades because they were tuba players, or were there other causes?*

ment in extracurricular activities *causes* students to earn high grades? Not necessarily. It might be that there are other factors—such as a general desire to succeed—that encourage or cause *both* high grades and extracurricular involvement. Thus, we cannot conclude on the basis of the correlation alone that one causes the other. As you will see, experiments allow us to draw conclusions about cause and effect.

Reading Check **Define** What are some of the limits of correlation?

SECTION 3 Assessment

Reviewing Main Ideas and Vocabulary

1. **Recall** What is the longitudinal method?

2. **Summarize** What are some of the drawbacks to the case-study method?

3. **Summarize** What are the advantages of each of the six methods of observation?

Thinking Critically

4. **Support a Position** Suppose you want to find out if there is a correlation between age and preferred volume level for listening to music for people between the ages of 15 and 55. Which observational method might you use? Explain your choice.

5. **Compare** What is the difference between the naturalistic-observation method and the laboratory-observation method?

6. **Analyze** Using your notes and a graphic organizer like the one below, explain the various aspects of correlation.

Correlation	
Positive correlation	
Negative correlation	
Limits of correlation	

FOCUS ON WRITING

7. **Descriptive** Choose some topic that you would like to learn about using the naturalistic-observation method. Spend 15 minutes observing your chosen topic. Then write a paragraph in which you describe what you have observed.

Environmental Psychology

Environmental psychology is a relatively new field that focuses on the interaction between people and their surroundings. It draws on anthropology, geography, urban design, and architecture. Researchers in this field observe people in real-life settings. By using this method, they can make recommendations about shaping the environment.

Eaton Centre in Toronto, Canada

The beginnings of the environmental psychology movement can be found in the work of Roger Barker, who ran a research facility in Oskaloosa, Kansas. Barker founded the center in 1948. He carefully observed life in the small Kansas town. He observed that people in stores behaved like customers, people in schools behaved like students, and people in church behaved like congregants. That is, behavior appropriate to a place seems to be to some extent encoded in the setting. Barker called this idea that people are unconsciously controlled by the rules of the setting "behavior setting."

If Barker represents the early days of the environmental psychology movement, the Graduate Center of the City University of New York (CUNY) represents more recent developments. It was among the first academic institutions in the United States to offer a Ph.D. in environmental psychology. The CUNY program takes a multidisciplinary approach to the interaction of people with the urban environment. Among the issues dealt with are homelessness, conflicts in urban planning, neighborhood participation, community housing, the design of public institutions, and transportation (Chapin, Hart, Katz, Low, 2007).

Today, environmental psychologists attempt to influence the work of architects, engineers, designers, and urban planners in order to improve the interaction of people and place. Environmental psychology has had a big impact on one particular setting—commercial venues where the idea is to design the setting so that people are encouraged to spend their money. Such settings include stores, malls, stadiums, casinos, and airports. Increasingly, the retail sector relies on research, focus groups, and observations provided by environmental psychology (Gifford et al., 2007).

Many environmental psychologists believe that density and crowding can cause stress and negative moods. Therefore, they advise planners and designers to reduce the effects of crowding in the design and planning of urban space. They recommend windows, high ceilings, doors to provide crowd control, and creating smaller spaces within an open office plan—all to reduce the impression of crowding. Noise is another factor that planners attempt to reduce in order to lower stress (Gifford et al., 2007).

Most of the research that is done in environmental psychology is done not in the lab but in the field. Environmental psychologists meet with many different groups, including architects, residents, urban planners, politicians, and so forth in order to get input for new projects and plans. For example, in a neighborhood about to undergo urban renewal, researchers might meet with residents to find out what they want and how they would like to see their space take shape.

Grand Century Plaza in Hong Kong, China

Thinking Critically

1. **Analyze** Who do you think would be likely to support research undertaken by environmental psychologists?

2. **Discuss** What are the circumstances in which shoppers are more likely to act as eager rather than skeptical or reluctant consumers?

Current Research **THINK** central thinkcentral.com

Experimental and Ethical Issues

Before You Read

Main Idea

The experimental method is used by researchers to answer questions about cause and effect. In addition, psychologists must consider the ethical issues involved in their experiments.

Reading Focus

1. How would you describe the primary purpose of the experimental method?

2. What is the purpose of single- and double-blind studies?

3. Why do researchers measure central tendency and dispersion?

4. What are three overriding ethical issues in psychology?

5. Why do scientists sometimes conduct research with animals?

Vocabulary

variables
independent variable
dependent variable
experimental group
control group
placebo
single-blind study
double-blind study
standard deviation
ethics

TAKING NOTES Use a graphic organizer like this one to take notes on the experimental method and ethical issues.

| Exper. Method |
| 1. |
| 2. |
| 3. |
| Ethical Issues |
| 1. |
| 2. |
| 3. |

RESEARCH AND ANIMAL RIGHTS

PSYCHOLOGY CLOSE UP

Are the rights of animals considered in research experiments? A recent court case in Alamogordo, New Mexico, involved the treatment of three chimpanzees—Rex, Ashley, and Topsy—in laboratory research. Veterinarians at the Charles River Laboratories routinely oversaw animal experiments mainly involving chimpanzees. Defendants in the case abandoned critically ill or injured chimpanzees to security guards who had no training in how to care for the animals. Some animals died of neglect.

The central issue was whether or not veterinarians are exempt from prosecution under the New Mexico cruelty statute if the vets are engaged in animal research experiments. Many observers believe that vets should be prosecuted for cruelty to animals in laboratory research. Among those who attempted to file friend of the court briefs with the New Mexico Supreme Court were Albuquerque Mayor Martin Chavez and Jane Goodall, the field scientist who revolutionized primate research. The abuse of these animals led the New Mexico legislature to amend the state's cruelty statute and remove the blanket exemption for research labs, making them prosecutable for animal cruelty.

There are many ethical issues involved in the treatment of both animals and people in research, including psychological research. Besides cruelty to animals, these issues include the treatment of people, informed consent, and deception. ■

A researcher conducts a sign-recognition experiment with a chimpanzee.

The Experimental Method

The method researchers use to answer questions about cause and effect is the experiment. In an experiment, participants receive what is called a treatment, such as a change in room temperature or a new drug. Researchers then carefully observe the participants to determine how the treatment influences their behavior (if at all).

As with other research methods, the experimental method has some limitations. For example, the conditions created in an experiment may not accurately reflect conditions in real life.

Almost by their very nature, experiments must simplify things somewhat in order to yield useful information about cause and effect. Nevertheless, experiments do yield useful information much of the time, and for that reason, psychologists frequently turn to the experimental method as they conduct their research.

Independent and Dependent Variables

Experiments contain **variables,** which are factors that can vary, or change. In an experiment, the **independent variable** is the factor that researchers manipulate so that they can determine its effect.

Suppose researchers are testing the hypothesis that warm temperatures cause aggression in humans. In that experiment, temperature is the independent variable because that is what researchers are manipulating to observe its effect.

In the same experiment, level of aggression is the dependent variable. As you might guess from its name, a **dependent variable** depends on something—the independent variable. The researchers want to find out whether level of aggression depends on temperature.

Experimental and Control Groups

Ideal experiments use experimental and control groups. Members of an **experimental group** receive the treatment. Members of a **control group** do not. Every effort is made to ensure that all other conditions are held constant for both the experimental group and the control group.

This method makes it possible for researchers to conclude that the experiment's results are caused by the treatment, not by something else. One of the fundamental flaws of the Hawthorne plant study was the lack of a control group.

Researchers randomly assign participants to one group or the other. For example, in an experiment about students' grades and extracurricular involvement, some students would be randomly assigned to participate in extracurricular activities. These students would make up the experimental group.

Others would be randomly assigned *not* to participate in extracurricular activities. These students would be the control group.

Once researchers ensured that all other factors—such as ethnic group or educational background—were the same for the two groups, they could then compare the groups to see whether involvement in extracurricular activities makes a difference in the grades participants earn.

When an experiment uses control groups as well as experimental groups, it is called a controlled experiment. An example of a study in which it is useful to have a control group concerns a key question for psychologists: Does psychotherapy work? In other words, do people who undergo therapy feel better? Does their behavior change?

Millions of people seek help from psychologists. Many patients believe their therapists have helped them. For example, a former patient might say, "I was in terrible shape before therapy, but I feel much better now."

Yet we do not know what would have happened if this person had not sought help. Perhaps they would have improved on their own, without professional intervention.

Many people feel better about their problems as time goes on, with or without therapy. In other words, an individual's involvement in therapy is not part of a controlled experiment. There is no control group—an identical person who has *not* gone to a therapist. Of course, we could never find such a person because no two people are exactly the same.

However, researchers can make up for this by conducting an experiment on the effects of therapy using a large number of people. In such an experiment, some people would be randomly assigned to an experimental group and would receive therapy. Others with the same problems as those in the first group would be assigned to a control group and would not receive therapy. Even though the people in the experimental group would not be identical to the people in the control group, individual differences would average out as long as the groups were large enough. Thus, researchers could determine whether people who receive therapy fare better than those who do not receive therapy through the use of a controlled experiment such as the one described above.

The Placebo Effect The question of whether psychotherapy works is further complicated by the fact that people who seek psychotherapy usually expect it to work. Imagine that a person who has a problem is about to see a therapist about it. Chances are, the person is expecting that the visit will be helpful. Otherwise, why would the person choose to visit a therapist?

In research studies and in our daily lives, our expectations affect what happens to us. Feeling better simply because we expect to feel better—and for no other reason—is an example of the placebo (pluh-SEE-boh) effect. A **placebo** is a substance or treatment that has no effect apart from a person's belief in its effect.

For example, one type of placebo is a tablet that appears to contain a real drug but actually has no medicinal value. Someone who has a headache and takes the tablet to feel better might start to feel better even though the tablet does not contain any medicine—as long as the person thinks that it does indeed contain medicine.

Reading Check **Define** In an experiment, what are variables?

Single- and Double-Blind Studies

Expectations can create bias toward certain points of view. If a person expects that a drug may have certain effects, he or she will be biased toward paying close attention to any sensations that are similar to the effects of the drugs.

How, then, can researchers deal with the effects of expectations? How can they learn whether the participants' preconceptions about a new drug are biasing their perceptions of its effects?

Single-Blind Studies One way that researchers can avoid the influence of expectations is by keeping participants unaware of, or blind to, the treatment they are receiving. In a **single-blind study,** participants do not know whether they are in the experimental group or the control group.

For example, in a single-blind drug study participants are divided into four groups. People in one group receive the drug and are told that they are receiving the drug. Members of the second group receive the drug and are told that they are receiving a placebo. The third group receives a placebo but is told that it is receiving the drug. People in the fourth group receive a placebo and are told that they are receiving a placebo.

What does it mean if the people taking the new drug improve faster, regardless of what they have been told, but people who take the placebo do not? It means the drug is effective. What does it mean if all the people who are told they are taking the drug get better faster, regardless of whether they are taking the drug or the placebo?

ACADEMIC VOCABULARY

preconceptions
opinions formed in advance of adequate knowledge or experience

SINGLE-BLIND AND DOUBLE-BLIND EXPERIMENTS

	Researcher	Participants	Experiment Organizer
Single-Blind Experiment	aware	unaware	aware
Double-Blind Experiment	unaware	unaware	aware

In both single-blind and double-blind experiments, researchers must guard against bias in favor of certain points of view by keeping participants unaware of their treatment.

Skills Focus **INTERPRETING CHARTS** Who is aware of the treatment or lack of treatment the participants are receiving?

It means that they improve because of their expectations—because of a belief that they are taking a helpful drug—and not because of the drug itself. In this case, the drug in and of itself has few if any benefits and is thus similar to the placebo.

Double-Blind Studies Participants may not be the only people involved in an experiment who have expectations. Researchers may also have expectations, such as a belief about the effectiveness of a particular treatment. It is therefore useful if the researchers are also unaware of who has had the treatment and who has had the placebo.

A study in which both participants and researchers are unaware of who receives the treatment is called a **double-blind study.** However, the experiment organizer remains aware of who has had the treatment and who has had the placebo. The organizer is, in fact, often a safety committee that oversees such studies.

Double-blind studies are required by the Food and Drug Administration before new drugs can be sold. People in these studies are assigned at random to take the real drug or the placebo. Neither the participants nor the people who measure the results know who is taking what.

Thus, the people who measure effects in double-blind studies can remain unbiased. After the measurements are made, an impartial panel (made up of people who do know who had the drug and who did not) determines, on the basis of the measurements of the unbiased observers, whether the effects of the drug differed from the effects of the placebo.

Reading Check **Compare** What is the difference between a single-blind and double-blind study?

Central Tendency and Dispersion

Researchers organize data to generalize about it. Teachers do this when they analyze test scores. A common technique is to measure central tendency, a number that describes the average score of a distribution. When the teacher adds all scores and divides the sum by the number of students who took the test, he or she finds the mean, or average score, which is most often used as the central tendency.

Other methods of arriving at the central tendency include finding the median and the mode. If scores are organized from lowest to highest, or highest to lowest, the median score is the middle score. Half of the grades are below this score and half are above. The mode is the most frequent score.

To understand the distribution or dispersion of data, researchers must document the range of scores, or how variable the scores are. The two most frequently used measures of variability are range and standard deviation. To find the range, the lowest score in the data is subtracted from the highest. This simple technique gives a crude measure of range.

Standard deviation is a measure of distance of every score to the mean. The larger the standard deviation the more spread out the scores are. If five students got 7 out of 10 questions correct on a test, two students got 10 correct, and one got 5 correct, the mode is 7, the median is 7, and the mean is 7.5.

To compute the standard deviation, subtract the mean from each score. For example, 10 minus 7.5 equals 2.5. This is a positive deviation because the score is above the mean. However, 7 minus 7.5 is negative .5, and 5 minus 7.5 is negative 2.5. Test scores that have a large range have a relatively higher standard deviation while test scores bunched together, as in this case, have a relatively small standard deviation.

Reading Check **Recall** What is the relationship between the standard deviation and the mean?

STANDARD DEVIATION BELL CURVE GRAPH

Mean

Frequency

Scores in standard deviation units

2.15%   13.59%   34.13%   34.13%   13.59%   2.15%

-3   -2   -1   0   1   2   3

Skills Focus INTERPRETING GRAPHS What score represents the mean in the curve above?

Ethical Issues

Ethics are standards for proper and responsible behavior. Psychologists follow ethical standards to promote the dignity of the individual, foster human welfare, and maintain scientific integrity. An important aspect of psychologists' work is to lessen human suffering. Along these lines, ethical standards prevent scientists from undertaking research or treatments that will be harmful to human participants.

Specific ethical guidelines have been established by the American Psychological Association (APA). You can find these guidelines in the back of the book. Psychologists are required to be familiar with these guidelines. The APA is a scientific and professional organization of psychologists.

Research with People Ethical standards limit the type of research that psychologists may conduct. Imagine trying to study whether early separation of children from their mothers impairs the children's social development. Scientifically, such a study might collect important psychological data. But it would be unethical to purposely separate infants from their mothers to study the effects of such a separation. Such a separation would violate the ethical principle that study participants must not be harmed. Thus, psychologists would not seriously consider running an experiment that involves intentional separation because of the harm it would be likely to inflict.

One alternative research approach to such a study might be to observe the development of children who have already been separated from their mothers since an early age. However, it could be difficult to draw specific conclusions from this type of research for a number of reasons.

The same factors that led to the separation—such as the death of the parents—may have influenced a child's development as much as (or perhaps more than) the separation itself. Even if there were a positive correlation between separation from the mother and the child's impaired social development, psychologists could not prove cause and effect. That is, they could not prove that one was caused by the other.

Resolving Ethical Issues

The American Psychological Association (APA) has a detailed statement of principles and code of conduct. The principles are divided into ten major categories. Listed below are eight ways to resolve ethical issues from the first category on ethical standards. For the complete Ethical Principles of Psychologists and Code of Conduct, see the reference section at the back of the book.

Misuse of work Psychologists take reasonable steps to correct misuse of their work.

Legal and ethical conflicts Psychologists take steps to resolve conflicts between their professional ethical responsibilities on the one hand and official laws and regulations on the other.

Ethical conflicts with organization Psychologists clarify any conflict between the APA ethics code and the demands of any other organization with which they are affiliated or for whom they happen to be working.

Informal resolution of violations Psychologists attempt to resolve an ethical violation by another psychologist by first bringing it to the attention of that person in an attempt to informally resolve the problem.

Reporting violations Psychologists take further action if an ethical violation has harmed or is likely to harm a person or organization and does not lend itself to an informal resolution of the problem.

Cooperation Psychologists cooperate in ethics investigations.

Complaints Psychologists do not file or encourage the filing of reckless ethics complaints. Rather, they carefully consider the circumstances of the situation.

Unfair discrimination Psychologists do not deny others professional advancement based solely upon their having been the subject of an ethics complaint if the complaint is unjustified or unsubstantiated.

Skills Focus INTERPRETING CHARTS

What do you think might be the purpose of these standards?

Informed Consent
Participants in psychological studies must sign consent forms. *What is the purpose of a consent form?*

What are the ethical standards researchers adhere to? The APA guidelines provide a number of provisions that detail what is needed to make a study ethical. These guidelines include two important principles: confidentiality and informed consent.

Confidentiality Psychologists treat the records of research participants and clients as confidential. In other words, the records are private. This is because psychologists respect people's right to privacy. In addition, people are more likely to disclose true information and feelings when they know that what they say will remain confidential.

In certain very rare circumstances, such as when a client reveals plans to harm someone, a psychologist may disregard confidentiality in order to protect the well-being of the client or of other people. Such situations, however, are definitely the exception rather than the rule. Even when they do arise, psychologists must carefully consider whether breaking confidentiality is the appropriate thing to do.

Informed Consent The APA has distinct restrictions against research studies that could pose a serious threat to the physical or psychological health of participants or that might have long-term, irreversible effects on them. However, the APA acknowledges that some worthwhile studies may cause participants to experience some discomfort or other short-term negative effects. To help avoid situations in which people volunteer to participate in research without knowing that such effects are possible, the APA generally requires that the participants provide informed consent.

Informed consent means that people agree, or consent, to participate in a research study only after they have been given a general overview of the research and have been given the choice of whether or not to participate. The provision of information and the opportunity to choose give people some degree of control and make participation less stressful.

Deception On the other hand, some psychological experiments cannot be run without deceiving people. For instance, new drug experiments and other blind studies cannot be conducted without keeping participants unaware of the treatment they are receiving or of the nature of the study. In order for the study to be valid, some participants must be deceived. In drug experiments, many participants might be told they are taking a real drug when they are actually taking a placebo.

Psychologists have debated the ethics of deceiving participants in research. According to the APA's statement of ethical principles, psychologists may use deception only when they believe that the benefits of the research outweigh the harm, that individuals would have been willing to participate if they understood the research benefits, and when participants receive an explanation of the study after it's over.

Explaining what happened in the study once it is over helps avoid misunderstandings about the research. Explanations also reduce participants' anxieties and let the participants maintain their dignity.

Ethics in Using Data Another area in which psychologists follow strict rules about ethics is in how they produce, store, and present their data. When researchers conduct a study, they need to be as objective as possible in planning the study, in collecting the data, and in analyzing the data. Without this objectivity, the researchers may bias the study, perhaps unintentionally, in favor of their hypothesis.

Even more importantly, when information collected by researchers contradicts their hypothesis, they must be willing to discard their hypothesis in light of the evidence.

It might be tempting to toss out all the evidence that contradicts the hypothesis and present to others only the evidence that supports the hypothesis. But this would be misleading and thus unethical. It might also become an obstacle to others' attempts to study psychology.

Reading Check **Define** Why is confidentiality so important in psychology?

Research with Animals

Needless to say, the experiments referred to earlier in the chapter, in which the scientists studied fish, were conducted with animals. Most studies that use animals (such as those in which researchers have rats run through mazes to find out how they learn) do not harm the animals at all. The idea of using a mirror to find out about the fighting fish was a much more ethical method than using another fighting fish. The scientists were able to move the mirror, but if they had used another real fish, the two fish might have fought to the death.

Sometimes, however, psychologists and other scientists conduct research that may be harmful to animals. Such research studies often use animals because they cannot be carried out with people for ethical reasons. Experiments on the effects of early separation of children from their mothers are an example. These experiments could not be done with

people, but they have been done with monkeys and other animals. Such research has helped psychologists investigate the bonds of attachment between parents and children.

There are other examples of psychological studies that rely on animals in order to avoid harming humans. Psychologists and biologists who study the brain sometimes destroy parts of the brains of laboratory animals to learn how those parts influence their behavior. This and other types of research on animals have benefited humans. Advances in the treatment of mental disorders, strokes, visual and memory defects, headaches, and high blood pressure can be traced to animal research.

Psychologists use animals only when there is no alternative and when they believe that the benefits outweigh the harm. Only a small percentage of psychological studies involve animals. Some researchers argue that many advances in medicine and psychology could not have taken place without harming some animals.

Yet many people believe that it is no more ethical to harm animals than it is to harm humans. Although the APA has rules of ethics for how animals used in research should be treated, controversy continues to surround the use of animals in scientific research.

Reading Check **Recall** Why are rules needed for the treatment of animals in experiments?

Complete a Webquest at thinkcentral.com on animal research.

Online Quiz THINK central thinkcentral.com

SECTION 4 Assessment

Reviewing Main Ideas and Vocabulary

1. **Define** What is a controlled experiment?

2. **Summarize** What is the purpose of ethical standards in the field of psychology?

3. **Explain** Why are confidentiality and informed consent important to psychological research?

Thinking Critically

4. **Draw Conclusions** Why might a double-blind study yield more reliable results than a single-blind study?

5. **Support a Point of View** Do you believe it is ethical or unethical to deceive people about the purposes of research studies?

6. **Analyze** Using your notes and a graphic organizer, explain the role of variables, experimental and control groups, and the placebo effect in the experimental method.

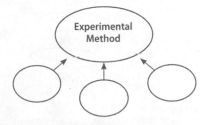

FOCUS ON WRITING

7. **Persuasive** In a paragraph, explain why you think research involving animals should be either abandoned or expanded.

Experiment
Applying What You've Learned

The Hypothetical Snack Bar

Among students at our school, are stated preferences for cola soft drinks and tortilla chips consistent with preferences when these items are taste-tested?

1. Introduction

The premise of the experiment is to conduct a double-blind taste test study. Before you start, record your favorite flavor of soda among those you are going to test. Then record your favorite flavor of tortilla chip among those you are going to test. You are trying to prove or disprove your hypothesis.

Set up two tables in the classroom, one for the soda experiment and one for the tortilla chip experiment. The subjects in the soda experiment will be the testers in the tortilla chip experiment; the subjects in the tortilla chip experiment will be the testers in the soda experiment.

2. Conducting the Cola Experiment

There will be a shield between the subject and the tester. The subjects will also be blindfolded when they sit down at the table.

- Two students, acting as assistants, pour the soda into plastic cups.

- The cups will be labeled in such a way that only the assistants know which soda is in which cup.

- The sodas must be the same color, either all colored or all clear.

- The tester will not be able to tell which cup holds which soda; therefore, it is a double-blind study and there can be no bias on the part of the researchers.

- The tester is given three cups of soda by the assistants, who have recorded which soda is in which cup.

- The subject tastes each of the sodas and indicates which is his or her preference. The tester records the results and, when the study is complete, the results are analyzed by the assistants.

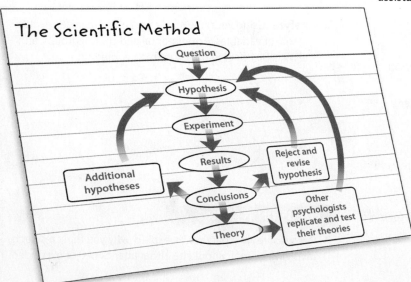

The Scientific Method

Question → Hypothesis → Experiment → Results → Conclusions → Theory

Additional hypotheses

Reject and revise hypothesis

Other psychologists replicate and test their theories

3. Conducting the Tortilla Chip Experiment

There will be a shield between the subject and the tester. The subjects will also be blindfolded when they sit down at the table.

■ You will follow the same steps with the tortilla chips as with the cola drinks.

■ The bowls will be labeled in such a way that only the assistants know which chips are in which bowl.

■ The chips should be the same brand but three different flavors. Try to get chips that have the same color coating on them so the tester cannot tell the difference. This will satisfy the requirements for a double-blind study.

■ The tester will not be able to tell which bowl holds which chips; therefore, it is a double blind study and there can be no bias on the part of the researchers.

■ The tester is given three servings of chips by the assistants who have recorded which chips are in which bowl.

■ The subject tastes each of the chips and indicates which is his or her preference. The tester records the results and, when the study is complete, the results are analyzed by the assistants.

■ You can extend the experiment by using cut-up pieces of candy bars or snack crackers in different flavors. The experiments are run the exact same way as the soda and tortilla chip tests.

4. Discussion

This experiment covers target population, how to conduct a study, single-blind and double-blind studies, and several other topics covered in the chapter. Hold a group discussion that focuses on the following questions:

■ Was the hypothesis proved or disproved?

■ Which subject matter that you studied in the chapter was touched on by these experiments?

■ What did you learn from this experiment?

Comprehension and Critical Thinking

SECTION 1 *(pp. 34–37)*

1. a. Identify What is the first step in scientific research?

   b. Explain What is a hypothesis and how is it often worded?

   c. Elaborate Explain the importance of replication in scientific research.

SECTION 2 *(pp. 38–42)*

2. a. Define What is a bias?

   b. Compare and Contrast What are some of the advantages and disadvantages of the survey method?

   c. Elaborate Why must psychologists select samples scientifically?

SECTION 3 *(pp. 44–49)*

3. a. Recall What is the cross-sectional method?

   b. Explain What is the difference between positive correlation and negative correlation?

   c. Evaluate If correlations do not explain cause and effect, why are they useful?

SECTION 4 *(pp. 51–57)*

4. a. Describe What is the experimental method?

   b. Compare and Contrast What is the difference between an experimental group and a control group?

   c. Evaluate Under what circumstances do you think a psychologist might justifiably break the promise of confidentiality?

INTERNET ACTIVITY ✷

5. Surveys are often used to help predict future events, such as election outcomes. How might these surveys affect the outcome of the events? Choose a recent election, such as a 2008 state primary election to choose a presidential candidate or the national election for president. Use the Internet to research how pre-election surveys and polls might have affected election results. Write a short report that summarizes your findings.

Reviewing Vocabulary

Match the terms below with their correct definitions.

6. hypothesis   **12.** placebo

7. sample   **13.** standard deviation

8. longitudinal method   **14.** ethics

9. correlation   **15.** control group

10. experiment   **16.** single-blind study

11. variables

A. method researchers use to answer questions about cause and effect

B. researchers select a group of participants and then observe them over a period of time

C. part of a target population studied by researchers

D. substance or treatment that has no effect apart from a person's belief in it

E. educated guess or answer to a research question

F. factors that can vary or change in an experiment

G. measure of how closely two things are related

H. standards for proper and responsible behavior

I. a measure of distance of every score to the mean

J. participants do not know whether they are in the experimental group or the control group

K. members of a study who do not receive treatment

Psychology in Your Life

17. Do you have a family pet, perhaps a cat or a dog? What would you think of your pet being used in an animal experiment that focused on family pets? Write an essay in which you defend or argue against the use of animal subjects in psychological research. Do some background reading so that you can support your position with facts. Read your essay to the class as part of a class discussion about the ethics of research with animals.

SKILLS ACTIVITY: ANALYZING PRIMARY SOURCES

Read the following excerpt, which is taken from the Ethics Code of the American Psychological Association. Then answer the questions that follow.

> **"**Psychologists strive to benefit those with whom they work and take care to do no harm. In their professional actions, psychologists seek to safeguard the welfare and rights of those with whom they interact professionally and other affected persons, and the welfare of animal subjects of research. When conflicts occur among psychologists' obligations or concerns, they attempt to resolve these conflicts in a responsible fashion that avoids or minimizes harm. Because psychologists' scientific and professional judgments and actions may affect the lives of others, they are alert to and guard against personal, financial, social, organizational, or political factors that might lead to misuse of their influence.**"**
>
> —American Psychological Association *Ethics Code*

18. Identify Main Ideas What is the essential ethical value or point of this excerpt?

19. Draw Conclusions Why must psychologists consider the welfare and rights of their clients?

WRITING FOR AP PSYCHOLOGY

Use your knowledge of psychological methods to answer the question below. Do not simply list the facts. Present a clear argument based on your critical analysis of the question, using the appropriate psychological terminology.

20. Briefly describe each of the following terms commonly used in established psychological procedures or methods. Describe how these terms help to ensure that psychological research is conducted in a scientific manner.

- mean
- median
- mode
- range
- standard deviation

Connecting Online

Visit **thinkcentral.com** for review and enrichment activities related to this chapter.

Quiz and Review

ONLINE QUIZZES
Take a practice quiz for each section in this chapter.

WEBQUEST
Complete a structured Internet activity for this chapter.

QUICK LAB
Reinforce a key concept with a short lab activity.

APPLYING WHAT YOU'VE LEARNED
Review and apply your knowledge by completing a project-based assessment.

Activities

eACTIVITIES
Complete chapter Internet activities for enrichment.

INTERACTIVE FEATURE
Explore an interactive version of a key feature in this chapter.

KEEP IT CURRENT
Link to current news and research in psychology.

Online Textbook

 Learn more about key topics in this chapter.

Experimental Psychologist

Generally considered the most scientific of psychological disciplines, experimental psychology involves research into the basic biological processes related to behavior, thoughts, and emotions.

Some experimental psychologists conduct research only with people. Others work with animals, such as dolphins.

Experimental psychologists follow a set of strictly controlled scientific procedures to learn about the relationships among two or more variables. Their research usually emphasizes physiological studies of the nervous system, the brain itself, and the basic processes of thinking, feeling, remembering, and perceiving external stimuli. Experimental psychologists lay the groundwork for more practical kinds of research and counseling. This basic research, which may seem to have no practical value at the time it is conducted, has led other researchers to develop useful techniques for reducing stress, increasing motivation, enhancing memory, and encouraging longer attention spans, for example.

In conducting their research, experimental psychologists often work with animals. They may compare the behavior of one species with that of another. In many cases, experimental psychologists use primates because their behavior is so similar to that of humans. The ethical use of animals in research procedures is a matter of ongoing debate. The benefits from using them, however, generally outweigh the potential harm. Also, experimental psychologists are careful to ensure that the animals receive humane treatment. Guidelines aid psychologists as they design animal research projects.

Temperament may be one of the most important factors when considering a career in experimental psychology, because it takes a certain type of person to think in these process-oriented terms. Like those in other basic research fields, experimental psychologists tend to be detail-oriented, patient individuals who easily become absorbed in their work, and do not require regular, close contact with other people. They tend to be independent, abstract thinkers. A doctoral degree is mandatory for the most engrossing work in experimental psychology. Candidates must have a strong preparation in the hard sciences, with a concentration in neuroanatomy, physiology, biology, molecular biology, and genetics.

Most graduate programs prefer candidates who have already demonstrated some competence in research and laboratory skills before entering the doctoral program. If a career in experimental psychology appeals to you, it would be wise to gain some exposure to research science as an undergraduate or even while still in high school.

Applying APA Style

APA Style **THINK** central   thinkcentral.com

Many articles in professional journals report the research of experimental psychologists. In keeping with the guidelines from the **American Psychological Association (APA)**, these articles follow a similar style for citing source materials.

The APA prefers citations within the text when referencing the source material used for direct quotes and paraphrased information. These citations appear in the body of the text and include the author's last name and the year of publication: (Martin, 2007). For direct quotes, page numbers are also included: (Newman, 2008, p. 208). In-text citations are a sign of quality scholarship. They also help authors avoid plagiarism and help readers locate the complete article.

Through Think Central you can find more on in-text citations from the APA style guidelines. Review the APA guidelines. Then make a list of different types of in-text citations and provide an example for each type.

Citation Type	Example
one author	Goode, 2004
two authors	
three authors	
direct quote	

Body and Mind

THE BRAIN OF PHINEAS GAGE

Phineas Gage's skull was pierced by an iron rod.

The Granger Collection, New York

The ability of the brain to withstand accidents is nothing less than remarkable. In some instances, people have not only survived severe injuries to the brain, but they have continued to live fairly normal lives. Sometimes, though, the victims are not quite the same as before the accident. Consider the case of Phineas Gage.

Mr. Gage was a promising railroad worker. His character was outstanding and he was well liked. But all that changed on September 13, 1848. While Gage was tamping down the blasting powder for a dynamite charge with an iron rod, the powder accidentally ignited. The inch-thick metal rod, which weighed more than 13 pounds, shot out of the hole. It rammed through Gage's brain and out the top of his head.

The rod landed many yards away. Gage fell back in a heap, but he was not dead. His coworkers watched in shock as, a few moments later, he stood up and spoke. They drove him by oxcart to a local doctor, John Harlow. As the doctor marveled at the hole through Gage's head, Gage asked the doctor when he could go back to work.

Two months later, the physical effects of Gage's wound had healed. Everyone, including the doctor, was surprised that Phineas Gage had survived the accident. He walked about, spoke normally enough, and was aware of his surroundings. However, Gage had changed. He no longer was a dependable worker. He had also become foul-mouthed and ill-mannered. It was clear that the accident had serious psychological consequences.

Gage died 13 years later during an epileptic seizure. Dr. Harlow persuaded Gage's family to donate his skull to the Warren Medical Museum at Harvard University. Generations of biologists and psychologists have studied the skull and wondered how Gage's changes in personality might have been caused by damage to his brain.

Biologists Hanna and Antonio Damasio explain that the way in which the rod entered the brain spared the areas involved in language and movement. Thus, Gage was able to speak normally and walk about easily. However, the rod had severely damaged an area in the brain related to personality. According to the Damasios, people who suffer damage to the same part of the brain today experience similar changes in personality. These people are often unable to censor their thoughts before speaking. As a result, they blurt out thoughts that they would have kept to themselves before their brains were injured.

Other researchers have found similar changes in patients' personalities after injuries to the same area of the brain. Some patients develop rule-breaking and impulsive behaviors. For example, they may

CHAPTER 3
BIOLOGY AND BEHAVIOR

begin to interrupt conversations. They are also less likely to make spontaneous facial expressions. The combination of excessive talking and lack of expression can make these individuals seem like entirely different people.

Brain injuries can result from many different types of accidents. During the war in Iraq, roadside bombs seriously injured the brains of thousands of soldiers. These injuries and one man's road to recovery were described by ABC News reporter Bob Woodruff, who suffered a traumatic brain injury in Iraq while covering the fighting. His book *In An Instant* provides details about the struggle to survive and to recover from traumatic brain injury. In this chapter you will learn more about the biology of the brain, its parts, and how it functions.

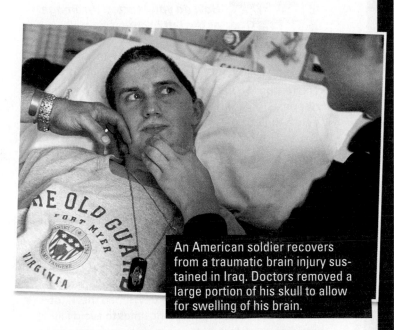

An American soldier recovers from a traumatic brain injury sustained in Iraq. Doctors removed a large portion of his skull to allow for swelling of his brain.

What do you think?

1. How did Phineas Gage's personality change after his brain injury?

2. What are some other possible circumstances in which individuals experience brain trauma?

Chapter at a Glance

SECTION 1: The Nervous System

- The nervous system functions as a communication system for the body. Messages are transmitted by neurons to axons and dendrites.

- The nervous system is made up of the central nervous system and the peripheral nervous system, which transmits messages between the central nervous system and all parts of the body.

SECTION 2: The Brain: Our Control Center

- The brain is composed of three major sections: the hindbrain, the midbrain, and the forebrain.

- The cerebral cortex is the part of the brain that controls thinking, memory, language, emotions, complex motor functions, perceptions, and much more.

SECTION 3: The Endocrine System

- The endocrine system secretes hormones that stimulate growth and many kinds of reactions, such as activity levels and moods.

- The major endocrine glands include the pituitary, the thyroid, the adrenals, the testes, and the ovaries.

SECTION 4: Heredity: Our Genetic Background

- Heredity plays a key role in the development of individuals' traits. Heredity is transmitted through genes, which are found in chromosomes.

- Kinship studies allow researchers to determine the influence of heredity and environment on individuals.

The Nervous System

Before You Read

Main Idea

The nervous system contains billions of cells called neurons. Neurons communicate with one another through the central and peripheral nervous systems.

Reading Focus

1. What are neurons, and how do they work?

2. How do neurotransmitters work as chemical messengers?

3. What does the central nervous system control?

4. How is the peripheral nervous system structured?

Vocabulary

central nervous system
peripheral nervous system
neurons
cell body
dendrites
axon
myelin
axon terminals
synapse
neurotransmitters
spinal cord
somatic nervous system
autonomic nervous system

TAKING NOTES Use a graphic organizer like this one to take notes on the nervous system.

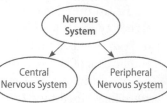

FIGHT OR FLIGHT

PSYCHOLOGY CLOSE UP

How do you react to the image at the left? Do you inwardly cringe even though you know it is just a photograph? Humans have physical and psychological reactions to dangerous situations. This response is commonly called the "fight or flight" response, that is, the body is ready to fight or to flee from a threat. When this response is activated, the heart rate increases, more blood flows to major muscle groups, and the body has a burst of energy and strength to help it either fight or run away. Eyesight sharpens and sensory awareness increases. In the case of an attack from this dog, you may assess whether your safety would best be met by running away from the animal or by defending yourself from its vicious jaws. Most reactions occur in an instant, without actual conscious thought.

In the early 1900s, physiologist Walter Cannon first argued that animals likely developed the "fight or flight" response in prehistoric times to avoid falling victim to predators. In our modern lives only rarely do we face a snarling dog, but we do face situations that cause the body to automatically respond to stress. In this section you will read about the system that allows the body to do this—the nervous system. ■

Neurons

The human nervous system is involved in thinking, dreaming, feeling, moving, and much more. It is working when we are active or still, awake or asleep. The nervous system regulates our internal functions. It is also involved in how we react to the external world. Even learning and memory are made possible by the nervous system. When we learn a new behavior or acquire new information, the nervous system registers that experience and changes to accommodate its storage.

The nervous system has two parts: the central nervous system and the peripheral nervous system. The **central nervous system** consists of the brain and the spinal cord. The **peripheral nervous system** is made up of nerve cells that send messages between the central nervous system and other parts of the body. In order to understand how the central and peripheral nervous systems work, we must first understand how nerve cells communicate with one another and how their messages travel through the body.

Each of us has more than 100 billion neurons, most of which are found in the brain. **Neurons** are nerve cells that run through our entire bodies and communicate with each other. Neurons send and receive messages from other parts of the body, such as muscles and glands. These messages relate to events: the sensation of a pinprick, the first steps of a child, the writing of a poem, the memory of a past event.

Recent research has shown that the brain has the ability to reorganize itself by altering the connections between neurons to make up for injury or disease, or to adjust to changes in the environment. This phenomenon is known as neuroplasticity. These changes can occur in response to new experiences at different times throughout an individual's life.

Components of a Neuron Neurons are somewhat like trees in structure. Parts of neurons resemble branches, trunk, and roots. And, as in forests, many nerve cells lie alongside one another like a thicket of trees. Unlike trees, however, neurons can also lie end to end. Some neurons' "roots" are intertwined with the "branches" of neurons that lie below.

Every neuron consists of three basic components: a cell body, dendrites, and an axon. The **cell body** produces energy that fuels the neuron's activity. Branching out from the cell body are thin fibers called **dendrites** that receive information from other neurons and pass the message through the cell body. While a dendrite carries information to the cell body, an **axon** transmits messages away from it.

Complete a Webquest at thinkcentral.com on brain plasticity.

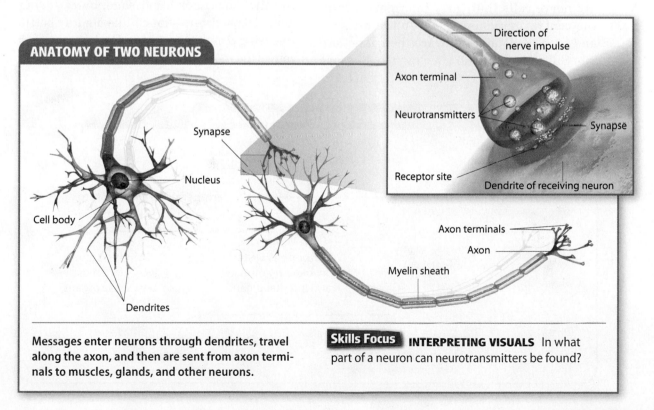

ANATOMY OF TWO NEURONS

Synapse

Nucleus

Cell body

Dendrites

Direction of nerve impulse

Axon terminal

Neurotransmitters

Synapse

Receptor site

Dendrite of receiving neuron

Axon terminals

Axon

Myelin sheath

Messages enter neurons through dendrites, travel along the axon, and then are sent from axon terminals to muscles, glands, and other neurons.

Skills Focus INTERPRETING VISUALS In what part of a neuron can neurotransmitters be found?

A neuron has many dendrites but usually only one axon. Axons vary greatly in length. Some are just a tiny fraction of an inch, while others stretch to several feet. Some neurons in your legs are several feet long.

Many axons are covered with **myelin,** a white fatty substance that insulates and protects the axon. This myelin sheath, or casing, also helps to speed up the transmission of the messages sent by neurons. At the end of the axon, smaller fibers branch out. These fibers are called **axon terminals.**

The Communication Process Messages are sent from the axon terminals of one neuron to the dendrites of other neurons. In order for a message to be sent from one neuron to another neuron, it must cross the **synapse.** The synapse is a junction between the axon terminals of one neuron and the dendrites of another. Messages travel in only one direction. Thus, messages enter the dendrites and travel through the cell body and axon to the axon terminals. From there, they cross synapses to the dendrites of other neurons.

The information that is sent depends on the location of the neuron in the body and the event that produced the message. Sensory neurons are nerve cells that carry information received by the senses to the central nervous system. Motor neurons, on the other hand, are nerve cells that carry information from the central nervous system to the muscles and the glands and influence their functioning. Suppose you stub your big toe. Sensory neurons take the message to the brain. Motor neurons take messages back to your foot so that you pull it up. These messages can move at speeds exceeding 200 miles per hour.

Occasionally, something happens to disrupt the message-sending process. A hard blow to the head from a car accident or a sports mishap, for example, can cause a concussion—an injury in which the soft tissue of the brain hits against the skull. This concussion may cause memory loss. Sometimes, the person is affected for only a few seconds. Other times, the person may experience effects for a much longer time. For example, a football player suffers a concussion during a game. He remembers being at the game, but he cannot remember what happened during the game. He may never be able to recall the event again. Research shows that memory is in large part a biological process.

Reading Check **Identify Supporting Details** How does each of the main parts of a neuron function?

Neurotransmitters: The Body's Chemical Messengers

Neurons send messages across synapses through the release of **neurotransmitters.** Neurotransmitters are chemicals that are stored in sacs in the axon terminals. A neuron fires, or sends a message, by releasing neurotransmitters—much like a spray bottle releasing droplets of water. Each message is converted into an electrical impulse that trav-

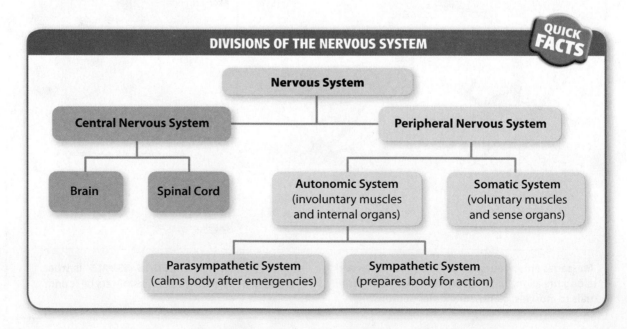

DIVISIONS OF THE NERVOUS SYSTEM — QUICK FACTS

Nervous System

- Central Nervous System
  - Brain
  - Spinal Cord
- Peripheral Nervous System
  - Autonomic System (involuntary muscles and internal organs)
    - Parasympathetic System (calms body after emergencies)
    - Sympathetic System (prepares body for action)
  - Somatic System (voluntary muscles and sense organs)

els the length of the neuron. The message is then transmitted to the next neuron by other neurotransmitters, and the process continues until the message arrives at its destination. This whole process takes only a fraction of a second, and neurons can fire hundreds of times every second.

Neurotransmitters are involved in everything people do. Whenever you wave a hand, yawn, or think about a friend, neurotransmitters are involved. Some diseases and psychological disorders may also be caused by the presence of too many or too few of various neurotransmitters.

There are several types of neurotransmitters. Each has its own structure and fits into a receptor site on the next neuron, similar to how a key fits into a lock. Researchers have identified dozens of neurotransmitters and their functions. For example, acetylcholine is involved in the control of muscles. It is used by the motor neurons of the spinal cord and stimulates skeletal muscles. Acetylcholine is also involved in learning and memory. When the amount of acetylcholine decreases, the formation of memories is impaired. Scientists believe that too little acetylcholine may be associated with Alzheimer's disease.

Another neurotransmitter, dopamine, is involved primarily in motor behavior. A deficiency in dopamine levels plays a role in Parkinson's disease, which is characterized by trembling hands, problems with balance, and uncoordinated, rigid movements. On the other hand, an excess of dopamine may contribute to the brain disorder schizophrenia. Other neurotransmitters include noradrenaline, which is primarily involved in preparing the body for action, and serotonin, which is involved in emotional arousal and sleep. Too little of both may be a factor in depression.

Although we are often unaware of the processes in our bodies, we can be sure that our bodies are hard at work whether we are running or sitting still. At any given moment, millions of neurons are shooting neurotransmitters across synapses and sending complicated messages to various parts of the body. These messages are carried via the spinal cord and the peripheral nervous system.

Reading Check **Find the Main Idea** How do neurotransmitters function?

The Central Nervous System

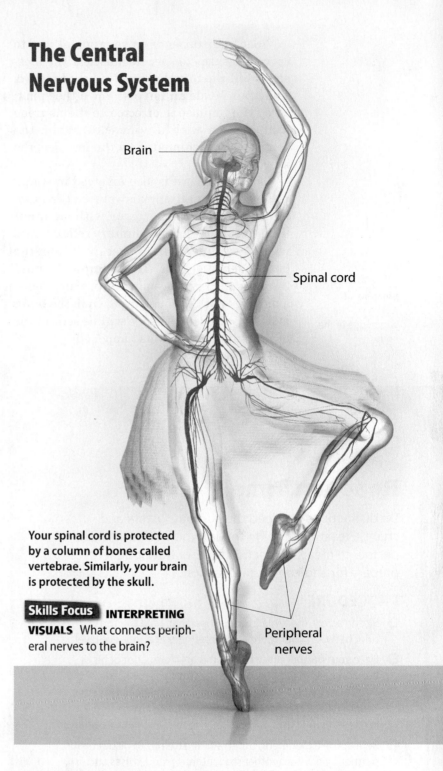

Brain

Spinal cord

Your spinal cord is protected by a column of bones called vertebrae. Similarly, your brain is protected by the skull.

Skills Focus **INTERPRETING VISUALS** What connects peripheral nerves to the brain?

Peripheral nerves

The Central Nervous System

The illustration above shows the central nervous system, which consists of the neurons of the spinal cord and the brain. The **spinal cord** is a column of nerves about as thick as a thumb that extends from the brain down the back. It is protected by the bones of the spine and transmits messages between the brain and the muscles and glands in the body.

Your brain depends on your spinal cord to carry messages to specific muscles. The messages tell the muscles exactly how to move. The brain sends an impulse down the spinal cord. The impulse is directed to the neurons that connect with the muscles. When the receptors are stimulated by the impulse, the muscles move.

The spinal cord is also involved in spinal reflexes. A spinal reflex is your body's automatic response to a trigger without input from the brain. This involuntary reflex occurs when nerve impulses are received from the body's sense organs. These impulses pass immediately into the spinal cord, which sends a message out. Although input from the brain is not required, a message will be sent to the brain telling it what has happened.

For example, if a person touches a hot stove, a message goes immediately from his or her hand to the spinal cord. A message to remove the hand is then sent back to motor neurons in the hand. The removal of the hand is a spinal reflex. The person may also register pain in his or her brain, but the pain is not what causes the reflex. In fact, pain might not even occur until after the person removes his or her hand.

Many of our simple actions are reflexive. They are the way the body protects itself from harm. Have you ever wondered why you blink when you get a speck of dust in your eye? Or why some people sneeze when they sniff pepper? These are reflexive actions designed to protect your eyes or prevent irritants from entering your lungs. Physicians sometimes test people's reflexes to make sure their nervous systems are functioning properly. When a doctor taps just below your knee cap to make your leg move, the purpose is to check the knee-jerk reflex, that is, to check that neurons are responding the way they are supposed to. The tap stimulates sensory neurons in the tendon of the thigh muscle. A message then gets sent to the spinal cord that the tendon has been stretched. In reaction, the thigh muscle contracts, causing the leg to straighten from the knee with a sudden kick.

Reading Check **Summarize** What are the functions of the central nervous system?

The Peripheral Nervous System

The peripheral nervous system lies outside the central nervous system and is responsible for transmitting messages between the central nervous system and all other parts of the body. The two main divisions of the peripheral nervous system are the somatic nervous system and the autonomic nervous system.

The Somatic Nervous System The **somatic nervous system** transmits sensory messages to the central nervous system. Its function is to carry messages from the voluntary muscles and sense organs. Activated by touch, pain, changes in temperature, and changes in body position, the somatic nervous system enables us to experience the sensations of heat and cold and to feel pain and pressure. For example, we can feel the softness of a cat's fur,

Quick Lab

Reaction Time

Do distractions overload the nervous system and change reaction time? In this lab you will work with a partner to measure reaction time, or how long it takes to prepare for and complete an action.

PROCEDURE

❶ Sitting across the table from your partner, hold the top of a ruler between your thumb and forefinger at about eye level.

❷ Have your partner place the thumb and forefinger of his or her dominant hand about an inch away from each side of the bottom of the ruler. Count 10 seconds, then release the ruler. Your partner should catch it, and hold it in place. Record the level of the ruler above the table in inches. Repeat three times.

❸ Repeat the experiment, but this time attempt to distract your partner by having another student make loud noises and sudden gestures. Record the level in inches. Repeat three times.

ANALYSIS

1. Average the distance from the table for the first three catches. Did the distance increase or decrease with each catch?

2. Compare the average with the last three catches. Did the distractions change the distance?

3. Which conditions produced the fastest reaction times? What do you think accounts for the difference?

Quick Lab **THINK** central   thinkcentral.com

warmth if the cat is sitting on our lap, and pain if the cat scratches us. The somatic system also alerts us that parts of the body have moved or changed position. It sends messages to the muscles and the glands and helps us maintain posture and balance.

The Autonomic Nervous System The word *autonomic* means "occurring involuntarily," or automatically. The human **autonomic nervous system** regulates the body's vital functions, such as heartbeat, breathing, digestion, and blood pressure. We generally do not have to think about these activities—they occur automatically and are essential for keeping us alive. Involuntary muscles and internal organs are governed by this system.

The autonomic nervous system has two divisions: the sympathetic and the parasympathetic nervous systems. Psychologists are interested in the autonomic nervous system because of the role it plays in feeling emotions. The responses of the autonomic nervous system are particularly important when a person experiences something stressful in his or her environment.

The sympathetic system is activated when a person is going into action, perhaps because of some stressful event. It prepares the body either to confront the situation or to run away. This is the "fight or flight" response.

When a person suddenly comes face to face with a snake, for example, the sympathetic nervous system is called into action. Should he or she stay or run away? The sympathetic nervous system prepares the body for this decision by suppressing digestion, increasing the heart and respiration rates, and elevating the blood pressure. In other words, the body is preparing the muscles most needed to respond to an emergency situation and strenuous activity. Do you ever feel queasy when you are in a stressful situation—such as when you are about to take a big test? This is because your sympathetic nervous system has kicked into action and has suppressed your digestive processes.

In contrast to the sympathetic system, the parasympathetic nervous system is sometimes called the "rest and digest" response. The parasympathetic system restores the body's reserves of energy after intense activity. Heart rate and blood pressure normalize,

breathing slows, and digestion returns to normal. The actions of both systems take place automatically. You do not have to consciously think about your body's responses. Imagine how difficult your life would be without the responses of the autonomic nervous system. You would have to make a decision about every action your body takes, even in dangerous situations.

If you are having trouble remembering which system is which, keep in mind that "sympathetic" and "stress" both start with the letter *s*, while "parasympathetic" and "peace" both begin with the letter *p*. The sympathetic nervous system reacts to stress; the parasympathetic nervous system restores peace to your body's systems.

Reading Check **Identify Supporting Details** What are the systems that make up the peripheral nervous system?

SECTION 1 Assessment

Reviewing Main Ideas and Vocabulary

1. **Identify** What are the main divisions of the nervous system?

2. **Contrast** How do the functions of the autonomic nervous system differ from the functions of the somatic nervous system?

3. **Describe** What is the role of the sympathetic nervous system in the "fight or flight" response?

Thinking Critically

4. **Explain** How do messages travel from one neuron to another?

5. **Elaborate** In what way do the parasympathetic and sympathetic nervous systems work together?

6. **Compare** Using your notes and a graphic organizer like the one below, compare the functions of each major part of the nervous system discussed in this section.

System	Function

FOCUS ON WRITING

7. **Descriptive** Recall a time in your life when you experienced a stressful situation such as a job or scholarship interview or even a bad dream. Write a paragraph describing how you felt nervous and relate those feelings to the action of the sympathetic nervous system.

The Brain: Our Control Center

Before You Read

Main Idea

The human brain has many parts that work together to coordinate body movement, create thought and emotions, and shape behaviors.

Reading Focus

1. What were some of the early beliefs about the brain?
2. What are the parts of the brain, and how do they function?
3. How is the cerebral cortex divided?
4. Which methods do scientists use to study the brain?

Vocabulary

medulla
pons
cerebellum
reticular activating system
thalamus
hypothalamus
limbic system
cerebrum
cerebral cortex
corpus callosum
association areas

TAKING NOTES Use a graphic organizer like this one to take notes on the parts of the brain.

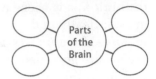

Parts of the Brain

RIGHT BRAIN, WRONG FACE

PSYCHOLOGY CLOSE UP

What if you could only see the right side of your face? Neurologist Oliver Sacks tells the story of Mrs. S, one of his most curious cases. Mrs. S had suffered a massive stroke that damaged the right side of her brain—the side of the brain that controls a person's ability to see things that are on one's left. As a result, *left* did not exist for Mrs. S. For example, when she ate, Mrs. S could only see the food on the right side of her plate. To complete a meal, Mrs. S would rotate her chair to the right, keeping her eyes turned right until she could see the rest of her dinner. When she looked at herself

in a mirror, she only saw the right half of her face. Visitors were often surprised when they met Mrs. S and she wore make-up only on the right side of her face.

Mrs. S suffered from hemi-inattention, a rare condition that makes it impossible to understand information processed by the right half of the brain. When doctors devised a way for Mrs. S to see her "missing half," she became extremely distressed. What she saw and how she experienced her body no longer matched her self-image. The way the left and right sides of the brain function separately and together controls our view of ourselves and of the world. ■

Early Beliefs About the Brain

Every person is unique in part because of the capacities for learning and thought made possible by the human brain. But we have gained our knowledge of the brain only recently. In ancient times, people did not attribute human psychological processes such as thinking to the working of the brain. They thought that what was inside a person's body was not very different from what was inside an animal's body. Therefore, they reasoned, the abilities that make people different from animals—such as creativity and imagination—could not be explained in biological terms. Instead, people widely believed that the body was inhabited by souls or demons.

The ancient Egyptians believed that a little person dwelled within the skull and regulated behavior. Greek philosopher Aristotle thought that the soul resided in the heart. The English language still reflects the belief in the heart as the seat of will, thought, hunger, and joy. We use expressions such as "deep in one's heart," "to know something by heart," and "to have a change of heart."

Today, however, we recognize that the mind, or consciousness, dwells within the brain. We now have greater understanding of the brain and the links between biological processes and psychological phenomena.

Reading Check **Sequence** How have ideas about the human brain changed over time?

Parts of the Brain

The human brain is composed of many parts that work together to organize our movements, create our thoughts, form our emotions, and produce our behaviors. Scientists have identified the localized functions of different parts of the brain.

The brain is divided into three sections: the hindbrain, the midbrain, and the forebrain. The hindbrain is the lower portion of the brain and is involved in many vital functions such as heart rate, respiration, and balance. It is called the hindbrain because it is at the back of the brain as it rests in the skull. The midbrain includes areas that are involved in vision and hearing. The forebrain, the front area of the brain, is involved in complex functions such as thought and emotion.

The Hindbrain The medulla, the pons, and the cerebellum are important structures of the hindbrain. The **medulla** is involved in vital functions such as heart rate, blood pressure, and breathing. The **pons** is located in front of the medulla and is involved in regulating body movement, attention, sleep, and alertness.

Cerebellum is the Latin word for "little brain." The **cerebellum** looks like the larger part of the brain (the cerebrum), under which it rests, but it is much smaller. It is involved in balance and coordination. A person whose cerebellum is injured may have trouble with coordination. The person may walk unsteadily and even occasionally fall down.

The Midbrain The midbrain is located between the hindbrain and the forebrain. Areas within the midbrain are involved in vision and hearing. Eye movement, for example, is controlled by an area in the midbrain. In addition, the midbrain contains part of the **reticular activating system.** The reticular activating system begins in the hindbrain and rises through the midbrain into the lower part of the forebrain. This system is important for attention, sleep, and arousal. Stimulation of the reticular activating system makes us alert. It affects arousal by increasing heart rate and blood pressure, and it increases brain activity. Some drugs, such as alcohol, reduce the activity of the reticular activating system, thus affecting alertness and reaction time.

Sudden, loud noises stimulate the reticular activating system and can awaken a sleeping person. However, the reticular activating system can screen out some noises. A person who lives in the city may not be awakened by the sounds of traffic roaring by. This same person may, however, awaken to sounds that are more out of the ordinary, such as a bird singing, even if these sounds are fairly soft.

The Forebrain Four key areas of the forebrain are the thalamus, the hypothalamus, the limbic system, and the cerebrum. Certain parts of the forebrain are very well developed in human beings. The forebrain is the part of the brain that makes it possible for humans to engage in complex thinking processes.

Thalamus is a Latin word meaning "inner chamber." The **thalamus** is a critical structure of the brain because it serves as a relay station for sensory stimulation.

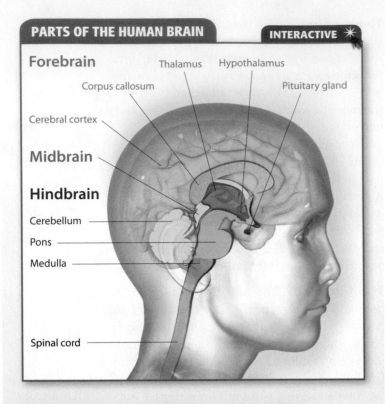

PARTS OF THE HUMAN BRAIN

INTERACTIVE

Forebrain
- Corpus callosum
- Cerebral cortex
- Thalamus
- Hypothalamus
- Pituitary gland

Midbrain

Hindbrain
- Cerebellum
- Pons
- Medulla

- Spinal cord

SENSORY AND MOTOR AREAS OF THE BRAIN

- Primary motor cortex
- Primary somasensory cortex
- Frontal lobe
- Parietal lobe
- Occipital lobe
- Vision
- Temporal lobe

Interactive Feature THINK central thinkcentral.com

The average human adult brain has more than 10 billion cells. Although the brain makes up about 2 to 3 percent of a person's body weight, it requires about 20 percent of the blood's oxygen supply.

Skills Focus INTERPRETING VISUALS What parts of the brain make up the forebrain?

Most of the messages coming from the sense organs go through the thalamus on the way to the higher levels of the brain (those areas responsible for mental processes such as thinking and reasoning). The thalamus transmits sensory information to the areas of the brain that interpret and respond to the information. The thalamus also relays sensory input from the eyes and the ears to the appropriate parts of the brain for interpretation of the input.

Hypo– is a Greek prefix meaning "under." Thus, the **hypothalamus** lies below the thalamus. The hypothalamus is tiny, but it is extremely important because it is involved in many aspects of behavior and physiological functions. It is vital to the regulation of body temperature, the storage of nutrients, and various aspects of motivation and emotion. It is also involved in hunger, thirst, sexual behavior, caring for offspring, and aggression. Disturbances within the hypothalamus can lead to unusual drinking and eating behaviors.

Among animals, stimulation of parts of the hypothalamus triggers behaviors such as fighting, mating, and even nest building. Although the hypothalamus is also important to humans, our behavior is less mechanical than other animals and tends to be influenced by cognitive functions such as thought, choice, and value systems.

The **limbic system** forms a fringe along the inner edge of the cerebrum. It gets its name from the Latin word *limbus*, which implies the idea of a circle or ring. The limbic system forms a kind of border around the brain stem. It is involved in learning and memory, emotion, hunger, sex, and aggression. A branch of psychology called evolutionary psychology has studied this area extensively. Evolutionary psychologists believe that the limbic system controls behaviors that are necessary for the survival of humans and other mammals. For example, it allows a person to distinguish between agreeable and disagreeable situations. The brain forms emotional memories of situations that help the person respond and adapt to the situation. Psychologists believe these areas are very specialized and only activate when triggered.

If a particular part of the limbic system is damaged, people can recall old memories but do not create new memories. For example, a man with damage to that area may have vivid childhood memories of playing with his sister but may not remember that the same sister visited earlier that day. Researchers have also found that destruction of another specific area of the limbic system can lead animals to show passive behavior. Destruction of still another area of the limbic system causes some animals to behave aggressively, even when there seems no reason to do so.

The **cerebrum** (Latin for "brain") is the crowning glory of the brain. Only in human beings does the cerebrum make up such a large part of the brain. It accounts for about 70 percent of the brain's total weight. The cerebrum is the site of most conscious and intellectual activities. The surface of the cerebrum is wrinkled with ridges and valleys. This surface is the cerebral cortex. The **cerebral cortex** is the outer layer of the brain, just as bark is the outer layer of a tree. (*Cortex* is the Latin word for "bark.")

The cerebral cortex is the part of the brain that we tend to think of when we talk about the brain. It is the part that makes us uniquely human—the part that thinks. In addition to thinking, the cerebral cortex also deals with memory, language, emotions, complex motor functions, perception, and much more.

Reading Check **Contrast** How do the functions of the midbrain and the forebrain differ?

The Cerebral Cortex

The cerebral cortex is composed of two sides—a left side and a right side. Each side is called a hemisphere. (The Greek *hemi-* means "half." Thus, each half of the brain is half a sphere, just as each half of Earth is a hemisphere.) To visualize the cerebral cortex, think of a walnut. The shell of the walnut is like the skull. Just as the walnut has two sides that are connected, so does the brain. In the brain, the structure that connects the two hemispheres is called the **corpus callosum.**

Information received by one side of the body is transmitted to the *opposite* hemisphere of the brain. For example, if you touch something with your left hand, that information is sent to the right side of your brain. And if you touch something with your right hand, the left hemisphere of your brain receives the information. The corpus callosum aids in getting information from one side of the brain to the other.

Each hemisphere of the cerebral cortex is divided into four parts called lobes. The frontal lobe lies behind the forehead, and the parietal lobe lies to the top and rear of the head. The temporal lobe lies to the side, just below the ears. The occipital lobe is located at the back of the head.

Some sensations, such as visual sensations, are received primarily in one lobe. However, each lobe does not necessarily act independently from the others. Some functions require the interplay of several lobes. The involvement of the cerebral cortex in the senses and motor behavior is a good illustration of this interaction.

Senses and Motor Behavior The occipital lobe is the primary visual area of the cerebral cortex. When light strikes the eyes, neurons in the occipital lobe fire, enabling us to see. We also "see" flashes of light if neurons in the occipital lobe are stimulated by electrodes.

Damage to different parts of the occipital lobe can create unusual conditions. People with damage to one area may be able to recognize an object, but they may be unable to differentiate it from another object that is similar. For example, if shown a key, they may know that they see a key, but they may not be able to tell it apart from another key.

Brain Facts

- Neurons create and send more messages than all the phones in the entire world. Combined, the neurons create enough electricity to power a 10-watt light bulb.

- Sensory neurons send information to the brain at a speed of more than 150 miles per hour.

- Motor neurons relay information at a speed of more than 200 miles per hour.

- The adult human brain weighs about 3 pounds—about the same as this textbook—and it contains about 100 billion neurons.

- If the cerebral cortex was unfolded, it would cover a typical classroom desk. The surface area of the cerebral cortex is large enough to hold more than 10 billion neurons.

- The average human brain is about 75 percent water.

- During the first month of life, the number of synapses in an infant's brain increases from 50 trillion to 1 quadrillion.

People with damage to another area may be able to report that they see a face, but they may not be able to identify exactly whose face it is that they see.

The hearing, or auditory, area of the cortex lies in the temporal lobe. Sounds are relayed from the ears to the thalamus to the auditory area. When this occurs, we hear sounds. If a specific area of the temporal cortex is damaged, a person may not be able to recognize very common sounds.

Messages received from the skin's sensory receptors are projected to the sensory cortex in the parietal lobe. These sensations include warmth, cold, touch, and pain. Different neurons fire depending on whether you have scratched your nose, touched the burner of a hot stove, or been stung by a bee.

Association Areas Much of the cerebral cortex is composed of areas that involve sensory and motor functions. Other areas, called **association areas,** shape information into something meaningful. For example, certain neurons in the visual area of the occipital lobe fire when we see vertical lines. Others fire in response to horizontal lines. Association areas put it all together. As a result, we see a box or an automobile or a road map instead of a confusing display of verticals and horizontals.

The association areas in the frontal lobes, near the forehead, could be called the brain's executive center. It appears to be where we solve problems and make plans and decisions.

Executive functions also require memory, like the memory in your computer. Association areas also provide the core of your working memory. They are connected with sensory areas in the brain and can tap whatever sensory information is needed or desired. The frontal region of the brain thus retrieves visual, auditory, and other kinds of memories and manipulates them—similar to the way in which a computer retrieves information from files in storage and manipulates it in working memory. Other association areas make possible the psychological functions of language.

Language Abilities Although the left and the right hemispheres of the brain have many of the same functions, they differ in several ways. For example, for nearly all right-handed people, language functions are based in the left hemisphere. Language functions are also based in the left hemisphere of about two out of three left-handed people.

Within the hemisphere containing the language functions, two key language areas are Broca's area and Wernicke's area. Damage to either area is likely to cause an aphasia, a difficulty with specific aspects of understanding or producing language.

Wernicke's area, which is located in the temporal lobe, pieces together sounds and sights. People with damage to this area may find it difficult to understand speech, and their speech often is meaningless. For example, when asked to describe a picture of two boys stealing cookies behind a woman's back, one person responded: "Mother is away her working her work to get her better, but when she's looking the two boys looking the other part. She's working another time."

Broca's area is located in the frontal lobe near the section of the motor cortex that controls the areas of the face used for speaking. When Broca's area is damaged, people speak slowly and laboriously, using simple sentences.

Left and Right Hemispheres The same hemisphere that contains most language functions is usually more involved in logic, problem solving, and mathematical computation than is the other hemisphere. The right hemisphere is relatively more concerned with the imagination, art, feelings, and spatial relations. People often speak of certain abilities as belonging to the right brain or to the left brain. Thus, people who are very logical are said to be "left-brained," while people who are creative are called "right-brained." This idea, however, has become exaggerated. Although some differences do exist, the hemispheres do not act independently of each other.

Much of what psychologists have learned about left- and right-hemisphere functioning comes from people who have had split-brain operations. In a split-brain operation, the corpus callosum, which connects the two hemispheres, is cut. This rarely performed procedure is sometimes used to help people with serious neural disorders such as severe epilepsy. People with epilepsy experience seizures, which are bursts of abnormal neuron firings that generally occur in one hemisphere and then spread to the other. Cutting the corpus callosum can reduce the severity and frequency of the seizures by preventing them from spreading. After the surgery, patients usually function quite effectively despite their hemispheres' inability to communicate with each other.

Still, the surgery does have effects on other brain functions. For example, someone who has undergone the procedure may be able to describe verbally an object she holds in her right hand but not one she holds in her left hand. This is because if an object is held in the right hand, the information is sent to the left hemisphere, which (in most people) contains language abilities. However, if the same object is held in the left hand, this information is sent to the right hemisphere, which has little language ability. Remember that in a brain with an intact corpus callosum, the hemispheres usually work together. Thus, most people can describe objects held in either hand.

Reading Check **Summarize** What are the main functions of each part of the cerebral cortex?

Methods of Studying the Brain

Much of our earlier understanding of the brain came from studies of people with head injuries. Today, researchers increase their knowledge of the brain and its functions by using a variety of techniques to study damaged and intact brains.

Studying the Human Brain

Researchers rely on a number of different methods for studying how the brain and its various parts work.

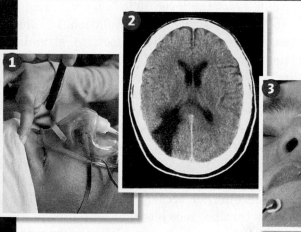
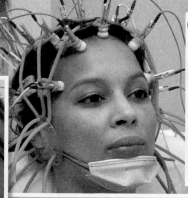
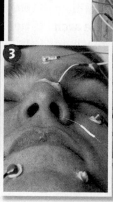
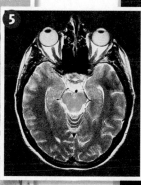

❶ **Accidents** Accidents that cause brain injuries provide researchers with opportunities for learning about how different parts of the brain function.

❷ **Lesions** By creating a lesion, or deliberately destroying a part of an animal's brain, researchers can track how the damage affects certain behaviors.

❸ **Electrical Stimulation** By electrically stimulating the brain, researchers have been able to determine which areas of the brain respond to visual, auditory, or sensory sensations.

❹ **Electroencephalogram** Electrical brain wave activity is transmitted by electrodes and enables researchers to diagnose certain disorders.

❺ **Brain Imaging** Scans such as MRI, CAT, PET, and fMRI allow researchers to create images of the brain and record certain brain functions, such as the ability to see a photograph.

Skills Focus INTERPRETING CHARTS What can scientists learn from accidents?

Accidents One way that researchers are able to see how the brain is related to psychological functions is through the study of brain damage due to accidents.

Brain damage from head injuries can result in confusion, loss of vision or hearing, and loss of memory. In some cases, the loss of large portions of the brain may result in relatively little loss of function. Yet the loss of vital smaller parts can result in language problems or memory loss. In other words, the location of the damage may have a greater effect than the amount of the damage.

The case of Phineas Gage is an example of how brain injuries can lead to a new understanding about the functions of the brain. Neurologist Antonio Damasio cites Gage's story as the historical beginning of the biological study of the brain.

Lesions Scientists can also study a brain by cutting, removing, or destroying parts of it. By observing an animal's behavior after a part has been removed, scientists can determine what types of behavior that area of the brain controls. For example, removal of a part of the brain may cause an animal to become more aggressive or more passive. Obviously, ethical considerations prevent this type of research on humans, but research can take place on laboratory animals. In addition, new imaging techniques, such as scans, allow researchers to observe changes in the behavior or bodily functions of humans with brain lesions.

Electrical Stimulation Electrical stimulation of the brain has shown that specific areas are associated with specific types of sensations (such as seeing light or feeling a tap on the arm) or motor activities (such as walking). In a classic experiment, physiologist José Delgado showed how electrical stimulation of the brain could make an animal change its behavioral patterns. The researcher implanted an electrode into a bull's brain. When the brain was stimulated, the bull dramatically stopped charging and circled to the right. In humans, electrical stimulation has been used to relieve pain and to control violent behavior.

In another study, James Olds and Peter Milner implanted electrodes in rats' brains to learn about the functions of the hypothalamus. When the rats pressed a lever, the electrodes stimulated a portion of the hypothalamus. As it turned out, the rats found this stimulation pleasurable—so pleasurable that the rats would press the lever up to 100 times a minute just to receive the stimulation. In some cases, hungry rats chose electrical stimulation over food. The part of the hypothalamus where the electrodes were implanted became known as a "pleasure center."

Electrical stimulation of the brain is not always reliable as a research tool. Stimulation in the same place can produce different effects at different times. On one occasion, a rat may eat when a portion of the brain is stimulated, but on another occasion it may drink. The areas that produce pleasant and unpleasant sensations in people may also vary from person to person and from day to day.

The Electroencephalograph The electroencephalograph (EEG) is a device that records the electrical activity of the brain. Electrodes attached to the scalp detect small amounts of electrical activity called brain waves. Researchers have learned that the brain has overall activity that rises and falls in predictable patterns. Some brain wave patterns are associated with wakefulness, relaxation, or sleep. Others show active thinking or certain bodily functions. EEG readings are used to help diagnose some kinds of psychological disorders and to help locate tumors.

Experimenting with the Brain
Researchers can trigger rats to eat more or less by electrically stimulating different parts of a rat's brain.

Brain Imaging Images of the brain can provide information about brain damage and other abnormalities. Imaging techniques are also used for early diagnoses of cancers and other problems. Surgeons use imaging to aid them during difficult and intricate surgeries.

In computerized axial tomography (CAT) scans, a moving ring passes X-ray beams around and through the head. The density of the brain tissue determines how much radiation is absorbed. Computers measure the amounts of radiation and piece together a three-dimensional view of the brain that can be displayed on a video monitor.

Similar to CAT scans, magnetic resonance imaging (MRI) is a noninvasive medical procedure. During an MRI, a person lies in a very powerful magnetic field. Radio waves then cause parts of the brain to give off extra energy. This energy is measured from multiple angles. A computer translates the information into a visual image of the brain's anatomy. It can also be used to produce detailed images of other organs, soft tissues, bones, and virtually all other internal body structures. An MRI is more powerful than a CAT scan and can show details more clearly. An MRI is more effective at revealing small injuries and abnormalities in hard-to-see areas.

While CAT scans and MRIs show snapshots of the brain, other new technologies allow researchers to see the brain at work. Top among these technologies are the positron emission tomography (PET) scan and a fast kind of MRI called the functional MRI (fMRI). In a PET scan, a person is injected with radioactive sugar. As the sugar reaches the brain, more of it is used in the locations where brain activity is greater. A computer uses the sugar levels to create an image showing the amount of activity in different areas of the brain.

The fMRI can show which parts of the brain are active when we perform different activities, such as listening to music or working on a math problem. If you raise your hand, the fMRI image will show activity in the part of the brain associated with that movement. If you start to sing a song, other parts of the brain will light up. Research with PET scans and fMRIs support the view that much of our problem solving takes place in the frontal lobes of the brain.

Using these methods, scientists have learned that the mind is a product of the brain. Today the scientific community agrees that for every mental event there are accompanying, underlying biological events. Imaging techniques have allowed us to explore more deeply how the nervous system, particularly the brain, functions while we are thinking, feeling, and moving. Moreover, the study of brain abnormalities has revealed that when parts of the brain undergo damage, other areas of the brain can sometimes take over the functions of the damaged areas.

Reading Check **Compare** How does the information researchers gain from accidents compare to brain imaging techniques?

SECTION 2 Assessment

Online Quiz THINK central thinkcentral.com

Reviewing Main Ideas and Vocabulary

1. **Contrast** How did ancient Egyptian and Greek ideas about the human capacity for thought differ?

2. **Recall** Why do scientists say that the cerebral cortex is the part of the brain that makes us unique as humans?

3. **Infer** Which methods of studying the brain are best for seeing brain function as it happens?

Thinking Critically

4. **Compare and Contrast** How are left-brained and right-brained people thought to be different?

5. **Predict** What might happen to a person's capacity for language if his or her cerebral cortex was damaged?

6. **Summarize** Using your notes and a graphic organizer like the one below, summarize the parts of the brain and the functions each performs.

Hindbrain	Midbrain	Forebrain

FOCUS ON WRITING

7. **Descriptive** Imagine that your are explaining the parts of the brain to a student in elementary school. Write a descriptive paragraph that would help the student understand the parts of the brain and the functions they fulfill.

The Endocrine System

Before You Read

Main Idea
The endocrine system produces hormones that affect growth, development, and some behaviors.

Reading Focus
1. What are three major glands of the endocrine system, and how do they affect the body?
2. What are the testes and ovaries, and what are their functions?

Vocabulary
endocrine system
hormones

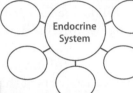

TAKING NOTES Use a graphic organizer like this one to take notes on the endocrine system and its functions.

Endocrine System

STEROID ABUSE AND TRAGEDY

PSYCHOLOGY CLOSE UP *Could tinkering with the body's endocrine system cause a violent rampage?* The memorial in this photograph is for professional wrestler Chris Benoit and his family, all of whom died in a double murder-suicide in 2007. Benoit had a prescription for anabolic steroids, synthetic hormones that build muscle and strength. Police speculated that Benoit killed his family as a result of steroid abuse. Steroids can have devastating side effects: irritability and uncontrolled anger, depression, and suicidal thoughts.

Violence wasn't typical of Benoit's nature, so the wrestler's father agreed to have his son's brain analyzed. The results showed that Benoit's brain was similar to that of an 85-year-old Alzheimer's patient. Although repeated concussions from his wrestling bouts probably caused the damage, the steroids could have contributed to an agitated mental state and horrible acts of violence. Most hormones, however, are essential and beneficial. In this section, you will learn about the endocrine system, the body's system for manufacturing and regulating these powerful chemicals. ■

Three Endocrine Glands

The **endocrine system** consists of glands that secrete substances, called **hormones,** into the bloodstream. The word *hormone* is derived from the Greek *horman,* meaning "to stimulate" or "to excite." Hormones stimulate growth and many kinds of reactions, such as changes in activity levels and physical moods. Because hormones affect behavior and emotional reactions, psychologists who study the biology of behavior are also interested in the endocrine system.

Hormones travel in the bloodstream throughout the body. Like neurotransmitters, hormones have specific receptor sites. The various hormones circulate throughout the body and act only on hormone receptors on the body part that they influence. Hormones are produced by several different glands. Three important glands in the endocrine system are the pituitary gland, the thyroid gland, and the adrenal glands.

The Pituitary Gland The pituitary gland lies just below the hypothalamus in the middle of the brain. It is about the size of a pea, but it is so important that it has been referred to as "the master gland." The pituitary gland, which is stimulated by the hypothalamus, is responsible for the secretion of many different hormones that affect various aspects of behavior. Some pituitary hormones stimulate other endocrine glands such as the adrenals, thyroid, and ovaries or testes.

Human growth hormone, for example, regulates the growth of muscles, bones, and glands. Children whose growth patterns seem abnormally slow often catch up to others the same age when doctors give them human growth hormone.

Some hormones affect females in relation to pregnancy and mothering. Prolactin stimulates production of milk in nursing women. Oxytocin is responsible for stimulating labor in pregnant women. Sometimes when a pregnant woman is overdue, an obstetrician causes labor to begin by injecting the woman with oxytocin hormone.

Oxytocin and prolactin have been shown in some lower mammals to be connected to maternal behaviors, such as caring for young. The role of these hormones in human maternal behaviors, however, remains unclear.

The Endocrine System

The glands of the endocrine system secrete hormones that stimulate various body functions.

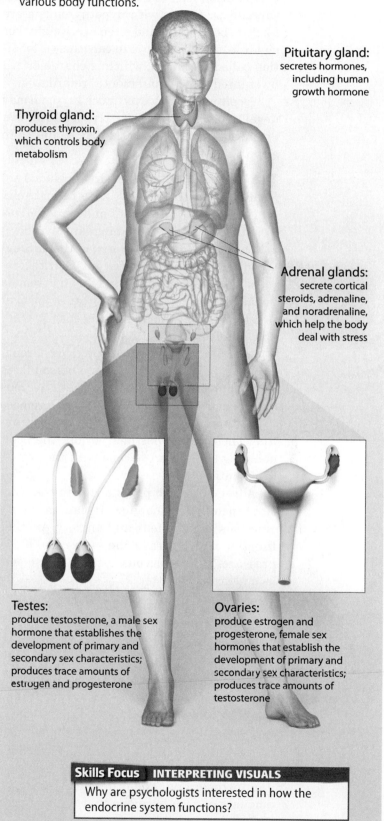

Pituitary gland: secretes hormones, including human growth hormone

Thyroid gland: produces thyroxin, which controls body metabolism

Adrenal glands: secrete cortical steroids, adrenaline, and noradrenaline, which help the body deal with stress

Testes: produce testosterone, a male sex hormone that establishes the development of primary and secondary sex characteristics; produces trace amounts of estrogen and progesterone

Ovaries: produce estrogen and progesterone, female sex hormones that establish the development of primary and secondary sex characteristics; produces trace amounts of testosterone

Skills Focus   INTERPRETING VISUALS

Why are psychologists interested in how the endocrine system functions?

The Thyroid Gland The thyroid gland produces the hormone thyroxin. Thyroxin affects the body's metabolism—its rate of converting food to energy. The production of too little thyroxin can lead to a condition called hypothyroidism. People with hypothyroidism are likely to be sluggish and often overweight. For children, too little thyroxin can cause a condition called cretinism, which is characterized by stunted growth and mental retardation.

People who produce too much thyroxin may develop hyperthyroidism. Hyperthyroidism is characterized by excitability, inability to sleep, and weight loss.

The Adrenal Glands The adrenal glands are located above the kidneys. The Latin prefix *ad–* means "toward" or "at," and *renal* derives from the Latin *renes,* meaning "kidneys."

The outer layer, or cortex, of the adrenal glands secretes cortical steroids. Cortical steroids increase resistance to stress and promote muscle development. They also cause the liver to release stored sugar, making energy available for emergencies.

The adrenal glands also produce adrenaline and noradrenaline. When a person faces a stressful situation, the sympathetic nervous system causes the adrenal glands to release a mixture of adrenaline and noradrenaline. These hormones help arouse the body, enabling the person to cope with the stressful situation.

Adrenaline also plays a role in the emotions people experience. It can intensify emotions such as fear and anxiety. Another function of noradrenaline is to raise blood pressure. In the nervous system, it also acts as a neurotransmitter.

Reading Check **Summarize** What body processes do the pituitary, thyroid, and adrenal glands influence?

Ovaries and Testes

Other glands are the ovaries (in females) and the testes (in males). These glands produce the hormones that influence sexual development and functions. Both glands produce the same hormones—estrogen, progesterone, and testosterone. The difference lies in the amounts of each hormone that are produced in females and males.

Estrogen and Progesterone Estrogen and progesterone are female sex hormones, although low levels are found in males. The ovaries in females produce these hormones. Estrogen is also produced in smaller amounts by the testes in males.

Estrogen is actually a group of chemically similar hormones. In humans and other animals, estrogen hormones foster the growth and development of female sexual characteristics, such as breast enlargement and rounded hips. Progesterone has multiple functions. It stimulates growth of the female reproductive organs and helps prepare the body for pregnancy.

Together, estrogen and progesterone regulate the menstrual cycle, and their levels vary greatly during that cycle. Changes in levels of estrogen have been linked to premenstrual syndrome (PMS) in some women. PMS is a collection of symptoms (such as irritability, depression, and fatigue) that some women experience before menstruating. At the same time, monthly increases in progesterone may cause other symptoms associated with PMS, such as a rise in body temperature.

As women grow older, their ovaries secrete smaller and smaller amounts of estrogen. In time, estrogen levels in the blood become so low that they no longer trigger the menstrual cycle. At this point a woman is said to have entered menopause, and she is no longer fertile. During menopause, many women may receive medical treatment with estrogens to relieve hot flashes and other menopausal symptoms.

Estrogen has psychological effects as well as biological effects. Higher levels of estrogen seem to be connected with optimal cognitive functioning and feelings of well-being among women. Women are also more interested in sexual activity when their estrogen levels are high—particularly during ovulation, when they are fertile.

Testosterone Testosterone is the primary male sex hormone, although females have small amounts of this hormone as well. Testosterone is produced by the testes in males. Small amounts of it are also secreted by the ovaries in females. Testosterone plays an important role in development.

In the prenatal period, testosterone influences development of the sex organs in the fetus. About eight weeks after fertilization, if testosterone is secreted by the fetus, it stimulates development of male sex organs. If testosterone is not secreted, female sex organs develop.

In adolescence, testosterone aids the growth of muscle and bone as well as the development of primary and secondary sex characteristics. Primary sex characteristics are directly involved in reproduction. Secondary sex characteristics, such as beard growth, distinguish males and females but are not directly involved in reproduction.

Testosterone is a kind of steroid. Steroids affect muscle mass, heighten resistance to stress, and increase the body's energy supply. Steroids also stimulate the sex drive and can raise self-esteem.

Recently, the production of synthetic human growth hormones and steroids known as <u>anabolic</u> steroids has gained the attention of behavioral psychologists. Because our society is highly competitive, some people are tempted to use steroids to enhance their performance or body appearance. Such use, however, has serious medical and ethical implications. These substances can produce changes not only in physical aspects of the body, but also in behaviors, moods, anger levels, aggressive behavior, and depression. Researchers have also reported links between steroid use and sleep disturbances, liver damage, heart disease, and other medical problems. Because some athletes use steroids to enhance their

athletic ability, steroids also cause ethical problems. They give athletes who use them an unfair advantage over those who do not.

Reading Check **Identify Supporting Details** What hormones are produced by the ovaries and the testes?

TEENS AND ANABOLIC STEROID USE

Use of anabolic steroids among teenagers has decreased over the last 10 years. However, teens who continue to use steroids do not always know what can happen as a result. Here are some effects of the use of anabolic steroids on the bodies of teenagers.

Sex of User	Effect
Male	• May have breast development • Risk of hair loss and male-pattern baldness
Female	• Risk male-type facial and body hair growth, and male-pattern baldness • May experience a deepening of the voice
Both Sexes	• May have stunted growth, or worsening acne • May develop liver tumors or abnormalities that affect the heart • May exhibit violent or aggressive behavior or mood swings

Skills Focus **INTERPRETING CHARTS** What are the effects of steroid use on both male and female users?

ACADEMIC VOCABULARY

anabolic a phase of metabolism in which substances are synthesized into living tissue

---

SECTION 3 Assessment

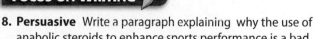

Reviewing Main Ideas and Vocabulary

1. **Recall** What are the functions of hormones?

2. **Explain** Why is the pituitary gland often called "the master gland"?

3. **Draw Conclusions** How are the adrenal glands and the sympathetic nervous system related?

Thinking Critically

4. **Compare** In what way are neurotransmitters and hormones similar?

5. **Explain** How does the endocrine system affect sexual development?

6. **Elaborate** What are some possible ways the endocrine system might affect behavior?

7. **Categorize** Using your notes and a graphic organizer like the one below, list the endocrine glands and their function.

Pituitary	Thyroid	Adrenal	Ovaries	Testes

FOCUS ON WRITING

8. **Persuasive** Write a paragraph explaining why the use of anabolic steroids to enhance sports performance is a bad idea for athletes.

Heredity: Our Genetic Background

Before You Read

Main Idea
Heredity is the transmission of characteristics from parents to offspring. Both heredity and environment shape an individual's personal traits.

Reading Focus
1. What are the roles of genes and chromosomes in heredity?
2. What are the main points of the nature-nurture issue?
3. What are kinship studies?

Vocabulary
heredity
genes
chromosomes

TAKING NOTES Use a graphic organizer like this one to understand the role of heredity and environment in shaping personality.

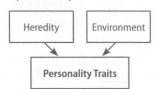

Heredity → Personality Traits ← Environment

Identical Strangers

PSYCHOLOGY CLOSE UP

Why were identical twins separated at birth? Imagine getting a phone call in which the caller says, "Hi, I just found out you are my twin." Such a call took place between Paula Bernstein and Elyse Schein after 35 years of being separated. As they got to know each other, the twins learned they had much in common. For example, both were interested in film: one sister was a filmmaker and the other wrote about films. Both had even suffered from depression in college.

Bernstein and Schein were separated shortly after birth and sent to different adoptive families. They were part of a secret study that focused on the effects of nature versus nurture—or heredity versus environment—on twins. Even the adoptive parents were unaware of the study's purpose. (Today, separation of siblings for adoption is illegal in most states.) Although it cannot be verified, many people think the study was designed to explore the inheritability of mental illness. The girls' mother had schizophrenia. The study was stopped in 1980 and the results sealed until 2066, so the twins may never know the exact nature or results of the study.

Studies of twins, especially of identical twins, enable researchers to investigate the influence of heredity and environment on individuals. As you will see, genetic makeup has a huge influence on the way each individual develops. ■

Heredity, Genes, and Chromosomes

Heredity is the transmission of characteristics from parents to offspring. Psychologists study heredity, along with the brain and the endocrine system, as a means of understanding why people behave as they do. Heredity plays a key role in the development of traits both in people and in animals. The traits we inherit help shape our behavior.

Heredity is key in the transmission of physical traits such as height, hair texture, and eye color. Heredity is also related, to some extent, to some psychological traits. Researchers have found that some psychological traits, such as shyness, leadership ability, aggressiveness, and even an interest in art, are influenced by heredity, although environmental factors also play an important role. Still, heredity has been shown to be one factor involved in many psychological disorders, including anxiety and depression, schizophrenia, bipolar disorder, and alcoholism.

Genes are the basic building blocks of heredity. Traits are determined by pairs of genes, with one gene in each pair inherited from each parent. Some traits, such as blood type, are controlled by a single pair of genes. Complex psychological traits, such as intelligence, involve combinations of genes as well as environmental factors.

Genes are found in threadlike structures called **chromosomes,** which are composed of deoxyribonucleic acid (DNA). DNA is in the form of a double helix. Most normal human cells contain 46 chromosomes that are organized into 23 pairs. In each of the 23 pairs, one chromosome comes from the father and the other comes from the mother. Each chromosome contains instructions for the development of particular traits in the individual.

Genetic disorders can be caused by a <u>mutation</u> of a gene, or a disorder may be inherited. A mutated gene may be passed on from parent to child for many generations. For example, hemophilia, a blood disorder, was passed to members of several royal European families for many generations. Sickle-cell anemia is a genetic mutation that is commonly found among African Americans.

Of the 23 pairs of chromosomes, 22 are similar in males and females. The twenty-third pair, the sex chromosomes, determines

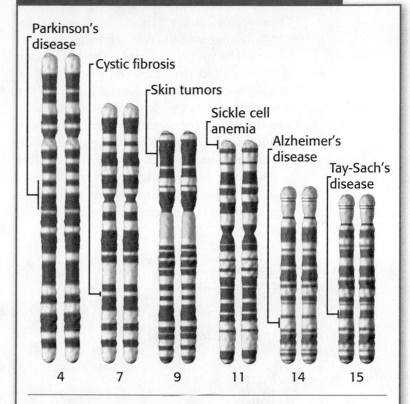

MAPPING GENETIC DISORDERS ON CHROMOSOMES

Parkinson's disease
Cystic fibrosis
Skin tumors
Sickle cell anemia
Alzheimer's disease
Tay-Sach's disease

4   7   9   11   14   15

This computer illustration shows how scientists have been able to locate genetic disorders on numbered pairs of chromosomes.

whether we are female or male. In males, the twenty-third pair consists of an X chromosome (so called because of its X shape) and a Y chromosome (because of its Y shape). Females have two X chromosomes, so they always pass an X chromosome on to their offspring. The chromosome that comes from the father, therefore, determines the sex of the offspring. If the father contributes an X chromosome, then the offspring is female. If the father contributes a Y chromosome, however, then the offspring is male.

When a child is born without all 46 chromosomes in each cell, physical and behavioral disorders may result. One of the most common disabilities of this type occurs when there is an extra, or third, chromosome on the twenty-first pair. When this happens, a baby will be born with Down syndrome. People with Down syndrome usually have some level of mental disability and may also have heart and respiratory problems.

Reading Check **Contrast** How are genes different from chromosomes?

ACADEMIC VOCABULARY

mutation a sudden and random change in the genetic material of a cell

Nature and Nurture

Throughout history, philosophers and scientists have debated the role of biology in determining who we are as people. This discussion is often called the "nature-nurture" issue. *Nature* refers to what people inherit—the biological groundwork that prepares a person to develop in certain ways. Nature can include such things as physical appearance, intelligence, and abilities in certain areas like math or the arts or language. *Nurture* refers to environmental factors—what a person is exposed to in life. Nurture includes a variety of factors such as family, education, culture, living conditions, everyday individual experiences, and other factors that make up one's environment.

People who support the "nature" side of the issue argue that people's traits and personality are primarily determined by their biological makeup. The argument is that our inherited characteristics determine the kind of people we are. Supporters of the "nurture" side argue that the environment we live in and our everyday experiences—not our biological inheritance—determine how we behave and think.

Parenting—Nature or Nurture?

The discussion among researchers and psychologists about nature versus nurture has always been a spirited one. Although few are completely on one side or the other, researchers have a tendency to favor one view over the other. The three experts here present their thoughts on the influence of nature and nurture with regard to parenting. *Which of the opinions come closest to your point of view? Explain.*

"Many parenting studies measure a correlation between parenting practices and children's outcomes and conclude that parenting made the difference . . . [However] It poses a question, how do we explain this very large component of personality that's not genetic but that just surely doesn't come from growing up in a particular home?"

—Steven Pinker, Harvard professor and author of *The Blank Slate: The Modern Denial of Human Nature*

"It's the assumption that what makes children turn out the way they do, aside from their genes, the environmental part of child development, is the experiences they have with their parents. It's really in the second half of the twentieth century that this idea of parental importance has become so popular and, in my view exaggerated."

—Judith Harris, author of *The Nurture Assumption*

"Nature/nurture work more as a dance . . . like Fred Astaire and Ginger Rogers. Once the dance starts it's how they interact together. . . . The potential is only defined by the gene interaction with the environment, and it may be that the environment sets the constraints just as . . . much as the genes do."

—Stanley Greenspan, M. D., child psychiatrist

Both of these views are extreme. Today most psychologists agree that the influences of both nature and nurture determine our psychological traits. Biology influences us to act in certain ways, but our environment—along with personal factors such as values and decision making—can modify these plans. It is the interaction of heredity and environment that determines who we are. A person who has the genetic potential to write a brilliant novel will never write that novel if he or she never learns to read or write. Likewise, an athlete who has the genetic potential to win a gold medal in figure skating will never win an Olympic medal if he or she has never been to a skating rink.

Although most psychologists agree that genes and the environment interact, the extent of the role that heredity plays is still a controversial topic. Some psychologists believe that many of our traits, including intelligence, are determined largely by genetics. Others have criticized this view and are concerned about its implications. The heredity view can be interpreted to suggest that we cannot control our destiny because it is determined by our biology. Taken to the extreme, the heredity view might suggest, for example, that we should not try to change something about ourselves with which we are not satisfied.

Most psychologists are careful to note that heredity is not destiny. They emphasize that the environment does play a role in determining how a person develops. A new factor has recently been introduced into the debate over nature-versus-nurture—the influence of parenting. Some psychologists suggest that peers and genes are more important in the development of a child than are parents. These psychologists believe that children are strongly influenced by the environment outside the home as well as inside it.

Reading Check **Analyze** Why do psychologists agree that "heredity is not destiny"?

Kinship Studies

The most common scientific way to sort out the roles that heredity and environment play in determining a trait is to conduct kinship studies. Kinship refers to the degree to which people are related—the more closely related, the more genes they will have in common.

Identical twins share 100 percent of their genes. A parent and child share 50 percent of their genes, as do full brothers and sisters, on average. Aunts and uncles related by blood share an average of 25 percent of their genes with nieces and nephews, and first cousins share an average of 12.5 percent.

Psychologists use this information to determine how much a trait is influenced by genetics and how much by environment. They study certain traits or behavioral patterns in individuals and then compare them to those of relatives. If genes are involved in a certain trait, then people who are more closely related, and who share more genes, should be more likely to exhibit the trait than do people who have less overlap in genes or who are not related. Two common types of kinship studies are twin studies and adoptee studies.

Twin Studies The study of identical and fraternal twins is a useful way to learn about the relative influences of nature and nurture. Because identical twins share the same genetic makeup, differences between identical twins would seem to be the result of the environment. For example, if one identical twin loves jazz, but the other twin prefers rock, that difference would appear to be due to the twins' different experiences in the environment—not their heredity.

In contrast, fraternal twins, like other brothers and sisters of the same parents, share an average of 50 percent of their genes. Thus, differences between fraternal twins might stem from either heredity or the environment. The premise behind twin studies is that if identical twins are more similar on a certain trait than are fraternal twins, then that trait is more influenced by genetics.

Researchers have found that in addition to physically resembling each other, identical twins resemble one another more strongly than fraternal twins in certain other traits, including shyness and activity levels, irritability, sociability, and happiness. Thus, these traits appear to be influenced by heredity.

Identical twins are also more likely than fraternal twins to share physical and psychological disorders, such as autism, substance dependence, and schizophrenia. Autism is a disorder characterized by limited social and communication abilities.

In a study on autism, both twins were likely to be autistic in 96 percent of the identical twin pairs. In contrast, both twins were likely to be autistic in only 24 percent of the fraternal twin pairs. This evidence strongly suggests a role for heredity in autism.

Adoptee Studies One problem with twin studies is that identical twins tend to be treated similarly and are exposed to similar environments. Because they share the same environment and heredity, it is sometimes difficult to determine whether their similarities are due more to nature or nurture.

One way to try to eliminate the effects of common backgrounds is to study children who have been adopted. Children who have been separated from their parents at an early age and then raised elsewhere provide special opportunities for sorting out the effects of nature and nurture. Psychologists look for the relative similarities between children and their adoptive and biological families. If the children act more like their biological families—with whom they share genes—than their adoptive families—with whom they share the environment—then their behavior may be largely influenced by heredity.

Twins Reared Apart One of the most useful types of kinship studies examines twins who have been reared apart. Twins reared apart are less likely than twins reared together to share common experiences. Thus, similarities are more attributable to genetic factors.

In a major study that began in 1979, Thomas Bouchard and his colleagues examined twins who were reared apart. They found that many psychological and personality traits—including intelligence, traditionalism (following rules), risk avoidance, aggression, and leadership—are influenced by heredity. In one study, Bouchard found a pair of identical twins who had been raised separately. Both had police training and had married women named Linda, and both chewed their fingernails.

Twins reared apart even share many of the same mannerisms, such as how they sit or stand. In one study, one pair of twins each wore seven rings, two bracelets on one wrist, and a bracelet and watch on the other wrist. Most researchers, however, acknowledge that the environment also has an important effect on the development of traits and mannerisms.

The results of twin studies were expected to yield important information. However, most of the studies were suspended for ethical reasons. For example, in the study that split Paula Bernstein and Elyse Schein, adoptive families were not notified that the children were a part of a scientific study. People also questioned the deliberate separation of children from siblings and the failure to inform the children or adoptive families of other siblings. Today, many states insist that siblings being adopted go to the same family.

Reading Check **Find the Main Idea** Why are studies of twins useful to psychologists?

SECTION 4 Assessment

Online Quiz **THINK** central thinkcentral.com

Reviewing Main Ideas and Vocabulary

1. **Recall** What is heredity?

2. **Identify** What factors are included in the idea of nurture?

3. **Summarize** What can psychologists learn from conducting kinship studies?

Thinking Critically

4. **Draw Conclusions** Why are psychologists interested in the nature-nurture issue?

5. **Explain** How do psychologists view the role of environment in determining individual traits?

6. **Rank** What do you think are the most compelling reasons for and against conducting studies of twins?

7. **Compare and Contrast** Using your notes and a graphic organizer like the one below, discuss the influence of nature and nurture on an individual.

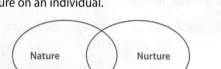

Nature   Nurture

FOCUS ON WRITING

8. **Persuasive** Re-read the quotes on the influence of parenting on children in the feature titled "Parenting—Nature or Nurture?" Write a paragraph supporting or refuting the ideas of one of the people quoted.

The Genographic Project

Have you wondered where your ancestors came from? Some families can trace their history back several centuries. But where were your ancestors 1,000 or 10,000 years ago? A remarkable program called the Genographic Project aims to map the migratory history of all humankind. What can it tell us about what we have inherited from our ancestors?

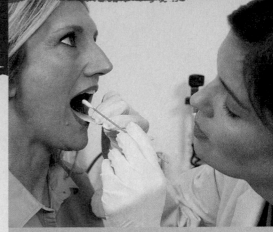

The Genographic Project relies on DNA samples voluntarily contributed by hundreds of thousands of people.

The Genographic Project is an attempt to study patterns and evidence from our past. The project conducts sophisticated analyses of DNA voluntarily contributed by hundreds of thousands of people from around the world, including samples from indigenous and traditional populations on six continents. Ten regional scientific teams collect and analyze data from their region.

Scientists believe that all human beings trace back to Africa, but what is not clearly known is how we migrated and populated the world. Another question is this: If we all share a common ancestor, why do we look so different from each other? Other questions arise about the impact of culture on our genetic background. For example, what influence did conquerors such as the Mongols or the Romans have on local populations?

An early finding from the study has shed light on the question about conquerors and invaders. Researchers studied men in Lebanon, a country in a region that has been invaded or ruled by several different cultures. The DNA of 926 men from Christian, Muslim, and Druze communities was analyzed. A genetic marker commonly found in European populations was found in Lebanese Christian men. This was probably the result of European Christian Crusaders, who began invading the region, once called the Levant, in the 1100s.

Among Lebanese Muslim men, a marker appeared that is typical of the populations of the Arabian Peninsula. Most likely these markers were a result of Muslim expansion in the 600s and 700s. Other markers revealed that Lebanese populations are closely related, suggesting that, before the arrival of Arabs and Europeans, the population was more homogenous (Zalloua et al., 2008).

The genetic markers linking Lebanese men to European and Arab ancestry tell one of many human migration stories. The ultimate goal of the Genographic Project is to uncover a web of migration stories that will explain how humans populated the world and show how closely the human family is related.

ORIGINS OF CRUSADER CHROMOSOMES IN LEBANON

North Sea

English

German

EUROPE

ASIA

ATLANTIC OCEAN

French

Italian

Italian

Black Sea

Caspian Sea

1097

Mediterranean Sea

Lebanon

670

636

AFRICA

643

Red Sea

623

Arabian Peninsula

Persian Gulf

Legend:
- Origins of Crusader armies
- Combined Crusaders
- The Levant
- → European Crusaders
- → Islamic Expansion
- 623 Date (AD)

Thinking Critically

1. **Infer** Why would the results of this study be of interest to psychologists?
2. **Discuss** How do you think you would react if you found out that your ancestors came from a place much different from where you originally believed?

Source: Data from National Geographic Society

Building the Human Brain

Reading and Activity Workbook

Use the workbook to complete this lab.

What are the major parts of the brain, and how do they work?

1. Introduction

The purpose of this lab is to help you understand one of the greatest mysteries that has ever existed: the human brain. You will work with a partner to build a three-dimensional mobile of the human brain. Building the human brain will help you identify the brain's major parts and learn the function of each part.

At the end of this lab, your knowledge of the brain will be put to the test. You will be faced with a series of fill-in-the-blank statements, each concerning a damaged region of the brain. Your challenge will be to correctly identify which region of the brain has been damaged. To complete this lab, follow the steps below.

■ Following your teacher's instructions, organize the class into groups of two students.

■ Read all of the steps of the lab. Then work with your partner to review the chapter material on the brain. Write down a few main points about each part of the brain.

■ Conduct additional library or Internet research on the parts of the human brain and their functions, if your teacher instructs you to do so.

■ Gather the materials you will need to complete your lab: coat hanger, string, magazines, Internet access, colored pencils, markers, glue, and scissors. You and your partner are now ready to create your model.

2. Diagramming the Brain

Working with your partner, create two diagrams of the brain. One diagram should outline the major lobes of the brain and the other diagram should clearly label the middle and lower brain structures. Be sure to identify all of the items listed below in your maps. When you finish, attach each diagram to one side of the coat hanger.

Diagram 1	**Diagram 2**
frontal lobe	pons
parietal lobe	medulla
occipital lobe	reticular formation
temporal lobe	cerebellum
sensory cortex	thalamus
motor cortex	hypothalamus
Broca's area	
Wernicke's area	

3. Crafting Your Mobile

Create an illustration or select an image or an object to represent the function of each part of the brain. Then attach your image or object to the mobile by tying it with string to the bottom of the hanger. Attach a label to each item so that you remember why you and your partner selected that item. For example, you might select a picture of an eye ball and label it "occipital lobes" to represent the occipital lobes, whose primary function is visual interpretation. When you have completed this task, you and your partner should have 14 items, drawings, or objects hanging from your mobile.

4. The Final Challenge: Mind over Matter

Using the knowledge gained from creating your mobile along with information from the chapter, work with your partner to answer the following questions. Write your answers on a single sheet of paper that you can turn in to your teacher along with your mobile.

1. Tom has been in a coma since his car accident last month. The area responsible for waking him is known as the _____ .

2. Antonio suffered a head injury playing baseball and is no longer able to produce words and sentences that make sense to others. This is most likely a result of damage to the _____ .

3. After suffering a stroke, Jessica is read the following statement: A lion killed the tiger. When asked which animal died, Jessica is unable to answer even though she can read the sentence out loud. Damage has most likely occurred to the _____ .

4. Maria has been diagnosed with a brain tumor that makes her prone to fits of aggressive outbursts. The tumor is most likely located on her _____ .

5. After suffering from a brain injury, David can no longer make decisions for himself and finds it very difficult to make plans for his future. This is most likely due to damage in the _____ .

6. Sarah has recently been diagnosed with the early stages of Alzheimer's disease. She is suffering memory loss due to damage in her _____ .

7. Due to complications from diabetes, Trevor has recently had his leg amputated. He now suffers from phantom limb sensations, feeling as if he must move his foot to make himself more comfortable. This is a result of messages still being received in the part of the brain called the _____ .

8. Britney was admitted to the hospital for spinal meningitis. If her brain continues to swell, it will cut off her breathing center, otherwise known as the _____ .

9. Having fallen off of a ladder and hit the back of his head, Marcus is no longer able to distinguish faces of loved ones from faces of strangers. He has most likely damaged the region of his brain called the _____ .

10. Due to a problem during neurosurgery, Allison has suffered some dramatic side effects. Once a slim 120 pounds, she now eats continuously and weighs over 300 pounds. Doctors have concluded they may have damaged the region of her brain known as the _____ .

5. Discussion

What did you learn from this lab? Your teacher will call the class together to hold a discussion that focuses on the questions below. Be prepared to use your mobile to help explain your answers to the class.

■ Overall, how successful were you and your partner at mapping the different parts of the brain?

■ Did attaching images and objects to your mobile help you better remember the functions of different parts of the brain? If so, what part of your brain do you think is responsible for this?

■ Were some parts of the brain particularly difficult to illustrate? If so, which ones, and why do you think they were hard to illustrate?

■ Were some parts of the brain particularly easy to illustrate? If so, which ones, and why do you think they were easy?

■ In your opinion, which part and function of the brain do you think is most important to human survival? Explain.

■ Is there any part of the brain that you think you could live without? Describe how your life might change if your brain lost the function of that part.

Comprehension and Critical Thinking

SECTION 1 *(pp. 66–71)*

1. a. Identify Main Ideas Why is the nervous system referred to as a communication system?

b. Explain How are messages transmitted from one neuron to another?

c. Elaborate How do the sympathetic and parasympathetic systems respond to stress?

SECTION 2 *(pp. 72–79)*

2. a. Recall List the three parts of the brain and one function of each.

b. Explain In what ways does the reticular activating system function?

c. Predict How might damage to the occipital lobe affect an individual?

SECTION 3 *(pp. 80–83)*

3. a. Identify Main Ideas Why are psychologists who study the biology of behavior interested in the endocrine system?

b. Sequence How do the adrenal glands and the nervous system respond when an individual faces a stressful situation?

c. Evaluate What are the effects of the endocrine system on human development?

SECTION 4 *(pp. 84–88)*

4. a. Describe What role does heredity play in human behavior?

b. Contrast How are twin studies different from adoptee studies?

c. Elaborate What are some of the possible consequences of abnormalities in chromosomes?

Reviewing Vocabulary

Match the terms below with their correct definitions.

5. peripheral nervous system
6. neurotransmitter
7. synapse
8. autonomic nervous system
9. cerebrum
10. cerebral cortex
11. reticular
12. endocrine system
13. genes
14. PET

A. system that regulates the body's vital functions

B. the outer layer of the brain

C. basic building blocks of heredity

D. chemicals that transmit messages in the nervous systems

E. system that transmits messages between the central nervous system and all other parts of the body

F. system of glands that secrete hormones into the bloodstream

G. the junction between an axon terminal and a dendrite

H. a scan that observes the brain at work

I. resembling an intricate or complex net

J. the forebrain with two hemispheres

INTERNET ACTIVITY ✳

15. How are traumatic brain injuries treated today? With the increased use of improvised explosive devices (IEDs) in war zones, there has been a major increase in traumatic brain injuries in the military. Use the Internet to research the effect of blast waves on the brain and the treatments being used to treat the injuries. Write a report describing the injuries and methods being used to treat them.

Psychology in Your Life

16. Imagine you have stubbed your toe. Think about the function of the nervous system in your body's responses. Write a paragraph describing what happens as your nervous system responds to this minor injury. With your paragraph, include a diagram showing the activity and systems involved in the response.

SKILLS ACTIVITY: INTERPRETING GRAPHS

Study the bar graph below. Then use the information to help you answer the questions that follow.

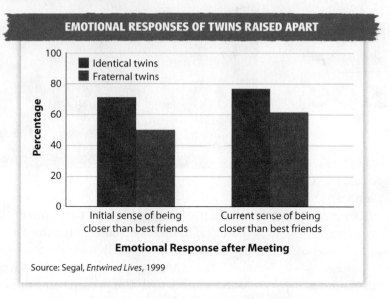

EMOTIONAL RESPONSES OF TWINS RAISED APART

- Identical twins
- Fraternal twins

Percentage

Emotional Response after Meeting

Initial sense of being closer than best friends

Current sense of being closer than best friends

Source: Segal, *Entwined Lives*, 1999

17. Contrast How are the responses of identical and fraternal twins different?

18. Infer What additional information would make this graph more useful?

19. Evaluate What might this data suggest about the role of heredity or environment in the responses of separated twins?

WRITING FOR AP PSYCHOLOGY

Use your knowledge of methods for studying the brain to answer the question below. Do not simply list facts. Present a clear argument based on your critical analysis of the question, using appropriate psychological terminology

20. Make a judgment about the value of the basic methods of studying the brain. Identify which methods are more likely to provide researchers with information that will benefit brain research.

- Five methods of research
- One area in which each method is most valuable in providing information
- Create a list of criteria for ranking the methods and a ranking order based on the criteria

Connecting Online

Visit **thinkcentral.com** for review and enrichment activities related to this chapter.

THINK central

Quiz and Review

ONLINE QUIZZES
Take a practice quiz for each section in this chapter.

WEBQUEST
Complete a structured Internet activity for this chapter.

QUICK LAB
Reinforce a key concept with a short lab activity.

APPLYING WHAT YOU'VE LEARNED
Review and apply your knowledge by completing a project-based assessment.

Activities

eACTIVITIES
Complete chapter Internet activities for enrichment.

INTERACTIVE FEATURE
Explore an interactive version of a key feature in this chapter.

KEEP IT CURRENT
Link to current news and research in psychology.

Online Textbook

Click for More

Learn more about key topics in this chapter.

OUT OF DARKNESS and Silence

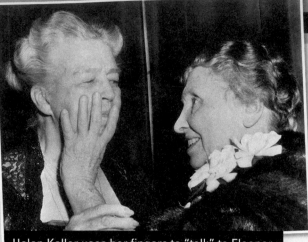

Helen Keller uses her fingers to "talk" to Eleanor Roosevelt at a party in 1954.

Our knowledge of the world comes to us through our senses. What happens, then, if we lose one or more of those senses? Perception may not be lost if other senses can compensate for the missing sense or senses. The life of Helen Keller serves as an excellent example of this compensation.

Helen Keller was born in Tuscumbia, Alabama, in 1880. When she was 19 months old, she was walking and had just started to learn a few words. Suddenly she became very ill. Despite the doctor's prediction that she would die, Keller survived, but she had become both deaf and blind.

It is hard to imagine what it must be like to wake up one day and find nothing but silence and darkness where once you heard sounds and saw objects and people. Not surprisingly, the young Keller became difficult to manage. Fearful, she clung to her mother's apron, and at times she had violent temper tantrums.

When Keller was almost seven, her life changed dramatically. Anne Sullivan arrived in Tuscumbia to teach Keller. Sullivan, who had been nearly blind herself, had attended the Perkins Institution for the Blind in Boston. Although two operations had restored much of her eyesight, she understood what it was like to be blind, and she was eager to teach her new pupil.

The situation did not look promising at first. Keller was rude to her new teacher, and she would not sit still to have Sullivan use the manual alphabet. In the manual alphabet, which is still used with people who are deaf and blind, the "speaker"

makes the signs right into the hand of the "listener," using the sense of touch to communicate. At first, Sullivan tried the word *doll* when she gave the child a doll as a gift. Keller simply took the present and ran off. Eventually, however, she began to imitate Sullivan, but she still had difficulty connecting the words with the actual objects.

One day, Sullivan put her pupil's hand under running water and repeatedly spelled the word *water* into the girl's palm. Suddenly Keller realized that w-a-t-e-r was the "cool something" that was running over her hand, and a breakthrough occurred. Within one hour, she learned 30 new words.

From that beginning came a long life of both learning and teaching. The easiest words to learn were those that described objects or things Keller could taste or smell. It was harder for the young girl to understand that her feelings also had names.

For the first few years, Sullivan was Keller's only teacher. Keller was soon eager to learn more. At the age of 10, Keller decided that she needed to learn to speak. To do so, she took lessons from a teacher of people who were deaf. Eventually, Keller learned to speak by "hearing" the vibrations made when she placed her fingers on Sullivan's larynx. Keller also learned to "listen" to others speak by putting her middle finger on the speaker's nose, her forefinger on the speaker's lips, and her thumb on the speaker's larynx.

CHAPTER 4

SENSATION AND PERCEPTION

Keller wanted to attend Radcliffe College, but to do so she had to complete regular high school. Sullivan accompanied her to class and signed the lectures into Keller's hand. Keller passed her exams and was admitted to Radcliffe. Later, Keller and Sullivan traveled and lectured around the world. They never rested in their efforts to improve the lives of people with hearing and visual disabilities.

Most people who are deaf and blind today agree that Helen Keller, who died in 1968, is an inspirational role model. She met with many U.S. presidents and other important leaders, focusing attention on the challenges faced by the deaf and blind. Many of the recent advances in sight and hearing loss prevention are a result of her tireless calls to action.

Inspired by Keller's legacy, Filipino students developed a device that converts text messages into Braille, the writing system of the blind.

What do you think?

1. How do people compensate for lost senses?

2. How do you think you might deal with losing one or more of your five senses?

Chapter at a Glance

SECTION 1: Understanding Sensation and Perception

- The stimulation and interpretation of our senses are limited by variable thresholds.
- Our senses adapt to changing conditions and environments.
- Physical and psychological factors affect our perception of stimuli.

SECTION 2: Vision

- Light enters the eye, which relays information to the brain and allows us to see.
- People with normal color vision can see all colors in the spectrum of visible light.
- People who do not have normal color vision are said to be "color blind."

SECTION 3: Hearing

- The ear allows us to hear and locate sounds, which have their own pitch and loudness.
- Deafness may be inherited or caused by disease, injury, or old age.

SECTION 4: Other Senses

- We perceive smell and taste by sensing the molecules of certain substances.
- Sensory receptors on our skin allow us to sense pressure, temperature, and pain.
- Body senses help us keep our balance and stand upright.

SECTION 5: Perception

- Perception allows us to organize and make sense of our sensory impressions.
- Cues help people perceive movement and motion and judge depth and perspective.
- The brain can trick the eye through visual illusions.

Understanding Sensation and Perception

Before You Read

Main Idea

Sensation is the process by which our five senses gather information and send it to the brain. Perception is the way in which we interpret this information.

Reading Focus

1. What processes and concepts affect the stimulation of the senses?
2. How does the process of sensory adaptation work?
3. What is signal-detection theory?

Vocabulary

sensation
perception
absolute threshold
difference threshold
sensory adaptation
signal-detection theory

TAKING NOTES Use a graphic organizer like this one to take notes on aspects of sensation and perception.

Sensation	Perception

Sensory OVERLOAD

PSYCHOLOGY CLOSE UP

Can you ever see, hear, and feel too much? Imagine stepping outside your door and being bombarded by a multitude of sights, sounds, and smells. Cars, people, and dogs overwhelm your senses. The sounds they make are unbearably loud. Even the scents of the flowers next door assault your nose. This is how the world might appear to you if you had autism spectrum disorder. Many people with autism suffer from this kind of sensory overload. They often avoid taking part in social activities because they can become disoriented by all the sensory input. When the noise and confusion become too much for them to bear, they may tune out and retreat within themselves.

This hypersensitivity can't be cured, but it can be treated. Psychologists have come up with different forms of therapy to try to desensitize autistic children. For example, hypersensitivity to touch can be decreased by applying deep pressure stimulation. In this form of therapy, the psychologist wraps the child in a mat and applies slow but steady pressure to the mat. The indirect "hug" has a calming effect on the child and reduces the oversensitivity of the child's nervous system.

All of us interpret the world through our senses. Most people, however, automatically filter out the unimportant information. In this section, you will learn what protects our senses from overload. ■

Stimulation of the Senses

Sensation is the stimulation of sensory receptors and the transmission of sensory information to the central nervous system (the spinal cord and brain). Sensory receptors are located in sensory organs such as the eyes and ears. The stimulation of the senses is automatic. It results from sources of energy like light and sound or from the presence of chemicals, as in smell and taste.

Perception is the psychological process through which we interpret sensory stimulation. Imagine that you are standing at one end zone of a football field while a play is going on. Some of the players are close and rushing toward you; other players are at the other end of the field. Those players who are far away look very small compared to those players who are barreling down on you. Still, you know that the quarterback, who has just thrown a pass from the other end of the field, is not actually tiny. How do you know? The answer is that you know through experience. Perception reflects learning, expectations, and attitudes.

Our senses are constantly absorbing information from our environment. However, we do not recognize most of this information. The stimulation and interpretation of our senses are affected by concepts known as absolute threshold and difference threshold.

Absolute Threshold Have you ever had your hearing tested? If so, try to remember the experience. There you were, sitting in a booth or quiet room with earphones on your head. At first, you heard nothing, and perhaps you began to wonder what was going on. Then suddenly you heard a beep. You had just discovered your absolute threshold for hearing that kind of sound. **Absolute threshold** is the weakest amount of a stimulus that can be sensed. Even before you heard that first beep, the person testing you was trying different beeps, but you simply could not hear them. The first one you heard was the weakest one you were capable of hearing. We only sense those sounds, sights, smells, tastes, and pressures that we can perceive.

Did you know that dogs can hear certain whistles that people cannot? This is because a dog's absolute threshold for certain sounds is different from that of a human being. In fact, many animals are much more sensitive than humans to sensory stimuli.

Absolute thresholds for humans have been determined for the senses of vision, hearing, smell, taste, and touch. However, our absolute thresholds for a particular stimulus differ, not only from animals, but also from person to person. Some people are more sensitive to certain sensory stimuli than others are. These differences can stem from both psychological and biological factors.

ABSOLUTE THRESHOLDS FOR SENSORY PERCEPTION

QUICK FACTS

This chart shows the absolute threshold for each of our five senses.

Sense	Stimulus	Receptors	Absolute Threshold
Vision	Electromagnetic energy	Rods and cones in the retina	A candle flame viewed from a distance of about 30 miles on a dark night
Hearing	Sound waves	Hair cells of the inner ear	The ticking of a watch from about 20 feet away in a quiet room
Smell	Chemical substances in the air	Receptor cells in the nose	About one drop of perfume diffused throughout a small house
Taste	Chemical substances in saliva	Taste buds on the tongue	About 1 teaspoon of sugar dissolved in 2 gallons of water
Touch	Pressure on the skin	Nerve endings in the skin	The wing of a fly falling on a cheek from a distance of less than half an inch

If absolute thresholds differed much from what they are, we might sense the world very differently. For example, if our ears were more sensitive, we might hear collisions among molecules of air. If our sense of smell were as sensitive as a dog's, we might be able to track down someone just by sniffing a piece of his or her clothing.

Difference Threshold For us to function well in the world, we need absolute thresholds low enough to see, hear, smell, taste, and feel what is going on around us—but not so low that our senses are overloaded with information we cannot use. We also need to be able to detect small differences between stimuli—what makes one stimulus different from another stimulus. In other words, we need a means of recognizing when someone turns the volume of the television up. The minimum amount of difference that can be detected between two stimuli is known as the **difference threshold.**

As another example, imagine that someone shows you two dark-blue paint chips. You may think they are the same color, even if they are slightly different. But now imagine that one of the paint chips is removed and replaced with another chip that is just a bit lighter or darker. Do the two paint chips still seem the same color? No. The smallest amount of difference you can see in order to distinguish between the two shades of blue is your difference threshold. Just as with absolute threshold, people's individual difference thresholds vary slightly.

Reading Check **Analyze** What is the relationship between the absolute threshold and the difference threshold?

Sensory Adaptation

When you first walk into a darkened movie theater, you may be able to see little except the colorless shapes of the other moviegoers. As time passes, however, you can see the faces of people around you and the features of the theater. Once your eyes adapt to the darkness, you are able to find your seat and avoid stepping on the toes of the other people seated in your row.

Our sensory systems adapt to a changing environment. **Sensory adaptation** is the process by which we become more sensitive to weak stimuli and less sensitive to unchanging stimuli. For example, as time goes by in the darkened movie theater, you're able to see the people around you much better—the people are weak stimuli. On the other hand, as we adapt to lying on the beach, we become less aware of the unchanging stimulus of the lapping of the waves. Similarly, city dwellers adapt to the sounds of traffic (unchanging stimuli) except for the occasional car backfire or fire engine siren. However, some stimuli do not display this kind of adaptation. For instance, we do not usually adapt quickly to pain. Unfortunately, that particular stimulus may persist for a long period of time.

Reading Check **Draw Conclusions** What sensory adaptation probably occurs after you rest your hand on a table's surface for a few minutes?

Signal-Detection Theory

As you might imagine, it is easier to hear a friend talking in a quiet room than in a room where many people are carrying on loud conversations. And when your nose is congested due to a cold, your dinner may seem to have little flavor. In the first case, the setting has made a difference in your sensation and perception. In the second case, your physical condition has made the difference. **Signal-detection theory** is a method of distinguishing sensory stimuli that takes into account not only the stimuli's strengths but also such <u>variable</u> elements as the setting, your physical state, your mood, and your attitudes.

Signal-detection theory also considers psychological factors such as motivations, expectations, and learning. For example, even if the place where you are now reading is buzzing with distracting signals such as a breeze against your face, the shadow of passing clouds, or the voices of passersby, you will be able to ignore those influences as long as you are motivated to keep reading. Similarly, people who smell perfumes for a living have learned through years of experience how to detect subtle differences others would not be able to smell.

We focus on whatever we consider important. Suppose that you attend a recital at school. A student you do not know plays the piano. Your mind may wander as you listen. But other people in the audience may have a different response. For example, do you think the student's parents let their minds wander? You can be pretty sure that they do not—the performance is much more important to them than it is to other members of the audience. There are also cases in which we think we perceive a stimulus and there is none. For example, suppose you are expecting an important visitor. While you're waiting, you might find that you jump up and open the door from time to time because you think you hear a knock—only to find that no one is there.

According to signal-detection theory, we do not always passively receive information from our senses. Under certain psychological factors, we make active decisions about what we perceive. Psychologists have conducted studies to determine the impact of these factors by focusing on stimuli that are difficult to detect. In one such study, psychologists asked participants to detect on a monitor the sound of a bomber jet. They were told that there would be a penalty for false alarms and for misses. But a miss meant a failure to detect the bomber and would result in possible deaths. As a result, the people in the study were more likely to register false alarms than misses.

Reading Check **Summarize** What factors can affect the signals we perceive?

SECTION 1 Assessment

Online Quiz THINK central thinkcentral.com

Reviewing Main Ideas and Vocabulary

1. **Define** What is absolute threshold?

2. **Identify Cause and Effect** What happens when you walk from the light into a darkened room?

3. **Draw Conclusions** How do you think you would respond to a fly buzzing in a room while you are taking an important exam?

Thinking Critically

4. **Infer** How do sensation and perception affect people's understanding of their environment?

5. **Evaluate** Why is it important that we have different thresholds for different stimuli?

6. **Predict** Predict how you might perceive your environment if you were alone in a spooky house. Why do you think that would be so?

7. **Analyze** Using your notes and a graphic organizer like the one below, write down examples of the auditory and visual signals that you are likely to pay attention to at a concert. Indicate what factors are involved in focusing your attention.

Signal	Factor

FOCUS ON WRITING

8. **Descriptive** In a paragraph, describe what life would be like if human beings lacked sensory adaptation. Be sure to describe what would happen if our eyes could not adjust to changing light conditions.

Animal Senses

Over the centuries, people have reported that animals appear to have a sixth sense for detecting earthquakes, hurricanes, volcanic eruptions, and tsunamis before the earth starts shaking. In more recent times, animals' acute senses have been used to help the disabled, find missing persons, and sniff out bombs and drugs.

Sheep can recognize about 50 sheep and 10 human faces and remember them for two years. Specialized areas of the sheep brain, similar to those in humans, encode facial identity. By studying these areas, scientists may help people who have lost the ability to recognize faces as a result of brain injury.

In December 2004, a tsunami from a massive earthquake in the Indian Ocean struck dozens of Asian and African countries. By the year's end, the death toll was estimated at more than 200,000. The devastating tsunami caught the people off guard but not many of the animals.

Along the western coast of Thailand, elephants giving rides to tourists began to trumpet agitatedly hours before the tsunami hit. About that time the massive earthquake that would send the big waves rushing toward shore was fracturing the ocean floor. An hour before the waves slammed into the area, the elephants began wailing. Just before the waves struck, the elephants trooped off to higher ground.

Service dogs like this one become more protective of their charges before the onset of an epileptic seizure.

Other animals, too, sensed the impending disaster. Dogs refused to go outside. Flamingos on the coast of India abandoned their sanctuary and headed into safer forests before the waves hit. In Sri Lanka, a large wave smashed into the Yala National Park. Yet, wildlife officials were surprised to find that hundreds of elephants, tigers, leopards, and other animals had escaped the wave unharmed.

Animals, in general, seem more in tune with the environment than humans. They may not know what is happening during a natural disaster, but they seem to know instinctively how to react. Rats, for example, evacuate buildings. Flocks of sparrows take flight. Dogs howl. Some animals are apparently supersensitive to sound; others to temperature, touch, or vibration. This sensitivity appears to give them advance warning of natural disasters.

Alan Rabinowitz of the Wildlife Conservation Society in New York says that many animals can detect subtle or abrupt changes in the environment that humans cannot. "Some animals have acute senses of hearing and smell that allow them to determine something coming towards them long before humans," Rabinowitz points out.

Those acute senses are now helping people. It may be a dog's keen sense of smell that allows it to predict epileptic seizures in children. In one study, a number of dogs accurately predicted the seizures by licking, whimpering, or standing next to the child. Some researchers believe that dogs detect a change in smell; many epileptics experience increased sweating before a seizure.

Dogs can also sniff out survivors after a disaster. About 72 hours after a devastating earthquake in China in May 2008, rescue workers had given up hope of finding any more survivors in a collapsed school. But suddenly a search dog barked and pointed to a spot amid the rubble. Two hours later, the workers uncovered a girl who was still alive.

These talented canines may have to make room for an animal with an even more extraordinary sense of smell—the wasp. In a recent study, the insects were quickly trained to detect many different odors. In time, trained wasps may be used to sniff out bombs and drugs and even detect tumors, ulcers, and other diseases by smell alone.

Thinking Critically

1. **Summarize** In what ways do people benefit from animals' super senses?
2. **Discuss** How might animals supplement disaster warning systems?

Vision

Before You Read

Main Idea
Light interacting with the eye allows us to see. People with normal vision can adapt to changing light conditions and can see any color in the spectrum of visible light.

Reading Focus
1. How does light work?
2. What are the main parts of the eye?
3. What allows us to have color vision?
4. What causes color blindness?

Vocabulary
pupil
lens
retina
photoreceptors
blind spot
visual acuity
complementary
afterimage

TAKING NOTES Use a graphic organizer like this one to take notes on the anatomy, adaptability, and color vision of the eye.

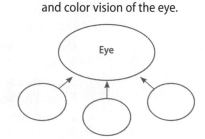

COLOR
Psychology

PSYCHOLOGY CLOSE UP

What color are you feeling? Are you green with envy? Are you feeling blue? Do you see red? For centuries, people have believed that colors could inspire different emotions. Green and blue, for instance, are known as cool colors and are supposed to have a calming effect. You've probably heard of the "green room," where guests relax before they appear on a television program. At the other end of the spectrum, warm colors—like red—are thought to evoke intense feelings of aggression, excitement, or anger.

Color psychology is often used in advertising and in the design of consumer goods. Red is eye-catching, but it is also said to make people feel hungry, which may account for its frequent application in food packaging. The ancient Chinese and Egyptians also believed that color had healing powers. They developed a therapy, called chromotherapy, that is still used by some practitioners of alternative medicine today.

Most psychologists, however, do not take color psychology seriously. They point to the fact that response to color is different in different cultures. They also note that the effects of color on emotion are only temporary: the calming effect of a blue room, for example, wears off pretty quickly. But color is still an important part of our world. Imagine how our vision would be affected without it. ■

Light

Those of us fortunate enough to have good vision usually consider information from vision to be more essential than that from our other senses. In fact, vision dominates our other senses to the point that we often make what we hear and feel conform to what we see. In psychology, this concept is known as "visual capture." To understand vision, it is important to know how light works.

Light is electromagnetic energy. It is described in wavelengths. The electromagnetic spectrum is made up of light that is visible to humans and light that is not. In fact, the light that humans can see makes up only a small part of the spectrum. The wavelengths of cosmic rays are only a fraction of an inch long. The wavelengths of some radio waves extend for miles. The wavelengths of visible light are in between.

You have probably seen sunlight broken down into colors as it filters through water vapor—this is what makes a rainbow. Sunlight can also be broken down into colors by means of a glass structure called a prism. The main colors of the spectrum, from shortest to longest wavelengths, are red, orange, yellow, green, blue, indigo, and violet.

Reading Check **Summarize** What is light?

The Eye

When you take a picture with a nondigital camera, light enters through an opening and is focused onto a sensitive surface—the film. Your eye is very similar. As in a camera, light enters the eye and then is projected onto a surface. The amount of light that enters is determined by the size of the opening in the colored part of the eye. This opening is called the **pupil.** When you look into someone's eyes, the black circles you see in the middle are the pupils. They may look solid to you, but actually they are openings. The size of the pupil adjusts automatically to the amount of light entering the eye.

Once light has entered the eye, it encounters the lens. The **lens** adjusts to the distance of objects by changing its thickness. These changes project a clear image of the object onto the retina. The **retina** is the sensitive surface in the eye that acts like the film in a camera. However, the retina consists of neurons—not film. Neurons that are sensitive to light are called **photoreceptors.** Once the light hits the photoreceptors, a nerve carries the visual input to the brain. In the brain, the information is relayed to the visual area of the occipital lobe.

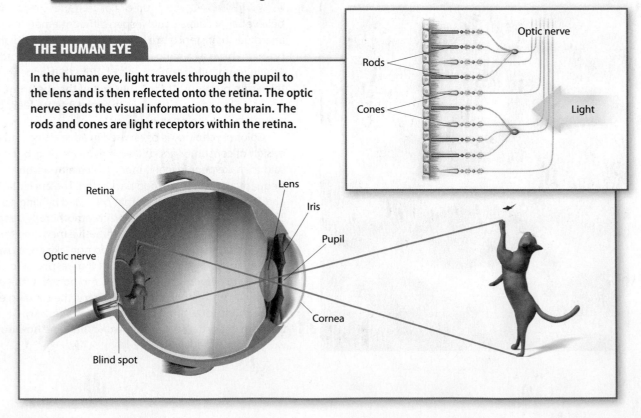

THE HUMAN EYE

In the human eye, light travels through the pupil to the lens and is then reflected onto the retina. The optic nerve sends the visual information to the brain. The rods and cones are light receptors within the retina.

Optic nerve

Rods

Cones

Light

Retina

Lens

Iris

Pupil

Optic nerve

Cornea

Blind spot

The Blind Spot When light hits the point where the optic nerve leaves the eye, the eye registers nothing because that area lacks photoreceptors. Thus it is called the **blind spot.** We all have one. If we did not have a blind spot, we would never be able to "see" anything—no visual input would reach the brain through the optic nerve for interpretation.

Rods and Cones There are two kinds of photoreceptors: rods and cones. Rods are sensitive only to the brightness of light. They allow us to see in black and white. Cones provide color vision. Rods are more sensitive to light than are cones. Therefore, as the lighting grows dim, as in a movie theater when the lights go down, objects lose their color before their outlines fade from view.

Dark and Light Adaptation When you first enter a movie theater, it may be too dark for you to find a seat. As time passes, however, you come to see the seats and the other people more clearly. This adjustment to lower lighting is called dark adaptation. Your ability to see in low light continues to improve for up to 45 minutes.

But what happens when you first move from the dark into the light? Imagine turning on the lamp next to your bed in the middle of the night. At first, you blink, and it almost hurts, but within only a minute or two, you have adapted. Adaptation to bright light happens much more quickly than adaptation to the dark.

Visual Acuity The sharpness of vision is called **visual acuity.** Visual acuity is determined by the ability to see visual details (in normal light). When people have their eyes examined, they have to read the letters on a chart. This chart is used to measure visual acuity. If you were to stand 20 feet from the chart and could only read the top letters, we would say that your vision is 20/100. This means that what a person with normal vision could see from a distance of 100 feet away, you could see from no more than 20 feet away. In such a case, you would be nearsighted—you would have to be particularly close to an object to make out its details. A person who is farsighted, on the other hand, needs to be farther away from an object than a person with normal vision to see it clearly.

THE COLOR WHEEL

Gray is in the middle of the wheel because when complementary colors of light mix, they form gray.

You may have noticed that older people often hold newspapers or books farther from their eyes than do younger people. As people reach middle age, their lenses become relatively brittle. Therefore, it is more difficult for them to focus, especially on nearby objects. As a result, many older people are farsighted.

Reading Check **Compare** In what way is the eye like a camera?

Color Vision

The world is full of brilliant colors. The wavelength of light determines the color. People with normal color vision see any color in the spectrum of visible light.

The Color Wheel The color wheel is made up of the colors of the spectrum bent into a circle. The colors across from each other are called **complementary.** For example, red and green are a complementary pair. If we mix complementary colors together, they form gray. You may have learned in art class that mixing blue and yellow creates green, not gray. But this is true only with *pigments,* or substances such as paints. Here we are talking about *light,* not about pigments.

Cones and Color Vision Cones, one of the two types of photoreceptors in the retina of the eye, enable us to perceive color. Some cones are sensitive to blue, some to green, and some to red. When more than one kind of cone is stimulated at the same time, we perceive other colors of the spectrum, such as yellow and violet.

This is similar to the way color television sets convey colors to the viewer. Although you may not be aware of it, the images you see on a television screen actually consist of thousands of very small dots, called pixels. Each of these dots is either blue, green, or red—the same colors that are perceived by the different types of cones in the eye. There are no yellow, purple, or even black or white dots in the television images. These and other colors are created only through various combinations of blue, green, and red dots.

Our color vision differs from that of many animals. That is because color vision evolved in animals that were active during the daytime. Some animals, such as some types of fish, do not have color vision at all; they do not have any cones in the retina of their eyes. As you have learned, humans have three types of cones. Other animals—such as dogs and cats—have two types. As a result, these animals see far fewer colors than we do. On the other hand, animals such as birds and some insects have four or more cones. They experience a wide variety of colors, including those in the ultraviolet range, which humans cannot see.

Afterimages Think of a time when you were blinded by a car's headlights or stared briefly at a light bulb. When you looked away, you probably saw a ghostly image floating before your eyes. What you saw is an afterimage. An **afterimage** is the visual impression that remains after the original image is removed. You perceive an afterimage when you have viewed a color for a while and then the color is removed. When you stare at a single intense color for a period of time, the cones of your eyes become tired. As a result, the afterimage you perceive of that color is its complementary color. The same holds true for black and white. Staring at one will create an afterimage of the other.

Most afterimages only last up to a minute—usually only a few seconds. After such a short amount of time, most of the nerve cells in the eyes have readjusted. In addition, the size of an afterimage depends on the distance from which it is viewed. If you view an afterimage on a nearby screen or surface, it will appear relatively small. If you view an afterimage on a more distant wall, it will appear much larger.

Reading Check **Identify Cause and Effect** What happens after you look intensely at a single color?

Quick Lab

Afterimages

An afterimage is a type of optical illusion. In this lab, you will experiment with afterimage by staring at the strangely colored flag above.

PROCEDURE

❶ Place a piece of blank white paper on your desk.

❷ Stare at the center of the flag above for 30 seconds. Try not to look away.

❸ After 30 seconds, direct your gaze to the piece of paper.

❹ Repeat the experiment, but this time, look at a distant wall after you've stared at the flag.

ANALYSIS

1. Describe what you saw when you looked at the piece of paper.

2. Why did you see those colors?

3. How long did the afterimage last when you looked at the piece of paper? at the wall?

4. Compare the size of the afterimage you saw on the paper with the one you saw on the wall. Which was bigger?

Quick Lab **THINK** central   thinkcentral.com

Color Blindness

If you can see the colors of the visible spectrum, you have normal color vision. People who do not have normal color vision are said to be "color blind." These people are partially or totally unable to distinguish color due to an absence of, or malfunction in, the cones. People who are totally color blind are sensitive only to light and dark and see the world as most people do on a black-and-white television set. Total color blindness is rare.

Partial color blindness, on the other hand, is fairly common. People who are partially color blind see some colors but not others. Particularly common is red-green color blindness, in which a person has difficulty seeing shades of red and green. About 99 percent of those who are color blind have this form. A blue-yellow form of color blindness also exists but is rather rare.

Color blindness is almost always inherited. Males are more likely to inherit the trait. About 8 percent of males worldwide are color blind as opposed to less than 1 percent of females.

There is no cure for color blindness, but it does not really cause any great impairment. For most people, color blindness is mostly an annoyance. Imagine the challenges of dressing every day or trying to read a map. On the other hand, the condition can be occasionally dangerous, as when a driver cannot distinguish traffic signals. But most people with

color blindness simply learn the position of the signals: red on the top, yellow in the center, and green on the bottom.

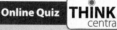 **Draw Conclusions** What difficulties might a person with red-green color blindness encounter when cooking red meat?

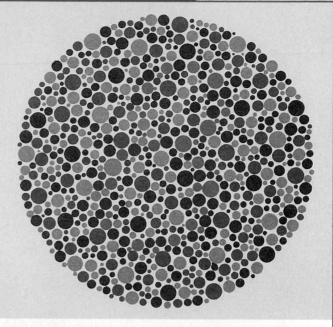

TEST FOR COLOR BLINDNESS

This image resembles a test for color blindness. In the actual test, which would be conducted by a trained professional, a person with normal color vision would see an 8, a person with red-green color blindness would see a 3, and a person with total color blindness would see no number.

SECTION 2 Assessment

Online Quiz THINK central thinkcentral.com

Reviewing Main Ideas and Vocabulary

1. **Recall** What different types of vision do rods and cones provide?

2. **Define** What is an afterimage?

3. **Identify** What is yellow's complementary color?

Thinking Critically

4. **Explain** What is the blind spot and why is it important?

5. **Draw Conclusions** Which colors of the rainbow would most people with color blindness be unable to see?

6. **Predict** What might happen if our eyes were unable to control the amount of light that entered them?

7. **Analyze** Using your notes and a graphic organizer like the one below, list the chain of events that occurs when light enters the human eye.

☐ → ☐ → ☐ → ☐ → ☐

FOCUS ON WRITING

8. **Descriptive** Imagine that you became completely color blind. How might your life be different from the way it is now? How would you have to adjust? Write a brief description of the ways in which your life would change.

Hearing

Before You Read

Main Idea
The ear is the human instrument for sensing sounds. When parts of the ear are damaged, deafness can occur.

Reading Focus
1. What two characteristics does every sound have?
2. What are the main parts of the ear, and how do they work?
3. What are some of the causes of deafness?

Vocabulary
cochlea
auditory nerve
conductive deafness
sensorineural deafness

TAKING NOTES Use a graphic organizer like this one to take notes on aspects of hearing.

Sound	Ear	Deafness

Hearing in COLOR

PSYCHOLOGY CLOSE UP

What does color sound like? A purple song. A scratchy flavor. A sight that is literally painful. Most of us maintain a strict separation of our senses, but others experience them blended together. This rare group may not just hear a melody but see it in living color.

These people—who number roughly 1 in 2,000—have a condition known as synesthesia. Their experience is real, not imagined. So when some synesthetes hear a word, they actually see a particular color in their mind's eye. When others watch a violent movie, they flinch with real pain at every blow. The condition seems to run in families. As a child, Russian writer Vladimir Nabokov once told his mother that the colors painted on his wooden alphabet blocks were "all wrong." She agreed: she saw them as different colors as well.

In recent years, researchers have observed brain activity in synesthetes as they respond to sounds that is not present in people without the condition. Psychologists have also discovered that synesthetes demonstrate greater empathy for others: they really feel another's pain. In any case, most synesthetes embrace their condition and don't consider it unusual. During a lecture, a scientist mentioned synesthesia and the ability of those with the condition to see colors moving in time to music. A student in the audience raised her hand. "Doesn't everyone?" she asked. ■

Some synesthetes agree that certain sounds always elicit the same color. They tend to see the notes of the harp, for instance, in a golden color.

Sound

Do you know how you are able to hear your phone ringing? a baby crying? leaves rustling in the wind? Sound travels rapidly through the air in waves. It is caused by changes in air pressure that result from vibration. Anything that makes a sound—the soft whisper of your voice, the hum of a tuning fork, the loud strumming of a guitar—causes vibrations. Each of these vibrations is called a cycle or a sound wave. Every sound has its own pitch and loudness.

Pitch Sound waves can be very fast, occurring many times per second. The pitch of a particular sound—how high or low the sound is—depends on its frequency, or the number of cycles per second. The more cycles per second, the higher the pitch of a sound.

Try this experiment. Cut a rubber band into two segments—one long, one short—and then stretch each one out and twang it. The shorter one has a higher sound, right? In the same way, women's voices usually have a higher pitch than those of men because women's vocal cords tend to be shorter and therefore vibrate at a greater frequency. Similarly, the strings of a violin are shorter and vibrate at a higher frequency than the strings of a cello, which are longer. Therefore, the violin's sound is higher in pitch than the sound made by the cello.

The human ear can hear sound waves that vary from 20 to 20,000 cycles per second. Many animals, including dogs and dolphins, hear sounds well beyond 20,000 cycles per second. This ability developed in many species as a means of detecting danger, communicating, and navigating. Although we cannot hear them, the sounds emitted by dolphins help them locate objects. The sound pulses echo back from fish and other objects.

Loudness What is the softest sound you can hear? What is the loudest? The loudness of a sound is determined by the height, or amplitude, of sound waves. The higher the amplitude of the wave, the louder the sound. The loudness of a sound is measured in decibels, a unit that is abbreviated *dB*. Zero dB is considered the threshold of hearing. Zero dB is about as loud as the ticking of a watch 20 feet away in a very quiet room.

DECIBEL RATINGS FOR SOME FAMILIAR SOUNDS

Zero decibel is the threshold for hearing. Prolonged exposure to sounds greater than 85 dB will cause some hearing loss. Sounds of 130 dB can cause immediate hearing loss.

Sound	Pain Level	Decibels
• Jet engine (close) • Shotgun blast	Severe Pain	150 140
• Rock concert • Thunder	Pain Threshold	120 110
• Subway train • Average car	Loud	90 80
• Conversation at 3 feet • Leaves rustling	Moderate	60 40
• 2 people whispering • Watch ticking	Hearing Threshold	20 0

Loudness, however, can be a subjective term. Of course, loudness is primarily related to a sound's measurement in decibels, but other factors include the duration of the particular sound and the ear's sensitivity to it. The addition of another sound also affects the perception of loudness. As a result, loudness can vary according to the situation and differs somewhat from person to person.

Reading Check **Find the Main Idea** How do we hear sound?

The Ear

Just as the eye is the human instrument for seeing, the ear is the instrument for sensing all the sounds around us. Humans and other vertebrates have a pair of ears, one on either side of the head. This symmetrical placement of the ears allows us to localize sound sources. In fact, the entire ear is shaped to recognize and capture sound waves. However, it is the brain and nervous system that actually "hear" the sounds.

The word *ear* can refer to the entire organ or to just the part that we can see. What we normally think of as the ear is actually the outer ear. This visible part—also referred to as the pinna—is basically a flap of tissue. The outer ear collects sound. We also have a middle ear and an inner ear.

ACADEMIC
VOCABULARY

membrane a thin
layer of tissue that
covers or lines an
organ

Anatomy The eardrum is the gateway from the outer ear to the middle ear. It is a thin <u>membrane</u> that vibrates when sound waves strike it. As it vibrates, it transmits the sound to three small bones in the middle ear: the hammer, the anvil, and the stirrup. (The stirrup is the smallest bone in the human body.) These bones then also begin to vibrate and transmit sound to the inner ear.

The inner ear, which is protected by the hardest bone in the body, consists of the cochlea (KOH-klee-uh). The word *cochlea* comes from the Greek word for "snail" because, in fact, it is shaped just like the shell of a snail. The **cochlea** is a bony tube that contains fluids as well as neurons that move in response to the vibrations of the fluids. The movement generates neural impulses that are transmitted to the brain via the **auditory nerve.** Within the brain, auditory input is projected onto the hearing areas of the cerebral cortex.

Locating Sounds Did you ever sit in front of a stereo, and for some reason, all the sound seemed to come from one side instead of from straight ahead? What you probably did was adjust the balance knob until the sound seemed equally loud in each ear.

Balancing a stereo set is similar to locating sounds. If a sound seems louder from the right, you think it is coming from the right because you are used to a sound from the right side reaching the right ear first.

But what if a sound comes from directly in front of you, from behind, or from above? All such sounds are equally loud and distant from each ear. So what do you do? Simple—you usually turn your head just a little to determine in which ear the sound increases. If you turn to your right and the loudness increases in your left ear, the sound must be in front of you. Of course, you also use information from vision and other cues to locate the source of sounds. If you hear the roar of jet engines, most of the time you can be fairly certain that the airplane is overhead.

Reading Check **Summarize** How does the cochlea carry sound to the brain?

Deafness

Not everyone perceives sound. Millions of Americans are deaf. Deafness may be inherited or caused by disease, injury, or old age.

Conductive Deafness If we see an older person with a hearing aid, we can assume that he or she is probably suffering from conductive deafness. **Conductive deafness** occurs because of damage to the middle ear. Since this part of the ear amplifies sounds, damage to it prevents people from hearing sounds that are not loud enough. Fortunately, people with conductive deafness are often helped by hearing aids. These aids provide the amplification that the middle ear does not.

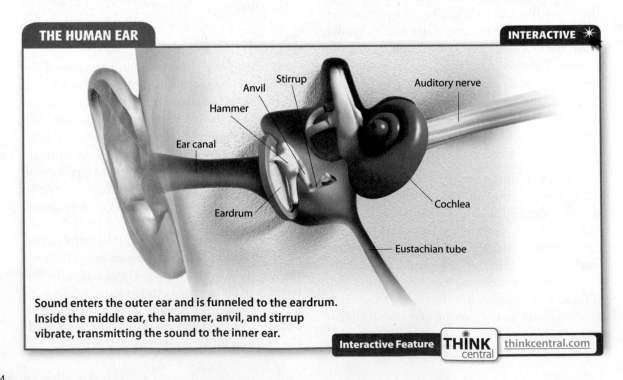

THE HUMAN EAR   INTERACTIVE ✳

Stirrup

Anvil

Hammer

Auditory nerve

Ear canal

Eardrum

Cochlea

Eustachian tube

Sound enters the outer ear and is funneled to the eardrum. Inside the middle ear, the hammer, anvil, and stirrup vibrate, transmitting the sound to the inner ear.

Interactive Feature **THINK** central   thinkcentral.com

Sensorineural Deafness Many people do not perceive sounds of certain frequencies. This is a sign of sensorineural deafness. **Sensorineural deafness** can be mild, moderate, or severe and is usually caused by damage to the inner ear. Most often, the neurons in the cochlea are destroyed. Sometimes sensorineural deafness is due to damage to the auditory nerve, either through disease or through prolonged exposure to very loud sounds.

Have you ever attended a concert and left with a ringing sensation in your ears? This may have meant that neurons had been destroyed in your ears. The same thing can happen to workers who operate certain drilling equipment or drive loud vehicles. The next time you are exposed to loud sounds, remember that it is a good idea to use earplugs.

Special devices called cochlear implants can help people with sensorineural deafness. These "artificial ears" contain microphones that sense sounds and electronic equipment that stimulates the auditory nerve directly. However, if the auditory nerve itself is damaged, the device cannot help.

Deafness in the World Today In recent years, people who are deaf have been able to come more into the mainstream of sensory experience as a result of their own efforts, the efforts of others, and new technology. For example, Scottish musician Evelyn Glennie, who has been deaf since the age of 12, became the first deaf person to sustain a career as a full-time solo percussionist. She uses as many as 60 instruments in a live performance and plays in her bare feet so she can feel the music. Of course, Glennie and generations of other severely disabled people have been inspired by Helen Keller. Keller was a tireless advocate for both the deaf and the blind. Throughout her life she appeared before legislatures, lectured, and wrote articles on behalf of the deaf-blind.

Some deaf people, however, do not wish to enter into the mainstream of sensory experience. They believe that deafness is a difference rather than a disability. In addition, they fear that attempts to help them overcome their deafness and communicate using spoken language may threaten their own expressive language and vibrant culture.

In recent years, society has become more sensitive to the needs of the deaf and has shown greater respect for their culture. Interpreters are often on hand to translate speeches into languages (such as American Sign Language) for audience members who are hearing impaired. More and more schools are offering courses in American Sign Language. Also, many television shows are now "closed captioned," which means that special decoders make captions of dialogue visible on the screen. And, as you have just read, scientists are always trying to find new ways to counteract damage inside the ear.

CASE STUDY CONNECTION

Helen Keller
Helen Keller's tireless efforts helped improve the prospects of deaf-blind people and inspired generations.

Reading Check **Contrast** What are some of the differences between conductive and sensorineural deafness?

SECTION 3 Assessment

Online Quiz **THINK** central thinkcentral.com

Reviewing Main Ideas and Vocabulary

1. **Recall** What determines the loudness of a sound, and how is loudness measured?

2. **Define** Describe the eardrum and explain its function.

3. **Identify** When is a cochlear implant an ineffective treatment for a deaf person?

Thinking Critically

4. **Infer** How might you locate a sound that comes from behind you?

5. **Identify Cause and Effect** Why can damage to the auditory nerve result in deafness?

6. **Support a Position** Do you consider deafness a disability or a difference? Explain your ideas.

7. **Sequence** Using your notes and a graphic organizer like the one below, trace the path of sound to the brain.

Brain

FOCUS ON WRITING

8. **Expository** Write a list of guidelines designed to help protect people's hearing. For example you might indicate some noises to avoid and what to do when loud sounds are unavoidable.

The Bionic Ear

For those who are severely hard of hearing or profoundly deaf, the world is a mostly silent place. But in 1985, when the cochlear implant was approved for testing, the technology held out great hope for the deaf. Since its introduction, however, the device has been a source of controversy and has divided the deaf community.

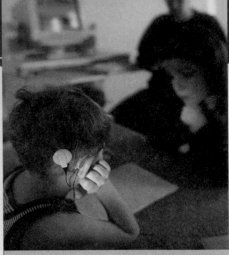

Children who receive an implant during the period when they would normally learn speech and language skills usually hear very well with a cochlear implant.

A cochlear implant is a small electronic device that is surgically placed behind the patient's ear. Unlike a hearing aid, which amplifies sound, the implant bypasses the ear and directly stimulates the auditory nerve. The device generates signals that the auditory nerve conveys to the brain, which recognizes them as sounds.

The implant is made up of the following parts: a microphone, which picks up sounds from the environment; a speech processor, which filters the sounds; a transmitter and receiver/stimulator, which receive signals from the processor and convert them into electric impulses; and an electrode array, which sends the impulses to the auditory nerve.

The device does not restore normal hearing. Rather it helps the recipient experience the sensation of sound. The recipient must learn how to understand the sounds. This can be a long process, involving intensive work with speech experts. According to one study, however, patients who receive implants in both ears are better able to perceive sound and speech (Bichey et al., 2008).

Babies and young children are the best candidates for cochlear implants. They can readily learn the speech, language, and social skills necessary to join the hearing world. Adults who have lost all or most of their hearing later in life also adapt well to the implant. They can be taught to connect the signals the device generates with the sounds they still remember.

The adjustment is far more difficult for adults who have always been deaf. When the implant is activated for these patients, they often react with bewilderment and irritation to the noises they can suddenly hear. Some even question whether anyone should receive an implant.

In fact, the implant inflamed the debate over deafness as a disability or a difference. Some deaf people questioned the psychological impact of the device on children who, they claimed, would not belong in either the deaf or hearing world.

In recent years, however, opposition to the implant has decreased. Today many members of the deaf community encourage parents to raise their implanted children "bilingually"—teaching them both spoken English and sign language. A 2007 study supports the idea that implants have not harmed young recipients. Teenagers given implants as children overwhelmingly reported having a positive identity and feeling a part of both the hearing and deaf communities (Wheeler et al., 2007).

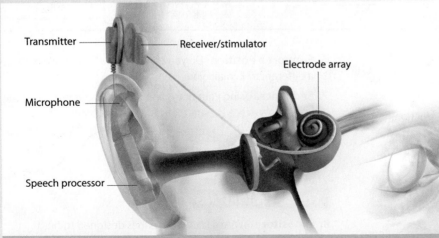

Transmitter

Receiver/stimulator

Electrode array

Microphone

Speech processor

The microphone, speech processor, and transmitter are placed behind the ear. The receiver/stimulator and electrode array are implanted in the skull and inner ear.

Thinking Critically

1. **Contrast** How does a cochlear implant differ from a hearing aid?

2. **Discuss** How do you think you would feel about cochlear implants if you were deaf?

Other Senses

Before You Read

Main Idea
In addition to vision and hearing, people possess the senses of smell and taste. We also have skin and body senses.

Reading Focus
1. How do people sense smell and taste?
2. What are the skin senses?
3. What body senses allow us to stand upright and coordinate our movements?

Vocabulary
olfactory nerve
gate theory
vestibular sense
kinesthesis

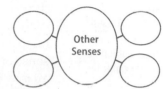

TAKING NOTES Use a graphic organizer like this one to take notes on our other senses: smell, taste, skin senses, and body senses.

Other Senses

Supertasters

PSYCHOLOGY CLOSE UP

What's on the tip of your tongue? You bite into a slice of orange and savor its slight tartness. Someone else eats a piece of the same fruit and purses his lips at the extremely bitter taste. We all perceive tastes somewhat differently, but about 25 percent of the population is particularly sensitive to a chemical called PROP, which causes them to experience taste with significant intensity. These people are sometimes known as supertasters.

Having super-sensitive taste buds can affect your health. Because they tend to dislike vegetables as a result of a perceived bitterness, supertasters may have a higher risk of some cancers. In fact, researchers have found that those who are highly sensitive to bitter tastes have an increased number of cancerous polyps in their colons. On the other hand, supertasters are also typically averse to the excessive sweetness in high-fat foods and so may be at less risk for obesity and heart disease.

In taste studies, psychologists have discovered that a traditional scale just doesn't work when supertasters are among the participants. A "strong" taste for a supertaster is exponentially more intense than a "strong" taste for those with normal taste buds. Researchers have been able to reduce the distortion by using a scale that refers to the strength of specific tastes. So, how salty is that pretzel you're about to eat? It's on the tip of your tongue. ■

Imagine how supertasters would react to this. The salty seared tuna topped with strips of seaweed—not to mention the raspberry sauce—would send their taste buds reeling.

Smell and Taste

Smell and taste are called the chemical senses. With vision and hearing, physical energy in the form of light and sound waves stimulates our sensory receptors. With smell and taste, however, we sense molecules of substances.

Smell People do not have as strong a sense of smell as many animals. Dogs use seven times as much of the cerebral cortex for smell as people do. Some dogs are used to sniff out drugs or explosives in suitcases or to track lost children or objects.

ACADEMIC VOCABULARY

resilient marked by the ability to recover quickly

But smell is important to people too. It is the sense that helps recall the most memories. Also, without smell, you would not be able to taste as much as you do. For example, if your sense of smell were not working, an onion and an apple would taste very much alike to you.

Odors of substances are detected by receptor neurons high in each nostril. Receptor neurons react when molecules of the substance in the form of a gas come into contact with them. The receptors send information about the odors to the brain via the **olfactory nerve**.

Our sense of smell adapts quickly. We adapt rapidly even to annoying odors. This may be fortunate if you are in a locker room. It may not be fortunate if harmful fumes, such as those from cars, are present—you may lose awareness of the smoke or fumes even though the danger remains. One odor can also be masked by another, which is how commercial air fresheners work.

Taste Why would your dog gobble up a piece of a candy bar but your cat turn up its nose at it? It's because dogs can taste sweetness, but cats lack that ability.

Most researchers agree on at least four basic taste qualities—sweet, sour, salty, and bitter. Some argue for a fifth basic taste called umami (oo-MAH-mee). A Japanese word, *umami* means "meaty" or "savory." Other researchers suggest there are even more basic tastes. Regardless of the number of basic tastes, the flavor of a food is more complex than taste alone. Flavor depends on odor, texture, and temperature as well as taste. For example, as you have read, apples and onions taste similar, but their flavors differ greatly. If it were not for odor, heated tenderized shoe leather might pass for steak.

We sense taste through receptor neurons located on taste buds on the tongue. Some people have low sensitivity for sweetness and may have to use twice as much sugar to sweeten their food as others who are more sensitive to sweetness. People who claim to enjoy very bitter foods may actually be "taste blind" to them. Sensitivities to different tastes can be inherited.

By eating hot foods and scraping your tongue, you regularly kill off many taste cells. But you need not be alarmed. Taste cells reproduce rapidly enough to completely renew themselves in a week.

The taste system is thus one of the most resilient of all the body's sensory systems. It is very rare for anyone to suffer a complete, permanent taste loss.

Reading Check **Identify Supporting Details** What are the four basic taste qualities?

The Skin Senses

What we normally call touch is better called the skin senses because touch is a combination of pressure, temperature, and pain. Humans have distinct sensory receptors for pressure, temperature, and pain, but some nerve endings may receive more than one type of sensory input. Our skin senses are vitally important to us. Studies have shown that premature infants grow more quickly and stay healthier if they are touched. And older people seem to do better if they have a dog or cat to stroke and cuddle; petting an animal can actually lower one's blood pressure.

Pressure Your body is covered with hairs, some of them very tiny. Sensory receptors located around the roots of hair cells fire where the skin is touched. Other structures beneath the skin are also sensitive to pressure. Different parts of the body are more sensitive to pressure than others. The fingertips, lips, nose, and cheeks are more sensitive than the shoulders, thighs, and calves.

The sense of pressure undergoes rapid adaptation. For example, when you first hold hands with someone, you are aware of the pressure. After a while, however, you become so used to the feeling of another person's fingers in your hand that you don't notice the pressure anymore. You have adapted.

Temperature Sensations of temperature are relative. When your body temperature is at a normal 98.6°F, you might perceive another person's skin as being warm. When you are feverish, though, the other person's skin might seem cool.

The receptors for temperature are neurons just beneath the skin. When skin temperature increases because you touch something warm, receptors for warmth fire. Decreases in skin temperature, such as those that occur when you put a cool, moist cloth on your forehead, cause receptors for cold to fire.

We adapt to differences in temperature. Have you ever walked out of an air-conditioned building into the hot sunshine? At first, the heat really hit you, but soon the sensation faded as you adapted to the warmth. In the same way, when you first jump into a swimming pool, the water may seem cold. Yet, after a few moments, the water feels warmer as your body adjusts to it.

Pain Headaches, backaches, and toothaches are only a few of the types of pain most of us experience from time to time. More serious health problems—such as arthritis, cancer, or wounds—also cause pain. Not all areas of the body are equally sensitive to pain. The more pain receptors located in a particular area of our skin, the more sensitive that area is.

Once a person gets hurt, everything happens very quickly. Pain originates at the point of contact. The pain message is sent from there to the spinal cord and to the thalamus in the brain. Then it is projected to the cerebral cortex, where the person registers the location and severity of the pain. Chemicals called prostaglandins help the body transmit pain messages to the brain. Aspirin and ibuprofen are common pain-fighting drugs that work by curbing production of prostaglandins.

Simple remedies like rubbing and scratching an injured area sometimes help relieve pain. Why? One possible answer lies in the gate theory of pain. **Gate theory** suggests that only a certain amount of information can be processed by the nervous system at a time. Rubbing or scratching the area transmits sensations to the brain that compete with the pain messages for attention. Thus, many neurons cannot get their pain messages to the brain. It is as if too many calls are flooding a switchboard. The flooding prevents many or all of the calls from getting through.

A fascinating fact in psychology is that many people experience pain in limbs that are no longer there. More than half of combat veterans with amputated limbs report feeling pain in the missing, or "phantom," limbs. The pain appears to involve activation of nerves in the stump of the missing limb, along with activation of neural circuits that have memories connected with the limb.

Reading Check **Summarize** How do our bodies deal with changing pressure and temperature?

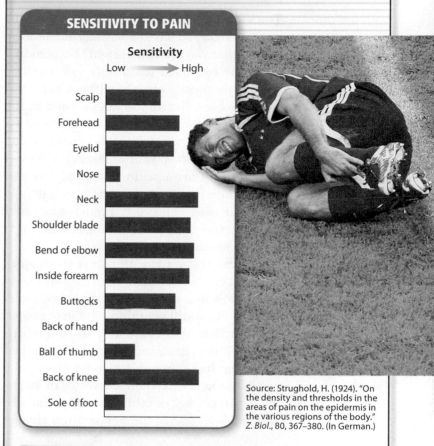

Statistically Speaking...

Pain Distribution Our ability to experience pain helps protect us from further injury. As this graph shows, however, some parts of the body are more sensitive to pressure and pain than others.

SENSITIVITY TO PAIN

Sensitivity
Low → High

- Scalp
- Forehead
- Eyelid
- Nose
- Neck
- Shoulder blade
- Bend of elbow
- Inside forearm
- Buttocks
- Back of hand
- Ball of thumb
- Back of knee
- Sole of foot

Source: Strughold, H. (1924). "On the density and thresholds in the areas of pain on the epidermis in the various regions of the body." *Z. Biol.*, 80, 367–380. (In German.)

Skills Focus **INTERPRETING GRAPHS** Which part of the body is most sensitive to pain? Which is least sensitive?

Complete a Webquest at thinkcentral.com on treating "phantom" limb pain.

Body Senses

Body senses are the senses that people are least aware of. But do not let that fool you. Without body senses, you would have to pay attention just to stay in an upright position, to lift your legs to go downstairs, or even to put food in your mouth.

The Vestibular Sense Stand up. Now close your eyes. Do you have to look in a mirror to be certain that you are still upright? No, of course not. Your **vestibular sense** tells you whether you are physically upright without having to use your eyes. Sensory organs located in the ears monitor your body's motion and position in relation to gravity. Your vestibular sense enables you to keep your balance. It tells you whether you are upside down and lets you know when you are falling. It also tells you how your body is moving through space and whether your body is changing speeds, such as in an accelerating automobile.

You can test your vestibular sense by spinning in a circle a few times and then suddenly stopping. When you stop, you probably feel as though you're still spinning—but in the opposite direction. Your brain may try to compensate for the sensation and cause you to feel dizzy. You have probably also confused your vestibular sense if, when showering or swimming, you got hot or cold water into your ear. When this happens, the temperature change in the sensory organs in your ear may cause your vestibular sense to think that you are spinning. As a result, you may feel dizzy.

Kinesthesis Ask some friends to close their eyes. Then ask them to touch their noses with their index fingers. How close to their noses did they come? Many of them were probably right on the mark, while others could only come close.

How did they locate their noses? Their eyes were closed, so they could not see their hands. They touched their noses through kinesthesis. **Kinesthesis** is the sense that informs people about the position and motion of their bodies. The word *kinesthesis* comes from the Greek words "to move" (*kinein*) and "perception" (*aisthēsis*). In kinesthesis, sensory information is fed to the brain from sensory organs in the joints, tendons, and muscles.

Kinesthesis is an essential component of everything we do. It allows us to perform the following actions:

- navigate our way through a room without bumping into furniture or people
- coordinate our movements and control our fine-motor skills
- feel our muscles contract during exercise without having to look at them.

Reading Check **Draw Conclusions** What prevents you from falling over when you stand up?

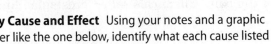

SECTION 4 Assessment

Reviewing Main Ideas and Vocabulary

1. **Contrast** What is the difference between taste and flavor?

2. **Identify** What is another name for skin senses?

3. **Summarize** Identify the chemical, skin, and body senses.

Thinking Critically

4. **Infer** How might an apple and an onion taste to you when your nose is congested? Explain why.

5. **Draw Conclusions** What might happen if you pinch your arm after you stub your toe?

6. **Evaluate** What do you think might be going on psychologically when a person with an amputated leg feels pain in the missing limb?

7. **Identify Cause and Effect** Using your notes and a graphic organizer like the one below, identify what each cause listed triggers in the senses.

Causes		Effects
1. Smell perfume 2. Bite into a lemon 3. Bump your elbow 4. Walk down the street	Senses	1. 2. 3. 4.

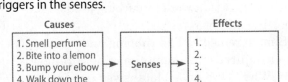

FOCUS ON WRITING

8. **Narrative** Write a brief conversation between a person who has body senses and one who does not. Have the person without body senses tell about his or her adventures at a party.

Perception

Before You Read

Main Idea
Perception is the way in which we organize our sensory impressions. Movement, depth, and constancy are some of the ways in which we make sense of these impressions.

Reading Focus
1. What are the main rules of perceptual organization?
2. How is movement perceived?
3. What cues do we use for depth perception?
4. What are perceptual constancies?
5. Why do we see visual illusions?

Vocabulary
closure
proximity
similarity
continuity
common fate
stroboscopic motion
monocular cues
binocular cues
retinal disparity

TAKING NOTES Use a graphic organizer like this one to take notes on perceptual organization, movement, depth, and constancy.

Depth Misperception

PSYCHOLOGY CLOSE UP

How do you feel when you look down? Does your heart pound with terror when you stand at the top of an escalator? When you look over the railing of a bridge, do you feel as if the ground is stretching away to infinity and beyond—or worse, as if it's rushing up to smack you in the face? If so, you may have poor depth perception. But you almost certainly have a fear of heights, or acrophobia.

For centuries, acrophobes have either avoided high places or tried to swallow their fears. But in recent years, psychologists have come to the rescue with a form of therapy involving virtual reality. In a typical treatment, participants stand at a railing and don the headgear. The virtual scene they see is the view from a balcony, but rendered in the dimensions of width, height, and depth. "It was completely realistic," one participant claimed. "I felt as though I was standing on the edge."

Of course, the feeling that the experience is real is the key to the treatment's success. Participants need to feel actual fear—complete with sweating and racing heart—to overcome it. Over the course of several sessions, they move on to virtual higher heights once their anxiety at a lower level diminishes. And the therapy seems to work. One man said that he now rides a glass-enclosed elevator without fear. He can even look down. ■

Rules of Perceptual Organization

Every minute of every day, countless impressions are made on our various senses. Imagine the confusion if we did not find ways to organize all that information. Perception is the way we organize and make sense of all our sensory impressions.

Gestalt psychologists applied the principle that "the whole is more than the sum of its parts" to the study of perception. Using this principle, they noted many different ways in which people make sense of sensory information. These ways are called the rules of perceptual organization and include closure, figure-ground perception, proximity, similarity, continuity, and common fate.

Closure Look at the pattern below on the left. Do you see random blotches of ink or a dog sniffing the ground? If you perceive the dog, it is not just because of the visual sensations provided by the drawing. Those are actually quite confusing. Despite the lack of clarity, however, you can still see a dog. Why? The answer is that you are familiar with dogs and that you try to fit the pieces of information into a familiar pattern.

What you are doing with this picture is filling in the blanks. Gestalt psychologists refer to this as the principle of closure. **Closure** is the tendency to perceive a complete or whole figure even when there are gaps in what your senses tell you.

Figure-Ground Perception Now take a look at the drawing on the right. What do you see? In the center of the drawing, you probably see a vase. If you look again, though, you may see more than a vase. Can you see the two profiles that form the sides of the vase?

This drawing is one of psychologists' favorite illustrations demonstrating figure-ground relationships. Figure-ground perception is the perception of figures against a background. When you saw a vase, it was a light-colored figure against a dark background. The profiles, on the other hand, were dark figures against a light background.

We experience figure-ground perception every day. If we look out a window, we may see people, buildings, cars, and streets or perhaps grass, trees, birds, and clouds. We see these objects as figures against a background, such as white clouds against a blue sky or a car in front of a brick building. What we perceive as the figure and what we perceive as the background influence our perception.

Other Rules of Organization Without reading any further, describe the drawing labeled A on the following page. Did you say that the drawing consisted of six lines, or did you say that it was three pairs of lines? If you said three pairs of lines, you were influenced by the **proximity,** or nearness, of some of the lines to each other. There is no other reason to perceive them in pairs since all of the lines are the same in every other respect.

CLOSURE

FIGURE-GROUND PERCEPTION

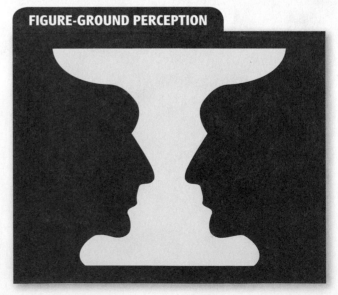

Now describe the drawing labeled B. Did you perceive it as a six-by-six grid or as three columns of *x*'s and three columns of *o*'s? If you said three columns, then you were grouping the columns according to the law of **similarity,** which says that people think of similar objects as belonging together.

What about the drawing labeled C? Is this drawing a series of half-circles, with every other one turned down? Or did you see a wavy line and a straight line? If you saw the wavy line and the straight line, you were probably organizing your perceptions according to the rule of **continuity.** People usually prefer to see smooth, continuous patterns (like lines and waves), not disrupted ones (like a series of alternating half-circles).

Finally, there is the law of **common fate.** Have you ever noticed how when you see things moving together, you perceive them as *belonging* together? For example, a group of people running in the same direction would appear to have the same purpose. You assume that they are part of the same group and that they are all running to the same place—in other words, that they have a common fate.

Reading Check **Find the Main Idea** What principle did psychologists apply when they developed the rules of perceptual organization?

Movement

Our world is not static. People, animals, and objects are constantly moving around us. When we sense this movement, we need to be able to make sense of it. We also need to organize our perceptions of movements that only seem to occur but are actually illusions.

Perception of Movement Try the following experiment. The next time you are in a car or a bus that is stopped at a traffic light, pay attention to what happens when the vehicle in the next lane begins to move forward. Do you think at first that your vehicle, not the other one, is moving? Is it unclear whether your car or bus is moving backward or the other one is moving forward?

To sense movement, humans need to see an object change its position relative to other objects. We all know now that Earth is moving, but, of course, we don't really feel it. To early

OTHER RULES OF ORGANIZATION

A. Proximity

B. Similarity

C. Continuity

scientists, on the other hand, whose only instrument for visual observation was the naked eye, it seemed logical that the sun circled Earth. After all, that is what they seemed to be seeing. To observe that it is Earth that moves around the sun, we would have to be somewhere in outer space. We cannot observe it while standing on Earth itself.

So how do you decide which vehicle is moving at the traffic light? One way is to look for objects that you know are stable, like structures on the side of the road—buildings, signs, or trees. If you are steady in relation to them, then your vehicle is not moving. This also sheds light on how participants in events perceive the action from different points of view, physically and psychologically. Those favoring one side over another tend to be biased in their reporting of events. For example, the viewpoint of someone driving a car that runs a red light may differ from that of someone driving a car in another direction.

Stroboscopic Motion We have been talking about perception of real movement; that is, movement that actually occurs. Psychologists have also studied *illusions* of movement. One such illusion of movement is called stroboscopic motion. In **stroboscopic motion,** the illusion of movement is produced by showing the rapid progression of images or objects that are not moving at all. Have you ever seen one of those little books designed to be flipped through quickly so that the figures on the pages appear to move? These books work because of stroboscopic motion.

Movies work in a similar way. Despite the name *movie,* movies do not consist of images that move. Instead, the audience is shown 16 to 22 pictures, or frames, per second. Each frame is just slightly different from the previous one. Showing the frames in rapid succession creates the illusion of movement. Why? Because of the law of continuity, humans prefer to see things as one continuous image. Perception smooths over the interruptions and fills in the gaps.

Reading Check **Summarize** How does the law of continuity affect stroboscopic motion?

Depth Perception

Imagine trying to go through life without being able to judge depth or distance. Like someone walking into a darkened theater, you might bump into other people or step on their toes. You would have trouble going up or down stairs without stumbling. Depth, in this case, has little to do with the way people sometimes use the word *deep.* It is not, for instance, the depth of a lake or a hole. Depth here means "distance away." For example, without really thinking about it, you decide how far away a glass of juice is from you. Can you just reach out and pick it up, or do you have to get out of your chair? You perceive the depth of objects through both monocular and binocular cues.

Monocular Cues for Depth **Monocular cues** need only one eye to be perceived. Artists use monocular cues to create an illusion of depth. These cues create the illusion of three dimensions, or depth, on two-dimensional, or flat, surfaces. Monocular cues cause certain objects in a piece of artwork to appear more distant from the viewer than others. These cues include perspective, clearness, overlap, shadow, and texture gradient.

If you take two objects that are exactly the same size and place one of them far away from you and the other nearby, the object that is farther away will stimulate a smaller area of your retina than the one that is near. Even though the objects are the same size, the amount of sensory input from the more distant object is smaller because it is farther away. The distances between far-off objects also appear to be smaller than the same distances between nearby objects. For this reason, the phenomenon known as perspective occurs. Perspective is the tendency to see parallel lines as coming closer together, or converging, as they move away from us. However, experience teaches us that objects that look small when they are far away will seem larger when they are close, even though their size does not actually change. In this way, our perception of a familiar object's size also becomes a cue to its distance from us.

The clearness of an object also helps in telling us how far away it might be. Nearby objects appear to be clearer, and we see more details. Faraway objects seem less clear and less detailed. Thus, the clearer a familiar object seems to be, the closer it is to us.

Overlap is another monocular cue that tells us which objects are far away and which ones are near. Overlap is the perception of one object as being in front of another. Nearby objects can block our view of more-distant objects. Look at the pairs of circles labeled A on the following page. Experience teaches us to perceive partly covered objects as being farther away than the objects that block them from view. As a result, the uncovered circles probably look closer to you.

Shadows and highlights also give us information about objects' three-dimensional shapes and where they are placed in relation to the source of light. Look at the other pair of circles labeled B on the following page. What do you see on the left compared to the right? You probably see a two-dimensional circle on the left and a three-dimensional sphere on the right. What is the difference between the two? The figure on the right shows a circle with a highlight on its surface and a shadow underneath. Because of these cues, you perceive the figure on the right to be closer to you.

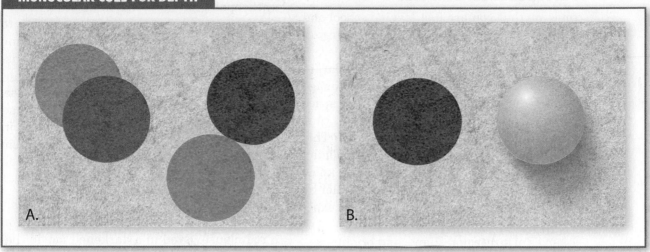

A.

B.

Still another monocular cue is texture gradient. Texture, of course, is the surface quality and appearance of an object. A gradient is a progressive change. Texture that is farther away from us appears to be denser than texture that is closer, and we see less detail. Therefore, closer objects are perceived as having a more varied texture than objects that are farther away. So, for example, a wall seen up close seems rougher and more textured than it does when seen from far away.

The most complex of monocular cues of depth is called motion parallax. Parallax refers to the change in the position of a heavenly body due to Earth's orbit. This cue is more complex because it involves not a stationary picture but the image of something as the viewer moves. Motion parallax is the tendency of objects to seem to move forward or backward depending on how far away they are from the viewer.

If you have the opportunity to take a drive in the countryside, pay attention to what happens to various objects as you move past them. You will notice that distant objects, such as mountains, the moon, and stars, appear to move forward with you and even follow you. Objects at an intermediate distance seem to stand still. Nearby objects, such as roadside markers, rocks, and trees, go by quite rapidly. If you did not know better, you might think that they were moving backward. Through experience, we realize that objects that appear to move with us are at a greater distance than those that pass quickly.

Binocular Cues for Depth Whereas monocular cues can be perceived with just one eye, both eyes are required to perceive **binocular cues** for depth. Two binocular cues for depth are retinal disparity and convergence.

Hold a finger at arm's length. Now slowly bring it closer until it almost touches your nose. If you keep your eyes relaxed as you do this, you will seem to see two fingers. An image of the finger will be projected onto the retina of each eye. Each image will be slightly different because the finger will be seen at different angles. This difference is referred to as **retinal disparity.** The closer your finger comes, the farther apart the "two fingers" appear to be. Thus, the amount of retinal disparity we detect gives us a cue about the depth of an object. However, retinal disparity serves as a cue to depth only for objects that are within a few feet of us, but not for objects that are farther away.

The other binocular cue we use is called convergence. Convergence is associated with feelings of tension in the eye muscle. When we try to maintain a single image of the approaching finger, our eyes must turn inward, or converge on it, giving us a cross-eyed look. The closer we feel our eyes moving toward each other, the nearer the object they are looking at is—and the more tension we feel in our eyes. Like retinal disparity, convergence has stronger effects when objects are close.

Reading Check **Contrast** What is the difference between monocular and binocular cues?

Perceptual Constancies

Imagine that you are just leaving school and that you see your friends waiting for you under a tree some distance away. As you walk over to them, they get closer and look larger because, as you have just learned, the image of your friends takes up more and more space on your retina. Why do you not think your friends are literally growing in inches? This would certainly appear to be the case judging from the sensory input. The reason you know your friends are not actually getting taller by the second is experience. Each person's experience creates perceptual constancies—constancies of size, color, shape, and brightness.

Size Constancy The image of a dog seen from a distance of 20 feet occupies about the same amount of space on the retina as an inch-long insect seen close up. Yet we do not perceive the dog to be as small as the insect. Similarly, we may say that people on the ground look like ants when we are at the top of a tall building, but we know they remain people even if the details of their forms are lost in the distance.

Through experience, people acquire a sense of size constancy. Size constancy is the tendency to perceive an object as being of one size no matter how far away the object is. Through experience, humans learn about perspective—that the same object seen at a great distance from the viewer will appear much smaller than when it is nearby.

How do we know that size constancy is something we learn? Some evidence comes from a study of the Mbuti people of Africa, who live in a dense forest. When British anthropologist Colin Turnbull took one of the Mbuti guides out of the forest and onto a wide plain, they happened to see some buffalo in the distance. The Mbuti guide mistook the buffalo for insects and would not believe Turnbull when he told him otherwise. The reason? Experience. The Mbuti man had seen buffalo before. However, having lived in a dense forest, he was not used to seeing them at great distances. He had therefore not developed size constancy.

Color Constancy Imagine that you are wearing a tan sweatshirt and your friend has on a red blouse. Even in a darkened movie theater, you both still know that your shirts are tan and red. Because of your previous experience, you perceive your shirts as remaining tan and red even though both appear gray in the darkness of the theater. Color constancy is the tendency to perceive objects as keeping their color even though different light might change the appearance of their color.

Shape Constancy Take a glass and look at it from directly above. You see a circle, right? Now move back slightly; it becomes an ellipse. So why would you still describe the rim of the glass as being a circle? Because of shape constancy—the knowledge that an item has only one shape no matter what angle you view it from. In the same way, a door appears to be a rectangle only when you view it straight on. When you open it, the left or right edge comes closer and appears to be larger, changing the retinal image of the door to a trapezoid. Yet because of shape constancy, you continue to think of doors as being rectangular.

Brightness Constancy Brightness constancy is the tendency to perceive an object as being equally bright even when the intensity of the light around it changes. Look at the drawing on this page. Does the gray square in the black frame look brighter than the one in the white frame? If it does, it is because we judge the brightness of an object by the brightness of other objects around it. For example, a black object really looks almost gray in very bright sunlight, but we perceive it as black because everything else around it is much brighter.

Reading Check **Identify Supporting Details**
How do people develop perceptual constancies?

BRIGHTNESS CONSTANCY

Visual Illusions

Do your eyes sometimes "play tricks on you"? Actually, your eyes are not to blame, but your brain's use of perceptual constancies is responsible. Your brain can trick your eye through visual illusions.

The drawings on this page show two visual illusions often used by psychologists. The drawing labeled A shows the Müller-Lyer illusion. Look at the two lines at the top of the illustration. Do you think they are the same length? To most people, the line on the right, with its reversed arrows, looks longer. Why? Again, because of experience. In this culture, we are used to living in rooms in buildings. The line on the right may remind us of how a far corner of a room looks, while the line on the left reminds us of the outside near corner of a building. The rule of size constancy is that if two objects seem to be the same size and one is farther away, the farther object must be larger than it actually seems. How did psychologists come to the conclusion that we are reminded of buildings and rooms in this illusion? Because they found that the illusion does not work in cultures in which people do not live in the same types of structures that we do.

Now look at the drawing labeled B, which shows the Ponzo illusion. Which of the two horizontal lines do you think is longer? Do you

VISUAL ILLUSIONS

A. Müller-Lyer Illusion

B. Ponzo illusion

perceive the top line as being longer? Actually, they are the same length. The rule of size constancy may also afford insight into this illusion. Perhaps the converging lines strike you as receding into the distance. If so, you assume from experience that the horizontal line at the top is farther down the track—farther away from you. The rule of size constancy is at work again.

Reading Check **Make Generalizations** How does culture influence our perception of visual illusions?

SECTION 5 Assessment

Reviewing Main Ideas and Vocabulary

1. **Recall** What is figure-ground perception?

2. **Summarize** What techniques do artists use to convey perspective in their work?

3. **Explain** Describe size constancy.

Thinking Critically

4. **Predict** How might someone from another culture who had never viewed anything from a high elevation perceive objects on the ground seen from the top of a skyscraper?

5. **Evaluate** Why do you think people try to fit the pieces of information they perceive into a familiar pattern?

6. **Elaborate** Suppose you are on a train and another pulls alongside of you at the same speed. How do you think you would perceive the situation?

7. **Sequence** Using your notes and a graphic organizer like the one below, list the organization methods that we use to perceive a group of people as they approach from a distance.

Group ●——|——|——|——|——► You

FOCUS ON WRITING

8. **Persuasive** Some psychologists claim that we only perceive that to which we pay attention. Other psychologists say that we perceive a great deal more than we pay attention to. With which viewpoint do you agree? Write a paragraph in which you support your position with a real-life example.

Sensory Thresholds and Perceptual Organization

Reading and Activity Workbook

Use the workbook to complete this lab.

What sensory impressions do you perceive—and which ones do you filter out?

1. Introduction

In this chapter, you have learned about sensory thresholds, the signal-detection theory, and rules of perceptual organization. You have read about how these concepts help people filter and make sense of the countless sensory impressions that bombard them every day. In this lab, you will get together with a group of classmates and record the sensations you perceive in a normal setting. By doing so, you will come to appreciate firsthand the impact these concepts have on your life.

After you have conducted the lab, you will discuss your experiences with your fellow group members. Then all groups will take part in a class discussion. You will compare your perceptions and discuss what you did and didn't perceive. To complete the lab, follow the steps below.

- Your teacher will divide the class into small groups and assign each a location to record impressions. Some groups will be assigned to the classroom, others to the school hallway, and still others will go outside on the school grounds.

- Your teacher will pass out materials that you will use, including art paper, markers, and colored pencils.

- With your group, discuss the following rules of perceptual organization: closure, proximity, similarity, continuity, common fate, size constancy, color constancy, brightness constancy, and shape constancy. Take notes that you can refer to during the lab.

2. Record and Illustrate

Before you begin the lab, select one person in your group to be the sensory recorder. The task of the sensory recorder will be to sit quietly and record all the sensations he or she hears, sees, or smells during the lab. The other group members will be illustrators. The task of the illustrators will be to draw pictures of the people, objects, and scenes they see during the lab that demonstrate some of the rules of perceptual organization.

Once everyone's role has been determined, proceed to your assigned location. Keep the following tips and steps in mind as you carry out the lab.

- Maintain a little distance from your other group members so that you don't distract each other. If you are spread out, you will also have slightly different perspectives and so will record a variety of sensations and images.

- As much as possible, do not talk to your fellow group members during the lab.

- Note to the sensory recorder: Most of the sensations you will perceive will probably consist of everyday sounds, sights, and smells. Be sure to record them as well as any other more unusual sensations.

- Note to the illustrators: Use your art materials to produce illustrations of five of the concepts you reviewed with your group. Each illustration should be on a separate piece of paper and should fill the page. Write the name of the concept illustrated on the back of the paper.

- Spend about 30 minutes absorbing impressions. Note that your senses are likely to dull as time passes in the same location.

3. Group Discussion

After the lab has been completed, get together with your group and discuss your experiences. Use the following to guide your discussion.

■ Share your illustrations. Did illustrators draw different objects, people, and scenes? What do you think accounts for this?

■ Have the sensory recorder read what he or she experienced during the lab. Did the recorder notice some sensations that illustrators do not recall? Why do you think that is so?

■ For the sensory recorder: How difficult was it to concentrate on all your senses at once for an extended period of time? Did you notice some everyday sensations during the lab that you ordinarily would not? Why do you think that was the case?

■ For the illustrators: Which perceptual concepts did all of you illustrate? Which ones did some of you illustrate? Which ones were not illustrated at all? Do you think some occur more frequently in daily life, or are some simply more difficult to detect?

4. Class Discussion

Now get together with the other groups in your class. Groups will take turns presenting their illustrations and recordings. As each group presents, the other groups will try to identify the concepts illustrated, explaining their reasoning. Finally, discuss the following questions.

■ Did some recorders and illustrators in the same locations notice things that other recorders and illustrators did not?

■ What role did signal-detection theory probably play in what the recorders and illustrators noticed?

■ How do you think sensory thresholds affected what you noticed?

■ In a school setting, which sense would you consider to be most important and why?

■ What would life be like if you suddenly lost the ability to distinguish shape constancy, closure, or any other perceptual organization concept?

Which rule of perceptual organization do these drawings illustrate? How do you know that the people in each drawing are the same height?

Comprehension and Critical Thinking

SECTION 1 (pp. 96–99)

1. a. Define What is sensory adaptation?

b. Contrast What is the difference between sensation and perception?

c. Make Judgments Why might signal-detection theory not apply to a person with autism?

SECTION 2 (pp. 101–105)

2. a. Recall How do pupils adjust to the amount of light available?

b. Explain How do we perceive colors other than blue, green, and red?

c. Elaborate How might you characterize the typical person with color blindness?

SECTION 3 (pp. 106–109)

3. a. Describe Why do women's voices tend to be higher than men's?

b. Identify Cause and Effect What might happen as a result of damage to the middle ear?

c. Evaluate Why do you think the inner ear is protected by the hardest bone in the body?

SECTION 4 (pp. 111–114)

4. a. Identify Main Ideas How are odors communicated to the brain?

b. Summarize Why are body senses important?

c. Predict What might happen to babies who are never held or touched?

SECTION 5 (pp. 115–121)

5. a. Identify Which school of psychology developed the principle of closure?

b. Infer How do our culture and experience affect our tendency to see visual illusions?

c. Elaborate Give an example of a situation in which monocular cues could be used to determine how far away an object is.

Reviewing Vocabulary

Fill in each blank with the term that correctly completes the sentence.

6. The weakest amount of a stimulus that can be sensed is called its _____ .

7. _____ is the process by which we become more sensitive to weak stimuli and less sensitive to unchanging stimuli.

8. The area in the eye that lacks photoreceptors is the _____ .

9. The visual impression that remains after the original image is removed is a(n) _____ .

10. _____ occurs because of damage to the middle ear.

11. _____ suggests that only a certain amount of information can be processed by the nervous system at a time.

12. _____ is the sense that informs people about the position and motion of their bodies.

13. Lenses that have lost their elasticity may be described as being _____ .

14. _____ need only one eye to be perceived.

INTERNET ACTIVITY ✳

15. Research to learn more about the deaf community. Find out what audism means to community members and why they compare this attitude to racism and sexism. Also, briefly study sign language and its rules and grammar. Write a paragraph describing what you learned and present it to your class. If possible, present a word or two in American Sign Language.

Psychology in Your Life

16. Conduct an experiment to show the relationship between taste and smell. Ask several friends to participate. Select four foods that are similar in texture, such as an apple, an onion, a pear, and a potato. Peel and cut the food into pieces. Blindfold the participants and ask them to hold their noses. Guide each person's hand to each bit of food and ask him or her to taste it and guess what it is. Write a report describing how accurately the participants guessed the same foods.

SKILLS ACTIVITY: INTERPRETING PRIMARY SOURCES

Read the following excerpt in which Constance Classen discusses the ways different cultures understand the senses. Then answer the questions that follow.

> 66 Different cultures present strikingly different ways of 'making sense' of the world. The Ongee of the Andaman Islands in the South Pacific, for example, live in a world ordered by smell. According to the Ongee, odour is the vital force of the universe and the basis of personal and social identity. Therefore, when an Ongee wishes to refer to 'me,' he or she points to his or her nose, the organ of smell. Likewise, when greeting a friend, an Ongee will ask 'How is your nose?' 99
>
> —Constance Classen, *Worlds of Sense: Exploring the Senses in History and Across Cultures*

17. **Draw Conclusions** What conclusions can you draw about smells on the Andaman Islands?

18. **Analyze** What point does Classen make about culture in this excerpt?

19. **Make Judgments** Which sense do you regard as the most important in your culture? Provide an example to support your answer.

WRITING FOR AP PSYCHOLOGY

Use your knowledge of perception to answer the question below. Do not simply list facts. Present a clear argument based on your critical analysis of the question, using the appropriate psychological terminology.

20. Briefly discuss each principle of perceptual organization below. For each one, explain the role psychology plays in the principle.
- closure
- similarity
- common fate

Biofeedback
AND CONSCIOUSNESS

Suppose someone told you to lift your arm. Could you do it? Of course—all you would have to do is decide to do it. Lifting your arm is an example of *voluntary* behavior. Walking and talking are other examples. You can walk and talk simply by deciding that you are going to do so.

Suppose someone told you to lower your blood pressure or your heart rate. Perhaps you could, but not directly. To lower your heart rate, you might sit down and take it easy. But blood pressure and heart rate are *involuntary* forms of behavior.

Or are they? A few decades ago, psychologists thought they knew the difference between voluntary and involuntary behaviors of the body. They thought voluntary behaviors were conscious. People could make them happen simply by directing their attention to the act. Psychologists thought other behaviors were involuntary. They could not be consciously controlled.

Then, in 1969, psychologist Neal E. Miller made an exciting discovery. He was able to train laboratory rats to increase or decrease their heart rates voluntarily. But why would rats do such a thing in the first place? Miller already knew that there is a pleasure center in the hypothalamus of a rat's brain. When a rat was given a small burst of electricity in this center, the rat felt pleasure, and it wanted more.

Because the rats would do whatever they could to continue feeling this pleasure, they quickly learned that whenever they pressed a lever in their cage, they received this bit of pleasure-producing electric shock. As a result, Miller's rats pressed this lever to the point of exhaustion.

Miller designed a study to find out what else the rats could do for pleasure. He implanted electrodes in the rats' pleasure centers. Then some of the rats were given shocks whenever their heart rates increased. Other rats received shocks when their heart rates decreased. After a training session that took only 90 minutes, the rats learned to change their heart rates by as much as 20 percent.

Miller's research was an example of biofeedback training (BFT). If it could be done with rats, could people, too, control bodily behavior thought to be involuntary? Instead of implanting electrodes in people's brains, researchers used monitors to let people know when, for example, their heart rates were slower. Thus, biofeedback is a system for monitoring and feeding back information about certain biological processes. A biofeedback system does not actually control any of the bodily behaviors. Instead,

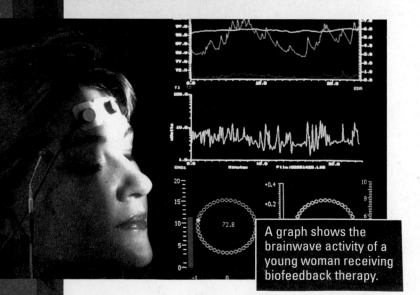

A graph shows the brainwave activity of a young woman receiving biofeedback therapy.

CHAPTER 5
CONSCIOUSNESS

Yoga is used as a technique to treat physical problems.

like a mirror, the biofeedback monitor reflects a person's own efforts and enables him or her to see how various voluntary behaviors affect the involuntary ones.

Studies have shown that biofeedback has numerous other applications. For example, biofeedback is moderately effective in reducing the intense pain of migraine headaches and other painful conditions.

Since Miller's studies in the 1960s and 1970s, biofeedback has had a resurgence as part of 21st-century alternative medicine that includes meditation, hypnosis, and yoga. Biofeedback is used to treat problems like high blood pressure, seizures, migraine headaches, and digestive disorders.

Biofeedback, along with other examples of alternative medicine mentioned above, has shed some light on the nature of consciousness. In this chapter you will look at various aspects of consciousness, including sleep and dreams, altered states of consciousness, and drugs and consciousness.

What do you think?

1. How can people learn to control involuntary behavior?

2. If you could use biofeedback to control an involuntary behavior, what would it be?

Chapter at a Glance

SECTION 1: The Study of Consciousness

■ Consciousness, like intelligence or emotion, is a construct; that is, it is a concept that cannot be seen, touched, or measured directly.

■ Consciousness has a number of different meanings, including sensory awareness, direct inner awareness, and a sense of self.

■ There are several levels of consciousness, including the preconscious, unconscious, and nonconscious.

SECTION 2: Sleep and Dreams

■ The sleep cycle is made up of four stages of sleep and REM sleep.

■ Sleep serves important physical and psychological needs.

■ Common sleep problems include insomnia, nightmares, night terrors, sleepwalking, sleep apnea, and narcolepsy.

SECTION 3: Altered States of Consciousness

■ Altered states of consciousness can be achieved while awake through biofeedback, meditation, and hypnosis.

■ There are many myths surrounding hypnosis.

■ Although there are controversies related to the use of hypnotism, hypnosis can be used to recall memories, reduce pain, and quit bad habits.

SECTION 4: Drugs and Consciousness

■ Depressants slow down the nervous system, stimulants increase the activity of the nervous system, and hallucinogens produce hallucinations.

■ Treatments for drug abuse include detoxification, maintenance programs, counseling, and support groups.

The Study of Consciousness

Before You Read

Main Idea

Consciousness, the awareness of things that are both inside and outside ourselves, is an elusive but essential subject of study for psychologists.

Reading Focus

1. Why is consciousness a psychological construct?

2. What are the general meanings of consciousness?

3. What distinguishes the different levels of consciousness from full conscious awareness?

Vocabulary

consciousness
selective attention
preconscious
unconscious
nonconscious
altered state of consciousness

TAKING NOTES Use a graphic organizer like this one to identify the different levels of consciousness.

1.	
2.	
3.	
4.	

THE STREAM OF CONSCIOUSNESS

PSYCHOLOGY CLOSE UP

What are you aware of right now? William James was one of the pioneers of psychology. In his book *Principles of Psychology* (1890), he coined the term "stream of consciousness" to describe the shifting and elusive nature of consciousness. The phrase highlights the fact that consciousness changes constantly, like a stream flowing swiftly along, carrying various bits of flotsam and jetsam. Then 20th-century literary modernists such as James Joyce in *Ulysses*, Virginia Woolf in *To the Lighthouse*, and

William Faulkner in *The Sound and the Fury* used stream of consciousness as a literary technique. In their writings, these authors tried to render the flow of impressions in one's consciousness by using snatches of thought and the free association of ideas and images.

Although consciousness will always be an elusive subject compared to other fields of psychological research, psychologists continue to study it. New techniques have been devised in an attempt to better understand the meaning of consciousness. ■

Consciousness as a Construct

Consciousness means the awareness of things that are both inside and outside ourselves. But what is consciousness? You are probably certain that you are conscious right now. You are conscious, or aware, that you are reading this page. But what about tonight, when you are asleep? Sleeping is related to consciousness. There are also several altered states of consciousness, such as those that occur when a person is in a hypnotic trance or is under the influence of certain drugs.

Today, most psychologists believe that we cannot capture the richness of human experience without talking about consciousness. However, psychologists have not always thought that consciousness should be part of the study of psychology.

In 1904 William James wrote an article titled "Does Consciousness Exist?" In this article, James questioned the value of studying consciousness because he could not think of a scientific way to observe or measure another person's consciousness. His point was that even though we can see other people talking or moving around, we cannot actually measure their consciousness. Although James later modified his position, his original position was influential.

John Watson, the founder of behaviorism, agreed with James. In 1913 Watson wrote an article called "Psychology as the Behaviorist Views It." In this article, he stated, "The time seems to have come when psychology must discard all references to consciousness." Watson, like James, questioned whether consciousness could be studied scientifically. He chose instead to focus only on observable behaviors.

Not all psychologists dismissed the possibility of studying consciousness. Today many psychologists believe that consciousness can be studied because it can be linked with measurable behaviors, such as talking, and with brain waves.

Consciousness is a psychological construct, as are intelligence and emotion. That is, none of these concepts can be seen, touched, or measured directly. However, they are known by their effects on behavior and they play roles in psychological theories. For example, we can theorize about how sleep or alcohol affects consciousness and devise ways of testing our theories. When people behave in certain ways, we may conclude that the behaviors result from, say, intelligence even though there is no way to be certain. Although consciousness cannot be seen or touched, it is real enough to most people.

Reading Check **Summarize** Why do some psychologists think consciousness can be studied?

Meanings of Consciousness

Generally speaking, consciousness means awareness. But there is more than one type of awareness. Thus, the term *consciousness* is used in a variety of ways. Sometimes consciousness refers to sensory awareness. At other times, consciousness may mean direct inner awareness. A third use of the term *consciousness* refers to the sense of self that each person experiences.

Consciousness as Sensory Awareness When you see a raindrop glistening on a leaf, when you hear your teacher's voice, or when you smell pizza in the cafeteria, you are *conscious* of all of these sensations around you, including sights, sounds, and smells. Your senses make it possible for you to be aware of your environment. Therefore, one meaning of consciousness is sensory awareness of the environment. In other words, you are conscious, or aware, of things outside yourself.

Focusing on a particular stimulus is referred to as **selective attention.** To pay attention in class, you must screen out the rustling of paper and the scraping of chairs. To get your homework done, you must pay more attention to your assignments than to your hunger pangs or the music playing in your headphones. Selective attention makes our senses keener. We may even be able to pick out the speech of a single person across a room at a party.

We tend to be more conscious of some things than others. For example, we tend to be particularly conscious of sudden changes, as when a cool breeze enters a sweltering room. We also tend to be especially conscious of unusual stimuli—for example, a dog entering the classroom. Intense stimuli—such as bright colors, loud noises, or sharp pains—also tend to get our attention.

ACADEMIC VOCABULARY
theorize propose a theory about; speculate about

Consciousness as Direct Inner Awareness

Imagine jumping into a lake or a swimming pool on a hot day. Can you feel the cool, refreshing water all around you? Although this image may be vivid, you did not really experience it. No sensory organs were involved. You are conscious of the image through what psychologists call direct inner awareness.

Any time you are aware of feeling angry, any time you remember a best friend you had when you were younger, any time you think about abstract concepts such as fairness, you do so through direct inner awareness. In other words, you do not hear, see, smell, or touch thoughts, images, emotions, or memories. Yet you are still conscious of them. This meaning of consciousness, then, is being aware of things inside yourself.

Consciousness as Sense of Self

Have you ever noticed how young children sometimes refer to themselves by their names? For example, they do not say, "I want milk" but "Taylor wants milk." It is only as they grow older that they begin to understand that they are unique individuals, separate from other people and from their surroundings.

From then on, they have a sense of self, no matter how much they or the world around them might change. In some uses of the word, *consciousness* is this sense of self in which we are aware of ourselves and our existence.

Reading Check **Identify** What are the three uses of the term consciousness?

Different Levels of Consciousness

So far, we have discussed only one of the levels of consciousness—the level at which people are aware of something and are aware of their awareness. But many psychologists speak of other levels of consciousness. These include the preconscious level, the unconscious level, and the nonconscious level. At these levels of consciousness, awareness is considerably more limited.

The Preconscious Level What if someone asked you what you wore to school yesterday? Or what you did after school? Although you were not consciously thinking about any of this information before you were asked about it, you will probably be able to come up with the answers.

Preconscious ideas are not in your awareness now, but you could recall them. You can make these preconscious bits of information conscious by directing your inner awareness, or attention, to them.

The Unconscious Level Sigmund Freud theorized that people have an unconscious mind. Information stored in the **unconscious** (sometimes called the subconscious) is unavailable to awareness under most circumstances. In other words, this information is hidden from the conscious mind.

FREUD'S LEVELS OF CONSCIOUSNESS

CONSCIOUS LEVEL
Perceptions
Thoughts

PRECONSCIOUS LEVEL
Memories   Stored knowledge

UNCONSCIOUS LEVEL

Selfish needs   Violent motives

Immoral urges   Fears

Irrational   Shameful   Unacceptable
wishes   experiences   desires

To Freud, consciousness is like an iceberg. Many memories, impulses, and feelings exist below the level of conscious awareness.

Skills Focus INTERPRETING VISUALS On what level did Freud place irrational wishes?

For example, imagine that you are planning to go to a party. Without realizing why, you find yourself continually distracted from getting ready. First, perhaps, you cannot find the shoes you were planning to wear. Then maybe you become involved in a lengthy phone call to a friend.

Can you guess why you were having trouble getting ready to go? It may be that you did not want to go to the party. But according to Freud, this desire to avoid the party was unconscious—you were unaware of it.

Freud believed that certain memories are painful and that some of our impulses, such as aggressiveness, are considered unacceptable. He stated that we use various mental strategies, called defense mechanisms, to push painful or unacceptable ideas out of our consciousness. In this way, we protect ourselves from feelings of anxiety, guilt, and shame.

In Freud's view, consciousness is like an iceberg. There are many layers to it, and much of it lies hidden beneath the surface. In his book *The Interpretation of Dreams* (1899), Freud argued that dreams express unconscious wishes.

For example, a child may dream of hitting a home run that sends three runners around the bases, thereby clinching a World Series title for the hometown team. Or a young girl may dream of driving the winning car in the Memorial Day Indianapolis 500.

The Nonconscious Level Many of our basic biological functions exist on a **nonconscious** level. For example, even if you tried, you could not sense your fingernails growing or your hair growing.

You know that you are breathing in and out, but you cannot actually feel the exchange of carbon dioxide and oxygen. You blink when you step from the dark into the light, but you cannot feel your pupils growing smaller. It may be just as well that these events are nonconscious. After all, how much can a person hope to keep in mind at once?

Altered States of Consciousness The word *consciousness* sometimes refers to the waking state—the state in which a person is awake. There are also **altered states of consciousness,** in which a person's sense of self or sense of the world changes. When you doze off, you are no longer conscious of what is going on around you even though, when awakened, you may claim you haven't missed a thing.

Sleep is one altered state of consciousness. Other altered states of consciousness can occur through meditation, biofeedback, and hypnosis. The rest of this chapter explores, among other topics, these altered states of consciousness, including the effects of drugs on consciousness.

Reading Check **Find the Main Idea** What are Freud's three levels of consciousness?

SECTION 1 Assessment

Online Quiz THINK central thinkcentral.com

Reviewing Main Ideas and Vocabulary

1. **Recall** Why did William James question the value of studying consciousness?

2. **Explain** What are two examples of ideas that are not in your awareness right now but that could be recalled if needed?

3. **Summarize** In what way is consciousness a psychological construct?

Thinking Critically

4. **Contrast** How does an altered state of consciousness differ from the three levels at which awareness is limited?

5. **Analyze** Do you think that a person can study or understand the consciousness of another person? Why or why not?

6. **Analyze** Using your notes and a graphic organizer like the one below, explain the different levels of consciousness.

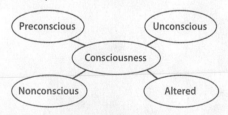

FOCUS ON WRITING

7. **Descriptive** Review the information on levels of consciousness and the illustration of consciousness as an iceberg. Write a paragraph in which you develop a different analogy about consciousness.

Sleep and Dreams

Before You Read

Main Idea

Sleeping and dreaming are essential to human health, although many questions remain. Some people are troubled by various sleep problems.

Reading Focus

1. What is the sleep cycle?
2. How have psychologists explored the importance of sleep and dreams?
3. What are sleep problems?

Vocabulary

circadian rhythm
rapid-eye-movement sleep
insomnia
night terror
sleep apnea
narcolepsy

TAKING NOTES Use a graphic organizer like this one to make notes about sleep and dreams.

Sleep Cycle

Sleep and Dreams

Importance of Sleep

Sleep Problems

FROM NIGHTMARE TO Novella

PSYCHOLOGY CLOSE UP

How did a dream become a classic horror story? Robert Louis Stevenson was a Scottish writer who wrote such classic works as *Treasure Island* and *Kidnapped*. One of his books has a strange history.

Stevenson wanted to write a book that would show the interaction of good and evil in human nature. He struggled with the problem of how best to treat this theme. According to legend, the answer came to him in a dream one night in 1885. Stevenson had a nightmare; his cries wakened the household. In the dream he had a vision of a good doctor being transformed into an evil man by taking a potion. When awakened from his nightmare, Stevenson supposedly said: "Why did you wake me? I was dreaming a fine bogey tale." That fine bogey tale became one of the classics of horror fiction—*The Strange Case of Dr. Jekyll and Mr. Hyde*.

Stevenson's dream shows the importance of dreaming to our waking lives. Dreams can express fears, wishes, goals, and aspirations. Many believe they can even provide solutions to problems that seemed insoluble during the day. ■

The Sleep Cycle

Are you aware that you spend about one third of your life asleep? Why do we sleep? Why do we dream? Why do some of us have trouble getting to sleep or experience nightmares?

Much of how people, animals, and plants function is governed by **circadian rhythms,** or biological clocks. The word *circadian* comes from the Latin words *circa,* meaning "about," and *dies,* meaning "a day." The circadian rhythms in humans include a sequence of bodily changes, such as those in body temperature, blood pressure, and sleepiness and wakefulness, that occurs every 24 hours. The human circadian rhythms usually operate on a 24-hour day.

The most-studied circadian rhythm is that of the sleep-wake cycle. Because people normally associate periods of wakefulness and sleep with the rotation of Earth, a full sleep-wake cycle is 24 hours. However, when people are removed from cues that signal day or night (such as clocks, radio or TV shows, sunrise, and sunset), their cycle tends to expand to about 25 hours. Researchers are unsure why this happens. This and many other issues concerning sleep have been, and continue to be, the subject of much research.

The Stages of Sleep Sleep researchers have discovered that we sleep in stages. Sleep stages are defined in terms of brain-wave patterns, which can be measured by an electroencephalograph (EEG). Brain waves are cyclical, and they vary on the basis of whether we are awake, relaxed, or sleeping. Four different brain-wave patterns include the following: beta waves, alpha waves, theta waves, and delta waves.

When we are awake and alert, the brain emits beta waves, which are short and quick. As we become drowsy, the brain waves slowly move from beta waves to alpha waves, which are a little slower than beta waves. During this relaxed state, we may experience visual images such as flashes of color or sensations such as feeling as if we are falling. This state is followed by five stages of sleep.

Stage 1 is the stage of lightest sleep. As we enter stage 1 sleep, our brain waves slow down from the alpha rhythm to the slower pattern of theta waves. This transition may be accompanied by brief images that resemble vivid photographs. Because stage 1 sleep is light, if we are awakened during this stage, wc will probably recall these images and feel as if we have not slept at all.

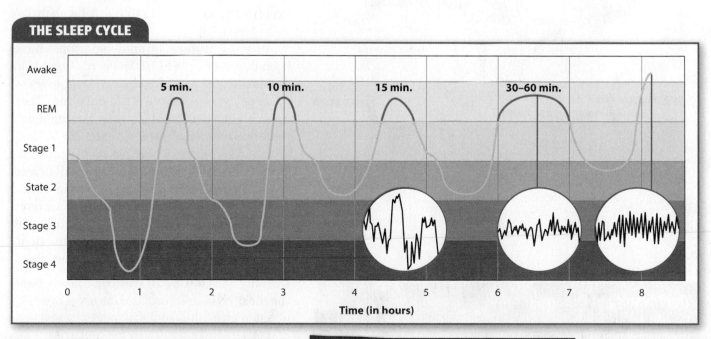

THE SLEEP CYCLE

This is a typical sleep pattern. Most people go through the cycle five times in eight hours. As the night progresses, stages 3 and 4 become shorter, and REM sleep becomes longer. Brain waves are shown in the circles.

Skills Focus INTERPRETING VISUALS

During which hours of sleep does REM sleep last the longest?

If we are not awakened, we remain in stage 1 sleep no more than 30 to 40 minutes. Then we move into sleep stages 2, 3, and 4. During stages 3 and 4, sleep is deep, and the brain produces delta waves—the slowest of the four patterns. Stage 4 is the stage of deepest sleep; it is the one during which someone would have the greatest difficulty waking us up.

REM Sleep After perhaps half an hour of stage 4 sleep, we begin a relatively quick journey back to stage 3 to stage 2 to stage 1. About 90 minutes will have passed since we fell asleep. Now something strange happens. Suddenly, we breathe more irregularly, blood pressure rises, and the heart beats faster. Brain waves become similar to those of stage 1 sleep. Yet this is another stage of sleep— the stage called **rapid-eye-movement sleep,** or REM sleep, because beneath our closed lids, our eyes are moving rapidly. The preceding four stages are known as non-rapid-eye-movement, or NREM, sleep because our eyes do not move as much during them.

During a typical eight-hour night of sleep, most people go through these stages about five times, each of which constitutes one sleep cycle. As the night goes on, periods of REM sleep become longer.

Reading Check Recall Which is the deepest stage of sleep?

The Importance of Sleep and Dreams

People need sleep to help revive the tired body and to build up resistance to infection. Sleep also seems to serve important psychological functions. It may help us recover from stress. It also helps us to consolidate certain memories from the previous day.

What would happen if people forced themselves to go without sleep? Randy Gardner, age 17, tried to find out as part of a science project. Under a physician's supervision, Randy stayed awake almost 11 days. He became irritable, could not focus his eyes, and had speech difficulties and memory lapses. William Dement, a sleep researcher, tracked Gardner's recovery. He found that Gardner slept an extra 6.5 hours for the first three days following the experiment. On the fourth night he slept 2.5 extra hours.

In some studies, animals or people have been deprived only of REM sleep. People and animals deprived of REM sleep tend to show what psychologists call REM-rebound. They catch up on their REM sleep by having much more of it when they sleep later on. REM sleep seems to serve particular psychological functions. Animals and people who are deprived of REM sleep learn more slowly than usual. They also forget more rapidly what they have learned. Other research findings suggest that REM sleep may help brain development in infants and "exercise" brain cells in adults.

Dreams It is during REM sleep that we have the most vivid dreams. Dreams are a mystery about which philosophers, poets, scientists, and others have theorized for centuries.

Dreams can be in black-and-white or in full color. Some dreams seem very realistic. You may have had a dream of going to class

The Mystery of Dreams
The mystery of dreams has occupied artists and thinkers for centuries. This image has qualities of both fantasy and realism that are often found in dreams. It might seem spooky or serene to you.
If dreams often express wishes or fears, what wish or fear might the above dreamlike image express?

Do You Remember Your Dreams?

Most people remember at least some of their dreams. They might remember their dreams in detail or just remember the high points. Other dreams they might have trouble recalling.

PROCEDURE

❶ Try to remember your dreams for one night. One technique might be to tell yourself to try to remember your dreams just before you go to sleep.

❷ Assign key words to your separate dreams for the night while you're in a still-sleeping, just-beginning-to-wake state before you get out of bed.

❸ Record your information for one night's worth of dreams and report back to the class the next day. Be sure to make a list of the key words that you came up with for your dreams.

ANALYSIS

1. What do you remember about your dreams?

2. How much uninterrupted sleep accompanied each dream?

3. Discuss with classmates if there seems to be any connection or pattern between dreams and the amount of uninterrupted sleep.

4. During REM sleep, people have the most vivid dreams. These dreams are most likely to have clear images and plots that make sense, even if the events are not realistic. Do you think any of the dreams you recorded occurred during REM sleep? Why or why not?

and suddenly realizing that there was going to be a test. You had not studied. You started to panic. Then you woke up. The dream felt very real. Other dreams are disorganized and seem less real.

We may dream every time we are in REM sleep. During REM sleep, dreams are most likely to have clear imagery and plots that make sense, even if some of the events are not realistic. During NREM sleep, plots are vaguer and images more fleeting.

If the events in a person's dream seemed to last 10 minutes, that person was probably dreaming for 10 minutes. That is, people seem to dream in "real time." Although some dreams involve fantastic adventures, most of the dreams people have are extensions of the activities of the day.

We sometimes have difficulty recalling the details of our dreams. This may be because we are often unable to hold on to information from one state of consciousness (in this case, sleeping/dreaming) when we move into another (in this case, wakefulness).

The Freudian View Have you ever heard the song "A Dream Is a Wish Your Heart Makes" from the Disney film *Cinderella*? Is it true that your dreams reveal what you really want? Sigmund Freud thought so; he theorized that dreams reflect a person's unconscious wishes and urges—"wishes your heart makes."

However, some unconscious wishes may be unacceptable, even painful. Those, Freud thought, would be the ones that would most likely appear in dreams, although not always in direct or obvious forms. Freud believed that people dream in symbols. He thought that these "symbolic" dreams give people a way to deal with painful material that they cannot otherwise deal with consciously.

The Biopsychological Approach Some psychologists believe that dreams begin with biological, not psychological, activity. According to this view, during sleep, neurons fire in a part of the brain that controls movement and vision. These neuron bursts are random, and the brain tries to make sense of them. It does so by weaving a story—the dream.

The biopsychological approach explains why people dream about events that took place earlier in the day. The most current activity of the brain concerns the events or problems of the day. Thus, the brain uses everyday matters to give structure to random bursts of neurons during REM sleep.

Today most psychologists caution that there are no hard-and-fast rules for interpreting dreams. And we can never be sure whether a certain interpretation is correct.

Reading Check **Recall** When do we have the most vivid dreams?

Complete a Webquest at thinkcentral.com on sleep problems.

Sleep Problems

Even when we need sleep, we may have trouble sleeping soundly. When these troubles last for long periods of time or become serious, they become sleep problems.

Insomnia The inability to sleep is called **insomnia,** from the Latin *in-*, meaning "not," and *somnus*, meaning "sleep." The most common type of insomnia is difficulty falling asleep. People with insomnia are more likely than others to worry and to have "racing minds" at bedtime. For many people, insomnia comes and goes, increasing during periods of anxiety or tension and decreasing or disappearing during less stressful periods.

People can actually make insomnia worse by *trying* to get to sleep. The effort backfires because it increases tension. We cannot force ourselves to fall asleep. We can only set the stage by lying down and relaxing when we are tired. Yet millions of people go to bed each night dreading the possibility that they will not be able to fall asleep.

Some people use sleeping pills to cope with insomnia, but many psychologists believe that the safest, simplest, most effective ways of overcoming insomnia do not involve medication. Psychologists recommend that people with insomnia try the following techniques:

- Tense the muscles, one at a time, then let the tension go. This helps relax the body.
- Avoid worrying in bed. If worrying persists, get up for a while.
- Establish a regular routine for getting up and going to sleep each day.
- Use pleasant images to relax.

Many psychologists also note that occasional insomnia is fairly common and is not necessarily a problem. It becomes a problem only if it continues for long periods of time.

Nightmares and Night Terrors You have probably experienced nightmares in your lifetime. Some nightmares are specific to a particular activity or profession. For example, the "actor's nightmare" involves being on stage with no idea what play is being performed, much less what any of the lines are.

In the Middle Ages, nightmares were thought to be the work of demons. Today we know that nightmares, like most other dreams, are generally products of REM sleep. In one study, college students kept dream diaries and reported having an average of two nightmares a month. Upsetting events can produce nightmares. People who are anxious or depressed are also more likely to have nightmares.

Night terrors (also called sleep terrors) are similar to, but more severe than, nightmares. Dreamers with night terrors feel their hearts racing, and they gasp for air. They may suddenly sit up, talk incoherently, or thrash about.

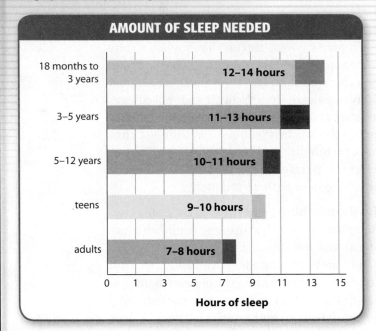

Statistically Speaking...

Sleep Problems The bar graph shows the amount of sleep recommended for specific age groups by sleep experts. Listed below the bar graph are the percentages of people with specific sleep problems.

AMOUNT OF SLEEP NEEDED

Age group	Hours of sleep
18 months to 3 years	12–14 hours
3–5 years	11–13 hours
5–12 years	10–11 hours
teens	9–10 hours
adults	7–8 hours

Hours of sleep (0 1 3 5 7 9 11 13 15)

74% Percentage of Americans who do not get enough sleep

10–50% Percentage of children who have nightmares

10–30% Percentage of children who have sleepwalking episodes

Skills Focus **INTERPRETING DATA** Why do you think such large segments of the population do not get enough sleep?

Sources: National Sleep Foundation; Diagnostic and Statistical Manual of Mental Disorders

They do not fully wake up. In the morning, they may recall a feeling or an image from the night terror. Memories of night terror episodes usually are vague.

Night terrors also differ from nightmares in when they occur. Night terrors tend to occur during deep sleep (stages 3 and 4), whereas nightmares occur during REM sleep. Night terrors happen during the first couple of sleep cycles, nightmares more toward morning. Night terrors are most common among young children and may reflect immaturity of the nervous system.

Sleepwalking Many children walk in their sleep. Sleepwalkers may roam about almost nightly during stages of deep sleep. They may respond to questions while they are up and about, but when they wake up they typically do not remember what they did or said. Contrary to myth, there is no evidence that sleepwalkers become violent or upset if they are awakened. However, because sleepwalkers are not fully conscious and thus may be prone to accidentally hurting themselves, they should be supervised if possible. Most children outgrow sleepwalking as they mature.

Sleep Apnea We all have occasional apneas, or interruptions in breathing. **Sleep apnea** is a breathing interruption that occurs during sleep. People with sleep apnea do not automatically start breathing again until they suddenly sit up and gasp for air. Once they begin breathing again, they fall back asleep. They usually do not wake up completely, so they may not even be aware of what has happened during the night. However, they often feel tired during the day.

Sleep apneas occur when a person's air passages are blocked. Thus, they are sometimes accompanied by snoring. A nasal mask that provides a steady air flow can help prevent breathing interruptions.

About 10 million Americans have apnea, and it is associated with obesity as well as snoring. Apnea is more than a sleep problem. It can lead to high blood pressure, heart attacks, and strokes.

Narcolepsy **Narcolepsy** is a rare sleep problem in which people suddenly fall asleep, no matter what time it is or where they are. One minute they are awake. The next, their muscles completely relax, and they are in REM sleep. Drug therapy and frequent naps have been used to treat narcolepsy.

Although people usually awaken from an episode of narcolepsy feeling refreshed, such episodes may be dangerous. For example, they can occur while driving or operating machinery. No one knows for sure what causes narcolepsy, but it is believed to be a genetic disorder of REM-sleep functioning.

Reading Check **Summarize** What are some of the main types of sleep problems?

SECTION 2 Assessment

Online Quiz THINK central thinkcentral.com

Reviewing Main Ideas and Vocabulary

1. **Summarize** What are the five stages of sleep?
2. **Define** What is NREM sleep?
3. **Recall** Why might narcolepsy be dangerous?

Thinking Critically

4. **Compare and Contrast** How are nightmares and night terrors similar and different?
5. **Explain** What are some of the recommended techniques for dealing with insomnia?

6. **Analyze** Using your notes and a graphic organizer like the one below, describe common sleep problems.

Insomnia
Nightmares
Sleep walking
Apnea
Narcolepsy

FOCUS ON WRITING

7. **Descriptive** Write a paragraph in which you describe vivid images from a dream or nightmare that you have experienced.

Sleep Deprivation in Teens

Lack of sleep affects both the mind and the body. Sleep deprivation can produce mental states of fatigue, drowsiness, and irritability. In addition, lack of sleep can contribute to physical symptoms such as weight gain, heart disease, and other symptoms and ailments. Teenagers who do not get enough sleep can also develop these problems.

A young tennis player experiences the effects of sleep deprivation.

The television show *60 Minutes* aired a segment on "The Science of Sleep" on March 13, 2008. Leslie Stahl interviewed Eve Van Cauter, M.D., an endocrinologist at the University of Chicago School of Medicine. In her laboratory, Van Cauter studies the effects of sleep and sleeplessness on the body. Her studies have revealed links between lack of sleep and increased rates of obesity, diabetes, heart disease, high blood pressure, and stroke (Van Cauter, University of Chicago Medical Center, 2004).

Van Cauter's work confirms and builds upon work done by the National Sleep Foundation. According to a study done by the group in 2004, here are signs of sleep deprivation:

- difficulty waking in the morning
- irritability in the afternoon
- falling asleep during the day
- oversleeping on the weekend
- difficulty concentrating
- waking up often and having trouble going back to sleep

It is estimated that adolescents need 9.2 hours of sleep a night. Some estimates claim that about a third of young adults are very sleepy during the day. According to a recent study, 26 percent of high school students sleep less than 6.5 hours on school nights, while only 15 percent sleep 8.5 hours or more (Carpenter, 2001).

About 14 percent of adolescents are overweight (National Center for Health Statistics, 2001). The extra weight in conjunction with the lack of adequate sleep creates a vicious circle. The incidence of sleep apnea among young people is liable to increase as the number of overweight teenagers increases. The symptoms of sleep apnea at night include snoring, breathing pauses during sleep, restlessness, mouth breathing, and difficulty getting up in the morning. The symptoms during the day include hyperactivity, inattention, behavior problems, and sleepiness.

Lack of adequate sleep among teens puts them at risk not only for physical ailments but also for intellectual and emotional difficulties, including poor school performance and accidents. Sleepiness causes over 100,000 car accidents each year, and teenage drivers are at fault in many of these crashes. Sleeplessness is a high risk factor for adolescent alcohol and drug abuse (Carpenter, 2001).

One possible solution to insufficient sleep by teenagers might be to change the starting time for school. Some Minnesota schools have moved start times from 7:20 AM to 8:30 AM. And here are some other ways for teenagers to get a good night's sleep:

- Avoid caffeine in the evening.
- Try to go to bed at the same time and get up at the same time.
- Try only to sleep in bed; no TV watching or reading.
- If you have trouble sleeping, then get up and read.

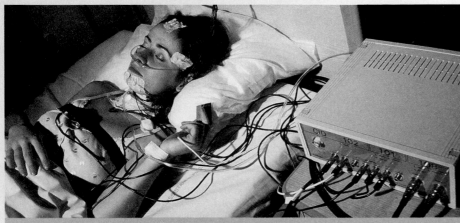

This young woman is attached to various monitors as part of a study on sleep apnea using electroencephalography.

Thinking Critically

1. **Summarize** What are some of the signs of sleep deprivation?
2. **Discuss** What might be the advantages of starting school later?

Current Research **THINK** central thinkcentral.com

Altered States of Consciousness

Before You Read

Main Idea
A variety of techniques have been developed in order to achieve altered states of consciousness.

Reading Focus
1. How do meditation and biofeedback work?
2. What is hypnosis?
3. How can hypnosis be used?

Vocabulary
meditation
biofeedback
hypnosis
posthypnotic suggestion

TAKING NOTES Use a graphic organizer like this one to explain the techniques and methods of both meditation and biofeedback.

Meditation	Biofeedback

Mesmer AND MAGNETISM

PSYCHOLOGY CLOSE UP

Are you feeling drowsy yet?
Franz Mesmer (1734–1815) was a German physician who was an important figure in the early history of hypnotism. He developed a theory called "animal magnetism." According to this theory, an invisible bodily fluid reacted to magnetic fields. Mesmer argued that disease resulted when the invisible fluid could not circulate freely. He "mesmerized" his patients by passing magnets over their bodies to supposedly unblock obstacles to circulation. He believed that balance could be restored by putting his patients in trance states.

Mesmer's theory of animal magnetism was soon discredited. However, his skill at putting his patients into trances evolved into a tool of hypnosis, which has been useful in treating bad habits such as smoking and overeating.

Hypnosis is one way of achieving an altered state of consciousness when awake. In this section, you will learn about hypnosis and other types of altered consciousness, including meditation and biofeedback. ■

In this poster advertising a hypnotist, people under his influence engage in odd behavior: a woman plays a table, a man rides a chair like a racehorse, and so forth.

Meditation and Biofeedback

People who are asleep and dreaming are in an altered state of consciousness. Other altered states of consciousness occur when we are awake. Two methods for achieving these states are meditation and biofeedback.

Meditation A method some people use to try to narrow their consciousness so that the stresses of the outside world fade away is called **meditation.** Many techniques have been used to meditate. The ancient Egyptians gazed upon an oil-burning lamp. The yogis of India stare at an intricate pattern on a vase or carpet. Other meditators repeat pleasing sounds called mantras, such as *om* or *sheereem*, and mentally focus on these sounds.

All of these methods of meditation share a common thread—they focus on a peaceful, repetitive stimulus. This focus helps one narrow his or her consciousness and relax. By narrowing their consciousness, people can suspend planning, worrying, and other concerns. Meditation is an important part of some religions. Buddhism, for example, makes meditation a central part of its practice.

Some people claim that meditation helps them achieve "oneness with the universe," pleasure, or some great insight. These claims have never been scientifically proven, but evidence does suggest that meditation can help people relax. Studies have found that meditation can also help some people lower their high blood pressure.

Biofeedback A system that provides, or "feeds back," data about something happening in the body is called **biofeedback.** Through biofeedback training, people have learned to control certain bodily functions, such as heart rate. Some people have used biofeedback to learn to create the brain waves produced when relaxing—alpha waves—as a way of coping with tension. Using biofeedback, people have learned to treat tension headaches and also to lower their heart rates or blood pressure. However, as with all treatments, biofeedback should be attempted only under the direct supervision of a medical professional.

Biofeedback has also been used to help in the treatment of attention-deficit/hyperactivity disorder (ADHD). A person who has attention-deficit/hyperactivity disorder is frequently inattentive or impulsively hyperactive to the point where he or she has trouble completing daily activities. The causes of ADHD are unknown. However, treatment is available for those who have ADHD. Some medications and biofeedback have proven to be helpful to some people by increasing their ability to concentrate.

Reading Check **Compare** What do meditation and biofeedback have in common?

Hypnosis: Myths and Realities

Hypnosis is another method for altering consciousness. Perhaps you have seen movies in which one character hypnotized another or seen audience members hypnotized in a magic show. If so, chances are you found that these people seemed unable to open their eyes, could not remember their own names, acted out scenes from childhood, or behaved in other odd ways. But hypnosis is not always what it seems to be in movies or magic shows.

The word *hypnosis* is derived from the Greek *hypnos*, meaning "sleep." Some psychologists believe that **hypnosis** is an altered state of consciousness during which people respond to suggestions and behave as though they are in a trance. Other psychologists, however, wonder whether hypnosis is truly an altered state of consciousness.

Studies have shown that some of the same effects achieved by hypnosis can also occur without hypnosis. Furthermore, brain-wave patterns (as measured by an EEG) of people in hypnotic states look about the same as brain-wave patterns that are produced in the waking state.

The History of Hypnosis Hypnosis began with the ideas of German physician Franz Mesmer in the late 1700s. He studied medicine at the University of Vienna, and it was there that he developed his theories of magnetism. Mesmer thought that all the various parts of the universe were connected by forms of magnetism.

To cure his patients, he would pass magnets over their bodies. Some of them would fall into a trance, then awaken feeling better. Eventually, though, scientists decided that Mesmer's so-called cures had very little scientific basis.

ACADEMIC VOCABULARY

stimulus something that causes a response

CASE STUDY
CONNECTION

Biofeedback
Biofeedback training enables people to control bodily functions previously regarded as not subject to conscious control.

Myths and Facts About Hypnosis

There are many false beliefs about hypnotism. Some of the most common myths are listed below, along with the facts.

Myths	Facts
You can be hypnotized against your will.	No one can be hypnotized unless he or she is willing to be.
When hypnotized, you can't open your eyes.	Being hypnotized dulls but does not fundamentally affect the normal functioning of all of the senses.
You cannot remember your own name.	You can remember everything you normally remember.
You act out scenes from childhood.	You don't typically act out scenes at all.
You behave in unusual ways.	You usually behave quite normally.
You will do anything.	You are unlikely to do anything you wouldn't normally do.
You go into a sleep state.	You stay conscious and relatively alert.

Hypnotism, however, may have more validity than Mesmer's magnet treatment. Today hypnotism may be used in a variety of ways. For example, some doctors use hypnosis as an anesthetic in certain types of surgery. Some psychologists use it to help clients reduce anxiety, manage pain, or overcome fears. Hypnosis is also used in the birthing process to reduce stress and anxiety.

Nevertheless, there is still a great deal about hypnosis that is not understood. Thus, hypnosis should always be left in the hands of professionals.

Achieving Hypnosis Professional hypnotists may put people in a hypnotic trance by asking them to focus on something specific—a spot on the wall, an object held by the hypnotist, or merely the hypnotist's voice. Hypnotists usually suggest that people's arms and legs are becoming warm, heavy, and relaxed. They may also tell people that they are becoming sleepy or are falling asleep.

But hypnosis is not sleep. People who are sleeping have very different brain waves from people in trances. But hearing the word *sleep* often helps a person enter a hypnotic trance.

People who are easily hypnotized are said to have hypnotic suggestibility. They can focus on the instructions of the hypnotist without getting distracted. Suggestible people also usually *like* the idea of being hypnotized and do not resist. In general, people can only be hypnotized if they allow themselves to be.

Explaining Hypnosis Psychologists offer various explanations for the behavior of people under hypnosis. Sigmund Freud was trained as a physician in Vienna. He moved to Paris to study under the neurologist Dr. Jean Martin Charcot, who used hypnosis to treat the mentally ill.

When Freud returned to Vienna, he used hypnosis to treat patients and relied on it in exploring the unconscious. According to Freud, hypnotized people permit themselves to put fantasy and impulse before fact and logic. Therefore, they believe what the hypnotist tells them. They may also enjoy the experience of letting the hypnotist tell them what to do.

According to another view, called role theory, people who are hypnotized are playing a part as if they are in a play. However, unlike actors in a play, hypnotized people may believe that what they are doing is real. Research suggests that many people in hypnotic trances may *not* be faking it. Rather, they become engrossed in playing the part of a hypnotized person. They use their imaginations to try to experience what the hypnotist tells them to experience.

There is no one generally accepted explanation for hypnosis. Most researchers agree that it can and does work with certain patients.

Reading Check **Recall** Whose ideas began the technique of hypnosis?

The Uses of Hypnosis

Psychologists continue to debate whether hypnosis has a scientific basis. They also continue to research what hypnosis can and cannot do. Some of the research on hypnosis has addressed the effects of hypnosis on memory, on feelings of pain, and on the quitting of habits such as smoking or overeating. It is also used to help calm patients. Another research question is why some people are more suggestible than others.

Hypnosis and Memory Police have used hypnosis to jog the memories of witnesses to a crime. At times this approach has worked with dramatic success. Nevertheless, studies have shown that unhypnotized people are just as likely as hypnotized people to remember details of a crime. More important, hypnotized people are just as likely to make *mistakes* about those details as are others. Many psychologists thus argue that material recalled under hypnosis should not be used as testimony in trials.

One interesting finding about hypnosis and memory has to do with memory of events that occur during the hypnotic trance itself. If directed by the hypnotist, some people will not recall what happened while they were hypnotized. Some of the more suggestible may not even remember that they were hypnotized at all.

Hypnosis and Pain Prevention Under certain circumstances and with careful application, hypnosis has been used to help people prevent pain. For example, dentists have used hypnosis successfully to help people avoid feeling pain during certain procedures.

Some people are so suggestible that they can even undergo surgery without anesthesia if they are hypnotized and told they feel no pain. Some studies have shown that a similar effect can be achieved through relaxation techniques and breathing exercises.

Hypnosis and Quitting Bad Habits To help someone quit a habit such as overeating, a therapist may use **posthypnotic suggestion.** In this technique, the therapist gives instructions during hypnosis that are to be carried out after the session has ended.

Often, psychologists link the habit with something repulsive, something that would make the person feel ill or disgusted. Then whenever that person begins the habit, such as lighting up a cigarette, that sickening image appears in his or her mind.

Sometimes hypnotists give more positive posthypnotic suggestions—for example, telling a person that he or she can now resist sweets. But the effectiveness of hypnosis for helping people quit smoking is uncertain.

Reading Check **Summarize** How have the police made use of hypnosis?

SECTION 3 Assessment

Reviewing Main Ideas and Vocabulary

1. **Recall** What common techniques do most methods of meditation share?

2. **Summarize** What is hypnotic suggestibility?

Thinking Critically

3. **Explain** How does biofeedback work?

4. **Draw Conclusions** Why do you think hypnosis is not used more often to relieve pain or change bad habits?

5. **Explain** What is posthypnotic suggestion, and how does it work?

6. **Analyze** Using your notes and a graphic organizer like the one below, explain the uses of hypnosis.

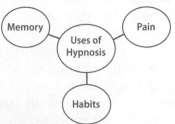

FOCUS ON WRITING

7. **Persuasion** In a paragraph, try to persuade one of your friends that he or she should be hypnotized for a specific reason.

Multicultural Perspectives on Consciousness

Visions, dreams, meditation, and hallucinations are important components of many cultures, reflecting the human desire to reach beyond what the senses can perceive directly. The methods for reaching these altered states of consciousness, however, are as diverse as the people who inhabit this planet.

Accompanied by music, whirling dervishes spin around until they are in a trance.

Australian Aborigines Aborigines in Australia believe that there are two worlds: the ordinary, physical world of daily life and another world called Dreamtime. Ritual songs, dances, stories, and dreams create the Dreamtime world. Frans Hoogland, a Dutchman who lived for 15 years among the Aborigines, described the process as beginning with a kind of emptiness or void. Then through the techniques of singing and dancing the participants create sound, beginning to give a shape to a new reality. The vibrations created by the singing and dancing, and the stories as well, help to make the spirit world of Dreamtime come into existence. For the Aborigines, dream and actuality are just different states of the same consciousness.

Mevlevi The Mevlevi are members of a Muslim sect in the country of Turkey. Like the Aborigines, the Mevlevi use dancing to create an altered state of consciousness. The Mevlevi are known as whirling dervishes because they whirl until they are in a trance. They believe that the trance brings them closer to Allah, or God, and spiritual truth.

Hinduism Some religions use meditation to achieve an altered state of consciousness. According to the yoga school, a part of Hinduism, every human being consists of two parts. The first is a person's body, mind, and conscious self. The second is the soul—or pure, empty consciousness. The yoga school uses exercises, postures, and meditations to teach the understanding of the soul.

Buddhism Buddhists meditate to achieve a state of enlightenment called nirvana. They believe that nirvana can be achieved through control of the mind, or mental discipline. Certain yoga techniques help followers achieve this control.

Inca People in some cultures use drugs to produce a religious trance. The Inca in the Andean highlands of South America use a drug called *yage* to hallucinate while a shaman, or holy man, watches them. The hallucinations range from pleasurable to terrifying. The Inca will endure even the terrifying visions because they believe that terror is something that needs to be overcome in order to communicate with the spirit world.

Huichol The Huichol Indians in central Mexico make a sacred pilgrimage to a place hundreds of miles from their homes. Once they arrive, they fast, pray, dance, and chant. The next day, they hunt for peyote, a strong stimulant that comes from a cactus plant. Then they sit with their shaman-priest, talk, eat peyote, and begin to hallucinate. They believe that the hallucinations help them achieve a state of fusion with their ancestors and the universe. The shaman must be present to help them return from the experience.

Aborigines in Australia perform ritual songs and dances in order to summon the spirit world into existence.

Thinking Critically

1. **Analyze** Why do you think some cultures view altered states of consciousness as something to be avoided?

2. **Discuss** Other cultures view altered states as something to be sought out. Why might this be so?

Drugs and Consciousness

Before You Read

Main Idea

Depressants, stimulants, and hallucinogens are all drugs that can affect consciousness. Drug abuse can be dealt with by a number of available treatments.

Reading Focus

1. How do depressants affect the body?
2. What are stimulants?
3. What are hallucinogens?
4. How do some treatments for drug abuse work?

Vocabulary

addiction
depressants
intoxication
narcotics
stimulant
amphetamine
hallucination
delusion
hallucinogen
detoxification

TAKING NOTES Use a graphic organizer like this one to take notes on three major categories of drugs.

| Depressants: |
| Stimulants: |
| Hallucinogens: |

Keeping a DEADLY SECRET

Everyday *Reach for a* **LUCKY** *instead of a* *sweet*

LUCKY STRIKE "IT'S TOASTED" CIGARETTES

ROSALIE ADELE NELSON. *Original "Lucky" Girl*
"To keep slender. I reach for a Lucky instead of a sweet"

"It's toasted" – No Throat Irritation – No Cough

PSYCHOLOGY CLOSE UP

Why did tobacco companies keep the results of nicotine studies hidden from the public? For many years tobacco companies claimed not to know that the nicotine in cigarettes caused serious health problems. Some ads, such as the one above from the 1920s, even touted health benefits of cigarettes. By the 1970s, however, the companies decided that they needed to fund research to disprove the claims of cigarette smoke's toxic effects. The companies wanted at least to marshal some evidence to refute the claims of scientists opposed to smoking. However, the cigarette companies wanted to keep their research secret. In fact, one major American cigarette company went so far as to set up a research facility in Germany to ensure that the research done there could not be linked to the company. This secret connection was concealed not just from the public but also from many of the company's own employees. Several other tobacco companies also made concerted efforts to conceal the addictive and deadly properties of tobacco and nicotine.

Nicotine is a powerful but legal addictive drug that affects consciousness. Both legal and illegal drugs can affect consciousness. ■

Depressants

Some drugs slow down the nervous system, while others spur it into rapid action. Some drugs, such as alcohol and nicotine (the drug found in tobacco), have been shown to be connected to serious diseases. Many drugs are addictive. **Addiction** to a drug means that after a person takes that drug for a while, the body craves it just to feel normal. Alcohol, nicotine, and many other drugs are addictive. In addition to physical addiction, people can become psychologically dependent upon drugs. Even if the body does not crave the drug, the person depends on it for a sense of well-being.

Drugs also have a number of effects on consciousness. They may distort people's perceptions, change their moods, or cause them to see or hear things that are not real. Categories of drugs that affect consciousness include depressants, stimulants, and hallucinogens.

Depressants are drugs that slow the activity of the nervous system. They generally give people a sense of relaxation but can have many negative effects. Depressant drugs include alcohol and narcotics such as barbiturates and opiates.

Alcohol Alcohol is the most widely used drug in the United States. Alcohol is a depressant. Small amounts of alcohol may have little effect, or they may be relaxing. High doses of alcohol can put a person to sleep. Too much alcohol can be lethal, either in the long term or the short term—people have died from drinking too much at one time.

Alcohol also intoxicates. **Intoxication** is another word for drunkenness. The root of the word *intoxication* is *toxic*, which means "poisonous." Intoxication slurs people's speech, blurs their vision, makes them clumsy, and makes it difficult for them to concentrate. They may bump into things or be unable to write. It also affects their judgment. In fact, they may not even realize that they are intoxicated. Therefore, they may try to do things that require a clear mind and good coordination, such as driving a car, when they are incapable of doing these things correctly. Alcohol is involved in more than half of all fatal automobile accidents in the United States.

Some drinkers do things they would not do if they were sober. Why? When drunk, people pay less attention to the consequences of their behavior. Alcohol can also bring feelings of elation that wash away inhibitions. Furthermore, it provides an excuse for behaviors that sober people know are unwise. Drinkers may place the blame for their behavior on the alcohol. But, of course, drinkers *choose* to drink. Thus, people remain responsible for actions taken while intoxicated.

Regardless of why people start drinking, regular consumption of alcohol can lead to addiction. Once people become addicted to alcohol, they may continue drinking to avoid withdrawal symptoms such as tension and trembling. Heavy drinking has been linked to liver problems, heart problems, and cancer.

Narcotics The word *narcotic* comes from the Greek *narke*, meaning "numbness" or "stupor." **Narcotics** are addictive depressants that have been used to relieve pain and induce sleep. Many narcotics—such as morphine, heroin, and codeine—are derived from the opium poppy plant.

Morphine is a narcotic that was used during the Civil War to deaden the pain from wounds. Therefore, addiction to morphine became known as "the soldier's disease."

Heroin, also introduced in the West in the 1800s, was hailed as the "hero" that would cure addiction to morphine. It was named heroin because it made people feel "heroic." This drug, which is now illegal, is a powerful narcotic that can give the user feelings of pleasure. However, coming off heroin can plunge the user into a deep depression. Furthermore, high doses impair judgment and memory and cause drowsiness and stupor. High doses of heroin can also depress the respiratory system so much that they lead to loss of consciousness, coma, and even death.

Heroin can also lead to death because it is often taken intravenously—that is, injected with a needle into a vein. Sometimes such needles are shared among users. If one user is infected with the virus that causes AIDS, needle sharing can infect other users as well.

People who are addicted to narcotics experience withdrawal symptoms when they try to stop using them. These withdrawal symptoms may include tremors, cramps, chills, rapid heartbeat, insomnia, vomiting, and diarrhea.

Reading Check **Recall** What are narcotics?

Stimulants

Stimulants, in contrast to depressants, increase the activity of the nervous system. They speed up the heart and breathing rate. Stimulants include nicotine, amphetamines, methamphetamines, and cocaine.

Nicotine Nicotine, the drug found in tobacco leaves, is one of the most common stimulants. The leaves are usually smoked in the form of cigarettes, cigars, and pipe tobacco. They can also be chewed, as in chewing tobacco.

Nicotine spurs the release of the hormone adrenaline, which causes the heart rate to increase. As a stimulant, nicotine may make people feel more alert and attentive, but research has shown that it does not improve the ability to perform complex tasks, such as solving difficult math problems.

Nicotine reduces the appetite and raises the rate at which the body changes food to energy. For these reasons, some smokers do not try to quit for fear that they will gain weight. But weight gain can be controlled by diet and exercise.

Through regular use, people can become addicted to nicotine. In fact, evidence suggests that cigarette smoking is as addictive as the use of heroin. People who stop smoking can experience symptoms such as nervousness, drowsiness, loss of energy, headaches, light-headedness, insomnia, dizziness, cramps, heart palpitations, tremors, and sweating. Nonetheless, many people have successfully quit smoking.

Smoking has also been associated with serious health risks. All cigarette advertisements and packs sold in the United States carry a message: "Warning: The Surgeon General Has Determined That Cigarette Smoking Is Dangerous to Your Health." Still, each year, more than 400,000 Americans die from smoking-related diseases. This is more than the number who die from motor-vehicle accidents, abuse of alcohol and all other drugs, suicide, homicide, and AIDS combined.

Smokers are 12 to 20 times more likely than nonsmokers to die of lung cancer. Moreover, the substances in cigarette smoke have been shown to cause several other kinds of cancer in laboratory animals. Cigarette smoking is also linked to death from heart disease, chronic lung and respiratory diseases, and other illnesses. Pregnant women who smoke risk miscarriage, premature birth, and babies with birth defects. Perhaps due to the risks involved in smoking, the percentage of American adults who smoke has declined from more than 40 percent in the 1960s to less than 25 percent today.

Research indicates that secondhand smoke, the cigarette smoke exhaled by smokers, can even increase the health risk of nonsmokers who inhale it. Secondhand smoke is connected with lung cancer, breathing problems, and other illnesses. It accounts for thousands of deaths per year. Because of the effects of secondhand smoke, smoking has been banned from many public places, such as government buildings, airports, and restaurants.

Amphetamines Another kind of stimulant is provided by **amphetamines.** They are especially known for helping people stay awake and for reducing appetite. Amphetamines are made from the chemical alpha-methyl-beta-phenyl-ethyl-amine, which is a colorless liquid made up of carbon, hydrogen, and nitrogen.

Amphetamines were first used by soldiers during World War II to help them remain awake and alert during the night. Sometimes called "speed" or "uppers," amphetamines can produce feelings of pleasure, especially in high doses.

Amphetamines can be taken in the form of pills. They can also be injected directly into the veins in the form of liquid methedrine, the strongest form of the drug. People who take large doses of amphetamines may stay awake and "high" for days. Such highs must come to an end, however. People who have been on prolonged highs usually "crash." That is, they fall into a deep sleep or depression. Some people even commit suicide when crashing.

High doses of amphetamines can cause restlessness, insomnia, loss of appetite, and irritability. They also affect consciousness. For example, people who have taken amphetamines sometimes experience frightening hallucinations. A **hallucination** is a perception of an object or a sound that seems to be real but is not real. One hallucination that people under the influence of amphetamines commonly experience is that bugs are crawling all over them.

MAJOR DRUG TYPES AND THEIR EFFECTS

Drugs can affect consciousness. Here are some of the major types, how they are taken, and a few of their possible intoxication effects and health consequences.

Name	How Used	Possible Intoxication Effects	Health Consequences
Depressants • Alcohol	• liquid that is drunk	• loss of inhibitions	• loss of coordination, confusion
• Narcotics (heroin, morphine, codeine)	• smoked, injected, swallowed, snorted	• relief from pain, sleepiness	• relief from pain, sleepiness
Stimulants • Nicotine	• smoked, chewed	• loss of appetite, hyperactivity, elevated blood pressure	• nervousness, lung damage
• Caffeine	• drunk or eaten	• increased alertness and energy	• jitteriness, irritability
• Amphetamines	• pills, injection, smoked, snorted	• wakefulness, reduced appetite	• depression, restlessness, insomnia
• Cocaine	• snorted, injected, smoked	• reduced appetite, relief from pain, increased confidence	• insomnia, nausea, convulsions
Hallucinogens • Marijuana	• smoked, swallowed, eaten	• enhanced emotions, sensory illusions	• impaired perception and coordination
• LSD	• pill	• intense hallucinations	• flashbacks, memory loss, violent outbursts
• Mushrooms	• swallowed	• sensory illusions	• flashbacks
• Mescaline	• swallowed, smoked	• distortions of reality	• panic
• Peyote	• swallowed	• dizziness	• self-injury
• Ecstasy	• swallowed	• increased sensory awareness, mild hallucinations, increased energy	• impaired memory, hyperthermia, rapid heartbeat

Skills Focus **INTERPRETING CHARTS** What are some of the long-term consequences of drug abuse?

Interactive Feature thinkcentral.com

Use of amphetamines can also cause the user to have delusions. A **delusion** is a false idea that seems real. If you thought you could fly (without the aid of an airplane), that would be a delusion. Overdoses of amphetamines are sometimes connected with delusions of being in danger or of being chased by someone or something.

One type of amphetamine has become an especially serious problem in recent years. Illegal methamphetamine—commonly called meth, crystal, or ice—is usually in the form of white or yellowish white crystals called "rocks" that are crushed and then either smoked, injected, or inhaled through the nose (that is, snorted).

ACADEMIC
VOCABULARY

euphoria a
feeling of great
happiness or
well-being

Methamphetamine's intense effects include euphoria, loss of appetite, increased alertness, and hyperactivity. These effects can give people a false sense of confidence that results in risky behavior.

Repeated use of methamphetamine causes severe damage to the body, including gum damage and advanced tooth decay, a condition known as "meth mouth." Permanent brain, kidney, and liver damage, and even death are also possible.

Methamphetamine is extremely addictive, and tolerance develops very rapidly. The illegal laboratories where the drug is produced, called meth labs, present their own dangers. The by-products of meth production include poisonous gas, toxic chemicals, and highly explosive substances. These labs often catch fire, endangering innocent people and their property.

Cocaine Cocaine is a stimulant derived from the leaves of the coca plant, which grows in the tropics of South America. Cocaine produces feelings of pleasure, reduces hunger, deadens pain, and boosts confidence. Because cocaine raises blood pressure and decreases the supply of oxygen while speeding up the heart rate, it can sometimes lead to serious consequences, even death.

Cocaine has been used as a painkiller since the early 1800s. It came to the attention of Sigmund Freud in 1884. Freud, then a young neurologist, first used the drug to overcome depression. He even published an article on cocaine called "Song of Praise." But Freud's excitement about cocaine's healing powers was soon cooled by his awareness that the drug was dangerous and addictive.

Overdoses of cocaine can cause symptoms including restlessness, insomnia, trembling, headaches, nausea, convulsions, hallucinations, and delusions. A very harmful form of cocaine is known as crack. Crack is very powerful. Moreover, crack is impure, and because of these impurities it is even more dangerous than other forms of cocaine. Because of the strain crack and other forms of cocaine can put on the heart, overdoses of these drugs are sometimes fatal.

Reading Check **Summarize** What are three types of stimulants?

Hallucinogens

A **hallucinogen** is a drug that produces hallucinations. In addition, hallucinogens may cause relaxation or feelings of pleasure. Hallucinogens can also cause feelings of panic.

Marijuana Marijuana is produced from the leaves of the *cannabis sativa* plant, which grows wild in many parts of the world. Marijuana may produce feelings of relaxation and mild hallucinations. Hashish, or "hash," comes from the sticky part of the plant. Hashish is stronger than marijuana.

Marijuana impairs perception and coordination, making it difficult to operate machines. It also impairs memory and learning. In addition, marijuana can cause anxiety and confusion. It increases the heart rate up to 140 to 150 beats per minute and in some people raises blood pressure.

Marijuana has effects on consciousness. People who are very intoxicated with marijuana may think time is passing more slowly than usual. A song might seem to last an hour rather than a few minutes.

Some people experience increased consciousness of bodily sensations such as heartbeat. Experiencing visual hallucinations is also fairly common while under the influence of marijuana.

Strong intoxication gives some marijuana smokers frightening experiences. Sometimes marijuana smokers become confused and lose their sense of self—their consciousness of who and where they are. Some fear they will lose themselves forever. Consciousness of a rapid heart rate leads others to fear that their hearts will "run away."

LSD Lysergic acid diethylamide (LSD) is a hallucinogen. LSD is sometimes simply called acid. It is much stronger than marijuana and can produce intense hallucinations. Some of these hallucinations can be quite bizarre. Some users of LSD claim that it expands consciousness and "opens new worlds."

LSD's effects are not predictable. Some LSD experiences are so frightening that the users, in a state of panic and confusion, injure themselves seriously or even commit suicide. In addition, some users of LSD experience lasting side effects such as memory loss, violent outbursts, nightmares, and panic.

Other Hallucinogens Mushrooms that contain the compound psilocybin have effects similar to LSD. Mushrooms are either eaten raw or with food. Psilocybin produces altered perceptions of sight, sound, taste, smell, and touch.

Other effects can include confusion, anxiety, and panic. The user may also have flashbacks. It is difficult to distinguish psilocybin from truly poisonous mushrooms. If a user takes the wrong kind, death can result.

Peyote is another hallucinogen. It comes from cactus plants native to Mexico. Its hallucinogenic properties are due to the alkaloid mescaline in the cactus. Peyote has been used in the religious rituals of Indian peoples of the southwestern United States as well as Mexico.

Ecstasy is sometimes called a club drug because it became popular at parties and clubs. Normally taken as a pill, it produces hallucinations, increased energy, loss of judgment, and serious physical side effects, such as nausea and high blood pressure.

Reading Check **Recall** What are LSD's effects?

Treatments for Drug Abuse

Treatment for drug abuse varies, depending on the drug. One form of treatment is detoxification. **Detoxification,** the removal of the harmful substance from the body, weans addicts from the drug while restoring their health. This treatment is most commonly used with people addicted to alcohol and narcotics.

Types of Drug Treatment

Detoxification Removal of harmful substances from the body

Maintenance Programs Controlled amounts of drug given to participants

Counseling Group or individual sessions

Support Groups People with similar problems sharing common experiences

Maintenance programs are another treatment sometimes used for people addicted to narcotics. Participants are given controlled amounts of the drug or some less addictive substitute. This treatment is controversial because the users never become completely free of drugs.

Counseling is a form of treatment that can be conducted either individually or in a group. Both individual and group methods are used for treating stimulant and depressant abuse.

Support groups consist of people who share common experiences, concerns, or problems. These individuals meet in a group setting to provide one another with emotional and moral support. Alcoholics Anonymous is a support group that encourages members to live without alcohol for the rest of their lives.

Reading Check **Summarize** What is the process of detoxification?

Online Quiz THINK central thinkcentral.com

SECTION 4 Assessment

Reviewing Main Ideas and Vocabulary

1. **Describe** What are the symptoms of intoxication?

2. **Recall** What are some of the effects of cocaine?

3. **Compare and Contrast** How are marijuana and hashish alike and different?

Thinking Critically

4. **Analyze** What are some of the effects of nicotine?

5. **Evaluate** Do you think people use drugs to heighten consciousness or to escape from it?

6. **Analyze** Using your notes and a graphic organizer like the one below, describe some of the effects of depressants, stimulants, and hallucinogens on consciousness.

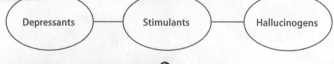

Depressants — Stimulants — Hallucinogens

FOCUS ON WRITING

7. **Expository** Write a paragraph about why and how the use of morphine became widespread.

Experiment
Applying What You've Learned

Student Achievement and Sleep Deprivation

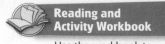
Reading and Activity Workbook
Use the workbook to complete this experiment.

What is the connection between adequate sleep and student academic achievement?

1. Introduction

A good deal of research has been done on student achievement and sleep deprivation. Some high schools across America have even revised their school schedule to accommodate the need for sleep among teenagers.

First, choose a partner. You and your partner can then recruit classmates, peers, or schoolmates to participate in your experiment. Then design an experiment testing sleep deprivation and memory. You can design a memory task as your dependent variable to test the effects of sleep deprivation on performance. For example, you might have students recite from memory the fifty state capitals in the United States. Include the following components in your experiment and be prepared to debrief the class following the conclusion of the experiment.

- An operational definition of your experiment (hypothesis)
- Dependent variable: memory task
- Independent variable
- Control group
- Experimental group
- Random assignment

2. Steps of the Experiment

Step 1: Operational definition: state the hypothesis in an if/then format and explain how you intend to measure change.

Step 2: Once your hypothesis has been formulated, then you are ready to undertake the following procedures:

- List the population being studied in the experiment.
- Be able to explain your sample in terms of size, educational background, gender, and age.
- Establish a control group and an experimental group.
- Define the independent and dependent variables.
- Establish what variables will remain constant throughout the experiment other than the independent variable.
- Conduct the experiment and test your memory task with the participants you have selected. For example, have them try to recall the state capitals of the 50 states when they are fully rested, partially rested, and not rested because of sleep deprivation.
- Explain the findings for the experimental and control groups.
- Consider whether there might be any confounding variables.
- How did you control for experimenter bias?
- Did you have any ethical concerns?
- You are encouraged to be creative in interrupting your sleep schedules. You might set the alarm for every 90 minutes, leave the television on, or leave music and lights on to see if they affect your sleep and performance.

3. Assessment

You will be required to give a brief presentation to the class revealing your findings. Include the following elements in your presentation:

■ What did you learn in the course of conducting the experiment?

■ What surprised you the most in conducting the experiment?

■ What would you change if you conducted the experiment again?

4. Discussion and Writing

Now get together with a small group of classmates. Compare your experiences in the experiment with those of the group. Discuss the experiment, focusing on the following questions:

■ Was your operational definition of the experiment (the hypothesis) well formulated?

■ What were the variables in your experiment?

■ Who made up the control group?

■ Who made up the experimental group?

Now the group can write up a report of its responses to the above questions. Then the various groups should compare their reports, discussing points of agreement and disagreement.

Sleep Deprivation Experiment

- Hypothesis: A lack of sleep has a negative effect on the ability to remember facts.

- Dependent variable: memory task such as reciting state capitals of all 50 states.

- Sample make-up:

- Control group:

- Experimental group:

- Confounding variables:

- Experimenter bias:

- Ethical concerns:

CHAPTER 5 Review

Comprehension and Critical Thinking

SECTION 1 (pp. 128–131)

1. a. Define Why is consciousness described as a construct?

b. Categorize What sorts of stimuli attract our selective attention?

c. Elaborate Give some examples of altered states of consciousness.

SECTION 2 (pp. 132–137)

2. a. Identify What are circadian rhythms?

b. Explain How do circadian rhythms influence human behavior?

c. Elaborate Which brain wave patterns occur during sleep stages 1 through 4?

SECTION 3 (pp. 139–142)

3. a. Describe In what way is biofeedback training useful?

b. Explain Evidence suggests meditation can help people achieve which two things?

c. Evaluate Give some of the pros and cons of using biofeedback instead of medication to reduce high blood pressure.

SECTION 4 (pp. 144–149)

4. a. Define How would you define addiction?

b. Explain What is a hallucination?

c. Make Judgments Why might some people drink or use other drugs even though they know that the drugs can be harmful?

Psychology in Your Life

5. Why do you think many people use medication to try to overcome insomnia? Why might medication not be an effective cure? Think about a situation in which you might have experienced a sleep disorder. Then write a short paragraph describing the situation and your possible course of action.

Reviewing Vocabulary

Match the terms below with their correct definitions.

6. consciousness

7. altered state of consciousness

8. REM sleep

9. insomnia

10. sleep apnea

11. meditation

12. biofeedback

13. depressant

14. stimulant

15. addiction

16. euphoria

17. detoxification

A. breathing interruption that occurs during sleep

B. the inability to sleep

C. drug that increases the activity of the nervous system

D. drug that slows the activity of the nervous system

E. a system that provides information about something happening in the body

F. sleep stage characterized by irregular breathing, increased blood pressure, and faster heart rate

G. method some people use to try to narrow their consciousness so that stresses of the outside world fade away

H. a state of consciousness in which a person's sense of self or sense of the world changes

I. awareness of things inside and outside ourselves

J. the removal of a harmful substance from the body

K. after a person takes a drug for a while, the body craves it to feel normal

L. a feeling of great happiness or well-being

INTERNET ACTIVITY ✳

18. How do sleep problems affect teenagers? Choose one sleep disorder covered in this chapter (such as insomnia, nightmares, sleepwalking, apnea, or narcolepsy) and use the Internet to research how the disorder affects teenagers. Look for information on how common the disorder is among teens, recent statistics and data, and common treatments. Write a short report summarizing your findings.

SKILLS ACTIVITY: INTERPRETING GRAPHS

Study the graph below. It shows the time spent sleeping by various percentages of the population. Then use the information in the graph to help you answer the questions that follow.

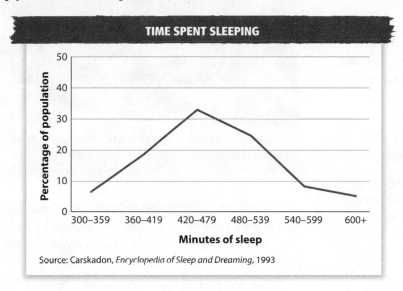

TIME SPENT SLEEPING

Source: Carskadon, *Encyclopedia of Sleep and Dreaming*, 1993

19. Identify How many minutes do most people spend sleeping per night?

20. Identify How many minutes of sleep do the fewest number of people manage to get each night?

21. Draw Conclusions What statement can be made about people who get less than 300 minutes of sleep and people who get more than 600 minutes of sleep?

WRITING FOR AP PSYCHOLOGY

Use your knowledge of drugs and consciousness to answer the question below. Do not simply list facts. Present a clear argument based on your critical analysis of the question, using the appropriate psychological terminology.

22. Briefly explain the health consequences of each of the drug types listed below.

- depressants
- stimulants
- hallucinogens

Connecting Online

Visit thinkcentral.com for review and enrichment activities related to this chapter.

Quiz and Review

ONLINE QUIZZES
Take a practice quiz for each section in this chapter.

WEBQUEST
Complete a structured Internet activity for this chapter.

QUICK LAB
Reinforce a key concept with a short lab activity.

APPLYING WHAT YOU'VE LEARNED
Review and apply your knowledge by completing a project-based assessment.

Activities

eACTIVITIES
Complete chapter Internet activities for enrichment.

INTERACTIVE FEATURE
Explore an interactive version of a key feature in this chapter.

KEEP IT CURRENT
Link to current news and research in psychology.

Online Textbook

 Learn more about key topics in this chapter.

Rehabilitation Counselor

How can a combat veteran come to terms with the loss of his legs? What skills might a person who has lost her eyesight develop so that she can be self-supporting? These are questions that a rehabilitation counselor might try to answer. Rehabilitation counseling is a subspecialty within counseling psychology. It is a subspecialty that demands dedication, patience, and stamina.

This army veteran works with a rehabilitation counselor to ease his adjustment to using a prosthetic leg.

Like clinical psychologists, counseling psychologists work with people experiencing distress. Counseling psychologists, however, tend to treat people who are confronted with stressful situations, rather than people who have more severe mental disorders. For example, the suicide of a family member may prompt a person to seek out a counseling psychologist's support and perspective for a few months. That client does not have a mental disorder, however.

In a similar way, people who have endured a severe physical illness or trauma might seek out the help of a rehabilitation counselor. These professionals work with individuals who have physical challenges. They help them adapt to their disabilities and become more self-sufficient. Rehabilitation counselors work with people of all ages, whether handicapped after an accident, an illness, or from birth. Their primary job is a tough one: helping people face the hard reality of having physical limitations while remaining both realistic and hopeful about the client's potential.

Rehabilitation counselors help prepare clients for jobs that they can do. They may also arrange for additional training. Part of their job may be recruiting potential employers for their clients.

A master's degree in rehabilitative counseling (often offered within university departments of education or health/kinesiology) is required for certification by the Commission on Rehabilitation Counselor Certification. Coursework ranges from case management to ethics. Candidates for certification must pass an exam.

Rehabilitation counselors work in a wide range of situations, from hospitals and rehabilitation agencies to college campuses. This can be an extremely rewarding career, though also a frustrating one, like any career that requires frequent contact with bureaucracy. Rehabilitation counselors must also deal with their clients' own frustrations and setbacks—but sometimes they can share in their clients' triumphs.

Applying APA Style

APA Style **THINK** central thinkcentral.com

Rehabilitation counselors publish articles in professional journals. These articles follow a style for using and citing Internet sources that is approved by the **American Psychological Association (APA)**.

When using electronic sources, direct readers to specific documents, rather than home pages. Be sure the addresses are correct and that the referenced document has not been deleted or moved.

Many electronic sources do not provide page numbers. To cite specific excerpts in the body of a text, include the author's last name, the year of the publication, and the paragraph number, preceded by the paragraph symbol or the abbreviation *para*: (Newman, 2007, para 3).

Through Think Central you can find more on Internet citations from the APA style guidelines. Review the APA

guidelines. Then make a list of different types of references and in-text citations for electronic sources and provide an example for each type.

Electronic Source	Example
No visible page or paragraph number visible	Redmond, 2005, Introduction, *para 2*
Paragraph number visible	

UNIT 3 Learning and Cognition

THE Little Albert EXPERIMENT

In the Little Albert experiment, a small child was taught to fear something that he had enjoyed before the experiment.

In 1920, psychologists John B. Watson and Rosalie Rayner published an article describing an experiment they had done on an infant named Albert. The story of the experiment had such an impact on the field of psychology that the boy became known as "Little Albert" and the experiment became a classic. Even today, psychologists and psychology students are familiar with it. The Little Albert experiment also raised important ethical questions and illustrates the degree to which ethical standards in psychological research have changed since 1920.

What was the experiment? It was a small but significant demonstration that emotional reactions such as fear can be acquired through a form of learning known as classical conditioning.

Albert was the 11-month-old son of one of Watson's and Rayner's acquaintances. Watson and Rayner observed that Albert did not become easily frightened. They also observed that he had a white laboratory rat for a playmate. To demonstrate that fears can be learned through associations, Watson

and Rayner decided to see if they could condition, or teach, Albert to fear the white rat rather than be amused by it. All they had to do, they reasoned, was pair the rat with something that Albert would find instinctively frightening.

One of the things that an 11-month-old finds instinctively frightening is loud, unexpected noises such as the clanging of steel bars. To teach Albert to fear rats, the researchers clanged steel bars behind his head every time he played with the rat. The small child reacted by crying and becoming afraid. Sure enough, after seven pairings of rat and loud noises, Albert showed a fear of the rat even when there were no more loud clanging noises.

When the rat was presented to Albert, he would become distressed, cry, and turn away. The rat had at first brought pleasure to Little Albert. Now, through no fault of its own, it had become a source of fear and trembling. Through association, the animal had taken on the meaning of the jangling, jarring steel bars to Little Albert.

Before the experiment, Albert showed no fear of rats. But after the experiment, rats and other furry objects scared him.

CHAPTER 6
LEARNING

Little Albert's newfound fear, however, did not stop with the rat. It spread, or generalized, to objects similar in appearance to the rat. For example, when the researchers later showed Albert a rabbit, a furry dog, and a fur coat, he showed fear toward each of them. Because of his experiences with the rat and the steel bars, Albert had learned to fear other objects that were white and furry. Shortly after the experiment was conducted, Little Albert was removed from the study.

Was it ethical for Watson and Rayner to conduct their experiment on such a small child—especially when the experiment involved repeatedly frightening him and teaching him to fear something that had previously given him pleasure? Today psychologists would say no, the Little Albert experiment was very unethical. For one thing, the researchers repeatedly frightened a very small child. For this reason and for others, the ethical standards followed by Watson and Rayner fall far short of the current standards used today by the American Psychological Association (APA). As a result, the experiment would never be duplicated today.

Despite these ethical questions, however, the Little Albert experiment does illustrate some important concepts of learning. The experiment showed that through the principles of classical conditioning, a person can be taught to fear something based on association and can generalize that fear to other similar objects.

What do you think?

1. How did Watson and Rayner condition Little Albert to fear white rats?

2. Do you think you have learned to fear or enjoy certain things because of conditioning or association? Explain.

Chapter at a Glance

SECTION 1: Classical Conditioning

■ Russian physiologist Ivan Pavlov pioneered research into a form of learning known as classical conditioning. In classical conditioning, one stimulus causes a response that is usually caused by another stimulus.

■ Classical conditioning can help people adapt to the environment and can help eliminate troubling fears or other behaviors.

SECTION 2: Operant Conditioning

■ Psychologist B. F. Skinner helped pioneer research into a form of learning known as operant conditioning, in which individuals learn from the consequences of their actions.

■ Operant conditioning depends on the use of reinforcements and a schedule to execute them.

■ The principles of operant conditioning can be applied to help people or animals learn to combine a series of simple steps or actions to form complex behaviors.

SECTION 3: Cognitive Factors in Learning

■ Cognitive psychologists focus on the mental aspects of learning and are interested in what people or animals know, not just what they do.

■ Cognitive learning is based on the idea that people and animals can learn by thinking or by watching others.

■ Some techniques for behavioral modification are based on the ideas of operant conditioning and cognitive factors.

SECTION 4: The PQ4R Method: Learning to Learn

■ The PQ4R method is a study method based on the work of educational psychologist Francis P. Robinson. Robinson believed that students will learn more when they take an active approach to learning.

■ The PQ4R method includes these six steps: preview, question, read, reflect, recite, and review.

Classical Conditioning

Before You Read

Main Idea
Classical conditioning is a form of learning that involves the use of a stimulus to generate a specific response.

Reading Focus
1. What are the basic principles of classical conditioning?
2. How might classical conditioning help people or animals adapt to the environment?
3. What are some applications of classical conditioning?

Vocabulary
conditioning
classical conditioning
unconditioned stimulus
unconditioned response
conditioned response
conditioned stimulus
taste aversion
extinction
spontaneous recovery
generalization
discrimination
flooding
systematic desensitization
counterconditioning

TAKING NOTES Use a graphic organizer like this one to take notes on classical conditioning.

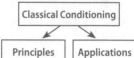

```
         Classical Conditioning
            ↙          ↘
    Principles      Applications
```

Makes My Mouth Water

PSYCHOLOGY CLOSE UP

Why do people have an immediate, physical response to a picture of pizza? If you are like most other people, this photograph of a pizza can make your mouth water. It may even cause a rumble in your stomach. But why? After all, it is just a picture.

Your response to the picture is a learned response based on your experience. If you had never tasted pizza, you almost certainly would not have the same reaction. But since you have eaten pizza before, just the thought of it can trigger a physical reaction in you. You have learned to associate the thought of a pizza with the actual experience you would have eating it. This reaction is part of a learning experience called classical conditioning, which you will learn about in this section.

There are many examples of classical conditioning. For example, If you have a dog or cat, it may come running into the kitchen whenever it hears a can opener. That is because your pet has learned to associate the sound of the can opener with food. People have also learned to respond to certain stimuli through association. For example, when the bell rings at school, what do you do? ■

Looking at a photograph of pizza can cause us to react as if it was real.

Principles of Classical Conditioning

Have you ever heard a song that you really liked that was popular a few years ago? Did the song "take you back" and make you feel a rush of sensations that you used to feel when the song was popular? If so, this reaction was probably a result of associations between the song and events in your life at the time the song was popular. In other words, the song served as a stimulus. A stimulus is something that produces a reaction, or a response, from a person or an animal. In this case, the response consisted of the feelings brought about by hearing the song.

Here is a simple experiment that also demonstrates associations. Think of a food you especially like. Is your mouth watering? If it is, you are experiencing the results of **conditioning,** a type of learning that involves stimulus-response connections. In particular, your reaction demonstrates a type of conditioning known as classical conditioning. **Classical conditioning** is a simple form of learning in which one stimulus (in this case, the thought of the food) calls forth the response (your mouth watering) that is usually called forth by another stimulus (the actual food). This occurs when the two stimuli have been associated with each other.

Pavlov's Dogs Some of the earliest findings about classical conditioning resulted from research somewhat similar to your own experiences in thinking of food. However, the early research was with dogs, not people. Russian physiologist Ivan Pavlov (1849–1936) discovered that dogs, too, learn to associate one thing with another when food is involved.

Pavlov did not set out to learn about learning. Rather, he was interested in the relationship between the nervous system and digestion. In particular, Pavlov was studying salivation, or mouth-watering, in dogs. He knew that dogs would salivate if meat was placed on their tongues because saliva aids in the eating and digestion of the meat. In other words, meat on the tongue is a stimulus for the production of saliva.

But Pavlov discovered that the dogs did not always wait until they had received meat to start salivating. For example, they salivated in response to the clinking of food trays brought into the laboratory. Why? Because

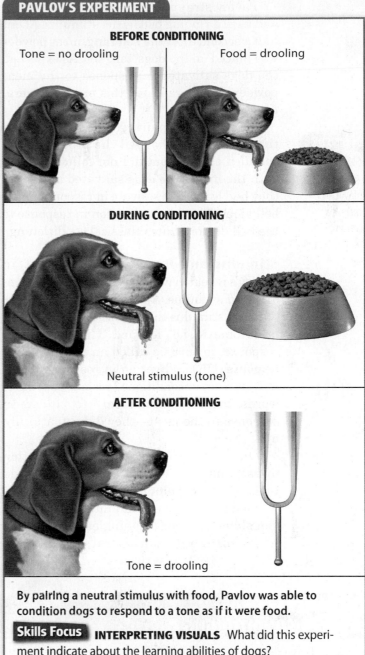

PAVLOV'S EXPERIMENT

BEFORE CONDITIONING

Tone = no drooling   Food = drooling

DURING CONDITIONING

Neutral stimulus (tone)

AFTER CONDITIONING

Tone = drooling

By pairing a neutral stimulus with food, Pavlov was able to condition dogs to respond to a tone as if it were food.

Skills Focus   INTERPRETING VISUALS   What did this experiment indicate about the learning abilities of dogs?

the dogs had learned from experience that this event—the clinking of the trays—meant that food was coming.

Pavlov decided that the salivation was worth looking into. If dogs could learn to salivate in response to clinking food trays because they were associated with the bringing of meat, could dogs also learn to salivate in response to any stimulus that signaled meat? Pavlov predicted that they could. He set out to show that he could train his dogs to salivate in response to any stimulus he chose.

Pavlov strapped the dogs into harnesses and used a ringing bell as the stimulus. About half a second after the bell rang, meat powder was placed on the dogs' tongues. As expected, the dogs salivated in response to the meat powder. Pavlov repeated this process several times.

After several pairings of the meat and the bell, Pavlov changed the procedure: he sounded the bell but did not follow the bell with the meat. The dogs salivated anyway—they had learned to salivate in response to the bell alone. The dogs' salivation in response to the bell demonstrates classical conditioning.

Stimulus and Response The meat in Pavlov's research was an example of an unconditioned stimulus. An **unconditioned stimulus** (US) is a stimulus that causes a response that is automatic, not learned. That automatic response, in turn, is called an **unconditioned response** (UR). Salivation in response to the meat was an unconditioned response. In other words, the dogs did not *learn* to salivate in response to the meat—they did so naturally, by instinct.

On the other hand, the dogs' salivation in response to the bell was a conditioned response. A **conditioned response** (CR) is a learned response to a stimulus that was previously neutral, or meaningless. In Pavlov's research, the bell was a neutral stimulus (NS).

CASE STUDY
CONNECTION

Little Albert
The Little Albert experiment is a famous example of classical conditioning in humans.

That is, before Pavlov associated it with the meat, it might have made the dogs' ears perk up, but it would not have made the dogs salivate because it had nothing to do with food. Through repeated association with meat, however, the bell became a learned stimulus, or a **conditioned stimulus** (CS), for the response of salivation.

The Little Albert experiment is another example of classical conditioning. The clanging of the steel bars was the unconditioned stimulus (US) that led to the unconditioned response (UR) of fear. The rat was the conditioned stimulus (CS) that, through association with the clanging of bars, also led to fear, now the conditioned response (CR).

Reading Check **Summarize** How does classical conditioning occur?

Adapting to the Environment

Classical conditioning helps animals and people adapt to their environment. For example, a bear cub may learn to associate a particular scent (CS) with the appearance of a dangerous animal (US). The cub can then hide or run away (CR) when it catches the scent.

Taste Aversions One form of classical conditioning that is useful to people is called a taste aversion. A **taste aversion** is a learned avoidance of a particular food. Have you ever eaten a food that made you ill? You probably stayed away from that food for a long time. If so, you developed a taste aversion to it.

Taste aversion is an example of one-trial learning. With other forms of classical conditioning, an association must be made several times before the conditioned response occurs. For example, Pavlov had to pair the bell with meat several times before the dogs began to salivate at the sound of the bell. In taste aversions, however, just one pairing of food and illness may be all that is necessary to create the aversion.

Extinction When conditions in the environment change, responses may also change. For example, an animal threatening to a bear cub may lose its menace once the bear matures.

When a conditioned stimulus (such as the scent of an animal) is no longer followed by an unconditioned stimulus (a dangerous animal), it loses its ability to bring about a

KEY CONCEPTS OF CLASSICAL CONDITIONING

QUICK FACTS

Before conditioning begins, an unconditioned stimulus (US) brings forth an unconditioned response (UR). During conditioning, a neutral stimulus (NS) is paired with the unconditioned stimulus (US). In the resulting conditioning, the neutral stimulus becomes a conditioned stimulus (CS). The conditioned stimulus then brings forth a conditioned response (CR).

Unconditioned Stimulus (US) causes an automatic response

Unconditioned Response (UR) an automatic response to a stimulus

Neutral Stimulus (NS) does not cause a response

Conditioned Stimulus (CS) a learned stimulus

Conditioned Response (CR) learned response to a neutral stimulus

conditioned response. This process is called **extinction.** Extinction occurs when the conditioned stimulus (CS) is disconnected from the unconditioned stimulus (US). As a result, the conditioned stimulus (CS) no longer causes the conditioned response (CR) to occur.

Pavlov found that with repeated ringing of the bell (CS) not followed by meat (US), the dogs eventually stopped salivating (CR) when they heard the bell (CS). The dogs had learned that the bell no longer meant that food was on the way. The conditioned response of salivating at the sound of the bell was extinguished.

Spontaneous Recovery An extinguished response, however, is not necessarily gone forever. With **spontaneous recovery,** organisms sometimes display responses that were extinguished earlier. The revival of the response follows a period in which the conditioned stimulus does not occur. For example, after the response of salivating at the sound of the bell had been extinguished in Pavlov's dogs, a day or two passed during which the dogs did not hear the bell at all. Then after this rest period, the bell was rung again. Even though the salivation response had previously been extinguished, it was now back in a bit weaker form—the dogs still produced saliva, but they produced less of it.

Think again of the song that brought back old feelings. If the song became popular again and you started hearing it every day, you probably would no longer experience the same rush of feelings when you heard it. But if a month passed without your hearing the song at all, the next time you heard it, those old feelings would probably return.

Generalization and Discrimination The act of responding in the same ways to stimuli that seem to be similar is called **generalization.** In a demonstration of generalization, Pavlov first conditioned a dog to salivate when it was shown a circle. The dog was shown a circle (CS) and was then given meat (US). After several pairings, the dog salivated when presented with only the circle. Pavlov next demonstrated that the dog would also salivate in response to the sight of other geometric figures, including ellipses and squares. The more closely the figure resembled a circle, the more drops of saliva flowed.

The dog's weaker response to figures that looked less like a circle was an example of discrimination. **Discrimination** is the act of responding differently to stimuli that are not similar to each other. Both generalization and discrimination help people and animals adapt to their environments. For example, a bear cub who has a bad experience with a wolf may generalize from that experience that all big furry animals that growl (other than adult bears) should be avoided. On the other hand, the bear cub probably discriminates between the wolf and a mouse. The mouse might be furry, but it is not big and does not growl. Thus, it is not a danger. A child who has been frightened by a dog may generalize and stay away from all dogs. But because of discrimination, the child continues to play with his or her stuffed animals, even if they are dogs.

Reading Check **Describe** Give three examples of ways that classical conditioning can help people adapt to their environment.

Applications of Classical Conditioning

Classical conditioning can help people learn to overcome their fears of different objects and situations. Many fears—such as a fear of heights or of snakes—are out of proportion to the actual risk of danger that they present. Some people fear looking out of windows in tall buildings, even though they cannot fall.

Applying Classical Conditioning
Through principles of classical conditioning, people can be taught to overcome certain fears, such as the fear of snakes.

Many people fear snakes, even snakes that are small and nonpoisonous. Two methods of reducing fears are based on the principle of extinction. These methods are known as flooding and systematic desensitization.

Flooding and Systematic Desensitization

In the method called **flooding,** a person is exposed to the harmless stimulus until fear responses to that stimulus are extinguished. For example, a person with a fear of snakes might be put in a room with lots of harmless snakes crawling around. A person with a fear of heights might be taken to the tops of tall buildings.

Although flooding is usually effective, it tends to be quite unpleasant. When people fear something, forced exposure to it is the last thing they want. For this reason, psychologists prefer to use a different method, known as systematic desensitization, to help people overcome their fears. With **systematic desensitization,** people are taught <u>relaxation techniques</u> and then, while they are relaxed, they are exposed gradually to the stimulus they fear. The goal of systematic desensitization is to teach the individual how to cope with their fears as they are gradually exposed to the stimulus.

For example, someone who fears snakes is shown pictures of snakes while in a relaxed state. Once the person can view pictures of snakes without losing the feeling of relaxation, he or she might then be shown some real snakes from a distance. Then, after some more time, the snakes are brought closer and closer, and eventually the person no longer fears snakes. Although systematic desensitization usually takes longer to work than flooding, it is not as unpleasant for the person experiencing it.

Counterconditioning Can cookies help children overcome their fears? In the 1920s, University of California professors Mary Cover Jones and Harold Jones reasoned that if fears could be conditioned by painful experiences, perhaps they could be treated by pleasant ones. In **counterconditioning,** a pleasant stimulus is paired repeatedly with a fearful one, counteracting the fear.

The Joneses tried out their idea with a two-year-old boy named Peter who feared rabbits. The Joneses gradually brought a rabbit closer to Peter while they fed Peter candy and cookies. Peter seemed nervous about the rabbit, but he continued to eat his treats. Gradually, the animal was brought even closer. Eventually, Peter ate treats and petted the rabbit at the same time. Apparently, his pleasure at eating the sweets canceled out his fear of rabbits.

Reading Check **Identify** What are three applications of classical conditioning?

Complete a Webquest at thinkcentral.com on systematic desensitization.

ACADEMIC VOCABULARY

relaxation technique any method or activity that helps a person to relax

---

SECTION 1 Assessment

Online Quiz THINK central thinkcentral.com

Reviewing Main Ideas and Vocabulary

1. **Contrast** How are an unconditioned stimulus and a neutral stimulus different?

2. **Explain** What is meant by extinction and spontaneous recovery?

3. **Describe** Give an example of discrimination in classical conditioning.

Thinking Critically

4. **Compare and Contrast** How are flooding, systematic desensitization, and counterconditioning similar? How are they different?

5. **Develop** In what ways are students classically conditioned in school settings?

6. **Draw Conclusions** Describe and explain learning as an adaptation to the environment.

7. **Sequence** Using your notes and a graphic organizer like the one below, show how classical conditioning takes place.

FOCUS ON WRITING

8. **Descriptive** Review the basic concepts of classical conditioning. Then think about an example of classical conditioning in your life, and write a paragraph describing how you became conditioned. Be sure to identify the stimuli and the responses.

Learning from a Virtual Rat

To research learning and conditioning, psychologists often design laboratory experiments with animals such as rats. But experiments with live animals can be costly and time-consuming. Why not take advantage of computer technology and use a virtual rat?

"Sniffy the Virtual Rat" is a computer program designed by psychologists Tom Alloway and Jeff Graham and computer programmer Greg Wilson. The program allows students to design realistic laboratory experiments in a virtual environment with a virtual rat. In the process, students not only learn how to design a sound experiment, they also learn the principles of classical conditioning.

Why use a virtual rat instead of real one? A virtual rat has several advantages. First, maintaining a laboratory with animals is too costly for many schools and colleges. Second, virtual rats never get tired and are always hungry. As a result, they can save researchers and students time and effort. Finally, one study showed that using a virtual rat significantly enhanced students' understanding (Venneman and Knowles, 2005).

To create "Sniffy," the researchers first studied live rats carefully. They found that a rat has about 80 individual moves. Out of that number, the researchers chose 30 moves for their virtual rat. Next, they studied how rats learn and created a computer program that mimicked a rat's intelligence. After several months of work, they had a trainable electronic rat—Sniffy.

The Sniffy computer program allows students to design and conduct classical conditioning experiments. Students can gain firsthand experience with the techniques and procedures used by psychologists in animal psychology experiments. In addition to receiving basic classical conditioning, Sniffy can be trained to perform several different tricks. For example, he can learn to sit up, beg, and groom his face.

Another advantage that Sniffy has over real rats is that he has been programmed to "learn" more quickly than a live animal. As a result, research time can be artificially sped up, so the results of an experiment can be analyzed quickly.

It generally takes beginner rat trainers between 40 minutes and an hour to get Sniffy to do what they want. Then students can analyze the behavioral data from their experiment, draw inferences and conclusions from it, and report on their findings. But here is the best part—there is no cleanup involved!

Thinking Critically

1. **Explain** What are some advantages to using a virtual rat like Sniffy?

2. **Discuss** What drawbacks might there be to using a virtual rat in an experiment instead of a real one?

Operant Conditioning

Before You Read

Main Idea
Operant conditioning occurs when people or animals have learned to respond to a certain situation with specific behaviors.

Reading Focus
1. How are operant conditioning and reinforcement related?
2. What are the main types of reinforcers?
3. How do rewards and punishments shape learning?
4. How do schedules of reinforcement influence learning?
5. What are some applications of operant conditioning?

Vocabulary
operant conditioning
reinforcement
primary reinforcers
secondary reinforcers
positive reinforcers
negative reinforcers
schedule of reinforcement
continuous reinforcement
partial reinforcement
shaping
chaining

TAKING NOTES Use a graphic organizer like this one to take notes on operant conditioning.

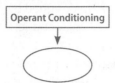

TWIGGY
the Water-Skiing Squirrel

PSYCHOLOGY CLOSE UP

How can a squirrel learn how to water ski? Twiggy the squirrel is a world-famous novelty act. Twiggy is a Florida gray squirrel that learned how to water ski behind a remote-controlled toy powerboat. The original Twiggy was found by Chuck and Lou Ann Best after a hurricane in 1978. The Best family raised the squirrel as a pet. As they played in their swimming pool, Twiggy would ride on their shoulders. One day, Chuck jokingly suggested that they teach Twiggy to water ski.

First, Twiggy was trained to balance on little foam blocks. Then, the squirrel learned how to hold onto a miniature set of handlebars. Eventually, Twiggy would hold on even while being pulled. Lou Ann Best has trained several squirrels, all named Twiggy, to water ski. According to Lou Ann, "You really can't discipline them. It's a lot of love and repetition that gets them to where they are supposed to know what to do."

The type of training used to teach Twiggy to water ski is called operant conditioning. With operant conditioning, a complex behavior can be broken down into a series of small steps that are eventually linked together in one larger behavior. Humans and animals participate in this kind of learning to acquire important skills. ■

Twiggy takes a ride behind a remote-controlled powerboat. Twiggy is a popular attraction at many boat shows.

Operant Conditioning and Reinforcement

In classical conditioning, we learn to associate one stimulus with another. Pavlov's dogs learned to associate a ringing bell with food. Because of classical conditioning, the response made to one stimulus (for example, food) is then made in response to the other (for example, the bell).

Classical conditioning, however, is only one type of learning. Another type of learning is operant conditioning. In **operant conditioning,** people and animals learn to do certain things—and not to do others—because of the results of what they do. In other words, they learn from the consequences of their actions. They may learn to engage in behavior that results in desirable consequences, such as receiving food or social approval. Or they might learn to avoid behaviors that result in negative consequences, such as pain or failure.

In classical conditioning, the conditioned responses are often involuntary biological behaviors, such as salivation or eye blinks. In operant conditioning, however, voluntary responses—behaviors that people and animals have more control over, such as studying— are conditioned. In operant conditioning, an organism learns to do something because of its effects or consequences.

To study operant conditioning, psychologist B. F. Skinner devised an animal cage that has been dubbed the "Skinner box." A Skinner box is ideal for laboratory experimentation. Treatments can be introduced and removed, and the results can be carefully observed.

In a classic experiment, a rat in a Skinner box was deprived of food. The box was designed so that when a lever inside was pressed, some food pellets would drop into the box. At first, the rat sniffed its way around the box and engaged in random behavior. The rat's first pressing of the lever was accidental. But food appeared.

Soon the rat began to press the lever more frequently. It had learned that pressing the lever would make the food pellets appear. The pellets reinforced the lever-pressing behavior. **Reinforcement** is the process by which a stimulus (in this case, the food) increases the chances that the preceding behavior (in this case, the lever pressing) will occur again.

After several reinforced responses, the rat pressed the lever quickly and frequently, until it was no longer hungry.

In operant conditioning, it matters little why the person or animal makes the first response that is reinforced. It can be by chance, as with the rat in the Skinner box, or the person or animal can be physically guided into the response. In training a dog to sit on command, the dog's owner may say, "Sit!" and then push the dog's rear end down. Once the dog is sitting, its response can be reinforced with a pat on the head or a food treat.

People can simply be told what they need to do when they are learning how to do things such as boot up a computer. In order for the behavior to be reinforced, however, people need to know whether they have made the correct response. If the computer does not start up the learner will probably think he or she has made a mistake and will not repeat the response. But if the computer does start up, the response will appear to be correct, and the learner will repeat it. Knowledge of results is often all the reinforcement that people need to learn new skills.

Reading Check **Describe** How does reinforcement result in operant conditioning?

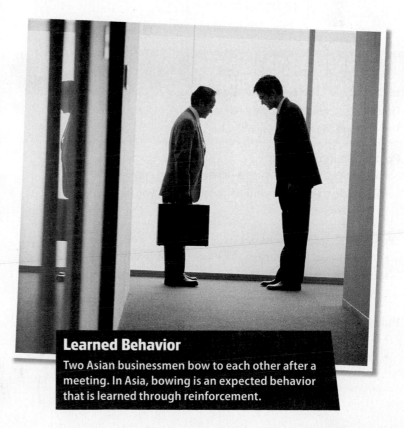

Learned Behavior
Two Asian businessmen bow to each other after a meeting. In Asia, bowing is an expected behavior that is learned through reinforcement.

Types of Reinforcers

The stimulus that encourages a behavior to occur again is called a reinforcer. There are several different types of reinforcers. Reinforcers can be primary or secondary. They can also be positive or negative.

Primary and Secondary Reinforcers Reinforcers that function due to the biological makeup of an organism are called **primary reinforcers.** For example, food, water, and adequate warmth are all primary reinforcers. People and animals do not need to be taught to value food, water, and warmth.

The value of **secondary reinforcers,** however, must be learned. Secondary reinforcers initially acquire their value through being paired with established reinforcers. Money, attention, and social approval are usually all secondary reinforcers. Money, for example, is a secondary reinforcer because we have learned that it may be exchanged for primary reinforcers such as food and shelter.

Secondary reinforcers may acquire their value through a long chain of associations. For example, good grades can lead to a good college, which can lead to a good job, which can lead to more money and social approval. As a result, good grades may come to be desired in and of themselves.

Positive and Negative Reinforcers Reinforcers can also be positive or negative. **Positive reinforcers** increase the frequency of the behavior they follow when they are applied. Food, fun activities, and social approval are good examples of positive reinforcers. In positive reinforcement, a behavior is reinforced because a person (or an animal) receives something he or she wants following the behavior.

Different reinforcers work with different people. For people who enjoy sports, for example, the opportunity to participate in a sport is a positive reinforcer. For people who do not enjoy sports, however, the opportunity to participate in a sport would not be an effective reinforcer. Similarly, what serves as a reinforcer at one time for a person may not be as effective at another time for that same person. When a person is hungry, food will work well as a positive reinforcer. But once the person has eaten and is full, food will no longer have an effect.

Unlike positive reinforcement, with negative reinforcement a behavior is reinforced because something unwanted *stops* happening or is removed following the behavior. **Negative reinforcers** increase the frequency of the behavior that follows when they are removed. Negative reinforcers are unpleasant in some way. Discomfort, fear, and social disapproval are negative reinforcers.

Daily life is filled with examples of negative reinforcement. When we become too warm in the sun, we move into the shade. When a food particle is stuck between our teeth, we floss to remove it. Both of these situations involve some uncomfortable stimulus—a negative reinforcer—that we act on to make the discomfort disappear. When a specific behavior reduces or removes the discomfort, that behavior is reinforced, or strengthened. For example, if a child does not want to perform a certain activity, he or she may scream, yell, or whine until the parent relents. The child's action has been reinforced and likely the behavior will be repeated when the child refuses to do something else demanded by the parent.

Reading Check **Summarize** Describe the four main types of reinforcers.

KEY CONCEPTS OF OPERANT CONDITIONING

Operant conditioning occurs when a learner's behavior is followed by a consequence, or reinforcement.

Positive Reinforcement
- Increases the frequency of a behavior when applied
- Example: if you finish your homework early, you get to go to the movies as a reward

Negative Reinforcement
- Increases the frequency of a behavior when removed
- Example: to stop the buzzing sound in your car, you have to roll up the window

Punishment
- Decreases the frequency of a behavior
- Example: your parents take your cell phone away for one day each week to lower your phone bill

Rewards and Punishments

Many people believe that being positively reinforced is the same as being rewarded and that being negatively reinforced is the same as being punished. There are some differences, however, particularly between negative reinforcement and punishment.

Rewards Rewards, like reinforcers, increase the frequency of a behavior, and some psychologists do use the term *reward* interchangeably with the term *positive reinforcement*. But Skinner preferred the concept of reinforcement to that of reward because the concept of reinforcement can be explained without trying to "get inside the head" of an organism to guess what it will find rewarding. A list of reinforcers is arrived at by observing what kinds of stimuli increase the frequency of a behavior.

Punishments While rewards and positive reinforcers are similar, punishments are quite different from negative reinforcers. Both negative reinforcers and punishments are usually unpleasant. But negative reinforcers increase the frequency of a behavior by being removed. Punishments, on the other hand, are unwanted events that, when they are applied, decrease the frequency of the behavior they follow.

Some school districts tie participation in athletic programs to academic grades, and both punishment and negative reinforcement are involved. To the athlete on the team who does not achieve the required grades, being removed from the team is a punishment. But once the student is off the team, the disappointment over being banned from participation is a negative reinforcer. The student may work harder to raise his or her class grades in order to rejoin the team, thus ending the disappointment.

Strong punishment can rapidly end undesirable behavior. But punishment tends to work only when it is guaranteed. If a behavior is punished some of the time but goes unnoticed the rest of the time, the behavior will probably continue.

Most psychologists feel it is preferable to reward children for desirable behavior rather than punish them for unwanted behavior.

When Punishment Is a Problem

Psychologists point to several reasons for minimizing the use of punishment. They believe that in most cases, punishment is not the best way to deal with a problem.

Punishment can create anger and hostility. Children who are punished may take out their anger on others.

Punishment does not in itself teach alternative acceptable behavior. A child may learn what not to do in a particular situation, but not what to do instead.

Severely punished people may try to leave the situation rather than change their behavior. A child who is often punished may respond by simply running away.

Punishment may have broader effects than desired. This can occur when people do not know why they are being punished and what is wanted of them.

Punishment is sometimes accompanied by unseen benefits that make the behavior more, not less, likely to be repeated. For instance, some children may learn that the most effective way to get attention from their parents is to misbehave.

Punishment may be imitated as a way of solving problems. For example, children hit by angry parents may learn not only that they have done something wrong but also that people hit other people when they are upset.

Skills Focus	INTERPRETING CHARTS

Which of these reasons do you feel is the strongest for not using punishment to shape behavior?

For example, parents and other authority figures should pay attention to children and praise them when the children are behaving well. If good behavior is taken for granted, and only misbehavior receives attention, misbehavior may get reinforced.

Psychologists also point out that children need to be aware of the desired behavior. In addition, they need to be capable of performing it. For example, consider a situation in which parents punish a child for not listening to directions only to find out much later that the child has a hearing problem and could not hear the directions.

Reading Check **Contrast** Explain how punishments are different from negative reinforcers.

Schedules of Reinforcement

A major factor in determining just how effective a reinforcement will be in bringing about a behavior has to do with the **schedule of reinforcement**—when and how often the reinforcement occurs.

Continuous and Partial Reinforcement We have been discussing **continuous reinforcement,** or the reinforcement of a behavior every time the behavior occurs. For example, the rats in the Skinner box received food every time they pressed the lever. If you go to a friend's house and your friend is there every time, you will probably continue to go to that same location each time you want to see your friend because you have always been reinforced for going there. New behaviors are usually learned most rapidly through continuous reinforcement.

It is not, however, always practical or even possible to reinforce a person or an animal for a behavior every single time the behavior occurs. Moreover, a person or animal who is continuously reinforced for a behavior tends to maintain that behavior only as long as the reinforcement is still there. If for some reason the reinforcement stops occurring, the behavior disappears very quickly. For example, if you go to your friend's house only to be told that your friend no longer lives there, you almost certainly will not return to that house again in search of your friend.

The alternative to continuous reinforcement is called partial reinforcement.

In **partial reinforcement,** a behavior is not reinforced every time it occurs. People who regularly go to the movies, for example, may not enjoy every movie they see, but they continue to go because they enjoy at least some of the movies. Behaviors learned through partial reinforcement tend to last longer after they are no longer being reinforced at all than do behaviors learned through continuous reinforcement.

There are two basic categories of partial reinforcement schedules. The first category concerns the amount of time (or interval) that must occur between the reinforcements of a behavior. The second category concerns the number of correct responses that must be made before reinforcement occurs (the ratio of responses to reinforcers).

Interval Schedules If the amount of time—the interval—that must elapse between reinforcements of a behavior is greater than zero seconds, the behavior is on an interval schedule of reinforcement. There are two different types of interval schedules: fixed-interval schedules and variable-interval schedules. These schedules affect how people allocate the persistence and effort they apply to certain tasks.

In a fixed-interval schedule, a fixed amount of time—say, five minutes—must elapse between reinforcements. Suppose a behavior is reinforced at 10:00. If the behavior is performed at 10:02, it will not be reinforced at that time. However, at 10:05, reinforcement again becomes available and will occur as soon as the behavior is performed. Then the next reinforcement is not available until five minutes later, and so on. Regardless of whether or how often the desired behavior is performed during the interval, it will not be reinforced again until five minutes have elapsed.

The response rate falls off after each reinforcement on a fixed-interval schedule. It then picks up as the time when reinforcement will be dispensed draws near. For example, in a one-minute fixed-interval schedule, a rat may be reinforced with food the first time it presses the lever after a minute has elapsed since the previous reinforcement. After each reinforcement, the rat's rate of lever pressing slows down, but as a minute approaches, lever pressing increases in frequency. It is as if the rat

PARTIAL REINFORCEMENT SCHEDULES

INTERVAL SCHEDULES

Schedule	Examples
Fixed-Interval Schedule An exact amount of time passes between each reinforcement.	• Studying for a weekly quiz • Getting your paycheck every two weeks
Variable-Interval Schedule A varying amount of time passes between each reinforcement.	• Checking e-mail • Winning a video game

RATIO SCHEDULES

Schedule	Examples
Fixed-Ratio Schedule Reinforcement occurs after a fixed number of responses.	• Getting one free meal after the purchase of ten • Losing your driver's license after five violations
Variable-Ratio Schedule Reinforcement occurs after a varying number of responses.	• Playing the lottery • The number of shots to score a goal in a soccer game

Partial reinforcement schedules can be based on time (interval) or response rate (ratio).

has learned that it must wait a while before reinforcement is available. Similarly, if you know that your teacher gives a quiz every Friday, you might study only on Thursday nights. After each quiz, you might not study again until the following Thursday. You are on a one-week fixed-interval schedule.

Farmers and gardeners are quite familiar with one-year fixed-interval schedules. If a particular type of fruit ripens only in the spring, for example, the farmer probably will not check to see if the fruit is ripe in the autumn or winter. However, as spring begins, the farmer will probably check more and more frequently to see if the fruit is ripe. Once all the fruit has ripened and been picked, the farmer will stop checking until the next spring.

In a variable-interval schedule, varying amounts of time go by between reinforcements. For example, a reinforcement may occur at 10:00, then not again until 10:07 (7-minute interval), then not again until 10:08 (1-minute interval), and then not again until 10:20 (12-minute interval).

In variable-interval schedules, the timing of the next reinforcement is unpredictable. Therefore, the response rate is steadier than with fixed-interval schedules. For example, if your teacher gives unpredictable pop quizzes, you are likely to do at least some studying fairly regularly because you do not know when the next quiz will be. And since there is always the chance that it could be tomorrow, you want to be prepared.

Ratio Schedules If a desired response is reinforced every time the response occurs, there is a one-to-one (1:1) ratio of response to reinforcement (one response, one reinforcement). If, however, the response must occur more than once in order to be reinforced, there is a higher response-to-reinforcement ratio. For example, if a response must occur five times before being reinforced, the ratio is 5:1. As with interval schedules, there are fixed-ratio schedules and variable-ratio schedules.

In a fixed-ratio schedule, reinforcement is provided after a fixed number of correct responses have been made. The rat in the box would have to press the lever, say, five times, and always exactly five times, in order to receive the food. Some stores use fixed-ratio schedules to encourage people to buy more. A video rental store, for instance, may promise customers a free video rental after payment for five rentals.

With a fixed-ratio schedule, the person or animal tends to try to get its fixed number of responses "out of the way" as quickly as it can to get to the reward. With the free video rental offer, for example, a customer may rent the five required videos as soon as possible to get the free one sooner. If the ratio is very high, however, it is often less effective, particularly with people.

With a variable-ratio schedule, reinforcement can come at any time. Sometimes the rat might have to press the lever 5 times to get the food; at other times, 8 or even 14 times.

ACADEMIC VOCABULARY

ratio the relationship in quantity, amount, or size between two or more things

The rat cannot predict how many times the lever must be pressed because the number changes each time.

This unpredictability maintains a high response rate. Slot machines tend to work on variable-ratio schedules. Even though the players do not know when (or even if) they will win, they continue to drop coins into the machines. And when the players do win, they often continue to play because the next winnings might be just a few lever-pulls away.

Extinction in Operant Conditioning In operant conditioning, as in classical conditioning, extinction sometimes occurs. In both types of conditioning, extinction occurs because the events that had previously followed a stimulus no longer occur.

In operant conditioning, the extinction of a learned response results from repeated performance of the response without reinforcement. In Skinner's experiment with the rats, lever pressing was followed by—and reinforced by—food. But if a rat presses a lever repeatedly and no food follows, it will eventually stop pressing the lever. The lever-pressing behavior will have been extinguished.

Reading Check **Infer** Why are both variable-interval schedules and variable-ratio schedules successful?

Applications of Operant Conditioning

As we have seen, even people who have never had a course in psychology use operant conditioning every day to influence other people. For example, parents frequently use rewards, such as a trip to the park or ice cream, to encourage children to perform certain tasks, such as cleaning their rooms. Some specific applications of operant conditioning in education include shaping, chaining, and programmed learning.

Shaping and Chaining If you have ever tried to teach someone how to do a complex or difficult task, you probably know that the best way to teach the task is to break it up into parts and teach each part separately. When all the parts have been mastered, they can be put together to form the whole task. Psychologists call this shaping. **Shaping** is a way of teaching complex behaviors in which one first reinforces small steps in the total activity.

Learning to ride a bicycle, for example, involves the learning of a complex sequence of behaviors and can be accomplished through shaping and chaining. In **chaining,** each step of a sequence must be learned and must lead to the next until the final action is achieved. The steps create a response chain. Sometimes several response chains must be learned to complete a desired action. For example, in learning to ride a bike a person must learn to move the bike forward by using the pedals. You may have seen a parent help a young child by holding the seat as the child learns to pedal. Then they must learn to balance the bicycle, and then to steer it. At first, each of these steps seems difficult, and people must pay close attention to each one. After many repetitions, though, and much praise and reassurance from the instructor, each step—and eventually bicycle riding itself—becomes habitual.

Cheerleader Chaining
Many long hours of practice allow these cheerleaders to perform complicated physical feats. *How is this an example of chaining?*

Chaining can occur either in a forward or backward response chain. In a forward chain, each step leads to a final goal. If you are learning to tie your shoes you eventually reach the point at which you have performed all the tasks in the chain and your shoes are tied. In backward chaining, you start with the final action and dissect each step it takes to get to that point. For example, suppose you want to know the steps in putting on a jacket. In backward chaining, you start with the jacket on and go backward through the steps necessary to put on the jacket.

Psychologists have used chaining to teach complex behavior patterns to animals. For example, they have trained rats to pedal toy cars by first reinforcing the rats' behavior of turning toward the cars. Next they wait until the rats approach the cars before providing further reinforcement. Then they wait until the rats touch the cars, and so on. In this way, rats have been trained to run up ramps, cross bridges, and climb ladders. This type of learning has also been used to train service animals to help people with disabilities.

Programmed Learning B. F. Skinner developed an educational method called programmed learning that is based on shaping and chaining. Programmed learning assumes that any task, no matter how complex, can be broken down into small steps. Each step can be shaped individually and combined to form the more complicated whole.

In programmed learning, a device called a teaching machine presents the student with the subject matter in a series of steps, each of which is called a frame. Each frame requires the student to make some kind of response, such as answering a question. The student is immediately informed whether the response is correct. If it is correct, the student goes on to the next frame. If the response is incorrect, however, the student goes back over that step until he or she learns it correctly.

These days, teaching machines are most likely to be computers that are programmed so that the material can branch off in several different directions, depending on where the student needs instruction and practice. The use of computers in learning is called computer-assisted instruction.

Programmed learning does not punish students for making errors. Instead, it reinforces correct responses. Teaching machines are infinitely patient with the learner. They are also highly efficient. Eventually, all students who finish the program earn "100 percent"—but they do so by learning in small steps at their own pace.

Reading Check **Identify Supporting Details** What are three examples of applications of operant conditioning?

SECTION 2 Assessment

Online Quiz THINK central thinkcentral.com

Reviewing Main Ideas and Vocabulary

1. **Identify** What are the basic types of reinforcers?

2. **Recall** What factors determine how effective a reinforcement will be?

3. **Contrast** What is the difference between interval schedules and ratio schedules?

4. **Explain** How are shaping and chaining linked?

Thinking Critically

5. **Contrast** How are negative reinforcers and punishment different?

6. **Analyze** What roles do reinforcement and punishment play in determining one's persistence and effort?

7. **Compare** Using your notes and a graphic organizer like this one, compare the different types of reinforcers that can be used in operant conditioning.

Reinforcer	Characteristics

FOCUS ON WRITING

8. **Descriptive** Choose a task that you would like to teach someone using shaping and chaining. Then write a description of each of the steps involved in the entire process.

Cognitive Factors in Learning

Before You Read

Main Idea

Cognitive learning focuses on the mental aspects of learning, such as obtaining, processing, and organizing information. Cognitive psychologists are interested not only in what people do, but also what they know.

Reading Focus

1. What is latent learning?
2. In what situations does observational learning take place?
3. What learning principles are involved in behavior modification?

Vocabulary

latent learning
observational learning

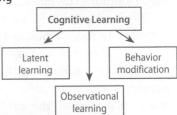

TAKING NOTES Use a graphic organizer like this one to take notes on cognitive learning.

Cognitive Learning
→ Latent learning
→ Observational learning
→ Behavior modification

It's Not Christmas WITHOUT Tamales

Several generations prepare tamales for a holiday celebration.

PSYCHOLOGY CLOSE UP

What do tamales have to do with Christmas? In some parts of Texas, Hispanic families celebrate the December holiday season by making tamales, a tradition that has been handed down for many years. To prepare the tamales, family members gather for the day. Generally, grandmothers and mothers are the chief tamale makers, and younger women are the assistants. The young people observe the whole process, including cooking the meat, preparing the dough, assembling the tamales, and then cooking them. This insures that when the assistants are older, they will know exactly how to make the tamales. In this way, a family tradition is passed down from generation to generation.

Tamale making is a good example of what psychologists call observational learning, or learning that is acquired by observing and imitating others. Observational learning is common in our everyday lives. If you think about it, you have probably learned many things by observing and imitating others, from how to hold a fork or brush your teeth to more specialized tasks such as how to text message, access your e-mail, or behave at a social event. Psychologists have studied exactly how we learn through observation. ■

Latent Learning

For B. F. Skinner, what was important was what organisms actually do, not what they say or think they might do. Skinner was interested only in organisms' behaviors.

Cognitive psychologists, however, prefer to speak about what people and animals *know* because of learning—not just what they do. Cognitive psychologists see learning as purposeful, not mechanical. They contend that a person can learn something simply by thinking about it or by watching others. They view people and even some animals as searching for information, weighing evidence, and making decisions. One kind of cognitive learning is called **latent learning**—learning that remains hidden until it is needed.

How do you know where objects are in your home, in your school, or in your neighborhood? You probably have a mental picture, or "cognitive map," of the area. Because you are familiar with your school, for example, you know the location of your locker, the main office, the cafeteria, the gym, and your psychology classroom. Chances are that no one has reinforced your creation of a mental picture of the school's layout; you have simply created it on your own.

In the past, many psychologists argued that organisms only learn behaviors that are reinforced. Today, however, most psychologists believe that much learning occurs without reinforcement. Support for this view comes from the work of E. C. Tolman. Tolman showed that rats will learn about their environments even in the absence of reinforcement. He trained some rats to run through mazes to reach food. Other rats were simply permitted to explore the mazes. They received no food or other rewards. After the unrewarded rats had run around in the mazes for 10 days, food was placed in a box at the far end of the mazes. After only one or two reinforced efforts, the previously unrewarded rats reached the food as quickly as the rewarded rats.

Tolman determined that the rats had learned about the layouts of the mazes even when they were not rewarded for their learning. Tolman distinguished between what organisms learn and what they do. Rats would learn about the mazes even when they roamed about without a goal. However, they had no reason to run efficient routes to the far end of the mazes until they were rewarded for doing so. Therefore, even though they had knowledge of the most rapid routes all along, this knowledge had been hidden, or latent, until the rats had reason to use it—when there was food at the end.

On your way to school each morning, you may pass a particular street corner at which you have never had any reason to stop. But if a friend wants to meet you at that corner on Saturday, you will know how to get there, even though you may never have stopped there before. This is another example of latent learning.

Reading Check **Recall** When is latent learning revealed?

Observational Learning

How many things have you learned from observing other people, from reading books, and from watching films and television? No doubt you have picked up a few ideas about how to act in certain situations. Certainly, cooking programs on television are based on the premise that people learn by watching or being told how others do things. People also learn to predict likely outcomes of actions by watching others.

In his research on social learning, psychologist Albert Bandura (1925–) has shown that we acquire knowledge and skills by observing and imitating others. Such learning is called **observational learning.**

Modeling One type of observational learning is modeling. Modeling is basically a type of imitation. A person will observe a certain behavior and later be able to reproduce it. For example, suppose you did not know how to get a bottle of water from a vending machine. You could observe people at a vending machine and determine what actions are needed to get a bottle of water from the machine. Or, suppose you are a new student in a class. You might model your behavior after other students. For example, you might learn that it is acceptable behavior to speak up in class by watching other students. In learning that classroom discussion is encouraged, you would have demonstrated the ability to learn by a process known as <u>vicarious</u> reinforcement.

ACADEMIC VOCABULARY

vicarious experienced indirectly through the experience of another

Observational learning and modeling account for much human learning. Children learn to speak, eat, and play at least partly by observing their parents and others do these things. Modern advertising also uses elements of observational learning—people often decide what products to purchase based on advertisements they have seen. You learn to pronounce words in your foreign-language class by hearing your teacher pronounce them. We may not always be able to do something perfectly the first time we try it, but if we have watched others do it first, we probably have a head start over people who are coming into it without any previous exposure.

The Effects of Media Violence One example of observational learning—and its effects—has to do with media violence. Television is one of our major sources of informal observational learning, and children are routinely exposed to scenes of violence just by turning on the TV set. If a child watches two to four hours of TV a day, she or he will have seen 8,000 murders and another 100,000 acts of violence by the time she or he has finished elementary school. Are G-rated movies safe? Perhaps not. One study found that virtually all G-rated animated films have scenes of violence, with a mean duration of 9 to 10 minutes per film. Many video games are also full of violent activity.

Most health professionals agree that media violence contributes to aggression. A joint statement issued by the American Psychological Association (APA) and several medical associations made the following points:

- Media violence supplies models of aggressive "skills" which children may learn by watching. Media violence also provides viewers with aggressive scripts—that is, ideas about how to behave in situations like those they have observed.

- Children who see a lot of violence are more likely to view violence as an effective and acceptable way of settling personal conflicts.

Statistically Speaking...

Video Game Violence and Children

Children and adolescents view violence not only on television but also in movies, music videos, and video games. Some studies have examined the impact of video games and violence on children and adolescents.

74% Percentage of school-age children who own video game equipment and play an average of 53 minutes per day

89% Percentage of video games that contain some kind of violence

17% Percentage of video games where violence is the primary focus

13–22% Estimated increase in violent behavior of adolescents due to playing violent video games

Skills Focus INTERPRETING DATA Why do you think so many video games contain violence?

Sources: National Youth Violence Prevention Resource Center; American Academy of Pediatrics

Interactive Feature THINK central thinkcentral.com

- Viewing violence can lead to emotional desensitization toward violence in real life. It can decrease the likelihood that one will take action on behalf of a victim of violence.
- Viewing violence may lead to real-life violence. Children exposed to violent programming at a young age have a higher tendency for violent and aggressive behavior later in life.

Just as observational learning may contribute to violent behavior, it may also be used to prevent it. Television networks, for example, have recently made some attempts to limit the amount of violence in programs intended for children. But it is probably not practical to hope to shield children from all violence—after all, even religious texts, the evening news, and classic works such as Shakespeare's *Macbeth* contain scenes of violence. Instead, young people can be informed that most people resolve their conflicts without resorting to violence. Children also can be told that the violence they see on TV shows is not real; it usually involves camera tricks, special effects, and stunts.

A person who has observed a behavior in others does not necessarily begin to display that behavior. There is a difference between what people learn and what they do. Of all the children who are exposed to media violence, only a few of them become violent. Furthermore, it may be that people who choose to watch violent television programs are more likely to be violent in the first place. It is difficult to prove a cause-and-effect relationship based only on correlation. If young people consider violence wrong for them, they will probably not be violent, even if they know how to be violent. The same applies to other behaviors as well.

Reading Check **Describe** What are three examples of observational learning?

Behavior Modification

The principles of cognitive learning can be used to change or modify people's behaviors. Psychologists and others have used these principles to encourage classroom discipline, create token economies, and use personal contracts to change behavior.

Quick Lab

Learning to Dance

Modeling is a type of observational learning that we use to learn many different activities. Do you think you can use modeling to teach others how to dance?

PROCEDURE

❶ Create a set of dance steps with a partner or small group to go along with some selected music. Practice the dance steps and their sequence.

❷ Try to teach another group the dance steps you created by modeling them. Have one member of your group demonstrate the steps. Have the rest of your group observe the learners and take notes on their actions. Did they watch carefully? Did they ask questions or ask to see the steps repeated?

❸ Ask the other group to perform the dance steps you have modeled for them, and take notes on your observations. Were all the steps reproduced in the manner they were presented?

ANALYSIS

1. Draw some conclusions about modeling from your before-and-after observational notes. How effective was modeling in teaching the other group your dance steps?

2. Have a discussion with the other group about how they think they learned the steps and patterns. How did observational learning play a role?

Quick Lab **THINK** central thinkcentral.com

Classroom Discipline Sometimes when we think we are reinforcing one behavior, we are actually unknowingly reinforcing the opposite behavior. For example, teachers who pay attention to students who misbehave may unintentionally give these students greater status in the eyes of some of their classmates. Some teacher training programs show teachers how to use principles of learning to change students' negative patterns of behavior. Teachers are taught to pay attention to students when they are behaving appropriately and to ignore misbehavior that is not harmful to themselves or to others. If misbehavior is ignored, or unreinforced, it should become extinct, according to the theory.

Teacher attention and approval may have more influence in elementary school than in high school. Among adolescents, peer approval can be more powerful than teacher approval and may reinforce misbehavior.

Moreover, ignoring adolescents' misbehavior may only encourage other students to become disruptive also.

Instead of ignoring misbehaving students, teachers may decide to separate them from the rest of the class or group. Teachers and parents frequently use a technique called time-out to discourage misbehavior. Time-out involves placing students in dull, confining environments for a short period of time, such as 10 minutes, when they misbehave. Students who are isolated cannot obtain the attention of peers or teachers, and no reinforcing activities are available.

Token Economies Another method of behavior modification involves the use of token economies. In token economies, people are "paid" to act correctly by earning rewards such as points, plastic chips, or other tokens that can be cashed in for treats, merchandise, or privileges the individual wants. As a result, people may stop doing a certain behavior, or they might begin to perform a desired behavior. For example, a child might receive points for gaining good grades in school, staying out of fights, or arriving at school on time. The points can then be traded for snacks, clothing, or special privileges such as extra computer time. These rewards are the reinforcers. The desired behaviors are rewarded and hopefully result in changes in behavior.

Token economies have been used in schools, prisons, and public housing complexes to change an overall atmosphere and reinforce desired behaviors. Critics of token economies, however, argue that the technique does not effectively change behaviors and that when the token system ends, the unwanted behaviors reappear.

Personal Contracts It is also possible to set up your own behavior modification program by using a personal contract. First, you will need to identify a behavior that you want to change. For example, maybe when you are nervous you tap your foot repeatedly, or perhaps you are always late when meeting friends. Next, set a goal for a new behavior. Finally, create a system of rewards or punishments for yourself to encourage the new behavior.

For example, suppose you tap your foot too much and want to stop that behavior. You might decide to place a rubber band around your wrist. Then, each time you become aware of tapping your foot you snap the rubber band against your wrist. The snapping makes you aware of your behavior, stings a little, and may lead you to tap your foot less often. In this case you have used a punishment to change your behavior. You could also use a reward. Suppose you decide that if you promptly meet your friends five consecutive times you can buy yourself a new shirt. This is behavior modification by using a reward. By using either rewards or punishments, you can alter your behavior.

Reading Check **Explain** How are learning principles used to modify behavior?

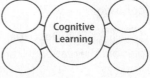

SECTION 3 Assessment

Reviewing Main Ideas and Vocabulary

1. **Describe** What is modeling?

2. **Define** What are token economies?

3. **Explain** Why does observational learning account for much human learning?

Thinking Critically

4. **Elaborate** Give an example of an event in your life in which you applied latent learning.

5. **Develop** What is your opinion about violence in video games and its effect on young people?

6. **Predict** Which technique of behavior modification—reward or punishment—do you think would have the most success?

7. **Make Generalizations** Using your notes and a graphic organizer like the one here, briefly explain the basic techniques used in cognitive learning.

Cognitive Learning

FOCUS ON WRITING

8. **Descriptive** Think of a student behavior that exists at your school and that a teacher or the principal might want to change. Then devise a way to change that behavior by using behavior modification techniques. Write out your plan in a short paper.

Pathways to Rewards

Pathways to Rewards is a program that seeks to help improve the lives of public housing residents in Chicago. The program uses the principles of token economies and has proved to be highly successful in helping people modify their behavior through a system of individual goals and rewards.

The Pathways to Rewards program for residents of Henry Horner Homes, a public housing project in Chicago, was devised to provide structure, support, and incentive for family members of all ages to set and work toward individual goals. These goals may include finding a new job, learning new skills, taking part in extracurricular activities like art or sports, or simply getting more involved and active in the community.

Each month, individuals meet with staff members of the Pathways to Rewards program to set their personal goals and to establish the steps needed to reach those goals. For example, if someone's goal is to find a new job, the plan might include preparing a résumé and submitting five job applications during the month. For a teenager, a goal might be to improve academic grades. The plan might specify getting at least a B on the next math test, spending more time studying, or going to an after-school tutoring program. For younger children, a goal might be to attend an after-school music class.

The program works like a frequent flyer program—participants accrue points for achieving their monthly goals. As individuals meet their goals, they earn points toward rewards of their choice. Points can be used for small rewards or accumulated over time for a larger reward. Rewards include items such as assistance paying utility bills, health club memberships, DVD players, bicycles, and gift cards. To keep earning points, individuals must continually set new and more challenging goals.

Each quarter, program participants celebrate the successful achievement of their goals at a community rewards banquet. These banquets provide public recognition and praise for the success of individuals participating in the program. The Pathways to Rewards staff hand out certificates to each adult and each child who has reached a goal since the last banquet. By celebrating individual achievement, the gathering provides social modeling for the entire community.

In addition to motivating people with the points program, Pathways to Rewards tries to translate individual achievement into community-wide "norms of progress." The program works to establish a new set of community-valued behaviors based on the expectation that everyone can take steps to improve their lives. And it is working. As of the end of 2007, 58 percent of those eligible to participate had chosen to enroll and had met 5,371 separate goals.

The Pathways to Rewards program rewards the achievements of residents of the Henry Horner Homes housing project in Chicago.

Thinking Critically

1. **Infer** Why do you think this program is successful?

2. **Discuss** Some people have criticized the Pathways to Rewards program as being bribes for good behavior. How do you view this criticism?

The PQ4R Method: Learning to Learn

Before You Read

Main Idea
The PQ4R method for studying is a system of active learning based on the work of an educational psychologist.

Reading Focus
1. When should you preview and question new material?
2. Why is it important to read, review, recite, and reflect on material?

Vocabulary
distributed learning
massed learning

TAKING NOTES Use a graphic organizer like this one to take notes on the PQ4R method.

The PQ4R Method	
Step	Actions
1.	
2.	
3.	
4.	
5.	
6.	

The Easy Way Out?

PSYCHOLOGY CLOSE UP *Have educational psychologists created an easy way to study and learn new material?* If you are like most students, you have probably wished at some point in your life that a quick and easy way of studying could be found. After all, wouldn't it be great if you could just rub a magic lamp, wish for success, and then skip all of the hard work that it takes to graduate from school and achieve success?

As you well know, there is no easy way out when it comes to studying and learning. Lots of study methods have been devised, and special machines have even been created to help students learn, but it still requires a great deal of time and effort. Although there is no magical solution, educational psychologists have created an effective study method based on principles of operant and cognitive learning. It is called the PQ4R method. ■

Preview and Question

If you put a sponge in a bathtub, it will soak up water. Many students assume that simply by attending class they will somehow soak up the subject matter of that course. Not so. Students are not sponges, and subjects are not water.

Students learn more when they take an active approach to learning. One such active approach is called the PQ4R method. Based on the work of educational psychologist Francis P. Robinson, the PQ4R method has six steps, previewing, questioning, reading, reflecting, reciting, and reviewing, which you can see on the chart on this page.

Following the steps of the PQ4R method can help you get the most from your textbooks. The first two steps, preview and question, take place before you even start reading.

Preview Previewing the subject matter in a textbook means getting a general picture of what is covered before you begin reading a chapter. If you are in the library or the bookstore looking at books to decide what to read, you may flip rapidly through the pages to get some idea of what the books are about. Thumbing through the pages is one way of previewing the material.

Many textbooks are designed to encourage students to preview chapters before reading them. This book, for instance, has Main Ideas, Reading Focus questions, Vocabulary terms, note-taking activities, section headings and subheadings, Reading Check questions, section assessments, and chapter reviews. If drama and suspense are your goals, read each chapter page by page. But if learning the material and retaining it is your goal, it may be more effective to first read the opening questions, skim the pages, and glance at the questions in the section assessments and chapter reviews.

Familiarity with the overall picture will give you a cognitive map of a chapter. Your map will have many blank areas, but it will have an overall structure. You can fill in the details of the map as you read through the chapter page by page.

Question Learning is made easier when we have goals in mind. When we want to learn something, we become active learners.

THE PQ4R METHOD

The PQ4R method is a system of active learning that has six steps.

1. Preview
Get a general picture of the material before you begin.

2. Question
Change headings into questions.

3. Read
Look for the answers to your questions as you read.

4. Reflect
Try to relate the material to past learning or to personal experience.

5. Recite
Speak the answers to your questions aloud to solidify the information in your mind.

6. Review
Review the material regularly.

One way to create goals is to phrase questions about the subject matter in each chapter. You may wonder what is a good way to come up with questions without reading the chapter first. Look at each heading. Write down all the headings in a notebook. If the book you are reading does not have helpful headings, you might try looking at the first sentence of each paragraph instead. Phrase questions as you proceed. With practice, you will develop questioning skills, and your questions will help you grasp the subject matter.

These sample questions are based on the major and minor headings in the first section of this chapter: What is classical conditioning? What are the basic principles of classical conditioning? You may have come up with different questions after reading the headings. There is always more than one "right" question. As you study, you will learn what works for you.

Reading Check **Compare** How are the steps of previewing and questioning similar?

Read, Reflect, Recite, and Review

After you have previewed the material and questioned what the learning goals are, it is time to read the material and study it more closely. To do that, you can follow the next four steps of the PQ4R method.

Distributed Learning

Studying regularly with others is an example of distributed learning, which distributes the time spent learning so you are not trying to learn everything at once.

Massed Learning

Cramming for a test is not an effective way to study. Studies show that massed learning, or cramming, is rarely successful.

Read Once you have formulated your questions, read the chapter with the purpose of answering them. Doing this will help you focus on the key points of the material. As you answer each question, jot down a few key words in your notebook that will remind you of the answer when you recite and review later. You may find it helpful to keep two columns in your notebook: one column for the questions themselves and the other column for the key words that relate to the answer to each question.

Reflect Reflecting on subject matter is an important way to understand and remember it. As you are reading, think of examples or create mental images of the subject matter.

One way to reflect is to relate new information to old information. For example, you may remember some facts about B. F. Skinner from the first chapter in this textbook. What you learned about him there can serve as a springboard for you to learn about him and about his work in greater detail in this chapter. Take advantage of what you already know.

Another way to reflect is to relate new information to events in your personal life. For instance, you can reflect on classical conditioning by thinking of times when you have experienced it. Then you will find it easier to remember that classical conditioning involves learning through the association of stimuli with each other.

Even if you cannot think of any way to relate the material to your own life, you probably know other people who provide examples of the kinds of behavior discussed throughout this book. To help yourself understand and remember the subject matter of psychology, think of ways in which the behavior of people described in the text and by your teacher is similar to—or different from—the behavior of people you know.

Recite Do you remember when you learned the alphabet? If you were like many children, you probably learned it by saying it—or singing it to the tune of the "Alphabet Song"—over and over again. This is an example of how reciting something can help a person learn. The same thing can work with your textbook. (You will have to make up your own song, however.)

Once you have read a section and answered your questions, reciting the answers will help you understand and remember them.

You can recite aloud or repeat words silently to yourself. You can do your reciting alone or with others. Many students learn by participating in study groups. They quiz each other with their questions, taking turns reciting the answers. Study groups may help you understand new material by having classmates explain it to you in a way that you easily understand. Study partners may share some of their personal reflections with you, which might help you make clearer associations with the material.

Review Learning takes time. As a result, we usually have to repeat or re-read things before we know them well.

To review something effectively, you can use "distributed" learning. **Distributed learning** means studying something regularly so the learning is distributed over several days or weeks. Distributed learning is more effective than **massed learning,** or trying to learn something all at once. Massed learning is also known as "cramming." Distributed learning usually takes no more work than cramming, but it means that you have to plan ahead and try to stick to some sort of schedule.

Review the material you are studying according to a reasonably regular schedule, such as once a week. Reviewing leads to relearning, and relearning on a regular schedule is easier than learning something the first time. By reviewing material regularly, we understand and remember it better.

It may seem like a large time commitment to study regularly when there is no apparent immediate need to do so, but it will reduce the amount of time you need to study right before a test. It may also help reduce the amount of anxiety you feel about the test the day before (negative reinforcement) because you know that you have already mastered at least some of the material. And it also helps keep you prepared for pop quizzes.

Once you have set aside enough time to review the material, you will need to figure out what techniques will help you most. One way to review the material is to go back to the questions and key words in your notebook. Cover up the answer column and read the questions in the left column as though they were a quiz. Recite your answers and check them against the key words in the right column. When you forget an answer or get an answer wrong, go back and re-read the subject matter in the textbook.

Another way of reviewing the subject matter, as already mentioned, is for you and your classmates to quiz each other. Reviewing the material as a group can help everyone understand the material on a deeper level. By taking a more active approach to learning, you may find that you are earning higher grades and gaining more enjoyment from the learning process.

Reading Check **Summarize** What are the "four Rs" in the PQ4R method?

SECTION 4 Assessment

Online Quiz **THINK** central   thinkcentral.com

Reviewing Main Ideas and Vocabulary

1. **Recall** Why should you use the PQ4R method to create questions from your chapter headings?

2. **Identify** Which of the steps in the PQ4R method helps you relate new information to old information?

Thinking Critically

3. **Explain** Why is distributed learning better than massed learning?

4. **Develop** Prepare a learning and studying schedule based on the PQ4R method for yourself for one of your classes.

5. **Analyze** Which parts of the PQ4R method are examples of types of operant conditioning?

6. **Sequence** Using your notes and a graphic organizer like the one below, explain the process of studying using the PQ4R method. Then circle the step that you think is the most critical to learning and retaining information.

FOCUS ON WRITING

7. **Expository** Suppose you have been asked to write a summary of effective study methods for new students at your school. Write a short summary that includes information from this section.

Reinforcement and Discouragement

How can positive reinforcement and discouragement affect people's behavior and performance?

Reading and Activity Workbook

Use the workbook to complete this experiment.

1. Introduction

In this experiment, you will study the effects of positive reinforcement and discouragement on behavior. You will work with your classmates to conduct an experiment on the number of sit-ups that students complete in three different situations: with no feedback; with positive reinforcement; and with discouragement. After you have completed the experiment, you will analyze the data and discuss the results as a class. To complete this experiment, follow the steps below.

■ With your classmates, review the steps of the scientific method. Then review the material in this chapter on operant conditioning. Write down the definition of positive reinforcement, along with a few main points about it.

■ For this experiment, the research question has been established for you: what effects do positive reinforcement and discouragement have on behavior? Discuss this question with your classmates.

■ Next, form a hypothesis. The hypothesis in this experiment might be that positive reinforcement will increase the number of sit-ups that students complete and discouragement will decrease the number. Or, it might be that positive reinforcement and discouragement will have no significant effect on the number of sit-ups students are able to perform. As a class, determine what your hypothesis is and write it down.

2. Preparing for the Experiment

In preparation, you and your teacher will need to find research subjects, assign roles, find a location, and create a schedule for conducting the experiment.

■ With your teacher, identify about 30 students from another class to serve as research subjects. The research subjects must commit to participate for about one hour on three separate days. You might want to find a physical education class that will agree to participate.

■ For the experiment to be valid, the participants must not be told its purpose. Instead, tell them that the purpose of the experiment is to analyze how someone's heart rate increases immediately after exercising. (At the conclusion of the experiment, participants will be informed of the real purpose and results of the experiment.)

■ Once you have enough participants, assign them randomly to three different groups—Group A, Group B, and Group C. In addition, give each participant a unique number for the study, such as Participant 1, Participant 2, and so on.

■ Next, assign roles for you and your classmates to fill during the experiment. The chart below shows the roles that are needed. There will be three stations for the experiment each day, and you will need one Timer, Assistant, Recorder, and Pulsetaker for each station. You will also need several Encouragers for one station and several Discouragers for another.

ROLES AND RESPONSIBILITIES	
Role	**Task**
Timers	Call "start" and "stop" as participants complete sit-ups
Assistants	Help hold participants' feet down as they complete sit-ups
Recorders	Count and record the number of sit-ups each participant completes
Pulsetakers	Pretend to take each participant's pulse before and after sit-ups
Encouragers	Give encouragement and positive reinforcement during sit-ups
Discouragers	Give discouragement to participants as they complete sit-ups

EXPERIMENT SCHEDULE

	Group A	Group B	Group C
Day 1	Control group	Gets positive reinforcement	Gets discouragement
Day 2	Gets positive reinforcement	Gets discouragement	Control group
Day 3	Gets discouragement	Control group	Gets positive reinforcement

◾ You will also need to find a suitable location to hold the experiment. It is important that the three stations are located far apart so the participants cannot see or hear what is going on at another station. For example, you might want to locate one station in the gym, another station outside, and the final station in a separate room.

◾ Finally, you will need to schedule the three days on which the experiment will be conducted and inform the participants of the appropriate time and meeting place.

3. Conducting the Experiment

To conduct the experiment, set up the three stations and follow the Experiment Schedule above. On Day 1, the three groups will attend the three stations as follows.

◾ Group A will be the control group. Have each participant in the group enter the station one at a time. The Pulsetaker will pretend to take the participant's pulse. The Timer will then call "start" and the participant will perform as many sit-ups as possible in two minutes. The Timer will then call "stop." The Assistant will help hold the participant's feet down as he or she performs sit-ups, and the Recorder will record the number of sit-ups performed. No talking will occur while the participant is doing the sit-ups. As soon as the two minutes are over, the Pulsetaker will again pretend to take the participant's pulse.

◾ Group B will receive encouragement and reinforcement. Each participant will be asked to complete as many sit-ups as he or she can during the two-minute period, just as in the control group. However, while the sit-ups are being performed, several Encouragers will give each participant positive reinforcement by saying things like, "Good job," and "Keep it up—you can do it!"

◾ Group C will receive discouragement. Each participant will be asked to complete as many sit-ups as they can during the two-minute period, just as in the control group. However, while the sit-ups are being performed, several Discouragers will say things like "This is stupid" and "You don't really need to try if you don't want to."

◾ On Days 2 and 3, the three groups will rotate to the different stations according to the Experiment Schedule.

4. Analysis and Conclusion

After the experiment is over, it is time to analyze the data with your classmates and draw some conclusions.

◾ Compare each participant's performance at each station. In general, did performance go up with positive reinforcement and go down with discouragement? If so, by how much? If there was a difference, was it significant? You might want to try to calculate the average increase for each participant after positive reinforcement and average decrease after discouragement.

◾ After your analysis, invite the study participants into your classroom for a discussion. Begin by informing them of the true purpose of the experiment. Next, share the results and analysis with them and ask for their thoughts on the experiment. Did they feel like positive reinforcement helped them perform better? Was discouragement a significant deterrent? How did they feel at each of the stations during the experiment?

◾ Finally, revisit your hypothesis and draw some conclusions about the effects of positive reinforcement and discouragement on behavior. Based on your results, can you make any generalizations about the effects of positive reinforcement and discouragement in general?

Comprehension and Critical Thinking

SECTION 1 (pp. 158–162)

1. a. Identify Main Ideas How do both people and animals learn responses through classical conditioning?

b. Describe How do generalization and discrimination help people and animals adapt to their environments?

c. Make Judgments Which application of classical conditioning do you think is most likely to be unpleasant? Why?

SECTION 2 (pp. 164–171)

2. a. Define What is the basic difference between positive and negative reinforcers?

b. Contrast How does a fixed-interval schedule of reinforcement differ from a fixed-ratio schedule?

c. Support a Position What is your opinion about the use of punishment as a method of altering behavior?

SECTION 3 (pp. 172–176)

3. a. Recall What are two types of learning that involve cognitive factors?

b. Explain How does latent learning take place?

c. Support a Position What is your opinion about the effects of media violence on children?

SECTION 4 (pp. 178–181)

4. a. Identify What are the six steps of the PQ4R method?

b. Summarize Briefly explain the purpose of each step in the PQ4R method.

c. Analyze Why do you think an active approach to learning can help people learn and retain information more effectively?

Reviewing Vocabulary

Identify the term or phrase from the chapter that best fits each of the following descriptions.

5. a type of learning that involves stimulus-response connections

6. a type of learning in which people or animals learn to do or not do certain things because of the results

7. a learned avoidance of a particular food

8. learning that remains hidden until it is needed

9. a stimulus that causes a response that is automatic and not learned

10. a way of teaching complex behaviors in which one first reinforces the small steps in an activity

11. any method or activity that helps a person relax

12. stimuli that increases the frequency of a desired behavior

13. a type of learning in which one stimulus calls forth the response that is usually called forth by another stimulus

14. the act of responding in the same ways to stimuli that seem to be similar

15. a timetable for the frequency of reinforcement

INTERNET ACTIVITY ✳

16. The theories of psychologist Lev Vygotsky, in addition to those of Albert Bandura, have influenced our understanding of learning in children. Use the Internet to find the basic ideas of both Vygotsky and Bandura. Then write a page comparing and contrasting their views on how learning takes place in the lives of children.

Psychology in Your Life

17. Think about a time in your life in which you learned something through observational learning. What did you learn? Was simple observation sufficient, or did you need more than that? Write a short summary explaining what you learned and how important observational learning was to your understanding.

SKILLS ACTIVITY: INTERPRETING CARTOONS

Study the cartoon below. Then use the information to help you answer the questions that follow.

Dr I P PAVLOV

"I DON'T KNOW ABOUT YOU, BUT THAT BELL'S STARTING TO PUT ME OFF MY FOOD!"

© Cartoon Stock

18. Infer What effect is the conditioned stimulus having in this cartoon?

19. Elaborate How would you explain this cartoon to an individual who knew nothing about classical conditioning?

WRITING FOR AP PSYCHOLOGY

Use your knowledge of learning theory to answer the question below. Do not simply list facts. Present a clear argument based on your critical analysis of the question, using appropriate psychological terminology.

20. Think about the impact role models have on individuals. Explain how the following psychological theories of learning might explain the impact that role models have on certain individuals.

- Observational learning
- Modeling
- Reinforcement

Connecting Online

Visit thinkcentral.com for review and enrichment activities related to this chapter.

THINK central

Quiz and Review

ONLINE QUIZZES
Take a practice quiz for each section in this chapter.

WEBQUEST
Complete a structured Internet activity for this chapter.

QUICK LAB
Reinforce a key concept with a short lab activity.

APPLYING WHAT YOU'VE LEARNED
Review and apply your knowledge by completing a project-based assessment.

Activities

eACTIVITIES
Complete chapter Internet activities for enrichment.

INTERACTIVE FEATURE
Explore an interactive version of a key feature in this chapter.

KEEP IT CURRENT
Link to current news and research in psychology.

Online Textbook

Click for More

Learn more about key topics in this chapter.

H.M. and his MISSING Memories

In the twentieth century, surgeons experimented with brain surgery to reduce seizures in epilepsy patients. In these now-rare surgeries, one or both of the patient's temporal lobes were removed to stop the seizures. Today we know that the temporal lobe has important functions in memory, speech, and hearing. The early surgeries on seizure patients were key to this discovery.

One of the most famous of these surgery cases was a man known as H.M. This patient suffered from severe epileptic seizures that began at the age of 16 and worsened as he reached adulthood. By the time he was 27, he could no longer live a normal life. At that point, he agreed to undergo temporal lobe surgery. During the procedure, surgeons also removed part of his hippocampus—a small structure that lies within the temporal lobes.

Following the operation, H.M.'s personality and mental functioning seemed to be normal. However, as time went on, it became increasingly difficult for him to

Viewing a familiar scene can trigger memories of people and events that you associate with that place.

process new information. His memory of events during the year leading up to the operation was weak, and his ability to learn and store new information was almost nonexistent. For example, two years after the surgery, H.M. thought he was still 27 years old. His memory was so poor that he forgot something as soon as he was distracted.

When he moved with his family to a new home, H.M. could not remember his new address or how to reach it. When his uncle died, he expressed appropriate grief at the loss. However, he soon began asking about his uncle and wanted to know why he did not visit. Each time he was told that his uncle was dead, H.M. grieved as if he were hearing the information for the first time.

Formal testing showed that H.M. could remember verbal information for as long as 15 minutes if he was allowed to rehearse it. However, the operation had made H.M. unable to transfer information from his short-term memory to his long-term memory. As soon as his short-term memory capacity reached its limit, or he was distracted from rehearsing new information in his short-term memory, he would forget the

CHAPTER 7

MEMORY

information. His capacity to remember non-verbal material was even more impaired. With or without distractions, he forgot even simple figures, such as circles, squares, and triangles.

Despite his severe memory loss, H.M. retained a limited capacity to learn, although the learning process was very slow and difficult. For example, H.M. had to exert great effort and undergo 155 trials to learn to navigate a very short visual maze, one which most people mastered after only a couple of trials. Surprisingly, a week later H.M. remembered what he had painstakingly learned. Two years later he still retained some of what he had learned: It took him only 39 trials to relearn his way through the maze—116 fewer than he had needed originally.

H.M. showed learning ability in other situations as well. When asked to trace a drawing of a star by looking at its reflection in a mirror, he completed the task successfully. In addition, he retained what he had learned. For example, on the second and third days, he performed as well on the first trial of the day as he had on the last trial of the day before. That was evidence that there was no memory loss from day to day. Apparently, H.M.'s short-term memory was intact, but he was unable to save items from short-term memory into long-term memory. His motor skills were unimpaired.

From cases such as that of H.M., psychologists have begun to shed light on the mysteries of memory. They have learned that memory is a complex set of functions performed by specific areas of the brain.

What do you think?

1. Of the many abilities that make up what we know as memory, which did H.M. lose and which did he retain?

2. Do you think the surgery that cured H.M. of seizures made his life better?

Chapter at a Glance

SECTION 1: Memory Classifications and Processes

■ Memory can be classed as explicit or implicit. Two main types of explicit memory are episodic and semantic.

■ Memory of sensory input involves three distinct functions: encoding, storage, and retrieval.

SECTION 2: Three Stages of Memory

■ In sensory memory, each of the senses records its input in a distinct register.

■ Sense data that receive attention are retained in short-term memory.

■ Information from short-term memory can be stored in long-term memory if it is encoded and linked to other stored information.

■ Information can be quickly retrieved from long-term memory because long-term memory is structured, or organized.

SECTION 3: Forgetting and Memory Improvement

■ The three basic remembering tasks are recognition, recall, and relearning.

■ Much of what we think of as remembering actually involves reconstructing ideas based on associations.

■ Forgetting, or memory failure, can be caused by a malfunction in encoding, storage, or retrieval.

■ Forgetting can occur at any stage of memory.

■ Knowledge of how remembering and forgetting occur has led to practical techniques for improving memory.

Memory Classifications and Processes

Before You Read

Main Idea
Memory is the process of encoding, storing, and retrieving information. Memory includes factual and general information, experiences of events, and skills.

Reading Focus
1. What are the three kinds of memory?
2. How does encoding of memories work?
3. What are the processes of memory storage?
4. What factors affect memory retrieval?

Vocabulary
memory
episodic memory
semantic memory
explicit memory
implicit memory
encoding
storage
maintenance rehearsal
elaborative rehearsal
retrieval
context-dependent memories
state-dependent memories

TAKING NOTES Use a graphic organizer like this one to take notes on the types and processes of memory.

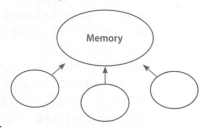

Memories of Tea AND Cakes

PSYCHOLOGY CLOSE UP

How did a small cake and a cup of tea elicit memories of a garden? Marcel Proust was a French writer obsessed with memories. Proust's genius was his ability to detail the thoughts and emotions he experienced as he remembered people, scenes, and events from his childhood. In his multi-volume book *Remembrance of Things Past*, Proust spends many pages telling about dunking a madeleine—a cake-like cookie—in a cup of tea and the cascade of feelings and images that passed through his mind as a result.

> *Once I had recognized the taste of the crumb of madeleine soaked in her decoction of lime-flowers which my aunt used to give me . . . immediately the old grey house upon the street, where her room was, rose up like the scenery of a theatre to attach itself to the little pavilion, opening on to the garden, which had been built out behind it for my parents.*

The mysteries of memory have fascinated people throughout history. How is it that we can have vivid memories of events that occurred many years ago, but we sometimes cannot remember what happened yesterday? How can we feel certain that we remember events that never actually happened? Why can two people experience the same event but remember it completely differently? In this section you will learn some of what researchers have discovered about what memory is and how it works. ■

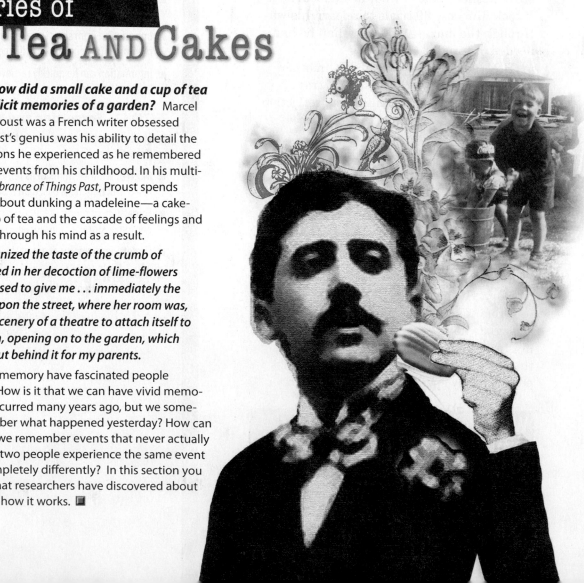

Three Kinds of Memory

What is memory? **Memory** is the process by which we recollect prior experiences and information and skills learned in the past. There are different kinds of memory. One way to classify memory is according to the different kinds of information it contains: events, general knowledge, and skills.

Episodic Memory **Episodic memory** is memory of a specific event. The event took place in the person's presence, and the person experienced the event. Your memories of what you ate for dinner last night and of your last quiz are examples of episodic memory.

Some events are so important that it seems as if a flash goes off and we photograph the scene in every detail. These are called flashbulb memories. For instance, you will probably never forget the first time you felt like you were in love. Maybe you can recall how the sky and the trees looked that day. Maybe you were a bit kinder to everyone. Maybe you laugh now when you recall that you were convinced that all of life's problems suddenly seemed solved.

On the other hand, you will probably never laugh when you recall the events of September 11, 2001. You may remember exactly where you were and what you were doing when you heard that one tower of the World Trade Center in New York City was in flames. Most people who witnessed the events of that day remember turning on their TV and watching in horror as the second tower was struck by an airplane, and it became clear that terrorism was at work. Our minds can still see the lower part of Manhattan covered with black smoke and ashen debris after the towers collapsed, and the bewildered people rushing away from the horrible scene.

There are several reasons why certain memories become etched in our minds when the "flashbulb" goes off. One reason is the distinctness of the memories. We pay more attention to events that have special meaning for us. Such events usually arouse powerful feelings. Also, we tend to think about flashbulb memories often, especially if they are positive ones—a first love, the birth of a child, or a special accomplishment.

Sometimes places or events make an impression on us—and thus become flashbulb memories—because they are connected to other events that were important at the time, such as a major disaster or tragedy. When we think of the important event later, it triggers memories of things that were connected to it. For example, many older Americans have flashbulb memories of the 1963 assassination of President John F. Kennedy.

Semantic Memory Your memory of facts, words, concepts, and so on—most of what you would say you know—is **semantic memory.** The word *semantic* means having to do with meaning and language. Much of what you learn in your classes at school becomes part of your semantic memory. For example, you probably learned and remember that George Washington was the first president of the United States.

Unlike with episodic memory, we usually do not remember when we acquired the information in our semantic memory. We probably cannot remember precisely when we first learned about George Washington, for instance. So, too, you remember the alphabet and that human beings breathe oxygen, but you probably do not remember where, when, or how you learned those things.

Episodic and semantic memories are both examples of **explicit memory.** Things that are explicit are clear, or clearly stated or explained. An explicit memory is memory of specific information. That information may be autobiographical (episodic), or it may refer to general knowledge (semantic).

Implicit Memory The opposite of *explicit* is *implicit,* and another kind of memory is **implicit memory.** Things that are implicit are implied, or not clearly stated. Implicit memories include practiced skills and learned habits. Knowing how to throw a ball, for example, is learned implicitly: you know how to throw, but you could not list out every step in the throwing motion, nor could you describe exactly how you change your motion to throw near or far. Other skills learned implicitly include riding a bicycle, skipping rope, typing, and playing a musical instrument. Once such a skill has been learned, it usually stays with you for many years, perhaps even a lifetime—even if you do not use it very often.

Reading Check **Summarize** What are the three main types of memory?

Encoding

You have just read about three different types of memory. There are also three major processes of memory. The first is encoding.

Imagine writing an essay or a story on a computer. You use the keyboard to type information in the form of letters. The information is stored on a hard drive. But if you were to look at the hard drive under a microscope, you would not be able to see the letters you typed. This is because the computer translates the information into a form in which it can be used. The translation of information into a form in which it can be used is called **encoding.** For both computers and humans, encoding is the first stage of processing information.

Initially, we receive information through our senses physically—such as when sound waves cause the eardrum to vibrate. In encoding we convert the stimulus into psychological formats that can be represented mentally. To do so, we use different types of codes. To see what kind of code you use, write this string of letters on a piece of paper:

OTTFFSSENT

Look at the string for 30 seconds and memorize as much of it as you can. Then continue reading this section to find out which type of code—visual, acoustic, or semantic—you used to remember the letters.

Visual and Acoustic Codes When you tried to memorize the letters, did you attempt to see them in your mind as a picture? If you did, you used a visual code. That is, you tried to form a mental picture of the letters in your mind.

Another way that you may have tried to remember the letters might have been to read the list to yourself and repeat it several times. That is, you may have said the letters (either out loud or silently) one after another: O, T, T, and so on. This way of trying to remember the letters uses an acoustic (or auditory) code. An acoustic code records the letters in your memory as a sequence of sounds.

Semantic Codes Still another way that you may have tried to remember the list might have been to try making sense of the letters, that is, to figure out what they might mean. For example, you may have noticed that the last four letters spelled the word *sent*. You may then have tried to see if the letters made up a phrase or sentence with the word *sent* in it. The word *semantic* means "relating to meaning," so this type of code is called a semantic code. A semantic code represents information in terms of its meaning.

What you may not have realized when you examined the list is that the letters OTTFFSSENT stand for the first letter of the series of numbers from one (O) through ten

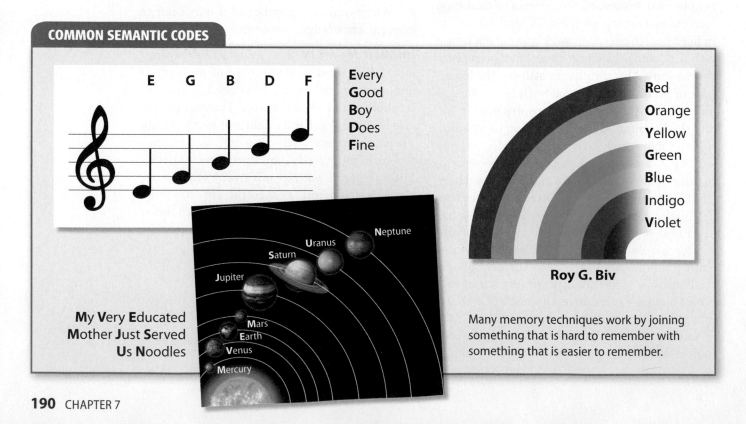

COMMON SEMANTIC CODES

E G B D F

Every
Good
Boy
Does
Fine

My Very Educated
Mother Just Served
Us Noodles

Neptune
Uranus
Saturn
Jupiter
Mars
Earth
Venus
Mercury

Red
Orange
Yellow
Green
Blue
Indigo
Violet

Roy G. Biv

Many memory techniques work by joining something that is hard to remember with something that is easier to remember.

(T)—that is, One, Two, Three, Four, Five, Six, Seven, Eight, Nine, Ten. Obviously, if you had known that in the first place, remembering the letters would have been much easier. By using semantic (meaningful) codes, you can memorize items more easily and will probably remember them for a longer amount of time than you would otherwise.

Reading Check **Identify** What different types of coding does the mind use?

Storage

After information is encoded, it must be stored. **Storage,** the second process of memory, is the maintenance of encoded information over a period of time. As with encoding, human storage of information is not all that different from a computer's storage of information. With a computer, however, the user must instruct the machine to save information in its memory. Otherwise, the information will be lost when the user shuts down the computer. People who want to store new information in their memory use a variety of strategies. These strategies are related closely to the strategies people use for encoding.

Maintenance Rehearsal Suppose you wanted to remember a name, address, or phone number. How would you do it? One way would be to keep repeating it to yourself to keep it alive in your memory. If a long time passed before you could find your address book and a pen, you might need to repeat it several times. Such mechanical or rote repetition of information in order to keep from forgetting it is called **maintenance rehearsal.** The more time spent on maintenance rehearsal, the longer the information will be remembered. Actors know this well. That is why they rehearse their lines until the lines are second nature.

Maintenance rehearsal requires only "surface processing"; in other words, it does not make information meaningful by connecting it to past learning. For that reason, it is actually a poor way to put information in permanent storage.

Elaborative Rehearsal A more effective way to remember new information is to make it meaningful through "deep processing," that is, by relating it to information you already know well. This method, called **elaborative rehearsal,** is widely used in education because it has proved to be a much more effective method than maintenance rehearsal. For example, language arts and foreign language teachers recommend elaborative rehearsal when they encourage students to use new vocabulary words in sentences instead of just repeating the individual words alone.

Organizational Systems Stored memories become organized and arranged in your mind for future use. If you are a fairly organized person, you probably have a particular place in your home for each of your possessions. When you bring items home, you probably do not just throw them on the floor or stick them haphazardly in a closet; instead, you sort them and put them in their places. That way you have a better chance of finding them when you need them. You have probably learned from experience that not knowing where your possessions are means that you end up spending a lot of time looking for them when you need them.

In some ways, your memory resembles a vast storehouse of files and file cabinets in which you store what you learn and need to remember. The more you learn, the more files you need and the more elaborate your filing system becomes. When you started attending school, for instance, the first facts you learned about American history may have been about Pocahontas, the Pilgrims, or George Washington. At first, your "American history" file probably had only a few pieces of information in it.

However, as you progressed and learned more about American history, you had to expand your filing system. As you learned about other presidents, you found new ways to file the information in your memory. You may have filed the presidents in chronological order, that is, in the order in which they held office. In that file you put Washington first, followed by others such as Jefferson, Lincoln, and Theodore Roosevelt. You may also have filed more recent presidents according to the events in American history with which they are associated, such as Franklin Roosevelt with the New Deal and World War II, Richard Nixon with Watergate, and George W. Bush with the war in Iraq.

As your memory develops, it organizes the information you learn into files and then into files within files. Your memory organizes the new information it receives into certain groups, or classes, according to common features. For example, all mammals share certain features. They are warmblooded, and they nurse their young. If you knew that whales are warmblooded and nurse their young, you probably filed them in your memory as mammals. If you did not know those facts, you might have filed them as fish because they swim and live in the water.

Classes can contain smaller classes and can also be part of a larger class. For example, the class mammals includes monkeys, rats, and other warmblooded, nursing creatures. At the same time, mammals are part of a larger class—animals. Much of our semantic memory that is stored as we get older and acquire more knowledge is organized into groups or classes.

Filing Errors Our ability to remember information—even when we are healthy and functioning well—is subject to error. Some memory errors occur because we "file" information incorrectly. Psychologists have discovered that when we classify pieces of information accurately—that is, when we place items in the correct files—we have a much better chance of recalling them accurately. Nevertheless, filing systems are not perfect. Have you ever misplaced a paper? For example, have you ever brought home a science paper and mistakenly filed it in your history folder? Our mental filing systems sometimes make similar errors.

Reading Check **Explain** How does elaborative rehearsal help your memory use organizational systems?

Retrieval

The third memory process is called retrieval. **Retrieval** consists of locating stored information and returning it to conscious thought. Retrieving information stored in our memory is like retrieving information stored in a computer. To retrieve information stored in a computer, we have to know the name of the file and the rules for retrieving it. Retrieval of information stored in our memory requires a similar knowledge of proper procedures.

Some information in our memory is so familiar that it is readily available and almost impossible to forget. Examples of this type of information include our own names and those of our friends and family members. But when it comes to trying to remember lines from a play or a mathematical formula, retrieval may be more difficult.

Do you remember the list of letters discussed earlier in the section? What were they? Write them down now. . . .

Now think about how you retrieved that string of letters from your memory. Notice that the method of retrieval you used depends on the way you encoded the string to begin with. For instance, if you used an auditory code, then, when you tried to recall the string of letters, you thought to yourself something like "ought-fissent," hearing the sounds in your mind, and then you tried to spell that string of sounds. But you might easily have made a mistake.

However, if you remember the semantic code that the letters stand for the numbers 1 through 10, you can accurately recall, or retrieve, the letters. Using this semantic code may be more complex than hearing the list in your mind, and it might take you a little longer to reconstruct the list of letters, but using the 1–10 device gives you a much better chance of remembering the letters—and of remembering them for a longer time.

Before reading on, take this very brief spelling quiz: Which of the following words is spelled correctly—*retrieval* or *retreival*? Even if you know how the word is pronounced, saying the word to yourself (using an acoustic code) will not help you remember the correct spelling, which is retri*e*val. How might you go about remembering the correct spelling? Repeating it over and over (maintenance rehearsal) is certainly one way. However, a much better way would be to remember a spelling rule, such as "*i* before *e* except after *c*," as a semantic code. That rule enables you to reconstruct the correct spelling without having to memorize the order of the letters.

Context-Dependent Memory Have you ever been to a place that brought back old memories? Perhaps you went back to your elementary school or to a neighborhood where you once lived. The memories that came back to you in that place are called **context-dependent memories.** The context of a memory is the situation in which a person first had the experience being remembered. Such memories are dependent on the place where they were encoded and stored. If you had not returned to the place where your memories were encoded, you probably would not have retrieved them.

A fascinating experiment in context-dependent memory involved students who belonged to a swimming club. Some students were asked to memorize lists of words while they were in the swimming pool. Other students tried to memorize the lists while they were out of the water. Later, the students who had studied the lists in the water did a better job of remembering them when they were in the water again. Students who had studied out of the water, on the other hand, remembered more words when they were dry. These findings suggest that the ability to retrieve memories is greater when people are in the place or situation in which they stored the memories to begin with.

Another study of context-dependent memory found that students did better on tests when they studied in the room where the test was given. If possible, try to do some studying for your tests in the classrooms where you will take the tests. Of course, you should study in a variety of other settings as well to help you retain the material after the tests are over.

When police and lawyers ask witnesses to describe a crime, they ask the witnesses to describe the scene as clearly and with as much detail as possible. By doing this, witnesses are better able to recall details that they might otherwise have forgotten. Police sometimes take witnesses to the scene of the crime in the hope that such visits will improve their memories of what they witnessed.

You might remember going to a party at which you heard a song that suddenly brought back memories of being in the seventh grade. That is because seventh grade is when you heard the song (probably many times), encoded it, and stored it in your memory. Hearing the song again brought back context-dependent memories connected to that earlier period in your life. In fact, one reason some people like to hear familiar music is that it brings back old and happy memories.

Three Basic Processes of Memory

In order to be remembered, sensory input must go through the three basic processes of memory: encoding, storage, and retrieval.

1. Encoding
- Encoding is translating sensory information into a form in which it can be stored.
- Encoding is the first process of remembering.
- Visual coding enables information to be stored as pictures.
- Acoustic coding enables information to be stored as sounds.
- Semantic coding enables information to be stored as meanings.

2. Storage
- Storage is the maintenance of encoded information over time.
- Storage is the second process of remembering.
- Storage is achieved through two types of rehearsal: maintenance rehearsal and elaborative rehearsal.
- Maintenance rehearsal uses repetition to aid storage.
- Elaborative rehearsal aids storage by fitting new information into an organizational system.
- Elaborative rehearsal is generally more secure than maintenance rehearsal.

3. Retrieval
- Retrieval is locating stored information and returning it to conscious thought.
- Retrieval is the third and final process of remembering.
- A memory is context-dependent if it can be retrieved more readily when the person is in a similar situation or environment as when the information was learned.
- A memory is state-dependent if it can be retrieved more readily when the person is in a similar emotional state as when the information was learned.

State-Dependent Memory Not only do people tend to retrieve memories better when they are in the same place they were in when they first stored the memories, but people also retrieve memories better when they are in the same emotional state they were in when they first stored the memories. Memories that are retrieved because the mood in which they were originally encoded is re-created are called **state-dependent memories.** For example, feelings of happiness tend to bring back memories from other times when we were happy, while feelings of sadness can trigger memories from other sad times.

ACADEMIC VOCABULARY

phenomenon an observable event or occurrence

To demonstrate this phenomenon, psychologist Gordon Bower conducted experiments in which study participants were instructed, while in a hypnotic trance, to experience happy or sad moods. Then, while still in the trance, the participants tried to memorize a list of words. People who had studied the list while in a happy mood were better able to recall it when they were put into a happy state again. People who had studied the list while in a sad mood showed better recall when placed back in a sad mood. Bower's explanation of these results is that mood influences memory.

Not only is memory better when people are in the same mood as when the memory was acquired, it is also better when people are in the same state of consciousness. Drugs, for example, alter one's state of consciousness and thus result in state-dependent memories. Things that happen to a person while under the influence of a drug may be remembered most accurately when the person is again under the influence of that drug.

On the Tip of the Tongue Memories can sometimes be difficult to retrieve. Trying to retrieve memories that are not very well organized or are incomplete can be highly frustrating. Sometimes we come so close to retrieving information that it seems as though the information is on the "tip of the tongue." Psychologists call this the tip-of-the-tongue phenomenon or the feeling-of-knowing experience. You feel you know something. In fact, you are sure you know it. However, you just cannot seem to verbalize it.

Because the files in our memory have labels, so to speak, that include both the sounds and the meanings of words, we often try to retrieve memories that are on the tip of the tongue by using either acoustic or semantic cues. Sometimes we try to summon up words that are similar in sound or meaning to a word that is on the tip of the tongue. We might make a remark like: "I can't think of her name. It starts with an M. Mary? Maria? Something like that."

Reading Check **Contrast** What clues can help you remember a context-dependent memory? a state-dependent memory?

SECTION 1 Assessment

Online Quiz THINK central thinkcentral.com

Reviewing Main Ideas and Vocabulary

1. **Summarize** What happens in each of the three main stages or processes of memory?

2. **Identify** What are the two types of explicit memory?

3. **Describe** How do organizational systems help the mind store memories? How do they help the mind retrieve memories?

Thinking Critically

4. **Contrast** What are the differences between maintenance rehearsal and elaborative rehearsal?

5. **Analyze** Explain why both episodic and semantic memories are classified as explicit.

6. **Compare and Contrast** In this section, human memory is likened to computer memory and to a filing system. In what ways might human memory be *unlike* these things?

7. **Analyze** Using your notes and a graphic organizer like the one here, identify the different memory tasks that the brain must perform. Give an example of each combination of memory stage and type of memory content.

Processes	Types		
	Episodic	Semantic	Implicit
1.			
2.			

FOCUS ON WRITING

8. **Expository** Think of a time you had a tip-of-the-tongue experience. Describe what you did to try to retrieve the memory, and explain why you think this worked or did not work.

Unreliable Memories, Unreliable Witnesses

"Misleading details can be planted into a person's memory for an event that actually occurred. It also is possible to plant entirely false memories," according to Elizabeth Loftus and Daniel Bernstein (Bernstein et al., 2005). For example, they persuaded adults to avoid eating eggs by getting them to remember—falsely—that eggs had made them sick in childhood. False memories about eggs may seem trivial, but what if the false memories are of suffering child abuse or witnessing a murder?

Elizabeth Loftus has been studying the reliability of memory for over 30 years.

Elizabeth Loftus's work has been key in showing how memories are constructed or reconstructed from a variety of sources. In one major study on false memory, Loftus found that about one-fifth of subjects could be influenced to "recall" false childhood memories of being lost in a shopping mall (Loftus, 1995). Loftus has shown not only that false memories exist but also that feeling sure about a memory does not prove that it is reliable.

One factor in false memory is source confusion—the inability to recall the source of a piece of information. If you cannot recall how you got an idea, you cannot know if the idea itself is reliable. Any idea in short-term memory, whether true or false, can be processed for storage in long-term memory and can be elaborated and modified to "make sense" alongside your other beliefs.

Researchers Valerie Reyna and Chuck Brainerd conceive two types of memory (Brainerd and Reyna, 2005). A "verbatim trace" is a precise representation of what you actually experienced. A "gist trace" represents the meaning of an experienced event and so is much more liable to error. Scans of brain activity during memory tasks showed that these two types of memory are recorded in two different parts of the brain. Further, children depend more heavily on the part of the brain that records verbatim traces. Since the capacity for gist trace develops over time, Reyna and Brainerd conclude that children's testimony can sometimes be more reliable than adults'.

Studies like these lead scientists to expect that brain scans may someday test the reliability of witnesses. We already know that different portions of the brain are activated depending on whether a person has seen the exact same thing before. If a person is shown an object unique to a crime scene, neuroimaging can (in theory) prove whether the person was there.

In the meantime, psychological research is helping train police investigators to avoid interviewing techniques that can mislead witnesses. One example is pressing for additional details when a witness has already expressed uncertainty.

Modern knowledge about the unreliability of memory means that even the testimony of the most honest witness must be carefully scrutinized.

Thinking Critically

1. **Explain** How can you tell if a "memory" is false or inaccurate?
2. **Discuss** According to Loftus, "Who we are may be shaped by our memories, but our memories are shaped by who we are and what we have been led to believe." What do you think she means?

Three Stages of Memory

Before You Read

Main Idea

The three stages of memory storage are sensory input, short-term or working memory, and long-term memory.

Reading Focus

1. What are the three types of sensory memory?

2. How does short-term memory work?

3. How do schemas affect long-term memory?

Vocabulary

sensory memory
iconic memory
eidetic imagery
echoic memory
short-term memory
primacy effect
recency effect
chunking
interference
long-term memory
schemas

TAKING NOTES Use a graphic organizer like this one to note ideas about each stage of memory.

Stages of Memory		
Sensory	Short-Term	Long-Term

a **rose** *to remember*

i before e, except after c
Her hair was long, and the sun was in her eyes.
She was wearing a red dress,
milk, eggs, bread . . .

PSYCHOLOGY CLOSE UP

How could roses affect one's ability to remember facts? In an interesting study, research subjects played a game in which they had to remember the locations of pairs of cards. They were presented with a burst of rose scent each time they learned a pair correctly. One half hour after the game they were sent to sleep. While the subjects were in the deepest phase of sleep, researchers exposed some of them to more pulses of rose scent. The next day, the participants played the game again. Those who had smelled the roses while asleep averaged a 97 percent score, while those who had smelled nothing averaged 86.

The subjects were not wakened by the scent, and they did not remember smelling anything while asleep. The apparent explanation is that while they were sleeping, their brains were still processing memories of the game. Somehow, the scent helped in this process of creating long-term memories.

Using functional MRI, the researchers further discovered that smelling roses during other phases of sleep did not enhance memories of the game. In addition, if instead of card pairs, subjects were asked to remember a finger-tap sequence, the scent did not affect their memory. These results suggest that we process different types of memories during different phases of sleep. They also suggest that we process memories in multiple steps or stages, even when we are not aware of doing so. ■

Sensory Memory

Sensory memory is the first stage of information storage. It consists of the immediate, initial recording of data that enter through our senses. If we were to see a scene in a brief flash—if a strobe light flashed once in a dark room, for instance—the visual impression would decay within a fraction of a second. Such an impression is called a memory trace. Except when we are asleep, we receive a continuous and potentially overwhelming stream of memory traces. If we want to remember what we perceive, we have to do something with the information very quickly.

Psychologists believe that each of our five senses has a register. For example, the mental pictures we form of visual stimuli are called *icons*. Icons are held in a sensory register called **iconic memory.** Iconic memories are accurate, photographic images. However, these iconic memories are extremely brief—just a fraction of a second. The rare ability to remember visual stimuli over long periods of time (what most of us think of as photographic memory) is called **eidetic imagery.** About 5 percent of children have eidetic imagery. This keen ability usually declines with age, however. By adolescence, it is nearly gone.

Mental traces of sounds, called *echoes,* are held in a mental sensory register called **echoic memory.** While icons are held only for a fraction of a second, echoes can last for several seconds. For this reason, acoustic codes are easier to remember than visual codes. That is, it is easier to remember a spoken list of letters than to remember a mental picture of the letters.

Reading Check **Infer** Why do scientists believe there are five sensory memory registers?

Short-Term Memory

If you pay attention to iconic and echoic memories held ever so briefly in a sensory register, you can transfer that information into your **short-term memory** (STM). The information will remain there after the sensory memory trace has faded away. Short-term memory is also called working memory.

We use our short-term memory a great deal of the time. Whatever you are thinking about is in your short-term memory. When you are trying to solve a math problem, the elements of the problem are in your short-term memory. When you meet someone new, you put the person's name in your short-term memory, perhaps by using the name or by repeating it to yourself several times. When a teacher changes the date on which a paper is due, you place that information in your short-term memory until you can write it down or store it in long-term memory. If you look up a number in the phone book, you need to keep it in your short-term memory until you dial it. If you have to walk across the room to reach the phone, you might repeat or rehearse the number on your way. If the number is busy, you need to keep it in your short-term memory even longer as you wait a few minutes before dialing again.

Information in short-term memory begins to fade rapidly after several seconds. If you want to remember it longer, you need to keep rehearsing the information or take other steps to prevent it from fading. People can sometimes keep visual images in short-term memory, but it is usually better to encode information as sounds that can be rehearsed or repeated.

The Primacy and Recency Effects When we try to remember a series of letters or numbers, our memories of the first and last items tend to be sharper than our memories of the middle items. The tendency to recall the initial items in a series is called the **primacy effect.** (The root *prim–* means "first.") No one has proven a definitive explanation of the primacy effect. Perhaps we remember the first items better because being first is itself a distinctive feature that attracts our attention, or perhaps it is because there is less competition or interference from surrounding items.

The tendency to recall the last items in a series is called the **recency effect.** The recency effect has not been explained definitively, either. Possible explanations are similar to those for the recency effect: being last would appear to be a distinctive feature that draws attention, and the last item in a list is not surrounded by other items that compete with it for attention. Additionally, earlier items in the list cannot interfere with later items, so the last item has less opportunity to become displaced.

Chunking When we try to keep something in our short-term memory by rehearsing it, it usually helps to organize the information into manageable units that are easy to remember. The organization of items into familiar or manageable units is known as **chunking.** Return for a moment to OTTFFSSENT. If you tried to remember it letter by letter, there were 10 distinct pieces, or chunks, of information to retain in your short-term memory. When you tried to repeat the list as consisting of 10 meaningless chunks, you probably had a difficult time. It is not easy to repeat 10 meaningless letters, let alone remember them.

If you tried to encode OTTFFSSENT as sounds—something like "ought-fissent"—you reduced the number of chunks you needed to remember from 10 to one or two. (Of course, you also needed to remember the variations in spelling.) Psychologist George Miller found that the average person's short-term memory can hold a list of seven items—the number of digits in a local telephone number. Nearly everyone can remember a ZIP code, which is five numbers long. Some people can remember a list of nine items, but very few people can remember more than nine.

Businesses try to obtain telephone numbers with as many zeros or repeated digits as possible because such numbers are easier to remember. Numbers with zeros and repeated digits contain fewer chunks of information. Alternatively, a business may try to get a telephone number that can be spelled out as a word or phrase. Thus, people need only remember the word or phrase, not the seven numbers. For instance, a clinic that helped people quit smoking was able to get a telephone number that spelled out the phrase NO SMOKE. This phrase worked well as a semantic code.

You may be wondering how people remember long-distance telephone numbers—since with area codes included, such phone numbers are 10 digits long. Actually, most people do not try to remember the numbers as a series of 10 separate items. Rather, they try to remember the area code as a single, separate chunk of information. They become familiar with the area codes of surrounding areas and of places where their long-distance friends and relatives live. When they know where someone lives, they sometimes already know and remember the area code.

If you had known that OTTFFSSENT stood for the first letters of the numbers 1 through 10, you could have reduced the number of chunks of information you needed to hold in short-term memory from 10 down to 1. That one chunk would have been a single rule: make a list of letters in which each letter is the first letter of the numbers 1 through 10.

Interference Short-term memory is like a shelf that can hold only so much. Once a shelf is full, if you try to squeeze something else onto it, you will end up shoving something else off. Only a limited amount of information can be retained in short-term memory at a time. **Interference** occurs when new information appears in short-term memory and takes the place of what was already there.

A classic experiment by Lloyd and Margaret Peterson showed how new information can cause problems with what is stored in short-term memory. The Petersons asked college students to remember three-letter combinations, such as ZBT. Because most students can remember seven chunks of information, this task was fairly easy. Nearly 100 percent of the students could recall the three-letter sequences when asked to repeat them immediately. But then the Petersons asked the students to count backward from a number such as 142 by threes (142, 139, 136, 133, and so on). After a certain amount of time passed, the students were then asked to stop counting backward and to report the letters they had been asked to remember. After only three seconds of this interference, the percentage of students who could recall their letters dropped by about half. After 18 seconds had elapsed, practically nobody could recall the letters. The numbers that entered the students' short-term memory while they were counting backward had displaced the letters in nearly all cases.

Short-term memory is very useful, but it is only a temporary solution to the problem of remembering information. It allows us just enough time to find a way to store chunks of information more permanently. Short-term memory is the bridge between sensory memory and long-term memory.

Reading Check **Find the Main Idea** Why is short-term memory also called working memory?

What Can You Remember?

You can take this short memory test by yourself or work with a partner. You will need a watch or clock with a second hand.

PROCEDURE

❶ Before you begin, use your hand or another book to hide the photograph on the right.

❷ Expose the photograph for five seconds and look at it; then hide it again.

❸ List as many objects from the photograph as you can, and describe everything you remember about each.

ANALYSIS

1. How many items in the picture were you able to identify? Could you describe them in accurate detail?

2. What exactly did you think about as you tried to remember? For instance, did you ask yourself questions? Did you use spatial cues?

3. Did you "remember" any objects or people that were not in the picture? How do you think this happened?

Quick Lab **THINK** central | thinkcentral.com

Long-Term Memory

Long-term memory (LTM) is the third, and final, stage of information storage. If you want to remember something more than just briefly, you have to take certain steps to store it in your long-term memory. Mechanical or rote repetition (maintenance rehearsal) is one way of transferring information from short-term memory to long-term memory. Relating new information to information that you already know (elaborative rehearsal) is another technique.

New information is constantly being transferred into your long-term memory. In fact, your long-term memory already contains far more information than an encyclopedia or a computer's hard drive. It holds names, dates, places, the memory of how you kidded around with the student in front of you in second grade, and the expression on your mother's face when you gave her the picture you drew of her in fourth grade. Your long-term memory contains more words, pictures, sounds, smells, tastes, and touches than you could ever possibly count.

Memory as Reconstruction Some psychologists once thought that nearly all the perceptions and ideas people had were stored permanently in their memory. Supporters of this view often pointed to the work of Wilder Penfield, a brain surgeon. Many of Penfield's patients reported that they had experienced images that felt like memories when, during surgery, parts of their brain were stimulated electrically. From this information, some observers inferred that experiences become a physical part of the brain and that proper stimulation can cause people to remember them. Today, psychologists recognize that electrical stimulation of the brain does not necessarily bring about the accurate replay of memories. Memory expert Elizabeth Loftus, for example, notes that the memories evoked by Penfield's instruments had little in the way of detail and were often factually incorrect.

We now know that memories are not recorded and played back like videos or movies. Rather, they are reconstructed from the bits and pieces of our experience. When we reconstruct our memories, we shape them according to the personal and individual ways in which we view and understand the world. Thus, we tend to remember things in accordance with our beliefs and needs. In this way, we put our own personal stamp on our memories. We may even censor some details that make us uncomfortable. This is one of the reasons brothers and sisters can have differing memories of the same family events: each sibling has interpreted the information differently.

Schemas The mental representations that we form of the world by organizing bits of information into knowledge are known as **schemas.** Elizabeth Loftus and J. C. Palmer conducted a classic experiment on the role of schemas in memory. They showed people a film of a car crash. Then they asked them to complete questionnaires about the film. One question asked for an estimate of how fast the cars were going when they collided. However, the researchers varied how they phrased the question for different participants. Some participants were asked how fast the cars were going when they "hit" each other. Other participants were asked how fast the cars were going when they "smashed" into each other.

The participants who had been asked how fast the cars were going when they "hit" each other estimated an average speed of 34 miles per hour. Those who responded to the word "smashed," on the other hand, estimated an average speed of 41 miles per hour. In other words, which schema people used—"hit" or "smashed"—influenced how they mentally reconstructed the crash.

The participants were questioned again a week later. They were asked if they had seen any broken glass. The correct answer was "no"; there was no broken glass in the film. Of participants who had been told that the cars had "hit" each other, 14 percent incorrectly said yes, there was broken glass. Of those who had been told that the cars had "smashed" into each other, however, 32 percent incorrectly reported seeing broken glass. Schemas influence both the ways we perceive things and the ways our memories store what we perceive.

Capacity of Memory Our long-term memory holds the equivalent of vast numbers of videos and films of our lifetime of experience. All of them are in color (as long as we can perceive color). They also come with stereo sound (as long as we can hear), with smells, tastes, and touches thrown in. This light-and-sound show would never fit on any stage. But all of it is contained comfortably within our long-term memory. And there is room for more, much more. How much more? Psychologists have yet to discover a limit to how much can be stored in a person's long-term memory.

Although there is apparently no limit to how much we can remember, we do not store all of our experiences permanently. Not everything that reaches our short-term memory is transferred to our long-term memory. Our memory is limited by the amount of attention we pay to things. We are more likely to remember the things that capture our attention. The memories we store in our long-term memory are the incidents and experiences that have the greatest impact on us.

Reading Check **Summarize** How do schemas help us remember?

Online Quiz **THINK** central thinkcentral.com

SECTION 2 Assessment

Reviewing Main Ideas and Vocabulary

1. **Summarize** How does attention affect what goes into short-term and long-term memory?

2. **Recall** What experimental evidence supports the existence of interference?

3. **Analyze** Why is short-term memory also referred to as working memory?

4. **Define** What is chunking?

Thinking Critically

5. **Interpret** What do scientists mean when they say that memory is reconstructive?

6. **Infer** Recall the Psychology Close Up at the beginning of this section. What memory process was going on during deep sleep?

7. **Evaluate** What experimental evidence discussed in this section do you think best supports schema theory?

8. **Sequence** Using your notes and a graphic organizer like the one here, describe the processes that transform raw sensory input into remembered experiences and information.

FOCUS ON WRITING

9. **Narrative** Choose any simple fact. Describe how you think it went through the three stages of memory and became something you know.

Forgetting and Memory Improvement

Before You Read

Main Idea

The three tasks of remembering are recognition, recall, and relearning. Failure of any of these results in forgetting.

Reading Focus

1. How does forgetting happen?

2. What are the three basic memory tasks?

3. How are the three ways of forgetting different?

4. What are some techniques for improving memory?

Vocabulary

recognition
recall
relearning
decay
retrograde amnesia
anterograde amnesia
infantile amnesia

TAKING NOTES Use a graphic organizer like this one to list different types of forgetting and note how each occurs.

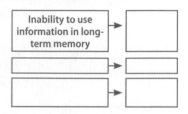

Inability to use information in long-term memory	→	
	→	
	→	

from Memory

Never to be Forgotten

Actual Site

PSYCHOLOGY CLOSE UP

What memories make the greatest impression?

Everyone has memories they say they will never forget. But Franco Magnani seems to have more of these than most people. When Magnani was in his thirties, he began painting extremely realistic pictures of his hometown of Pontito in the Tuscany region of Italy. This is remarkable because he left Pontito as an adolescent and has not been back since. Nor did he have any photographs or drawings of Pontito. His paintings are done entirely from his childhood memories, and the images reflect the perspective of a child.

The inspiration for Franco's "memory paintings" are his vivid, detailed, three-dimensional visual memories of his childhood home. When he is having these visions, he turns his head to "see" what is around the corner or behind him. Magnani's visions began as dreams during a serious illness and then increased in frequency. Eventually, Magnani was having daydreams while at his job as a chef—hallucinations, almost. At a certain point, he felt compelled to paint what he was seeing. "Like a flash," he says, "I'd see intricate details of my village. It was so acute, I'd want to leave the stove, go home, [and] start sketching." In this section you will read more about how and why people forget and remember. ■

Forgetting

Forgetting is the flip side of remembering. Forgetting may seem simple enough. If you do not think about something, you forget it, right? Not really; it is not that simple.

Forgetting can occur at any one of the three stages of memory—sensory, short-term, or long-term. Information encoded in sensory memory decays almost immediately unless you pay attention to it and transfer it into short-term memory. A memory trace in a visual sensory register decays in less than a second, and a sound recorded in echoic memory lasts no more than a few seconds.

Information in short-term memory does not last long, either. It will disappear after only 10 or 12 seconds unless you find a way to transfer it into your long-term memory. Information stored in short-term memory is lost when it is <u>displaced</u>, or crowded out, by new information.

ACADEMIC VOCABULARY

displace move from an original or natural place

The most familiar and significant cases of forgetting involve the inability to use information in long-term memory. If you think of the mind as a file cabinet, you can imagine how forgetting could be due, for instance, to a lost or damaged file or an initial filing error. Because long-term memory holds such vast amounts of material and the material is represented in an abstract form, forgetting and other memory errors (such as recalling information incorrectly) are not uncommon. Sometimes new information becomes mixed up with material you already know.

As well, old learning can interfere with new learning. For example, if you study a new foreign language, your knowledge of a language you already know or are studying at the same time can interfere with your new learning. This is more likely to happen if the languages are somewhat similar. Consider the French, Spanish, and Italian languages. The three have many similar word roots and spellings: for instance, *amour* (French), *amar* (Spanish), and *amore* (Italian) all mean "love." If you have ever tried to learn two or more of these languages, especially at the same time, you know how easy it is to confuse them.

Reading Check **Contrast** How does forgetting information in short-term memory differ from forgetting information in long-term memory?

Basic Memory Tasks

Do you know what DAL, RIK, and KAX are? They are nonsense syllables—meaningless sets of two consonants with a vowel in the middle. Nonsense syllables provide psychologists with a way to measure three basic memory tasks: recognition, recall, and relearning.

The first researcher to use nonsense syllables to study memory was German psychologist Hermann Ebbinghaus (1850–1909). His experiments are regarded as the first scientific study of forgetting, and psychologists today continue to use nonsense syllables in their studies. Because nonsense syllables are meaningless, remembering them depends on acoustic coding (saying them out loud or in one's mind) and rote repetition (maintenance rehearsal). These tasks play a part in recognition, recall, and relearning.

Recognition One of the three basic memory tasks is **recognition,** which involves identifying objects or events that have been encountered before. It is the easiest of the memory tasks. In some experiments on recognition, psychologists ask people to read a list of nonsense syllables. The participants then read a second list of nonsense syllables and are asked to identify any syllables in the second list that appeared in the first list. In this instance, forgetting is defined as failure to recognize a syllable that has been read before.

A classic study by Harry Bahrick and his colleagues examined recognition using a different technique. Bahrick took pictures from the yearbooks of high school graduates and mixed them in with four times as many photos of strangers. Recent graduates correctly picked out their former classmates 90 percent of the time. Graduates who had been out of school for 40 years recognized their former schoolmates less often, but not by too much— 75 percent of the time. Keep in mind that only one photo in five was actually of a former schoolmate. Thus, if the graduates had been guessing, they would have picked out former schoolmates only 20 percent of the time. The participants recognized the photos of their former classmates far more easily than they recalled their classmates' names. The study showed that the ability of people to recognize familiar faces remains strong and lasting.

Statistically Speaking...

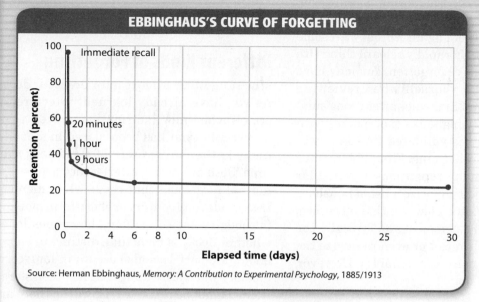

EBBINGHAUS'S CURVE OF FORGETTING

Retention (percent)

Immediate recall

20 minutes

1 hour

9 hours

Elapsed time (days)

Source: Herman Ebbinghaus, *Memory: A Contribution to Experimental Psychology*, 1885/1913

The Speed of Forgetting

The ability to recall nonsense syllables drops sharply during the first hour of learning. After the first hour, memory loss becomes more gradual. Ebbinghaus measured the rate at which test subjects forgot a list of nonsense syllables. Subsequent research has shown that when the information to be learned is meaningful and significant—when there is a reason to learn and remember it—forgetting slows considerably.

Skills Focus **INTERPRETING GRAPHS** Given a list of nonsense syllables, what is the likelihood of remembering any particular syllable the next day?

Interactive Feature thinkcentral.com

Recall The second memory task is recall. To **recall** something means to bring it back to mind. In recall, you do not immediately recognize something you have come across before. Rather, you have to "search" for it and possibly try to reconstruct it in your mind.

Hermann Ebbinghaus sometimes studied his own recall ability by reading aloud to himself with a metronome (an instrument that marks out exact time by ticking) a list of nonsense syllables. He would then test how many of the syllables he could recall. Typically, Ebbinghaus could recall seven of the syllables after reading a list one time. As noted earlier, this is the number of items most people can keep in short-term memory.

If a person memorizes a list of nonsense syllables and is asked to repeat back the list immediately, there is generally no memory loss. But the ability to recall drops off quickly: about half of the items are forgotten within the first hour. After that first hour, memory loss becomes more gradual. For instance, the amount of material a person remembers is cut

in half again in about a month. The person continues to forget as time goes on, but the rate of forgetting slows down considerably.

Psychologists also use paired associates to measure recall. Paired associates are lists of two nonsense syllables. In this method, people read a list pair by pair. Later, they are given the first member in each pair and are asked to recall the second one. That is, the people try to retrieve one syllable with the other serving as the cue.

Learning the vocabulary of a foreign language is something like learning paired associates. For example, a student studying Spanish might try to remember a Spanish word by pairing it with an English word that has a similar meaning. The student might remember that the Spanish word *mano* means "hand" by creating a meaningful link between the words. She or he could do that by remembering that the English word *manually* means "by hand." Otherwise, the only way to remember the foreign word is by mechanical repetition (maintenance rehearsal).

Relearning The third basic memory task is **relearning.** Sometimes we do not remember things we once knew. For example, people who have been out of school for 25 years might not remember any algebraic formulas. However, they could probably relearn them very quickly if they studied them again. Often, with some effort, we can fairly rapidly relearn things we once knew but have forgotten. You may have experienced this yourself when reviewing math facts or grammar rules after a long summer vacation. Ebbinghaus's experiments with nonsense syllables validated this as a general idea about relearning. First, Ebbinghaus recorded how many repetitions a particular person needed to memorize a list of nonsense syllables. Then, after a few months had passed, he checked on the person again. Typically, the person could not recall or even recognize the original list of nonsense syllables. However,

Ebbinghaus found that the person was able to relearn the list more quickly than she or he had learned it the first time.

Reading Check **Analyze** What do experiments with nonsense syllables prove about recognition, recall, and relearning?

Different Kinds of Forgetting

Much forgetting is due to interference or decay. As you have already learned, interference occurs when new information shoves aside or disrupts what has been placed in memory. **Decay** is the fading away of a memory over time. Both decay and interference are part of normal forgetting that occur when memory traces fade from sensory or short-term memory (although some researchers have questioned whether decay is an actual, distinct phenomenon). Memory loss also occurs in long-term memory when something that has been stored there cannot be retrieved. However, there are more extreme kinds of forgetting.

Repression According to Sigmund Freud, the founder of psychoanalytic theory, we sometimes forget things on purpose without even knowing we are doing it. Some memories may be so painful and unpleasant that they make us feel anxiety, guilt, or shame. To protect ourselves from such disturbing memories, said Freud, we forget them by pushing them out of our consciousness. Freud called this kind of forgetting repression. For example, a person might forget to go to a dentist appointment because he or she expects the experience to be unpleasant. Non-Freudians usually explain repression in terms of interference.

Amnesia Amnesia is severe memory loss. It is often caused by trauma to the brain—such as from a fall or a blow to the head, electric shock, brain surgery, stroke, shock, fatigue, or illness. There are several types of amnesia, but all of them are extremely rare. Nonetheless, study of people suffering from amnesia has been very important in developing an understanding of how memory works.

People afflicted by **retrograde amnesia** forget the period leading up to a traumatic event. For example, athletes knocked unconscious during a game often have no memory of what happened before the play in which they were injured. Some cannot even remember starting

Repressed Memories

"First, we'll look for repressed memories of malpractice suits."

Skills Focus **INTERPRETING CARTOONS**

Why would a psychotherapist be interested in a patient's repressed memories?

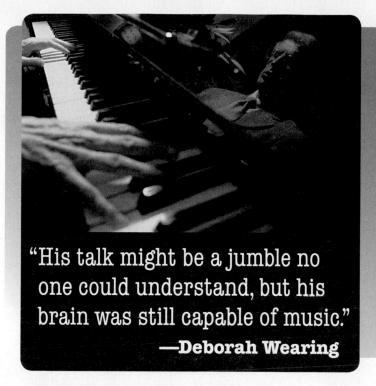

"His talk might be a jumble no one could understand, but his brain was still capable of music."
—Deborah Wearing

Memorable Melodies

An infection in pianist Clive Wearing's brain disabled his episodic and auto-biographical memory. He suffered near-total retrograde amnesia—he lost virtually all memory of his life before the infection—and total anterograde amnesia, losing the ability to store new long-term memories. Yet Wearing's skills, such as his abilities to read music and to play the piano, remained intact. *How does Clive Wearing's memory loss compare to H.M.'s?*

the game. In the most severe cases of retrograde amnesia, the person cannot remember a period of several years prior to the traumatic incident. One man suffered retrograde amnesia after receiving a head injury in a motorcycle accident. When he woke up after the accident, he had no memory of anything that had happened since he was 11 years old.

More commonly, trauma to the brain causes memory loss of events that take place after the trauma. This type of memory loss, in which the person loses the ability to store new memories, is called **anterograde amnesia.** Certain kinds of brain damage, such as damage to the hippocampus, have been linked to anterograde amnesia. Transient global amnesia is profound anterograde amnesia that begins abruptly and usually lasts less than a day.

Infantile Amnesia Unlike these extreme and rare forms of forgetting, there is one type of amnesia that we all experience. Some people think that they can remember events that took place in their infancy, but actually they cannot.

After many years of hearing his patients talk about their childhoods, Freud found that they could not remember things that had happened to them before the age of three. This forgetting of early events he called **infantile amnesia.**

People who think that they can remember their birth have probably constructed the memory from other memories. For example, they may remember being told about their birth by a parent or another family member. Or they may remember the birth of a younger sibling and then use that information to create a memory of their own birth.

The reason for infantile amnesia is not that the events happened a long time ago. People in their 80s have many precise memories of their life between the ages of 6 and 10, even though the events they remember occurred 70 years earlier. College freshmen, meanwhile, have difficulty remembering events that occurred before the age of 6, even though these events occurred only 13 or 14 years earlier. Therefore, failure to recall events from infancy or early childhood is not simply a matter of decay.

Freud explained infantile amnesia in terms of repression. He believed that young children often have aggressive and sexual feelings toward their parents but that they forget these feelings as they get older. The fact that people also tend to forget boring and bland events from their early childhoods is seen by some as casting doubt on Freud's theory.

Infantile amnesia reflects biological and cognitive factors. One biological factor is the development of the hippocampus, which does not become mature until about the age of two.

CASE STUDY
CONNECTION

Anterograde Amnesia H.M.'s memory problems began after part of his hippocampus was surgically removed.

Forgetting is the inability to remember. Because memory is such a complicated process, there are many ways in which it can go wrong, and there are many possible causes and types of forgetting.

Type	Description
Decay	Fading away of a memory over time
Interference	Displacement, disruption, or distortion of previously existing memories by new memories
Repression	Subconscious forgetting to ease anxiety, guilt, shame, or other emotional trouble
Amnesia	Severe memory loss
Retrograde amnesia	Loss of memory of events that occurred prior to the trauma
Anterograde amnesia	Loss of the ability to store new long-term memories

Another biological factor is that memory formation is somewhat inefficient for a few years until myelination of nerve cells is complete.

There are also cognitive reasons for infantile amnesia:

- Infants are not particularly interested in remembering the past year.
- Infants, unlike older children and adults, tend not to weave together episodes of their lives into meaningful stories. Information about specific episodes thus tends to be lost.
- Infants do not make reliable use of language to symbolize or classify events. Their ability to encode sensory input is therefore limited.

Note that infantile amnesia refers to episodic memory—memory of specific events. We certainly learn and remember many other things during infancy and early childhood using semantic and implicit memory. For example, we learn who our parents are and to have strong feelings for them. We learn and remember the language spoken at home. We learn how to encourage other people to care for us. We learn how to get from one part of the home to another. We remember such information and skills quite well.

Reading Check **Recall** What are the five types of forgetting discussed in this section?

Improving Memory

Memory can be improved. As a result of studies of memory and forgetting, psychologists have been able to identify different strategies people can use to improve their memory.

Drill and Practice One basic way to remember information is by going over it again and again, that is, by repetition, or drill and practice. Repetition is one fairly effective way to transfer information from sensory memory to short-term memory and from short-term memory to long-term memory. You can remember facts in psychology and other courses by pairing different pieces of information with each other and then drilling yourself on the connections between the items.

A trick for remembering the names of people you meet is to use the names right away. This will help you remember them later. If you are introduced to a new person, for example, say his or her name aloud when you are introduced. You might find it even more helpful to write the name down, if you can, at the end of the conversation.

Relate to Existing Knowledge Elaborative rehearsal—relating new information to what you already know—requires you to think more deeply about the new information. If new information becomes connected in a variety of ways to what is already stored in your long-term memory, your brain will have more ways of finding it later. As a result, you may remember the new information better.

Elaborative rehearsal can be helpful in many situations. For example, if you were trying to remember the spelling of the word *retrieve,* you would probably do it by recalling the rule "*i* before *e* except after *c.*" But how would you remember the spelling of the word *weird,* which does not follow the rule? You could use elaborative rehearsal on the word by recalling that it does not follow the "*i* before *e*" rule because it's a "weird" word.

Constructing links between items is another way elaborative rehearsal can help improve memory. You may find it easier to remember vocabulary words from a foreign language if you construct a meaningful link between each foreign word and its English equivalent. One way to create such a link is to find part of the foreign word and construct a sentence or phrase that includes that part of the word in English. For example, suppose that you are trying to remember that a *peso* (PAY-soh) is a unit of Mexican money. You might note that *peso* contains the letters *pe*, and then construct the following sentence: "*Pe*ople pay with money." Then, when you come across the word *peso*, you recognize the *pe* and retrieve the sentence that serves as the link. From that sentence, you can then reconstruct the meaning of the word *peso*.

Form Unusual Associations It is sometimes easier to remember a piece of information if you can make an unusual or even humorous association between that piece of information and something else. For example, suppose that you wanted to memorize the symbol for the chemical element tin. You could remember that *Sn* is the symbol for tin by thinking of a *sn*ake in a *tin* can.

Sometimes people can enhance memory by forming a group of unusual associations. Suppose that you need to buy groceries but do not have time to write out a shopping list. How will you remember what items to buy? First, think of a group of related images, such as the parts of your body. Then, picture each dish you plan to cook as hanging from a different body part. For example, you might envision lasagna hanging off your left shoulder. When you are at the supermarket, mentally go through the body parts you have designated and see what is connected to each. When you get to the left shoulder and envision the lasagna, tick off the items you need to buy in order to make the lasagna: noodles, tomato paste, and so on.

Use Mnemonic Devices Methods for improving memory are called mnemonics (nee-MAHN-iks) or mnemonic devices. Many mnemonic devices combine chunks of information into a catchy or easily recognizable format, such as an acronym, phrase, or jingle. Others involve clever ways of combining different types of information, such as joining a mental picture with a mental caption, or pairing data from two different senses.

In biology, for example, you can remember that dromedary camels have one hump, and Bactrian camels have two humps. How? Just turn the uppercase letters D and B on their sides and count the "humps" in each one.

If you meet a lot of people you may benefit from using mnemonic devices to remember names. For instance, if you meet someone named Ben, you could imagine his face attached to a body like a rubber toy that wiggles and *ben*-ds from side to side. If his name is Ben Hamilton, you might imagine this figure being buried by a *ton* of *ham* falling from the sky.

Complete a Webquest at thinkcentral.com on constructing a "memory palace."

Reading Check **Make Generalizations** How can you make new information easier to remember?

Online Quiz THINK central thinkcentral.com

SECTION 3 Assessment

Reviewing Main Ideas and Vocabulary

1. **Define** What is a sensory register?

2. **Describe** How do memories decay?

3. **Interpret** Explain Freud's concept of repression.

4. **Identify** What are three methods for improving memory?

Thinking Critically

5. **Identify Cause and Effect** Why is elaborative rehearsal generally a more effective memory strategy than maintenance rehearsal?

6. **Explain** Why do you think relearning something you have forgotten would be easier than learning it for the first time?

7. **Contrast** How is remembering a list of nonsense syllables different from remembering a list of your classmates?

8. **Predict** How could you tell if a patient suffering from anterograde amnesia was having failures of encoding, storage, or retrieval?

9. **Categorize** Using your notes and a graphic organizer like this one, classify the different types of amnesia and forgetting as due to biological or mental causes.

Biological   Mental

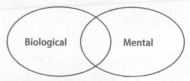

FOCUS ON WRITING

10. **Narrative** Imagine the thoughts of someone who suffers from some form of amnesia. Write a journal or diary entry from this person's point of view.

Experiment
Applying What You've Learned

Effective Memory Improvement

Which method of memorization is most effective?

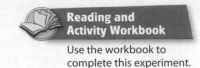

Reading and Activity Workbook

Use the workbook to complete this experiment.

1. Introduction

In this experiment, you and your classmates will evaluate the methods of memory improvement discussed in this chapter by using those methods and comparing their effectiveness. To complete this experiment, follow the steps below.

■ You will work in small groups to collect data; then, all the groups will combine their data. To ensure that all the tests are run in the same way, you will first work as a class to outline the main steps of the experiment.

■ To prepare for this planning discussion, review what you learned earlier about the steps of scientific research. Make a list of each of the main steps and the purpose of each step.

■ Following your teacher's instructions, you will organize into smaller student groups to write memory tests, conduct your experiments, and analyze your data. Your teacher will assign each group one or more of the three memorization strategies described in Section 3: (1) drill and practice, (2) relate to existing knowledge, and (3) form unusual associations.

■ After completing the group work, you will rejoin the rest of the class, compile everyone's data, and discuss the results.

2. Planning Your Experiments

Here are some suggestions to help you plan the experiments.

❶ **Frame a Research Question** To start forming a research question, begin by brainstorming. It might be helpful to create web diagrams on the board or screen. In the center oval, list one of the memorization techniques discussed in the chapter, and then add branches for ideas about when that technique would be useful. Here's an example:

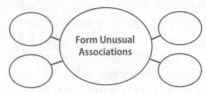

Form Unusual Associations

❷ **Form a Hypothesis** If you have difficulty forming a hypothesis, start making statements based on your research question that start with "I guess . . . " or "I think . . . ," such as, "I think elaborative rehearsal would be effective for remembering Civil War battles." After you have formed this statement, remove the starting "I think" statement and you have written yourself a hypothesis.

❸ **Plan How to Test the Hypothesis** You will use the testing method of observation. It is important to have a clear, detailed list of experimental steps before you begin. It is also important that all the groups use the same format for recording data so everyone's results can be combined and analyzed at the conclusion of the experiment. As you plan your experiment, consider these issues.

■ Determine your dependent and independent variables.

■ Will you be looking for a causal explanation or a correlation?

■ For what factors do you need to control? How will you control for them?

■ Decide how you will sample participants—your subjects. Following your teacher's guidance, you may perform the experiments using the individuals in your group, another group in the class, or another class in the building as your participants.

3. Designing and Conducting Your Memory Test

❶ **Develop the Memory Test** Address these questions as you develop your test:

- What and how much will you ask your research subjects to remember?

- How much memorization time will you give subjects?

- How will you guide your subjects to use the proper strategies?

- How much time will you allow to separate the memorizing and the testing?

❷ **Conduct Your Tests and Record Data** You'll need a table in which to record the data you collect. Each group should use the same table. See the example at right.

4. Analyzing and Interpreting the Results

❶ **Compile and Analyze the Data** When all of the groups are ready to come back together, make a version of the data table on the board and compile all the data. Analyze your findings by asking some of the following questions:

- What are some similarities in the data? some differences?

- What did we learn from the experiment?

- Were there any other variables that might have affected the data?

- Did the results bring up any other researchable questions?

❷ **Draw Conclusions** Look back at your hypothesis; say it to yourself again while looking at the data. Was your hypothesis verified, or borne out? If yes, then your conclusions have already been drawn! If your hypothesis was not supported by the data, ask yourself if there are any new conclusions that you can draw from the data. You might use the "I guess . . . " or "I think . . . " statements again to get you started.

Sample Data Sheet

Research Group: _Matt R., Chenise L., Sheila P._

Memory Methods Used

Try 1: _____

Try 2: _____

Try 3: _____

Subject	Try 1	Try 2	Try 3
1.	3/5	1/5	3/5
2.	2/5	2/5	2/5
3.			
4.			
5.			

5. Discussion

Once you have finished the experiment, it is a good idea to look back and evaluate the entire experience. You can use some of the following questions in your discussion:

- What was the most challenging part of writing out procedures for the experiment? What do you think made this challenging? Could there have been a better way to create procedures?

- Do you consider the results to be valid and useful for supporting or refuting the original hypothesis? Why or why not? What could have been done differently in order to make the results more valid?

- How will the conclusions that you've drawn help you in studying or in some other aspect of your life? Do these conclusions apply to all people or just to those in your class?

- Were there any other tools (such as the Internet, a larger population from which to choose participants, more time, etc.) that could have helped in conducting the experiment? How would these have assisted you, and how might they have affected the data?

Comprehension and Critical Thinking

SECTION 1 *(pp. 188–194)*

1. a. Define Define explicit and implicit memory. What types of knowledge are associated with each of these types of memory?

b. Identify Cause and Effect How does encoding affect memory storage? How does memory storage affect memory retrieval?

c. Elaborate Explain the relationship between a semantic code and an organizational system.

SECTION 2 *(pp. 196–200)*

2. a. Identify What is a sensory register? How is a sensory register different from short-term memory?

b. Interpret What is meant by the claim that memory is reconstructive? Why is this claim significant?

c. Evaluate What evidence suggests that short-term memory is limited to a few items? How convincing is this evidence?

SECTION 3 *(pp. 201–207)*

3. a. Recall What are the three basic tasks of memory? Define each of them.

b. Explain How do mnemonic devices work?

c. Support a Position Do you think there are any sorts of forgetting that cannot be explained by interference? Explain.

INTERNET ACTIVITY ✳

4. From preparing for tests, to building business relationships, to driving a taxicab, many tasks in life are helped by effective memorization. A great many techniques have been proposed, some going back thousands of years. Use the Internet to research three different memorization techniques. Answer these questions:

- Which techniques are based on scientific research?
- For what uses or situations is each technique intended or best suited?
- Do the different memorization techniques have anything in common?

Reviewing Vocabulary

Identify the term from the chapter that best fits each of the following descriptions.

5. loss of ability to store new long-term memory

6. translation of information into a form in which it can be stored and recovered

7. an organized representation of some portion of experience, used for interpreting new information

8. identification of an object or event that has been previously encountered

9. memories that are easier to recollect in a particular setting or circumstance

10. to force out or push out

11. visual images that are retained for only a fraction of a second

12. organizing bits of information into familiar units

13. technique for remembering by combining new information to be remembered with information already remembered

14. tacit knowledge of skills, which cannot be stated clearly or procedurally

15. inability to remember experiences from early childhood

16. inability to remember events from a time leading up to a traumatic event

17. areas in which immediate sense data are initially recorded

18. studying by repetition

Psychology in Your Life

19. Make a plan for studying for your next psychology test or for an upcoming test in another subject. Identify the different types of knowledge you will be expected to have. Think about how to use maintenance rehearsal, elaborative rehearsal, and various sorts of coding. Decide what you need to recognize and recall and what you may need to reconstruct. Write up your plan in the form of a chart or checklist.

SKILLS ACTIVITY: INTERPRETING GRAPHS

Study the bar graph below. Then use the information to help you answer the questions that follow.

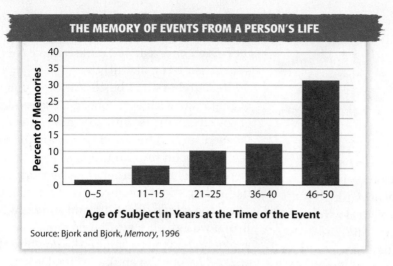

THE MEMORY OF EVENTS FROM A PERSON'S LIFE

Age of Subject in Years at the Time of the Event

Source: Bjork and Bjork, *Memory*, 1996

20. Identify What percent of new memories do adolescents retain?

21. Interpret Read the labels carefully and think about what the graph shows. Write one short sentence summarizing the pattern shown by the graph.

22. Identify Cause and Effect What facts help to explain the pattern shown by the graph?

23. Evaluate Based on the data in this graph, would you say that humans have good memories? Explain why or why not.

WRITING FOR AP PSYCHOLOGY

Use your knowledge of memory to answer the question below. Do not simply list facts. Present a clear argument based on your critical analysis of the question, using appropriate psychological terminology.

24. Explain how defects or deficiencies in each of the following parts or systems can produce memory failures, and describe the symptoms that would appear.

- temporal lobe
- parietal lobe
- thalamus
- reproductive system

Connecting Online

Visit thinkcentral.com for review and enrichment activities related to this chapter.

Quiz and Review

ONLINE QUIZZES
Take a practice quiz for each section in this chapter.

WEBQUEST
Complete a structured Internet activity for this chapter.

QUICK LAB
Reinforce a key concept with a short lab activity.

APPLYING WHAT YOU'VE LEARNED
Review and apply your knowledge by completing a project-based assessment.

Activities

eACTIVITIES
Complete chapter Internet activities for enrichment.

INTERACTIVE FEATURE
Explore an interactive version of a key feature in this chapter.

KEEP IT CURRENT
Link to current news and research in psychology.

Online Textbook

 Learn more about key topics in this chapter.

CAN ANIMALS Talk to Us?

Language is one of the factors that sets human beings apart from other creatures. Sure, parrots can say a few words like "Polly wants a cracker." And your dog may respond to commands such as "Sit!" But animals cannot truly use language.

Or can they?

Over the past few decades, various researchers have attempted to teach language to chimpanzees and other apes. One of the earliest efforts was aimed at getting a chimp to speak human words. But several years of work that yielded few positive results led to the conclusion that chimps cannot produce verbal speech. But just because chimps cannot talk does not necessarily mean that they are incapable of understanding language. Subsequent efforts therefore focused on teaching chimps to use symbols, such as those of American Sign Language (ASL).

Washoe, a female chimpanzee, was one of the first chimps reported to use language. By the age of 5, Washoe could use more than 100 ASL signs. These included signs for actions *(come, give, tickle)*, objects *(apple, flower, toothbrush),* and even for more abstract concepts such as *more.*

Moreover, Washoe could combine the signs to form simple sentences. The sentences were similar to those of two-year-old children: "More tickle," "More banana," "More milk." As time passed, Washoe signed longer sentences such as "Give me toothbrush hurry." However, Washoe had trouble with word order. One day she might sign, "Come give me toothbrush." The next she might sign, "Hurry toothbrush give me." Even one-year-old children use correct syntax more consistently.

Researchers had better luck in terms of grammar with a bonobo, a close relative of the chimpanzee, named Kanzi. Kanzi learned several hundred words and to correctly respond to commands in which these words were put together in ways that Kanzi had not previously heard. For example, he knew the words *dog, bite,* and *snake.* When Kanzi was given a stuffed dog and a stuffed snake and asked to "make the dog bite the snake," he put the snake to the dog's mouth, even though he had never before heard this sentence. Kanzi's grammatical ability, however, never surpassed that of the average two-and-a-half-year-old child.

In a different type of research, psychologist Dr. Irene Pepperberg worked for 30 years with a parrot named Alex. Alex learned about 100 words, which he was able to put into categories. He learned colors and shapes and even a few numbers. Alex created his own words for objects by combining words he already knew. For example, Alex called an apple a "ban-erry." The bird seems to have felt that the apple tasted something like a banana, and that it

Like the chimpanzee Washoe and the bonobo Kanzi, this orangutan has learned to use sign language to communicate some basic concepts.

Watch the Video
Explore topics on thinking and language.

Alex works with psychologist Irene Pepperberg to identify colors and letters.

resembled a cherry. Critics, however, said that Alex learned by rote and did not truly use language.

So the question remains: Can animals use language? The answer seems to hinge on the definition of language. It seems clear that animals can learn to use signs and symbols and can follow some commands given to them. So if this is considered language, then yes, animals can use language.

Most psychologists use a more restrictive definition of language: the combination of symbols into original, grammatical sentences. If we use this definition, the answer becomes less clear. Whatever the final answer, though, the experiments with animals and language also raise new questions about animal intelligence. What is going on in their brains when they communicate—by whatever method—with people? Are they thinking? How does their thinking differ from ours? What is thinking, and how is it connected to language?

What do you think?

1. What did Washoe, Kanzi, and Alex learn to do?
2. How do you think language should be defined?

CHAPTER 8
THINKING AND LANGUAGE

Chapter at a Glance

SECTION 1: Understanding Thinking

■ Thinking is the mental activity that allows us to understand, process, and communicate information.

■ The basic units of thought include symbols, concepts, and prototypes.

■ There are three kinds of thinking: convergent, divergent, and metacognition.

SECTION 2: Problem Solving

■ Problem solving involves a series of processes, including analyzing the problem, breaking it into component parts, and establishing goals.

■ Algorithms and heuristics are general approaches to problem solving.

■ There are specific methods of problem solving, including systematic searching, trial and error, difference reduction, means-end analysis, working backward, and use of analogy.

SECTION 3: Reasoning and Decision Making

■ Reasoning is the use of information to reach conclusions. There are two main types of reasoning: deductive and inductive.

■ People use a variety of methods to make decisions, including using a balance sheet and some types of heuristics.

SECTION 4: Language

■ Language is the communication of ideas through symbols that are arranged according to rules of grammar.

■ Language contains three basic elements: phonemes, morphemes, and syntax.

■ Children everywhere learn language in the same sequence of steps. Heredity and environment both affect language learning.

■ Bilingualism is the ability to understand and speak two languages.

Understanding Thinking

Before You Read

Main Idea

Thinking is the mental activity that allows humans to process, understand and communicate information. There are three types of thinking: convergent, divergent, and metacognitive.

Reading Focus

1. What are some basic elements related to thinking?
2. How do the three types of thinking differ?

Vocabulary

thinking
symbol
concept
prototype
convergent thinking
divergent thinking
metacognition

TAKING NOTES Use a graphic organizer like this one to take notes on the nature of thinking.

Thinking

A Life-Saving $ymbol

PSYCHOLOGY CLOSE UP *How do you know a sign warns of danger even though you don't read Turkish?* Look at the signs to the right. Are your eyes drawn immediately to the scary-looking skull with the red arrows? Would you touch something that bore such a sign? Of course not! The skull and jagged arrows are universal symbols that we can easily read as threatening death by electrocution.

There are many such symbols in our lives. They help us navigate in our world. So, for instance, finding the right restroom in a country where you don't speak the language is made easier by simplfied male and female figures on the doors. If you are driving down the highway and see the sign with the car falling into water, you know to avoid a potential hazard ahead, perhaps a washed-out bridge. When standing at a crosswalk, you know that the orange hand tells you to wait.

Your reaction to these symbols is instant. They act like wordless thoughts in your mind—thoughts that you can act on immediately. But symbols do more than keep us on the right road and out of danger. They are also essential elements in the thinking process. ◼

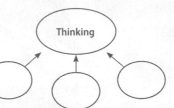

ÖLÜM TEHLİKESİ

卫生间

Do you know what these signs are telling you? Symbols are useful not only on signs. When we think, we use symbols.

Basic Elements of Thinking

This chapter is about thinking. When you are awake, you are probably thinking nearly all the time. But the type of thinking you are doing may vary from moment to moment. Maybe you are just reflecting on how much fun you had with your friends last night. You may be solving a problem, such as a geometry theorem or how to convince your parents to let you go on that weekend trip. Or you may be reasoning—using information to draw a conclusion. Perhaps you are making a decision, such as which after-school job to pursue. Problem solving, reasoning, and decision making are three types of thinking explored in this chapter. And because thinking often relies on language, this chapter also deals with language.

Thinking is the mental activity that is involved in the understanding, processing, and communicating of information. It is a complex process. Thinking is made possible through units of thought that include symbols, concepts, and prototypes.

Symbols When we think, we use symbols to represent the things about which we are thinking. A **symbol** is an object or an act that stands for something else. As you are probably aware, symbols are a part of our daily lives. Your school mascot and the American flag are both examples of symbols. Different types of symbols are found in mathematics. Plus and minus signs, for example, are both symbols: the plus sign signifies "add," and the minus sign signifies "subtract."

Letters and words are also symbols. After all, a word actually stands for something else—it is not the thing itself. For example, the word *plate* is not itself a plate—it only refers to an object that is called a plate in the English language.

Even your mental images are a type of symbol. If you picture a dog in your mind, that image stands for a dog, but of course it is not itself a dog. If it were not for symbols, we would be unable to think about things that were not present.

Concepts What do dogs, horses, and elephants have in common? You may say that they are all animals, or that they are all mammals. When we think, we tend to mentally group together objects, events, or ideas that have similar characteristics, as dogs, horses, and elephants do. Such a grouping is called a **concept**. "Animal" and "mammal" are both examples of concepts.

Much thinking involves categorizing new items and manipulating the relationships among them. Think of a new kind of animal, for instance—just make one up. What makes it an animal? You have used the concept "animal" to create a new item that fits into the "animal" category. Now imagine your new animal in a tree eating a piece of fruit. You are thinking about relationships among concepts (your animal, the tree, and the fruit).

People organize concepts in hierarchies, series of levels that go from broad to narrow. As we saw above, dogs, horses, and elephants can be grouped both as animals and as mammals. The "animal" concept is higher up in the hierarchy than is the "mammal" concept because it is broader, or contains more elements. Sparrows, goldfish, and spiders are all animals, but they are not mammals.

People learn concepts through experience. Simple concepts such as "ball" and "vegetable" are taught by means of examples. We point to a baseball or a basketball and say, "ball" or "This is a ball" to a child. We point to broccoli or carrots and say, "Eat your vegetables." Communication of the meaning of abstract concepts such as fairness, beauty, and goodness may require detailed explanations, a variety of personal experiences, and many examples. Even then, people may still disagree about what is fair, beautiful, or good.

Prototypes Often when we think about a concept, we have an image in our minds of a particular example of that concept, even though a concept is a category and contains many different examples. For instance, picture a shoe in your mind. What does the shoe you pictured look like? Does it have shoelaces, straps, or neither? Does it have a heel, or is it flat-soled?

The shoe you imagined was a **prototype**—an example of a concept that best <u>exemplifies</u> the characteristics of that concept. A prototype does not have to be an actual, experienced example, such as a particular shoe you have seen. Instead, a prototype can be more like an average of all experienced examples.

ACADEMIC VOCABULARY

exemplify to show or illustrate by example

Your prototype probably contains elements of many different shoes you have seen.

A prototype may provide standards of comparison for a concept. Which do you think is a better example of a shoe: a tennis shoe or a bedroom slipper? You probably said a tennis shoe. Why? Because a tennis shoe is probably closer to your "shoe" prototype than is a bedroom slipper. Most people think of shoes as items that are worn outside or in public, and bedroom slippers usually are worn only around the house. But a bedroom slipper is still a type of shoe.

Prototypes help us categorize our world and process information about it. Without prototypes, we might have to examine every unfamiliar element in our experience as a totally new thing. When we encounter an object or an experience that does not fit into the usual aspects of the prototype, we must either create a new concept or redefine what we are experiencing.

Reading Check **Identify** What are three basic elements related to thinking?

Three Kinds of Thinking

Researchers who study thought processes are interested not only in the elements that play roles in thinking, but also in the ways that we think. Psychologists have determined that in general we think in three ways: convergent, divergent, and metacognitive.

These ways of thinking can all be used to tackle a mental task. Sometimes one form is more efficient than the others. Often all three ways of thinking are involved. Suppose, for example, that you are thinking about taking a vacation with your family. You might use convergent thinking to decide if you want to go to the mountains or the seashore. Divergent thinking might be more helpful for coming up with different places you might want to go or activities to do within a certain place. Finally, metacognition involves the way you may plan the whole vacation. Do you think you will get the best information by calling a travel agent, using the Internet, or talking to friends? You may return to either convergent or divergent thinking as you complete your plans.

Three Kinds of Thinking

You use three basic types of thinking. You probably go back and forth from one type to another effortlessly throughout the day.

Convergent Thinking The thinker uses just the available facts to find the single best solution for how to get to school.

Divergent Thinking Here, she lets her mind come up with many more options for answering the question.

Metacognition When using metacognition, the thinker considers her own thought processes.

Convergent With **convergent thinking,** thought is limited to available facts. When using convergent thinking, we look at a problem or task and narrow the options to one solution. This type of thinking is important in solving specific problems and setting and achieving goals. For example, if you are looking for your house key on your key chain, you eliminate all the keys that you know are not house keys. You will pick out the correct key to open the door. Developing rules and following them is another example of convergent thinking. If you are working a math problem you use convergent thinking to find the correct answer. The next time you are taking a multiple-choice test you will use convergent thinking to narrow the choices presented to the one most likely to be correct.

Many school assignments and tests focus on this type of learning. However, convergent thinking is not particularly creative. Perhaps that is why creative thinkers often do not do well on standardized tests. Albert Einstein and Thomas Edison, two of the greatest scientific minds of the modern world, were creative thinkers, not convergent thinkers. In fact, Edison did poorly in public school. His mind wandered, and a teacher is said to have questioned his mental capacity. In high school Einstein clashed with authorities and resented the rigidity of the school curriculum. Later he wrote that the spirit of learning and creative thought were lost in strict rote learning—a type of convergent thinking—practiced at the school.

Divergent Edison and Einstein would have done better at schools where divergent thinking was encouraged. **Divergent thinking** allows the mind to associate more freely to various elements of a problem. One follows "leads" that run in different directions. Divergent thinking is at the base of creativity. Unlike convergent thinkers, divergent thinkers like open-ended questions and like to seek unique solutions to them.

Psychologist J. P. Guilford, who did groundbreaking work in this area, identified four different aspects of divergent thinking. The thinker is able to rapidly produce a large number of ideas or solutions to a problem, is flexible in approaching the problem, has ideas different from most other people, and has the ability to think through the details of an idea and carry it out.

An English psychologist named Liam Hudson devised a test for creative thinking that he administered to schoolboys. One of the questions he asked was, "How many uses can you think of for a brick?" Most of the boys could only think of three or four answers in a period of three minutes. The divergent thinkers were far more creative and generated 10 or more solutions. As you can imagine, businesses and many different fields of study need divergent thinkers to bring new ideas into their operations.

Divergent thinking sometimes occurs as day-dreaming or fantasies. A thought may emerge that you were never conscious of thinking. Have you ever worked on a problem, gotten stuck, and simply walked away only to find that when you returned to the problem later you had a solution? That is a type of divergent thinking in action.

Metacognition A third way of thinking is called metacognition. **Metacognition** consists of planning, evaluating, and monitoring mental activities. In other words, it is thinking about thinking. The concept of metacognition is not new. In the 300s BC, the Greek philosopher Aristotle was actually discussing metacognition when he pondered how people use their senses and their thought processes. Psychologist John H. Flavell brought the term into popular use in 1979.

Metacognition has two different aspects: metacognitive knowledge and metacognitive experiences. Metacognitive knowledge consists of knowing how you or others think, knowing what a task requires, and knowing what strategies to use to perform it. For example, you may realize that you learn best when you study with a friend and you quiz each other. Metacognitive experiences, on the other hand, consist of activities such as reflecting on your own thoughts. You would be having a metacognitive experience if you wonder why you thought that the answer on a history test was France even though you had known earlier that it was Germany.

A person using metacognition may work in one of three categories or stages in solving a problem. One is developing a plan, which could be called the knowledge of task category.

In this category, the individual asks himself or herself a series of questions.

- What do I already know about the topic?
- What is my goal?
- What should I do first?
- What strategies will work best to do this task?
- How much time do I have to complete the task?
- How will I be evaluated?

Suppose you must prepare a plan for a Web site for your science class. Using metacognition you will think about a topic and what you know about it and where you can get more information on it. You might think about what you know about planning a Web site and how long it will take to put your ideas together. If you are working with other people you may divide up the work so that each of you has tasks that are best suited to your talents. You may find out what points you will be graded on for the project. Finally you will need to plan stages of the project so you can complete the job on time.

The second category of metacognition involves monitoring yourself to judge progress toward your goal. In this category, the individual asks another series of questions.

- How am I doing?
- Am I on the right track?

- What more might I need to know?
- How is my pacing going? Do I need to adjust my time line?
- Do I need to try something different?

At this stage in your Web site project you should be determining if you are on track and using the right set of learning strategies to get the job done. You should also have some idea if you will finish on time. If your timing is off you may need to make adjustments in the scope of the project or dedicate more time to its completion.

As you finish the project you will evaluate how you actually performed. Once again you will ask yourself a series of questions.

- How well did I do?
- What could I have done differently?
- Can I apply any of what I learned in doing this task to other problems?

Reflecting on what you have done in completing the task is important because you consider both how you did it and how you may be able to apply that knowledge to another task. In applying metacognitive thought you will become more aware of your own learning processes, how to regulate them, and how to learn more effectively.

Reading Check **Contrast** In what ways are the three ways of thinking different?

SECTION 1 Assessment

Online Quiz **THINK** central thinkcentral.com

Reviewing Main Ideas and Vocabulary

1. **Define** What is thinking?

2. **Identify** What are three basic units of thought, and how do they work?

3. **Explain** How are divergent thinking and creativity related?

Thinking Critically

4. **Analyze** How are concepts and prototypes related?

5. **Explain** What activities take place when an individual uses metacognition?

6. **Predict** In what types of situations would convergent thinking be useful?

7. **Compare and Contrast** Using your notes and a graphic organizer like the one here, explain the three ways of thinking and how they differ.

Types of Thinking	Characteristics

FOCUS ON WRITING

8. **Expository** Review the text on the topic of metacognition and on the PQ4R method you learned in an earlier chapter. In a paragraph identify which aspects of the PQ4R method incorporate metacognition.

Automatic Thought Processes

How we think has long been of interest to psychologists. How much of our thinking is done consciously? Do we really think about every single thing we do? Do we deliberately make choices in all our actions? Current research indicates that the answer is no. (Hassin, et. al, eds., 2006)

About a century ago, Sigmund Freud and Carl Jung proposed that many of our thought processes occur without our conscious intention. Their theories lost prominence, however, as academic psychologists concentrated on concepts of behavior and learning that could be tested in the lab. Now those subconscious processes are receiving new attention.

Yale psychologist John Bargh, for example, believes that some of our thinking is nonconscious and automatic. That is, the thought processes are set into motion by features of the environment, and the brain responds without conscious thought. (Bargh and Chartrand, 1999)

We are quite aware of some thought processes. For example, a job applicant might think carefully about how to behave in an interview. But there are other situations in which we have not thought about our behavior. For example, have you ever judged people by the clothing they are wearing? How does this happen?

Bargh believes that our brain has processes in which it codes environmental events and directs us to respond in a certain way. For example, an individual is likely to behave similarly to others in a group. We generally act in this way because we don't like being the "one who sticks out in a crowd." Psychologists speculate that at one point in our lives we think about the goal of being similar to others. Gradually this behavior

Automatic thought processes often lead us to make snap decisions about people, based on various cues. if you were this worker's employer, what do you think you would assume about his abilities?

becomes internalized and consciously thinking about the behavior stops. The brain automatically takes control and creates the behaviors necessary to fit in with the crowd. This whole process affects our behavior.

An experiment demonstrated the automatic thought process. Test subjects were given a series of words related to stereotypes of old people—"Florida," "sentimental," and "wrinkled," for examples. As the test takers left the room after the experiment, they walked more slowly.

Some researchers call this type of automatic thinking "thinking lite." It seems to take about one third less

effort to think in this way than regular thinking. This allows the brain to be engaged in more conscious ways with other tasks. Bargh suggests that these processes are "mental butlers" that know us so well that they anticipate and take care of some tasks for us, without being asked.

Thinking Critically

1. **Evaluate** Think about a situation you had not encountered before. How did your behavior at that time reflect the theory about automatic thought?

2. **Discuss** What are some dangers of automatic thought?

Problem Solving

Before You Read

Main Idea
Solving problems can be done in logical and planned ways to achieve the best results.

Reading Focus
1. What are two basic approaches to problem solving?
2. How can certain methods help with problem solving?
3. Why do obstacles to problem solving occur?
4. What is the connection between problem solving and creativity?

Vocabulary
algorithm
heuristic
difference reduction
means-end analysis
mental set
functional fixedness
recombination
incubation effect

TAKING NOTES Use a graphic organizer like this one to take notes on problem-solving processes and methods and the role of creativity.

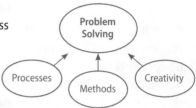

SAVING THE Cougar Ace

The hundreds of tons of fuel on board the *Cougar Ace* could have created an environmental disaster when the huge ship tipped over.

PSYCHOLOGY CLOSE UP

How do you pick up a ship? As it approached North America from Japan in July of 2006, a heavily loaded freight ship named the *Cougar Ace* was required to release water from its ballast tanks to prevent contaminating American waters. It is a tricky maneuver, since the water going out has to be replaced immediately with local water to keep the ship stable. Something went dreadfully wrong—perhaps a big wave hit. The water transfer was interrupted, and within minutes the ship keeled over onto its side. It appeared the ship would sink with all its cargo of almost 5,000 automobiles.

A team from a company specializing in saving ships came to the rescue. As the team plotted to move tons of water to where it needed to be, the members were very aware that one mistake could sink the ship completely.

A range of skills would come into play, from computer modeling to rock climbing. It was a slow and delicate process, but the team managed to set the ship upright. Although the cargo eventually had to be scrapped, the ship and the local marine environment had been saved.

Few of us face such huge problem-solving challenges. But we can all learn more about the problem-solving process and how to enhance our own problem-solving skills. ■

Approaches to Problem Solving

People solve many different kinds of problems every day. For example, a student may need to know the formula for the area of a circle or how many protons oxygen contains.

Other problems concern fitting things into a busy schedule or paying for what we need. Still other problems are social problems.

Solving problems involves a series of processes including analyzing the problem, breaking it into component parts, and establishing goals. Intermediate goals address parts of the problem that must be solved to arrive at the terminal goal—that is, the final solution to the problem.

On the following two pages you will find a series of problems. Go ahead and turn to those pages and try to solve them now. If you have difficulty with any of them, don't worry—you will learn the answers as you read.

In many cases, people do not go straight from a problem to its solution in one giant leap. Rather, they move toward the solution in a series of steps. Ideally, each step taken moves the problem solver closer to the solution. But how do people know what steps to take? If they do not know the solution, how can they know where to start?

Through experience, people know that different types of problems must be approached in different ways. By simply identifying the type of problem it is, people have an idea of which method to use—which steps to take—in solving the problem.

Algorithms Some types of problems are best approached with the use of an algorithm. You may have heard this term in math classes, but it also has a broader definition. An **algorithm** is a specific procedure that, when used properly and in the right circumstances, will always lead to the solution of a problem.

Formulas are examples of algorithms. If you know the radius (r) of a circle and you want to find the area (A) of that circle, you can apply the formula $A = \pi r^2$ to get the correct answer. As long as you know the formula and how to use it correctly, you need know nothing else to solve the problem.

Many algorithms are more complex and time-consuming than simple formulas, however. One such complex algorithm is called a systematic search. In a systematic search, each possible solution to a problem is tried and tested according to a certain set of rules.

For example, suppose that you are working on a crossword puzzle. You are trying to fill in a word for which you have all but one letter—say, **C L _ F F**. Using a systematic search, you would try putting every letter of the alphabet, starting with **A**, in that blank middle space until you found the letter that formed a word that fit the clue. In other words, first you would try **C L A F F**, then you would try **C L B F F**, then **C L C F F**, and so on, until you came to the right letter, which would be an **I**. Now you have the correct answer (**C L I F F**). It might take some time, but as long as you had all the other letters in the word correct and as long as you were able to recognize the word once you found it, this method would be guaranteed to work.

Heuristics While algorithms are guaranteed to work, they are not always practical. Suppose, for example, that you were missing not one, but two letters of your crossword puzzle word—**C _ _ F F**. In order to have success with the systematic search, not only would you have to try every letter of the alphabet in each of the two spaces, but you would have to fill in one of them with a placeholder while you tried letter after letter in the other space.

In other words, first you would have to fill the first blank space with an **A**, then you would have to run through all 26 letters in the second blank space. And when that did not work, you would have to try a **B** in the first space, and then run through all the letters *again* in the second space. By the time you arrived at **C L I F F**, you would have already run through 294 other possible solutions.

Needless to say, although this algorithm would eventually lead to success, it would not be a very efficient way to do a crossword puzzle, nor would it be very interesting or rewarding. This is why, for many types of problems, people use heuristics rather than algorithms. **Heuristics** are rules of thumb that often, but not always, help us find the solution to a problem. They are shortcuts.

In the first crossword puzzle problem, where only one letter is missing, you probably would use the following heuristic: in a five-letter word in which four of the letters are consonants, the fifth letter has to be a vowel.

Thus, instead of trying *eight* possible combinations before you arrived at the letter I, you would try only *two:* A and E (the only vowels that precede I in the alphabet). In the second crossword puzzle problem, in which two letters are missing, a heuristic might involve deciding that certain letters of the alphabet (B, C, D, F, and so on) would be unlikely to follow the first letter C, and thus you would not even try them as possibilities. Rather, you might focus on the letters that you know are likely to follow C.

Heuristics are faster than algorithms, but they are not as reliable. For example, we might forget that if C is the first letter of a word, the letter L (a consonant rather than a vowel) might be the second. And in some <u>circumstances</u>, we might miss some more unusual words. Think about a word that looks like this C _ _ C H. You mostly likely would not try a Z in the first blank space because the letter Z usually does not directly follow the letter C. Maybe as a last resort you would try the systematic approach and finally come up with the word C Z E C H—a resident of the Czech Republic or a Slavic language!

Reading Check **Recall** What are two basic processes used in problem-solving?

ACADEMIC VOCABULARY

circumstances
situations or conditions

Problem-Solving Methods

Algorithms and heuristics are general approaches to problem solving. There are also specific methods of problem solving. Systematic searching, which we have already discussed, is one of these methods. Others include trial and error, difference reduction, means-end analysis, working backward, and use of analogy.

Trial and Error Trial and error is somewhat similar to systematic searching, except that it is more haphazard and less reliable. In trial and error, we often do not keep track of which possibilities we have already tried.

Sometimes we have to resort to trial and error in solving a problem. If we know what our goal is, but we have absolutely no idea how to reach it, all we can do is try different things and see what happens with each one. Eventually, we might arrive at our goal, but success is more or less by chance.

If you have ever tried to work on a maze puzzle, you probably found that the only thing you could do was just to pick one possible route and see where it took you. When you hit a dead end, you came back and tried something else until it proved to be an error.

Five Problems to Solve

Try solving these problems. You will learn the answers as you read the section.

Problem 1 Naomi, Marquita, and Kim want to get ready for a party together. The party is across the street from Naomi's home, so they meet there an hour before the party. When they are ready to leave for the party, though, it is raining heavily. None of them wants to get wet, of course, but the girls have only one umbrella, and it is big enough to protect only two people from the rain. How can all three of the girls get to the party without getting drenched?

Problem 2 Imagine that you are a doctor. One of your patients has a brain tumor that must be destroyed if the patient is to survive. Certain rays will destroy the tumor if they are intense enough. To reach the tumor, however, the rays need to pass through the healthy tissue that surrounds it, and at the intensity needed to destroy the tumor, the rays will also destroy the healthy tissue. How can you use the rays to destroy the tumor without damaging the healthy tissue?

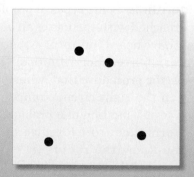

Problem 3 Trace this dot formation or copy it exactly onto a sheet of paper. Then connect all four dots with two straight lines without lifting your pencil from the paper.

Difference Reduction In a method called **difference reduction,** we identify our goal, where we are in relation to it, and the direction we must go to move closer to it. In other words, we want to *reduce the difference* between our present situation (problem unsolved) and our desired situation (problem solved).

Suppose you are standing blindfolded on the side of a hill. Your goal is to get to the top of the hill, but because you cannot see, you do not know which way to go. So what do you do? You take a step. If you feel yourself moving downward, then you know that you are going the wrong way and that you must change direction. But if you feel a pull in your legs that means you are moving upward, you know you are getting closer to the top of the hill. You have identified which direction to go in to move closer to your goal.

The difference-reduction method is a heuristic, however, and thus is not always reliable. Sometimes we may think we have reached our goal when we have not. Suppose, for instance, that the hillside levels off for a bit before it continues upward to the top. You may think you have reached the top when you arrive at this level place, and you may stop there. You do not know that there is more hill ahead.

Furthermore, sometimes we have to take what seems to be a step away from our goal in order to achieve that goal. For example, to organize your desk, you might have to take everything out of the drawers first, to categorize the contents—even though this would seem to be a step in the wrong direction (since at first, things will become messier rather than neater). After you have organized your things you will be able to reach your goal of a tidy and neat desk space. Similarly, what seems to be moving us closer to a goal may actually be moving us farther away.

Problem 1 highlights some of the pitfalls of the difference-reduction method. In order for Naomi, Marquita, and Kim to get to the party dry, two of them (say, Marquita and Kim) must cross the street to the party first, leaving the third one (Naomi) back at Naomi's home. But then either Marquita or Kim must *leave* the party and go back with the umbrella for Naomi. In other words, they must temporarily increase, rather than decrease, the difference between the goal (all three of them at the party) and their present situation (two of them at the party but one of them not). One of the two currently at the party must temporarily leave the party.

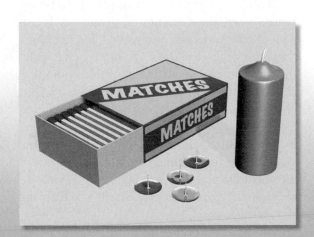

Problem 4 Imagine that you are in a room with a candle, a box of matches, and some thumbtacks. Your task is to use these objects to attach the candle to the wall. How do you do it?

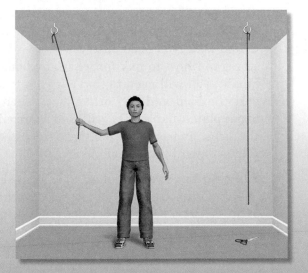

Problem 5 Imagine that you are in a room in which two strings are hanging from the ceiling. Your task is to tie the two strings together, but they are so far apart that you cannot reach both of them at the same time. The only other object in the room is a pair of safety scissors. How can you tie the strings together?

Means-End Analysis Another heuristic problem-solving technique is called means-end analysis. In **means-end analysis,** we know that certain things we can do (means) will have certain results (ends). Using a picnic for a crowd as an example, you know that the amount of food and supplies required means you will need a car to get them to the picnic site. Taking everything on a bike won't work.

As with the difference-reduction method, means-end analysis aims to reduce the difference between where we are and where we want to be. But means-end analysis goes beyond difference reduction in its awareness that a particular action will have a particular effect. The difference-reduction user asks, "What direction do I move in order to get from here to there?" The means-end-analysis user asks, "What can I do to get from here to there?"

Users of means-end analysis often break a problem down into parts and then try to solve each part individually, recognizing that solving each of the parts will contribute to solving the entire problem.

Suppose you are in charge of getting food for a picnic. First you will have to decide what foods will be served at the picnic. Next you will need to figure out how to obtain these food items—a trip to the grocery store will be necessary. Then you will have to figure out which store to go to, how to get there, how to find what you need once you arrive at the store, and how to pay for what you bought. Finally, you will need to find a way to transport the food and any other items such as paper plates, napkins, a grill, and charcoal to the picnic location. Each of these steps is one means toward the end of having a picnic.

Working Backward Related to means-end analysis is the technique known as working backward. As in means-end analysis, working backward involves breaking a problem down into parts and then dealing with each part individually. In working backward, however, the problem solver starts by examining the final goal, then works back from the final goal to the present position to determine the best course of action.

This method is particularly useful when we know what we want to accomplish but are not sure how best to begin. Working backward helps ensure that we start off on the right path and avoid having to retrace our steps if we discover that the path we have chosen does not lead where we want to be.

Suppose that you need to drive to a city nearby, but discover that the route you planned to take is closed for construction. It is unlikely that you would just drive around until you found a street that might lead to the location you are trying to reach. That would be time consuming and costly.

A better approach might be to get a map and work backward from the final destination. Start off by identifying the street on which the address is located. Then find the street that is nearest to that one, and so on, working back to your location. This way you can avoid getting stuck in the middle of a strange city.

If you have a big project due at some time in the future, you may set out dates to have specific tasks done by working backwards. Suppose you have a paper due at the end of a grading period. You may decide that by the week before it is due you will have a rough draft finished. Working backward you will be able to establish when you must finish any necessary research and preliminary writing. Using this approach avoids the last minute struggle to finish because you did not plan appropriately.

Analogies People also solve some problems by analogy. An analogy is a similarity between two or more items, events, or situations. When people have successfully solved one problem, they may try to use the same approach in solving another problem if it is similar enough to the first one. For example, if you observe that studying early and getting a good night's rest helps you do well on a test for one class, you may try that technique again the next time you have a test, even if the next test is in a different class. Many analogies, however, are much less obvious, and the trick is to find one that works.

Problem 2 (the ray-tumor problem) is not an easy one, and people typically have difficulty solving it. However, when they are provided with a story to use as an analogy, they often can solve the problem. Such a story might be as follows:

A group of terrorists barricaded themselves in a building in the middle of a town. Government officials considered it necessary to capture the terrorists, even though the operation would require a large force of agents to storm the building. Furthermore, the terrorists had planted mines on all of the streets that led to the building. If the entire force passed over any one of the streets, the mines would explode, killing not only the agents but also the people who lived in the surrounding area. Thus, the officials decided to divide the force into smaller units and send each unit on a different street leading to the building. Timing was arranged so that all of the units arrived at the building at the same time, and the terrorists were captured.

If you still cannot figure out the solution to the problem, look at the solution to the right.

A famous example of problem solving by analogy involves the ancient Greek scientist Archimedes (ahr-kuh-MEE-deez). As legend has it, Archimedes had been trying to find a way of measuring the volume of the king's crown, but the crown's irregular shape made it difficult, and Archimedes could not figure out what to do.

One day, as Archimedes climbed into his bath, some water overflowed from the filled tub onto the floor. Suddenly, Archimedes saw an analogy between what had just happened and the crown problem he was working on, and the solution to the problem came to him. He could measure the volume of the crown by placing it in a water-filled bowl and then collecting and measuring the amount of water that overflowed. Archimedes had realized that the volume of water displaced by an object equals the volume of the object—whether the object is a human body or a king's crown. He was said to be so happy that he shouted "Eureka!" which means, "I have found it."

Reading Check **Identify** What are five problem-solving methods?

Obstacles to Problem Solving

Sometimes we have trouble finding the solution to a problem simply because the problem is difficult or perhaps because we have little experience in solving that type of problem. At other times, particular obstacles get in our

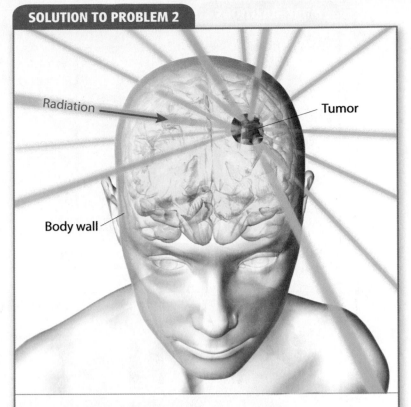

SOLUTION TO PROBLEM 2

Radiation

Tumor

Body wall

Weak rays sent from several points meet at the tumor site. Radiation will be intense at this site, thereby destroying the tumor. But because the individual rays are weak, they will not damage the healthy tissue.

way of solving a problem. Two of these obstacles are known as mental set and functional fixedness.

Mental Set As we know from our discussion on problem solving by analogy, people often try to solve new problems in ways that worked for similar problems. The tendency to respond to a new problem with an approach that was successfully used with similar problems is called **mental set.** While mental set can sometimes help us solve a problem, it can also sometimes get in the way.

Image that you are given an algebra quiz of six word problems. They all deal with different scenarios, so you suspect that you might use a different formula for each problem. But as you work through problems 1 through 5, you find that all of them use the same formula: $x = A - B + 2C$. So you assume that problem 6 will also use that same formula, and you use it to solve problem 6. However, because you had a mental set, you did not realize that problem 6 actually had a simpler solution.

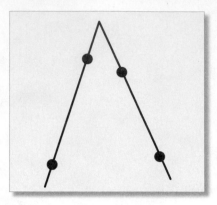

Solution to Problem 3 The lines connecting the four dots must extend beyond the dots.

Solution to Problem 4 To solve this problem, you have to overcome functional fixedness and think of the box as a platform, not as a container.

Solution to Problem 5 To solve this problem, tie the scissors to one of the strings and set the string swinging. Then catch the swinging string.

Mental set can limit our problem solving abilities in other areas also. For example, did you solve Problem 3? If not, mental set may have been responsible. From past experience, you probably perceived the four dots as the corners of a quadrilateral, and thus it may not have occurred to you that the lines could go beyond the dots. This is an example of how an incorrect assumption, caused by mental set, can elude us.

Here is another example. Do you consistently win against a certain opponent in a sport or game? Perhaps it is because your defeated opponent uses the same tactics every time, such as repeating the same defense formation. Athletic coaches often analyze the plays of other teams to see if they can detect mental set in the opponent's game plan and prepare their own teams to detect such play.

Functional Fixedness Another obstacle to problem solving is called functional fixedness. **Functional fixedness** is the tendency to think of an object as being useful only for the function that the object is usually used for.

Problems 4 and 5 are challenging because of functional fixedness. In Problem 4, the solution is to tack the box of matches to the wall and then use it to support the candle. But people have trouble arriving at this solution because they think of the box as a container and not as something they can actually use to support the candle. In other words, they are fixed on the function of the box as a container because that is usually what it is.

Similarly, in Problem 5, the solution is to tie the safety scissors to one of the strings as a weight. Then you can start the weighted string swinging so that it will reach you as you hold the other string. But again, most people are fixed on the function of the scissors as something to cut with, not as a weight to make the string swing.

In each of these examples, functional fixedness interfered in coming to a solution to the problem. To practice avoiding functional fixedness, you may want to look around your home or school and imagine other creative ways to use familiar objects.

Reading Check **Compare** In what way is functional fixedness a type of mental set?

Problem Solving and Creativity

Functional fixedness can often be overcome by creativity—the ability to come up with new or unusual ways of solving a problem. Creativity requires divergent thinking rather than convergent thinking. As you read earlier, with convergent thinking, thought is limited to available facts. With divergent thinking, however, there are many options and possible solutions to a problem. The various "leads" run in many directions; perhaps one of them leads to a solution.

Sometimes successful problem solving may require both divergent and convergent thinking. At first, divergent thinking produces many possible solutions. Convergent thinking then helps one to select the most probable solutions and to reject the others.

Flexibility Flexibility is the ability to adapt to new, different, or changing situations. Flexibility leads to original thinking. Think of the problem involving attaching the candle to the wall. Viewing the box of matches as a support platform rather than as a container, for example, is creative because this is not how matchboxes are usually used.

Test yourself on your flexibility by thinking up different use for a pencil or a metal nail file. With flexibility you move beyond functional fixedness to see new ways of using an object or approaching a problem. For example, did you think of the pen as a way to prop open a window or to puncture the shrink-wrap on the latest DVD you purchased? Could a nail file serve as an emergency screwdriver? The next time you get stuck on a problem ask yourself if you can be more flexible in your approach. Flexibility may allow you to come up with a creative solution.

Recombination Have you ever done a jumble word puzzle—one in which you rearrange the letters of one word to create another one? If so, you have practiced **recombination.** Recombination is the mental rearrangement of elements of a problem. For example, think about a musical selection. Music is made up of notes arranged in a scale. But the combination of those notes creates distinctive sounds. The same notes could be recombined to sound like a completely new piece of music. All the composer needs to do is use a different rhythm, different types of instruments, and softer or louder tones. Many creative works involve recombinations of familiar elements.

Insight and Incubation Archimedes' experiment with the crown and the water was an example of problem solving by analogy. It was also an example of insight, or sudden understanding. Usually we solve a problem by breaking it down into steps. Sometimes, however, we seem to arrive at the solution to a problem all of a sudden, as Archimedes did. Often we have little conscious awareness of how we found the solution—it just seems to come to us on its own.

Have you ever pondered a problem for a while, then had the solution come to you suddenly? Did it seem to come in a flash? When this happens, we have experienced insight. Often we express our delight and surprise by exclaiming "Aha!" or something similar. As a result, experiences of insight are also known as "Aha!" experiences.

Psychologist Wolfgang Köhler pioneered studies into this type of experience. During World War I, Köhler was marooned on one of the Canary Islands, off the northwest coast of Africa. While stranded, Köhler worked with a colony of chimpanzees that the Prussian Academy of Science kept there. His research with these animals demonstrated to him that much learning is achieved by insight.

In one of Köhler's experiments, a chimpanzee was placed in a room in which some bananas were hanging from the ceiling. The chimp clearly wanted the bananas and tried to reach them by jumping. But the bananas were too high up to be reached this way. The chimp walked around, looked at the bananas, walked around some more, noticed some boxes that were also in the room, and sat down for a while. The chimp seemed to be doing nothing related to the problem of reaching the bananas. Then, all of a sudden, the chimp got up, stacked the boxes, and climbed up on them to reach the bananas. Apparently, the chimp had suddenly seen the situation in a new way. That is, the chimp had had a flash of insight.

Köhler's findings suggested that animals and people set up problems in their minds and play with them until they are solved. Once the parts of the problem fit together in the right way, the solution seems to come in a flash.

A Chimpanzee's Insight

This series of contemporary photos documents the chimpanzee's problem-solving abilities. *What process allowed the chimp to solve the problem?*

Sometimes, we need to get away from a problem for a while before a solution comes to us. When we arrive at the solution to a problem that we have not been consciously working on, we have experienced the **incubation effect.** One type of incubator warms eggs so that they will hatch at the right time. Incubation in problem solving means standing back from a problem for a period of time while some unconscious process within us continues to work through it. Later, the answer may occur in a flash—it will have "hatched" on its own.

Because of the incubation effect, psychologists sometimes recommend that people take a break from work on a difficult problem. Go for a walk, call a friend, or read a few chapters from a mystery novel. After taking such a break, you may come back to the problem refreshed, and a new point of view or approach may have developed.

Reading Check **Describe** What are some methods for solving problems creatively?

Online Quiz THINK central thinkcentral.com

SECTION 2 Assessment

Reviewing Main Ideas and Vocabulary

1. **Define** What are algorithms and heuristics?

2. **Contrast** How is the difference-reduction method different from the means-analysis method of problem solving?

3. **Explain** How might a mental set interfere with successful problem solving?

Thinking Critically

4. **Analyze** Why might a person be forced to use a trial and error method to solve a problem?

5. **Make Generalizations** When might both divergent and convergent thinking be used in problem solving?

6. **Evaluate** Do you think there are certain situations in which insight and the incubation effect are more likely to come into play than in others? Explain your answer.

7. **Elaborate** Using your notes and a graphic organizer like the one below, identify and explain the factors of creativity.

Creativity

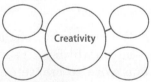 **FOCUS ON WRITING**

8. **Expository** Solve this problem: "A plane crashes on the border between Mexico and the United States. Where should the survivors be buried?" Then explain your analysis of the problem.

Reasoning and Decision Making

Before You Read

Main Idea

Deductive and inductive reasoning are used in the decision-making process. Various strategies can help us make decisions.

Reading Focus

1. What is deductive reasoning?
2. What are the steps in inductive reasoning?
3. When can weighing costs and benefits be helpful?
4. What are some shortcuts in decision making?

Vocabulary

reasoning
deductive reasoning
premise
inductive reasoning
availability heuristic
representativeness
  heuristic
anchoring heuristic

TAKING NOTES Use a graphic organizer like this one to take notes on reasoning and decision-making strategies.

Types of reasoning	Decision making strategies

A pitcher studies all aspects of the situation before deciding what kind of pitch to throw.

PSYCHOLOGY CLOSE UP

How does a pitcher make quick decisions? In virtually every sport, players must make split-second decisions throughout a game. A pitcher will not only assess the tendencies of the batter he is facing, but also the situation on the bases and, especially, the signals from the catcher. But if he thinks the catcher is giving a bad signal, the pitcher may shake it off or call for a conference on the mound. The pitcher makes all these decisions very rapidly.

In our lives too, we make split-second decisions, such as whether or not to react to a rude comment. We also make decisions in slower and more measured ways. You may be considering several different colleges to attend after high school. How do you select one? Just like the pitcher, you will consider a range of data about the various schools. Chances are you will also use reasoning strategies to make a final choice. In this section we will look at reasoning and decision-making strategies that we use almost every day—whether quickly or slowly. ■

Deductive Reasoning

Reasoning is the use of information to reach conclusions. There are two main types of reasoning: deductive reasoning and inductive reasoning. In **deductive reasoning,** the conclusion is true if the premises are true. A **premise** is an idea or statement that provides the basic information that allows us to draw conclusions. Here is an example of deductive reasoning:

1. South Korea is in Asia.
2. The city of Seoul is in South Korea.
3. Therefore, Seoul is in Asia.

The first two statements of this example are the premises, while the third statement is the conclusion. The conclusion is said to be *deduced* from the premises; if South Korea is in Asia and Seoul is in South Korea, then Seoul must be in Asia.

In deductive reasoning, the conclusion is always true when the premises are true. However, if the premises are incorrect, then the conclusion may be incorrect as well. For example:

1. Countries that are near each other have similar languages.
2. Japan and Korea are near each other.
3. Therefore, Japan and Korea have similar languages.

The first premise—that countries that are near each other have similar languages—is faulty. Countries that are near each other do not necessarily have similar languages. Thus, the conclusion is incorrect. Japan and Korea are near each other, but their languages are not very similar.

Reading Check **Identify** What is one problem with using deductive reasoning?

Inductive Reasoning

In deductive reasoning, we usually start out with a general statement or principle and reason down to specifics that fit that statement or principle. In **inductive reasoning,** we reason from individual cases or particular facts to reach a general conclusion.

In inductive reasoning, the conclusion is sometimes wrong, even when the premises are correct. For example, in the set above, the assumption that countries that are near each

other have similar languages was probably based on inductive reasoning. The thinking may have been:

1. Spain and Portugal are near each other, and they have similar languages.
2. Sweden and Norway are near each other, and they have similar languages.
3. Therefore, countries that are near each other have similar languages.

But even though *some* countries that are near each other do indeed have similar languages, this does not mean that *all* countries that are near each other do. In effect, the statement that countries that are near each other have similar languages was really only a hypothesis, or an educated guess, rather than a conclusion. In the previous example the hypothesis is shown to be wrong—Japan and Korea are near each other yet do not have similar languages.

Assume for a moment that the hypothesis was correct—that countries that are near each other have similar languages. How could that hypothesis be proved? Only by comparing the languages of every single country in the world and showing that all countries that are near each other have similar languages. However, it was quite easy to prove that the hypothesis was wrong by providing only one example of countries that are near each other and have different languages.

It is often impossible to prove an assumption reached by inductive reasoning to be true. We can only prove it false. But people often fail to realize this. As a result, they seek to prove, or confirm, their hypotheses rather than disprove them.

Even though inductive reasoning does not allow us to be certain that our assumptions are correct, we use inductive reasoning all the time. And until we prove a hypothesis false, we assume it to be true. For example, if we have read two books by a particular author and enjoyed both books, we conclude that a third book by the same author also will be enjoyable. Until we find a book by that author that we do not enjoy, we will probably go on reading that author's books. Inductive conclusions do not follow logically from premises, as deductive conclusions do. Yet they are accurate often enough that we can rely on them in our daily lives.

Most sciences, including psychology, rely on inductive reasoning. Scientists gather specific pieces of information, and then come up with general theories that explain the information. However, no matter how much information scientists have to support a particular theory, they can never know for sure if the theory is true for all times and all situations. There might still be some information not yet collected that would prove the theory false.

Reading Check **Contrast** How is inductive reasoning different from deductive reasoning?

Weighing Costs and Benefits

Life is filled with decisions. Most of these decisions are fairly minor in the general scheme of things. Should you take a jacket with you? Do you want the burger or the salad?

Other decisions, of course, are major. Should you go to college or get a job right after high school? Which political candidates should you support?

Making decisions means choosing among goals or courses of action to reach goals. When we are making careful decisions, we weigh the pluses and minuses of each possible course of action. We think about the importance of our goals, and we consider our abilities to overcome whatever obstacles may lie ahead. To make good decisions, we often need to gather more information about our goals and our abilities to attain them.

The use of a balance sheet—a listing of various reasons for or against making a particular choice—can help us make sure that we have considered all the available information. A balance sheet might be a list of the costs and the benefits of taking an action. For example, if you are trying to decide whether to participate in a certain extracurricular activity, you might make a list of the advantages (such as gaining experience and having fun) and the disadvantages (such as losing time that might be needed for studying) of doing so.

A balance sheet can also be useful when a person is trying to decide between two or more alternatives. Listing all the alternatives and the reasons for each one may help the person visualize which of the alternatives is the better course of action. The balance sheet may also help indicate areas where more information is needed.

USING A BALANCE SHEET

Take a year off to travel
✓ A chance to see other parts of the world and meet new people
✓ Travel is cheaper for students.
– Travel would use up money that had been set aside for college.

Go directly to college
✓ Get to know new people and make contacts for future jobs
✓ Will still remember how to study efficiently
✓ Get started on career more quickly
– Miss out on travel

Information still needed to finalize decision
? What do my parents think?
? How much would a year of travel cost?
? If I travel, would any of my friends be able to come along?
? How important is travel experience to my future career?

A balance sheet can help you make big decisions. Here are some factors a student might consider when trying to decide what to do after graduation from high school.

A word of caution, though, is appropriate here. When using a balance sheet, one should not simply total the number of pluses and minuses and make a decision based on the numbers! The balance sheet can clarify the issues, but some of the issues may be much more significant than others.

Reading Check **Recall** What is one method for making good decisions?

Shortcuts in Decision Making

Weighing the costs and benefits may be the best thing to do whenever we want to be sure to make the right decision. But weighing costs and benefits can be time-consuming and is not always practical. Furthermore, in order to weigh costs and benefits, we need to know what they are, but we often have to make decisions based on somewhat limited information. In such cases, we use heuristics. That is, we take shortcuts.

The Availability Heuristic One way that people make decisions is on the basis of available information in their immediate consciousness. This is called the **availability heuristic.**

For example, what percentage of the students at your school would you estimate are involved in extracurricular activities? Unless you go to a very small school, your answer to this question will probably reflect your personal knowledge of students who do and do not participate in extracurricular activities. Knowledge of these individuals is available to you. Rather than going out of your way to find out whether all the students you do *not* know participate in activities, you base your answer on what you already know.

Thus, if most of the students you know participate in extracurricular activities, you may think that most of the students in the entire school do too. But this is not necessarily true—the sample of students you know may not be representative of all students.

Events that are more recent or better publicized than others also tend to be more available. For example, whenever a plane crashes, the event is very well publicized. Car accidents, however, cause far more deaths than airplane crashes in the United States. But because of the publicity given to the airplane crashes, people are more likely to fear flying than they are to fear driving. They overestimate the risk of flying and underestimate the risk of driving.

The media also tend to focus on acts of violence, such as murder. As a result, people tend to overestimate the amount of violence in the United States.

The Representativeness Heuristic Imagine that you are taking a true-false quiz. The quiz has six items. Which of the following answer sequences do you think is most likely to appear on the quiz?

T T T T T T

F F F T T T

T F F T F T

You probably said the third one. Why? For one thing, you know that six "trues" in a row are unlikely (assuming your teacher is not trying to play games with you). Second, you probably assume that your teacher wrote a quiz that had a random mix of true and false answers. The sequence **T F F T F T** looks random. The **T T T T T T** and **F F F T T T** sequences

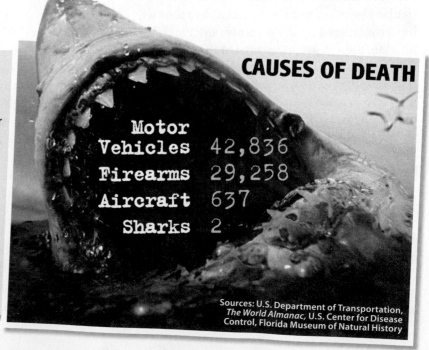

Availability Heuristic

Assessing Risks The availability heuristic allows people to make decisions or judgments based on information that is immediately known to them. This information may or may not reflect reality, however. For example, people visiting a beach may worry about being killed by a shark because they recently heard about a deadly attack. Look at the figures at right listing select causes of death for the year 2004. How valid is the fear of being killed by a shark?

CAUSES OF DEATH

Motor
Vehicles   42,836
Firearms   29,258
Aircraft   637
Sharks   2

Sources: U.S. Department of Transportation, *The World Almanac*, U.S. Center for Disease Control, Florida Museum of Natural History

do not. Most people would thus select the **T F T T F T** sequence because it looks *representative*. It seems to represent a random sequence.

Based on the **representativeness heuristic,** people make decisions about a sample according to the population that the sample appears to represent. In the entire population of true-false tests you have seen, more answer sequences have looked like the third one (on your sample quiz) than like either of the other two. Thus, the third answer sequence best *represents* the type of sequence you have come to expect, based on your previous experiences with true-false tests.

The representativeness heuristic can be misleading, however. Assuming that your teacher really has written a quiz with a random mix of true and false answers—with a 50-50 chance of either a true or a false answer on any given quiz item—each of the three sequences listed above is *equally likely*. For each item, the chance that the answer will be true is one in two, just as the chance that the answer will be false is also one in two. The likelihood of attaining any specific sequence—whether **T T T T T** or **T F F T F T**, say—is the same (1 in 64, in fact).

So what does this have to do with decision making? Well, imagine taking that quiz again. Suppose that you know the answers to the first five items and that they are all true. But the sixth item has you stumped, and you have to guess at the answer. Do you guess true, which would mean six "trues" in a row? Or do you guess false because you figure that it is unlikely that six "trues" in a row would occur? The temptation may be strong to go with the "false." But if the answers were assigned randomly, it really doesn't matter. Regardless of the answers to the previous five items, the answer to the final item has a 50-50 chance of being true and a 50-50 chance of being false. You might as well flip a coin.

The Anchoring Heuristic Another shortcut that people sometimes take in making decisions is called the anchoring heuristic. When using the **anchoring heuristic,** people make decisions based on certain ideas or standards they hold, ideas or standards that serve as an anchor for them. For example, people often decide to go along with the things they

learn early in life. Early learning serves as an anchor in thinking.

If you have grown up in a family in which everyone else votes in elections, you probably expect to vote too. That expectation is an anchor in your life. Beliefs about politics, religion, and ways of life are common anchors. When something happens that makes people question the beliefs they have grown up with, they may change their beliefs a bit. When people form judgments or make estimates, they begin with an initial view, called a presumption. The initial view serves as the anchor. As they receive additional information, they make adjustments. But such adjustments are often difficult for people to make, and sometimes people are unwilling to make them.

Reading Check **Identify Main Ideas** What are three shortcuts in decision making?

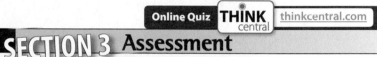

SECTION 3 Assessment

Reviewing Main Ideas and Vocabulary

1. **Define** What is a premise?
2. **Explain** What is the purpose of a balance sheet?
3. **Identify** Which heuristic is based on information in a person's immediate consciousness?

Thinking Critically

4. **Explain** Why is it impossible to prove an assumption reached by inductive reasoning to be true?
5. **Analyze** What is the biggest problem with using a representative heuristic?
6. **Draw Conclusions** How does one's upbringing as a child influence decision making?
7. **Contrast** Using your notes and a graphic organizer like the one here, contrast the three heuristic methods for making decisions.

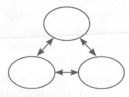

FOCUS ON WRITING

8. **Descriptive** Think of a decision you made recently. Identify the type of reasoning you used and which heuristics you may have employed. Write a description of the issue and its context and the methods you used to make your decision.

Language

Before You Read

Main Idea

Language is a complex human activity that allows humans to communicate with others over time and space. It has specific elements, and people acquire language in specific steps.

Reading Focus

1. What are some of the basic concepts of language?

2. How do the basic elements of language build on each other?

3. What are the stages of language development?

4. Why is bilingualism a significant aspect of modern society?

Vocabulary

language
psycholinguistics
language acquisition device
phoneme
morpheme
syntax
semantics
overregularization

TAKING NOTES Use a graphic organizer like this one to take notes on language.

A Mystery LANGUAGE

PSYCHOLOGY CLOSE UP

What language is written on the Phaistos Disk? Scholars have asked that question since this 6.2-inch clay object was found on the island of Crete in 1908. Although since then doubt has been cast on the object's authenticity, many scholars think the disk does display an ancient written language. For a hundred years, scholars have tried without success to decipher the script incised on the disk. One thing they have determined is that the characters were pressed into the clay with some kind of stamp.

The unreadable message spirals like a snake from the rim to the center. Both sides of the disk are covered with symbols. There are a total of 242 symbols—45 different kinds. The symbols are arranged into 61 groups separated by lines. Are the symbols letters or syllables? Do the grouped symbols make up words or sentences? We really don't know.

Such an object raises many questions. If this disk truly represents a lost language, who spoke it? What did it sound like? What were the first words of babies born into this language's culture? How did people learn to write this language? Although mysteries will remain, we can be sure that the study of languages—both familiar and puzzling—will continue for many years to come. ■

Some evidence indicates that the Phaistos Disk was made between 1850 and 1600 B.C.

Basic Concepts of Language

Language is the communication of ideas through symbols that are arranged according to rules of grammar. Language makes it possible for people to share knowledge. People can use language to describe what they ate for breakfast or what they thought of the movie they just saw. They can use language to set down the learning of past generations and store it for people who will live hundreds of years in the future. Language also permits people to use the eyes and ears of other people to learn more than they ever could from their own individual experiences.

Our language ability sets us apart from other species. Although there are many ways to communicate, human beings are the only species to use language so creatively. In the Case Study for this chapter, you read about animals who did, in fact, use words and phrases and even did so in unique ways. However, most psychologists would argue that the animals did not create original, grammatical sentences that would be considered the baseline for accomplishing the use of language.

Human language is an incredibly complex mental process. Our words and sentences are composed of many parts. The way the brain processes speech sounds, the way words relate to each other, the combination of words for sentences, and the meaning of words and sentences are all a part of the psychology of language, called **psycholinguistics.**

Although early philosophers may not have used the term psycholinguistics, language and its processes have fascinated people for centuries. Areas of interest include the processes by which humans acquire, use, and understand language. Researchers ask questions like, "How does the brain actually put together the sounds and patterns of speech into something that the individual understands?" Another question is, "How do we put words in the proper order to create understanding?" But perhaps the most basic questions in psycholinguistics are, "Why do we have language?" and "Where does our facility with language come from in the first place?"

Hereditary Influences In the mid-1950s an American linguist, Noam Chomsky, proposed a theory to answer basic questions of human language acquisition. Chomsky said that we are all born with an innate ability to learn languages. He said we are also born with a knowledge of basic grammatical structure. That is, the human ability to use syntax is "hard-wired" into the brain. According to Chomsky, this inborn ability to put together language in sentences helps explain the amazing rapidity with which children learn languages. One line of argument that supports Chomsky's theory is the fact that children make certain characteristic errors as they learn their first language, while they do not make other types of errors.

This natural tendency to acquire language can be called a **language acquisition device** (LAD). The LAD enables the brain to understand and use grammar. It enables people to turn ideas into sentences. People may not be ready for chemistry and algebra until high school, but the LAD makes people most capable of acquiring language between about 18 to 24 months of age and puberty. One- and two-year-olds seem to learn languages with ease. In many cases, they learn more than one language and become bilingual.

Environmental Influences People may have an inborn ability to learn language, but environmental influences are also important. Learning theorists claim that language learning is similar to other kinds of learned behavior. Children learn language, at least in part, by observing and imitating other people. For example, all babies vocalize in nonsense syllables, a process called babbling. But during their first year, babies start to babble the sounds they hear around them from speakers of the local language and drop other sounds not spoken in that language.

Billions of children have acquired the languages of their parents and have then proceeded to hand them down to their children. In this manner, languages pass, with small changes, from generation to generation.

Discussions about basic language acquisition are far from over. Chomsky has many critics, behaviorist psychologists being the most vocal among the critics. But we will leave the arguments for now to look more closely at language itself.

Reading Check **Contrast** What are the two main sources of language acquisition?

ACADEMIC VOCABULARY

acquisition
attainment or achievement

CASE STUDY CONNECTION

Animals and Language The human ability to create original, grammatical sentences is unique.

Dynamic Semantics

Punctuation and pronunciation affect semantics. In this lab, sentences take on different meanings based on the punctuation or pronunciation used.

PROCEDURE

❶ Write the following on the board.

Woman without her man is lost.

❷ Have volunteers punctuate the sentence. There are at least two ways the sentence can be punctuated. Read the punctuated sentences aloud.

❸ Have volunteers read the following question as either a student asking another student about her idea for a science project or an annoyed mother who has found her child making a mess. Are there more ways to say the sentence that affect the meaning?

What are you doing?

ANALYSIS

1. Study the ways the first sentence was punctuated. Ask the volunteers how they decided the meaning of the sentence. Discuss how views about women and men may have influenced the semantics of this sentence.

2. Listen to the difference in the tones of voice in the vocal exchange. Discuss how the feelings of the two people may have influenced the way the lines were delivered.

3. Summarize how more than just words influence the meaning of language.

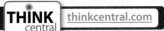
Quick Lab THINK central thinkcentral.com

The Basic Elements of Language

Languages contain three basic elements: phonemes (sounds), morphemes (basic units of meaning), and syntax (grammar). Combinations of these units create the words, phrases, and sentences that we use to communicate ideas. The meaning of words and sentences can vary according to semantics.

Phonemes The basic sounds of a language are called **phonemes.** (Languages that do not consist of sounds, such as American Sign Language, do not have phonemes.) Humans can produce about 100 different sounds. Some languages only have about a dozen phonemes, however. There are 26 letters in the English alphabet, but there are many more than 26 phonemes. English uses about 43 phonemes.

Phonemes include consonants, such as the *d* and *g* in *dog*. They also include vowels, such as the *o* in *dog* and the *o* in *no*. Even though *no* and *dog* each contain an *o*, the *o* sound is different in each word, and thus the two *o* sounds are two different phonemes. Other phonemes in English cannot be represented by a single letter—for example, the sound *sh*.

English contains some phonemes and phoneme distinctions that are not found in other languages. French has no equivalent for the English *th,* for example, which is why native French speakers often use a *z* sound to approximate the *th* in an English word: "Zee book is on zee table." Chinese does not distinguish between a *p* sound and a *b* sound. Japanese does not distinguish between *r* and *l*.

Morphemes The units of meaning in a language are called **morphemes.** Morphemes are made up of phonemes. Some morphemes, such as *car* and *bike,* are words in and of themselves. Other morphemes are prefixes (for example *pre,* which means "before"), while still others are suffixes (for example, *-ness,* which can convert an adjective into a noun). Many words use combinations of morphemes. English uses morphemes such as *z* and *s* to make objects plural. Adding the *z* morpheme to *car* makes the word plural; adding the *s* morpheme to *bike* makes it plural.

In English, the past tense of regular verbs is formed by adding the *ed* morpheme to the end of the present-tense verb. The past tenses of *walk* and *talk,* for example, are *walked* and *talked*. Verbs such as *to be, to run,* and *to think* do not follow this rule, however. Thus they are considered irregular verbs.

Syntax The way in which words are arranged to make phrases and sentences is **syntax.** The rules for word order are the grammar of a language. English syntax usually follows the pattern of subject, verb, and object of the verb:

Alberto (subject)→cooked (verb)→dinner (object).

Many other languages have a different word order. Whereas in English the verb usually goes in the middle of the sentence, between the subject and the object, in German the verb often is placed at the end of a sentence. In the vast majority of languages, however, the subject precedes the object. And in no languages does the object appear first in a sentence.

Semantics To examine another essential concept related to language, compare these two sentences:

It will be a long time before dinner is served.

The members of Alberto's family long for a tasty dinner.

In the first sentence, *long* is an adjective. The sentence means that there is still much time before dinner. In the second sentence, on the other hand, *long* is a part of a verb—"to long for." The word *long,* therefore, clearly has more than one meaning.

The study of meaning is called **semantics.** Semantics involves the relationship between language and the things depicted in the language. Words that sound alike, such as *right* and *write,* can have different meanings, depending on how they are used. So can words that are spelled alike, as we saw with *long.*

How a sentence is structured also affects meaning. Compare these two sentences:

Alberto's chicken is ready to eat.

Alberto's family is ready to eat.

The first sentence probably means that Alberto has prepared the chicken and that it is ready to be eaten. The second sentence looks similar, but it most likely means that Alberto's family is hungry—that the members of his family want to eat as soon as possible.

Sentences have a surface structure and a deep structure. The surface structure is what you see, the actual words of a sentence. Both "ready to eat" sentences have the same surface structure. The deep structure of a sentence is its deeper meaning, the message the speaker is trying to communicate. The "ready to eat" sentences differ in meaning.

Some sentences have an unclear surface structure—you cannot be certain of the deep structure based on the surface structure. An example is the sentence, "Do you hear me?" The questioner may want to know if you are detecting sound or if you are truly hearing the message being delivered. The meaning here is only detectable in the context of the moment in which the statement is being made. In this case, the meaning of the word *hear* is at the base of understanding the question.

Reading Check **Describe** What are the three basic elements of language?

The Stages of Language Development

How do people learn languages? Children develop language in a sequence of steps. The sequence is the same for nearly all children no matter where they live or what language they learn. It begins with crying, cooing, and babbling, then moves into the learning of words, and finally, the learning of grammar.

Crying, Cooing, and Babbling Crying, cooing, and babbling are not considered true language because they do not use symbols with specific meanings. Nevertheless, crying is an effective form of verbal expression—it usually gets the attention of caregivers.

During their second month, babies begin to coo. Coos are vowel-like and resemble "oohs" and "ahs." Cooing seems to express feelings of pleasure. Tired, hungry babies do not coo. Cries and coos can communicate discomfort, hunger, or enjoyment.

At about six months of age, infants begin to babble. Unlike crying and cooing, babbling has the sounds of speech. Babies often babble consonant and vowel combinations, as in *ba, gaz,* and even the highly valued *mama* and *dada.* At first, however, combinations that actually have meaning, such as *mama* and *dada,* are just coincidental.

Crying, cooing, and babbling are basic human abilities. Children from cultures whose languages sound different all babble similar sounds, including sounds they have not heard. In fact, children babble phonemes found in languages spoken around the world. By 9 or 10 months of age, however, children pick out and repeat the phonemes used by the people around them. Other phonemes start to drop away.

Researchers have found that babies understand much of what other people are saying before they can talk. They demonstrate understanding with their actions and gestures.

Words, Words, Words After babbling comes the learning of words—the start of true language. Most children acquire new words slowly at first. After they speak their first word, there may be a gap. In fact, it may take another three or four months before they have a 10-word vocabulary. At about 18 months, children are saying about two dozen words.

Most early words are nouns—names for things. Research indicates that reading to children increases their vocabulary. It is thus a good idea for parents to pull out the storybooks and read to their children. Studies suggest that reading to children improves their awareness of phonemes and improves the child's decoding skills. It also leads to higher reading achievement and advanced oral language development, especially in the elementary grades.

Children sometimes overreach—they try to talk about more things than they have words for. Often they extend the meanings of words to refer to things for which they do not have words. This behavior is called overextension. For example, if a child sees a cow but does not know the word *cow,* she or he might call the cow a doggie.

Development of Grammar The first things children say are usually brief, but they have the meanings of sentences. That is, these utterances have a grammar. Even one word can express a complete thought, such as "Sit!" Children just starting to use language use only the words essential to communicating.

Sometimes a word will have more than one meaning, depending on the circumstances. For example, *doggie* can mean "There is a dog," "That stuffed animal looks like my dog," or "I want you to give me the dog!" Most children readily teach their parents what they mean with their utterances. They are delighted when parents do as requested and may howl when they do not.

As they approach their second birthday, most children begin to use two-word sentences. "That doggie" might seem like just a phrase but is really a sentence in which *is* and *a* are implied: "That (is) (a) doggie." Two-word utterances such as this appear at about the same time in all languages.

Even brief two-word utterances show understanding of grammar. A child who wants his or her mother to sit in a chair says, "Sit chair," not "chair sit." Similarly, the child says, "my doggy," not "doggy my," to show possession. "Mommy go" means Mommy is leaving. "Go Mommy" expresses the desire to have Mommy leave.

Between the ages of two and three, children's sentences expand to include missing

Complete a Webquest at thinkcentral.com on how grammar differs among various languages.

INTERACTIVE

Stages of Language Development

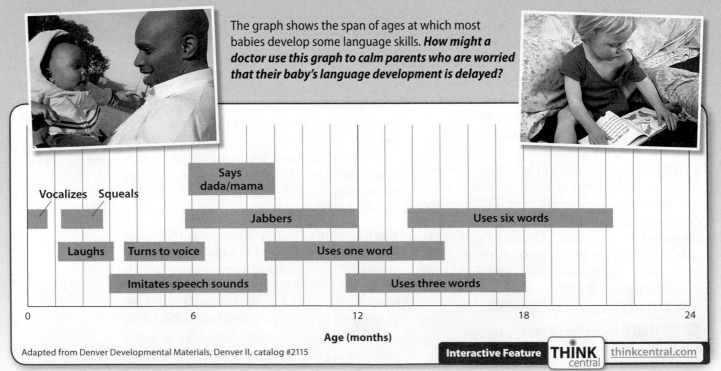

The graph shows the span of ages at which most babies develop some language skills. *How might a doctor use this graph to calm parents who are worried that their baby's language development is delayed?*

Vocalizes | Squeals

Says dada/mama

Jabbers

Uses six words

Laughs | Turns to voice

Uses one word

Imitates speech sounds

Uses three words

| 0 | 6 | 12 | 18 | 24 |

Age (months)

Adapted from Denver Developmental Materials, Denver II, catalog #2115

Interactive Feature THINK central thinkcentral.com

words. They add articles (*a, an, the*), conjunctions (*and, but, or*), possessive and demonstrative adjectives (*your, her, that*), pronouns (*she, him, it*), and prepositions (*in, on, over, around, under, through*).

One interesting aspect of how children learn grammar has to do with irregular words. English has many irregular verbs and nouns. For example, the past tense of *am* is *was,* the past tense of *sit* is *sat,* and the plural of *child* is *children.* Children first learn irregular words by imitating their parents. Two-year-olds often use them correctly. But then a seemingly odd thing happens. Even though the children have used these words correctly, they soon begin to use them incorrectly.

What has happened is that they have learned the rules for forming the past tense and plurals (in English, adding *d* or *ed* morphemes to make a word past tense and adding *s* or *z* morphemes to form plurals). Once they have learned these rules, they begin to make errors. For example, three- to five-year-olds may say, "I runned away" instead of "I ran away." They are likely to talk about the "sheeps" or "gooses" they "seed" on the farm.

Children make these errors because they have applied the normal rules to all words, even the words for which the rules do not work—a process called **overregularization.** Although it may seem like a bad thing when children begin to incorrectly use words that they previously used correctly, overregularization represents an advance in the development of grammar. In another year or two, children will learn the correct forms of the irregular words as well as the regular ones, and overregularization will stop.

Reading Check **Sequence** In what order do children learn language?

Bilingualism

Many people, of course, learn more than one language. To speak two languages fluently is to be bilingual. In general, learning a second language during childhood is much easier than learning it later in life. This fact supports the theory that there is a period in childhood during which language acquisition is easiest and most effective.

Although the majority of people in the United States speak only English, the number

Statistically Speaking...

POLLING PLACE
投票站 CASILLA ELECTORAL
投票所 LUGAR NG BOTOHAN
투표소 PHÒNG PHIẾU

A Multilingual Country Hundreds of languages are spoken in the United States. The figures below show about how many people speak one of the top six languages at home, as of 2005.

268,111,000	Total population 5 years old and older
216,176,000	speak English only
32,184,000	speak Spanish or Spanish Creole
2,300,000	speak Chinese
1,383,000	speak French, including Patois and Cajun
1,377,000	speak Tagalog (a language of the Philippines)
1,142,000	speak Vietnamese

Thinking Critically Some Americans fear that the English language is in danger of losing prominence in this country. Do you think the figures support this concern? Why or why not?

Source: Statistical Abstract of the United States 2008

of those who are bilingual is growing. In this respect, this country is becoming more like other parts of the world. Many people in other countries speak two or more languages. Some countries have minority populations whose languages differ from the official tongue. A large percentage of Europeans learn English and the languages of neighboring nations.

Consider the Netherlands. Dutch is the native language, but children are also taught French, German, and English in the public schools.

For more than 40 million people in the United States, English is a second language. Millions of speakers converse each day in Asian, African, and European languages.

A century ago a common belief held that children reared in bilingual homes would be slowed in their cognitive and language development. The attitude was that people who knew two languages were crowding their mental abilities because cognitive capacity is limited. However, the U.S. Bureau of the Census reports that more than 75 percent of Americans who first spoke another language in the home also speak English "well" or "very well." Moreover, a careful analysis of older studies in bilingualism shows that the bilingual children often lived in poor families and had little education. Yet these bilingual children were compared to middle-class children who spoke English. In addition, achievement and intelligence tests were given in English, which was the second language of the bilingual children. Lack of education and poor testing methods, rather than bilingualism, accounted for the apparent differences in achievement and intelligence.

Today most psychologists believe that it is good for children's cognitive development to be bilingual—in Spanish, Russian, Chinese, or any other language. Bilingualism expands children's awareness of different cultures and broadens their outlooks on life. For example, bilingual children are more likely to understand that the symbols used in language are arbitrary. Children who speak only English are more likely to think that the word *dog* is somehow connected directly with the nature of the animal. Bilingual children therefore have somewhat more cognitive flexibility. In addition, learning a second language has been shown to increase children's expertise in their first (native) language.

Although bilingualism is a growing trend in this country, it still evokes strong emotions and occasional controversy. For example, in 2008, two Vietnamese American cousins, who were at the top of their class, spoke a few sentences of Vietnamese during their graduation speeches. The lines in Vietnamese expressed appreciation to their parents, who were in the audience and had limited English proficiency. A school board member protested, prompting the school board to consider requiring that graduation addresses be in English only.

In addition, various groups have tried to require that English be used for all public occasions in this country. No language is designated as the "official" language of the United States.

Reading Check **Make Generalizations** What are some advantages to bilingualism?

SECTION 4 Assessment

Reviewing Main Ideas and Vocabulary

1. **Identify Main Ideas** What are some examples of the uses of language?

2. **Recall** How do people learn language?

3. **Define** What are semantics?

Thinking Critically

4. **Explain** What is overregularization?

5. **Analyze** What is the purpose of grammar?

6. **Support a Position** Write a paragraph supporting or disagreeing with the following statement: "All children in U.S. public elementary schools should learn a second language." Use information from the section to uphold your views.

7. **Compare and Contrast** Using your notes and a graphic organizer like the one below, compare and contrast the three basic elements of language.

Element	Characteristics

FOCUS ON WRITING

8. **Descriptive** Think of a part of your life in which you use specialized language, such as in a sport or while learning to play a musical instrument. Identify five words unique to that experience and write a dictionary entry for each one. Then describe how you acquired this specialized language.

Disappearing Languages

By the year 2100 about half of the world's 7,000 or so languages are likely to have disappeared. As a result, information about cultures, their history, the environment, and the different ways that people think will also disappear.

The Mohawk tribe, of which this child is a member, is one of the cultures in the United States whose language is disappearing.

Languages die as the few remaining people who speak them die. Some of the languages that are disappearing are currently spoken by only a handful of people, many of whom are very old. If the younger members of a culture group do not learn the language, it will be gone forever.

There are five regions where languages are disappearing most rapidly. Two are in the United States: the upper Pacific Coast and the Southwest, including Oklahoma. In these regions, Native American languages are being lost. The other three regions are northern Australia, central South America, and eastern Siberia. These regions also have large numbers of indigenous people.

Why do languages die out? There are several reasons. In some of these areas, the speakers of native languages have been forced to speak the language of a dominant culture. For example, a few decades ago teachers and officials punished Native American children if they spoke their own language instead of English.

A more common reason at work today is the influence of dominant cultures and languages, called "predator" languages by some linguists. English is certainly one of them, since it dominates the Internet and global communications in science, entertainment, and business. Among other predator languages are Chinese, Spanish, Hindi, and Swahili. All of these languages are spoken by hundreds of millions of people.

A third reason is that people naturally want to pursue a better way of life for themselves and their families. Using the language of commerce and education is one path to prosperity.

Why does it matter if languages disappear? In fact, a great deal is at stake. For one thing, when a language is lost, so is an entire culture. Many of the dwindling languages have rich traditions of stories, songs, and histories that were never written down. Also, valuable information about the environment that is still undocumented by science can be lost if peoples who lived close to the natural world can no longer share that knowledge in their own language.

Perhaps the most significant issue, however, is the loss of different ways of thinking and of different ways of using language. For instance, the Karkardian language of the Caucasus Mountains has 48 consonants but, according to some linguists, no vowels at all. The Boro language of India and Bangladesh has some remarkable verbs. Examples include *onsra,* "to love for the last time," and *egthu,* "to create a pinching sensation in the armpit." Mohawk, spoken by a North American tribe, has extremely complex verbs. If you want to say "I am currently bringing the sugar to someone," you use a single word: *tkhetsikhetenhawihtennihs.*

In many countries, there are efforts to save or even revive dying languages. Since 2000, instruction in Welsh has been compulsory in Wales. In the Yukon area of Canada, elders of the Yupiit tribe contribute to a collection of their language's vocabulary and grammar. Many other such programs are ongoing around the world.

Despite such efforts, languages will disappear. We will all be poorer for the loss.

Ryan Bransetter, who traces part of his heritage to the Walla Walla tribe, learns the tribe's language from Cecilia Bearchum at an Oregon reservation.

Thinking Critically

1. **Summarize** What are three reasons why languages are dying?

2. **Discuss** Do you think that the English language reveals unique features of our culture? If so, what are they?

Children, Thinking, and Language

Help new parents understand how their child will think, solve problems, and use language in these processes.

Reading and Activity Workbook

Use the workbook to complete this lab.

1. Introduction

In this lab you will create a pamphlet designed to help parents understand how their children think and solve problems and the importance of language in this process. You will work in two different groups. In the first group you will become experts about one particular aspect of thinking and language. (See some suggestions for topics in Step 2, Conducting Your Research.) In the second group you will share your expertise with other group members and construct your pamphlet.

◾ Following your teacher's instructions, organize the class into five equal-sized groups.

◾ Your teacher will assign each group one of the following topics: Thinking, Problem Solving, Creativity, Decision Making, Language.

◾ Work with students in your group to become experts on your assigned topic. Write down important terms, concepts, and ideas. All group members should have the same information at the conclusion of this portion of the activity. It is very important that you share information and ideas and write down what you know and learn. You will take this information to a different group and your classmates in that new group will expect you to be the expert on your topic.

◾ You may also conduct media center research to gather more information about your assigned topic.

2. Conducting Your Research

Parents have many concerns about how well their children will acquire language and use language to think. For example, some children start to speak much later than their peers. Others may not acquire the basic language skills that they will need if they are to learn how to read and solve various problems throughout life. You will want to conduct research to identify and elaborate on these and other concerns.

There are some steps that parents can take to ensure that their children develop all the language skills they will need to be successful. Regular visits to a physician familiar with language development are important. Other examples include reading to the children and speaking to them using many different words and a calm tone of voice. Include these and similar strategies in your research.

3. Sharing Your Expertise

You will be assigned a new group in which every member was assigned a different area of expertise. This may be done easily if each expert group numbers off from 1 to 5. By doing this, you should have one expert from each topic in your new group. In your new group, each expert will teach other group members about her or his topic. In teaching your group members, be sure to include:

◾ The name of your topic

◾ Important terms and concepts regarding your topic

◾ How your topic is important (think how individuals would be different if your topic did not exist)

◾ Examples of how your topic works

4. Making the Pamphlet

Once all group members have shared their information, it is time to make your pamphlet. The purpose of your pamphlet is to educate parents about how children think, solve problems, and learn language. Your pamphlet must be divided into five sections (one for each topic) and have a cover. The cover must include a title, your names, and a graphic or illustration. Each section must include:

- Three to five sentences or bullet points with key information/main ideas

- At least two terms related to the topic (these may be embedded in the sentences)

- An example of how the topic works (for example, if your topic is problem solving, you may provide an example of how to solve a problem)

- A graphic or illustration that enhances understanding about the topic

5. Exchange Pamphlets

Once all the groups have finished their work, exchange pamphlets with another group. Review the new pamphlet and note information that you did not include in your own. Also, pay close attention to the examples and illustrations provided by the other group.

6. Discussion

What did you learn from this lab? Hold a group discussion that focuses on the following questions:

- Overall, how successful was the class at creating pamphlets that could educate parents about thinking and language?

- Which topics were easiest to understand and explain?

- Which topics were most difficult to understand and explain?

- What examples were most helpful? Why?

- What illustrations were most helpful? Why?

- How might parents use this knowledge as they make decisions regarding their children?

- What are the greatest challenges individuals face as they attempt to solve problems?

- As we communicate in many different settings (face to face, telephone, writing, e-mail, instant messaging, texting), in what ways might you expect language to change during your lifetime?

- Do these multiple means of communication make language more or less important? Explain.

Comprehension and Critical Thinking

SECTION 1 *(pp. 214–218)*

1. a. Identify What are three units of thought that make language possible?

   b. Contrast How are convergent and divergent thinking different?

   c. Elaborate How do you use metacognition when you study for a final exam? Give specific examples.

SECTION 2 *(pp. 220–228)*

2. a. Define What is an algorithm?

   b. Explain Why is trial and error often not an effective or efficient problem-solving method?

   c. Support a Position Defend or refute this statement: "Insight is totally unpredictable."

SECTION 3 *(pp. 229–233)*

3. a. Recall What is reasoning, and what are the two main types?

   b. Explain What are some of the factors you might record if you were using a balance sheet when trying to decide between attending a community college or a four-year college?

   c. Elaborate Why must premises always be correct? What could happen if they are incorrect?

SECTION 4 *(pp. 234–240)*

4. a. Define What is a LAD, and what does it do?

   b. Compare and Contrast What is the difference between phonemes and morphemes? What do they have in common?

   c. Identify Cause and Effect What are some reasons why parents may become very anxious about a child's language acquisition?

Reviewing Vocabulary

Match the terms below with their correct definitions.

5. language   **10.** heuristics

6. recombination   **11.** premise

7. mental set   **12.** exemplify

8. semantics   **13.** symbol

9. morpheme   **14.** functional fixedness

A. an object or an act that stands for something else

B. the tendency to think of an object as being useful only for the function that the object is usually used for

C. to show or illustrate by example

D. the tendency to respond to a new problem with an approach that was successfully used with similar problems

E. unit of meaning in a language

F. rules of thumb, or shortcuts

G. an idea or statement that provides the basic information that allows us to draw conclusions

H. the study of meaning

I. the communication of ideas through symbols that are arranged according to rules of grammar

J. the mental rearrangement of elements of a problem

INTERNET ACTIVITY ✴

15. What are the issues surrounding bilingualism in your community or state? What positions do people on both sides of the issue take? Are their supporting arguments valid? Use the Internet to research these questions. Write a short report that summarizes your findings.

Psychology in Your Life

16. Think of a problem facing your school or community for which there are two or more possible solutions or courses of action. Create a balance sheet listing each possible course of action and its pros and cons. Then write a brief report explaining what your final decision is, how you reached that decision, and how the balance sheet helped you arrive at your decision.

SKILLS ACTIVITY: INTERPRETING CARTOONS

Certain symbols are in common use because their meaning is instantly understandable. Study the cartoon and answer the questions that follow.

17. Analyze What does the cartoonist assume that you know?

18. Explain In what way does the cartoon contradict your assumptions about symbols?

WRITING FOR AP PSYCHOLOGY

Use your knowledge of language acquisition to answer the question below. Do not simply list facts. Present a clear argument based on your critical analysis of the question, using the appropriate psychological terminology.

19. Which factor or factors do you think have the most powerful impact on language acquisition?

- inherent language acquisition device
- hereditary influences
- environmental influences

Connecting Online

Visit thinkcentral.com for review and enrichment activities related to this chapter.

Quiz and Review

ONLINE QUIZZES
Take a practice quiz for each section in this chapter.

WEBQUEST
Complete a structured Internet activity for this chapter.

QUICK LAB
Reinforce a key concept with a short lab activity.

APPLYING WHAT YOU'VE LEARNED
Review and apply your knowledge by completing a project-based assessment.

Activities

eACTIVITIES
Complete chapter Internet activities for enrichment.

INTERACTIVE FEATURE
Explore an interactive version of a key feature in this chapter.

KEEP IT CURRENT
Link to current news and research in psychology.

Online Textbook

 Learn more about key topics in this chapter.

What Makes a creative GENIUS?

Martha Graham's bodily-kinesthetic intelligence helped her to explore new pathways in modern dance.

Harvard psychologist Howard Gardner believes that there are several kinds of intelligence. Above and beyond the sorts of intelligence useful in school, Gardner suggests that other kinds of intelligence are necessary for success in other areas.

Gardner's perspective on intelligence stems in part from his life-long love of the arts. As a student of psychology, Gardner noticed that the arts and creativity generally received little attention. He decided to investigate their relationship to intelligence by studying some of the most creative people of the 1900s.

In 1993 Gardner published his findings in a book titled *Creating Minds.* In it, Gardner describes the characteristics and circumstances that shaped the lives and work of seven major figures: Sigmund Freud, Albert Einstein, Pablo Picasso, Igor Stravinsky, T. S. Eliot, Martha Graham, and Mohandas Gandhi. Each of these people was outstanding in his or her field, and each one also happens to represent one of the intelligences in Gardner's theory.

Sigmund Freud, as you know, was a famous psychologist whose intelligence provided insight into his own deepest feelings. Albert Einstein, the physicist who established the theory of relativity, had a special ability in math. Pablo Picasso—a painter, sculptor, and potter—had outstanding spatial-relations intelligence. Igor Stravinsky, a composer, had extraordinary musical ability. T. S. Eliot, a poet, had linguistic intelligence. Martha Graham, a dancer, had special body-kinesthetic intelligence. Mohandas Gandhi possessed exceptional sensitivity to the feelings and needs of others, which helped him to become an influential leader in India.

Using the information he learned about these creative people, Gardner developed EC. *EC* stands for Exceptional Creator, an imaginary person who combines the common characteristics of creators. As embodied by an imaginary woman, the characteristics are as follows:

- EC comes from outside a major city but not so far removed that she is uninformed.
- EC's family is neither wealthy nor poor but is reasonably comfortable.
- EC's upbringing is fairly strict, and her closest friend is outside her immediate family.
- EC's family is not especially educated, but they value learning.
- EC discovers her talent at an early age.
- As an adult, EC feels the need to test herself against others in her field, and she moves to the city.
- Once she makes a major breakthrough in her field, EC becomes isolated from her peers.
- EC works nearly all the time and makes tremendous demands on herself.
- EC is self-confident, stubborn, and able to deal with adversity.
- EC has a second major breakthrough in her field about 10 years after the first.
- EC lives a long time, gains many followers, and makes contributions in her field until her death.

CHAPTER 9
INTELLIGENCE

Most of the famous creators Gardner studied had to struggle to win acceptance for their ideas. When acceptance came too easily, some even made a special effort to be unconventional because they felt it made them more creative.

Gardner points out that each and every characteristic will not be true for all creative individuals. However, as a general profile, quite a few of the details should hold true. As you will learn in this chapter, creativity is not the same as intelligence. But the seven major figures Gardner profiled possessed both exceptional creativity and exceptional intelligence.

Artist Pablo Picasso's high spatial-relations intelligence led him to invent new styles and helped him to create masterpieces of visual art.

Chapter at a Glance

SECTION 1: What Is Intelligence?
■ Intelligence is different from achievement.
■ Psychologists have developed several different theories of intelligence.

SECTION 2: Measurement of Intelligence
■ Psychologists use tests to measure a person's intelligence.
■ Intelligence tests must be both reliable and valid.
■ Problems with the use and design of intelligence tests have led to some controversies.

SECTION 3: Differences in Intelligence
■ Most people have average intelligence.
■ There are several levels of mental retardation.
■ The gifted have high intelligence and special talent.
■ Creativity is independent of intelligence.

SECTION 4: What Influences Intelligence?
■ Genetic factors have a strong influence on intelligence.
■ A nurturing environment promotes intellectual development in children.
■ Advanced age limits some aspects of intelligence.

What do you think?

1. What seven types of intelligence did Gardner's Exceptional Creators demonstrate?

2. What living person do you consider an Exceptional Creator? How does he or she exhibit the common characteristics of creators?

What Is Intelligence?

Before You Read

Main Idea
Psychologists have many different theories of intelligence.

Reading Focus
1. How is human intelligence a puzzle?
2. What are some of the leading theories of intelligence?

Vocabulary
achievement
intelligence

TAKING NOTES Use a graphic organizer like this one to take notes on intelligence.

Theory	Description

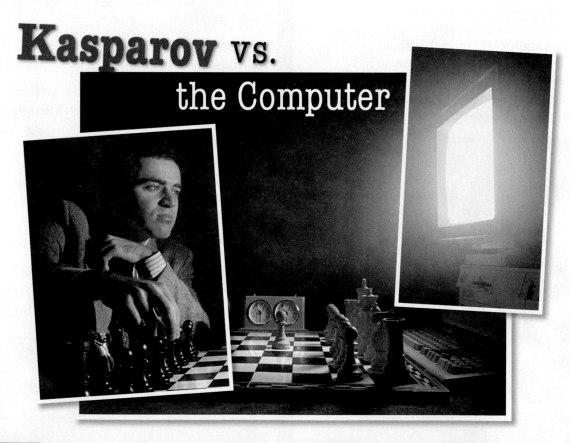

Kasparov vs. the Computer

PSYCHOLOGY CLOSE UP

Can a computer be a Grand Master?
Garry Kasparov reigned as world chess champion from 1985 to 2000. One of his rare defeats during this period came in a 1997 match against an IBM supercomputer known as Deep Blue. In a 1996 match, Kasparov had beaten Deep Blue handily: three wins, two draws, and one loss. But through five games of the rematch, Deep Blue held Kasparov to one win, three draws, and one loss. In the sixth game, a tired Kasparov accidentally reversed two steps in a well-known defensive maneuver. Deep Blue immediately took advantage by taking Kasparov's queen. Kasparov soon admitted defeat.

Deep Blue was an example of artificial intelligence (AI), a broad field that involves the creation of "thinking machines." These machines include everything from industrial robots to speech-recognition devices to game-playing computers. A computer designed specifically for one particular intellectual task, as Deep Blue was, is called an expert system.

Although it could be an expert, can any computer be truly intelligent? Some computers do one particular task better than humans. But no computer can perform as many different tasks as the human brain. After retiring from competitive chess in 2005, Kasparov turned his attention to Russian politics. Deep Blue was built only to beat Kasparov. After its victory, IBM disassembled the machine. ■

The Intelligence Puzzle

Intelligence is one characteristic that sets humans apart from other forms of life. Although other animals display intelligence, humans' capacity to adapt to changing conditions sets them apart from other animals.

The human ability to think about abstract ideas, such as space and time, also sets us apart from all other species. Intelligence has even expanded our senses, enabling us to invent microscopes and telescopes to see things too small or distant for the naked eye to detect. This chapter examines how intelligence is defined and measured. It also discusses differences in intelligence and considers the factors that influence intelligence.

The nature of intelligence varies. People can be very intelligent and not know many facts about academic subjects because they have not studied. People can also know a great deal because they have worked hard, even if their intelligence is not particularly high. But what exactly is intelligence?

Understanding Achievement According to psychologists, one thing intelligence is *not* is **achievement,** which refers to knowledge and skills gained from experience. In other words, achievement focuses on the things that you know and can do. Thus, achievement involves specific content, such as Spanish, calculus, history, psychology, biology, art, or music.

The relationship between achievement and experience is obvious. If you have spent many hours reading about the Civil War, for example, then you will probably do well on a test about that period in U.S. history. You will have gained knowledge on the subject of the Civil War. But if you were tested on the Revolutionary War instead, you might not do as well.

Although intelligence is not the same as achievement, intelligence can provide the *basis* for achievement. Intelligence makes achievement possible by giving people the ability to learn.

For example, consider two students who are both fascinated by mathematics. Suppose that they both take exactly the same math classes and spend the same amount of time studying the subject. The only difference between the two is that student A is more intelligent than student B. Despite the equality of opportunity and effort, student A will gain more knowledge and skills from the mathematics classes than student B. Intelligence helps student A achieve more than student B.

Understanding Intelligence Now we know what intelligence is *not*. But what is it? **Intelligence** can be defined as the abilities to learn from experience, to think rationally, and to deal effectively with others. Within that definition, psychologists have differing theories about what exactly makes up intelligence.

Reading Check **Analyze** What is the difference between achievement and intelligence?

Theories of Intelligence

Some people have very strong science or math skills. Others are talented in music or art. Still others have the ability to get along well with other people. Are all of these abilities signs of intelligence? Is any of them? How many factors are involved in intelligence?

Throughout human history, many philosophers and scientists have speculated about the answers to these questions. The Greek philosopher Plato devoted much of his writing to examining the nature of intelligence and the human mind. French philosopher Blaise Pascal suggested that there were two types of intelligence: mathematical and intuitive. In the 1800s, the rise of psychology as a science led to new theories of intelligence.

Spearman's Two-factor Theory Around 1900, psychologist Charles Spearman observed that people who do well on one type of intelligence test tend to do well on others, too. He suggested that general intelligence, which he labeled *g*, underlies all of our intellectual abilities. The *g* factor represents the abilities to reason and to solve problems.

The SATs, which break intellectual skills into verbal, quantitative, and writing subtests, reflect a more or less unified factor, which some psychologists refer to as *g*. At the same time, all people are better at some things than others—such as math, music, or writing. For this reason, Spearman suggested that specific, or *s*, factors account for people's specific abilities. Taken together, *g* and *s* explained Spearman's observations.

Thurstone's Theory of Primary Mental Abilities Many psychologists accepted Spearman's two-factor theory of intelligence. One who took exception was L. L. Thurstone, a specialist in psychological testing. In the 1930s Thurstone argued that Spearman's tests were flawed. Thurstone's own tests showed that instead of one general intelligence, there were seven "primary mental abilities": word fluency, verbal comprehension, spatial visualization, <u>facility</u> with numbers, memory, reasoning, and perceptual speed. Further testing led him to include something similar to Spearman's g in his theory.

ACADEMIC VOCABULARY

facility ability or aptitude

Gardner's Theory of Multiple Intelligences Later psychologists began to wonder whether all forms of intelligence could be measured through testing. Psychologist Howard Gardner considered a wide variety of studies and cultures to develop a new theory. In 1983 Gardner proposed a set of seven intelligences, which he later expanded to nine.

- verbal, or linguistic, intelligence
- logical-mathematical intelligence
- visual-spatial intelligence
- bodily-kinesthetic intelligence (such as dancers and athletes have)
- musical-rhythmic intelligence
- interpersonal intelligence (sensitivity to other people's feelings)
- intrapersonal intelligence (insight into one's own inner feelings)
- naturalist intelligence (understanding of nature and the laws that govern natural behavior)
- existential intelligence (insight into the larger philosophical issues of life)

Gardner refers to these talents or abilities as intelligences because they can be quite different from one another. In addition, he proposes that the different intelligences are independent of each other.

For example, one student might have strong scientific ability but little talent at music. Another student might have special musical-rhythmic ability but few athletic skills. A student athlete might have highly developed bodily-kinesthetic skills but limited scientific abilities.

Critics of Gardner's theory of multiple intelligences state that exceptional abilities in the musical or bodily-kinesthetic areas are not really what is meant by intelligence. His critics argue that those skills are special talents and that being talented is not the same thing as being intelligent.

Sternberg's Triarchic Theory In 1985 psychologist Robert Sternberg published his triarchic theory of intelligence. This theory breaks intelligence into the following three factors:

- analytical intelligence (the type of intelligence we use in academic courses)
- creative intelligence
- practical intelligence

Some people might excel in their schoolwork, while other people might be more creative or have more practical intelligence, or "street smarts." Practical intelligence includes abilities such as knowing how to discuss a grade with a teacher or what to do if you discover that you have lost your wallet.

Sternberg's Triarchic Model

Sternberg divided intelligence according to the way people process information. Everyone is capable of using the three types of intelligence to some degree. But each person tends to excel at one type. This chart shows some tasks performed by each type of intelligence.

Analytical Intelligence
- calculating expenses and profits
- diagramming a sentence
- measuring the results of a chemistry experiment

Creative Intelligence
- painting a portrait
- writing a song
- cooking a meal with the ingredients on hand

Practical Intelligence
- changing a tire
- negotiating with an employer
- leading a group on a tour of your school

Skills Focus INTERPRETING CHARTS What kind of intelligence are you using when you answer test questions? Explain.

Some students with limited analytical skills do very well in school—and afterward—because they are creative or have street smarts.

We often use more than one of Sternberg's three factors at the same time. If you were doing an experiment for an upcoming science fair, you might use practical intelligence to plan your time and to obtain the materials you need. You would use your analytical intelligence to interpret the results of your experiment. In addition, you would use your creative intelligence to design the display for your project.

Emotional Intelligence Psychologists Peter Salovey and John Mayer became interested in why smart people are not always as successful as might be expected. In 1990 they proposed yet another kind of intelligence: emotional intelligence. The theory gained popularity in 1995 with the publication of the book *Emotional Intelligence* by psychologist Daniel Goleman. Emotional intelligence, said Goleman, consists of five factors that are involved in success in school or on the job:

- **Self-awareness**: the ability to recognize our own feelings. If we know how we feel, we can better cope with our feelings.

- **Mood management**: the ability to distract oneself from an uncomfortable feeling. Although we may not be able to prevent feelings of anger or sadness, we do have some control over how long the feelings last. Rather than dwell on bad feelings, we can distract ourselves or make changes to improve our situation.

- **Self-motivation**: the ability to move ahead with confidence and enthusiasm. People who are self-motivators sometimes accomplish more than less motivated people who obtain higher scores on intelligence tests.

- **Impulse control**: the ability to delay pleasure until the task at hand has been accomplished. A student who resists the temptation to watch television until her or his homework is done may do better in school than a student who puts off homework until later.

- **People skills**: the ability to empathize, understand, communicate, and cooperate with others. People skills help us get along with others, and getting along with others helps us in school and on the job.

A "class clown" may have exceptional people skills. According to the new theory, such people could be considered emotionally intelligent. Emotional intelligence captured the interest of many psychologists and led to new research on the subject.

Reading Check **Summarize** Name and describe the theory of intelligence that suggested that there was a single, basic intelligence.

Online Quiz **THINK** central thinkcentral.com

SECTION 1 Assessment

Reviewing Main Ideas and Vocabulary

1. **Define** What is intelligence?

2. **Identify** What seven forms of intelligence did Thurstone propose?

Thinking Critically

3. **Summarize** How did Spearman use *g* and *s* to explain intelligence?

4. **Explain** What did Spearman and Thurstone's theories of intelligence have in common that later psychologists began to question?

5. **Support a Position** Do you agree that all nine of Gardner's intelligences are really forms of intelligence? If so, choose one of the non-academic intelligences and explain why it qualifies as a form of intelligence. If not, choose one and explain why you think it is not a form of intelligence.

6. **Compare** Using your notes and a graphic organizer like the one below, align Gardner's nine intelligences with Sternberg's triarchic model.

Gardner	Sternberg

FOCUS ON WRITING

7. **Descriptive** Decide which of Sternberg's three types of intelligence is your strongest. Write a paragraph describing a situation in which you displayed this form of intelligence.

Measurement of Intelligence

Before You Read

Main Idea

Psychologists have developed different kinds of intelligence tests. To be useful, the tests must be reliable and valid.

Reading Focus

1. What are the two most widely used intelligence tests?

2. How are test reliability and validity measured?

3. What are some controversies and problems associated with intelligence tests?

Vocabulary

mental age
intelligence quotient
transformed score
reliability
test-retest reliability
validity

TAKING NOTES Use a graphic organizer like this one to take notes on intelligence testing.

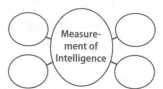

Measurement of Intelligence

WHEN THE "CONSTANTLY-TESTED" GENERATION GROWS UP...

I SEEK WISDOM AND I BROUGHT MY NUMBER-TWO PENCIL!

www.caglecartoons.com

Mike Keefe THE DENVER POST 03/25/06

People Just Keep Getting SMARTER

PSYCHOLOGY CLOSE UP

Why do scores keep rising on intelligence tests? Educators, politicians, and the media frequently worry over declining academic standards and students who don't care. But psychologist James Flynn discovered something that might brighten the worriers' mood: people actually seem to be getting smarter, not dumber.

While researching intelligence tests used by the U.S. military, Flynn discovered something odd. Each time the tests were updated, some recruits would take both the old and the new version. And each time, their average score was higher on the old test than on the new test. Since IQ scores reflect the intelligence of the general population, the recruits compared more favorably against people from several years before than against people today. In other words, average intelligence was rising.

To confirm his findings, Flynn looked at results from several types of intelligence tests and many different cultures. Regardless of the type of test or the nationality of the test taker, he found that people seemed to be getting smarter. After publishing his results, the trend became known as the Flynn Effect.

Why is this happening? Flynn considered and ruled out several theories. Better nutrition doesn't seem to be the answer; neither does better schooling. One of the sturdiest hypotheses is that as our society becomes more complex and more technological, our brains are faced with more challenges from an early age. This rich environment may help us make the most of our mental capabilities. ■

Two Intelligence Tests

You have probably taken many tests throughout your school career. Some of the tests you have taken or will take are achievement tests—they show what you have learned. Other tests are aptitude tests, which are intended to predict your ability to learn new skills. There are also tests that are designed to measure intelligence. The most widely used intelligence tests are the Stanford-Binet Intelligence Scale and the Wechsler scales.

The Stanford-Binet Scale In the early 1900s, leaders of the French public school system were interested in finding a test that could identify children who were likely to need special educational attention. In response, French psychologist Alfred Binet devised the first modern intelligence test. The original version of the test was first used in 1905.

Binet assumed that intelligence increased with age, so his test contained questions for children of different age levels. Older children were expected to answer more difficult questions. Children earned "months" of credit for correct answers.

Binet's test yielded a score called a mental age. A child's mental age is not the same thing as his or her chronological age. **Mental age** (MA) shows the intellectual level at which a child is functioning. For example, a child with an MA of six is functioning, intellectually, like the typical six-year-old, even if the child is not six years old. An MA of nine is above average for a seven-year-old. The same MA of nine is below average for an 11-year-old.

In 1916 Binet's test was brought to the United States and revised by Louis Terman of Stanford University. For this reason, the test became known as the Stanford-Binet Intelligence Scale (SBIS).

The version of the Stanford-Binet test used today provides an intelligence quotient, not an MA. An **intelligence quotient** (IQ) is a number that reflects the relationship between a child's mental age and his or her actual, or chronological, age (CA). The IQ is a *quotient* because we use division to obtain the number. The IQ was initially computed using the formula IQ = (mental age divided by chronological age) × 100, or

$$IQ = \frac{\text{Mental Age (MA)}}{\text{Chronological Age (CA)}} \times 100$$

For example, a child with an MA of nine and a CA of nine would have an IQ of 100.

STANFORD–BINET INTELLIGENCE SCALE

These items are similar to those that appear on the Stanford-Binet Intelligence Scale. That test includes tasks for age levels from two to adult. The Stanford-Binet test produces an intelligence quotient, or IQ, that compares mental age to chronological age.

Age Level	Sample Item 1	Sample Item 2
2 years	Children know basic vocabulary words. When the examiner says, "Show me the hands" (or other part), they can point to the proper parts of a doll.	Children can match a model by building a tower made up of four blocks.
4 years	Children show language and classifying ability by filling in a missing word: "Father is a man; mother is a _____."	Children show general understanding by answering questions such as: "Why do people have cars?"
9 years	Children can point out absurdities. "Sally has a bicycle with square wheels. What is silly about that?"	Children show language ability by responding to queries such as: "What number rhymes with *sea*?"
Adult	Adults show vocabulary knowledge and conceptual thinking by explaining the differences between word pairs such as "honor" and "glory."	Adults show spatial skills by answering questions such as: "If a car turned to the left to head south, in what direction was it heading before it turned?"

Skills Focus **INTERPRETING CHARTS** At what age are children expected to recognize absurdities?

Interactive Feature THINK central   thinkcentral.com

Children who answer test items as competently as older children have IQs above 100. An 8-year-old who does as well as the average 10-year-old will attain an IQ of 125. Children who do not do as well as typical children their age attain IQ scores below 100.

The intelligence quotient is an example of a **transformed score**—any score that has been changed from a raw score in a systematic way. Psychologists transform raw scores so that test results can be more easily compared.

The Wechsler Scales The Stanford-Binet is the "classic" individual intelligence test. Today, however, David Wechsler's scales are more widely used. Wechsler developed intelligence tests for children and adults. The most widely used test is the revised Wechsler Adult Intelligence Scale (WAIS-R).

The Wechsler scales consist of several subtests. Each subtest measures a different intellectual skill. Some of Wechsler's subtests measure verbal skills. Others <u>assess</u> performance skills. In general, verbal subtests involve words and ideas; performance subtests focus on spatial relations. Both verbal and performance subtests require reasoning ability. The Wechsler scales reveal relative strengths and weaknesses as well as overall intellectual functioning.

The Wechsler scales differ from the Stanford-Binet test in several important ways. The Wechsler scales do not use the concept of mental age, although they still use the term IQ. The Stanford-Binet test measures verbal ability, whereas the Wechsler scales measure both verbal and nonverbal abilities. Because the Wechsler tests yield three scores (verbal, nonverbal, and combined), they can be used to identify particular learning disabilities. For example, if an individual's verbal score is significantly lower than his or her nonverbal score, this might indicate a reading disability.

Scores on the Wechsler tests are based on a comparison of a person's answers with the answers of others in the same age group. The average score for any age level is 100. About 50 percent of scores fall within a broad range of 90 to 110. About 2 percent of people who take the tests score above 130, and about 2 percent score below 70.

Reading Check **Identify** What is now the most widely used intelligence test?

Reliability and Validity

The results of intelligence tests affect people's lives, so psychologists hold the tests to high standards. Intelligence tests (and other types of psychological tests) must meet two criteria: they must be *reliable* and *valid*.

Test Reliability Imagine that every time you measured the width of your desk with a tape measure, it showed a different result. If this happened, we would say that the tape measure was an unreliable form of measurement. The **reliability** of a test refers to its consistency. A test or any other method of assessment is reliable if it gives a highly similar score every time it is used. A reliable intelligence test should obtain similar IQ scores for the same individual on different testing occasions.

There are different ways of showing a test's reliability. One of the most common is called **test-retest reliability.** Test-retest reliability is determined by comparing scores earned by the same person on the same test taken at different times. The Stanford-Binet and Wechsler tests are both highly reliable. For example, if you took the Stanford-Binet in your first year of high school and again in your senior year, your IQ score would probably be nearly the same both times.

Keep in mind that "nearly the same" does not mean "identical." Scores for the same person on different testing occasions may vary somewhat. A person may be more motivated or attentive one day than another. Also, scores may improve as subjects become familiar with the test format. In addition, intelligence is not fixed—it varies over time. Some intellectual skills may increase with education; some may decline with age, injury, or health problems.

Test Validity A test has **validity** if it measures what it is supposed to measure. To see whether a test is valid, test scores are compared with outside standards or norms. A proper standard for checking the validity of a musical aptitude test might be the ability to learn to play a musical instrument. Tests of musical aptitude therefore should predict ability to learn to play a musical instrument.

What standards might be used to check the validity of intelligence tests? Most people agree that intelligence plays a role in academic success. Intelligence test scores should

The Wechsler scales consist of subtests that measure different skills. These are examples of items similar to those that appear on the various subtests.

Verbal Subtests

General Information
1. How many legs does a dog have?
2. How many nickels make a quarter?
3. What is ice made of?
4. Who wrote *Harry Potter*?
5. What is salt?

Similarities
1. How are a wolf and a fox alike?
2. How are a saw and a hammer alike?
3. How are a day and a week alike?
4. How are a circle and a square alike?

General Comprehension
1. What should you do if you see someone forget her coat when she leaves a restaurant?
2. Why does some food need to be stored in a refrigerator?
3. Why is copper often used in electrical wires?

Vocabulary
This test consists simply of asking "What is a _____?" or "What does _____ mean?" The words cover a wide range of difficulty.

Arithmetic
1. Sam had two pieces of fruit, and Joe gave him four more. How many pieces of fruit did Sam now have?
2. Four women divided 12 eggs equally among themselves. How many eggs did each person receive?
3. If two buttons cost 20 cents, how much would a dozen buttons cost?

Performance Subtests

Digit Symbol
The subject is tested on the ability to associate meaningless figures with specific numbers.

Block Design
The subject is tested on the ability to recreate geometric designs using colored blocks.

Picture Completion
The subject is asked to identify what is missing from a picture like this.

Picture Arrangement
The subject is tested on the ability to arrange pictures such as these in a sequence so that they tell a story.

---

therefore predict school grades. They do so moderately well. Intelligence is also thought to contribute, in part, to job success. Scores on intelligence tests have been shown to predict adult occupational status reasonably well. Thus, these intelligence tests seem to be reasonably valid. However, because there is considerable disagreement about what intelligence is, some psychologists believe that it is difficult to make definitive statements about the validity of IQ tests.

Reading Check **Infer** What scores would you expect if a person took an unreliable test several different times?

Controversies and Problems

Intelligence testing has become an accepted part of our culture. But the history of intelligence testing is full of controversies, some of which have yet to be resolved. In addition, psychologists point to problems with intelligence tests that may affect results.

Controversies In the late 1800s many began to see intelligence testing as a way to improve society. Movements sought to elevate the most intelligent people to positions of importance. But they also wanted to reduce the numbers of the least intelligent people.

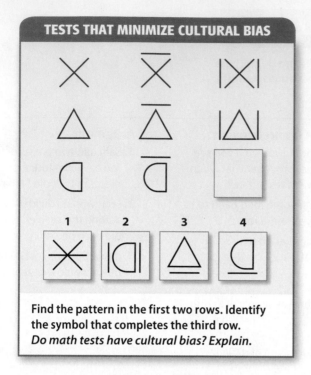

TESTS THAT MINIMIZE CULTURAL BIAS

1   2   3   4

Find the pattern in the first two rows. Identify the symbol that completes the third row.
Do math tests have cultural bias? Explain.

of that group would find such tests more difficult. For example, a question about building an igloo would be easier for Inuit, who live in the Arctic, but more difficult for most other people. In theory, tests that are free from cultural bias ought to be possible. The challenge is to develop questions that test a particular skill regardless of the test-taker's culture.

Problems Intelligence tests are not perfect. Some test takers do better than others, but not necessarily because they are more intelligent. Other factors—such as education or economic background—can make a difference.

Motivation to do well also contributes to performance on intelligence tests. Faced with frequent failure, a person may begin to expect to fail. Without the motivation to try his or her best, failure becomes more likely.

Expectations are especially important when test takers are members of a group with negative stereotypes. When people know about a negative stereotype that applies to them—regardless of the truth of the stereotype—the expectation can be self-confirming. This is called stereotype threat. Studies have shown that reminding subjects about a negative stereotype before they take a test can result in performance that does not match true abilities. Conversely, subjects who are reminded of positive stereotypes tend to perform better than expected.

Reading Check **Identify Supporting Details**
What are two ways in which an intelligence test might show cultural bias?

In the early 1900s the United States used intelligence tests to determine which immigrants would be allowed into the country. Those who did not score well were deported. During the same period, many states sterilized people who were found to be "mentally defective." The horrors perpetrated by Nazi Germany in the name of social purity brought an end to these misuses of intelligence tests.

Another controversy around intelligence testing is cultural bias. Critics charge that some tests give an advantage to a particular group because they are created by members of that group. People who are not members

---

Online Quiz **THINK** central   thinkcentral.com

Reviewing Main Ideas and Vocabulary

1. **Define** What is mental age?
2. **Explain** Why is IQ called a *quotient*?
3. **Recall** What two criteria must all intelligence tests meet?

Thinking Critically

4. **Evaluate** If a 10-year-old boy takes the Stanford-Binet test and scores as well as a 12-year-old, what would his IQ be?
5. **Explain** How is test-retest reliability determined?
6. **Interpret** How is the following question culturally biased? *Lawrence and Molly go to the opera once a month. About how many arias do they hear each year?*

7. **Compare and Contrast** Using your notes and a graphic organizer like the one below, compare the Stanford-Binet test to the Wechsler scales.

Similarities	Differences

FOCUS ON WRITING

8. **Persuasive** A politician proposes a new law to require voters to have an average score or higher on an intelligence test. Anyone with a below-average score cannot vote. Write a letter to the editor explaining the pitfalls of this proposal.

Differences in Intelligence

Before You Read

Main Idea

Most people have average intelligence. A few have either very high or very low intelligence.

Reading Focus

1. What is average intelligence?

2. How is mental retardation defined?

3. Does giftedness just mean being very smart?

4. What is creativity?

Vocabulary

mental retardation
gifted
prodigy
creativity

TAKING NOTES Use a graphic organizer like this one to take notes on differences in intelligence.

Average   Gifted

Creative

PSYCHOLOGY CLOSE UP

Does autism help Temple Grandin understand animals?

Autism is a complex neurological disorder that affects millions of people. Generally, autistic people have difficulty interacting with others and may focus intensely on one object or subject. For many years, autism was treated as a kind of mental retardation. As the disorder has become better understood, psychologists have realized that some autistic people have normal intelligence. And a few people with autism display extraordinary gifts.

Temple Grandin, for example, has autism and a gift for understanding animals. She first realized this ability as a teenager. She felt more at ease among the animals at her aunt's ranch than among people. Grandin pursued her interest in animals and eventually earned advanced degrees in animal science.

While completing her degrees, Grandin began visiting a meat-packing plant, where she observed that the animals were in distress. She realized that the design of the chutes and pens was one of the chief causes of stress for the animals. The manager of the plant, who had gotten to know Grandin through her many visits, offered her the chance to redesign the layout to make it easier on the animals. Her design succeeded, and she began a career designing more animal-friendly environments.

Temple Grandin credits the support she received at every step of her life for helping her make the most of her talents. As more autistic people receive such support, their intelligence will shine through. ▣

Intelligence AND Autism

Average Intelligence

Despite the limits of intelligence tests, they do have some uses. One of the primary functions of intelligence tests is to help identify people whose intelligence is out of the ordinary—at either end of the scale. The education system best suits people of average intelligence. Those with extremely high or extremely low intelligence need special accommodations.

The average IQ score is 100. This is by design. Test-makers administer drafts of their tests to sample populations in order to confirm that the tests are reliable and valid. They use the results to calibrate how the tests are scored. The mean average score becomes the mid-point, or 100. When the general population takes the test, a person's score should reflect her or his intelligence in relation to all the other people taking the test.

About half of the people in the United States attain scores in the broad average range from 90 to 110. Nearly 95 percent attain scores between 70 and 130.

What about the other 5 percent? People who attain IQ scores of 70 or below are defined by psychologists as having mental retardation. People who attain scores of 130 or above are regarded as gifted. In both cases, special help is needed.

Reading Check **Find the Main Idea** What is the average score on an intelligence test?

Mental Retardation

While having an IQ score at or below 70 is the technical definition of **mental retardation,** there are other indicators as well. Mental retardation is also associated with problems in communication, taking care of oneself, social skills, self-direction, travel in the community, and vocational training. There are several levels of mental retardation.

Mild Retardation About 80 percent of people with retardation are classified as mildly retarded, with IQs ranging from 50 to 70. Such people often are not obviously retarded, but as children they have more difficulty than most other children in learning to walk, in feeding themselves, and in learning to talk. Most children with mild retardation are able to learn to read and do arithmetic. As adults, they often are able to take care of themselves and hold jobs. They may, however, need occasional guidance and support.

Moderate Retardation People with IQ scores from 35 to 49 have moderate retardation. They can learn to speak, to feed and dress themselves, and to work under supportive conditions. They usually do not learn to read or to solve math problems. Children with Down syndrome are most likely to be classified in the moderately retarded range.

WEBQUEST
Complete a Webquest at thinkcentral.com on mental retardation.

Statistically Speaking...

IQ Scores Psychologists refer to this bell-shaped graph as a "normal distribution." Many traits, including intelligence, are distributed along normal curves.

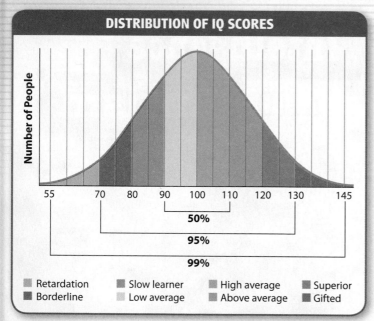

DISTRIBUTION OF IQ SCORES

- Retardation
- Borderline
- Slow learner
- Low average
- High average
- Above average
- Superior
- Gifted

50% Percentage of people whose intelligence scores range from 90 to 110

5 to 10 Estimate of how many points intelligence scores rise every 10 years

100 million Approximate number of standardized tests given to U.S. students each year

Skills Focus **INTERPRETING GRAPHS** Why is the bell curve tallest at the center?

Although adults with moderate retardation are usually not capable of self-maintenance, they can participate in simple recreation and travel alone in familiar places.

Severe Retardation People with severe mental retardation—IQs of 20 to 34—usually require constant supervision. They may have some understanding of speech and be able to respond. Although they can perform daily routines and repetitive activities, they need continuing direction in a protective environment. Some children in this category can learn some basic self-help tasks, such as self-feeding.

Profound Retardation People with profound retardation—IQs below 20—barely communicate. They may show basic emotional responses, but they cannot feed or dress themselves and are dependent on other people for their care throughout their lives.

Causes of Retardation Retardation can be caused by any of several factors. Accidents that result in brain damage and difficulties during childbirth can cause retardation. Pregnant women who abuse alcohol or drugs, are malnourished, or who have other health problems may give birth to children who are mentally retarded. Retardation also can be caused by genetic disorders or abnormalities, such as Down syndrome.

Reading Check **Identify** What are the four levels of mental retardation?

Giftedness

Technically speaking, people who are gifted have IQ scores of 130 or above. However, giftedness (like retardation) may be more than just a matter of IQ. In general, to be **gifted** is to possess outstanding talent or to show the potential for performing at remarkably high levels of accomplishment when compared with other people of the same age, experience, or environment.

The most gifted children are sometimes called child prodigies. A **prodigy** develops special skill in a particular talent or discipline in childhood. Prodigies perform at a level comparable to, or above, most adults in that field. Many prodigies benefit from parents who encourage and help develop their child's talent. Some famous prodigies are listed here.

Famous Prodigies

Visual Arts

Gian Lorenzo Bernini Bernini first learned to sculpt in the workshop of his father, a sculptor. By the age of 14, Bernini was crafting portrait busts for wealthy patrons. He created his first masterpieces in his early 20s. As a sculptor, architect, and painter, Bernini established the baroque style.

Music

Wolfgang Amadeus Mozart Mozart's father, Leopold, trained him as a musician from an early age. Mozart wrote his first composition at age 5 and gave his first public performance when he was 6. He had written 8 symphonies by the time he was 12. Mozart composed some of the world's greatest music.

Sports

Venus and Serena Williams The Williams sisters' father, Richard, raised them to be tennis stars. They each began winning amateur tournaments at the age of 10 and turned professional at age 14. Venus, the older sister, ranked 25th in the world by age 17. Serena ranked 21st in the world by age 16. They have both won many Grand Slam tournaments.

Math

Ruth Lawrence After being tutored at home by her father, Ruth Lawrence entered Oxford University at age 11. Two years later, she graduated with honors with a degree in mathematics. The next year, she had earned a second degree in physics. By the time Lawrence was 17, she had earned a doctorate in math.

Some researchers believe that motivation and creativity contribute to giftedness. Others emphasize the importance of insight. And many educators consider children with outstanding abilities to be gifted. The abilities can be in specific areas such as music, language arts, mathematics, or science. Children may be gifted in terms of leadership abilities or creativity, or they may exhibit excellence in the visual or performing arts.

On the basis of research and experience, educators generally recognize the importance of identifying gifted children early and providing them with rich, varied learning opportunities. Special schooling helps gifted children to develop their potential.

Reading Check **Summarize** What does it mean to be gifted?

Creativity

Giftedness is often linked with creativity. **Creativity** is the ability to invent new solutions to problems or to create original or ingenious materials. For example, some of Albert Einstein's best work grew out of his ability to visualize difficult problems. He developed the theory of special relativity by imagining what light would look like if an observer could move at the speed of light. Einstein himself recognized the value of creativity. He once said, "The true sign of intelligence is not knowledge but imagination."

Although creativity may be a part of giftedness, a person can be highly creative without being gifted. In fact, a person can even be substantially below average in intelligence and yet have very high creativity.

English psychiatrist Lorna Selfe identified one such person, a girl named Nadia. Nadia had <u>diminished</u> mental skills and could not speak. However, she had a remarkable talent for drawing, and her creative ability was indisputable. Nadia exemplified savant syndrome—a person who has autism or mental retardation yet exhibits extraordinary skill, even brilliance, in a particular field. About 10 percent of people with autism display special skills, but fewer than 1 percent of people with other mental disabilities do.

Research suggests that highly intelligent people are more likely than the average person to be particularly creative. Yet just as a high level of creativity does not guarantee high intelligence, high intelligence does not guarantee high creativity. For example, a Canadian study of gifted children ages 9 to 11 found that they generally were more creative than children who were average in intelligence. However, this was only true for the group as a whole. Some of the gifted individuals were no more creative than the children who were average in intelligence.

Reading Check **Draw Conclusions** Are all creative people highly intelligent? Explain.

Online Quiz THINK central thinkcentral.com

SECTION 3 Assessment

Reviewing Main Ideas and Vocabulary

1. **Define** What is a prodigy?

2. **Recall** What is the technical definition of mental retardation?

Thinking Critically

3. **Support a Position** Does it make sense for the education system to be tailored to the needs of people of average intelligence? Why or why not?

4. **Identify Cause and Effect** What are some of the possible causes of mental retardation?

5. **Elaborate** How could someone be highly intelligent without being considered gifted?

6. **Explain** How could someone be highly creative without being highly intelligent?

7. **Categorize** Using your notes and a graphic organizer like the one below, describe the four levels of mental retardation.

Level of Retardation	Characteristics

FOCUS ON WRITING

8. **Expository** Imagine that someone creating an intelligence test accidentally used only extremely smart people to calibrate the test. Explain what would happen when the test was administered to the general population.

What Influences Intelligence?

Before You Read

Main Idea

Both heredity and environment influence a person's intelligence.

Reading Focus

1. How does your genetic make-up influence your intelligence?
2. How does your environment influence your intelligence?
3. What are some of the connections between aging and intelligence?

Vocabulary

heritability
fluid intelligence
crystallized intelligence

TAKING NOTES Use a graphic organizer like this one to take notes on influences on intelligence.

Genetics	→	
Environment	→	
Age	→	

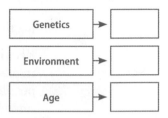

Hungry to Learn

PSYCHOLOGY CLOSE UP

Can hunger make you smarter? The brain is part of the body, so the state of your body affects your intelligence. One commonly-recognized example of this is the effect of over-eating. Everyone knows you shouldn't eat a big meal before an important test—you'll be too sleepy to do your best.

Scientists have found that the opposite approach might help. When the stomach is empty, it produces ghrelin, a hormone that signals that it's time to eat. But ghrelin also boosts learning, memory, and spatial reasoning. Mice that were injected with ghrelin performed better than other mice when running mazes and performing other tests of their intelligence.

Does this mean you should starve yourself before your next big exam? Probably not. First of all, the scientists point out that more research needs to be done to establish whether hunger would help improve human intelligence. Secondly, the brain needs food to function. Too little nourishment might boost ghrelin levels, but it would also starve the brain of fuel. As with so many things, moderation is probably the best choice: take your test fed, but not full. ■

Genetic Influences on Intelligence

Through the 1900s, a great debate took place in the scientific world. Scientists wondered whether we are more influenced by our genetics or by our environment. The question applies to many human characteristics but few more so than intelligence. We will look first at the genetic side of the debate.

Are all people born with the same amount of intelligence? How do genetic factors affect the level of intelligence we have? Researchers who study the genetic factors in intelligence have used kinship studies and adoptee studies to explore questions such as these.

Kinship Studies If genetic factors are involved in intelligence, then closely related people should be more alike in terms of intelligence test scores than distantly related or unrelated people. For this reason, psychologists have studied intelligence test scores of related people. Identical twins have often been used in these studies. Because they have exactly the same genetic makeup, their test scores should be identical if intelligence is solely inherited. Any difference in scores would mean that other factors are also involved.

ACADEMIC VOCABULARY
colleagues
co-workers or associates

Psychologist Thomas Bouchard and his colleagues compiled the results of more than 100 studies on the relationship between heredity and intelligence. They found that the intelligence test scores of identical twins are more similar than those of any other group of people. This finding holds true even when the twins are reared apart and grow up in different environments. Similarities in intelligence test scores between pairs of fraternal twins, other brothers or sisters, and parents and children are moderate. Similarities in intelligence between children and foster parents and between cousins are weak. What does all this mean? It means that genes do seem to play some role in intelligence. But how great a role does inheritance play?

Heritability is the extent to which variations in a trait from person to person can be explained by genetic factors. Most studies suggest that the heritability of intelligence ranges from 40 to 60 percent. That is, about half of the differences in intelligence test scores among people can be accounted for by heredity.

Adoptee Studies Some studies have compared the intelligence test scores of adopted children to those of their biological parents and their adoptive parents. If children are separated from their biological parents at early ages but their intelligence test scores remain very similar to those of their biological parents, it is probably because of genetic influences.

On the other hand, if the intelligence test scores of adopted children are more like those of their adoptive parents, it is probably because of environmental influences. Most studies of adopted children have found that their intelligence test scores are more like those of the biological parents than those of the adoptive parents. Thus, there seems to be further evidence of heredity's role in intelligence.

Other psychologists, however, argue that an overemphasis on heredity can undermine parental and educational efforts to help children learn. Parents and educators are most effective when they believe their efforts will improve children's knowledge and skills. Because parents and educators cannot change children's genetic codes, it is useful for them to assume that effective parenting and teaching can make a difference.

Reading Check **Draw Conclusions** Whose intelligence test score will probably be closest to yours: a parent, a cousin, or a neighbor? Explain.

Environmental Influences on Intelligence

Bouchard and his colleagues found that for each type of kinship, from identical twins to parents and children, intelligence test scores are more alike for pairs of people who were reared together than for pairs who were reared apart. This result holds for identical twins, other brothers and sisters, and even people who are unrelated. These findings suggest that environmental factors also affect intelligence. A variety of studies have examined the influence of home environment, parenting style, schooling, and other environmental factors on intelligence.

Home and Parenting Studies have shown that home environment and styles of parenting influence the development of intelligence.

Boosting Brainpower

Many factors influence how well our brains work. A quick survey may reveal how common behaviors affect your academic performance.

PROCEDURE

❶ Take out a blank piece of paper but do not put your name on it. Answer the following questions about the past week:

How many hours did you spend exercising?

How many hours of sleep did you get?

How many caffeinated beverages did you consume during or before school?

How many hours did you play a musical instrument?

What were your scores on quizzes and tests?

❷ Collect the answers, and order them by test scores.

❸ Enter the results in a table with a column for each answer and a row for each student.

ANALYSIS

1. As a class, analyze the results, and see if you can correlate any of the four factors with higher test scores.

2. Now do the same with lower test scores.

3. If you find a clear link between behaviors and test scores, write a short press release describing your findings. If not, discuss whether any of these behaviors affect academic performance.

Quick Lab THINK central thinkcentral.com

The following factors have been demonstrated to help improve intellectual functioning in children.

- The parents are emotionally and verbally responsive to their children's needs.
- The parents provide enjoyable and educational toys.
- The parents are involved in their children's activities.
- The parents provide varied daily experiences during the preschool years.
- The home environment is well-organized and safe.
- The children are encouraged to be independent—to make their own decisions and to solve their own problems whenever possible.

Preschool Programs Many preschool programs are designed to provide young children with enriched early experiences. These experiences are intended to develop intelligence and to prepare children for school. Many such programs exist, but one particularly well-known program is Head Start. Begun in 1965, Head Start was designed to give economically disadvantaged children a better start in school.

Communities across the United States operate Head Start centers under the guidance of the U.S. Department of Health and Human Services. Parental involvement is an important feature of Head Start. This program includes health, education, and social services for participating children and their families. In local Head Start centers, children become familiar with books. They also play word and number games; work with puzzles, drawing materials, toy animals, and dolls; and interact with teachers in a school-like setting.

Preschool programs such as Head Start have been shown to increase the intelligence test scores, achievement test scores, and academic skills of participants. Preschool programs also appear to have long-term benefits. Graduates of these programs are less likely to repeat a grade or to be placed in classes for slow learners. They are more likely to finish high school, to attend college, and to earn high incomes. Participation in such programs even decreases the likelihood of juvenile delinquency and reliance on welfare programs.

Reading Check **Summarize** What did Bouchard find that demonstrates the importance of environment on intelligence?

Aging and Intelligence

Psychologists are also concerned about factors that affect intelligence among adults, especially older adults. Most older people show some drop-off in intelligence as measured by scores on intelligence tests. The decline is usually most notable in timed test questions—questions that must be answered within a certain amount of time. On the other hand, vocabulary skills can continue to expand for a lifetime.

Slowed response times are part of a decline in **fluid intelligence.** These mental capacities allow us to respond quickly to novel situations or problems. What remains more stable, though, is **crystallized intelligence**—the sum of our knowledge about the world. Crystallized intelligence can continue to grow throughout our lives.

Biological changes contribute to some of the decline in fluid intelligence. However, older people who retain their health have very high levels of intellectual functioning. One study, conducted in Seattle, has been following intellectual changes in adults since 1956. The Seattle study has found that intellectual functioning in older people is linked to several environmental factors:

- level of income
- level of education
- a history of stimulating jobs
- intact family life
- attendance at cultural events, travel, and reading
- marriage to a spouse with a high level of intellectual functioning
- a flexible personality

In general, the more of these factors that are present in people's lives and the higher and stronger the factors are, the higher the level of intellectual functioning.

All things considered, intellectual functioning in people of all ages appears to reflect many genetic, physical, personal, and social factors. The fact that a person's genetically determined intellectual potential cannot be predicted makes it difficult to resolve the debate about the roles that genetics and environment play in intelligence. However, no matter what genes a person may have inherited, that person's intelligence is not fixed or unchangeable. People can, depending on their education and other factors, improve their intellectual functioning. Genetic factors give each person a range of possibilities. The environment influences the expression of these possibilities. Intelligence remains a complex concept that challenges psychologists, educators, and many others.

Reading Check **Contrast** What is the difference between fluid and crystallized intelligence?

SECTION 4 Assessment

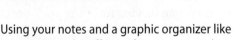
Online Quiz THINK central thinkcentral.com

Reviewing Main Ideas and Vocabulary

1. Define What is heritability?

2. Identify Main Ideas What are the two broad categories of influences on intelligence?

3. Recall What type of intelligence tends to decline in older adults?

Thinking Critically

4. Identify Cause and Effect Why are the IQ scores of identical twins closer than the IQ scores of any other group of people?

5. Explain What effect do preschool programs such as Head Start have on intelligence scores?

6. Summarize Using your notes and a graphic organizer like the one below, summarize the effects of environmental influences on intelligence.

Home and Parenting	Preschool

FOCUS ON WRITING

7. Descriptive Imagine that your local government has asked for your help in designing a new program for senior citizens. They want the program to help senior citizens maintain their mental acuity, and they suggest basing it on the Seattle study. Briefly describe how your program would work.

Emotional Intelligence Influences Success

Emotional intelligence includes the ability to resist temptation.

If you are really smart, are you guaranteed to achieve success? Or does it take more than just book smarts to succeed? Despite the emphasis still placed on traditional measures of intelligence, researchers have found that other types of intelligence are just as important to success at school and work. In particular, emotional intelligence—the ability to understand your own emotions and those of others—turns out to play a significant role in success.

Throughout most of the 1900s, when people thought of intelligence, they thought of the sort measured by the Stanford-Binet and similar tests. The results of standard intelligence tests seemed like a clear indicator of potential success in school and work.

The real world is not so simple, however. The people who score highest don't necessarily achieve the greatest success. It isn't that traditional intelligence isn't important—it takes a certain level of intelligence to be a doctor, for example—but the smartest people aren't necessarily the most successful. Studies have found that IQ can account for as little as 10 percent of a person's success at work.

Why is this? Psychologists began to investigate, and they found some surprising results.

The executive recruiting firm Egon Zehnder International studied the experience, intelligence, and emotional intelligence of executives from around the world. They found that executives with low emotional intelligence were the most likely to fail, regardless of their experience and intelligence. Conversely, those with high emotional intelligence were the most likely to succeed (Fernández-Aráoz, 2007).

One study of insurance salespeople found that optimism and pessimism can affect success. Among new salespeople, the optimists sold 37 percent more in their first two years than the pessimists. The company then decided to hire a group of salespeople who had failed the usual entrance exam but scored high on optimism. Those salespeople outsold the company average by 27 percent.

Some studies show that IQ and emotional intelligence are related. At Stanford University, researchers asked four-year-old subjects to stay alone in a room with a marshmallow while the researcher left the room. If they could resist eating the marshmallow until the researcher returned, they could have a second marshmallow. Fourteen years later, the kids who had been able to wait for the second marshmallow scored about 200 points higher on the SAT than the kids who gave in to temptation.

Success at school and work requires more than just emotional intelligence. But emotional intelligence seems to play a significant role.

Emotional intelligence has been shown to be an important factor of success in the workplace.

Thinking Critically

1. **Interpret** How is emotional Intelligence related to IQ?

2. **Discuss** Name some careers for which emotional intelligence might be important. Explain your answer.

Profile of a Genius

What are the most important qualities for a genius to have? Who has met the profile of a genius?

Reading and Activity Workbook
Use the workbook to complete this lab.

1. Introduction

Often when we hear the word *genius*, the image of Albert Einstein immediately comes to mind. But wasn't he simply a physics genius? Or perhaps if genius in music is mentioned, then Mozart or Beethoven might take the spot. And Leonardo da Vinci is often considered an all-around genius. With so many methods of qualifying what makes a person a genius, it has become a challenge to decide who is one and who is not.

This lab will help you create a profile of a genius using the information learned in this chapter. Working in small groups, you will consider multiple factors before creating a profile, such as: which theory of intelligence you agree with, what method of testing is most indicative of genius, and what kind of upbringing might influence a person's intelligence. Once you have made these decisions, then your group can begin working on drafting a profile of the qualities you expect a genius to possess.

■ Working in small groups organized by your teacher, begin going through each aspect of intelligence addressed in this chapter: theories, testing, and influences. Write down your group's opinions on each of these three areas to use as a foundation when composing the profile of a genius.

■ In your groups begin using the information regarding intelligence to form a profile of a genius. Remember that even though there may be slight differences in opinion, you must come up with one profile as a group.

■ Present your group's profile to the class. The other groups will have an opportunity to agree with or to challenge your decisions, so be prepared to defend your choices!

■ After everyone has shared their profiles, you will look at descriptions of individuals considered to have genius qualities and choose which group's profile they best match.

2. Writing a Profile

After your group has decided which theory (or theories) of intelligence you agree with, the ideal methods to test an individual, and what form of upbringing would be most likely to lead to genius-like qualities, then you can start working on a profile of a genius. Your profile will be similar to a job description. Many examples of job descriptions can be found on the Internet by searching for the words: job descriptions.

❶ **Create Basic Headings:** The first step in writing a profile is deciding what your main headings are going to be. On the next page, there are some from which you can choose. You don't have to use all of them, and there are others that you can create on your own.

❷ **Fill In Specific Information:** Once you have chosen the main headings for the profile, write in bulleted specifics for each of the headings. Try to list at least three items per heading. See the example of Education on the next page.

❸ **Defend Your Reasoning:** Choose the group member whose paper is going to be presented to the class. Then, using another group member's copy of the profile, prepare your defenses for each of your choices. Remember that the other groups will be able to question your decisions, so it's best to be prepared ahead of time. If your group has enough members, assign one group member to each heading to defend it, should questions arise.

3. Presenting the Profile

Once the groups have all finished their profiles, have one group at a time present their work before the class. Each group listening must ask at least one clarifying question, refute a group's choice, or make a suggestion when listening to the presentations of the other groups.

4. Put the Geniuses to the Test

Once you have finished sharing each of your profiles with the class, put some of the individuals commonly referred to as geniuses to the test. Information can be found by simply using their names as an Internet search.

❶ Find information on the genius of your choice on the Internet or in your library. Some examples of geniuses are shown on this page. There are many other individuals that you might be interested in profiling.

❷ Have the class identify which group's profile best fits the genius. Search through their biographies for similar headings or subheadings.

❸ Identify how many categories of the profile match this individual. Calculate a percentage of corresponding qualities.

❹ Label the individual as GENIUS or AVERAGE.

EDUCATION:
- Finished high school before 15 years of age
- Attended Ivy League college or university
- Obtained master's and PhD with honors before 20 years of age

Your genius profile should include headings such as "Education." For each heading, make a list of specific accomplishments you would expect from a genius.

EXAMPLES FOR PROFILES

Basic Profile Headings
- Definition
- Distinguishing Characteristics
- Standards
- Knowledge of . . .
- Ability to . . .
- Experience
- Education
- Upbringing
- Test Scores
- Personal Attributes
- Interpersonal Skills
- Leadership Skills
- Awards
- Certifications
- Hobbies

Examples of Geniuses
- Confucius
- Leonardo Da Vinci
- Wolfgang Amadeus Mozart
- George Washington Carver
- Marie Curie
- Albert Einstein
- Srinivasa Ramanujan
- Stephen Hawking
- Marilyn Vos Savant
- Kim Ung-yong
- Alia Sabur

Comprehension and Critical Thinking

SECTION 1 *(pp. 248–251)*

1. a. Describe What is *g,* and who developed the term?

b. Analyze Why is achievement not necessarily a sign of intelligence?

c. Support a Position Which theory of intelligence do you think is the most accurate? Use specific examples to explain your answer.

SECTION 2 *(pp. 252–256)*

2. a. Recall What is the most common way to determine an intelligence test's reliability?

b. Evaluate Why are the Wechsler scales more widely used than the Stanford-Binet test?

c. Interpret Other than vocabulary and problem-solving methods, what else might cause intelligence tests to be culturally biased?

SECTION 3 *(pp. 257–260)*

3. a. Identify Give one unique characteristic of each of the following individuals:

- person with moderate retardation
- person with profound retardation
- gifted person
- creative person

b. Elaborate What is the relationship between creativity and intelligence?

c. Explain Why is the average IQ score always 100?

SECTION 4 *(pp. 261–264)*

4. a. Identify Main Ideas List three examples of things that parents can do to help improve the intelligence of their children.

b. Identify Cause and Effect What have kinship and adoptee studies revealed about the genetic role in intelligence?

c. Evaluate How might attending cultural events help someone who is age 70 or older maintain a high level of intellectual functioning?

Reviewing Vocabulary

Fill in each blank with the term that correctly completes the sentence.

5. The abilities to learn from experience, to think rationally, and to deal effectively with others is called _____ .

6. _____ with numbers is one of Thurstone's primary mental abilities.

7. _____ shows the intellectual level at which a child is functioning.

8. An _____ is a number that reflects the relationship between a child's mental age and his or her chronological age.

9. The _____ of a test refers to its consistency.

10. A test has _____ if it measures what it is supposed to measure.

11. A _____ develops special skill in a particular talent or discipline in childhood.

12. _____ is the extent to which variations in a trait from person to person can be explained by genetic factors.

13. Mental capacities that allow us to respond quickly to novel situations or problems are called _____ .

14. _____ is the sum of our knowledge about the world.

INTERNET ACTIVITY ✳

15. Fetal alcohol syndrome (FAS) is a cause of mental retardation. Use the Internet to find out more about FAS. Look for information on why it is never safe for pregnant women to drink, how many children suffer from FAS, and other recent news and statistics. Then make a poster or other display warning about the dangers of drinking alcohol during pregnancy.

Psychology in Your Life

16. How many of the nine intelligences proposed by Howard Gardner do you use in this class? List the nine, and describe how you have used each to learn about psychology. For any that you have not used in a significant way, develop a way to incorporate them into the classroom.

Study the bar graph below. Then use the information in the graph to help you answer the questions that follow.

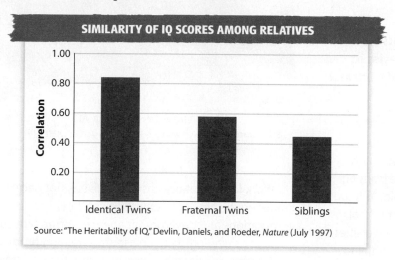

SIMILARITY OF IQ SCORES AMONG RELATIVES

Source: "The Heritability of IQ," Devlin, Daniels, and Roeder, *Nature* (July 1997)

17. Identify Which of the relatives shown in the graph have the most similar intelligence scores?

18. Make Generalizations What does this graph suggest about the effect heredity has on intelligence?

19. Predict If you added a bar showing the correlation of IQ scores for identical twins raised in separate households, how tall would it be relative to these three bars? Why?

WRITING FOR AP PSYCHOLOGY

Use your knowledge of intelligence and intelligence testing to answer the question below. Do not simply list facts. Present a clear argument based on your critical analysis of the question, using the appropriate psychological terminology.

20. Describe how psychologists determine whether an intelligence test meets the three criteria listed below. For each criterion, include a brief definition of the term, the standards used to determine whether a test meets the criterion, and why it is important for intelligence tests to possess that quality.

- reliable
- valid
- culturally unbiased

Connecting Online

Visit thinkcentral.com for review and enrichment activities related to this chapter.

THINK central

Quiz and Review

ONLINE QUIZZES
Take a practice quiz for each section in this chapter.

WEBQUEST
Complete a structured Internet activity for this chapter.

QUICK LAB
Reinforce a key concept with a short lab activity.

APPLYING WHAT YOU'VE LEARNED
Review and apply your knowledge by completing a project-based assessment.

Activities

eACTIVITIES
Complete chapter Internet activities for enrichment.

INTERACTIVE FEATURE
Explore an interactive version of a key feature in this chapter.

KEEP IT CURRENT
Link to current news and research in psychology.

Online Textbook

Click for More   Learn more about key topics in this chapter.

Educational Psychologist

Should classrooms consist only of students of the same age? How should a school district revise its curriculum to meet the changing needs of students? How can computers facilitate learning?

These are examples of the questions that educational psychologists try to answer. In general, they study how people learn. They perform research—both in and out of the classroom—geared to aiding the learning process and improving education as a whole. Although educational psychologists typically work for school districts, they are frequently employed by universities, where they engage in research and assist in training teachers and school counselors.

Unlike school psychologists, educational psychologists are more involved in theoretical issues that affect learning rather than with individual students. Their research often involves measuring a group's abilities and achievements by administering, and sometimes creating, standardized tests. Educational psychologists then use the results of these tests to help place students in specific programs and to develop curricula in schools.

Educational psychologists may focus on several other issues. They may, for example, study the psychological factors that affect a student's test-taking ability or school performance in general. They may research the effects that cultural and gender differences have on learning or the range of instruction methods available to teachers.

Educational psychologists may study various learning environments, such as this small all-girls classroom.

Work for educational psychologists is not necessarily limited to the academic environment, however. Large corporations and government agencies often hire educational psychologists to devise staff training programs.

A bachelor's degree in psychology is the first step in the long, complex process of becoming an educational psychologist. Candidates are urged to gain teaching experience on the elementary, middle school, or high school level before pursuing a doctoral program within a university's education or psychology department. Since the work of educational psychologists involves evaluating and interpreting research data, the training requires proficiency in mathematics, statistics, and computer science. Depending on the graduate program, the final degree earned will be a Doctor of Education (Ed.D.) or a Doctor of Philosophy (Ph.D.) Although educational psychology is a difficult profession to break into, it is an attractive career for those who wish to influence the course of the educational system itself.

Applying APA Style

APA Style · THINK central · thinkcentral.com

People in many lines of work read the articles that educational and other psychologists publish. So, clear communication is essential. Correct grammar aids communication. The **American Psychological Association (APA)** has guidelines for correct grammar.

The APA addresses common grammar errors that appear in manuscripts submitted to APA journals. One common error has to do with subject-verb agreement. A verb has to agree in number with the subject of the sentence. For example, in the sentence "One of the musicians play tomorrow," the verb play does not agree in number with the singular subject, "one." The subject-verb agreement is correct here: "One of the musicians plays tomorrow."

Through Think Central you can find more information on avoiding the most common grammar errors from the APA style guidelines. Review the APA guidelines. Then write several examples of sentences using incorrect grammar along with corrected sentences. An example is provided for you.

Incorrect Grammar	Correct Grammar
The sisters, together with their mother, exercises daily.	The sisters, together with their mother, exercise daily.

UNIT 4 Development

CASE STUDY

BULLYING:
A Schoolyard Epidemic

Bullying in schools has many causes that are rooted in issues of development. Its effects also are potentially devastating to victims' development.

Nine-year-old Stephanie did not want to go to school. It turns out that Stephanie had had a disagreement with Susan, another girl at school. Susan had then threatened to beat Stephanie mercilessly if Stephanie showed up at school again. To highlight her warning, Susan had shoved Stephanie across the school hall. Stephanie was a victim of bullying, and Susan was a bully.

Was there something unusual about this situation? Not really. Although boys are more likely than girls to be bullies, many girls engage in bullying, too. Overall, an estimated 70 to 75 percent of students are bullied at some point. Moreover, an estimated 10 percent of students are exposed to extreme bullying.

Bullying has devastating effects. Students come to think of school as a violent place rather than a safe place for learning. Even bullies come to see the school as a violent environment. Bullying also impairs adjustment to middle school and high school, where older children sometimes bully younger children. In particular, bullying impairs adjustment for children who speak another language in the home. Those children tend to experience bullying more often than other children.

Many but not all bullies have some characteristics in common. First, their achievement tends to be lower than average. Perhaps peer approval—or the ability to control other students—becomes more important to bullies than learning or grades. Second, bullies are more likely to come from homes where there is violence between the parents.

In addition, numerous studies have investigated the personalities of bullies. One study compared bullies to nonaggressive students from similar backgrounds. This study found that bullying was more

THE STATS ON BULLYING

The #1 most common form of violence is bullying.

28% of 12- to 18-year-olds reported being bullied in 2005, up from 5% in 1999.

Nearly 160,000 young people miss school every day due to fear of attack or intimidation by other students.

9% of 10- to 17-year-olds say they were abused at least once by "cyberbullies."

Source: Center for Disease Control (CDC);
National Center for Education Statistics

CHAPTER 10
INFANCY AND CHILDHOOD

often associated with delinquent behavior, attention deficit hyperactivity disorder, and depression. Bullies were also more likely to assume that others wanted to harm them, even when the assumption had no basis.

Is there a cure for bullying? School systems and families have a stake in controlling it. Setting strict limits on bullies can sometimes help. Yet, much bullying—if not most—goes unreported. Some children do not report bullying because they are embarrassed. Other children do not report bullying because they fear retaliation. Many children simply learn to accommodate or avoid bullies until they are out of school.

A short film released in 2008, *Stories of Us: Bullying*, gives teachers a tool for talking about the subject in a way that kids can respond to. Middle school students in Champaign, Illinois acted in the film and played major roles in writing the script. The students who contributed ideas and dialogue for the script quickly realized that they had been guilty of many similar acts—starting rumors and gossiping, cyberbullying, intimidation, and so on. Because of the students' input, the film has a realistic quality and a powerful message.

The subjects of bullying and development are intertwined in a number of ways. Bigger, more physically developed children often bully younger, smaller kids. Bullies, as you read, often come from homes where their social development has been damaged by violence. In addition, bullying can destroy victims' self-esteem at a time when children need positive interactions the most.

What do you think?

1. How does bullying affect students and the school atmosphere?

2. Does bullying occur in your school? What can school officials, parents, and students do to limit or stop it?

Chapter at a Glance

SECTION 1: Developmental Psychology

- Developmental psychology is the study of how people grow and change throughout their lives.

- Developmental psychologists are concerned with many issues. One issue is the extent to which heredity (nature) and environment (nurture) affect development. Another is whether people develop in distinct stages or whether development is more gradual and steady.

SECTION 2: Physical Development

- Children grow physically from the time they are conceived through infancy and childhood.

- Reflexes, motor development, and perceptual development are all important aspects of physical development.

SECTION 3: Social Development

- Through the process of social development, infants and children learn to relate to other people.

- Attachment bonds infants and children to those close to them, and the quality of this attachment affects how they develop.

- Parenting styles cover a wide range, but some styles are more likely to produce well-adjusted children who place a high value on themselves. The value one places on one's self is called self-esteem.

SECTION 4: Cognitive Development

- Cognitive development is the development of people's thought processes.

- The psychologist Jean Piaget divided cognitive development into four stages: the sensorimotor stage, the preoperational stage, the concrete-operational stage, and the formal-operational stage.

- The psychologist Lawrence Kohlberg's theory of moral development has three stages: the preconventional level, the conventional level, and the postconventional level. Each of these three levels is further divided into two levels.

Developmental Psychology

Before You Read

Main Idea

The field of developmental psychology examines physical, social, and cognitive development. Heredity and environment control different aspects of development to varying degrees.

Reading Focus

1. Why and how do psychologists study development?

2. How do both heredity and environment contribute to the development process?

3. How would you describe development as a process of stages versus continuity?

Vocabulary

developmental psychology
maturation
critical period

TAKING NOTES Use a graphic organizer like this one to take notes on developmental psychology.

Developmental Psychology		

Sun, Sand, and Psychology

PSYCHOLOGY CLOSE UP

What can you learn about developmental psychology at the beach?

A day at the beach—what a fine opportunity to get some sun, relax, have a swim, and observe human development. It may sound strange, but people-watching at the beach is the perfect way to survey human development. As you sit on your towel, you notice a family to your right. A baby wakes, crying. Mom picks her up, gives her a bottle and a snuggle, and the baby is totally content. Nearby, Dad watches over their 5-year-old son. The two construct a sand castle. The boy's castle wall repeatedly falls over, and he begins to whimper. "I can't do it—I can't do anything right," he says. Dad offers encouragement and helps rebuild the wall. To your left, a group of teenagers plays volleyball. A boy and girl sit apart from the group and have an intimate talk. Another boy about their age walks past, looking lonely and clearly longing to join in.

What signs of development do these people show? The infant simply shows a need for comfort and nourishment. Her brother shows a desire to accomplish things, but doubts his abilities. Mom and Dad try to act in their children's best interests and make sacrifices for them. The teenagers develop close relationships—both friendly and romantic. But the one boy is struggling to find his place among his peers. As people grow older, they steadily develop and their lives become richer and more complex. ■

The Study of Development

Developmental psychology is the field in which psychologists study how people grow and change throughout the life span—from conception, through infancy, childhood, adolescence, and adulthood, and until death. Psychologists are interested in studying the two stages discussed in this chapter—infancy and childhood—for many reasons. One is that early childhood experiences affect people as adolescents and adults. Another is that by studying early stages of development, psychologists can learn about developmental problems, what causes them, and how to treat them. For example, why do some children have low self-esteem? Psychologists can also learn about what types of experiences in infancy and childhood foster healthy and well-adjusted children and adults.

Studying development is also interesting in and of itself. Developmental psychologists study not only people of different ages but also different types of development. These include physical development, social development, and cognitive development.

Because developmental psychologists study people across the life span, they are interested in seeing how people change over time. Psychologists use two methods to study change: the longitudinal method and the cross-sectional method.

Using the longitudinal method, developmental researchers select a group of participants and then observe that same group for a period of time, often years or even decades. The advantage of a longitudinal study lies in being able to observe, compare, and contrast the behaviors of each individual participant over time, as he or she matures and changes. The longer period of time needed for these studies is both a benefit and a drawback. Over time, some subjects may withdraw from the study for any number of reasons. Another possible drawback is that simply being part of a study over a number of years may affect or alter participants' behaviors.

The cross-sectional method eliminates some of the problems of the longitudinal method. In cross-sectional studies, researchers select a sample that includes people of different ages (rather than following individuals as they pass through those age groups). They then compare the participants in the different age groups. This type of study is less time-consuming (and also less expensive), but as with the longitudinal method, some advantages come with built-in drawbacks. The fact that individuals are born at different points in time introduces the possibility that they might have grown up with different educational methods, medical treatments, and cultural influences.

Reading Check **Draw Conclusions** What are two reasons that psychologists are interested in studying infancy and childhood?

Heredity and Environment

Developmental psychologists are concerned with two general issues. The first involves the ways in which heredity and environmental influences contribute to human development. The second issue involves whether development occurs gradually or in stages.

Psychologists have long debated the extent to which human behavior is determined by heredity (nature) or environment (nurture). This debate has been particularly relevant to the study of development. Some aspects of behavior originate in the genes people inherit from their parents. In other words, certain kinds of behavior are biologically "programmed" to develop as long as children receive adequate nutrition and social experience. Researchers use kinship studies, including studies of twins separated at birth, to try to gauge the importance of heredity and environment on human development.

In the field of human development, heredity manifests itself primarily in the process called maturation. **Maturation** is the automatic and sequential process of development that results from genetic signals. For instance, because of maturation, infants generally sit up before they crawl, crawl before they stand, and stand before they walk. This sequence happens automatically and on its own genetically determined timetable. Each infant has his or her own timetable, and there is a wide range of what is considered "normal" when it comes to reaching stages within the sequence. No matter how much one might try to teach these skills to infants, they will not do these things until they are "ready."

Nature, Nurture, and Feral Children

A Chilean boy, Axel Rivas, shows a painting of the pack of dogs with whom he lived. "They are my family," he told authorities. Stories of children living wild and raised by animals have always fascinated people. These stories challenge basic ideas of humanity. Are we born human, or are we made human? *How do feral children fit into the heredity versus environment debate?*

blank slate—a clean blackboard—on which the infant's experiences will be written. In this view, nurture, or the environment, will have the greatest effect on the newborn's development.

Watson and other behaviorists presented environmental explanations for behavior. They thought that the influence of nurture was much stronger than that of nature. The influences of nurture, or the environment, are found in factors such as nutrition, family background, culture, and learning experiences in the home, community, and school.

Today nearly all psychologists would agree that both nature and nurture play key roles in children's development. For example, while few psychologists today believe that maturation plays the major role in *all* areas of development, they certainly think it is central in some, such as physical development and motor development.

Reading Check **Summarize** Name and describe three major issues that are part of the heredity versus environment debate.

Stages Versus Continuity

Another topic of debate among psychologists is whether human development occurs primarily in stages or as a continuous process. In other words, is development like climbing a set of stairs to reach the top (each stair being a distinct level), or is it like walking up an inclined plane or hill (a gradual increase up to the top, without distinct levels)?

A stage, like one step in a staircase, is a period or a level in the development process that is distinct from other levels. Certain aspects of physical development appear to take place in stages. For example, young children go through sitting, crawling, standing, and walking stages—in that order. When people move from one stage to another, their bodies and behavior can change dramatically.

Maturational theorists, such as Gesell, generally believe that most development occurs in stages. Rapid changes usher in dramatically new kinds of behavior, causing entry into the next stage. For instance, when an infant's legs become strong enough to support him or her, the infant stands and soon begins to walk. A new stage of life has begun, and the child changes from infant to toddler.

This concept of "readiness" relates to an important term in the study of development: critical period. A **critical period** is a stage or point in development during which a person is best suited to learn a particular skill or behavior pattern. For example, much research suggests that there may be a critical period for language development in humans. Young children seem to learn language more easily than older children and adults.

Psychologist Arnold Gesell (1880–1961) proposed that maturation played the most important role in development. He focused on many areas of development, including physical and social development. Behavioral psychologists, such as John Watson, took a different view from Gesell's. Behaviorism originated in the 1600s with English philosopher John Locke, who believed that the mind of the infant is like a *tabula rasa* (Latin for "blank slate"). That is, when an infant is born, her or his mind is like a

Jean Piaget is one of the most famous stage theorists. His field was cognitive development. As a young researcher working on intelligence testing, he noticed patterns in children's thinking that led him to a lifelong study of how children think. His studies led him to conclude that everyone develops in the same way, through four stages. Different children reach stages at different times, but everyone goes through the stages in the same order. Erik Erikson is another well-known stage theorist. He focused on the role of social relationships in the development of the personality. Erikson believed people pass through eight stages in the healthy development of their personalities, and that each stage was a task to be mastered before moving on.

Not all psychologists, however, agree that development occurs in stages. For example, J. H. Flavell and his colleagues argue that cognitive development is a gradual process. According to Flavell, cognitive development is an example of continuous development, which, like walking up a slope, happens gradually. For instance, the effects of learning cause gradual changes, such as the improvement over time in a child's ability to walk or the addition of new words to a child's vocabulary.

Continuous development can occur almost unnoticed. A child's steady growth in weight and height from the ages of about 2 to 11 years is an example of continuous development that happens so gradually we usually are not aware of the changes as they are occurring.

Development in Stages

Stages Theories based on the existence of stages hold that development occurs in a predetermined sequence of steps. One cannot jump or skip steps, and everyone takes the steps in the same order. For example, Jean Piaget theorized that children are able to understand certain things between the ages of 2 and 7 but move on to a whole new knowledge set between 7 and 12. Piaget's theory sees cognitive development as a result of preprogrammed heredity.

Continuous Development

Continuity Theories based on the idea of continuity hold that stages of development do not exist. For example, behaviorists, such as John Watson, believe that children pick up knowledge constantly through observation and learning. Each new bit of acquired knowledge builds upon what is learned before. Behaviorist theories, therefore, stress the importance of environment over that of heredity in cognitive development.

However, it is not always clear whether development occurs in stages or in a steady progression. Psychologists continue to debate the issue.

Reading Check **Recall** Which mode of development (stages or continuity) is more aligned with heredity, and which is more aligned with environment?

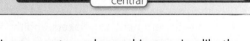

SECTION 1 Assessment

Reviewing Main Ideas and Vocabulary

1. **Recall** What is meant by the term *critical period*?

2. **Describe** Is maturation a product of heredity or environment? Why?

3. **Summarize** How do stage theorists think that people develop?

Thinking Critically

4. **Contrast** Explain how longitudinal and cross-sectional studies are different.

5. **Explain** Which element, nature or nurture, do behaviorists such as John Watson believe most influence development? Explain.

6. **Analyze** Using your notes and a graphic organizer like the one below, explain how heredity and stages are related and how environment and continuity are related.

Heredity	Stages	Environment	Continuity

FOCUS ON WRITING

7. **Expository** What do you think is a more powerful influence on how people develop: heredity or environment? Write two paragraphs explaining your view and include at least two examples from real life that back up your view.

Physical Development

Before You Read

Main Idea

In the womb and in infancy and childhood, humans go through a series of physical developments that are generally sequential.

Reading Focus

1. How is physical growth important from conception through childhood?

2. What are reflexes, and how are they beneficial?

3. What is motor development?

4. What do infants learn through the process of perceptual development?

Vocabulary

infancy
childhood
reflex

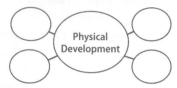

TAKING NOTES Use a graphic organizer like this one to take notes on physical development.

Physical Development

SIZED TO FIT

PSYCHOLOGY CLOSE UP

How did seat belts highlight differences in physical development?
How many times were you told as a child, "You can't do that until you're bigger"? What your parents (or that sign at the amusement park) meant was that you hadn't physically developed enough to do something safely. As we grow physically, we hit milestones that allow us to perform certain tasks or use certain technologies safely. Some technologies are even designed to keep people safe, but they may fail when levels of physical development are not taken into account.

In the United States, as recently as the 1970s, neither adults nor children wore any kind of safety restraints while riding in cars. By the early 1980s, an education campaign by the government, car makers, and the insurance industry made it clear: seat belts saved lives. But, as states began to pass laws and more people buckled up, something strange happened. Young children wearing seat belts in accidents were increasingly hospitalized with abdominal and even some spinal injuries. The problem: seat belts were designed with full-grown adults in mind, not smaller kids. The solution: booster seats for children ages 4–14 to compensate for their smaller size and to make the seat belts fit properly. As you'll see in this section, children develop physically in size and in other ways. ■

YOU MUST BE THIS TALL TO RIDE THIS ATTRACTION

↓ FLOWBOARD ↓

↑ 52" ↑

Physical Growth

A newborn enters the world possessing certain physical characteristics and equipped with certain abilities. For example, an infant is born measuring a certain length and weighing a certain amount. Both height and weight will increase with time and nourishment. The infant is also born with certain reflexes. Changes in reflexes and gains in height and weight are examples of physical development. Motor development and perceptual development are other examples.

Babies grow at an amazing rate, but the most dramatic gains in height and weight occur even before an infant's birth. During the first eight weeks of the mother's pregnancy, the tiny embryo in the mother's uterus develops fingers, toes, eyes, ears, a nose, a mouth, a heart, and a circulatory system. Both the liver and the kidneys begin their functions. Throughout this critical period, the embryo is extremely vulnerable. Drugs, alcohol, and other harmful chemicals can profoundly affect its normal development.

At eight weeks, the 1 1/2-inch-long embryo enters the fetal stage. Throughout this stage the fetus slowly begins to exhibit the characteristic appearance and even behavior of a baby. During the fourth month, the fetus nearly doubles in length, and the mother will soon begin to feel it moving. It can open and close its mouth and swallow as well. In months five and six, the fetus's skin finishes developing, and its hair and nails are becoming visible. It can open and close its eyes and even experiences periods of sleep and wakefulness. It is in general from this stage forward that the organs of the various body systems, such as the respiratory system, are developed to the point that they can sustain the life of the baby in case it is born prematurely.

During the nine months of pregnancy, the embryo develops from a nearly microscopic cell to a baby about 20 inches in length. A newborn weighs a billion or more times what it weighed at conception.

During **infancy**—the period from birth to the age of two years—dramatic gains continue in height and weight. Infants usually double their birth weight in about five months and triple it by one year. They grow about 10 inches in height in the first year. During the

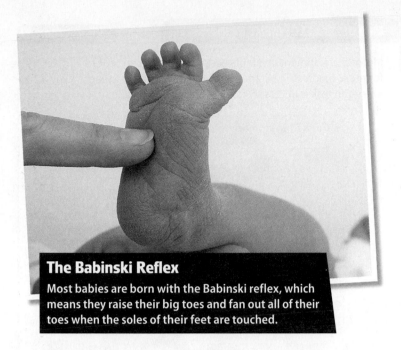

The Babinski Reflex
Most babies are born with the Babinski reflex, which means they raise their big toes and fan out all of their toes when the soles of their feet are touched.

second year, infants generally gain another four to six inches in height and another four to seven pounds in weight.

After infancy comes **childhood,** the period from two years old to adolescence. Following the second birthday, children gain on average two to three inches and four to six pounds each year until they reach the start of adolescence.

Reading Check **Recall** Give three examples of developments that occur during the fetal stage.

Reflexes

A **reflex** is an involuntary reaction or response, such as swallowing. Some of these reflexes the infant keeps; others such as sucking disappear when they are no longer needed. Soon after a baby is born, the doctor or nurse places a finger against the palm of the baby's hand. Babies are not told how to respond and do not "know" what to do, of course. Even so, they usually grasp the finger firmly. Grasping is a reflex. Reflexes are inborn, not learned, and they occur automatically, without thought.

Some reflexes are essential to our survival. Breathing is such a reflex. Although it is a reflex, we can also breathe consciously if we wish—slowly or quickly, deeply or shallowly. The breathing reflex works for a lifetime. Sneezing, coughing, yawning, blinking, and many other reflexes also continue for a lifetime.

ACADEMIC VOCABULARY

respiratory system the system of organs and passages involved in the intake and exchange of oxygen and carbon dioxide between a living organism and its environment

Motor development in infants occurs in an ordered set of stages for most children. The stages build on one another, so each newly mastered task is necessary for the next to be possible.

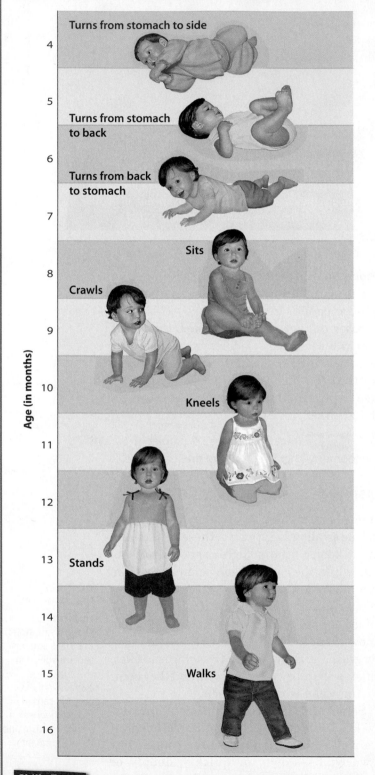

Turns from stomach to side

Turns from stomach to back

Turns from back to stomach

Sits

Crawls

Kneels

Stands

Walks

Age (in months)

Skills Focus INTERPRETING VISUALS About how long does it take for babies to learn to walk, and what skills do they typically learn first?

Interactive Feature **THINK** central thinkcentral.com

Rooting is another reflex that babies are born with. Because of the rooting reflex, babies turn toward stimuli that touch their cheeks or the corners of their mouths. Once infants locate the source of a stimulus, they automatically begin sucking and swallowing. The sucking and swallowing reflexes are essential to an infant's survival; without them, newborns would not eat. Babies reflexively suck objects that touch their lips and reflexively swallow food in their mouths.

Babies also reflexively withdraw from painful stimuli. They pull up their legs and arch their backs in response to sudden sounds or bumps. This is known as the Moro, or startle, reflex. Babies also raise their big toes when the soles of their feet are touched, a behavior that is called the Babinski reflex. They also eliminate wastes by reflex.

As children develop, many reflexes, such as rooting and sucking, disappear. Other reflexes, such as swallowing, remain. And some reflexes, such as elimination of wastes, come under voluntary control. These changes are all part of the maturation process.

Reading Check **Describe** How do newborns respond to their environment? Give two examples.

Motor Development

It might seem that, at first, babies are just bundles of reflexes and random movements. Soon, however, as their muscles and nervous systems mature, newborns' random movements are replaced by purposeful motor activity. The development of purposeful movement is called motor development. It is divided into two areas: gross motor development and fine motor development.

Gross motor development refers to babies' progress in coordinating major muscle groups, such as the arms, the legs, and the trunk. Rolling over, sitting up, crawling, and walking are all examples of gross motor skills. The development of these skills almost always proceeds in known and predictable stages. For example, almost all babies roll over before they sit up unsupported, and they crawl before they are able to stand up and later walk. Milestones in infants' and children's motor development are shown in the diagram at left.

Fine motor development refers to coordination of the hands, face, and other smaller muscles. As with gross motor skills, the development of fine motor skills begins with simple gains and proceeds in stages. At around four months, many babies can grab and shake toys. By nine months, some can pick up small objects between their thumb and index finger. Others will begin to show signs of right- or left-handedness. By a year, they may stack blocks or turn the pages of a book.

The point at which these various behaviors occur, however, is different from infant to infant and even from culture to culture. For example, in Uganda, infants usually walk before they are 10 months old, whereas in the United States, babies often do not start walking until around one year of age. Why might this be? Perhaps it is because, while American babies spend much of their time lying in cribs, Ugandan babies spend much of their time being carried on their parents' backs. This contact with the parents, the sense of movement, and the upright position the babies maintain as they are being carried may help them learn to walk earlier.

Reading Check **Identify** What are the two types of motor development?

Perceptual Development

Imagine what the world must seem like to a newborn. Prior to birth, the baby has spent several months in a warm, dark place. Now suddenly, it finds itself in a bright, noisy world full of sensory stimuli. Perceptual development is the process by which infants learn to make sense of the sights, sounds, tastes, and other sensations to which they are exposed.

Infants tend to prefer new and interesting stimuli. They seem to be "preprogrammed" to survey their environment and to learn about it. For example, a study by Robert Fantz found that two-month-old infants preferred pictures of the human face to any other pictures, such as newsprint, a bull's-eye, or colored disks without patterns.

Researchers have, however, discovered that infants' perceptual preferences are influenced by their age. For example, 5- to 10-week-old babies look longest at patterns that are fairly complex. It does not matter whether

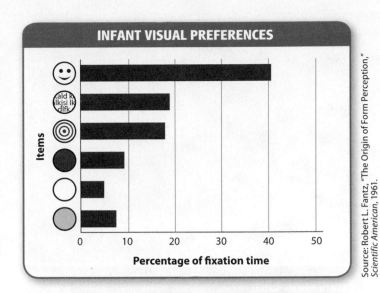

INFANT VISUAL PREFERENCES

Percentage of fixation time

Source: Robert L. Fantz, "The Origin of Form Perception," *Scientific American*, 1961.

Skills Focus **INTERPRETING CHARTS**
Judging by the babies' preference, what age would you say they are?

the pattern looks like a human face. What most interests them is the variety and complexity of the pattern. At this age, eyesight is not fully developed, so infants prefer to look at the most complex things they are capable of seeing reasonably well. By 15 to 20 weeks, patterns begin to matter. Babies then begin to stare longer at facelike patterns.

These studies illustrate how nature and nurture work together. At first, infants seem to have an inborn preference for moderately complex visual stimuli. That is a result of nature. Their preference for human faces seems to appear only after they have had some experience with people. So that preference results from the infant's interaction with his or her environment.

Other studies have focused on depth perception in infants. In some of these studies, researchers use what has become known as the "visual cliff." The visual cliff is a special structure, a portion of which has a surface that looks like a checkerboard. Another portion is a sheet of glass with a checkerboard pattern a few feet below it. It creates the illusion of a drop-off of a few feet—like a cliff.

One classic study with the visual cliff found that very young infants seem to be unafraid when they are placed at the edge of the apparent drop-off. But by nine months, however, infants respond with fear to the drop-off.

The Visual Cliff

Most infants who can crawl refuse to cross the part that appears to be a cliff even if their mothers call them. *What do the results of visual cliff experiments say about infants' visual abilities over time?*

sight. When it comes to hearing, most newborns stop whatever they are doing to turn toward unusual sounds. They respond more to high-pitched sounds than to low-pitched ones, although they seem to be soothed by the sounds of someone singing softly or speaking in a low-pitched tone. No wonder parents often sing lullabies to help their infants go to sleep.

By the 1990s all babies born in the United States were screened for hearing impairment before leaving the hospital. About 1 in 1,000 children have some degree of hearing loss. This loss ranges in severity from total deafness to partial hearing loss with some special educational needs. Children with serious hearing impairment benefit greatly from early detection. Beginning treatment early in life helps them to better acquire language and speech skills.

Newborns immediately distinguish strong odors. They spit, stick out their tongues, and wrinkle their noses at pungent odors and nasty tastes (as the rest of us do). But they smile and show licking motions in response to the sweet smells of chocolate, strawberry, and vanilla. They also like sweet-tasting liquid but refuse to suck salty or bitter liquids. It looks like a "sweet tooth" is part of human nature.

Another classic study found that by the time infants learn to crawl, most of them will refuse to move onto the glass portion even when their mothers call them from the other side. Perhaps crawling and exploring the world have taught the older infants that drop-offs are dangerous. Experience may have contributed to their ability to perceive depth.

Vision, of course, is only one type of perception. In general, infants' hearing is much better developed at birth than is their eye-

Reading Check **Recall** What elements make up perceptual development?

SECTION 2 Assessment

Online Quiz **THINK** central   thinkcentral.com

Reviewing Main Ideas and Vocabulary

1. **Define** What is a reflex? Give two examples.

2. **Recall** What are the two types of motor developments? What makes them different?

3. **Define** What is meant by the term *perceptual development*?

Thinking Critically

4. **Explain** In your own words, explain what the visual cliff experiment demonstrates about perceptual development.

5. **Draw Conclusions** Which real-life example from the section shows that some motor developments are influenced more by environment than by heredity?

6. **Evaluate** Why might it be advantageous for infants to react negatively to foul odors and bad tastes?

7. **Compare and Contrast** Using your notes and a graphic organizer like the one below, describe how motor development and perceptual development are similar and different.

Similarities	Differences
1.	
2.	

FOCUS ON WRITING

8. **Expository** Write a paragraph giving at least two theories of why babies seem pre-programmed to survey their environment and to learn about it.

Raising a Better Child

In the past, ideas about how to raise children generally came from one's family, religion, and other institutions within the community. Beginning around the 1900s, however, the theories of psychologists increasingly began to inform American parenting strategies. Why did parents look beyond traditional sources to learn how to raise their children?

The social upheavals of the last hundred years provide clues to the answer. Because people began to live farther away from their relatives, grandparents were no longer nearby to offer helpful parenting suggestions or quick advice. The U.S. economy became more complicated and competitive, and often both parents were forced to, or chose to, work outside the home. Mass media and consumerism became huge influences on children. With this very brief sampling of the social changes of the twentieth century, it is no wonder American parents struggle to cope.

Today, at any library or bookstore, the number of books promising to improve both parents and children is mind-boggling. This suggests that many parents are unsure about the "right" way to raise children.

One popular idea, dubbed the "Mozart effect," involves the music of the brilliant 18th-century Austrian composer, Wolfgang Amadeus Mozart. Playing Mozart's complex and beautiful music for children, the theory says, helps tiny brains make all-important neural connections that boost life-long intelligence. This movement began with a 1993 study in which college students listened to a Mozart sonata. Later, researchers found that some students had increased spatial-reasoning skills.

The results, however, lasted only 15 minutes after the students stopped listening to the sonata. It is hard to say how the narrow results of this study expanded into books and CDs to play for babies. Better-supported research, however, shows that when preschool and elementary school kids learn to read music or study an instrument, their spatial-reasoning skills show lasting improvements.

Another idea getting media attention deals with the importance of play. Some researchers say that today's children are hurt by not playing enough or in the same ways that children did in the past. These psychologists propose that play for children today relies too heavily on purchased objects—toys, computers, video games—with built-in rules. Imaginative, unsupervised, active play with other children, researchers say, helps in the development of self-regulation. Their studies suggest that kids who engage in this kind of play control their emotions and have greater self-motivation and discipline in adulthood.

Clearly, among the avalanche of parenting books and theories in the marketplace, some have more merit than others. Parents need to do their homework when looking for help with their kids.

Some research shows that active, imaginative play helps kids develop useful, lifelong skills.

Thinking Critically

1. **Explain** What does the large number of child-rearing books suggest about the challenges that parents face?

2. **Discuss** How do you think the ways that you played as a child have affected you?

Social Development

Before You Read

Main Idea

Social development in infants and children has much to do with parents' behaviors, histories, personalities, and abilities. Other caregivers are involved in raising many American children.

Reading Focus

1. Why is attachment vital to human relationships?

2. How do styles of parenting differ?

3. What are some issues associated with child abuse and neglect?

4. How does outside child care affect children's development?

5. What is the importance of self-esteem to developing children?

Vocabulary

attachment
stranger anxiety
separation anxiety
contact comfort
imprinting
authoritative
authoritarian
self-esteem
unconditional
   positive regard
conditional
   positive regard

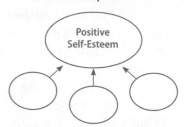

TAKING NOTES Use a graphic organizer like this one to take notes on social development.

Positive Self-Esteem

Teaching Baby Birds to Fly Right

Whooping cranes hatched from eggs in captivity learn their migration route from an ultralight aircraft.

PSYCHOLOGY CLOSE UP

What can baby cranes tell us about social development? In 1950, the last whooping cranes that nested in Louisiana died. This tragedy left only one natural flock of these majestic birds in North America. This flock, which migrates yearly between northern Canada and southern Texas, had only 21 birds in 1955. If a calamity struck this population, wild whooping cranes would disappear from North America forever. What could save the wild cranes?

One answer is a project involving biologists in comically awkward whooping crane outfits and volunteers flying ultralight aircraft. Each year, a new group of crane hatchlings arrives at a wildlife refuge in central Wisconsin. Biologists care for the hatchlings following strict rules: they can not talk, and they must wear the outfits to keep the young birds from imprinting on people. Whooping cranes imprint on—become permanently attached to—the first moving object they see upon hatching. This process tells them what they are for the rest of their lives. The cranes then learn to follow the ultralight aircraft, beginning on the ground before they can fly. When the hatchlings have matured and fall arrives, it is time for them to follow the aircraft to Florida. If the birds had imprinted on a person, they might break off their migration to land at a football game or a backyard barbecue. The proper attachment of the hatchlings to their own kind helps ensure the future of the flock. ■

Attachment

Social development involves the ways in which infants and children learn to relate to other people. For example, infants usually can be comforted by being held, and they soon respond to their mothers' voices. At first, they might cling to their mothers, but after a few months they venture out to explore the world and to make contact with strangers. Infants tend to play with toys by themselves, even when other children are around. As they grow older, however, they begin to play with others. All of these and other changes are part of social development.

Attachment is an important factor affecting social development. Feelings of **attachment** are the emotional ties that form between people. Feelings of attachment keep people together. Because infants are basically helpless and are totally dependent on others to fulfill their needs, feelings of attachment are essential to their survival. Infants and children try to stay in contact with the people to whom they are attached.

Development of Attachment Psychologist Mary Ainsworth studied attachment in infants around the world. What she observed in every place she studied was that, at first, infants prefer being held or even just being with someone—anyone—over being alone. By about four months of age, however, infants develop specific attachments to their main caregivers—usually their mothers. This attachment grows stronger by six to seven months. Once they reach this point, infants and children try to maintain contact with their mothers and cry or complain when they are separated.

By the age of about eight months, some infants develop a fear of strangers. This fear is known as **stranger anxiety.** Infants who experience stranger anxiety cry and reach for their parents if they are near strangers. Their anxiety is somewhat less if the person to whom they are attached is holding them. The closer they are to the strangers, however, the more upset they become. They are most distressed when the strangers actually touch them.

At about the same age, infants may also develop separation anxiety. **Separation anxiety** causes infants to cry or behave in other ways that indicate distress if their mothers leave them. Why do infants become so attached to their primary caregivers? Research suggests that at least two factors are involved: contact comfort and imprinting.

Contact Comfort For a long time, psychologists thought that infants became attached to those who fed them. But then psychologist Harry F. Harlow observed that infant monkeys without mothers or companions became attached to pieces of cloth in their cages—even though, of course, the pieces of cloth did not provide food. The monkeys held on to their pieces of cloth and were upset when the cloth was taken away. Harlow conducted several experiments to find out why, and what types of objects to which the monkeys would and would not become attached.

In one study, Harlow put infant monkeys in cages, each of which had two "mothers."

Harlow's Experiment in Contact Comfort

Harlow's baby monkeys were nourished by their wire "mothers." Even so, the monkeys chose to cling to the soft cloth mothers, which seemed to give them comfort. *What does the baby monkeys' behavior say about the importance of contact versus nourishment?*

One object was made from wire and held a baby bottle. The other, which had no bottle, was made of soft terry cloth. The monkeys spent most of their time clinging to their cloth "mother," even though it did not feed them. Harlow thus concluded that the monkeys had a basic need for **contact comfort,** which is the instinctual need to touch and be touched by something soft, such as skin or fur. This need seems to be even stronger than the need for food. In other words, the monkeys and perhaps human babies may cling to their mothers because of the need for contact comfort rather than just because they are hungry. Based on such findings, researchers have concluded that attachment grows more from bodily contact than from feeding.

Bonds of attachment between mothers and infants also appear to provide a secure base from which the infants can explore their environments. Harlow and Zimmerman placed toys, such as stuffed bears and wooden insects, in cages with infant monkeys. Some of the cages had wire "mothers," and the others had terry cloth "mothers." The monkeys who were alone or with wire mothers cringed in fear as long as the bears or insects were in the cage. Infant monkeys in cages with terry cloth mothers, on the other hand, cringed for a while but eventually began to explore the bears or insects. The terry cloth mothers apparently gave the infant monkeys a sense of security that enabled them to explore the world around them.

Imprinting For many animals, attachment is an instinct. Instinctive behavior develops during a critical period shortly after birth. Ducks, geese, and some other animals become attached to the first moving object they see. The moving object is said to become imprinted on the infant animal. **Imprinting** is the process by which some animals form immediate attachments during a critical period.

Researchers have shown that animals can become imprinted on some rather unusual objects. Using imprinting, researcher Konrad Lorenz acquired a family of goslings for himself. How did he do it? He was present when the goslings hatched, and he then allowed them to follow him. The critical period for imprinting in geese and some other animals begins when they can first move about on

their own. Lorenz's "family" followed him wherever he went. They ran to him when they were frightened. They honked loudly when he left them alone—just as human infants cry when they are left by the people to whom they are attached.

Although the development of attachment may also be instinctive in people, human attachments develop somewhat differently than attachments among ducks and geese. For example, children do not imprint on the first person they see or are held by. For humans, it takes several months before infants become attached to their main caregivers. There is also no known critical period for attachment in humans. Children can become strongly attached to their adoptive parents even when they are adopted after infancy.

Secure Versus Insecure Attachment When mothers or other primary caregivers are affectionate and reliable, infants usually become securely attached. Infants with secure attachment are very bonded to their caregivers. They cry or protest if the parent or caregiver leaves them. When the caregiver returns, the infants welcome that person back and are happy again.

When caregivers are unresponsive or unreliable, the infants are usually insecurely attached. They often do not seem to mind when the caregivers leave them. When the caregivers return, the infants make little or no effort to seek contact with them. Some insecure infants may cry when picked up, as if they are angry with the caregiver.

Secure infants may mature into secure children. Secure children are happier, friendlier, and more cooperative with parents and teachers than insecure children are. They get along better with other children than insecure children do. Secure children are also less likely to misbehave and more likely to do well in school than insecure children.

Autism Autism is a developmental disorder that prevents children from forming proper attachments with others. It presents a wide range of social, cognitive, behavioral, and physical problems. People with autism have certain brain abnormalities that likely came about during pre-natal development. As a result, they have difficulty processing sensory information, which severely damages their

Autism Diagnosed cases of autism are growing, though the increase may be due, in part, to greater knowledge and better diagnostic techniques. Autism can devastate families, and its impact on society is growing.

3.7 to 1 The ratio of males to females diagnosed with autism

300,000 The number of U.S. children age 4–17 diagnosed with autism through 2004

94% The percentage of parents of autistic children who reported that their child needed special services for a medical, behavioral, or other health condition

Sources: Centers for Disease Control and Prevention: Parental Report of Diagnosed Autism, 2003–2004

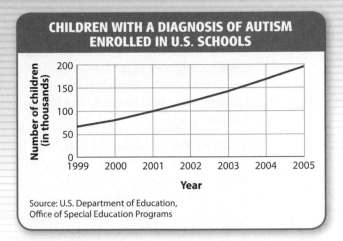

CHILDREN WITH A DIAGNOSIS OF AUTISM ENROLLED IN U.S. SCHOOLS

Source: U.S. Department of Education, Office of Special Education Programs

Skills Focus **INTERPRETING GRAPHS** How many years did it take for the number of children with autism to double, reaching 200,000?

ability to relate to their environment as a whole. For example, some people with autism experience pain at the slightest touch, while others have no reaction to painful stimuli. Autism severely limits its sufferers' ability to communicate with others. Speech is often limited to strange noises or endlessly repeated words or phrases, or it is nonexistent.

People with autism have a very wide variety of symptoms that can be very severe or very subtle. As a result, some people with mild cases go undiagnosed for years. Doctors cannot diagnose autism through a medical test. It can only be detected by watching how a child behaves and how he or she communicates and interacts with others.

Parents and doctors often recognize symptoms of autism during infancy and early childhood. Infants may go limp or become stiff and rigid when their parents hold them. Some infants cry when they are picked up, while others take no notice of affection from their parents. Generally, signs of attachment—smiling, eye contact, playfulness—are absent. In addition, an autistic child may show no signs of stranger anxiety. Later in infancy and into childhood, certain physical behaviors, such as arm flapping and walking on toes, can occur.

Austistic children may also begin to develop certain obsessive or ritualistic behaviors, or they may become self-destructive—banging their heads or biting themselves.

Reading Check **Define** What is contact comfort and how does it relate to the idea of attachment?

Styles of Parenting

Styles of parenting differ along two separate dimensions. One dimension is warmth-coldness; the other is strictness-permissiveness. Warm parents can be either strict or permissive, as can cold parents. The terms *warm, cold, strict,* and *permissive* are at the extreme ends of these dimensions. This means that, for example, parents are neither absolutely cold nor absolutely warm. The vast majority of parents are somewhere in the middle but closer to one extreme or the other.

Warm or Cold? Warm parents show a great deal of affection to their children. For example, they hug them, and smile at them often. They show their children that they are happy to spend time with them and enjoy their company. Cold parents may not be as affectionate toward their children or appear to enjoy them as much.

Research suggests that children fare better when their parents are warm to them. The children of warm parents are more likely to be well adjusted. They are also more likely to develop a conscience—a sense of moral goodness or a sense of responsibility when they do wrong. Children of cold parents, on the other hand, are usually more interested in escaping punishment than in doing the right thing for its own sake.

Strict or Permissive? If you have younger siblings, you probably know that children do many things that anger or annoy other people. For example, they may make noise when other people are trying to sleep or concentrate on a difficult task. Children may also engage in behaviors that are unhealthy to themselves. They may have poor eating habits or watch too much television. They may neglect their schoolwork or play with dangerous objects.

Some parents are extremely strict when it comes to such behaviors. They impose many rules and supervise their children closely. Permissive parents, on the other hand, impose fewer rules and watch their children less closely. Permissive parents tend to be less concerned about neatness and cleanliness than are strict parents.

Parents may be strict or permissive for different reasons. Some extremely strict parents cannot tolerate disorder. Others fear that their children will run wild and get into trouble if they are not taught self-discipline. Some parents are permissive because they believe that children need freedom to express themselves if they are to become independent. Other parents are permissive because they are less concerned or have little time to monitor their children's activities. Without clear and consistent guidance, these children may become confused about which behaviors are acceptable and which are not.

Strictness can have positive and negative results, depending on how it is used. Strictness is not necessarily the same as meanness; parents can be strict but still love their children. Research suggests that consistent and firm enforcement of rules can foster achievement and self-control, especially when combined with warmth and support. But physical punishment or constant interference may lead to disobedience and poor grades in school.

Authoritative (meaning "with authority") parents combine warmth with age appropriate rules and responsibilities. The children of authoritative parents are often more independent and achievement oriented than other children. They also feel better about themselves. Parental demands for responsible behavior combined with affection and support usually pay off.

Be careful not to confuse the term *authoritative* with the word *authoritarian,* which means "favoring unquestioning obedience." **Authoritarian** parents believe in obedience for its own sake. They have strict guidelines that they expect their children to follow without question. Children of authoritarian parents may become either resistant to other people or dependent on them. They generally do not do as well in school as children of authoritative parents. They also tend to be less friendly and less spontaneous.

Reading Check **Describe** Can a parent be warm but strict or cold but permissive? Explain how parenting styles can be a mix of things.

Child Abuse and Neglect

Most parents are kind and loving to their children. Yet child abuse—physical, sexual, and psychological—is relatively widespread. The incidence of child abuse is seriously underreported because children themselves often are unable, unwilling, or afraid to go to the

---

STYLES OF PARENTING

Styles of parenting lie somewhere in the categories of strict-permissive and cold-warm. Each pair of words in the chart, such as *demanding* and *lenient* or *detached* and *affectionate*, represent ends of a continuum. Most parents do not lie at these extreme ends, but generally fall somewhere in the middle.

Strict	Permissive	Cold	Warm
Demanding	Lenient	Indifferent	Supportive
Controlling	Democratic	Careless	Protective
Dictatorial	Inconsistent	Detached	Affectionate
Antagonistic	Overindulgent	Negligent	Caring

Skills Focus **INTERPRETING CHARTS** Do you think it is possible for parents to be strict but warm or permissive but cold? Explain your answer using terms from the chart.

Identifying Parenting Styles

How are different parenting styles expressed in the communications between parents and children? And do interpretations of parenting styles vary? Do all children perceive parents' communications in the same way?

PROCEDURE

❶ Organized the class into four groups—one for each style of parenting. Group one will be for *strict,* group two for *permissive,* group three for *cold,* and group four for *warm.*

❷ On a small sheet of paper, write a statement or question that you think parents who conform to your group's assigned parenting style might say to their children. Try to make your statements or questions true to life. Label your paper with the parenting style, but do not write down your name. Remember that although most parents lean toward one of these parenting styles, very few are at the extremes.

❸ Fold up your papers and collect them in a box.

❹ Have the teacher draw statements from the box and read them aloud. Your teacher should not tell which style is represented. As a class, discuss in which category each statement belongs.

ANALYSIS

1. Does the class agree on which statements belong in which category? Discuss possible reasons for disagreement.

2. Discuss the possibility that a child might see his or her own parents' style as the norm, even if it falls close to one extreme or another.

Quick Lab **THINK** central thinkcentral.com

---

authorities, and abusive parents sometimes try to protect one another. In 2006, about 3.3 million allegations of child abuse or neglect were made in the United States. About 905,000 children were found to be victims, which comes to approximately 12.1 children per 1,000. In the same year, there were an estimated 1,530 child abuse fatalities, of which 78 percent were children under the age of four.

Physical child abuse refers to a physical assault of a child, including actions such as striking, kicking, shaking, and choking. In 13 states, any child born showing evidence of having been exposed to alcohol or illegal drugs is also legally a victim of child abuse. Child sexual abuse is the sexual victimization or exploitation of a child by an older child, an adolescent, or an adult. More than 80 percent of the time in cases of sexual abuse, the child knows the perpetrator. It is often someone such as a relative, a childcare provider, a family friend, or a teacher.

Neglect is failure to give a child adequate food, shelter, clothing, emotional support, or schooling. More health problems and deaths result from neglect than from abuse.

Why do some parents abuse or neglect their children? Psychologists have found the following factors to be associated with child abuse or neglect:

- stress, particularly the stresses of unemployment and poverty
- a history of physical or sexual abuse in at least one parent's family of origin
- acceptance of violence as a way of coping with stress
- lack of attachment to the child
- substance abuse
- rigid attitudes about child rearing

Studies show that children who are abused run a higher risk of developing psychological problems than children who did not grow up in an abusive environment. For example, they tend to be unsure of themselves. They are thus less likely than other children to venture out to explore the world around them. They are more likely to suffer from a variety of psychological problems, such as anxiety, depression, and low self-esteem. They are less likely to be close to their peers and more likely to engage in aggressive behavior. As adults, they are more likely to act in violent ways toward their dates or spouses.

Child abuse tends to run in families. There are many possible reasons for this pattern. For one thing, children may imitate their parents' behavior. If children see their parents coping with feelings of anger through violence, they are likely to follow suit.

Complete a Webquest at thinkcentral.com on child abuse and neglect.

They are less likely to seek other ways of coping, such as humor, verbal expression of negative feelings, deep breathing, or silently "counting to 10" before reacting. These strategies help by giving the feelings of anger time to subside. When parents attempt to cope with anger and stress by abusing alcohol, it can lead to child abuse as well. Alcohol abuse runs in families, and alcoholism is thought to have a genetic component.

Children also often adopt their parents' ideas about discipline. Abused children may come to see severe punishment as normal. As a result, when they have children, they may continue the pattern of abuse and neglect.

This pattern does not mean, however, that all people who were abused as children will in turn become abusers themselves. Most children who are victims of abuse do not later abuse their own children. One study found that mothers who had been abused as children but who were able to break the cycle of abuse with their own children were likely to have received emotional support from a non-abusive adult during childhood. They were also likely to have participated in therapy and to have a nonabusive mate.

Reading Check **Describe** Why is a parent with a history of child abuse in his or her own family more likely to become a child abuser?

Child Care

In the United States today, most parents—both fathers and mothers—work outside the home. More than half of mothers of children younger than one year of age are working mothers. For this reason, millions of preschoolers are cared for in day-care facilities. Some parents and psychologists are concerned about the effects of day care on the development of children.

The effects of day care depend in part on the quality of the day-care center. One study found that children in day-care centers with many learning resources, many caregivers, and a good deal of individual attention did as well on cognitive and language tests as children who remained in the home with their mothers. A Swedish study actually found that on tests of math and language skills, children in the best day-care centers out-performed children who remained in the home.

Studies of the effects of day care on parent-child attachment have yielded mixed results. Children in full-time day care show less distress when their mothers leave them and are less likely to seek out their mother when they return. Some psychologists worry that this distancing from the mother could mean that the child is insecurely attached. But other psychologists suggest that children may simply be adapting to repeated separations from and reunions with their mothers.

Statistically Speaking...

Daycare Whether a child receives nonparental care depends to some degree on questions of age, income, and education.

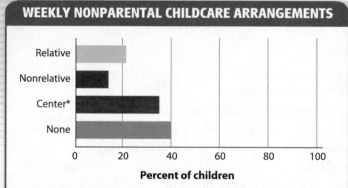

WEEKLY NONPARENTAL CHILDCARE ARRANGEMENTS

Percent of children

*Center-based arrangements include day-care centers, Head Start programs, preschools, pre-kindergartens, and other early childhood programs.

Source: U.S. Department of Education, National Center for Education Statistics, 2005

53% Percent of one-year-olds who have nonparental child care; jumps to 85% at age five

53% Percent of households with an income of $10,000 or less per year that have nonparental child care; rises to 72% for households over $75,000

43% Percent of mothers with a high school diploma or GED have children in child care; 74% of mothers with graduate or professional degrees have children in child care

Skills Focus **INTERPRETING GRAPHS** Why does the percentage of children in child care add up to more than 100 percent?

Source: The National Center for Education Statistics, National Household Education Surveys Program, 2005

Day care seems to have mixed effects on other aspects of children's social development. Children in day care are more likely to share their toys and be independent, self-confident, and outgoing. However, some studies have found that children in day care are less cooperative and more aggressive than are other children. Perhaps some children in day care do not receive the individual attention they need. When they are placed in a competitive situation, they become more aggressive to try to meet their needs. Yet some psychologists interpret the greater aggressiveness of children in day care as a sign of independence rather than social maladjustment.

All in all, it would appear that nonparental care in itself may not affect child development very much. The quality of care seems to be more important than who provides it.

Reading Check **Recall** Explain why the effects of day care on children are said to be mixed.

Self-Esteem

Self-esteem, the value or worth that people attach to themselves, begins to develop in early childhood. It is important because it helps to protect people against the stresses and struggles of life. Everyone experiences failure now and then, but high self-esteem gives people the confidence to know that they can overcome their difficulties. Although high self-esteem is important, recent research questions its aggressive promotion, at the expense of other virtues, in modern child rearing.

Influences on Self-Esteem What factors influence self-esteem? Secure attachment plays a major role. Young children who are securely attached to their parents are more likely to have high self-esteem.

How parents react to their children can also make a difference. Research suggests that authoritative parenting contributes to high self-esteem in children. Children with high self-esteem tend to be close to their parents because their parents are loving and involved in their lives. Their parents also teach and expect appropriate behavior and thus encourage them to become competent individuals.

Psychologist Carl Rogers noted that there are two types of support parents can give to their children—unconditional positive regard or conditional positive regard. **Unconditional positive regard** means that parents love and accept their children for who they are—no matter how they behave. Children who receive unconditional positive regard usually develop high self-esteem. They know that even if they do something wrong or inappropriate, they are still worthwhile as people.

On the other hand, children who receive conditional positive regard may have lower self-esteem. **Conditional positive regard** means that parents show their love only when the children behave in certain acceptable ways. Children who receive conditional positive regard may feel worthwhile only when they are doing what their parents (or other authority figures) want them to do.

Once these children grow up, they often continue to seek the approval of other people. Excessive need for approval from other people is linked to low self-esteem. It is unrealistic for people to expect everyone to like and respect them. If they understand that it is natural for others to not always appreciate them, they may have higher self-esteem in the long run.

A sense of competence also increases self-esteem. By the age of about four, children begin to judge themselves according to their cognitive, physical, and social competence. Children who know that they are good at something usually have higher self-esteem than others. Children may feel good about themselves if they are good at puzzles or counting (cognitive skills), if they are good at tying their shoelaces or swinging (physical skills), or if they have friends (social skills).

Gender and Self-Esteem By the ages of about five to seven, children begin to value themselves on the basis of their physical appearance and performance in school. Girls tend to display greater competence in the areas of reading and general academic skills. Boys tend to display competence in math and physical skills.

Does this mean that girls are genetically better in reading and boys better in math? No. It may be that the reason girls and boys show greater competence in these areas is that people around them have suggested that this is what girls and boys are *supposed* to be good at. So girls predict that they will do better on tasks that are considered to be "feminine."

Boys predict that they will do better when tasks are labeled "masculine." When people feel they will do well at a particular task, they often do. People generally live up to the expectations that they have for themselves and that others have for them.

CASE STUDY
CONNECTION

Bullying Kids who bully their classmates may be driven by multiple factors, but low self-esteem does not appear to be one of them. Too often, however, low self-esteem is the result for victims of bullying.

Age and Self-Esteem Children gain in competence as they grow older. Through experience they learn more skills and become better at them. Even so, their self-esteem tends to decline during the elementary school years. Self-esteem seems to reach a low point at about age 12 or 13 and increases again during adolescence. What explains this pattern? It appears that young children assume that others see them as they see themselves. Thus, if they like themselves, they assume that other people like them too. As children develop, however, they begin to realize that some people might not see them the way they see themselves. They also begin to compare themselves to their peers. If they see themselves as less competent in some areas, their self-esteem may decrease.

The Self-Esteem Trap By the 1970s, the dominant feeling among psychologists and in U.S. culture at large was that boosting people's self-esteem could greatly improve the state of the society. Greater self-esteem would help people solve their personal problems and love themselves and their neighbors. It was thought of by many as a potential cure-all for society's ills. Parents and teachers were taught that failure, ranking, and unequal rewards for competition were potential death blows to self-esteem. Showering children with praise regardless of performance on a task was the order of the day.

In 2000, a group of psychologists surveyed the published research on the subject and presented findings on the benefits of high self-esteem. The conclusions were surprising. High self-esteem in children did not lead to higher grades. Kids with high self-esteem did have higher grades. But that was because getting good grades promoted high self-esteem, not the other way around. Also, high self-esteem did not make violent kids any less so or keep kids from becoming bullies. The evidence showed that, in general, bullies think highly of themselves. The stereotype of the bully as sullen, self-hating, and desperate for praise was not borne out by the research.

Other results were more predictable. People with high self-esteem were generally happier and more resilient in the face of problems, and they showed more initiative. They were also more likely to stand up to bullies themselves. Although these are positive things, it seems that focusing on building self-esteem at the expense of other qualities, such as self-control or self-discipline, may be misguided.

Reading Check **Recall** When and how does a person's sense of self-esteem develop?

Online Quiz **THINK** central   thinkcentral.com

SECTION 3 Assessment

Reviewing Main Ideas and Vocabulary

1. **Identify Main Ideas** Name and describe the two types of anxiety that strike infants around the age of eight months.

2. **Recall** What does it mean for a child to be insecurely attached, and what can be the result for the child?

3. **Explain** What is the link between autism and a lack of attachment between infant and parent?

Thinking Critically

4. **Draw Conclusions** Why do you think children who have been abused are more likely to suffer from psychological problems, such as anxiety, depression, and low self-esteem?

5. **Elaborate** How do you think boys and girls can be helped to display competence in areas that they presently do not?

6. **Analyze** Using your notes and a graphic organizer like this one, list things related to attachment and parenting that might be related to positive self-esteem.

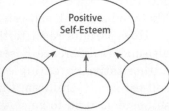

FOCUS ON WRITING

7. **Narrative** Write two paragraphs about parenting styles. In the first, say what combination of parenting qualities you think is best for bringing up a child. In the second, say what combination of parenting qualities you are likely to exhibit based on your personality. Do the two match?

Inside the Autistic Mind

People with autism have a difficult road in life. The list of possible problems associated with autism is long and troubling. Autistic people often exhibit obsessive/compulsive and self-injurious behavior. Many have impaired intellectual abilities and motor skills. All autistic people have moderate to severe issues with communication and socialization. Recent research is looking deep into the brains of people with autism to help explain and attempt to deal with this strange and serious condition.

Researchers at York University in Toronto, Ontario, are trying to observe differences in the brain functions of people with autism versus those of people whose development is more typical. The researchers are doing this by observing brain activity in mother-child pairs where the child has autism.

The mother-child pairs play, socialize, and share—things that require joint attention and social-emotional engagement. While they do this, their brain activity is monitored using the sensing devices pictured below. The subjects wear nets containing electroencephalography (EEG) sensors that read electrical activity produced by the brain. Other mother-child pairs, in which the child is not autistic, play and socialize in a similar way, and their brain activities are monitored as well.

Another area of research has to do with mirror neurons—a new class of brain cells identified only recently. The discovery of mirror neurons, like many scientific discoveries, was quite accidental. Researchers studying brain function of macaque monkeys noticed that certain neurons fired when a monkey performed a certain task, such as reaching for a peanut. Later, as a researcher reached for a peanut to hand to the monkey, the very same neurons fired. In other words, the same neurons fired in the monkeys' brains whether they were performing a certain act or watching that same act being performed. By firing when the monkey is just observing, these neurons "mirror" observed movement.

Over time, researchers demonstrated that this same mirror neuron system exists in humans as well. For most people, scientists believe, the mirror neuron system is what allows them to acquire language, understand and imitate the actions of others, and demonstrate empathy.

Studies of the mirror neuron systems of people with autism show intriguing results. The mirror neuron systems of people with autism responded when they performed an activity, but not when they observed the activity. These findings may help explain why individuals with autism have trouble comprehending and responding appropriately to others (Oberman et al, 2005).

The findings of these two areas of research may help doctors diagnose autism earlier. In addition, they may help in the development of new and better therapies.

Thinking Critically

1. **Analyze** Why do you think the mothers are involved in the first study described?
2. **Discuss** Why do you think mirror neuron problems lead to empathy and language shortcomings?

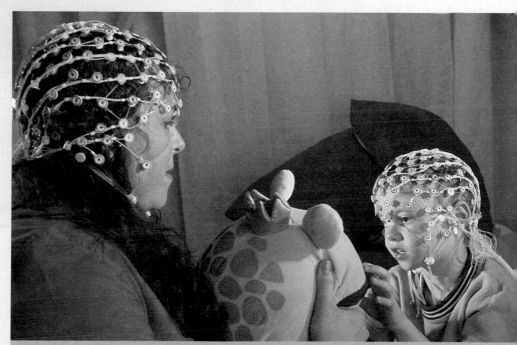

Researchers monitor the brain functions of children with autism and their mothers. They hope to develop treatments and diagnostic techniques from their findings.

Cognitive Development

Before You Read

Main Idea

The study of cognitive development looks at how people's thought processes change and evolve over time. Jean Piaget and Lawrence Kohlberg are two influential theorists in this area.

Reading Focus

1. What are the stages of Piaget's theory of cognitive development?

2. How did Kohlberg use a moral dilemma to illustrate his theory of moral development?

Vocabulary

sensorimotor stage
object permanence
preoperational stage
concrete-operational stage
formal-operational stage
preconventional moral reasoning
conventional moral reasoning
postconventional moral reasoning

TAKING NOTES Use a graphic organizer like this one to take notes on cognitive development.

Piaget	Kohlberg

Five-year-old LOGIC

WHY DO TREES HAVE LEAVES?
WHERE DOES THE SUN GO AT NIGHT?
WHERE?
WHY IS GRASS GREEN?
WHY IS THE SKY BLUE?
HOW?
WHY?

PSYCHOLOGY CLOSE UP

Have you ever spent some quality time with a five-year-old? Most five-year-olds are a ton of fun to be around. They're energetic, creative, and inquisitive—boy, are they inquisitive. Sometimes you think the questions will never stop. They also employ a peculiar brand of logic. Order a pizza for two five-year-olds some day, and you'll find out. Sit them at the kitchen table together, and let them watch while you select two identically sized slices of pizza. Cut one slice into bite-sized pieces and leave the other one whole. Give the whole piece to one child and the cut-up piece to the other one. There will certainly be a problem. The child with the whole piece will probably start to gloat: "I got more than you!" The child with the cut-up slice will pout: "Why did you give me less?" They react this way even though they watched you get two identical slices!

The pizza argument is just one example of five-year-old logic. Children's thought processes and how they develop are the subjects of this section. ■

Piaget's Theory of Cognitive Development

In addition to social development, psychologists are interested in studying cognitive development, or the development of people's thought processes. Jean Piaget (1896–1980) is probably the best-known researcher in the area of children's cognitive development. When Piaget was in his early 20s, he was employed at the Binet Institute in Paris. At the institute he worked on the Binet intelligence test, trying out potential test questions on children.

Before long, Piaget realized that the children he questioned gave certain types of wrong answers and that these wrong answers fit patterns from child to child. Piaget was so interested in these patterns that the study of children's thinking became his life's work.

Assimilation and Accommodation Piaget believed that human beings organize new information in two ways: through assimilation and through accommodation. Assimilation is the process by which new information is placed into categories that already exist. For example, a little girl might know the word *doggie* because her family has a pet collie. If she sees a Great Dane on the street and says "doggie," she has assimilated the new information about the Great Dane into the category "dog"—even though the Great Dane looks and may act differently from her collie.

If the same child sees a cat and says "doggie," an adult will most likely correct her. Through such corrections, she will learn that the category "dog" does not apply to cats, and a new category is needed. This adjustment is an example of accommodation—a change brought about because of new information.

Piaget theorized that children's thinking develops in a sequence of stages. Some children are more advanced than others at a given age, but the developmental sequence is the same for everyone. Piaget identified four stages: sensorimotor, preoperational, concrete operational, and formal operational.

The Sensorimotor Stage The behavior of newborns is mainly reflexive. They are capable only of responding to their environment and cannot initiate behavior. Instead of acting, infants react. By about one month of age, however, infants begin to act with purpose. As they coordinate vision with touch, for example, they will look at objects they are holding.

The first stage of cognitive development is characterized mainly by learning to coordinate sensation and perception with motor activity. Infants begin to understand that there is a relationship between their physical movements and the results they sense and perceive. That is why Piaget called this stage the **sensorimotor stage.**

Infants who are three and four months old are fascinated by their own hands and legs. They are easily amused by watching

PIAGET'S STAGES OF COGNITIVE DEVELOPMENT

Stage	Age	Characteristics
Sensorimotor Stage	0–2	• Learning to coordinate sensation and perception with motor activity • Development of object permanence
Preoperational Stage	2–7	• One-dimensional thinking • Displays of egocentrism, artificialism, and animism
Concrete-Operational Stage	7–12	• Signs of adult thinking about specific objects but not abstract ideas • Reduced egocentrism
Formal-Operational Stage	12+	• Capable of abstract thinking • Able to deal with hypothetical situations, strategize, and plan ahead to solve problems

Skills Focus **INTERPRETING CHARTS** In what stage do people move from understanding objects to understanding complex ideas? Explain.

themselves open and close their fists. If they hear an interesting sound, such as a rattle, they might do something to sustain the sound. By four to eight months, infants are exploring cause-and-effect relationships. They might, for example, hit mobiles that hang over their cribs so that the mobiles will move.

Perhaps you have heard the expression "Out of sight, out of mind." Before infants are six months old, objects out of their sight are truly out of their minds. The infants do not realize that objects out of sight still exist. They might stare at a rattle, but if you were to put the rattle behind a piece of paper, they would not look or reach to find it. By eight months to a year, however, infants understand that things that have been taken away still exist. A 10-month-old probably would search for a rattle that was hidden behind a screen. Piaget called this **object permanence**—the understanding that objects exist even when they cannot be seen or touched.

According to Piaget's theory, object permanence occurs because infants are able to hold an idea in mind. For example, they learn that "rattle" is a shiny, noisy object. They can mentally picture a rattle even when it is no longer in view. Therefore, they know to look for it when it is hidden behind a screen.

The Preoperational Stage The sensorimotor stage ends at about the age of two years, when children begin to use words and symbols (language) to represent objects. At this point, children enter the **preoperational stage.**

Preoperational thinking is very different from more mature forms of thinking. Children's views of the world are different from those of adolescents and adults. Preoperational children think in one dimension—they can see only one aspect of a situation at a time. This is evident in the fact that they do not understand the law of conservation. The law says that key properties of substances, such as their weight, volume, and number, stay the same even if their shape or arrangement are changed. That is, the basic properties are *conserved*. Children in the preoperational stage cannot comprehend all the aspects at once, so they focus only on the most obvious one—the way a substance looks.

When preoperational children are shown two identical tall, thin glasses of water, each filled to the same level, they know that both glasses hold the same amount of water. However, if water from one of the tall glasses is poured into a short, squat glass, the children say that the other tall glass contains more liquid than the short one. They say this even if they have *watched* the water being poured. Because they can focus only on what they are seeing at a given moment—and on one dimension at a time—they incorrectly think that the tall glass now contains more water than the short glass. Their thinking is that it looks as if there is less water in the short glass (because the water level is lower) and therefore it must be so. Children in the preoperational stage do not realize that increases in one dimension (such as width) can make up for decreases in another (such as height).

Another characteristic of children in the preoperational stage is egocentrism—the inability to see another person's point of view. Preoperational children assume that other people see the world just as they do. They cannot imagine that things might happen to others that do not happen to them. They think that the world exists to meet their needs. Egocentrism is a consequence of the preoperational child's one-dimensional thinking. Egocentrism is not the same as selfishness. When a preschooler sits down in front of the TV blocking everyone else's view, he or she is not being rude. The child simply thinks you can see exactly what he or she can see.

Preoperational children are also artificialistic and animistic. That is, they think that natural events such as rain and thunder are made by people (artificialism). They also think objects such as the sun and the moon are alive and conscious (animism).

EXAMPLES OF PREOPERATIONAL THINKING

At the preoperational stage, children are self-centered. They also think that objects are alive, and people are responsible for the workings of nature.

Kind of Thinking	Sample Questions	Typical Answers
Egocentric	Why does the sun shine? Why is grass green? What are TV sets for?	To keep me warm Because that's my favorite color To watch my favorite cartoons
Artificialistic	Why do stars twinkle? Why do trees have leaves? Where do boats go at night?	Because they're happy To keep them warm They go to sleep, like me
Animistic	Why is the sky blue? Where do mountains come from? What is the wind?	Somebody painted it A giant built them A person blowing

Thinking Critically How might children in the concrete-operational stage answer the questions in the "Egocentric" area of the chart?

The Concrete-Operational Stage Most children enter the **concrete-operational stage** at about the age of seven. In this stage, children begin to show signs of adult thinking. Yet they are logical only when they think about specific objects and concrete experiences, not about abstract ideas. This is one reason why many teachers assign them hands-on projects. Seeing, touching, and manipulating objects often help concrete-operational children understand <u>abstract</u> concepts.

Children at the concrete-operational stage can focus on two dimensions of a problem at the same time. For this reason, they understand the laws of conservation. They understand that a short, wide glass might contain the same amount of water as a tall, thin glass. They can therefore recognize that a gain in width compensates for a loss in height.

Concrete-operational children are less egocentric than children in earlier stages. They can see the world from another person's point of view. They understand that people may see things differently because they have different experiences or are in different situations.

The Formal-Operational Stage The final cognitive stage in Piaget's theory begins at about age eleven or twelve and continues through adulthood. It is the **formal-operational stage,** which represents cognitive maturity.

People in the formal-operational stage think abstractly. They realize that ideas can be compared and classified mentally just as objects can. For example, they understand what is meant by the unknown quantity x in algebra. They can work on geometry problems about lines, triangles, and squares without concerning themselves with how the problems relate to the real world. They can also deduce rules of behavior from moral principles. They focus on many aspects of a situation simultaneously when reasoning and solving problems.

During the formal-operational stage, people are capable of dealing with hypothetical situations. They realize that they may be able to control the outcome of a situation in several different ways. Therefore, if one approach to solving a problem does not work, they will try another. They think ahead, imagining the results of different courses of action before they decide on a particular one.

Criticism of Piaget's Theories A number of psychologists have questioned the accuracy of Piaget's views. Some believe his methods caused him to underestimate the abilities of children. Recent research using different methodology indicates that preschoolers are less egocentric than Piaget's research suggested. Some psychologists also assert that several cognitive skills appear to develop more continuously than Piaget thought. Nonetheless, his theories are still respected.

Reading Check **Recall** What are the stages of Piaget's theory of cognitive development?

Kohlberg's Theory of Moral Development

Psychologist Lawrence Kohlberg (1927–1987) devised a cognitive theory about the development of children's moral reasoning. Kohlberg used the following story in his research:

A woman was near death from a special kind of cancer. There was one drug that the doctors thought might save her. It was a form of radium that a pharmacist in the same town had recently discovered. The drug was expensive to make, but the pharmacist was charging 10 times what the drug cost him to make. He paid $200 for the radium and charged $2,000 for a small dose of the drug. The sick woman's husband, Heinz, tried to borrow the money, but he could raise only about $1,000. He told the pharmacist that his wife was dying and asked him to sell it cheaper or let him pay later. But the pharmacist rejected the man's plea saying that he had discovered the drug and intended to make money from it. Heinz became desperate and broke into the man's store to steal the drug for his wife.

Should Heinz have stolen the drug? Was he right or wrong? Kohlberg believed there was no simple answer. Heinz was involved in what Kohlberg called a moral dilemma. In this case, laws against stealing contradicted Heinz's strong human desire to save his wife.

Kohlberg was not particularly interested in whether children thought Heinz was right or wrong. More important to Kohlberg were the reasons why children thought Heinz should or should not steal the drug. Kohlberg classified these reasons according to levels of moral development.

ACADEMIC VOCABULARY

abstract not part of concrete existence; theoretical

As a stage theorist, Kohlberg believed that the stages of moral development always follow a specific sequence. Children advance at different rates, however, and not everyone reaches the highest stage. Kohlberg theorized that there are three levels of moral development and two stages within each level.

The Preconventional Level According to Kohlberg, through the age of nine, most children are at the preconventional level of moral development. Children who use **preconventional moral reasoning** base their judgments on the consequences of behavior.

In stage 1, children believe that what is "good" is what helps one avoid punishment. Therefore, children at stage 1 would argue that Heinz was wrong because he would be caught for stealing and sent to jail.

At stage 2, "good" is what satisfies a person's needs. Stage 2 reasoning holds that Heinz was right to steal the drug because his wife needed it.

The Conventional Level People who are at the level of **conventional moral reasoning** make judgments in terms of whether an act conforms to conventional standards of right and wrong. These standards derive from the family, religion, and society at large.

At stage 3, "good" is what meets one's needs and the expectations of other people. Moral behavior is what most people would do in a given situation. According to stage 3 reasoning, Heinz should steal the drug because a good and loving husband would do whatever he could to save the life of his wife. But stage 3 reasoning might also maintain that Heinz should not steal the drug because good people do not steal. Both conclusions show conventional thinking. Kohlberg found stage 3 moral judgments most often among 13-year-olds.

Stage 4 moral judgments are based on maintaining the social order. People in this stage have high regard for authority. Stage 4 reasoning might insist that breaking the law for any reason sets a bad example and undermines the social order. Stage 4 judgments occurred most often among 16-year-olds.

The Postconventional Level Reasoning based on a person's own moral standards of goodness is called **postconventional moral reasoning.** Here, moral judgments reflect one's personal values, not conventional standards.

Stage 5 reasoning recognizes that laws represent agreed-upon procedures, that laws have value, and that they should not be violated without good reason. But laws cannot bind the individual in exceptional circumstances. Stage 5 reasoning might suggest that it is right for Heinz to steal the drug, even though it is against the law, because the needs of his wife have created an exceptional situation.

Stage 6 reasoning regards acts that support human life, justice, and dignity as moral and good. People at stage 6 rely on their own consciences. They do not necessarily obey laws or agree with other people's opinions. Using

KOHLBERG'S STAGES OF MORAL DEVELOPMENT

QUICK FACTS

Level	Stage	Moral Reasoning Goal	What is Right?
Preconventional	1	Avoiding punishment	Doing what is necessary to avoid punishment
	2	Satisfying needs	Doing what is necessary to satisfy one's needs
Conventional	3	Winning approval	Seeking and maintaining the approval of others using conventional standards of right and wrong
	4	Law and order	Moral judgments based on maintaining social order High regard for authority
Postconventional	5	Social order	Obedience to accepted laws Judgments based on personal values
	6	Universal ethics	Morality of individual conscience, not necessarily in agreement with others

Piaget or Kohlberg?

Skills Focus **INTERPRETING CARTOONS** Does the behavior of these kids reflect a stage of development from Piaget or Kohlberg? Explain.

stage 6 reasoning, a person might argue that the pharmacist was acting out of greed and that survival is more important than profit. So Heinz had a moral right to steal the drug to save his wife. Postconventional reasoning rarely occurs in adolescents and is found most often in adults.

Bias in Kohlberg's Theory Some studies have found that according to Kohlberg's stages, boys appear to reason at higher levels of moral development than do girls. Does this mean that boys are morally superior to girls? No. It may mean instead that Kohlberg's stages and scoring system were biased to favor males.

Psychologist Carol Gilligan argues that the differences between boys and girls are created because of what adults teach children about how they should behave as boys or girls. For example, girls are often taught to consider the needs of others over simple right or wrong. Therefore, a girl might worry that both stealing the drug and letting Heinz's wife die are wrong. Such reasoning—involving empathy for others—would be classified as stage 3.

Boys, however, are often taught to argue logically rather than with empathy. Therefore, a boy might set up an equation to prove that life has greater value than property. This would be considered reasoning at stage 5 or even stage 6.

Gilligan suggests, however, that girls' reasoning is at as high a level as that of boys. Girls have, in fact, thought about the same kinds of issues boys considered. In the end, they have chosen to be empathetic, not

because their thinking is simpler, but because it is very complex—and because of what they have been taught is appropriate for girls.

Reading Check **Describe** How does moral reasoning change throughout Kohlberg's stages?

Online Quiz **THINK** central thinkcentral.com

SECTION 4 Assessment

Reviewing Main Ideas and Vocabulary

1. **Define** What is object permanence?

2. **Explain** What does a child consider to be "good" in stage 2 of Kohlberg's theory?

3. **Summarize** What is the major case for bias in Kohlberg's theory?

Thinking Critically

4. **Contrast** Contrast Piaget's ideas of assimilation and accommodation. What makes them different?

5. **Elaborate** Why do children in the concrete operational stage of development have problems dealing with the algebraic idea of an unknown quantity?

6. **Compare and Contrast** Using your notes and a graphic organizer like the one shown, compare and contrast the theories of Piaget and Kohlberg. In what ways are they different, and where do they seem to overlap?

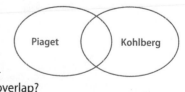

FOCUS ON WRITING

7. **Descriptive** People at stage 6 moral reasoning do not obey laws that go against their conscience. Write a paragraph giving your opinion of what the world would be like if everyone acted in this way.

Prenatal and Postnatal Development

Reading and Activity Workbook

Use the workbook to complete this lab.

How do fetuses and infants develop in the United States and in other parts of the world?

1. Introduction

In this chapter, you have learned about the range of ways in which children develop. In particular, you learned about the physical development of children, beginning in the womb and continuing through the blossoming of fine motor skills. Physical development is for the most part dictated by heredity. It is primarily a natural, biological process with some built-in variation that reflects each individual's genetic makeup. You also read, however, that cultural factors have a role to play in physical development. In Uganda, for example, infants walk two months earlier, on average, than do children in the United States. Possible reasons given for this include the amount of time and the manner in which Ugandan babies are carried by their parents—environmental factors.

In this lab, you will look more closely at both fetal and infant development. Aside from the biological elements of physical development, you will also try to find more examples of how environment plays a role in the process.

■ Your teacher will organize the class into two groups. Group A will research prenatal (before birth) physical development. Group B will research postnatal (after birth) physical development.

■ Once the research is complete, each group will give oral presentations of their findings.

When this project is complete, you should have a much greater knowledge of early human development not just in the United States, but in other cultures as well.

2. Form Groups and Research

Once your teacher has organized the class into group A and group B, it is time to assign duties within the group.

Group A, which will research prenatal development should organize itself into three teams. Each team will research a three-month period of the nine months of prenatal development.

■ Get started by reviewing the pertinent information in Section 2.

■ Use the Internet and the library to find information on your period of development.

■ Find out what organs, systems, and other notable body parts are present (or not present) at the stage you're researching.

■ Of what activities is the fetus capable during the time assigned to you? Can it move? What body systems are functioning?

Group B, which will research postnatal development, should organize itself into four teams. Each team will research a six-month period of the first two years of postnatal development.

■ Get started by reviewing the pertinent information in Section 2.

■ Use the Internet and the library to find information on your period of development.

■ Find out what reflexes are present. A few are listed in the chapter, but you should find others.

■ What internal development continues after birth? Are many organs and systems still less than completely developed?

■ To what extent are the sensory organs developed, and when do they become useful?

These are suggested areas of research, but each group should be creative in finding and presenting information. Try to have one or more visual aids to liven up your presentation.

3. Research International Issues

Now that each group's initial research is complete, it is time to widen the scope of your inquiry.

Different prenatal practices and problems in other parts of the world can affect prenatal development. Group A teams should each pick a health care or social problem that affects fetal development in another country.

■ What is the cause of the problem?

■ How does it affect the baby? the mother?

■ What, if anything, is being done to alleviate the problem?

Group B will research cultural differences in motor development. Each team should find a country where children develop differently, such as in the Uganda example from Section 2.

■ How is motor development different in this place?

■ Is the difference advantageous or detrimental?

■ What explains the difference?

4. Organize Your Findings and Give Your Presentation

Work as a team to get your information organized and ready as an oral presentation. The presentation should be no more than five minutes long, and several members of the group should participate as speakers. The teams should go in chronological order beginning with the Group A team that has conception to three months and ending with the Group B team that has 19 through 24 months.

5. Discussion

What did you learn from your research and from the other groups' reports? Hold a group discussion that focuses on the following questions:

■ What surprised you most about prenatal development?

■ Which issue that affects unborn children in different countries concerned you the most? Why?

■ Which age period of motor development did you find most interesting? Why?

■ Did any of the international differences in motor development come as a surprise to you? Explain.

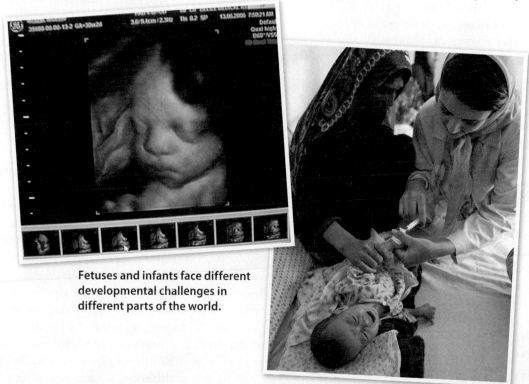

Fetuses and infants face different developmental challenges in different parts of the world.

Comprehension and Critical Thinking

SECTION 1 (pp. 274–277)

1. a. Define Why are psychologists interested in studying infancy and childhood?

b. Contrast In what ways do heredity and environment contribute to human development?

c. Support a Position Which theory makes more sense to you: development by stages or continuous development? Why?

SECTION 2 (pp. 278–282)

2. a. Recall Are reflexes a result of nature or nurture? Explain.

b. Explain What is the purpose of reflexes? Could an infant survive without them? Explain.

c. Evaluate Why do you think gross motor development begins before fine motor development?

SECTION 3 (pp. 284–292)

3. a. Define What is stranger anxiety?

b. Contrast Contrast authoritative and authoritarian parenting styles.

c. Elaborate Explain the difference between unconditional and conditional positive regard. What could be a possible negative outcome of unconditional positive regard for children?

SECTION 4 (pp. 294–299)

4. a. Describe What is the concrete-operational stage of Piaget's theory?

b. Sequence List the stages of Kohlberg's theory of moral development from the oldest level to the youngest, and briefly explain each.

INTERNET ACTIVITY ✳

5. A developmental disorder is any physical or psychological disorder that slows a child's development. In this chapter, you read about one developmental disorder, autism, but there are many others. Use the Internet to research another developmental disorder. Some examples are cerebral palsy, fragile X syndrome, Down's syndrome, and Tourette's syndrome. Collect information on causes, symptoms, treatments, and any other facts you find interesting. Then write a paper on the disorder.

Reviewing Vocabulary

Fill in each blank with the term that correctly completes the sentence.

6. The process by which some animals form immediate attachments is known as _____.

7. A(n) _____ is an involuntary reaction or response.

8. _____ is the automatic and sequential process of development that results from genetic signals.

9. The instinctual need to touch and be touched by something soft is called _____.

10. Something that is _____ is theoretical, or not part of concrete existence.

11. _____ is the value or worth that people attach to themselves.

12. The understanding that objects exist even when they cannot be seen or touched is known as _____.

13. _____ is the field in which psychologists study how people grow and change throughout the life span.

14. Feelings of _____ are the emotional ties that form between people.

Psychology in Your Life

15. What would you do if you were faced with a moral dilemma? Consider the following story. Your best friend, Ellen, has been accepted to her parents' alma mater. Ellen and her parents have always dreamed that she would go to college there too. She's taking the same English course you took last year, and her final paper is due in one week. Her teacher, who replaced the teacher you had last year, has told her that the controversial topic she chose for her term paper is unacceptable. A month of research and writing has been wasted, and she will not be given extra time to finish. If she fails this class, her dreams and her parents' dreams will be crushed. Do you let her submit the paper you wrote last year as her own? Answer the question truthfully and gauge where you are in Kohlberg's framework. Tell the story to people of different ages to see where they stand as well.

SKILLS ACTIVITY: INTERPRETING GRAPHS

The graph below breaks down child abuse and neglect into age groups. According to the U.S. Department of Health and Human Services, just over 900,000 children in the United States were verified victims of abuse or neglect in 2006.

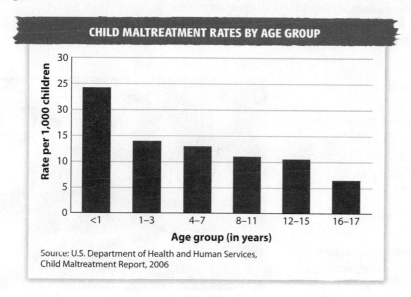

CHILD MALTREATMENT RATES BY AGE GROUP

Rate per 1,000 children

Age group (in years)

Source: U.S. Department of Health and Human Services, Child Maltreatment Report, 2006

16. Analyze In number of years covered, what is the smallest age range shown? Is it also smallest in number of victims per 1,000? Explain.

17. Compare What two age ranges, when their victims per 1,000 are added together, equal the age range with the most victims per 1,000?

18. Make Judgments Explain the overall trend shown in the chart. What does this trend indicate about who is most often and least often abused or neglected?

WRITING FOR AP PSYCHOLOGY

Use your knowledge of developmental psychology to answer the question below. Do not simply list facts. Present a clear argument based on your critical analysis of the question, using the appropriate psychological terminology.

19. In your own words, briefly describe each of the developmental psychology terms listed below. For each term, include real life examples that show how or when the term relates to real people and events.

- heredity versus environment
- attachment
- Piaget's theory of cognitive development

Connecting Online

Visit thinkcentral.com for review and enrichment activities related to this chapter.

THINK central

Quiz and Review

ONLINE QUIZZES
Take a practice quiz for each section in this chapter.

WEBQUEST
Complete a structured Internet activity for this chapter.

QUICK LAB
Reinforce a key concept with a short lab activity.

APPLYING WHAT YOU'VE LEARNED
Review and apply your knowledge by completing a project-based assessment.

Activities

eACTIVITIES
Complete chapter Internet activities for enrichment.

INTERACTIVE FEATURE
Explore an interactive version of a key feature in this chapter.

KEEP IT CURRENT
Link to current news and research in psychology.

Online Textbook

Click for More
Learn more about key topics in this chapter.

CASE STUDY

Teenage Employees
AROUND THE WORLD

Around the world, younger people are on the move, from country to country and from the countryside to the city. In fact, the United Nations estimates that part of the population growth through 2030 will occur as young people move to urban areas to find work.

Teens Around the World The main force driving this change is the globalization of the world's economy. This means that jobs are moving from the country to the city and from industrialized to less-industrialized countries. Young people are following these job opportunities.

As economies shift from an agricultural base to a service and industrial base, education and employment have become more and more interconnected. Because education is more important than ever, school enrollment has dramatically increased in the developing world.

Nonetheless, the International Labour Organization (ILO) estimates that approximately 191 million children between five and fourteen years old (16 percent of all children in this age group) were active in their countries' economies in 2004. And the percentage is much higher in certain developing countries.

Adolescents in rural areas are more likely to work and less likely to go to school than children in cities. In Bangladesh, 47.8 percent of girls aged 15–19 are in the labor force; for boys in the same age group, the percentage is 65.5. In India for the same age group, the figures are 26.2 percent for girls, and 43.8 percent for boys. In Thailand, the figures are 29.1 percent for girls and 37.7 percent for boys.

A waitress delivers an order to her customers.

Teens in the United States In the United States, research shows that many adolescents work in addition to going to school. About half of all high school sophomores, two-thirds of juniors, and almost three-fourths of seniors have a job during the school year. On average, girls and boys are equally likely to work, but boys tend to work longer hours.

Millions of teens who work in this country are legally employed. Yet, many other teens work illegally. Some of these other teens receive cash payments so that their

A young pottery worker carries clay in Cairo, Egypt.

CHAPTER 11

ADOLESCENCE

employers can avoid paying taxes or minimum wages. Other teens work too many hours, late hours, or at hazardous job sites.

Research also shows that the groups of teens who are working has changed. In the past, teenagers from low-income households were more likely to work than wealthier teens. Teens from low-income families often worked to help support their families. Today employment is more common among middle-class adolescents. One reason might be that middle-class families tend to live nearer to the locations where teens can easily find jobs, such as suburban malls.

Many middle-class adolescents do not work for the same reasons that teens from low-income families do. Teens from low-income families tend to work to help support their families or to save money for college. In contrast, most middle-class teens use their income for personal purchases, including clothing, music, sports equipment, TVs, and cars.

Working can benefit teens. By holding a job, adolescents can develop responsibility, learn the value of money and education, and acquire good work habits.

However, working can also have negative effects. Teens who work long hours sometimes report lower grades, higher rates of drug and alcohol use, more delinquent behavior, lower self-esteem, and higher levels of psychological problems.

You may have a job or may be considering getting one. Working and the problems that can come with a job are among the challenges facing adolescents today.

Chapter at a Glance

SECTION 1: Physical Development
- During the adolescent growth spurt, which lasts two to three years, the average teenager grows 8 to 12 inches in height.
- Many physical changes take place during adolescence.
- Maturation rates vary among adolescents.

SECTION 2: Social Development
- Adolescents typically experience a great deal of stress during their teen years, due both to biological and psychological causes.
- Relationships with parents change during adolescence.
- Adolescents turn increasingly to their peers for support during adolescence.

SECTION 3: Identity Formation
- One of the main psychological tasks of adolescence is finding an identity—a sense of who one is and what one stands for.
- There are four categories of adolescent identity status.
- Issues of gender and ethnicity play a major role in the formation of identity.

SECTION 4: Challenges of Adolescence
- Adolescents face many challenges during their teen years.
- Eating disorders can be one of the big problems of adolescence.
- Substance abuse can cause many diseases.
- Many issues surround adolescent sexuality.

What do you think?

1. How has adolescent employment changed in the United States?

2. Do you think the benefits of teens working long hours during the school year outweigh the disadvantages? Why or why not?

Physical Development

Before You Read

Main Idea
Adolescence is a time of great change, especially in terms of physical development.

Reading Focus
1. What are the three age category labels between childhood and adulthood?
2. What is the adolescent growth spurt?
3. What does sexual development encompass?
4. What differences in maturation rates occur among adolescents?

Vocabulary
adolescent growth spurt
puberty
primary sex characteristics
secondary sex characteristics
menarche

TAKING NOTES Use a graphic organizer like this one to take notes on sexual development.

Sexual Development	
Changes in males	Changes in females

A **Big** Appetite

PSYCHOLOGY CLOSE UP

Why am I always hungry? Jeremy, in the comic strip "Zits," is in many ways a typical teenager, experiencing a growth spurt and all that such a spurt implies. Jeremy has a big, indeed insatiable, appetite. He requires enormous quantities of food to fuel his growth spurt. For this reason, he and his friends like to patronize a restaurant that features an all-you-can-eat buffet. In addition to his big appetite, Jeremy has big feet, gangly limbs, and long, flailing arms that seem to be barely under his control.

Big biological changes occur in adolescence—bigger changes than at any time since infancy. Different parts of an adolescent's body grow at different rates. The nose, ears, or feet can grow bigger before the rest of the body has had time to catch up.

These changes can be stressful for the person experiencing them—which is why a sense of humor can come in handy in weathering the stresses of adolescent growth. You will read more about the adolescent growth spurt, sexual development, and maturation in this section. ■

From Child to Adult

In earlier times in Western societies (and in some developing countries today), the period of transition from childhood to adulthood was very brief. Most people took over the responsibilities of adulthood—going to work, caring for children, and so on—shortly after they reached sexual maturity. The transition to adulthood was often marked by an elaborate ceremony that symbolized the passage from childhood to adulthood.

Starting in the 1900s, however, that changed. In Western societies today, required education has been extended, and the status and duties of adulthood have been delayed. As a result, adolescence has come to cover most of the teen years and a little beyond. Today the period known as adolescence is sometimes subdivided into smaller categories. These categories include early adolescence (ages 11 through 14), middle adolescence (15 through 18), and late adolescence (18 through 21).

The biological changes that occur during adolescence are greater than those of any other time of life, with the exception of infancy. In some ways, however, the changes in adolescence are more dramatic than those that occur in infancy—unlike infants, adolescents are aware of the changes that are taking place and of what the changes mean. But no teenager can ever be quite sure how all these physical changes will turn out. There are many variables to consider. Different adolescents begin their growth spurts at different ages, and they grow at different rates. Even the different parts of an adolescent's body grow at different rates. Most adolescents worry about the final shape and size of their growing bodies.

Reading Check **Recall** What are the years of the three age categories of adolescence?

The Adolescent Growth Spurt

During adolescence the stable growth patterns in height and weight that mark early and middle childhood come to an end. Stability is replaced by an abrupt burst of growth. This **adolescent growth spurt** usually lasts two to three years. During this time of rapid growth, most adolescents grow 8 to 12 inches in height.

Statistically Speaking...

Physical Growth in Adolescents Throughout childhood, girls and boys are similar in height. At puberty, girls surge ahead. At about age 14, boys surge back ahead of girls.

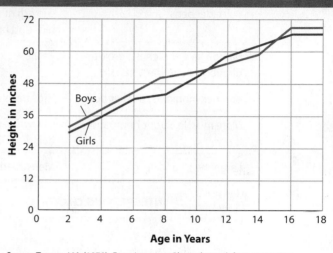

AVERAGE GROWTH RATES FOR BOYS AND GIRLS FROM CHILDHOOD THROUGH ADOLESCENCE

Source: Tanner, J.M. (1978). *Fetus into man: Physical growth from conception to maturity.* Cambridge, MA: Harvard University Press. (p. 118)

girls 8–11/boys 10–14
Age range during which growth spurt starts

girls 3.2"/boys 3.7"
Height gained in inches in growth spurt

girls 8–14/boys 9–14
Age range during which puberty begins

Skills Focus **INTERPRETING GRAPHS** At what two ages do the growth lines intersect for boys and girls?

Differences Between Boys and Girls Girls typically begin the adolescent growth spurt a little earlier than boys. For most girls, the growth spurt usually begins at about the age of 10 or 11. For boys, the adolescent growth spurt begins about 2 years later. As a result, girls tend to be taller and heavier than boys during early adolescence.

SEXUAL CHANGES

Both males and females undergo major physical changes in adolescence. These changes are caused by hormones.

Changes in Males	Changes in Females
Testes increase output of testosterone.	Ovaries secrete more estrogen.
Sexual organs grow.	Growth of breast tissue.
Voice deepens.	Growth of supportive tissue in hips and buttocks.
Hair on face and chest; growth of pubic and underarm hair	Pelvic region widens.
Broader shoulders, thicker body	Hips become rounder.
More muscle, larger heart and lungs	Growth of pubic and underarm hair
Larger heart and lungs.	Menstruation

Skills Focus INTERPRETING CHARTS What causes sexual changes?

These two photographs of the same person show the changes that occur between childhood and adolescence.

Then, during middle adolescence, most boys catch up and grow taller than their female classmates. However, the exact time when this growth will occur for any individual—boy or girl—is difficult to predict.

The Awkward Age This period of sudden adolescent growth can be awkward for both boys and girls because different parts of their bodies grow and mature at different rates. This growth spurt may cause adolescents to feel as if their hands or feet are too big or to worry that they "just don't look right."

Although some teenagers may feel that they look awkward, they actually tend to be well coordinated during adolescence. As adolescents become older and complete the growth spurt, their bodies usually reach their correct proportions.

Sometimes adolescents don't eat enough of the right foods to support the growth spurt. For example, calcium in the diet is important for proper bone growth. Menstruating girls need sufficient iron in their diets. For reasons such as this, proper nutrition is important during the adolescent years.

Reading Check **Define** What is the awkward age?

Sexual Development

Adolescence begins with the onset of puberty. **Puberty** refers to the specific developmental changes that lead to the ability to reproduce. This biological stage of development ends when physical growth does.

During puberty the reproductive organs of both males and females develop and dramatically change the adolescent body. Characteristics that are directly involved in reproduction are called **primary sex characteristics.** Characteristics that are not directly involved in reproduction, **secondary sex characteristics,** also develop during puberty. These secondary sex characteristics include changes such as the growth of hair on certain parts of the body, the deepening of the voice in males, and the rounding of the hips and breasts in females. These changes are linked to changes in hormone levels.

Changes in Males In boys, hormones from the pituitary gland cause the testes to increase output of the hormone testosterone. This causes boys' sexual organs to grow, their voices to deepen, and hair to grow on their genitals, faces and later on their chests.

During the period of rapid growth, boys develop broader shoulders and thicker bodies. They also develop more muscle tissue and larger hearts and lungs.

Changes in Females In girls, hormones from the pituitary gland stimulate the ovaries to secrete more estrogen. Estrogen spurs the growth of breast tissue and supportive tissue in the hips and buttocks. As a result, the pelvic region widens and the hips become rounder. Girls also produce small amounts of androgens, which are similar to testosterone, in the adrenal glands. Androgens stimulate the growth of pubic and underarm hair. Estrogen and androgens work together to spur the growth of the female sex organs.

The production of estrogen, which becomes cyclical in puberty, regulates the menstrual cycle. The first menstruation, or **menarche,** is a major life event for most girls, and most societies consider it the beginning of womanhood. It usually occurs between 11 and 14.

Reading Check **Recall** What are primary sex characteristics?

Differences in Maturation Rates

Some adolescents reach physical maturity at a relatively early age, while others reach it later. Research suggests that boys who mature early have certain advantages over boys who mature later. They tend to be more popular and to be leaders within their circle of friends. Their greater size and strength may give them a competitive edge in sports. They also tend to be more self-assured and relaxed. This may boost their self-esteem.

However, boys who mature early physically are not necessarily more mature than their peers in how they approach and handle problems. Also, coaches, friends, and others may pressure them to perform beyond their abilities. Although early-maturing boys may have some advantages over their peers who develop later, these advantages seem to fade over time. Some studies indicate that boys who mature later show better adjustment as adults. Of course, not all early maturing boys have problems, either as adolescents or as adults.

Early maturation is somewhat different for girls. Girls who mature early may feel awkward because they are taller than their classmates, both male and female. They may be teased about their height and secondary sexual characteristics.

Needless to say, not all girls who mature early encounter problems. In any case, the differences between early- and late-maturing girls usually do not last long. Once their peers catch up to them, the issue of differences in maturity generally disappears.

Reading Check **Find the Main Idea** What happens to the advantages of early maturation?

ACADEMIC VOCABULARY
cyclical recurring or moving in cycles

SECTION 1 Assessment

Online Quiz THINK central thinkcentral.com

Reviewing Main Ideas and Vocabulary

1. **Describe** Which age period does adolescence cover?

2. **Define** Give another name for the adolescent growth spurt.

3. **Summarize** What are some examples of secondary sex characteristics?

Thinking Critically

4. **Compare and Contrast** Name some of the main differences in the adolescent growth spurt between boys and girls.

5. **Finding the Main Idea** What are some long-term effects of early maturation for girls and for boys?

6. **Analyze** Using your notes and a graphic organizer like the one below, explain sexual development changes in males and females.

FOCUS ON WRITING

7. **Narrative** In a journal entry, write a paragraph in which you tell a brief story about why adolescence is the "awkward age." The story may be true or fictional.

The Adolescent Brain

The adolescent brain is a work in progress. Magnetic Resonance Imaging (MRI) studies have shown that the teenage brain continues to grow and develop through the teen years. With MRIs, researchers can see how the brain really works. They can see what parts of the brain use energy when performing a particular task.

One of the leading pioneers in research on the teenage brain is Dr. Jay Giedd at the National Institute of Mental Health (NIMH) in Bethesda, Maryland. Giedd also works with colleagues at McGill University in Montreal, Canada. Their research has confirmed that young people's brains are not fully developed until they reach their early twenties (Giedd et al., 2008).

Dr. Giedd studied the brains of 145 children using MRIs every two years during their childhood and adolescence. (MRIs do not require dyes or radiation and so are ethically acceptable.) Previously, most experts thought the brain's structure was pretty much set by the age of 5 or 6. But Giedd and other researchers have discovered changes in the structure of the brain that appear later in development (Spinks, 2003). Giedd's studies were longitudinal studies that followed some subjects from the age of three to the age of thirty.

Giedd and his colleagues found that the prefrontal cortex appears to grow again just before puberty. The prefrontal cortex is sometimes described as the CEO of the brain, controlling overall planning, impulse control, and judgment. Although adolescents are typically strong physically, the late development of the prefrontal cortex is one element in their relatively high rates of injury and accidents (Casey et al., 2008).

That is, because impulse control among adolescents is still relatively immature, adolescents make some unwise decisions. These decisions can result in injuries, violence, substance abuse, unintended pregnancies, and sexually transmitted diseases.

Giedd's studies help to explain why adolescents and young adults engage in riskier behavior than do younger or older people. Puberty pushes adolescents toward risky behavior and thrill seeking before the control system in the brain that regulates risky impulses has had time to fully mature. One of the most surprising findings of Giedd's work is that the production of gray matter in the brain does not stop in childhood but continues into the teens and even the twenties (Spano, 2002).

Some of the characteristic behaviors of adolescence, such as increased risk taking and poor judgment, may have as much to do with developmental events in the brain as with the hormonal changes of puberty. All this has produced an appreciation for the dynamic nature of the brain.

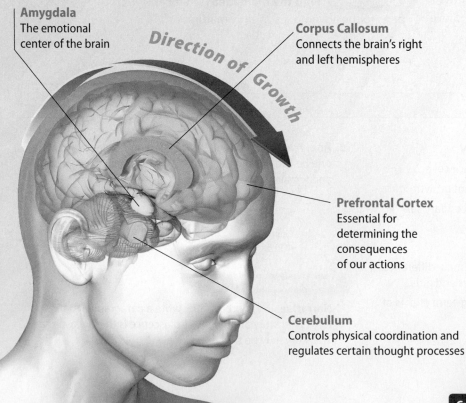

Amygdala
The emotional center of the brain

Direction of Growth

Corpus Callosum
Connects the brain's right and left hemispheres

Prefrontal Cortex
Essential for determining the consequences of our actions

Cerebullum
Controls physical coordination and regulates certain thought processes

Thinking Critically

1. **Categorize** Why do adolescents sometimes make unwise decisions?

2. **Discuss** What are some of the areas in which you think adolescents should be able to make their own decisions and judgments, based on what you have just read about brain development, impulse control, and risky behavior in adolescents?

Current Research **THINK** central thinkcentral.com

Social Development

Before You Read

Main Idea

Adolescence is a challenging time during which teenagers must learn new social skills and ways of interacting with others.

Reading Focus

1. What two factors make adolescence a time of stress and storm?
2. What is the main reason that relationships with parents change during adolescence?
3. Why are relationships with peers so important to adolescents?

Vocabulary

cliques
crowds
peer pressure

TAKING NOTES Use a graphic organizer like this one to take notes on adolescent relations with parents and peers.

Relations with parents	Relations with peers

Clueless OR COOL?

PSYCHOLOGY CLOSE UP

Why are relationships so difficult sometimes?
Probably at some time in your life you've wanted to join a particular group, club, or team. And you may or may not have been successful in gaining acceptance into the group. Teenagers typically choose friends who are like themselves in background, goals, and attitudes. Shared interests—such as sports, a favorite author or band, or hobby—may be enough to override differences in background or attitudes.

The unpleasant experiences of adolescence, such as bullying, teasing, and feelings of being excluded by in-crowds and cliques, are typical of the teenage years and are nearly universal. On the other hand, such experiences don't last forever, and with time most people manage to find a group of friends who are more accepting and less judgmental. ■

Storm and Stress

About 100 years ago, G. Stanley Hall, the founder of the American Psychological Association, described adolescence as a time of *Sturm und Drang*. These are German words that mean "storm and stress." Hall attributed the conflicts and distress some adolescents experience to biological changes.

Biology and Adolescence Research suggests that the hormonal changes of adolescence do have some effect on the activity levels, mood swings, and aggressive tendencies of many adolescents. However, contemporary studies suggest that cultural and social influences may have more of an effect on adolescent behavior than hormones do.

Psychology and Adolescence Adolescence is a psychological concept as well as a biological concept. Psychologically, the adolescent period ends when people become adults and take on adult responsibilities. How long adolescence lasts varies with each individual. For some people, adolescence may be quite extended; for others, it is quite short.

Certainly, adolescence can be a challenging time of life. Some teenagers may experience difficulties at home or at school that lead to psychological and social problems. Nonetheless, the vast majority of teenagers face the many challenges of adolescence and cope with them successfully. They form new friendships, increase their knowledge, build their self-awareness, and develop personal and social skills that enable them to become successful and competent adults.

Reading Check **Define** What do the German words *Sturm und Drang* mean?

Relationships with Parents

During adolescence, parent-child relationships undergo redefinition. However, the picture of adolescence as a state of constant rebellion against parents and society is exaggerated. The truth is that most of the changes that occur during adolescence are positive.

The Quest for Independence As adolescents strive to become more independent from their parents, however, some conflicts may arise. This striving for greater freedom often results in bickering, especially in early adolescence. Conflicts typically center on such issues as homework, chores, money, appearance, curfews, and dating. Arguments sometimes arise when adolescents maintain that personal choices, such as those that have to do with clothes and friends, should be made by them, not their parents.

The adolescent quest for independence may lead to less time spent with family, greater emotional attachment to people who are not family members, and more activities outside the home. In one study, children ranging in age from 9 to 15 carried electronic pagers for a week so that when signaled they could report to researchers what they were doing and with whom. The study showed that the older the children were, the less time they spent with their families.

A Lasting Bond Greater independence from parents does not mean that adolescents withdraw emotionally from their parents or fall completely under the influence of their peers. Most adolescents continue to love, respect, and feel loyalty toward their parents.

Adolescents who feel close to their parents tend to show greater self-reliance and independence than those who are distant from their parents. Adolescents who retain close ties with parents also tend to fare better in school and have fewer adjustment problems.

Despite a certain amount of parent-adolescent conflict, parents and adolescents usually share similar social, political, religious, and economic views. For example, adolescents tend to share the religion of one or both of their parents. Rarely will a teenager break completely with his or her family and adopt a different religion. Therefore, while there are frequent parent-adolescent differences of opinion about behavior and rules of conduct, conflict between the generations on broader issues is less common.

Adolescents tend to interact with their mothers more than they do with their fathers. Most adolescents also see their mothers as more supportive than their fathers, as knowing them better, and as more likely to tolerate their opinions. Teenagers are also more likely to seek and follow advice from their mothers than from their fathers.

Reading Check **Summarize** Why do adolescents often spend less time with their families?

Adolescents on Television

A variety of television shows feature adolescent characters. Some are supporting characters. Others are the main characters on shows that deal primarily with adolescents and the issues they face.

PROCEDURE

❶ Keep a log for a week of adolescent characters that you observe on television.

❷ Record in your log the qualities and defining characteristics of these characters.

❸ As you watch a number of shows in order to observe television's portrayal of adolescents and their world, record the names of the shows.

ANALYSIS

1. Make a list with your classmates of the shows that you observed and the names of the characters on these shows.

2. Make another list of the defining qualities of adolescents as portrayed on television.

3. Discuss with the class whether they think the portrayal of adolescents on television is accurate and fair. If the class feels that the portrayal is inaccurate or unfair, discuss why you think such a portrayal persists.

Quick Lab THINK central thinkcentral.com

Relationships with Peers

The transition from childhood to adolescence involves an increase in the importance of peers. While most adolescents maintain good relations with parents, <u>peers</u> become more important in terms of influence and emotional support.

Adolescent Friendships Friendship is a very important part of adolescence. Most adolescents tend to have one or two "best friends," but they have other good friends as well. Adolescents may spend several hours a day with their friends. When teenagers are not actually with their friends, they are often talking with them on the phone or texting them on their cell phones.

Adolescents value loyalty as a key aspect of friendship. They say that true friends "stick up for you in a fight" and do not "talk about you behind your back." In other words, having friends means more to adolescents than just having people to spend time with. Close friends provide support and understanding.

Adolescents usually choose friends who are similar to themselves in age, background, educational goals, and attitudes toward drinking, drug use, and sexual activity. In addition, adolescents' closest friends are usually of their own sex. The friendships of adolescent girls tend to be closer than those of boys. Girls are more likely than boys to share their secrets, personal problems, and innermost feelings. While boys also have close friendships, they tend to spend time together in larger, less intimate groups. These gender differences in patterns of friendship continue into adulthood.

Cliques and Crowds Adolescents not only have close friends; they also tend to belong to one or more larger peer groups. **Cliques** are peer groups of 5 to 10 people who spend a great deal of time with one another, sharing activities and confidences. Larger groups of people who do not spend as much time together but share attitudes and group identity are called **crowds.**

Adolescent cliques often include members of both sexes, which may lead to romantic relationships. Most young people also belong to a larger crowd with whom they go to parties, play basketball or baseball, and participate in other activities.

Some adolescents join certain cliques in their search for the stability and sense of belonging that come from being part of such a group. They may imitate their peers' speech and adopt some of their values. Teens in the same clique may follow similar fads in the way they dress or style their hair. They and the other members of the group may even become intolerant of "outsiders"—people not in the group.

ACADEMIC VOCABULARY

peers people who have equal standing with one another in rank, class, or age

Peer Influences Parents often worry that their adolescent children's needs for peer approval will influence them to engage in risky or unacceptable behavior. However, the assumption that parents and peers often pull an adolescent in different directions does not seem to be borne out by reality.

In fact, parental and peer influences often coincide to some degree. For example, research suggests that peers are more likely to urge adolescents to work for good grades and complete high school than they are to try to involve them in drug abuse, sexual activity, or delinquency.

Nevertheless, adolescents are influenced by their parents and peers in different ways. Adolescents are more likely to follow their peers in terms of dress, hairstyles, speech patterns, and taste in music. However, they are more likely to agree with their parents on issues such as moral values and educational and career goals.

In early adolescence, **peer pressure** is relatively weak, but it increases in middle adolescence, peaking at about the age of 15. Then, however, peer pressure seems to decrease after the age of 17.

Adolescents are strongly influenced by their peers for several reasons. They seek the approval of their peers and feel better about themselves when they receive such approval.

Peers provide standards by which adolescents can measure their behavior as they grow more independent of their parents. Also, because peers may share some of the same feelings, they can provide support in times of trouble or difficulty.

Dating and Romantic Relationships Many people begin dating during adolescence. Dating usually develops in stages. During the first stage, adolescents place themselves in situations where they will probably meet peers of the other sex—for example, at after-school events. In the next stage, adolescents participate in group dating, such as joining a mixed group at the movies. Finally, they may pair off as couples for traditional dating.

People date for several reasons. Obviously, people may date simply because they enjoy spending time with somebody they like. But dating may also help adolescents learn how to relate positively to other people. Furthermore, dating may help prepare adolescents for the more serious courtship activities that come later in life.

Among younger adolescents, dating relationships tend to be casual and short-lived. But in later adolescence, relationships tend to be more stable and committed.

Reading Check **Summarize** How do relationships with peers change during adolescence?

Online Quiz THINK central thinkcentral.com

SECTION 2 Assessment

Reviewing Main Ideas and Vocabulary

1. **Summarize** When does adolescence end?

2. **Recall** With which parent are adolescents more likely to interact?

3. **Define** How is a crowd different from a clique?

Thinking Critically

4. **Draw Conclusions** Why are adolescents influenced by their peers?

5. **Evaluate** Why might adolescence be considered a time of storm and stress?

6. **Analyze** Using your notes and a graphic organizer like the one below, explain adolescent relationships with peers.

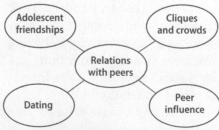

FOCUS ON WRITING

7. **Descriptive** Write a paragraph in which you describe what you feel is most stressful about adolescence.

Identity Formation

Before You Read

Main Idea
One of the main tasks of adolescence is the search for identity.

Reading Focus
1. How do psychologists view identity development?
2. What is identity status?
3. What roles do gender and ethnicity play in identity formation?

Vocabulary
identity crisis
identity status
identity moratorium
identity foreclosure
identity diffusion
identity achievement

TAKING NOTES Use a graphic organizer like this one to take notes on identity status.

Identity Status
1.
2.
3.
4.

TURNING A Life Around

PSYCHOLOGY CLOSE UP *How did one young man's experiences have a positive impact on his identity?* Tyrone Flowers had a difficult childhood and adolescence. His parents were only teenagers when Tyrone was born. He was raised by relatives, along with his brothers and sisters. He did without new clothes, and meals were irregular. He became violent and spent time in mental hospitals and detention centers and eventually, he got into a fight and was shot three times. The shooting meant that he would spend the rest of his life in a wheelchair.

Then Tyrone made a choice to turn his life around. He went to a community college, then to a university, and eventually to law school where he earned a law degree. Then he founded Higher M-Pact, a nonprofit community group in Kansas City, Missouri, to help young people at risk. The group does such things as hand out school supplies to children who need them.

Although Tyrone Flowers's story is a highly dramatic example, most adolescents go through the experience of having their identity, a sense of who they are and what they stand for, shaped by their circumstances and the choices they make. ◼

Tyrone Flowers overcame adversity and turned his life around by founding Higher M-Pact to help others.

Identity Development

Psychoanalyst Erik Erikson maintained that the journey of life consists of eight stages. At each stage, there is a task that must be mastered for healthy development to continue. Erikson said that young children must deal with issues of trust, autonomy (self-government), and initiative (taking the lead). Once children begin school, their main task becomes the development of competence, which is the sense that they can learn and achieve.

According to Erikson, the main task of the adolescent stage is the search for identity—a sense of who you are and what you stand for. Adolescents seek to identify their beliefs, their values, and their life goals. They also need to identify the areas in which they agree and disagree with parents, teachers, and friends.

Erikson believed that the task of establishing one's identity is accomplished by choosing and developing a commitment to a particular role or occupation in life. Accomplishing this task may also involve developing one's own political and religious beliefs.

To find an identity that is comfortable, adolescents may experiment with different values, beliefs, roles, and relationships. They may try out different "selves" in different situations. For example, the way they behave with their friends may be quite different from the way they behave with their parents. Adolescents who take on these different roles may sometimes wonder which of their selves is the "real" one. Adolescent identity is achieved when different selves are brought together into a unified sense of self.

Erikson thought that teens who do not succeed in forging an identity may become confused about who they really are and what they want to do in life. They may have difficulty making commitments and may drift from situation to situation. Since they do not create a solid sense of self, they may remain overly dependent on the opinions of others.

One key aspect of adolescent identity development is what Erikson called an identity crisis. An **identity crisis** is a turning point in a person's development when the person examines his or her values and makes or changes decisions about life roles. Adolescents can feel overwhelmed by the choices that lie before them and the decisions they must make.

In Piaget's four stages of cognitive development, the final stage is the formal-operational stage. It generally begins at puberty and continues through adulthood. Formal-operational thinking involves abstract thinking, such as hypothetical situations. It enables people to find reasonable solutions to problems and to predict the possible consequences of the decisions. Formal-operational thinking helps adolescents make important life choices. Because their thinking is no longer tied to concrete experience, adolescents can evaluate the options available to them even though they may not have personally experienced them.

Reading Check Recall According to Erikson, what is the main task of the adolescent stage of development?

Identity Status

According to psychologist James Marcia, the adolescent identity crisis arises as teenagers face decisions about their future work, moral standards, religious commitment, political orientation, or sexual orientation. Marcia studied the different ways that adolescents handle commitment and cope with the adolescent identity crisis. He concluded that there are four categories of adolescent **identity status,** or reaction patterns and processes. Adolescents do not remain in a single one of these categories throughout their entire adolescence, nor do they proceed through them in a particular order. Rather, they move in and out of the various categories, from one to another. The four categories are identity moratorium, identity foreclosure, identity diffusion, and identity achievement.

Identity Moratorium A moratorium is a "time out" period. Teens experiencing what Marcia termed **identity moratorium** delay making commitments about important questions. They are actively exploring various alternatives in an attempt to forge their identity. They may even experiment with different behaviors and personalities. Adolescents experimenting with different ways of life in their search for an identity may adopt distinctive ways of dressing or behaving.

Adolescents who remain in moratorium longer than other teens may become somewhat anxious as they struggle to find anchors in an unstable world. But they are heading in a general direction even if they do not know where their journey will end. They may end up attending college, joining the armed services, or doing something completely different to reach their final goals.

Identity Foreclosure To avoid an identity crisis, adolescents in the **identity foreclosure** category make a commitment that forecloses (or shuts out) other possibilities. These adolescents make a definite commitment, but the commitment is based on the suggestions of others rather than on their own choices. They adopt a belief system or a plan of action without closely examining whether it is right for them. They may simply follow the model set by their parents, peers, teachers, or other authority figures in order to avoid uncertainty.

Although following a path recommended by an adult eliminates the need to make some hard choices, some adolescents become foreclosed too early. After they find themselves dissatisfied with the direction of their lives, they may switch to the moratorium category.

Identity Diffusion Adolescents in the category of **identity diffusion** seem to be constantly searching for meaning in life and for identity because they have not committed themselves to a set of personal beliefs or an occupational path. They lack goals or interests and seem to live from crisis to crisis.

Identity diffusion typically occurs in middle school and early high school. However, if it continues into the eleventh and twelfth grades, identity diffusion can lead to an "I don't care" attitude. Some adolescents in this category become angry and rebellious.

Identity Achievement Adolescents in the **identity achievement** category have coped with crises and have explored options. They have then committed themselves to occupational directions and have made decisions about important life questions. Although they have experienced an identity crisis, they have emerged from it with solid beliefs or with a plan, for example to pursue a course of study that leads to a particular career. Identity-achieved teens have feelings of well-being, self-esteem, and acceptance. They are capable of setting goals and working toward attaining their goals.

Many young people do not reach identity achievement until well after high school. It is normal to change majors in college and to change careers. Such changes, which may be made several times, do not mean that these people are indecisive or that they have made wrong decisions. The changes may simply mean that these individuals are continuing to actively explore their options. College, vocational training, and jobs are broadening experiences that expose people to new ways of life, career possibilities, and belief systems. It is common to adjust one's personal goals and beliefs as one matures and views the world from a new or broader perspective.

Reading Check **Summarize** What is an identity moratorium?

Gender and Ethnicity in Identity Formation

All adolescents struggle at some point with issues concerning who they are and what they stand for. However, the nature of the struggle is somewhat different for males and females and for adolescents from different ethnic backgrounds.

INTERACTIVE ✳

IDENTITY STATUS CATEGORIES

QUICK FACTS

By studying how teenagers handle commitment and cope with the adolescent identity crisis, psychologist James Marcia identified four adolescent identity status categories.

Identity Moratorium
Searching for identity, exploring alternatives, delaying commitments

Identity Foreclosure
Conforming, accepting childhood identity and values, identifying with others, making commitments and plans without self-examination, becoming inflexible

Identity Diffusion
Making no commitment, no soul searching, no goals, angry and rebellious

Identity Achievement
Exploring options, committing to direction in life and occupation, finding own identity

Interactive Feature thinkcentral.com

Gender and Identity Formation According to Erik Erikson's theory, identity development during adolescence means embracing a philosophy of life and a commitment to a career. However, his views of the development of identity applied primarily to boys.

Erikson believed that people develop the capacity to form intimate relationships in the young adult stage of development. He also believed that the development of relationships was more important than occupational issues and values to women's identity.

Erikson, like Sigmund Freud, believed that women's identities were intimately connected with their roles as wives and mothers. Men's identities, on the other hand, were not assumed to depend on their roles as husbands and fathers.

Today many women work outside the home. Research shows that female adolescents are now more apt to approach identity formation like male adolescents. The concern of female adolescents about occupational plans is now about equal to that of males.

However, there is a difference. Female adolescents also express concern about how they will balance the day-to-day demands of work with those of family life. Their concern is well founded. Despite their involvement in the workplace, women in the United States still bear most of the responsibility for rearing the children and maintaining the home.

Ethnicity and Identity Formation Identity formation is often more complicated for adolescents from ethnic minority groups. These adolescents may be faced with two sets of cultural values. These two sets of values are those of their ethnic group and those of the larger society.

Sometimes these values are in conflict. In those cases, minority adolescents need to reconcile the differences and, frequently, decide where they stand.

Prejudice and discrimination can also contribute to the problems faced by adolescents from ethnic minority groups as they strive to forge a sense of identity. For example, the cultural heroes for these adolescents may not be recognized by members of other groups in society.

Adolescents whose father and mother are from different cultural backgrounds must also wrestle with balancing two cultural heritages. Parents from different ethnic groups may decide to spend their lives together. However, their cultures sometimes do not dwell contentedly side by side in the minds of their children. As a result of this discrepancy, the children may experience some degree of emotional conflict.

Reading Check **Compare and Contrast** For which group of adolescents is identity formation especially complicated?

Online Quiz THINK central thinkcentral.com

SECTION 3 Assessment

Reviewing Main Ideas and Vocabulary

1. **Define** What is an identity crisis?

2. **Summarize** What are the four main identity status categories?

3. **Recall** To which gender were Erikson's views of development intended to apply?

Thinking Critically

4. **Support a Point of View** Do you agree that the main task of adolescence is the formation of identity? Explain.

5. **Explain** What is Piaget's formal-operational stage of cognitive development?

6. **Analyze** Using your notes and a graphic organizer like the one below, explain the roles of gender and ethnicity in identity formation.

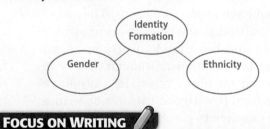

FOCUS ON WRITING

7. **Expository** Write a paragraph in which you explain what factors you think have been most important in forming your identity.

Rites of Passage

A rite of passage marks a person's entrance into a new stage of life. These ceremonies include baptisms, graduations, and marriages. For many people around the world, various rites such as school graduations and weddings signify the end of one period of life and the beginning of another.

A young man reads the Torah in Hebrew as part of his Bar Mitzvah ceremony.

Three Stages Most rites of passage are characterized by three stages. In the first stage, the participant is separated from his or her previous status. The next stage is a transitional stage in which the participant learns the behavior and ideas appropriate to his or her new status. In some African societies, for example, boys who are on the verge of adulthood are separated from others for days or even months while they learn tribal traditions and skills. After the completion of the second stage, the participant is formally admitted into his or her new status. This is often marked by an elaborate ceremony.

Graduation Ceremonies People often pass through the stages of a rite of passage as a group. For example, in many graduation ceremonies In the United States, the students sit together in a special area separated from families and friends. The walk across the stage to receive a diploma symbolizes the transition from student to graduate. In some ceremonies in which the graduates wear academic caps and gowns, the graduates move the tassels on their caps from one side to the other to signify their entrance into the new group.

Quinceañera In some societies, teenagers celebrate certain birthdays as rites of passage. For example, the fifteenth birthday is an important occasion for many Hispanic girls. It is celebrated by the girl, her family, and community members in an event called *quinceañera*. A ceremony, usually involving a church mass, is followed by a party.

Bar and Bat Mitzvahs Jewish adolescents mark their entrance into the adult religious community with a special ceremony called (for boys) a bar mitzvah, which means "son of the commandment," or (for girls) a bat mitzvah, which means "daughter of the commandment." When a Jewish child reaches age 13, he or she is expected to observe the religious customs and obligations of Jewish adulthood. After much preparation, Jewish teens read from the Torah.

Genpuku This was an ancient rite of passage—specifically, a coming of age ceremony—in Japan. Boys between the ages of 12 and 16 were taken to shrines where they were presented with a suit of armor, given an adult haircut, and also given an adult name.

Poy Sang Long This is a rite of passage among the Shan people of Myanmar and Thailand. Between 7 and 14 years of age, boys take vows as monks and participate in monastery life for a few weeks or months. The ceremony goes on for three days, with the boys being dressed up as princes in traditional clothes.

In some Hispanic cultures, a girl's 15th birthday marks her passage into adulthood.

Thinking Critically

1. **Analyze** Besides the examples mentioned above, what are some other rites of passage for adolescents in the United States?

2. **Discuss** How do these rites of passage help in the process of identity formation?

Challenges of Adolescence

Before You Read

Main Idea

Adolescence is a difficult time for most teenagers, with concerns about friendships, jobs, future careers, and body image among their many challenges.

Reading Focus

1. Why is adolescence a difficult time?
2. What eating disorders affect adolescents?
3. How can substance abuse be a challenge for adolescents?
4. What issues surround adolescent sexuality?
5. How does crime affect adolescents?

Vocabulary

anorexia nervosa
bulimia nervosa
juvenile delinquency
status offenses

TAKING NOTES Use a graphic organizer like this one to take notes on challenges of adolescence.

Challenges of Adolescence
Eating Disorders
Substance Abuse
Sexuality
Crime

Bringing Up Baby

PSYCHOLOGY CLOSE UP

How can a doll help prevent teen pregnancy? RealCare Baby is a program that helps teenagers realize the amount of work and responsibility involved in taking care of a baby. The baby is, in fact, crafted to look like a real infant. It cries frequently, just like a real baby. The purpose of the doll is to imitate a real human infant's need for constant attention and care. In the United States, approximately 31 percent of sexually active teenage girls become pregnant annually, twice as many as in Canada and eight times as many as in Japan. One of the main goals of the RealCare Baby program is to change these statistics in the United States.

A couple of days with the RealCare Baby doll usually helps most teenagers realize that they are not yet ready for the responsibilities of parenting. Issues revolving around sexuality and parenting are just some of the challenges that teenagers face in developing responsible behavior. ◼

A Difficult Time

Adolescence is a rewarding time of life for many young people. Yet, for others, adolescence is a difficult time. Some adolescents have problems that seem too large to handle. Nearly all teenagers know classmates who have school or family problems. Adolescents who are not accepted by their peers often experience loneliness and feelings of low self-esteem. Concerns about getting a good job, being able to support family members, and being accepted into college can be highly stressful.

Some young people may develop an eating disorder. Others may abuse alcohol or drugs. Still others may turn to crime and acts of mischief. Tragically, a few take their own lives.

Reading Check **Summarize** What are some causes of stress among adolescents?

Eating Disorders

The adolescent growth spurt makes it important that teenagers receive adequate nutrition. The average girl needs about 2,200 calories a day, and the average boy about 3,000. Adolescents also need protein, carbohydrates, fiber, vitamins, and minerals in their diet.

Adolescents who develop eating disorders get neither the calories nor nutrients their bodies need. Some teenagers starve themselves. Eating disorders affect many teenagers and young adults. More attention has been focused on eating disorders in recent years. The two main types of disorders are anorexia nervosa and bulimia nervosa. In the United States the typical person with anorexia or bulimia is a young white woman of higher socioeconomic status.

Anorexia Nervosa A life-threatening disorder characterized by self-starvation and a distorted body image is called **anorexia nervosa.** Adolescents with anorexia usually weigh less than 85 percent of what would be considered a healthy weight. By and large, eating disorders afflict women during adolescence and young adulthood. Women with anorexia greatly outnumber men with the disorder.

In the typical pattern, an adolescent girl notices some weight gain and decides that it must come off. But even after she loses the "excess" weight, dieting—and, often, exercise—continues even after she reaches an average weight, even after family members and others have told her that she is losing too much. Girls with anorexia usually deny that they are wasting away. Their body image is distorted. They focus on remaining pockets of fat—which may be nonexistent—while others see them as "skin and bones."

Women with anorexia may lose 25 percent or more of their body weight in a year. Their overall health declines. A British study found that for many women, anorexia is a prolonged problem. Of women contacted 21 years after being hospitalized for the problem, only half had fully recovered within 10 years. About 4 to 5 percent of women with anorexia die from causes related to the problem.

Bulimia Nervosa Recurrent cycles of binge eating followed by dramatic measures to eliminate food, such as vomiting, are characteristic of **bulimia nervosa.** Binge eating frequently follows a pattern of severe dieting. As with anorexia, the great majority of people with bulimia are female. In addition to vomiting, girls may seek to compensate for what they have eaten by fasting, strict dieting, and vigorous exercise. Girls with bulimia tend to be perfectionists in their attitudes about body shape and weight.

Origins of Anorexia and Bulimia To understand anorexia and bulimia, let us return to the fact that so many more women than men develop these problems. Theorists account for the gender gap in different ways. Some psychodynamic theorists suggest that anorexia represents a woman's effort to return to a stage before the onset of puberty and adolescence. Anorexia allows her to avoid growing up, separating from her family, and taking on adult responsibilities.

But the cultural aspects of eating disorders seem to be more important. Young people with eating disorders are often attempting to conform to an ideal body shape. Popular fashion models represent that ideal: they are taller and slimmer than the average woman. The feminine ideal has been becoming slimmer and slimmer. As the feminine cultural ideal grows thinner, some women with average or heavier-than-average figures can feel more and more pressure to slim down.

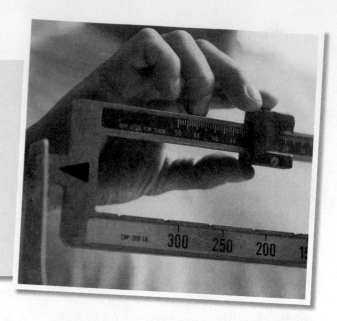

Eating Disorders

Definition: Eating disorders are life-threatening ailments characterized by self-starvation and a distorted body image, recurrent cycles of binge eating, and dramatic measures to eliminate food. They are especially destructive in adolescence because the growth spurt makes adequate nutrition vitally important.

Symptoms may include: excessive dieting and exercise, excessive weight loss, obsession with food

Behavior: bingeing, purging, fasting

Complete a Webquest at thinkcentral.com on substance abuse.

Many men with eating disorders are involved in sports or jobs that require them to maintain a certain weight, such as wrestling, dancing, and modeling. Men are more likely than women to control their weight through intense exercise. Men are also under social pressure to conform to an ideal body image.

Families also play a role in eating disorders. Parents of adolescent girls with eating disorders are relatively more likely to have problems with eating and dieting themselves, to think that their daughters should lose weight, and to consider their daughters to be unattractive. Some researchers speculate that adolescents may develop eating disorders as a way of coping with feelings of loneliness. Some cases of anorexia nervosa may even reflect exaggerated efforts to remain healthy by avoiding intake of fat and cholesterol, which are widely publicized as risk factors for heart problems.

Anorexia nervosa and bulimia nervosa both tend to run in families. Researchers have found evidence pointing to genetic factors involving perfectionism as increasing the risk of these disorders. Even so, they believe there is a role for cultural influences. Perhaps genetic factors contribute to a perfectionistic personality and then cultural and family influences direct the perfectionism toward concern about body shape.

Treatment Whatever the causes, eating disorders are a severe health problem, and people who have them require professional assistance to overcome them. Often a school psychologist or counselor can suggest possible courses of action.

Sometimes health professionals will give students with eating disorders a choice—either to enter a treatment program (where their caloric intake is closely monitored) or to remain in school as long as they stop losing weight and receive counseling. They may have to see a psychologist on a regular basis and have their weight checked weekly.

Reading Check **Define** What are anorexia and bulimia nervosa?

Substance Abuse

Substance abuse usually begins with experimentation in adolescence. Reasons include curiosity, peer pressure, parental abuse, rebelliousness, escape from boredom or pressure, and a search for excitement or pleasure.

Prevalence of Substance Abuse A government survey of more than 15,000 teenagers across the United States found that use of drugs and cigarettes increased over the 1990s. Cigarette smoking was up slightly, with 35 percent of teenagers reporting lighting up in the previous month. The number of teens who reported smoking marijuana in the previous month nearly doubled from about 15 percent in 1991 to 27 percent in 1999. However, a survey conducted by the National Institute on Drug Abuse concluded that the use of cigarettes and marijuana declined from 2001–2007. Alcohol is used occasionally by the majority of high school and college students.

Adolescents often try alcohol and other substances because their peers recommend them or their parents use them. Adolescents also frequently turn to alcohol and other substances to cope with stress. In the short term, use of a substance may win the approval of peers or improve one's mood. It may also reduce unpleasant sensations such as anxiety and tension. But binge drinking and long-term drinking are connected to aggressive behavior, poor grades, and car accidents.

More than 400,000 Americans die from smoking-related diseases each year, including lung cancer, emphysema, and heart attacks. Cocaine narrows blood vessels, thickens the blood, and quickens the heart rate. These events have caused the sudden deaths of a number of athletes who used cocaine to try to boost their performance. Marijuana contains more tars than cigarette smoke—a factor in lung cancer. Marijuana also elevates one's heart rate and blood pressure. Marijuana can also make it more difficult to retain information—that is, it can make it more difficult to learn both in and out of school.

Regular use of alcohol and some other substances—particularly nicotine, cocaine, barbiturates, and heroin—can cause teenagers to become addicted to them. Addicts experience intense cravings for the substances when their effects have worn off. They usually have to take more and more of the substance to achieve the same effects they once obtained with a small amount. The substance may eventually take control of the person's life.

Treatment Withdrawing from alcohol and other drugs can be a physically and psychologically painful experience for people of any age. After someone is admitted to a hospital or a treatment center, the first step in his or her treatment is detoxification—the removal of the toxic, or poisonous, substance from the body. During this process, the person is gradually and carefully taken off the drug.

Another important aspect of the treatment of adolescents with substance abuse problems is psychological. Therapists can help young people understand the meaning of their drug use and help teenagers recognize what is at the root of their problems.

Drug Prevention Most school drug-prevention programs are aimed at stopping the use of so-called gateway drugs. These drugs include alcohol, cigarettes, and marijuana.

Research on the effectiveness of prevention programs shows mixed results. Attempts to scare students by warning them about the dangerous consequences of using drugs can backfire, possibly because scare tactics can arouse their curiosity and disbelief. Peer counseling is often effective because students are more willing to believe other students who have actually used the substances.

Reading Check **Recall** What are some of the reasons that adolescents try alcohol?

Substance Abuse

Definition: Substance abuse is the use of alcohol, drugs, and other substances to alter mood, done to the point of physical or emotional damage. Addictions may be linked to genetics, but environment also plays a role. Not everyone who has a genetic inclination will develop an addiction, and not everyone who has an addiction is genetically predisposed.

Symptoms may include: addiction, aggressive behavior, accidents, impaired judgment, physical symptoms of specific diseases caused by different drugs, such as nicotine or alcohol

Behavior: aggression, forgetfulness, drunk driving, erratic judgment and actions

FACTORS CONTRIBUTING TO TEENAGE PREGNANCY

Several factors contribute to the likelihood of teenage pregnancy.

Problematic relationships
- fights with parents or rebellion against parents

Emotional problems
- feelings of emptiness or loneliness

Problems in school
- lack of educational goals

Loosening of prohibitions
- portrayal of sexual themes in media

Peer pressure
- friends engaging in sexual activity

Lack of knowledge
- misunderstanding or ignorance about the facts of reproduction

Sexuality

Many adolescents struggle with issues of how and when to express their sexual feelings. But they receive mixed messages. Their bodies may be giving them a powerful "go-ahead" signal at the same time that their parents and other adults are advising them of the dangers of early sexual relationships and encouraging them to practice abstinence.

Yet other messages may come from media images—models in advertisements, television shows that revolve around sex, and popular songs with lyrics that contain powerful sexual messages. Many teenagers may assume that sexual activity is more widespread among their peers than it actually is. The truth is, however, that many adolescents are not sexually active.

People today often start dating and establishing exclusive relationships at a younger age than people of earlier times. Adolescents who begin dating early are more likely to engage in sexual relations during high school. About 7.2 percent of American girls between the ages of 15 and 17 become pregnant each year. This amounts to more than 750,000 pregnancies a year.

Teenage pregnancies can be devastating for adolescent mothers, their children, and society at large. Life for many teenage mothers is an uphill struggle. Teenage mothers are more likely to live in poverty and lack hope for their futures than teenagers of the same age who do not have children.

Half of all adolescent mothers quit school and go on welfare. Few receive financial or emotional help from the fathers of their children. The fathers—sometimes also adolescents—often cannot support themselves, much less a family. Most adolescents share the view that teenage parenthood is very undesirable.

Some adolescent girls intentionally become pregnant to try to strengthen relationships with their boyfriends or to fill an emotional void by having a child. However, the relationships with the fathers usually come to an end. Premature motherhood tends to make emotional problems worse, not better. It also has serious implications for the offspring. Teen mothers are more likely to give birth to premature babies and to babies who are below average in weight.

Reading Check **Recall** What percentage of American girls between 15 and 17 become pregnant each year?

Crime and Avoiding Problems

The term **juvenile delinquency** refers to many illegal activities committed by children or adolescents. The most extreme acts of delinquency include robbery, rape, and homicide, which are serious crimes regardless of the offender's age. Less serious offenses, known as **status offenses,** are illegal only when they are committed by minors. Status offenses include truancy (that is, unexcused absence from school), drinking, smoking, and running away from home.

Some people assume that teenagers from poor neighborhoods are more likely to break the law than other teens. However, this is not true. Research shows that low income is not a factor. Another common belief is that children whose mothers work outside the home are more likely to engage in delinquent behavior. Research seems to indicate that this is not the case, however.

Many delinquent acts do not lead to arrest and prosecution but still have serious consequences for the teen. Status offenses tend to be handled by school officials, social workers, parents, and other such authorities who can impose various punishments without the police or the courts.

When adolescents *are* arrested and prosecuted, they are often referred to mental-health agencies and are not formally labeled as delinquents. Nonetheless, between 25 percent and 30 percent of the serious crimes in the United States are committed by teenagers under the age of 18.

Factors that contribute to juvenile delinquency are similar to those that contribute to substance abuse. They include the following factors:

- low self-esteem
- feelings of <u>alienation</u> and estrangement
- lack of affection, lax discipline, and use of severe physical punishment in the home
- behavior problems that began early
- poor grades and lack of educational or vocational goals
- pressure from peers
- having a parent or sibling who has been convicted of criminal behavior

Most adolescents who have clear educational and vocational goals manage to steer clear of such problems. Adolescents who fear the onset of a particular problem are usually better off if they can talk things over with a trusted adult—that might be a parent or another relative, a teacher, or a guidance counselor.

Unfortunately, many troubled adolescents do not get into programs developed to deal with juvenile delinquency until after the behavior pattern has become well established. Then it is more difficult to help them.

The most successful delinquency-prevention programs are those that address the problems early. These programs provide classes and support groups for parents, make home visits to families, and provide other services. And they encourage parents to become involved in the activities of their children in and out of school.

Research shows that children who participate in prevention programs do better in school, are more likely to graduate from high school, go on to college, and get a steady job than those children who do not participate. They also seem less inclined to commit crimes.

Reading Check **Summarize** What are some examples of status offenses?

ACADEMIC VOCABULARY

alienation
isolation, estrangement, dissociation

SECTION 4 Assessment

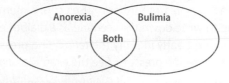

Reviewing Main Ideas and Vocabulary

1. **Recall** Approximately how many Americans die of smoking diseases each year?

2. **Summarize** Why do adolescents experiment with drugs?

3. **Contrast** How do status offenses differ from other acts of delinquency?

Thinking Critically

4. **Categorize** What are some of the types of challenges faced by adolescents today?

5. **Explain** What are three of the most common factors that contribute to juvenile delinquency?

6. **Analyze** Using your notes and a graphic organizer like the one here, explain the similarities and differences between anorexia and bulimia.

Anorexia   Bulimia

Both

FOCUS ON WRITING

7. **Narrative** Write a dialogue in which you and a friend discuss the best method of treatment for another friend's eating disorder or substance-abuse problem.

Peer Pressure

Can you resist peer pressure and stand up for your beliefs even if it means risking an awkward situation or confrontation?

Reading and Activity Workbook

Use the workbook to complete this simulation.

1. Introduction

This simulation will help you practice different ways of responding to peer pressure in a positive way. You will work in small groups to write peer-pressure scenarios. Then you will discuss these scenarios and role-play a different scenario in front of the class. Finally, you will hold a class discussion on how accurate the simulations were and how successful people were in standing up to peer pressure. To complete this simulation, follow the steps below.

- Following your teacher's instructions, organize the class into groups of four students.

- As a group, review the material in this chapter on peer pressure.

- Next, discuss a realistic and appropriate scenario in which one or more teenagers use peer pressure to try to get a friend to do something they do not want to do. Then write it down. Be prepared to discuss your scenario with the rest of the class.

- As a class, role-play the scenario described on the next page. Then hold a class discussion on the effectiveness of refusal skills.

2. Writing Your Scenario

The goal of this part of the activity is to simulate an appropriate response to peer pressure by writing a plausible scenario. Working with your group, write a scenario that simulates a peer-pressure situation. Select one member of your group to write down the scenario as a dialogue. Your scenario should clearly identify the teen being pressured and the peer exerting the pressure. See the example on this page.

After your group is through writing the scenario, hold a class discussion about what each group wrote. How realistic were the scenarios? In the sample dialogues, what techniques were used by peers to try to influence people's behavior?

Here is an example of a sample peer-pressure scenario that includes dialogue.

> **Peer:** Come on! Everyone's doing it! It's all over the school. Just try it!
>
> **Teen:** I don't care! I don't like it! It's wrong! I don't want to mess myself up.
>
> How would you respond to the peer's hectoring comments?
>
> **Peer:** Ah, it won't do you any harm. Everyone's going to call you "chicken," you know. Cluck, cluck!
>
> **Teen:** Stop it! I am not chicken! I just don't have to do it if I don't want to!
>
> **Peer:** Yeah, yeah, sure, whatever. Cluck, cluck!
>
> **Teen:** Stop it!
>
> **Peer:** Just don't try hanging with us any more. That's all I got to say!
>
> **Teen:** Come on! You're my friends!
>
> **Peer:** Of course we are! And would we steer you wrong?
>
> **Teen:** OK, I suppose.

3. Simulation

The chart below gives some refusal skills and sample responses of how to respond to peer pressure. As a class, follow the steps below to act out a simulation in which one teen attempts to use refusal skills to stand up to peer pressure.

❶ Read the list of refusal skills and sample responses in the chart below.

❷ Select three groups of four students to take turns role-playing a scenario in front of the class. In each group, one student will practice using refusal skills to avoid the pressure from three friends to drink alcohol, following the scenario below.

❸ Scenario: You have a couple of friends over to play video games. Your parents went out to dinner, so you have the house to yourselves. One friend finds beer in the refrigerator. She suggests that you and your friends drink some of it.

Refusal Skill	Sample Response
1. Blame someone else.	"My parents would ground me for life. Besides it's just not worth it."
2. Suggest something else to do.	"Let's order pizza and watch a movie."
3. Give a reason.	"No, thanks, I don't think that's cool."

4. Discussion

What did you learn from your simulation? Was the teen response effective? What might the teen have said instead? Hold a group discussion that focuses on the following questions:

■ Overall, how successful was the teen at resisting peer pressure?

■ Were the difficulties of coping with peer pressure accurately presented in the simulation? Why or why not?

■ Were some successful strategies for coping with peer pressure presented? What were they, and why do you think they were effective?

5. Writing

Finally, write a couple of paragraphs in which you describe what you think is the best way to respond to peer pressure.

Saying "no" to peer pressure is an important skill that everyone has to learn.

Comprehension and Critical Thinking

SECTION 1 *(pp. 306–309)*

1. a. Recall How much do most adolescents grow in height during the two or three years of the adolescent growth spurt?

b. Compare and Contrast What is the difference between primary and secondary sex characteristics?

c. Elaborate Why do some adolescents feel awkward during the adolescent growth spurt?

SECTION 2 *(pp. 311–314)*

2. a. Describe To what did G. Stanley Hall attribute the conflicts and stress of adolescence?

b. Analyze How is the behavior of adolescents influenced by fads and peers?

c. Develop What characterizes the adolescent quest for independence?

SECTION 3 *(pp. 315–318)*

3. a. Identify Main Ideas How is adolescent identity achieved?

b. Explain What does it mean to find one's identity?

c. Make Judgments How is the concept of moratorium related to finding an identity?

SECTION 4 *(pp. 320–325)*

4. a. Define What is substance abuse?

b. Categorize What are some factors contributing to the likelihood of teenage pregnancy?

c. Elaborate What is the detoxification process in the treatment of substance abuse?

Psychology in Your Life

5. Imagine that you are the writer of a newspaper column in which you answer letters from teens seeking advice. Think of a problem or issue that concerns you. Compose a letter briefly describing the background of the problem. Then write a response that suggests a way to deal with the situation.

Reviewing Vocabulary

Match the terms below with their correct definitions

6. puberty

7. primary sex characteristics

8. menarche

9. cliques

10. identity crisis

11. identity foreclosure

12. identity achievement

13. anorexia nervosa

14. peers

A. a turning point in a person's development when he or she makes important decisions or changes

B. peer groups who spend much time together

C. developmental changes that lead to the ability to reproduce

D. shutting out other possibilities to avoid an identity crisis

E. characteristics that are directly involved in reproduction

F. people who have equal standing with one another in rank, class, or age

G. a life-threatening disorder characterized by self-starvation and a distorted body image

H. category in which adolescents have coped with crises and have explored options

I. the first menstruation

INTERNET ACTIVITY ✷

15. Is peer counseling an effective way of helping teenagers deal with the challenges of adolescence? Choose a particular challenge, such as eating disorders, substance abuse, or sexuality. Then use the Internet to research how peer counseling might help teenagers deal with the problem. Look for information on how common the problem is among teens and recent statistics and data on peer counseling. Then write a short report that summarizes your findings.

SKILLS ACTIVITY: INTERPRETING GRAPHS

Study the graphs below. Then use the information in the graphs to help you answer the questions that follow.

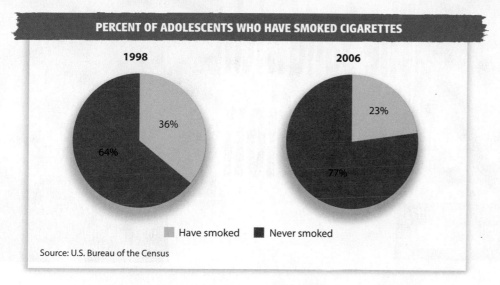

PERCENT OF ADOLESCENTS WHO HAVE SMOKED CIGARETTES

1998

36%

64%

2006

23%

77%

■ Have smoked   ■ Never smoked

Source: U.S. Bureau of the Census

16. Infer What happened to cigarette smoking among teenagers between 1998 and 2006?

17. Make Judgments How might a psychologist use this information to assist in creating an effective antismoking program?

WRITING FOR AP PSYCHOLOGY

Use your knowledge of adolescence to answer the question below. Do not simply list facts. Present a clear argument based on your critical analysis of the question, using the appropriate psychological terminology.

18. Think of a short story or novel you have read that features an adolescent as its main character. Try to connect the character to information you learned in this chapter about adolescent development and the challenges of adolescence. Write a profile of the character in which you consider the following issues.

- identity crisis
- peer pressure and cliques
- puberty

Connecting Online

Visit thinkcentral.com for review and enrichment activities related to this chapter.

Quiz and Review

ONLINE QUIZZES
Take a practice quiz for each section in this chapter.

WEBQUEST
Complete a structured Internet activity for this chapter.

QUICK LAB
Reinforce a key concept with a short lab activity.

APPLYING WHAT YOU'VE LEARNED
Review and apply your knowledge by completing a project-based assessment.

Activities

eACTIVITIES
Complete chapter Internet activities for enrichment.

INTERACTIVE FEATURE
Explore an interactive version of a key feature in this chapter.

KEEP IT CURRENT
Link to current news and research in psychology.

Online Textbook

 Learn more about key topics in this chapter.

The average woman will spend 17 years raising her children and 18 years taking care of her parents.

The Sandwich Generation

Some aging parents do not like to admit they need help and resist their children's efforts to take care of them.

Linda Williams is a wife and mother of three teenagers, but she's still a daughter, too. So when her 88-year-old mother could no longer take care of herself, Williams had the elderly woman move into her Chicago home. Williams became, in effect, a parent to her aging mother and joined the many middle-aged adults of the "sandwich generation"—those who care for their children as well as their parents.

A combination of circumstances has conspired to create the sandwich generation. For one thing, people are living longer. For another, young adults are marrying and starting their families later. There are also fewer professional caregivers available. As a result, people in middle adulthood often find themselves caught in the middle—between their parents and their children.

In fact, about 20 million Americans belong to the sandwich generation. According to the Pew Research Center, an estimated 1 of every 8 Americans aged 40 to 60 is raising children and taking care of their parents. And the numbers are growing. One report predicts that two-thirds of adults who are middle-aged today will wind up taking care of their own aging parents.

You may not be surprised to learn that the dual-parenting role takes a toll on the caregivers. Many have to cut back on their work hours or give up their jobs entirely to stay home and take care of their parents full-time. Stress is also a factor. A 2006 study found that the stress suffered by these middle-aged caregivers often compromises their health and leads to depression. They typically neglect their own needs and sometimes spend as many as 40 hours a week providing care.

The financial strain of looking after aging parents in the home can be another burden—but possibly a less costly one than paying for professional care outside the home. Those who choose to place their parents in an assisted-living facility pay an average of $3,000 a month. A private room in a nursing home can run more than $6,000 a month.

Of course, the primary caregivers aren't the only ones who suffer from the demands of the situation. With attention focused on parents and children, spouses may feel left out or abandoned. The children may be angered by the disruption in the household and end up resenting their grandparents.

CHAPTER 12

ADULTHOOD

The relationship between the adult children and parents can be damaged as well. After a lifetime of being her mother's child, for example, Williams felt disconcerted by the role reversal. "My mother had always been so independent," she said. "Now I sometimes find myself treating her like a child."

Journalist Carol Abaya knows what it's like to belong to the sandwich generation. After she had juggled the needs of her parents and her children for a number of years, Abaya began writing an advice column for other adults in the same situation. For many of these adult children, the hardest part is knowing when to step in and take control of their parents' lives. Abaya suggests talking to parents before they need help. She also advises getting to know the parents' neighbors and asking them to keep an eye on things.

In spite of the challenges, however, many of those in the sandwich generation report a sense of satisfaction about their new role. They feel good about fulfilling their obligation as children and, in many cases, renewing their emotional attachment to their parents. As Williams said, "Every day I get to spend with my mother is a gift."

This may be good news for the children of today's roughly 95 million middle-aged adults. As these adults age, they too will create huge demands for care. Their children may well be the second wave of the sandwich generation.

In this chapter, you will learn about other issues facing those in young, middle, and late adulthood. You will also find out how people can age successfully.

What do you think?

1. What strain can shouldering responsibility for both one's children and one's aging parents place on a family?

2. Do you think children should be expected to take care of their elderly parents? Why or why not?

Chapter at a Glance

SECTION 1: Young Adulthood

■ Young adulthood is characterized by becoming independent from parental authority and trying new ways of doing things.

■ Many young adults form lasting relationships and marry.

■ Although most young couples marry because they are in love, many marriages in the United States end in divorce.

SECTION 2: Middle Adulthood

■ One of the greatest challenges facing middle-aged adults is retaining the ability to create, originate, and produce.

■ During middle adulthood, many adults go through a period of reassessment and reevaluate what to do with the rest of their lives.

■ Many middle-aged adults have to adjust to the changing needs of their children and deal with their own physical changes.

SECTION 3: Late Adulthood

■ Regular exercise and a healthy diet can help older adults reduce the impact of the physical changes they undergo.

■ People age as their cells age and begin to malfunction.

■ Cognitive changes, including memory decline, occur in late adulthood, but most older adults do quite well intellectually.

■ Aging involves social changes that involve work, family, and living arrangements.

■ Older adults who age successfully continue to believe that life is meaningful and full.

SECTION 4: Death and Dying

■ A much criticized theory states that the stages of dying include denial, anger, bargaining, depression, and acceptance.

■ Dying people need support, relief from pain, and a dignified end.

■ Funerals help the living celebrate the life of the deceased and cope with sadness.

Young Adulthood

Before You Read

Main Idea

During young adulthood, most men and women become independent, begin careers, and develop meaningful relationships.

Reading Focus

1. What are some characteristics and goals of young adulthood?

2. Why are marriage and relationships important parts of young adulthood?

3. How does divorce affect parents and children?

Vocabulary

identity
patriarchy

TAKING NOTES Use a graphic organizer like this one to take notes on the characteristics and issues of young adulthood.

Young Adulthood

Characteristics

Issues

Married and in Sync

PSYCHOLOGY CLOSE UP

Why do some married couples come to look like each other? You've probably heard that dog owners tend to resemble their pets, but did you know that married couples can come to look like each other too? A psychology study found that, over time, many husbands and wives developed similar facial features. And it's not because they looked alike when they first got married.

So what's going on? The psychologists who conducted the study considered a number of factors, including the impact of a couple's similar diet, environment, and disposition. But they largely ruled these factors out in favor of a more emotional explanation: empathy. It seems that couples who truly sympathize with each other tend to mimic their significant other's facial expressions. The expressions create similar patterns of wrinkles and furrows and—eventually—similar faces. The study even found that many of these understanding couples reported greater happiness than other married pairs.

You may find the idea of growing to look like your future spouse a romantic or a horrifying proposition. In either case, once you enter young adulthood, it might be a good idea to study the face of the person you fall in love with very carefully. One day it may be just like looking into a mirror. ▪

Characteristics and Goals

Young adulthood, also called early adulthood, covers a span of approximately 20 years—from about age 20 to about age 40. Most people reach their physical peak in their 20s. During their 20s and early 30s, they are faster, stronger, better coordinated, and have more endurance than they have ever had or will ever have again. Many people also are at the height of their cognitive powers during this period.

Young adulthood is characterized by a desire to try new ways of doing things and by changing relationships with parents. In their late teens and early 20s, some people assume that they must live the way their parents do if they want to succeed in life. Some also assume that their parents will always be there to rescue them if their plans fail. As time passes, however, young adults learn to become independent and to take responsibility for themselves and the decisions they make.

Studies indicate that, in the United States, becoming independent from parental authority is a key goal of development for most young adult men. Women are generally less concerned with seeing themselves as separate, independent individuals. They tend to be more interested in creating relationships with others. Of course, these are generalizations only; many women in their 20s become independent and focus on their development as individuals. The creation and maintenance of relationships are also important concerns for many men.

Reassessment Adults in their 20s often believe they have chosen the course in life that is exactly right for them. As they reach their 30s, however, they often reevaluate the decisions they have made in an effort to determine whether their chosen course is really the one that is right for them. Some psychologists have labeled the late 20s and early 30s the "age 30 transition." People often ask themselves, "Why am I doing this?" or "Where is my life going?" Sometimes they find that the life paths they chose in their 20s are no longer the paths they truly want to follow.

This period of reassessment may bring about major life changes. Some people change jobs or start new careers. Many single people feel that this is the time to find a mate. People

who have been working in the home, perhaps raising children, may feel the urge to find a job outside the home. Couples who are without children may think about starting a family.

Women in particular may find themselves reassessing their lives in their 30s. Some women in their 30s begin to think about the biological changes that lie ahead. Many women become concerned about how many childbearing years they have left, especially if they have not already had children. Furthermore, during their early 30s, many women begin to feel that they have been controlled by others and that they have never had the chance to shape their own lives. Today, as in years past, it is still mostly women who take care of family and household chores. As a result, women in the workforce may feel overwhelmed by the double duties of caring for their families and maintaining jobs.

In addition, research suggests that some working women have mixed feelings about success on the job. Even though the great majority of women are in the workplace, some still feel they must sacrifice their family lives to advance their careers. Although working men also have less time to spend with their families, many people still consider it more acceptable for men to work long hours than for women to do the same.

Developmental Tasks of Young Adulthood

This chart lists some of the tasks that psychologist Erik Erikson associated with young adulthood.

- Exploring adult roles
- Becoming independent
- Developing intimate relationships
- Adjusting to living with another person
- Starting a family and becoming a parent
- Assuming the responsibilities of managing a home
- Beginning a career or a job
- Assuming some responsibilities in the larger community—for example, participating in local government or religious organizations
- Creating a social network of friends and co-workers

Settling Down After the upheaval of the early 30s, the mid- to late-30s are often characterized by settling down or "planting roots." People in their 30s may increase the financial and emotional investments they make in their lives. Many have been employed long enough to earn promotions and pay raises. They often become more focused on advancing their careers and gaining stability in their personal lives. Of course, not every individual necessarily experiences all of these tasks. Nor does every young adult follow them in a particular order. For example, many people today choose to remain single or to postpone or forgo having and rearing children.

Reading Check **Analyze** Why do many men and women reassess their lives in their 30s?

Marriage and Relationships

An important part of adolescence and young adulthood is the development of an **identity,** or who you are and what you stand for (your values). Identity brings the personal stability that is needed to form lasting relationships.

Relationships can be difficult to sustain when one or both of the people involved lack personal stability. However, young adults who have developed a firm sense of their own identity during adolescence may be ready to join their lives with those of other people through friendships and marriage. Psychologist Erik Erikson believed that people who do not develop intimate relationships may risk falling into a pattern of isolation and loneliness. An intimate relationship is not necessarily a physical relationship. Rather, it is a trusting, close friendship with another person in which one can be honest without fear of rejection.

In the United States, 75 percent to 80 percent of people get married at least once. However, more people have been delaying marriage in recent decades to pursue educational and career goals. Therefore, the median age of marriage has risen in the past 30 years from about 23 to 27 for men and from about 21 to 25 for women.

History of Marriage In most Western societies, men have traditionally played the dominant role in marriage as well as in the larger society. This system is known as **patriarchy.** Over the past several decades, however, this situation has changed, and spouses are now more likely to be considered equal partners.

Marital roles in modern society are still changing. Some couples continue to adhere to roles in which the husband is the breadwinner and the wife is the homemaker. Other couples have begun to share, and even sometimes reverse, these roles. And many single or divorced individuals are alone responsible for fulfilling these roles.

INTERACTIVE ✴

Marriage Practices Over Time

Throughout history, marriage has changed according to the needs of people and society. The only thing that hasn't changed is the idea of marriage as a bond between two people.
How do the marriage practices described reflect each time and place?

Kingdom of Israel According to the Hebrew Bible, a man was required to marry his deceased brother's widow if he died without a son.

Ancient Greece Girls in ancient Greece often married around the age of 15. Men married around the age of 30, after fulfilling their military service.

India Arranged marriages in India have been practiced for centuries. Today, parents may still choose a child's spouse—usually with the child's consent.

In the United States today, most people marry primarily for love. The concept of romantic love as a reason for marriage, however, did not become widespread in Western societies until the 1800s. In the 1600s and 1700s, most marriages were arranged by the parents of the bride and groom, generally on the basis of how the marriage would benefit the two families. This practice permitted the orderly transfer of wealth from one family to another and from one generation to the next. Another purpose of marriage was to provide a stable home life for children.

Today, however, companionship and intimacy are central goals in most marriages. Marriage generally provides feelings of security and opportunities to share experiences and ideas with someone special. A *New York Times* poll found that the great majority of people in the United States—about 86 percent—still see marriage as permanent.

Choosing Spouses Unlike in times past, in which marriages were arranged by the family, today young people in the United States typically select their own mates. Parents may, however, have at least some degree of influence over the choice.

People are also influenced in their marital decisions by factors such as ethnicity, level of education, social class, and religion. Generally, most people marry others who are similar to themselves. In fact, people in the United States rarely marry people of different races or socioeconomic classes. According to the U.S. Census Bureau, only 4 percent of U.S. marriages are interracial. More than 90 percent of married couples are of the same religion. Similarity in attitudes and tastes is a key contributor to attraction and intimate relationships.

People also tend to choose marriage partners who are near their own age. This is especially true for couples who marry in early adulthood. People who meet in school and then marry each other tend to be similar in age. Most bridegrooms are about two to five years older than the women they are marrying. People who marry later in life or who remarry after being divorced or widowed are less likely to select partners who are as close in age.

Marriages between similar people may have a greater chance at survival because the partners probably share many of the same values and attitudes. Dissimilar couples, however, can work to overcome the differences that divide them by developing shared interests and mutual respect. Evidence that similarity between spouses is beneficial in the long run—the entire course of the marriage—remains somewhat limited.

Reading Check **Compare** How does marriage today compare with marriage in the past?

ACADEMIC VOCABULARY

interracial involving or composed of different races

Medieval Europe Marriages among the nobility were arranged to secure wealth and power. In the 12th century, however, troubadours glamorized the idea of courtly love.

Pre-Civil War America A marriage ceremony between enslaved Africans often involved the ritual of jumping or stepping over a broomstick while friends and family watched.

Sudan In Sudan, many people still observe the tradition of having the groom's family pay for the bride's hand in marriage with cattle.

Korea A traditional Korean marriage represents the union of two families rather than the joining of two individuals. Today, many try to keep such traditions alive.

Interactive Feature thinkcentral.com

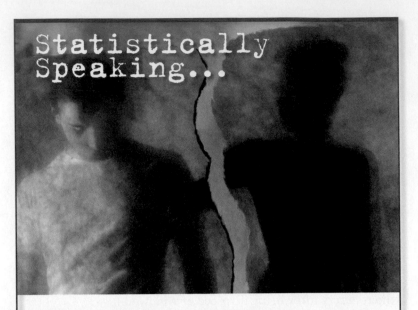

Statistically Speaking...

The Financial Impact of Divorce The financial consequences of divorce for women are much less severe than they used to be. Nonetheless, a significant gap still remains between a woman's individual, or per capita, income after divorce and a man's.

−14% Average decline in per capita income experienced by women who remain single after divorce

−3% Average decline in per capita income experienced by women who remarry after divorce

+80% Average increase in per capita income experienced by men who remain single after divorce

+40% Average increase in per capita income experienced by men who remarry after divorce

Skills Focus INTERPRETING DATA Why do you think a woman's per capita income declines after divorce? Why do you think a man's income rises?

Source: *Social Science Quarterly*, March 2001

Divorce

Although most couples get married because they are in love, many of the marriages in the United States end in divorce. The divorce rate rose steadily throughout most of the last century before leveling off in the 1980s. More than one quarter of children live in single-parent households.

Reasons for Divorce Why is divorce such a common occurrence? One reason may be that obtaining a divorce has become easier than it used to be. Many states now have "no-fault" divorce laws. That means that a judge can grant a divorce without having one or both partners blaming the other. If both partners agree on issues of child custody, financial support, and the distribution of the couple's assets, the marriage is legally dissolved.

The increased economic independence of women also may have made them less inclined to remain in a troubled marriage. Just a few decades ago, most women were homemakers with little or no work experience outside the home. Because there were relatively few employment opportunities for women at that time, many women probably doubted whether they would be able to support themselves and their children. Today, however, more women have jobs outside the home and are therefore more likely to have the economic independence that makes it easier for them to break away.

Of course, there are numerous other reasons why people get divorced, including spouse abuse, child abuse, infidelity, strains brought about by illness or financial hardship, and an inability to communicate effectively. Increasingly high expectations may also have made divorce more likely.

The Costs of Divorce Divorce has many financial and emotional costs. When a household splits, the financial resources are usually divided. Often, neither partner can afford to maintain the standard of living he or she had while married. Divorced mothers often face the primary responsibility for rearing the children and may need to increase income. Divorced fathers, meanwhile, may find it difficult to pay child support and alimony—financial support paid to a former spouse.

Yet, for some people, divorce is a time of personal growth and renewal. When partners are convinced they cannot save their marriage, divorce may enable them to establish new and more rewarding lives. Despite the difficulties in adjusting to a divorce, most divorced people eventually recover. The majority remarry. Yet research suggests that remarriages are even more likely than first marriages to end in divorce. This may be because divorced people are inclined to leave a troubled second marriage fairly quickly. People in first-time marriages, on the other hand, may be more inclined to persist even if the marriage is difficult.

The Children of Divorce Divorce can be difficult for the children, no matter what their age. Research shows that the children of divorced people are more likely to have behavioral problems, engage in substance abuse, and earn lower grades in school. Sometimes a stepfamily introduces new family relationships. Parents may have to work more to support the family financially and so have less time for the children. Nevertheless, most children overcome an initial period of stress and eventually adjust to their new situation. However, boys often have greater problems than girls in adjusting to parental conflict or divorce.

It also seems that it is not so much parental separation that affects the children as the breakdown in the quality of parenting that often follows separation. Alison Clarke-Stewart and her colleagues analyzed data from the National Institute of Child Health and Human Development Study of Early Child Care to examine the effects of marital separation on children during the first three years of life. The families studied included nearly 100 separated or divorced mothers and a comparison group of 170 two-parent families. In general, the children in the two-parent families obtained higher scores on achievement and ability tests, showed more social skills, and experienced fewer problems and greater security. However, when the researchers considered the mothers' levels of education and income, the differences between the children in one-parent versus two-parent families became less significant. Thus, the psychological development of the children in this study was not affected by parental separation or divorce. Instead, the children's psychological development was related to the mother's income, level of education, and well-being. The results of this study suggest that children may fare better in homes with well-adjusted divorced mothers than in homes with constantly bickering married parents. To protect the children, psychologists usually advise parents who are getting divorced to

- try to agree on how they will interact with the children,
- help each other maintain a good parent-child relationship, and
- avoid criticizing each other to or in front of the children.

Should parents in conflict stay together for the sake of the children? There is no easy answer to this question. Although divorce can have negative effects on children, so, too, do marital conflicts. Marital conflict or fighting may be a source of serious psychological distress in children and adolescents. In addition, marital conflicts make relationships between parents and children more difficult and may also be connected with later conflict in the children's own marriages.

Reading Check **Summarize** Why do people divorce?

SECTION 1 Assessment

Reviewing Main Ideas and Vocabulary

1. **Recall** What is a key goal of development for most young adult men?

2. **Identify Cause and Effect** Why has the average age of marriage risen over the last several decades?

Thinking Critically

3. **Explain** What role does identity play in a healthy relationship?

4. **Make Judgments** What might be considered ironic about the poll suggesting that the majority of Americans see marriage as permanent?

5. **Support a Position** Do you agree or disagree with the following statement: "Parents in conflict should remain together for the sake of the children"? Provide evidence to support your position.

6. **Rank** Using your notes and a graphic organizer like the one below, rank the goals of young adulthood by importance from your viewpoint.

FOCUS ON WRITING

7. **Descriptive** In a paragraph or two, describe what you think your life might be like as a young adult ten years from now.

Middle Adulthood

Before You Read

Main Idea

During middle adulthood, men and women continue to be creative in their careers, family life, and community. They also face new life changes as they grow older.

Reading Focus

1. What is generativity?
2. Why do many adults experience a midlife transition?
3. What life changes do people face in middle adulthood?

Vocabulary

generativity
midlife transition
midlife crisis
empty-nest syndrome
menopause

 Use a graphic organizer like this one to take notes on the challenges and issues of middle adulthood.

Middle Adulthood
Challenges · Issues

PSYCHOLOGY CLOSE UP

Is the midlife crisis a myth?

You may have heard the stereotypes: a man going through a midlife crisis buys himself a flashy, red sportscar; a woman dyes her hair and dresses like her daughter. Author Gail Sheehy popularized the term *midlife crisis* in the 1970s, and it became a catchword for any kind of setback in middle age. But does the midlife crisis really exist?

It almost certainly doesn't outside Western society. Other cultures simply don't recognize the concept. In China, for example, the cultural emphasis on family and community greatly reduces the importance placed on such an individual concern. And while studies of Hindu and Japanese cultures indicate that people may experience difficult transitions during middle adulthood, these are far from crises.

The crisis may not even exist in the United States. Recent studies reveal that only about 10 percent of middle-aged Americans claim to have experienced a psychological crisis caused by their age alone. There also appears to be a scientific basis for exploding the myth of the midlife crisis. Neuroscientists have discovered that the working of the brain's right and left hemispheres actually becomes better integrated during the middle adulthood years. Not only that, but negative emotions also diminish during this period. As you will learn in this section, middle adulthood can actually be a time for new beginnings. ■

Generativity

Middle adulthood spans the years from 40 to 65. By age 40, most people have begun to lose some of the strength, coordination, and stamina they had in their 20s and 30s. This decline is generally so gradual that it is hardly noticeable. It is often only of concern to people who rely on physical fitness for their livelihoods or interests. However, middle adulthood can also be the time when many people first *begin* to work on developing their physical potential. Even someone who has been inactive for years might decide at 45 to train for a marathon. People who work at their conditioning can maintain excellent health and strength throughout middle adulthood.

According to developmental psychologist Erik Erikson, the greatest challenge facing middle-aged adults is **generativity**—the ability to create, originate, and produce. According to Erikson, generativity adds meaning to the lives of adults, and it helps them to maintain and enhance their self-esteem.

Adults can be creative, or generative, in various areas of their lives, such as their careers, their families, and their communities. People in middle adulthood are often also in positions in which they can exercise a particularly important influence on the world around them. As experienced workers, they may improve methods and relationships in the workplace. As parents, they guide the next generation. As voters and residents, these adults can help make their communities safer, friendlier places. Erikson also believed that adults who are not generative become stagnant. Stagnation—lack of advancement or development—can result in feelings of emptiness and meaninglessness.

Reading Check **Identify Supporting Details**
How can adults maintain generativity?

Transition

Some psychologists have noted that many people experience a midlife transition around the ages of 40 to 45. The **midlife transition** is a period in middle adulthood when people's perspectives change in a major way. Some adults in their 40s are struck with the dramatic realization that they have lived about half their lives. They see themselves as being

Developmental Tasks of Middle Adulthood

According to Erik Erikson, the focus of these developmental tasks is improving one's quality of life and strengthening relationships, both personal and in the community.

- Helping one's children make the transition from home life to the outside world
- Strengthening the relationship with one's spouse
- Helping make the world a better place by assuming leadership roles in social and civic activities
- Achieving mastery in one's career
- Adjusting to the physical changes that occur in middle age
- Making decisions about how to spend one's second adulthood
- Pursuing one's passions
- Coping with one's aging parents

at a turning point. Previously, they had probably thought of their ages mostly in terms of how many years had elapsed since their birth. Once the midlife transition occurs, however, they begin to think of their ages in terms of how many years they may have left.

People in their 30s may still think of themselves as the older siblings of brothers or sisters in their 20s. Then, in their early 40s, a critical event often occurs. It may be a serious illness, a change at work, the death of a friend or a parent, or even just losing at basketball to one's child. Whatever the event, it triggers a 40-year-old's realization that he or she has made a generational shift. For example, the death of a parent may mean that the 40-year-old is now the head of the family. Similarly, losing at basketball to one's child may trigger the realization that "I'm not a kid anymore."

Women tend to undergo their midlife transitions about five years earlier than men do, at about age 35 instead of 40. What makes the mid-30s so special for women? For some women, 35 is about the age when they have sent their youngest child off to grade school, an event that can illustrate that their children are quickly growing up.

Many women, of course, are not finished (or have not begun) having children by the age of 35, and for women who become pregnant at age 35 or older, doctors advise routine fetal testing for Down syndrome and other chromosomal disorders. At around age 40, women are also encouraged to begin having regular mammograms—specialized x-rays for early detection of breast cancer—and are considered at greater risk for various types of cancer. These are all events that can cause women to reflect on their age and <u>mortality</u>.

ACADEMIC VOCABULARY

mortality
inevitable death

With the thought that their lives may be close to half over, many people—men and women—come face-to-face with their limitations. They may acknowledge that they may never realize the dreams they had when they were younger. For some adults, however, entering midlife may trigger a sense of urgency—a "last chance" to do certain things.

Midlife Crisis or Age of Mastery? In some people, the midlife transition triggers a second period of reassessment, often referred to as a **midlife crisis.** The middle-aged professional who sees younger people advancing at a faster rate may become seriously depressed. The parent with two or three teenagers may feel less needed by her or his children.

The concept of the midlife crisis has often been treated as something generally negative. It suggests that people are overwhelmed by the crushing realities and the limits of their lives. Yet journalist Gail Sheehy is quite positive about the years from 45 to 65. She calls these years the "age of mastery."

Sheehy maintains that during these years, people are frequently at the height of their creative and productive powers. Therefore, Sheehy believes, the key task for middle-aged adults is to decide what they will do with the remainder of their lives. Because people are living longer than people did in previous generations, most American adults have 30 to 40 healthy years left after they reach middle adulthood. Men and women can continue to have fulfilling lives if they find careers or hobbies that bring satisfaction and if they pursue these newfound interests wholeheartedly.

Middlescence But how do people go about recognizing and finding these interests? The term *middlescence* is sometimes used to describe a period of searching that in some ways resembles adolescence. Both middlescence and adolescence are periods of transition. Just as a key task of adolescence is the formation of identity in becoming an adult, middlescence involves a search for a new identity, or a *second* adulthood.

By the time they reach their early 40s, women have already dealt with some of the fears and uncertainties that are only just starting to confront men. As women emerge from middlescence in their 40s and 50s, they frequently experience a renewed sense of self. Many women in this age group feel confident and secure. They extend their interests. For example, they may become more involved in their communities. They are committed to what they are doing and feel productive, effective, and empowered.

Reading Check **Summarize** How do many adults respond to the midlife transition?

Baby Boomers

Definition: a term used to refer to those who were born during the post-World War II baby boom, in the years between 1946 and 1964; popular motto: "50 is the new 30"

Characteristics: youthful, active, free-spirited, optimistic, oriented to social causes, defiant, distrustful of government, self-indulgent

Impact: on economy—largest group of consumers, potential future burden on Social Security; on society—fought for individual rights; refusal to grow old may have inspired others

Life Changes

In middle adulthood, many men and women experience life changes. Some of these changes involve adjusting to the needs of children, who are themselves growing to adulthood. Others involve dealing with the physical changes that come with growing older.

The Empty-Nest Syndrome In the past, psychologists placed great emphasis on the so-called empty-nest syndrome. **Empty-nest syndrome** is the term applied to the feelings of emptiness and loss mothers and fathers sometimes feel after the children have left home to establish their own lives. For mothers who have never worked outside the home, it can be particularly difficult to adjust to the departure of the children whose upbringing has been a full-time job. After years of total commitment to being a wife and mother, some women seem to lose their sense of purpose and become depressed after their children go out on their own.

Contemporary research findings, however, reveal a much more optimistic picture. Once the "nest" is empty, many women report that they are happier with their marriages and other aspects of their lives than ever before. Many women mention positive changes, such as greater peace of mind, self-confidence, and personal stability. Many middle-aged women become more self-assertive and achievement-oriented. Furthermore, most women whose children have left home are already employed. With more energy and time to spend outside the home, many women become more influential in politics and careers. Many others return to school. And although there may be some problems of adjustment once children leave, those problems affect both parents, not just mothers.

There is much variation, of course. Some people in middle age feel hopeless and drained. But often middle age is a time of increased freedom. Many people have been successful enough to be free of financial worries. Many begin to travel extensively. They may have the leisure time to take up new hobbies or explore old interests. Therefore, middle age does not need to be a painful period. Rather, it can be a time to enjoy new freedoms and opportunities for self-development.

The Boomerang Generation

Definition: young adult children who, after leaving home to go to college, be on their own, or pursue a career, choose to return and live with their parents; also called "kidults"

Reasons for Return: few or low-paying jobs, high cost of housing, large student loan debts, desire to save money; close relationship with parents; fear of independence

Impact on Parents: positive—continued close relationship with child, help gained with household responsibilities and younger children; negative—loss of freedom, tension, economic burden, particularly when taking care of aging parents

Even those in the sandwich generation may feel a strong sense of satisfaction from their role as caregiver for both their children and parents. Studies have shown that some women even derive positive health benefits from the role.

Menopause Menopause, the end of menstruation, usually occurs in a woman's late 40s or early 50s, although it can occur earlier or later. It is caused by a decrease in the hormones estrogen and progesterone. After menopause, a woman no longer produces egg cells that can be fertilized. Other body changes also occur. Breast tissue decreases, and the skin becomes less elastic. In addition, there may be a loss in bone density that can lead to brittle bones—a condition called osteoporosis.

In some women, the hormonal changes of menopause may cause discomfort, such as hot flashes—sudden sensations of warmth, often accompanied by reddening and sweating, fatigue, and mood swings. However, in most cases, these symptoms are relatively mild. Some women cope with the more severe changes of menopause with hormone-replacement therapy—taking hormones to replace those the body no longer produces.

The psychological meaning of menopause to a woman is often more important than the physical changes she experiences. Some women feel that they are losing their identity as women and are likely to be more distressed by menopause than those who do not have such feelings. Women who feel that their primary purpose in life was having children are also likely to find menopause stressful.

CASE STUDY
CONNECTION

The Sandwich Generation
Those caring for both children and aging parents can reap health benefits.

MYTHS AND REALITIES ABOUT MENOPAUSE

The left side of this chart shows several of the myths about menopause. The realities of menopause are shown on the right.

Myth	Reality
After menopause, women need estrogen-replacement therapy.	Not necessarily. Some estrogen is still produced by the body. Women should begin estrogen-replacement therapy with caution, in any case, because of possible health risks.
Menopause is accompanied by depression and anxiety.	Not necessarily. However, hormonal changes in the body can affect a woman's moods.
At menopause, women suffer crippling hot flashes.	Not necessarily. Not all women experience hot flashes, and those who do can often be treated successfully.
Menopause ends a woman's sex drive.	Not at all. In fact, many women feel a renewal of sexual interest.
A woman's general level of activity is lower after menopause.	Not so. Many women report having more energy after menopause.

Many people—including both men and women—have negative impressions of menopause. For example, some people consider menopause to be abnormal or a disease. The reality, however, is often positive. Far from being a disease, menopause is normal and can be a healthy development in women's lives.

When people refer to a woman as "menopausal," they are usually talking about the mood swings and increased irritability that can occur. Unfortunately, this oversimplifies what menopause is all about for women, and it also reinforces the stereotype of menopause as a time when women are not in control of their emotions. Such stereotypes and myths often do not have anything to do with the biology or psychology of aging.

Do men undergo menopause? The quick answer is "of course not," since men have never menstruated. Yet occasionally you may hear or read about the so-called male menopause. Men do experience a hormone decline. At about age 40 or 50, testosterone levels in men begin to decline. They may fall to one third or one half of their peak levels by age 80. However, this is a gradual drop-off. It does not resemble the sharp plunge in estrogen levels that women experience.

The decline in a man's testosterone level may be connected with such other age-related changes as loss of strength, weight gain, reduced energy, and decreased fertility. Some of these changes, however, could just as well be due to a man's gradual loss of human growth hormone rather than to a decrease in the testosterone level.

Reading Check **Make Generalizations** Why do many people have a negative attitude toward menopause?

SECTION 2 Assessment

Online Quiz THINK central — thinkcentral.com

Reviewing Main Ideas and Vocabulary

1. **Identify Main Ideas** What may happen if middle-aged adults are not generative?

2. **Compare** In what ways can middle adulthood be similar to adolescence?

3. **Make Generalizations** How might parents feel when their children leave home?

Thinking Critically

4. **Analyze** How do you think the myths about menopause influence the way menopausal women are treated?

5. **Make Judgments** Is middle adulthood a greater challenge for men or for women, or is it equally challenging for both?

6. **Evaluate** Do you think middle age is a time of crisis or a period of new opportunities? Explain your answer.

7. **Identify Main Ideas** Using your notes and a graphic organizer like the one at right, list the positive and negative aspects of middle adulthood.

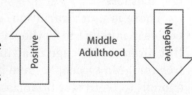

FOCUS ON WRITING

8. **Narrative** Write a brief dialogue between parents and their child who has come back home to live after college.

Late Adulthood

Before You Read

Main Idea

Late adulthood is a time of many changes—physical, cognitive, and social. The ways in which older adults handle all these changes can determine how successfully they age.

Reading Focus

1. What physical changes are part of late adulthood?

2. Why do people age?

3. What cognitive changes occur in late adulthood?

4. How do social changes affect older adults?

5. How can older adults age successfully?

Vocabulary

programmed theories
cellular damage theories
free radical
cross-linking
dementia
senile dementia
Alzheimer's disease
ego integrity

TAKING NOTES Use a graphic organizer like this one to take notes on the changes that occur in late adulthood.

Changes	Notes
Physical	
Cognitive	
Social	

PSYCHOLOGY CLOSE UP

What's the secret of long life?

Some researchers think they may have found it. They discovered four far-flung places where people live longer than they do anywhere else. These so-called Blue Zones are Loma Linda, California; Okinawa, Japan; Sardinia, Italy; and the Nicoya Peninsula in Costa Rica. In this steamy corner of Central America, researcher Dan Buettner came across someone who, he believed, was the prototype for all successful centenarians: a 100-year-old woman named Panchita.

The morning Buettner met Panchita, he was accompanied by her son, Tommy. As soon as they arrived at her home, Panchita began brow-beating her reluctant son to eat—even though he was 80 years old and a great-grandfather. She had already been up for hours, chopping wood, grinding corn by hand, and working in her yard.

When Buettner spoke to Panchita, he realized that she shared the characteristics of other centenarians he had met. She lived simply, retained strong ties with her family, was flexible but decisive, was highly likeable, and had a deep religious faith. And these qualities had been tested. Panchita had worked hard all her life and had raised her four children mostly by herself. Hardest of all, one of her sons had died when he was only 20. Yet in spite of her challenges and misfortunes, Panchita told Buettner, "I am a blessed woman today." And, oh yes: optimism is another secret to long life. ■

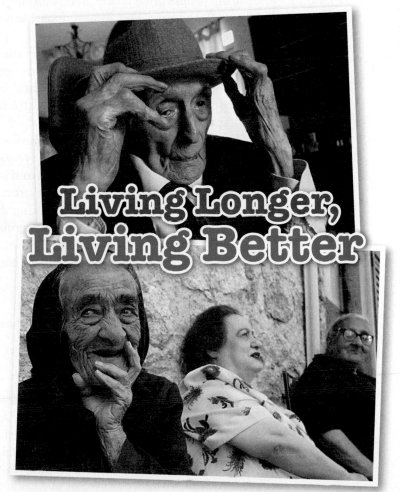

Living Longer, Living Better

Like Panchita, these centenarians from Sardinia (top and bottom left) have found the secret to a long and happy life.

Physical Changes

Age 65 marks the beginning of late adulthood. People are living longer than ever before. In 1900 only one American in thirty was over 65. By the year 2020 nearly one American in five will be age 65 or older.

Many physical changes take place in late adulthood. Wrinkles and skin folds appear as the skin becomes less elastic. Some of the senses become less sharp. In general, older people do not see and hear as well as younger people. A decline in the sense of smell leads many older people to add more spices to their food for flavor. The reflexes and the reaction time of older people also tend to be a little slower than those of younger people.

A few of the physical changes cause health problems. For example, as bones become more brittle, they fracture more easily, and the risk is greater that they will break if the person falls. As people grow older, their immune systems also become less effective as barriers against disease.

However, older adults can do many things to maintain their health, strength, and energy levels. Regular exercise and a healthful diet can contribute to making older adults feel well and also help them fight disease.

Exercise helps people maintain flexibility and fitness at any age—including the years of late adulthood. Because brittle bones and stiff joints are a natural part of the aging process, many older people may prefer walking and swimming to more weight-bearing exercises such as running and bicycling. The latter activities tend to cause more stress on bones and joints.

Reading Check **Identify Supporting Details**
What can older adults do to help maintain their health and strength?

ACADEMIC VOCABULARY

toxin a poison produced by certain animals, plants, and bacteria

Why People Age

As we age, our bodies change. But the rate of these changes differs from person to person. Why do some people seem to age faster than others? Many scientists hope that by understanding the process of aging, we may eventually be able to slow it down or even reverse some of its negative effects. Theories of aging fall into two categories: programmed theories and cellular damage theories.

Programmed Theories The developmental theories that maintain that aging is the result of genetics are called **programmed theories.** These theories of aging view people as having biological clocks that move forward at a predetermined pace. Studies show that people whose parents lived long lives are more likely to have long lives themselves. This suggests that genetics plays a significant role in the length of one's life.

Heredity influences our cells, our hormones, and our immune systems. The cells in our bodies divide and repair themselves only a specific number of times. After that, they become inactive and eventually die. Some researchers believe that the limitation on the number of times a cell can divide is less important than the fact that the cells are aging. As they age, cells become less able to repair themselves. This makes people vulnerable to diseases that involve cellular breakdown, such as cancer.

Heredity also affects our hormones. Hormonal changes in later life may leave the body more vulnerable to certain health problems, such as diabetes, osteoporosis, and heart disease. Researchers are investigating the possible role of certain hormones—such as melatonin and human growth hormone—in the aging process.

In addition, heredity influences the immune system. According to programmed theories, genetics may predetermine the decline in our immune systems. Such a decline makes the body less able to fight off disease.

Cellular Damage Theories In contrast to programmed theories, **cellular damage theories** of aging suggest that cells malfunction as a result of damage, not heredity. The damage may come from internal body changes or from external causes, such as trauma or toxins.

The cells in our bodies are affected by the environment. If they are exposed to poisons or cancer-causing agents for long periods of time, they become less able to repair themselves and more vulnerable to disease. As time passes, cells and vital organs are worn down, like machines whose parts eventually wear out from constant use.

Some scientists blame chemicals called free radicals for damage to our bodies. **Free radicals** are unstable molecules in our bodies.

They are normally produced as by-products of digestion. They may also be produced by exposure to environmental agents, including ultraviolet light, air pollution, pesticides, and even extreme heat. According to this view, aging occurs because free radicals accumulate in the body. These molecules eventually damage cells, causing people to age faster and to become vulnerable to various diseases.

Cross-linking may be yet another cause of aging. According to this view, proteins within a cell bind together, toughening body tissues. This toughening eventually leads to the breakdown of various bodily processes and causes aging.

Aging is a complex biological process. It may not be explainable by a single cause or theory. Aging may result from a combination of the processes described in this section, or it may involve factors we are not aware of yet. For these reasons, researchers continue to study aging.

Reading Check **Contrast** What is a major difference between programmed theories and cellular damage theories?

Cognitive Changes

Cognitive development is also affected by aging. Cognitive development in adulthood has many aspects—creativity, memory functioning, and intelligence. People can be creative for a lifetime. Pablo Picasso was still painting in his 90s, and Grandma Moses did not begin painting until she was 78. Architect Frank Lloyd Wright designed New York City's innovative Guggenheim Museum when he was 89 years old.

Although people can lead creative lives throughout old age, memory ability does decline with age. It is common for older people to have trouble recalling the names of things or people. Memory lapses can be embarrassing, and older people sometimes lose confidence in their memory. But declines in memory are not usually as great as people assume, and they can sometimes be reversed. Memory tests usually measure ability to recall meaningless information. Older people show better memory in areas in which they can apply their special experiences to new challenges. For example, who do you think would do a better job of learning and remembering how to

solve problems in chemistry—a young expert in history or a retired chemistry teacher?

All in all, most older people do quite well intellectually. Late adulthood is a time to discover new skills and ways of thinking. Unfortunately, some older people do have cognitive problems, such as senile dementia and Alzheimer's disease.

Senile Dementia The serious loss of cognitive functioning is called **dementia.** People with dementia show major losses in memory. They may also have speech problems or be unable to perform simple tasks, such as tying their shoes or buttoning a shirt, even if they are physically able to perform such tasks. They may also have difficulty concentrating or making plans.

Dementia that occurs after age 65 is called **senile dementia.** Only a minority of older people have senile dementia, sometimes called senility. Most cases occur in people over 80.

Alzheimer's Disease **Alzheimer's disease** is a progressive form of mental deterioration that affects about 10 percent of people over the age of 65 and nearly half of those over the age of 85. Although Alzheimer's is connected with aging, it is a disease and not a normal part of aging.

MYTHS ABOUT ALZHEIMER'S — QUICK FACTS

Many myths abound about Alzheimer's disease. In this chart, some of them are laid to rest.

Myth	Reality
Only older adults can get Alzheimer's.	Actually, Alzheimer's can also strike people in their 30s, 40s, and 50s.
Contact with the aluminum in cans and cookware can lead to Alzheimer's.	There is no evidence for this theory.
Flu shots increase the risk of Alzheimer's.	In fact, flu shots have been shown to reduce the risk of Alzheimer's.
Alzheimer's can be treated and cured.	Medication can slow the progression of the disease for a time, but there is no treatment or cure.
Alzheimer's is not fatal.	Unfortunately, Alzheimer's does kill its sufferers by slowly destroying brain cells and disrupting body functions.

Alzheimer's disease is characterized by general, gradual deterioration in mental processes such as memory, language, and problem solving. As the disease progresses, people may fail to recognize familiar faces or forget their names. Eventually, people with Alzheimer's disease become helpless. They become unable to communicate or walk and require help with eating and other simple tasks.

Alzheimer's disease is also characterized by reduced levels of the neurotransmitter acetylcholine (ACh) and by the buildup of a sticky plaque in the brain. The plaque is formed from fragments of a body protein. Normally, the immune system prevents the buildup of this plaque, but the immune system does not do its job effectively in the case of people with Alzheimer's disease. One form of drug therapy is aimed at boosting ACh levels by slowing its breakdown. This approach achieves modest benefits with many people. Another approach to the treatment of Alzheimer's is the development of a vaccine made of a harmful protein that will help the immune system to better attack the plaque.

Vascular Dementia Another common kind of dementia is vascular dementia. Vascular dementia can be caused by the bursting of a blood vessel in the brain (as during a stroke) or by a decrease in the blood supply to the brain. Such a decrease happens when fatty deposits collect in the blood vessels that go to the brain. The deposits cause the blood vessels to narrow, impeding the blood flow. Various infections can also cause dementia.

Reading Check **Summarize** What are the characteristics of Alzheimer's disease?

Social Changes

In addition to physical and cognitive changes, aging also involves many social changes. People have to make decisions about their retirement, how much time to spend with their children and grandchildren, and where they should live.

Retirement Many people dream of retirement, the period when they no longer need to wake up early in the morning and go to work. Other people dread the idea of retirement, wondering what they will do with all their free time. In many cases, retirement is voluntary.

But people in some jobs, including teachers in most school systems, must retire when they reach a certain age, usually 65 or 70. In other cases, older people find themselves forced out of jobs because of discrimination or for other reasons related to age.

Some people turn their attention to leisure activities when they retire. Others continue in part-time work, either paid or voluntary. Research indicates that there may be some common experiences involving retirement. When people first retire, they often undergo a "honeymoon" phase. They feel very positive about their newfound freedom, and they do many of the things they had dreamed about doing once they had the time. During this honeymoon period, people are often quite busy.

After a while, however, many people become disillusioned with retirement. Their schedules slow down, and they discover that the things they had fantasized about are less stimulating than they had thought they would be. Retirement can also place stress on a marriage because spouses may suddenly be spending a great deal more time together than they ever have before. As people encounter such experiences, they tend to develop a more realistic view of retirement. They may join volunteer groups and participate more in community activities. Sometimes elderly persons begin entirely new careers—painting or writing, for example. In general, people establish a new routine, and stability sets in.

Grandparenthood Grandparents often have more relaxed relationships with their grandchildren than they had with their children. Their perspectives may have become broader as they have grown older. Many have become more tolerant and understanding over the years. And because they do not usually have to shoulder the major responsibility for the grandchildren, grandparents can often just enjoy them. However, for a variety of reasons, increasing numbers of grandparents are in fact taking on the major responsibility for raising their grandchildren.

Adult children frequently value their parents for the roles they play with the grandchildren. For example, retired grandparents who live nearby can help baby-sit. Grandparents also often serve as sources of wisdom and love for grandchildren.

How Do You View the Elderly?

Much of what we think we know about older adults is influenced by their portrayal in movies and television. Test your knowledge here.

PROCEDURE

❶ Copy the following statements on a piece of paper and indicate whether you think each one is true or false.

    a. The elderly are poor drivers.

    b. Older workers are more productive than younger workers.

    c. Older people have no interest in sex.

    d. The elderly are mean and grouchy.

    e. Old age is like a second childhood.

❷ Ask your teacher for the correct answers.

All members of the Young@Heart rock band are at least 70 years old.

ANALYSIS

1. Get together with a partner and compare your answers.

2. Discuss the answers you got wrong. Why do you think you thought this way? Where do you think your ideas came from?

3. Consider what the quiz suggests about the elderly.

4. With your partner, discuss ways you can get to know more about the older people in your family and community.

Quick Lab **THINK** central thinkcentral.com

For many older adults, balancing a need for independence with a need to stay involved with their children and grandchildren is an important job. How often older adults see the children and grandchildren and whether they have the right to make "suggestions" become key issues. Although many older people worry that their families might no longer want them around, most older people see or talk to their children regularly.

Living Arrangements Some Americans hold certain stereotypes about older people's living arrangements. One stereotype portrays older people living with their children. Another has them in nursing homes and other institutions. Still another stereotype is that older people buy condominiums or move to retirement communities in areas with warmer climates.

On the contrary, most older people are independent. Many of them are financially secure and own their own homes. Most older people also remain in their hometowns rather than move to other areas of the United States. It is true that nearly 30 percent of older people will spend some time in a nursing home. However, the populations of nursing homes usually consist of people who are 80 or older.

Reading Check **Make Generalizations** What role can older adults play in their loved ones' lives?

Successful Aging

Some people age more successfully than others. Psychologists have found that "successful agers" have several characteristics that can inspire all people to lead more enjoyable and productive lives.

Ego Integrity Erik Erikson believed that people in late adulthood, like those in other stages of life, face certain developmental tasks. He believed that one challenge facing people in late adulthood is the maintenance of **ego integrity**—the belief that life is meaningful and worthwhile even when physical abilities are not what they used to be. A person with ego integrity is able to accept his or her approaching death with composure. This may be late adulthood's greatest challenge.

People spend most of their lives developing relationships and gathering possessions. Erikson believed that ego integrity enables people to let go of relationships and objects as the end of life approaches. Older people who do not maintain ego integrity risk falling into despair because they feel as if they are losing everything that matters to them. Ego integrity is connected with the wisdom to accept that one's life span is limited and to realize that nothing will last forever. Successful agers have this wisdom.

Aging and Adjustment Most people in their 70s report being largely satisfied with their lives. Despite the physical changes that occur with aging, more than 75 percent rate their health as good or excellent.

Older people tend to be more satisfied with their lives when they are in good health and when they are financially secure. In fact, there is a correlation between socioeconomic status and health. Economically disadvantaged people at any age are more likely to report ill health than people of higher socioeconomic status. People who are financially secure are usually able to afford better health care and preventive services. They tend to worry less, and thus their stress is reduced. It may also be true that throughout life, people who are healthy are able to work harder and earn higher incomes. Most older people have some degree of financial security, but about 10 percent of people age 65 or older do live below the poverty line.

Among older people, as among younger people, a strong connection exists between social support and personal well-being. Social support is provided by various relationships.

Spouses, children, and friends may all provide social support, helping out in both practical and emotional ways when necessary. This may help explain the research finding that older couples generally are happier than older single or widowed people. Once couples are retired, they tend to spend more time together. Their relationships thus take on greater importance in their lives. When one spouse dies, however, children often are able to give needed support to the surviving spouse.

Reshaping One's Life Another component of successful aging is reshaping one's life to focus on what is important. Laura Carstensen's research on people aged 70 and above revealed that successful agers formulate specific goals that bring them satisfaction. For example, rather than becoming involved with many different causes or hobbies, they may focus on one particular interest. Successful agers may have less time left than younger adults, but they tend to spend it more wisely.

Paul and Margret Baltes noted that successful agers no longer try to compete with younger people in certain activities, such as athletics or business. Rather, they focus on matters that allow them to maintain a sense of personal control. They also try to find ways to make up for losses in some of their abilities. If their memories are not quite what they used to be, they may make notes or use other types of reminders. If their senses are no longer as sharp as they once were, they use devices such as hearing aids or eyeglasses. Some older people even develop creative solutions to their problems. For example, the great pianist Arthur Rubinstein performed well into his 80s, even after he had lost much of his speed. To make up for this lack, he would slow down as he approached a passage in the music that required him to play faster. In this way, he gave the impression of speed during the more rapid passages.

A Positive Outlook A positive outlook is another component of successful aging. For example, some older people blame their occasional aches and pains on specific causes, such as a cold. Others simply blame old age itself. Not surprisingly, those who attribute their problems to specific causes are more optimistic that they will get better. Thus, they have a more positive outlook or attitude.

QUICK FACTS

Developmental Tasks of Late Adulthood

Erik Erikson believed that acceptance and adjustment are primary tasks of late adulthood.

- Adjusting to physical changes and keeping (or becoming) physically active
- Maintaining concern about other people so that one does not become preoccupied with one's own physical changes
- Shifting interests from work to retirement or leisure activity
- Adjusting to changes in financial status
- Establishing fulfilling living arrangements
- Learning to live with one's husband or wife in retirement (in that both spouses may now be together much of the time)
- Adjusting to the illness or the death of one's husband or wife

Researcher William Rakowski followed 1,400 people aged 70 and above who had common health problems, such as aches and pains. He found that those who blamed the problems on aging were more likely to die sooner than those who blamed the problems on specific factors. In fact, many studies have shown that older people who hear negative stereotypes about late adulthood actually begin to walk more slowly and become more forgetful. These negative images of aging can even affect their cardiovascular systems.

Self-Challenge Yet another component of successful aging is challenging oneself. Many people look forward to late adulthood as a time when they can rest from life's challenges. However, sitting back and allowing the world to pass by is a prescription for becoming passive and for not living life to its fullest extent. Some people view the later years as the beginning of the end of life, but they can be much more. In fact, the later years provide many opportunities for self-fulfillment.

This view was confirmed in a study conducted by Curt Sandman and Francis Crinella. They randomly assigned 175 participants, whose average age was 72, either to a foster-grandparent program or to a control group. They then followed the participants for 10 years. As compared to people in the control group, the foster grandparents faced greater physical challenges, such as walking a few miles each day. They also had new social experiences by getting to know the children and their families. The results of the study showed that people in the foster-grandparent program improved their overall cognitive functioning, including their memories. They even slept more soundly.

Withdrawing from life and avoiding challenges is clearly not the route to well-being and good health for the elderly. Focusing on what is important, maintaining a positive attitude, and accepting new challenges are as important for older people as they are for younger people.

The secret to successful aging does not require great lifestyle changes. And it is not necessarily related to one's educational level, marital status, or income. In studies, older adults themselves came up with their own recipe for success. The formula is simple and good advice for everyone, no matter what age. It includes

- increasing participation in activities,
- making more close friends,
- visiting with family, and
- spending quiet time reading and listening to music.

Reading Check **Identify Cause and Effect** What can happen when older adults do not have a positive outlook?

SECTION 3 Assessment

Online Quiz THINK central thinkcentral.com

Reviewing Main Ideas and Vocabulary

1. **Describe** What do programmed theories maintain about aging?

2. **Recall** Why do grandparents often enjoy rewarding relationships with their grandchildren?

3. **Explain** Why is ego integrity an important part of healthy aging?

Thinking Critically

4. **Draw Conclusions** What can older adults do to make sure they get the most out of their retirement years?

5. **Predict** How might older adults feel who are no longer able to drive and have to live with their children?

6. **Elaborate** What steps do you think young and middle-aged adults might take now to age successfully?

7. **Identify Cause and Effect** Using your notes and a graphic organizer like the one below, list the possible effects of each cause listed.

Older adult begins walking regularly	→	
Older adult stays involved with family	→	
Older adult avoids challenges	→	

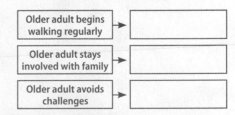

FOCUS ON WRITING

8. **Expository** Many older people experience memory losses. Write some guidelines that older people could use to keep track of their medication and remember important telephone numbers and directions to places they like to visit.

ADULTHOOD **349**

Living in the Moment

What do you want to do with the rest of your life? With your future stretching far into the distance, you probably have plenty of ideas. But suppose you didn't have so much time? How would your priorities change? How would you make the most of the time you have left? These are questions that those in late adulthood have to consider.

According to the theory of socioemotional selectivity, our perception of time plays an important role in the types of goals we set. Young adults, for example, tend to set long-term goals, such as acquiring knowledge, establishing a career, and developing relationships. Older adults, on the other hand, set short-term goals they can accomplish in the present. Above all, they pursue activities that are more emotionally oriented, such as spending time with close friends and family.

At the same time, older adults begin to restrict their social network. Because the elderly view their time as limited, they focus on important relationships and begin to let go of those that are more casual. Even though their social circles become smaller as they age, many older adults do not feel isolated. Studies show that they experience a great sense of well-being with the intimate relationships they maintain (Lang, et al., 1998).

As emotional relationships become more important, older adults also become better at controlling their emotions, particularly negative ones. According to one study, feelings of anger, depression, loneliness, and boredom tend to decrease as people age (Charles, et al., 2001). This decrease could be due to the fact that older adults have learned how to deal with intense emotions better than younger adults. Their fewer, but closer, relationships may also provide greater emotional support.

Although the socioemotional selectivity theory has the greatest implications for those in late adulthood, its effect is not limited to older adults. Apparently, age does not cause our goals to change focus. Any shift in our perspective of time can cause a shift in our goals and motivations. So, for example, those faced with a terminal illness or even students approaching graduation are likely to adopt present-oriented goals. Like older adults, they tend to strengthen their bonds with a tight-knit group of intimates.

Not everyone buys into the theory, however. Critics of it claim that generalizations about family relationships in late adulthood, in particular, are not always so clear cut. Some older adults, they say, maintain unhealthy ties with family members out of habit or necessity. And in some cases, the elderly may have little social contact with anyone due to illness or relocation.

In general, though, many older adults want to live in the moment. Some even make a list of all the things they want to do. And at the top of that list may be "Spend more time with the family."

In the movie *The Bucket List*, the characters played by Jack Nicholson *(right)* and Morgan Freeman set out to accomplish a list of goals before they die, but their relationship becomes more important than the list.

Thinking Critically

1. **Draw Conclusions** How might the fact that older adults' emotions seem to "mellow with age" enhance their well-being?

2. **Discuss** Think about a situation when your time with friends was limited. What were your main goals during this period?

Current Research **THINK** central | thinkcentral.com

SECTION 4

Death and Dying

Before You Read

Main Idea

People deserve to die with dignity and the support of those who love them. After someone dies, the living often depend on religious beliefs and traditional customs to cope with their sadness.

Reading Focus

1. What are the stages of dying?
2. How can people help a loved one die with dignity?
3. How do people deal with death?

Vocabulary

hospice
euthanasia
living will
bereaved

TAKING NOTES Use a graphic organizer like this one to take notes on dying and death.

Dying	Death

The **Last** Lecture

PSYCHOLOGY CLOSE UP

What message would you leave behind? On September 18, 2007, computer science professor Randy Pausch gave a lecture to an audience at Carnegie Mellon University in Pittsburgh. The lecture was titled "Really Achieving Your Childhood Dreams," but it came to be known as "The Last Lecture." Pausch had been diagnosed with pancreatic cancer and was told he had about six months to live. He began by talking about all the dreams he'd had as a child—the ones that came true, like writing an article for *World Book Encyclopedia*, and the ones that didn't, like playing In the NFL. He also talked about the people he'd helped during his career and those who had helped him. He didn't talk about his wife and children. That, he said, would be too painful.

Throughout the lecture, Pausch entertained and joked with the audience. When he first stepped on stage and received a standing ovation, he said, "Make me earn it." He showed the audience all the stuffed animals he'd ever won at amusement parks (one of his realized childhood dreams) and invited his listeners to take one. He brought out a huge birthday cake for his wife and led the audience in a chorus of "Happy Birthday to You." But at the end of the lecture, Pausch admitted that he'd misled his listeners. The lecture, he said, was really about how to live your life. And then he had one more admission: "The talk's not for you, it's for my kids. Thank you all. Good night." Less than a year after he delivered his last lecture, Randy Pausch died from cancer. He was just 47 years old. ■

Stages of Dying

We all must face death eventually. Yet most of us seem to want to turn away from such a thought. According to psychiatrist Elisabeth Kübler-Ross, people often avoid the subject of death. We seem to do all kinds of things to keep from confronting the reality of death. For example, prior to burial, funeral directors use cosmetics to make the deceased person look as if he or she is just asleep.

Because death often brings sadness, some people send their children away to friends or relatives so that they need not face the grief and anxiety around the home. Children may be prevented from visiting dying grandparents. But part of healing after a death is having the chance to say good-bye. Therefore, some psychologists suggest that trying to protect children by keeping them away from a dying loved one may actually make it harder for them to cope with their grief.

Kübler-Ross worked with people who had terminal illnesses. An illness is terminal when it seems certain to lead to death. Some types of cancers are terminal illnesses. Kübler-Ross theorized that there are five stages through which many dying people pass. She believed that many older people have similar feelings when they suspect that death is near, even if they have not been diagnosed with a terminal illness. The stages are as follows:

1. **Denial**. For example, the dying person might think, "It can't be me. The doctor's diagnosis must be wrong."

2. **Anger**. People in this stage might think, "It's unfair. Why me?"

3. **Bargaining**. For instance, "I'll be kinder if I can just live to see my only grandson graduate."

4. **Depression**. The person may despair and wonder, "What's the use of living another day?"

5. **Acceptance**. The person reasons, "I've had a good life. I'm ready to die."

Kübler-Ross's theory has met with considerable criticism. Some psychologists, such as Edwin Shneidman, agree that many terminally ill people have the kinds of feelings Kübler-Ross described. But Shneidman has not found that the feelings follow a particular sequence. Shneidman finds that people faced with approaching death show a variety of reactions. Some people have quickly shifting emotions that range from rage to surrender, from envying the young and healthy to yearning for the end. Some people accept death more easily; others feel despair. Still others feel terror. People's reactions to dying reflect their unique personalities and their philosophies of life.

Another problem with Kübler-Ross's theory is that it may tempt family members and health professionals to ignore the uniqueness of each individual's experiences at the end of life. If a dying person is angry or in despair, people may think that it is just a stage and not pay close attention to the dying person's feelings. In addition, people might try to encourage the dying person to work through the sequence of stages in the belief that by doing so the dying person will reach the acceptance stage sooner. However, what a dying person may really need is to be treated as a living individual with hopes and feelings, not as someone undergoing predictable stages of behavior.

Reading Check **Analyze** Why has Kübler-Ross's theory been criticized?

Dying with Dignity

Dying people, like other people, need security, self-confidence, and dignity. Dying people may also need relief from pain. One controversial issue is whether terminally ill individuals should be given painkilling drugs that are highly addictive. Physicians usually try to balance the patient's need for relief from severe and constant pain against the dangers of such drugs. However, some people feel that worrying about addiction does not make sense when a person is going to die soon.

Dying people, perhaps even more than other people, need to feel cared for and supported. Therefore, it is helpful for family members to encourage a dying person to talk about his or her feelings. Sometimes it is enough just to spend quiet time with the person. Family members and others can also help by assisting with financial and legal arrangements to pay for medical care and the distribution of property. The knowledge that one's final wishes will be carried out can help the dying person gain a sense of peace and completion.

Some dying people want to know all the details regarding their situation; others do not. Therefore, it is important for family members and health professionals to understand the extent of the person's need for details. It is also important to give the person accurate information about what she or he can expect to experience in terms of pain and loss of body functions and control. Old and dying people should not be treated like infants, but as adults who have dignity and a right to know what is going to happen to them.

The Hospice Alternative Some people enter a hospice before they die. A **hospice** is a home-like place where dying people and their families are given the physical and emotional support to help them cope with terminal illness. Unlike hospitals, hospices do not restrict visiting hours. Family members and friends work with trained staff to provide physical comfort and emotional support. Hospice care may also be given in the patient's own home by visiting hospice workers.

In a hospital, rules determine a patient's treatment—usually the patient has little say in the matter. In a hospice, however, dying people are allowed more control over their lives. They are encouraged to make decisions about their diets, activities, and medication. Relatives and friends often remain in contact with the hospice staff to cope with their own feelings of grief after the person has died.

Euthanasia The term **euthanasia** comes from the Greek language and means "easy death" (*eu* means "well"; *thanatos* means "death"). Some physicians may consider euthanasia when they are absolutely convinced that there is no hope for a person's recovery, such as when a person has been in a coma for a long time or when the pain of a terminal illness is unbearable. Euthanasia is illegal in most states, but many people support making euthanasia legal, with clear restrictions.

Opponents of euthanasia argue that no one has the right to take—or to help another person take—a life, even one's own life. Opponents also maintain that new medications and therapies are continually being developed and that a person who feels today that death is the best option might feel more optimistic next week. The pain and suffering may be temporary, but death is permanent.

End-of-Life Psychology

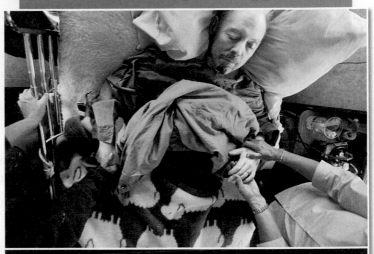

"Psychologists have tended to overlook end-of-life issues . . . but we can't afford to overlook them anymore."

So says psychologist Judith Stillion, who believes that a psychologist should be part of a dying patient's medical team. As a team member, a psychologist can discuss patients' psychological health with their physicians and nurses. Stillion hopes that such a team effort might prevent the dying from feeling alone.
Do you think that most dying patients would welcome psychological care? Why or why not?

The Living Will Many people write **living wills** to avoid being kept alive by artificial support systems when there is no hope for recovery. The living will is a legal document.

A living will is intended to spare people the perceived indignity and cost of being kept alive when there is no hope of survival and to spare their families from having to make the decision to remove a loved one from an artificial life-support system. The document does not go into effect until the person is incapacitated. Of course, whether to have a living will is a choice that each individual must make.

Complete a Webquest at thinkcentral.com on the controversy over euthanasia.

Reading Check **Summarize** How can people help a dying person achieve a sense of peace?

Dealing with Death

When a family member or friend dies, the living are left behind to deal with the death. The ritual of funerals and the support of others can help people cope with their sadness.

The Funeral The funeral is a traditional way for a community to acknowledge that one of its members has died. The rituals of the funeral also provide a framework for what to do and how to act when someone has died.

The specific kind of funeral chosen usually reflects religious beliefs and cultural practices. Some funeral services tie a person's death to the ongoing progression of time. Various professionals, such as undertakers and religious leaders, can be especially helpful concerning the final arrangements for the deceased.

Funerals are a way of saying good-bye. But they accomplish much more. As the deceased is physically removed and prepared for burial or cremation, his or her body is both physically and symbolically separated from the living. Some customs provide mourners time to view the body and meet with family members.

Funerals also provide a way to remember and celebrate the life of the deceased. Many funerals include a eulogy. Family and friends may share favorite memories of the deceased. Finally, there is the burial or the cremation of the body. This is when family and friends physically let go of the person who has died.

ACADEMIC VOCABULARY

eulogy a speech praising the person who has just died

Bereavement It is normal to feel sad when a family member or friend dies, but people may also experience a sense of relief that the person's suffering is finally over. Such feelings of relief often seem disturbing, but they are rather common. The people who are left behind are said to be **bereaved,** which means mourning over something or someone precious who has been taken away. People who are bereaved may have feelings of sadness and loneliness, numbness, anger, and even relief. When the dying person suffers greatly, family members may feel they have reached the limits of their ability to be helpful. Therefore, it is normal for them to feel a certain amount of relief when death finally comes.

Some bereaved people may join support groups or seek professional help in dealing with their grief. With or without such help, most bereaved people eventually recover from their losses. They may never forget the person they have lost, but they usually become less preoccupied by the loss itself. They resume their lives at home and at work. They may always miss the person who died, but most of the time they are able to resume normal functioning. Sometimes the survivors grow in compassion for others and gain a deeper appreciation of the value of life.

Reading Check **Identify Supporting Details** What is the purpose of a funeral?

SECTION 4 Assessment

Reviewing Main Ideas and Vocabulary

1. **Identify** What are some of the ways that people try to avoid facing death?

2. **Contrast** How does hospice care differ from hospital care?

3. **Infer** Why might it be important for people to write a living will before they die?

Thinking Critically

4. **Draw Conclusions** A common saying is "Funerals are for the living." What does this statement mean?

5. **Evaluate** How might helping a loved one die with dignity ease a family member or friend's grief?

6. **Support a Position** Do you agree with Kübler-Ross that dying has predictable stages, or do you agree with her critics? Defend your position.

7. **Categorize** Using your notes and a graphic organizer like the one below, list the ways that people might help someone who is dying.

Ways to Help the Dying

FOCUS ON WRITING

8. **Persuasive** Write a brief editorial in which you support or oppose euthanasia for people with extremely painful, terminal illnesses.

Cultural Perspectives on Grief and Death

People everywhere grieve when a loved one dies. However, the form that their grief takes and the rituals people observe in the face of death vary from culture to culture. To a great extent, our culture shapes us and the way we look at the world. The way we express grief and respond to death is no less a product of culture.

Day of the Dead Unlike many Americans, the people of Mexico do not avoid the subject of death. On the contrary, they dedicate a two-day long celebration to it called the Day of the Dead. Mexicans mark the festival on November 1 and 2 with fireworks, reunions at family plots, and special foods. And many of these foods are quite macabre: sugar skulls and coffins, sweet rolls topped with dough in the shape of bones, and breads molded into human figures. Families also prepare a feast on a special altar for the spirits of their dead loved ones, who are believed to return home for a visit. In addition to the food, some people thoughtfully include a wash bowl and towel so that the spirits can clean up before they eat. Families also place incense and candles on the altar to help the departed find their way home.

Concept of Death in Sub-Saharan Africa According to some traditional African religions, life does not end with death. The dead are believed to continue their existence in a spirit world, where they have the power to help or harm the living. Many African peoples observe certain religious rituals to make sure that the deceased has a safe passage to the afterlife. Some are so fearful of the dead that they remove the body from the home through a hole in the wall instead of the door. They then quickly cover up the hole so that the spirit cannot find its way back.

Chinese Funeral Customs Funerals and burials are serious matters in traditional Chinese society. Before the deceased is laid in the coffin, the body is washed and completely dressed, although never in red. Red, it is believed, will turn the deceased into a ghost. Throughout the funeral—which can last for 49 days—selected family members of the deceased wail loudly. Funeral guests light incense for the deceased and pay their respects to the family. They are also encouraged to donate gifts of money to the family to help with the costs of the lengthy funeral.

Chinese mourners burn paper money for the deceased to use in the afterlife.

At the burial site, the family burns paper models of household objects. These are thought to be the items the deceased will take to heaven.

Traditional Jewish Mourning A Jewish funeral traditionally begins with the relatives of the deceased tearing a black ribbon or garment to symbolize their grief. After a simple ceremony, pallbearers carry the coffin to the burial site, often stopping seven times for the recitation of a psalm. Then, before they leave the cemetery, mourners wash their hands in ritual cleansing. Finally, the family returns home where they mourn the dead for seven days—a ceremony called Shivah.

Skeleton figures in Mexico are shown doing ordinary things because tradition holds that people must remain who they are after death so they can return for the Day of the Dead.

Thinking Critically

1. **Compare** What similar attitude toward the dead do all of these cultural traditions reveal?

2. **Discuss** What different funeral traditions have you heard about?

Experiencing the Stages of Adulthood

Reading and Activity Workbook

Use the workbook to complete this simulation.

What would you like to say to your future self? How might you see yourself looking back as an older adult?

1. Introduction

In this chapter, you have learned about the goals and challenges people face at every stage of adulthood. Imagine that you could see yourself 50 years from now. What would you, as a teenager, want to ask your older self? What advice would your older self have for your present, younger self? In this simulation, you will have the opportunity to find out by writing two letters—one addressed to yourself in late adulthood, the other written from the point of view of your older self.

The simulation will help you think about what the stages of adulthood might hold for you. Trying to picture yourself as an older adult and imagining what challenges you might already have encountered may give you a glimpse into the future. To complete the simulation, follow the steps below.

■ Following your teacher's instructions, organize the class into groups of three to four students.

■ Within your group, discuss and generate ideas for your letters. Consider the issues and challenges you might face as you age.

■ Write your two letters. In the first letter, you will imagine what you will be like 50 years from now and write to that person. In the second letter, you will write an answer. You will pretend you are now in late adulthood and respond to your younger self.

■ Share your letters with your group. Discuss your ideas and insights into the stages of adulthood.

2. Generate Ideas

Before you begin the simulation, get together with the other members of your group and discuss what you have learned about the issues and challenges of each stage of adulthood. In your letters, you will discuss each stage's developmental tasks and incorporate the terms and concepts that psychologists use to describe the aging process. As you conduct the discussion, you might want to take notes that you can refer to when you carry out the simulation.

Generate ideas about what life might be like for you in young adulthood. Discuss how you might confront the following challenges.

■ Independence

■ Marriage

■ Divorce

■ Having children (or not)

■ Beginning a professional career

Generate ideas about what life might be like for you in middle adulthood. Discuss how you might confront the following challenges.

■ Generativity

■ Midlife crisis

■ Empty-nest syndrome

Generate ideas about what life might be like for you in late adulthood. Discuss how you might confront the following challenges.

■ Physical changes

■ Cognitive changes

■ Social changes

3. Write the Letters

After your group discussion, write the two letters on your own. Each letter should reflect a clear understanding of the challenges faced throughout the aging process.

Keep the following tips in mind as you write the first letter to your future self.

■ Remember that the person you are writing to is yourself—but 50 years older than you are now. To help focus on your future self, you might picture a relative or family friend who is currently a similar age.

■ Think about the issues that most concern you at each stage of adulthood. What would you like to know about these issues? What do you look forward to? What do you fear?

■ Describe your hopes and dreams. Ask your future self for advice on how you can achieve them.

Now keep the following tips in mind as you write your reply to the first letter.

■ Remember that your response should be written from the point of view of yourself as an older adult. Try to imagine what you might look like 50 years from now and what you might have experienced.

■ Imagine your life. Did you marry and have children? Did you have a successful career? What would you like to tell yourself to expect? What do you know now that you wish you knew earlier?

■ Think about your family's medical history. What conditions might you have encountered over the next 50 years—or successfully avoided? Based on your experience, what advice can you offer your younger self?

4. Share and Discuss the Letters

After you have finished writing your letters, get back together with your group. Take turns reading the letters aloud and discussing them. Use the following questions to guide your discussion.

■ How successful do you think you were at writing letters from these two different perspectives?

■ How did you decide what to put in your letters?

■ Which stage of adulthood do you think you will enjoy the most?

■ Which stage of adulthood do you think you will enjoy the least?

■ What single thing about adulthood do you expect to enjoy the most?

■ What did you learn about yourself from writing these letters?

■ Do you think this exercise will help you anticipate and deal with whatever may happen in the future?

Finally, read the three quotations about aging below. Consider your attitude toward aging now and as an older adult. Are your attitudes different? Do the younger and older versions of yourself agree or disagree with the quotations? Discuss the meaning of the quotations with the group and whether your attitude toward aging changed as a result of the simulation.

> The idea is to die young as late as possible.
> —*Ashley Montagu*

> Age is an issue of mind over matter. If you don't mind, it doesn't matter.
> —*Mark Twain*

> None are so old as those who have outlived enthusiasm.
> — *Henry David Thoreau*

Comprehension and Critical Thinking

SECTION 1 *(pp. 332–337)*

1. a. Identify What factors typically influence a young adult's choice of a spouse?

b. Contrast How do the characteristics and goals of men and women in young adulthood differ?

c. Make Judgments Do you think it is too easy today to obtain a divorce? Should it be harder? Support your opinion.

SECTION 2 *(pp. 338–342)*

2. a. Define What is stagnation?

b. Draw Conclusions Why do you think large numbers of middle-aged adults enroll in classes and programs offered by community organizations, schools, and colleges?

c. Elaborate How might a woman who did not bear any children react to menopause?

SECTION 3 *(pp. 343–349)*

3. a. Recall What role do free radicals play in the aging process?

b. Explain Why do some older adults become disillusioned with retirement?

c. Support a Position Do you agree with Erik Erikson that a person with ego integrity can accept his or her death with composure? Why or why not?

SECTION 4 *(pp. 351–354)*

4. a. Describe What can bereaved people do to help themselves deal with their grief?

b. Identify Cause and Effect What might be the psychological effect of preventing children from visiting a dying loved one?

c. Evaluate Why might a family choose to remove a loved one from a hospital and place him or her in a hospice?

Reviewing Vocabulary

Identify the term or phrase from the chapter that best fits each of the following descriptions.

5. progressive form of mental deterioration

6. feelings of emptiness after children have left home

7. inevitable death

8. speech praising person who has just died

9. system in which men play the dominant role in society

10. the end of menstruation

11. unstable molecules in our bodies

12. the ability to create, originate, and produce

13. belief that life is meaningful and worthwhile even in late adulthood

14. period in middle adulthood when people's perspectives greatly change

INTERNET ACTIVITY ✳

15. Find out about divorce practices in different cultures. As you research, look for answers to the following questions: Is divorce easy or difficult to obtain? What, if any, are acceptable reasons for divorce? How are children affected by divorce in this culture? How do other people in this culture view those who divorce? How do the divorce practices compare with those in the United States? Write a brief report, summarizing your findings.

Psychology in Your Life

16. Create a chart or other visual that summarizes the physical, mental, and social characteristics and issues of young adulthood, middle adulthood, and late adulthood. Then interview several people in each of the three stages. Do the characteristics represent what they are experiencing? Have they dealt with the issues listed at their stage of life? What further characteristics and issues would they add to the chart? After you have completed your interviews, write a paragraph in which you evaluate and summarize the responses.

SKILLS ACTIVITY: INTERPRETING PRIMARY SOURCES

Read the following excerpt from *On Death and Dying*, in which Dr. Elisabeth Kübler-Ross discusses the behavior of a dying patient. Then answer the questions that follow.

> **❝**Another patient was in utmost pain and discomfort, unable to go home because of her dependence on injections for pain relief. She had a son who proceeded with his plans to get married, as the patient had wished. She was very sad to think that she would be unable to attend this big day, for he was her oldest and favorite child. . . . She had made all sorts of promises if she could only live long enough to attend this marriage. The day preceding the wedding she left the hospital as an elegant lady. Nobody would have believed her real condition. She was the 'happiest woman in the whole world' and looked radiant. . . . I will never forget the moment when she returned to the hospital. She looked tired and somewhat exhausted and—before I could say hello—said, 'Now don't forget I have another son!'**❞**
>
> —Elisabeth Kübler-Ross, *On Death and Dying*

17. **Identify** According to Kübler-Ross's stages of dying theory, which stage had the patient in the excerpt reached?

18. **Sequence** According to Kübler-Ross's theory, what feelings will characterize the patient's next stage of dying?

19. **Evaluate** Why do you think that the patient thought it important to tell Kübler-Ross that she had another son?

WRITING FOR AP PSYCHOLOGY

Use your knowledge of the stages of adulthood to answer the question below. Do not simply list facts. Present a clear argument based on your critical analysis of the question, using appropriate psychological terminology.

20. Briefly discuss the psychological impact of the following on people at each stage of adulthood:
    * social network
    * career
    * aging

Developmental Psychologist

At what age do children develop the ability to think abstractly? Does isolation reduce short-term memory in nursing home residents? Why do infants need more sleep than older children?

If you find questions like these intriguing, you may want to become a developmental psychologist and study the behavioral changes that occur at various stages in a person's life. In the past, developmental psychology was limited to the study of developmental stages of children. For this reason, it was called "child psychology." Recently, however, researchers have become aware that people experience complex and interconnected physical, psychological, intellectual, and social changes throughout the entire life span. Another change in the field is that the father's role in a child's life now receives more attention than it did in the past.

Among the contemporary issues that interest developmental psychologists are changes in our ability to perform certain tasks as we age. Developmental psychologists also investigate language acquisition, changes in perception, creativity, sensory acuity, intellectual abilities, and emotions at different stages of life.

Most developmental psychologists focus on a certain period in the life span, such as infancy, childhood, adolescence, middle age, or old age. This last category, called gerontology, will be particularly important in the future, as the country's population ages.

Developmental psychologists are interested in all stages of human development, from infancy to old age.

Another topic of interest to developmental psychologists is the changing roles of men and women in society. These researchers study the impact of gender stereotyping and the implications of that stereotyping on a child's development.

Developmental psychologists usually work for universities, teaching and conducting research. Many combine academic careers with secondary careers in writing, as a natural outgrowth of their interests. Some developmental psychologists also work in clinical settings such as hospitals, prisons, nursing homes, schools, group homes, nursery schools, or hospices.

As our society changes, new and exciting issues will be raised. Developmental psychologists are likely to lead the way in answering these questions. The more we learn, the more we will understand human development and behavior.

Applying APA Style

APA Style **THINK**central   thinkcentral.com

Developmental psychologists often include tables, graphs, charts, and diagrams in their journal articles. Style guidelines from the **American Psychological Association (APA)** help them create graphics that are clear and accurate.

The APA refers to graphs, charts, and drawings as figures. According to APA style, figures should not duplicate information that is stated in the text, and they should contain only essential facts.

When presenting information in graphic form, choose the type of illustration that is most appropriate to the data. Bar graphs are best for comparing data and trends. Line graphs are helpful for showing changes over time. Circle graphs show the relationship among parts of a whole; they can display percentages effectively.

Through Think Central you can find more on creating figures from the APA style guidelines. Go to the site to review

the APA guidelines. Then make a list of different types of figures, and provide an example of the data each can present. An example is provided for you.

Type of Figure	Type of Data
bar graph	average annual rainfall in selected countries
line graph	
circle graph	

UNIT 5 Personality

THE Happiness OF NATIONS

We often hear statistics about how nations rank against each other. World's largest economy? The United States has the largest gross domestic product. Largest population? China has over 1.3 billion people. Largest area? Russia is almost twice the size of the next largest country, Canada.

But we rarely hear about how happy a nation's people are. Does it matter if your country ranks first in manufacturing or oil production if you and your fellow citizens are miserable?

Dutch social psychologist Ruut Veenhoven thought that national happiness deserved more attention. He set out to learn which nations had the happiest citizens and what made them that way. His efforts led to the World Database of Happiness, which compiles the results from studies of happiness. Countries are then ranked on a scale of 0 to 10, with 10 being happiest.

As the map below shows, Denmark, Switzerland, and Austria lead the list, with scores of 8.0 to 8.2. The next group of countries, which scored 7.6 to 7.8, is more diverse. These countries include Iceland, Finland, and other European nations, but also Australia, Canada, Guatemala, and Mexico. At the opposite end of the list are less contented countries such as Armenia, Moldova, and Tanzania. These countries have happiness scores from 3.2 to 3.7.

The United States scored 7.4, which puts it in the top 20 percent. As the world's wealthiest country, it might be expected to place higher. If money does not buy happiness, what's the secret?

HAPPINESS SCALE

Most Happy	8.0–10.0
	6.0–7.9
	4.0–5.9
	2.0–3.9
Least Happy	0–1.9
	Data not available

LIFE SATISFACTION IN EUROPE

Source: World Database of Happiness

CHAPTER 13
MOTIVATION AND EMOTION

The happiest countries had certain characteristics in common. They tended to be modern societies supportive of individualism. Freedom, in the form of personal and political liberty, was key. Perhaps surprisingly, the degree of income inequality and the amount of state-sponsored services did not seem to matter. But confidence in the honesty and efficacy of the government did.

So if the government of Moldova instituted the same policies as Denmark, would its people soon be just as happy as the Danes? They would be happier, but other factors still apply. Veenhoven found that the characteristics of the society in which you live and your position in that society affect your happiness. But so do your health, personality, and way of life. That helps to explain why there are still unhappy people in Denmark and the other highly-happy countries, as well as happy people in Tanzania and the other least-happy countries. Both your society and your psychology affect your happiness.

Politicians have begun to take note of Veenhoven's work. Most countries focus on improving economic growth, judged by gross domestic product (GDP) and similar measures. But King Jigme Singye Wangchuck of Bhutan declared that his country would instead devote its efforts to raising GNH—gross national happiness. British politician David Cameron created a Quality of Life Policy Group aimed at raising GWB—general well-being. The success of such efforts may hinge on how well policymakers understand motivation and emotion, which are the topics of this chapter.

What do you think?

1. What characteristics did the happiest countries share?

2. What would it take for gross national happiness to replace gross domestic product as the chief measure of national success?

Chapter at a Glance

SECTION 1: The Psychology of Motivation
- Motivations can be analyzed as needs and drives.
- Psychologists have developed several different theories of motivation, including instinct theory, drive-reduction theory, humanistic theory, and sociocultural theory.

SECTION 2: Biological Needs: Focus on Hunger
- Biological needs such as hunger involve both physiological and psychological factors.
- Obesity has many causes but also many solutions.

SECTION 3: Psychological Needs
- All people seek sensory stimulation.
- Some people feel driven to high achievement.
- People seek to balance their beliefs, actions, and thoughts.
- Humans are motivated to be social.

SECTION 4: Emotions
- Emotions have biological, cognitive, and behavioral components.
- Facial expressions of emotion are the same around the world.
- Psychologists have developed several different theories of emotion.

The Psychology of Motivation

Before You Read

Main Idea

Psychologists study motivation to explain why people behave the way they do.

Reading Focus

1. What does the psychology of motivation deal with?
2. What are the major theories of motivation?

Vocabulary

motive
need
drives
instincts
homeostasis
self-actualization

TAKING NOTES Use a graphic organizer like this one to take notes on the psychology of motivation.

The Psychology of Motivation	
Motivation	Theories

Confronting Fear and Failure

PSYCHOLOGY CLOSE UP

What makes rock climbers keep trying when they keep falling? Rock climbers frequently suffer falls that are often painful and potentially deadly. What motivates them to keep coming back?

Learning any new sport involves trying and failing, then learning from your mistakes. If the new sport is something like tennis or water polo, the consequences are small. You may hit a bad shot or pass the ball to the opposing team. But if you take up an extreme sport like rock climbing, watch out. The consequences of failure become much more significant.

Psychological researchers have identified several different factors that motivate rock climbers. Some rock climbers enjoy nature and appreciate being away from modern life. Others find motivation in competing with fellow climbers. Still others seek the mental strength to master their fears and the physical strength and skills needed to master the rock. And, of course, almost every rock climber could be counted among the thrill seekers.

Any one of these motivators, by itself, might not be enough to overcome fear of injury, especially after a climber experiences a bad fall. But in combination, these factors give many climbers the mental strength to get back on the rock. ■

Rock climbing is a dangerous sport that requires both mental and physical strength.

Motivation

Why do some people like to travel to faraway places or to try new foods? Why are other people happy to stay home and eat the same meals every week? The answer to these questions—and other questions about why people do the things they do—relates to motivation. A **motive** is a stimulus that moves a person to behave in ways designed to accomplish a specific goal.

Motives are considered theoretical states because they cannot be seen or measured directly. Psychologists assume that people and other organisms are motivated when they observe the people trying to reach their goals. The psychology of motivation deals with the *whys* of behavior.

Needs When psychologists speak of motives, they also often speak of needs. A **need** is a condition in which we require something we lack. People have both biological and psychological needs. People fulfill biological needs to survive. Examples of biological needs include the need for oxygen and food. Biological needs such as for food or sleep occur because of physical deprivation. That is, people feel hungry or sleepy when they have not eaten or slept for a while.

Achievement, self-esteem, a sense of belonging, and social approval are examples of psychological needs. Like biological needs, psychological needs motivate people to accomplish certain goals.

However, psychological needs differ from biological needs in two important ways. First, psychological needs are not necessarily based on deprivation. A person with a need to achieve an A on a test may already be an honor roll student. Second, unlike biological needs, which are inborn, psychological needs may be learned.

People possess common biological characteristics, thus they have similar physical needs. For example, all people must eat to survive; therefore all people need food. However, people have different psychological needs because they learn from a variety of experiences. Psychological needs are shaped by culture and learning, so people's psychological needs differ markedly. For example, some people prefer vegetarian diets because they believe it is morally wrong to kill animals for food.

Drives Biological needs and psychological needs give rise to **drives**—the forces that motivate an organism to take action. The biological need for food gives rise to the hunger drive. The biological need for water gives rise to the thirst drive.

Although hunger and thirst are aroused by biological needs, the *experience* of them is psychological. The longer we are deprived of something such as food or water, the stronger our drive becomes. For example, our hunger drive is stronger 6 hours after eating than it is 20 minutes after eating.

Reading Check **Identify Supporting Details** What are the two types of needs?

Theories of Motivation

Psychologists agree that motives prompt behavior, but they are not in agreement about the nature of motivation. The leading theories of motivation are instinct theory, drive-reduction theory, humanistic theory, and sociocultural theory.

Instinct Theory Behavior patterns genetically transmitted from generation to generation are known as **instincts.** Sometimes they are called fixed-action patterns. Researchers have discovered that many animals are born to act in certain ways in certain situations.

Siamese fighting fish reared in isolation display the same instinctive behavior as do those raised with other Siamese fighting fish. Males fan their fins and gills in the typical threatening posture when other males are introduced into their tanks. Similarly, bees perform an instinctive "dance" to relay the location of food to other bees. Scientists have found that bees from different parts of the world use essentially the same dances.

However, not all animal behavior is purely instinctive. Studies have shown that birds acquire the songs characteristic of their species only partly by instinct. Young birds need to hear the songs of their species in order to learn how to communicate effectively.

Psychologists once believed that human behavior, like that of animals, is instinctive. In the late 1800s and early 1900s, psychologists William James and William McDougall argued that people have instincts that foster survival and social behavior.

ACADEMIC VOCABULARY

isolation being alone or away from others

Today, however, most psychologists do not believe that human behavior is primarily motivated by instinct. If a behavior pattern is instinctive, they argue, it must be found throughout a species. However, there is so much variation in the way people behave that much of human behavior is unlikely to be instinctive.

Drive-reduction Theory Psychologist Clark Hull formulated the drive-reduction theory in the 1930s. Drive-reduction theory is based on learning as well as motivation. According to this theory, people and animals experience a drive arising from a need as an unpleasant tension. They learn to do whatever will reduce that tension by reducing the drive, such as eating to reduce their hunger drive.

Some drives, such as hunger, are caused by biological needs, which are inborn. Other drives, such as a drive for money, are learned from experience. According to drive-reduction theory, people will try to reduce these learned drives, just as they try to reduce their biological drives.

Basic drives, such as hunger, motivate us to restore an internal state of equilibrium, or balance. The tendency to maintain this state of equilibrium in the body is called **homeostasis.** Homeostasis works like a thermostat. When room temperature drops below a certain point—called the set point—the heat comes on. The heat stays on until the set point is reached. Similarly, according to the theory, when people are hungry, they will eat until they reach a level at which they are no longer hungry.

Drive-reduction theory seems to apply to many biological drives, including hunger and thirst. Yet people sometimes eat when they are not hungry. They also often act to increase rather than decrease the tension they experience. For example, some people enjoy riding roller coasters and driving fast cars. Yet these activities increase rather than decrease the tension they experience. Clearly, drive-reduction theory does not explain all motivation.

Humanistic Theory Some psychologists, known as humanists, argue that instinct theory and drive-reduction theory suggest that human behavior is mechanical and directed only toward surviving and reducing tension. According to humanistic psychologists, however, people are also motivated by the conscious desire for personal growth and artistic fulfillment. In fact, they argue, sometimes our drive to fulfill such needs outweighs our drive to meet more basic needs.

For example, some people seek artistic or political goals, even though they may have difficulty affording food or may have to give up a certain level of comfort or security to achieve their goals. Some artists, musicians, and writers commit themselves to their artistic goals even when they are unable to make a living by doing so.

Abraham Maslow, one of the pioneers of humanistic psychology, pointed out that some people are willing to tolerate pain, hunger, and other kinds of tension to achieve their artistic or political goals. An aspiring musician might spend countless hours practicing the violin and learning new songs. Instinct theory and drive-reduction theory might have difficulty explaining this behavior. But humanistic theory would suggest that the musician's desire to achieve artistic fulfillment makes her feel that it is worth sacrificing other desirable activities, such as spending time with her friends.

Maslow claimed that people strive to fulfill their capacity for self-actualization. The term **self-actualization** refers to the need to become what one believes he or she is capable of being. The desire to fulfill oneself takes one past the point of just satisfying one's physical needs. Maslow believed that striving to become something or to do something meaningful in one's life is as essential to human well-being as food.

Maslow organized human needs into a hierarchy—a ranking of items in order of importance. (See the chart on the next page.) At the bottom of the hierarchy are biological needs. Next comes the need for safety, followed by the need for love and belongingness, then the need for esteem. The need for self-actualization is at the top. Maslow believed that once a person's needs at one level are satisfied, the person will move on to try to satisfy needs at the next higher level. For example, once food and drink have satisfied a person's biological needs, that person will then seek means to satisfy safety needs, such as the needs for shelter and security.

Maslow believed that people rise naturally through the levels of this hierarchy as long as they do not encounter stiff obstacles along the way. Many people seek self-actualization through work, hobbies, and aesthetic experiences such as music, art, and poetry.

Critics of Maslow's hierarchy of needs argue that it does not apply to everyone. For example, some people show little interest in satisfying higher-level needs such as achievement and social recognition, even after their biological and safety needs have been met. But, one might ask, does their apparent lack of interest stem from not being motivated to seek achievement or from having met with overwhelming obstacles?

Sociocultural Theory Sociocultural theorists argue that even if basic drives such as hunger are inborn, cultural experiences and factors influence the behavior that people use to satisfy those drives. The foods people eat and the way they eat those foods are shaped by culture. Cultural experience affects whether people prefer hot dogs or tacos, coffee or tea, apples or pineapples. Cultural experiences also affect whether people prefer kissing lips or rubbing noses to express feelings of affection.

Reading Check **Compare** According to humanistic psychology, what is wrong with instinct theory and drive-reduction theory?

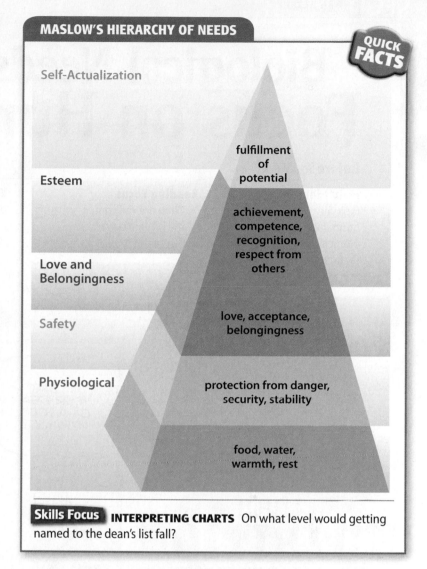

MASLOW'S HIERARCHY OF NEEDS

QUICK FACTS

- Self-Actualization — fulfillment of potential
- Esteem — achievement, competence, recognition, respect from others
- Love and Belongingness — love, acceptance, belongingness
- Safety — protection from danger, security, stability
- Physiological — food, water, warmth, rest

Skills Focus **INTERPRETING CHARTS** On what level would getting named to the dean's list fall?

SECTION 1 Assessment

Online Quiz **THINK** central thinkcentral.com

Reviewing Main Ideas and Vocabulary

1. **Define** What is a motive?

2. **Describe** How are needs and drives related?

3. **Recall** What word names our bodies' tendency to maintain a state of equilibrium?

Thinking Critically

4. **Explain** Why do psychologists think that little human behavior is instinctive?

5. **Elaborate** By the end of the school day, most students and teachers are eager to finish classes. Use drive-reduction theory to describe why this happens.

6. **Interpret** Using your notes and a graphic organizer like the one below, describe how the major theories of motivation explain thirst.

Theory	Explanation of Thirst

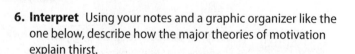

FOCUS ON WRITING

7. **Descriptive** Have you achieved self-actualization? Describe what you have done—or what you hope to do—that might reach that level on Maslow's hierarchy. Explain how your motivation was—or will be—distinct from the other levels.

Biological Needs: Focus on Hunger

Before You Read

Main Idea
Biological needs such as hunger involve both physiological and psychological factors.

Reading Focus
1. What are the components of the hunger drive?
2. What causes obesity?

Vocabulary
obese

TAKING NOTES Use a graphic organizer like this one to take notes on biological needs.

Hunger	Obesity

more **TASTE** than **NUTRITION**

PSYCHOLOGY CLOSE UP

Why do people keep eating junk food? It seems that every week another study shows how junk foods ruin our health. For example, on the Department of Health and Human Services list of leading causes of premature death in the United States, poor diet and lack of exercise are second only to tobacco use.

Despite such warnings, Americans can't seem to stop eating junk food. Hamburgers make up about 15 percent of all restaurant sales. U.S. consumers spend about $23 billion per year on ice cream and about $25 billion on candy.

Why are these bad-for-you foods so hard to resist? Part of the answer is biological. Most junk food contains high amounts of sugar or fat or salt, or some combination of the three. Each of these ingredients triggers reward receptors in our brains that tell us "good! good!" and "more! more!" Until recently, it made sense to follow those signals. There was no such thing as a donut. Fries did not exist. Unless you were very well-to-do, rich foods were rare treats.

Which points up another part of the problem: These days, junk food is easier to find than healthy food. There's a convenience store full of sodas and snacks on every corner, and rows of fast food restaurants line the streets.

In addition, junk foods tend to be cheaper than real foods. Agricultural subsidies reduce the prices of products made with corn syrup, sugar, and vegetable oils. And processed foods can sit on store shelves much longer than fresh fruits and vegetables.

But change seems to be on the horizon. Sales of most junk foods have stopped rising, and most fast food restaurants now offer some healthy options. ■

The Hunger Drive

Biological needs are based mainly on body tissue needs, such as the needs for food, water, air, temperature regulation, and pain avoidance. However, even basic biological needs can be complex because they involve psychological as well as physiological factors. People need food to survive, but food can mean much more than mere survival. Food can be a symbol of the closeness of the family or group of friends, or it can be something to make a stranger feel welcome. Food can also be part of a pleasurable social experience with others.

Hunger is regulated by both biological and psychological factors. In this section, we will look at the mechanisms in the body that are involved in the hunger drive. We will also examine the psychological influences that are involved in hunger.

The Role of the Mouth The acts of chewing and swallowing provide certain sensations that help satisfy the hunger drive. In a "sham feeding" experiment conducted in the 1940s, tubes were implanted in dogs' throats so that the food they swallowed was dropped out of their bodies instead of moving into their stomachs. Nevertheless, the dogs stopped feeding after a brief period. Based on the finding of this and other studies, researchers have concluded that chewing and swallowing apparently help reduce feelings of hunger in animals as well as in people.

The hunger drive is usually satisfied when the body digests food and the nutrients in the food enter the bloodstream. However, this takes time. Chewing and swallowing help let the body know that its hunger drive is being satisfied, thus saving us from eating more than is needed. Still, it is wise to stop eating *before* feeling completely full because it takes time for the digestive tract to metabolize food and provide signals to the brain that the need for food has been satisfied.

The Role of the Stomach It was once believed that the growls and contractions (called hunger pangs) of an empty stomach were the cause of hunger. Researchers did, in fact, find that when a person is hungry, his or her stomach does contract. However, they also found that the stomach contracts at other times as well. Furthermore, people who have

HUNGER—BIOLOGICAL FACTORS

Hypothalamus

Mouth

Stomach

Hunger is partly driven by complex physiological processes.

Skills Focus **INTERPRETING VISUALS** What larger organ is the hypothalamus a part of?

surgery to remove their stomachs still experience hunger. Thus, the researchers concluded that hunger pangs felt in the stomach play a role in hunger but are not the main factor involved in signaling hunger.

The Hypothalamus The level of sugar in the blood and the part of the brain known as the hypothalamus are key influences on feelings of hunger. When people have not eaten for a while, their blood sugar level drops. Information about the sugar level is then communicated to the hypothalamus, which is known to be involved in the regulation of body temperature and various aspects of psychological motivation and emotion.

Researchers have learned more about how the hypothalamus functions through research on laboratory animals. In these studies, researchers implanted electrodes on the hypothalami and observed the effects on the animals' behavior. They found that the side of the hypothalamus, called the lateral hypothalamus (LH), appears to function as a "start-eating" center. If the LH is electrically stimulated, the rat will begin to eat, even if it has just finished eating a large meal.

Conversely, if a lesion is made in the LH, the rat may stop eating altogether and eventually die of starvation if it is not force-fed.

The underside of the hypothalamus, called the ventromedial hypothalamus (VMH), apparently functions as a "stop-eating" center. When this center is electrically stimulated, the rat will stop eating. When this part of the hypothalamus is destroyed, the rat will continue to eat until it is several times its normal weight. The damage to the VMH interferes with the rat's ability to recognize that its hunger has been fulfilled, and the rat simply continues to nibble. Eventually, the rat's eating will level off and the rat will maintain the higher weight.

Psychological Influences Many biological factors affect the hunger drive. However, this is only part of the story. In human beings, psychological as well as biological factors affect feelings of hunger. For example, we usually eat more when we are in the presence of other people than when we are alone. You may not realize you are hungry until a friend mentions that he is hungry. Your friend, therefore, would have acted as a psychological influence on your hunger drive.

Learning that certain amounts of food or drink will produce a feeling of well-being and relaxation can cause people to eat and drink when they feel upset. For example, they may develop the habit of eating and drinking at the first sign of pressure or anxiety as a way to fend off feeling any negative emotions. People with a tendency to eat compulsively or drink alcohol excessively need to be alert to this tendency. Likewise, parents should consider whether it is wise to give children food as a reward for doing something good. Rewarding with food can cause a child to grow up associating food with parental approval, perhaps leading to dietary problems in later life.

Reading Check **Identify Cause and Effect** What happens when you keep eating until you feel totally full?

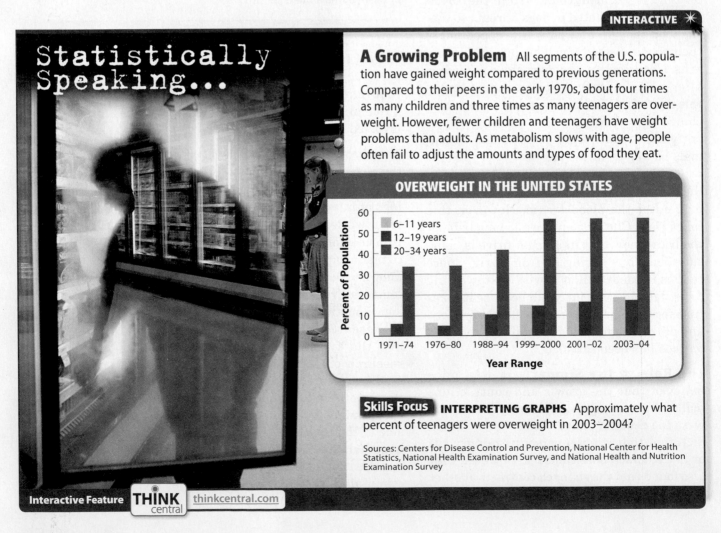

Statistically Speaking...

A Growing Problem All segments of the U.S. population have gained weight compared to previous generations. Compared to their peers in the early 1970s, about four times as many children and three times as many teenagers are overweight. However, fewer children and teenagers have weight problems than adults. As metabolism slows with age, people often fail to adjust the amounts and types of food they eat.

OVERWEIGHT IN THE UNITED STATES

- 6–11 years
- 12–19 years
- 20–34 years

(Bar graph: Percent of Population vs. Year Range — 1971–74, 1976–80, 1988–94, 1999–2000, 2001–02, 2003–04)

Skills Focus **INTERPRETING GRAPHS** Approximately what percent of teenagers were overweight in 2003–2004?

Sources: Centers for Disease Control and Prevention, National Center for Health Statistics, National Health Examination Survey, and National Health and Nutrition Examination Survey

Interactive Feature **THINK** central thinkcentral.com

Obesity

More than 6 out of 10 adult Americans are overweight. Moreover, 3 in 10 are **obese**—that is, weigh more than 30 percent greater than their recommended weight. Problems with unhealthy weight gain are on the rise in the United States. For example, in the early 1960s only about 45 percent of Americans were overweight. But by the early 2000s that figure had risen to about 66 percent.

Obese people suffer more illnesses than others, including heart disease, stroke, diabetes, gall bladder disease, gout, respiratory problems, and certain kinds of cancer. It has been estimated that over 110,000 people in the United States die each year because of health problems related to excess weight and inactivity. Weight control is elusive for most obese people. They often regain the weight they have lost after dieting successfully.

Causes of Obesity Why are so many people obese? As with the hunger drive in general, both biological and psychological factors appear to contribute to obesity. Obesity seems to run in families. But does this mean that it is inherited? Not necessarily. For example, obese parents may simply encourage their children to overeat by having fattening foods around the house and by setting an example. However, research suggests that heredity plays a major role in obesity. One study showed that adopted children tend to more closely resemble their biological parents than their adoptive parents in terms of body weight.

One of the ways in which heredity may contribute to obesity is that certain people with a particular gene may not receive the biological signal that they have eaten enough to <u>sustain</u> them. Thus, they end up eating more than they need to.

Genes also help determine the number of fat cells a person has. People with a greater number of fat cells feel hungry sooner than people with fewer fat cells, even if they are of the same weight. When overweight people take off extra pounds, they do not reduce the number of fat cells in their body. Instead, the fat cells shrink. As they shrink, they signal the brain, triggering the hunger drive. For this reason, many people who lose weight complain that they feel hungry all the time.

People metabolize food—or burn calories—at different rates and in accordance with the amount of muscle and fat in their bodies. Since fatty tissue converts food to energy more slowly than muscle does, people with more body fat metabolize food more slowly than people who weigh the same but have a lower percentage of body fat.

Men tend to have more muscle and less fat in their bodies than women. The average man is approximately 40 percent muscle and 15 percent fat. The average woman is 30 to 35 percent muscle and 25 percent fat. Therefore, men tend to burn calories more quickly than women of the same weight. For this reason, men generally are able to lose weight more easily than women, and they can usually eat more than women can without putting on extra pounds.

Psychological factors also play a role in obesity. For example, people tend to eat more when they are under stress or experiencing certain negative emotions, such as anxiety. Ironically, the stress of trying to diet can make some people want to eat even more.

Personal circumstances also affect people's ability to control their weight. For example, many people tend to overeat and ignore their diets when they are attending family gatherings, watching television, or experiencing tension at school, home, or work.

Losing Weight Psychologists have worked with other professionals to devise strategies to help overweight people lose weight. Some of these strategies appear in the multitude of books on losing weight. Others have been adopted by businesses that operate weight loss programs or meal services.

Not everyone who is a few pounds overweight should try to slim down. For example, women in the United States today are often under social pressure to conform to an unnaturally slender feminine ideal. As a result, they tend to set unrealistic weight-loss goals.

Any teenager who considers going on a diet should proceed with caution because adolescents need a good deal of nourishment—perhaps more than any other age group. Adolescents should discuss the benefits and hazards of dieting with their parents and with a health professional, such as a doctor or school nurse.

ACADEMIC VOCABULARY

sustain to keep alive or to supply with nourishment

A sound diet is one that is sensible, realistic, and well planned. Healthful weight-control programs do not involve fad diets such as fasting, eliminating carbohydrates, or eating excessive amounts of one particular food. Instead, they involve changes in lifestyle that include improving nutritional knowledge, decreasing caloric intake, exercising, and substituting healthful foods for harmful foods.

Most people in the United States eat too much fat and not enough fruits and vegetables. Junk foods like french fries, hamburgers, donuts, and candy tend to be particularly high in fat. Eating foods that are low in fat sets a good precedent for a lifetime of healthful eating. It is good for the heart and can also help in losing weight. Losing weight means "burning" or using more calories than you eat. Foods that are high in fat also tend to be high in calories. Nutritional knowledge helps people manage their consumption of food to take in fewer calories. Taking in fewer calories does not just mean eating smaller portions. It means switching to some lower-calorie foods—relying more on fresh, unsweetened fruits and vegetables (eating apples rather than apple pie), fish and poultry, and skim milk and cheese. It means cutting down on butter, margarine, oils, and sugar.

The same foods that help control weight—whole grains, fruits, and vegetables—also tend to be high in vitamins and fiber and low in fats. Such foods may also reduce the risk of heart disease, cancer, and other illnesses.

Dieting plus exercise is more effective than dieting alone for shedding pounds and keeping them off. Exercise burns calories and builds muscle tissue, which metabolizes more calories than fatty tissue does.

Keeping Weight Off Many people who lose weight struggle not to regain weight. Some studies suggest that the majority of dieters regain the weight they lose within five years. Maintaining a new, more healthy weight requires ongoing work.

Psychologists found several key similarities in people who succeeded in losing weight and not regaining it. Before losing weight, most lacked confidence but also lacked awareness of bad health habits. Deciding to lose weight and adopting new, more healthy behaviors gave these people a boost of self-confidence. Support from friends or family helped them ingrain the new habits as well as bounce back from periods of failure. Most importantly, the people who succeeded in keeping the pounds from coming back recognized that they were not just going on a one-time diet. They had adopted a new, life-long approach to eating and exercising.

Reading Check **Identify Supporting Details** Why do men generally find it easier to lose weight than women?

SECTION 2 Assessment

Online Quiz THINK central thinkcentral.com

Reviewing Main Ideas and Vocabulary

1. **Identify Main Ideas** Why is the hunger drive not purely biological?

2. **Define** What is obesity?

3. **Recall** What part of the hypothalamus governs when to start eating? What part governs when to stop eating?

Thinking Critically

4. **Compare** What is the difference between being obese and being overweight?

5. **Predict** If fresh, nutritious foods became as cheap and readily available as junk food, what would happen to average weight in the United States?

6. **Elaborate** In terms of the hunger drive, where does physiology end and psychology begin? Use the example of someone who has lost weight and now often feels hungry.

7. **Explain** Using your notes and a graphic organizer like the one here, explain the roles of the mouth, stomach, and hypothalamus in the hunger drive.

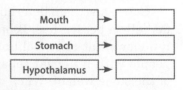

Mouth →

Stomach →

Hypothalamus →

FOCUS ON WRITING

8. **Persuasive** Imagine that 10 years from now you will be overweight. Write a letter to your future self explaining how to lose the weight and keep it off.

Psychological Needs

Before You Read

Main Idea
Psychological motivations include stimulus motives and achievement motivation. Several different theories attempt to explain what drives people.

Reading Focus
1. What are stimulus motives?
2. Why doesn't everyone have achievement motivation?
3. What motivates people to make things fit?
4. How does the desire for affiliation motivate people?

Vocabulary
stimulus motives
sensory deprivation
achievement motivation
extrinsic rewards
intrinsic rewards
cognitive consistency
balance theory
cognitive-dissonance theory
affiliation

TAKING NOTES Use a graphic organizer like this one to take notes on psychological needs.

Psychological Needs

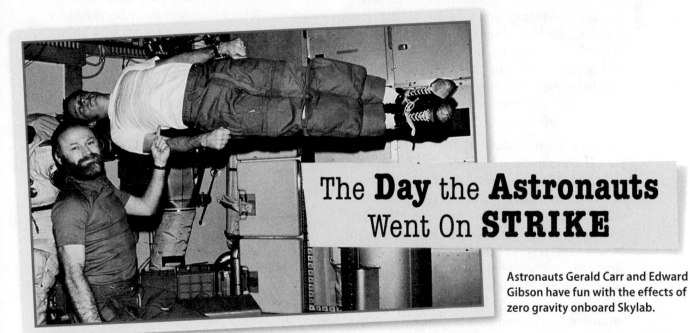

The Day the Astronauts Went On STRIKE

Astronauts Gerald Carr and Edward Gibson have fun with the effects of zero gravity onboard Skylab.

PSYCHOLOGY CLOSE UP

Was it mutiny or a well-deserved rest? Skylab was the first U.S. space station. Astronauts Gerald Carr, William Pogue, and Edward Gibson made up the third and last crew to visit Skylab. Their mission lasted from November 16, 1973, to February 8, 1974.

Skylab was designed for scientific work. NASA flight control had set a busy schedule, and the astronauts had trouble keeping up. Commander Carr hinted that the schedule was unrealistic. But flight control continued to shorten the time per task and began canceling rest days to pack in more work.

The astronauts did their best to complete their assignments, but it was wearing on them mentally. Gibson pointed out that the rush compromised the quality of the scientific results. Pogue told mission controllers that the lab was a mess because the schedule left no time to clean up after experiments. Flight control ignored the complaints.

Commander Carr faced a dilemma. He and his crew needed rest, and the schedule was unrealistic. Then he hit on an idea that might solve both problems. He shut down communications between Skylab and the ground for 24 hours. Carr, Pogue, and Gibson took a day off.

When Carr restored communications, the crew and the flight controllers had a frank discussion about the situation. NASA finally realized they needed to back off their frenzied work plan. Rested, the astronauts found their motivation restored. Having their psychological needs addressed made the rest of the mission go much more smoothly. ■

Stimulus Motives

Human beings and other organisms are motivated to reduce the tension or stimulation caused by biological drives such as hunger or thirst. The hungry person who "has a bite to eat" wants to reduce the feeling of being hungry. However, we experience psychological needs as well as biological needs. Some psychological needs motivate us to reduce tension or stimulation. Other psychological needs actually lead us to increase the amount of stimulation we experience.

Desires for stimulation are known as **stimulus motives.** Stimulus motives include sensory stimulation, activity, exploration, and manipulation of the environment. Some stimulus motives have clear survival value. Human beings and other organisms who are motivated to explore and manipulate their environments are more likely to survive. Learning about one's surroundings increases usable information concerning resources and potential dangers. Manipulation allows people to change the environment in useful ways, thereby increasing and enhancing their chances of survival.

Sensory Deprivation Some psychologists have tried to understand stimulus motives by seeing what happens when people are deprived of all stimulation. During the 1950s, student volunteers at McGill University in Montreal were paid $20 per day for participating in an experiment in which they did nothing—literally nothing. They were blindfolded and placed in small rooms. Their arms were bandaged so that they could feel no tactile sensations (sensations of touch), and they could hear nothing except the dull hum of the air conditioner. The intention of the experiment was to see how people would react to an absence of stimulation, a state referred to as **sensory deprivation.**

With nothing to do, some of the students slept. Those who remained awake began to feel bored and irritable. As the hours passed, the students felt more and more uncomfortable. Some reported having hallucinations. The study was scheduled to last for several days, but many students quit during the first day despite the monetary incentive and the desire to help in the research. Most of those who completed the study felt they had been through a terrible ordeal and, for several days after the experiment, found it difficult to concentrate on even simple matters. They reported feeling extreme boredom and disorientation for some time. The experiment demonstrated the importance of sensory stimulation to human beings.

Desire for Sensory Stimulation All people seek sensory stimulation, but it is clear that some need it more than others. Some people like being couch potatoes. They enjoy sitting and relaxing in front of a TV whenever possible. Other people prefer more active lifestyles. They are not happy unless they are out running or tossing a ball around.

You may know someone who is always on the run. This person may be happiest when hiking, riding a skateboard, or taking on other physical challenges. Many psychologists would call such a person a sensation seeker. A sensation seeker is somebody who regularly seeks out thrilling activities such as riding mountain bikes, roller coasters, or even skydiving. They feel at their best when they are doing something active or adventurous.

It is not clear why some people seek high levels of sensation and others prefer lower levels. Inborn factors may play a role. So may learning experiences. For example, a child or adolescent whose parents ride motorcycles or skydive will be exposed to these activities at an early age. He or she may be inclined to want to try these activities.

Exploration and Manipulation Anybody who has ever had the experience of bringing home a new cat knows that the animal's first reaction to totally new surroundings is to show anxiety. The frightened cat may hide under a bed or in a closet. However, eventually, the cat will feel adventurous enough to take a few tentative steps out. Then it will begin exploring its new surroundings. Within a few days, the cat will probably have explored every corner of the house. In this respect, cats and people appear to behave in similar ways. Most people are also motivated to explore their immediate surroundings.

Once people and animals become sufficiently comfortable with their environment, they seek novel stimulation. That is, they seek new and varied experiences. For example, laboratory monkeys learn to manipulate gadgets just for the sake of the novel stimulation.

Are You Driven to Succeed?

People with high achievement motivation tend to share certain characteristics. Answering the questions in this quiz may reveal to what degree achievement motivates you.

TEST

❶ Do you think more about your future than your past?

❷ Would you feel dissatisfied if no one but your friends and family ever heard of you?

❸ Do you approach life with careful planning?

❹ Do you feel unhappy when you don't earn high grades?

❺ Do you find it exciting to be in the spotlight?

❻ Is it difficult for you to forget about school on weekends?

❼ Do you consider yourself ambitious?

❽ Would you like to work on a project with a very talented person even if he or she was difficult to get along with?

PROCEDURE AND ANALYSIS

1. Answer each test question either "yes" or "no."

2. Count the number of questions you answered "yes" and the number you answered "no."

3. When everyone is done, create a table on the board with nine columns labeled "0" through "8."

4. Tally up the number of people who answered "yes" to all of the questions, and write that number under 8. Do the same for the rest of the possibilities.

5. Discuss the results. Ask students at either extreme—the ambitious 8s and the laid-back 0s—to discuss their different approaches to life.

Quick Lab | THINK central | thinkcentral.com

Other researchers have shown that laboratory rats who are not terribly hungry usually choose to explore unfamiliar parts of mazes rather than to head down familiar alleys directly to a food reward.

Do people and animals explore and manipulate their environment because these activities help them meet their needs for food and safety? Or do they explore and manipulate these objects simply for the sake of novel stimulation? Many psychologists believe that exploration and manipulation are reinforcing in and of themselves. Monkeys appear to enjoy "monkeying around" with gadgets. If you leave mechanical devices in their presence, the monkeys will learn how to manipulate them without any reward other than the pleasure of doing so.

Many human infants will play endlessly with "busy boxes"—boards or boxes with pieces that move, honk, squeak, rattle, and buzz. Most children seem to find pleasure in playing with new gadgets and discovering interesting new activities. This seems to support the view of psychologists who see the desire for novel stimulation as natural to both people and animals.

Reading Check **Identify Supporting Details**
How might exploration and manipulation help an animal to survive?

Achievement Motivation

People who are driven to get ahead, to tackle challenging situations, and to meet high personal standards of success are said to have high **achievement motivation.** For example, students who demonstrate high achievement motivation will work on difficult test items until they find the answer or run out of time. These students tend to earn higher grades than students with equal abilities but lower achievement motivation.

Adults with high achievement motivation may strive to move ahead in their careers. They may set challenging goals for themselves, broaden their skills, or simply recognize and take advantage of opportunities presented to them. Adults with high achievement motivation are more likely to be promoted and earn high salaries than less motivated people with similar opportunities.

Research shows that people with high achievement motivation enjoy personal challenges and are willing to take moderate risks to achieve their goals. However, such people also have a greater risk of heart disease and other stress-related illnesses.

Types of Goals Achievement motivation can be fueled by a variety of different sources. For some students, performance goals may be the reason for their achievement motivation.

Performance goals are specific goals such as gaining admission to college, earning the approval of parents or teachers, or even simply avoiding criticism. For example, a performance goal such as winning a science scholarship might motivate a student to study advanced biology.

Other students are driven mainly by learning goals. For some students, learning for learning's sake is the most powerful motivator. Psychologists call motivators such as these learning goals. People who demonstrate high achievement motivation may be influenced by more than one type of goal. In the previous example, in addition to striving to win the scholarship, the student probably also enjoys studying science.

Performance goals are usually satisfied by external or extrinsic rewards. **Extrinsic rewards** include good grades, a good income, and respect from others. On the other hand, learning goals are usually satisfied by internal or **intrinsic rewards,** such as self-satisfaction.

ACADEMIC VOCABULARY
consistent in agreement with, compatible

Development of Achievement Motivation

Where does achievement motivation come from? Parents and caregivers certainly play a crucial role. Their attitude toward achievement is instrumental in developing a child's motivation.

Research suggests that children with learning goals often have parents who encourage them to be persistent, to enjoy schoolwork, and to find their own ways to solve problems whenever possible. Such parents create opportunities to expose their children to new and stimulating experiences. Parents of children with performance goals, on the other hand, are more likely to reward their children with toys or money for good grades and to punish them for poor grades.

Research also shows that parents of children with high achievement motivation tend to be generous with their praise when their children do well. Such parents are also less critical of their children when they do poorly. The children themselves set high personal standards and relate their feelings of self-worth to their achievements.

Reading Check Identify Cause and Effect
What sorts of rewards usually satisfy performance goals?

Making Things Fit

The stimulus motives we have been discussing are examples of psychological needs aimed at increasing our level of stimulation. However, many psychological needs are aimed at reducing stimulation or tension, especially in interactions with other people. These types of psychological needs are based on people's need to maintain a balance between their personal beliefs, actions, and thoughts.

Cognitive Consistency Cognitive theorists, such as Leon Festinger and Sandra Bem, maintain that people are motivated to achieve **cognitive consistency.** That is, they seek to think and behave in a way that fits what they believe and how others expect them to think and behave. According to Festinger, people are primarily motivated to behave according to their beliefs. Therefore, a person who is politically liberal would find it difficult to support a conservative candidate. According to Bem, most girls and boys try to behave in ways that are consistent with what people expect of females and males in their society.

Most people prefer that the "pieces" of their lives fit together. They seek out as friends those who have values and interests similar to their own. As they grow older, most people try to find a set of beliefs that will help them understand the world in which they live. Most people feel better when the important relationships in their lives are stable and orderly. Two theories that address this need to create cognitive consistency are balance theory and cognitive-dissonance theory.

Balance Theory According to **balance theory,** people need to organize their perceptions, opinions, and beliefs in a harmonious manner. They want to maintain a cognitive balance by holding consistent views and by being with people who share their beliefs and values. When the people we like share our attitudes, there is a state of balance that gives us a feeling that all is well.

Imagine a group of high school students who are good friends. The group includes a mix of girls and boys, and each excels at a different subject. But why is this group of friends so close? According to balance theory, they have probably discovered that they share many of the same values, interests, and beliefs.

Balance theory also suggests that, when we care about a person, we tend to share her or his interests. Some of the group of friends, for example, may not have been very interested in attending a classical violin recital. However, one person in the group loves to perform music and invited the rest of the group to her violin recital. Because of their friendship, the group attended the recital. In this way, they were introduced to, and developed positive feelings about, something that one member liked.

Psychologists note that people who have strong feelings for each other, as one couple in the group does, might be upset to discover a major area of disagreement. Such a disharmony would place them in a state of imbalance. When someone we care about disagrees with us, an uncomfortable state of imbalance arises. We may attempt to end the uncomfortable state by trying to persuade the other person to change his or her attitude or by changing our feelings about the other person.

Relationships can usually survive disagreements about such things as different tastes in food or a difference of opinion about a movie. However, more basic conflicts such as over religion, politics, or personal values can create a state of imbalance.

When we dislike certain people or have no feelings toward them one way or another, their attitudes are not of much interest to us. Because we do not care about them, we are not greatly affected by the disharmony between their views and ours. We can be said to be in a state of nonbalance. Unlike imbalance, which tends to upset people, nonbalance usually leaves people feeling indifferent.

Cognitive-dissonance Theory Why do people find a state of imbalance uncomfortable? The answer is that people want their thoughts and attitudes (cognitions) to be consistent with their actions. Awareness that our cognitions are inconsistent (dissonant) with our behavior is unpleasant. It causes an inner tension, which can be uncomfortable. According to **cognitive-dissonance theory,** people are motivated to reduce this inconsistency.

Classic research on cognitive dissonance was conducted by psychologists Leon Festinger and James Carlsmith. Participants in their experiment were divided into two groups.

Both groups performed a boring task such as turning pegs. The people in one group were paid $20 to tell another person that the boring task was interesting. The people in the second group were paid $1 to say that the boring task was interesting. Afterward, the participants were asked to express their own actual feelings about the task. The people who received $1 rated the task as *more* interesting than the people who were paid $20.

According to cognitive-dissonance theory, this occurred because the people who received $1 felt an inconsistency—a dissonance—between their cognition ("That was a boring task") and their action ("I just told someone that task was interesting"). The people who received $20 could easily justify lying about how they really felt about the task because doing so was worthwhile, financially. The people who received just $1 could not use that excuse. Instead, they changed their attitude about the task. By convincing themselves that the task was more interesting than it really was, they were able to reduce the inconsistency between their cognition and their action.

What happens when two people in a relationship disagree about a key issue, such as religion? A strong disagreement about an important issue can injure or even end a relationship.

THEORIES OF MOTIVATION

Theories of motivation can be grouped into two broad categories.

Stimulus Motivators
- **Sensory stimulation** desire to gain experience through the senses
- **Activity** desire for physical movement
- **Exploration and manipulation** desire to investigate the surrounding world
- **Achievement motivation** desire to challenge oneself and to meet high standards of success

Reducing Tension Motivators
- **Balance theory** desire to coordinate internal perceptions, opinions, and beliefs with those of other people
- **Cognitive-dissonance theory** desire to keep our thoughts and attitudes consistent with our actions
- **Affiliation** desire to join with others and to be accepted by the larger group

Cognitive-dissonance theory suggests that people having such a basic disagreement may seek to reduce the dissonance by trying to pretend that the differences between them are unimportant or even by denying that the differences exist. They may avoid thinking about those differences and put off dealing with them as long as possible.

Reading Check **Draw Conclusions** What situations can create a state of imbalance?

Affiliation

If we never dealt with other people, imbalance or cognitive dissonance would never occur. But humans are social beings. The desire to join with others and be part of something larger than oneself is called **affiliation.** The desire to affiliate prompts people to make friends, join groups, and participate in activities with others. During adolescence, the motive for affiliation with one's peers is particularly strong. It is a time of life when one discovers how peers provide emotional support, useful advice, and pleasurable company.

Affiliation motivation helps keep families, groups, and nations together. However, some people are so strongly motivated to affiliate that they find it painful to be by themselves. Sometimes a strong need to affiliate may be a sign of anxiety.

Psychologist Stanley Schachter showed how anxiety increases the desire to affiliate. In a classic study, he manipulated people's anxiety levels. He told one group of people that they would be given painful electric shocks. He told another group of people that they would be given mild electric shocks. All participants were then asked to wait for the shock apparatus to be set up. They were given the choice of waiting alone or waiting in a room with other participants.

Almost two-thirds of those who expected the painful shock chose to wait with other participants. In contrast, only one-third of those who expected the mild shock chose to wait with other participants. Schachter concluded that anxiety tends to cause people to want to affiliate with other people.

Other studies have shown that the desire to affiliate with a group can lead people to disregard their own perceptions. For example, a test subject might be asked to count and remember the number of items on a table. In a waiting room, the actual test subject meets a group of actors pretending to be fellow test subjects. If all of the actors agree that there were a different number of items on the table, most test subjects will change their answer to align with the group.

Reading Check **Infer** Why doesn't everyone feel the same amount of desire to affiliate?

SECTION 3 Assessment

Online Quiz THINK central thinkcentral.com

Reviewing Main Ideas and Vocabulary

1. **Define** What are stimulus motives?

2. **Contrast** What is the difference between extrinsic rewards and intrinsic rewards?

3. **Recall** What term describes the desire to join a group?

Thinking Critically

4. **Interpret** What happens when someone experiences sensory deprivation for long periods? Why?

5. **Support a Position** Do all people with high achievement motivation want to prove they are better than everyone else? Explain why this is or is not the case.

6. **Elaborate** Tony leads the Hunting and Fishing Club. Sandy is the head of the Anti-Cruelty-to-Animals Society. Use balance theory to explain why Tony and Sandy are not friends.

7. **Compare and Contrast** Using your notes and a graphic organizer like the one below, explain the relationship between balance theory and cognitive-dissonance theory.

Similarities	Differences

FOCUS ON WRITING

8. **Descriptive** What motivates you? Look at the table on the previous page, and decide which of the seven types of motivation drives you the most. Using specific examples, describe how this motivator shapes your life.

Emotions

Before You Read

Main Idea
Emotions are states of feeling that influence thoughts and behaviors. Facial expressions reflect our emotions.

Reading Focus
1. What is the nature of emotion?
2. How do facial expressions differ across different cultures?
3. What are the major theories of emotion?

Vocabulary
emotions
opponent-process theory

TAKING NOTES Use a graphic organizer like this one to take notes on emotions.

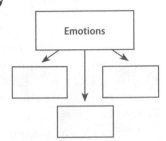

The Man With No EMOTIONS

PSYCHOLOGY CLOSE UP

What happens when a person becomes perfectly rational?
"Be rational about this." "Don't let your feelings get in the way." "Use your head." Our culture suggests that emotions interfere with making good decisions. But what would actually happen if a person lost the capacity to feel and became more like a computer? The results might surprise you.

Doctors discovered that a successful businessman had a brain tumor. Surgeons removed the tumor, but the tumor had destroyed part of the man's prefrontal cortex, a region of the brain associated with personality and social behavior. The man regained full mental functioning—almost. Tests showed that his memory and intelligence were as good as they had been before the operation. The one difference was emotion. He could feel nothing. Things that might make a person sad or angry or joyous left the man unmoved.

He tried to resume his life, but things did not go so well. Previously, the man had run his own business, but now he found himself unable to make the simplest decisions. He lost the ability to prioritize, and he lost track of time easily. His marriage fell apart and ended in divorce. His business ventures began to fail. He could see what was happening around him, but it didn't seem to matter. He felt nothing.

This example shows how important emotions are for clear thinking. Far from interfering with reasoning, emotions play an essential role in decision making. ■

The Nature of Emotions

Anxiety and elation are two commonly experienced emotions. **Emotions** are states of feeling. For most people, positive emotions such as happiness and love make life worth living. Persistent negative emotions such as fear and sadness can make life difficult.

Some emotions arise in response to a situation. For example, a musician giving a violin recital might feel anxious because she is uncertain about her ability to perform. Emotions can also motivate behavior. When the musician remembers that her friends and family members are in the audience, she might feel their support and play with improved confidence.

Emotions have biological, cognitive, and behavioral components. Strong emotions spark activity in the autonomic nervous system. For example, anxiety triggers activity of the sympathetic division of the autonomic nervous system. When people are anxious, their hearts race. They breathe rapidly, sweat heavily, and tense their muscles. The cognitive component of anxiety—the idea that something terrible might happen—may lead a person to try to escape from the situation. But where do emotions come from, and how many kinds do people experience?

The ancient Chinese believed that there are four inborn (instinctive) human emotions: happiness, anger, sorrow, and fear. Behaviorist John B. Watson believed that there are three instinctive emotions: fear, rage, and love. In 1932 psychologist Katherine Bridges proposed that people are born with one basic emotion: general excitement. This excitement then divides into other emotions as children develop.

Psychologist Carroll Izard suggests that all the emotions that people experience are present and distinct at birth. However, they do not all show up at once. Instead, they emerge as the child develops.

Many psychologists support Izard's view. In fact, they have found that infants show many emotions at ages earlier than those suggested by Bridges. In one study, the mothers of three-month-old babies were interviewed. Results of the study revealed that 99 percent of the mothers reported that their babies showed curiosity; 95 percent of the mothers reported that the babies displayed joy; 84 percent, anger; 74 percent, surprise; and 58 percent, fear.

Questions concerning how many emotions there are, how they develop, and how they affect our lives remain unanswered. Two emotions of great importance to most people, however, are happiness and anger.

Happiness William James said that the motive behind everything that people do is "how to gain, how to keep, how to recover happiness." Certainly our state of happiness or unhappiness affects nearly everything we do as well as our perception of our surroundings. People who are happy think the world is a happier, safer place, make decisions more readily, and report greater satisfaction with their lives than do people who are unhappy. When a person is unhappy, gloom seems to settle over everything he or she does. When his or her mood brightens, everything seems better—school, work, relationships, and self-image. It seems that happiness and unhappiness create their own momentum.

Moreover, many studies have found that the happier we are, the more likely we are to help others. When good things happen that lift our mood, we are more likely to volunteer our time to help other people.

Psychologists have made happiness a new measure of national well-being. The World Database of Happiness compiles studies of happiness done by many different researchers. Most of the studies are based on interview questions. For example, the World Values Survey, conducted by the University of Michigan, relies on two questions: "Taking all things together, would you say you are very happy, rather happy, not very happy, or not at all happy?" and "All things considered, how satisfied are you with your life as a whole these days?" Some scientists object that people's estimates of their own feelings are not objective measures.

Anger Anger is a common response to an insult or an attack. Anger can often make a person seem out of control. Angry people may even seek revenge. The Roman poet Horace called anger "a short madness."

What makes people angry? Psychologist James Averill asked study participants to keep a record of their experiences with anger.

WEBQUEST

Complete a Webquest at thinkcentral.com on how advertisers use emotion to sell products.

CASE STUDY
CONNECTION

The Happiness of Nations The World Database of Happiness attempts to track the happiness of people around the world.

The Six Basic Emotions

All people use the same facial expressions to show anger, disgust, fear, happiness, sadness, and surprise. *Which emotion does each face exhibit?*

Most of the participants reported becoming at least moderately angry several times a week, while others became angry several times a day. Usually the anger was directed against someone close—a friend or family member—and over some alleged offense, especially if the act seemed deliberate or thoughtless. However, small annoyances such as a loud noise, an unpleasant odor, or an accidental injury can also make a person angry.

What is an effective way to handle anger? Hold it in? Lash out at the offender? The participants in Averill's study reported that when they became angry they tended to react by being assertive rather than hostile. Their anger frequently prompted them to discuss the situation with the offending person, thus easing the unpleasant feelings. Such controlled reactions are almost always more effective at reducing anger than hostile outbursts or suppression of the feelings of anger.

Reading Check **Find the Main Idea** How many emotions do all psychologists agree on?

Facial Expressions

We often "read" people's faces. We can tell when people are happy from their smiles. We can see when they are fearful from their open mouths and the look in their eyes. We can read people's expressions and know when they are sad or surprised. Are these facial expressions of emotion instinctive, or do people learn to show these expressions to signify certain emotions on the basis of their cultural settings?

Cross-cultural evidence suggests that facial expressions are probably inborn. The ways in which people express many emotions appear to be the same around the world. Certain facial expressions seem to suggest the same emotions in all people. For example, smiling appears to be a universal sign of friendliness and approval. Baring the teeth may be a universal sign of anger. Charles Darwin, the naturalist who developed the theory of natural selection, believed that the universal recognition of facial expressions had survival value by communicating motivation.

For example, facial expressions could signal whether a group of approaching strangers were friendly or hostile.

But some anthropologists, including Margaret Mead, argued that emotions are not universal. They argued that emotions and the way we express emotions depend on what culture we come from. For example, in one culture burping after a meal might lead to feelings of disgust. In another culture, the same burp might be perceived as a compliment and lead to feelings of happiness.

Psychologists have been able to show that emotions and the way we express those emotions are indeed universal. In a classic study by psychologist Paul Ekman, people from around the world were asked to identify the emotions that were being expressed in a series of photographs. The photos were similar to the ones shown on the previous page. They showed people expressing anger, disgust, fear, happiness, sadness, and surprise. Researchers interviewed people ranging from college students at a European university to tribal members in the remote highlands of New Guinea. All of the groups agreed on the emotion that was being portrayed in each photograph. Even the New Guineans, who had had almost no contact with Americans or Europeans, saw the same emotions in the facial expressions.

Reading Check **Identify Supporting Details** Why do psychologists believe that facial expressions are universal?

Theories of Emotion

Emotions are states of feeling that influence thought and behavior. People respond emotionally to events and situations in a variety of ways. Psychologists have different theories about what emotions are, where they come from, and how they operate.

The Opponent-process Theory According to the **opponent-process theory,** originated by psychologist Richard Solomon, emotions often come in pairs, with one emotion being followed by its opposite. That is, one emotion—for example, extreme happiness—tends to be followed by feelings that are opposite—for example, extreme sadness—rather than by a <u>neutral</u> feeling.

Solomon and his colleague J. D. Corbitt suggested that people are inclined to maintain balance in their emotional lives. When this balance is upset by a strong emotional response to a particular situation, an opponent process, or an opposite emotional response, occurs. The opponent process eventually restores emotional balance.

For example, although a musician might have practiced in preparation for her recital, she could still feel anxious when she goes on stage. Once she begins to play, however, and focus on the music, her anxiety might disappear and be replaced by tremendous relief, even elation. The first emotion (anxiety) was followed by its opposite (relief).

The Commonsense Approach You and most of your classmates would probably agree with a "commonsense approach" to emotions. According to this view, when something happens to a person in a certain situation, the person quickly interprets the situation. The interpretation triggers body sensations that signal a feeling, or emotion. The emotion, in turn, triggers a behavior. For example, a person who is walking down the street and encounters a large snarling dog may sense that he or she is in danger. That person then feels anxious (body sensation) and quickly turns down the nearest side street to avoid the dog (behavior).

Many psychologists agree that thoughts (appraisal of the situation) come before our feelings and behavior. They maintain that people's appraisals of their situations are the keys to emotional response. That is, people's thoughts, feelings, and behavior are strongly intertwined, and their thoughts to some degree determine their emotional and behavioral responses.

Other psychologists, however, believe that it is important to understand the biology of emotion. According to these psychologists, the activities of the nervous system and hormones play a more important role in determining emotion than what people are thinking about their situations. Some psychologists even believe that people's behavior determines their thoughts and feelings. Three important theories of emotion are the James-Lange theory, the Cannon-Bard theory, and the theory of cognitive appraisal.

ACADEMIC VOCABULARY
neutral not aligned with any position

The James-Lange Theory In the late 1800s, philosopher and psychologist William James suggested that people's emotions follow, rather than cause, their behavioral reactions. That is, people act first and then react emotionally according to the way they acted. For example, a person crossing the street who looks up and sees a truck bearing down acts first to get out of the way, then feels fright. James would say that the emotions of fear and panic are the *result* of jumping out of the way of the truck, not the cause of the action. This theory was also proposed by the Danish biologist Karl G. Lange at about the same time. Hence, it is called the James-Lange theory of emotion.

According to James and Lange, certain situations trigger reactions, called instinctive bodily response patterns. These patterns include specific feelings and behaviors. For example, a physical threat can trigger one of two instinctive response patterns: fighting or fleeing from the situation. According to this view, people who would meet the threat by fighting would experience the emotion of anger *because* (and only *after*) they acted aggressively. People who would meet the threat by fleeing would experience the emotion of fear *because* (and *after*) they ran away from the situation. In other words, their behavior would come first, followed by the emotion that fit the behavior.

The James-Lange theory suggests that people can change their feelings by changing their behavior. Changing one's behavior to change one's feelings is an approach used in behavior therapy, a method that has sometimes been employed to treat certain psychological disorders.

The James-Lange theory has been criticized, however, because it downplays the role of human cognition. This theory views the cognitive appraisal of a situation as having little or no role in determining human behavior. The James-Lange theory also minimizes the role of personal values and choice as factors in human behavior.

The Cannon-Bard Theory Walter Cannon and Philip Bard were physiologists, scientists who study the functions of the human body. Their view of emotion was rooted in physiology. They suggested that emotions *accompany* the bodily responses that are aroused by an external stimulus. According to the Cannon-Bard theory, a situation triggers an external stimulus that is processed by the brain. The brain then stimulates bodily changes and cognitive activity (the experience of the emotion) simultaneously. Emotions are not produced by the bodily responses.

The central question raised by the Cannon-Bard theory is whether bodily responses and emotions do in fact occur at the same time. In some cases, it seems they do not. For example, pain or a threat may trigger bodily responses (such as rapid heartbeat) in someone before that person begins to experience distress or fear. Also, people who manage a "narrow escape" from a dangerous situation often become quite upset and shaken afterward, when they have had a chance to consider what might have happened to them. In such situations it seems that a two-stage reaction is involved—the bodily response is followed by the emotional reaction.

The Theory of Cognitive Appraisal Other theoretical approaches to emotion have focused on cognitive factors. One theory, called the theory of cognitive appraisal, argues that all emotions have similar bodily response patterns.

THEORIES OF EMOTION

Psychologists have developed several different theories to explain the relationship between emotions, thoughts, and behaviors.

James-Lange Theory
- The theory is named for William James and Karl G. Lange, who proposed similar theories at about the same time.
- Emotions follow behavior.
- People can change their feelings by changing their behavior.

Cannon-Bard Theory
- The theory is named for Walter Cannon and Philip Bard, who were physiologists.
- Emotions are triggered by external stimuli.
- Emotions and bodily responses occur simultaneously.

Theory of Cognitive Appraisal
- All emotions have similar bodily response patterns.
- People label their emotions based on their cognitive appraisal of the situation.

That is, the body reacts in physically similar ways even though different emotions are being experienced. This theory maintains that the way people label an emotion depends largely on their cognitive appraisal of the situation.

The cognitive appraisal that occurs is based on many factors. These factors include the person's analysis of the situation and the ways other people are reacting in the same situation. When other people are involved in the same situation, an individual will look at the way they are reacting and then compare his or her reaction to theirs to arrive at what seems to be the right response.

Critics of the theory of cognitive appraisal point out that studies designed to support the theory often yield different results when repeated. In science, research studies must be replicated with the same methods used and similar results obtained. Since several studies designed to prove cognitive appraisal theory produced different results, some psychologists have questioned the theory's validity.

Evaluation of the Theories The theory of cognitive appraisal is quite different from the James-Lange theory. The James-Lange theory asserts that each emotion has distinct and easily recognized bodily sensations. The theory of cognitive appraisal asserts that all emotions are rooted in common bodily sensations but argues that we label these sensa-tions differently according to the situation. The truth may lie somewhere in between.

In summary, it is possible that the bodily response patterns of different emotions are more distinct than the theory of cognitive appraisal suggests, but are not as distinct as James and Lange suggested. In addition, research with PET scans suggests that dif-ferent emotions involve different parts of the brain. Furthermore, lack of control over our emotions and ignorance of what is happen-ing to us appear to be distressing experiences. Thus, it seems that our cognitive apprais-als of our situations do affect our emotional responses but not to the extent envisioned by some cognitive-appraisal theorists.

People are complex, thinking beings who evaluate information both from their personal situations and from their bodily responses to their situations. Most likely, they process information from both sources to label their emotions and to decide what action to take. No one theory of emotion we have discussed applies to all people in all situations. That may not be a bad thing. People's emotions are not as easily understood or manipulated as some theorists have believed.

Reading Check **Summarize** What theory sug-gests that emotions happen after an instinctive bodily response?

Online Quiz THINK central thinkcentral.com

SECTION 4 Assessment

Reviewing Main Ideas and Vocabulary

1. **Define** What are emotions?

2. **Identify Main Ideas** What are the six basic emotions that people of all cultures identify as facial expressions?

3. **Recall** How does opponent-process theory explain the way emotions change?

Thinking Critically

4. **Interpret** How did Carroll Izard explain the way people develop emotions?

5. **Explain** Why do some anthropologists believe that emo-tions are not universal?

6. **Analyze** Have you ever heard a song that made you cry? Use the common sense approach to explain how the song affected your emotions.

7. **Categorize** Using your notes and a graphic organizer like the one below, categorize the way the three major theories view emotion.

Theory	Explanation of Emotion

FOCUS ON WRITING

8. **Persuasive** How many different emotions do you think there are? Do you, like John B. Watson, believe in three basic emotions, or do you think there are dozens? Use specific examples to support your viewpoint.

Evolutionary Psychology

Psychologists have always studied what makes us do what we do and feel the way we feel. Recently, some psychologists began approaching these questions from the perspective of human evolution. Instead of creating theoretical constructs such as the ego and the id, these psychologists tried to see how our behaviors may have helped our ancestors survive and reproduce. The new field became known as evolutionary psychology.

Evolutionary psychology attempts to understand human psychology through the lens of natural selection. As you may recall from biology, natural selection is a process that operates from generation to generation. Plants and animals that are well-adapted to their environment survive and pass their genes down to the next generation. Those that have characteristics ill-suited to their environment die and fail to breed.

Evolutionary psychologists apply these principles to human behavior. Psychological traits that helped humans survive and procreate got passed down to future generations;

traits that resulted in death or failure to procreate got eliminated. For example, fear of the dark: Early humans without this fear might have wandered into the dark and gotten eaten by predators. Other examples range from our tastes in food to our affection for children.

One subject that evolutionary psychologists have studied extensively is play. All children play. In fact, the young of most mammals engage in playful behavior. Playing around seems like purposeless fun, but not according to evolutionary psychology. Play is so widespread that it must have some evolutionary advantage.

Psychologist Thomas Power examined play in both humans and other animals. His study confirmed that play helps the young develop both mentally and physically. Among social animals, play helps teach rules and establish hierarchies.

Power also noticed that play does not end with childhood. Both human and non-human adults continue to play, both with the young and with each other. The evolutionary benefit seems two-fold: When adults play with the young, they help the young develop and learn social rules. Play among adults keeps them physically and mentally agile (Power, 2000).

Another mystery that evolutionary psychology has investigated is emotion. If rational thought is humanity's big advantage over the rest of the animals, why do we still have emotions? Psychologists Martie Haselton and Timothy Ketelaar found that emotions actually help people make the right decisions. They also found that emotions perform an essential role in interactions with other people.

However, our primitive emotions are not ideally suited to the modern world. For example, people generally show more fear of insects than of speeding cars and other modern hazards (Haselton and Ketelaar, 2005).

All children and many young animals engage in playful behavior.

Thinking Critically

1. **Explain** How does natural selection work?

2. **Discuss** What are some other psychological traits that might have had evolutionary advantages?

Identifying Motivations and Emotions

Reading and Activity Workbook

Use the workbook to complete this simulation.

What can you learn about motivation and emotion through developing fictional characters?

1. Introduction

Now that you have learned about motivations and emotions in the abstract, it's time to examine them in action. The following simulation will help you better understand the key ideas of this chapter. It will also help you experience and better understand motivations and their link to emotion.

You will work in small groups to develop four different characters: a student applying to college; his parents; and an admissions officer from the college. Then each character will be brought to life in front of the class through acting. Finally, the entire class will discuss the performances and analyze the motivations and emotions of the four characters.

2. Defining the Characters and Their Feelings

❶ The main character in the simulation is a student named Mark:

Mark Turner is a junior at City High School. He recently received his SAT score of 2100 in the mail but his current GPA is 2.2. Mark is very lazy in class and often does not complete his homework. However, he loves baseball and is a member of the school team. He is a good player but not good enough to get an athletic scholarship. Mark is also a member of the multicultural club, but he does not usually attend its meetings or special functions.

❷ Mark's parents are Tish and Robert:

Mark's mother, Tish, works in an office downtown. She manages a small department in a large company. Tish paid her own way through college and graduated near the top of her class. She believes her degree helped her to get a good job.

Mark's dad, Robert, works in construction. After he graduated from high school, he took a few classes at a community college. But when he began working he didn't have time for school, and he never earned a degree. Robert was a good baseball player, too, when he was younger.

Tish and Robert have been married for 18 years. Mark is their only child.

❸ The admissions officer is named Shelly:

Shelly Johnson has worked as an admissions officer at State College for 15 years. She graduated from a different college where she had been given a music scholarship. She still plays piano in a local jazz band, but her job as an admissions officer pays the bills. Shelly reviews thousands of applications every year. She rejects about half of them.

3. Acting Out the Scenarios

▪ Following your teacher's instructions, organize into three groups. Large classes may be divided into six groups.

▪ The first group will represent Mark. The second group will represent Mark's parents, and the third group will represent the college admissions officer.

▪ Each group will brainstorm to understand their characters better. Discuss the following questions and any others that might help to understand your character:

- Mark—Why do you behave the way you do? What could or should you say to defend what you do in school?

- Mark's parents—Why are you concerned about Mark? What could or should you say to Mark to encourage or motivate him?

- College admissions officer—What is it like to review thousands of applications? Does Mark seem to merit admission?

Improvise the following scenes using different actors each time. Have one person from the Mark group play Mark, two people from the parents group play Tish and Robert, and one person from the third group play Shelly. Clear a space for a stage, and arrange chairs and other props to simulate the setting of each scene.

- Mark comes home from baseball practice. His parents stop him before he goes to his room and ask him about his report card, on which he has gotten mostly Cs.

- That night, Tish and Robert discuss the situation by themselves. They try to figure out what they can do to encourage Mark to do better in school.

- The family visits State College and meets with Shelly, the college admissions officer. Mark wants to know about the baseball program. His parents want to know if Mark stands a chance of getting into the school.

- On the drive back, Mark and his parents discuss how the meeting went and what Mark's future holds.

4. Discussion

After all of the scenarios have been acted, discuss the characters and their feelings. Try to answer questions such as the following:

- What motives can be identified in each of the characters?

- What needs can be identified in each of the characters?

- What drives can be identified in each of the characters?

- How and where do the arguments in the scenario fit into Maslow's Hierarchy of Needs?

- Would specific performance goals help Mark to become a better student? Why or why not?

- Identify intrinsic and extrinsic rewards from the scenario. How do you think Mark would be best motivated?

- What emotions became obvious in the performance? What facial expressions did you notice? How much more emotion would be present if this were "real" rather than acted? Explain.

CHAPTER 13 Review

Comprehension and Critical Thinking

SECTION 1 (pp. 364–367)

1. a. Identify What term describes how the body maintains equilibrium, such as the need for sleep?

b. Contrast How do biological and psychological needs differ?

c. Support a Position Why is instinct theory not used to explain human motivation?

SECTION 2 (pp. 368–372)

2. a. Recall What role does the hypothalamus play in hunger?

b. Explain Why is knowledge of nutrition important as a strategy for weight loss?

c. Make Judgments How have psychological factors played a role in the epidemic of obesity in the United States?

SECTION 3 (pp. 373–378)

3. a. Describe Describe an example of a person with high achievement motivation.

b. Summarize What are two examples of stimulus motives, and why are such motives important?

c. Explain Why is sensory deprivation an important concept in the study of human motivation and emotion?

SECTION 4 (pp. 379–384)

4. a. Identify Main Ideas What is the commonsense theory of emotion?

b. Identify Cause and Effect What theory explains why a person might feel "on top of the world" one day and "down in the dumps" the next day?

c. Elaborate Use a specific example to illustrate the difference between the James-Lange and Cannon-Bard theories of emotion.

Reviewing Vocabulary

Fill in each blank with the term that correctly completes the sentence.

5. A need or desire that energizes and directs behavior is called _____.

6. _____ are complex, unlearned behaviors that are present throughout a species.

7. _____ people weigh more than 30 percent above their recommended weight.

8. _____ include sensory stimulation, activity, exploration, and manipulation of the environment.

9. A state in which there is little or no sensory stimulation is called _____.

10. Good grades are an example of _____, something external given in response to the attainment of a goal.

11. The theory of _____ says that people try to make their thoughts and behaviors match their beliefs and others' expectations.

12. People need air, water, and food in order to _____ themselves.

13. The desire to join with others and to be part of a larger whole is called _____.

14. _____ are states of feeling that involve physical arousal, expressive behaviors, and conscious experience.

INTERNET ACTIVITY ✴

15. Choose a comprehensive weight loss program like Weight Watchers. Use the Internet to research the program. Write a short report that explains how the program balances addressing the physiology and the psychology of weight loss.

Psychology in Your Life

16. Identify a person in your school or community who has worked hard to achieve a specific goal. Interview that person and try to determine the motivation behind his or her success. Also find out if the person gave up anything or had to overcome obstacles to achieve his or her goal. Write a brief report summarizing your findings.

SKILLS ACTIVITY: INTERPRETING PRIMARY SOURCES

The following excerpt is taken from an essay by Abraham Maslow, *Self-actualizing People: A Study of Psychological Health*. Read the excerpt, which describes people who are psychologically healthy. Then answer the questions that follow.

> **❝**It would convey the wrong impression to say that they are self-satisfied. What we must say rather is that they can take the frailties and sins, weaknesses, and evils of human nature in the same unquestioning spirit with which one accepts the characteristics of nature. One does not complain about water because it is wet, or about rocks because they are hard, or about trees because they are green. As the child looks out upon the world with wide, uncritical, undemanding, innocent eyes, simply noting and observing what is the case, without either arguing the matter or demanding that it be otherwise, so does the self-actualizing person tend to look upon human nature in himself and in others.**❞**
>
> — Abraham Maslow, *Dominance, Self-Esteem, Self-Actualization* (Brooks/Cole, 1973)

17. Identify Main Ideas According to Maslow, do self-actualized people feel as though they have perfected themselves?

18. Interpret Do self-actualized people have a realistic view of human nature? Explain.

19. Elaborate Drawing upon information in the excerpt, what is Maslow's concept of human nature?

WRITING FOR AP PSYCHOLOGY

Use your knowledge of motivation and emotion to answer the question below. Do not simply list facts. Present a clear argument based on your critical analysis of the question, using the appropriate psychological terminology.

20. What role does the body play in emotions? Use the following specific emotions in your answer:

- anger
- anxiety
- sorrow

YOU ARE WHAT MAKES YOU LAUGH

Studying what people find funny is just one way that psychologists gain insight into what makes us who we are—our personalities.

Everybody loves to laugh, and everybody loves a comedian. But what does your humor style say about your personality? Psychologist Rod Martin claims that humor is a form of communication and, as he states, "We all use it differently." Humor, he believes, can reveal how you feel about yourself and how you relate to others.

After conducting research on how people make others laugh, Martin discovered that a sense of humor doesn't necessarily mean that someone is fun-loving and good-natured. On the contrary, it could indicate that he or she actually has a hostile personality. For example, a person who uses put-down humor may do so as an acceptable way to channel aggression. Pointing out someone's flaws in a humorous way makes the victim of the joke look bad while making the joker look good. If the victim protests, the joker can claim to be "just kidding" and avoid responsibility.

The "hate-me" humor style may be considered the polar opposite of the put-down style. People who tell jokes at their own expense use this style. For the most part,

we tend to appreciate this self-deprecating type of humor because we can laugh along with the joker.

Occasional jokes in this style are fine and probably healthy. According to Martin, however, people who constantly humiliate themselves in front of others for laughs may do so as a result of their self-loathing. They may also alienate their audience once the playfulness wears thin. Besides, too many hate-me jokes can make people feel uncomfortable. Hate-me humor may even contribute to the joker's feelings of unworthiness and foster depression and anxiety—perhaps even drug abuse. The late comedian Chris Farley, who died of a drug overdose at the age of 33, employed this humor style.

Of course, not all humor styles reflect negative personality traits. Martin says that people who tell jokes to relieve a tense situation or lighten the mood often reveal a warm, good-natured personality. Their bonding style of humor is inclusive, suggesting that "we're all in this together." Popular comedian Ellen Degeneres demonstrates this humor style.

CHAPTER 14

THEORIES OF PERSONALITY

Similarly, we embrace the joker who laughs at life's absurdities. People who practice this style of humor don't take themselves too seriously, which may help them deal with the challenges in their lives.

Even a morbid sense of humor can be a positive personality trait. The ability to laugh in the face of danger actually suggests a healthy psyche. Doctors in the operating room often crack jokes to ease tension. Since the outbreak of the Iraq War, Iraqi civilians have at times used humor to cope with life in a war-torn nation. For example, they have celebrated a form of April Fool's Day in which they play macabre pranks on each other. Although it may not seem so, this is a positive form of humor that may promote both mental and physical health. When you can laugh at life, you are more able to ease stress levels and less likely to be angry, depressed, or anxious.

It turns out that what we find funny may also be tied to other aspects of our personalities. Neuroimaging has revealed that there is an area in the center of the brain that lights up when someone sees a smiling face or hears a joke. Studies have shown that this area lights up more often in people with outgoing personalities, who tend to laugh more, than in those with reserved personalities, who do not laugh as much.

In this chapter, you will learn about other approaches psychologists have taken to study personality. All of their theories have one thing in common: they try to explain why we are who we are.

What do you think?

1. According to psychologist Rod Martin, what personality traits might be revealed by someone who constantly tells jokes about other people?

2. Which type of humor style do you and your friends have? Do you agree that your humor style reflects your personality? Why or why not?

Chapter at a Glance

SECTION 1: The Trait Approach

■ Psychologists study personality to discover patterns of feelings, motives, and behavior that set people apart from one another.

■ Trait theorists attempt to understand personality by focusing on traits, or those aspects of personality that remain stable.

■ Psychologist Hans Eysenck used two basic dimensions of personality— introversion-extroversion and emotional stability-instability—to organize traits.

■ The Five Factor Model identifies five basic personality factors: extroversion, agreeableness, conscientiousness, emotional stability, and openness to experience.

SECTION 2: The Psychoanalytic Approach

■ According to the psychoanalytic approach, personality is shaped by inner struggles that all people experience.

■ The psychoanalytic approach is based on Sigmund Freud's theories about the structure of the mind, defense mechanisms, and the stages of personality development.

■ Many of Freud's intellectual heirs have made unique contributions to the psychoanalytic approach.

SECTION 3: The Learning Approach

■ The two branches of the learning approach, behaviorism and social-learning theory, focus on how experiences shape behavior.

■ Behaviorists assert that people learn socially desirable behaviors through a process called socialization.

■ Social learning theorists argue that people learn by observation.

SECTION 4: The Humanistic and Sociocultural Approaches

■ The humanistic perspective emphasizes the importance of free choice, self-awareness, self-fulfillment, self-esteem, and ethical conduct in personality development.

■ Psychologists following the sociocultural approach focus on how gender, ethnicity, and culture influence personality.

The Trait Approach

Before You Read

Main Idea

Psychologists who support the trait approach believe that personality traits are inborn and unchanging. Many trait theorists believe that people can be measured according to five basic personality factors.

Reading Focus

1. Who have been the most influential trait theorists?

2. What is the Five-Factor Model?

3. How do some psychologists evaluate the trait approach?

Vocabulary

personality
trait
introverts
extroverts

TAKING NOTES Use a graphic organizer like this one to take notes on aspects of the trait approach.

Theorist	Factors	Evaluation

Shy or in Need of Therapy?

PSYCHOLOGY CLOSE UP

Is being shy a mental illness? Northwestern University professor Christopher Lane tells a story about how his shy mother reacted to the crowds and chaos she experienced as a child during the World War II bombing of London. She pretended to be a horse and galloped about on all fours! Her parents didn't panic or assume that their child had a psychological disorder. They evidently felt that she was just shy and handled the tension in her own creative, imaginative way.

How might parents react to such behavior today? Some would rush their child to a psychiatrist for a diagnosis and medication. Extreme shyness, which was once considered a virtue, is now often diagnosed as "social anxiety disorder"—a disorder to be treated with therapy and drugs. Pharmaceutical companies have jumped at the chance to advertise shyness-curing medications to people who had not previously seen this personality trait as a disorder. In fact, one company spent $93 million on its ad campaign for such a drug.

Some people suffer from shyness so crippling that it is a genuine disorder. But, for most people, shyness is just an individual quirk—a personality trait. To gain insight into what makes each one of us unique, psychologists struggle to understand and explain personality traits and identify disorders such as shyness. ■

Trait Theorists

When people think of a person's personality, they usually think of the person's most striking characteristics, as in an "assertive personality" or an "artistic personality." Psychologists define **personality** as the patterns of feelings, motives, and behavior that set people apart from one another.

A **trait** is an aspect of personality that is considered to be reasonably stable. We assume that a person has certain traits based on how the person behaves. If you describe a friend as shy, it may be because you have seen your friend looking anxious and trying to escape social encounters. Traits are assumed to account for consistent behavior in different situations. You would probably expect your shy friend to act withdrawn in most social situations. If, on the other hand, you have a friend who is constantly making jokes, you would probably conclude that being outgoing and humorous are two of her traits.

Trait theorists have generally assumed that traits are somehow fixed or unchanging. However, the question of where traits come from has been pondered through the ages.

Hippocrates An early answer to where traits come from was offered by the Greek physician Hippocrates. The ancient Greeks believed that the body contains fluids called humors. Hippocrates suggested that personality traits are a result of different combinations of these bodily fluids.

Hippocrates believed that there are four basic fluids, or humors, in the body:

- yellow bile, which was associated with a choleric, or quick-tempered, disposition
- blood, which was linked with a sanguine, or warm and cheerful, temperament
- phlegm, which was linked with a phlegmatic, or sluggish and cool, disposition
- black bile, which was connected with a melancholic, thoughtful temperament

Certain diseases and disorders were believed to reflect a lack of balance in these humors. Methods such as bloodletting (the removal of blood from the body) were recommended to restore the balance of humors and one's health. Although there is no scientific evidence for Hippocrates' biological theory, words based on his ideas remain in use today.

Gordon Allport In the 1930s, psychologist Gordon Allport (1897–1967) cataloged some 18,000 human traits from a search through lists of descriptive words. Some of the words, such as *short* and *brunette,* describe physical traits. Others, such as *shy* and *emotional,* describe behavioral traits. Still others, such as *honest,* concern morality.

Allport assumed that traits can be inherited and that they are fixed in the nervous system. He conducted thorough and detailed studies of individuals, noting their outstanding traits as well as their behaviors. Allport's research led him to conclude that traits are the building blocks of personality. He asserted that a person's behavior is a product of his or her particular combination of traits.

Hans J. Eysenck British psychologist Hans J. Eysenck (1916–1997) focused on the relationships between two personality dimensions: introversion-extroversion and emotional stability-instability. He used these dimensions to organize various personality traits.

WEBQUEST

Complete a Webquest at thinkcentral.com on personality.

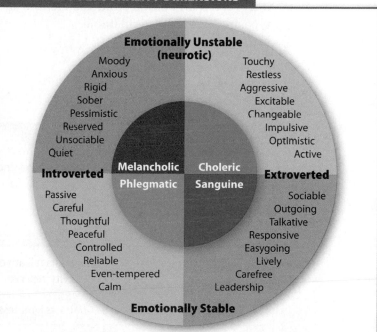

EYSENCK'S PERSONALITY DIMENSIONS

This diagram shows how closely Eysenck's personality dimensions relate to the four personality types identified by Hippocrates.

Skills Focus INTERPRETING VISUALS According to the diagram, which of Hippocrates's personality types are most unstable?

Source: Eysenck, H.J. and Eysenck, M.W. *Personality and Individual Differences.* Plenum Publishing, 1958.

In his model, Eysenck placed introversion and extroversion at opposite poles. **Introverts** tend to be imaginative and to look inward rather than to other people for their ideas and energy. **Extroverts,** on the other hand, tend to be active and self-expressive and gain energy from interaction with other people. The contrast between introversion and extroversion was first proposed by Carl Jung, whom you will read about later in this chapter. Also, stable people are usually reliable, composed, and rational. Unstable people can be agitated and unpredictable.

ACADEMIC VOCABULARY

dimensions the range over which or the degree to which something extends; scope

Eysenck placed personality traits according to where those traits appear within the <u>dimensions</u> of introversion-extroversion and emotional stability-emotional instability. For instance, an anxious person might be highly introverted and emotionally unstable. A reckless or impulsive person might be highly extroverted and unstable.

Eysenck's scheme is similar to the one suggested by Hippocrates. According to Eysenck's dimensions, the choleric type would be both extroverted and unstable; the sanguine type, extroverted and stable; the phlegmatic type, introverted and stable; and the melancholic type, introverted and unstable.

Reading Check **Contrast** How do introverts and extroverts tend to differ?

The Five-Factor Model

The "big five" may sound like a description of a basketball team. In psychology, however, the term refers to recent research suggesting that there may be five basic personality factors. These include the two found by Eysenck—extroversion and emotional stability—along with conscientiousness, agreeableness, and openness to experience. Many personality theorists, particularly Robert McCrae and Paul T. Costa, Jr., have helped in the development of the Five-Factor Model. Cross-cultural research suggests that the five factors appear to define the personality structure of American, German, Portuguese, Jewish, Chinese, Korean, and Japanese people. A study of more than 5,000 German, British, Spanish, Czech, and Turkish people suggests that the factors are related to people's basic temperaments, which are largely inborn. The researchers interpreted the results to mean that personalities mature naturally as part of the aging process, rather than in response to external, environmental conditions.

Research on the Five Factors A great deal of research has been conducted on the Five-Factor Model. For example, consider driving. Studies show that people who are given more traffic tickets and who get into more collisions tend to score lower on the factor of

THE FIVE-FACTOR MODEL

The Five-Factor Model describes what many psychologists consider to be the five basic factors or dimensions of personality. Each of the five factors consists of a range of specific personality traits.

Factor	Traits
1. Extroversion	Contrasts talkativeness, assertiveness, and activity with silence, passivity, reserve
2. Agreeableness	Contrasts kindness, trust, and warmth with hostility, selfishness, and distrust
3. Conscientiousness	Contrasts organization, thoroughness, and reliability with carelessness, negligence, and unreliability
4. Emotional Stability-Instability	Contrasts reliability and coping ability with nervousness, moodiness, and sensitivity to negative events
5. Openness to Experience	Contrasts imagination, curiosity, and creativity with shallowness and lack of perceptiveness

agreeableness than do people who receive fewer tickets. In other words, it is safer to share the road with agreeable people. People who score high on agreeableness get along with nearly everybody and tend to go along with what other people want. They also tend to score low on conscientiousness, because they do not examine other people too closely.

The Five-Factor Model also has been used to study political beliefs. For example, studies in the United States, Belgium, and Poland show people who are authoritarian or strongly conservative tend to score low on openness to experience. They tend to reject ideas that are not sanctioned by an authority figure.

Links to Disorders Researchers are also studying how the five factors relate to the ways in which people interact with their friends and families. In the field of psychological problems, researchers are studying links between the five factors and a variety of disorders. These include anxiety disorders, thinking that one is ill when there is no medical basis for the belief, depression and suicide attempts, schizophrenia, and personality disorders. The Five-Factor Model helps in describing these disorders. It remains to be seen how well the model will enable psychologists to explain the disorders and help people who experience them.

Psychologists continue to disagree about which personality factors are the most basic. However, nearly all psychologists would agree that the "big five" personality dimensions are important in defining a person's psychological makeup. Moreover, a person's position along these dimensions tends to be established at an early age and remain stable through life.

Reading Check **Identify Supporting Details** What does research on the five factors suggest about people's basic temperaments?

Evaluation of the Trait Approach

One shortcoming of the trait approach is its singular focus on describing traits. Moreover, the efforts of trait theorists to link personality traits to biological factors have not been successful. Today trait theory focuses on describing traits, rather than explaining their origins or investigating how people with undesirable traits can change for the better.

The work of trait theorists has, however, had a number of practical applications. In suggesting that there are links between personalities, abilities, and interests, trait theorists have alerted us to the value of matching people to educational programs and jobs on the basis of their personality traits.

The ability to objectively measure personality traits may be the greatest strength of the trait approach. However, such measurements are limited. For instance, an introverted person may act in an outgoing manner around family and friends, and an extroverted person may sometimes crave privacy. Trait theory also provides no explanation of how personality develops. As a result, some psychologists question its value in clinical applications.

Reading Check **Summarize** What are the strengths of the trait approach?

Online Quiz **THINK** central thinkcentral.com

SECTION 1 Assessment

Reviewing Main Ideas and Vocabulary

1. **Define** How do psychologists define personality?

2. **Summarize** What are the four personality types identified by Hippocrates?

3. **Draw Conclusions** According to Eysenck, which personality dimensions would be used to describe someone who is reserved, anxious, and depressed?

Thinking Critically

4. **Make Judgments** How do you think most entertainers would score on the Five-Factor Model?

5. **Evaluate** Which personality traits might be important for an elementary school teacher?

6. **Support a Position** Do you think that personality traits are inborn and cannot be changed? Explain your answer.

7. **Make Generalizations** Label the sections of a graphic organizer like the one at right Melancholic, Choleric, Phlegmatic, and Sanguine. Then use your notes to write down your own personality traits in the appropriate sections and make generalizations about your personality type.

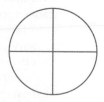

FOCUS ON WRITING

8. **Descriptive** Write one or two paragraphs describing the personality traits of a character in a favorite TV show or movie. Draw conclusions about where the character would fall within Eysenck's model.

The Psychoanalytic Approach

Before You Read

Main Idea

The psychoanalytic approach stresses the influence of the unconscious on personality. Freud, Jung, Adler, Horney, and Erikson are among the most important psychoanalytic theorists.

Reading Focus

1. What theories did Sigmund Freud develop about the mind?

2. Why do people use defense mechanisms?

3. What are Freud's main stages of personality development?

4. Who are other important psychoanalytic theorists?

5. How do psychologists evaluate the psychoanalytic approach?

Vocabulary

id
ego
superego
defense mechanisms
repression
rationalization
regression
projection
collective unconscious
archetypes
inferiority complex

TAKING NOTES Use a graphic organizer like this one to take notes on the theories of Freud, Jung, Adler, Horney, and Erikson.

Psychoanalyst	Theories
Freud	
Jung	
Adler	
Horney	
Erikson	

Old Questions
FOR THE Modern Mind

PSYCHOLOGY CLOSE UP

Can psychoanalysis stand the test of time? Have you ever admitted to making a Freudian slip? Do you try to keep your ego in check? If so, you have referred to two ideas from the work of Sigmund Freud. In fact, many of Freud's theories related to psychoanalysis have become part of modern culture—in our language, movies, politics, literature, and other aspects of daily life.

Courses about Freud in university psychology departments, however, are harder to find. A recent study of 150 prominent U.S. colleges and universities reported that of the 1,092 courses that referred to psychoanalysis, more than 86 percent were offered outside of psychology departments. In academic psychology, theories that can be tested in the laboratory receive much more attention than Freud's, which relied on conversations with and observations of his patients.

Is the swing away from Freud a problem? One University of Chicago philosopher, Jonathan Lear, thinks so. "Some of the most important things in human life are just not measurable," Lear says. He predicts a swing back to Freud when more empirical methods for exploring human existence are found wanting. In the meantime, the work of Freud and other people who have contributed to psychoanalysis can still raise interesting, useful questions about our innermost thoughts and feelings. ■

Am I still relevant?

Sigmund Freud

The psychoanalytic approach to personality teaches that all people—even the most well-adjusted—undergo inner struggles. According to this approach, people are born with certain biological <u>drives</u>, such as aggression, sex, and the need for superiority. These drives, however, may come into conflict with laws, social norms, and moral codes that have previously been internalized. At any moment, a person's behavior, thoughts, and emotions represent the outcome of inner contests between the opposing forces of drives and rules.

The "inner conflict" approach to personality theory owes its origin to Sigmund Freud (1856–1939). Freud was trained as a physician. Early in his practice in Vienna, Austria, he was astounded to find that some people had lost feeling in a hand or had become paralyzed in the legs even though nothing was medically wrong with them. When Freud interviewed these individuals, he found that many things in their lives were making them very angry or anxious. Yet they refused to recognize their emotional or social problems. They were at the mercy of powerful inner emotions, even though on the surface they seemed calm.

The Unconscious Freud believed that conscious ideas and feelings occupy only a small part of the mind. Many of people's deepest thoughts, fears, and urges remain out of their awareness. These urges are pushed into an unconscious part of the mind.

One way in which Freud explored the unconscious was through psychoanalysis. In psychoanalysis, people are encouraged to talk about anything that pops into their minds. They do so in a comfortable and relaxed setting. The people Freud observed—those who had lost feeling in their hands or legs—regained much of their functioning when they talked about the things that were on their minds. For this reason, psychoanalysis has been called a "talking cure."

Freud also explored the unconscious through dream analysis. He believed that people experience unconscious wishes in their dreams—often in disguised form. Freud would ask people to record their dreams upon waking. He would then help them explore the dreams' possible hidden meanings.

Another technique that Freud used was hypnosis. He felt that people in a hypnotic state had better access to their unconscious thoughts. Freud eventually abandoned hypnosis, however, because many people later denied the things they said when they were in a hypnotic state.

The Id Freud believed that the mind has three basic psychological structures. The first of these structures is called the id. The **id** behaves like a stereotypical two-year-old: "I want what I want, and I want it now." The id represents basic drives such as hunger. It demands pleasure through instant gratification and pays no attention to laws, social customs, or the needs of others. The id follows what Freud called the *pleasure principle*—the urge for an immediate release of energy or emotion that will bring personal gratification, relief, or pleasure.

According to Freud, the id is present at birth. Babies, he claimed, are completely id-driven. And it is an important structure in early life because it ensures that a baby's needs will be met.

The Ego The second psychological structure, which Freud called the **ego,** develops because a child's demands for instant gratification cannot be met immediately or because meeting these demands may be harmful. Freud wrote that the ego "stands for reason and good sense." It develops from the id and is guided by the *reality principle*—the understanding that, in the real world, we cannot always get what we want.

The ego seeks to satisfy the appetites of the id in ways that are consistent with reality. For example, the id lets you know that you are hungry, but the ego lets you know that certain ways of satisfying your hunger—such as cooking a hamburger—are more appropriate than others—such as eating raw hamburger. The ego also provides the conscious sense of self. Activities such as planning dinner and studying for a test are functions of the ego.

Although most of the ego is conscious, some of its business is carried out unconsciously. For instance, the ego acts as a censor that screens out the wild impulses of the id. When the ego senses that indecent or improper impulses are rising into awareness, it tries to repress or reject them.

ACADEMIC VOCABULARY

drive powerful needs or instincts related to self-preservation that motivate behavior

The Superego The third psychological structure Freud formulated is the **superego.** The superego develops throughout early childhood. It functions according to the *moral principle.* By incorporating the standards and values of parents and members of the community, the superego provides us with our moral sense. The superego acts as the conscience and floods the ego with feelings of guilt and shame when we think or do something that society defines as wrong.

The ego does not have an easy job. It is caught between the conflicting messages of the id and the superego. For example, the id may urge, "You want to go out with your friends. Don't study now!" while the superego warns, "You have to study or you will not pass the test." According to Freud, people with healthy egos—and thus healthy personalities—find ways to balance the id's demands and the superego's warnings. In this case, the healthy ego would probably conclude, "Study now, and after I do well on the test, I can spend time with my friends."

Reading Check **Identify Supporting Details**
How did Sigmund Freud think the human mind was organized?

Recovering Repressed Memories

MANKOFF

"Now, we can get all those repressed memories the easy way or the hard way."

Skills Focus **INTERPRETING CARTOONS**
What might this psychoanalyst say is the "easy way" to retrieve repressed memories?

Defense Mechanisms

According to Freud, **defense mechanisms** are methods the ego uses to avoid recognizing ideas or emotions that may cause anxiety. These defenses operate unconsciously.

Repression One of the main Freudian defense mechanisms is repression. **Repression** removes anxiety-causing ideas from conscious awareness by pushing them into the unconscious. To explain repression, Freud compared people's personalities to teakettles. Primitive urges such as aggression seek expression just like steam tries to escape from a boiling kettle. But acknowledging these urges could cause a person serious feelings of guilt, anxiety, and shame. Thus, the urges are repressed, keeping the lid on the boiling kettle.

Repression, however, is not always successful. When enough steam builds up inside, the teakettle pops its lid. When people "pop their lids," the results are outbursts of anger and the development of other psychological and emotional problems.

Rationalization Other defense mechanisms protect us from unacceptable ideas in a different manner. They do not completely repress such ideas, but they distort them in one way or another. One such defense mechanism is **rationalization**—the use of self-deception to justify unacceptable behaviors or ideas. For instance, a student who cheats during a test may explain, "I only cheated on a couple of questions—I knew most of the material."

Rationalization can protect one's self-esteem or self-concept. However, it can also mask the real reason for a particular behavior and so prevent the person from dealing with the situation.

Regression Freud believed that when an individual is under a great deal of stress, he or she will return to behavior that is characteristic of an earlier stage of development. He termed this behavior **regression.** For example, like a young child, an adolescent may pout and refuse to speak to her parents when forbidden to go out with friends. Similarly, an adult may become highly dependent on his parents following the breakup of his own marriage. Regressive behavior is usually temporary. It only becomes a problem when it is used frequently to avoid adult behavior.

Projection A motion picture projector thrusts an image outward onto a screen. Freud believed that people sometimes deal with unacceptable impulses by projecting these impulses outward onto other people. In other words, people see *their own* faults in other people. For example, hostile people, unable to think of *themselves* as hostile, may accuse other people of hostility. As a result of this **projection,** they may think of the world as a dangerous place.

Effects of Defense Mechanisms According to Freud, when used in moderation, defense mechanisms may be normal and even useful to protect people from painful feelings such as anxiety, guilt, and shame. Such defense mechanisms become unhealthy, he said, when they lead a person to ignore the underlying issues causing those feelings. However, Freud also noted that a person with a strong and healthy ego is able to balance the id and the superego without the use of such mechanisms. Therefore, the use of defense mechanisms may indicate the presence of inner conflict or personal anxiety.

Reading Check **Summarize** What are some common defense mechanisms?

Stages of Personality Development

Freud believed that an individual's personality develops through a series of five stages. These stages of development begin at birth and continue to shape human personality through adolescence. Freud claimed that people instinctively seek to preserve and extend life. He also thought that these instinctive efforts to survive are aided by a psychological energy he labeled libido. (*Libido* is the Latin word for "desire.") This theory is one of the most controversial personality theories.

Freud organized psychological development into five periods: oral, anal, phallic, latent, and genital. Children were said to encounter conflicts during each stage. If the conflicts were not resolved, Freud believed that the child might become fixated, or stuck, at an early stage of development. The child would then carry that stage's traits into adulthood. Thus, Freud believed that an adult's psychological problems might actually stem from unresolved childhood conflicts.

More Defense Mechanisms

Freud's daughter, Anna Freud, worked to explain defense mechanisms in depth, including the ones listed below.

Displacement Displacement is defined as the transfer of an idea or impulse from a threatening or unsuitable object to a less threatening object. For example, a football player who is yelled at by his coach may go home and yell at his little brother.

Reaction Formation People who use the defense of reaction formation act contrary to their genuine feelings in order to keep their true feelings hidden. For example, someone who is unconsciously attracted to another person may keep the impulses out of mind by being mean to that person.

Denial In the mechanism of denial, a person refuses to accept the reality of anything that is bad or upsetting. For example, people who smoke cigarettes may ignore the risks of lung cancer and heart disease from smoking because they think, "It can't happen to me."

Sublimation Individuals can channel their basic impulses into socially acceptable behavior through sublimation. For example, a hostile student may channel aggressive impulses into contact sports.

Skills Focus **INTERPRETING CHARTS** Which defense mechanisms might be healthy?

The Oral Stage In Freud's theory, psychological development begins in the first year of life. He noted that infants are continually exploring their world by picking up objects and putting those objects into their mouths. Infants also receive their main source of pleasure— food—with their mouths. For these reasons, Freud termed the first stage of development the oral stage. He theorized that the infant's survival is dependent on the attention of adults. A child whose caretakers do not meet his or her needs during this stage may become fixated at the oral stage. Some examples of this fixation might include smoking, overeating, excessive talking, and nail biting. In addition, as an adult, such a person might have clinging interpersonal relationships.

The Anal Stage During this stage, according to Freud, children between the ages of one and a half to two and a half learn that they can control their bodily functions, and the issue of self-control becomes vital. Conflict during the anal stage can lead to two sets of adult personality traits. So-called anal-retentive traits involve an excessive use of self-control, resulting in excessive needs for order and cleanliness. People with anal-expulsive traits, on the other hand, may be careless and messy.

The Phallic Stage The third year of life marks the beginning of the phallic stage. Young girls and boys begin to discover the physical differences between the two sexes and become more focused on their own bodies. Children may also develop strong attachments to the parent of the opposite sex. At the same time, they may view the same-sex parent as a rival for the other parent's affections. Freud argued that the complex emotions of the phallic stage can lead to several psychological disorders later in life, including depression and anxiety.

The Latency Stage By age five or six, Freud believed, children have been in conflict with their parents for many years. In response, children retreat from the conflict and repress all aggressive urges. This marks their entry into the latency stage. *Latent* means "hidden," and during the latency period, impulses and emotions remain hidden, or unconscious.

The Genital Stage Freud wrote that people enter the final stage of psychological development, the genital stage, at puberty. The adolescent does not generally encounter any new psychological conflicts during this period and does become more aware of his or her own gender identity. However, the conflicts of the early development stages resurface.

Reading Check **Sequence** At what age do each of the stages of development occur?

Other Important Theorists

Other important psychoanalysts contributed their own theories about personality development. Some of these theorists followed Freud; others made their own mark on the study of personality.

Carl Jung Sigmund Freud had several intellectual heirs. The best known of these theorists is Carl Jung (1875–1961). Jung was a Swiss psychiatrist who had been a colleague of Freud's. He fell into disfavor with Freud, however, when he developed his own psychoanalytic theory—known as *analytic psychology*—which places a greater emphasis on the influences of shared symbols and religion on human behavior.

Jung, like Freud, was intrigued by unconscious processes. But he dramatically altered Freud's theory of these processes. In addition to an individual unconscious that stores

Jung's Four Main Archetypes

Jung wrote extensively about four archetypes that he thought functioned as separate systems within an individual's personality.

Self the center of the human psyche and personality; unifies consciousness and unconsciousness; total unity; God; often symbolized by a circular image called a *mandala*, like the image at right

Shadow the darker side of human nature; embodies chaos and uncontrollable or unacceptable emotions; often represented by devil figures or mysterious enemies

Anima/Animus Anima: feminine qualities within a man's personality; Animus: masculine qualities within a woman's personality

Persona the public self; the image or character that a person wants to show to the outside world

Interactive Feature thinkcentral.com

material that has been forgotten or repressed, Jung argued that all people also possessed an inherited collective unconscious. According to Jung, the **collective unconscious** is a store of human concepts shared by all people across all cultures.

The structural components of the collective unconscious are basic, primitive concepts called archetypes. **Archetypes** are ideas and images of the accumulated experience of all human beings. Examples of archetypes include the supreme being, the young hero, the fertile and nurturing mother, the wise old man, the hostile brother, and even fairy godmothers, wicked witches, and themes of rebirth or resurrection. Jung found that each of these concepts appears in some form across most cultures and religions.

Jung argued that although these images remain unconscious, they often appear to us as figures in our dreams. He declared that these images influence our thoughts and feelings and that they help form a foundation on which personality develops. Despite his interest in the collective unconscious, Jung granted more importance to conscious thoughts than Freud did.

Jung believed that one archetype is the sense of self. According to Jung, the self is a unifying force of personality that gives people direction and provides them with a sense of their own completeness. Jung believed that every person's conscious sense of self can be characterized by four functions of the mind—thinking, feeling, intuition, and sensation. He argued that all four of these elements exist in every individual's unconscious. However, an individual can be identified by the function that becomes his or her primary form of expression. He thought that people could form healthy personalities by bringing together, or integrating, these conscious elements with the collective unconscious archetypes. His name for this integrating process is *individuation*.

Many psychologists consider Jung's theory of the collective unconscious to be mystical and unscientific. But Jungian theory has developed a tremendous following among the general public. Many people enter Jungian analysis to examine their dreams and to work toward individuation. Scholars explore the use of archetypal symbols as they appear in literature and the arts. In addition, Jung's focus on myth has made his theory of the collective unconscious very popular with those who study religion.

Reading Check **Find the Main Idea** What is Jung's theory of the collective unconscious?

Alfred Adler Alfred Adler (1870–1937) was one of the followers of Freudian psychoanalysis theory. Adler believed that people are basically motivated by a need to overcome feelings of inferiority. To describe these feelings of inadequacy and insecurity, Adler coined the term **inferiority complex.**

In some people, Adler theorized, feelings of inferiority may be based on physical problems and the need to compensate for them. This theory may have developed in part from Adler's own attempts to overcome repeated bouts of illness. As a child, Adler's legs were deformed by a disease called rickets and he nearly died from pneumonia.

Physical problems are not the only source of feelings of inferiority, according to Adler. He believed that all of us have some feelings of inferiority because of our small size as children. He thought that these feelings give rise to a drive for superiority. Adler also introduced the term *sibling rivalry* to describe the jealousies among brothers and sisters.

Adler, like Jung, believed that self-awareness plays a major role in the formation of personality. Adler's spoke of a creative self that is capable of free will and self-determination. The creative self is strives to overcome physical and environmental obstacle. For example, president Theodore Roosevelt exemplified Adler's belief in the individual's potential for self-creation. As a child, Roosevelt was frail and asthmatic. Through physical training, he overcame these challenges to become a strong and robust adult, and president of the United States.

Karen Horney In agreement with Freud, Karen Horney (1885–1952) believed that childhood experiences play a major role in the development of adult personality. She believed that the greatest influences on personality are social relationships—and the parent-child relationship.

Horney, like Freud, saw parent-child relationships to be of paramount importance. Small children are completely dependent.

Erik Erikson believed that social relationships are the most important factors in personality development. Here are the eight stages of Erikson's theory.

Stage 1:	Stage 2:	Stage 3:	Stage 4:
Trust versus Mistrust	**Autonomy versus Shame and Doubt**	**Initiative versus Guilt**	**Industry versus Inferiority**
Infancy (Age 0–1)	**Early childhood** (Age 2–3)	**Preschool years** (Age 4–5)	**Grammar school** (Age 6–12)
Coming to trust the mother and the environment—to associate surroundings with feelings of inner goodness	Developing the desire to make choices and the self-control to exercise choice	Adding planning and "attacking" to choice; becoming active and on the move	Becoming eagerly absorbed in skills, tasks, and productivity; mastering the fundamentals of technology

When their parents treat them with indifference or harshness, children develop feelings of insecurity that Horney termed *basic anxiety*. Because children also resent neglectful parents, Horney theorized that feelings of hostility would accompany the anxiety. She agreed with Freud that children would repress rather than express feelings of hostility because they would fear driving their parents away. In contrast to Freud, however, she also believed that genuine and consistent love could temper the effects of even the most painful childhoods.

Erik Erikson Like Horney, Erik Erikson (1902–1994) thought that social relationships are the most important factors in personality development. He placed great emphasis on the general emotional climate of the mother-infant relationship. Erikson also granted more powers to the ego than Freud had allowed. According to Freud's theory, people may think that they are making choices, but they may only be rationalizing the compromises forced upon them by inner conflict. According to Erikson's theory, on the other hand, people are entirely capable of consciously making real and meaningful choices.

Erikson, like Freud, devised a developmental theory of personality. Erikson, however, expanded on Freud's five stages of development and formulated a psychosocial theory of development consisting of eight stages. Whereas Freud's developmental stages end with adolescence, Erikson's theory is based on the idea that personality development is a lifelong process.

Erikson named his stages after the traits people might develop during each of them. For example, the first stage of psychosocial development is "trust versus mistrust." A warm, loving relationship with the mother (and others) during infancy may lead to a sense of basic trust in people and in the world. On the other hand, a cold, unfulfilling relationship might create a sense of mistrust that could damage other relationships if left unresolved. Erikson believed that most people maintain a blend of trust and mistrust.

Reading Check **Compare** How are the views on childhood of Adler, Horney, and Erikson similar?

Evaluation of the Psychoanalytic Approach

Although psychoanalytic concepts such as libido and id strike many psychologists as unscientific today, Freud was an important champion of the idea that human personality and behavior are subject to scientific analysis. In Freud's day, serious psychological problems were still seen as signs of weakness or so-called craziness. Freud's thinking contributed greatly to the development of compassion for people with psychological disorders.

Psychoanalytic theory also focused the attention of scientists and therapists on the far-reaching effects of childhood events. Freud and Erikson suggested that early childhood traumas can affect us throughout our lives. As a result, psychoanalytic theorists have heightened society's awareness of the emotional needs of children.

Stage 5: **Identity versus Role Diffusion** **Adolescence** (Age 13–18) Connecting skills and social roles to formation of personal and career objectives	Stage 6: **Intimacy versus Isolation** **Young adulthood** (Age 19–30) Committing oneself to another person; engaging in sexual love	Stage 7: **Generativity versus Stagnation** **Middle adulthood** Needing to be needed; guiding and encouraging the younger generation; being creative	Stage 8: **Integrity versus Despair** **Late adulthood** Accepting the end of one's own life cycle; achieving wisdom and dignity

Freud also helped us recognize that sexual and aggressive urges are common. He pointed out that there is a difference between recognizing these urges and acting on them. He realized that our thinking may be distorted by our efforts to avoid anxiety and guilt. To help people understand their motives, he devised an influential method of psychotherapy.

Psychoanalytic theories—particularly the views of Freud—have, however, been criticized on many counts. Even followers of Freud argued that he placed too much emphasis on unconscious motives and neglected the importance of social relationships. Opponents of Freud's theories also assert that most people consciously seek self-enhancement and intellectual pleasures and do not merely try to gratify the dark demands of the id.

Critics have also questioned Freud's methods for gathering evidence from clinical sessions. Using this method, therapists may subtly influence clients to say what the therapists expect to hear. Freud himself may have projected his own childhood experiences and feelings onto his clients. Also, Freud and many other psychoanalytic theorists gathered their evidence only from case studies of white, middle-class individuals who sought help for their psychological problems. Moreover, because people who seek therapy are likely to have more problems than the general population, Freud's clients may not have been the most representative sample from which to gather information.

Reading Check **Analyze** What important contributions has Freud made to psychology?

SECTION 2 Assessment

Online Quiz THINKcentral thinkcentral.com

Reviewing Main Ideas and Vocabulary

1. **Recall** What did Freud believe dreams could reveal?

2. **Analyze** What are the relationships between the id, ego, and superego?

3. **Infer** According to Freud, at what stage might people recognize a sexual preference?

Thinking Critically

4. **Draw Conclusions** Which defense mechanism might people use to justify stealing office supplies from an employer?

5. **Evaluate** According to Jung, why do certain archetypes appear in people's dreams?

6. **Support a Position** What is your opinion of Freud's theory about the stages of personality development? Explain whether you think his theory is valid.

7. **Compare and Contrast** Using your notes and a graphic organizer like the one opposite, choose two psychoanalysts discussed in this section and compare and contrast their theories.

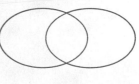

FOCUS ON WRITING

8. **Narrative** Write a brief dialogue between either a Freudian or a Jungian psychoanalyst and a client describing a dream.

Password to Personality

Nowadays, just about every computer-user creates passwords to guard personal secrets large and small. Most people pick their passwords in a split second. Others think long and hard to come up with what they think is an unbreakable code. Regardless of how you devise your own secret login, chances are it will be easier to crack than you think.

Recently, psychologists have confirmed something that computer hackers have known for a long time: most people create passwords that reflect their personal lives and interests. A recent psychological study suggests that passwords are like modern-day personality tests, revealing clues about a computer user's personality, as well as providing entry into his or her electronic world.

Under the direction of psychologist Helen Petrie, now professor of human-computer interaction at the University of York, the study surveyed 1,200 workers from 30 companies in the United Kingdom. The study found that passwords are unintentionally revealing because people tend to choose the first things that come into their minds. In this way, passwords tap into the unconscious, revealing ideas, things, and feelings that exist just below consciousness.

Moreover, when it came to picking passwords, the survey results revealed four distinct categories of computer users. About 48 percent of users fell into the family category. For passwords, these computer-users tended to choose a name, nickname, or birth date belonging to themselves or to someone special to them, such as a child, spouse, or pet. The study also found that people in the family category were occasional computer users with strong family ties.

Some 32 percent of the study's respondents fit into the fan category. "Fans" used the names of athletes, sports teams, movie stars, singers and fictional characters for passwords. According to Petrie, fans are typically young and want to identify with a brand or a celebrity lifestyle. Top choices for passwords in this category included singer Madonna, cartoon character Homer Simpson, actor George Clooney, and soccer player David Beckham.

Another 11 percent of respondents fit into a category that Petrie defined as "fantasists." These computer-users often picked passwords that expressed an interest in sex or a fantasy identity, such as "goddess," that the user was unlikely to ever live out. According to the study's results the majority of fantasists were men. However, 37 percent of fantasists identified themselves as women.

The most security conscious and computer literate respondents fit into the study's smallest category—the cryptics. Often identified as "geeks," the cryptics created obscure passwords by mixing letters, numbers, symbols, and punctuation to come up with passwords such as "PA*591!" Although uninteresting, these carefully selected passwords tend to be the safest choices.

If computer passwords are indeed a window into personality, one thing may hold true: people may be generally easier to read than they think. This should make computer hackers happy for a long time.

Psychologists have found that computer passwords reveal personality traits.

Thinking Critically

1. **Summarize** What personality characteristics characterize each of the four main types of password users?

2. **Discuss** How do you select your computer passwords? What do they reveal about your personality?

The Learning Approach

Before You Read

Main Idea
The learning approach has two branches: behaviorism and social-learning theory. Behaviorists believe that our actions are learned. Social-learning theorists think that we learn by observation.

Reading Focus
1. What are some of the beliefs behind behaviorism?
2. How do social-learning theorists approach learning?
3. Why are some psychologists dissatisfied with the learning approach?

Vocabulary
socialization
social cognitive theory

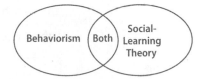

TAKING NOTES Use a graphic organizer like this one to compare behaviorism and social-learning theory.

Behaviorism — Both — Social-Learning Theory

 Personality Makeover

PSYCHOLOGY CLOSE UP

Who do you want to become? Are you shy and reserved? Would you like to be outgoing and the life of the party? Such a transformation might just be possible. Some personality psychologists claim that character traits can be learned. Apparently, your personality isn't set in stone.

Researchers studied the personality traits that most people admire, such as integrity, loyalty, kindness, and vitality, and the people who possess them. It turns out that the traits didn't necessarily come to these people naturally—they were behavioral habits that had to be learned. Of course, transforming your personality isn't easy, and it doesn't happen overnight. Psychologists compare the process to that of a chronically overweight person trying to shed the pounds. Changing one's personality isn't impossible, but it often forces people to step outside of their comfort zones.

With practice, though, the new personality can come to feel natural. Studies have shown that people who behave like extroverts are treated like extroverts. Positive reinforcement and experiences encourage the transition. Over time, the behavior becomes spontaneous. Eventually, it doesn't really matter whether you are actually shy by nature. You have learned to reshape your personality. ■

CASE STUDY
CONNECTION

You Are What
Makes You Laugh
A recent study
suggests that people
learn different
humor styles that
often reveal aspects
of their personality

ACADEMIC
VOCABULARY
utopian ideal

Behaviorism

The learning approach emphasizes the effects of experience on behavior. Some of the theorists who take this approach might assume that your sense of humor—to use an example—is largely a learned behavior. They might explain that you make jokes because you have learned that you will somehow be rewarded or positively reinforced for such behavior. Your family's laughter and obvious amusement would be examples of such positive reinforcement. The psychological approach that offers such an explanation is called behaviorism, and is a branch of the learning approach.

John Watson and B. F. Skinner The founder of behaviorism is John B. Watson. He claimed that external forces or influences—not internal influences such as traits or inner conflict—largely shape people's preferences and behavior. In the 1930s, Watson's approach was taken up by B. F. Skinner. Skinner agreed that we should pay attention to how organisms behave and avoid trying to see within people's minds, which he believed was unscientific. Skinner also emphasized the effects of reinforcement on behavior.

Socialization Most of us assume that our wants originate within us. But Watson and Skinner largely discarded ideas of personal freedom, choice, and self-direction. Skinner suggested that environmental influences, such as parental approval and social custom, condition or shape us into wanting some things and not wanting others. **Socialization** is the process by which people learn the socially desirable behaviors of their particular culture and adopt them as part of their personalities.

In his 1948 novel, *Walden Two*, Skinner described a utopian society in which people are happy and content because every member of the society contributes to and receives the benefits of the society. They have been socialized from early childhood to help other people and society at large. Because of childhood socialization, people in the fictional community want to be decent, kind, and unselfish. They see their actions as a result of their own free will. According to Skinner, however, no one is really free. In his view, we are shaped into wanting what is good for society at an early age.

Reading Check **Summarize** According to behaviorists, how do people learn acceptable behavior?

Have External Forces Influenced Your Personality?

Quick Lab

You may think that who you are and what you want is all your idea. But is it? In this lab, you will answer a series of questions that will help you consider whether outside forces may have influenced your behavior.

PROCEDURE

❶ Read the following questions and write your answers to them on a separate piece of paper.

   a. What do you want to do with your life?

   b. Has anyone you know well pursued a similar path?

   c. Has anyone you know well expressed approval of your choice?

❷ As you write your answers, try to recall exactly how your family and friends have reacted to your future plans. Be as objective as possible.

ANALYSIS

1. After you have answered the questions, discuss your responses with a partner.

2. Consider whether your plans are a natural outcome of your personality, talents, and preferences. Are your future plans a good fit for you?

3. If someone you know has followed a similar path, reflect on your relationship with this person. Do you admire this person? Have you ever imitated his or her behavior?

4. Think about the people in your life who approve of your future plans. Do you crave approval and positive reinforcement from them?

5. Has your environment influenced your future plans?

Quick Lab THINK central thinkcentral.com

Social-Learning Theory

Social-learning theory is another branch of the learning approach. Psychologists who support this theory might suggest that you learned how to be funny by observing how other people use humor. Proponents of social-learning theory include psychologist Albert Bandura. Social learning theorists, like Bandura, focus on the importance of learning by observation, and on the role of the cognitive processes that produce individual differences.

Albert Bandura For Albert Bandura, "learning would be exceedingly laborious, not to mention hazardous, if people had to rely solely on the effects of their own actions to inform them what to do." Bandura argued that practically any behavior that could be learned from direct experience, could also be learned by observing and modeling other people.

Bandura tested his theory in a famous experiment known as the "Bobo Doll" study. A bobo doll is an inflatable toy that stands upright on a rounded base and bounces back up when it is pushed. In his study, Bandura wanted to see whether people learn aggressive behavior from modeling. He had children, aged three to six, enter a playroom one by one with an adult. Half of the children witnessed the adult violently hit a bobo doll; the other half did not. Once left alone in playroom with a bobo doll, the children who had witnessed the aggressive behavior were far more likely to act violently toward the bobo doll than those who had not witnessed violent behavior.

In a later, related study, Bandura found that children who witnessed an adult being punished for aggressive behavior were less likely to copy the adult's behavior. The studies suggest that children learn what society deems acceptable behavior by watching and modeling others.

Social Cognitive Theory Bandura's findings formed the basis of his **social cognitive theory.** According to this theory, personality is shaped and learning is acquired by the interaction of the following:

- **personal factors,** which include one's thoughts, beliefs, values, expectations, emotional disposition, and biological and genetic makeup;
- **behavior,** or one's actions and experience;

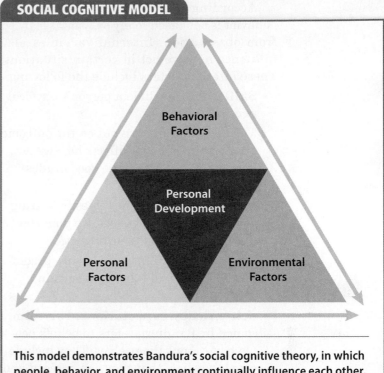

SOCIAL COGNITIVE MODEL

Behavioral Factors

Personal Development

Personal Factors

Environmental Factors

This model demonstrates Bandura's social cognitive theory, in which people, behavior, and environment continually influence each other.

Skills Focus INTERPRETING VISUALS What does the model suggest about how personality develops?

- **environmental factors,** which include the social, cultural, and political forces that influence behavior.

The theory presents a way to understand and predict human behavior. It states that a person's environment provides models for behavior. In other words, we watch another's behavior—and the reinforcements he or she receives as a result—and model our own behavior on what we have observed. Social-learning theorists refer to this process as purposeful learning.

Purposeful Learning To behaviorists, learning is the mechanical result of reinforcement. To social-learning theorists, on the other hand, people engage in purposeful learning. Unlike behaviorists, who believe that people are at the mercy of their environments, social-learning theorists argue that people can act intentionally to influence the environment. Individuals seek to learn about their environments and have a certain degree of control over reinforcement. Observational learning extends to reading about others or watching them in media such as television and film.

According to social-learning theorists, behavior is not based solely on what is learned from observation. Internal variables also influence how we act in certain situations. These internal factors include the following:

- **Skills:** Skills include a person's physical and social abilities.
- **Values:** The value we put on the outcome of a certain behavior affects how we act. For example, if you value good grades, you will study.
- **Goals:** We regulate ourselves by setting goals. Once the goal is set, we plan the most effective way to achieve it.
- **Expectations:** Expectations are predictions of what will happen in certain situations.
- **Self-efficacy expectations:** This term, coined by Bandura, refers to beliefs people have about themselves. They include people's beliefs that they can succeed and accomplish the goals that they set for themselves. For example, if you believe that you are a good public speaker, you will be motivated to speak before the class assembly. People with high self-efficacy expectations are also more likely to persist at difficult tasks.

Reading Check **Identify Supporting Details** What is social cognitive theory?

Evaluation of the Learning Approach

What are the strengths and weaknesses of learning theories? Learning theorists have made key contributions to the understanding of behavior, but their theories have left some psychologists dissatisfied. Psychoanalytic theorists and trait theorists focus on internal variables such as unconscious conflict and traits to explain behavior. Learning theorists emphasize the influence of environmental conditions on behavior. They have shown that people learn to do things because of reinforcement.

Behaviorism is limited in its ability to explain personality. Behaviorism does not describe, explain, or even suggest the richness of inner human experience. Behaviorism does not deal with thoughts, feelings, and people's complex inner maps of the world.

Social-learning theory does deal with these issues. But critics of social-learning theory argue that it has not come up with satisfying explanations for the development of traits or accounted for self-awareness. Also, social-learning theory—like behaviorism—may not pay enough attention to the role genetic variation plays in determining individual differences in behavior.

Reading Check **Contrast** In what way do learning theorists disagree with psychoanalytic theorists?

Online Quiz **THINK** central thinkcentral.com

SECTION 3 Assessment

Reviewing Main Ideas and Vocabulary

1. **Define** What is socialization?

2. **Identify Cause and Effect** According to behaviorists, what happens as a result of positive reinforcement?

3. **Infer** According to social-learning theorists, how might children's behavior be affected by domestic violence?

Thinking Critically

4. **Draw Conclusions** Many students strive to get good grades. How would social-learning theorists explain this behavior? How would behaviorists explain it?

5. **Evaluate** How would social-learning theorists claim that having an optimistic personality might influence behavior?

6. **Support a Position** Do you agree with the behaviorist view that true personal freedom does not exist? Why or why not?

7. **Analyze** Using your notes and a graphic organizer like the one at right, determine what social-learning theorists learned from Bandura's bobo doll study.

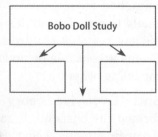

FOCUS ON WRITING

8. **Expository** Write a brief report in which you evaluate the learning approach for yourself. Discuss whether you think personality can be learned or observed.

The Humanistic and Sociocultural Approaches

Before You Read

Main Idea
Humanistic psychologists believe that people shape their personalities through free choice and action. Sociocultural psychologists focus on the roles of ethnicity, gender, and culture in personality formation.

Reading Focus
1. What is the focus of humanistic psychology?
2. Who is Carl Rogers?
3. How do psychologists evaluate the humanistic approach?
4. What is sociocultural psychology?
5. How does the sociocultural approach view personality development?

Vocabulary
self-concept
congruence
acculturation

TAKING NOTES Use a graphic organizer like this one to take notes on the characteristics of humanistic and sociocultural psychology.

Humanistic	Sociocultural

PSYCHOLOGY CLOSE UP

How do you want to be rewarded for a great performance? If you work hard to do your very best, would you rather receive flowers and applause from an audience or get a big paycheck? When you go to a rock concert, do the band members really care that you holler and clap when they begin your favorite song? Or are they just in it for the money? To our brains, the two types of rewards are actually similar.

Japanese researchers wanted to know the answers to the questions above. They asked what happens in the brain when someone is offered either cash or a compliment as compensation for a job well done. Test subjects played a gambling game, answered a personality questionnaire, or made a video. When these efforts were reviewed favorably by others and cash or compliments were offered in return, the researchers used functional magnetic resonance imaging (fMRI) to observe the activity in a reward-related area of the brain. Both types of reward caused activity in the reward area of the brain. The scientists concluded that the pleasure we receive from compliments means that we really do care what other people think of us.

Clearly, we get a psychological boost from having a good reputation, and we have a powerful need to belong. Issues related to how we see ourselves as individuals and as members of a group are of interest to psychologists who take humanistic and sociocultural approaches to personality. ■

You Deserve a **Reward**

Humanistic Psychology

Behaviorists argue that psychologists should not attempt to study self-awareness. Humanists, on the other hand, begin with the assumption that self-awareness is the very core of humanity. They focus on people's pursuits of self-fulfillment and ethical conduct. To humanistic psychologists, people are truly free to do as they choose with their lives. Moreover, because people are free to choose, they are fully responsible for the choices that they make.

Abraham Maslow Humanistic psychologist Abraham Maslow (1908–1970) believed that humans are separated from lower animals because they recognize a desire to achieve self-actualization—to reach their full potential. He also believed that because people are unique, they must follow their own paths to self-actualization. However, accomplishing this requires taking risks. Maslow argued that people who stick to what is tried and true may find their lives boring and predictable. For example, a gifted young musician may be very close to her friends, but she may also realize that she possesses a unique musical ability and so accepts a scholarship to a distant music college. According to Maslow's theory, her willingness to pursue her talent and her courage to leave her friends behind and go away to college are factors in her search for self-actualization.

Hierarchy of Needs Before self-actualization can be achieved, however, Maslow recognized that certain basic needs must first be met. He developed this concept by creating what he called a "hierarchy of needs." Maslow claimed that each need in the hierarchy had to be fulfilled before the next one could be addressed.

Below are the five levels of Maslow's hierarchy of needs, beginning with the first, most basic level.

- **Physiological needs:** water, air, food, and sleep. Maslow asserted that all other needs were secondary to these very basic and instinctive needs.
- **Security needs:** safety and security. These needs include shelter, employment, health insurance, and safe environments.
- **Social needs:** love, belonging, and acceptance. These include the needs for family, friends, and romantic attachments.
- **Esteem needs:** self-esteem, respect, social recognition, and accomplishment. These include the need for a career or hobby that provides an individual with a sense of self-worth.
- **Self-actualization needs:** self-awareness and personal growth. These include the need to achieve one's full potential.

According to Maslow, once the first three sets of needs have been met, esteem and self-actualization needs become increasingly important. However, Maslow stressed that the hierarchy is not rigid. People progress through the hierarchy sequentially, but not necessarily in the same way. For example, one person may feel a stronger need for social recognition than for romantic attachments. The hierarchy, like the humanistic psychologist who designed it, allows for an individual's freedom of choice in the quest for self-actualization.

Reading Check **Identify Supporting Details** What is self-actualization?

Carl Rogers

Carl Rogers (1902–1987), another advocate of the humanistic approach, believed that people are basically good and mentally healthy. Furthermore, he claimed that all people have within them the drive to grow and develop their potential. Building on Maslow's hierarchy, Rogers thought that we seek to fulfill all of our basic and personal growth needs because it is simply in our nature to do so.

Like Maslow, Rogers believed that people are to some degree the conscious architects of their own personalities. In Rogers's view, people shape their personalities through free choice and action. Because Rogers's theory revolves around people's sense of self, it is termed *self theory*.

Rogers placed great emphasis on the human ability to derive a **self-concept,** a view of oneself as an individual. He also believed that the self is concerned with recognizing personal values and establishing a sense of one's relationships to other people. The self is the center of each person's experience, an ongoing sense of who and what one is. It provides the experience of being human in the world, and it is the guiding principle behind both personality and behavior.

The Self-Concept and Congruence Our self-concepts are made up of our impressions of ourselves and our evaluations of our adequacy. Rogers believed that the key to happiness and healthy adjustment is **congruence,** or consistency between one's self-concept and one's experience. For example, if you consider yourself to be outgoing and friendly, this self-concept will be reinforced if you have good relationships with other people. This will probably lead to feelings of happiness and a sense that your self-concept is accurate. If, however, you have difficulty getting along with others, the inconsistency between your self-concept and your experience will probably cause you to feel anxious or troubled.

Self-Esteem and Positive Regard Rogers assumed that we all develop a need for self-esteem. At first, self-esteem reflects the esteem in which others hold us. For example, parents help children develop self-esteem when they show them unconditional positive regard. Parents show unconditional positive regard when they accept children as they are, no matter what the children's behavior is at any particular moment.

Parents show children conditional positive regard if they accept children only when they behave in a desired manner. Conditional positive regard may lead children to think that they are worthwhile only if they behave in certain ways.

Humanistic psychologists believe that each of us has a unique potential. Therefore, children who think that they are worthwhile only if they behave in certain ways will end up being disappointed in themselves. Humanistic psychologists believe that we cannot fully live up to the wishes of others and also remain true to ourselves.

The expression of the self does not always have to lead to conflict. Rogers was optimistic about human nature. He believed that we hurt others or act in antisocial ways only when we are frustrated in our efforts to develop our potential. When parents and others are loving and tolerant of the ways in which we are different, we, too, are loving.

However, Rogers believed that children in some families learn that it is bad to have ideas of their own, especially about political, religious, or sexual matters. When children

The Psychology of *The Sims*

Millions of people play *The Sims,* the popular computer game developed in the late 1990s. But did you know that the game's creator, Will Wright, based the Sims on humanistic psychology? Wright's game designers, like the one above, program the Sims characters to engage in activities—work, play, and romance—that help them fulfill themselves according to Maslow's hierarchy of needs. For example, Sims characters cannot enjoy a movie if they are hungry. In fact, the designers have created characters so true to life that many Sims fans create virtual versions of their own lives. *How might you help a Sim achieve self-actualization?*

perceive their parents' disapproval, they may come to see themselves as rebels and label their feelings as selfish, wrong, or evil. If they wish to retain a consistent self-concept and self-esteem, they may have to deny many of their genuine feelings. They may, in a sense, have to disown parts of themselves.

According to Rogers's theory, the path to self-actualization requires getting in touch with our genuine feelings and acting on them. This is the goal of person-centered therapy, Rogers's method of psychotherapy.

Reading Check **Identify Cause and Effect** What might happen as a result of a parent's conditional positive regard?

Evaluation of the Humanistic Approach

For most animals, to be alive is to move, to eat, to breathe, and to reproduce. However, humanistic psychologists think that humans are not merely animals. They believe that for human beings an essential aspect of life is conscious experience—the sense of one's self as progressing through space and time. Humanists grant consciousness a key role in our daily lives. This focus on conscious experience is one reason that humanistic theories have tremendous popular appeal.

Another reason for their popularity is that they stress human freedom. Psychoanalytic theories see us largely as products of our childhoods. Learning theories, to some degree, see us as products of circumstances. Both theories argue that our sense of freedom is merely an illusion. Humanistic theorists, however, say that our freedom is real.

The primary strength of the humanistic theories—their focus on conscious experience—is also their main weakness. Conscious experience is private and subjective. Therefore, some psychologists question the soundness of framing theories in terms of consciousness. Others, however, believe that the science of psychology can afford to relax its methods if loosening them will help it address the richness of human experience.

Critics also note that humanistic theories, like learning theories, have little to say about the development of traits and personality types. Humanistic theorists assume that we are all unique, but they do not predict the sorts of traits, abilities, and interests that people might develop.

ACADEMIC VOCABULARY
subjective not objective, personal

Reading Check **Summarize** Why are humanistic theories popular?

Sociocultural Psychology

The sociocultural perspective focuses on the roles that ethnicity, gender, socioeconomic status, and culture play in shaping personality, behavior, and mental processes. Many children in the United States are raised by parents who have grown up in another country. Nonetheless, these children are comfortable in American schools with their American friends. Sociocultural theorists would claim that both family and environmental influences are key factors in the development of the children's personalities.

Individualism versus Collectivism One aspect of culture that sociocultural theorists focus on is the level of individualism or collectivism in a society. Individualism is a trait valued by many people in the United States and in many European nations. Individualists tend to define themselves in terms of their personal identities. They usually give priority to their personal goals. When asked to complete the statement "I am . . . ," they are likely to respond in terms of their own personality traits or occupations. For example, they are likely to say, "I am friendly and outgoing" or "I am a computer programmer."

In contrast, many people from Africa, Asia, and Central and South America tend to be more collectivistic. Collectivists tend to define themselves in terms of the groups to which they belong and often give priority to the goals of their groups. They feel complete only in terms of their social relationships with others. When asked to complete the statement "I am . . . ," they are likely to respond in terms of their families, religion, or nation. For example, they are likely to say, "I am a father," "I am a Buddhist," or "I am Japanese."

The Western capitalist system fosters individualism. It assumes that individuals are entitled to amass personal fortunes if they have the drive and ability to do so. The individualist perspective is found in the self-reliant heroes of Western entertainment—from the gritty cowboy featured in scores of movies to such comic book superheroes as Batman. The traditional writings of many non-Western cultures, on the other hand, have praised people who put the well-being of the group ahead of their personal ambitions.

There are, of course, conflicting ideals—as well as individual differences—within cultures. In the United States, for example, children may be taught to be "Number One," but they are also taught to share with other children. But, on the whole, the contrast between the individualist Western world and the more collectivist nations of other parts of the world is a generally reliable measure of some personality differences between individuals from these regions.

Sociocultural Factors and the Self According to sociocultural theorists, social and cultural factors also affect the self-concept and self-esteem of the individual. Carl Rogers noted that our self-concepts tend to reflect how we believe other people see us. Members of ethnic groups who have been subjected to discrimination and poverty may have poorer self-concepts and lower self-esteem than people who have not experienced discrimination and poverty. Similarly, members of ethnic groups that have traditionally held power in society are likely to have a positive sense of self because they share in the expectations of personal achievement and respect that are typically given to members of such groups.

In some cases, however, things are not so simple. Many women in the United States, particularly white women, are unhappy with their appearance. This is in part because the media ideal is found in female models who are on average 9 percent taller and 23 percent slimmer than the average American woman. But, a survey found that African American girls are likely to be happier with their appearances than are white girls.

How do sociocultural theorists explain this difference? It appears that African American girls are taught that there is nothing wrong with them if they do not match the ideals of the majority culture. They come to believe that if the world treats them negatively, it is because of prejudice, not because of who they really are or what they do. White girls, on the other hand, may be more likely to look inward and blame themselves for not attaining the unreachable ideal.

Acculturation and Self-Esteem Personalities are influenced by more than personal traits and learning experiences. They are also influenced by cultural settings. For example, Korean American children may absorb traditional Korean values from their family members. At school, however, they are exposed daily to values that are uniquely American.

Acculturation is the process of adapting to a new or different culture. People who immigrate to the United States undergo acculturation. If they come from Africa, Asia, or Latin America, they are likely to find that differences in language are only the tip of the iceberg of cultural differences.

Statistically Speaking...

Cultural Views on Body Image The bar graph below shows the percentage of girls who are happy with their appearance. The yellow bars reveal the percentages of white girls, African American girls, and Hispanic girls in elementary school who claimed that it is "always true" that they are happy the way they are. The orange bars show the percentages of white girls, African American girls, and Hispanic girls in high school who made the same assertion.

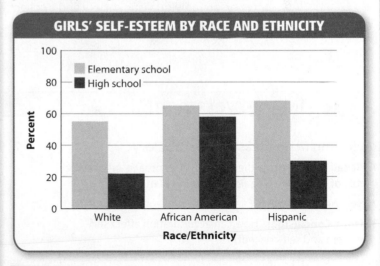

GIRLS' SELF-ESTEEM BY RACE AND ETHNICITY

Skills Focus **INTERPRETING GRAPHS** Based on the graph, how do girls' perceptions of their appearance change between elementary school and high school? Which cultural group indicates a greater acceptance of their appearance?

Source: *Shortchanging Girls, Shortchanging America.* Published by the American Association of University Women, 1994.

Acculturation occurs in various patterns. Some immigrants become completely assimilated, or absorbed, into the culture of the area to which they move. They may stop using both the language and customs of their country of origin. Others choose to maintain separation. They retain the language and customs of their country of origin and never become completely comfortable with those of their adopted country. Still others become bicultural. That is, they integrate both sets of customs and values.

Research suggests that people who are bicultural have the highest self-esteem. For example, Mexican Americans who are fluent in English are more likely to be emotionally stable than Mexican Americans who do not speak English as well. Adopting the ways of the new society without giving up a supportive cultural tradition and a sense of ethnic identity apparently helps people function most effectively. According to the sociocultural approach, for example, a Korean American woman who achieves musical and educational success and who has high self-esteem might reflect a balance between her traditional Korean heritage and her cultural surroundings in the United States.

Reading Check **Contrast** What are key differences between an individualistic society and a collectivistic one?

Evaluation of the Sociocultural Approach

The sociocultural perspective provides valuable insights into the roles of ethnicity, gender, culture, and socioeconomic status in personality formation. Sociocultural factors are external forces that are internalized and affect all of us. They run through us deeply, touching many aspects of our personalities. Without reference to sociocultural factors, we may be able to understand generalities about behavior and mental processes. We cannot, however, understand how individuals think, behave, and feel about themselves within a given cultural setting. The sociocultural perspective also enhances our sensitivity to cultural differences and allows us to appreciate much of the richness of human behavior.

The sociocultural approach has particular implications for education. It indicates that learning is not just a function of an individual's personality. Social and cultural contexts also have an impact on learning. As a result, some sociocultural psychologists believe that more attention should be paid to such learning tools as group activities, which may be heavily tied to social and cultural practices.

Reading Check **Make Generalizations** What implications might the sociocultural approach have for learning and education?

SECTION 4 Assessment

Online Quiz THINK central thinkcentral.com

Reviewing Main Ideas and Vocabulary

1. **Recall** According to the humanistic approach, what is the role of self and free choice in shaping human behavior?

2. **Summarize** What is Carl Rogers's concept of congruence?

3. **Draw Conclusions** How can acculturation affect self-esteem and self-concept?

Thinking Critically

4. **Contrast** How does humanistic psychology differ from psychoanalytic and learning approaches?

5. **Evaluate** What roles does self-esteem play in both humanistic and sociocultural psychology?

6. **Elaborate** Why might a person who abandons his or her culture of origin have lower self-esteem than a person who becomes bicultural?

7. **Rank** Using your notes and a graphic organizer like the one below, create your own hierarchy of needs. Place the five needs in the order that they are most important to you. Briefly explain what each need involves.

FOCUS ON WRITING

8. **Persuasive** Do you believe, like Carl Rogers, that each individual takes charge of his or her environment? State your opinion and defend it in a paragraph or two.

The Science of Well-Being

You might have come across the term "positive psychology" on TV, radio, or even in fashion magazines. But what is it really? What does it mean? In a nutshell, positive psychology is a science of the positive aspects of human life: happiness, well-being, and flourishing. Positive psychology is different from many self-help books, though. It aims to bring solid empirical research into areas such as personal strengths, wisdom, creativity, motivation, and the characteristics of positive groups and institutions.

For a long while it seems that the field of psychology has emphasized the shortcomings and struggles of individuals rather than their potentials (Seligman & Csikszentmihalyi, 2000). Positive psychology is different. In short, it is not concerned with how to move individuals from −8 to −2 for example, but with how to bring them from +2 to +8. In other words, its fundamental objective is to study what sort of life is worth living.

Despite being a young discipline, positive psychology has succeeded in making some groundbreaking discoveries. For example, researchers have found that happiness is partly innate and partly depends on us. All objective life circumstances combined account for not more than 10 percent of variance in well-being. The effects of being fired or promoted lose their impact on our happiness levels within three months. Winning the lottery often brings people misery and desiring money doesn't make one much happier either (Boniwell, 2006).

Even more fascinating is the possibility that well-being is tied to a long life. One study analyzed the application letters of young women entering convents at age of 18 for indicators of happiness. All of the young nuns had similar, moderate lifestyles. They didn't smoke or drink, had a balanced diet, and worked as teachers.

The study's results indicated that the happiness expressed by the applicants at age 18 could have been used to predict how long the nuns would live. Years later, when the nuns reached age 85, 90 percent of the nuns whose happiness was in the top 25 percent at the time of their application were still alive compared to 34 percent of those who were among the least happy. Even at the age of 94, over half of the happiest nuns were alive, while only 11 percent of those who were least happy were still alive. So the study suggests that happiness can buy us an extra 9.4 years of life (Danner, Snowdon and Friesen, 2001).

Recent research indicates that using simple well-being strategies can make people lastingly happy. For example, a randomized controlled trial carried out by Seligman and his colleagues demonstrated that spending some time in the evening thinking of three things that went well that day can increase one's happiness for up to six months (Seligman, 2005). That would seem to be a small investment of time for a big return of happiness!

According to positive psychologists, people can create their own happiness and well-being by thinking positive and healthful thoughts.

Thinking Critically

1. **Draw Conclusions** Why do you think happy people live longer?

2. **Discuss** With so much misery and suffering in the world, why should psychologists spend time and resources studying people who are already doing well?

Your Self: Applying Theories of Personality

Can theories of personality explain what makes you unique?

Reading and Activity Workbook

Use the workbook to complete this lab.

1. Introduction

This lab will help you review the different theories of personality presented in this chapter. First, you will review the key approaches and people discussed in this chapter. Then, you will be asked to select four of the approaches and apply them to your own personality. Working individually you will create a collage with four distinct regions. Each region will analyze your personality from the point of view of one of the four approaches you have selected. Then, each student will be asked to present his or her collage to the class. Finally, the entire class will evaluate each collage and try to determine which approaches are represented. To complete this lab, follow the steps below.

- Read all of the steps of the lab. Then select four of the approaches to personality discussed in this chapter to illustrate in your collage (See the chart on Key Approaches and People on the next page.)

- Review the chapter material on each of your four approaches. Write down a few main points about each approach, taking note of important ideas and people.

- Conduct additional library or Internet research if your teacher instructs you to do so.

- Gather the materials you will need to complete your lab: note cards, poster board, magazines, markers, scissors, and glue.

2. Profiling Your Personality

Who do you think you are? What features of your personality are well-known to your friends and family? Which of your personality traits are known only to a few people? All of us have distinct personality traits that distinguish us from others. Use a graphic organizer like the one below to brainstorm a list of personality traits that make you unique.

My Personality Profile	
I am . . .	I like to . . .
1.	1.
2.	2.
3.	3.

3. Creating Your Collage

Use your notes and your personality profile to create a collage that represents your personality from each of the four approaches to personality you selected. Follow the steps below to complete your collage.

❶ Divide a sheet of poster board into four distinct regions. Each region will represent a different approach to personality theory.

❷ In each region, create an illustration or select images and words to represent your personality from one approach to personality discussed in this chapter. For example, for the psychoanalytic approach, you could choose an iceberg to show the relationship between the conscious and the unconscious mind. The part of the iceberg above water could represent the conscious mind. In this part of the collage, you could place images representing aspects of your personality that others easily recognize. The iceberg below water could represent the unconscious. Here, you could place aspects of your personality you are less aware of.

❸ Once you have completed all four sections of your collage, write a paragraph explaining which approach to personality you think most clearly explains your personality and why.

4. Presenting Your Collage

Following your teacher's instructions hang your collages for the class to see. When called upon, present your collage to the class. Be careful not to reveal which approaches to personality you chose to illustrate. Invite your classmates to guess which approach is represented in each section of your collage. Finally, using points from the paragraph that you wrote, explain to the class which approach you think best describes your personality.

5. Discussion

What did you learn from this lab? Your teacher will call the class together to hold a discussion that focuses on the questions below. Be prepared to use your collage to help explain your answers to the class.

- Overall, how successful were you at applying the different approaches to personality to your own personality?

- Were some approaches to personality particularly difficult or easy to illustrate? If so, why?

- What major features of your personality were depicted in each part of your collage?

- In terms of depicting specific features of your personality, did you think any of the approaches were limited?

- In your opinion, which aspects of your personality are most important to survival? To self-fulfillment? Explain.

KEY APPROACHES AND PEOPLE

The Trait Approach
- Gordon Allport
- Hans Eysenck
- The Five Factor Model

The Psychoanalytic Approach
- Sigmund Freud
- Carl Jung
- Alfred Adler
- Karen Horney
- Erik Erikson

The Learning Approach
- Behaviorism
- John Watson
- B.F. Skinner
- Social Learning Theory
- Albert Bandura
- Social-Cognitive Theory

Humanistic Psychology
- Abraham Maslow
- Carl Rogers

Sociocultural Psychology
- Individualism
- Collectivism
- Sociocultural factors

CHAPTER 14 Review

Comprehension and Critical Thinking

SECTION 1 (pp. 392–395)

1. a. Recall Which factors would a person who is hostile, selfish, and unreliable score low on according to the Five Factor Model?

b. Explain How did Hans J. Eysenck build on Carl Jung's distinction between extroversion and introversion?

c. Support a Position Do you think that it is ever possible for a person to be too conscientious or too open to new experiences? Explain.

SECTION 2 (pp. 396–403)

2. a. Identify Main Ideas According to Carl Jung, what is the relationship between archetypes and the collective unconscious?

b. Sequence Describe Erikson's stages of psychosocial development.

c. Predict What do you think might happen to society if the structure of the human mind had an id, but not an ego or a superego?

SECTION 3 (pp. 405–408)

3. a. Identify According to social cognitive theory which factors shape personality development?

b. Contrast In what ways does behaviorism differ from social cognitive theory?

c. Evaluate What are the strengths and weaknesses of social-learning theory?

SECTION 4 (pp. 409–414)

4. a. Describe What roles do the self and free choice play in humanistic psychology?

b. Interpret How can the process of acculturation have both positive and negative effects on self-esteem?

c. Rank Which factors do you think have the greatest influence on shaping a teenager's personality: free choice and individual action, or sociocultural factors such as ethnicity, gender, and culture? Explain.

Reviewing Vocabulary

Match the terms with their correct definitions.

5. personality
6. trait
7. introverts
8. extroverts
9. defense mechanisms
10. rationalization
11. archetypes
12. socialization
13. self-concept
14. congruence

A. ideas and images of the accumulated experiences of all human beings

B. the consistency between one's self-concept and one's experience

C. methods used by the ego to avoid anxiety

D. people who tend to be active and self-expressive and gain energy from interacting with others

E. people who tend to be imaginative and look inward for ideas and energy

F. the patterns of feelings, motives, and behavior that set people apart from one another

G. the use of self-deception to justify unacceptable behaviors or ideas

H. a view of oneself as an individual

I. the process by which people learn socially desirable behaviors

J. an aspect of personality that is considered to be reasonably stable

INTERNET ACTIVITY ✳

15. What personality traits do psychologists possess? Choose two psychologists discussed in this chapter and conduct Internet research to find biographical information about each one. Then, using either Hans Eysenck's dimensions of personality or the Five-Factor Model, come up with a set of trait words for each psychologist.

Psychology in Your Life

16. Albert Bandura studied how children learn violence from adult models. Today many people are concerned about how the media and computer games model violence. Keep a diary for a week of your own television and gaming activity. Record how many acts of violence you see in each show or game. Write a paragraph summarizing your findings, and tell how you think exposure to violence might affect your attitudes or behavior.

SKILLS ACTIVITY: INTERPRETING PRIMARY SOURCES

Read the following excerpt, in which psychologist Alfred Adler discusses why he believes people strive for superiority. Then answer the questions that follow.

> **❝**Now I began to see clearly in every psychical phenomenon the striving for superiority. It runs parallel to physical growth. It is an intrinsic necessity of life itself. It lies at the root of all solutions of life's problems, and is manifested in the way in which we meet these problems. All our functions follow its direction . . . Willing, thinking, talking, seeking after rest, after pleasure, learning, understanding, work and love, betoken [show] the essence of this eternal melody. Whether one thinks or acts more wisely or less, one always moves along the lines of that upward tendency. In our right and wrong conceptions of life and its problems, in the successful or the unsuccessful solution of any question, this striving for perfection is uninterruptedly at work. **❞**
>
> —Alfred Adler, *Understanding Human Nature*

17. Explain What importance does Adler give the idea of "striving for superiority" in this excerpt?

18. Predict How might a behaviorist such as John B. Watson have responded to Adler's arguments in this excerpt?

WRITING FOR AP PSYCHOLOGY

Use your knowledge of personality to answer the question below. Do not simply list facts. Present a clear argument based on your critical analysis of the question, using the appropriate psychological terminology.

19. Briefly describe the main points of each of the approaches to personality listed below. For each approach, include a general description of who helped developed the approach and how it can be used to understand personality.
- The Five Factor Model
- Sigmund Freud's psychoanalytic approach
- humanistic approach

Connecting Online

Visit thinkcentral.com for review and enrichment activities related to this chapter.

Quiz and Review

ONLINE QUIZZES
Take a practice quiz for each section in this chapter.

WEBQUEST
Complete a structured Internet activity for this chapter.

QUICK LAB
Reinforce a key concept with a short lab activity.

APPLYING WHAT YOU'VE LEARNED
Review and apply your knowledge by completing a project-based assessment.

Activities

eACTIVITIES
Complete chapter Internet activities for enrichment.

INTERACTIVE FEATURE
Explore an interactive version of a key feature in this chapter.

KEEP IT CURRENT
Link to current news and research in psychology.

Online Textbook

 Learn more about key topics in this chapter.

TESTING YOUR Work Personality Type

Extroversion | Introversion | Sensing | Intuition

Thinking | Feeling | Judging | Perceiving

Have you ever wondered how you or someone else would classify your personality? Are you an extrovert or introvert? Your personality type may make you well suited for certain jobs and less suited for others.

Many people like to find out about themselves—to identify their characteristics and personalities. One of the most popular tests for that purpose is the Myers-Briggs Type Indicator® (MBTI®). Isabel Briggs Myers and her mother, Katharine Cook Briggs, began designing a personality test in the 1940s. Their goal was to create an objective test that would help employers hire people suited for particular kinds of jobs.

Even today, the MBTI is popular in career and business counseling. According to the Consulting Psychologists Press, the MBTI is "the most widely used personality inventory in history."

The MBTI is based on the personality theory of psychologist Carl Jung, who was one of Sigmund Freud's students. Jung believed that there are different personality types and that how a person acts is based on the person's personality type. He also suggested that a person's personality preferences are present early in life and become more apparent as the person matures.

Over 2 million people a year take the MBTI. Here are some typical questions:

1. Which rules you more? (a) your head (b) your heart

2. At a party, do you (a) interact with many, including strangers? (b) interact with a few, known to you?

After choosing between (a) and (b) answers for 126 questions, the test taker's preferences are evaluated along four dimensions. The dimensions are extroversion versus introversion (E vs. I); sensing versus intuition (S vs. N); thinking versus feeling (T vs. F); and judging versus perceiving (J vs. P). Preferences may be classified as

CHAPTER 15
PSYCHOLOGICAL TESTS

strong, moderate, or weak. The stronger one's preference, the more one will exhibit the characteristics of a dimension.

Each preference is characterized by a particular way of seeing situations and other people. For example, extroverted people enjoy interacting with others, while introverted people prefer solitary activities. So extroverted people are more likely to enjoy jobs such as police work, sales, teaching, and other occupations that involve constant, daily contact with other people. Introverted people, on the other hand, are more likely to prefer jobs such as research, writing, and various forms of art that allow them to work individually on projects.

Intuitive people value creativity, while sensation-oriented people prefer practicality. Thinking people prefer to be logical and analytical when making decisions, while the decision-making process for feeling people relies more on interpersonal involvement and subjective values. Judgers typically prefer an environment that is ordered and structured, while perceivers tend to be more flexible and spontaneous.

The total possible combinations add up to 16 types, such as INTJ, ISFP, ESTJ, ENFP, and so on. In theory, each person is one of those 16 types. According to people who support the MBTI's results, how an individual sees the world and how he or she behaves can be predicted on the basis of the person's personality type.

The MBTI is just one kind of psychological test. There are many others that you will undoubtedly encounter in life and that you will learn more about in this chapter.

What do you think?

1. What are the four dimensions that MBTI measures?

2. How might being labeled as having a certain type of personality affect you on the job?

Chapter at a Glance

SECTION 1: Psychology and Testing
- Psychological tests assess abilities, feelings, attitudes, and behavior.
- For a psychological test to be useful and accurate, it has to be standardized, reliable, valid, and have norms for scoring.
- Computers can be used to administer tests and help students prepare for tests.

SECTION 2: Measuring Achievement, Abilities, and Interests
- Three major kinds of tests measure achievement, aptitudes, and interests.
- Achievement tests measure people's skills and knowledge in specific academic areas.
- Aptitude tests measure a specific set of skills.
- Vocational aptitude tests help people figure out what their interests are.

SECTION 3: Personality Tests
- Objective tests present test takers with a standardized group of test items in the form of a questionnaire.
- Projective tests have no clearly specified answers and use an open-ended format.

SECTION 4: Taking Tests
- Students can follow some general tips to improve their performance on tests.
- Multiple-choice questions are common on standardized tests such as the SATs.
- There are ways for students to reduce test anxiety.

Psychology and Testing

Before You Read

Main Idea

Psychological tests include achievement tests, aptitude tests, interest tests, and personality tests.

Reading Focus

1. What are some uses of psychological tests?

2. What are four important features of a psychological test?

3. How can computers be used in testing?

Vocabulary

behavior-rating scales
self-reports
standardized test
validity scales
norms
norm group

TAKING NOTES Use a graphic organizer like this one to take notes on the four kinds of psychological tests discussed in this section.

1. Achievement:
2. Aptitude:
3. Interest:
4. Personality:

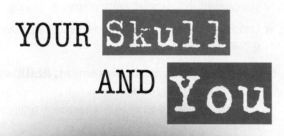

YOUR Skull AND You

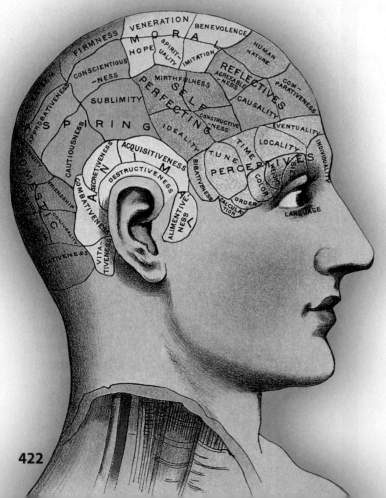

PSYCHOLOGY CLOSE UP

Do the bumps on your head say something about what is in your brain? Phrenology is the study of the skull, its shape and its bumps. This field was based on the mistaken belief that the bumps and protuberances of the skull somehow reveal character and mental capacity. Many people thought that the shape and bumps of one's skull correlate with parts of the brain believed to control various personality traits.

Franz Joseph Gall (1758–1828) argued that each mental ability is based in a specific part of the brain. He thought that the size of the specific brain region mirrored the importance of the ability in a particular person. Further, he said that this importance or prominence was reflected on the surface of the skull. Some of the specific traits that Gall and his followers looked for included so-called "criminal" traits. They identified specific areas of the skull as associated with, for example, combativeness and cautiousness.

Phrenology remained popular into the 20th century, although it had no scientific validity. Modern science has totally discredited Gall's theories. Now there are more reliable and scientific tests to assess various aspects of our minds and personalities. ▪

Uses of Psychological Tests

There are many different kinds of psychological tests. You have already learned about one kind of psychological test: intelligence tests. The psychological tests discussed in this chapter include achievement tests, aptitude tests, interest tests, and personality tests.

Tests to determine how much students have learned are called achievement tests. Tests for special aptitudes and interests are sometimes given to an individual to determine whether he or she is suited for certain occupations. There are also tests that identify the psychological traits that make up a person's personality. Therefore, tests that measure psychological traits are also known as personality tests. Personality tests measure almost every known personality trait. Some tests measure a dozen or more traits at one time. The Myers-Briggs Type Indicator is an example.

Psychological tests assess abilities, feelings, attitudes, and behaviors. The responses a person gives on test items can help psychologists to predict a person's future behavior, as well as possible career choices.

Psychological tests are hardly a new invention. It appears that over 2,500 years ago, during the golden age of Greece, people were selected for government service on the basis of psychological tests. Those early tests measured physical as well as mental abilities. Evidence also suggests that psychological tests were used to select civil-service employees some 2,000 years ago in China. The Chinese tests measured verbal and mathematical abilities as well as knowledge of law and geography.

Modern researchers have been using various types of psychological tests for about 100 years. Francis Galton, James Cattell, Alfred Binet, and other early psychologists began constructing modern psychological tests in the late 1800s.

Psychological tests can be used to help people make important decisions. Tests can help indicate whether a person is suited for a particular class in school or for medication to reduce agitation. Intelligence tests are often used to indicate whether children are likely to profit from special kinds of educational experiences. Transformed score tests such as the Scholastic Assessment Test (SAT) can help determine whether students are likely to succeed in college. As part of their admissions process, college admissions personnel also often ask high school teachers and guidance counselors to rate applicants on scales that measure such traits as willingness to work hard and cooperativeness.

More specialized tests are used to measure students' prospects for success in graduate schools such as business, law, and medical schools. Many graduate schools use the Graduate Record Examination (GRE). Similarly, medical schools use the Medical College Admission Test (MCAT).

Some psychological tests measure behavior directly. For example, **behavior-rating scales** are used to measure behavior in such places as classrooms and hospitals. With behavior-rating scales, trained observers may check off each occurrence of a specific behavior within a certain amount of time, say, 15 minutes. For example, an observer might count how many times a person gestures while talking to someone else. This might be a measure of how outgoing the person is.

Behavior-rating scales are growing in popularity today, particularly for use with children. However, most psychological tests rely on people's **self-reports** about their attitudes, feelings, and behavior—that is, what people say about themselves.

Reading Check **Analyze** What are behavior-rating scales used for?

Features of Psychological Tests

Psychological tests are sometimes frightening for the test takers and sometimes misleading for the evaluators. Tests such as the SAT can be particularly scary because the results on a test taken on one day can seem nearly as important as the grades earned over several years. The results can be misleading because a person may be ill or distracted on the day of the test and not perform as well as he or she might on another day.

For a psychological test to be useful and reasonably accurate, it has to have certain features, or characteristics. It has to be standardized, it has to show reliability and validity, and it has to have norms for scoring.

Standardization A **standardized test** is one that is administered and scored the same way every time. Psychologists and educators are trained in how to administer and score standardized tests accurately. For example, the two most widely used intelligence tests, the Stanford-Binet and Wechsler, are given individually. Test administrators are trained to ask the same questions in the same way. They also receive training in how to score the tests and interpret those scores.

Of course, some experts question the validity of IQ tests as general measures of intelligence. They believe that most IQ tests measure only analytical ability and that there are other abilities, such as creativity and practical skills, that the tests do not measure.

Other tests such as the SAT are given to thousands of students at a time. All students receive the same instructions, and computers grade the answers. Essay questions on a standardized test are not graded by a computer. However, instructions for administrators on how to score essay questions are very clear and precise. This clarity and precision help to ensure that the same criteria will be used to score essay questions. This is true regardless of who is doing the scoring, or where or when the scoring is being done.

Reliability and Validity You learned earlier that the *reliability* of a measure is its consistency. That is, an individual's score on a test should be the same or very nearly the same every time the individual takes that test. Test-retest reliability is demonstrated when a person receives similar scores on the same test taken on different occasions. *Validity* refers to the extent to which a test measures what it is intended to measure and predicts what it is intended to predict.

Test results can be distorted when people answer in ways they think will please the interviewer. People have also been known to exaggerate their problems on personality tests as a way to get attention.

In addition, people may answer in the way they think is "correct," even if there are no objectively right or wrong answers. To avoid such distortion, some psychological tests have validity scales built into them.

Validity scales involve questions that, if answered in a certain way, let the psychologist know that the test taker is not answering the questions honestly. Validity scales thus depend on the answers to a variety of interlinking questions.

For example, there may be several test items on which a psychologist would expect to see a pattern of similar answers. If no such pattern is found, those answers, taken together, may indicate that the test taker is not answering questions honestly. Validity scales are often helpful, as in identifying substance abuse. However, they are not foolproof.

Most tests you take in your classes are not psychological tests, and most are not constructed scientifically. Still, these tests should also be reliable and valid. Generally speaking, the longer a test is, the more valid it is. Would you rather have your grade on a math test depend on solving just one problem, or would you prefer it to be based on your solutions to 10 or 20 problems?

Some students believe that the scores they receive on tests taken in class are often not a valid measure of what they know. They argue that the tests do not really measure what they have learned because their nervousness interferes with their ability to perform well.

Norms Psychological tests are usually scored by comparing an individual's score to the norm. **Norms** are established standards of performance. They are designed to tell test administrators which scores are average, high, or low.

ESTABLISHING NORMS

Frequency

Mean

34.13%   34.13%

2.15%   2.15%

13.59%   13.59%

-3   -2   -1   0   1   2   3

Scores in standard deviation units

Skills Focus INTERPRETING GRAPHS At what position is the norm on the above graph located?

Norms for a test are usually established by administering the test to a large group of people who are similar to those for whom the test is intended. This group of test takers is called the **norm group.**

Imagine you are asked to create a psychological test for elementary school students. The tests would need to ask questions appropriate to the age of the children.

You would establish the norm by administering the test to thousands of elementary school students of the same age or grade level. This would be your norm group. The average score of the norm group would become the norm for that test. The scores of all other children taking the test in the future would be compared to that established norm.

Reading Check **Summarize** What is a standardized test?

Computers and Testing

Computers can be used to administer tests and to help students prepare for tests such as the SAT and the ACT. Many test preparation programs are now available from a variety of reputable sources. Some offer detailed tutorials; others offer customized study plans. Most contain hundreds of practice questions that familiarize students with a particular test and help reduce test anxiety. In addition,

such programs are upbeat and fun, making test preparation an enjoyable experience for students.

Computers have been testing people for more than 30 years. One computer program currently in use for this purpose is CASPER, which stands for Computerized Assessment System for Psychotherapy Evaluation and Research.

A CASPER interview lasts about 30 minutes. The interview explores a wide variety of topics, including family relationships, social activities, overall life satisfaction, and specific behavior patterns that may be suggestive of physical and psychological disorders. The test results obtained in a CASPER interview are provided to the client and therapist. Questions and responses are displayed on a monitor. To answer a question, the test taker presses a number on the keyboard. CASPER follows up with more questions.

How well do people respond to being tested by a computer? Research shows that people find the computer program user-friendly. In addition, standardization seems to be easier and more consistent with a computer. Computers can be programmed to ask specific questions in a prescribed sequence.

Reading Check **Summarize** What is one advantage of computer testing?

Reviewing Main Ideas and Vocabulary

1. **Recall** What do most psychological tests rely heavily upon for information about people's attitudes, feelings, and behavior?

2. **Define** What are norms?

3. **Identify** How might computers help students with test preparation?

Thinking Critically

4. **Explain** What does the concept of validity in a test specifically refer to?

5. **Categorize** What do psychological tests assess?

6. **Analyze** Using your notes and a graphic organizer, explain standardization, norms, reliability, and validity in tests.

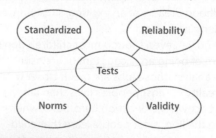

FOCUS ON WRITING

7. **Persuasive** Write a speech in which you argue either for or against the use of tests to identify personality types. Read your speech to the class.

Measuring Achievement, Abilities, and Interests

Before You Read

Main Idea
Achievement tests and aptitude tests are both commonly administered to students in high school.

Reading Focus
1. What do achievement tests measure?
2. What do aptitude tests measure?
3. How do people distinguish between achievement and aptitude?
4. What are two vocational interest inventories?

Vocabulary
achievement tests
aptitude tests
vocational interest inventories
forced-choice format

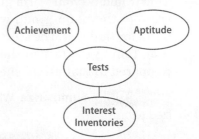

TAKING NOTES Use a graphic organizer like this one to take notes on different kinds of tests.

Achievement — Tests — Aptitude
Tests
Interest Inventories

Tinker, Tailor, Soldier, Spaceman

PSYCHOLOGY CLOSE UP

What do you want to be when you grow up? When you were younger, did you ever walk down the street with your parents only to be stopped by a kindly neighbor and asked what you wanted to be when you were older? Most children develop a standard response to such questions, usually born of a genuine interest in doing something exciting some day, such as flying to distant planets, putting out fires, rounding up stray cattle, helping sick people, or fighting the nation's enemies. And childhood play—with its costumes of astronauts, cowboys, fashion designers, firefighters, nurses, and so forth—only makes more real the childhood dreams of an exciting, satisfying, and challenging career.

And yet, even though most children don't dream of being an accountant or an insurance analyst, those jobs are much closer to the reality of most people's lives than are the jobs of cowpoke or action hero. Somewhere along the line, most people learn that childhood dreams and aspirations must be adapted to measured aptitudes, abilities, and interests. For most of us, we begin to get this dose of reality in school, where we are measured and tested in a number of ways to determine our interests and abilities. ◼

Achievement Tests

Achievement tests, aptitude tests, and tests of interests are all closely related. Most of the tests that you have taken in your classes at school have probably been achievement tests. There are also tests that measure people's abilities, or aptitudes. Still other tests help people identify their interests. Students have been taking achievement tests for many years. When a student is having difficulty deciding on a college major, a teacher or guidance counselor can focus on testing a student's abilities and interests.

Achievement tests measure people's skills and the knowledge they have in specific academic areas. A history test is an example of an achievement test. Throughout elementary and middle school, most students' basic skills are tested every year. They are tested in science, reading, math, and many other subject areas.

In high school, most students are tested repeatedly on their achievements in each of their courses. Factors such as intelligence and motivation play a role in achievement, but so does learning. For example, it should come as no surprise that students taking Spanish will have higher scores on a Spanish achievement test than students who are not taking Spanish, even though the students who haven't studied Spanish may be equal in intelligence and motivation.

College students who wish to go to graduate school may be required to take standardized achievement tests in their major field of study—Spanish, political science, math, or psychology, for example. The tests are designed to determine whether the students have enough knowledge in the specific area to succeed in graduate school.

Reading Check **Summarize** What are some examples of achievement tests?

Aptitude Tests

Achievement tests measure a narrow range of skills. Intelligence tests, on the other hand, measure overall learning ability. Aptitude tests fall somewhere in between. Aptitude tests measure more specific abilities or skills than intelligence tests but broader abilities or skills than achievement tests. **Aptitude tests** are generally used to determine whether a person is likely to do well in a given field of work or study.

The Scholastic Assessment Test is a general aptitude test. It is used to predict how well students are likely to do in college. The Law School Admission Test and the Medical College Admission Test are more specialized. These tests use percentile grade equivalent scores—the percent of scores at or below any given score—to predict how well students will do in law school and medical school, respectively. For example, success in medical school depends heavily on the ability to understand chemistry and biology. Therefore, the MCAT has many questions relating to these and related subjects.

Of course, aptitude is not the only factor that influences achievement in school. Some people score high on tests such as the SAT but earn comparatively low grades in college, while others with lower SAT scores may earn relatively higher grades in college. Other factors besides aptitude important for success in school include having a positive attitude toward school and placing a high value on education. It is also important to possess certain personality traits such as perseverance and optimism in order to succeed in school.

Reading Check **Identify Supporting Details** What is an example of an aptitude test?

Distinguishing Between Achievement and Aptitude

Sometimes it is difficult to distinguish between an achievement test and an aptitude test. Aptitude tests are intended to measure potential for learning in a specific area. An aptitude test is usually given to a person before that person has had any training in the specific area. It is used to predict how well the person will do in that particular area after receiving training.

However, current abilities and future success are often based on past achievements. For example, the SAT is intended to measure the ability to do well in college, but it is given in specific languages. Therefore, the ability to do well on the SAT depends on achievements in English or the language in which the individual takes the test.

ACADEMIC VOCABULARY

percentile one of a set of points on a scale arrived at by dividing a group into parts in order of magnitude

Choosing a Career

One of the most important tasks of the teen years is thinking about what sort of career you would like to have when you are out of school and an adult. Take a survey in your class to find out the top job choices of your classmates.

PROCEDURE

1 List your top five career choices.

2 Discuss with other students their top five choices.

3 Discuss what skills and talents are required for frequently-listed jobs.

ANALYSIS

1. Is it realistic for most students to expect to have a career in the top choices listed? Discuss.

2. Can everyone hope to be an astronaut or an NBA star? Discuss.

3. Discuss realistic plans to reach achievable goals.

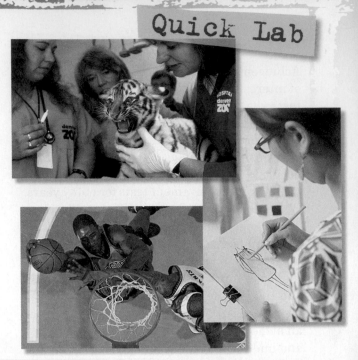

Quick Lab **THINK** central thinkcentral.com

Moreover, the SAT consists of verbal and quantitative parts. The verbal sections rely heavily on vocabulary—that is, knowledge of the meanings of words. The quantitative part relies heavily on mathematical knowledge. Skill in these areas—knowledge of vocabulary and mathematics—depends on the amount one has learned or achieved. Thus, the test does not simply measure aptitude.

However, because performance on the SAT does not depend on one specific course, the SAT used to be called the Scholastic *Aptitude* Test. Recently, in recognition of the role that achievement plays in the SAT, the test was renamed the Scholastic *Assessment* Test.

It may be that there is no such thing as a "pure" aptitude test. All aptitude tests rely on some kind of prior achievement.

Reading Check **Summarize** What two areas of knowledge does the SAT rely heavily upon?

Vocational Interest Inventories

People usually perform better in jobs that interest them. This is probably due to the fact that people tend to pay more attention and thus absorb more information if something has captured their attention. Moreover, people who share interests with those who are successful in a given job are more likely to succeed in that job.

Thus, many psychologists and educators use **vocational interest inventories** to help people determine whether their interests are similar to those of people in various lines of work. Two widely used interest inventories are the Kuder™ Preference Records and the Strong-Campbell Interest Inventory.

Kuder® Career Search A counselor may give a student a test called a Kuder Career Search. This test has a **forced-choice format,** which means that the test taker is forced to choose one of the answers, even if none of them seems to fit his or her interests precisely. For example, test takers are asked to indicate which of a group of activities they like most and which they like least. They are not allowed to answer "none of the above."

The Kuder asks test takers to choose between activities such as the following:

  a. hiking in the forest

  b. giving someone advice

  c. playing a musical instrument

The results are scored to show how much the person appears to be interested in areas such as science, music, art, literature, and outdoor work.

Campbell™ Interest and Skill Survey (CISS®) People taking a Kuder test can see where their interests lie and which areas they might want to look into for employment opportunities.

Obviously, a person who repeatedly indicates a preference for music-related activities is showing a definite interest in music. The CISS is not as obvious or direct as the Kuder Career Search. The CISS includes many different kinds of items.

The CISS compares the test taker's interests with the interests of people who enjoy and are successful in various kinds of work. For example, if most successful accountants enjoy reading and solving puzzles, then a test taker who indicates these same preferences might also be a successful accountant. Therefore, the content of the test questions themselves may not be as important as the combination of interests the test taker shares with people who are employed in certain occupations such as accounting or working with numbers.

Evaluation of Interest Inventories Interest inventories are of great value to students who do not have specific career goals. There are over 20,000 different occupations in the United States, and the task of trying to select one can be overwhelming to people who are unclear about their interests. Interest inventories can help point people in a direction they might find fulfilling.

On the other hand, interest in an area does not necessarily mean that one has the ability, or aptitude, to succeed in that area. Therefore, it is usually desirable to make vocational choices on the basis of one's abilities as well as one's interests.

No important life decisions should be made on the basis of a single psychological test. Tests provide only one source of information about an individual, and no test is perfectly reliable. Teachers' and counselors' personal knowledge of an individual should also be taken into account. People may also believe that the results of a single test may not be an accurate reflection of who they are.

Most students are usually pleased with the outcome of their interest tests because the scores often seem to fit their own images of themselves. If the test results seem wrong to them, it would be unwise to follow the directions suggested by the test results. For example, suppose the test showed that a particular student likes outdoor activities, which suggests a career that includes working outdoors. An individual may enjoy hiking and boating *occasionally* but also know that he or she would dislike having to work outside all day and every day. He or she would have to carefully consider the test results in light of what he or she knows about himself or herself. Taking additional interest tests might provide a clearer picture of the kind of career he or she would enjoy.

Reading Check **Summarize** What is a forced-choice format?

SECTION 2 Assessment

Online Quiz THINK central thinkcentral.com

Reviewing Main Ideas and Vocabulary

1. **Define** What kind of test is the SAT?

2. **Recall** How is the Kuder Career Search test structured?

3. **Describe** Why was the SAT recently renamed?

Thinking Critically

4. **Compare and Contrast** What is the difference between an achievement test and an aptitude test?

5. **Analyze** What is the purpose of vocational interest inventories?

6. **Summarize** Using your notes and a graphic organizer like the one below, summarize the ways in which achievement tests, aptitude tests, and interest inventories are used.

Tests	
Achievement	
Aptitude	
Interest Inventories	

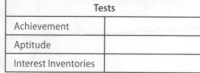

7. **Descriptive** In a paragraph, explain what you wanted to grow up to be when you were a child. Assess whether your career goals have changed as you have grown older.

Implicit Attitude Tests

Implicit attitude (or association) tests (IATs) are on the cutting edge of current psychological research. These tests measure not what people explicitly (clearly) say they believe about race and gender, but rather what their actions reveal them to implicitly, or unconsciously, believe. In other words, you might have prejudices you don't even know about.

In an article titled "Our Racist, Sexist Selves" that appeared in the *New York Times* on April 6, 2008, columnist Nicholas D. Kristof describes some of these implicit attitude tests. Kristof mentions a number of universities that offer online psychological tests. These implicit attitude tests reveal that many people have unstated and unacknowledged prejudices based on race and gender.

The University of Chicago, for example, has a test that measures implicit attitudes about race. In one test, the test taker comes face to face with white men and black men, some of whom are holding objects that could be cell phones or guns. The idea of the test is to shoot the gunmen but not the others. Test results reveal that both white and black test takers are quicker to shoot the black men than they are the white men.

Harvard also offers online psychological tests that test implicit attitudes on race. The results of these tests reveal the discrepancy between what people believe or think about themselves and their unconscious association of white with good and black with evil (Banaji, et al).

Project Implicit is a joint project of Harvard, the University of Virginia, and Washington University. The project involves a large-scale study of implicit preferences. Project Implicit's Implied Association Test attempts to demonstrate differences between explicit attitudes or beliefs on a subject and implicit or unconscious beliefs (Banaji, Nosek, and Greenwald, 2006). The topics explored by Project Implicit include disabilities, religion, body weight, and age.

Gender is another problematic arena of unconscious, unstated biases. Kristof points out that implicit attitude tests reveal that most people have biases not only against people of other races but also against women in positions of power and authority. In fact, some scholars think that prejudice based on race may be easier to overcome than prejudice based on gender (Eagly et al.).

Another area where implicit and explicit attitudes come into play is that of obesity. Most people explicitly claim not to be prejudiced when it comes to body type. But tests reveal a common prejudice against obesity shared by many people.

However, some recent research studies suggest that implicit attitude tests must be used with caution. One study has suggested that test taker performance on IATs can be affected if the participant thinks the test results will be made public.

Thus, one cautionary concern is what an IAT is really measuring. Another concern is the honesty of people's responses.

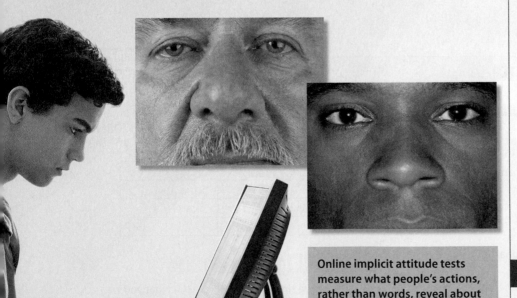

Online implicit attitude tests measure what people's actions, rather than words, reveal about their unconscious beliefs, attitudes, and prejudices.

Thinking Critically

1. **Explain** What do implicit attitude tests measure?

2. **Discuss** What are some ways implicit biases might be overcome?

Current Research **THINK** central — thinkcentral.com

Personality Tests

Before You Read

Main Idea

Objective tests and projective tests can help to describe and measure various aspects of personality.

Reading Focus

1. What are objective tests?
2. How would you describe projective tests?

Vocabulary

objective tests
projective tests
open-ended format

TAKING NOTES Use a graphic organizer like this one to take notes about objective tests.

MMPI-2	CPI

SENSE OF Humors

Black Bile

Yellow Bile

Blood

Phlegm

The Granger Collection, New York

These early paintings illustrate the idea of four personality types based on four humors (bodily fluids).

PSYCHOLOGY CLOSE UP

Why are people the way they are?

The Greek physician Hippocrates (460–c. 375 B.C.) developed the idea of four personality types based on four humors or bodily fluids: black bile (melancholic, sad), yellow bile (choleric, angry), blood (sanguine, active, energetic), and phlegm (phlegmatic, listless). Galen (A.D. 129–200), companion and physician to the Roman emperor Marcus Aurelius and personal physician to the emperor Commodus, was also the chief physician to the gladiators. Living about 600 years after Hippocrates, he refined the theory of humors. Galen wrote about 300 works, of which roughly half survive. His authority was widespread and practically absolute. His ideas spread throughout western Europe, as well as to the Byzantine Empire and Arabia.

The ideas of Hippocrates and Galen about humors as the basis of personality types prevailed for almost 2,000 years. It wasn't until centuries later, when the scientific method became accepted as the best way to assess information, that new experiments and studies eventually discredited the theory of humors as an explanation for personality types. ■

Objective Tests

An individual's personality consists of his or her characteristics, habits, preferences, and moods. Psychologists use personality tests to describe and measure various aspects of people's personalities. Sometimes, they also use personality tests to help diagnose psychological problems and disorders. There are two kinds of personality tests: objective tests and projective tests.

Objective tests present test takers with a standardized group of test items in the form of a questionnaire. The Minnesota Multiphasic Personality Inventory® (MMPI®) and the California Psychological Inventory™ (CPI™), discussed on the following pages, are examples of objective personality tests.

In terms of format, test takers are limited to a specific choice of answers—true or false, for example. Sometimes test takers are asked to select the preferred answer from groups of three. In either case, though, the test takers must choose from a list of answers provided for them.

Minnesota Multiphasic Personality Inventory

The MMPI is the psychological test most widely used in clinical work and in research that requires measurement of personality traits. First developed in the late 1930s, the MMPI was intended for use by clinical and counseling psychologists to help diagnose psychological problems in people. A revised version of the test was released in 2008.

The MMPI-2 contains 567 items presented in a true-false format. Psychologists can score the MMPI-2 by hand, but they usually score it by computer. Computers generate reports by comparing the individual's score to group norms stored in the computer's memory. While the computer is certainly an objective (unbiased) scorer, most psychologists believe that the scores should be supplemented and confirmed by interviews and observation.

The MMPI-2 is organized into ten clinical scales, up to eight validity scales, and numerous subscales. The clinical scales reveal psychological problems. They also indicate whether people have stereotypical masculine or feminine interests and whether they are outgoing or shy.

To create the clinical scales of the MMPI-2, the designers interviewed people who had already been diagnosed with various psychological disorders. A test-item bank of several hundred items was assembled. It was based upon questions that are frequently asked in clinical interviews. Here are some of the true-false items:

My father was a good man. **T F**
I am seldom troubled by headaches. **T F**
I have never done anything dangerous for the thrill of it. **T F**
I work under a great deal of tension. **T F**

People with various psychological disorders, such as depression or schizophrenia, will answer certain questions in predictable ways. For example, a person suffering from depression might answer "true" to such questions as "I often feel sad for no reason" or "Sometimes I think life simply isn't worth living."

These test items are then placed on scales to measure the presence of psychological disorders. A person taking the test may answer the questions in ways that are similar to the responses of people who are known to have a particular psychological disorder. If that is the case, then the psychologist administering the test is alerted to the possible presence of that disorder in the person.

The validity scales are designed to detect distorted answers, misunderstood items, or an uncooperative test taker. Some of the abbreviations include L for lie, F for infrequency, and K for correction. For example, people with high "T" scores may answer questions in a way that makes them seem excessively moral or well behaved. Such people might answer the item "I never get angry" with "true." People with high "F" scores, which measure infrequency, have a tendency to exaggerate complaints, or they may be trying to get attention by giving seemingly bizarre answers.

However, there are questions concerning the usefulness of the validity scales. For example, people with serious psychological disorders may indeed see the world in an unusual way. Therefore, if they obtain high F-scale scores, it may be because of their problems and not because they are exaggerating their situation.

California Psychological Inventory

Because the MMPI-2 was designed to diagnose and classify psychological disorders, some psychologists prefer not to use it to measure the personality traits of "normal" clients. Many of these psychologists instead use the California Psychological Inventory, or CPI. The format of the CPI is similar to that of the MMPI-2, but it is designed to measure 15 "normal" personality traits, such as dominance, sociability, responsibility, and tolerance.

In many ways, the CPI is a more valid instrument than the MMPI-2, even though it is not as widely used. The norm group for the CPI is much larger than that for the MMPI-2, and greater care was taken in controlling for factors such as age, socioeconomic status, and geographic location.

Furthermore, the CPI has a much higher test-retest reliability than the MMPI-2.

ACADEMIC VOCABULARY

socioeconomic
involving both social and economic factors

CLINICAL SCALES OF THE REVISED MMPI-2

The MMPI-2 is the most widely used psychological test in clinical work. Although originally intended for use by psychologists to diagnose psychological disorders, it has now become the most widely used instrument of personality measurement in psychological research. This list describes some of the specific disorders the MMPI-2 typically assesses.

Scale	Abbreviation	Possible Interpretations
Hypochondriasis	Hs	Has bodily concerns and complaints
Depression	D	Is depressed, guilty; has feelings of guilt and helplessness
Conversion hysteria	Hy	Reacts to stress by developing physical symptoms; lacks insight
Psychopathic deviate	Pd	Is immoral, in conflict with the law; has stormy relationships
Masculinity-Femininity	Mf	Has interests and behavior patterns considered stereotypical of the other gender
Paranoia	Pa	Is suspicious and resentful, highly cynical about human nature
Psychasthenia	Pt	Is anxious, worried, high-strung
Schizophrenia	Sc	Is confused, disorganized, disoriented; has bizarre ideas
Hypomania	Ma	Is energetic, restless, active, easily bored
Social introversion	Si	Is introverted, timid, shy; lacks self-confidence

It seems to be a better predictor of such things as school and job success, leadership, and reactions to stress.

Reading Check **Find the Main Idea** What are two examples of objective tests?

Projective Tests

Projective tests, unlike objective tests, have no clearly specified answers. Such tests use an **open-ended format** to gauge people's characteristics. People are presented with ambiguous stimuli such as inkblots, drawings of vague shapes, or pictures of people engaged in various activities. The test takers are then asked to report what the stimuli represent to them. They might also be asked to tell stories about the stimuli. Since the inkblots or drawings are open to interpretation, experts think that people's interpretations reveal something about their personalities. The Rorschach (RAWR-shahk) inkblot test and the Thematic Apperception Test (TAT) are two examples of widely used projective tests.

Rorschach Inkblot Test Have you heard of a personality test that asks people to tell what a drawing or an inkblot looks like? There are actually a number of such personality tests. The Rorschach inkblot test is the best known of them. The Rorschach test is named after its originator, Swiss psychiatrist Hermann Rorschach (1884–1922).

It is an interesting side note that when Rorschach was an adolescent, his nickname was Klex, which means "inkblot" in German. Look at the Rorschach inkblot shown on page 434. If you were taking the test, a psychologist would hand you a card with the inkblot and ask you what it looks like.

Because the Rorschach is a projective test, there is no list of clearly defined answers from which to choose. Instead, test takers provide their own responses to each inkblot. However, some answers are more in keeping with the features of the blot than others. An inkblot could be a bat or a flying insect, an animal with a pointed face, a jack-o'-lantern, or many other things.

Complete a Webquest at thinkcentral.com on Rorschach inkblot tests.

Rorschach Inkblot Test

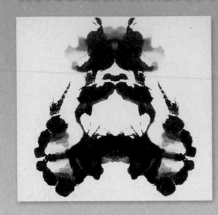

In the Rorschach Inkblot Test, people react to what they see. They project their interpretations onto an image that is presented to them. While there is no correct answer to a Rorschach inkblot test, certain answers are more in keeping than others with the features of the blot.

Rorschach's parents are so fixed on the test that they interpret everything—even spilled milk—as significant.

Answers such as "my mother's face" or "the devil in flames" are not readily suggested by the features of the inkblot. Therefore, a pattern of responses such as these is much more likely than other patterns to suggest the possible presence of a personality disorder in the test taker.

Many attempts have been made to standardize the Rorschach. People's responses to the cards are usually interpreted according to factors such as location, determinants, content, and form level.

- **Location** is the part of the blot to which the person responds. Does he or she respond to the whole card or to a detail?
- **Determinants** include features of the blot such as shading, texture, or color. People who are highly influenced by the texture and color are thought to be more emotional than those who do not focus on these aspects of the blot. Answers that incorporate many features of the blot are thought to reflect high intelligence.
- **Content** refers to the precise object the test taker reports seeing. Is he or she seeing a bat, a jack-o'-lantern, or a human figure?
- **Form level** indicates whether the answer is in keeping with the actual shape of the blot. Generally speaking, answers that fit the shape of the blot suggest that the individual sees the world the way most people do. (Some psychological disorders, such as schizophrenia, are characterized by bizarre perceptions.)

Supporters of the Rorschach test claim that it provides useful information that might not be obtained elsewhere. However, some researchers raise serious questions about the reliability, accuracy, and validity of the Rorschach test. Because no two professionals interpret Rorschach responses in quite the same way, they argue that the test results can be arbitrary or biased to support the professional's point of view.

Thematic Apperception Test The Thematic Apperception Test, or TAT, was developed in the 1930s by psychologists Henry Murray and Christiana Morgan at Harvard University. It is widely used in clinical practice and in motivation research. The TAT consists of drawings that, like the Rorschach inkblots, invite a variety of interpretations. Test takers are given the cards one at a time.

They are then asked to create a story for each card. For example, people are asked what might have led to the scene depicted on the card, what the person in the picture is doing, and how the story will end.

The idea behind the TAT is that people's needs and values emerge from the stories they tell. This can be especially true of attitudes toward other people, such as parents and romantic partners. The TAT is also used to measure achievement motivation, the desire to do one's best and to realize one's goals.

For example, a TAT card might show an image of two women. However, it may be a little unclear exactly what their connection is. Are they mother and daughter? Do they have a close relationship? Are they friends? Here are two stories about the image shown at right:

Story 1 The mother and daughter are both annoyed. They dislike family gatherings. They have little in common and have nothing to say to one another, so they avoid even making eye contact. They are anxious for the awkward moment to be over.

Story 2 The mother and daughter are enjoying a quiet moment together. As they've gotten older, they don't have as much time to spend with one another. But they've remained close and have shared many special times. They feel lucky to have each other's support and love.

Psychologists are trained to derive attitudes and achievement motivation scores from stories such as these. As you might have guessed, the second story suggests a more positive attitude and achievement motivation than the first story.

Reading Check **Summarize** What are two examples of projective tests?

THEMATIC APPERCEPTION TEST   **INTERACTIVE**

Test takers are asked to create a story for a variety of cards with images that invite interpretation.

Skills Focus **INTERPRETING VISUALS** What story might you be able to tell about the two figures pictured above?

Interactive Feature THINK central   thinkcentral.com

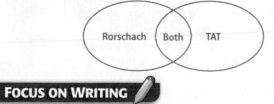

Online Quiz THINK central   thinkcentral.com

SECTION 3 Assessment

Reviewing Main Ideas and Vocabulary

1. **Describe** What is the function of the validity scales in the MMPI-2?

2. **Recall** What are the two types of personality tests?

3. **Define** What is an open-ended format?

Thinking Critically

4. **Explain** How are the two types of personality tests used?

5. **Support a Position** Because there are no standardized criteria for scoring answers on projective tests such as the Rorschach and the TAT, how accurate do you think they are? Support your answer.

6. **Compare** Using your notes and a graphic organizer like the one below, describe similarities in projective tests such as the Rorschach and the TAT.

Rorschach   Both   TAT

FOCUS ON WRITING

7. **Narrative** Write a paragraph in which you write a brief story to go with the inkblot or the TAT image in this section.

Taking Tests

Before You Read

Main Idea

Taking tests can be a nerve-racking experience, but there are ways to improve your performance.

Reading Focus

1. What are some tips for taking tests?
2. Multiple-choice questions are found on what sorts of tests?
3. What are some warning flags in true-false questions?
4. What strategies can you use for short-answer and essay questions?
5. How can you reduce test anxiety?

Vocabulary

cramming
cognitive restructuring

TAKING NOTES Use a graphic organizer like this one to take notes on tips for taking tests.

Tips For Taking Tests	
1. Multiple Choice	
2. True/False	
3. Short Answer	
4. Essay	

Test-Taking TERROR

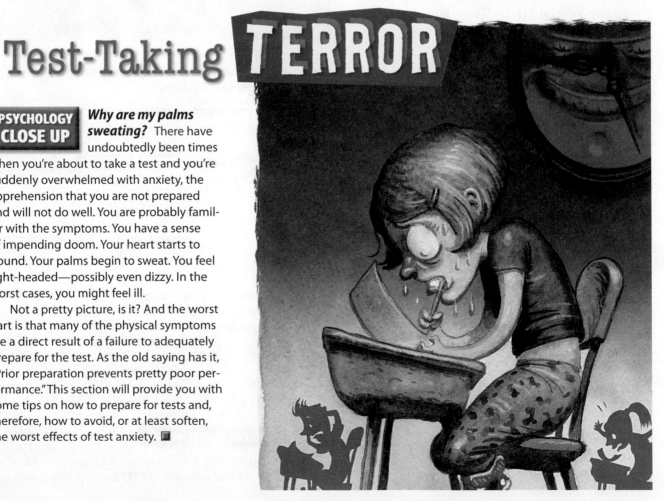

PSYCHOLOGY CLOSE UP

Why are my palms sweating? There have undoubtedly been times when you're about to take a test and you're suddenly overwhelmed with anxiety, the apprehension that you are not prepared and will not do well. You are probably familiar with the symptoms. You have a sense of impending doom. Your heart starts to pound. Your palms begin to sweat. You feel light-headed—possibly even dizzy. In the worst cases, you might feel ill.

Not a pretty picture, is it? And the worst part is that many of the physical symptoms are a direct result of a failure to adequately prepare for the test. As the old saying has it, "Prior preparation prevents pretty poor performance." This section will provide you with some tips on how to prepare for tests and, therefore, how to avoid, or at least soften, the worst effects of test anxiety. ■

Tips for Taking Tests

Many students think, "I know the material from my classes, but I just don't do well on tests." Sometimes they are right. But often they are wrong. When students are sure that they know something but cannot quite retrieve it—when it seems to be on the tip of their tongues—it may be that they did not learn it as well as they think they did. For them, much of the cure lies in developing better study habits.

Some students, however, do know the material and yet they still perform poorly on tests. This section offers some general tips on taking tests, as well as specific ways of coping with certain types of test questions.

Teachers generally determine the types of tests they give and when they give them. Midterm and final exams are usually a matter of school or department policy. And standardized tests, such as the SAT, are scheduled for certain dates throughout the year. You might think you have little control over the tests you take, but in reality there are many things students can do to help take charge of tests.

Gather Information Learn where and when the next test will be given. Find out about the types of questions that will be asked and the topics you should study. Most teachers and other test administrators do not mind your asking questions about tests. Some teachers may say that "everything" will be on the test, but others may offer specific information about what they consider important.

In addition, ask students who have already taken the course where test questions tend to come from. Do they tend to come from the textbook or from class notes?

Practice Plan regular study periods. Use your reading assignments and class notes to create test questions that might be similar to those on the exam. Create a study group, and practice answering these test items with group members. Define key terms on your practice test. Outline the answers to possible essay questions. Try to answer all the questions and exercises in your textbook—even the ones that were not assigned as homework. Some of them may appear on the test. Even if they do not appear on it, they will provide useful practice.

Make the most of your study group. Pool your knowledge. Quiz one another and read the answers to your essay questions aloud. This is a good way to prepare yourself for writing the essays on the actual test. In the process, you will probably discover the areas that need further study.

Be Test-Wise Small oversights can cause you problems on a test. For example, be sure you read the directions carefully and follow them precisely. Bring the right materials to class. Be sure your pencils are sharpened or that your pens have blue or black ink. Have some paper available, if only to use as scrap paper. Ask your teacher if you may use a pocket dictionary to check your spelling on essays. Teachers may also let you bring calculators and formulas to science and math tests.

Reading Check **Recall** What is an example of being test-wise?

Multiple-Choice Questions

Multiple-choice items are common on many types of tests. They are used in standardized tests, such as the SAT, and they are also used in classroom quizzes and exams. Educators and psychologists often use multiple-choice questions because they encourage the student to focus on the right answer (and reject the wrong ones). They can also be graded quickly and objectively.

Here are some hints for doing well on multiple-choice tests:

- *Try to answer the question before you look at the choices.*
- *Consider every possible choice.*
- *Look for answers that are opposites. When you see two answers that are opposite in meaning, one of them is likely to be the correct choice.*
- *Look for the best choice listed.*
- *Mark difficult questions so that you can come back to them later.*
- *Guess only when the odds of gaining points outweigh the odds of losing points.*
- *Change your answer if you think you have made a mistake.*

Reading Check **Analyze** Why should you look for answers that are opposites?

Statistically Speaking...

Taking Multiple-Choice Tests You can make the odds work in your favor on a multiple choice exam. How? By taking into account some of the percentages listed below, which were compiled by researchers at Rutgers University, as well as other scholars. By playing these odds, you can become a more intelligent test-taker.

50% If you can eliminate two choices, you have increased your odds to one in two, or 50 percent.

57.8% Percentage of answers that go from wrong to right when changed

20.2% Percentage of answers that go from right to wrong when changed

22.8% Percentage of answers that go from wrong to wrong when changed

Skills Focus INTERPRETING CHARTS Based on these percentages do you think it's a good or bad idea to change the occasional answer on a multiple choice test?

Source: http://lrc.rutgers.edu/pdf/multiplechoiceexams.pdf

True-False Questions

True-false questions can be tricky. After all, if half the questions are true and half are false, it is possible that you could earn a grade of 50 percent simply by guessing. The following pointers can help you maximize your performance on true-false items:

- *For the item to be true, every part of it must be true.*
- *Be wary of items that use absolutes such as* all, always, *or* never.

- *Items that provide more information and are longer than others tend to be true.*

Keep in mind that these are only rules of thumb, however. They are not foolproof instructions. Your best strategy is still to study thoroughly and know the answers on your own.

Reading Check **Analyze** What are the odds of answering a true-false question correctly?

Short-Answer and Essay Questions

Short-answer items ask the test taker to give a brief response to a question. Here are some pointers for short-answer questions:

- *Answer in brief but complete sentences.*
- *Include significant terms in your answer.*
- *Avoid simply restating the question in different terms or making circular arguments.*
- *Use detail if time and space allow.*

The first step in answering an essay question is making certain you have understood the question. Read the directions carefully and look for key words to guide your answer. Ignoring them increases the chances that you will omit important points from your answer.

Before beginning to write your essay, make a quick outline on a piece of scrap paper to help you organize your thoughts. The outline should help you keep track of the main points you wish to make in your answer. Mark where you will start and where you will end. Jot down key terms that represent ideas you wish to expand on in your essay. If you run out of time before you complete the essay, attach the outline to show where you were headed. It may help your grade (and it certainly will not hurt it).

Express your strongest ideas first. When you lead with the concepts you know best, you build a foundation for a strong argument.

How long should your essay be? A good rule of thumb is "Don't count words; just answer the question." Teachers will reward you for being on the mark as long as you have provided sufficient support for your argument.

Reading Check **Summarize** What is the first step in answering an essay question?

Test Anxiety

Some students become anxious before and during exams. The anxiety they experience consists of feelings of dread and foreboding. Test anxiety ranges from increased tension to actual physical symptoms, such as rapid breathing, pounding heartbeat, light-headedness or dizziness, and nausea.

Anxiety may be very uncomfortable, but it is not always a bad thing. It is normal to feel somewhat anxious as a test approaches. Anxiety shows that we understand the importance of the occasion and that failure may have serious consequences. But some test-anxious students allow negative thoughts and self-doubts to distract them, preventing them from focusing on the test itself.

Be Prepared One way to overcome test anxiety is to be prepared. If you study carefully and review the material regularly, you can be confident that you will recall what you have learned.

Review the material regularly before a test and avoid **cramming,** or preparing hastily for an examination. Learning takes time. Studying a reasonable amount every day is far more effective than cramming suddenly the night before. You can begin to cope with possible test anxiety right from the beginning of the semester—by planning a regular study schedule and sticking to it.

Overlearn Overlearning means reviewing the material, even after you think you have mastered it. Overlearning accomplishes two objectives: remembering the subject matter longer and building confidence.

Think Helpful Thoughts There are some strategies for ending upsetting thoughts and focusing on the task at hand—the test. What are the negative thoughts that occur to you at test-taking times? Write them down. Once you are aware of these negative thoughts, then you can replace them with positive ones.

This method of coping is called cognitive restructuring. **Cognitive restructuring** means consciously changing the thoughts one has in a particular situation. Cognitive restructuring consists of the following four steps:

1. Identify self-defeating thoughts, paying special attention to exaggerated ones.
2. Replace self-defeating thoughts with positive messages to yourself.
3. Imagine yourself in the testing situation and practice positive thinking.
4. Reward yourself for thinking positively.

If you consistently practice cognitive restructuring, you will become less anxious and more confident about taking tests. Your grades may reflect the changes.

Reading Check **Summarize** What is cognitive restructuring?

ACADEMIC VOCABULARY

foreboding sense of impending evil or misfortune

SECTION 4 Assessment

Online Quiz THINK central | thinkcentral.com

Reviewing Main Ideas and Vocabulary

1. **Describe** How can making an outline help you answer an essay question more effectively?
2. **Recall** What two objectives does overlearning accomplish?
3. **Describe** Why can test anxiety be a good thing?

Thinking Critically

4. **Summarize** What does practicing for a test involve?
5. **Identify Cause and Effect** What type of stress do some students feel before or during tests, and how might this stress affect their scores?

6. **Categorize** Using your notes and a graphic organizer like the one below, describe the four steps of cognitive restructuring.

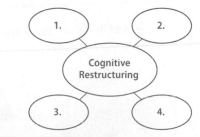

FOCUS ON WRITING

7. **Narrative** Write a paragraph in which you describe your worst case of test anxiety.

Writing a Personality Quiz

What do your answers to questions on a personality quiz say about you? Can your answers reveal your gender?

Reading and Activity Workbook

Use the workbook to complete this lab.

1. Introduction

In this chapter you have learned about different kinds of personality tests. These include both objective tests that present test takers with a standardized group of test items, and projective tests that have no clearly specified answers.

The goal of this activity is to simulate a personality quiz by writing test items for such a test. The class will work in two groups—all the girls will be in one group, and all the boys will be in another. Each group will attempt to write questions for a personality quiz. The goal is to have the answers to the questions reveal the gender of the quiz taker.

Each group should make a list of the questions they would ask to determine the personality of a member of the opposite sex. Here are some sample questions:

- What is your favorite color?
- If you were a tree, what kind would you be?
- If you could be any kind of animal, what would you be?
- What is your favorite leisure time activity?

2. Writing the Quiz

Working in groups according to your teacher's instructions, write a personality quiz that simulates a real personality test. Here are some steps to follow in order to narrow down your list of questions to the best ones.

- Which questions are appropriate?
- Are the proposed questions valid or not? Why?
- What other questions might you ask?
- Is there likely to be a difference in the type of questions from a gender standpoint between the two groups? Should there be such a difference? If not or if so, why?
- From the 15 or 20 questions that your group has come up with, choose the top five questions.
- Next to the top five questions list the reasons why each is valid.

If you could be an animal, what would you be?

OR

What kind of tree would you be?

OR

3. Class Presentation

Once you have written questions, the next step in the process is to present your questions to the class.

- First, each group should write down their answers to the top five questions. Then discuss as a class how you came up with the questions.

- Have the first group, male or female, present their questions to the class.

- Group members will explain how they came up with their questions to determine personality.

- Then have the second group do the same, explaining their questions to the class.

- Explain how the questions reveal personality, especially gender traits.

4. Written Presentation

After class presentations, each student will write a couple of paragraphs describing what he or she has learned.

- Explain what you have learned from the exercise of drafting questions for a gender-revealing personality quiz.

- How might a personality quiz reveal the gender of the quiz taker?

5. Discussion

What did you learn from this simulation? Hold a group discussion that focuses on the following questions.

- Overall, how successful was the class at writing quiz items that revealed gender and personality?

- Were some items particularly easy to write? If so, which ones and why?

- Were some items particularly difficult to write, and why?

- What kinds of quiz items do you think are most effective, and why?

The answers that students give to the questions on a quiz can reveal aspects of their personalities, interests, and attitudes.

Comprehension and Critical Thinking

SECTION 1 (pp. 422–425)

1. a. Describe What kinds of psychological tests are described in this chapter?

b. Explain What is a norm group?

c. Elaborate Which feature or characteristic of psychological tests seems to be more consistent with the computer?

SECTION 2 (pp. 426–429)

2. a. Define What is a vocational interest inventory?

b. Make Generalizations How are aptitude tests generally used?

c. Make Judgments Why is it important not to depend too much on the results of interest inventories?

SECTION 3 (pp. 431–435)

3. a. Recall What does TAT stand for?

b. Explain How were the clinical scales of the Minnesota Multiphasic Personality Inventory originally created?

c. Develop In terms of the MMPI-2, how is someone suffering from schizophrenia characterized?

SECTION 4 (pp. 436–439)

4. a. Describe Which ideas should you lead with in writing an essay?

b. Summarize What steps might a student take to overcome test anxiety?

c. Support a Position Do you think it is possible for psychologists to accurately measure a person's personality using only multiple-choice and true-false questions? Explain your answer.

INTERNET ACTIVITY

5. The importance and the validity of the SAT (Scholastic Assessment Test) have been the subject of debate for the past several years. Use the Internet to research some of the issues surrounding the SAT. Then write an essay stating your position on the use of the SAT as a part of the college admission process. Include references to your research to support your position.

Reviewing Vocabulary

Match the terms below with their correct definitions.

6. behavior-rating scales
7. self-reports
8. standardized test
9. norms
10. achievement tests
11. aptitude tests
12. forced-choice format
13. projective tests
14. scales

A. a test that is administered and scored the same way every time

B. established standards of behavior

C. tests generally used to determine whether a person is likely to do well in a given field of work or study

D. standards of measurement or judgment

E. reports in which people comment on their own attitudes, feelings, and behavior

F. format in which the test taker is required to choose one of several answers, even if none of them seem to fit his or her personality

G. tests with no clearly specified answers

H. tests that measure behavior in such places as classrooms and hospitals

I. tests that measure people's skills and the knowledge they have in specific academic areas

Psychology in Your Life

15. Why do you think people in the same occupation often share the same interests, even outside interests not directly related to their jobs? What are some of your interests and with whom do you share those interests? Write a brief report in which you describe some of your interests and the sorts of occupations in which you think you might find colleagues with the same interests.

SKILLS ACTIVITY: INTERPRETING CARTOONS

Study the cartoon below. Then use the information to answer the questions that follow.

Close to Home © 1993 John McPherson. Reprinted with permission of Universal Press Syndicate.

© 1997 John McPherson/Dist. by Universal Press Syndicate.

The year the SAT creators decided to mess with students' minds.

16. **Analyze** Why do the students assume that there is something wrong with the test?

17. **Identify Main Idea** What does this cartoon suggest about test creators?

WRITING FOR AP PSYCHOLOGY

Use your knowledge of psychological tests to answer the question below. Do not simply list facts. Present a clear argument based on your critical analysis of the question, using the appropriate psychological terminology.

18. Briefly describe what you regard as the most useful tips for taking each of the following kinds of tests.
   - multiple-choice
   - true-false
   - short-answer
   - essay

Connecting Online

Visit **thinkcentral.com** for review and enrichment activities related to this chapter.

THINK central

Quiz and Review

ONLINE QUIZZES
Take a practice quiz for each section in this chapter.

WEBQUEST
Complete a structured Internet activity for this chapter.

QUICK LAB
Reinforce a key concept with a short lab activity.

APPLYING WHAT YOU'VE LEARNED
Review and apply your knowledge by completing a project-based assessment.

Activities

eACTIVITIES
Complete chapter Internet activities for enrichment.

INTERACTIVE FEATURE
Explore an interactive version of a key feature in this chapter.

KEEP IT CURRENT
Link to current news and research in psychology.

Online Textbook

Click for More Learn more about key topics in this chapter.

WOMEN IN COMBAT

In 2008 Monica Lin Brown, a U.S. Army medic, became the second woman since World War II to be awarded the Silver Star. The Silver Star recognizes gallantry in combat. Brown earned the medal while in a patrol convoy in Afghanistan. One of the vehicles was struck by a roadside bomb. As soon as the bomb struck, Brown dashed from her unharmed vehicle to attend to her wounded comrades. As Taliban fighters sprayed machine gun and mortar fire, she shuttled five men to safety, repeatedly risking her life to return for each of the wounded soldiers and shielding them from bullets and shrapnel with her own body.

Some days later, Brown was removed from her unit to a safe post, against her wishes. The reason: Brown is a woman. U.S. law prohibits women from serving in units whose primary mission involves direct ground combat.

The ban on women in combat has a long history. Officially, women were completely excluded from U.S. military service until World War II. Since then there have been numerous changes in both the law and in military regulations. As of 2008, women remained restricted from about 8 percent of Army occupations.

Still, the Iraq War that began in 2003 has often seen female soldiers such as Brown in combat situations. One reason is that the Army has skirted the restriction on women in combat by labeling women GIs as "attached to" rather than "assigned to" combat units. And mixed-gender National Guard units have been deployed alongside but not as part of infantry units.

According to Army reports, female combat troops are prepared and are needed. Nevertheless, Congress has retained the restriction.

Some people argue that women are not physically strong enough to perform crucial battlefield tasks such as carrying wounded soldiers to safety. Author Erin Solaro, a veteran U.S. Army Reserve officer, admits that the average female recruit is smaller than the average male recruit and has less upper body strength. Still, Solaro argues that properly trained women are strong enough to fulfill all the duties of combat.

Law professor Kingsley Browne claims that having women as comrades has a negative effect on men's morale. According to Browne, men do not trust women in dangerous situations. "Even if women actually were as courageous as men, they are not expected to be. That lower expectation of their courage—irrespective of their actual levels of courage—would almost inevitably result in reduced combat performance."

Days after being awarded the Silver Star, Monica Browne was reassigned to duty in a military hospital. Here she treats an Afghan civilian.

CHAPTER 16
GENDER ROLES

College students can serve in the Reserve Officers Training Corps (ROTC), which offers leadership opportunities to men and women equally.

So is male bias the reason for treating women unequally? According to a 2008 report sponsored by the U.S. Army War College, "There is not the slightest doubt that women can perform their assigned duties in the combat zone, including engaging in combat actions essential to their personal and unit's self-defense, with skill and valor equal to their male comrades." Yet male officers still have "continuing ambivalence about assignment [of women] to direct combat units."

If women were inherently gentle and afraid, or if it were men's duty to protect women, then women would not belong in combat. So what one thinks about these issues depends on one's expectations about how men and women do and ought to behave. This chapter is about gender in our society, how it is acquired, and how it guides behavior.

What do you think?

1. What reasons have been offered for excluding women from combat?

2. Do you think women should be allowed to serve in combat situations? Why or why not?

Chapter at a Glance

SECTION 1: Gender Roles and Differences

■ Gender roles are different sets of behaviors that a culture considers appropriate for males and females.

■ Gender stereotypes are oversimplified, fixed beliefs about what behaviors are appropriate for males and females.

■ Men and women typically exhibit physical, cognitive, behavioral, and personality differences.

■ Differences between men and women are both inherited and learned.

■ For the most part, the range of differences among all men or among all women is greater than the differences between the typical or average man and woman.

SECTION 2: Gender Typing

■ Gender typing refers to children's self-identification with a gender and their acquisition of gender traits and roles.

■ Biological factors in gender typing include genetics and hormones.

■ Psychoanalytical theory, social learning theory, and schema theory explain gender typing in distinct ways.

SECTION 3: Variations in Gender Roles

■ Gendered behavior differs within societies at different times.

■ Gendered behavior differs between different societies.

Gender Roles and Differences

Before You Read

Main Idea

Some psychological differences between males and females are the product of biology and some are learned.

Reading Focus

1. What is a gender role? What is a gender stereotype?

2. What differences characterize men and women?

3. Do gender roles cause or reflect personality differences between men and women?

Vocabulary

gender
gender roles
gender stereotypes
nurturance

TAKING NOTES Use a graphic organizer like this one to take notes about differences between males and females.

Perceived Characteristic or Difference	Evidence

BREAKING the GLASS CEILING

Andrea Jung (left) runs Avon, a $10 billion company with more than 5 million sales representatives and about 42,000 employees.

PSYCHOLOGY CLOSE UP

How do gender roles affect career success? The term "glass ceiling" refers to invisible barriers that prevent women from reaching the top positions in the business world. For example, of the 500 largest U.S. companies in 2008, only 12—about 2.5 percent—were headed by women.

The women's movement that came to prominence in the 1970s encouraged many women to pursue careers either before or instead of marrying and starting a family. Yet even today women are greatly over-represented in a few occupations that have little opportunity for advancement: secretary/office clerk, nurse, daycare provider, schoolteacher, and housecleaner. Notably, these occupations tend to involve traditional women's work such as caring for children and keeping house.

People disagree about how to explain why limits on women's achievement in the business world persist. Some people have attributed these limits to differences in men's and women's intellectual or emotional abilities and styles. Others place the blame on subtle or not-so-subtle social pressure, or to prejudice and discrimination. Others say it is simply a matter of personal interests and choices.

Andrea Jung, chairman and CEO of Avon Products, attributes her success to many factors—including leadership, knowledge, and creativity. But she also stresses the importance of finding a woman executive to be her mentor. ◼

Understanding Roles and Stereotypes

We all have physical characteristics that make us different from other people. Height, hair color, eye color, and many other physical traits help to differentiate who we are. Possibly the most fundamental physical characteristic of any human being is his or her gender. **Gender** refers to the sex of an individual, either male or female. Like hair color and eye color, gender is a biological trait that is fixed by the genes before birth.

Gender Roles Closely related to the concept of gender is the idea of **gender roles**—widely accepted societal expectations about how males and females should behave. Gender roles enable us to identify whether a person in our society is a man or a woman. Gender roles also define appropriate and normal masculine and feminine behavior in a particular culture. Unlike gender itself, gender roles are not genetically determined. Rather, gender roles appear to be a product of both biological and social factors.

Although one speaks of "playing a role," people do not *play* gender roles in the same way that they play roles on the stage. That is to say, they do not usually see themselves as pretending to be someone they are not. Instead, for most people, gender roles are simply a part of who they are and how they see themselves.

Psychologists are careful to distinguish two ways in which gender roles function. When we observe and describe differences between boys and girls or men and women, we are using gender roles descriptively: "Men are like this . . . , women are like this . . ."

Gender roles can also function normatively, as norms or standards for judging people: "This is how women ought to act"; "These colors are for girls . . ."; "These games are for boys . . ."

When gender roles are used as norms, people who violate gender roles are sometimes insulted, mocked, or <u>ostracized</u> by others. To avoid disapproval, boys often choose to avoid activities they might enjoy or even excel at but which are "for girls," and girls often choose to avoid activities they might enjoy or even excel at but which are "for boys."

Gender Stereotypes The normative function of gender roles is crucial for how we learn the gender roles in our society. But gender roles can become so rigid that they develop into **gender stereotypes,** which are fixed and oversimplified beliefs about the ways in which men and women ought to behave.

Many gender stereotypes in the United States are linked to traditional views of men as breadwinners and women as homemakers. In U.S. society, the feminine gender stereotype is warm, emotional, dependent, gentle, helpful, patient, submissive, and interested in the arts. The masculine gender stereotype is independent, competitive, tough, protective, logical, and competent at business, math, and science. Women are traditionally expected to care for the children and cook the meals.

Similar gender stereotypes are widespread in industrialized societies. For example, in their survey of 30 countries, John Williams and Deborah Best found that men are more likely to be judged to be wise, courageous, aggressive, dominant, arrogant, and unemotional. Women are more likely to be seen as dependent, submissive, weak, emotional, foolish, and sensitive.

Even emotions are given gender stereotypes. Subjects in one study believed that women more often than men experienced the emotions of sadness, fear, and sympathy. But they thought that men were more likely to feel anger and pride.

Gender stereotypes have tended to keep women in the home. Women of course bear children, but they also are traditionally expected to have the further primary responsibility for raising their children, to naturally be good at childcare, and to enjoy it. On the other hand, popular humor makes fun of men's presumed incompetence in raising children and maintaining a clean, neat home.

When it comes to working outside the home, today many jobs are still stereotyped as primarily for women—for example, nursing and teaching in elementary school. However, large numbers of women have entered some professions previously limited to men, such as medicine and law.

Reading Check **Compare and Contrast** What is the difference between a gender role and a gender stereotype?

Complete a Webquest at thinkcentral.com on stereotypes of boys and girls.

ACADEMIC VOCABULARY

ostracize to reject or exclude

Physical and Cognitive Differences

What differences actually exist between women and men? There are obvious physical differences between the sexes, but other, less obvious disparities also seem to exist. These include differences in personality and behavior and differences in cognitive, or intellectual, abilities. As we shall see, psychologists disagree about the extent to which these differences are biologically based as opposed to learned through experience.

Physical Differences Several physical differences between the sexes are usually apparent because males and females differ in primary and secondary sex characteristics. Primary sex characteristics refer to the organs of the reproductive system. For example, women have ovaries and men have testes. Secondary sex characteristics include such traits as deeper voices and greater amounts of facial hair in men and smaller body size and wider hips in women. These traits are controlled by sex hormones, which in turn are determined primarily by genetics.

This is not to say that every woman has less facial hair than every man or that every man has a deeper voice than every woman. These statements about secondary sex characteristics describe the average man or woman.

Cognitive Differences It was once believed that men were more intelligent than women because men had greater knowledge of world affairs and skill in science and industry. Although most men could demonstrate greater knowledge and skill in these areas, this ability did not reflect differences in intelligence. Rather, these differences arose from the exclusion of women from world affairs, science, and industry.

Modern scientific assessments of intelligence do not show gender differences in overall cognitive abilities. However, girls seem to acquire language somewhat faster than boys do. Reviews of the research suggest that girls are somewhat superior to boys in verbal abilities, such as composing sentences and paragraphs, finding words that are similar in meaning to other words, spelling, pronunciation, and knowledge of foreign languages. Also, in the United States far more boys than girls have reading problems, such as reading below grade level. Men headed for college seem to catch up in verbal skills.

On the other hand, men seem to be somewhat superior in the ability to manipulate visual images held in memory and in visual-spatial abilities of the sort used in mathematics, science, and even map reading. Psychological tests of spatial ability have assessed skills such as finding figures embedded within larger designs and mentally rotating figures in space. One study compared the navigation strategies of 90 male and 104 female college students. In giving directions, college men more often described distances in terms of miles and directional coordinates in terms of north, south, east, and west. College

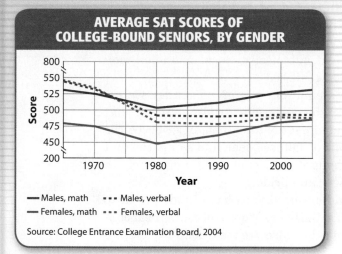

Statistically Speaking...

AVERAGE SAT SCORES OF COLLEGE-BOUND SENIORS, BY GENDER

— Males, math   - - - Males, verbal
— Females, math   - - - Females, verbal

Source: College Entrance Examination Board, 2004

SAT Scores and College Graduations Men still outscore women on the SAT®, the most common college admissions test. But according to graduation totals, women are more successful in college.

57% Percent of bachelor's degrees conferred on men, 1970

57% Percent of bachelor's degrees conferred on women, 2005

Skills Focus INTERPRETING GRAPHS How have the differences between average males' and females' SAT scores changed over time?

Sources: College Entrance Examination Board, 2004; Statistical Abstract, 2008.

women were more likely to refer to landmarks and turns to the right or left. Notice that either set of directions can be effective—the point is that men and women seem to demonstrate and to rely on different sets of abilities.

In the past, boys regularly surpassed girls in measured computational abilities, but in 2008, a review of the research found that this difference has virtually disappeared. Studies still find that males excel in mathematical problem solving in high school and college, and boys generally outperform girls on the mathematics section of the SAT®.

Explaining Gender Differences At present, real gender differences do appear to exist. However, psychologists note the following:

- In most cases, the differences are small, and they appear to be getting smaller as more women pursue course work in a wider range of fields. More girls are excelling in mathematics and science and pursuing careers in fields previously dominated by men, such as architecture, medicine, scientific research, and finance.

- These gender differences are *group* differences. There is greater variation in these skills between individuals *within* the groups than between the groups. Many men's verbal skills surpass those of the "average" woman, and millions of women exceed the "average" man in math and spatial abilities.

- Some differences may reflect cultural influences. For example, spatial and mathematical abilities may be stereotypically masculine. However, women who are given just a few hours of training in spatial skills—for example, rotating geometric figures or studying floor plans—perform at least as well as men on tests of these skills.

- Women now obtain most of the bachelor's degrees in biology and nearly half of the degrees in chemistry and math. Gains in computer science and engineering have also been dramatic. These trends contradict the stereotype that mathematics and the sciences are male domains.

Reading Check **Identify Cause and Effect**
What are the two general causes of physical and cognitive differences between men and women?

"We couldn't connect. He kept spouting technobabble, and I, of course, kept coming back with psychobabble."

© The New Yorker Collection, February 23, 1998, by Sidney Harris. All Rights Reserved.

Skills Focus **INTERPRETING CARTOONS**
How does this cartoon reflect gender stereotypes?

Differences in Personality and Behavior

Many gender differences are found in personality and behavior. Women, for example, tend to exceed men in trust and **nurturance,** or affectionate care. Men tend to exceed women in such traits as assertiveness and tough-mindedness. Other gender differences in personality and behavior include differences in communication styles, levels of aggression, and traits desired in a mate.

Communication Styles A common masculine stereotype is that of the "strong, silent type." While many people believe that women talk more than men do, research suggests that the opposite is actually true. Girls do tend to be more talkative than boys during early childhood, but by the time they enter school, boys usually dominate classroom discussions.

Males and Aggression

Is sport simply a nonlethal outlet for male aggression? Aboriginal Maori men of New Zealand traditionally performed a dance called a *haka* before battle. Its purposes were to intimidate the enemy and to make the men fight more aggressively. In the photo, the New Zealand national rugby team performs a *haka* before a tournament game. Some American football teams have adopted the tradition.

Do you think the haka *is an appropriate outlet for aggression?*

"The tendency to aggression is an innate, independent, instinctual disposition in man."
—Sigmund Freud

Indeed, as girls mature, they do less of the talking in most mixed-sex groups. By adulthood, men generally spend more time talking than women do in many situations. Men are also more likely to introduce new topics and to interrupt others.

Men tend to talk less than women do about their feelings and personal experiences. Women often talk with other women—mothers, sisters, roommates, and friends—about intimate matters. Men talk about intimate matters much less often. When they do, they generally do so with women rather than with other men, perhaps because women tend to be better at using and understanding nonverbal communication. Women are also more likely to offer understanding and support.

Whether these gender differences in communication styles are biologically based or socially learned is still unclear. Male and female children tend to be treated differently from birth in both the number and nature of verbal and nonverbal communications directed toward them.

Aggression In most cultures, it is primarily the men who fight in war and compete in sports and games. This is, in part, because men tend to be physically larger and stronger than women, as previously mentioned. Yet men may be more suited to these activities for another reason as well—their generally higher level of aggression.

Aggression includes hostile or threatening verbal actions, such as challenges, threats, boasts, and demands; physical actions such as grabbing or destroying someone's property; and actual physical attacks such as hitting and shoving. Most psychological studies of aggression have found that men tend to be more aggressive than women. Not only are men more likely than women to act aggressively, particularly if provoked, but they are also more likely to use physical forms of aggression. It has been suggested that, just as aggression helps other male animals engage in ritualized combat to compete for mates, human male aggression is responsible for competitive sports. Women act aggressively less often, and when they do they tend to use indirect forms of aggression.

Although it is clear that men tend to be more aggressive than women, the origins of this gender difference are not as clear. Some experts believe that gender differences in aggression are primarily due to biological differences between men and women. For example, aggressive behavior has been linked with high levels of testosterone.

Although biology may help explain gender differences in aggression, it is likely that the differences are also at least partly due to predominant male and female gender roles. In many societies, men are expected and socialized—or taught through the influence of social pressures—to be tougher, more assertive, and more aggressive than women.

Mate Selection Many physical features, such as cleanliness, good complexion, clear eyes, strong teeth, healthy hair, firm muscle tone, and a steady gait, are found to be universally appealing to both genders. However, studies on mate selection find that men tend to be more swayed than women by a partner's physical appearance. In a survey of more than 13,000 people in the United States, psychologist Susan Sprecher and her colleagues asked a series of questions relating to characteristics that people find appealing in a mate. They found that women were more willing than men to marry someone who was not good-looking but were less willing to marry someone who was unlikely to hold a steady job. Women also tended to place greater emphasis than men on character traits such as dependability, kindness, and fondness for children.

A 2008 study by psychologists Todd Shackelford, David Schmitt, and David Buss came to similar conclusions. They found that women attached more importance to a potential mate's social status, financial resources, dependability, education, and intelligence than men did; men put more weight than women did on good looks, health, and a desire for home and children.

Some psychologists believe that men and women originally valued different characteristics in potential mates because they are the traits that help ensure successful reproduction. However, this explanation cannot be proved conclusively. Gender differences in socialization may also influence which traits men and women look for in a mate. Regardless of the cause, however, the differences between the sexes in the traits considered important in a mate are real and can be found in many different cultures.

As discussed earlier, actual differences in cognitive abilities, personality, and behavior are quite small and may be diminishing. Furthermore, many differences between men and women appear to be due largely to environmental influences and cultural expectations and not to inborn biological differences.

Reading Check **Identify Supporting Details**
What are some apparent differences between males and females?

SECTION 1 Assessment

Reviewing Main Ideas and Vocabulary

1. **Define** What is the difference between gender and gender roles?

2. **Identify Main Ideas** How do gender roles affect personality?

3. **Compare and Contrast** State the main similarity and the main difference between a gender role and a gender stereotype.

4. **Identify** What is nurturance? How does it relate to women's traditional gender roles?

Thinking Critically

5. **Analyze** Provide an example of your personal interests, behavior, or personality and decide whether it is stereotypical for your gender.

6. **Evaluate** Use your notes and a graphic organizer like the one shown to categorize gender traits discussed in the chapter. For each, decide if it is a trait you would like to have and whether you think it is a desirable trait in a friend. Do you see any patterns in how you judge the genders?

Trait in Self		Trait in Friend	
Positive	Negative	Positive	Negative

FOCUS ON WRITING

7. **Expository** Write a paragraph or two discussing one or more of the effects of gender stereotypes. Illustrate your points with examples from the lives of people you know.

The Emotional Development of Boys

Since the late 1990s, numerous researchers have shown interest in how boys learn what it is to be a man. And what they are finding is not good. Society's messages to boys have been called desensitizing and isolating and have been blamed for acts of violence by boys and men.

In 1982, psychologist Carol Gilligan's *In a Different Voice* rocked the academic world by putting forth the claim that, up until that point, developmental psychology had been based on sexist assumptions and sexist research. Gilligan proposed a new approach to moral and emotional development and a new way of conducting psychological research. She would try to understand girls on their own terms, rather than labeling them as inferior because they thought differently than boys. Gilligan's theory and her methodology became the focus of a huge body of research.

And then someone asked, "What about boys?" Gilligan had shown how even preschool-age girls engage in subtle emotional reasoning. Why couldn't boys do it, too?

There were critics who saw this as a sexist attempt to shift focus back onto the male. But others found value in research showing how a strict division of gender roles shortchanges both men and women by cutting them off from the full variety of human experience. These researchers say that society's messages about boys' and men's identities result in a constrained emotional development.

According to child psychologist Michael Thompson, the standard of maleness is "strength, stoicism, and avoiding anything feminine." (Kindlon & Thompson, 1999) Boys learn to be tough and to hide weaknesses, and they learn to avoid intimacy, sympathy, and empathy. This precludes them from having close friendships. As well, it cuts them off from other teenage boys with whom they share experiences.

Other research has found that teachers pay more attention to boys, who are more likely than girls to interrupt and cause disturbances (Sadker & Sadker, 1994). Thus, much of the attention paid to boys is negative.

Taken together, these lessons breed antisocial behavior, self-doubt, loneliness, depression, and even violence. Child psychologist Dan Kindlon calls this "emotional miseducation." (Kindlon and Thompson, 1999)

The main influence on boys' emotional development is the models provided by other men (Garbarino, 1999). This includes not only fathers but also men from popular entertainment such as professional athletes, movie heroes, and pop singers. And it includes peers who not only model masculinity but also ridicule boys who display signs of sensitivity or caring. It even includes mothers and wives, who often unwittingly discourage "weakness" in their sons and husbands. (Kindlon & Thompson, 1999)

When a boy is taught to be tough, does he also learn to ignore his feelings?

Thinking Critically

1. **Analyze** What traits do you think make for an ideal male role model?

2. **Discuss** What would you suggest to improve the ways in which boys and girls learn gender roles?

Current Research THINK central thinkcentral.com

Gender Typing

Before You Read

Main Idea
Several different theories attempt to explain how children acquire their gender roles.

Reading Focus
1. What is gender typing?
2. How do biological views help explain gender typing?
3. What psychological views relate to gender typing?

Vocabulary
gender typing
lateralization
modeling
gender schema

TAKING NOTES Use a graphic organizer like this one to take notes on the key concepts and claims of each theory about gender typing.

Theory	Concepts and Definitions	Claims
biology		
psychoanalysis		
social learning		
schema		

Do you think this toy truck is for a boy or a girl? Why?

PSYCHOLOGY CLOSE UP **Does advertising teach gender differences, or does it reflect them?** As advertising has become more pervasive in children's lives, many people are taking a closer look at its effects on children's ideas about gender. Surveys of television viewing conducted by the A. C. Nielsen company show that preschool boys and girls have different TV-viewing preferences. Television executive Rich Cronin believes that girls are more interested in relationship-oriented entertainment, while boys are more interested in action-oriented programs. Companies use this information to design and market different products for boys and girls.

Psychologists know that gender identity begins developing before age 3. Thus, at the same time as youngsters are developing their ideas about what it is to be a man or woman in our society, advertising is competing with parents and schools to influence them. To what extent does advertising simply provide young consumers information about products designed for them? And to what extent does it teach young boys and girls which products and styles are appropriate for their gender? What does a two-year-old girl learn about gender differences as she watches advertisements for dolls and action figures? In this section you will read about how a child learns to take on a set of gender roles. ■

Understanding Gender Typing

As you have learned, differences in average measured abilities such as physical strength, intellectual abilities, and communication style do appear to exist between the genders. But these differences are not detectable at birth. So, how do they develop into complex, deeply-ingrained gender roles? Several different theories have been proposed to explain gender role development, which is also known as **gender typing.**

Research has shown that children as young as two-and-a-half years of age have begun to develop ideas about what traits and behaviors characterize males and females. These findings suggest that gender typing takes place at an early age. A number of theories have been proposed to explain gender typing. These theories fall into two general categories. One group explains gender typing as a biological process, governed by natural chemical differences between the male and female bodies. The other theory explains gender typing as a psychological process, involving learning, socialization, and interpersonal relations.

Reading Check **Define** What is gender typing?

Biological Views

Biological views of gender typing focus on the role of such factors as genes and hormones in the development of gender-related behavior.

Genetics Scientists believe that traits that help individuals survive and reproduce tend to be passed on to future generations. The extent to which genes guide behavior is hotly debated. Nonetheless, some anthropologists have argued that the traits that ensured the survival and reproductive success of early humans made early men successful hunters and warriors and early women successful child-rearers. For men, these traits would have included good visual-spatial skills and aggression. For women, such traits would have included good nonverbal communication skills and nurturance.

The genetic theory has been adjusted as anthropologists have found new evidence about prehistoric societies. The evidence indicates that ancient gender roles may not have been as rigid as scholars once supposed. For instance, men and women probably shared responsibilities for farming, hunting, and child-rearing. In any case, according to the

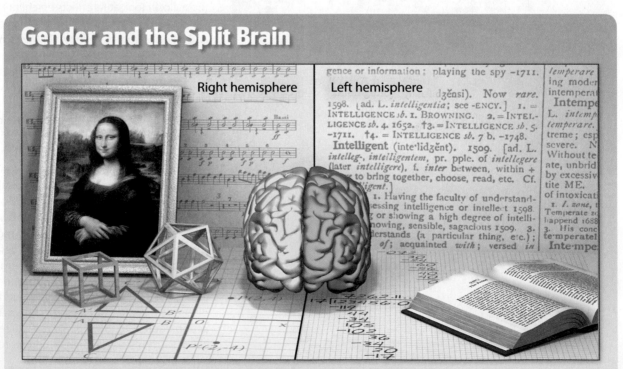

Gender and the Split Brain

Right hemisphere

Left hemisphere

Generally, the left hemisphere specializes in verbal, logical, and mathematical thinking, and the right hemisphere specializes in visual-spatial thinking. The two hemispheres develop somewhat differently in men and women.

How could you investigate whether men and women think differently?

theory, genes that produce behaviors that improve survival would have been passed on to future generations, and those behaviors would eventually come to characterize humans as a species.

The genetic view of gender role origins is on the whole controversial. Proponents cite studies of many nonhuman animals that appear to prove that many behaviors are genetically determined. However, critics argue that biological makeup does not predetermine human behavior. In their view, genes are important determinants of physical traits such as strength, but complex social behaviors such as aggression involve learning and cultural influences as well as heredity. They point to cross-cultural research that shows variation in gender roles across societies and within individual societies over time. This variation suggests that gender roles are largely learned and not inherited.

Hormones Some psychologists believe that gender typing occurs because men and women differ in the organization and functioning of their brains. According to this view, sex hormones sculpt the brains of men and women differently before birth. To understand this theory, one needs some background knowledge of brain structure and function.

The two hemispheres, or right and left sides, of the brain are somewhat specialized to carry out different functions. The majority of cognitive functions are performed by both hemispheres; however, they are performed more quickly and efficiently by one hemisphere than by the other. In most people, the right hemisphere is better at performing visual-spatial tasks, whereas the left hemisphere is better at verbal tasks. Producing speech is one of the few cognitive tasks that are the *sole* responsibility of one hemisphere or the other. This specialization of the two sides of the brain is called **lateralization.** Lateralization occurs during fetal development and is apparently influenced by sex hormones. Thus, lateralization may occur differently in boys and girls.

There is some evidence to suggest that testosterone leads to relatively greater growth of the right hemisphere as compared with the left hemisphere. This evidence is consistent with research indicating that females tend to show less lateralization than males. Taken

Quick Lab

Gender Division in the Home

As American lifestyles have changed since the mid-1900s, men's responsibility for homemaking duties has, in general, increased. But there is wide variation in both what men do and in what they are expected to do.

PROCEDURE

❶ Make a list of common tasks around the home: for example, washing clothes, shopping for groceries, and paying bills.

❷ Make two copies of your list. Use one to record your personal predictions about whether each task is more commonly men's or women's responsibility. Keep this list private until after you complete Step ❹.

❸ Use the other copy of your list to collect data from peers. Ask your classmates whether each job on the list is done in their home by men, boys, women, or girls.

❹ Compare the data you collected with those of your peers.

ANALYSIS

1. Based on your results, do you think there are such things as typical men's and women's work?

2. Discuss whether your results match your personal expectations (from Step ❷).

3. Based on your data, how firm is the gender division of labor? That is, how much or how little overlap is there in the work that males and females do? Are your results surprising?

Quick Lab **THINK** central thinkcentral.com

together, these studies could help explain why males seem to be better at visual-spatial tasks, which tend to be processed by the right hemisphere, and why females seem to be better at verbal tasks, which tend to be processed by the left hemisphere of the brain.

Some psychologists also believe that gender typing may be a result of subtle prenatal changes to the brain caused by sex hormones. For example, they suggest that boys' inclinations toward aggression and rough-and-tumble play might be due to the influence of testosterone on the brains of developing male fetuses. However, other psychologists argue that social influences are more important than hormones in shaping gender typing.

Reading Check **Identify Supporting Details** How do genes and hormones affect gender typing?

Psychological Views

Although many psychologists believe that genes and sex hormones play some role in gender typing, others believe that psychological processes play a more important role. Among the psychological theories that have been suggested to explain how gender typing comes about are psychoanalytic theory, social-learning theory, and gender-schema theory.

Psychoanalytic Theory Sigmund Freud's psychoanalytic theory argues that gender typing can be explained in terms of gender identification, which occurs between the ages of three and five.

At the beginning of this period, Freud argued, children seek the attention of the parent of the opposite sex and perceive the parent of the same sex as a rival for that attention. By the end of the period, however, children no longer feel this way and instead identify with the parent of the same sex.

According to Freud, it is through this process of identification with the same-sex parent that a child comes to develop the behaviors that are associated with his or her own sex. The child internalizes the standards of the same-sex parent and eventually adopts that parent as a role model for behavior.

There are some problems with this theory. According to Freud, the complex feelings that children have for the parent of the opposite sex are not resolved until children reach age five. However, as noted previously, children tend to display gender roles much earlier. Even in infancy, boys have been found in some studies to be more independent than girls. Also, between the ages of one and three, many girls show preferences for dolls and soft toys, whereas many boys prefer hard transportation toys. The appearance of gender differences in very young children does not disprove Freud's explanation of gender typing, but it does raise difficult questions for the theory.

Social-Learning Theory According to social-learning theory, gender role behavior, like other behavior, is acquired through two different learning processes—reinforcement and modeling.

Reinforcement occurs when a behavior has <u>propitious</u> consequences. Because it is rewarded, the behavior is more likely to be repeated. In contrast, behaviors that are not rewarded and behaviors that are punished are less likely to be repeated, because they are not reinforced.

Social-learning theorists argue that reinforcement of appropriate gender role behavior starts very early. Almost from the moment of birth, the way babies are treated may depend on their sex. When children are old enough to understand language, parents and others begin to instruct them about how they are expected to behave. Parents tend to talk and read more to baby girls, for example, and fathers often engage in more rough-and-tumble play with boys.

Parents are also likely to reward a child for behavior that they consider appropriate for the child's gender and to punish or at least fail to reward the child for behavior they consider inappropriate. For example, studies have found that parents tend to react positively when children play with toys considered gender appropriate. On the other hand, parents often react negatively when children play with toys considered gender inappropriate. Fathers especially are likely to react negatively when their sons play with toys considered more appropriate for girls, such as dolls. They may frown, make sarcastic comments, and even physically separate the child from the toy. Girls, however, are less likely to receive negative reactions from their fathers for playing with toys considered more appropriate for boys, such as trucks.

From an early age, boys are also more likely to be given toy cars, toy guns, and athletic equipment. Girls, on the other hand, are more likely to receive dolls and other soft toys. When playing with their children at home, parents also tend to reach first for toys considered appropriate for the child's sex, even when the child owns toys that are generally considered appropriate for both sexes.

Studies of aggression provide some good examples of how behavior is learned through reinforcement. In one study, one-year-old boys and girls were found to be equally likely to use aggressive actions, such as pushing or grabbing, in order to obtain what they wanted. They were also equally likely to use communication, such as whining or gesturing. Yet adults' reactions to the children's efforts differed depending on the children's sex. The

ACADEMIC VOCABULARY

propitious favorable, advantageous

adults tended to respond positively when the girls tried to communicate and solve the dispute in a nonaggressive manner but showed little response when the boys behaved this way. On the other hand, the adults tended to ignore aggression in the girls and respond positively to it in the boys.

Not surprisingly, by age two the girls in the study no longer acted aggressively. They had apparently learned through reinforcement to communicate their wants verbally. The boys had learned the opposite lesson, and their level of aggression remained high. As a result of such differences in reinforcement, girls tend to develop more anxiety about aggression and greater inhibitions against displaying it.

Even in the absence of reinforcement, social learning can occur through observation and imitation of others. This process is known as **modeling.** Children learn about both male and female gender role behavior by observing males and females with whom they commonly interact. However, the children are more likely to model or imitate individuals of the same sex as themselves, particularly a parent of the same sex. Children are also more likely to receive positive reinforcement for imitating the behavior of a parent of the same sex.

Observational learning and imitation were illustrated in a classic experiment by David Perry and Kay Bussey. In their study, eight- and nine-year-old boys and girls watched adult models indicate their preferences for one of the items in each of 16 different pairs of items. The adults chose among such pairs as toy cows versus toy horses and oranges versus apples. The children in the study did not realize that the adults' preferences were purely arbitrary. When the children were asked to indicate their own preferences for the items in the pairs, the boys' choices matched the adult men's choices 14 out of 16 times, and the girls' choices matched the adult women's choices 13 out of 16 times. Thus, both boys and girls tended to model their behavior after role models of their own sex, even though the behavior was actually arbitrary and unrelated to gender.

If gender roles are learned, as social-learning theory suggests, then they should be flexible, or capable of changing. Indeed, there are indications that this is the case. Today, as more women are working outside the home, gender roles do seem to be changing. Another indication of gender role change is that parents are more likely now than in the past to encourage their daughters to play sports and follow careers. They are also more likely to encourage their sons to be nurturing and cooperative.

Gender-Schema Theory Social-learning theory has made important contributions to our understanding of how reinforcement and modeling promote gender-typed behavior. A somewhat different view of gender typing is provided by gender-schema theory.

According to this theory, children themselves play an active role in developing gender-appropriate behavior. Children form their own concepts about gender and then shape their behavior so that it conforms to their gender concepts. Specifically, children develop a gender schema in order to organize their perceptions of the world.

A **gender schema** is a cluster of ideas about physical qualities, behaviors, and personality traits associated with one sex or the other.

THEORIES FOR EXPLAINING GENDER TYPING

QUICK FACTS

Both biological and psychological explanations have been suggested for gender typing.

Theory	Explanation
Genetics (biological)	The genes that determine sex also determine gendered behavior.
Hormones (biological)	Hormonal differences between boys and girls cause different patterns of development.
Psychoanalytic Theory (psychological)	Boys and girls identify with and so learn gender roles from their same-sex parent.
Social-Learning Theory (psychological)	Gender differences are modeled by parents and reinforced by positive and negative reactions.
Gender-Schema Theory (psychological)	Children form gender-based self-conceptions, which guide their behavior.

Skills Focus INTERPRETING CHARTS Might more than one of these theories be true?

The theory holds that gender is such a strong force in our society that children come to organize their perceptions along gender lines.

Gender-schema theorists suggest that as soon as children learn whether they are boys or girls, they begin to seek information concerning gender-typed traits. Even very young children start to mentally group people of the same sex according to the traits they believe are representative of that gender.

Once their gender schema is formed, children strive to live up to it. They begin to judge themselves according to the traits they believe are relevant to their sex, using their gender schema as a standard for comparison. In so doing, children blend their developing self-concepts with the prominent gender schema of their culture. For example, boys may react aggressively when provoked because they perceive that is what society expects males to do. Girls, on the other hand, may try to cooperate because they perceive that society expects such behavior from females.

Across both genders, children's self-esteem depends in part on how similar their own personalities, behaviors, and physical appearances are to those of the prominent gender schema. In other words, boys who see themselves as fitting their culture's ideals of masculinity are more likely to develop higher self-esteem than boys who do not. Similarly, girls who see themselves as fitting their culture's ideals of femininity are more likely to develop higher self-esteem than girls who do not.

Children's gender schema also determines how important particular traits are to them. Consider the dimensions of strength-weakness and kindness-cruelty. Children are likely to learn that the strength-weakness dimension is more important to males, whereas the kindness-cruelty dimension is more important to females. Thus, a boy is more likely to be concerned about how strong he is, whereas a girl is more likely to be concerned about being kind.

In summary, both the biological view and the psychological view of gender typing can help us understand why males and females behave as they do. This is because differences in gender roles are likely to be influenced by differences in biology, life experiences, and cultural expectations. Each of these factors plays a role in determining how individual males and females behave.

Regardless of how gender typing occurs, perhaps it should not be viewed as inevitable. While most human societies have found it appropriate for males and females to have very different roles, many people today believe that strict gender roles no longer suit our basic values or our way of life.

Reading Check **Summarize** How do social learning theory and schema theory explain gender typing?

SECTION 2 Assessment

Online Quiz **THINK** central thinkcentral.com

Reviewing Main Ideas and Vocabulary

1. **Recall** What are the five different theories of gender typing?

2. **Compare and Contrast** Compare and contrast lateralization of brain function in men and women.

3. **Describe** According to schema theory, what functions does a gender schema serve?

Thinking Critically

4. **Contrast** Describe some differences in your gender schema for men and for women.

5. **Elaborate** What criticisms have been made of the psychoanalytic theory of gender typing? What responses might a psychoanalytic thinker make?

6. **Explain** According to social learning theory, what role does modeling play in gender typing?

7. **Analyze** Which gender traits are explained by biology, and which are the product of learning? Use a graphic organizer like the one shown to evaluate the theories.

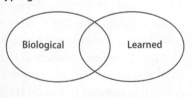

FOCUS ON WRITING

8. **Narrative** Write a brief story about a boy who receives a "girl's toy" for a present or about a girl who receives a "boy's toy" for a present. Use narrative or dialog to indicate the main character's feelings.

Variations in Gender Roles

Before You Read

Main Idea
Gender roles differ in different societies and change over time.

Reading Focus
1. How have gender roles varied over time?
2. What aspects of gender vary among different cultures?

Vocabulary
ethnography

TAKING NOTES Use a graphic organizer like this one to note variations from stereotypical gender characteristics.

Stereotype	Counter-Example?

Why is that MAN in the KITCHEN?

PSYCHOLOGY CLOSE UP

How many stay-at-home dads do you know? According to stereotypes, the kitchen is Mom's domain, and Dad cooks only outdoors on the barbecue. But the world does not always fit our stereotypes. While a single-family home with a stay-at-home dad Is far from the norm across the United States, there are many more such households today than there were a century ago. As of 2005, the U.S. Census Bureau estimated that there were about 143,000 stay-at-home dads in the United States, out of over 66 million married fathers.

Still, changes in gender roles do not make gender differences evaporate. Stay-at-home dad Michael Paranzino tells his daughter, "Moms might make the clothes match, but Daddy doesn't." Researchers want to know how children's conceptions of gender might be different when they grow up with a stay-at-home father rather than a stay-at-home mother or (what is more common) no stay-at-home parent. Do boys grow into more-caring men if their father is their primary caretaker? Do girls who grow up with a stay-at-home dad develop different expectations about potential husbands? In this section you will read about how gender roles vary from society to society and how they change within a society through time. ■

Variation in Gender Roles Through Time

Both social-learning theory and gender-schema theory propose that learning plays the key part in gender role development. They suggest that gender roles are not inborn or fixed at birth but may vary from person to person. Research has shown that gender roles can vary from culture to culture. In other words, what is considered gender-appropriate behavior in one society may be viewed differently in another cultural setting. In Western society, gender roles have changed dramatically over time, as is demonstrated by women's increasing participation in activities long considered appropriate only for men—business, sports, politics, and the military, to name a few.

Throughout most of history, women in most parts of the world were expected to be the child rearers, and men were expected to provide food and safety for women and children. With this division of labor as a base, men and women also had additional, related duties. These differences in gender roles were based in part on the different biological characteristics of the two sexes. Women were more restricted in their activity and mobility by childbearing and the need to nurse their young children. So, for instance, women attended to each other's births and continued to care for children as they grew. Men, being larger, stronger, and biologically less tied to childbearing and child rearing, were considered better suited for hunting and similar activities. Because women did not engage in battle, men became military and political leaders.

Women were also expected to be less aggressive than men in mate selection. Rather than initiating relationships with men, many women adorned themselves to appear more attractive.

Thus, throughout much of the past, gender roles were both more distinct and more rigid than they are in contemporary Western society. Not only did men and women engage in different activities, but their interactions were sometimes restricted as well. Some historians have gone so far as to say that there were distinct female and male worlds, but this is an exaggeration.

Gender in the Modern United States In the mid-20th century, the accepted pattern was for a woman to marry, stay at home, and care for the house and children. According to the dominant ideas of the time, the ideal woman was a devoted wife who kept a clean house and had dinner waiting when her husband returned from work. She was expected to put

CASE STUDY
CONNECTION

Women in Combat
American women have a much greater role in the military today than in the last century, although as Monica Brown knows, limits remain.

INTERACTIVE ✳

Women's Roles Over Time

The ways in which women's roles have changed over time suggest that many gender traits are learned products of culture and not purely the result of biology. *How have women pioneered changes in gender roles?*

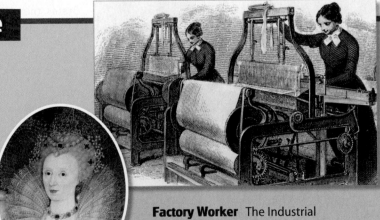

Political Leader Queen Elizabeth I of Britain (1533–1603) did not fit the expectations for women of her day. She was educated and intelligent, a shrewd politician, an able military leader, and she refused numerous marriage proposals.

Factory Worker The Industrial Revolution brought both men and women into factory jobs. Although women were paid poorly and conditions were harsh, factory work eventually led to more employment opportunities.

the needs of her husband and children ahead of her own. The idea that a woman should put her own career or personal ambitions ahead of marriage and raising a family was not very widespread. Women who did not marry were frowned upon, as were mothers who worked outside the home and men who did not have steady work.

American society has changed since the early 1960s. In 2000, 70 percent of women were either employed or seeking employment. And roughly 57 percent of mothers were going to work within 6 months after giving birth.

Today, many women are working and marrying later or remaining unmarried. The number of women living alone went from 11.5 percent in 1970 to more than 15 percent in 2005. Compared to 1976, in 2004 nearly twice as many women aged 40–44 had never had children. In 2005, less than one-fourth of households were married couples with minor children, compared to 40 percent in 1970.

Many married women work because their families cannot afford to live on one income alone. In some families, the wife works to support the family while the husband remains at home with the children. These choices are far more widely accepted today than they were in the 1970s.

In other ways, too, male and female gender roles in the United States today are much more flexible than they were just a few decades ago. In many marriages, for example, husbands and wives share household chores, child rearing, and wage earning equally. However, women who work outside the home are largely expected to retain long-established feminine gender roles in the household.

Other sorts of gender differences have also been in the process of change. Girls' and women's participation in sports has grown to almost that of men. Meanwhile, it has also become more acceptable for boys and men to opt out of sports. Both men and women wear either short or long hair, earrings, face makeup, and tattoos. Men and women equally wear pants, although skirts and dresses for men would appear to have remained largely taboo.

Reading Check **Identify Supporting Details** In what ways have gender differences in the United States changed?

Cultural Variation

Gender roles not only vary through time but also vary from culture to culture. A famous work of **ethnography** by anthropologist Margaret Mead explored this issue. In the 1930s, Mead studied three different groups of people—the Mundugumor, the Arapesh, and the Tchambuli—on the South Pacific island of New Guinea.

Interactive Feature THINK central thinkcentral.com

Celebrity "The Divine Sarah," Sarah Bernhardt (1844–1923) was said to be as famous as the Eiffel Tower in her day. Bernhardt's love affairs and habit of wearing men's clothing caused scandals, as did her playing men's roles on the stage.

Wartime Industrial Worker During World War II large numbers of women moved into industrial occupations. They made tools, planes, weapons and ammunition, machinery, and consumer goods while men served in the military.

Politician, Attorney, Jurist In 1981 Sandra Day O'Connor became the first woman appointed to the U.S. Supreme Court. Her previous jobs included private practice attorney, justice of the Arizona Court of Appeals, and state senate majority leader.

Construction Tradeworker The integration of women into male-dominated trades such as carpentry and plumbing is underway. Equality has not yet arrived, but some women have risen to supervisory positions.

According to Mead, the Mundugumor were a warlike people, and both men and women were very aggressive. Mundugumor women looked down on bearing and rearing children because this interfered with their ability to go to battle. In contrast, the neighboring Arapesh were gentle and peaceful, and Arapesh men and women played an equal role in caring for the children and maintaining the land.

The Tchambuli differed from both the Mundugumor and Arapesh in their gender roles. Mead reported that Tchambuli men spent most of their time caring for children, gossiping, bickering, primping, and haggling over prices. Tchambuli women, on the other hand, spent most of their time catching the fish that made up the bulk of the Tchambuli diet. Tchambuli women also kept their heads shaved, disliked wearing ornaments, and were more aggressive than the men.

Margaret Mead's interpretation of her New Guinea study has been criticized as being too subjective, or biased by her personal views concerning gender roles. Still, the data Mead collected clearly suggest that what is considered appropriate behavior for men and women can differ from one culture to another. Thus, the data may support the claim that many gender differences are learned, not inborn.

Since Margaret Mead published her early research in the 1920s and 1930s, the idea that gender norms and roles vary across cul-

ACADEMIC VOCABULARY

deliberation discussion of reasons in order to reach a decision

tures has become widely accepted. Historians, archaeologists, and ethnographers have studied ancient as well as contemporary cultures around the world and have found variety in what is considered normal.

For instance, in ancient Egypt it was accepted that either a man or a woman could be the ruler, whereas no woman could rule in such ancient Mesopotamian societies as Assyria and Akkad.

In some North American native societies, the roles of men and women were different from those of the early English and Spanish explorers and settlers. Men and women of the Seneca, for instance, were equal participants in tribal votes and deliberations. In some tribes, a council of mothers had to ratify decisions on going to war. In most tribes, married couples retained separate ownership of all property, and often even maintained separate homes.

Another example is the Scythians, a nomadic society of Central Asia around the 7th and 8th centuries B.C. Recent archaeological evidence suggests that Scythian women were warriors who rode and fought on horseback alongside men and probably inspired the legends of the Amazons.

Reading Check **Identify Main Ideas** What do cultural differences suggest about how gender roles are acquired?

SECTION 3 Assessment

Online Quiz THINK central   thinkcentral.com

Reviewing Main Ideas and Vocabulary

1. **Recall** How do gender roles differ in the three New Guinea societies that Margaret Mead studied?

2. **Identify Supporting Ideas** In what ways have American society's gender roles changed over time?

3. **Draw Conclusions** What do the data from ethnographic research suggest is a significant determinant of gender roles?

Thinking Critically

4. **Interpret** How is it thought that biologically defined capacities for child bearing and nursing affected gender roles of early human societies?

5. **Make Generalizations** In what ways do contemporary American two-parent families divide responsibilities?

6. **Categorize** Using a graphic organizer like the one shown, make two lists of gender roles according to whether the roles do or do not vary across times and cultures.

Vary	Do Not Vary

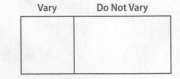

FOCUS ON WRITING

7. **Persuasive** Write a brief essay explaining why you think strict, rigid gender roles are a good thing or a bad thing for a society.

Gender Roles Around the World

Margaret Mead showed that, to some degree, men's and women's roles are a cultural product and not solely determined by biology. The obvious next question is, "To what degree?" One way in which social and behavioral scientists since Mead have tried to answer this question is by further ethnographic studies to assess the ways in which gender roles vary.

In 2008, Jose Zapatero announced the first Spanish cabinet to have a majority of women, including Carme Chacon, 7 months pregnant, as defense minister.

One of the key scenes where gender roles play out is in employment. Across societies there are marked differences in women's expected roles in the economy. For example, over 67 percent of East Asian women participate in the labor market, compared to around 36 percent in South Asia. Since the participation rate for men in both regions is between 80 and 85 percent, the difference cannot be attributed to economic conditions.

Another area of difference is in the type of jobs held by men and women. One study found that women held 59 percent of administrative and managerial jobs in Sweden, in contrast to 6 percent in Turkey and 4 percent in Korea.

Cultures also differ in how they distinguish appropriate public behavior for men and women. In some societies governed strictly by Islamic law, such as Afghanistan, women remain in the home; they go out in public only in special circumstances and only if their head and face are covered; and they receive only enough education to enable them to study the Qur'an. The rules of *hijab*—an Arabic word meaning "covering" or "concealment"—are different in each society because gender roles developed from a mixing of Islamic teachings and various local customs. In Turkey, for instance, it is illegal to wear the headscarf in schools or universities. The purpose of this rule is to protect those women who would choose not to cover their heads from being pressured or threatened.

Men's and women's roles across cultures have become more alike as societies around the world have become more industrialized, participate more in a world economy, and are increasingly inundated by worldwide news and entertainment sources. This change means that in many developing countries, gender roles in the industrialized, cosmopolitan cities differ greatly from those in more isolated rural areas.

At public events in Afghanistan, women are veiled, and men and women are separated by a wall.

Thinking Critically

1. **Summarize** In what ways do women's roles in different societies differ?

2. **Discuss** To what extent do you think men and women choose their gender roles?

Simulation
Applying What You've Learned

Identifying Gender Stereotypes

Reading and Activity Workbook

Use the workbook to complete this simulation.

How accurate are gender stereotypes? If you saw an actor portray an anonymous character, do you think that you could tell whether the character was supposed to be a man or a woman? Here's a chance to find out.

1. Introduction

What does she really mean when she says, "Let's just be friends"?

When he says he'll call me and it's been 3 hours, does that mean that he's really not going to call me?

We've all either experienced for ourselves or known others who have experienced frustrations trying to understand individuals of the other gender. But how accurate are the typical stereotypes? In this simulation you will role-play to portray the different genders. To complete the simulation, follow the steps below.

▪ As a class you will make a list of roles or characters that include both stereotypical gender traits and less-common gender traits.

▪ Then you will pair off and create a scenario for your two roles/characters.

▪ Finally, you will enact your scenario for the class. Your classmates will try to guess the genders of your two characters.

2. Initial Preparation

▪ As a class, brainstorm as many gendered roles as you can think of. Try to list roles that are stereotypical—for example, a stay-at-home mother—as well as nonstereotypical variations such as a stay-at-home father like the one discussed in Section 3. Record everyone's ideas on the board.

▪ Once you are done, have a small work group write the descriptions on note cards or small pieces of paper.

▪ Following your teacher's instructions, each student will draw a card from the pile and then find a partner. You and your partner will plan and enact a scenario together.

3. Creating the Scenarios

Once you have your card with your role, meet with your partner and create a scenario in which you each portray gender stereotypes. Your teacher will tell you how much time you will have to plan and practice your scenario. Here are some things to consider when working out your scenario:

▪ Separately, think of at least five things about your character's personality and situation that will enable the class to guess your character's gender. Consider:

- Family responsibilities
- Career opportunities
- Financial requirements
- Contemporary or historical time period
- Cognitive differences
- Aggression
- Communication
- Dating
- Cultural surroundings

▪ Create a scenario in which both you and your partner can showcase the main aspects of the gender type that you are portraying. This situation can be realistic: for example, a married mother and a divorced mother discussing child-care issues as they ride the elevator up to work; or the situation can be improbable: for example, a stay-at-home father and a Mundugumor woman window shopping as they power walk in the mall.

■ Make sure that your scenario provides a lot of clues to help the rest of the class guess your roles. But also try to make it a little difficult for the class to guess. If you have a nontraditional gender type, be sure to include some of the nontraditional qualities.

■ Write out a basic script that you and your partner will follow. This will help you to make sure that you are including each of the aspects that make your character's gender identifiable. It will also help you assure that you are including something to make the identification a bit of a challenge for the class. Each of you should have a copy of the script so that you do not have to share it when you are in front of the class.

■ Practice your script at least once before getting up in front of the class. Look for anything that might be confusing, and double check that there are several instances that include clues for the class to guess.

4. Presenting and Observing the Scenarios

Following your teacher's instructions, pairs will take turns getting up in front of the class and enacting the scenario that they have created.

■ As each group performs its simulation, look for identifying markers that will help to identify gender roles. Remember that sometimes the gender stereotypes will affect your thinking, so try to look for both traditional and nontraditional gender roles.

■ If there is time after each pair has presented their scenario, match up any two willing participants to portray their gender types extemporaneously. This can be interesting to see how two differing gender types would interact.

■ You can also try impromptu scenarios with three or four characters.

5. Discussion

■ Were the stereotypical gender types easier to identify than those that were nontraditional? Why or why not?

■ What were the aspects that made it easiest to identify a gender role? Family obligations? Aggression levels? Cognitive differences? Why would these affect the ease with which someone could identify a gender role?

■ What was revealed in scenarios that showed interactions between traditional and nontraditional gender roles? What seemed to cause tension or conflict? What personality traits were conducive to positive interactions?

■ What do these scenarios reveal about the information presented in this chapter? Was the information in the chapter reliable when applied to these scenarios? What would you consider to be unrealistic about these scenarios? What was authentic?

Comprehension and Critical Thinking

SECTION 1 *(pp. 446–451)*

1. a. Identify What are some ways in which familiar male and female stereotypes are inaccurate?

b. Explain How do psychologists believe biology can explain some gender differences?

c. Make Judgments Which aspects of gender roles do you think are biologically determined and which are cultural?

SECTION 2 *(pp. 453–458)*

2. a. Describe How might hormones affect lateralization differently in men and women?

b. Explain How might social learning theory explain why boys tend to speak more than girls in elementary classrooms?

c. Elaborate How do you think a gender schema would be learned?

SECTION 3 *(pp. 459–462)*

3. a. Recall What are some ways in which gender roles have changed from ancient to modern times?

b. Compare What aspects of gender roles in the United States today seem unchanged from prehistoric times?

c. Predict In what ways do you think American gender roles might change in the next few decades?

INTERNET ACTIVITY ✴

4. Use the Internet to research this question: Does advertising teach gender roles or does it only reflect a society's existing gender roles? Investigate studies of the effects of advertising on children. Also read reviews of and commentary on the issue. Write a short report that summarizes your findings.

Reviewing Vocabulary

Fill in each blank with the term that correctly completes the sentence.

5. A child's _____ are the two sets of traits and behaviors he or she uses to classify people into male and female.

6. The scientific study of human cultures is called _____.

7. The male and female _____ are biological traits fixed before birth.

8. Some researchers have argued that _____, or loving care and attention, is a genetically-acquired trait in women.

9. Oversimplified generalizations about the characteristics of males and females, or _____, often turn out to be mistaken.

10. People who violate expected behavior for their gender are sometimes _____, or shunned and excluded.

11. _____ are the differing sets of behaviors that a culture considers appropriate for males or females.

12. _____ is the name for the process by which people learn to conform to their society's gender roles.

13. A council of advisers _____ when they discuss reasons in order to reach a decision.

14. The process of learning behavior through the observation and imitation of others is called _____.

15. Prior to birth, the brain undergoes _____, in which the left and right hemispheres develop specializations in certain functions.

Psychology in Your Life

16. Think of a way in which a school or government treats males and females differently. For instance, you might be aware of a rule that is applied differently to boys and girls, or you might think of ways in which similar behaviors by boys and girls are judged differently depending on who exhibits the behavior. Write a letter to a local school or government official explaining *either* why you support this difference *or* why you think the policy should be changed.

SKILLS ACTIVITY: INTERPRETING GRAPHS

This bar graph shows how much of their playtime children spend with other children of the same gender and with children of the other gender. Notice that the graph does not give any information about how much children play, nor does it give any information about differences between boys' and girls' playmates. Study the graph. Then, answer the questions that follow.

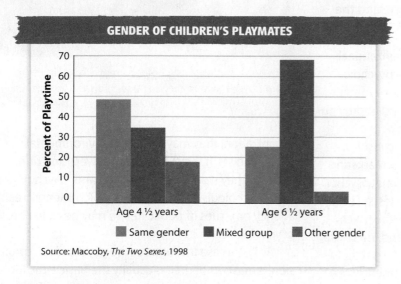

GENDER OF CHILDREN'S PLAYMATES

Y-axis: Percent of Playtime (0, 10, 20, 30, 40, 50, 60, 70)

X-axis: Age 4 ½ years, Age 6 ½ years

Legend: ■ Same gender ■ Mixed group ■ Other gender

Source: Maccoby, *The Two Sexes*, 1998

17. Contrast Of the two age groups shown in the graph, which age group plays more in mixed-gender groups?

18. Make Generalizations On the whole, how do the rates of same-gender and mixed-gender play change between the fifth and seventh years of childhood?

WRITING FOR AP PSYCHOLOGY

Use your knowledge of gender to answer the question below. Do not simply list facts. Present a clear argument based on your critical analysis of the question, using the appropriate psychological terminology.

19. DSM-IV defines *gender identity disorder* as "a strong and persistent cross-gender identification" accompanied by "persistent discomfort" with his or her sex.

- Identify two different psychological theories, and tell how each theory could explain the nature and causes of gender identity disorder.
- Evaluate the two explanations.

Connecting Online

Visit thinkcentral.com for review and enrichment activities related to this chapter.

THINK central

Quiz and Review

ONLINE QUIZZES
Take a practice quiz for each section in this chapter.

WEBQUEST
Complete a structured Internet activity for this chapter.

QUICK LAB
Reinforce a key concept with a short lab activity.

APPLYING WHAT YOU'VE LEARNED
Review and apply your knowledge by completing a project-based assessment.

Activities

eACTIVITIES
Complete chapter Internet activities for enrichment.

INTERACTIVE FEATURE
Explore an interactive version of a key feature in this chapter.

KEEP IT CURRENT
Link to current news and research in psychology.

Online Textbook

Click for More — Learn more about key topics in this chapter.

Organizational Psychologist

How can a company arrange cubicles to maximize space without isolating employees? How would a department layoff affect employee morale and the company as a whole?

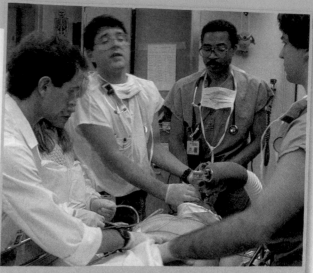

An organizational psychologist may work with hospital employees to help them deal with on-the-job stress.

Psychology enters the workplace with organizational, or industrial, psychologists. Organizational psychologists are usually employed by business or government to devise ways of increasing productivity and improving working conditions—while saving money.

Organizational psychologists generally consult with various divisions of one or more companies. Marketing departments often consult with organizational psychologists to conduct surveys and focus group tests. These efforts can help marketing divisions assess the psychological profile of their intended audience and, therefore, affect advertising campaigns. Organizational psychologists may also help human resource departments create new questions for interveiwers or suggest ways to improve employee morale. The psychologists may be called upon by executives to assess the company's time-management program.

The more the workplace changes, the more need there will be for organizational/industrial psychologists to smooth transitions. And so far, there is no sign that change in the workplace will slow down.

Like counselors, organizational/industrial psychologists assume the titles indicated by their specific work situations. For example, if they work for a conservation organization, they may be called environmental psychologists. If they work for an advertising firm, perhaps they would be called consumer psychologists. And psychologists working for a governmental health agency on issues of public health may be called health psychologists.

As is the case throughout the psychological profession, a master's degree is usually the basic educational requirement for more challenging positions. Doctorates are becoming more prevalent.

Although organizational/industrial psychology is one of the less visible careers in psychology, it is one of the most far-reaching in terms of the work's impact on the public. The career choices available to anyone qualified for the field are quite extensive. There are no fewer choices than there are types of industries. The field is most appealing to people who are good at spotting trends, are outgoing, and can get along with a range of individuals and groups.

Applying APA Style

 APA Style THINK central thinkcentral.com

Organizational psychologists work with a wide range of employees. Their reports and recommendations must be clear. The **American Psychological Association (APA)**, provides guidelines for eliminating stylistic problems that can make one's written work unclear.

Redundancy—using words with the same meaning as other words in a sentence—can occur when a writer is trying to emphasize a point. For example, "tired and weary" is a redundant phrase.

Another common stylistic flaw is overuse of the passive voice. When you can, say who or what is responsible for the action. "Dr. Carter delivered the results" is clearer than "The results were delivered."

Through Think Central you can find more information on eliminating redundancy and using active and passive voice from the APA style guidelines. Go to the site to review the APA guidelines. Then write several examples of redundancy along with more concise versions. List passive and active sentences also. An example is provided for you.

Redundant	Concise
enormously large	enormous

Health and Adjustment

1 OUT OF 4 Americans WILL experience A psychological disorder

Are you taking your medication?

He's losing touch with reality.

I need to relax.

I feel like I'm losing control.

let's talk more about that.

where did I bury that thought?

Group Therapy

The Slow-Food, Low-Stress♥Diet

SPᵀᴱˢ FRANÇAISES

Although about 75 percent of the French regularly eat at home, they also enjoy leisurely meals in restaurants.

How would you like to eat all the fatty, butter-rich foods you'd like and not gain weight? That seemed to be what the French diet promised. In spite of consuming meals heavy in cheese, pastries, and chocolate, the French appeared to remain slimmer than the average American. They also reported a lower incidence of heart disease. This maddening phenomenon became known as the French paradox.

The paradox came to the public's attention in 1991 on the television program *60 Minutes.* During the program, French scientist Serge Renaud claimed that an ingredient in red wine, which the French consumed regularly, somehow reduced drinkers' cholesterol levels. By extension, it also protected them from heart disease.

Renaud's assertion was a boon to winemakers around the world. Wine consumption in the United States immediately soared by 44 percent. But other research soon debunked Renaud's theory. No one, however, denied that the French managed to stay slimmer than Americans.

So how do they do it? Today some researchers think they know the answer: The French simply take the time to enjoy their food. The average American bolts down a hamburger, eats in the car, or gobbles a sandwich while writing e-mails or watching television. By contrast, the French typically spend two hours eating lunch. They set their forks down between bites and savor their food. And eating is a social activity—a time to talk and relax with friends and family.

Paradoxically, although the French spend more time eating than Americans, they actually consume less food. They may eat several courses, but the portions are smaller. And while the French eat three meals a day, they don't typically snack in between. They also don't reach for seconds.

CHAPTER 17
STRESS AND HEALTH

In addition, the French emphasize quality over quantity. Foods tend to be unprocessed and fresh. While it's true that they consume a diet rich in fat, the fats are found mostly in dairy products. Dairy fats, it turns out, are healthier and make you feel full longer.

Yet what may separate the French from us the most is their relaxed attitude toward food and eating. The French eat what they want and don't feel guilty about it. Psychologist Paul Rozin surveyed people of several different nationalities, including American and French, on their attitudes toward food. The Americans, he found, were much more likely than the French to worry about food and obsess over diets. Revealingly, in a word-association test, "chocolate cake" prompted Americans to respond with "guilt"; the French, with "celebration." The Americans associated "heavy cream" with "unhealthy," while the French linked the confection with "whipped."

Thus it would seem that our eating habits are not only unhealthy, they are adding to our overall stress levels. There again we might imitate the French. Their custom of making a meal a social occasion may foster peace of mind, which relieves stress and can lower the risk of heart disease.

So the next time you sit down to dinner, try turning off the television and talking to your dinner companions. Enjoy a leisurely meal and the conversation. At the end of the dinner, indulge in a few small bites of chocolate cake and try not to feel guilty about it. Your stress-free attitude—and even the cake—may be good for your health.

What do you think?

1. What are some of the key factors that might explain the French paradox?

2. Do you think Americans are ever likely to change their eating habits and adopt the French diet? Why or why not?

Chapter at a Glance

SECTION 1: Understanding Stress

■ Stress is the arousal of one's mind and body in response to demands made upon them.

■ Sources of stress include frustration, daily hassles, and life changes.

■ Different types of conflict contribute to stress.

■ Some people create their own stress through their personality type.

SECTION 2: Stress: Responses and Effects

■ Maintaining a positive attitude and a sense of humor are among the ways that people can reduce the effects of stress.

■ Stressful situations produce the three stages of the general adaptation syndrome.

■ Chronic stress can suppress the activity of the body's immune system.

SECTION 3: Psychological Factors and Health

■ Both biological and psychological factors play important roles in health problems.

■ Headaches are among the most common stress-related health problems.

■ People can make behavioral changes to help reduce the risks of heart disease.

■ People with cancer must cope with the biological aspects of their illness as well as with its psychological effects.

SECTION 4: Ways of Coping with Stress

■ Defensive coping methods as a means of handling stress are self-defeating and usually harmful.

■ Effective active coping methods for dealing with stress include changing stressful thoughts, relaxing, and exercising.

Understanding Stress

Before You Read

Main Idea

Many different situations and events can produce both good and bad stress. Some personality types may even create their own stress.

Reading Focus

1. What are the two different kinds of stress?
2. What are the main sources of stress?
3. Why does conflict cause stress?
4. How does personality type affect stress?

Vocabulary

stress
eustress
distress
stressor
approach-approach conflict
avoidance-avoidance conflict
approach-avoidance conflict
multiple approach-avoidance conflict

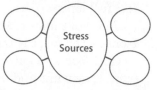

TAKING NOTES Use a graphic organizer like this one to take notes on the sources of stress.

Stress Sources

The STRESS of Being Perfect

PSYCHOLOGY CLOSE UP

Are you a slave to success? Does this description sound like anyone you know: She has to get all A's, be president of the debate club, get the lead role in the school play, and win at everything. If you do know such a person, you know a perfectionist, and he or she is probably living with severe stress.

Perfectionism actually dooms those who pursue it. The drive to be perfect creates an unending source of negative emotions because perfectionists focus on mistakes and failures. So instead of feeling free to try new experiences and learn new tasks, they rigidly control their behavior. As a result, perfectionists may never discover what they really want to do or who they really are.

Unfortunately, perfectionism seems to be on the rise, and psychologists think they know why: pushy parents. Many parents today micromanage their children's lives and demand perfection. They may think they are doing their children a favor by setting high goals for them, but these parents are actually raising a generation that is liable to become increasingly frustrated, anxious, and depressed.

Ironically, the strive for perfection results in just the opposite. It stifles creativity and prevents real success. So if your parents are stressing you out by refusing to accept second-best, ask them if they got all A's in school. If they didn't—and even if they did—give yourself a break, and start looking at failure as another chance to learn. ■

Different Kinds of Stress

In physics, stress is defined as pressure, or a force. Examples of physical stress include rocks crushing the earth or water pressing against a dam. Psychological stresses can also "crush" and "press" people. People may feel crushed by the burden of making an important decision, or they may feel pressed by a lack of time in which to complete a major task.

In psychology, **stress** is the arousal of one's mind and body in response to demands made upon them. Stress forces an organism to adapt, to cope, to adjust. The word *stress* is used differently by different psychologists. Some psychologists describe stress as an event that causes tension. Others describe stress as a person's response to a disturbing event. Still others define stress as a person's perception of an event.

Not all stress is bad. Stress can increase sharpness and motivation and can keep people alert and involved. This kind of positive stress is called **eustress.** Positive stress can be a sign that a person is taking on a challenge or trying to reach a goal. For example, you might experience eustress as you participate in a classroom activity, whether you are leading or following the activity.

Negative stress—called **distress**—is linked to intense pressure or anxiety that can have severe psychological and physical effects. When stress becomes too severe or prolonged, it can strain people's ability to adjust to various situations. Negative stress can dampen people's moods, impair their ability to experience pleasure, and even harm the body.

High school and college students often experience stress that is related to family problems, relationships, pressures at school, loneliness, and general nervousness. In fact, stress is one of the main reasons that college students seek help at counseling centers.

Reading Check **Identify Supporting Details** Why isn't all stress bad?

Sources of Stress

The event or situation that produces stress is called a **stressor.** However, what is a stressor for one person may not be a stressor for another. For example, two people might react to a long bus trip quite differently. For one it might be

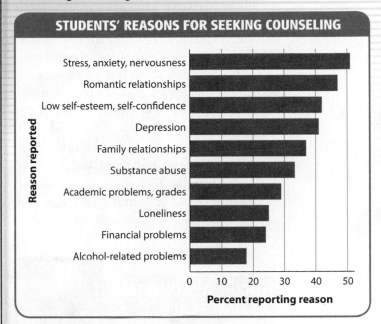

Statistically Speaking...

Stress and Other Pressures
This bar graph shows some of the reasons college students give for seeking counseling.

STUDENTS' REASONS FOR SEEKING COUNSELING

Reason reported (y-axis):
- Stress, anxiety, nervousness
- Romantic relationships
- Low self-esteem, self-confidence
- Depression
- Family relationships
- Substance abuse
- Academic problems, grades
- Loneliness
- Financial problems
- Alcohol-related problems

Percent reporting reason (x-axis): 0, 10, 20, 30, 40, 50

Skills Focus **INTERPRETING GRAPHS** Which of the reasons shown might add to students' stress?

Sources: "College Youth Haunted by Increased Pressures" by B. Murray, 1996, *APA Monitor*, 26 (4), 47; "College students and Alcohol Abuse Statistics," American Psychiatric Association, HealthyMinds.org.

a relaxing vacation, while for another person it could be stressful and unpleasant. However, some stressors are common to most people. For example, a loud, continuous drilling noise outside one's window would be irritating to just about everyone.

When stressors and stresses pile up on each other, we can reach a point where we have difficulty coping. To avoid reaching that point, it is important to recognize some of the causes of stress.

Frustration One of the most common sources of stress is frustration—being blocked from obtaining a goal. Examples include being delayed from keeping an appointment, lacking enough money to buy an item we need or want, or forgetting something important.

Sometimes life seems full of frustrations. Although many frustrations are minor, the more serious ones can be extremely stressful—for example, working for weeks on an important project, only to lose it and have to create it all over again.

Daily Hassles The everyday frustrations we all experience are called daily hassles. They come in different forms, but they have one thing in common—they all create stress. When daily hassles become severe or frequent enough, they can threaten a person's well-being. Psychologist Richard Lazarus and his colleagues found that there are eight main types of hassles:

- household hassles, including preparing meals, cleaning, and shopping
- health hassles, including illness, anxiety about medical or dental treatment, and the side effects of medications
- time-pressure hassles, including the feeling that there are too many things to do, too many responsibilities, and not enough time to do what needs to be done
- inner-concern hassles, including feelings of low self-esteem and loneliness
- environmental hassles, including noise, crowding, pollution, traffic, and crime
- financial hassles, including concerns about paying current bills, repaying loans, and saving for the future
- work hassles, including unhappiness with one's job and problems with co-workers
- future-security hassles, including concerns about job security, taxes, investments, and retirement income

These hassles can result in feelings of tension, nervousness, worry, and sadness.

Life Changes Life changes—such as moving, serious illness, or a death in the family—are another source of stress. Life changes differ from daily hassles in two important ways: (1) Many life changes are positive and desirable; (2) Life changes tend to happen less often.

Researchers Thomas Holmes and Richard Rahe attempted to rank various life changes according to the amount of stress each produced. The researchers asked people to rate each of the life changes on a scale of 1 to 100 in terms of how much stress they experienced and how much adjustment they needed to make. Holmes and Rahe used the figures to create the Social Readjustment Rating Scale.

Even life changes that are enjoyable can produce stress because they require a certain amount of adjustment. According to Holmes and Rahe, too many life changes, even good ones, can cause stress that leads to high blood pressure and other health problems.

Daily hassles and life changes—especially unpleasant ones—influence the quality of a person's life. They can cause a person to worry excessively and can dampen his or her spirits. Stressors can also lead to health problems that range from minor athletic injuries to serious illnesses. Holmes and Rahe found that people who experienced many life changes within a year's time were much more likely to develop medical problems than those who did not.

Reading Check **Make Generalizations** How can sources of stress influence a person's life?

INTERACTIVE

SOCIAL READJUSTMENT RATING SCALE

This scale ranks various life changes according to the amount of stress each produces.

Rank	Life Event
1	Death of spouse
2	Divorce
3	Marital separation
4	Jail term
5	Death of close family member
6	Personal injury or illness
7	Marriage
8	Fired at work
9	Marital reconciliation
10	Retirement

Sources: Reprinted with permission from T. H. Holmes and R. H. Rahe (1967). The social readjustment rating scale. *Journal of Psychosomatic Research*, 11, 213–218.

Interactive Feature THINKcentral thinkcentral.com

THE FOUR TYPES OF CONFLICT

Psychologists have identified four types of conflict, a source of stress.

Type of Conflict	Definition	Example
Approach-approach	A choice between two equally attractive alternatives	Choosing between cake and ice cream for dessert
Avoidance-avoidance	A choice between two equally unattractive alternatives	Going to the dentist or letting a toothache get worse
Approach-avoidance	A choice of whether or not to do something when part of the situation is attractive but the other is not	Deciding whether to buy a new DVD player that would cost a lot of money
Multiple approach-avoidance	A choice between alternatives that have both good and bad aspects	Deciding whether to stay at home to study for a test or to go out to the movies with friends

Conflict

Another source of stress is conflict, being pulled in two or more directions by opposing forces or motives. Conflict can be frustrating, especially when a person is facing a difficult decision, such as choosing which college to attend. The pressure to make the right choice only adds to the stress involved in making such a major decision.

A person thinking about going to college or entering the armed services may feel conflicting emotions. He or she may be excited about the prospect of learning new information and developing new skills for the future. However, college is expensive, and a person who plans to attend college must think about how to pay for it. The person may also have mixed feelings about leaving home.

Psychologists have identified four types of conflict. These are approach-approach conflicts, avoidance-avoidance conflicts, approach-avoidance conflicts, and multiple approach-avoidance conflicts.

Approach-Approach Conflict An **approach-approach conflict** is the least stressful type of conflict because the choices are positive. In this situation, each of the goals is both desirable and within reach. For example, suppose you were accepted by several colleges. You would then be faced with an approach-approach conflict because you would have to choose which college to attend.

An approach-approach conflict is usually resolved by making a decision. However, after the decision is made, the person may still have persistent self-doubts about whether he or she has made the right decision. The decision maker may not feel settled until he or she is in the new situation and knows that things are working out. For example, even after you decide which college you will attend, you may still feel uncertain until you settle into your dorm, meet your roommates, and begin classes.

Avoidance-Avoidance Conflict An **avoidance-avoidance conflict** is more stressful. People in this type of conflict are forced to choose "the lesser of two evils"—that is, to choose between two unsatisfactory alternatives. People are motivated to avoid each of two negative goals, but the problem is that avoiding one requires approaching the other. For example, suppose you were faced with the choice of dropping a course in which you were doing poorly and risked receiving a poor grade. However, by dropping the course, you would not have enough credits to graduate. Both alternatives have a negative side.

Approach-Avoidance Conflict A single goal can produce both approach and avoidance motives. This is called an approach-avoidance conflict. People face an **approach-avoidance conflict** when a choice is both good and bad at the same time. For instance, you might want to attend a college that has an excellent reputation and exactly the program you are looking for, but the college is very far away and visiting home would be difficult and costly.

Multiple Approach-Avoidance Conflict The most complex form of conflict is a **multiple approach-avoidance conflict.** In this kind of conflict, each of several alternative courses of action has its advantages and disadvantages. You face this type of conflict when you have to decide which college courses to take. The factors to consider may include your level of interest in the subject, the reputation of the teacher, the usefulness of the course to your overall plan, and the difficulty of the course.

When deciding what to eat in a restaurant, you might have to choose between food that is healthful but not very tasty, tasty food that is not very healthful, and food that is both tasty and healthful but is too expensive. In such a dilemma, you would be faced with a multiple approach-avoidance conflict.

When conflicting motives are strong, people may encounter high levels of stress and confusion about what course of action to choose. They need to make a decision to reduce the stress, yet decision-making itself can be quite stressful, especially when there is no clear right choice. Some people cope with such difficult decisions by making a two-column list, jotting down all the reasons for and against a particular choice. The thought that goes into making the list sometimes helps people decide what to do.

ACADEMIC VOCABULARY

dilemma situation requiring a choice between options that are equally undesirable

Reading Check **Analyze** Which type of conflict might cause the most amount of stress?

Personality Types

Some people actually create their own stress. Psychologists have classified people into two basic personality types: type A (intense) and type B (laid-back). Type A people are always on the go; they put pressure on themselves and thus are constantly under stress. They are highly driven, competitive, and impatient. Type A people always feel rushed and pressured because they operate at full speed and become annoyed when there is even the slightest delay. Type A people never seem to have enough time, especially since they often try to do several things at once. They walk, eat, and talk faster than other people, and they are generally quick to become angry.

Type B people, in contrast, are more relaxed. They are more patient, do not become angry as easily, and are typically less driven than type A people. While type A people often earn more money than type B people do, type A people pay a high price for their success. They must live with the heightened stress they create for themselves. Research shows that type A personalities run a much greater health risk than type B people. If they do not loosen up and relax, but instead continue their type A behavior, they are in greater danger of suffering coronary heart disease.

Reading Check **Contrast** How does the behavior of type A and type B people differ?

SECTION 1 Assessment

Online Quiz THINK central thinkcentral.com

Reviewing Main Ideas and Vocabulary

1. **Identify** What is a stressor?

2. **Summarize** What are the eight main types of daily hassles?

3. **Explain** Why is an approach-approach conflict the least stressful type of conflict?

Thinking Critically

4. **Draw Conclusions** Suppose you won the lottery. Why might that event cause you stress?

5. **Predict** Do you think the stress level of a person with a type A personality might decrease or increase if he or she were forced to retire? Explain your answer.

6. **Support a Position** Parents report high stress levels for their children—even very young children. What steps do you think parents could take to alleviate this stress?

7. **Identify Cause and Effect** Using your notes and a graphic organizer like the one below, identify possible effects of the stress shown.

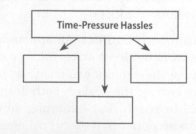

Time-Pressure Hassles

FOCUS ON WRITING

8. **Descriptive** Describe a time you faced a multiple approach-avoidance conflict. What different courses of action did you have to consider? How did you resolve the conflict?

Stress: Responses and Effects

Before You Read

Main Idea

People respond to stress in different ways, but stressful situations produce similar responses in the body. Stress—especially chronic stress—can even compromise the body's immune system.

Reading Focus

1. What factors influence our response to stress?
2. What is the general adaptation syndrome?
3. How does stress affect the immune system?

Vocabulary

self-efficacy expectation
general adaptation syndrome (GAS)

TAKING NOTES Use a graphic organizer like this one to take notes on the responses to and effects of stress.

Responses	Effects

A Healthy Dose of PESSiMiSM

PSYCHOLOGY CLOSE UP

Can you ever be too optimistic? It turns out you can. Too much optimism and good fortune can actually overtax the immune system. Furthermore, stress can actually strengthen it.

Does all this seem counterintuitive? After all, positive emotions and events are supposed to be healthy, and stress is supposed to suppress the immune system—but apparently not always. Consider the case of Brian. A gifted writer, Brian fulfilled a lifelong dream when a book he wrote was accepted by a major publishing company. Instead of being thrilled, however, Brian went into a tailspin: depression, followed by alcoholism, obesity, and heart disease. Brian suffered from low self-esteem. Although he had optimistically dreamed of such success, he probably never really expected to achieve it. Psychologists believe that only emotionally healthy people can handle enormous success. For the Brians among us, stress—in the form of disappointment and unfulfilled dreams—may actually be healthier.

A daily dose of stress may also help us fight disease. In a study, rats that received electric shocks to their tails every day were better able to fight off a bacterial infection than rats that did not receive the shocks. The researchers concluded that short-term stress can actually boost immunity.

Psychologists do distinguish between short-term stress and chronic stress, however. In this section, you will find out what prolonged stress can do to your body and your health. It isn't pretty. ■

The glass on the left represents the view of optimists, who would describe it as half full. The glass on the right represents the view of pessimists, who would describe it as half empty.

Responses to Stress

Psychological factors play an important role in people's responses to stress. People with different types of personalities respond to stress in different ways. People who are more relaxed and free of conflict are less likely than others to become sick when they do experience prolonged stress.

The stress of an event depends largely on what the event means to the person involved. Going to college may be important to you, but leaving home and being away from your family and friends may also mean a great deal to you. Moving can be a positive or a negative event, depending on whether one moves to where one wants to be and on the difficulties of packing, unpacking, and paying for the move. Even a positive move, such as moving to a larger house, creates some stress. However, a negative move, such as being evicted from one's home, is much more stressful because of the fear, anxiety, anger, and depression it can trigger.

Biological factors also account for some of the differences in people's responses to stress. Research suggests that some people inherit the tendency to develop certain health problems under stress. Yet most people can do things to influence or reduce the effects of their stress. Factors that influence the effects of stress include self-efficacy expectations, psychological hardiness, a sense of humor, predictability, and social support.

Self-Efficacy Expectations Do you remember the children's story "The Little Engine That Could"? In an effort to pull a heavy load up a great hill, the engine repeated to itself, "I think I can, I think I can." The engine succeeded because of its self-efficacy expectations. **Self-efficacy expectations** are the beliefs people have that they can accomplish goals that they set for themselves. The goal might be to write a persuasive essay, dunk a basketball, or learn to solve math problems. Believing one can do it helps one reach the goal.

Self-efficacy expectations are closely related to self-confidence. Self-confidence affects people's abilities to withstand stress. For example, when people are in frightening situations, self-confidence reduces the level of adrenaline in the bloodstream. As a result, people are less likely to experience panic and nervousness. People with more self-confidence—a strong belief that they can handle difficult situations—are also less likely than those with less self-confidence to be upset by stress. In other words, a self-confident person is more likely to keep cool under pressure.

Psychological Hardiness Psychological hardiness is a personality characteristic that helps people withstand stress. The research on psychological hardiness is based on the pioneering work of Suzanne Kobasa and her colleagues. They studied business executives who were able to resist illness despite heavy workloads and stress on the job. The researchers found that these psychologically hardy executives differed from other executives in three important ways.

- **Commitment.** The hardy executives were highly committed to their jobs; they believed that their work was meaningful, though it was also demanding and stressful; they regarded their stress as a source of motivation rather than as something that was victimizing them.

- **Challenge.** The hardy executives sought out challenges; they preferred change to stability even though the changes often required great adjustment; they regarded change as interesting and rewarding rather than threatening.

- **Control.** The hardy executives viewed themselves as being in control of their lives and able to influence and control the rewards and punishments they received; they did not feel helpless in the face of the forces that were involved in shaping their lives.

Other researchers have also found that believing that one is in control of a situation tends to enhance the body's ability to withstand stressful events.

Sense of Humor Do you know the old saying "Laughter is the best medicine"? The idea that humor lightens the burdens of life is one that dates back to ancient times. One study found that students who had a sense of humor and saw humor in difficult situations experienced less stress than students who were not able to find humor in the same situations.

Some research suggests that emotional responses, such as happiness and even anger, may have beneficial effects on the immune system as well. Since humor and laughter are connected with feelings of happiness, they probably really are good "medicine" for the body.

Predictability Having the ability to predict a stressor seems to reduce the amount of stress it causes. Predictability allows people to brace themselves for an event and, in many cases, to plan various ways to cope with it. Since having control of the situation helps reduce stress, having prior information about the expected stressor gives people a feeling that they will be able to deal with it. For example, ill people who ask about the medical procedures they will undergo and the pain they will experience tend to cope with the stress better than ill people who do not know what to expect.

Social Support The presence and interest of other people provide the social support that helps people cope with stress. Like psychological hardiness, social support helps insulate people from the effects of stress. People who lack social skills and spend most of their time alone seem more likely to develop infectious diseases when they are under stress.

There are several ways to provide social support to people who are under stress.

- Express your concern by listening to people's problems and offering sympathy, understanding, and reassurance.
- Provide physical relief by offering the material support and services that help people adjust to stress—for example, financial assistance, food, and shelter.
- Offer information, including advice, that helps people cope with stress.
- Provide feedback to help people understand or make sense of what they have experienced.
- Socialize, which includes talking, playing, or just being with the people who are under stress.

Research clearly suggests the value of social support. For example, older people who have social support recover more rapidly from physical problems than older people who have no support. People who have buddies who join them on an exercise program are more likely

A Laugh a Day Keeps the Doctor Away

"My brother thinks he's a chicken—we don't talk him out of it because we need the eggs."
—**Groucho Marx**

When writer Norman Cousins was diagnosed with a painful illness that is similar to arthritis, his doctor prescribed high doses of painkillers. But Cousins came up with medication of a different kind: He watched Marx Brothers movies. He found that laughing at the movies eased his pain and helped him sleep better. In very little time, he was able to get off the painkillers. *Why do you think laughter can reduce pain?*

than others to stay with the activity. Social support also appears to shield people and help them recover from feelings of depression.

Social support helps many immigrants to cope with the stresses of adapting to life in the United States. It helped Midwest families cope with the stresses of severe flooding in 2008 and enabled Chinese villagers to deal with a major earthquake that same year. Social support also helps people remain healthy and in good spirits when caring for other people who have serious health problems.

Reading Check **Draw Conclusions** What role might attitude play in responding to stress?

The General Adaptation Syndrome

How is it that daily hassles, life changes, conflict, and other sources of stress often make people ill? Stress researcher Hans Selye suggested that the body under stress is like a clock with an alarm that does not shut off.

Selye observed that different stressful situations each produced similar responses by the body. Whether the source of stress was a financial problem, a physical threat, or a bacterial invasion, the body's response was always the same. Selye labeled this response the **general adaptation syndrome (GAS).** The GAS has three stages: an alarm reaction, a resistance stage, and an exhaustion stage.

The Alarm Reaction The alarm reaction is initiated when a stressor is perceived. This reaction mobilizes the body for defensive action. In the early 1900s, physiologist Walter Cannon described this alarm system as the fight-or-flight reaction.

Animals and human beings experience this fight-or-flight reaction in similar ways. Consider an animal's reaction when a stranger approaches or when the animal notices some other change in its environment that signals possible danger. A person might react the same way. Imagine that as you are about to go to sleep, you hear a loud noise in another room. Like the animal, you also become alert to your environment and sensitive to any sight, sound, or other stimulus around you that might indicate danger. Your body is in the fight-or-flight mode that occurs when danger is perceived to be present.

During the alarm reaction, the sympathetic nervous system is activated. This produces a flood of stress hormones that act to prepare the body to deal with the stressor. Adrenaline and noradrenaline arouse the body to help it cope with threats and stress. Corticosteroids and ACTH protect the body from allergic reactions (such as difficulty breathing). Once the stressor or threat is removed, the body returns to its previous state.

The Resistance Stage If the alarm reaction mobilizes the body and the stressor is not removed, people enter the resistance stage of the GAS. During this stage, people attempt to find a way to cope with the stressor to avoid being overwhelmed by their negative reactions. The body tries to regain its lost energy, repair damage, and restore balance. However, people may still feel enough of a strain to continue to experience some physical symptoms.

The Exhaustion Stage If the stressor is still not removed, people may enter the exhaustion stage of the GAS. At this stage, the adrenal and other glands activated by the fight-or-flight reaction can no longer secrete hormones. People's muscles become worn out. Their heart and breathing rates slow down.

As the resources available to combat stress become depleted, people reach a breaking point. Continued stress during the exhaustion stage may cause people to develop health problems ranging from allergies and hives to ulcers and heart disease—and even death.

Reading Check **Summarize** What are the three stages of the general adaptation syndrome?

ACADEMIC VOCABULARY
secrete to release a liquid substance

Fight-or-Flight Reaction

Definition: an alarm reaction that mobilizes the body for defensive action when a person first perceives a stressor

Characteristics: air passages widen to allow more air intake; hair stands on end; level of blood sugar increases; heart rate increases; muscles tighten up; blood pressure rises; senses sharpen and become more alert; steroids and adrenaline are secreted

Effects: blood flows away from surface areas to major muscle groups, flooding them with energy; body receives a burst of energy; person is ready to "fight"—confront the stressor—or take "flight"—run away from the stressor

Effects of Stress on the Immune System

Stress also affects our ability to cope with disease. Research shows that chronic stress suppresses the body's immune system.

The Immune System You might think that some people are not exposed to the kinds of organisms that cause serious health problems. But actually, that is not true. Most people are exposed to a great variety of disease-causing organisms. However, an intact immune system fights off most of them.

How does the immune system fight against disease? The immune system prevents disease by producing white blood cells that destroy disease-causing microorganisms (bacteria, fungi, and viruses), worn-out body cells, and cells that have become malignant (cancerous). White blood cells first recognize and then destroy foreign bodies and unhealthy cells.

Some white blood cells produce antibodies. Others destroy the foreign bodies by surrounding and digesting them. The immune system "remembers" these invaders and maintains antibodies in the bloodstream to fight them, often for years.

Stress and the Immune System One of the reasons that stress eventually exhausts people is that it stimulates their bodies to produce steroids, which suppress the functioning of the immune system. Persistent secretion of steroids interferes with the formation of antibodies, which are crucial in fighting germs. In the case of some serious diseases, such as cancer, the added stress that results from having a life-threatening disease contributes to the suppression of the immune system, thus leading to further health problems.

A study of dental students showed the effects of stress on the immune system. To test the functioning of each student's immune system, researchers measured the level of antibodies in the students' saliva at different times during the school year. The lower the level of antibodies, the lower a person's immune-system functioning.

Students showed lower immune-system functioning during more stressful school periods. The study also showed that students with many friends had healthier immune systems than students with fewer friends. The study suggests that social support may have been a factor in insulating some students from the detrimental effects of stress.

Other studies have found that the stress of examinations weakens the capacity of the immune system to combat certain viruses, such as the Epstein-Barr virus, which causes fatigue and other health problems. In another study, researchers found that training aimed at improving coping skills and relaxation techniques improved the functioning of the immune systems of the participants.

These studies indicate that stress causes the immune system to function less effectively. They also indicate that social support, which reduces stress, makes the immune system function better.

Reading Check **Analyze** How does the immune system protect people against disease?

Complete a Webquest at thinkcentral.com on how to strengthen the immune system.

Online Quiz **THINK** central   thinkcentral.com

SECTION 2 Assessment

Reviewing Main Ideas and Vocabulary

1. **Recall** How does self-confidence affect people's ability to withstand stress?

2. **Summarize** What are five ways to provide social support to those under stress?

3. **Identify Cause and Effect** What may be the result of continued stress during the exhaustion stage?

Thinking Critically

4. **Explain** What might happen to the immune system after stress becomes prolonged?

5. **Evaluate** Why do you think that a person's stress can be alleviated simply by being in contact with other people?

6. **Develop** What advice for maintaining his or her immune system would you give to a student who is in a high-stress situation?

7. **Sequence** Using your notes and a graphic organizer like the one below, identify the events that might occur when someone is under extreme stress.

FOCUS ON WRITING

8. **Narrative** Write a short, fictional scene in which you tell what happens when a camper hears a noise outside his tent. Be sure to describe the camper's fight-or-flight reaction.

Psychological Factors and Health

Before You Read

Main Idea

Both biological and psychological factors play an important role in medical problems, including headaches, heart disease, and cancer.

Reading Focus

1. How do biological and psychological factors affect health?
2. What are the most common types of headaches?
3. What factors contribute to heart disease?
4. How is cancer linked to stress?

Vocabulary

health psychology
migraine headache

TAKING NOTES Use a graphic organizer like this one to take notes on the role played by biological and psychological factors in headaches, heart disease, and cancer.

	Biological Factors	Psychological Factors
Headaches		
Heart disease		
Cancer		

MIGRAINE ART

PSYCHOLOGY CLOSE UP

Can you see my pain? Migraine sufferers describe their pain as agonizing and nightmarish. One man said that he felt like he was "being beaten up" during an attack. And the punishment must seem endless—the headaches can last 72 hours.

Instead of just talking about their pain, however, some sufferers translate what they feel onto a canvas. Some artists focus on what they see just before the onset of a migraine, during the so-called aura phase. Many see zigzag lines or lose visual perspective—people and objects become fuzzy and indistinct. Above all, these artists try to convey the head-exploding pain of a migraine.

Although migraine art has become increasingly popular, experts believe it is nothing new. Some of the mystical "visions" conveyed in paintings from the medieval period may actually represent the hallucinations experienced during a migraine attack. The German abbess Hildegard of Bingen is probably the most famous of these mystical artists. Born in 1098, Hildegard claimed at a young age to have had visions of God. In time, she described and illustrated what she saw. Neurologist Oliver Sacks believes that the representations of her visions reflect classic migraine symptoms.

In many respects, of course, we have come a long way since the Middle Ages. But there is still no cure for migraines. Sufferers hope that the interest in migraine art will help researchers learn more about headaches and migraines and so result in better understanding and treatment. ◼

During the aura phase, migraine sufferers often see shimmering lights that move across their field of vision. Here, Hildegard illustrates the light as a multitude of falling stars that shine brightly before burning out.

Biological and Psychological Factors

Why do some people develop cancer or have heart attacks? Why do others seem immune to these health problems? Why do some people seem to fall prey to just about everything that is going around, while others ride out the longest winters with hardly a sniffle?

Biological factors play an important role in physical illness. For example, family history of a particular disease can certainly increase a person's susceptibility to that disease. Other biological factors that are involved in the development of illness include exposure to disease-causing microorganisms, inoculations against certain diseases, accidents and injuries, and age.

A family history of health problems, such as heart disease and cancer, may tempt some people to assume there is little they can do to influence their health. But one's family history (or genetic inheritance) merely suggests a potential for developing an illness. Health writer Jane Brody noted that a bad family medical history should not be considered a sign of doom. She noted that, instead, it should be welcomed as an opportunity to keep the harmful genes from expressing themselves.

While biological factors are important, many health problems are affected by psychological factors, such as one's attitudes and patterns of behavior. Psychological states of anxiety and depression can impair the functioning of the immune system and make people more vulnerable to physical health problems.

Health psychology is concerned with the relationship between psychological factors and the prevention and treatment of physical illness. In recent years, health psychologists have been exploring the various ways in which states of mind influence physical well-being. Because of the growing recognition of the link between psychological factors and health, an estimated 3,500 health psychologists are now on the faculties of medical schools. Health psychologists have made important contributions to the understanding and treatment of many different kinds of medical problems, including headaches, heart disease, and cancer.

Reading Check **Analyze** How can a bad family medical history be a positive opportunity?

Headaches

Among the most common stress-related health problems are headaches. People under stress will sometimes get a headache as a direct result of feeling tense. It is estimated that 20 percent of Americans experience intense stress-induced headaches.

Types of Headaches There are several types of headaches. The most frequent kind is the muscle-tension headache. When people are under stress, the muscles in their shoulders, neck, forehead, and scalp tend to tighten up. Prolonged stress can lead to prolonged muscle contraction, which causes muscle-tension headaches. Such headaches are characterized by dull, steady pain on both sides of the head and by feelings of tightness or pressure.

The next most common kind of headache is the **migraine headache.** Migraine headaches usually have a sudden onset and are identified by severe throbbing pain on one side of the head. Migraines affect 1 American in 10. They may last for hours or days. Some people have warning "auras" before attacks. These warnings include visual distortions or the perception of unusual odors. The migraines themselves may be accompanied by sensitivity to light, loss of appetite, nausea, vomiting, loss of balance, and changes in mood.

Brain imaging suggests that when something triggers a migraine, neurons at the back of the brain fire in waves that ripple across the top of the head and then down to the brainstem, which has many pain centers. Triggers for migraines include barometric pressure, pollen, and some drugs. Other triggers are aged cheese and the hormonal changes connected with menstruation.

Psychological factors also trigger or worsen migraines. For example, the type A behavior pattern apparently contributes to migraines. In one study, 53 percent of people who had migraine headaches showed the type A behavior pattern, compared with 23 percent of people who had muscle-tension headaches.

Regardless of the source of the headache, people can unwittingly propel themselves into a vicious cycle. Headache pain is a stressor that can lead to an increase in, rather than a relaxing of, muscle tension in the neck, shoulders, scalp, and face.

CASE STUDY
CONNECTION

The Slow-Food, Low-Stress Diet
About 33 percent of American adults are obese, as opposed to about 10 percent of the French.

Treatment Aspirin, acetaminophen, and many prescription drugs are used to fight headache pain. Some inhibit the production of the prostaglandins that help initiate transmission of pain messages to the brain. Newer prescription drugs can help prevent many migraines. Behavioral methods can also help. Progressive relaxation focuses on decreasing muscle tension and has been shown to be highly effective in relieving muscle-tension headaches. Biofeedback training has also helped many people with migraine headaches. However, these methods should only be attempted under the supervision of a trained health-care professional.

Reading Check **Identify Cause and Effect** How can headache pain result in a vicious cycle?

Heart Disease

Researchers are not certain how stress increases the risk of heart disease. Chronic stress can be a contributing factor by causing blood pressure and cholesterol to rise. Prolonged stress may also lower the immune system's response to harmful hormones.

Risk Factors Nearly half the deaths in the United States each year are caused by heart disease, making it a major national health problem. There are many risk factors associated with heart disease.

- **Family history (genetics).** People with a family history of heart disease are more likely than others to develop heart disease themselves.

- **Physical conditions.** Obesity, high serum cholesterol levels, and hypertension all contribute to heart disease. About one American in five has hypertension, or abnormally high blood pressure. Although there appears to be a genetic component to hypertension, many other factors are also involved. These factors include smoking, obesity, and excessive salt in one's diet. Blood pressure also rises when people become angry or are on guard against threats.

- **Patterns of consumption.** Heavy drinking, smoking, overeating, and eating food high in cholesterol can also contribute to heart disease. Americans' typically stressful attitude toward food and eating—unlike that of the French—contributes to the risk of heart disease.

- **Type A behavior.** People who exhibit type A behavior are more likely than people who exhibit type B behavior to develop heart disease.

- **Anger and hostility.** A constant need to control angry and hostile impulses increases the risk of developing heart disease.

- **Job strain.** Overtime work, assembly-line labor, and exposure to conflicting demands on the job can all contribute to heart disease.

- **Lack of exercise.** People who do not get regular exercise are more likely to suffer from coronary heart disease than those who exercise regularly.

Alternative Medicine

Herbal Remedies: plant extracts used as medicine; popular remedies include ginseng (to increase energy) and ginkgo (to improve memory); not regulated by the Food and Drug Administration

Acupuncture: ancient Chinese medical procedure involving the insertion of hair-thin needles in the skin *(shown at right)*; used to ease post-surgery pain as well as pain of arthritis, backache, headache, and asthma; usually safe when applied by licensed practitioners

Reflexology: massage technique usually applied to feet and hands; areas of the feet and hands supposed to correspond to other areas of the body; pressure believed to reduce stress and improve health

Behavioral Changes Various medical treatments, such as surgery and medication, are available for heart disease. However, people can also benefit from behavioral changes that reduce its risks. Among these behavioral changes are the following:

- **Quitting smoking.** The links between smoking and heart disease (and lung cancer) make quitting smoking the single best way to reduce the risks of serious health problems.
- **Controlling weight.** Maintaining a healthy weight appropriate to one's body proportions can help reduce the risk of heart disease.
- **Reducing hypertension.** Relaxation training, meditation, exercise, weight control, and a reduction in the intake of salt all help control blood pressure.
- **Lowering serum cholesterol levels.** Behavioral methods for lowering cholesterol include cutting down on foods high in cholesterol and saturated fats and exercising regularly.
- **Changing type A behavior patterns.** Learning to slow down and relax can decrease the risk of heart attacks. This is especially true for people who exhibit type A behavior and who have had previous heart attacks.
- **Exercising regularly.** A moderate program of exercise can help protect people from heart disease.

Reading Check **Summarize** What can people do to help reduce the risk of heart disease?

Cancer

Cancer is a disease that involves the rapid and abnormal growth of malignant cells. Cancerous cells can take root anywhere—for example, in the blood, skin, digestive tract, lungs, or reproductive organs. If not controlled early, cancer cells can spread and establish masses, or tumors, elsewhere in the body. People actually develop cancer cells frequently, but the immune system normally succeeds in destroying them. Individuals whose immune systems are weakened by physical or psychological factors appear to be more likely candidates than others for getting cancer.

Personality Type and Cardiac Risk

Type D: a personality type that is prone to distress; "D" stands for "distressed"

Characteristics: emotional profile—angry, hostile, worried, depressed, gloomy; psychological profile—negative view of self, suppresses feelings, pessimistic, overreacts to stressful situations, lonely, isolated

Cardiac Risk: greater risk of dying once heart disease develops; about four times more likely than non-D personality types to suffer a second heart attack

Risk Factors People may inherit a tendency to develop certain kinds of cancer. The genes involved may remove the normal controls on cell division, allowing cancer cells to multiply wildly. Certain kinds of behavior also increase the risk of cancer. These behaviors include smoking, sunbathing (ultraviolet light can cause skin cancer), and eating animal fats. Substances in cigarette smoke may damage genes that would otherwise block the development of many types of cancers. Psychological problems such as prolonged anxiety and depression may also heighten the risk.

Research suggests that stress may be an additional risk factor for the development of cancer. In one study, researchers separated mice into two groups. One group was regularly subjected to stressful conditions, while the other group was not. The immune systems of the mice in the group that were exposed to stressful conditions showed a reduced ability to kill cancer cells compared to the mice that were not exposed to stressful conditions. Other experiments with animals have suggested that once cancer has taken root, stress can affect the course of its development.

Psychological Aspects People with cancer must cope with the biological aspects of their illness, ranging from possible weakness and pain to the side effects of their medications. They also face many psychological effects of cancer, such as anxiety about the medical treatment itself and about the possible approach of death. Additionally, severe depression and feelings of vulnerability often accompany the diagnosis of cancer.

Unfortunately, many people who are diagnosed with cancer are also burdened by the necessity of dealing with the insensitivity of others. Some people may actually criticize the person with the illness for feeling sorry for himself or herself or for "giving up" the fight against the disease.

Painful side effects sometimes accompany the treatment for certain types of cancer. For example, nausea frequently occurs during chemotherapy. People receiving chemotherapy are sometimes taught relaxation and guided imagery techniques, which have been shown to significantly reduce the nausea and vomiting associated with chemotherapy.

Studies of children and adolescents with cancer have found that playing video games also reduces the discomfort of chemotherapy. By allowing the children to focus their attention on battling computer-generated enemies, such games help keep the children distracted from the discomfort caused by the treatment.

Positive Attitude Cancer requires medical treatment, and in some cases there are too few available treatment options. However, the attitudes people have about their cancer do seem to make a difference. A 10-year follow-up of women with breast cancer found a significantly higher survival rate among women who met their diagnosis with a "fighting spirit" rather than with resignation. A desire to fight the illness is apparently a key component of successful treatment. Social support also increases the survival rate of people who have cancer.

Psychologists have found that the feelings of hopelessness that sometimes accompany the diagnosis of cancer may hinder recovery because they can suppress the person's immune system. In addition, hospitalization itself is stressful because it removes people from the familiar surroundings of home and the sources of social support. Furthermore, being in the hospital and subject to hospital routines—for any reason—reduces one's sense of control.

In some cases, there may not be a great deal that a person with cancer can do to affect the eventual outcome of the disease. However, there are numerous ways to reduce the risk of developing cancer in the first place. The most effective way is to avoid behavioral risk factors for cancer by reducing the intake of fats and increasing the intake of fruits and vegetables. Limiting the amount of stress one is exposed to and having regular medical checkups are also vital factors in the reduction of the risk of developing cancer.

Reading Check **Identify Supporting Details** What psychological effects might those with cancer face?

ACADEMIC VOCABULARY

chemotherapy treatment of disease using chemicals to kill cells

---

SECTION 3 Assessment

Online Quiz THINK central thinkcentral.com

Reviewing Main Ideas and Vocabulary

1. **Recall** What is health psychology concerned with?

2. **Identify** What is the most frequent type of headache?

3. **Explain** How can one deal with the side effects of cancer?

Thinking Critically

4. **Draw Conclusions** Who is more likely to suffer from headaches: the type A personality or the type B personality? Explain your answer.

5. **Evaluate** How can psychological methods be used to help people prevent or deal effectively with health problems?

6. **Support a Position** Do you think that companies that provide health and life insurance should be allowed to charge higher rates to people under high levels of stress? Support your answer.

7. **Identify Cause and Effect** Using your notes and a graphic organizer like the one below, list some of the biological and psychological effects of stress.

FOCUS ON WRITING

8. **Persuasive** Write a short letter in which you encourage someone who is at risk for cancer or heart disease to make behavioral changes and have a positive attitude. Explain how the person can benefit from these adjustments.

Ways of Coping with Stress

Before You Read

Main Idea

People handle stress using both defensive and active coping methods. Defensive coping methods are often self-defeating, while active coping methods are far more effective.

Reading Focus

1. What are some defensive coping methods?
2. How do active coping methods help ease stress?

Vocabulary

defensive coping
active coping

TAKING NOTES Use a graphic organizer like this one to compare defensive and active coping methods.

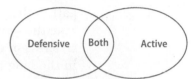

Defensive — Both — Active

Business Samurai

PSYCHOLOGY CLOSE UP

Why won't Japanese business-men take a break? You may think Americans are stressed out by work, but compared with Japanese businessmen, we're pretty laid-back. Known as "business samurai" in Japan, these men maintain an extreme work ethic. Like the feudal soldiers they are named for, the businessmen pledge unwavering loyalty to their employers— their modern-day lords—and literally work until they drop.

About 59 percent of Japanese businessmen admit to severe fatigue as a result of work, but they refuse to seek help. Work obsession is considered a virtue in Japanese culture; asking for help is considered a weakness.

However, Japanese men are literally working themselves to death. About 10,000 die every year as a result of stress, called *karoshi* in Japan. Concerned wives call crisis hot-lines for help, but their efforts have little effect.

To cope with and reduce their stress, many business samurai drink alcohol, but this only masks the problem. As a result, some Japanese psychologists report that rates of anxiety, depression, and even suicide have skyrocketed among middle-aged men.

These men need a mental health break. As you will learn in this section, there are coping methods Japanese businessmen—or anyone—can use to alleviate stress. But first they have to be willing to lay down their swords. ▣

Defensive Coping

Because stress harms people's physical and psychological well-being, it is important to know how to cope with or reduce the stress in one's life. **Defensive coping** is one way to handle stress and reduce the immediate effects of a stressor, but it is probably not the most desirable way. Defensive coping may involve socially unacceptable behavior (substance abuse or aggression), running away from one's problems (withdrawal), or self-deception (use of defense mechanisms).

ACADEMIC VOCABULARY

interpersonal relating to the interactions between individuals

Defensive coping may give people time to gather their resources, but it does not eliminate the source of stress or improve the effectiveness of one's response to stress. In fact, in the long run, defensive methods are self-defeating and usually harmful.

Substance Abuse Some adolescents and adults use alcohol, tranquilizers, and other drugs to try to reduce feelings of stress. People may become psychologically dependent on these substances as they try to decrease their awareness of stress or to disguise what has become, for them, an unpleasant reality. That dependence only makes a problem worse because it makes people less able and less willing to deal with it.

Aggression Some people use aggression and violence to cope with stressful situations, such as those that involve feelings of frustration or a difference of opinion with another person. However, violence rarely, if ever, provides solutions to people's problems. In fact, aggressive behavior often heightens interpersonal conflict because it may motivate an injured party to seek revenge.

Withdrawal Some people withdraw from a stressful situation because they are frightened, feel helpless, or believe that any decision they make will be a mistake. Withdrawal can be emotional (loss of interest in life, turning away from friends and family), or it can be physical (moving to a new location to avoid dealing with an old problem).

Suicide is the ultimate form of withdrawal. Some people experience so much stress and feel so hopeless about ever solving their problems that they believe the only way out is to commit suicide. Of course, suicide does not solve or reduce problems. It usually only increases the pain of those who are left to deal with its aftermath.

Defense Mechanisms Sigmund Freud believed that defense mechanisms protect the ego from anxiety that may be produced by an awareness of unacceptable ideas or impulses. Defense mechanisms become problematic when they are the only means used to cope with stress.

Reading Check **Find the Main Idea** Why are defensive coping strategies not the most desirable ways to deal with stress?

Active Coping

Active coping involves changing the environment or situation (in socially acceptable ways) to remove stressors, or changing one's response to stress so that stressors are no longer harmful. Methods of active coping include changing stressful thoughts, relaxing, and withstanding stress through exercise and deep breathing. These methods are far more effective than defensive coping strategies.

DEFENSE MECHANISMS

This chart identifies and provides examples of some common defense mechanisms.

Type	Definition	Example
Denial	The refusal to accept the reality of something that is bad or upsetting	An overworked employee is unwilling to admit to feeling stressed by his job out of a fear of appearing weak or incompetent.
Repression	The removal of anxiety-causing ideas from conscious awareness by pushing them into the unconscious	A soldier squashes his feelings of anxiety about going into combat.
Projection	The attribution of an undesirable impulse, thought, or feeling to other people	An angry student, frustrated by a discussion in class and unable to think of herself as angry, accuses her classmates of behaving angrily.

Skills Focus **INTERPRETING CHARTS** In each example, what might be the result of using the defense mechanism?

Calming Stressful Thoughts

Stressful thoughts can make an already stressful situation worse. People can actively cope with stress by becoming aware of these thought patterns and changing them. In this lab, you will practice changing stressful thoughts to calming ones.

PROCEDURE

❶ Get together with a partner.

❷ Read the stressful thoughts below and discuss the calming thoughts you might replace them with. For example, you might change "I feel like I'm losing control" to "This is painful and upsetting, but I don't have to go to pieces."

   a. "This will never end."

   b. "How can I go out there? I'll look like a fool."

   c. "My heart feels like it could leap out of my chest."

   d. "There's nothing I can do!"

❸ Ask your teacher for some possible answers.

ANALYSIS

1. With your partner, study the possible answers. Were the calming thoughts you came up with similar to these?

2. What do all of the calming thoughts have in common? Do you think they would really ease someone's stress?

3. Take turns discussing the stressful thoughts you have experienced when you have been under stress. Suggest calming thoughts that might replace them.

4. Consider the benefits of changing stressful thoughts. What effect do you think the practice could have on your emotional and physical well-being?

Quick Lab **THINK** central thinkcentral.com

Changing Stressful Thoughts Have you ever thought to yourself, "I feel like I'm losing control"? Such thoughts can actually increase the amount of stress you experience. However, people who have stressful thoughts can learn to recognize and change them before becoming overwhelmed by them. Through careful study, people can learn to identify self-defeating thoughts. Whenever a person feels tense or anxious, he or she should pay close attention to such thoughts and transform them into calming ones. A sign that this is working is evident when the person begins to automatically have calming thoughts rather than stressful ones.

Relaxation Techniques Stress can cause strong bodily reactions, such as muscle tension, rapid breathing, high blood pressure, sweating, and a rapid heart rate. These reactions are signs that something is wrong. They should prompt people to survey the situation and try to make things right. Psychologists and other researchers have developed a number of techniques for reducing the bodily changes that are brought on by stress. These techniques include meditation, biofeedback, and progressive relaxation.

Meditation is a form of relaxation that involves focusing one's attention on a single point of reference and eliminating all other thoughts from the mind. It can be practiced anywhere and does not require any special equipment. Many people find that meditation decreases their stress and brings real peace of mind. Research has also shown that meditation can improve the emotional and physical well-being of patients who suffer from conditions that may be worsened by stress, such as asthma, chronic pain, and depression.

Some people have difficulty recognizing their bodies' responses to stress. A form of mind-body therapy called biofeedback can help. During a biofeedback session, a therapist applies sensors to the patient's body that monitor responses to stress. For example, a sensor may signal when the patient's muscles contract during a headache. This information can help the patient recognize the physical cues that accompany a headache so that he or she can then focus on relaxing the muscles.

Progressive relaxation helps lower stress in the body by reducing muscle tension. Reducing tension also affects the heart and breathing rates. Progressive relaxation teaches people how to relax by having them purposely tense a specific muscle group and then relax it. You can practice this technique while sitting in a chair by first tightening one fist, then the other, and gradually releasing the pressure. This process of tightening and then releasing muscles helps people distinguish between feelings of tension and feelings of relaxation.

Changing stressful thoughts and lowering the level of bodily reactions to stress reduce the effects of stressors and give the person more time to develop a plan for effective action. When there is no way to reduce or eliminate the stressors, thinking calming thoughts and relaxing the body will increase the ability to endure stress.

Exercise Exercise fosters physical health, enhances people's psychological well-being, and helps people cope with stress. Stress-reducing exercise includes activities such as running and jogging, running in place, brisk walking, swimming, bicycle riding, jumping rope, and playing team sports.

Sustained physical activity reduces the incidence of heart attacks. In one long-term research project, Ralph Paffenbarger and his colleagues studied 17,000 people. They examined the relationship between the incidence of heart attacks and the levels of physical activity in the people they studied. The incidence of heart attacks began declining when the physical activity level rose to that of burning as few as 500 calories a week.

Inactive people run the highest risk of heart attacks. People who burn at least 2,000 calories a week through sustained physical activity live two years longer, on average, than less active people. Sustained exercise also appears to strengthen the functioning of the immune system.

Breathing When people are under stress, their breathing tends to become quick and shallow. By practicing controlled, regulated breathing techniques, people can calm themselves and reduce the physical symptoms of stress. Controlled breathing can even help relieve some stress-related health problems, including panic attacks and digestive disorders. The next time you are stressed out, try the following breathing exercise.

- Sit with your back straight.
- Place your tongue against the back of your teeth.
- Keeping your mouth closed, slowly inhale through your nose and mentally count to five.
- Hold your breath while you count to seven in your head.
- Exhale making a whooshing sound through your opened mouth for a count of eight. You should feel your lungs release the air.
- Repeat the exercise three more times.

This breathing exercise can actually calm the nervous system. You can use it whenever you are faced with a stressful situation. You can also use it to help you fall asleep.

Reading Check **Identify Supporting Details** How can active coping methods relieve some health problems?

Online Quiz THINK central thinkcentral.com

SECTION 4 Assessment

Reviewing Main Ideas and Vocabulary

1. **Identify** When might someone use withdrawal as a way of coping with a stressful situation?

2. **Contrast** What is the difference between defensive and active coping methods?

3. **Summarize** What are some examples of effective active coping methods?

Thinking Critically

4. **Predict** What do you think might happen when a person lashes out physically during a confrontation? What might be a better response?

5. **Make Judgments** Do you think only people with certain personality traits use defensive coping methods, or do you think anyone might use them from time to time? Support your answer.

6. **Compare** Using your notes and a graphic organizer like the one below, list the characteristics that the active coping methods have in common.

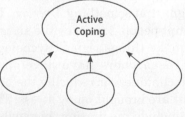

Active Coping

FOCUS ON WRITING

7. **Descriptive** Write a paragraph about a time when you used an active coping method to deal with a stressful situation.

Coping with Catastrophe

On September 11, 2001, Americans and people all over the world watched as the unthinkable happened. Of course, the tragedy most affected those who lost family members and friends. But even people who only witnessed the attacks on television suffered real symptoms of stress—what some psychologists call "second-hand stress."

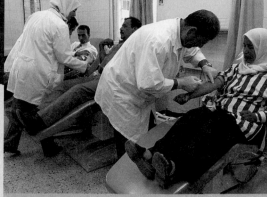

On September 12, 2001, Palestinians in Gaza showed their sympathy for the 9/11 victims by donating blood.

In a study led by psychologist Roxane Silver, researchers discovered that many of these people experienced symptoms similar to post-traumatic stress disorder (Silver, et al., 2002). Weeks after the attacks, they continued to replay in their minds the images they had seen on television. And these images still inspired strong feelings of fear and anxiety.

Comparable reactions occurred in the aftermath of Hurricane Katrina in 2005. Many people who compulsively followed the coverage of the tragedy experienced the fight-or-flight reaction, which causes blood pressure and heart rate to rise. For some with impaired immune systems, the response does not turn off. Serious health problems can occur as a result.

So how can we reduce this second-hand stress? Some psychologists suggest that we simply take a break from the news, by either avoiding it entirely for a few days or by limiting viewing to a half hour or so a day. But other psychologists say that turning away and ignoring the horrific news is just a form of denial and has limited value in really reducing stress.

In her study, Silver found that active coping strategies were most effective in coming to terms with 9/11. Those who donated blood or money to help the victims reportedly felt less helpless. Actively coping with the tragedy helped these people overcome their symptoms of post-traumatic stress disorder or avoid them altogether.

Silver's findings seem to have been supported by the experience in China following its devastating May 2008 earthquake. People from all over the country demonstrated great compassion and charity. Shortly after the earthquake, Chinese volunteers traveled long distances to the small towns and villages affected to help dig their compatriots out of the rubble and generally lend a hand. In fact, so many volunteers flooded the areas that local authorities had to close some of the roads.

The Chinese people also coped with the tragedy by making donations. Millions lined streets to donate blood, money, and clothes. Private citizens and companies contributed hundreds of billions of dollars. In fact, the disaster galvanized the Chinese people, and their response to it helped them heal. Their active coping not only decreased their stress but also brought them closer together. Some believed that the massive relief effort gave China a renewed sense of unity (Elegant, 2008).

Just about a month after the earthquake in China, areas of several midwestern states were ravaged when record floods hit the region. Again, people not directly affected by the disaster generously offered their help. Some came to the areas to fill sandbags; others sent food, clothing, and money to families who lost everything in the floods. "I just felt better doing something," said one volunteer. And that about sums it up.

When parts of Iowa flooded in June 2008, volunteers filled sandbags to help hold back the water.

Thinking Critically

1. **Analyze** How does helping disaster victims reduce second-hand stress?

2. **Discuss** Think of a time when you helped someone overcome difficulties. What did you do? How did it make you feel?

Current Research **THINK** central thinkcentral.com

Simulation
Applying What You've Learned

Stress and Active Coping Methods

What is the most effective way to cope with a stressful situation?

Reading and Activity Workbook

Use the workbook to complete this simulation.

1. Introduction

We deal with stress every day. As you have learned in this chapter, stress can result from minor, everyday problems, or it can be tied to a major, life-changing event. In this simulation, you will get together with a group of classmates to develop and perform a simulation in which you role-play a stressful situation. In your simulation, you will also demonstrate how to deal with the situation by using effective coping methods. To complete the simulation, follow the steps below.

■ Following your teacher's instructions, organize the class into six student groups.

■ Your teacher will assign each group one of the following six stressful situations:

❶ Frustration: You are delayed in traffic and miss an important appointment.

❷ Daily hassle: The wheels of your car have been stolen.

❸ Life change: You are about to move to a new state.

❹ Avoidance-avoidance conflict: You dread going to the dentist, but your toothache is getting worse.

❺ Approach-avoidance conflict: You want to buy a new DVD player, but it will cost a lot of money.

❻ Multiple approach-avoidance conflict: You need to stay at home to study for a test, but your friends have invited you to go to a movie with them.

■ Work with your group to write the simulation for the situation you have been assigned.

■ Student groups will take turns performing their simulations before the rest of the class. During each performance, the audience will take notes.

■ Take part in a group discussion on the simulations, and then apply what you have learned to create a list of tips on coping with stress.

2. Prepare the Simulation

With your group, discuss the source of stress or type of conflict that you have been assigned. Review what you learned about this stressor or conflict in the chapter. Then discuss and develop the situation you are going to role-play. Follow these steps as you develop your simulation:

■ Decide what role each member of the group will play. You might have one student play the role of the person dealing with the stress, several others play the roles of friends and advisers, and one play the role of a narrator.

■ Talk about how the person at the center of the situation should react to the stress. For example, he or she might reduce the stress by demonstrating a sense of humor or taking deep breaths.

■ Agree on how the friends and advisers will react. What active coping methods will they suggest? Be sure the methods are effective and suitable for the situation.

■ If you have a narrator, discuss how he or she will introduce and set up the situation.

■ Work together to write dialogue for the simulation. The dialogue should sound natural and realistic. Include stage directions that indicate how each speaker should act and move throughout the simulation. Note that the performance of the simulation should be about five minutes in length.

■ Make a photocopy of the simulation for each actor.

■ Practice the simulation a couple of times. The first time, do a read-through while sitting in your chairs. The second time, try enacting the simulation. You might want to continue practicing until all group members feel confident with their roles.

3. Perform the Simulation

Once all the groups have prepared their simulations, they will take turns performing them. During your group's performance, keep the following in mind:

■ You can read from your photocopy of the simulation, but try to look at the other role-players from time to time for realism.

■ Speak loudly enough so that audience members do not have to strain to hear you.

■ Act your role in a serious manner.

■ Be supportive of your group members if they falter.

As an audience member, be attentive and courteous. Take notes on the following as you watch each performance:

■ The stressor or conflict being demonstrated

■ The depiction of the stressful situation

■ The effectiveness of the coping methods used to deal with the situation

■ Some different ways the situation might have been handled

■ Whether the situation seemed familiar and what other situations it reminded you of

■ How you reacted in a similar situation

4. Discussion

After all of the simulations have been performed, join in a class discussion. Talk about the performances, focusing on the following questions:

■ What did you think of the performances?

■ Did each one represent a stressful situation realistically?

■ What were some of the effective coping methods the groups presented?

■ What, if anything, would you have done differently?

■ Which coping methods do you find most effective in your daily life?

■ Can you think of a time in which you or someone you know effectively coped with a situation similar to one of those presented?

■ Can you think of a time in which you or someone you know could have coped more effectively with a stressful situation?

■ Do you think you can apply what you have seen to dealing with some of the stressful situations in your daily life?

Finally, as a class, come up with a list of tips on coping with stress. Your list might include the following:

■ The coping methods used in the stressful situations performed

■ The coping methods you have used successfully in other stressful situations

■ Other ideas on defusing or avoiding stressors

What type of stressful situation is this? What might the man do to cope with it?

CHAPTER 17 Review

Comprehension and Critical Thinking

SECTION 1 (pp. 472–476)

1. a. Describe What contributes to the stress experienced by many high school students?

b. Explain Why can positive life changes produce stress?

c. Elaborate Think of a character—in television, movies, or fiction—who exemplifies the type B personality. How does this character demonstrate type B behavior?

SECTION 2 (pp. 477–481)

2. a. Recall How does the body react during the alarm reaction stage of the general adaptation syndrome?

b. Summarize How do self-efficacy expectations affect the way a person responds to stress?

c. Evaluate Why might a diagnosis of cancer further impair a person's immune system?

SECTION 3 (pp. 482–486)

3. a. Identify What are some behavioral methods for reducing the pain of headache?

b. Make Generalizations What generalizations can you make about the risk factors for heart disease?

c. Make Judgments Why do you think some people criticize cancer patients for feeling sorry for themselves? Do you think they are trying to help? Explain your answer.

SECTION 4 (pp. 487–490)

4. a. Identify Main Ideas Why do some defensive coping methods only make a problem worse?

b. Identify Cause and Effect How does changing stressful thoughts help increase the ability to endure stress?

c. Predict What do you think might happen to a high school student whose only means of coping with a problem is to lock herself in her room?

Reviewing Vocabulary

For each of the following questions, choose the letter of the best answer.

5. Which of the following refers to an event or situation that produces stress?
  A. dilemma   **C.** distress
  B. eustress   **D.** stressor

6. Which type of conflict forces people to choose between the lesser of two evils?
  A. approach-approach   **C.** approach-avoidance
  B. avoidance-avoidance   **D.** multiple approach-avoidance

7. Which response to stress is closely related to self-confidence?
  A. self-efficacy expectations   **C.** sense of humor
  B. psychological hardiness   **D.** predictability

8. What is the name for the body's response to a stressful situation?
  A. self-efficacy expectations   **C.** defensive coping
  B. general adaptation syndrome   **D.** active coping

INTERNET ACTIVITY ✳

9. Research to find out how stress in the workplace, along with other stress, can affect a person's health and well-being. What kinds of situations contribute to job stress? How do employers try to deal with job stress? Write a report summarizing your findings.

Psychology in Your Life

10. The Social Readjustment Rating Scale focuses primarily on life changes experienced by adults. Get together with a small group of classmates and create a social readjustment scale for teens. Make a list of 10 events and assign a rating to each item on the basis of a consensus of group members. For example, you might list excessive homework or parental restrictions on your scale. Once you have compiled your list, share and discuss it with your class. Do your classmates agree with your scale?

SKILLS ACTIVITY: INTERPRETING PRIMARY SOURCES

Read the following excerpt, in which Anne Petersen and Ralph Spiga look at school as one of the sources of adolescent stress. Then answer the questions that follow.

> **"**Indeed, the school may provide major stress during the adolescent years. In early adolescence, young people in our society move from a single classroom, with one teacher and the same group of classmates, into a middle school or junior high school, where they pass from class to class, most often with different teachers and different students. For many young people, this transition may be smooth, but for others it appears to be untimely and stressful. . . . Little research has focused on the transition from eighth or ninth grade into senior high school. Research with early adolescents, however, would suggest that this change also involves stress.**"**
>
> —Anne C. Petersen and Ralph Spiga,
> "Adolescence and Stress," from *Handbook
> of Stress: Theoretical and Clinical Aspects*

11. **Identify Main Ideas** According to this excerpt, what is a key source of school-related stress for adolescents?

12. **Draw Conclusions** Why might the transition into middle school be "untimely" for some adolescents?

13. **Develop** How might educators make school transitions less stressful for adolescents?

WRITING FOR AP PSYCHOLOGY

Use your knowledge of the general adaptation syndrome to answer the question below. Do not simply list facts. Present a clear argument based on your critical analysis of the question, using the appropriate psychological terminology.

14. Briefly discuss what happens during each stage of the syndrome listed below. Explain the role stress plays in each stage.
    - the alarm reaction
    - the resistance stage
    - the exhaustion stage

Connecting Online

Visit thinkcentral.com for review and enrichment activities related to this chapter.

Quiz and Review

ONLINE QUIZZES
Take a practice quiz for each section in this chapter.

WEBQUEST
Complete a structured Internet activity for this chapter.

QUICK LAB
Reinforce a key concept with a short lab activity.

APPLYING WHAT YOU'VE LEARNED
Review and apply your knowledge by completing a project-based assessment.

Activities

eACTIVITIES
Complete chapter Internet activities for enrichment.

INTERACTIVE FEATURE
Explore an interactive version of a key feature in this chapter.

KEEP IT CURRENT
Link to current news and research in psychology.

Online Textbook

Learn more about key topics in this chapter.

NOT GUILTY by Reason of Insanity

The majority of people with serious psychological disorders are not dangerous to others. Some, however, do commit violent crimes. Of these, some are found not guilty of the crimes of which they are accused "by reason of insanity." Typically, these people are sent to psychiatric institutions instead of prison. They may be released when they are judged no longer to be a threat to others.

A well-known use of the insanity plea occurred in the case of John Hinckley Jr., who tried to assassinate President Ronald Reagan in 1981. Not only did Hinckley attempt to murder the president, but he did so in front of millions of television witnesses. Nevertheless, Hinckley was found not guilty by reason of insanity after expert witnesses testified that he had the serious psychological disorder called schizophrenia.

Another famous case is that of Andrea Yates, who on June 20, 2001, drowned all five of her young children. Yates freely confessed to the murders. She told a psychiatrist that she feared her children were "doomed to perish in the fires of hell"—a fate

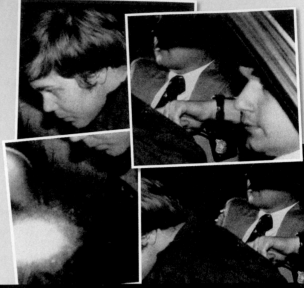

John Hinckley Jr. was arrested immediately after his attempted assassination of President Reagan on March 30, 1981.

from which she hoped to save them. When Yates went to trial, the jury rejected the insanity defense and convicted her of first-degree murder. However, Yates won a new trial in 2006, and this time was found not guilty by reason of insanity.

In using an insanity defense, lawyers apply a modified version of the M'Naghten Rule, which states that if it can be proved that at the time of committing a criminal act a person either did not understand the nature of the act or did not know that it was wrong, then the person is insane and not responsible for the act. The M'Naghten Rule goes back to 1843, when a Scot named Daniel M'Naghten tried to kill the British prime minister, Sir Robert Peel. M'Naghten believed that he was the target of an international conspiracy that included Sir Robert and the pope. In the assassination attempt, M'Naghten killed Peel's secretary instead of the prime minister. M'Naghten was arrested and tried but was judged not guilty. The jury declared that M'Naghten was insane and thus not responsible for the crime.

Typically, when an accused person pleads insanity, prosecuting attorneys try to show

At her second trial, Andrea Yates was found not guilty by reason of insanity.

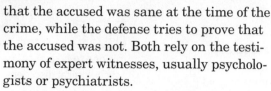
CHAPTER 18

PSYCHOLOGICAL DISORDERS

that the accused was sane at the time of the crime, while the defense tries to prove that the accused was not. Both rely on the testimony of expert witnesses, usually psychologists or psychiatrists.

Many people claim that the insanity defense allows criminals literally to "get away with murder." However, the defense is actually used rarely and is often unsuccessful. Recent changes have made it more difficult to use the insanity plea successfully. For example, it is now up to the defense to prove that the defendant's mental illness is one that qualifies under the insanity plea.

"Insanity" is a legal concept, not a psychological one, and to be legally usable, it must be all or nothing—one is either sane or insane. In reality, most psychological disorders are a matter of degree. The distinction is important. One can be mildly depressed, for example, but according to the law, one cannot be mildly insane. Because of the insanity plea's all-or-nothing nature, deciding on someone's sanity can be a very difficult decision for judges and juries.

Our legal system requires a wide range of people to make decisions about the mental health of others. How equipped are jurors to make these decisions? How informed are we about what separates mental illness from mental health? For example, the case of Andrea Yates poses some basic questions that are not easily answered: Is a woman who drowns all her children to "save" them automatically insane, even though she knew that her action was wrong in the eyes of the law? Just what is mental illness?

What do you think?

1. In general, what criteria must a defendant meet to be ruled legally insane?

2. Do you support the use of the insanity defense? Why or why not?

Chapter at a Glance

SECTION 1: Understanding Psychological Disorders

- Psychological disorders are behavior patterns or mental processes that cause serious personal suffering or interfere with a person's ability to cope with everyday life.

- Psychological disorders are classified in the *Diagnostic and Statistical Manual of Mental Disorders*, also known as the *DSM*.

SECTION 2: Anxiety and Mood Disorders

- Anxiety disorders occur when people feel fear or nervousness out of proportion to the actual threat.

- Mood disorders are characterized by mood changes that are inappropriate for the situation to which they are responding.

SECTION 3: Dissociative and Somatoform Disorders

- Dissociative disorders are characterized by the separation of certain personality components or mental processes from conscious thought.

- Somatoform disorders are expressed in the form of actual physical symptoms.

SECTION 4: Schizophrenia

- Schizophrenia is usually considered the most serious psychological disorder and can be very disabling.

- Schizophrenia is characterized by a loss of contact with reality.

- The three types of schizophrenia are paranoid, disorganized, and catatonic schizophrenia.

SECTION 5: Personality Disorders

- Personality disorders are patterns of inflexible traits that disrupt social life or work and may distress the affected individual.

- Four common personality disorders are paranoid, schizoid, antisocial, and avoidant.

Understanding Psychological Disorders

Before You Read

Main Idea

Psychological disorders are relatively common. They cause personal suffering to millions of people and interfere with their ability to cope with everyday life.

Reading Focus

1. What are psychological disorders, and how common are they?

2. What are the four major symptoms that can help identify psychological disorders?

3. How do psychologists classify psychological disorders?

Vocabulary

psychological disorders
culture-bound syndromes

TAKING NOTES Use a graphic organizer like this one to take notes on psychological disorders.

```
        Psychological
         Disorders
       /     |      \
What they are  Identifying  Classifying
              disorders    disorders
```

Misunderstanding Mental Illness

PSYCHOLOGY CLOSE UP

Why were people with mental illnesses seen as criminals? Until about a century ago, mental illness was a mystery. To both the public and to the medical profession, people who behaved strangely were often seen as evil or cursed, not ill. Doctors sometimes proposed causes for the illnesses that we now consider absurd, such as reading too many novels. Because they did not understand mental disorders, doctors and other officials often treated mental patients very harshly, severely restricting their freedom and even punishing them as if they were criminals. One common method of control was the straitjacket, which is a garment with extra-long sleeves that wrap around the patient's body. The straitjacket was actually more humane than the ropes and metal chains with which some patients were shackled.

Now we know that psychological disorders are indeed illnesses. Mental health professionals have described almost 400 such disorders. Their causes, however, are sometimes disputed. You will read more about psychological disorders in this section. ■

This straitjacketed mental patient was photographed in 1946.

What Are Psychological Disorders?

You have already learned that psychology is the scientific study of behavior and mental processes. **Psychological disorders** are behavior patterns or mental processes that cause serious personal suffering or interfere with a person's ability to cope with everyday life.

Many people believe that psychological disorders are uncommon, affecting relatively few individuals. It is true that the great majority of people are never admitted to mental hospitals, and most people never seek the help of psychologists or psychiatrists. And although many people have relatives they consider eccentric, few people have family members they consider to be truly abnormal.

Estimates suggest, however, that about one in four adults in the United States have experienced some type of psychological disorder. In addition to the many people with substance abuse problems, 26 percent of people in the United States experience some type of psychological disorder in a given year. In any given month, the figure is approximately 13 percent. For people aged 15–44, psychological disorders are the leading cause of disability in the United States.

Reading Check **Summarize** What is a common misconception about psychological disorders?

Identifying Psychological Disorders

Deciding whether particular behaviors, thoughts, or feelings are "normal" or "abnormal" can be difficult. What is normal is often equated with what is average for the majority of people. Using this definition of normality, deviation from the majority becomes the primary criterion for abnormality.

People with psychological disorders usually do not differ much from so-called normal people. In fact, the primary difference is the simple exaggeration of certain behaviors or mental processes. For example, laughing is a normal and healthy response to humorous situations. However, someone who laughs all the time, even in a tragic situation where everyone else is sad might be considered abnormal.

Certain behavior patterns and mental processes may suggest that an individual has a psychological disorder. The word *suggest* is important here, because diagnosing an individual with a psychological disorder is often difficult, and reaching a correct diagnosis is not always a simple process.

However, psychologists generally use several criteria to determine whether a person's behavior indicates the presence of a psychological disorder. These <u>criteria</u> include how typical the behavior is of people in general, whether the behavior is maladaptive, whether the behavior causes the individual emotional discomfort, and whether the behavior is socially unacceptable.

ACADEMIC VOCABULARY

criteria the standards on which a judgment or decision may be based

INTERACTIVE ✳

Statistically Speaking...

Psychological Disorders in the United States
Drug and alcohol addiction, depression, and anxiety disorders are the most common psychological disorders.

26.2% Percentage of American adults who suffer from a diagnosable mental disorder in a given year

6% Percentage of Americans who suffer from a serious psychological disorder

47.1 million Annual number of visits to office-based physicians due to psychological disorders in the United States

6.9 days Average hospital stay for patients with psychological disorders in the United States

90% Percentage of people that kill themselves who suffer from a diagnosable psychological disorder

Skills Focus **INTERPRETING DATA** What is one possible result of not diagnosing and treating a serious mental disorder?

Sources: National Institute of Mental Health; National Center for Health Statistics

Interactive Feature **THINK** central   thinkcentral.com

Typicality The normality of a behavior or mental process is often determined by the degree to which it is average, or typical, of the behavior or mental processes of the majority of people. There are, however, problems with defining normality in terms of what is typical of most people. The fact that a behavior is not typical of most people does not mean it is abnormal. Scientific and artistic geniuses, such as Marie Curie and Pablo Picasso, certainly are not typical of people in general. That does not mean, however, that such people are abnormal. In addition, people who are quite normal may have lifestyles that differ widely from the rest of the community. Additional measurements must be taken into account to assess people with different styles and habits.

Maladaptivity Many psychologists believe that what makes a behavior abnormal is the fact that it is maladaptive. That is, the behavior impairs an individual's ability to function adequately in everyday life. Behavior that causes misery and distress rather than happiness and fulfillment may be considered maladaptive. Alcohol abuse is one such behavior. Alcohol abuse often has strong negative effects on the drinker's health, work, and family life. Abuse of alcohol may discourage the drinker from seeking healthier solutions to the problem of anxiety as well as create additional problems of its own.

Behavior that is hazardous to oneself or to others may also be considered maladaptive. This type of maladaptive behavior may include threatening or attempting suicide as well as threatening or attacking other people. Maladaptive behaviors can put the person with a disorder on the wrong side of the law.

It is important to note, however, that most people who commit violent crimes do not have diagnosable psychological disorders. This is because most criminals are fully aware of what they are doing. That is, they know that their behavior is illegal and that they can be held responsible for it. Equally important, the majority of people with psychological disorders, even severe psychological disorders, are not violent or dangerous.

Emotional Discomfort Psychological disorders such as anxiety and depression cause most people serious emotional discomfort.

For example, people who are depressed often suffer feelings of helplessness, hopelessness, worthlessness, guilt, and extreme sadness. They may lose interest in virtually everything they once enjoyed and believe that life is no longer worth living. Such feelings are so stressful that they may lead the affected individual to consider suicide. Thus, severe emotional discomfort may be a sign of a psychological disorder.

Socially Unacceptable Behavior Behavior that violates a society's accepted norms may also be an indication of a psychological disorder. However, whether a behavior is socially unacceptable may depend on the particular culture in which it occurs. What is considered normal behavior in one culture may be considered not normal in another. Therefore, the cultural context of a behavior must be taken into account before deciding that the behavior indicates a psychological disorder.

The importance of culture is demonstrated by **culture-bound syndromes,** which are clusters of symptoms that are considered recognizable diseases only within specific cultures or societies. Many behaviors associated with culture-bound syndromes would be considered abnormal by people who were unaware of the cultural context. For example, many people in Middle Eastern cultures believe that certain unusual behaviors, such as head-banging, are due to possession of the body by a spirit. In the local cultural context, spirit possession is considered to be a rational explanation for the behavior, and the affected individual is not thought to have a mental illness. However, in the United States, such an unusual behavior might be considered a sign of a psychological disorder.

On the other hand, there are some culture-bound syndromes that are clearly disorders, as interpreted both by the home culture and by mainstream Western society. Their causes may be unique to the culture, though. Some culture-bound syndromes have serious physical symptoms and results. There are many types of culture-bound syndromes, some of which are described in the feature at the end of this section.

Reading Check **Find the Main Idea** What are four features that might indicate a psychological disorder?

Classifying Psychological Disorders

Most psychologists believe that it is important to have a widely agreed upon classification of psychological disorders. Unless there is agreement about how to classify psychological disorders, it is difficult to know how many people have a given disorder or what other factors, such as socioeconomic status, heredity, or gender differences, may be associated with it. It is also important to classify psychological disorders so that individuals can be correctly diagnosed and treated.

The most widely used classification system for psychological disorders is the *DSM*, or *Diagnostic and Statistical Manual of Mental Disorders*, published by the American Psychiatric Association. The most recent version of the manual, the *DSM-IV-TR™*, was published in 2000.

Major Categories of Psychological Disorders

The *DSM-IV-TR™* lists 16 basic categories of psychological disorders, of which 13 are described here. You will learn about six of these general categories: anxiety, mood, dissociative, somatoform, and personality disorders; and schizophrenia.

Disorders usually first diagnosed in infancy, childhood, or adolescence include mental retardation, attention deficit disorders, and autism spectrum disorders.

Delirium, dementia, and amnesia, and other cognitive disorders result from brain damage, degenerative diseases such as Alzheimer's disease, or exposure to toxic substances or drugs.

Substance-related disorders are associated with the excessive use of or withdrawal from drugs such as alcohol, nicotine, amphetamines, cocaine, hallucinogens, opiates, or caffeine.

Schizophrenia and other psychotic disorders are characterized by delusions, hallucinations, and severe disruptions in thoughts and emotions.

Anxiety disorders include phobias, generalized anxiety disorder, panic attacks, post-traumatic stress disorder, and obsessive-compulsive disorder.

Mood disorders include major depression, bipolar disorder, postpartum depression, and chronically depressed mood.

Dissociative disorders are characterized by the separation of certain mental processes or personality traits from conscious thoughts, including dissociative amnesia and dissociative identity disorder (multiple personality disorder).

Somatoform disorders involve physical symptoms for which no biological cause can be found.

Sexual and gender identity disorders include sexual dysfunctions and the need for unusual or bizarre acts to achieve sexual satisfaction.

Eating disorders are characterized by abnormal eating patterns, including anorexia nervosa (self-starvation caused by an irrational fear of becoming overweight) and bulimia nervosa (episodes of binge eating and vomiting).

Sleep disorders include disorders associated with sleeping patterns, including insomnia and sleepwalking.

Impulse control disorders not elsewhere classified are characterized by an inability to resist an impulse to perform actions that are harmful to the individual or to others, including compulsive gambling, stealing (kleptomania), and setting fires (pyromania).

Personality disorders are characterized by maladaptive patterns that cause distress or interfere with one's ability to function, including antisocial and paranoid personality disorders.

Skills Focus   INTERPRETING CHARTS

What kinds of disorders are typically diagnosed early in one's life?

People use the *DSM* for various purposes. Psychiatrists and other mental health professionals use its terminology to communicate about patient needs and treatment. Insurance companies may require that patients match *DSM* diagnoses to cover treatment costs. Researchers investigating certain disorders or specific diseases may recruit patients whose symptoms match the *DSM* criteria for that disease.

The way psychological disorders are classified has changed significantly from earlier *DSM* systems. Until 1980, when the third edition of the *DSM* was published, psychological disorders were classified on the basis of their presumed causes. For many decades, the most widely accepted causes were those suggested by Freud's psychoanalytic theory.

Many psychologists criticized early versions of the *DSM* because very diverse psychological disorders were grouped together under the labels "neuroses" and "psychoses." As a result, beginning with the *DSM-III* in 1980, psychological disorders have been categorized on the basis of observable signs and symptoms rather than presumed causes.

The *DSM* is subject to ongoing revision. New categories are added and old ones removed as knowledge of psychological disorders increases. For example, post-traumatic stress disorder (PTSD) was added to the *DSM* only after the Vietnam War, when many soldiers were found to suffer from the disorder. More recent research into PTSD in Iraq war veterans may be included in the revision of the *DSM* text that is scheduled for 2012.

With each new revision of the *DSM*, the number of psychological disorders has grown. Currently, the manual contains almost 400 types of disorders. Critics worry that some of the disorders being added are simply everyday problems, as opposed to the more serious disorders such as schizophrenia and PTSD.

The remainder of this chapter focuses on six major types of psychological disorders: anxiety disorders, mood disorders, dissociative disorders, somatoform disorders, schizophrenia, and personality disorders. Many of the symptoms of these disorders are simply exaggerations of normal thoughts, feelings, or behaviors. As a result, as you read about the different symptoms, you may feel that you have one or more of the disorders being described. Such a feeling is common among most people who read about psychological disorders for the first time. Keep in mind that only trained professionals can diagnose psychological disorders, and they can do so only after careful evaluation.

Reading Check **Summarize** What are some ways in which the *DSM* has been revised?

SECTION 1 Assessment

Online Quiz **THINK** central thinkcentral.com

Reviewing Main Ideas and Vocabulary

1. **Define** What are psychological disorders?

2. **Summarize** How did the arrangement of the criteria for the classification of psychological disorders change in 1980?

Thinking Critically

3. **Elaborate** Why must psychologists be aware of culture-bound syndromes when determining what is abnormal?

4. **Categorize** Give an example of a feeling or a behavior that would be considered normal in one circumstance but might be considered a sign of a psychological disorder in another circumstance.

5. **Predict** What are the common pitfalls that students of psychology may face when learning about psychological disorders?

6. **Analyze** Using your notes and a graphic organizer like the one below, explain the problems that can arise when using the following criteria to determine the presence of a psychological disorder.

Criteria	Problems
1. Typicality	
2. Maladaptivity	
3. Emotional discomfort	
4. Social unacceptability of behavior	

FOCUS ON WRITING

7. **Persuasive** In a paragraph, explain why the changes made in the organization of the *DSM* in 1980 were a benefit to psychologists and their patients.

Culture-Bound Syndromes

In certain cultures, one can find combinations of psychiatric and physical symptoms recognized as diseases only in that culture. Some of the symptoms of these maladies coincide with disorders in the *DSM*. Others, however, are quite specific to the individual culture. These culture-bound syndromes are often treated with folk remedies.

Sufferers of *susto* may seek help from a *curandero* in a healing ritual.

Hikikomori *Hikikomori* are Japanese people who have withdrawn from social life. The Japanese Ministry of Health, Labour and Welfare has defined the affliction, also called *hikikomori,* as refusing to leave one's parents' house and isolating one's self from society for six months or longer. The extreme competitiveness of Japanese education and society have been cited as contributing to *hikikomori.*

This 19-year-old *hikikomori* has shut himself away in his parents' tiny apartment since he was 11 years old.

Latah In Malaysia and some other areas, *latah* is the name both for a condition and someone who suffers from it. The condition is characterized by having a severe reaction to being startled. When surprised, *latahs,* usually women, may mimic the speech of people around them and obey any order. If a *latah* does something wrong during such an episode, she is ordinarily not held responsible.

Ghost sickness Ghost sickness has occurred among the Navajo of the American Southwest. The symptoms include bad dreams, loss of appetite, a feeling of suffocation, hallucinations, fainting, and a pervasive feeling of terror. A preoccupation with death and the dead is blamed for the symptoms. Ghosts, called *chindi,* or witches are believed to cause the fixation.

Hwa-byung In Korea, some people suffer from *hwa-byung,* which means "anger illness" or "fire illness." Many physical symptoms result from the panic and depression believed to be due to the suppression of anger. These physical symptoms may include a heavy feeling in the chest, insomnia, fatigue, or indigestion. Western psychiatrists would probably diagnose a *hwa-byung* patient as suffering from anxiety or depression.

Amok In Malaysia, a previously peaceful man who suddenly tries to kill or injure others is said to be struck by *amok,* from a Malay word that means "rushing in a frenzy." Men who "run amok"—the syndrome does not occur in women—may be overwhelmed by some kind of shame and feel they can no longer live with such dishonor. A person in the grips of this syndrome may continue to attack until he is restrained, exhausted, or killed by bystanders.

Susto Hispanic groups in the United States and parts of Latin America report a disorder called *susto.* Sufferers experience acute unhappiness following a frightening event. The victim believes that her soul has left her body. Physical symptoms, such as muscle pain and insomnia, may accompany the misery. A *curandero,* or healer, may be called to perform a ceremony that will return the soul to its rightful place. *Susto* may be similar to post-traumatic stress disorder (PTSD).

Zar There is a religious custom and a syndrome in the Middle East and North Africa known as *Zar.* During a Zar ritual, of which music is an important aspect, a person (usually a woman) is supposedly possessed by a spirit. The "possessed" person shouts, laughs, bangs her head, and displays other odd behaviors. The Zar custom may offer an emotional release for women in male-dominated societies.

Thinking Critically

1. **Summarize** What are some of the physical symptoms associated with culture-bound syndromes?

2. **Discuss** Do you think Western medical schools should include culture-bound syndromes in their psychiatry programs? Why or why not?

Anxiety and Mood Disorders

Before You Read

Main Idea

Anxiety disorders cause people to experience irrational or excessive fear. Mood disorders cause people to experience mood changes that are inappropriate to the situation.

Reading Focus

1. What are some characteristics of anxiety?
2. What are five major types of anxiety disorders?
3. How do psychologists explain anxiety disorders?
4. How do the two main types of mood disorders compare?
5. Which theories explain the origins of mood disorders?

Vocabulary

phobia
social phobia
panic attack
agoraphobia
obsessive-compulsive disorder (OCD)
post-traumatic stress disorder (PTSD)
depression
bipolar disorder
mania

TAKING NOTES As you read, take notes on the types and characteristics of anxiety and mood disorders.

Type of Disorder	Characteristics
1.	
2.	
3.	

A Footballer's Fixations

PSYCHOLOGY CLOSE UP

Why does an English soccer star need three refrigerators?
When David Beckham joined the Los Angeles Galaxy, many American sports fans knew of his phenomenal talent on the soccer field, his prominent place on the fashion scene, and his glamorous wife. What they did not know is that Beckham suffers from obsessive-compulsive disorder, often abbreviated as OCD. This mental condition drives Beckham to require his surroundings be arranged just so. For example, when he stays in a hotel room, he cannot rest until all the leaflets and books are stowed out of sight. At home, he has three refrigerators, so that drinks, salad fixings, and other foods are stored separately. If there are three soft drink cans in the fridge, he has to put one away so that an even number of cans remains. Beckham has said "I have to have everything in a straight line or everything has to be in pairs."

OCD is one of the anxiety disorders that afflict millions of people. For many of these people, their disorders go undiagnosed and untreated. ■

Before the 2006 World Cup, soccer star David Beckham disclosed that he suffers from obsessive-compulsive disorder (OCD).

Does Public Speaking Make You Nervous?

One of the most common phobias that people have is the fear of public speaking. Standing and speaking in front of a group is not a strenuous activity, so why does it cause so much anxiety?

PROCEDURE

❶ While seated calmly at your desk, take your pulse for ten seconds.

❷ Stand up at the front of the class and read the following statement:

People who experience obsessions are usually aware that the obsessions are unjustified. This distinguishes obsessions from delusions.

❸ Return to your desk and immediately take your pulse for ten seconds.

ANALYSIS

1. Calculate the number of beats per minute for your resting heart rate.

2. Calculate the number of beats per minute after your speech.

3. Compare the two heart rates.

4. Describe any other changes that you noticed as your body dealt with the stress of speaking in front of the class.

5. Discuss with the rest of the class how the anticipation of public speaking affected you, what physical responses you felt during the exercise, and why you think public speaking can cause so much anxiety.

 Quick Lab THINK central thinkcentral.com

What Is Anxiety?

Anxiety refers to a generalized state of dread or uneasiness that occurs in response to a vague or imagined danger. It differs from fear, which is a response to a real danger or threat. Anxiety is typically characterized by nervousness, inability to relax, and concern about losing control. Physical signs and symptoms of anxiety may include trembling, sweating, rapid heart rate, shortness of breath, increased blood pressure, flushed face, and feelings of faintness or lightheadedness. All are the result of overactivity of the sympathetic branch of the autonomic nervous system.

Everyone feels anxious at times—for example, before a big game. In such situations, feeling anxious or worried is an appropriate response that does not indicate a psychological disorder. However, some people feel anxious all or most of the time, or their anxiety is out of proportion to the situation provoking it. Such anxiety may interfere with effective living, the achievement of desired goals, life satisfaction, and emotional comfort. When these problems occur, anxiety is considered a sign of a psychological disorder. Anxiety-based disorders are among the most common of all psychological disorders in the United States.

Reading Check **Analyze** How are anxiety disorders different from normal anxious reactions?

Types of Anxiety Disorders

Anxiety disorders classified in the DSM-IV include phobic disorder, panic disorder, generalized anxiety disorder, obsessive-compulsive disorder, and stress disorders. A description of each follows.

Phobic Disorder The word **phobia** derives from the Greek root *phobos*, which means "fear." Specific phobia, which is the most common of all the anxiety disorders, refers to a persistent excessive or irrational fear of a particular object or situation. To be diagnosed as a phobic disorder, the fear must lead to avoidance behavior that interferes with the affected person's normal life.

Almost any object or situation may lead to a phobic reaction. Several phobias, however, are especially common. The most common include:

- zoophobia: fear of animals
- claustrophobia: fear of enclosed spaces
- acrophobia: fear of heights
- arachnophobia: fear of spiders

Other relatively common phobias include fear of thunderstorms, blood, snakes, dental procedures, driving, and air travel.

When people with specific phobias are confronted with the object or situation they fear, they are likely to feel extremely anxious.

 Complete a Webquest at thinkcentral.com on phobic disorders.

As a result, they tend to avoid what they fear. Someone with hematophobia (a fear of blood) might avoid needed medical treatment. Someone with aviaphobia (a fear of air travel) might turn down a job promotion because the new position involves air travel. For example, an aviaphobic businesswoman panicked before a flight to an important meeting in Philadelphia. She got off the plane, rented a car, and drove to Philadelphia, but she still missed the meeting. She later resigned from her job as a result. Thus, although most people with specific phobias never seek treatment for their disorders, a specific phobia can seriously disrupt a person's life.

Social phobia is characterized by persistent fear of social situations in which one might be exposed to the close scrutiny of others and thus be observed doing something embarrassing or humiliating. Some people with social phobias fear all social situations; others fear specific situations, such as public speaking, eating in public, or dating.

People with social phobias generally try to avoid the situations they fear. They may invent excuses to avoid going to parties or other social gatherings, for example. If such avoidance is impossible, the situations are likely to cause great anxiety. In addition, the avoidance behavior itself may greatly interfere with work and social life.

Panic Disorder and Agoraphobia People with panic disorder have recurring and unexpected panic attacks. A **panic attack** is a relatively short period of intense fear or discomfort characterized by shortness of breath, dizziness, rapid heart rate, trembling or shaking, sweating, choking, nausea, and other distressing physical symptoms. It may last from a few minutes to a few hours. People having a panic attack may believe they are dying or "going crazy." Not surprisingly, they usually have persistent fears of another attack.

For most people who suffer panic disorder, attacks have no apparent cause. However, many people with panic disorder also have agoraphobia. **Agoraphobia** is a fear of being in places or situations in which escape may be difficult or impossible. People with agoraphobia may be especially afraid of crowded public places such as movie theaters, shopping malls, buses, or trains.

Agoraphobia is a common phobia among adults. In fact, according to the *DSM-IV,* people with one or both disorders make up from 50 to 80 percent of the phobic patients seen in clinical practice.

Most people with agoraphobia have panic attacks when they cannot avoid the stressful situations they fear. They are afraid they will

Arachnophobia

Definition: a simple phobia characterized by an irrational, excessive, and persistent fear of spiders

Symptoms: may include feelings of panic, excessive sweating, rapid breathing, a quickened heartbeat, nausea, or dizziness

Impact on daily life: avoiding encounters with spiders by refusing to go barefoot, checking when showering or getting into and out of bed, fumigating the home, or sealing windows with tape

Other Specific Phobias

Amaxophobia
fear of riding in a car

Astraphobia
fear of thunder, lightning, and storms

Chromophobia
fear of colors

Coulrophobia
fear of clowns

Gephyrophobia
fear of bridges

Microphobia
fear of small things

Octophobia
fear of the number 8

Paraskavedekatriaphobia
fear of Friday the 13th

Selenophobia
fear of the moon

Taphophobia
fear of being buried alive

Trypanophobia
fear of needles or injections

OCD: Compulsive Hoarding

Definition: a type of obsessive-compulsive disorder characterized by the compulsive acquiring and keeping of a large number of possessions, leading to significant distress or impairment in daily living

Symptoms: may include compulsive need to acquire more possessions, inability to discard possessions, deep shame and embarrassment

Impact on daily life: saving items that are broken or useless, buying and storing large amounts of items but never using them, pulling useful materials from the trash on a regular basis but never putting them to use, acquiring huge numbers of small animals (such as cats) and being unable to keep them in clean conditions

---

have a panic attack in a public place where they will be humiliated or unable to obtain help. Panic disorder and agoraphobia both lead to avoidance behaviors. These behaviors can range from avoiding crowded places to never leaving home at all. Thus, these disorders can be very serious.

Generalized Anxiety Disorder According to the *DSM-IV*, generalized anxiety disorder (GAD) is an excessive or unrealistic worry about life circumstances that lasts for at least six months. The worries must be present most of that time in order to warrant a diagnosis of GAD. Typically, the worries focus on finances, employment, interpersonal problems, accidents, or illness.

GAD is one of the most common anxiety disorders, yet few people seek psychological treatment for it because it does not differ, except in intensity and duration, from the normal worries of everyday life. It is difficult to distinguish GAD from other anxiety disorders, and many people with GAD have other anxiety disorders as well, most often phobic disorders.

Obsessive-Compulsive Disorder Among the more <u>debilitating</u> of the anxiety disorders is **obsessive-compulsive disorder (OCD).** Obsessions are unwanted thoughts, ideas, or mental images that occur over and over again. They are often senseless or repulsive, and most people with obsessions try to ignore or suppress them. The majority of people with obsessions also practice compulsions, which are repetitive ritual behaviors, often involving

checking or cleaning something. Compulsive acts may reduce the anxiety the the obsessions produce.

The following examples are typical of people with OCD. One person is obsessed every night with doubts that he has locked the doors and windows before going to bed. He feels driven to compulsively check and recheck every door and window in the house, perhaps dozens of times. Only then can he relax and go to sleep. In another example, a team of researchers reported the case of a woman who was obsessed with the idea that she would pick up germs from nearly everything she touched. She compulsively washed her hands over and over again, sometimes as many as 500 times a day.

People who experience obsessions are usually aware that the obsessions are unjustified. This distinguishes obsessions from delusions. Although obsessions are a sign of a less serious psychological disorder than delusions, they still can make people feel extremely anxious, and they can seriously interfere with daily life. Compulsions may alleviate some of the anxiety associated with obsessions, but the compulsions themselves are time-consuming and usually create additional interference with daily life.

Stress Disorders Stress disorders include post-traumatic stress disorder (PTSD) and acute stress disorder. The two disorders have similar symptoms, but they differ in how quickly the symptoms appear after the traumatic event that triggers the disorder. They also differ in how long they last.

ACADEMIC VOCABULARY
debilitating
weakening, making life much more difficult.

TYPES OF ANXIETY DISORDERS

Anxiety is a state of dread or uneasiness that occurs in response to danger. A person with an anxiety disorder experiences anxiety out of proportion to the actual or perceived threat.

Phobic Disorder
A persistent, excessive, or irrational fear of an object or a situation. Acrophobia is a fear of heights; claustrophobia is a fear of enclosed spaces. Fear of public speaking is an example of a social phobia.

Panic Disorder and Agoraphobia
Recurring, unexpected panic attacks characterized by rapid heart rate. Agoraphobia is a phobic disorder in which people fear they will be caught in crowded, public places when they have an attack.

Generalized Anxiety Disorder
Excessive or unrealistic worry that appears to be present nearly all the time.

Obsessive-Compulsive Disorder
Unwanted thoughts or ideas, combined with impulses that are difficult or impossible to resist, such as repeated hand washing, connected with the idea that one's hands remain unclean.

Stress Disorders
Intense, persistent feelings of anxiety that follow traumatic events. PTSD may be accompanied by flashbacks, nightmares, and avoidance of stimuli connected with the traumatic event.

Post-traumatic stress disorder (PTSD) refers to intense, persistent feelings of anxiety that are caused by an experience so traumatic that it would produce stress in almost anyone. Experiences that may produce PTSD include rape, child abuse, assault, severe accident, airplane crash, natural disasters, and war atrocities. It appears to be a common result of extensive trauma. For example, up to one fourth of the people in areas hit by Hurricane Katrina in 2005 suffered some symptoms of PTSD.

People who suffer from PTSD may exhibit any or all of the following symptoms:

- flashbacks, which are mental reexperiences of the actual trauma
- nightmares or other unwelcome thoughts about the trauma
- numbness of feelings
- avoidance of <u>stimuli</u> associated with the trauma
- tension, irritability, poor concentration

ACADEMIC VOCABULARY

stimuli outside factors that directly influence a person

The symptoms may occur six months or more after the traumatic event, and they may last for years or even decades. The more severe the trauma, the worse the symptoms tend to be.

Acute stress disorder is a short-term disorder with symptoms similar to those of PTSD. Also like PTSD, acute stress disorder follows a traumatic event. However, unlike with PTSD, the symptoms occur immediately or at most within a month of the event. The anxiety also lasts a shorter time—from a few days to a few weeks. Not everyone who experiences a trauma, however, will develop PTSD or acute stress disorder.

Reading Check **Summarize** What are the five types of anxiety disorders?

Explaining Anxiety Disorders

Several different explanations for anxiety disorders have been suggested. As is true for most of the psychological disorders discussed in this chapter, the explanations fall into two general categories: psychological views and biological views.

Psychological Views For anxiety disorders and the other disorders discussed in this chapter, psychoanalytic views are presented even though they are no longer widely accepted. These views are included because they influenced later theories and had a major impact on the classification of psychological disorders until recently, as discussed earlier.

According to psychoanalytic theory, anxiety is the result of "forbidden" childhood urges that have been repressed, or hidden from consciousness. If repressed urges do surface, psychoanalysts argue, they may do so as obsessions and eventually lead to compulsive behaviors. For example, if one is trying to repress "dirty" sexual thoughts, repetitive hand washing may help relieve some of the anxiety.

Learning theorists believe that phobias are conditioned, or learned, in childhood. This may occur when a child experiences a traumatic event—such as being lost in a crowd or frightened by a bad storm—or when a child observes phobic behavior in other people. If a parent screams or faints when a child climbs onto a large box, for example, the child may learn an unreasonable fear of heights—even moderate heights. Or if a parent warns a child that all dogs are dangerous and must not be touched, the child may learn to fear all dogs. Learning theorists argue that such conditioned phobias may remain long after the experiences that produced them have been forgotten.

Learning theorists also assert that people will learn to reduce their anxiety by avoiding the situations that make them anxious. For example, a student who feels anxious speaking in front of others in class may learn to keep quiet because it reduces his or her feelings of anxiety. However, by intentionally avoiding the anxiety-producing behavior, the student has no chance to learn other ways of coping with or unlearning the anxiety. As a result, the anxiety may worsen or be generalized to other situations that involve speaking in front of others.

Cognitive theorists, on the other hand, believe that people make themselves feel anxious by responding negatively to most situations and coming to believe they are helpless to control what happens to them. This creates great anxiety.

Biological Views Research indicates that heredity may play a role in most psychological disorders, including anxiety disorders. For example, one study showed that if one of a pair of identical twins exhibited an anxiety disorder, there was a 45 percent chance that the other twin would also exhibit the disorder. This was true even of twins raised in different families. By contrast, the chance of fraternal twins both developing anxiety disorders was only about 15 percent. Similarly, adopted children are more likely to have an anxiety disorder if a biological parent has one than if an adoptive parent does. Both types of studies suggest that genetics plays at least some role in the development of anxiety disorders.

How did genes get involved? Some psychologists believe that people are genetically inclined to fear things that were threats to their ancestors. These psychologists argue that people who rapidly acquired strong fears of real dangers—such as large animals, snakes, heights, and sharp objects—would be more likely to survive and reproduce. To the extent that the tendency to develop such fears is controlled by genes, they conclude, the tendency would be passed on to future generations, causing the disorders to be relatively common today.

Interaction of Factors As with many other disorders, the causes of anxiety disorder may be mixed. Some cases of anxiety disorder probably reflect the interaction of biological and psychological factors. People with panic disorder, for example, may have a biologically based tendency to overreact psychologically to physical sensations. The initial physical symptoms of panic—such as rapid heart rate and shortness of breath—cause these people to react with fear, leading to even worse panic symptoms. They may think they are having a heart attack and experience severe psychological stress. Anxiety about having another panic attack becomes a psychological disorder itself—one that originated in a biological reaction.

Regardless of their cause, anxiety disorders are both common and disabling. In serious cases, they lead to tremendous restrictions and limitations in lifestyle, relationships, and work. They can also lead to great personal distress. In extreme cases, the sufferer can be practically paralyzed with fear. Fortunately, most people who suffer from anxiety disorder respond well to treatment, which is covered in the next chapter.

Reading Check **Find the Main Idea** How do learning theorists explain anxiety disorders?

Perspectives on Anxiety Disorders

Psychoanalytic View Anxiety represents the "leakage" of forbidden aggressive or sexual ideas or urges that were repressed during childhood.

Learning View Phobias are conditioned, or learned in childhood, either through direct experience or observation. People avoid threatening situations to reduce anxiety.

Biological View Anxiety disorders tend to run in families, suggesting a role for genetic factors. Anxiety disorders may be the exaggerated remains of adaptive fears.

Cognitive View People exaggerate threats and believe they are helpless to deal with them.

Types of Mood Disorders

Most people have mood changes that reflect the normal ups and downs of daily life. They feel down when things go wrong, such as failing an important test, and they feel up when good things happen, such as when their team wins a championship.

Some people, however, experience mood changes that seem inappropriate for or inconsistent with the situations to which they are responding. They feel sad when things are going well, or they feel elated for no apparent reason. People who have abnormal moods such as these may have a mood disorder.

Mood disorders fall into two general categories. **Depression** typically involves feelings of helplessness, hopelessness, worthlessness, guilt, and great sadness. **Bipolar disorder** involves a cycle of mood changes from depression to wild elation and back again.

Mood disorders—particularly depression—are very common psychological disorders. In any six-month period, about 8 percent of women and 4 percent of men are likely to be diagnosed with some form of depression. The *DSM-IV* classifies mood disorders into several different types of depressive and bipolar disorders.

Major Depression Major depression is by far the most common of all psychological disorders. Depression may affect more than 100 million people worldwide. Some 8 to 18 percent of the general population will experience major depression in their lifetime.

According to the *DSM-IV*, major depression is diagnosed when an individual experiences at least five of the following symptoms:

1. persistent depressed mood for most of the day
2. loss of interest or pleasure in all, or almost all, activities
3. significant weight loss or gain due to changes in appetite
4. sleeping more or less than usual
5. speeding up or slowing down of physical and emotional reactions
6. fatigue or loss of energy
7. feelings of worthlessness or unfounded guilt
8. reduced ability to concentrate or make meaningful decisions
9. recurrent thoughts of death or suicide

For a diagnosis of major depression to be made, at least one of the individual's five symptoms must be one of the first two symptoms in the list. Also, the symptoms must be present for at least two weeks and occur nearly every day during that period.

Severely depressed individuals may become consumed by feelings of worthlessness or guilt. Severe depression calls for immediate treatment—as many as 15 percent of severely depressed individuals eventually commit suicide.

Major Depression

Definition: a disorder characterized by persistent sad, anxious, or "empty" feelings that interfere with daily living

Symptoms: may include feelings of hopelessness or worthlessness, irritability, restlessness, loss of interest in once-pleasurable activities, fatigue, difficulty concentrating, changes in appetite, persistent aches or pains

Behaviors: may include withdrawal from social activities, insomnia or excessive sleeping

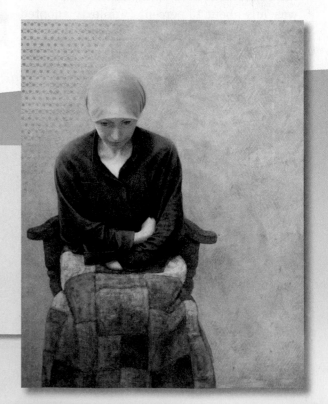

Bipolar Disorder Once called manic depression, bipolar disorder is characterized by dramatic ups and downs in mood. Periods of **mania,** or extreme excitement characterized by hyperactivity and chaotic behavior, can change into depression quickly and for no apparent reason.

The manic phase is characterized by a mood that is persistently and abnormally elevated. In some people, however, this phase may be characterized by irritability instead of elation. Manic moods are also characterized by at least some of the following traits:

- inflated self-esteem
- inability to sit still or sleep restfully
- pressure to keep talking and switching from topic to topic
- racing thoughts (referred to as "flight of ideas")
- difficulty concentrating.

Individuals in the manic phase may appear highly excited and act silly or argumentative. In severe cases, they may have delusions (beliefs that have no basis in reality) about their own superior abilities. They may also experience hallucinations (sensory perceptions that occur in the absence of sensory stimuli) such as hearing imaginary voices or seeing things that are not really there. These individuals may also engage in impulsive behaviors, such as going on spending sprees, quitting their jobs to pursue wild dreams, or making foolish business investments. Thus, the manic phase of bipolar disorder can be very disruptive to an individual's life.

Postpartum Depression Some women suffer a type of depression, called postpartum depression (PPD), after giving birth. Symptoms may include feelings of hopelessness and inadequacy in childcare skills. This condition can have a negative effect not just on the woman's health, but also on parent-infant bonding. Not long ago, PPD was kept hidden and considered a source of shame. Now, however, doctors and hospitals act aggressively to prevent and treat PPD.

Reading Check **Analyze** What are some ways that mood disorders can disrupt one's daily life?

Explaining Mood Disorders

Psychological and biological theories have been proposed to explain why such a large number of people experience mood disorders. These theories are explained here.

Psychological Views The psychoanalytic view of depression connects past events to the present. It says that people prone to depression suffered a real or imagined loss of a beloved object or person in childhood.

Thoughts and Depression

Psychologists note that many people create or worsen feelings of depression through irrational thoughts. In this way, they make it seem as if they cannot change things for the better. This chart shows the kinds of thoughts that can increase depression, along with more realistic thoughts that can help people take control of their lives.

A depressed person might think . . .	A rational alternative would be . . .
"There's nothing I can do."	"I can't think of anything to do right now, but if I work at it, I may."
"I'm no good."	"I did something I regret, but that doesn't make me evil or worthless as a person."
"This is absolutely awful."	"This is pretty bad, but it's not the end of the world."
"I just don't have the brains for this course."	"I guess I really need to go back over the basics in the course. Whom can I turn to for help?"
"I just can't believe I did something so terrible!"	"That was a bad experience. Well, I won't be likely to try that again soon."
"I can't imagine ever feeling right."	"This is painful, but if I try to work it through step by step, I'll probably see my way out of it eventually."

Explaining Depression

"Son, it's important to remember that it's O.K. to be depressed."

Skills Focus | **INTERPRETING CARTOONS**

What does this cartoon imply about the causes of depression?

According to this view, the child feels anger toward the lost object or person but, instead of expressing the anger, internalizes it and directs it toward himself or herself. This leads to feelings of guilt and loss of self-esteem, which in turn lead to depression.

Learning theorists have suggested other explanations for depression. Some believe that learned helplessness makes people prone to depression. Psychologist Martin Seligman demonstrated the concept of learned helplessness in a classic but now widely criticized experiment. In his experiment, Seligman taught dogs that they were helpless to escape from electric shock. First, he placed a barrier in the dogs' cage to prevent them from leaving when shocks were administered. Later the barrier was removed. However, when shocks were again administered, the dogs made no effort to escape. They had apparently learned there was nothing they could do to prevent the pain.

This learned helplessness has been compared to the helplessness often seen in people who are depressed. Learning theorists argue that people prone to depression have learned through experience to believe that previous events in their lives were out of their control. This leads them to expect that future events will be out of their control as well. As a result, whenever a negative event occurs, these people feel helpless, and this leads to depression.

In contrast, cognitive theorists have suggested that some people are prone to depression because of their habitual style of explaining life events. According to attribution theory, people assign different types of explanations to events—internal or external, stable or unstable, and global or specific. These attributional styles affect people's self-esteem and self-efficacy. These styles also relate to expectancy—what people expect based on prior experiences. Suppose, for example, that someone goes on a date that does not work out. Different ways to explain the uncomfortable evening might include the following:

- "I really messed up" (internal explanation, places blame on self).
- "Some people just don't get along" (external explanation, places the blame elsewhere).
- "It's just my personality" (stable explanation, suggests problem cannot be changed).
- "It was that lousy head cold I've had all week" (unstable explanation, suggests problem is temporary).
- "I have no idea what to do when I'm with other people" (global explanation, suggests problem is too large to deal with).
- "I have difficulty making small talk" (specific explanation, suggests problem is small enough to be manageable).

Research shows that people who are depressed are more likely than other people to blame their failures on internal, stable, and global causes—causes they feel helpless to change. Cognitive theorists argue that such explanations give rise to feelings of helplessness, which in turn lead to depression.

Another cognitive theory was proposed by Aaron Beck, who suggested that people who are depressed have a negative view of themselves, their experiences, and their future. According to Beck, this is because people who are depressed have negative self-schemas—self-judgments developed from negative experiences in early childhood. This leads them to filter out positive information and perceive negative information as more negative than it really is. Such negativity, Beck argued, makes people prone to depression.

Biological Views Other researchers have investigated biological factors in mood disorders. Mood disorders, like anxiety disorders, tend to occur more often in the close relatives of affected individuals than they do in the general population. Between 20 and 25 percent of people with mood disorders have a family member who is affected by a similar disorder. Moreover, identical twins of affected individuals are more likely to be affected than fraternal twins. These studies seem to indicate that mood disorders have a genetic component.

Scientists believe that two neurotransmitters, or chemical messengers, in the brain—serotonin and noradrenaline—may at least partly explain the connection between genes and mood. Serotonin and noradrenaline both play a role in mood regulation. Low levels, or deficiencies, of serotonin may create a tendency toward mood disorders in general. Deficiencies of serotonin combined with deficiencies of noradrenaline, however, may be linked to depression specifically. These findings have been important in the development of a wide range of drug therapies for the treatment of mood disorders.

Biological and Psychological Factors As we have seen before, a combination of factors may be at work in the explanation of mood disorders. Many cases of depression may reflect the interaction of biological factors such as neurotransmitter levels and psychological factors such as learned helplessness. This has been demonstrated with laboratory animals. Seligman and Weiss found that dogs that learned they were helpless to escape electric shocks also had less noradrenaline activity in their brains. Helplessness is thus linked to specific neurotransmitter deficiencies. The relationship may result in a vicious cycle. A depressing situation may slow down the activity of noradrenaline in the brain; in turn, the chemical changes may then worsen the depression. Breaking that cycle may be the key to successful treatment.

Reading Check **Explain** How was Martin Seligman's experiment with dogs related to theories about mood disorders?

SECTION 2 Assessment

Reviewing Main Ideas and Vocabulary

1. **Explain** How does anxiety differ from fear?

2. **Describe** What is the relationship between panic disorder and agoraphobia?

3. **Recall** What are five symptoms of major depression?

4. **Contrast** What is the difference between depression and bipolar disorder?

Thinking Critically

5. **Evaluate** Why are studies of twins important for determining whether a disorder has a biological basis?

6. **Develop** Describe and explain self-esteem, self-efficacy, and expectancy from the perspective of attribution theory.

7. **Analyze** Using your notes and a graphic organizer like the one here, explain why such a large number of people experience mood disorders, particularly depression.

Theories	Explanation
Psychoanalytic	
Learning	
Cognitive	
Biological	
Biological and Psychological	

FOCUS ON WRITING

8. **Narrative** Review the information about anxiety disorders in this section. Then try to imagine what life is like for a person who suffers from obsessive-compulsive disorder. Write a diary entry from that person's point of view, in which you describe how the disorder affects tasks and events of daily life. Or, select a different anxiety disorder and write a similar diary entry.

Post-Traumatic Stress Disorder and Iraq War Veterans

In Iraq and Afghanistan, dangers could wait behind any doorway. Such uncertainties have added to soldiers' stress.

Few of us will ever experience the horrors of war directly—the physical agony, the fear, the grief of seeing friends killed, the moral dilemmas that soldiers face. For those who survive these ordeals, the trauma of combat may not be left behind on the battlefield. Instead, some veterans experience vivid flashbacks and nightmares that replay the wartime shocks over and over. Many of these vets are diagnosed with post-traumatic stress disorder (PTSD).

A high incidence of PTSD has been reported among soldiers returning from the war in Iraq and Afghanistan. Added to the usual stress of combat are various factors that have increased the disorder's appearance. Some of those factors are the difficulty of distinguishing between enemies and allies and the threat of unseen improvised explosive devices (IEDs). In addition, many of the veterans are members of the National Guard and military reserves. Being called into combat has already disrupted their previously civilian lives, and the extra stress of PTSD adds dramatically to their troubles.

Researchers are attempting to understand the reasons and implications of what some observers call a PTSD epidemic. One study focused on more than 100,000 veterans who sought medical care at U.S. Department of Veterans Affairs (VA) facilities. About one fourth were diagnosed with a mental disorder. The study found that younger vets, from 18 to 24 years old, are more likely to be diagnosed with PTSD than older veterans (Seal et al., 2007).

The connection between increased PTSD risk and combat-related head injuries was the subject of another study. Of particular concern were the soldiers who had lost consciousness during the injury episode. They were especially prone to post-traumatic stress. The study's authors found that many symptoms previously ascribed to brain injury, including memory loss, irritability, and insomnia, are actually the result of PTSD—a welcome conclusion, because PTSD is more treatable than brain injury (Hoge et al., 2008).

Other researchers have examined the overwhelming impact of so many PTSD cases on the armed forces' mental health facilities. More than 300,000 servicemen and women have returned from Iraq and Afghanistan. A survey indicates that about 20 percent of those involved in combat suffer from severe mental disorders (Tanielian and Jaycox, 2008). Currently, they can receive up to five years of free health care from the VA for any mental disorder related to combat. Since PTSD often shows up long after the end of the trauma, increased mental healthcare for veterans will be necessary for many years to come.

Some veterans hesitate to seek help for PTSD, thinking that having the disorder means they are weak. PTSD is treatable, especially through early intervention.

Thinking Critically

1. **Draw Conclusions** Why do you think younger veterans are more likely to be diagnosed with PTSD?

2. **Discuss** Given the current research on PTSD, what steps do you think the U.S. Department of Veterans Affairs should take to deal with the effects of PTSD in returning soldiers?

Dissociative and Somatoform Disorders

Before You Read

Main Idea

Dissociative disorders cause people to lose their memory or identity. Somatoform disorders cause people to express psychological distress through physical symptoms.

Reading Focus

1. What is dissociation, and what are the four dissociative disorders?

2. How do theorists explain the origins of dissociative disorders?

3. What is somatization, and what are the most common types of somatoform disorders?

4. How do theorists explain the origins of somatoform disorders?

Vocabulary

dissociation
depersonalization
somatization

TAKING NOTES Use a graphic organizer like this one to take notes on the types and characteristics of dissociative and somatoform disorders.

Dissociative Disorders	Somatoform Disorders

LOST in New York City

PSYCHOLOGY CLOSE UP

How could a man forget his entire life? On July 3, 2003, a man with bumps and cuts on his head woke up on a train near Coney Island, at the edge of New York City. He did not know where he was, why he was on the train, or how he became injured. He had no idea who he was.

Eventually, a police officer helped identify the frightened man as Doug Bruce, a British resident of New York who years before had abandoned a successful career as a stockbroker to become a photographer. No clues emerged, however, about how Bruce lost his memory to a condition called total retrograde amnesia. Bruce experienced things as if for the first time that we take for granted—rain, fireworks, the ocean, sports, re-runs of TV cop shows.

Doug Bruce's story was filmed for a documentary titled *Unknown White Male*. Some observers doubt that his amnesia is real. To date, however, the "old" Doug Bruce has not reappeared, and the source of "new" Bruce's amnesia remains a mystery. ◼

Dissociative Disorders

The term **dissociation** refers to the separation of certain personality components or mental processes from conscious thought. In some situations, dissociation is normal. Someone may be so engrossed in reading a book or watching a television program, for example, that he is unaware that his name is being called. Someone else may become so involved in watching the road that she misses the sign for her exit on the freeway. Perhaps the most common form of normal dissociation is daydreaming, in which the person's thoughts may be "a million miles away." In each of these cases, dissociation usually does not indicate a psychological disorder.

However, when dissociation occurs as a way to avoid stressful events or feelings, it can be a sign of a psychological disorder. People with dissociative (di-SOH-shee-uh-tiv) disorders may lose their memory of an event or even forget their identity. A common theory is that dissociation occurs when individuals are faced with urges or experiences that are very stressful. By dissociating, they are able to remove themselves from the source of stress and lessen their feelings of anxiety.

There are no current statistics on the prevalence of dissociative disorders. In part, this is because the *DSM-IV* classifies them somewhat differently than they were classified in the past. However, dissociation is a common psychological symptom.

Dissociative Amnesia Formerly called psychogenic amnesia, dissociative amnesia is characterized by a sudden loss of memory, usually following a particularly stressful or traumatic event. A person experiencing dissociative amnesia typically cannot remember any events that occurred for a certain period of time surrounding the traumatic event. Less commonly, a person may forget all prior experiences and may be unable to remember his or her name, recognize friends and family, or recall important personal information. Dissociative amnesia may last for just a few hours, or it may persist for years. Memory is likely to return just as suddenly as it was lost, and the amnesia rarely recurs.

The term *psychogenic* means "psychological in origin." Dissociative amnesia cannot be explained biologically—as the result of a head injury, for example. Most often, a traumatic event, such as witnessing a serious accident, precedes the amnesia. The incidence of dissociative amnesia rises markedly during wartime and crises such as natural disasters.

Dissociative Fugue Dissociative fugue—previously called psychogenic fugue—is characterized not only by forgetting personal information and past events but also by suddenly relocating from home or work and taking on a new identity. Like dissociative amnesia, dissociative fugue usually follows a traumatic event that is psychologically very stressful. It is reported most frequently during wartime and natural disasters.

When individuals with dissociative fugue travel away from their home or workplace, they may take on a new name, residence, and occupation. They may become socially active in their new identity and not appear to be ill in any way. When the fugue comes to an end, they no longer remember what happened during the fugue state.

Dissociative Identity Disorder Formerly called multiple personality disorder, dissociative identity disorder involves the existence of two or more personalities within a single individual. The various personalities may or may not be aware of the others, and at least two of the personalities take turns controlling the individual's behavior.

Each personality is likely to be different from the others in several ways, including in such observable traits as voice, facial expression, and handedness, as well as self-perceived age, gender, and physical characteristics. The personalities may even have different allergies and eyeglass prescriptions. They may also behave very differently from one another.

People who are diagnosed with dissociative identity disorder usually were severely abused in childhood. They typically suffered severe physical, sexual, or psychological abuse. Less often, dissociative identity disorder is preceded by other types of trauma.

Depersonalization Disorder A condition called **depersonalization** refers to feelings of detachment from one's mental processes or body. People with this disorder describe feeling as though they are outside their bodies, observing themselves at a distance.

Depersonalization is a common symptom of other psychological disorders in addition to being a disorder in its own right. After depression and anxiety, it is the most common complaint among psychiatric patients. Like the other dissociative disorders, depersonalization disorder is likely to be preceded by a stressful event.

Reading Check **Compare** What is the basic feature that dissociative disorders have in common?

Explaining Dissociative Disorders

Dissociative disorders have been explained primarily by psychological views. According to psychoanalytic theory, people dissociate in order to repress unacceptable urges. In dissociative amnesia or fugue, for example, the person forgets the disturbing urges. In dissociative identity disorder, the person expresses undesirable urges by developing other personalities that can take responsibility for them. In depersonalization, the person goes outside the self, away from the turmoil within.

According to learning theorists, individuals with dissociative disorders have learned not to think about disturbing events in order to avoid feelings of guilt, shame, or pain. They dissociate themselves from the stressful events by selectively forgetting them. This is reinforced by the reduced anxiety they feel when the trauma is forgotten.

Neither cognitive nor biological theorists have offered a complete explanation of dissociative disorders. At present, there is no convincing evidence that either biological or genetic factors play a role in the development of dissociative disorders.

Reading Check **Summarize** Which type of theories can explain dissociative disorders?

Somatoform Disorders

Somatization, which comes from the Greek word for "body," refers to the expression of psychological distress through physical symptoms. People with somatoform disorders have psychological problems (such as depression) but experience inexplicable physical symptoms (such as paralysis).

It is important to distinguish between somatoform disorders and malingering, or the conscious attempt to "fake" an illness in

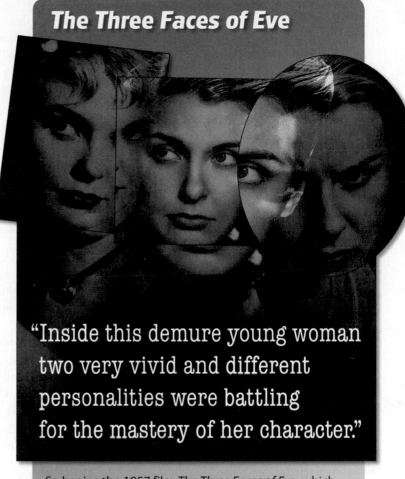

The Three Faces of Eve

"Inside this demure young woman two very vivid and different personalities were battling for the mastery of her character."

So begins the 1957 film *The Three Faces of Eve,* which was based on a real case of dissociative identity disorder. As the story progresses, a third personality emerges. In fact, the woman whose case inspired the film experienced 21 different personalities.
Do you think Hollywood accurately portrays serious psychological disorders such as dissociative identity disorder? Why or why not?

order to avoid work, school, or other responsibilities. People with somatoform disorders do not intentionally fake their illnesses. They honestly feel pain, for example, or believe they cannot move their limbs.

Because of the nature of the condition, reliable statistics on the incidence of somatoform disorders are not available. Many diagnoses of somatoform illness later prove to be incorrect when patients are found to have actual medical illnesses. On the other hand, cases of somatoform disorders may go undiagnosed because of the focus on physical, as opposed to psychological, symptoms.

Conversion Disorder People with conversion disorder experience a change in or loss of physical functioning in a major part of the body for which there is no known medical explanation. For example, they may suddenly develop the inability to move their legs, even though no medical explanation for the disability can be found. These behaviors are not intentionally produced. That is, the person is not faking it.

Conversion disorder is complicated because many people who experience the disorder show little concern about their symptoms, no matter how serious or strange they may be. This lack of concern may help in the diagnosis of conversion disorder.

Hypochondriasis Also called hypochondria, hypochondriasis (hy-poh-kahn-DRY-uh-sis) is defined as a person's unrealistic preoccupation with thoughts that he or she has a serious disease. People with hypochondriasis become absorbed by minor physical symptoms and sensations, convinced that the symptoms indicate the presence of a serious medical illness. They maintain their erroneous beliefs despite reassurances from doctors that there is nothing physically wrong with them. Some people with hypochondriasis visit doctor after doctor, seeking the one physician who will find the cause of their symptoms.

Reading Check **Summarize** What are the two main types of somatoform disorders?

Explaining Somatoform Disorders

Explanations for somatoform disorders in general, and specifically conversion disorder and hypochondriasis, are primarily psychological. According to psychoanalytic theory, somatoform disorders occur when individuals repress emotions associated with forbidden urges and instead express them symbolically in physical symptoms. The physical symptoms thus represent a compromise between the unconscious need to express feelings and the fear of actually expressing them.

More recently, other psychologists have argued that people with conversion disorder "convert" psychological stress into actual medical problems. There may be a direct connection between the body part affected and the cause. For example, a fighter pilot may lose the ability to see at night as a response to great anxiety he felt about flying nighttime bombing missions. Another individual may suffer paralysis of the legs after nearly being in a car accident.

Some behavioral theorists have suggested that somatoform symptoms can serve as a reinforcer if they successfully allow a person to escape from anxiety. There are also some indications that biological or genetic factors may play a role in the development of somatoform disorders.

Reading Check **Analyze** What does it mean to convert psychological stress into an actual physical problem?

SECTION 3 Assessment

Reviewing Main Ideas and Vocabulary

1. **Describe** What are the four dissociative disorders?

2. **Contrast** How does somatization differ from malingering?

Thinking Critically

3. **Evaluate** In some cultures, people are encouraged to go into trancelike states. Should this kind of dissociation be considered a sign of a psychological disorder? Why or why not?

4. **Infer** How do you think learning theorists might explain somatoform disorders?

5. **Analyze** Using your notes and a graphic organizer like the one below, explain how conversion disorder and hypochondriasis are different.

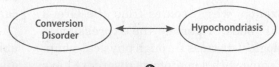

FOCUS ON WRITING

6. **Descriptive** How might dissociative disorders cause difficulties for law enforcement? Describe a scenario for each of the dissociative disorders in which the disorder complicates a legal case or situation.

Schizophrenia

Before You Read

Main Idea
Schizophrenia is the most serious psychological disorder, causing thought disruption and a decreased ability to function normally.

Reading Focus
1. What are the basic symptoms of schizophrenia?
2. What are the three major types of schizophrenia?
3. How do psychological and biological explanations of schizophrenia differ?

Vocabulary
schizophrenia
catatonic stupor

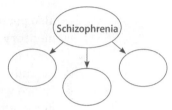

TAKING NOTES Use a graphic organizer like this one to take notes on the characteristics of the different types of schizophrenia.

An Artist's Troubled Mind

As artist Louis Wain (center) sank into schizophrenia, his painting style changed.

PSYCHOLOGY CLOSE UP

What can paintings of cats reveal about a human mind? In the late 1800s, Londoners were entranced with Louis Wain's humorous paintings of pets dressed as people and mimicking human activities. Wain specialized in cats —cats drinking tea, cats attending the opera, cats playing cards, cats doing all kinds of funny things. Later, Wain painted cats on their own, just being cats. Gradually, Wain's cat portraits became more odd, with wild eyes and spiky fur. At the same time, Wain was sinking into schizophrenia, a mental disorder marked by a separation from reality. Wain's increasing illness is reflected in the growing strangeness of his art. Eventually, his cats became just the starting point for frantic abstract designs. Louis Wain spent his last years in an asylum for the mentally ill, painting the asylum's flowers and cats. ■

What Is Schizophrenia?

Schizophrenia, usually considered the most serious of the psychological disorders, is characterized by loss of contact with reality. Schizophrenia can be very disabling and can lead to the affected person's inability to function independently. Typically, schizophrenia first appears in young adulthood, but it may occur at other ages. Although it usually develops gradually, it can also appear suddenly. Schizophrenia can now be treated more effectively, although if untreated it can worsen over time.

The most striking symptoms of schizophrenia include hallucinations, delusions, and thought disorders. In most cases, the hallucinations are auditory—voices telling the individual what to do or commenting on the individual's behavior. Sometimes they may tell the individual to harm herself or himself or others. Robert Bayley, a schizophrenia sufferer, described his hallucinations this way: "The visions are extremely vivid . . . Paving stones transform into demonic faces . . . Buildings and rooms spin and weave and their walls close in as I look on, paralyzed by fear . . . The voices either ramble in alien tongues or scream orders to carry out violent acts. They also persecute me by way of unwavering commentary and ridicule to deceive, derange, and force me into a world of crippling paranoia."

Individuals with schizophrenia may experience what are called delusions of grandeur. For example, they may believe that they are historical figures, famous celebrities, or on a special but secret mission to save the world. Sometimes the delusions are of persecution. For example, a person with schizophrenia might believe that he is being pursued by spies or some other shadowy enemy. Other delusions may include beliefs that one has committed unpardonable sins or even that one does not really exist.

Thought disorders involve problems in the organization or the content of mental processes. The thoughts of a person with schizophrenia may skip from topic to topic in an apparently illogical way. This is reflected in the person's speech, which sounds disorganized and confused. A person with schizophrenia may also repeat the same word or phrase over and over, repeat words or phrases that another person has spoken, or invent new words.

People with schizophrenia have other symptoms that affect their ability to function. These symptoms include social withdrawal, impaired social skills, and loss of normal emotional responses. Some people with schizophrenia may even go into a **catatonic stupor**—an immobile, expressionless, comalike state.

Understandably, these symptoms cause tremendous stress to individuals with schizophrenia and their families. It has been estimated that as many as 20 percent of people with schizophrenia attempt suicide and that 10 percent actually do kill themselves.

Schizophrenia is found in all cultures, and its symptoms have been recognized for centuries. A large number of people have schizophrenia—an estimated 2.4 million in the United States alone.

Reading Check **Summarize** What is the basic characteristic of schizophrenia?

Perceptions of Schizophrenia

Descriptions of what we might now call schizophrenia first appeared in an Egyptian medical document written in about 1550 BC. The ways in which people have viewed and reacted to schizophrenia have varied widely over the centuries. *How has our understanding of the causes of schizophrenia changed over time?*

The Muslim World
In response to what they read in the Qur'an, Islamic doctors took a clinical and humane approach to mental illnesses such as schizophrenia.

The Granger Collection, New York

The Ancient World Mental disorders were widely seen as a result of the gods' anger, and sufferers were treated harshly as a result. Some thinkers, such as Hippocrates, viewed such disorders as true illnesses.

European Middle Ages
Schizophrenia was often viewed as witchcraft or possession by demons. Many sufferers were tortured and executed.

Types of Schizophrenia

Individuals with schizophrenia vary greatly in their symptoms, although virtually all have thought disorders. Most people with schizophrenia exhibit a combination of symptoms.

The *DSM-IV* classification of schizophrenia and other psychotic disorders is based primarily on the duration and recurrence of symptoms. The types of schizophrenia include paranoid, disorganized, and catatonic schizophrenia.

Paranoid Schizophrenia People with paranoid schizophrenia have delusions or frequent auditory hallucinations, all relating to a single theme. These people may have delusions of grandeur, persecution, or jealousy. For example, individuals with paranoid schizophrenia may be convinced that people have been plotting against them even when there is no evidence of such a plot.

A person with paranoid schizophrenia may be distrustful of everyone except a spouse or a special friend. He or she may even accuse people who are trying to help of being part of a covert conspiracy. Although people with this type of schizophrenia tend to have less disordered thoughts and obviously bizarre behavior than do people with other types of schizophrenia, they may be agitated, confused, and afraid.

Disorganized Schizophrenia People with disorganized schizophrenia are incoherent in their thought and speech and disorganized in their behavior. They usually have delusions or hallucinations as well, but these tend to be fragmentary and unconnected, unlike the more ordered and systematic delusions of those with paranoid schizophrenia.

People with disorganized schizophrenia are also either emotionless or show inappropriate emotions. Typically, they act silly and giddy, and they tend to giggle and speak nonsense. They may neglect their appearance and hygiene. Sometimes they may even lose control of their bladders and bowels.

The following case description illustrates several symptoms of disorganized schizophrenia. A 40-year-old man was brought to the hospital by his distraught mother, who reported that she had become deeply afraid of her son. It was the twelfth time he had been checked into the hospital. The man was dressed in a dirty, tattered overcoat, a baseball cap, and house slippers. He spoke with a childlike quality and walked with exaggerated movements. His emotions ranged from anger (hurling obscenities) to silliness (giggling for no apparent reason).

Since stopping his medication about a month before his hospitalization, the man had been hearing voices and acting more strangely.

Early Modern Europe Schizophrenia and other mental illnesses were still seen as afflictions to be punished. The patients were often kept in chains like criminals. Outsiders paid a penny to watch the patients at Bethlem Hospital in London.

The Age of Enlightenment Mental illness began to be seen as a disease instead of a curse.

Late 1800s Emil Kraepelin was the first psychiatrist to classify schizophrenia as a distinct mental disorder. Sigmund Freud began to develop his theories for analyzing mental illnesses, including schizophrenia.

The Granger Collection, New York

1930s and 1940s Many people, including doctors, saw schizophrenia as a hereditary defect to be removed from society. Thousands of mental patients were sterilized. In Nazi Germany, an unknown number of people with schizophrenia were killed.

Later 20th Century Schizophrenia was widely accepted as a disease that can respond to a range of therapies, including medication.

He told the interviewer that he had been "eating wires and lighting fires." His speech was generally incoherent and contained many rhyming phrases.

Catatonic Schizophrenia The most obvious symptom of catatonic schizophrenia is disturbance of movement. Activity may slow to a stupor and then suddenly switch to agitation. Individuals with this disorder may hold unusual, uncomfortable body positions for long periods of time, even after their arms and legs swell and stiffen. They may also exhibit waxy flexibility, a condition in which other people can mold them into strange poses that they continue to hold for hours.

Reading Check **Summarize** What are the three types of schizophrenia?

Explaining Schizophrenia

Many different theories have been proposed to explain schizophrenia. These theories include both psychological and biological views.

Psychological Views According to the psychoanalytic perspective, schizophrenia is the result of the overwhelming of the ego by urges from the id. The urges threaten the ego and cause intense conflict. In response, the individual regresses to an early phase of the oral stage of development in which the infant has not yet learned that it is separate from the mother. In this condition, fantasies become confused with reality, leading to hallucinations and delusions. Like many psychoanalytic theories, this one has fallen into disfavor over the years.

Other psychological views focus on the family environment as the root of schizophrenia. One such theory suggests that a family in which a parent frequently expresses intense emotions and has a pushy, critical attitude puts children at risk of developing schizophrenia. While it is possible that such a family environment may increase the chances of onset or relapse in individuals who have schizophrenia, family environment does not actually cause the illness.

Biological Views Schizophrenia appears to be a brain disorder, and many studies have been done to determine how the brains of people with schizophrenia differ from those of other people. One avenue of brain research connects the major problems found in schizophrenia—problems in attention, memory, abstract thinking, and language—with differences in the frontal part of the brain. There is some evidence that there are differences in the size and structure of certain brain areas in people with schizophrenia.

At his trial, John Hinckley Jr.'s lawyers fought to introduce a CAT-scan of Hinckley's brain as evidence that he had schizophrenia. The defense lawyers believed that the scan would help prove that Hinckley's brain was abnormal and show a biological basis for his schizophrenia. After hearings on the matter, the judge allowed the scan as evidence. It showed that Hinckley's brain had widened *sulci,* the folds and ridges on the brain's surface. According to psychiatrists, widened *sulci* are far more common in people with schizophrenia than in other people.

Research also suggests that people with schizophrenia may have experienced a loss of synapses, the structures that connect neurons and make it possible for neurons to communicate with one another. What might cause these differences in brain structure? Research evidence suggests that there are three biological risk factors for schizophrenia: heredity, complications during pregnancy and birth, and birth during winter. Schizophrenia, like many other psychological disorders, runs in families. People with schizophrenia constitute about 1 percent of the population. However, children with one parent who has schizophrenia have about a 10 percent chance of being diagnosed as having schizophrenia themselves, and children with two such parents have about a 35 to 40 percent chance. When one identical twin has schizophrenia, the other has about a 40 to 50 percent chance of also being diagnosed with it. Many studies have been carried out to try to isolate the gene or genes involved in schizophrenia. Some studies have found locations for multiple genes on several chromosomes. Recent research suggests that particular genes may provide a vulnerability to schizophrenia. Further advances in genetic research techniques may shed more light on this possibility.

Many people with schizophrenia experienced complications during their mother's pregnancy and their birth. For example, the mothers of many people with schizophrenia had influenza during the sixth or seventh month of pregnancy. People with the disease are also somewhat more likely to have been born during the winter than would be predicted by chance. Maternal starvation has also been related to schizophrenia. These biological risk factors suggest that schizophrenia involves abnormal prenatal brain development.

Problems in the central nervous system may involve neurotransmitters as well as brain structures, and research has focused on one particular neurotransmitter: dopamine. According to the dopamine theory of schizophrenia, the brains of people with schizophrenia use more dopamine than average, although they may not produce more. Why? They may have more dopamine receptors in the brain than other people do, or their dopamine receptors may be hyperactive.

Multifactorial Model The multifactorial model of schizophrenia illustrates how biological and psychological factors may interact in the development of the disorder. In this model, genetic factors create a vulnerability, or susceptibility, to schizophrenia. Among people who are genetically vulnerable, other factors, such as prenatal problems or trauma during birth, may lead to brain injury and the development of schizophrenia. Once the disorder develops, its course may be negatively affected by a troubled family environment.

The multifactorial model also suggests that even severely dysfunctional environmental factors alone are not enough to lead to the development of schizophrenia. Thus, people who are not genetically vulnerable are unlikely to develop the disorder, regardless of the environmental risk factors to which they have been exposed.

Reading Check **Analyze** What are some indications that schizophrenia has a physical basis?

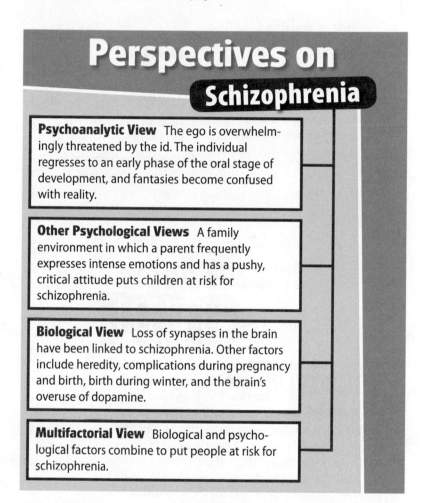

Perspectives on Schizophrenia

Psychoanalytic View The ego is overwhelmingly threatened by the id. The individual regresses to an early phase of the oral stage of development, and fantasies become confused with reality.

Other Psychological Views A family environment in which a parent frequently expresses intense emotions and has a pushy, critical attitude puts children at risk for schizophrenia.

Biological View Loss of synapses in the brain have been linked to schizophrenia. Other factors include heredity, complications during pregnancy and birth, birth during winter, and the brain's overuse of dopamine.

Multifactorial View Biological and psychological factors combine to put people at risk for schizophrenia.

SECTION 4 Assessment

Online Quiz **THINK** central thinkcentral.com

Reviewing Main Ideas and Vocabulary

1. **Recall** What are four symptoms of schizophrenia?

2. **Contrast** How does paranoid schizophrenia differ from disorganized schizophrenia?

3. **Describe** How would you describe the varying activity levels of a person experiencing catatonic schizophrenia?

Thinking Critically

4. **Summarize** What are some biological explanations for the origins of schizophrenia?

5. **Evaluate** What are the major psychological views that attempt to explain schizophrenia?

6. **Draw Conclusions** Using your notes and a graphic organizer like this one, explain why a multifactorial model of schizophrenia may help in explaining the disorder.

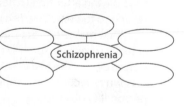
Schizophrenia

FOCUS ON WRITING

7. **Persuasive** Write a letter to a friend in which you suggest that he or she be examined by a psychiatrist for help with symptoms that resemble those of schizophrenia. Include a description of the friend's actions and their consequences.

Personality Disorders

Before You Read

Main Idea
Personality disorders are characterized by patterns of unchanging personality traits that disrupt people's social lives and work lives.

Reading Focus
1. What are personality disorders, and how do they differ from other psychological disorders?
2. What are ten types of personality disorders?
3. How do psychological and biological views explain the origins of antisocial personality disorder?

Vocabulary
personality disorders

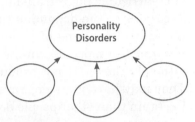
TAKING NOTES Use a graphic organizer like this one to take notes on personality disorders.

Personality Disorders

It's **all** about HER!

PSYCHOLOGY CLOSE UP
Why does Lisa demand so much attention? Perhaps you know someone like Lisa. At parties, she always steers the conversation back to herself. She makes sure everyone knows how important, accomplished, and intelligent she is. If Lisa doesn't get the admiration she thinks she deserves, she'll move on to another group and take over their conversation. She thinks nothing of telling—not asking, telling—someone to get her a plate of food or something to drink. Talking to Lisa after the party, you can see another side of her personality. Even though there were plenty of guys paying attention to her, she still envied Julia for talking to the new Swedish exchange student.

What makes Lisa act the way she does? She may actually have a personality disorder named after Narcissus, a youth in a Greek myth who fell in love with his own reflection. That condition is called narcissistic personality disorder. ■

What Are Personality Disorders?

Personality disorders are patterns of inflexible traits that disrupt social life or work and may distress the affected individual. The American Psychiatric Association defines a personality disorder as "an enduring pattern of inner experience and behavior that deviates markedly from the expectations of the culture of the individual who exhibits it." These patterns usually show up by late adolescence and affect all aspects of the individual's personality, including thought processes, emotions, and behavior.

It is important to note the distinction between personality disorders and other psychological disorders that they may resemble. Psychological disorders, such as major depression or a phobic disorder, for example, are illnesses that an individual experiences as episodes. Such illnesses can be clearly distinguished from the individual's personality. In contrast, personality disorders are enduring traits that are major components of the individual's personality.

Reading Check **Contrast** How are personality disorders different from other disorders that they may resemble?

Types of Personality Disorders

The chart on this page shows the *DSM-IV* classification of personality disorders. They are described here in detail.

Paranoid Personality Disorder People with paranoid personality disorder tend to be suspicious of others and to interpret others' motives as harmful or evil. They tend to perceive other people's behavior as threatening or insulting, even when it is not. They are difficult to get along with—argumentative, yet cold and aloof. It is not surprising that people with this disorder often lead isolated lives.

Unlike individuals with paranoid schizophrenia, people with paranoid personality disorder are not confused about reality. However, their view of reality is distorted, and they are unlikely to see their mistrust and suspicions as unfounded or abnormal.

Schizoid Personality Disorder People with schizoid personality disorder have no interest in relationships with other people. They also lack normal emotional responsiveness. They

do not have tender feelings for, or become attached to, other people; spending time with others just seems pointless. Thus, people with schizoid personalities tend to be loners, with few if any friends.

These symptoms are similar to some of the symptoms of schizophrenia. Unlike people with schizophrenia, however, people with schizoid personality disorder do not have delusions or hallucinations. They stay in touch with reality.

Schizotypal Personality Disorder Symptoms of this disorder include odd behaviors, unconventional beliefs, and a need for social isolation. Although the disorder is similar to schizoid personality disorder, people with the schizotypal disorder avoid relationships because of a fear of not fitting in, not because they are uninterested in others.

PERSONALITY DISORDERS AND THEIR CHARACTERISTICS

Personality disorders are inflexible and lasting patterns of behavior that hamper social functioning. Listed here from the *DSM-IV-TR* are the 10 specific personality disorders and their main characteristics.

Personality Disorder	Main Characteristics
Paranoid	Suspiciousness and distrust about others' motives
Schizoid	Detachment from social relationships
Schizotypal	Acute discomfort in close relationships; eccentricities of behavior
Antisocial	Disregard for the rights of others
Borderline	Instability in interpersonal relationships and self-image
Histrionic	Excessive emotionality, need for attention
Narcissistic	Grandiosity, need for admiration, lack of empathy
Avoidant	Social inhibitions, feelings of inadequacy
Dependent	Submissive, clinging
Obsessive-Compulsive	Obsession with orderliness, perfectionism, and control

Skills Focus **INTERPRETING CHARTS** What is one characteristic that a person with antisocial personality disorder might have in common with someone who has narcissistic personality disorder?

Antisocial Personality Disorder People with antisocial personality disorder show a persistent behavior pattern of disregard for, and violation of, the rights of others. Typically, they do not feel remorse for their antisocial behaviors, and they continue the behaviors despite the threat of social rejection and punishment.

In childhood and early adolescence, a person with antisocial personality disorder may run away from home, hurt other people or animals, lie, or steal. In adulthood, the person may be aggressive and reckless, have a hard time holding a job, incur large debts, or break the law.

Borderline Personality Disorder Instability of mood, chaotic personal relationships, and a disturbed sense of self are among the symptoms of borderline personality disorder. Self-mutilating behaviors, such as cutting, can be evidence of the disorder. The name comes from an early description of the disorder as being on the "borderline" between neurosis and psychosis.

Histrionic Personality Disorder People with this disorder are overly emotional and dramatic and seek constant attention. Inappropriate seductiveness and being easily influenced by other people are also common symptoms. Although people with histrionic personality disorder may be outwardly successful in work and social situations, their personal relationships are often troubled, partly because the disorder limits one's ability to cope with loss or failure. Such failures are often blamed on others.

Narcissistic Personality Disorder People with this disorder believe that they deserve excessive admiration. They may be preoccupied with fantasies of their own success, power, intelligence, or beauty. In addition, they show little empathy toward other people, treating them with arrogance and exploiting them.

Avoidant Personality Disorder People with avoidant personality disorder desire relationships with other people, but they are prevented from forming these relationships by tremendous fear of the disapproval of others. Thus, they act shy and withdrawn in social situations. They are always afraid they will say or do something that is foolish or even embarrassing.

The symptoms of avoidant personality disorder are similar to those of social phobia, and people with avoidant personality disorder virtually always have social phobias as well. However, not all people who have social phobias have avoidant personality disorder. The latter seems to be a more severe condition.

Dependent Personality Disorder This disorder is characterized by being overly dependent on other people. Among the symptoms are difficulty in making decisions without extensive advice, reluctance to take responsibility for one's own life, difficulty expressing disagreement, lack of initiative, and fear of being left to take care of oneself. People with dependent personality disorder often seek a new relationship immediately after the end of another so that they are not left alone.

Obsessive-Compulsive Personality Disorder While similar to obsessive-compulsive disorder, this personality disorder is different. Obsessive-compulsive personality disorder is characterized by inflexibility and fixation on rules, procedures, and orderliness. People with the disorder can be particularly anxious about time, relationships, cleanliness, and money. They often work many more hours than their financial situation demands. They do not, however, perform the constant, meaningless rituals that are common in obsessive-compulsive disorder.

Reading Check **Analyze** What are some ways that personality disorders can make life difficult?

Explaining Personality Disorders

Most personality disorders were not classified until 1980, with the publication of the third edition of the *DSM*. However, both psychological and biological theories have been suggested to explain some of them. Here we will concentrate on antisocial personality disorder.

Psychological Views Freud's psychoanalytic theory regarding the antisocial personality type states that a lack of guilt underlies the antisocial personality. This lack of guilt is due to a problem in the development of the conscience, or superego. Research has found that children who are rejected by adults and harshly punished rather than treated with affection tend to lack a sense of guilt.

Some learning theorists have suggested that childhood experiences "teach" children how to relate to other people. If children are not reinforced for good behavior and only receive attention when they behave badly, they may learn antisocial behaviors. Such behaviors may persist into adulthood. Other learning theorists maintain that antisocial personality disorder develops when a child lacks appropriate role models and when the role models they do have act aggressively.

Cognitive theorists argue that antisocial adolescents tend to see other people's behavior as threatening, even when it is not. They use this faulty view of other people's actions to justify their own antisocial behavior.

Biological Views Genetic factors are apparently involved in the disorders. For example, antisocial personality disorder tends to run in families. Adoptee studies reveal higher incidence of antisocial behavior among the biological parents than among the adoptive relatives of individuals with the disorder.

The genetics of antisocial personality disorder may involve the frontal part of the brain, an area that is connected with emotional responses. There is some evidence that people with antisocial personality disorder have fewer neurons in the frontal part of the brain than other people. The fewer neurons could make the nervous system less responsive. As a result, such people would be less

Perspectives on a Personality Disorder

Psychoanalytic View Lack of guilt due to a problem in the development of the conscience causes the antisocial personality.

Other Psychological Views Childhood experiences teach children how to relate to other people. If children get attention only when they behave badly or don't have appropriate role models, they may develop antisocial behaviors.

Biological View Heredity plays a role in antisocial disorders, as does having fewer neurons in the frontal part of the brain.

likely to show guilt for their misdeeds and to learn to fear punishment. But a biological factor by itself is unlikely to cause the development of an antisocial personality.

Although the origins of personality disorders are still unresolved, treatment of these disorders is more straightforward. Methods of treatment for psychological disorders are the focus of the next chapter.

Reading Check **Analyze** How may childrearing affect the development of antisocial personality disorder?

SECTION 5 Assessment

Reviewing Main Ideas and Vocabulary

1. **Define** How would you define a personality disorder?

2. **Contrast** How does paranoid personality disorder differ from paranoid schizophrenia?

3. **Explain** What is the difference between schizoid personality disorder and schizophrenia?

4. **Describe** What are three behaviors of an individual with antisocial personality disorder?

Thinking Critically

5. **Evaluate** Why do you think people with antisocial personality disorder are often more difficult to treat than people with other types of personality disorders?

6. **Support a Position** Which seems more sound to you—the psychological or biological theory about the origins of antisocial personality disorder? Explain your answer.

7. **Draw Conclusions** Using your notes and a graphic organizer like this one, explain the major difference between personality disorders and other disorders that they may resemble.

Disorder	Definition
Psychological disorders (such as schizophrenia or phobic disorders)	
Personality disorders (such as paranoid personality disorder or antisocial personality disorder)	

8. **Narrative** Review the Psychology Close Up feature about the girl with narcissistic personality disorder. Write a similar profile of someone with one of the other personality disorders. Designate which disorder you are describing.

Diagnosing Psychological Disorders

Reading and Activity Workbook

Use the workbook to complete this lab.

Can you diagnose a psychological disorder based on a written description of someone's symptoms?

1. Introduction

This lab will help you review the major psychological disorders covered in this chapter. You will work in small groups to review one of the six general types of disorders that you learned about. Then your group will select at least two specific disorders and write fictional case studies describing someone who suffers from each disorder. Finally, the entire class will evaluate each case study and try to diagnose the disorder being described. To complete this lab, follow the steps below.

■ Following your teacher's instructions, organize the class into six student groups.

■ Your teacher will assign each group one of the six general types of psychological disorders covered in this chapter—anxiety disorders, mood disorders, dissociative disorders, somatoform disorders, schizophrenia, and personality disorders.

■ Work with the students in your group to review the chapter material on the general type of disorders that you were assigned, along with the specific disorders that fall within that category. (See the chart titled Major Psychological Disorders on the next page.) Write down a few main points about both the general type of disorders and the specific disorders.

■ Conduct additional research on your assigned disorders, if your teacher instructs you to do so. Your group is now ready to write the case studies.

2. Writing the Case Studies

Working as a group, select at least two specific disorders from your assigned type of psychological disorders. Then, write case studies for these disorders. Each case study should be written on a single sheet of paper and should include each of the items shown in the sample case study below. After your group is finished writing the case studies, give them to your teacher.

❶ A fictional name and age;

❷ A description of the person's physical, mental, or behavioral symptoms, with relevant details;

❸ A description of how the person's disorder affects his or her life;

❹ An "answer"—the specific psychological disorder that the case study describes.

Sample Case Study

❶ **Andrew, Age 37**

Andrew Miller was a delivery driver for an office equipment company. Three years ago Andrew was making a delivery when he was involved in a horrific car accident. As he was exiting the highway, a four-car collision occurred right in front of Andrew's van that he was unable to avoid. Andrew smashed into the car in front of him, killing one person and rolling his van over. He was thrown out of his vehicle and suffered a broken arm, three broken vertebrae, and multiple cuts and lacerations. He was lucky to survive. Immediately after the accident, Andrew ran to the person he hit and tried to help her, but she

❷ died at the scene.

Andrew spent two weeks in the hospital, where he underwent several surgeries before being discharged. However, Andrew does not remember his time in the hospital. He also cannot remember anything about the accident or even several days before it, despite his best attempts. Six months after the accident, Andrew has

❸ almost fully recovered physically, but still says that the time period surrounding his accident is "a complete blank."

What psychological disorder does Andrew suffer from?

❹ **Answer:** Dissociative Amnesia

3. Diagnosing the Disorders

Before you and your classmates try to diagnosis the psychological disorders described in the case studies, briefly review the disorders covered in the chapter. To review the disorders and complete the diagnoses, follow these steps:

■ Have someone from each group share with the rest of the class the main points about the general type of disorder assigned to their group, along with information on the specific disorders. This will serve as a quick review for the entire class.

■ Your teacher will then randomly select the case studies and read them aloud to the class.

■ After each case study is read, jot down on a piece of paper which psychological disorder you think the case study describes and why. Refer to the chart titled Major Psychological Disorders on this page for a complete list of the disorders covered in this chapter.

■ Your teacher will then ask the class to vote on which psychological disorder is being described. After the vote, briefly discuss each case study as a group to determine the correct answer. (Do not vote on or discuss the case studies that your group wrote unless your teacher calls on you.)

4. Discussion

What did you learn from this lab? Hold a group discussion that focuses on the following questions:

■ Overall, how successful was the class at diagnosing the psychological disorders described in the case studies?

■ Were some disorders particularly easy to diagnose? If so, which ones, and why do you think they were easy?

■ Were some disorders particularly difficult to diagnose? If so, which ones, and why do you think they were difficult?

■ How do you think this lab would have been different if some of the case studies described people with multiple psychological disorders? Do you think that would have made the lab more realistic?

■ How might being able to personally observe and interview the people described in the case studies have helped with a diagnosis?

MAJOR PSYCHOLOGICAL DISORDERS

Anxiety Disorders
- Specific Phobias
- Panic Disorder
- Agoraphobia
- Generalized Anxiety Disorder
- Obsessive-Compulsive Disorder (OCD)
- Post-Traumatic Stress Disorder (PTSD)

Mood Disorders
- Major Depression
- Bipolar Disorder
- Postpartum Depression

Dissociative Disorders
- Dissociative Amnesia
- Dissociative Fugue
- Dissociative Identity Disorder
- Depersonalization Disorder

Somatoform Disorders
- Conversion Disorder
- Hypochondriasis

Schizophrenia
- Paranoid Schizophrenia
- Disorganized Schizophrenia
- Catatonic Schizophrenia

Personality Disorders
- Paranoid Personality Disorder
- Schizoid Personality Disorder
- Schizotypal Personality Disorder
- Antisocial Personality Disorder
- Borderline Personality Disorder
- Histrionic Personality Disorder
- Narcissistic Personality Disorder
- Avoidant Personality Disorder
- Dependent Personality Disorder
- Obsessive-Compulsive Personality Disorder

CHAPTER 18 Review

Comprehension and Critical Thinking

SECTION 1 *(pp. 498–502)*

1. a. Describe How common are psychological disorders in the United States?

b. Summarize What are the four main criteria that psychologists use to determine the presence of a psychological disorder?

c. Support a Position Of the four main criteria used to diagnose disorders, which do you think is the most significant? Why?

SECTION 2 *(pp. 504–513)*

2. a. Define What is an anxiety disorder? What is a mood disorder?

b. Analyze Why do you think major depression is the most common psychological disorder?

c. Make Judgments In your opinion, when do normal feelings of anxiety and uneasiness about a situation cross the line to become an anxiety disorder?

SECTION 3 *(pp. 515–518)*

3. a. Recall What are dissociative and somatoform disorders?

b. Contrast Give an example of a normal form of dissociation in everyday life, and contrast with an example of a dissociative disorder.

c. Evaluate Why do you think it is so difficult to get reliable statistics on the incidence of somatoform disorders?

SECTION 4 *(pp. 519–523)*

4. a. Describe What are some of the causes of schizophrenia?

b. Infer Why might dissociative identity disorder be confused with schizophrenia?

c. Make Judgments Do you think the psychological views on the causes of schizophrenia are valid? Support your answer with facts from the text.

SECTION 5 *(pp. 524–527)*

5. a. Identify Main Ideas How can personality disorders be distinguished from other psychological disorders?

b. Contrast What are the differences between schizoid personality disorder and avoidant personality disorder?

Reviewing Vocabulary

Match the terms below with their correct definitions.

6. psychological disorder
7. criteria
8. anxiety
9. phobia
10. depression
11. bipolar disorder
12. schizophrenia
13. catatonic stupor
14. personality disorder

A. feelings of helplessness, hopelessness, worthlessness, guilt, and great sadness

B. an immobile, expressionless, comalike state

C. behavior patterns or mental processes that cause serious personal suffering or interfere with a person's ability to cope with everyday life

D. patterns of inflexible traits that disrupt social life or work and may distress the affected individual

E. a serious psychological disorder characterized by a loss of contact with reality

F. the standards on which a judgment or decision may be based

G. a cycle of mood changes from depression to wild elation and back again

H. a general state of dread or uneasiness that occurs in response to a vague or imagined danger

I. a persistent excessive or irrational fear

INTERNET ACTIVITY

15. How do psychological disorders affect teens? Choose one disorder covered in this chapter, such as depression or phobic disorder, and use the Internet to research how the disorder affects teenagers. Look for information on how common the disorder is among teens, recent statistics and data, and common treatments. Write a short report that summarizes your findings.

Psychology in Your Life

16. What should you do if you encounter someone who you suspect suffers from a psychological disorder? Should you talk to the person or contact an adult or a mental health professional for help? Think about a realistic situation in which you might find yourself dealing with someone who has a psychological disorder. Then, write a short paragraph describing the situation and your possible course of action.

SKILLS ACTIVITY: INTERPRETING GRAPHS

The bar graph below shows how some factors, including family history, increase the risk of a child developing schizophrenia later in life. The number 1 represents the norm, and each number above 1 represents a 100 percent increase in the risk. Therefore, a child born in winter has about a 10 percent higher risk of developing schizophrenia than average. Study the graph and answer the questions that follow.

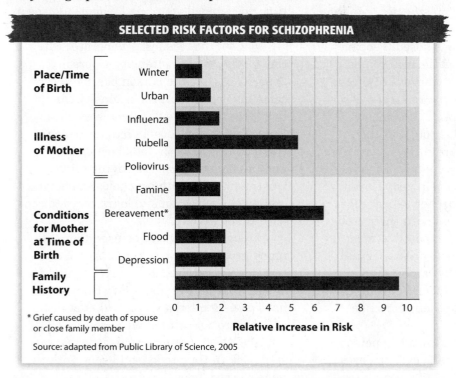

SELECTED RISK FACTORS FOR SCHIZOPHRENIA

Place/Time of Birth
- Winter
- Urban

Illness of Mother
- Influenza
- Rubella
- Poliovirus

Conditions for Mother at Time of Birth
- Famine
- Bereavement*
- Flood
- Depression

Family History

0 1 2 3 4 5 6 7 8 9 10
Relative Increase in Risk

* Grief caused by death of spouse or close family member

Source: adapted from Public Library of Science, 2005

17. Analyze Of the factors listed, which besides family history increases the odds the most?

18. Compare Which mother's illness increases a child's odds of developing schizophrenia by about 10 percent? by 200 percent?

19. Develop How does this graph suggest that events beyond the mother's control can increase the risk of schizophrenia?

WRITING FOR AP PSYCHOLOGY

Use your knowledge of psychological disorders to answer the question below. Do not simply list facts. Present a clear description based on your critical analysis of the question, using the appropriate terminology.

20. Briefly describe each of the disorders listed below. For each disorder, include a general description of the disorder, a review of the symptoms, and a description of the possible causes.

(A) Post-traumatic stress disorder (PTSD)

(B) Major depression

(C) Schizophrenia

VIRTUAL THERAPY

The curtain opens and you step out onto the stage. Before you even start speaking, you are certain the audience is bored. People stretch and cough. Is that a snore you hear? The palms of your hands turn sweaty. Your stomach flutters. Suddenly, you feel dizzy, like you might pass out at any moment.

The anxiety you feel is real, but the scene is not. What you are seeing is a virtual scene created by a company. The virtual scene is designed to help people overcome stage fright. Researcher Albert Rizzo notes, "To help people deal with their problems, you must get them exposed to what they fear most." Companies create virtual scenes and experiences by combining video clips of real people with special effects. In this way, people can face their fears in a controlled environment.

To experience a virtual scene, a person wears a helmet with screens over the eyes to create a 3-D effect. A motion sensor in the helmet changes the scene with the wearer's head position. For example, if you were wearing one of these helmets, each time you turned your head, you would see a different part of the virtual scene.

With virtual scenes, an operator can control the level of intensity a person experiences. As the person begins to overcome his or her fear, the intensity can be increased. For example, people who fear flying can experience a virtual airplane flight that is smooth and short or bumpy and prolonged. People receiving virtual treatment work with psychologists before and after the sessions to learn ways to cope with their anxiety.

Virtual therapy can be used to tackle many problems: stage fright, fear of elevators, fear of heights, fear of flying, and fear of bad weather are just a few. Engineers have even created a virtual re-enactment of the terrorist attacks on September 11, 2001. With this re-enactment, people can step back in time to learn to cope with their memories of the attacks.

Virtual Iraq is an experimental treatment program that has been designed to help soldiers work through the trauma

A young man undergoes virtual therapy under the supervision of a trained therapist.

CHAPTER 19

METHODS OF THERAPY

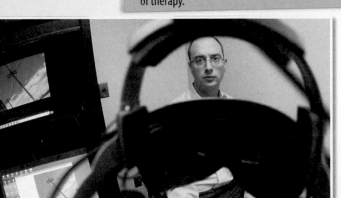

U.S. Army clinical psychologist Greg Reger is shown
with a headset. It is used in an experimental virtual-
reality computer simulation designed to treat soldiers
suffering from post-traumatic stress disorder (PTSD).

induced by combat in Iraq. Symptoms experienced by the soldiers include nightmares,
flashbacks, obsessive thoughts, detachment, and anger. Some soldiers completely
withdraw from society.

During the treatment, the soldier
attempts to deal with PTSD by means of
a computer-simulated environment. He or
she wears a helmet with video goggles and
earphones. A modified version of a popular
war video game is also part of the program.
Sights, sounds, and smells are created to
help manage the painful memories of combat in Iraq.

The U.S. Department of Defense is testing Virtual Iraq as one of three virtual
reality programs it is developing for the
treatment of post-traumatic stress disorder.
If the virtual reality therapy proves itself
in clinical tests, it will likely become widely
used in the treatment of PTSD in returning
Iraqi war veterans. In this chapter you will
learn more about different kinds of therapy.

What do you think?

1. Why might virtual therapy have some limitations to its
usefulness?

2. Why might people be more willing to face their fears in a
virtual setting than in a real one?

Chapter at a Glance

SECTION 1: What Therapy Is and Does

■ The various methods of psychotherapy seek to help troubled
individuals.

■ There are a variety of methods and types of professionals
involved in psychotherapy.

■ Individual therapy and group therapy both have advantages.

SECTION 2: The Psychoanalytic and Humanistic Approaches

■ Psychoanalysis is a method of therapy that was developed by
Sigmund Freud.

■ Some of the techniques of psychoanalysis include free association, dream analysis, and transference.

■ The primary goal of humanistic therapy is to help individuals
reach their full potential.

SECTION 3: Cognitive Therapy and Behavior Therapy

■ The aim of cognitive therapy is to help people learn to think
about their problems in more productive ways.

■ The goal of behavior therapy is to help people develop more
adaptive behavior.

SECTION 4: Biological Therapy

■ Biological therapy relies on medication, electric shock, and surgery to help people deal with psychological disorders.

■ Because these treatments are medical in nature, they must be
administered by a physician.

■ Electroconvulsive therapy and psychosurgery are both controversial procedures.

What Therapy Is and Does

Before You Read

Main Idea
Therapy falls into two basic categories: psychologically based therapy and biologically based therapy. Both forms of therapy can help people increase awareness and change behavior.

Reading Focus
1. What are the main goals of psychotherapy?
2. What are the three main categories of professionals who practice psychotherapy?
3. How do individual and group therapy compare?

Vocabulary
psychotherapy
self-help group

TAKING NOTES Use a graphic organizer like this one to take notes on the various types of mental health professionals.

Types of Mental Health Professionals	

Treating the Mentally Ill

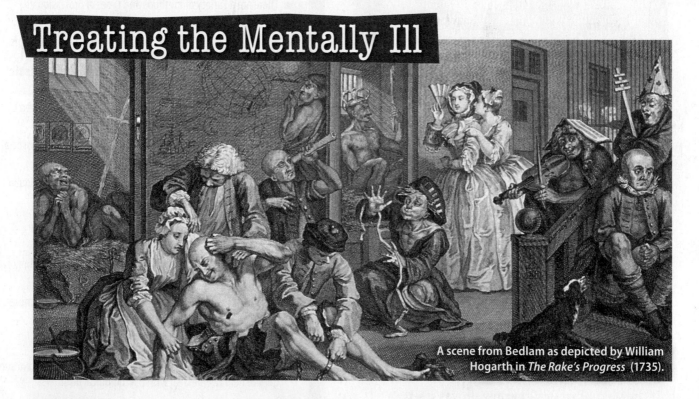

A scene from Bedlam as depicted by William Hogarth in *The Rake's Progress* (1735).

PSYCHOLOGY CLOSE UP

How did the name of a hospital become a synonym for uproar and disorder? Bedlam was the byname for the first hospital for people with mental illnesses established in England. It was founded in 1247 as a priory (a monastery or convent). The founder was Simon FitzMary, a former sheriff of London. St. Mary of Bethlehem (also called Bethlem) was first mentioned as a hospital in 1330. Patients resided there by 1403.

In 1547, Henry VIII gave Bethlem Hospital and its revenues to the City of London as a hospital for the mentally ill. Eventually it became notorious for the brutal treatment of its residents. Visitors would come on holiday outings to mock the appearance and behavior of the patients. Residents endured unsanitary conditions and beatings, as well as other harsh treatment. Eventually the word *bedlam* came to be used for all asylums and is still used to describe an uproar.

Today, the treatment of people with psychological disorders has improved. Sophisticated methods of therapy help individuals with psychological problems to function in society rather than be separated from society. ■

Achieving the Goals of Psychotherapy

Methods for treating psychological problems and disorders fall into two general categories: psychological methods, or methods of psychotherapy, and biological methods. The methods of psychotherapy aim to change the thought processes, feelings, or behavior of the individual. These methods are based on psychological principles. In contrast, biological therapies attempt to alleviate psychological problems by affecting the nervous system in some way. This chapter examines different methods of therapy for psychological problems. Often therapists blend these methods.

Therapy is a general term for the variety of approaches that mental health professionals use to treat psychological problems and disorders. Psychologically based therapy, known as **psychotherapy,** involves verbal interactions between a trained professional and a person (the client or patient) who is seeking help for a psychological problem. Biologically based therapies involve the use of drugs or other medical procedures to treat psychological disorders.

Although the various methods of psychotherapy use different approaches, they all seek to help troubled individuals. They do this by giving individuals hope for recovery; helping individuals gain insights or new perspectives on their problems; and providing the individual with a caring, trusting relationship with a mental health professional.

Providing hope for recovery is very important because most people who seek therapy have problems they believe they cannot handle alone. They may have low self-esteem and lack the confidence to recognize that their situation can improve. Just the belief that therapy will help them is enough to put many people on the road to recovery. This reaction is similar to the placebo effect, about which you learned earlier.

Helping the individual gain insight or a new perspective is important because many psychological problems are the result of negative outlooks and misinterpretations. For example, someone who is depressed is likely to have poor self-esteem. This person may be able to see only the negative side of every situation and may feel responsible for that nega-

tivity. Changing this individual's outlook and perceptions may help to relieve the depressed mood and to improve his or her self-esteem.

Providing a caring, trusting relationship is important because people with psychological problems often feel isolated, afraid, and distrustful of others. Psychotherapy encourages individuals to talk freely about their feelings and problems. Therefore, a trusting relationship with the therapist is essential to the process. Establishing such a relationship between client and therapist is a key goal of psychotherapy.

In addition to providing hope, a new perspective, and a trusting relationship, all psychotherapy methods share the goal of bringing about changes in individuals seeking help. In the case of an individual who is depressed, for example, the psychotherapist tries to help the client develop a more positive outlook and higher self-esteem. In the case of a person experiencing a phobia, the psychotherapist helps the individual become desensitized, or less likely to react, to the object of fear.

The most commonly used methods of psychotherapy are psychoanalysis, humanistic therapy, cognitive therapy, and behavior therapy. The chart on the next page summarizes the main features of these methods.

Each method of psychotherapy has a different goal and different ways of achieving that goal. Some psychotherapists use just one method. Others use an eclectic approach; that is, they choose from a variety of methods, depending on what works best for the individual client. Which method is the most effective often depends on the nature of the psychological problem.

This raises the issue of the effectiveness of psychotherapy in general. Although some people find that psychotherapy does not help them, many people seem to benefit from it. However, it is difficult to know how those who benefit would have done in the absence of treatment.

Some people feel better about themselves as time goes on, even without treatment; others find solutions to their problems on their own, without benefit of therapy. Nonetheless, research on the effectiveness of psychotherapy is encouraging.

Reading Check **Find the Main Idea** What is one of the key goals of psychotherapy?

ACADEMIC VOCABULARY

eclectic selecting elements from a variety of sources, systems, or styles

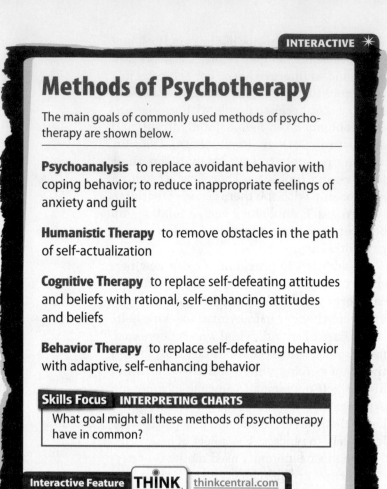

INTERACTIVE ✳

Methods of Psychotherapy

The main goals of commonly used methods of psychotherapy are shown below.

Psychoanalysis to replace avoidant behavior with coping behavior; to reduce inappropriate feelings of anxiety and guilt

Humanistic Therapy to remove obstacles in the path of self-actualization

Cognitive Therapy to replace self-defeating attitudes and beliefs with rational, self-enhancing attitudes and beliefs

Behavior Therapy to replace self-defeating behavior with adaptive, self-enhancing behavior

Skills Focus **INTERPRETING CHARTS**

What goal might all these methods of psychotherapy have in common?

Interactive Feature **THINK** central **thinkcentral.com**

Psychotherapy in Practice

Many types of professionals are involved in the treatment of psychological problems and disorders. However, it is primarily psychologists, psychiatrists, and social workers who practice psychotherapy.

Types of Mental Health Professionals

Counseling psychologists generally treat people with less serious psychological problems, such as adjustment problems. These psychologists often work in schools and other educational institutions, where they counsel people about their personal problems.

Clinical psychologists help people with psychological problems adjust to the demands of life. Their clients' problems may range from anxiety to loss of motivation. Many clinical psychologists work in hospitals or clinics, while others work in community mental health centers or in private practice.

Psychiatrists are medical doctors, and many have private practices. Because they are physicisns, psychiatrists are the only mental health professionals in most states who can prescribe medication and administer other types of biological therapy. Other professionals who think their clients might benefit from medication must consult with a psychiatrist. A psychologist or social worker, for example, might refer a client to a psychiatrist.

Other professionals who help people with psychological problems include psychiatric social workers and psychiatric nurses. Both have special training in psychology and usually work with other medical or mental health professionals. Psychiatric social workers may work in community mental health clinics, general hospitals, and hospitals for the mentally ill. They may also practice psychotherapy in a private office where they counsel individual clients as well as families.

Teachers, guidance counselors, clergy, and family doctors may also help individuals with problems. Such professionals may have little formal training in psychology. However, they are often the people that troubled individuals turn to first for help. A student, for example, might go to a teacher for advice on dealing with test anxiety, or ask a guidance counselor for help in making a career decision.

Selecting the Right Professional Those seeking help for a psychological problem should familiarize themselves with the various practitioners and the type of treatment each offers. One way that people can gain that information is to ask questions.

- What is the professional's field? For example, people with psychological problems should see people who belong to a profession, such as psychology, psychiatry, medicine, social work, or nursing.

- What degrees does the professional hold? Psychiatrists have medical degrees; psychologists usually have doctoral degrees; and social workers usually have master's degrees. The appropriate degrees ensure the professional is trained to help people.

- Is the professional licensed by the state? All states require licensing of psychologists and psychiatrists. Some states also require the licensing of social workers and nurses. To be issued a state license, professionals must pass exams or demonstrate expertise in other ways.

- What are the therapist's plans for treatment, and how long will treatment likely take? There is variation in the nature and duration of treatment for different methods of psychotherapy. The individual should know in advance what to expect from the treatment method.
- What is the estimated cost of treatment? Psychotherapy can be expensive, and it is not always covered by health insurance plans. Although cost should not have to be the deciding factor in choosing a therapist, for some people it must be, simply because they cannot afford to go into debt to receive treatment.

Reading Check **Identify Supporting Details** Why must psychiatrists also be physicians?

Individual Versus Group Therapy

Therapists use methods of psychotherapy with individuals or groups. Frequently, people who seek help for psychological problems have a choice between individual and group therapy. To make the best choice, it is important to be aware of the advantages of each type.

Advantages of Individual Therapy Some people do better with individual therapy because they need more personal attention than they would receive as part of a group. Moreover, some people feel uncomfortable talking about their problems in front of other people. These individuals are likely to talk more openly and freely if they are alone with their therapist.

Advantages of Group Therapy Group therapy can, however, have certain advantages over individual therapy. In fact, many people who begin seeing a therapist individually eventually switch to group therapy.

One advantage of group therapy is that it helps individuals realize that they are not alone. People can see other group members struggling with problems similar to their own. In this way, members of the group can often benefit from the insights gained by other group members who have gone through similar struggles.

Group members can support each other because they have had similar experiences— they have "been there" themselves. Group therapy also gives individuals a chance to practice coping and other social skills in a supportive environment.

One of the most significant advantages of group therapy is that it shows individuals that therapy can work to help them with their problems. People see other members of the group recovering, and this gives them hope of recovery for themselves.

From a practical standpoint, group therapy enables the therapist to work with several people at once. In addition, it often allows a therapist to immediately see people who might otherwise have to be placed on a waiting list to receive individual help. It is also more affordable for clients because they share the cost of the therapist's time and do not have to bear the full cost of the session.

Types of Group Therapy There are several types of group therapy, including couples therapy, family therapy, and therapy for people who share similar problems. These problems might include an eating disorder, a substance-abuse issue, money problems, or the grief created by the loss of a loved one. Couples therapy tries to help two people improve or find more satisfaction in their relationship with each other.

TYPES OF PROFESSIONAL THERAPISTS

Several types of professionals practice psychotherapy. Five are listed here, along with their training, examples of their workplaces, and typical therapeutic activities.

Counseling Psychologist, Ph.D., Psy.D., or Ed.D.
Educational institutions such as colleges and high schools, or in businesses; refers clients with serious problems to clinical psychologist

Clinical Psychologist, Ph.D., Psy.D., or Ed.D.
Works in hospitals and clinics; assists and treats people with psychological problems

Psychiatrist, M.D.
Able to prescribe medicine and perform operations

Psychiatric Social Worker, M.S.W.
Counsels people with everyday personal and family problems

Psychiatric Nurse, R.N.
Dispenses medicine and acts as a contact person between counseling sessions

Couples therapy helps people communicate more effectively by helping them learn new ways to listen to each other and to express their feelings. Such therapy also helps couples discover ways to resolve conflicts and handle intense emotions.

Family therapy aims to help troubled families by improving communication and relations among family members. It also seeks to promote the family's emotional growth.

Family therapy is based on the assumption that the lives of family members are intertwined. Therefore, the family as a whole is likely to suffer when one member has a problem that goes untreated. Inevitably, such an untreated problem will affect other members of the family. Children, for example, might begin to display symptoms that come to the notice of teachers and other students in their school.

For example, a parent may be addicted to alcohol and become abusive when intoxicated. The abuse may lead to low self-esteem, anxiety, and depression in other family members. Or a family might seek family therapy to help them cope with a family member's schizophrenia. Others might seek family therapy to help them adjust to a divorce.

Self-help groups are composed of people who share the same problem, such as overeating, drug addiction, or compulsive gambling.

Members of a self-help group meet regularly—often without a therapist—to discuss their problems, share solutions, and give and receive support.

Again, take the problem of alcoholism. There are a variety of treatment options for alcoholics. Treatment programs include both inpatient and outpatient care. Inpatient centers provide a sheltered place to go through withdrawal while getting counseling.

One of the best-known self-help groups is Alcoholics Anonymous (AA). AA has served as a developmental model for many other self-help programs. The AA method for recovery involves 12 steps. Through regular meetings and shared experiences, AA members bring themselves and each other closer to a life that is free of alcohol and full of emotional, physical, social, and spiritual well-being.

Al-Anon and Alateen are programs that provide treatment and support for the families of alcoholics. Al-Anon is designed to help family members talk about and share advice on the problem of living with an alcoholic. Alateen is specifically designed to help teenagers cope with this situation. There are local chapters of AA, Al-Anon, and Alateen in just about every community in the United States.

Reading Check **Identify** What are the advantages of a self-help group?

SECTION 1 Assessment

Reviewing Main Ideas and Vocabulary

1. **Identify** Which method of therapy attempts to remove obstacles in the path of self-actualization?

2. **Recall** Which therapy involves verbal interactions between a trained professional and a client who is seeking help for a psychological problem?

3. **Describe** Which mental health professional may prescribe medications?

Thinking Critically

4. **Summarize** What is the goal of couples therapy?

5. **Draw Conclusions** What questions should one ask when selecting a psychotherapist?

6. **Evaluate** Using your notes and a graphic organizer like the one below, explain the advantages and disadvantages of each type of psychotherapy

(Individual:)—(Therapy)—(Group:)

FOCUS ON WRITING

7. **Expository** Write a paragraph in which you explain which method of psychotherapy you think would be most useful for most people, and why.

The Psychoanalytic and Humanistic Approaches

Before You Read

Main Idea

Psychoanalysis and humanistic therapy are two important methods of treatment.

Reading Focus

1. How did Freud view the role of psychoanalysis?
2. What are some of the methods of psychoanalysis?
3. What is the goal of humanistic therapy?

Vocabulary

free association
resistance
dream analysis
manifest content
latent content
transference
humanistic therapy
person-centered therapy
nondirective therapy
active listening

TAKING NOTES Use a graphic organizer like this one to take notes on the methods of psycho-analysis.

Methods of Psychoanalysis	
Free Association	
Dream Analysis	
Transference	

LOOKING FOR
Hidden Meanings

PSYCHOLOGY CLOSE UP

What do dreams mean? Have you ever had a recurring dream, one that kept coming back to haunt your sleep, maybe a couple of times a week or even nightly? For example, a six-year-old boy reported a recurring dream in which he was standing at one end of a dark corridor. From the other end, silhouetted against a bright light, a tall dark figure approached him. The man who walked toward him had only one arm, and in his hand he carried a shovel. The boy stood paralyzed, unable to move. Then just before the dark figure reached him, and before the boy could see his face, the boy floated up to the ceiling. Although the dark figure grabbed for him in an attempt to pluck him down from the ceiling, the boy bobbed up and out of reach.

You may have had a recurring dream, too. A very common one is the final exam dream, in which you arrive for an important test, only to find that you are not prepared. Perhaps you studied the wrong material, or you brought the wrong supplies, or you are not appropriately dressed or not dressed at all.

In some methods of therapy, dreams may provide a way into unconscious hopes and fears. Some psychologists think that dreams express both apparent and hidden fears and desires. ■

Freud and Psychoanalysis

Psychoanalysis, the model of therapy developed by Sigmund Freud, literally means "analysis of the psyche (mind)." Psychoanalysis was the first formal method of psychotherapy used in Western countries. For many years, it was the only method used. In recent decades, however, it has become less popular.

Freud believed that most psychological problems originate in early childhood experiences and inner conflicts. These conflicts can cause people to develop unconscious sexual and aggressive urges that, in turn, cause anxiety. For Freud, guilt occurs when the urges enter conscious thought or when the individual acts upon them. Guilt also leads to more anxiety.

Psychoanalysts try to reduce anxiety and guilt by helping clients become aware of the unconscious thoughts and feelings that are believed to be at the root of their problems. Psychoanalysts call this self-awareness *insight*. Once insight has been gained, clients can use the knowledge to resolve problems.

Reading Check **Find the Main Idea** For Freud, what was the source of most psychological problems?

Methods of Psychoanalysis

Some of the techniques psychoanalysts use to help clients gain insight include free association, dream analysis, and transference.

Free Association The primary technique of psychoanalysis is **free association.** In free association, the analyst asks the client to relax and then to say whatever comes to mind. Free association developed from Freud's early use of hypnosis to tap into his clients' unconscious thoughts and feelings. The use of free association instead of hypnosis enables the client to participate more actively in the analysis.

The topic of the free association might be a memory, dream, fantasy, or recent event. The assumption is that, as long as the client associates freely, unconscious thoughts and feelings will "break through" and show up in what the client says. The client is encouraged to say whatever comes to mind, no matter how trivial, embarrassing, or painful the ideas may seem. In fact, psychoanalysts believe that the more hesitant the patient is to say something,

ACADEMIC VOCABULARY

repressed
excluded from the conscious mind

the more likely it is that the hesitancy reflects an unconscious thought or feeling.

Resistance is the term psychoanalysts use to refer to a client's reluctance to discuss issues raised during free association. Therapists using free association think that resistance reflects a defense mechanism, such as the repression or denial of painful feelings.

The role of the analyst in free association is to point out the types of things the client is saying—or resisting saying—and to help the client interpret the meaning of the utterances or lack thereof. Psychoanalysts believe that free association allows the client to express troubling thoughts and feelings in a safe environment where those thoughts and feelings may be explored. Through such means, clients gain insight into their problems.

Dream Analysis Freud believed that dreams express unconscious thoughts and feelings. He called them the "royal road into the unconscious." In a technique called **dream analysis,** the analyst interprets the content of dreams to unlock these thoughts and feelings.

Freud also distinguished between the manifest and latent content of dreams. **Manifest content** refers to the actual content of the dream as it is remembered by the client. **Latent content** refers to the hidden meaning in the dream, which the therapist interprets from the manifest content. For example, a client may dream about falling from a mountain and being unable to grab anything to break his fall (manifest content). The therapist might interpret the dream to mean that the client has repressed feelings that his life is out of control (latent content).

Transference As analysis proceeds, many clients begin to view their relationship with their analyst as being similar to one they have or had with another important person in their lives, often a parent. They experience similar feelings toward the analyst and expect the analyst to feel and behave as the other person did. In other words, the client is transferring feelings and expectations from one person to another. This process is called **transference.**

Psychoanalysts make use of transference to help the client express and analyze unconscious feelings he or she has toward that other important person. In fact, establishing a transference relationship is a major goal of

Free Association

In free association, the analyst tells the client to relax and say whatever pops into his or her mind. If someone says the word "dog" to you, "cat" might pop into your mind, or "shoe" might call up "sock."

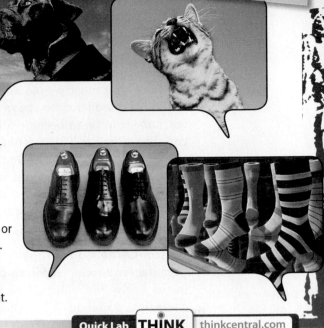

PROCEDURE

❶ Pair off with another student.

❷ Make up a list of words that deal with an important topic such as the environment or political elections.

❸ One of you reads each word while the other comes up with a one-word response.

ANALYSIS

1. Make a list with your classmates of words that have to do with the environment or politics. For example, for the environment, your list might include "global warming," "greenhouse gases," and so forth.

2. Make another list of their responses or associations to the first list of words.

3. As a group, discuss what your associations reveal about your attitudes toward politics and the environment.

Quick Lab THINK central thinkcentral.com

psychoanalysis. Psychoanalysts believe that transference exposes unresolved problems in earlier relationships. The client can then work through these problems, with the help of the analyst, in order to solve similar problems in current relationships.

Evaluation of Psychoanalysis Many psychologists believe that Freud placed too much emphasis on sexual and aggressive urges. Some argue that he underestimated the importance of conscious ideas and changes in behavior. Despite these criticisms, however, a classic review of dozens of studies concluded that people who had received psychoanalysis showed greater well-being than 70 to 75 percent of those who had not received treatment. Psychoanalysis has proved especially useful in the treatment of anxiety, mild depression, and difficulty in handling social relationships. However, it is generally not useful for the treatment of major depression, bipolar disorder, or schizophrenia.

The techniques of traditional psychoanalysis often require clients to meet with their analyst four or five times a week, for a period of months or years. For some clients, this provides a supportive, long-term relationship that fosters emotional growth and insight. For others, however, the cost of therapy in time, money, and emotional distress is too great to make psychoanalysis a real option.

Psychoanalysis does not work for everyone. For example, it is not the most effective type of psychotherapy for individuals who are less verbal. Nor does it work as well for people who are too seriously disturbed to gain insight into their problems.

Brief Psychoanalysis Over the past several decades, shorter terms of psychoanalysis have become more common. In traditional psychoanalysis, a client and therapist may meet almost daily over the course of several years. By contrast, in brief psychoanalysis, client and analyst typically meet just 10 to 20 times over the course of a few months to a year. The shorter treatment makes brief psychoanalysis available to a wider range of people.

The techniques used in brief psychoanalysis are generally the same techniques that are used in traditional psychoanalysis. The primary difference between the two approaches is that brief psychoanalysis has a more limited focus. Whereas traditional psychoanalysis examines the client's entire personality, brief psychoanalysis concentrates on fixing a specific problem. For brief psychoanalysis to be effective, clients usually must be motivated and actively involved in applying the insights in therapy to the events in their lives.

Reading Check **Summarize** What main goal do the techniques of psychoanalysis serve?

Humanistic Therapy

The primary goal of **humanistic therapy** is to help individuals reach their full potential. It does this by helping individuals develop self-awareness and self-acceptance. The method assumes that most people are basically good and have a tendency to strive for self-actualization—that is, to become all that they are capable of being. The method also assumes that people with psychological problems just need help tapping their inner resources so they can grow and reach their potential. Person-centered therapy is the most widely used method of humanistic therapy.

Person-Centered Therapy The psychologist Carl Rogers developed **person-centered therapy** in the early 1950s. According to Rogers, psychological problems arise when people act as others want or expect them to act. The role of person-centered therapy is to help clients find their true selves and realize their unique potential.

Person-centered therapy is sometimes called client-centered therapy. The use of the term *client* instead of *patient* reflects the status given to individuals seeking help. Clients are seen as equals in a working relationship with the therapist. Clients are encouraged to take the lead in therapy, talking openly about whatever may be troubling them. This method is called **nondirective therapy** because it is not directed by the therapist.

Active listening is a widely used communication technique in which the listener repeats, rephrases, and asks for clarification of the speaker's statements. The goal is to convey to the speaker that words are heard and thoughts and feelings are understood. The therapist remains nonjudgmental and supportive, regardless of what the client says, providing what Rogers calls *unconditional positive regard*. The support of the therapist helps the client accept himself or herself and his or her true feelings. Self-esteem also rises, giving the client confidence.

Person-centered therapy is practiced widely by school and college counselors. It helps students deal with anxiety, depression, and other psychological problems and helps students make decisions. Counselors provide a supportive atmosphere in which students feel free to explore and make their own choices.

Evaluation of Humanistic Therapy In a review of several studies, nearly three-fourths of people obtaining person-centered therapy showed greater well-being, on average, than people who did not receive therapy. Like psychoanalysis, person-centered therapy seems to be most helpful for highly motivated people. Humanistic therapy works best for people who experience anxiety, mild depression, or problems in their social relationships.

Reading Check **Summarize** What is nondirective therapy?

SECTION 2 Assessment

Reviewing Main Ideas and Vocabulary

1. **Recall** What is another term for a client's self-awareness achieved in psychoanalysis?

2. **Define** What is dream analysis?

3. **Describe** What is the goal of active listening?

Thinking Critically

4. **Infer** According to psychoanalytic theory, what effect do unconscious thoughts and feelings have on a person's ability to form meaningful personal relationships?

5. **Analyze** What role does the therapist play in person-centered therapy?

6. **Evaluate** Using your notes and a graphic organizer like the one below, evaluate psychoanalysis and humanistic therapy.

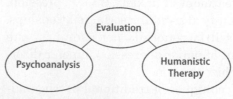

FOCUS ON WRITING

7. **Descriptive** Write a paragraph in which you describe a dream that you think reveals both an apparent meaning and a hidden meaning.

Public Therapy

In my mind at the time, if I got to the roof, Hollywood would send a helicopter to rescue me.

I introduce myself as Tiffany, but you can call me Princess. I love all eyes on me.

The quotes at the right are from just a few of the troubled guests who have appeared on *Dr. Phil*, a TV talk show hosted by psychologist Phil McGraw, Ph.D. Many other guests have willingly paraded symptoms of their mood, anxiety, and personality disorders before a sometimes jeering, cheering, or laughing audience.

On *Celebrity Rehab*, drugged-out and alcoholic semi-celebrities tell Dr. Drew Pinsky—and the American public—not just about their addictions, but also about the traumas that they blame for the addictions. On his radio show, "Dr. Drew" and his co-host use the weird problems of their callers for comedy effect.

Amateurs with no qualifications have also found remarkable success offering public therapy in the most unlikely settings. Sitting on a street corner next to a sign that reads "Talk to Me," a couple have invited discussion of everything from drug addiction to failing marriages with thousands of strangers. A woman with no credentials as a counselor opened a New York stage show in which she conducted 13-minute "therapy" sessions with volunteers from the audience. In Milwaukee, a couple set up a counseling service in the restrooms of nightclubs. Some clubbers skipped the dance floor and went straight to the restroom for advice.

What is going on here? Why has psychological therapy, which traditionally has been a private matter between patient and therapist, become so public? Why are people not just willing, but eager to discuss their problems, including serious psychological disorders, in front of anyone? Why do they accept advice from strangers? Has the openness about highly personal disorders gone too far?

A psychologist who has appeared on various TV talk shows observed that these public displays are intended to entertain, and in so doing they sometimes exploit people with serious problems. He makes the further point that people who are seriously interested in exploring their problems should seek help in therapy. But if they're only interested in exhibitionism or revenge, they are more likely to go on a talk show. He also cited the lure of celebrity, no matter how brief, as a reason why people beg producers to allow them to appear on these shows.

One reason for the public display of personal burdens may be the way that modern society, despite all its electronic networks, has actually isolated many people. Those who spend all their free time on their computers or cell phones texting their friends may not engage in an actual face-to-face conversation for days at a time. It is no wonder, then, that the street-corner "therapists" feel that people come to them for "plain old-fashioned conversation."

Perhaps another reason people accept "therapy" from strangers is the popularity of the self-help movement. These people may see the glut of self-help books as an indication that anyone can offer valid therapies, no matter what their qualifications. And advice from a restroom analyst is so much faster and cheaper!

Street psychologists bring therapy to the people.

Thinking Critically

1. **Analyze** What are some of the hazards and possible benefits of public therapy?

2. **Discuss** Why do you think therapy has become public for many people?

Cognitive Therapy and Behavior Therapy

Before You Read

Main Idea
Cognitive therapy and behavior therapy help people develop new ways of thinking and behaving.

Reading Focus
1. What is the aim of cognitive therapy?
2. What is the aim of behavior therapy?

Vocabulary
rational-emotive behavior therapy
aversive conditioning
successive approximations

TAKING NOTES Use a graphic organizer like this one to take notes on cognitive therapy and behavior therapy.

Two Kinds of Therapy
Cognitive Therapy:
Behavior Therapy:

"Wish I Could Be There"

PSYCHOLOGY CLOSE UP

How do people overcome their phobias? Allen Shawn, son of former *New Yorker* editor William Shawn and brother of playwright and actor Wallace Shawn, has published a memoir about his life titled *Wish I Could Be There*. Shawn has agoraphobia. That is, he is afraid of public spaces and also of isolation. He avoids fields, parking lots, tunnels, unknown roads, subways, elevators, and bridges. Shawn has nonetheless learned to work around his phobias. He is a composer and writer on the faculty of Bennington College in Vermont.

Shawn's memoir demonstrates in great detail how his phobias have harmed and constrained his life. Still, through therapy Shawn has managed to live a productive if not "normal" life. At Roosevelt Hospital in New York, he underwent group treatment in a program that involved weekly meetings. Activities included group discussions, relaxation exercises, working through a handbook, individual sessions with trained helpers, and outings with other people with phobias. Allen Shawn is one of many people for whom therapy is a means to deal with fears and lead a more contented life. ■

Cognitive Therapy

Cognitive therapy and behavior therapy are considered together because both methods share the same goal—to help clients develop new ways of thinking and behaving. Both cognitive and behavior therapists encourage clients to focus on their thoughts and actions. Advocates of these two theories contend that only by modifying self-defeating thoughts and behavior patterns will the client truly be able to solve his or her own problems. Thus, the aim of these therapies is to eliminate troubling emotions or behaviors rather than to help patients gain insight into the underlying cause of their problems, which is a key goal of psychoanalysis and humanistic therapy.

The aim of cognitive therapy is to help people learn to think about their problems in more productive ways. Cognitive psychologists focus on the beliefs, attitudes, and thought processes that create and compound their clients' problems. They believe that some people develop ways of thinking that are illogical or based on faulty assumptions. Such ways of thinking can lead to emotional and behavioral problems for these people.

Cognitive therapists help people change their ways of thinking. These therapists also try to help people develop more realistic and logical ways of thinking. Cognitive psychologists argue that once people have changed their ways of thinking, they become more capable of solving their emotional and behavioral problems.

The two most widely used cognitive therapy methods are rational-emotive therapy and psychiatrist Aaron Beck's model of therapy, sometimes called cognitive restructuring therapy. Both of these methods aim at modifying people's ways of thinking as a means of improving their emotional health. However, the two methods differ somewhat in the aspects of thinking they maintain must be changed and in the approach they take to bringing about those changes.

Rational-Emotive Behavior Therapy

First developed by psychologist Albert Ellis in the 1950s, **rational-emotive behavior therapy** (REBT) is based on Ellis's belief that people are basically logical in their thinking and actions. However, the assumptions upon which they base their thinking or actions are sometimes incorrect. According to Ellis, people may develop emotional problems when they base their behavior on these kinds of faulty assumptions.

People are often unaware of their false assumptions, even though the assumptions influence their conscious thoughts and actions. The role of the therapist in REBT is first to identify and then to challenge the false assumptions. To teach individuals to think more realistically, REBT therapists use techniques such as role-playing and modeling. Role-playing helps individuals see how their assumptions affect their relationships. Therapists use modeling to show individuals other, more realistic assumptions they might adopt.

Individuals in rational-emotive behavior therapy may also receive homework assignments. For example, they may be asked to read relevant literature, listen to tapes of psychotherapy sessions, or carry out experiments designed to test their assumptions. The more faithfully patients complete their homework, the more likely it is that their therapy will succeed.

Beck's Cognitive Therapy

Another form of cognitive therapy was introduced in the 1960s by psychiatrist Aaron Beck. In contrast to REBT's focus on faulty assumptions, the focus of Beck's cognitive therapy is on restructuring illogical thought processes. Beck has noted several types of illogical thought processes that may lead to emotional problems. Some of these include the following.

- **Arbitrary inference**, or drawing conclusions for which there is no evidence
- **Selective abstraction**, or drawing conclusions about a situation or event on the basis of a single detail and misinterpreting or ignoring other details that would lead to a different conclusion
- **Overgeneralization**, or drawing a general conclusion from a single experience

Instead of confronting and challenging clients about the errors in their ways of thinking, as the REBT therapist does, the therapist using Beck's approach gently guides clients in testing the logic of their own thought processes and developing more logical ways of thinking.

One technique for doing this is to train clients to observe and record their thoughts in response to the events of daily life. Therapists can later review events with clients and help them see the illogical thought processes that are causing them emotional problems.

Evaluation of Cognitive Therapy Cognitive therapy tends to be a short-term method, making it a realistic option for more people than traditional psychoanalysis. Clients generally meet with their therapist once a week for 15 to 25 weeks.

Studies of cognitive therapy show that modifying irrational beliefs of the type described by Albert Ellis helps people with problems such as anxiety and depression. Modifying self-defeating beliefs of the sort outlined by Aaron Beck also frequently alleviates those conditions. Cognitive therapy also helps people with personality disorders.

Cognitive therapy is helpful for people with major depression who had been considered responsive only to medicine and other kinds of biological therapies. Many studies show that cognitive therapy is as effective or even more effective than antidepressant medication. For one thing, cognitive therapy provides <u>coping skills</u> that reduce the risk of recurrence of depression once treatment ends. A combination of cognitive therapy and antidepressant medication may be superior to either treatment alone in the case of people with persistent depression.

Reading Check **Find the Main Idea** Other than Beck's model, what is the most widely used cognitive therapy method?

Behavior Therapy

The goal of behavior therapy, which is also called behavior modification, is to help people develop more adaptive behavior. Some people seek behavior therapy to eliminate undesirable behaviors, such as overeating or smoking. Others seek behavior therapy to acquire desirable behaviors, such as skills needed to develop relationships or confront phobias.

Behaviorists believe that both desirable and undesirable behaviors are largely learned and that people with psychological problems have learned unhealthy ways of behaving. The aim of behavior therapy is to teach people more desirable (or healthier) ways of behaving. To behaviorists, the reasons for the undesirable behavior are unimportant. Changing the behavior is what matters.

Many behavioral techniques fall into two categories: counterconditioning, which helps people to unlearn undesirable behaviors, and operant conditioning, which helps in the learning of desirable behaviors. The choice of behavioral techniques for an individual client depends largely on the nature of the individual's psychological disorder.

Counterconditioning If undesirable behaviors are conditioned, or learned through reinforcement, then presumably they can be unlearned, or counterconditioned. Counterconditioning pairs the stimulus that triggers an unwanted behavior (such as fear of spiders) with a new, more desirable behavior. Counterconditioning techniques include systematic desensitization, modeling, and aversive conditioning.

Systematic desensitization was developed by psychiatrist Joseph Wolpe in the 1950s as a treatment for phobias and other anxiety disorders. The assumption underlying systematic desensitization is that a person cannot feel anxious and relaxed at the same time. The therapist trains the client to relax in the presence of an anxiety-producing situation.

This is done in a systematic way. First, the therapist teaches the client how to relax completely. Once this has been accomplished, the therapist gradually exposes the client to the object or situation that causes the phobic response. For a person who fears spiders, the therapist might first ask the person to simply imagine a spider. If the thought of a spider makes the client feel anxious, the client is told to stop thinking about the spider and relax again. This is done repeatedly until the thought of a spider no longer causes anxiety.

Gradually, the stimulus is increased—the person might be shown pictures of spiders, asked to hold a toy spider, and then asked to handle a real spider. In each case, the person is trained to respond with relaxation until the stimulus no longer provokes anxiety.

Systematic desensitization may be combined with other counterconditioning measures, such as modeling and aversive conditioning. Modeling involves observational

ACADEMIC VOCABULARY
coping skills skills to contend with difficulties successfully

CASE STUDY
CONNECTION

Overcoming Fears
Virtual therapy is another more recent technique for learning to deal with irrational fears. Virtual scenes can be created to help people slowly overcome their fears of, for example, spiders.

learning. The client observes and then imitates the therapist or another person coping with the feared object or situation. For the person with a fear of spiders, the therapist might ask the person to observe someone watching a spider make a web. The client would then be encouraged to behave in the same way.

Aversive conditioning is, essentially, the opposite of systematic desensitization. In aversive conditioning, the therapist replaces a positive response to a stimulus with a negative response. For example, for a person who wants to stop smoking, the therapist might replace the pleasant feelings associated with smoking with unpleasant ones. The person might be asked to smoke several cigarettes at once through a device that holds two or more cigarettes. This overexposure to cigarette smoke makes smoking unpleasant. With repetition, the person may come to avoid smoking.

People who learn more desirable behaviors through counterconditioning often experience a boost in their self-esteem as well. Furthermore, by confronting, challenging, and overcoming their fears or bad habits, such people will increase their opportunity to lead less restrictive lives.

Operant Conditioning The behavioral technique of operant conditioning is based on the assumption that behavior that is reinforced tends to be repeated, whereas behavior that is not reinforced tends to be extinguished. Behavioral therapists reinforce desirable behaviors with rewards and at the same time withhold reinforcement for undesirable behaviors. In other words, therapists teach clients in a given situation, or antecedent, to behave in a certain way to achieve a desired consequence. The rewards for desirable behavior might be praise or treats, for example, depending on the client and the setting.

Operant conditioning has sometimes proved effective in more severe cases, such as schizophrenia and childhood autism, that were previously resistant to other types of treatment. Operant conditioning is often used in institutional settings, such as mental hospitals. In such settings, the therapist may set up a token economy, that is, a system of rewards. When people in these settings begin to demonstrate appropriate behavior, they are rewarded with a plastic coin or token. The tokens can be accumulated and exchanged for real rewards, such as snacks, extra television time, a trip to town, or a private room.

The staff at one mental hospital used operant conditioning to convince withdrawn schizophrenic patients to eat their meals. The more the staff coaxed the patients to eat—sometimes even hand-feeding them—the worse the problem became. The extra attention from the staff was apparently reinforcing the patients' lack of cooperation: The greater the refusal to eat, the more attention the patients received.

The solution was to stop reinforcing the uncooperative behavior and instead reinforce cooperative behavior. Patients who arrived late at the dining hall were locked out, and hospital staff were prevented from helping patients at mealtime. Thus, uncooperative behavior was no longer rewarded with extra attention. Only those who cooperated received food. As a result, the uncooperative patients quickly changed their eating habits.

AVERSIVE VS. OPERANT CONDITIONING

	Goal	Technique	Rationale
Aversive	End harmful behavior	Associate harmful behavior with painful stimulation	Associating a behavior with aversive stimulation makes the behavior offensive
Operant	Encourage adaptive behavior	Reinforce adaptive behavior or avoid reinforcement of maladaptive behavior	Reinforcement increases the frequency of behavior and lack of reinforcement extinguishes behavior

Sometimes people find it difficult to adopt a new behavior all at once, finding it easier to change their behavior gradually. Another method of operant conditioning, called successive approximations, is useful in such situations. The term **successive approximations** refers to a series of behaviors that gradually become more similar to a target behavior. Through reinforcement of behaviors at each stage, the target behavior is finally achieved.

Suppose, for example, a student wants to increase his study time to two hours a day. On the first day, he studies for half an hour and then gives himself a reward. Each night he adds five minutes to his study time and gives himself a reward until he reaches his goal.

The relationship between antecedents, behavior, and consequences can be seen when operant conditioning is used for social skills training. People with severe psychological problems may lack social skills because of isolation and social withdrawal. In fact, lacking the social skills needed for independent living is one of the major symptoms of schizophrenia. A therapist might assist a client by teaching him or her to say "hello" in a friendly way when meeting someone. This technique would help the client function more comfortably in society—that is, it would help the client achieve a desired consequence.

Behavior therapists help people build their social skills by advising clients on their behavior, modeling effective behaviors, and encouraging clients to practice effective behaviors. Such techniques have proved successful in helping students build social relationships. They have also been used to help people with severe psychological disorders. With social skills training, a person who otherwise would be dependent on others might be able to hold a job and live on her or his own.

Evaluation of Behavior Therapy Behavior therapy tends to be somewhat more effective overall than psychoanalysis or person-centered therapy. It is also a short-term therapy, sometimes bringing about lasting results in just a few months.

Behavior therapy is especially effective for well-defined problems such as phobias, post-traumatic stress disorder, and compulsions. It has helped people overcome depression, social problems, and problems with self-control (as in quitting smoking or drinking). In addition, behavior therapy has proved very useful for managing the care of people living in institutions, including people with schizophrenia or developmental disabilities.

There is a new, integrated approach to treatment called cognitive-behavior therapy. It attempts to change the way a person both thinks and behaves.

Reading Check **Summarize** What are some of the techniques of counterconditioning?

Online Quiz THINK central thinkcentral.com

Reviewing Main Ideas and Vocabulary

1. **Describe** What is the focus of Beck's cognitive therapy?

2. **Define** What is aversive conditioning?

3. **Recall** What technique did Joseph Wolpe develop as a treatment for phobias and other anxiety disorders?

Thinking Critically

4. **Explain** What might be an example of behavior and consequences in a behavioral situation?

5. **Summarize** What techniques do cognitive and behavior therapists use to help people?

6. **Compare and Contrast** Using your notes and a graphic organizer like the one below, explain the basic similarities and differences between counterconditioning and operant conditioning.

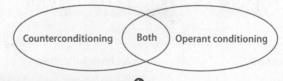

Counterconditioning | Both | Operant conditioning

FOCUS ON WRITING

7. **Descriptive** Describe how one treatment in this section can be used to relieve a certain kind of phobia.

Biological Therapy

Before You Read

Main Idea

Biological therapy relies on methods such as medication, electric shock, and surgery to help people with psychological disorders.

Reading Focus

1. How are the major categories of drugs used in drug therapy?
2. What is electroconvulsive therapy?
3. How would you define psychosurgery?

Vocabulary

antianxiety drug
antidepressant drug
lithium
antipsychotic drug
electroconvulsive therapy
psychosurgery
prefrontal lobotomy

TAKING NOTES Use a graphic organizer like this one to take notes on various kinds of drug therapy.

Drug Therapy
Antianxiety:
Antidepressant:
Lithium:
Antipsychotic:

A CRUEL PROCEDURE

PSYCHOLOGY CLOSE UP

Why was an ice pick ever considered a surgical tool? A lobotomy is a surgical procedure in which nerve pathways linking one or more lobes to the rest of the brain are cut. The method was invented in the 1930s and became widely used during the 1940s and 1950s. Lobotomies were supposed to reduce the agitation and violence of people with serious disorders, but sometimes their use was seriously abused. In 1960, a 12-year-old boy named Howard Dully was lobotomized by Dr. Walter Freeman. Now a bus driver in California, Dully has over the past couple of years attempted to discover what happened to him and why.

Dully's stepmother claimed he was a discipline problem and managed, with the surgeon's collaboration, to convince the boy's father to agree to the surgical procedure. It now seems clear that he was lobotomized for nothing more serious than the normal behavior of a young boy. The psychiatrist who performed the operation, Walter Freeman, thought that mental illness was correlated with emotions and that cutting the brain would cut away overactive feelings or emotions. He performed lobotomies on some 2,500 patients in 23 states. Today this brutal procedure is rarely performed. ■

Dr. Walter Freeman performed a lobotomy on Howard Dully (above) when Dully was only 12 years of age.

Drug Therapy

The methods of psychotherapy described so far rely on verbal interactions between the psychotherapist and the individual seeking help. As you have seen, psychotherapists may give their clients emotional support, advice, and help in understanding and changing their thoughts and behaviors.

Biological therapy, on the other hand, attempts to alleviate psychological problems by affecting the nervous system. Biological therapy relies on methods such as medication, electric shock, and even surgery to help people with psychological disorders. All of these biological methods affect the brain in a variety of ways.

Because these treatments are medical in nature, they must be administered or prescribed by psychiatrists or other physicians. Psychologists do not prescribe drugs or administer biological treatments, but they may help decide whether a certain kind of biological therapy is appropriate for the treatment of a particular individual.

Drug therapy is the most widely used biological treatment for psychological disorders. It works well for several different problems. Four major types of medication are commonly used: antianxiety drugs, antidepressant drugs, lithium, and antipsychotic drugs. All of these medications can be obtained only with a prescription.

Antianxiety Drugs Also called minor tranquilizers, **antianxiety drugs** are used as an outpatient treatment to help people who suffer from anxiety disorders or panic attacks. They are also prescribed for people who are experiencing serious distress or tension in their daily lives.

Antianxiety drugs work by depressing the activity of the nervous system. They lower the heart rate and respiration rate. They also decrease feelings of nervousness and tension. Although antianxiety medications help control the symptoms of anxiety, they are not a permanent cure for anxiety disorders. Thus, most people use them for a short period of time. The longer a person takes an antianxiety medication, the less effective the drug may become. Higher doses may be needed in order to achieve the same effect.

The major side effects of antianxiety medications are feelings of fatigue. It is also possible to become dependent on antianxiety drugs. People who are dependent on these drugs may lose the ability to face the stresses and strains of everyday life without them.

Antidepressant Drugs People who suffer from major depression are often treated with **antidepressant drugs.** Antidepressant drugs are also sometimes used in the treatment of such problems as eating disorders and panic disorders.

Antidepressants work by increasing the amount of one or both of the neurotransmitters. These are norepinephrine (noradrenaline) and serotonin. They tend to be most helpful in reducing the physical symptoms of depression. They increase activity levels and reduce the severity of eating and sleeping problems.

In order to work effectively, antidepressant medications must build up in the body to a certain level. This may take anywhere from several days to a matter of weeks. Severely depressed people who are at risk of suicide are sometimes hospitalized until the medication reaches the level required to improve their depressed mood. This is to prevent them from taking an overdose of the medication, which could be lethal.

In addition, antidepressants sometimes have negative side effects, such as escalated heart rate and excessive weight gain. For these and other reasons, some psychologists believe that antidepressant medications should be reserved for people who fail to respond to psychotherapy.

Mood Stabilizing Drugs Some drugs are prescribed to stabilize patients' mood disorders. One of the most popular is lithium. The ancient Greeks and Romans may have been the first people to use a compound of the metal **lithium** to treat psychological disorders. They discovered that mineral water helped many people with what used to be called manic depression but is now called bipolar disorder. The mineral water may have contained lithium.

Today lithium carbonate is given in tablet form to help people with bipolar disorder. Lithium seems to flatten out their cycles of mania and depression. Scientists do not understand completely how lithium does this. Lithium is known, however, to affect the functioning of several neurotransmitters.

Lithium may have side effects, such as shakiness, memory impairment, and excessive thirst. Memory problems are reported to be the major reason that people stop using the drug.

Antipsychotic Drugs People who are diagnosed with schizophrenia are likely to be prescribed **antipsychotic drugs.** These drugs are also called major tranquilizers.

Antipsychotic medications are effective for reducing agitation, delusions, and hallucinations. Their use has enabled many thousands of people with schizophrenia to live outside of mental hospitals.

Schizophrenia is associated with high levels of dopamine activity. Antipsychotic medications work by blocking the activity of dopamine in the brain. Unfortunately, prolonged use of these medications can lead to problems in balance and coordination and produce tremors and twitches.

Nonetheless, controlling the symptoms of schizophrenia with medication often allows those with schizophrenia to lead more normal lives. They can live more independently—even hold jobs—and maintain better social relationships. Greater independence and better social relationships increase self-esteem and social support, both of which are likely to have a positive effect on emotional health and the control of schizophrenia.

Reading Check **Find the Main Idea** What psychological disorder is lithium used to treat?

Statistically Speaking...

The Homeless and Therapy A large percentage of the homeless population has severe psychological disorders. Some are on antipsychotic drugs that have allowed them to be deinstitutionalized, that is, live outside of mental hospitals.

20–25% Percentage of the single adult homeless population that suffers from mental illness

5–7% Percentage of homeless people with mental illness who require hospitalization

30% Percentage of homeless with addiction disorders

33% Percentage of homeless population with untreated psychiatric illnesses

Skills Focus **INTERPRETING CHARTS** What might have been the effect on society at large of the use of antipsychotic drugs to treat mental patients?

Sources: National Coalition for the Homeless

Electroconvulsive Therapy

Electroconvulsive therapy (ECT), commonly called electric-shock therapy, was introduced as a treatment for psychological disorders in the 1930s by Italian psychiatrists Ugo Cerletti and Lucio Bini. Before ECT is given, anesthesia is administered to render the person unconscious throughout the procedure. Then an electric current is passed through the person's brain. The electric current produces convulsions (violent <u>involuntary</u> contractions of muscles) throughout the body. In some cases, muscle relaxant drugs are given to prevent injury during the convulsions.

When ECT was introduced, it was used for many psychological disorders, including schizophrenia. Once antipsychotic drugs became available, ECT was used much less often. In fact, in 1990 the American Psychiatric Association recommended that ECT be used primarily for people with major depression who do not respond to antidepressant drugs.

ECT is controversial for many reasons. For one thing, many professionals are distressed by the thought of passing an electric shock through a patient's head and producing convulsions. There are also side effects, including memory problems.

ACADEMIC VOCABULARY

involuntary
against one's will

However, research suggests that for most people, cognitive impairment after ECT tends to be temporary. One study followed up on 10 adolescents who had received ECT an average of three and a half years earlier. Six of the ten had complained of memory impairment immediately after treatment, but only one complained of continued problems at the follow-up.

Psychological tests did not reveal any differences in cognitive functioning between severely depressed adolescents who had received ECT and others who had not. Despite the controversies surrounding ECT, it appears to help many people who do not respond to antidepressant drugs. Nonetheless, it is a drastic treatment that is used only in the most extreme cases.

Reading Check **Identify Cause and Effect** Why did the use of ECT drop off?

Psychosurgery

Psychosurgery is brain surgery that is performed to treat psychological disorders. The best-known technique, **prefrontal lobotomy,** has been used to reduce the agitation and violence of people with severe psychological disorders.

The method was developed by Portuguese neurologist António Egas Moniz in the 1930s. The procedure involves cutting the nerve pathways in the brain between the prefrontal lobes and the thalamus. However, the treatment produces several serious side effects, including distractibility, reduced learning ability, overeating, apathy, social withdrawal, seizures, reduced creativity, and occasionally even death. At the beginning of this section, you read about Howard Dully, who had a lobotomy at the age of 12. Since the procedure, he has suffered from feeling different, abnormal, and ashamed.

It is not surprising that prefrontal lobotomy is an even more controversial procedure than ECT. Experts challenged the original rationale behind the surgery, and early success rates were exaggerated by advocates of the procedure. Because of the side effects of the surgery and the availability of antipsychotic drugs, prefrontal lobotomies are now performed only rarely.

Drug therapies, and to a limited extent ECT, seem to be effective for some psychological disorders that do not respond to psychotherapy. It is important to realize, however, that medications and electric shocks cannot help a person develop more rational ways of thinking or solve relationship problems. Changes such as these are likely to require psychotherapy.

Reading Check **Summarize** What is the best-known technique of psychosurgery?

Complete a Webquest at thinkcentral.com on lobotomies.

Online Quiz THINK central thinkcentral.com

SECTION 4 Assessment

Reviewing Main Ideas and Vocabulary

1. **Describe** How are antianxiety drugs used?

2. **Identify** Which treatment for psychological disorders was introduced in the 1930s by Ugo Cerletti and Lucio Bini?

3. **Identify Main Ideas** What are some of the side effects of lobotomies?

Thinking Critically

4. **Explain** What are the three major biological treatments for psychological disorders?

5. **Draw Conclusions** Why is electroconvulsive therapy a controversial treatment for psychological disorders?

6. **Categorize** Using your notes and a graphic organizer like the one below, describe the type of biological therapy that might be used for each of the following: panic disorder, bipolar disorder, schizophrenia, and severe depression.

Biological Therapy
Drug Therapy:
ECT:
Psychosurgery:

FOCUS ON WRITING

7. **Narrative** Have you ever seen a film or television show in which a person has been subjected to ECT? Write a paragraph in which you describe the movie or TV show. If you haven't seen such a show, write a story about what you imagine the procedure to be like.

The Over-Prescription of Drugs

Antipsychotic drugs are being prescribed for young and old at an increasingly high rate, even though the effects of these drugs on the young in particular have not been studied carefully. Dr. William Cooper is a Vanderbilt University pediatrician and a co-author of a study of antipsychotic drug use. He believes that antipsychotic drugs are being prescribed without a full understanding of their possible risks and side effects (Cooper et al., 2004).

The Vanderbilt study focused on the use of antipsychotic drugs among low income children. It found that for patients covered by Medicaid there was an incentive to prescribe medication because Medicaid provides complete coverage for drug therapy.

The behavioral problems that drugs are being used to treat include attention deficit hyperactivity disorder (ADHD), conduct disorders, autism, and depression. The study found, however, that the medications had not been studied carefully enough to prove that they work safely in children.

This study raises questions about the financial motives of those involved in prescribing antipsychotic drugs. Pharmaceutical companies stand to make billions of dollars if their products become even more widely used among the general population of children and adults. Those most at risk because of the overuse of antipsychotic drugs include children in the juvenile justice system, in a state's custodial care program, and the disabled.

A Duke University Medical Center study found that there is an increased use of antipsychotic drugs in pediatric populations. One of the concerns raised by the Duke study was the use of drug therapy to treat behavioral problems. The study found that antipsychotic drugs were used among 267.1 per 100,000 subjects aged 19 and younger (Curtis and Masselink, et al., 2005). Eighty percent of the young patients who were put on antipsychotic drugs were males.

For both adults and children, there are potential side effects to these medications. These negative side effects include weight gain, nervous problems, heart rhythm irregularities, diabetes, tooth decay, and sleepiness. Another risk among those on antipsychotic drugs is depression.

And the overprescription of drugs is not just a problem among young patients. It has become so common that the Food and Drug Administration recently issued a warning that people taking antidepressants must be closely monitored for an increased risk of suicide. The advisory issued by the agency asked the drug manufacturers to put detailed warnings about an increased risk of suicidal behavior on the labels of ten antidepressants: Prozac, Zoloft, Paxil, Wellbutrin, Luvox, Celexa, Lexapro, Effexor, Serzone, and Remeron. The warning included both children and adults.

Pharmaceutical companies stand to make billions of dollars if their products become even more widely used.

Despite the concerns that have been raised, antipsychotic drugs continue to be widely used to treat behavior disorders. One reason is that many managed care plans provide complete coverage for drug therapy but limited coverage for psychiatric evaluation. This creates a financial incentive to use drug therapy.

Thinking Critically

1. **Explain** What are some of the side effects of antipsychotic drugs in children?

2. **Discuss** How many commercials for drugs do you see on television, and what role might that play in the over-prescription of drugs?

Identifying the Methods of Therapy

Reading and Activity Workbook

Use the workbook to complete this simulation.

As you have seen in the chapter, there are many methods of therapy. Which approach do you think is best?

1. Introduction

This simulation will help you review the different approaches to therapy and the methods implemented by clinical psychologists. You will work individually to review the approaches and then in small groups you will write therapy-session skits. After each therapy session is acted out, the class will guess what approach and method were being implemented. To complete this simulation, follow the steps below.

■ On your own, review the approaches to therapy covered in this chapter.

■ Work in groups to write a simulated therapy session using one of the methods of therapy described in this chapter.

■ After observing your classmates' simulations, determine what method of therapy is being implemented and from what approach that therapy comes.

2. Reviewing the Methods of Therapy

On your own, review the different approaches and methods of psychotherapy. As you review these approaches, take notes that include the following information:

■ Name of the therapy

■ Psychological approach of the therapy

■ Important terms and concepts

■ Goal of the therapy

For example, for psychoanalysis, your notes should look like this:

■ Name of therapy: Psychoanalysis

■ Approach: Psychoanalytic approach

■ Terms and concepts: free association, resistance, transference, dream analysis

■ Goal: to reduce anxiety by developing awareness of unconscious conflict

3. Creating Your Simulation

The goal of this part of the activity is to simulate a therapy session implementing one of the methods you have just reviewed. Working in groups organized according to your teacher's instructions, write a skit that simulates a therapy session. First, review the terms and concepts that are important when using this therapy as well as its goal. Next, determine which two members of your group will act out the simulation. Finally, write your skit. As you write your skit, each simulated therapy session should include the information listed below.

A. A clear identification of who is the client and who is the therapist

B. A clear description of why the client is in therapy

C. Terminology that indicates clearly the method of therapy in practice

Sample:

Therapist: Hi, I'm glad that you came to visit me today

Client: Thank you. I wish I didn't have to be here.

Therapist: Why don't you explain to me why you are here?

Client: I've been experiencing a lot of anxiety lately. I've been getting angry really easily and I'm not sure why.

Therapist: Well, why don't you try to relax on the couch over there? When you are ready, just tell me the first thing that comes to mind.

4. Determining Methods of Therapy Being Simulated

After observing each simulation, be prepared to guess which type of therapy was being implemented. Do not blurt out your guesses while the skit is being performed. Give everyone a chance to process the information. For each skit, be prepared to answer the following questions:

▦ Which type of therapy was being simulated?

▦ From which approach does that therapy come?

▦ What language was used during the session, and what does it indicate about the type of therapy?

▦ What was the goal of the session?

5. Discussion

What did you learn from this simulation? Hold a group discussion that focuses on the following questions:

▦ Overall, how successful was the class at determining which method of therapy was being practiced?

▦ Were some methods of therapy particularly easy to determine? If so, which ones and why?

▦ Were some methods of therapy particularly difficult to guess? If so, which ones and why?

▦ Which methods of therapy do you think are most effective?

▦ How do you think therapists determine which method to practice in a given situation?

APPROACHES AND METHODS OF THERAPY

- Psychoanalysis
- Humanistic therapy
- Person-centered therapy
- Nondirective therapy
- Rational-emotive behavior therapy
- Beck's cognitive therapy
- Counterconditioning
- Operant conditioning
- Drug therapy
- Electroconvulsive therapy
- Psychosurgery

A client reclines on a couch and talks about his problems while his therapist takes notes.

Comprehension and Critical Thinking

SECTION 1 (pp. 534–538)

1. a. Define Which is the only type of professional therapist who can prescribe medication?

b. Explain How does psychotherapy help troubled individuals?

c. Elaborate Why is providing a trusting relationship important in psychotherapy?

SECTION 2 (pp.539–542)

2. a. Identify Who developed person-centered therapy in the early 1950s?

b. Explain What is free association?

c. Evaluate What is an example of a transference relationship and why might a therapist encourage such a relationship?

SECTION 3 (pp.544–548)

3. a. Identify Who developed rational-emotive behavior therapy?

b. Compare and Contrast What is the difference between the two counterconditioning techniques of systematic desensitization and aversive conditioning?

c. Elaborate Other than the examples given in the text, what is an example of the use of systematic desensitization?

SECTION 4 (pp. 549–552)

4. a. Describe What disorders are antidepressant drugs used to treat?

b. Explain When do therapists use electroconvulsive therapy?

c. Develop What are the advantages of treating depression with cognitive therapy instead of with antidepressant drugs?

Reviewing Vocabulary

Match the terms below with their correct definitions.

5. psychotherapy

6. free association

7. latent content

8. humanistic therapy

9. active listening

10. aversive conditioning

11. coping skills

12. antianxiety drug

13. psychosurgery

A. the hidden meaning in a dream

B. therapy intended to help individuals reach their full potential

C. brain surgery performed to treat psychological disorders

D. drugs prescribed to help people with anxiety disorders

E. ability to contend with difficulties successfully

F. therapy in which a positive response to a stimulus is replaced with a negative response

G. psychologically based therapy

H. psychoanalytic technique in which the analyst asks the client to relax and then to say whatever comes to mind

I. communication technique in which the listener repeats, rephrases, and asks for clarification of the statements made by the speaker

INTERNET ACTIVITY ✳

14. How might the social and cultural conditions of Freud's time have influenced his ideas? Use the Internet to research how the social and cultural conditions of Vienna, Austria, in the late 1800s and early 1900s influenced Freud's ideas about the causes of psychological problems. Write a brief summary of what you learn.

Psychology in Your Life

15. How might belief in the assumption that "I must be loved by everyone to be happy" lead to unreasonable expectations and feelings of depression? Think about a situation in which someone you know seems to be operating on that assumption. Then write a short paragraph describing the situation and what course of action you might recommend to that person.

SKILLS ACTIVITY: INTERPRETING CARTOONS

Study the cartoon below. Then use the information to help you answer the questions that follow.

Victoria Roberts

"She said, 'I'll go if you go,' and I said, 'I'll go if you go,' and here we are."

16. Explain In the typical psychoanalytic encounter, how many people are in the room, and who are they?

17. Elaborate What does the cartoon suggest about people's attitude toward therapy?

 WRITING FOR AP PSYCHOLOGY

Use your knowledge of methods of therapy to answer the question below. Do not simply list facts. Present a clear argument based on your critical analysis of the question, using appropriate psychological terminology.

18. Briefly describe each of the following aspects of person-centered therapy.
- nondirective
- active listening
- unconditional positive regard

Connecting Online

Visit **thinkcentral.com** for review and enrichment activities related to this chapter.

Quiz and Review

ONLINE QUIZZES
Take a practice quiz for each section in this chapter.

WEBQUEST
Complete a structured Internet activity for this chapter.

QUICK LAB
Reinforce a key concept with a short lab activity.

APPLYING WHAT YOU'VE LEARNED
Review and apply your knowledge by completing a project-based assessment.

Activities

eACTIVITIES
Complete chapter Internet activities for enrichment.

INTERACTIVE FEATURE
Explore an interactive version of a key feature in this chapter.

KEEP IT CURRENT
Link to current news and research in psychology.

Online Textbook

 Learn more about key topics in this chapter.

Clinical Psychologist

A child displaced by Hurricane Katrina works with Karla Leopold, an art therapist, in Baker, Louisiana.

Clinical psychologists work in a wide range of settings to help people with various psychological problems. This flexible career is growing in popularity with psychology graduates.

About half of all graduate degrees in psychology are awarded in the field of clinical psychology. Therefore, you could say that clinical psychology is the most popular branch of psychology. Some clinical psychologists work with individuals who suffer from severe psychological disorders, while others limit their practices to treating people with less severe behavioral or adjustment problems. In the course of their work, clinical psychologists may deal with such diverse problems as severe depression, juvenile delinquency, drug abuse, marital problems, or eating disorders.

Many clinical psychologists with doctoral degrees have private practices, where they see clients who voluntarily come to them for treatment. Others, however, work in veterans' hospitals, mental health clinics, or prisons, where they are generally assigned to a specific number of patients.

Some clinical psychologists teach—primarily in universities or medical schools—where they pass on their experience and knowledge to others, rather than apply their skills directly. They also add to knowledge in the field by conducting research and publishing their findings. Some clinical psychologists conduct workshops and train business leaders or other professionals.

Clinical psychologists may be self-employed. Or, they may be hired by government, business, schools, universities, hospitals, or nonprofit organizations. They may be either consultants or full-time employees. Because clinical psychology is extremely flexible, it is becoming more competitive, as is admission to strong graduate programs.

You may confuse clinical psychologists with psychiatrists. The distinction is a significant one. In treating their patients, clinical psychologists may conduct interviews, practice methods of psychotherapy, and administer and interpret psychological tests. They do not, however, prescribe medication or administer other kinds of biological therapy.

Psychiatrists, on the other hand, are medical doctors who specialize in the treatment of psychological disorders. By law, only psychiatrists can prescribe medication to their clients.

Applying APA Style

 APA Style THINK central thinkcentral.com

Many clinical psychologists publish articles in professional journals in which they discuss people who have various psychological disorders and physical disabilities. In keeping with guidelines from the **American Psychological Association (APA)**, the writers try to eliminate negative or insulting language—whether intentional or unintentional—when referring to these persons. For example, psychologists speak of a person with schizophrenia rather than of a schizophrenic. The implication is that the person being discussed is first and foremost a human being. The person's disorder is secondary.

Through Think Central you can find APA style guidelines and more on using respectful language when discussing people with psychological disorders. Review the APA guidelines. Then write several phrases that are not respectful along with phrases that show proper respect. An example is provided for you.

Problematic Phrase	Preferred Phrase
mentally ill person	person with a mental illness

UNIT 7 Social Psychology

SHAPING
THE BLACK EXPERIENCE

W. E. B. Du Bois

W. E. B. Du Bois was one of the most influential educators, writers, and social leaders in American history. He was born in Massachusetts in 1868, just five years after President Abraham Lincoln issued the Emancipation Proclamation.

In 1903 Du Bois published a classic work titled *The Souls of Black Folk*. The book is partly autobiographical, and in the following excerpt, Du Bois reveals how he felt when he first learned, as a schoolboy, that he was "different from the others" and "shut out from their world."

"It is in the early days of rollicking boyhood that the revelation first bursts upon one, all in a day, as it were. I remember well when the shadow swept across me. I was a little thing, away up in the hills of New England. . . In a wee wooden schoolhouse, something put it into the boys' and girls' heads to buy gorgeous visiting-cards—ten cents a package—and exchange. The exchange was merry, till one girl, a tall newcomer, refused my card. . . Then it dawned upon me with a certain suddenness that I was different from the others; or like, mayhap, in heart and life and longing, but shut out from their world by a vast veil. I had thereafter no desire to tear down that veil, to creep through; I held all beyond it in common contempt, and lived above it in a region of blue sky and great wandering shadows. That sky was bluest when I could beat my mates at examination-time, or beat them at a foot-race. . ."

The U.S. government has passed many laws against discrimination, and progress in race relations has been achieved since Du Bois published his book. However, racial prejudice still exists. The National Association for the Advancement of Colored People (NAACP) and other groups continue to work to eliminate discrimination in American society.

Almost 100 years after Du Bois's classic work, Neil de Grasse Tyson published *The Sky Is Not the Limit*. This story tells how and why an African American kid from the Bronx came to be a Ph.D. astrophysicist and one of the most sought-after and respected scientific experts and public intellectuals of his generation.

In his book, de Grasse Tyson tells about an undergraduate classmate at Harvard who told him that "blacks in America do not have the luxury of your intellectual talents being spent on astrophysics." Was he wasting his talents? While still working on his doctoral dissertation, de Grasse Tyson made his first television appearance— explaining the significance of several explosions detected on the Sun. Later, as he watched himself on TV, he saw something he found remarkable:

SOCIAL COGNITION

"A scientific expert on the Sun whose knowledge was sought by the evening news. The expert on television happened to be black. . . At no [time] could I recall a black person (who is neither an entertainer or an athlete) being interviewed as an expert on something that had nothing whatever to do with being black."

His uncertainty about his intellectual pursuits was gone. He found that he could best serve the African American community by combating what he calls "the latent supposition that blacks as a group are just not as smart as whites." Neil de Grasse Tyson could use his expertise to set an admirable example and refute a deeply held stereotype. Such stereotypes and related topics are the subjects of this chapter.

Neil de Grasse Tyson

What do you think?

1. What do you think Du Bois meant when he said he was "shut out from their world by a vast veil"?

2. Do you feel there is still prejudice, like the attitude de Grasse Tyson faced, about people's intellectual abilities?

Chapter at a Glance

SECTION 1: Attitudes

■ Attitudes are beliefs and feelings that can affect how people behave in certain situations.

■ Attitudes develop in a number of ways throughout people's lives. Sometimes behaviors follow attitudes, and sometimes attitudes follow behaviors.

SECTION 2: Persuasion

■ Persuasion is the direct attempt to influence others' attitudes.

■ People can be persuaded via the central route, using evidence and logic, or via the peripheral route, using positive and negative associations and cues.

SECTION 3: Prejudice

■ A prejudice is a generalized attitude toward a specific group of people. Prejudiced attitudes are based on stereotypes, which can then lead to discrimination.

■ People can overcome prejudice by learning about others and by speaking up when others communicate or behave in prejudicial ways.

SECTION 4: Social Perception

■ People form attitudes about one another based on their social perceptions. First impressions play a large role in this process.

■ In general, people tend to judge the behaviors of others more harshly than they do their own behavior. They also tend to attribute different motives to others than they do to themselves.

■ The multiple forms of nonverbal communication have important parts in social perception.

SECTION 5: Interpersonal Attraction

■ Attraction is the process by which people are drawn to others who appeal to them in a number of ways.

■ People are attracted by physical appearance and by similarity in personal background and attitudes.

■ Attraction often leads to friendship or to romantic relationships.

Attitudes

Before You Read

Main Idea
Attitudes are an important aspect of our psychological lives because they are a major motivator for how we behave and view the world.

Reading Focus
1. What are some basic concepts in understanding attitudes?
2. How do attitudes develop?
3. How are attitudes and behaviors related?

Vocabulary
attitude
cognitive evaluation
cognitive anchor

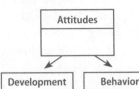 Use a graphic organizer like this one to take notes on attitudes.

Attitudes → Development / Behavior

Attitudes in Action

PSYCHOLOGY CLOSE UP

Why might you ignore your own beliefs? We all have certain attitudes that influence how we behave and how we view the world. You might have acquired some of your attitudes as a young child. Others may have developed later in life as you observed your friends' behavior or thought about something you saw, heard, or read. Regardless of how you developed your attitudes, though, you might not always behave according to your beliefs.

This contradictory behavior can be puzzling. Take the act of blood donation, for example. A person may have a positive attitude toward giving blood because he or she knows that it can help sick or injured people. But what if

the person is afraid of needles? For some people, a fear of needles can outweigh any positive attitude toward blood donation.

You're more likely to act according to your attitudes if your beliefs are very strong or if you have a strong personal interest in something. The Greenpeace workers shown in the photograph above, for example, are probably firm believers in the Greenpeace mission—to protect the natural environment and solve environmental problems. In this case, their attitudes about the importance of environmental protection are strong enough to motivate their behavior. In this section, you will learn more about the effects of attitudes on behavior. ■

Understanding Attitudes

Attitudes are beliefs and feelings about objects, people, and events that can affect how people behave in certain situations. A person's attitude about strangers, for example, can influence how that person feels and behaves around people he or she does not know. If a person believes that strangers are dangerous, that person is likely to feel afraid around strangers and may try to avoid situations where he or she is likely to meet new people. On the other hand, if a person believes that strangers are people just like him or her, that person is more likely to feel open to strangers and try to know them better.

Attitudes are a major aspect of social cognition. In fact, our attitudes may be the primary motivator for how we behave and how we view the world. They affect who we are friends with, how we vote, where we live, what we eat, what kind of work we choose, and many other decisions that are central to who we are.

Attitudes are such an important aspect of our psychological lives because they foster strong emotions, such as love or hate. Attitudes can also vary greatly. A person belonging to a particular cultural group may have attitudes that have been shaped by the traditional physical environment of that group. The field of social psychology is devoted to studying human interactions, of which attitude development is prominent. Social psychologists also study areas such as communication, competition, leadership, and cooperation.

Under certain circumstances, a person's attitudes can change. They tend to remain stable, however, unless that person is strongly encouraged to change them. This section examines several aspects of attitudes—how they develop, how they affect behavior, and how behavior affects them.

Reading Check **Define** What are attitudes?

How Attitudes Develop

People often have attitudes about things they have never experienced directly. People may be opposed to war or capital punishment, for example, even though they have no personal experience of either event. Where do such attitudes come from?

Attitudes develop in several ways. Conditioning, observational learning, cognitive evaluation, and the use of cognitive anchors all play roles in the development of attitudes.

Conditioning Learning through conditioning plays an important role in acquiring attitudes. Children are often reinforced for saying and doing things that are consistent with the attitudes held by their parents, teachers, and other authority figures. For example, parents who believe that it is important to share with others may praise, or reinforce, a child who shares a toy with a friend. Through such conditioning, the child acquires an attitude about the importance of sharing.

Observational Learning People also acquire attitudes through observation. For example, teens may observe that classmates who dress, talk, or act in certain ways seem to be admired by their peers. These teens may adopt the same ways of dressing, talking, or acting because they have learned through observation that doing so might lead to acceptance and approval. Commercial advertising relies heavily on observational learning to shape our attitudes. For example, by seeing commercials on TV, we learn that one brand of cola is cooler or more fun than the other.

Cognitive Evaluation People often evaluate evidence and form beliefs on the basis of their evaluations. This process, which is known as **cognitive evaluation,** also plays a role in the development of attitudes. People evaluate evidence that comes from many sources.

Part of the process of cognitive evaluation is learning to examine data carefully. When a news story, a politician, or a company provides information—a set of statistics or the results of a scientific study—the end user should ask if the information was gathered properly. For example, bias can be introduced into a survey by asking leading questions, or certain groups of people can be left out of the survey group, and so on. These types of bias can accidentally or purposely skew the survey's results.

Another question to consider is what, if anything, does the person or organization presenting the information have to gain if readers believe it? If, for example, a gum maker's company lab says their gum improves chewers' overall health, is it necessarily true or false?

You cannot know for certain, but there is good reason for healthy skepticism. The fact that the company runs the lab and stands to profit from one result more than another raises issues involving scientific independence and interference.

People are especially likely to evaluate evidence if they think they will have to justify their own attitudes to other people. For example, a teen who wants an after-school job may evaluate the evidence about working if he knows he will have to justify it to his parents. He may ask friends who have part-time jobs how they handle the extra responsibility.

Cognitive Anchors and Animal Rescue

"We made a promise that what happened in Hurricane Katrina would never happen again."

Amanda St. John, founder of the animal rescue group MuttShack, and her dedicated volunteers helped save over 3,000 abandoned pets in New Orleans after Katrina hit. Sadly, many thousands more could not be saved. Kindness to animals is a cognitive anchor Ms. St. John and her volunteers share—one that drives their desire to help animals in need. *How might MuttShack volunteers interpret an event such as Hurricane Katrina differently than other people?*

Cognitive Anchors A person's earliest attitudes tend to serve as **cognitive anchors,** or persistent beliefs that shape the ways in which he or she sees the world and interprets events. Cognitive anchors tend to keep a person's attitudes from changing. This is less true for attitudes that are only slightly different from the ones we hold. People may make several small changes in attitude over time that together add up to a significant change. People who hold on to cognitive anchors for decades, however, rarely adopt significantly new attitudes. In other words, no amount of cognitive evaluation is likely to cause your grandfather to stray from the baseball team he has supported since childhood.

Reading Check **Identify Main Ideas** What are two of the four ways that people's attitudes develop?

Attitudes and Behavior

The definition of *attitudes* suggests that people's behaviors are always consistent with their attitudes. However, the link between attitudes and behavior is not always strong. In fact, people often behave in ways that contradict their attitudes. For example, many people know that smoking cigarettes and drinking alcohol excessively are harmful to their health, yet they still smoke and drink excessively. Likewise, most people realize that it is dangerous and illegal to drink and drive, yet some do it just the same.

When Behavior Follows Attitudes People are more likely to behave in accordance with their attitudes if the attitudes are specifically tied to the behaviors. For example, someone who believes that aerobic exercise is necessary to prevent heart disease is more likely to exercise regularly than someone who believes that only a healthy lifestyle is important for good health. Similarly, strong attitudes are better predictors of behavior than weak attitudes. Students who believe strongly in the value of hard work, for example, may be more likely to study than students who believe less strongly in the benefits of hard work.

People are also more likely to behave in accordance with their attitudes when they have a vested interest, or a personal stake, in the outcome of a behavior. People are more likely to go to the polls and vote on an issue, for example, if the issue affects them directly. That is one reason why issues such as tax reform often have high voter turnouts.

Attitudes are more likely to guide behavior when people are aware of them, particularly if the attitudes are put into words and spoken. Verbalizing and repeating an attitude makes it come to mind quickly, and attitudes that come to mind quickly are more likely to influence how people act. People are also more likely to be aware of attitudes that affect them emotionally. Someone who loves animals is likely to be aware of his attitude about animal rights, for example. Likewise, someone who is angered by destruction of the environment is likely to be aware of her attitudes about recycling and conservation.

When Attitudes Follow Behavior Most of the time attitudes come first and behavior follows. However, sometimes the reverse is true. In some situations, attitudes follow behavior.

Attitudes are especially likely to follow behavior when people begin to behave, or are encouraged to behave, in ways that conflict with their attitudes. In such situations, people may suffer cognitive <u>dissonance</u>, an uncomfortable feeling of tension that may accompany a contradiction between attitudes and behaviors. In order to reduce the tension they feel, people may try to justify their behavior and change their attitudes to fit their acts.

Most people can relate to a classic example of cognitive dissonance: buyer's remorse. Let's say you have your eye on a used car—a cool old European van from the 1970s. You have fallen in love with the way it looks and the idea of piling your friends into it and driving around town. Once you buy it, though, you start to realize a few things. It does not have air bags or any other safety features to speak of, it is very uncomfortable on long trips, and there is no air conditioning. You experience cognitive dissonance because you were in love with this vehicle and now you are starting to have negative feelings.

How do you eliminate the dissonance? You might tell yourself that safety was never really your thing anyway; you like to live on the edge. Also, this car is mainly for short trips, so it doesn't really matter if you're uncomfortable on the occasional road trip. And who needs air conditioning? It's more fun to have the windows down and blast your music anyway. All of these are ways to overwhelm your negative thoughts and get back to the positive feelings you had before. You could also eliminate the dissonance by selling the car and buying one that meets more of your needs. But that is a much more difficult solution.

> **Reading Check Recall** How do attitudes and behavior shape one another?

ACADEMIC VOCABULARY

dissonance lack of agreement or consistency; conflict

SECTION 1 Assessment

Reviewing Main Ideas and Vocabulary

1. **Define** What are attitudes?

2. **Recall** How does conditioning help to shape people's attitudes?

3. **Explain** How does verbalizing an attitude make it more likely that the attitude will guide your behavior?

Thinking Critically

4. **Compare** In your own words, describe observational learning and cognitive anchors as influences on attitude formation. Are they at all similar? Why?

5. **Rank** Give three examples of cognitive anchors that you recognize in yourself. Now rank them from one to three on likeliness that your attitude could be changed (with 3 being most likely). Explain your rankings and whether you think any of these attitudes could actually ever be changed.

6. **Analyze** Using your notes and a graphic organizer like the one below, explain whether you think cognitive anchors are likely to be subjects of cognitive dissonance.

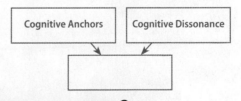

| Cognitive Anchors | Cognitive Dissonance |

FOCUS ON WRITING

7. **Narrative** Think about a time when you experienced cognitive dissonance but changed your attitudes to fit with your behavior. Write one paragraph describing the situation and another analyzing the situation. Do you feel good about how you changed your attitude?

Attitudes and Achievement

How do you feel about school? Do you put considerable care and effort into your studies? Are you enthusiastic about what you're learning in your classes? Do you feel confident that you'll be successful academically? According to a recent study, your attitude and behavior can have a direct impact on your academic achievement.

Many researchers have conducted studies to find out what factors boost academic achievement. One recent study explored the effect of two factors on academic achievement, particularly in reading and mathematics (Akey, 2006). Researchers looked at students' engagement in school, or their level of participation and interest, and at students' own view of their academic success.

The study involved about 450 high-school students. Researchers used test score records and student surveys to obtain the data for the study. The survey questions focused on students' attitudes toward and behavior in school.

Like previous research has found, this study demonstrated that students who were more engaged in their schoolwork and who had a more positive view of their ability to be successful in their studies achieved greater academic success. However, unlike previous research, the study found that students' belief in their ability to succeed had a much greater impact on academic achievement than how involved students were in their schoolwork.

Not surprisingly, researchers have found that the two factors are closely linked. Students who believe they have the ability to succeed are generally more involved in school. On the other hand, those who believe they lack the ability to succeed generally make few attempts to get involved in school-related activities.

Based on the findings, how can schools help to foster academic achievement? The study suggests that schools should be set up specifically to support and instill feelings of success in students. The study found that caring, supportive teachers play a key role by providing an atmosphere in which students feel confident about their ability to succeed.

High expectations and clearly defined rules and guidelines also contribute to academic achievement. Students attending schools with high expectations tend to have greater academic success. Having clear expectations helps students become confident in their ability to succeed and increases their involvement in school-related activities.

Students generally become more involved in schoolwork when activities include student interaction. Activities that encourage interaction, such as debates and group projects, rather than activities that require students to work in isolation, result in more engaged students.

The findings imply that the earlier schools instill in students confidence in their ability to succeed, the better off students will be. With a positive attitude and greater involvement in schoolwork, students are more likely to experience academic success.

Students are able to achieve award-winning results when schools have high expectations that students believe they can meet.

Thinking Critically

1. **Explain** How can schools instill in students an attitude of belief in their academic abilities?

2. **Discuss** Which of the two factors examined in the study do you think is more important to academic achievement? Why?

Current Research **THINK** central thinkcentral.com

Persuasion

Before You Read

Main Idea

People use a range of persuasive techniques to try to change other people's attitudes. These techniques can be direct, relying on logic or evidence, or indirect, relying on emotions or perception.

Reading Focus

1. What are the main methods of persuasion?
2. How do the message and the messenger relate to persuasion?
3. How do the situation and the audience affect persuasion?
4. How can one resist persuasive messages?

Vocabulary

persuasion
central route
peripheral route
two-sided argument
emotional appeal
sales resistance

TAKING NOTES Use a graphic organizer like this one to take notes on persuasion.

Persuasion

Persuading Others to **LIKE** You

PSYCHOLOGY CLOSE UP

What face do you want the world to see? Is there an image of yourself you like to project? How can you persuade others that the image you project is the real you? One way is through the social networking Web site Facebook.

The Psychology of Facebook, a course at Stanford University, was developed by persuasion psychologist Professor B. J. Fogg. The course examines various aspects of the popular site as a persuasive tool. One aspect is the use of profile pictures, the photograph on the front page of the Facebook entry. If a personal photograph is not attached to the allocated space, a question mark appears instead. Fogg proposes the idea that just the uncomfortable feeling of being identified with only a question mark persuades the user to attach his or her personal photograph.

The class also addresses the question of why individuals choose a particular photograph. What impression are they trying to project? Do they want to be regarded in a certain light—as strong, fun-loving, or serious? Fogg asks students to describe the image of themselves that they would want to communicate through their profile picture. The students' responses indicate that choosing the appropriate photograph is critical for projecting the impression the individuals want to impart and for persuading others to see them in a certain light. In this section you will learn more about methods of persuasion. ■

Methods of Persuasion

Attitudes tend to remain constant unless people are motivated to change them—for example, if they are persuaded to do so. **Persuasion** is a direct attempt to influence other people's attitudes or views. Parents, for example, may try to persuade their children to adopt the same values that they hold. Children, on the other hand, may try to persuade their parents to allow them more freedoms and privileges.

There are two basic ways to persuade people. The **central route** uses evidence and logical arguments to persuade people. Advertisements might point out the superior quality of a product, such as the superior taste and nutritional content of a breakfast cereal. Or a parent might use statistics on bicycle accidents to persuade a child to wear a helmet.

The **peripheral route** is indirect. It attempts to associate objects, people, or events with positive or negative cues. For example, an advertisement for athletic shoes might feature a famous athlete. The aim is to influence people to associate their positive feelings for the famous individual with the product or the message that is being endorsed. The most persuasive messages use both routes.

Reading Check **Recall** What are the two central routes of persuasion?

ELEMENTS OF PERSUASION

Persuasion is the attempt to influence or change people's attitudes or views. There are two basic ways to persuade people, and within each there are a number of elements and techniques.

Central Route	This direct method uses evidence and logical arguments to persuade people.
Peripheral Route	This indirect method attempts to make positive or negative associations using objects, people, or events.
The Message	The message stands alone in the central route. In a two-sided argument, for example, the message is straightforward but attempts to discredit opposing views.
The Messenger	The messenger plays an important role in the peripheral route. Messages delivered by trustworthy, attractive, or familiar people can help persuasive messages succeed.

Message and Messenger

In the central route, the message itself is most important. In the peripheral route, the message is important, but it does not stand alone. The messenger also plays an important role.

People present persuasive messages in a number of time-tested and very creative ways. For example, two-sided arguments tend to be more effective than one-sided arguments, especially when the audience is uncertain about its position on the issue. "Glittering generalities" can be offered as evidence which, when examined closely, doesn't amount to much. Also, emotional appeals can be very convincing.

Repetition Research shows that repeated exposure to a stimulus eventually results in a more favorable attitude toward that stimulus. For example, people respond more favorably to abstract art or classical music after being repeatedly exposed to it.

Advertisers, political candidates, and others who want to persuade people use repetition to encourage people to adopt a favorable attitude toward their product or ideas. Many television commercials are repeated over and over so that potential consumers will react favorably to the products—and buy them—when they see these items in the store. One might think that such repetition would offend or annoy viewers (and to some extent it does), but research suggests that commercials are more effective when they are repeated regularly. Similarly, political candidates who appear regularly in television commercials tend to receive more votes than candidates who appear less often in commercials.

Two-Sided Arguments A type of persuasive message that can be particularly effective is the **two-sided argument.** With this type, the messenger presents not only his or her side of the argument but also the opposition's side to discredit the opposition's views. For example, a cereal advertiser admits that its brand of cereal is not as sweet as competing brands and then explains how the less sweet taste is evidence that the product is more nutritious. Admitting weaknesses in this way makes the message seem more honest.

Presenting the other side can also undercut the opposition's stance. A two-sided argument

NO ONE EVER THINKS THEY'LL WAKE UP HERE. METH WILL CHANGE THAT.

MONTANA METH PROJECT

METH
not even once.

Appealing to Emotions

Public safety messages, such as this one, often appeal to emotions because they often deal with potentially tragic subjects and situations. The emotional appeal can also shock the viewer into agreement. *What emotional appeal is being used here? Is it effective? Why or why not?*

can convince the listener that he or she has already heard all the important points, even though only one side has been presented.

Emotional Appeals **Emotional appeals** persuade by arousing such feelings as loyalty, admiration, desire, jealousy, or fear rather than by convincing through evidence and logic. Thus, an emotional appeal is a peripheral route in persuasion.

Arousing fear is a particularly effective method of persuasion. Smokers are more likely to be convinced to quit smoking, for example, when they are presented with frightening photos of blackened lungs rather than dry, unemotional statistics on lung cancer. A politician may stir up fears to distract from real, more mundane problems. In general, appeals based on fear tend to be most effective when they are strong, when the audience believes them, and when the audience believes it can avoid the danger by changing its behavior.

Glittering Generalities The use of vaguely positive words and images in a message promotes good feelings, but what does it really say? Political campaigns often employ glittering generalities. Candidates might be described as "good for America," "the right person for our community," or a "person who

gets things done." None of these things cites specific evidence of ability or promises any notable result for the future.

Commercial advertisements also employ a wide range of glittering generalities when delivering their messages. For example, a soap maker may say that their product gives you "that mountain-fresh feeling." There's something vaguely appealing about that, but what does it really tell a potential buyer? A sausage maker's claim of "down-home goodness" conjures the image of a hearty breakfast on the farm, but does the message transmit any truly useful information?

Role of the Messenger Some people are more persuasive than others. Research shows that people are persuasive if they are

- experts. This makes the audience more likely to follow their advice.
- trustworthy. This makes the audience more likely to believe what they say.
- physically attractive. This makes the audience likely to pay attention to them.
- similar to their audience in ethnicity, age, and other physical characteristics. People are more likely to imitate others who appear similar to themselves.

Complete a Webquest at thinkcentral.com on sales resistance.

Messengers who stand to gain from their persuasive efforts are less likely than others to be effective. For example, if the president of a company says his or her company's product is the best one on the market, people are generally less likely to be persuaded by his or her arguments. An independent scientist, on the other hand, is a more convincing messenger.

Reading Check **Describe** In what kind of persuasion is the messenger important?

Situation and Audience

When a person is in a good mood, he or she is less likely to evaluate messages carefully. As a result, people tend to be more receptive to persuasion when they are feeling good. Thus, putting people in a good mood—with a compliment, for example—tends to boost the acceptance of persuasive messages.

Most messages are aimed at a specific audience. A political candidate is trying to reach the voters in his or her district, for example. Differences in age, sex, and other characteristics of the intended audience influence how the message should be delivered to be most persuasive. Emotional appeals may work better with children, for example, whereas logic may be more effective with adults.

Reading Check **Describe** How might the use of the situation and the audience easily be combined to aid in persuasion?

Resisting Persuasive Messages

Some people are less easily persuaded than others. For example, some people have developed an attitude called **sales resistance.** People possessing sales resistance have no trouble turning down requests to buy products or services. Other people have little or no sales resistance. They find it difficult to refuse a sales pitch or other types of requests.

Research suggests that two personality factors may be involved in sales resistance—self-esteem and social anxiety. People who find it easy to refuse requests tend to have high self-esteem and low social anxiety. They believe in themselves, stand up for what they want, and are not overly concerned about what other people think of them.

People who find it difficult to say no, on the other hand, are likely to have lower self-esteem and greater social anxiety. They may worry what salespeople will think of them, for example, or be concerned that the people requesting donations will be insulted if they refuse to give. People with low self-esteem and high social anxiety are also likely to be easily persuaded in situations other than sales and donations. For example, they may be more easily persuaded to engage in activities that go against their attitudes, beliefs, and values, such as using alcohol or other drugs.

Reading Check **Identify Main Ideas** How is self-esteem related to sales resistance?

Online Quiz THINK central thinkcentral.com

SECTION 2 Assessment

Reviewing Main Ideas and Vocabulary

1. **Recall** What is the significance of the audience when it comes to persuasion?

2. **Describe** What factors keep some people from developing sales resistance? Explain.

3. **Explain** Does delivering the same message over and over again aid in persuasion? What is this technique called, and how does it work?

Thinking Critically

4. **Contrast** Give brief explanations of the central route and the peripheral route of persuasion. How are they different?

5. **Support a Position** In your opinion, which of the two types of persuasion, the central route or the peripheral route, is more reputable? Give reasons to support your opinion.

6. **Analyze** Using your notes and a graphic organizer like this one, explain how both the central and peripheral routes relate to situation and audience.

Situation		Audience	
Central	Peripheral	Central	Peripheral

FOCUS ON WRITING

7. **Descriptive** Write two paragraphs, one using glittering generalities and another using an emotional appeal. One should be a pitch to sell a medicine for arthritis, and the other should sell voters on a congressional candidate.

Prejudice

Before You Read

Main Idea

Prejudice occurs when people prejudge and stereotype other groups, and it can result in discrimination. Prejudice has deep-seated social and psychological causes that can be overcome.

Reading Focus

1. What attitudes and actions are part of the prejudicial view?

2. What are some of the causes of prejudice?

3. What are some ways that individuals can help overcome prejudice?

Vocabulary

prejudice
discrimination
scapegoat

TAKING NOTES Use a graphic organizer like this one to take notes on prejudice.

The Prejudicial View	Causes of Prejudice	Overcoming Prejudice

FIGHTING FIRES and PREJUDICE

PSYCHOLOGY CLOSE UP *Is there anything wrong with this picture?* Chances are, you do not see anything out of the ordinary in this photograph of female firefighters. But some people believe that women simply are not capable of being firefighters—or of being construction workers, police officers, soldiers, or any number of other traditionally male occupations. Indeed, women firefighters are a relatively recent phenomenon; there were few women firefighters in the United States before the mid-1970s, when lawsuits, government action, and changing attitudes helped open the doors to the nation's firehouses.

Even after women began proving their abilities as firefighters, they often faced prejudice and discrimination from their male co-workers, ranging from crude jokes to harassment to denial of training or promotion. In fact, one survey by the International Association of Women in Fire and Emergency Services found that 88 percent of women firefighters had experienced sexual harassment at some point in their careers. Even in the most progressive departments, like the one in San Diego, California, where this photograph was taken, women are still a minority and often face hazing. Prejudice based on sex, race, ethnicity, religion, or another category can have a profound effect on the people being discriminated against as well as on society at large. In this section, you will learn more about the causes and effects of prejudice. ■

The Prejudicial View

A type of attitude that causes a great deal of harm is prejudice. **Prejudice**—a generalized attitude toward a specific group of people—literally means "prejudgment." People who are prejudiced judge other people on the basis of their group membership rather than as individuals. People who are prejudiced may decide, for example, that one person is deceitful because he or she belongs to a particular ethnic group or that another person is highly intelligent because that individual belongs to another ethnic group. Prejudicial attitudes are based on stereotypes, and they often lead to harmful behavior known as discrimination.

Stereotypes Stereotypes are unchanging, oversimplified, and usually distorted beliefs about groups of people. People tend to develop or adopt stereotypes as a way to organize information about their social world. Stereotypes make it easier to interpret the behavior of others, even though the interpretations are often wrong. For example, if we expect an older man to be sexist because a sexist attitude is part of our stereotype of older males, then we are more likely to interpret his words and deeds as sexist.

Another reason people tend to develop stereotypes is because they assume that those who are different from themselves are similar to each other in many ways. Traits seen in some members of a group are incorrectly assumed to characterize all members of the group. An Asian American may think, for example, that all European Americans or all African Americans have similar personality traits, behavior patterns, or attitudes.

Stereotypes are harmful because they ignore people's individual natures and assign traits to them on the basis of the groups to which they belong. One of the many problems with stereotyping is that the traits assigned are usually negative. However, stereotypes can also include positive traits—such as the belief that members of a particular group are hard workers.

Statistically Speaking...

Opinions on Immigration In recent years, Americans' opinions of immigrants have become more negative. Some people harbor negative stereotypes about immigrants, generally in relation to employment and crime.

12% Percentage of Americans who feel that immigrants have a positive effect on job opportunities for them and their families

34% Percentage of Americans who feel that immigrants have a negative effect on job opportunities for them and their families

4% Percentage of Americans who feel that immigrants make the crime situation better

58% Percentage of Americans who feel immigrants make the crime situation worse

Source: Gallup, Inc.

AMERICANS' VIEWS OF ILLEGAL IMMIGRANTS

Over time, do immigrants pay their fair share of taxes, or do they cost taxpayers too much by using public services (hospitals, schools)?

Respondents by ethnic group, 2006

Respondents by ethnic group, 2008

■ Pay fair share ■ Cost taxpayers ■ No opinion

Source: Gallup, Inc.

Thinking Critically In your opinion, why did one ethnic group's opinions vary so greatly from the opinions of the others?

Interactive Feature THINK central thinkcentral.com

Stereotype threat is a phenomenon that occurs when members of a group are aware of a stereotype that says they cannot perform a certain task—along the lines of "white men can't jump." When they try to perform this task, knowledge of the stereotype causes them to perform worse than they normally would.

For example, researchers performed a study to investigate the stereotype that white athletes have more "sports intelligence," while African American athletes have more "natural athletic ability." When white and black athletes performed a physical task without reference to this stereotype, they both performed well. But when researchers told the subjects that the task measured "natural athletic ability," the white athletes performed less well. When researchers told subjects that the task measured "sports intelligence," the African American athletes' performance declined.

Stereotypes limit possibilities by discouraging the expression of the full range of an individual's talents, interests, and feelings. Even positive stereotypes can be harmful because they may put pressure on people to live up to unrealistic expectations.

Discrimination Prejudice often leads to negative behavior in the form of discrimination. **Discrimination** refers to the unfair treatment of individuals because they are members of a particular group. For example, people may be denied jobs, housing, voting privileges, or other rights because of their skin color, sex, or religion. But these are not the only forms of discrimination. In 2008, researchers showed that discrimination against overweight people is on the rise and now occurs more often than racial discrimination. Victims of every type of discrimination often begin to see themselves as inferior. Thus, they are likely to have low self-esteem. People with low self-esteem tend to have low expectations for themselves, thus reducing their chances for success.

Reading Check **Compare** What is the connection between stereotyping and discrimination?

Causes of Prejudice

Why are some people prejudiced and others are not? Psychologists and other researchers have studied the origins of prejudice and have found many potential causes.

Exaggerating Differences One reason some people are prejudiced is that they exaggerate how different others are from themselves. People tend to prefer (as friends and acquaintances) those who are similar to themselves and who share their attitudes. People who differ in one or several ways—in skin color or religion, for example—are often assumed to have attitudes and customs that are more different than they really are.

Justifying Economic Status People also tend to develop prejudices against those who belong to a different, often lower earning, economic group. Those in higher socioeconomic groups often justify their own economic superiority by assuming that people who have a lower economic status are inferior to them. They may believe that people who are worse off than themselves work less hard or are less motivated to succeed. Such beliefs may be used as an excuse for—and thus help maintain—existing injustices.

CASE STUDY
CONNECTION

The Black Experience
Neil de Grasse Tyson overcame stereotypical views of how he should use his intellect and became a leader in the African American community.

Protesting Hate Crimes
People protest a racist incident at Columbia University in 2007. A hangman's noose was placed on an African American professor's door. *Why do you think that people of all races protest against racism?*

Social Learning Children, like adults, acquire many attitudes from other people. They are especially likely to acquire the attitudes of their parents. Children tend to imitate their parents, and parents often reinforce their children when they do. In this way, parents who are prejudiced often pass along their prejudicial attitudes to their children.

Victimization Sometimes people who are the victims of prejudice feel empathy for others who are discriminated against. However, this is not always the case. In fact, some victims of prejudice try to gain a sense of power and pride by asserting their superiority over people that are even worse off than themselves. Thus, victimization may lead to further prejudice.

Scapegoating A **scapegoat** is an individual or group that is blamed for the problems of others because the real cause of the problems is either too complex, too powerful, or too remote to be confronted. The term *scapegoating* refers to aggression against the targeted group.

The scapegoat group is likely to have certain characteristics that make it a safe and highly visible target. Typically, scapegoats are people who are too weak to defend themselves or who choose not to return the attack. They are also likely to stand out because of their differences from majority groups.

Probably the best-known and most extreme example of scapegoating is the victimization of European Jews in the 1930s and 1940s. Nazi dictator Adolf Hitler blamed Jewish people for Germany's serious economic troubles. Under Hitler's leadership, millions of Jews were killed.

Reading Check **Identify** Name and describe three potential causes of prejudice.

Overcoming Prejudice

Although prejudice is difficult to overcome, it can be done. Increased contact among members of different groups is one of the best ways for people to develop less prejudicial attitudes. For example, when people work together to achieve common goals, they are likely to learn about one another as individuals, and this may weaken the stereotypes.

On an individual level, one can reduce prejudice by speaking up when other people act or talk in ways that reflect prejudicial attitudes. Individuals can also set an example of tolerance and understanding for others by their own words and actions.

Finally, prejudicial attitudes do not have to lead to discriminatory behavior. A person who is prejudiced can make a conscious effort to treat all people courteously and fairly. This, in turn, may help reduce the person's own prejudicial attitudes.

Reading Check **Recall** How can increased contact between groups help to lessen prejudice?

SECTION 3 Assessment

Online Quiz **THINK** central thinkcentral.com

Reviewing Main Ideas and Vocabulary

1. **Recall** How does a prejudiced person judge other people?

2. **Describe** How does stereotype threat affect individuals who are the subject of stereotypes?

3. **Define** What does the term *scapegoat* mean?

4. **Identify Cause and Effect** Explain the cause-effect relationship between prejudice and discrimination.

Thinking Critically

5. **Explain** Do prejudicial attitudes always lead to discriminatory behavior? Explain.

6. **Elaborate** Why do you think increased contact helps to overcome prejudice?

7. **Draw Conclusions** Using your notes and a graphic organizer like this one, use the strategies from "Overcoming Prejudice" to explain how to combat specific causes of prejudice.

Strategies for Overcoming Prejudice		
•		
•		
•		
Exaggerating Differences	Social Learning	Scapegoating

FOCUS ON WRITING

8. **Descriptive** Think of a story of discrimination from a novel or movie or from history or your community. Write a paragraph briefly describing the story. Then write a second paragraph linking the story to how and why prejudice and discrimination develop and how they can be overcome.

Seeds of Peace

What is the best way for people from regions of the world in conflict to change their attitudes about each other? The organization Seeds of Peace believes the solution lies in coming face to face with the people long considered to be enemies. Every summer, Seeds of Peace brings young people from war-torn regions of the world to a camp in Maine. The goal is for the participants to rise above deep-seated hatreds and overcome prejudices and negative attitudes.

Kids from the Middle East and the United States work together during a problem-solving exercise.

The Seeds of Peace is a nonprofit organization focused on helping teenagers from the world's conflict regions develop conflict-resolution skills. The organization was created by the late John Wallach, who witnessed and reported on regional conflicts during his 30-year career as a journalist. At a dinner party in 1993, Wallach proposed his program to the Israeli foreign minister, the Egyptian ambassador, and a representative of the Palestinian Liberation Organization (PLO). He challenged them to send groups of teenagers to participate in a summer camp in Otisfield, Maine. There, the teenagers would live and learn together. The camp opened that summer.

At first, the program included only Israeli and Arab teens from ten nations in the Middle East. Although the program initially focused on the Arab-Israeli conflict, it eventually included teens from other major conflict regions, such as South Asia and the Balkans.

The main focus of Seeds of Peace is to help participants develop the leadership skills required to advance reconciliation and coexistence in their troubled homelands. The camp hopes to do this by helping campers develop empathy and respect for those they consider different from themselves. Participants also develop much-needed communication and conflict-resolution skills.

The lakeside camp in Maine sits on 67 beautiful, wooded acres. The camp is often the first opportunity for these teenagers to meet the people whom they view as their enemies. For three weeks, the teenagers are paired with those they have been taught to hate. They live together in cabins, share meals, and participate in sports and creative activities. The teens also learn about each other through attendance at different types of religious services.

Facing and interacting with the very people they are supposed to hate provides the teens with opportunities to view each other as individuals. They examine issues that divide them. By engaging in activities and discussions, the teens have the opportunity to focus more on the similarities that unite them as individuals. And they learn that individuals can disagree on issues but still be friends.

The goal of the increased contact and interaction is to change long-held attitudes and prejudices and to break down stereotypes. Many participants form friendships that last beyond the camp. Often, after they have left the camp, they view it as one of the most important and memorable experiences of their lives.

Campers get acquainted and gain confidence in each other by doing "trust falls."

Thinking Critically

1. **Explain** How do participants learn about one another as individuals?

2. **Discuss** Why do you think the Seeds of Peace summer camp helps participants dispel prejudicial attitudes?

Social Perception

Before You Read

Main Idea

Social perception refers to how we see and what we feel about others. Social perception is heavily influenced by first impressions, differing vantage points, and nonverbal cues.

Reading Focus

1. To what extent do people form perceptions based on first impressions?

2. What does attribution theory say about how we perceive ourselves and others?

3. How does nonverbal communication influence our perceptions of others?

Vocabulary

social perception
primacy effect
recency effect
attribution theory
fundamental attribution error
actor-observer bias
self-serving bias

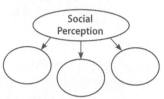

TAKING NOTES Use a graphic organizer like this one to take notes on social perception.

Social Perception

Can **Deception** Fool **Perception?**

PSYCHOLOGY CLOSE UP

Can your face give you away? Have you ever told a lie, only to have someone say, "I can tell by your face that you're lying"? A study by Canadian researchers showed that although people can be skillful at lying, it is hard to hide completely the emotions revealed on your face. One researcher concluded that "unlike body language, you can't monitor or completely control what's going on on your face."

The researchers focused on a case involving a Canadian man named Michael White. In 1995, White made a sobbing public appeal for the return of his missing wife. A few days later, claiming to be frustrated by the slow police search, White angrily said he would search for his wife himself and led searchers to her body. He was eventually convicted of his wife's murder. Upon carefully analyzing White's earlier emotional plea, the researchers detected flashes of anger and disgust on his face, signs that had not been noticed before. Most people saw only the expressions of concern and fear.

These involuntary facial movements and expressions are an example of nonverbal communication, which you'll read about in this section. ■

Forming Perceptions

Social perception refers to the ways in which people perceive one another. Social perception affects the attitudes people form toward one another.

A person will often wear his or her best clothes to a job interview or for a first date. Likewise, defense attorneys encourage their clients to dress well when they are in the courtroom and within view of the jury. The reason? People think that their first impressions of other people are accurate, and first impressions are often based on how a person looks. The tendency for people to form opinions of others on the basis of first impressions is called the **primacy effect.**

First impressions are important because they may have lasting effects on our relationships with others. If our first impression of a new acquaintance is negative because the person appears to be self-centered, for example, then we are unlikely to want to know the person better. However, if our first impression is positive—the person seems friendly and interesting—then we are more likely to want to develop a relationship with that person.

How people interpret the future behavior of others is also influenced by their first impressions. For example, someone who impresses us as intelligent and well educated is more likely to be taken seriously in future encounters than someone who comes across as superficial and silly.

The **recency effect** occurs when people change their opinions of others on the basis of recent interactions instead of holding on to their first impressions. If someone you initially thought was quiet tells long, loud stories the next three times you see him or her, the recency effect might come into play.

Reading Check Contrast How are the primacy and recency effects different?

Attribution Theory

People often explain the behavior of others and their own behavior differently. According to **attribution theory,** people tend to explain behavior in terms of either dispositional, or personality, factors or in terms of situational, or external, factors. For example, suppose you meet someone at a party who seems reluctant to talk to other people. You may assume that this person is either shy or conceited. This assumption would be a dispositional attribution. On the other hand, you may assume that this person is usually friendly but simply does not know anyone at the party. This would be a situational attribution.

Fundamental Attribution Error The tendency to overestimate the effect of dispositional causes for another person's behavior, and to underestimate situational causes, is referred to as the **fundamental attribution error.** It is a common mistake that affects many of our interactions with other people.

Actor-Observer Bias For the most part, people tend to attribute the behavior of others to dispositional, or internal, factors and to attribute their own behavior to situational, or external, factors. This tendency is called the **actor-observer bias.** Actor-observer bias occurs because we tend to judge others only by the behavior we witness, and people's behavior may not always be a true reflection of their personalities.

Suppose you observe a stranger acting in a rude manner. If this is your only encounter with the person, you are likely to assume that the stranger has a rude disposition—that is, that he or she is a rude person. In most other situations, however, the same person might behave in a very polite fashion. Observing the stranger in most other situations, then, would lead to the assumption that he or she has a polite, respectful disposition. This may in fact be the case. The person might have acted rudely only because of the circumstances. Perhaps the person was provoked. Or maybe he or she was irritable due to lack of sleep or a tough day at work.

Self-Serving Bias People are more likely to attribute their own successes to dispositional, or personality, factors. They are also more likely to attribute their failures to situational factors. This is called a **self-serving bias.** The self-serving bias allows individuals to place the blame for their failures on circumstances outside their control. At the same time, however, it enables them to take full credit for their successes.

Reading Check Explain What are dispositional factors and situational factors?

ACADEMIC VOCABULARY

bias a personal and sometimes unreasoned judgment

Nonverbal Communication

Research suggests that nonverbal communication, including body language and facial expressions, says more about us than we might wish. Can you read your classmates' nonverbal cues? Can you tell when they are not telling the truth? Read this Quick Lab to find out.

PROCEDURE

1. Write a five-sentence story about something you did recently—a trip to the store or a night out with friends, for example. Four of the sentences should be true, but one should be untrue. Don't give away your lie; make sure it's not too obvious. Highlight the sentence that isn't true.

2. Take a few minute to memorize your story.

3. Break into pairs. Sit face to face and take turns telling your story to each other. Don't make faces or try to throw off your listener. Tell it straight. If your listener wants to hear it again, read it a second time.

4. After hearing the story and gauging your partner's body language and facial expressions, take one guess at which sentence was untrue. On a sheet of paper, record the person's name and whether you guessed right.

5. Repeat steps 3 and 4 with three other classmates.

ANALYSIS

1. How many did you get right out of four?

2. As a class, discuss how nonverbal communication affected people's attempts to hide the truth. Also, if some classmates were not caught in their lies, discuss how they hid them from everyone else.

Quick Lab THINK central thinkcentral.com

Nonverbal Communication

It is not only what people say and do but how they say and do it that influences our perceptions of them. Forms of nonverbal, or unspoken, communication include facial expressions, gestures, posture, and the distance we keep from others. These and other forms of "body language" affect our perceptions of people, largely because they often indicate feelings. Feelings of sympathy or anger, for example, may be inferred from a concerned look or frown.

Some nonverbal forms of communication are learned early. Even young children can "read" a tone of voice, a facial expression, or other forms of nonverbal communication. Thus, before they understand all the words their parents are speaking, they can tell from nonverbal communication how their parents are feeling.

Without necessarily being aware of it, people use nonverbal communication to send messages to other people. They may even use nonverbal communication to mask their true feelings. For example, a parent who wishes to hide his fear or worry from his child might use nonverbal forms of communication, such as smiles and a relaxed bearing, to convince the child that all is well.

Physical Contact Touching is one way in which people communicate nonverbally. However, not all people use physical contact to communicate with others. For example, American women are more likely than American men to touch the people with whom they are interacting.

Touching can be an effective means of communication. In one experiment, college students who had filled out several personality questionnaires were asked by the experimenter to stay and help in another study. Students who were touched during the request were more likely to help in the subsequent study. In another study, waitresses received larger tips when they touched customers on the hand or shoulder while making change.

A study in a nursing home found that the ways in which people respond to touch depend on many factors. In the study, whether the residents responded to the touching favorably or unfavorably depended on the status of the staff member doing the touching, the type of touch, and the part of the body that was touched. Touching was not appreciated when it was inappropriate or forceful.

Eye Contact People can learn a great deal about the feelings of others from eye contact. When someone who is talking looks directly into the eyes of the listener, for example, the talker is usually telling the truth. Avoidance of eye contact, on the other hand, may indicate that the talker is lying. This is why a message is more believable and persuasive when the messenger makes eye contact with the audience.

One type of eye contact is gazing, or looking at someone with a steady, intent look that conveys eagerness or attention. Gazing usually is interpreted as a sign of friendliness, and it may greatly influence relationships.

Another type of eye contact is staring, or looking fixedly with wide-open eyes. Staring is usually interpreted as a sign of anger. Being the object of staring makes most people uncomfortable, and they may try to avoid the stare. For example, one study found that drivers who were stared at by other drivers at an intersection crossed the intersection faster when the light changed.

Cultural Considerations There is, however, considerable cultural variation in the use of nonverbal communication. The way Americans communicate nonverbally with one another is not necessarily the same way that people communicate in other parts of the world.

The distance people keep from one another varies in different cultures around the world. In general, Americans like to have a good deal of space. We generally position ourselves "at arm's length," or about two feet apart, from acquaintances. On the other hand, a person from Japan may feel that this is too close, preferring a distance of about three feet, while a person from Costa Rica will be quite comfortable with less than two feet of space.

Without taking cultural differences into account, it might be easy for an American to attribute the greater space needed by a Japanese person as a sign of coldness or arrogance. Likewise, the closeness of the Costa Rican might come off as aggression.

What is normal in terms of physical touching and eye contact also varies greatly between cultures. There is great variation within every culture, though. For example, even though most Americans prefer a good deal of personal space, it is not unusual to meet someone who stands only eight inches from you while chatting.

Regardless of what culture they live in, most people send unspoken messages that can greatly influence how other people see them—whether they know it or not. Thus, becoming more aware of nonverbal communication can increase our understanding of others.

Reading Check **Identify** What are three kinds of nonverbal communication that affect how people perceive one another?

SECTION 4 Assessment

Online Quiz THINK central thinkcentral.com

Reviewing Main Ideas and Vocabulary

1. **Define** What does social perception mean?

2. **Recall** What is the term for people's tendency to form opinions of others based on first impressions?

3. **Explain** The actor-observer bias describes what two basic human tendencies?

Thinking Critically

4. **Contrast** How are the primacy effect and the recency effect different?

5. **Develop** If you read that people in a country you were about to visit were more likely to touch people when communicating, would that change your behavior during your visit? Explain.

6. **Explain** Using your notes and a graphic organizer like this one, write two examples that illustrate the actor-observer bias.

Actor-Observer Bias	

FOCUS ON WRITING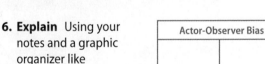

7. **Expository** Write a paragraph or two explaining why you think people perceive their own actions and those of others as described by attribution theory. Who benefits and to what end? Use examples you have witnessed or in which you have participated.

Interpersonal Attraction

Before You Read

Main Idea
People are attracted to others for many reasons. Personal appearance and personality traits play significant roles, as do similarity and reciprocity.

Reading Focus
1. How do concepts of physical appearance vary?
2. Why are similarity and reciprocity essential to attraction?
3. What is the difference between friendship and love?

Vocabulary
attraction
matching hypothesis
reciprocity
triangular model of love
intimacy
passion
commitment

TAKING NOTES Use a graphic organizer like this one to take notes on interpersonal attraction.

Physical Appearance	Similarity and Reciprocity	Friendship and Love

EYE OF THE BEHOLDER

Wodaabe men show off their eyes and white teeth—two important facets of their culture's ideal of male beauty—with their facial expressions.

PSYCHOLOGY CLOSE UP

Is beauty really in the eye of the beholder? What people consider attractive certainly varies among cultures. For the Wodaabe, a nomadic people in the west African countries of Niger and Nigeria, men are central to the group's ideas of beauty. Every year, young Wodaabe men take part in a festival called Gerewol. An important aspect of the festival is the beauty contests, in which the men show off their good looks to the Wodaabe women, who act as judges. Beauty for Wodaabe men consists of having large round eyes, a long straight nose, white teeth, and light skin.

The Wodaabe concept of beauty contrasts with such concepts in the West, where the beauty of women often receives more attention. Western cultures generally attribute beauty to women, rarely to men. Women are described as "beautiful," whereas, "handsome" describes men's physical appearance.

Whether or not you consider a certain individual attractive depends on what physical qualities you value. Although some concepts of what constitutes physical attractiveness are universal, many ideas of beauty vary from culture to culture. Wherever we live, concepts of beauty affect our personal relationships. ■

Physical Appearance

Attraction is the process by which people are drawn to others who appeal to them in a number of ways. Attraction to another person often leads to friendship or love. Factors that attract us to particular people as potential friends or partners include physical appearance, similarity to ourselves, and evidence that our attraction is returned.

Physical appearance tends to influence our choice of friends and partners. What qualities make someone physically attractive? There is no single answer. Some people may find a slim body build most attractive, while others may prefer a more muscular build. Some people find blond hair most attractive; others may prefer black hair. Still others don't care about hair color but prefer curly hair. Clearly, people's ideas of attractiveness differ.

Universals of Beauty Although there is variation among people in the types of traits they consider attractive, some aspects of attractiveness appear to be widely shared or even universal. For example, a smiling person is generally perceived to be more attractive than a person who is frowning.

Studies have also found that certain types of facial features are attractive to most people. In one study, both British and Japanese people were asked to identify the types of features they found most attractive in women. People from both cultures identified large eyes, high cheekbones, and narrow jaws as the most attractive types of facial features.

Another study investigated the kinds of faces that infants find most attractive. This was judged by the amount of time the infants spent looking at the faces of strangers—the longer the gaze, the greater the presumed attraction. As early as the age of two months, infants in the study seemed to prefer faces that were also rated by adults as most attractive. This evidence suggests that we do not "learn" what is attractive by being socialized in a particular culture. Other research, however, indicates that people do learn what features are considered attractive.

Differences in Body Shape Preference Although preferences for certain facial features may be universal, preferences for body shape vary greatly. There is, in fact, a great deal of variation in people's standard for attractiveness of body shape—both in the shape we prefer in others and the shape we perceive ourselves as having.

This was demonstrated in a study of college men and women. The men in the study tended to believe their own body shape closely approached the "ideal" shape that women find attractive. However, the women tended to believe that they were heavier than the "ideal" shape men find attractive.

The results of this study are important. They suggest that females are more likely than males to incorrectly think they are too heavy to be attractive. Not surprisingly, women are more likely than men to go on weight-loss diets, and they have far higher rates of eating disorders.

Evidence suggests that in the United States, many men prefer their partners to be shorter than themselves, whereas many women prefer their partners to be taller. On the job as well as in relationships, tallness tends to be perceived as an asset for men, whereas height in women tends to have less impact on their jobs.

This is not to say, however, that physical appearance will determine an individual's ability to succeed on the job or in relationships. The initial attraction one feels for another person may be based on the person's physical appearance. However, other traits usually become more important as people get to know one another better. Traits such as honesty, loyalty, warmth, and sensitivity tend to be more important than physical appearance in forming and maintaining long-term relationships.

Reading Check **Describe** What part of attraction is more universal, and what parts are more particular to individual preferences?

Similarity and Reciprocity

You may be familiar with the saying "Birds of a feather flock together." This saying suggests that we are usually attracted to people who are similar to us. On the other hand, another popular saying asserts "Opposites attract." Which of these two contradictory statements is true? Generally speaking, the answer is that we are more attracted to people who are similar to us.

Perceptions of Beauty

Customs governing how people beautify themselves differ widely among societies. The use of cosmetics and decoration with natural materials are common practices. Some societies have gone further, altering the skin or even bone structure. Clearly, some aspects of who and what is attractive are learned. **Which aspects of what our culture considers beautiful do you think are learned, and which are not?**

Scarification Scarification is practiced in some African societies. Often the process is undertaken at important stages in a girl's or a woman's life, such as puberty or marriage. The scarring is often done in intricate patterns to accentuate a person's beauty. The scars can also be markers of fertility, courage, and family or group identity.

Heian Japan In the Heian period in Japan (794–1185), makeup was an important part of the beauty regimen. Women whitened their faces with rice powder. They also shaved their eyebrows and replaced them with two inked thumbprints high on the forehead near the hairline. In addition, women artificially blackened their teeth.

Mayan Head Shaping Among the Maya of Central America, parents used boards and straps to flatten the foreheads of infants. One study of pre-Columbian Mayan remains showed head shaping in nearly 90 percent of the remains.

The Yanomamö Women among the Yanomamö people of South America beautify themselves with polished sticks inserted into facial perforations. They may also wear flowers, palm fronds, or other leaves or plants. Facial painting is reserved for special occasions, such as feasts.

Similarity in Physical Attractiveness According to the **matching hypothesis,** people tend to choose as friends and partners those who are similar to themselves in attractiveness. One reason for this may be the fear of rejection—the belief that someone more attractive will not be interested in them.

Similarity in Other Characteristics People's friends and partners also tend to be similar to them in race, ethnicity, age, level of education, and religion. One reason we choose friends and partners with backgrounds that are similar to our own is that we tend to live among people who are similar to ourselves. Thus, these are the people we are most likely to meet, to know, to date, and possibly to marry.

Another reason people tend to choose friends and partners with similar backgrounds is that such people often have similar attitudes as well—and people tend to be attracted to others with attitudes similar to their own. In fact, similarity of attitudes is a key contributor to attraction in both friendships and romantic relationships. Attitudes toward religion and children tend to be the most important factors in people's attraction to potential partners.

Reciprocity When we have feelings of attraction or affection for another person, we want that person to return those feelings. **Reciprocity** is the mutual exchange of feelings or attitudes. It applies to situations in which the person we like likes us back. In other words, our feelings are returned, or reciprocated. Like similarity, reciprocity is a powerful contributor to feelings of attraction.

Reciprocity of feelings is a major factor in forming romantic relationships, but it may also apply to casual encounters. Research shows that people are more open, warm, and helpful when they are talking with strangers who seem to like them.

Reading Check **Describe** Why is similarity important in developing relationships?

Friendship and Love

Friends are people for whom one has affection, respect, and trust. Most people value friends because of the rewards that friendship offers. For example, friends are concerned about one another and help and support one another when they can. As friendships develop, people may evaluate, consciously or unconsciously, how well the relationship is providing the rewards they seek in the friendship.

The people we choose as friends tend to be people with whom we have frequent contact, such as a fellow student. The people we find attractive and the people who approve of us are the people we are likely to choose as friends. In addition, they are likely to be similar to us in many ways, such as in attitudes, values, and their selection of other friends.

Friendship is different from love. We use the word *love* in several ways. Love refers to the feelings of attachment between children and parents, siblings, and other family members. Love also refers to feelings of patriotism for one's country or to feelings of passion about strongly held values, such as freedom. Most commonly, however, love refers to the feelings of mutual attraction, affection, and attachment shared by people who are "in love."

To better understand the relationships of people in love, psychologist Robert Sternberg developed the **triangular model of love.** Sternberg identifies seven types of love relationships: romantic love, liking, companionate love, empty love, fatuous love, infatuation, and consummate love. Each of the seven is characterized by at least one of three components: intimacy, passion, or commitment.

Intimacy refers to closeness and caring. It is reflected by mutual concern and by the sharing of feelings and resources. **Passion** refers to feelings of romantic and sexual attraction. In addition to verbal expressions of love, passion is reflected by many types of nonverbal communication, such as gazing, hugging, and kissing. **Commitment** refers to a couple's recognition that they are "in love" and want to be together, "for better or for worse."

Several of the seven forms of love are characterized by only one of the three components. For example, infatuated love is passion without intimacy or commitment, while empty love is commitment without passion or intimacy. Several others combine two aspects. Romantic love is intimacy and passion without commitment, for example. According to Sternberg, only consummate love, which is an ideal that is difficult to attain, is characterized by all three components.

Most couples start out with feelings of physical attraction that may develop into passion. If they are compatible, their intimacy and passion may grow. Eventually, they may decide to make a commitment to each other. Thus, from dating to a steady relationship to marriage, love changes as our relationships endure, deepen, and become a more important part of our lives.

Reading Check **Analyze** What are two ways in which friendship and love are related?

SECTION 5 Assessment

Online Quiz  thinkcentral.com

Reviewing Main Ideas and Vocabulary

1. **Recall** Are people's feelings about attractiveness inborn or learned? Explain.

2. **Define** What is the matching hypothesis? Give a reason why it influences attitudes and actions the way it does.

3. **Compare and Contrast** How does the way that women view their body shape compare with the way that men view their body shape? How does this affect women?

Thinking Critically

4. **Draw Conclusions** Why is reciprocity of feeling so important—even for casual encounters?

5. **Support a Position** Why do you think it is that, although physical attraction is initially crucial, traits such as honesty and loyalty later become more important to a relationship?

6. **Analyze** Using your notes and a graphic organizer like this one, show how similarity and reciprocity can lead to friendship and love.

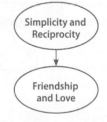

FOCUS ON WRITING

7. **Expository** If the importance of similarity to the development of relationships is so important, what do you think accounts for the endurance of the saying "Opposites attract"? What advantage can you find to people who are opposites getting married, for instance? Answer each question with a short paragraph.

Types of Persuasion

Can you correctly predict whether central or peripheral route persuasion is more effective?

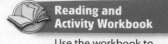

Reading and Activity Workbook

Use the workbook to complete this experiment.

1. Introduction

One of the topics you learned about in this chapter is persuasion. You read that there are two basic routes that one can take when trying to persuade someone to respond in a certain way—the central route and the peripheral route. But which technique works better? In this experiment, you will try to determine if the central or peripheral route is more effective. By doing so, you may learn valuable lessons that you can use in your daily life. For example, the ability to persuade others successfully can be a useful skill as you move on to college or the working world. In addition, the ability to see through the persuasive techniques of others can help you become a more informed, sophisticated consumer and citizen. In this experiment, you will:

- organize into small groups as directed by your teacher

- review the elements of the experimental method

- create advertisements

- develop a hypothesis

- show your advertisements to different groups of people

- record your test subjects' reactions

- record your data

- analyze your findings

After you have conducted the lab, you will discuss the results with your fellow group members. Then all groups will take part in a class discussion.

2. Creating the Ads

Take some time to review the chapter material on persuasion. Also, review the diagram titled The Experimental Method on the next page. Then you will be ready to move forward with your experiment.

Organize into groups as directed by your teacher. If possible, organize the groups so that at least one person in each group has an art background. Each group will create two full-page magazine-type ads for a certain product. Both ads will be for the same product, but one will use the central route, and the other will use the peripheral route of persuasion. You will need paper, markers, or other art supplies. Follow these steps:

- First, each group will decide on a product that lends itself to both types of persuasion in an ad. If you need ideas, look at the ads as you flip through one of your favorite magazines.

- Distribute tasks among group members. An ad needs visuals, words (copy), and a layout, so everyone can pitch in.

- While the central route technique is fairly straightforward, you will need to decide what type of peripheral route technique you will use—emotional appeal, glittering generalities, or another type.

Work together to create your ads and make them both as appealing as possible. You want everyone who sees them to be swayed by their content, so be creative.

3. Forming and Testing Your Hypothesis

Which method do you think will be more successful? In your group, discuss your views about the effectiveness of advertising and vote on which ad will be more successful. Record your hypothesis, along with a list of reasons why your group supports it. If any members of your group strongly disagree with the group decision, they can record a dissenting hypothesis.

Each group will develop a questionnaire that challenges the test participants to think about how the ad is trying to persuade them. For example, you might ask:

- What about the ad appeals or does not appeal to you?

- How do you feel about the product when viewing the ad?

- Does the ad engage you intellectually or emotionally?

- Does the ad's message speak to you as a consumer? Why or why not?

- Would the ad make you more or less likely to buy the product advertised?

Your teacher will organize students from other classes to be your test subjects. Give each subject a color copy of each ad and a questionnaire. Collect the questionnaires when the subjects are finished.

4. Analyzing Data and Evaluating Results

Compile the results of your experiment. Which type of ad was more persuasive? Did the results confirm or refute your hypothesis? Within your group, discuss the questionnaire responses. Then discuss the results as a class. Use the following questions to guide your discussion:

- Which persuasive method was most effective?

- How did the choice of product relate to each method's effectiveness? Did some products lend themselves to one method of persuasion more than to the other?

- For any group whose hypothesis was not borne out by test results, why do you think this happened? Use the questionnaire answers for clues.

- If you were to do this sort of experiment again, how would you change the method to improve it?

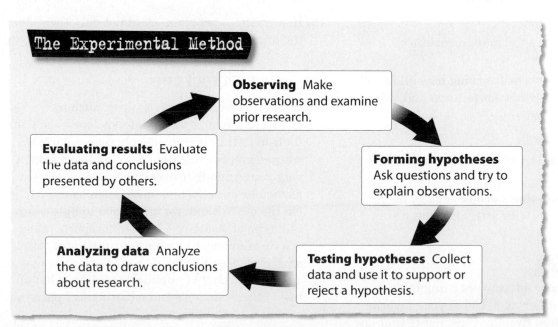

The Experimental Method

Observing Make observations and examine prior research.

Forming hypotheses Ask questions and try to explain observations.

Testing hypotheses Collect data and use it to support or reject a hypothesis.

Analyzing data Analyze the data to draw conclusions about research.

Evaluating results Evaluate the data and conclusions presented by others.

This is one view of the experimental method. Note that results turn into new observations, and new hypotheses can be formulated and tested.

Comprehension and Critical Thinking

SECTION 1 *(pp. 562–565)*

1. a. Define What is cognitive evaluation? Give an example.

b. Analyze Is observational learning likely to alter people's beliefs in long-term cognitive anchors? Explain.

c. Elaborate How might a person's physical environment—the climate or the local terrain, for example—shape his or her attitudes?

SECTION 2 *(pp. 567–570)*

2. a. Recall What sort of people develop effective sales resistance?

b. Infer What is it about glittering generalities that make them persuasive? Give at least two possible answers.

SECTION 3 *(pp. 571–574)*

3. a. Define What is a stereotype?

b. Sequence Put the terms *discrimination*, *social learning*, and *stereotyping* in the order that they affect a person's attitudes and actions.

c. Support a Position How does speaking up when people talk in ways that express prejudicial attitudes help reduce prejudice?

SECTION 4 *(pp. 576–579)*

4. a. Describe What are the main elements of attribution theory?

b. Explain How does a self serving bias allow individuals to escape blame for failures and take credit for successes?

SECTION 5 *(pp. 580–583)*

5. a. Recall Are some aspects of beauty universal? Explain.

b. Infer Why do you think people tend to be attracted to others with attitudes that are similar to their own?

INTERNET ACTIVITY ✷

6. What methods are advertisers using to persuade you and other teens? Visit your favorite Web sites and find five advertisements that use a method of persuasion you can identify from your reading of Section 2. Write a short report detailing your findings.

Reviewing Vocabulary

Fill in each blank with the term that correctly completes the sentence.

7. An individual or group that is blamed for the problems of others is known as a _____.

8. The _____ occurs when people change their opinions of others on the basis of newer interactions instead of holding on to their first impressions.

9. _____ are beliefs and feelings about objects, people, and events that can affect how people behave in certain situations.

10. Closeness and caring that is reflected by mutual concern and by the sharing of feelings and resources is called _____.

11. A direct attempt to influence other people's attitudes or views known as _____.

12. _____ is the mutual exchange of feelings or attitudes.

13. A lack of agreement or consistency—a conflict— can also be referred to as _____.

14. _____ refers to a couple's recognition that they are "in love" and want to be together, "for better or for worse."

15. In a _____ people present not only their side of the argument but also the opposition's side.

Psychology in Your Life

16. What are some of your cognitive anchors? Everyone has attitudes that developed early in their lives that become deeply rooted parts of who we are. For example, we may learn from a very young age to love certain kinds of dogs, a particular climate, or a sport, such as tennis. On the other hand, we may learn to hate a certain type of weather, a particular sports team, or a style of music. Examine your attitudes closely and think about some of the central cognitive anchors that help to define you. Make a list of five of these anchors and write a short paragraph explaining each one.

SKILLS ACTIVITY: INTERPRETING CARTOONS

Look at the cartoon below. Then use the information to answer the questions that follow.

SORRY, YOU ARE SIMPLY NOT THE RIGHT MAN FOR THE JOB.

© Cartoon Stock

17. **Describe** The man in the cartoon has decided that only men are fit for this job. What kind of attitude is this?

18. **Analyze** Give a possible scenario describing how the man's behavior was influenced by social learning.

19. **Develop** Name and describe two ways in which the woman might overcome the discrimination she is experiencing.

WRITING FOR AP PSYCHOLOGY

Use your knowledge of social perception to answer the question below. Do not simply list facts. Present a clear argument based on your critical analysis of the question, using the appropriate psychological terminology.

20. What is attribution theory? Explain how dispositional and situational factors are central to the theory. Also, explain and give examples of the following elements of attribution theory:
   - actor-observer bias
   - fundamental attribution error
   - self-serving bias

Connecting Online

Visit thinkcentral.com for review and enrichment activities related to this chapter.

THINK central

Quiz and Review

ONLINE QUIZZES
Take a practice quiz for each section in this chapter.

WEBQUEST
Complete a structured Internet activity for this chapter.

QUICK LAB
Reinforce a key concept with a short lab activity.

APPLYING WHAT YOU'VE LEARNED
Review and apply your knowledge by completing a project-based assessment.

Activities

eACTIVITIES
Complete chapter Internet activities for enrichment.

INTERACTIVE FEATURE
Explore an interactive version of a key feature in this chapter.

KEEP IT CURRENT
Link to current news and research in psychology.

Online Textbook

Click for More

Learn more about key topics in this chapter.

ACTS of Altruism

Sometimes, in extraordinary circumstances, people are willing to sacrifice their own well-being, even their lives, to help other people who are in peril. History provides a number of inspiring examples of such people who were willing to put the welfare of others before their own welfare. Two such people were Raoul Wallenberg and Paul Rusesabagina.

Raoul Wallenberg was a Swedish businessman and the foreign representative of a Central European trading company. In 1944 the Nazis sent troops into Hungary for the purpose of rounding up the country's Jewish population. This was part of the Nazi campaign to destroy the Jewish people in Europe.

Wallenberg, because of his knowledge of the country, asked to be assigned as a diplomat to Budapest, Hungary. During his time in Budapest, he managed to save thousands of Hungarian Jews.

He secured passage out of the country for some Jews by means of counterfeit documents such as passports. He also bribed government officials to look the other way so that Jews could leave Hungary.

In addition, Wallenberg provided sanctuary for some Jews by setting up residence houses for them under the protection of the Swedish flag. These were houses that the Nazis could not enter under the rules of diplomatic immunity.

Wallenberg's story has a mysterious but unhappy ending. By 1945 Germany was on the brink of defeat, surrounded by British and American soldiers to the west and Soviet soldiers to the east. In 1945 Budapest fell to the invading Soviet armies. Shortly thereafter, Wallenberg was arrested by Soviet authorities and charged with espionage. He was taken to Moscow and eventually disappeared into the Soviet prison system. According to some accounts, he died of a heart attack in prison in 1947. Other reports from prisoners in the system claimed that he was alive as late as 1975.

However and whenever he died, Wallenberg risked his life to save the lives of approximately 100,000 Jews. Although he lost his freedom and his life, he won the admiration of the world.

Paul Rusesabagina is another extraordinary individual who risked his own life to save the lives of others. His story takes place in Rwanda, a country located in east central Africa.

In 1994 a long dispute between the two ethnic groups of Rwanda—the Hutus and the Tutsis—exploded into a 100-day frenzy of slaughter and genocide conducted by the Hutus against the Tutsis. The murders left nearly one million people dead.

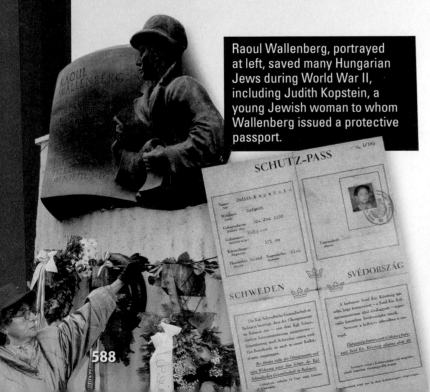

Raoul Wallenberg, portrayed at left, saved many Hungarian Jews during World War II, including Judith Kopstein, a young Jewish woman to whom Wallenberg issued a protective passport.

CHAPTER 21

SOCIAL INTERACTION

Paul Rusesabagina was a hotel manager in Rwanda who saved hundreds of lives when Hutu militias went on a rampage.

Rusesabagina was the manager of the Hotel des Milles Collines, in Rwanda's capital city, Kigali. His father was a Hutu and his mother was a Tutsi. As the hotel manager, he provided shelter to more than 1,200 refugees, mostly Tutsis as well as some moderate Hutus.

When the Hutu militias began to attack the United Nations peacekeepers, most of them were withdrawn and the situation became even more dangerous. Genocide raged outside the grounds of the hotel, with machete-wielding mobs hacking their victims to death. Rusesabagina was able to hold the rampaging Hutu militias at bay.

He was able to use his influence and connections to keep the militias and mobs from entering the hotel. Rusesabagina's bravery saved hundreds of lives at great risk to himself.

In this chapter you will learn more about aggression and altruism. You will also learn about group behavior, conformity, and obedience.

What do you think?

1. Which groups did Wallenberg and Rusesabagina help?

2. Would you risk your life to save other people? Can you imagine circumstances under which you would do so? What are those circumstances?

Chapter at a Glance

SECTION 1: Group Behavior

- People behave differently in groups than they do as individuals.

- Being a member of a group does not always improve individual performance.

- Many important decisions are made by groups rather than by individuals.

- People tend to take greater risks as part of a group than they would if they were acting alone.

SECTION 2: Conformity and Obedience

- People who conform bring their behavior into line with that of a group.

- Solomon Asch investigated the extent to which people conform to social norms.

- One of the most obvious influences on people's behavior is the power of people in authority to compel them to obey.

SECTION 3: Aggression and Altruism

- Aggression, words or actions that are intended to harm other people, is a widespread social problem.

- Freud believed that aggressive urges are unavoidable reactions to the frustrations of daily life.

- Cognitive psychologists maintain that aggressive behavior is influenced by people's values.

- An unselfish concern for the welfare of other people is the hallmark of altruistic behavior.

Group Behavior

Before You Read

Main Idea
People behave differently in groups than they do as individuals. Often, they are willing to take greater risks in a group.

Reading Focus
1. What is social facilitation?
2. How would you define social loafing and risky shift?
3. What are some characteristics of group decision-making?
4. What is group polarization?
5. How would you describe group leadership?

Vocabulary
social facilitation
evaluation apprehension
social loafing
diffusion of responsibility
risky shift
social decision schemes
group polarization
authoritarian leaders
democratic leaders
laissez-faire leaders

TAKING NOTES Use a graphic organizer like this one to take notes on the different kinds of social decision schemes.

First Shift
Social Decision Schemes
Majority Wins
Two-thirds Majority
Truth Wins

We're Number One! We're Number One!

PSYCHOLOGY CLOSE UP

Why would sports fans riot, even though their team had won?

Many people like to feel that they belong to a group that is dedicated to a higher purpose. Examples of such groups might include religious organizations, political parties, or even, on a less serious level, sports teams. And as members of such a group, sports fans, for example, are far more likely to engage in behavior that they would think twice about as individuals.

For example, Boston Red Sox fans, like sports fans everywhere, identify themselves with the fortunes of their team. Its ups and downs provide moments of exaltation and moments of despair for the fans. And whether it's celebrating the thrill of victory or the agony of defeat, fans can sometimes overreact in expressing their sense of solidarity with the team's fortunes.

In 1986 the Red Sox suffered a stinging defeat. In 2004, they won the World Series. In both cases, in defeat and in victory, the fans celebrated with riots that involved burning cars and general mayhem in the streets. It's safe to say that most members of the crowd that indulged in such problematic behavior would not, as individuals, have engaged in such acts. That's because people behave differently in crowds. ■

Social Facilitation

How people behave as part of a group often differs from how they behave as individuals. People may try harder, take greater risks, or make different decisions when they are with others than they would if they were alone. The ways in which groups affect individual behavior are discussed in this section.

Social facilitation refers to the concept that people often perform better when other people are watching than they do when they are alone. The presence of other people seems to facilitate and encourage one's performance.

Social facilitation is not limited to people. Psychologist Robert Zajonc found that dogs and cats—and even cockroaches—do things faster when they are in a group than when they are alone. This finding suggests that social facilitation may be a basic animal response. Zajonc proposed that animals respond in this way because the presence of others increases their level of excitement.

Evaluation apprehension, or the concern about the opinion of others, is another reason that the presence of other people may improve performance. Evaluation apprehension may motivate people to try harder so that others will think more highly of them.

Reading Check **Summarize** Who or what does social facilitation affect?

Social Loafing and Risky Shift

Being a member of a group does not always improve one's performance. When people are working together toward a common goal rather than working on individual tasks, they may "slack off" and not try as hard. This behavior is referred to as **social loafing.** Social loafing is especially likely to occur when people see that other members of the group are not pulling their share of the load.

The phenomenon of social loafing may occur because of **diffusion of responsibility**—the tendency for people to feel less responsible for accomplishing a task when the effort is shared among members of a group. As part of a group, individuals are likely to feel less accountable for their own actions. Therefore, they are less likely to worry about what others think of them, because they have less

evaluation apprehension. They may even feel that their contribution to the group's effort is not very important.

A related social phenomenon is the **risky shift**—the tendency for people to take greater risks when they are part of a group than they would as individuals acting on their own. People may feel more powerful (or less vulnerable) as part of a group. This is because the responsibility for a particular situation or action is shared with the other group members. The risky shift may help explain such events as prison riots and mob attacks.

Reading Check **Find the Main Idea** What is diffusion of responsibility?

Group Decision-Making

Many important decisions are made by groups rather than by individuals. Committees, for example, are often appointed to study and make decisions about specific issues. Juries decide on the guilt or innocence of people accused of crimes. Friends may decide as a group which movie to see. These are examples of group decision-making.

Because many decisions are made by groups, psychologists have studied how being part of a group affects the process. They have identified a number of **social decision schemes,** or rules that govern group decision-making. These include the majority-wins scheme, the truth-wins scheme, the two-thirds-majority scheme, and the first-shift scheme.

Majority-Wins Scheme In the majority-wins scheme, the group agrees to a decision that was initially supported by a majority of group members. For example, a group of five friends might be trying to decide what to do on the weekend—say, whether to go to a movie or to the mall. At first, three of the five friends might opt for the movie and the other two friends for the mall. However, after discussing the two choices, all five friends might agree to go to the movie, the option that was initially supported by the majority.

The majority-wins scheme applies most often to situations in which there are no right or wrong choices. Rather, the preference of the majority guided the decisions of the other friends.

Truth-Wins Scheme Often, the members of a group come to realize that one option is better than others after they learn more about the different choices available. This is referred to as the truth-wins scheme. Suppose that in the example just given, the five friends learn that the movie they hoped to see has been canceled and that another movie is being shown, one that interests them less. After gathering and sharing the information, the group might decide to go to the mall instead, a decision that is based on a clearly better choice between their two options.

Two-Thirds–Majority Scheme Some groups concur with a decision after two-thirds of their members come to an agreement about the correct choice. This is called the two-thirds-majority scheme. It often applies to decisions made by juries. When two-thirds of a jury initially vote for conviction, the remaining third may go along with the decision of the others.

First-Shift Scheme The first-shift scheme applies to groups that are deadlocked, or split fifty-fifty, about a decision. If one person changes his or her mind, or shifts from one side to the other, others may shift to the opposite side as well. For example, a jury might be deadlocked, with half believing the defendant is guilty and half believing the defendant is innocent. Those jurors who thought the defendant was guilty might follow the lead of the

ACADEMIC VOCABULARY

concur to be of the same opinion; agree

first juror who changes his or her vote from guilty to not guilty, even in the absence of new information about the case.

Reading Check **Summarize** Which scheme applies to groups that are deadlocked?

Group Polarization

Members of a group usually share similar attitudes. Indeed, shared attitudes are often what attract people to particular groups in the first place.

For example, teens who are concerned about the plight of stray animals might join an organization that has the goal of ending euthanasia at the local animal shelter. Teens who are not as concerned about animals, on the other hand, are unlikely to join such a group.

The shared attitudes that group members hold are likely to grow stronger over time. This strengthening of a group's shared attitudes is called **group polarization.** It occurs as group members discuss and act upon the attitudes they share.

Polarization can be positive or negative. If high-prejudice group members are prejudiced against people of other races or religions, for example, then group polarization is likely to increase their prejudice. If, on the other hand, low-prejudice group members are tolerant of people who are different, then polarization may make them even more tolerant.

Reading Check **Draw Conclusions** What is an example of negative group polarization?

Group Leadership

All groups, regardless of their nature, have leaders who serve several important functions in their groups. Leaders help group members identify goals and establish and implement plans for reaching them. Leaders may also offer emotional support to group members.

Some leaders are appointed by outsiders; others are chosen by a vote of group members. The president of an organization might be elected by a vote of group members. The president, in turn, might appoint a member of the group to head a committee to complete a particular task. Organizations such as businesses, schools, and the military usually have clear chains of command, or leadership.

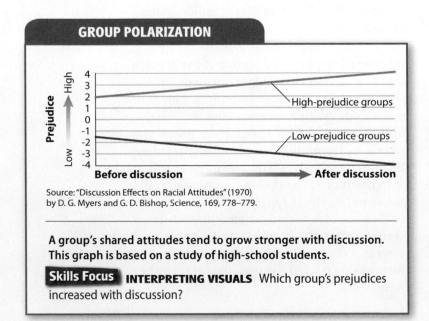

GROUP POLARIZATION

Source: "Discussion Effects on Racial Attitudes" (1970) by D. G. Myers and G. D. Bishop, Science, 169, 778–779.

A group's shared attitudes tend to grow stronger with discussion. This graph is based on a study of high-school students.

Skills Focus **INTERPRETING VISUALS** Which group's prejudices increased with discussion?

Informal groups may not have official leaders. However, some members are likely to have more influence than others.

Group leaders often have certain personality traits and social skills that enable them to influence the decisions and behavior of others. For example, leaders tend to be more self-confident, outgoing, and intelligent than other group members.

Despite these similarities, leaders may differ in how they operate. In other words, they may have different styles of leadership. Leaders may be authoritarian, democratic, or laissez-faire.

Authoritarian Leaders **Authoritarian leaders** exert absolute control over all decisions for the group. They tell other group members what to do and demand that group members obey their orders. Military leaders, for example, give orders to those of lesser rank and expect their orders to be carried out immediately and without question. This obedience is felt to be necessary to military discipline.

Democratic Leaders Military leaders tend to be authoritarian toward those below them in the chain of command, but they are more democratic when they are planning strategies with other officers. **Democratic leaders** encourage group members to express and discuss their ideas and, in addition, to make their own decisions.

Such leaders may try to build a consensus—that is, to encourage agreement on a decision. Alternatively, they may request that group members take a vote and follow the decision of the majority.

Laissez-Faire Leaders The term *laissez-faire* is French for "to let (people) do (as they choose)." Like democratic leaders, **laissez-faire leaders** encourage group members to express and explore their own ideas. However, laissez-faire leaders take a less active role in the decision-making process. They tend to stand back and allow group members to move in whatever direction they wish, even if the group seems to be making poor choices.

Comparing Leadership Styles No one style of leadership is best for every group or situation. In times of crisis, authoritarian leaders may be more effective because they can make decisions quickly.

In other situations, democratic or laissez-faire leaders may be more effective. Their styles of leadership allow group members to express themselves and grow as individuals. Such leadership may be important when the group is searching for new ways to solve a problem or when trying to help group members meet challenges in their lives.

Reading Check **Analyze** What is an authoritarian leader?

SECTION 1 Assessment

Online Quiz THINK central thinkcentral.com

Reviewing Main Ideas and Vocabulary

1. **Define** What is social loafing?

2. **Describe** What is the social decision scheme in which the members of a group come to realize that one option is better than others?

3. **Identify** What is a laissez-faire leader?

Thinking Critically

4. **Compare and Contrast** What is the difference between social facilitation and social loafing?

5. **Categorize** What are the four social decision schemes?

6. **Elaborate** Using your notes and a graphic organizer like the one below, describe three different styles of leadership.

Group Leadership
Authoritarian:
Democratic:
Laissez-faire:

FOCUS ON WRITING

7. **Expository** In a paragraph, explain why you prefer to follow one certain kind of leader rather than another. Cite examples of different leaders you have dealt with in different situations to support your explanation.

Conformity and Obedience

Before You Read

Main Idea
The pressure to conform is an indirect social influence on behavior. The power of people in positions of authority is a more direct social influence.

Reading Focus
1. Why are groups and social norms important?
2. What were Asch's studies of conformity?
3. Why do people conform?
4. What was the purpose of Milgram's studies of obedience?
5. Why do people obey?

Vocabulary
conform
social norms
explicit norms
implicit norms
foot-in-the-door effect

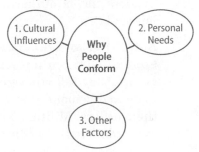

TAKING NOTES Use a graphic organizer like this one to take notes on why people conform.

Why People Conform
1. Cultural Influences
2. Personal Needs
3. Other Factors

Going Along With the Crowd

Members of Reserve Police Battalion 101

PSYCHOLOGY CLOSE UP

Why did 500 ordinary men commit mass murder?

Christopher Browning's book *Ordinary Men: Reserve Police Battalion 101 and the Final Solution in Poland* describes the events and motives that caused 500 middle-class, middle-aged German men to terrorize Jews in Poland in July of 1942. It was easier for most of these policemen to join in the killing than to break ranks and refuse to participate. By November of 1943 these ordinary civilians had murdered about 85,000 Jewish people.

Before the killing began the commanding officer, Major Trapp, explicitly offered to excuse any man who did not want to participate in the impending mass murder. Trapp's offer thrust responsibility onto each man individually. Still, between 80 to 90 percent of the men participated in the killing, finding it too difficult not to conform. Unlike soldiers, these policemen had the burden of choice. They were not "just following orders." Rather, the pressure to conform to their peers' expectations was paramount.

In his book, Browning notes that no member of Reserve Police Battalion 101 who refused to participate was physically harmed or punished. Instead, outright refusal to participate brought more subtle consequences, such as the threat of isolation from the group. ▪

Importance of Groups and Social Norms

As you learned in the first section of this chapter, people behave differently around other people than they do when they are by themselves. How people behave toward others depends upon a variety of factors, such as those discussed below.

Sometimes people behave aggressively toward others; sometimes they try to help others. Other people can also influence us. They might do this by giving us orders or pressuring us to adapt to their standards of behavior.

The least direct social influence on behavior is the pressure to **conform,** or to modify one's attitudes and behavior to make them consistent with those of other people. People who conform bring their behavior in line with that of a group. The group may be a formal organization, such as a school club, or a loose collection of people, such as several friends who always hang out together. You and others in your circle of friends are an example of such a group.

Being accepted by a group can be important because groups help people satisfy many needs. Groups can fulfill an individual's needs for belonging, affection, and attention. Meeting such needs is one reason why many teens join clubs at school, sports teams, academic clubs, and other social organizations.

Groups are also important because they offer support to individuals when they are facing difficult problems. People who are grieving the loss of a loved one, for example, may benefit by joining a support group. And, groups may help people accomplish things they could not accomplish on their own. For instance, workers may join together to form a labor union in order to fight for better working conditions, shorter hours, or higher wages.

Belonging to a group usually means following, or conforming to, the group's social norms. **Social norms** are the standards of behavior that people share. They serve as guidelines for what people should and should not do or say in a given situation. For example, social norms tell people what to eat, what to wear, and when and where to make a joke. They also tell us how to dress, how to greet a business associate at a party, and how to behave in public.

Social norms can be explicit or implicit. **Explicit norms** are spoken or written rules. Examples of explicit norms include traffic rules and school dress codes. **Implicit norms** are unspoken, unwritten rules. Examples of implicit norms include modes of dress or ways of greeting that are unique to a particular group. Although implicit norms are unstated, they nonetheless guide people's words and actions.

Social norms can be useful or harmful. They are useful if they help promote the safety and well-being of individuals or groups. Bathing regularly and not talking in a theater during a movie are examples of useful social norms. Social norms are harmful when they promote risky behavior. Smoking cigarettes—a norm in some groups—is an example of harmful social norms.

Reading Check **Find the Main Idea** What are implicit norms?

Asch's Studies of Conformity

To what extent will people conform to social norms? Psychologist Solomon Asch addressed this question in a series of well-known experiments in 1955. Asch wanted to determine whether people would go along with group opinion even when the group opinion differed from their own, and even when the group opinion was very obviously wrong. The results of Asch's studies on conformity turned out to be quite surprising.

Procedure Asch asked participants in the study to look at three lines of varying length and to compare them with a standard line. The participants were asked to indicate which of the three lines was the same length as the standard line.

Each participant was tested in a group of several other people. However, the other group members were really Asch's associates. They were simply posing as study participants.

For the first few comparisons, all of Asch's associates gave the correct answer. However, for many of the remaining comparisons, all of the associates gave the same wrong answer. For example, they might have said that line 1 was the same length as the standard line, even though line 1 was clearly shorter than the standard line.

Complete a Webquest at thinkcentral.com on Asch's studies of conformity.

Conformity

How do you conform to the group? Some people conform in their dress, as shown at right. Others conform in their preferences in music or movies. We all conform—even the nonconformists—but how exactly is the question.

PROCEDURE

❶ Form groups of four or five students.

❷ In your group, list several categories in which each individual feels the need to conform—clothing, food tastes, music, movies, socializing, and so forth.

❸ Then for each category, write a list of the top five ways each person in the group conforms. Select one person in the group as your speaker.

ANALYSIS

1. Have the spokesperson for each group present the categories the group listed to the class.

2. Select someone to write each group's categories on the board.

3. Beneath each category, list the top five ways that students conform. Synthesize the findings of each group and come up with one list under each category of the top five ways of conforming.

4. Discuss the results. Do you think you are more individualistic than the results show?

Quick Lab **THINK** central thinkcentral.com

Results When Asch's associates gave an answer that was obviously wrong, many study participants conformed to the group opinion and gave the same wrong answer. About three-fourths of study participants went along with group opinion at least once, one-third went along with the group at least half the time, and one-fourth went along with the group virtually all the time. Study participants who conformed to group opinion later admitted that they knew the answers they gave were incorrect, but they went along with the group so as not to appear different from the others.

Asch's studies show that most people are all too willing to go along with the crowd. His research into conformity revealed that people will conform to those around them so as not to appear different.

> **Reading Check** **Identify Cause and Effect** Why did participants conform to group opinion?

Why People Conform

"Going along with the crowd" is probably at least as common in everyday life as it was in Asch's experiments. Most people avoid talking, acting, or dressing differently from other members of the groups to which they belong. Why is conformity so common? Several factors may contribute to the tendency to conform.

Cultural Influences Some cultures are collectivistic. This means that these cultures place greater emphasis on the group than on the group's individual members. In many Asian cultures, for example, the individual is seen primarily as part of the family and society rather than as a separate and distinct person. In such cultures, individuals show a greater tendency to conform to the group. In fact, they may feel extremely uncomfortable if they are singled out as somehow different from the other members of the group, even if that distinction is positive.

Need for Acceptance Some people conform to social norms in order to be liked and accepted by others. This need to conform stems from the belief that people who dress, talk, or act differently from other people stand out from the crowd and thus draw negative attention to themselves. In actuality, however, this is not always true.

People who depend the most on the acceptance and approval of others tend to be those with low self-esteem and high social anxiety. They may value being liked more than they value being right. They may also be very self-conscious about standing out from others, fearing that others will ridicule or reject them if they appear different.

Other Factors Several other factors contribute to the tendency to conform to social norms. For example, the chances of conforming to a group's norms increase as the group grows in size—at least up to about eight members. Further increases in size (past eight members) seem to have little effect on the tendency to conform.

Individuals are more likely to conform to the group when all other members of the group are unanimous in their words and actions. However, if even one person disagrees with the rest of the group, others in the group also are less likely to conform.

Reading Check **Find the Main Idea** What are some other factors besides cultural influences and need for acceptance that make conformity so common?

Milgram's Studies of Obedience

One of the most obvious and direct social influences on people's attitudes and behavior is the power of people in positions of authority. Parents often order their children to clean their own rooms or do their homework. Judges order lawbreakers to pay fines or perform community service. People in positions of authority expect that their requests and demands will be obeyed.

And, in fact, most children obey their parents, teachers, and other adults. Most adults obey police officers, judges, and other authority figures. Such obedience is necessary to protect the safety and well-being of the community and its people.

Throughout history, however, many people have also obeyed orders to commit immoral acts, such as killing innocent people. In the 1900s alone, Turks killed Armenians, Nazis killed Jews in Europe, Serbs killed Muslims in Bosnia, and Hutus killed Tutsis in Rwanda. In each case, those who did the killing justified their acts by saying they were "just following orders."

Are people who commit immoral acts unusual or abnormal? Or would most people be obedient in a similar situation? Yale University psychologist Stanley Milgram, whose own parents were killed by the Nazis during World War II, investigated this question in a series of studies conducted in the 1960s and 1970s. The purpose of Milgram's research was to determine whether the average person would obey the commands of authority figures.

Procedure In the first phase of his research, Milgram placed advertisements in local newspapers, seeking male volunteers to participate in a study of learning. In response, 40 men, ranging in age from 20 to 50, volunteered for the study. The volunteers represented a wide range of educational levels—from people who had not completed elementary school to others who had earned graduate degrees. Study participants also represented a variety of occupations, including teachers, engineers, laborers, and salespeople.

Instead of revealing the true nature of the study, Milgram told participants that its purpose was to investigate the effects that punishment has on memory. Some participants, Milgram explained, would be "teachers," and others would be "learners." In reality, all the volunteers who answered the advertisement were assigned to the teacher group, whereas those in the learner group were Milgram's associates.

Study participants were told that learners were expected to learn word pairs that would be read to them from a list. After the learners had heard the entire list, the teachers read the words one at a time. Each learner was then asked to provide the word that was paired with the word read by the teacher. If a learner made the correct choice, nothing happened, and teacher and learner went on to the next test item. However, if a learner made an incorrect choice, the teacher was to deliver an electric shock. With each mistake a learner made, the teacher was to increase the amount of voltage.

Learners were strapped into chairs and electrodes were attached to their wrists. The teachers sat at a console in an adjacent room. On the console were levers labeled with the voltage they controlled (from 15 to 450 volts) and the seriousness of the shocks they delivered (from slight to severe). Although the teachers were led to believe that the learners received shocks for each incorrect answer, the equipment did not really deliver shocks. The learners were never hurt or put at risk in any way.

Teachers were first given a sample shock of 45 volts so that they would have some idea of what learners supposedly would be experiencing. A shock of 45 volts is not harmful, but it was unpleasant enough to convince teachers that high-voltage shocks would be painful, even dangerous. Teachers were told that they could quit at any time.

However, if they hesitated to deliver a shock or to go on with the experiment, they were urged by repeated commands from the researcher to continue. The researcher also offered reassurances that the shocks, although painful, would cause no permanent damage.

Results As learners made errors, teachers delivered greater and greater voltage in each shock. At 300 volts, learners pounded on the other side of the wall, even screamed in make-believe pain.

Yet 35 of the 40 participants continued with the experiment. Nine participants refused to continue somewhere between the 300-volt and the 450-volt level.

However, the rest, almost two thirds of the participants, obeyed instructions to give shocks throughout the entire range of voltage, up to 450 volts, even though these participants later said that they had been afraid of harming the people receiving the shocks.

Were the people who volunteered for Milgram's study abnormally insensitive, even cruel? Apparently not. They showed signs of great distress as the shocks they delivered increased in voltage. They sweated, bit their lips, trembled, stuttered, groaned, and dug their fingernails into their palms. Some even had fits of nervous laughter. Many also told the researcher that they wanted to stop. Nonetheless, most continued to deliver shocks of increasing voltage to the learners in the study.

Milgram repeated the experiment with other participants, including women and college students, and in other settings, including a storefront on a city street. In each phase of the research, at least half the participants obeyed the researcher and administered the entire series of electric shocks.

Most of us would like to believe that people seldom obey orders to do things that conflict with their own attitudes. However, Milgram's studies of obedience showed that the majority of people will obey those kinds of orders, even though doing so may cause them great emotional distress.

Reading Check **Analyze** About what percentage of participants gave shocks throughout the entire range of voltage?

Why People Obey

Why did the participants in Milgram's studies obey the researcher? What causes people, in general, to obey? Several causes have been identified.

One reason people tend to be obedient is that they have been socialized from childhood to obey authority figures, such as parents, teachers, members of the clergy, and police officers. Study participants saw the researchers in Milgram's studies as authority figures, so they obeyed orders to give shocks to the learners. To do otherwise would have conflicted with deeply held attitudes about correct behavior.

There are a number of reasons why the participants in Milgram's experiments tended to see the researcher as an authority figure. The researcher's age, for example, might have influenced some people to see in him a figure of authority. His gender, especially considering that the studies he conducted began in the early 1960s, might also have influenced some people.

REASONS PEOPLE OBEY

People obey authority figures for a variety of reasons. Here are some of the most important.

Socialization
People have been socialized since childhood to obey authority figures.

Foot-in-the-Door Effect
People have a tendency to give in to major demands once they have given in to minor ones.

Confusion About Attitudes
People become confused about their beliefs if they are disturbed by what is happening around them.

Buffers
If people are protected from the consequences of their actions they are more likely to follow orders.

Furthermore, there is the fact of his profession, that he was a psychologist. And finally, there is the fact that he held a professional position at a prestigious school, Yale University.

Another reason people tend to be obedient to authority figures is the **foot-in-the-door effect.** This behavior is the tendency for people to give in to major demands once they have given in to minor ones. The foot-in-the-door effect is an example of how people may gradually change their attitudes to justify their behavior.

After participants in Milgram's studies had delivered small shocks to learners, it was easier for them to deliver increasingly larger shocks. In a similar way, soldiers become accustomed to obeying commands concerning relatively unimportant matters, such as how to dress, when and where to eat, and how to perform routine drills. Later on, they are more likely to obey commands relating to much more important matters that may involve risking their lives or taking the lives of other people.

People who are aware of their attitudes are more likely to behave in accordance with those attitudes. As people become disturbed by what is happening around them—by the learners' screams and wall-pounding in Milgram's studies, for example—they are likely to become less aware of, or at least more confused about, their own beliefs. Thus, they may be more likely to behave in ways that are in conflict with their attitudes.

When people are buffered, or protected, from observing the consequences of their actions, they are more likely to follow orders, even immoral ones. In the first phase of Milgram's research, for example, teachers and learners were placed in separate rooms.

Thus, the teachers could not see how their actions were affecting others. In later phases of the research, teachers and learners were placed in the same room so that the teachers could see the pain they were inflicting on the learners. Without the buffer of a wall to separate them from the people they thought they were hurting, compliance with the researcher's demands dropped from 65 percent to about 40 percent.

Today many soldiers are similarly buffered from their enemies. Their only contact with opposing forces may be a blip on a radar screen. Attacking their enemies may involve little more than pressing a button that launches a missile.

The results of Milgram's studies suggest that obeying orders to kill enemies in this way may be easier than obeying orders to kill other human beings at close range.

Reading Check **Describe** What are buffers?

ACADEMIC VOCABULARY
compliance acting in accord with a wish, request, or demand

SECTION 2 Assessment

Online Quiz THINK central thinkcentral.com

Reviewing Main Ideas and Vocabulary

1. **Define** What are explicit norms?

2. **Describe** What does it mean to conform?

3. **Recall** Who studied whether the average person would obey authority figures?

Thinking Critically

4. **Compare and Contrast** What is the most significant difference between explicit and implicit norms?

5. **Draw Conclusions** What did Milgram's studies reveal about obedience to authority?

6. **Elaborate** Using your notes and a graphic organizer like the one below, explain why people obey.

Why People Obey
Socialization
Foot-in-the-Door
Confusion About Attitudes
Buffers

FOCUS ON WRITING

7. **Persuasive** Your behavior is probably shaped by both conformity and authority. Which do you think is more powerful in shaping your behavior? Write a paragraph in which you argue that either conformity or authority is the more difficult pressure to resist.

Cults and Conformity

A cult is a religious sect that is generally considered by the mainstream society to be extreme. Cult followers often live in an unconventional manner under the guidance of an authoritarian, charismatic leader. Cults often pressure members to make what is private (for most people) public. Privacy is forbidden in most cults. Many cults enforce conformity.

Marshall Applewhite, founder and leader of the Heaven's Gate cult

In the late 1970s the People's Temple, led by Jim Jones, was a dangerous doomsday cult. Jones predicted a violent day of judgment was close at hand. Jones claimed to be an incarnation of Jesus and Buddha, among others. He became a messiah-like figure in the People's Temple.

Jones believed that he would die with his 900 followers and move to another planet where they would all live in peace. Most decided to commit mass suicide by drinking a beverage laced with cyanide. Others were murdered. In all, 914 people died.

The Branch Davidians, led by David Koresh, was another cult that demanded absolute and unthinking obedience from its followers. Koresh and his followers believed they were living in the "end times" when divine judgment would come to pass. Eventually Koresh and about 80 followers died in a siege of the Branch Davidian compound near Waco, Texas, by the Bureau of Alcohol, Tobacco, and Firearms and FBI.

Heaven's Gate was a cult based near San Diego, California, and led by a man named Marshall Applewhite. Applewhite drew parallels between himself and Jesus. Group members gave up all they owned and lived a life free of material possessions. In 1997, Applewhite persuaded his followers to commit suicide in order to allow their souls to board a spaceship that he claimed was concealed behind the Hale-Bopp comet.

How are we to understand such groups? Philip Zimbardo, a social psychologist, believes that we should be asking what was so appealing about the group that so many people joined it voluntarily? In other words, what needs was the group fulfilling that were not being met by society? (Zimbardo, 1997)

These three cults have a number of factors in common. They are sometimes referred to as Doomsday or Armageddonist cults. Such cults possess the following characteristics.

- They claim a rigid division between the chosen people of the cult and the rest of the world.
- They complain that the world is against the cult.
- They have a vision of an apocalyptic showdown between the cult and the rest of the world.
- They have a vision of the cult leader as a messiah or world dictator.

H. Keith Henson, a psychologist, has explained the hold that cults exercise on their members in terms of "capture-bonding," or the social reorientation that one might feel when captured from one warring tribe and taken to another. An example of this is the so-called Stockholm Syndrome, in which people begin to identify with their captors (Henson, 2002).

Thinking Critically

1. **Compare** What are some similarities shared by cults?

2. **Discuss** What effect might the pressures to conform to a cult have on the individual?

The Reverend Sun Myung Moon, leader of the Unification Church, claims to be the second coming of Christ. Here he conducts a blessing ceremony, or mass wedding, for his followers.

Current Research **THINK** central · thinkcentral.com

Aggression and Altruism

Before You Read

Main Idea

Aggression refers to words or actions that can hurt people. Altruism refers to words or actions that can help people.

Reading Focus

1. How does biology influence aggression?

2. What are some features of the psychoanalytic and cognitive views of aggression?

3. How do learning and sociocultural theorists think about aggression?

4. What is altruism?

5. What factors affect altruism?

Vocabulary

catharsis
altruism
bystander effect

TAKING NOTES Use a graphic organizer like this one to take notes on the various reasons or views used to explain aggression.

Explaining Aggression	
Sociocultural	
Learning	
Cognitive	
Biological	
Psychoanalytic	

CONFLICT Resolution

PSYCHOLOGY CLOSE UP

How can both sides win? Inevitably, when people live and work closely together, conflicts arise. Have you ever spent time at a summer camp? Have you ever lived in a dormitory and had to deal with people's different schedules and likes and dislikes? Imagine that you are living in a dormitory along with a hundred other students. Music is blaring and the television is blasting at all hours of the day and night. Dirty laundry piles up in the corner of the room. Dirty dishes are left on all available surfaces rather than washed and put away. Food is left out to spoil and to lend its own distinct aroma to the general atmosphere of the dorm.

In such close quarters, conflicts sometimes erupt, and a compromise has to be devised that is fair to all concerned. In a situation such as a dormitory, there is often a designated person who acts as a mediator to settle disputes. Sometimes that person is an older student who is a resident of the dorm and helps to solve problems. Or it might be an expert brought in from the outside who can be trusted to be objective and not to take sides. Such a neutral person facilitates communication between two or more parties to help them resolve an issue. In this way, aggression can be constructively channeled into creative solutions to problems. ■

Biological View of Aggression

Aggression refers to words or actions that are meant to hurt other people. It is a serious and widespread social problem. For example, murder is the second-leading cause of death in the United States among young people between the ages of 15 and 24, and more than a million children each year are victims of abuse. Children not only suffer from the results of aggression; they seem to be fascinated by it. For example, children are drawn to video games in which they can manipulate figures to kill or torture others.

Why are people aggressive? Several reasons have been suggested. They include biological, psychoanalytic, cognitive, learning, and sociocultural views.

The brain and hormones appear to be involved in aggression. In response to certain stimuli, many lower animals react with instinctive aggression. For example, the male robin responds aggressively to the red breast of another robin. A brain structure (the hypothalamus) appears to be involved in this instinctive reaction.

Electrical stimulation of part of the hypothalamus triggers aggressive behavior in many kinds of animals. However, humans have more complex brains, and other parts of the brain apparently dampen possible aggressive instincts.

The male sex hormone testosterone is also involved in aggression. Testosterone appears to be connected with the tendency to try to dominate and control other people. Men have higher testosterone levels than women do and are also usually more aggressive than women, particularly in contacts with male strangers.

Studies show, for example, that aggressive 9- to 11-year-old boys are likely to have higher testosterone levels than less aggressive age-mates. Also, members of "wild" college fraternities have higher testosterone levels, on average, than members of "well-behaved" fraternities. Testosterone levels also vary with the occasion: men's testosterone levels tend to be higher when they are winning—whether at football or chess.

Throughout the animal kingdom, more aggressive individuals are more likely to survive and transmit their genes to future generations. Aggression may be "natural" in people as in other species, but intelligence is also a key to survival in the case of humans. The capacity to outwit other species may be more important to human survival than aggressiveness. Now that people have organized themselves into societies in which many acts of aggression are outlawed or confined to sports, intelligence and organizational skills may be more important than aggressiveness to human survival.

Reading Check **Identify** What is the male sex hormone involved in aggression?

Psychoanalytic and Cognitive Views

Sigmund Freud believed that aggressive urges are unavoidable reactions to the frustrations of daily life. Freud's views influenced the psychoanalytic view of aggression. Cognitive psychologists believe that people's behavior, including aggressive behavior, is not influenced by inherited tendencies or repressed urges.

Psychoanalysis and Aggression According to Freud and the psychoanalytic view, it is normal for people to have urges to hurt other people who do not meet their wishes or demands. Such urges tend to be repressed, however, because people fear hurting others (especially their parents) and, in turn, being rejected by them.

Freud also believed that repressed aggressive urges are likely to find other outlets. The urges might be expressed indirectly—for example, by the aggressive individual destroying other people's possessions or disobeying their orders. Alternatively, the urges might be expressed directly but toward strangers later in life.

Freud believed that the best way to reduce the tension caused by repressed aggressive urges and to prevent harmful aggression toward other people is to allow, or even encourage, less harmful expressions of aggression. For example, verbal aggression in the form of sarcasm or the expression of angry feelings might vent some of the aggressive feelings in the unconscious without causing bodily harm to other people. So might cheering on one's team or watching aggressive sports such as boxing or wrestling. Psychologists refer to such venting of aggressive impulses as **catharsis.**

Does catharsis really act as a safety valve, reducing feelings of tension and lowering the chances of harmful aggression toward others? Some studies have found that catharsis does seem to play this role.

Other studies, however, have found that "letting off steam," either verbally or by watching aggressive sports, seems to encourage people to be more, not less, aggressive. Thus, it is unclear whether catharsis increases or decreases aggressive behavior.

Cognitive Psychology and Aggression

Cognitive psychologists maintain that aggressive behavior is influenced by people's values, perceptions, and choices. In this view, people act aggressively because they believe that aggression is justified and necessary—either in general or particular situations.

Some cognitive psychologists have suggested that frustration and suffering trigger feelings of anger and that these feelings cause people to act aggressively. However, they also argue that people do not act aggressively automatically and without thought. Rather, people decide whether they will act aggressively on the basis of such factors as their previous experiences with aggression and their interpretation of other people's behavior.

How people interpret the behavior of others may be important in this regard. Some people interpret other people's behavior as intentionally insulting or cruel, even when it is not. This interpretation may stir up feelings of anger that in turn lead to aggression.

Reading Check **Summarize** What is catharsis?

Learning and Sociocultural Views

Learning <u>theorists</u> believe that people learn to repeat behaviors that are reinforced. Thus, when aggressive behavior is reinforced, people learn to behave aggressively. Sociocultural theorists argue that some cultures encourage independence and competitiveness and that this, in turn, promotes aggression. Other cultures emphasize cooperation.

ACADEMIC VOCABULARY

theorist one who speculates, or formulates a theory

INTERACTIVE ✳

Statistically Speaking...

TV Viewing and Violence Television viewing seems to play a role in teaching children aggressive behavior. Children spend a great deal of time watching acts of violence portrayed on television.

8 Hours per day television is on in the average American household

8,000 Number of murders seen on television by average child by age 11

75% Percentage of killers who get away with murder on television

5.7% Percentage of teens who watched less than an hour of televsion per day who committed a violent act

18.4% Percentage of teens who watched 1 to 3 hours of television per day who committed a violent act

25.3% Percentage of teens who watched more than three hours per day who committed a violent act

Skills Focus **THINKING CRITICALLY** What other factors besides television viewing may affect these numbers?

Source: *The Washington Post*, March 28, 2002

Interactive Feature **THINK** central thinkcentral.com

Learning Theorists Learning theorists believe that one reason that aggression may be reinforced is that it helps people to get their own way. For example, teens who bully other people may be able to control others with force or threats of force. Although other people may stay out of their way, bullies are also likely to be rejected as friends by most of their peers. Thus, it is questionable whether such behavior is really reinforced.

However, there is little question that other types of aggressive behavior are reinforced. In many sports, aggression helps players win games. Winning, in turn, gains them the admiration of fans and often, at least in professional sports, large paychecks.

Learning theorists also believe that people learn many behaviors by observing others. People observe aggressive behavior on television, in the movies, and in video games. Many people also observe aggressive behavior in their own homes and neighborhoods. Thus, most people observe aggression and learn from their observations.

The role that television violence plays in teaching children aggressive behavior has received a considerable amount of attention. This is because most children spend a great deal of time watching television—more time, in fact, than they spend in school. Evidence suggests that by the time the average child reaches middle school, he or she has viewed more than 8,000 murders and 100,000 other acts of violence on television.

Most experts agree that watching violence on television leads people to act more aggressively. The Statistically Speaking feature on page 603 shows some of the data that support this conclusion. The seriousness of criminal acts committed by age 30 seems to correspond to the amount of television watched before age eight.

Watching violence on television may influence people to become more aggressive because television may reinforce an individual's ideas about violence and thus lessen his or her inhibitions against aggression. Children may also learn to imitate the acts of violence they see on television.

Sociocultural Theorists Sociocultural theorists argue that the United States is a good example of a country that promotes competitiveness and aggression. Most Americans place a high value on individual rights and freedoms. They also emphasize competition.

When so much importance is attached to the individual, getting along with others becomes less important. When one person is strongly encouraged to win over others, hostility and aggression may result.

Other cultures place greater value on the welfare of the group and encourage people to cooperate. This may reduce levels of aggression. Children in countries such as Japan and Korea, for example, tend to be less aggressive than children in the United States. That is because their cultures encourage courtesy, respect, cooperation, and deference to others, all of which promote a sense of community and mutual self-interest and respect.

Reading Check **Contrast** What are examples of competitive and cooperative societies?

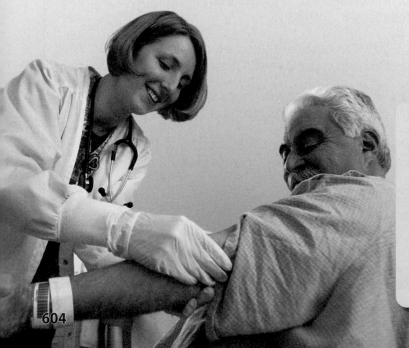

Altruism and Careers

Overview: There are certain occupations that regularly call upon the altruism of their members.

Careers: firefighters, police officers, doctors, nurses, lifeguards, caretakers in nursing homes

Behavior: On a daily basis, people in altruistic careers may have to rescue people from fires, save people from drowning, provide first-aid treatment, take care of people who come to the emergency rooms of hospitals, or take other actions.

Altruism and Others

Aggressive people show little regard for other people or their feelings. **Altruism,** on the other hand, is an unselfish concern for the welfare of other people. Altruistic people sacrifice their own well-being to help others in need.

Evolutionary psychologists believe that altruism, like aggression, is linked to genetics. Although altruistic behavior benefits other people, evolutionary psychologists believe it can also help people pass on their genes to future generations. At least it can do so if the altruistic behavior is directed toward relatives—that is, toward people who have many of the same genes as the altruist.

By helping their relatives survive and reproduce, evolutionary psychologists argue, early humans indirectly passed on their genes to the next generation. In this way, genes for altruism have come to be part of the human gene pool. Thus, according to the evolutionary view, humans are altruistic by nature.

The evolutionary explanation of altruism has been criticized for many of the same reasons that the evolutionary explanation of aggression has been criticized: no clear-cut genetic basis for altruistic behavior has been found, and the tendency to act altruistically varies too widely to be under genetic control. The evolutionary view has also been criticized as not explaining why people act altruistically toward those to whom they are not related.

Reading Check **Summarize** Who believes that altruism is linked to genetics?

Factors Promoting and Inhibiting Altruism

Research has shown that several factors influence whether a person will help others. One factor is the person's state of mind. Many studies have found that people are more likely to help others when they are in a good mood. Being in a good mood seems to make people feel more generous and eager to help others. It also may make people feel more powerful and better able to provide aid to those in need.

People who have problems themselves may also be more likely to act altruistically, perhaps because their own problems make them sensitive to the troubles of others. People who are empathic—that is, able to put themselves in another's place—may be more likely to be altruistic for the same reason.

Being competent to help others seems to increase the chances that people will act altruistically. For example, registered nurses are more likely than people with no medical training to come to the aid of accident victims. Similarly, police officers, who are trained to intervene in violent and dangerous situations, are more likely than the average person to help people in trouble. A good student might feel competent to help others with their schoolwork. A good athlete might volunteer to help others on his or her team. A good musician might volunteer to help others in the band so that the school band can make a good showing at a state competition. In all these situations, competent people are acting altruistically.

CASE STUDY
CONNECTION

Acts of Altruism
Both Raoul Wallenberg and Paul Rusesabagina had some power and authority in the worlds in which they were functioning and displaying altruistic behavior.

Altruism and Athletes

Overview: Athletes are sometimes viewed as self-centered, but many, such as Tiger Woods, Mia Hamm, Peyton Manning, and Warrick Dunn, show their altruism by working for charitable causes.

Athlete: Peyton Manning, the quarterback for the Indianapolis Colts, is involved in a number of charitable causes.

Behavior: Peyton Manning has been active in the fight against pediatric cancers. Manning and a young cancer patient display a banner with the new name of an Indianapolis facility honoring Manning's work in helping to fund new treatments for children.

605

People with a strong need for approval also may be more likely to act altruistically. By doing so, they hope to gain the approval of others. In addition, a sense of personal responsibility may increase the chances of altruistic behavior. Teachers and camp counselors, for example, are responsible for those in their care, and they are more likely to act altruistically toward them than others are.

Inhibiting Factors There are also several factors that seem to make people reluctant to help others in distress. In some cases, people may not be aware that another person is in trouble. In fact, the less sure they are that another person needs help, the less likely they are to offer assistance.

Some people may fail to act altruistically because they think there is nothing they can do to help. Others may be afraid of making a social blunder and being ridiculed. Finally, people may fail to act altruistically, particularly in dangerous situations, because they fear injuring themselves in the attempt.

Bystander Effect The chances of people helping someone in need also depend on how many other people are present to help. Research has shown that people are less likely to give aid when other bystanders are present. This is called the **bystander effect.**

A classic experiment by psychologists John Darley and Bibb Latané is one of many studies that have documented the bystander effect. In one phase of the study, participants were placed in separate cubicles and asked to talk with one another over an intercom. One of the participants was actually an associate of the researchers. When his turn came to talk, he called for help and then made sounds that suggested he was having an epileptic seizure.

Some study participants had been led to believe that they alone could hear the person having the seizure. Others had been led to believe that from one to four other participants could hear him as well. About 85 percent of participants who thought that no one else could hear the person came to his aid. However, when participants thought that others could also hear the individual in trouble, fewer of them tried to help. In fact, the more people who were presumed to be able to hear him, the less likely participants were to become involved.

It seems that diffusion of responsibility limits altruistic behavior. When people are members of a group, they are likely to stand back and wait for others to help the person in need. However, when other people are not around, they are more likely to act in an altruistic manner.

Reading Check **Find the Main Idea** What is the bystander effect?

SECTION 3 Assessment

Online Quiz THINK central thinkcentral.com

Reviewing Main Ideas and Vocabulary

1. **Identify** What is the biological view of aggressive behavior?

2. **Describe** According to learning theorists, how do children learn aggressive behavior?

3. **Recall** What brain structure seems to be involved in instinctive aggression?

Thinking Critically

4. **Identify Cause and Effect** Why is it important to understand the causes of aggression?

5. **Categorize** Describe two situations, one in which bystanders are likely to help a person in trouble and one in which bystanders are less likely to help. Explain your answer.

6. **Compare and Contrast** Using your notes and a graphic organizer like the one below, explain the factors promoting and inhibiting altruism.

Factors Affecting Altruism	
Promoting:	Inhibiting:

FOCUS ON WRITING

7. **Narrative** In a couple of paragraphs, write an account of your involvement, or that of a friend or family member, in a situation that required conflict resolution.

The Individual and the Group

Sociocultural theorists argue that some cultures, such as that of the United States, encourage competitiveness. Other cultures, such as those of Thailand, Japan, and Korea, emphasize cooperation. Studies have shown a correlation between cooperation and reduced levels of aggression and between competition and higher levels of aggression.

Thailand In Thailand, more than 90 percent of the people are Buddhists. Most villages have a Buddhist temple that serves as the center of social life. An ancient tradition of Buddhism in Thailand stresses the importance of being a monk. This has led to a unique custom in Thailand. During their late teens or early twenties, many Thai men become monks for a short time. They go to live in a monastery where they meditate and study Buddhist teachings. They shave their heads, wear saffron robes, and give up their worldly possessions. This process of socialization helps them leave their individuality behind and adapt to the values of the group. By so doing, they put themselves in touch with the deepest values of the community and the society at large. After his time as a monk, a young man is considered ready for adult life.

Buddhist monks in Thailand pray together.

Japan In general, Japanese culture emphasizes group membership. Many corporations blur the line between the individual and the group, and between private life and work. For example, employees from the lowest-level worker to the company president might all wear company uniforms to emphasize group solidarity. Employees might start each day by singing the company song and spend leisure time at company-sponsored events. In the evening, employees may go home to company houses. The Japanese view of the relationship between individual and group involves cooperation, courtesy, and mutual respect.

Korea The teachings of Confucius have influenced Korea. Confucius stressed the importance of social order and good government. His ideas have influenced the way many Koreans view the role of the individual as essentially one of conforming to the norms of the wider social group to which he or she belongs. Social order is not the only value taught by Confucius that is important to most Koreans. Education is also highly valued in the Confucian tradition, and this too can be observed in the way education is conducted in South Korea. The needs of the group, or the class, are placed above those of any one individual in the group.

The figure of the lone cowboy on horseback has become a symbol of America.

United States Much of the rest of the world views the United States as "cowboy country," where the individual is supreme. The cowboy is commonly seen as representative of very deep-seated American values such as individual rights, independence, and a kind of winner-take-all mentality. The cowboy is willing to take an unpopular stand against the herd mentality of the group. These are stereotypes, of course, of American attitudes and behavior, but they have great currency around the world. In the view of outsiders, Americans are sometimes said to have a "me first" attitude.

Thinking Critically

1. **Draw Conclusions** What do you think might be the effect on the individual worker of being provided with benefits such as housing?

2. **Discuss** What are some of the costs and benefits of both cultural styles? How does the United States go against the stereotype?

Revisiting Milgram

Stanley Milgram conducted his studies of obedience in the 1960s and 1970s. Are Milgram's studies still relevant in the world of the 21st century?

Reading and Activity Workbook

Use the workbook to complete this experiment.

1. Introduction

When reading about Stanley Milgram's studies of obedience, many people think, "I wouldn't do that." Maybe that's true. Maybe times have changed or people have changed since Milgram's studies were conducted. Your task is to design a new experiment that could test Milgram's original findings. You will work in small groups and follow the scientific method as you design your experiment. You will not actually perform your experiment, but you will present your proposal to the class for discussion and comment. To complete this experiment, follow the steps below.

■ Following your teacher's instructions, organize the class into groups of three or four students.

■ In your group, review the scientific method as it applies to the Milgram study. How did he accomplish each step in the process—form a hypothesis, determine needed information, gather information, evaluate results, draw conclusions, and replicate the results?

■ Discuss the concepts of sample/population and ethics as they apply to the Milgram study.

2. Designing Your Experiment

Milgram hypothesized that the average person has a tendency to obey an authority figure. Your task is to design an experiment that tests this same hypothesis in a new way. Working as a group, write down responses to each of the following:

■ Your hypothesis (same as Milgram's): The average person tends to obey an authority figure.

■ What information do you need to test your hypothesis?

■ Design a new experiment to test your hypothesis (gather information). Be creative. You must investigate Milgram's hypothesis but try to do so in a new and unique way. You will have an experimental group (Milgram used teachers), a control group (Milgram did not use a control group), an independent variable (participants being told by an authority figure to continue despite their belief they were hurting someone), and a dependent variable (obedience).

■ Here are some specific ideas for designing your experiment.

❶ Choose an experimental group. It might be younger siblings or possibly another class.

❷ Choose an authority figure. It might be an adult such as a teacher or another school figure such as a guidance counselor or a school therapist.

❸ Imagine situations in which an authority figure might make specific requests of the participants in the experiment. For example, the experimental group might be asked to be silent for an hour, to sit in a specific position or posture for a half hour, to come early to school, or to stay late after school.

❹ Consider the ethical standards of your experiment.

■ What results do you expect? What concerns might someone have upon reading about your experiment?

■ Assuming your hypothesis is proven correct, what conclusions may we draw about human behavior?

■ If your experiment was conducted in another country, do you think that you would get the same results? What if your experiment was conducted 50 years ago or 50 years in the future?

3. Presenting Your Experiment

All good science must undergo the scrutiny of others who are knowledgeable about the subject. Describe your experiment to the class and be sure to address the following:

■ What concerns do your classmates have in terms of design, sample/population, control, generalizability of test results, and ethics?

■ How would your classmates improve on your experimental design?

■ If your classmates were an ethical review board, would they approve your study?

4. Discussion

■ Overall, how successful was the class at designing experiments that would test Milgram's original hypothesis?

■ What did the best experiments have in common?

■ What were some common weaknesses in the various experimental designs?

■ How might you apply the understandings you have developed as a result of the Milgram study to the world today? Why does it matter?

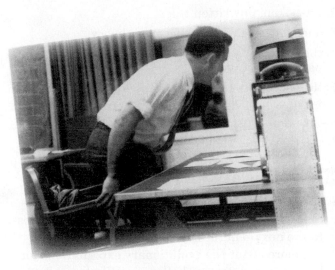

This is the machine that was used in Stanley Milgram's classic study of obedience.

One of the few participants in Milgram's study who refused to continue with the experiment is shown in this photo.

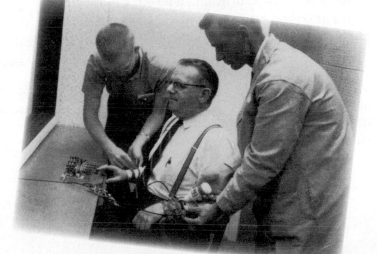

One of Milgram's associates has electrodes attached to his wrists.

Comprehension and Critical Thinking

SECTION 1 *(pp. 590–593)*

1. a. Define What is the first-shift scheme?

b. Explain What is an example of positive group polarization?

c. Make Judgments What is the relationship between diffusion of responsibility and risky shift?

SECTION 2 *(pp. 594–599)*

2. a. Describe How does socialization affect people's behavior?

b. Analyze What happens to people's beliefs if they are disturbed by what is happening around them?

c. Elaborate What is the difference between obedience and conformity?

SECTION 3 *(pp. 601–606)*

3. a. Identify Main Ideas How would an evolutionary psychologist and learning theorist explain the tendency for people to obey authority figures?

b. Draw Conclusions Why do some psychologists believe that catharsis can help prevent aggression?

c. Elaborate How is the bystander effect related to diffusion of responsibility?

Psychology in Your Life

4. Request permission to attend a meeting of a school or community organization. During the meeting, take notes on how the group's leader conducts the meeting. Afterward, review your notes and decide what style of leadership was used. How might the meeting have been conducted if another style of leadership had been used instead? Write a brief summary of what you have learned.

Reviewing Vocabulary

Match the terms below with the correct definitions.

5. social facilitation

6. evaluation apprehension

7. social loafing

8. risky shift

9. majority-wins schemes

10. group polarization

11. social norms

12. implicit norms

13. theorist

A. the tendency to slack off when part of a group

B. group decision-making process in which the group makes decisions in accordance with what the majority wants

C. the strengthening of a group member's attitudes

D. unspoken, unwritten rules

E. one who speculates, or forms a theory

F. the tendency for people to take greater risks as part of a group

G. the concept that people often perform better when other people are watching

H. the standards people share

I. concern about the opinion of others

INTERNET ACTIVITY ✳

14. How might aggression or altruism help individuals survive, reproduce, and contribute their genes to the next generation? Use the Internet to find out more about the evolutionary explanations for human aggression and altruism. What evidence supports the claims that the behavior helps individuals spread their genes? What evidence refutes the claims? Describe the evidence in a short written report.

SKILLS ACTIVITY: INTERPRETING GRAPHS

Study the graph below. Then use the information in the graph to help you answer the questions that follow.

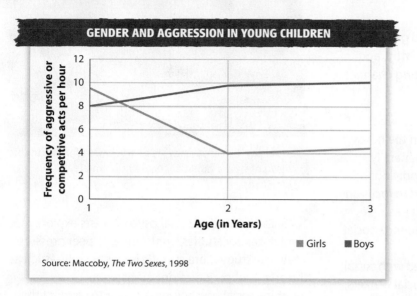

GENDER AND AGGRESSION IN YOUNG CHILDREN

Source: Maccoby, *The Two Sexes*, 1998

15. Compare Which group becomes less aggressive with age, and when does a big difference appear compared to the other group?

16. Interpret What information would you request from the psychologist to learn more about this study and its usefulness?

WRITING FOR AP PSYCHOLOGY

Use your knowledge of obedience and conformity to answer the question below. Do not simply list facts. Present a clear argument based on your critical analysis of the question, using the appropriate psychological terminology.

17. Briefly describe how teens in your community are pressured to conform to their peers. Discuss each of the issues listed below.

- social norms
- explicit norms
- implicit norms

Connecting Online

Visit thinkcentral.com for review and enrichment activities related to this chapter.

Quiz and Review

ONLINE QUIZZES
Take a practice quiz for each section in this chapter.

WEBQUEST
Complete a structured Internet activity for this chapter.

QUICK LAB
Reinforce a key concept with a short lab activity.

APPLYING WHAT YOU'VE LEARNED
Review and apply your knowledge by completing a project-based assessment.

Activities

eACTIVITIES
Complete chapter Internet activities for enrichment.

INTERACTIVE FEATURE
Explore an interactive version of a key feature in this chapter.

KEEP IT CURRENT
Link to current news and research in psychology.

Online Textbook

Learn more about key topics in this chapter.

Social Psychologist

How do individuals behave in social and group situations? Do boys and girls play differently, and if so, why? Do people's styles of interacting change in the workplace?

These are questions for social psychologists, who study the effects of group membership on the behavior of individuals. Their primary focus is, generally, how behavior in social situations affects individuals. However, social psychologists usually tend to focus on external influences and environments. For example, they focus on such issues as attitudes, influence, social cognition, and interaction.

Social psychologists are often confused with social workers. Both focus on social behavior. Social workers, however, are more involved with individuals. Their work is more practical and less research-oriented than the work of the social psychologist. There is also an overlap with the field of anthropology. Anthropologists also study social behavior, but they are more concerned with the social customs, rituals, and interactions of various groups of people. Finally, social psychology is also closely related to sociology. There is, however, a distinct difference between the two. Social psychologists focus on the effects of group membership on the behavior of an individual person. Sociologists, on the other hand, are more concerned with the group as a whole—its structure and characteristics.

Social psychologists may study how membership in this crowd of sports fans affects the individual fan.

Some issues that social psychologists explore may involve gender studies, conformity, or peer pressure. They may study more specific issues as well—such as the effects of prejudice on self-esteem.

Many social psychologists prefer to conduct their research in naturalistic settings. Although they have less control over the variables than they would in a lab, the results are based on real-life factors. Other social psychologists work and study in research facilities, government agencies, universities, or industry.

Preparations for the profession can vary. Social psychologists often first obtain a bachelor's degree in psychology, anthropology, or sociology. A doctoral degree offers maximum career flexibility.

The options in the field are vast and rewarding. People who enjoy observing others are most likely to be happy in this stimulating field of psychology.

Applying APA Style

APA Style THINK central thinkcentral.com

Social psychologists publish articles in professional journals. Their work may also appear in other publications. So that their writing is clear, social psychologists follow the style guidelines for punctuation approved by the **American Psychological Association (APA)**.

Punctuation establishes the pace of a sentence. Punctuation also helps prevent misunderstanding of text. For example, the colon is often misused. The APA guidelines state that a colon can be used between an introductory clause that is a complete sentence and the phrase or clause that extends or explains it. An example is "He has only one goal: passing his driver's test." If the clause following the colon is a complete sentence, it should begin with a capital letter. So, "They agreed on one point: Everyone brings a snack" is correct.

Through Think Central you can find more on correct punctuation from the APA style guidelines. Go to the site to review the APA guidelines. Then write several examples of correct punctuation. An example is provided for you.

Punctuation	Correct Usage
comma	The event occurred on May 6, 2008.
semicolon	
dash	

REFERENCE SECTION

Landmark Studies in Psychology

Ethical Principles of Psychologists and Code of Conduct

The Little Albert Experiment

Background *In psychology's early years, Sigmund Freud's theory that human behavior was largely a product of unconscious, internal processes dominated the field. In tandem with Ivan Pavlov's work, the study described here resulted in an alternative theory called behaviorism. It held that human behavior was learned primarily through experiences with the outside environment.*

Little Albert learned to fear white, fluffy objects.

Study Methodology

John B. Watson, the experiment's main author, sought to find out if he could teach a human infant to fear things that the child previously had viewed as benign. His subject was a baby boy known as "Baby Albert B." or "Little Albert." Watson began by identifying several things that did not scare Baby Albert. These neutral stimuli (so called because they do not provoke a reaction) included a white rat, a white rabbit, a fake white beard, and white cotton. Albert expressed interest in these objects and even reached for them. Why they were similarly white and somewhat furry will become clear later.

The core of the experiment involved setting the baby next to one of the neutral stimuli, the rat, and then making a loud noise, which is known to cause instinctive fear in humans. Watson chose banging on a metal bar with a hammer behind the baby. That noise is an example of an unconditioned stimulus, one for which the reaction it causes, or stimulates, does not need to be learned. After repeating this step a total of seven times over two separate sessions, Watson then moved to the experiment's next step, setting Albert next to the rat without the noise.

Results and Interpretation

The baby reacted just as Watson had expected. Although there was no loud noise, Albert immediately recoiled in fear of the rat even though at the start of the experiment he had shown no such fear. Thus, Watson had demonstrated that he could teach, or condition, a human to have a particular emotional response—in this case, fear—to a particular thing, or stimulus—in this case, the rat.

Watson followed up this part of the experiment by trying to transfer the newly taught fear to another object that at the experiment's start had not scared the baby. Sure enough, when a white rabbit was placed next to Albert, he also reacted with fear. This transfer of a conditioned response to a larger set of similar stimuli is called *generalization*.

Watson's study had additional findings. First, he showed that the objects continued to induce fear outside the laboratory, but to a lesser degree. He also went back and reproduced the response a month later, showing that the learning lasted for some time.

Watson's basic insight—that even emotions can be learned—has held up over time. Subsequent experiments, however, have shown that conditioning can be lost over time through a process called *extinction*. Moreover, researchers today would strongly reject on ethical grounds an experiment making a human baby the subject of such harmful treatment.

Watson, J. B., and Rayner, R. (1920). Conditioned emotional responses. *Journal of Experimental Psychology* 3, 1–14.

Thinking Critically

1. **Identify** What is behaviorism?
2. **Predict** How might a therapist have helped Albert to enjoy white rats and rabbits again later in life?

Pavlov and Conditioned Reflex Theory

Background *This experiment conducted by the Russian scientist Ivan P. Pavlov led to his development of the conditioned reflex theory. That theory—also called classical conditioning—explains how noninstinctual behaviors are learned, one of the basic concerns of psychology.*

Pavlov trained dogs to associate a sound with food.

Study Methodology

Ivan Pavlov, who was a physiologist, not a psychologist, came up with this experiment while conducting another one using dogs to study the mechanics of food digestion. In that experiment, Pavlov connected a tube to the dogs' salivary glands and then collected and measured the amount of saliva the dogs produced when given food. During the course of that experiment, Pavlov observed an unexpected result that could not be explained as an instinctual physiological response. Namely, nonfood stimuli that regularly took place during feedings—footsteps, for instance—began to cause the dogs to salivate even in the absence of food. The hypothesis that this was learned, not instinctual, behavior prompted Pavlov to set up a new experiment.

To study the noninstinctual behavior he observed during his earlier experiment, Pavlov created a controlled environment that separated the dogs from all stimuli other than that introduced by the experimenter. The experiment itself consisted of playing a metronome, a device used to keep time in music, at the same time as feeding the dogs. This sequence was repeated for several days. Then, Pavlov began playing the metronome by itself without feeding the dogs.

Results and Interpretation

As Pavlov theorized, playing the metronome always at the same time as the feedings caused the dogs to salivate profusely whenever they heard the metronome, regardless of whether food was present. Pavlov then went on to produce similar results with odors and visual cues instead of sounds.

Pavlov interpreted the experimental results as proof of two types of behavior. The first, called an unconditioned reflex, was instinctual behavior that need not be learned. Such behavior was triggered by what he called an unconditioned stimulus—in this case, food. Pavlov called the second type of learned behavior a conditioned reflex. It is learned by repeatedly pairing a neutral stimulus—in this case, a metronome—with an unconditioned stimulus (food). By doing so, the neutral stimulus is converted into what Pavlov called a conditioned stimulus.

Pavlov's use of empirical experimentation to discover the conditioned reflex helped bring much-needed respect to the emerging field of psychology. Moreover, the experiment led Pavlov himself to switch from physiology to psychology, making him one of the discipline's pioneers. Pavlov was so influential that numerous other experiments have cited this one—more than a thousand just since 2000.

Pavlov, I. P. (1927). *Conditioned Reflexes*. London: Oxford University Press.

Thinking Critically

1. **Identify** What basic question did Pavlov's experiment address?
2. **Explain** How is a neutral stimulus converted into a conditioned stimulus?

The Rorschach Test

Background *This study by the psychiatrist Hermann Rorschach started as an experiment aimed at comparing how people with different mental illnesses interpreted abstract forms made from a blob of ink. By the end of the study, Rorschach had concluded that the inkblots could also be used to diagnose psychological problems.*

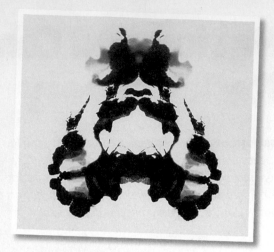

What do you see in this inkblot?

Study Methodology

Have you and a friend ever looked at the same cloud formations but seen very different things? If so, in a way you have already been introduced to the Rorshach inkblot test.

Hermann Rorschach's experiment started with the theory that when a person tries to make sense of an abstract image, its ambiguity causes the person to look inward and project meaning onto it, since it does not correspond to an actual thing. Thus, the meaning a person projects onto the ambiguous image provides a clue into the person's unconscious.

The tool used in Rorschach's experiment was an inkblot made by dropping ink on a piece of paper and then folding the paper in half. The result was a random symmetrical image that was ambiguous enough to be suggestive of various objects, in a similar way as a cloud may look like other objects. (Rorschach found that symmetrical inkblots tended to be more suggestive of other images.)

The subjects for the study consisted of a mix of people, some with mental disorders such as schizophrenia. Other subjects had no diagnosed disorders. The basic procedure was to show each subject a series of 10 inkblots, some of different ink colors, and ask what each looked like. Rorschach used a number of different criteria to interpret the subjects' responses, such as how long it took them to respond, whether color or movement was part of their description, and, of course, what the test subject thought the inkblot looked like.

Results and Interpretation

Two major findings came out of Rorschach's experiment. First, he found that certain responses tended to correlate with specific mental conditions. For instance, "normal" subjects seldom failed to provide an answer, while subjects with schizophrenia often refused to do so. People who were depressed gave fewer answers than those who were not. People with depression saw more animals than did other participants. The second major finding was that the inkblot test, which Rorschach called the form interpretive test, could be used to help diagnose psychological disorders.

It should be noted that subsequent studies have tended to question the effectiveness of the inkblot test as a diagnostic tool, although some more recent studies have found it helpful in diagnosing some specific conditions. Nonetheless, the test is still used by many psychotherapists, especially in the initial stages of therapy, as a way of gaining insight into the patient's mental state.

Rorschach, H. (1942). *Psychodiagnostics: A diagnostic test based on perception.* New York: Grune and Stratton.

Thinking Critically

1. **Identify** What was the initial purpose of Rorschach's experiment, and what other unplanned result caused a major change in psychology?

2. **Explain** According to Rorschach, what is it about ambiguous images that makes them a window into internal mental states?

Defense Mechanisms

Background *Sigmund Freud shaped the study of psychology more than any other person. However, Freud's methodology was often unscientific. Other psychologists have explored and expanded upon his work, including his daughter, Anna Freud. Her work included a study of the Freudian concept of defense mechanisms.*

Anna Freud, with her father and niece

Study Methodology

Sigmund Freud claimed that the human personality consisted of three components. He called these components the ego, the superego, and the id. When they work well together, a person is balanced, makes good decisions, and exhibits normal behavior. At times, however, the components do not work together well. For example, the id, which seeks pleasure, may overwhelm the ego, which assesses real-world conditions. This imbalance can lead to *free-floating anxiety,* a sense of anxiety that does not seem to have a clear cause.

Freud argued that humans try to resolve their anxiety by way of defense mechanisms. These are tools that the mind uses to restore balance between the id, ego, and superego. People use defense mechanisms to deceive the self or distort reality so that the anxiety diminishes. In her work, Freud's daughter Anna refined the concept of defense mechanisms. Anna Freud took a more systematic approach to her studies, using research and observation. For example, she studied the effects of stress on children housed in orphanages that she and her colleagues had founded.

Results and Interpretation

Anna Freud identified 10 defense mechanisms, including repression, regression, projection, reaction formation, and sublimation. Repression is the denial of feelings that create anxiety. Regression is the return to an earlier stage of development. For example, an insecure child might imitate the behaviors of an infant such as thumb-sucking. Projection is the process of projecting one's anxieties onto someone else. For example, a wife who is considering divorce may accuse her husband of wanting to end the marriage. A person employing reaction formation lessens anxiety by expressing a reaction opposite to the one actually felt. Finally, sublimation is the use of healthy and productive activities to relieve anxiety. Freud believed that sublimation was a healthy response to psychological distress.

Anna Freud's concept of defense mechanisms is perhaps impossible to prove empirically. However, psychologists have found the concept useful for describing and understanding many varieties of human behavior.

Freud made another major contribution to psychology. Her work with children helped establish developmental psychology as a legitimate field of study.

Freud, A. (1946). *The ego and the mechanisms of defense.* New York: International Universities Press.

Thinking Critically

1. **Identify** List five defense mechanisms that Anna Freud identified.

2. **Explain** Why did Freud claim that sublimation was a healthy response to anxiety?

Skinner's Superstitious Pigeons

Background *This study by B. F. Skinner involved teaching pigeons superstitious behavior—that is, behavior believed to produce a consequence that in reality it does not. It was one of several studies that led Skinner to develop his theory of radical behaviorism, which posits that all, as opposed to some, human behavior stems from experience rather than from internal thoughts, as Freud argued.*

Skinner in his lab with colleagues and pigeons

Study Methodology

B. F. Skinner conducted his study with what he called a conditioning chamber. Also known as the Skinner box, it consisted of a cage with a food dish inside that could be filled either by the lab animal via a lever inside the cage, or as in this case, from the outside by the experimenter. Skinner started his study by putting eight pigeons in separate conditioning chambers and then feeding them at regular 15-second intervals for several days. Next, Skinner slowly lengthened the feeding interval to one minute for one of the birds. In the last stage of the experiment, Skinner stopped feeding the birds altogether.

Results and Interpretation

During the 15-second interval, most of the birds displayed a variety of new repetitive behavior patterns such as spinning clockwise and pecking the floor. In the second stage, the bird whose feeding interval had been lengthened continued to display the behavior pattern it had adopted earlier, but in a more exaggerated and frantic way. In the final stage of the experiment, where the feeding stopped entirely, all the birds gradually stopped their behavior pattern. However, the bird whose feeding interval was lengthened in the experiment's second stage repeated the behavior pattern some 10,000 times before giving up.

Skinner interpreted these behavior patterns as resulting from the birds' belief that their actions caused the food to appear, even though the food was going to drop into the feeding bowls no matter what they did. In short, the birds were exhibiting superstitious behavior.

Through this and similar experiments, Skinner came up with a mechanism he called *operant conditioning* to explain how behavior patterns are learned through experience. According to the theory, a behavior is learned when it produces positive results. Skinner called this *reinforcement.* Conversely, a behavior is not learned when the consequences are negative. Skinner called this process *punishment.* Finally, Skinner found that a behavior had to be maintained by means of regular reinforcement or it would eventually stop. These processes are called *maintenance* and *extinction,* respectively.

The pigeons study has inspired many other experiments. For example, a researcher used a similar method for studying how boys with attention deficit/hyperactiviy disorder (ADHD) responded to discontinued reinforcement when playing a game. Like the pigeons, the boys exhibited superstitious behavior.

Skinner, B. F. (1948). *Superstition in the pigeon. Journal of Experimental Psychology* 38, 168–172.

Thinking Critically

1. **Identify** How do Skinner's ideas differ from Freud's in terms of how human behavior develops?

2. **Analyze** Why did the pigeon whose feeding interval was lengthened react as it did?

REM Sleep and Dreaming

Background *Every person dreams, although some people may not recall dreaming. The universality of dreaming has led psychologists to wonder how important it is. Do we need to dream? William Dement tried to determine the value of dreaming by studying what happens when people do not dream.*

Dreams can be pleasant or frightening.

Study Methodology

William Dement built his study upon the result of a 1953 study. Eugene Aserinsky and Nathaniel Kleitman had noted that while infants slept, there were periods of eye movement. Aserinsky wondered if these eye movements were related to dreaming. He and his colleague studied 20 adults. When the sleeping volunteers exhibited eye movement, they were awakened. Most reported that they were dreaming at that time. This study showed that dreaming occurred during a sleep period called REM (rapid eye movement) sleep.

The Aserinsky study made it possible to pinpoint when a sleeping person was dreaming—during REM sleep. William Dement used this information to learn if dreaming was necessary. The sleeping habits of eight volunteers were monitored for several nights. Then for the next three to seven nights, the volunteers were awakened whenever they went into REM sleep. They were then allowed some nights of uninterrupted sleep, a period Dement called the recovery phase. In the final phase of the experiment, volunteers were awakened only after REM sleep ended. In other words, they were allowed to finish dreaming before they were awakened.

Results and Interpretation

On average, Dement's volunteers dreamed 80 minutes per night. During the recovery phase, which took place after several nights of no REM sleep, volunteers averaged 112 minutes of dreaming. It appeared that when subjects lost dream time, they needed to make up for that lost time. Scholars now call this the REM-rebound effect.

Dement also noticed that during the period of no-REM sleep, the test subjects went into REM sleep more often. For example, one subject had to be awakened seven times the first night that volunteers were denied REM sleep. By the last night of that phase of the experiment, that subject had to be awakened 23 times to stop REM sleep from occurring.

These results led Dement to conclude that dreaming is necessary. In fact, Dement wrote a book for the nonscientist in which he proposed more attention be paid to our need for a good night's sleep during which we can dream. Dement even called ours a "sleep-sick society."

Aserinsky, E., and N. Kleitman, N. (1953). Regularly occurring periods of eye mobility and concomitant phenomena during sleep. *Science* 118, 273–274.
Dement, W. (1960). The effect of dream deprivation. *Science* 131, 1705–1707.

Thinking Critically

1. **Explain** How did Dement know that his test subjects were dreaming?

2. **Define** What is the REM-rebound effect? What does the effect indicate about the importance of REM sleep?

Piaget and Object Permanence

Background *The Swiss psychologist Jean Piaget is credited with founding the field of psychology called human development. This field is devoted to the study of the stages of mental development that all humans pass through in their lifetimes.*

Playing peekaboo can illustrate a child's understanding of object permanence.

Study Methodology

Jean Piaget's main line of research involved outlining a process of childhood cognitive development that went through four stages. This particular experiment, which led to the discovery of a concept called object permanence, illustrates his overall research method.

Piaget was working at a boys' school run by Alfred Binet, grading intelligence tests, when he noticed that the children's wrong answers seemed to follow a pattern. They consistently made errors that older children and adults did not make. Piaget theorized that children's learning processes are naturally different from those of adults. He decided to study those processes using an unusual, unstructured approach that consisted of using open-ended games and informal interviews to observe behavior. In another unusual step, for much of his research he used his own children as subjects.

Piaget's object permanence experiment involved observing his infant children's interactions with objects. His goal was to find out when an infant begins to recognize that an object that disappears from sensory awareness still exists—a concept he called object permanence. The experiment started with Piaget identifying when infants recognize that objects exist idependently. Once that point was reached, it involved showing an infant an object, hiding it, observing how the child reacted in terms of trying to find it, and then interpreting the observations of that behavior.

Results and Interpretation

Within the four overall stages of development, Piaget identified six substages, starting at birth and culminating in the development of object permanence at about age two. Piaget found that in the earliest stage, an infant views the outside world as an extension of himself or herself. By the middle substage, infants clearly recognize objects but do not understand that the objects continue to exist when out of sight. By the final substage, infants can find hidden objects. This ability, object permanence, is a major turning point that is essential to the development of complex reasoning skills.

Piaget's four-stage framework for childhood cognitive development—in which the development of object permanence is a crucial step—has served as a template for many subsequent studies in human development. It also has real-world relevance in terms of parenting and education because it helps educators and parents tailor the learning process to a child's stage of development.

Piaget, J. (1954). The development of object concept. In J. Piaget, *The construction of reality in the child*, pp. 3–96. New York: Basic Books.

Thinking Critically

1. **Identify** What is object permanence?

2. **Analyze** Why might the fact that Piaget used his own children as research subjects cause some psychologists to question his conclusions?

Asch on Group Conformity

Background *Everyone at some time has felt pressure to go along with the group. This study conducted by the social psychologist Solomon Asch was among the first to study systematically how group pressure to conform influences individual behavior.*

Source: Adapted from p. 32 of Asch, S. E. (1955). Opinions and social pressure. *Scientific American* 193(5), 31–35

Lines like those used in the Asch experiment

Study Methodology

Solomon Asch set about testing the power of conformity by creating what at first glance seemed to be a simple visual test. The test consisted of what appeared to be a group of eight participants comparing several sets of two cards. For each set, one card had a single line and the other had three differently sized lines, one of which was the same length as the line on the single-lined card. The subjects were then asked to identify which of the three lines on one card was the same length as the single line on the other card.

However, this seemingly straightforward test was actually a ploy that all but one of the eight subjects was in on. The "trick" behind the study was that every time a set of cards was shown to the seven "subjects" who were secretly cooperating with the experimenter, all of them picked the same wrong line on purpose. Asch set the experiment up in this way to see whether the one unknowing participant would conform to the group by choosing the same line everyone else did even though his own eyes told him it was the wrong answer.

Results and Interpretation

Around one-third of the subjects consistently went along with the group by choosing the wrong answer. About three-quarters of the subjects picked the wrong answer at least once. Clearly, group pressure was a significant influence on individual behavior. Moreover, in a follow-up experiment Asch demonstrated the

power of conformity from another angle. Using the same experimental design, Asch found that conformity fell to around 5 percent when just one of the seven "cooperating subjects" went against the group and chose the right answer.

Asch's experiment is important because it was the first to show just how powerful the pressure to conform is in molding individual behavior. Given that most individuals spend much of their lives within social groups, it is a finding that provides significant real-world insights into both the formation of individual behavior and group decision making.

Asch's study has also been influential within the field of psychology, inspiring numerous subsequent studies. One such line of research has found that there is an optimal group size for producing conformity. Conformity increases as the group's size increases until the group reaches about seven members. After that, it gradually decreases as more group members are added.

Asch, S. E. (1955). Opinions and social pressure. *Scientific American* 193(5), 31–35.

Thinking Critically

1. **Identify** What aspect of the study's design allowed the experimenter to produce the appearance of group conformity?

2. **Predict** How might an individual's level of attachment to a specific group influence the degree of individual conformity to that group?

Harlow's Study of Contact Comfort

Background *Because it is among the most powerful of emotions, love has attracted the attention of many psychologists. For most humans, the first person we love is our mother. Behavioral psychologists have argued that children love their mother because she meets primary needs such as food and security. Harry Harlow designed an experiment to determine if love itself is a primary need.*

Harlow and one of the laboratory monkeys

Study Methodology

How does one study an emotion as mysterious as love? Harry Harlow set out to do just that—study the kind of love that binds infants to their mothers.

Harlow used rhesus monkeys, which are biologically similar to humans, in his studies. The infant monkeys in his lab were raised by humans and protected from disease and dangers more effectively than they would have been in the wild by their mothers. He noticed that infant monkeys became very attached to cloth pads that lined the bottoms of their cages. In fact, if the cloth pad was removed from the cage, the monkey's health declined. When the cloth was restored, the monkey improved. Harlow wondered if these pads provided some comfort that the baby monkeys needed as much as food or water.

Harlow built two types of surrogate, or stand-in, mothers for the infant monkeys. Both models dispensed milk and provided heat. The first model was made of smooth wood covered with sponge rubber and soft cloth. The second was made of wire mesh. Eight infant rhesus monkeys were placed in a cage with access to both models. However, half the monkeys received milk from the cloth-covered surrogate, while the other half got milk from the wire-mesh surrogate. To learn more, at times Harlow placed an object that caused a fearful reaction (in this case, a wind-up toy bear) into the cages.

Results and Interpretation

No matter which model provided milk, the infant monkeys strongly preferred to spend time with the cloth-covered surrogate. Monkeys who received milk from the wire-mesh surrogate still spent most of their time with the cloth-covered "mother." When the scary bear was in the cage, all the monkeys rushed to the cloth-covered surrogate for comfort. Harlow also discovered that when a cloth-covered surrogate was in the cage, the infants were more willing to play with new objects placed in the cage. He concluded that the comfort the monkeys received from the soft cloth fulfilled some need. It provided them with a sense of security in the presence of danger and the confidence to explore their environment.

Harlow's experiment has implications not just for parents but for all people who care for children. It proved that physical contact with other people is important in all childcare settings, including the home, daycare centers, hospitals, and orphanages.

Harlow, H. F. (1958). The nature of love. *American Psychologist* 13, 673–685.

Thinking Critically

1. **Analyze** What criticisms of Harlow's experiments might other psychologists offer?

2. **Explain** Why did Harlow use rhesus monkeys in this experiment?

The Origin of Form Perception

Robert Fantz studied what holds infants' attention.

Background *Psychologists have long been fascinated by infants, and many studies focus on infants' abilities and development. However, studying infants is difficult, as they cannot communicate what they are thinking. Robert Fantz devised a study of infants' ability to perceive form, or patterns, shapes, and sizes.*

Study Methodology

By the middle of the twentieth century, psychologists agreed that human infants can perceive lights, colors, and movement. However, many scholars argued that infants could not perceive shapes and patterns.

To determine if human infants could see forms, Robert Fantz first performed an experiment with newly hatched chicks that had not yet encountered grain or seeds, their natural foods. He placed objects of different shapes and sizes in front of the chicks. He discovered that they pecked at round objects and spheres more than they did triangles and flat objects. That is, they pecked at objects shaped like seeds. The chicks could perceive forms.

Testing human infants was harder, because human babies have limited control over their body movements. Newborns cannot peck or point at things. Fantz realized, however, that they do stare. (In developmental psychology, the term for staring is *preferential looking*.) Fantz and his colleagues built a box with openings for presenting various objects. They first experimented by placing infant chimpanzees in the box to see if they stared at the objects. They did, so the researchers then placed babies ranging in age from 1 to 15 weeks into the box. The babies were presented with objects of various shapes and with different patterns on them in the box openings. The length of time that the infants stared at each form was recorded.

Results and Interpretation

Fantz discovered that infants stared longer at objects covered with complex patterns such as swirls or checkerboards than at objects without patterns. At eight weeks, the infants began preferring certain patterns. For example, they stared longer at a bull's-eye than at stripes.

The chicks had preferred forms that resembled seeds. What accounted for the shapes that attracted the attention of human infants? Fantz believed that humans were drawn to shapes that resembled human features. In a second experiment, he exposed infants to oval disks covered with black-and-white patterns. As Fantz had hypothesized, the more the pattern resembled a human face, the more interesting the infants found the pattern.

Fantz's research proved that infants' minds are not blank slates. They possess inborn abilities that shape how they respond to their environment. His study led other researchers to expand investigations into the ways that infants perceive the world around them.

Fantz, R. L. (1961). The origin of form perception. *Scientific American* 204 (May), 61–72.

Thinking Critically

1. **Explain** Why did Fantz measure how long infants stared at an object?
2. **Analyze** Why might human infants respond to patterns that resemble a human face?

The Bobo Doll Experiment

Background *One could argue that aggression has been at the root of many human troubles throughout our history, so it is not surprising that psychologists are interested in aggression. Is aggression a result of human biology? Is it a learned behavior? To help answer these questions, Albert Bandura and his colleagues at Stanford University studied aggression in children.*

Bandura in front of a photo from the Bobo doll experiment

Study Methodology

Albert Bandura maintained that aggression is a learned behavior. He theorized that children who observed aggression in an adult would model that behavior in similar circumstances. To test his hypothesis, Bandura studied 36 boys and 36 girls ranging in age from three to six years old. The children were organized into three groups. The first group served as the control group. The second group observed adults behaving aggressively, while the third group watched adults who were not aggressive. Each group contained the same number of boys and girls.

Each child was brought into a room that contained toys and activities. An adult in the room played with Tinkertoys™. In the group exposed to aggressive behavior, after one minute the adult would strike an inflated clown doll (called a Bobo doll) with a mallet, kick it, punch it in the nose, and sit on it. The adult was also verbally aggressive, shouting at the doll. Children who were to observe nonaggressive behavior watched an adult who played quietly with the Tinkertoys the entire time.

After watching the adult, each child was taken to a different room with attractive, appealing toys. The researchers reasoned that to incite aggression, the children should be angry. So to frustrate the children, researchers told the children they could not play with these toys. The children were then taken to another room that contained several toys, including a Bobo doll.

Results and Interpretation

The study revealed that the children who had witnessed adult aggression were more likely to strike the Bobo doll than were the children who had observed a nonaggressive adult. Boys were more likely to be aggressive than girls, especially if the boys had seen a male adult beat the Bobo doll. Girls were more likely to strike the doll if they had watched an aggressive female adult.

Bandura concluded that aggression was a behavior learned by observing someone else's aggressive behavior. In a later study he showed that children modeled their behavior on adults they saw in films rather than in person. This study raised concerns about young children who watch violence on TV shows. As a result, many studies on children and televised violence followed publication of the Bobo doll experiment. Congress has held hearings on media violence, and parental advisory rating systems developed from such public attention to learned aggression.

Bandura, A., Ross, D., and Ross, S. A. (1961). Transmission of aggression through imitation of aggressive models. *Journal of Abnormal and Social Psychology* 63, 575–582.

Thinking Critically

1. **Analyze** What does this study suggest about the impact of gender on modeling behavior?
2. **Predict** Would the outcome of the study have been different if it involved another human instead of a blow-up doll?

The Milgram Experiment

Background *The Milgram experiment is a landmark experiment in social psychology, the field devoted to the study of human behavior within groups. It was in part an attempt by its author, Stanley Milgram, to understand why otherwise normal people helped commit wartime atrocities.*

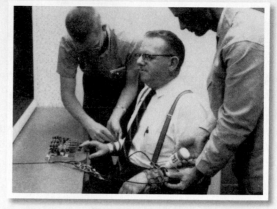

Experiment assistants and participant

Study Methodology

The experiment began with a hypothesis—that the urge to obey authority is strong enough to cause people to violate their own moral and ethical beliefs. However, designing an experiment to test that proposition posed a dilemma—how could it be done without actually harming someone in the process?

Stanley Milgram devised a clever, if still controversial, experiment. Its centerpiece was a fake, yet very convincing, machine supposedly capable of administering electric shocks at 30 increasingly stronger levels. During the experiment, the machine was controlled by the subject, who did not know that it was a fake. In the study, two other persons secretly acted out roles. One played an authority figure who directed the experiment. The other played a subject who was supposedly receiving electric shocks.

Milgram recruited 40 male subjects of different ages and occupations. They were told that they were participating in a study on the impact of punishment on learning and that their role was to question another subject (who, as mentioned, was collaborating with the experimenter) and administer increasingly higher-level shocks for each wrong answer. The sham subject then gave wrong answers on purpose. If the unknowing subject hesitated to administer the shock, he was ordered to do so by the person playing the authority figure. The more the subject hesitated, the stonger the commands became.

Results and Interpretation

With regular prompting from the fake authority figure, all the study's participants shocked the fake subject beyond the point where he appeared to be yelling in pain and became despondent and refused to answer. At this point, when the fake authority figure demanded they continue, 65 percent did so all the way to the highest shock level. The study showed that humans are highly susceptible to pressure from authority figures.

There was another major finding as well. Many of the study's unknowing subjects showed signs of extreme stress even as they obeyed their orders. This second finding continues to be a source of ethical debate among psychologists. In short, can deceiving study subjects and placing them under extreme stress ever be justified?

Milgram's study has obvious real-world implications. Given the apparent ease with which humans can ignore their own moral and ethical beliefs in the face of authority, one might argue that it is important to place strict guidelines on the use of authority.

Milgram, S. (1963). Behavioral study of obedience. *Journal of Abnormal and Social Psychology* 67, 371–378.

Thinking Critically

1. **Identify** In what two ways was the experiment problematic in terms of ethics?

2. **Analyze** How might the study have been an attempt to understand the sources of wartime atrocities?

Internal and External Control

Background *This experiment, conducted by Julian Rotter, is a landmark in the field of psychology devoted to study of the individual personality. The study demonstrated the existence of a specific personality trait influencing how much control individuals think they have over their lives.*

Does chance or choice control your life?

Study Methodology

When psychologists refer to personality, they mean the mix of behaviors, or traits, that make an individual unique. Julian Rotter theorized that one trait that makes up an individual's personality is whether the individual believes in what he called an internal locus of control or an external locus of control. Those in the first group tend to believe that they are in control of the events surrounding their lives, while those in the second tend to believe that events are outside of their control.

Rotter's study consisted of two steps. In the first step, he developed a test called the *I-E Scale* that he hoped would enable him to identify a subject as having either an internal or external personality. The scale consisted of having subjects read a series of paired statements. One statement attributed an outcome to individual effort, while the other attributed it to fate. For each pair, the subject identified the statement with which he or she agreed.

The second part of the study took place later and involved examining the results of subsequent studies by Rotter and others that used the I-E Scale. Rotter theorized that those studies' results would confirm the existence of the internal and external loci of control.

Results and Interpretation

The studies confirmed the results of Rotter's test. For example, in one gambling-related study, those who were identified as "internals" on the I. E. Scale were more likely than

"externals" to avoid bets with high odds on the grounds that they were not likely to win. In other words, they resisted the notion that they might get lucky and win. Similarly, another study found that in trying to achieve a goal, internals tended to be more highly motivated than externals. This was because they recognized that the outcome was in their own hands.

Rotter explained the development of the internal-external personality trait in terms of how the process of conditioned learning plays out for an individual over time. If, over the course of learning many behaviors, most of the things that reinforce those behaviors are viewed by the individual as a result of their own actions, then the individual develops an internal-locus-of-control personality. If, on the other hand, most of the reinforcements appear to come from things outside the person's control, the individual develops an external-locus-of-control personality.

Rotter, J. B. (1966). Generalized expectancies for internal versus external control of reinforcement. *Psychological Monographs* 80, 1–28.

Thinking Critically

1. **Identify** What is an external locus of control?

2. **Analyze** Why might someone whose personality demonstrates an internal locus of control be able to stop a bad habit, such as smoking, more easily than someone characterized by an external locus of control?

Learning to Feel Helpless

Background *One basic insight of psychology is that much of human behavior is learned. This experiment by the behavioral psychologist Martin Seligman showed that among the "bad" behavior patterns that can be learned is a mistaken belief in helplessness.*

Dogs learned helplessness in the Seligman experiment.

Study Methodology

The basic theory behind Martin Seligman's experiment was that repeated exposure to an unpleasant, inescapable situation can result in the mistaken feeling that other events are beyond one's control. To test the proposition, Seligman designed a two-part experiment. The subjects were 24 dogs divided into three groups of 8 dogs each. The "unpleasant situation" his subjects were exposed to was a mild electrical shock.

The first part of the study involved two of the three groups. It consisted of placing a pair of dogs, one from each group, into a harness. For each harnessed pair, the dog from one group could easily escape the shock by moving its head from side to side, while the dog from the other group could not escape the shock no matter what it did. (The harness was rigged so that the dog's shock ended when the other dog figured out how to stop the shock; that way, both dogs received the same amount of shock time.)

The second part of the study included the third group, which was a control group. Seligman administered shocks to all the dogs, one at a time, in a box that was set up so that the dog could jump over a partition and avoid the shock. For each of the dogs, Seligman recorded whether it learned to escape the shock and, if so, how long it took to learn the behavior.

Results and Interpretation

Seligman reasoned that if his theory was correct, then the dogs that could not escape the shock in the study's first part would be far less likely than dogs from the other two groups to learn how to escape the avoidable shock. Seligman's statistical analysis supported that hypothesis. Between 70 percent and 80 percent of the "no-escape" dogs from the first part of the experiment failed to escape the shock in the second part when they could have done so. Meanwhile, almost all the dogs in the other two groups—both the "escape" dogs in the first part and the third control group—escaped quickly and easily.

The results of this experiment led Seligman and others to argue that learned helplessness is one cause of mental illness. This conclusion can have a practical application in treating the depression and anxiety some people develop after natural disasters and other traumatic events beyond their control.

Seligman, M. E. P., and Maier, S. F. (1967). Failure to escape traumatic shock. *Journal of Experimental Psychology* 74, 1–9.

Thinking Critically

1. **Identify** What mental illness can develop from an individual's mistaken feeling of helplessness?

2. **Analyze** What ethical issue is involved in the experiment, and what factor is balanced against that ethical issue in order to justify such an experiment?

Facial Expressions and Culture

Background *Facial expressions are one cue that humans use to determine a person's mood. We make different faces when we are happy, sad, or angry. Psychologist Paul Ekman wondered if the meaning of facial expressions remained constant across cultures. In other words, do facial expressions express the same emotions across the globe, or do factors such as culture change their meaning?*

Smiles and laughter are universal.

Study Methodology

There are so many ways in which cultures are different, from concepts of beauty and rules of behavior to religious beliefs and basic philosophies. Is it likely that we all smile when we're happy and frown when we're sad?

Paul Ekman and his colleague Wallace Friesen conducted two studies to determine if the links between certain facial expressions and certain emotions were universal. In the first study, they showed photographs of human faces and asked volunteers to name the emotion reflected in the expression. Study participants were from Argentina, Brazil, Chile, Japan, and the United States. Every study participant identified the same emotion for every photograph.

The researchers realized, however, that their study was flawed. In an age of global media, people in industrialized countries had long been exposed to certain images. To test the hypothesis that certain facial expressions had universal meanings, they needed subjects who had not been exposed to media images. They found such people in 1971 in New Guinea, where members of the Fore tribe had had limited contact with modern cultures.

Ekman and Friesen divided the Fore into two groups. Members of the first group had had no contact with modern cultures. They spoke no English and had never seen a motion picture. Members of the second, much smaller group, were familiar with some aspects of modern culture.

Trained translators read brief stories to members of each group and asked them to pick out a photograph with a facial expression that corresponded to the events in the story. The stories were simple; for example, the "happiness" story was about someone whose friends have come for a visit. The photos were all of Westerners, not members of the Fore.

Results and Interpretation

The psychologists discovered that many facial expressions are universal. The Fore picked the same expressions to represent the same emotions that people from other countries had selected. The one exception was that of fear, which the Fore often confused with surprise.

These findings indicate that facial expression may be the result of survival mechanisms of early humans. For example, the expression that signaled fear warned other humans of danger and helped them to survive. Humans retain these expressions and their meanings even today.

Ekman, P., and Friesen, W. V. (1971). Constants across cultures in the face and emotion. *Journal of Personality and Social Psychology* 17, 124–129.

Thinking Critically

1. **Analyze** Why might it be difficult to re-create this study today?

2. **Infer** Besides those that show fear, what facial expressions may have provided evolutionary advantages, and in what way might they have done so?

The Stanford Prison Experiment

Interactions between guards and prisoners were a focus of the experiment.

Background *A team of researchers led by the social psychologist Philip Zimbardo designed this study as a way of testing the theory that the social setting—in this case an inherently oppressive prison environment—is an important factor in molding individual behavior.*

Study Methodology

The subjects in Philip Zimbardo's now-famous prison study were 24 male college students, all of whom had been tested and found to be healthy and psychologically normal. This ensured that none of the subjects started the experiment with "abnormal" individual personality traits that might taint the results.

At the start of the study, half the subjects were randomly assigned the role of prisoner. The other half became mock prison guards. After a staged arrest and booking process conducted with the help of the local police department, the "prisoners" were sent to a "jail" created in the basement of a campus building, where they were placed in the custody of the realistically dressed "guards" for what was to be a two-week mock imprisonment.

Results and Interpretation

Shortly after the experiment began, the behavior of both the prisoners and the guards underwent a dramatic change. Within the first two days, a prisoner "riot" took place, which was ruthlessly put down by the guards using icy blasts from a fire extinguisher. Thereafter, the prisoners became despondent and depressed. Several were so traumatized by the experience that they had to be released within the first few days.

As for the guards, many of them used their position of authority to physically and mentally abuse the prisoners. Moreover, while some guards did their jobs without resorting

to abuse, none of them tried to stop the more abusive ones. In one representative incident, the prisoners refused to help a fellow prisoner who was being abused by the guards. They voted not to give up their blankets in exchange for the release of the "misbehaving" prisoner from solitary confinement.

In the end, the shocking results of the Stanford prison experiment led to its termination in just six days instead of two weeks. The experiment showed how social factors, which in this case involved an uneven distribution of power and control between prisoners and guards, can trigger the rapid development of abnormal behavior patterns.

The Stanford experiment continues to be relevant today. The 2004 scandal involving the treatment of prisoners at the Abu Ghraib military prison in Iraq brought the Stanford study back into public awareness.

Zimbardo, P. G. (1972). The pathology of imprisonment. *Society* 9 (6), 4–8.
Haney, C., Banks, W. C., and Zimbardo, P. G. (1973). Interpersonal dynamics in a simulated prison, *International Journal of Criminology and Penology* 1, 69–97.

Thinking Critically

1. **Identify** What was the underlying theory of this experiment?

2. **Draw Conclusions** How might this experiment support the idea that improving the prison environment can have a positive impact on prisoners' behavior?

Identifying Mental Illness in a Mental Hospital

Background *In determining if a person suffers from mental illness, mental health care providers observe behavior. A person exhibiting abnormal behavior may be diagnosed as having a psychological disorder. In a 1973 study, David Rosenhan discovered that the link between abnormal behavior and a diagnosis of such a disorder may be the result of the provider's perceptions.*

How does the setting affect the diagnosis?

Study Methodology

David Rosenhan and seven volunteers participated in the study. Claiming to hear voices that said "empty," "hollow," and "thud," each participant applied for admission to a psychiatric hospital. The "patients" reported no other symptoms besides the voices. All were admitted—all but one with a diagnosis of schizophrenia. Once admitted, participants gave honest answers to the doctors' questions. Most important, participants always engaged in normal behavior, never pretending to be mentally ill. They cooperated with the staff and were model patients in all ways. (They all flushed any medication they received down the toilet, however.)

The participants took notes on their experiences. At first, they tried to hide this from the staff, but later recorded their observations openly, since the doctors interpreted the note-taking as another symptom of their disorder.

Results and Interpretation

The average hospital stay for the participants was 19 days. The shortest stay was 7 days. One participant was released after 52 days in the hospital. All seven who had been diagnosed with schizophrenia were released with a diagnosis of schizophrenia in remission.

Even though they exhibited normal behavior, doctors and other hospital staff treated the participants as if they were mentally ill. They typically ignored questions from the participants, rarely carrying on a conversation. One interesting aspect of the study was that the genuine patients were more likely than the hospital staff to suspect that the participants were not mentally ill. Some patients even accused the study volunteers of being investigative journalists. Rosenhan noted that even as hospital patients received little personal attention from doctors, the patients were given large quantities of medication.

Rosenhan concluded that hospital psychiatrists and staff assumed that any patient admitted to the hospital must be mentally ill. Doctors interpreted many normal behaviors as being abnormal. Patient behavior, then, was not the key to understanding the diagnosis. Instead, the setting in which the behavior took place determined how the staff perceived the patients.

Rosenhan repeated his study several times after publishing his article. The results were usually the same. His research has led to greater care in diagnostic procedures and has increased awareness of the dangers of applying labels to patients.

Rosenhan, D. L. (1973). On being sane in insane places. *Science* 179, 250–258.

Thinking Critically

1. **Analyze** Why do you think that patients in the mental hospital were more likely than doctors to recognize that study participants did not have psychological disorders?

2. **Predict** How might a mental health professional approach the problem of diagnosing mental illness after reading Rosenhan's study?

Multiple Intelligences

Background *For most of the twentieth century, psychologists used tests to measure intelligence. However, some critics noted that the tests were not reliable. Test scores were influenced by factors other than intelligence, such as race and social class. These concerns led Howard Gardner and other psychologists to search for new definitions of intelligence.*

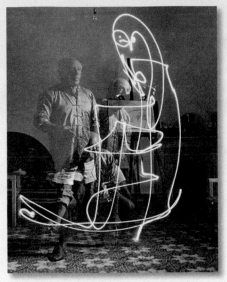

What type of intelligence did Pablo Picasso exhibit?

Study Methodology

To revise our understanding of intelligence, Howard Gardner studied how the brain works. He noted that different parts of the brain carried out different tasks. People who suffered from brain injuries often lost certain mental skills. He also studied prodigies, people who possess an outstanding ability in one area of life but are unremarkable in others. For example, an individual may be average in most ways yet have musical talent far beyond that of an average person.

From his studies, Gardner concluded that intelligence is not a single, unified level of ability. Instead, Gardner argued that human beings possess multiple intelligences. An individual may have great ability in one area, be average in other, and below average in yet another.

Gardner listed seven types of intelligence. Linguistic intelligence is skill with words and language. Musical intelligence is a heightened ability with music. People with high logical-mathematical intelligence are good with numbers and analysis. Spatial intelligence is the ability to mentally manipulate images. Dancers and athletes in particular possess body-kinesthetic intelligence. Intrapersonal intelligence is the ability to know one's own motivations and emotions, while interpersonal intelligence is the skill of identifying other people's feelings and desires.

Later, Gardner added an eighth intelligence—naturalist intelligence. A person with this quality is able to "recognize and classify plants, minerals, and animals, including rocks and grass and all variety of flora and fauna." He cited Charles Darwin as a good example.

To define an intelligence, Gardner established eight signs. Examples include evidence that the intelligence has developed over evolutionary time, and the ability to study the intelligence with psychological experiments.

Results and Interpretation

Published in 1983, Gardner's theory of multiple intelligences became popular with many scholars. It influenced educational systems as teachers sought to understand how students learn. Critics, however, have charged that there is no scientific basis for Gardner's theory. They point out that it is impossible to prove or disprove. Some critics claim that Gardner's categories do not reflect intelligence but, rather, different styles of thinking.

Gardner, H. (1983). *Frames of mind: The theory of multiple intelligences.* New York: Basic Books.

Thinking Critically

1. **Explain** How did Gardner's study of brain functioning lead to the theory of multiple intelligences?

2. **Support a Position** Besides Gardner's seven intelligences, what other types of intelligences might psychologists claim exist?

Cultural Values and Human Behavior

Background *Psychologists agree that the culture you live in influences your behavior. However, cultures are very complex, and it can be difficult to determine exactly how culture shapes behavior. Psychologist Harry Triandis studied different cultures and the ways in which they affect human behavior.*

The study examined Puerto Rican attitudes about values.

Study Methodology

Harry Triandis used the concept of the ingroup to organize cultures into two broad categories. In what Triandis called collectivist cultures, individuals are loyal to a specific ingroup to which they belong. An ingroup may be as small as a family or tribe or as large as a nation. The success and survival of the ingroup is more important than individual success. In return for their commitment to the ingroup, individuals receive emotional support and other assistance. Such loyalty to the ingroup persists even if the individual's relationship with the group becomes difficult or unpleasant.

Individualist cultures, in contrast, place more emphasis on personal satisfaction and success. The ingroup is not as important as it is in a collectivist culture. People may be a member of several ingroups but typically are not deeply loyal to any ingroup in particular.

To learn more, Triandis and his colleagues organized three studies. In each study, participants completed questionnaires that measured their attitudes toward values that were either individualistic or collectivist.

Results and Interpretation

The first study revealed that citizens of the United States emphasize individualistic values. The second study included Americans and participants from Japan and Puerto Rico. Triandis discovered that the Puerto Ricans and the Japanese had some collectivist and some individualist attitudes. Finally, the third study compared responses of Americans and Puerto Ricans. This study again indicated that Puerto Rican culture emphasized some collectivist attitudes. Puerto Ricans prized interactions with others and believed that groups provided positive support. Americans, however, were more concerned with self-reliance.

Triandis was able to map the two types of cultures. He found that individualist cultures are found in northern and western Europe and countries influenced by those regions. Some qualities that these countries share are a frontier, large numbers of immigrants, and both physical and social mobility. Besides the United States, Canada and Australia are examples. Most other regions Triandis labeled as collectivist.

Triandis's work proved to be very influential. Psychologists and sociologists have used his ideas to explore a variety of behaviors and attitudes. For example, studies indicate that people living in individualistic cultures are more likely to suffer from loneliness.

Triandis, H., Bontempo, R., Villarreal, M., Asai, M., and Lucca, N. (1988). Individualism and collectivism: Cross-cultural perspectives on self-ingroup relationships. *Journal of Personality and Social Psychology* 54, 323–338.

Thinking Critically

1. **Identify** What values might be important to people in individualistic cultures?
2. **Predict** How might divorce rates differ between individualistic and collectivist cultures?

The Minnesota Twins Study

Background *Scientists have long debated the forces that shape human personality. For most of the twentieth century, scholars argued that factors in one's environment—the influence of parents and teachers, for example—shape personalities. However, some psychologists wondered about the role of heredity and genetics in forming personality. Psychologists at the University of Minnesota designed an experiment to help determine whether nature (genetics) or nurture (environment) is more important in determining who we are.*

These twins were raised apart but share many characteristics.

Study Methodology

We may not like to think that heredity plays a significant role in our personalities. We would rather think that our ability to make friends or to persevere in the face of difficulty is due more to our virtues than to our genes.

To study the effects of genes on personality, psychologist Thomas Bouchard enlisted the participation of monozygotic twins. Commonly called identical twins, monozygotic twins share the same genetic makeup. Bouchard and his colleagues at the University of Minnesota opened a registry for twins born in Minnesota from 1936 to 1955. They organized the twins who registered into two groups. The first group consisted of monozygotic twins raised together (MZT). The second group was made up of monozygotic twins who had been separated at an early age and raised apart (MZA). Volunteers from each group were given a wide array of tests. Scholars studied the twins' health, religious beliefs, reaction times, and even listed their personal belongings. The testing took about 50 hours to complete.

The psychologists used the test results to create a database of information about the two groups of twins. The psychologists rated the level of shared personality traits among members of the MZT group. They then rated the similarity of the same traits of the MZA group. Comparing the results of the tests on the two groups allowed the psychologists to evaluate the role of heredity and environment in forming personalities.

Results and Interpretation

The study of the database showed that members of the MZA group and the MZT group had very similar test results. If environment were wholly responsible for personality, the twins raised apart would in some ways be very different from one another. However, twins raised apart were about as similar to one another in personality as were twins raised together. This outcome indicated that genes play a major role in the development of personality.

The study's authors did not completely dismiss the role of environment. For example, they noted that a person's intelligence quotient (IQ) could improve with proper training.

Critics claimed that other studies of twins have shown that environment plays a greater role than the University of Minnesota study found. Despite such criticisms, Bouchard and his fellow psychologists changed the debate over nature and nurture. Scientists continue to conduct research on the influence of genetics on personality.

Bouchard, T., Lykken, D., McGue, M., Segal, N., and Tellegen, A. (1990). Sources of human psychological differences: The Minnesota study of twins reared apart. *Science* 250, 223–229.

Thinking Critically

1. **Explain** Why did the Bouchard study use monozygotic twins?
2. **Predict** How might this study affect our understanding of the importance of genetics?

Ethical Principles of Psychologists
and Code of Conduct

PREAMBLE

Psychologists are committed to increasing scientific and professional knowledge of behavior and people's understanding of themselves and others and to the use of such knowledge to improve the condition of individuals, organizations, and society. Psychologists respect and protect civil and human rights and the central importance of freedom of inquiry and expression in research, teaching, and publication. They strive to help the public in developing informed judgments and choices concerning human behavior. In doing so, they perform many roles, such as researcher, educator, diagnostician, therapist, supervisor, consultant, administrator, social interventionist, and expert witness. This Ethics Code provides a common set of principles and standards upon which psychologists build their professional and scientific work.

This Ethics Code is intended to provide specific standards to cover most situations encountered by psychologists. It has as its goals the welfare and protection of the individuals and groups with whom psychologists work and the education of members, students, and the public regarding ethical standards of the discipline.

The development of a dynamic set of ethical standards for psychologists' work-related conduct requires a personal commitment and lifelong effort to act ethically; to encourage ethical behavior by students, supervisees, employees, and colleagues; and to consult with others concerning ethical problems.

GENERAL PRINCIPLES

This section consists of General Principles. General Principles, as opposed to Ethical Standards, are aspirational in nature. Their intent is to guide and inspire psychologists toward the very highest ethical ideals of the profession. General Principles, in contrast to Ethical Standards, do not represent obligations and should not form the basis for imposing sanctions. Relying upon General Principles for either of these reasons distorts both their meaning and purpose.

PRINCIPLE A: BENEFICENCE AND NONMALEFICENCE

Psychologists strive to benefit those with whom they work and take care to do no harm. In their professional actions, psychologists seek to safeguard the welfare and rights of those with whom they interact professionally and other affected persons, and the welfare of animal subjects of research. When conflicts occur among psychologists' obligations or concerns, they attempt to resolve these conflicts in a responsible fashion that avoids or minimizes harm. Because psychologists' scientific and professional judgments and actions may affect the lives of others, they are alert to and guard against personal, financial, social, organizational, or political factors that might lead to misuse of their influence. Psychologists strive to be aware of the possible effect of their own physical and mental health on their ability to help those with whom they work.

PRINCIPLE B: FIDELITY AND RESPONSIBILITY

Psychologists establish relationships of trust with those with whom they work. They are aware of their professional and scientific responsibilities to society and to the specific communities in which they work. Psychologists uphold professional standards of conduct, clarify their professional roles and obligations, accept appropriate responsibility for their behavior, and seek to manage conflicts of interest that could lead to exploitation or harm. Psychologists consult with, refer to, or cooperate with other professionals and institutions to the extent needed to serve the best interests of those with whom they work. They are concerned about the ethical compliance of their colleagues' scientific and professional conduct. Psychologists strive to contribute a portion of their professional time for little or no compensation or personal advantage.

PRINCIPLE C: INTEGRITY

Psychologists seek to promote accuracy, honesty, and truthfulness in the science, teaching, and practice of psychology. In these activities psychologists do not steal, cheat, or engage in fraud, subterfuge, or intentional misrepresentation of fact. Psychologists strive to keep their promises and to avoid unwise or unclear commitments. In situations in which deception may be ethically justifiable to maximize benefits and minimize harm, psychologists have a serious obligation to consider the need for, the possible consequences of, and their responsibility to correct any resulting mistrust or other harmful effects that arise from the use of such techniques.

PRINCIPLE D: JUSTICE

Psychologists recognize that fairness and justice entitle all persons to access to and benefit from the contributions of psychology and to equal quality in the processes, procedures, and services being conducted by psychologists. Psychologists exercise reasonable judgment and take precautions to ensure that their potential biases, the boundaries of their competence, and the limitations of their expertise do not lead to or condone unjust practices.

PRINCIPLE E: RESPECT FOR PEOPLE'S RIGHTS AND DIGNITY

Psychologists respect the dignity and worth of all people, and the rights of individuals to privacy, confidentiality, and self-determination. Psychologists are aware that special safeguards may be necessary to protect the rights and welfare of persons or communities whose vulnerabilities impair autonomous decision making. Psychologists are aware of and respect cultural, individual, and role differences, including those based on age, gender, gender identity, race, ethnicity, culture, national origin, religion, sexual orientation, disability, language, and socioeconomic status and consider these factors when working with members of such groups. Psychologists try to eliminate the effect on their work of biases based on those factors, and they do not knowingly participate in or condone activities of others based upon such prejudices.

ETHICAL STANDARDS

1. Resolving Ethical Issues

1.01 Misuse of Psychologists' Work

If psychologists learn of misuse or misrepresentation of their work, they take reasonable steps to correct or minimize the misuse or misrepresentation.

1.02 Conflicts Between Ethics and Law, Regulations, or Other Governing Legal Authority

If psychologists' ethical responsibilities conflict with law, regulations, or other governing legal authority, psychologists make known their commitment to the Ethics Code and take steps to resolve the conflict. If the conflict is unresolvable via such means, psychologists may adhere to the requirements of the law, regulations, or other governing legal authority.

1.03 Conflicts Between Ethics and Organizational Demands

If the demands of an organization with which psychologists are affiliated or for whom they are working conflict with this Ethics Code, psychologists clarify the nature of the conflict, make known their commitment to the Ethics Code, and to the extent feasible, resolve the conflict in a way that permits adherence to the Ethics Code.

1.04 Informal Resolution of Ethical Violations

When psychologists believe that there may have been an ethical violation by another psychologist, they attempt to resolve the issue by bringing it to the attention of that individual, if an informal resolution appears appropriate and the intervention does not violate any confidentiality rights that may be involved. (See also Standards 1.02, Conflicts Between Ethics and Law, Regulations, or Other Governing Legal Authority, and 1.03, Conflicts Between Ethics and Organizational Demands.)

1.05 Reporting Ethical Violations

If an apparent ethical violation has substantially harmed or is likely to substantially harm a person or organization and is not appropriate for informal resolution under Standard 1.04, Informal Resolution of Ethical Violations, or is not resolved properly in that fashion, psychologists take further action appropriate to the situation. Such action might include referral to state or national committees on professional ethics, to state licensing boards, or to the appropriate institutional authorities. This standard does not apply when an intervention would violate confidentiality rights or when psychologists have been retained to review the work of another psychologist whose professional conduct is in question. (See also Standard 1.02, Conflicts Between Ethics and Law, Regulations, or Other Governing Legal Authority.)

1.06 Cooperating With Ethics Committees

Psychologists cooperate in ethics investigations, proceedings, and resulting requirements of the APA or any affiliated state psychological association to which they belong. In doing so, they address any confidentiality issues. Failure to cooperate is itself an ethics violation. However, making a request for deferment of adjudication of an ethics complaint pending the outcome of litigation does not alone constitute noncooperation.

1.07 Improper Complaints

Psychologists do not file or encourage the filing of ethics complaints that are made with reckless disregard for or willful ignorance of facts that would disprove the allegation.

1.08 Unfair Discrimination Against Complainants and Respondents

Psychologists do not deny persons employment, advancement, admissions to academic or other programs, tenure, or promotion, based solely upon their having made or their being the subject of an ethics complaint. This does not preclude taking action based upon the outcome of such proceedings or considering other appropriate information.

2. Competence

2.01 Boundaries of Competence

(a) Psychologists provide services, teach, and conduct research with populations and in areas only within the boundaries of their competence, based on their education, training, supervised experience, consultation, study, or professional experience.

(b) Where scientific or professional knowledge in the discipline of psychology establishes that an understanding of factors associated with age, gender, gender identity, race, ethnicity, culture, national origin, religion, sexual orientation, disability, language, or socioeconomic status is essential for effective implementation of their services or research, psychologists have or obtain the training, experience, consultation, or supervision necessary to ensure the competence of their services, or they make appropriate referrals, except as provided in Standard 2.02, Providing Services in Emergencies.

(c) Psychologists planning to provide services, teach, or conduct research involving populations, areas, techniques, or technologies new to them undertake relevant education, training, supervised experience, consultation, or study.

(d) When psychologists are asked to provide services to individuals for whom appropriate mental health services are not available and for which psychologists have not obtained the competence necessary, psychologists with closely related prior training or experience may provide such services in order to ensure that services are not denied if they make a reasonable effort to obtain the competence required by using relevant research, training, consultation, or study.

(e) In those emerging areas in which generally recognized standards for preparatory training do not yet exist, psychologists nevertheless take reasonable steps to ensure the competence of their work and to protect clients/patients, students, supervisees, research participants, organizational clients, and others from harm.

(f) When assuming forensic roles, psychologists are or become reasonably familiar with the judicial or administrative rules governing their roles.

2.02 Providing Services in Emergencies

In emergencies, when psychologists provide services to individuals for whom other mental health services are not available and for which psychologists have not obtained the necessary training, psychologists may provide such services in order to ensure that services are not denied. The services are discontinued as soon as the emergency has ended or appropriate services are available.

2.03 Maintaining Competence

Psychologists undertake ongoing efforts to develop and maintain their competence.

2.04 Bases for Scientific and Professional Judgments

Psychologists' work is based upon established scientific and professional knowledge of the discipline. (See also Standards 2.01e, Boundaries of Competence, and 10.01b, Informed Consent to Therapy.)

2.05 Delegation of Work to Others

Psychologists who delegate work to employees, supervisees, or research or teaching assistants or who use the services of others, such as interpreters, take reasonable steps to (1) avoid delegating such work to persons who have a multiple relationship with those being served that would likely lead to exploitation or loss of objectivity; (2) authorize only those responsibilities that such persons can be expected to perform competently on the basis of their education, training, or experience, either independently or with the level of supervision being provided; and (3) see that such persons perform these services competently. (See also Standards 2.02, Providing Services in Emergencies; 3.05, Multiple Relationships; 4.01, Maintaining Confidentiality; 9.01, Bases for Assessments; 9.02, Use of Assessments; 9.03, Informed Consent in Assessments; and 9.07, Assessment by Unqualified Persons.)

2.06 Personal Problems and Conflicts

(a) Psychologists refrain from initiating an activity when they know or should know that there is a substantial likelihood that their personal problems will prevent them from performing their work-related activities in a competent manner.

(b) When psychologists become aware of personal problems that may interfere with their performing work-related duties adequately, they take appropriate measures, such as obtaining professional consultation or assistance, and determine whether they should limit, suspend, or terminate their work-related duties. (See also Standard 10.10, Terminating Therapy.)

3. Human Relations

3.01 Unfair Discrimination

In their work-related activities, psychologists do not engage in unfair discrimination based on age, gender, gender identity, race, ethnicity, culture, national origin, religion, sexual orientation, disability, socioeconomic status, or any basis proscribed by law.

3.02 Sexual Harassment

Psychologists do not engage in sexual harassment. Sexual harassment is sexual solicitation, physical advances, or verbal or nonverbal conduct that is sexual in nature, that occurs in connection with the psychologist's activities or roles as a psychologist, and that either (1) is unwelcome, is offensive, or creates a hostile workplace or educational environment, and the psychologist knows or is told this or (2) is sufficiently severe or intense to be abusive to a reasonable person in the context. Sexual harassment can consist of a single intense or severe act or of multiple persistent or pervasive acts. (See also Standard 1.08, Unfair Discrimination Against Complainants and Respondents.)

3.03 Other Harassment

Psychologists do not knowingly engage in behavior that is harassing or demeaning to persons with whom they interact in their work based on factors such as those persons' age, gender, gender identity, race, ethnicity, culture, national origin, religion, sexual orientation, disability, language, or socioeconomic status.

3.04 Avoiding Harm

Psychologists take reasonable steps to avoid harming their clients/patients, students, supervisees, research participants, organizational clients, and others with whom they work, and to minimize harm where it is foreseeable and unavoidable.

3.05 Multiple Relationships

(a) A multiple relationship occurs when a psychologist is in a professional role with a person and (1) at the same time is in another role with the same person, (2) at the same time is in a relationship with a person closely associated with or related to the person with whom the psychologist has the professional relationship, or (3) promises to enter into another relationship in the future with the person or a person closely associated with or related to the person.

A psychologist refrains from entering into a multiple relationship if the multiple relationship could reasonably be expected to impair the psychologist's objectivity, competence, or effectiveness in performing his or her functions as a psychologist, or otherwise risks exploitation or harm to the person with whom the professional relationship exists.

Multiple relationships that would not reasonably be expected to cause impairment or risk exploitation or harm are not unethical.

(b) If a psychologist finds that, due to unforeseen factors, a potentially harmful multiple relationship has arisen, the psychologist takes reasonable steps to resolve it with due regard for the best interests of the affected person and maximal compliance with the Ethics Code.

(c) When psychologists are required by law, institutional policy, or extraordinary circumstances to serve in more than one role in judicial or administrative proceedings, at the outset they clarify role expectations and the extent of confidentiality and thereafter as changes occur. (See also Standards 3.04, Avoiding Harm, and 3.07, Third-Party Requests for Services.)

3.06 Conflict of Interest

Psychologists refrain from taking on a professional role when personal, scientific, professional, legal, financial, or other interests or relationships could reasonably be expected to (1) impair their objectivity, competence, or effectiveness in performing their functions as psychologists or (2) expose the person or organization with whom the professional relationship exists to harm or exploitation.

3.07 Third-Party Requests for Services

When psychologists agree to provide services to a person or entity at the request of a third party, psychologists attempt to clarify at the outset of the service the nature of the relationship with all individuals or organizations involved. This clarification includes the role of the psychologist (e.g., therapist, consultant, diagnostician, or expert witness), an identification of who is the client, the probable uses of the services provided or the information obtained, and the fact that there may be limits to confidentiality. (See also Standards 3.05, Multiple Relationships, and 4.02, Discussing the Limits of Confidentiality.)

3.08 Exploitative Relationships

Psychologists do not exploit persons over whom they have supervisory, evaluative, or other authority such as clients/patients, students, supervisees, research participants, and employees. (See also Standards 3.05, Multiple Relationships; 6.04, Fees and Financial Arrangements; 6.05, Barter With Clients/Patients; 7.07, Sexual Relationships With Students and Supervisees; 10.05, Sexual Intimacies With Current Therapy Clients/Patients; 10.06, Sexual Intimacies With Relatives or Significant Others of Current Therapy Clients/Patients; 10.07, Therapy With Former Sexual Partners; and 10.08, Sexual Intimacies With Former Therapy Clients/Patients.)

3.09 Cooperation With Other Professionals

When indicated and professionally appropriate, psychologists cooperate with other professionals in order to serve their clients/patients effectively and appropriately. (See also Standard 4.05, Disclosures.)

3.10 Informed Consent

(a) When psychologists conduct research or provide assessment, therapy, counseling, or consulting services in person or via electronic transmission or other forms of communication, they obtain the informed consent of the individual or individuals using language that is reasonably understandable to that person or persons except when conducting such activities without consent is mandated by law or governmental regulation or as otherwise provided in this Ethics Code. (See also Standards 8.02, Informed Consent to Research; 9.03, Informed Consent in Assessments; and 10.01, Informed Consent to Therapy.)

(b) For persons who are legally incapable of giving informed consent, psychologists nevertheless (1) provide an appropriate explanation, (2) seek the individual's assent, (3) consider such persons' preferences and best interests, and (4) obtain appropriate permission from a legally authorized person, if such substitute consent is permitted or required by law. When consent by a legally authorized person is not permitted or required by law, psychologists take reasonable steps to protect the individual's rights and welfare.

(c) When psychological services are court ordered or otherwise mandated, psychologists inform the individual of the nature of the anticipated services, including whether the services are court ordered or mandated and any limits of confidentiality, before proceeding.

(d) Psychologists appropriately document written or oral consent, permission, and assent.

(See also Standards 8.02, Informed Consent to Research; 9.03, Informed Consent in Assessments; and 10.01, Informed Consent to Therapy.)

3.11 Psychological Services Delivered To or Through Organizations

(a) Psychologists delivering services to or through organizations provide information beforehand to clients and when appropriate those directly affected by the services about (1) the nature and objectives of the services, (2) the intended recipients, (3) which of the individuals are clients, (4) the relationship the psychologist will have with each person and the organization, (5) the probable uses of services provided and information obtained, (6) who will have access to the information, and (7) limits of confidentiality. As soon as feasible, they provide information about the results and conclusions of such services to appropriate persons.

(b) If psychologists will be precluded by law or by organizational roles from providing such information to particular individuals or groups, they so inform those individuals or groups at the outset of the service.

3.12 Interruption of Psychological Services

Unless otherwise covered by contract, psychologists make reasonable efforts to plan for facilitating services in the event that psychological services are interrupted by factors such as the psychologist's illness, death, unavailability, relocation, or retirement or by the client's/patient's relocation or financial limitations. (See also Standard 6.02c, Maintenance, Dissemination, and Disposal of Confidential Records of Professional and Scientific Work.)

4. Privacy And Confidentiality

4.01 Maintaining Confidentiality

Psychologists have a primary obligation and take reasonable precautions to protect confidential information obtained through or stored in any medium, recognizing that the extent and limits of confidentiality may be regulated by law or established by institutional rules or professional or scientific relationship. (See also Standard 2.05, Delegation of Work to Others.)

4.02 Discussing the Limits of Confidentiality

(a) Psychologists discuss with persons (including, to the extent feasible, persons who are legally incapable of giving informed consent and their legal representatives) and organizations with whom they establish a scientific or professional relationship (1) the relevant limits of confidentiality and (2) the foreseeable uses of the information generated through their psychological activities. (See also Standard 3.10, Informed Consent.)

(b) Unless it is not feasible or is contraindicated, the discussion of confidentiality occurs at the outset of the relationship and thereafter as new circumstances may warrant.

(c) Psychologists who offer services, products, or information via electronic transmission inform clients/patients of the risks to privacy and limits of confidentiality.

4.03 Recording

Before recording the voices or images of individuals to whom they provide services, psychologists obtain permission from all such persons or their legal representatives. (See also Standards 8.03, Informed Consent for Recording Voices and Images in Research; 8.05, Dispensing With Informed Consent for Research; and 8.07, Deception in Research.)

4.04 Minimizing Intrusions on Privacy

(a) Psychologists include in written and oral reports and consultations, only information germane to the purpose for which the communication is made.

(b) Psychologists discuss confidential information obtained in their work only for appropriate scientific or professional purposes and only with persons clearly concerned with such matters.

4.05 Disclosures

(a) Psychologists may disclose confidential information with the appropriate consent of the organizational client, the individual client/patient, or another legally authorized person on behalf of the client/patient unless prohibited by law.

(b) Psychologists disclose confidential information without the consent of the individual only as mandated by law, or where permitted by law for a valid purpose such as to (1) provide needed professional services; (2) obtain appropriate professional consultations; (3) protect the client/patient, psychologist, or others from harm; or (4) obtain payment for services from a client/patient, in which instance disclosure is limited to the minimum that is necessary to achieve the purpose. (See also Standard 6.04e, Fees and Financial Arrangements.)

4.06 Consultations

When consulting with colleagues, (1) psychologists do not disclose confidential information that reasonably could lead to the identification of a client/patient, research participant, or other person or organization with whom they have a confidential relationship unless they have obtained the prior consent of the person or organization or the disclosure cannot be avoided, and (2) they disclose information only to the extent necessary to achieve the purposes of the consultation. (See also Standard 4.01, Maintaining Confidentiality.)

4.07 Use of Confidential Information for Didactic or Other Purposes

Psychologists do not disclose in their writings, lectures, or other public media, confidential, personally identifiable information concerning their clients/patients, students, research participants, organizational clients, or other recipients of their services that they obtained during the course of their work, unless (1) they take reasonable steps to disguise the person or organization, (2) the person or organization has consented in writing, or (3) there is legal authorization for doing so.

5. Advertising and Other Public Statements

5.01 Avoidance of False or Deceptive Statements

(a) Public statements include but are not limited to paid or unpaid advertising, product endorsements, grant applications, licensing applications, other credentialing applications, brochures, printed matter, directory listings, personal resumes or curricula vitae, or comments for use in media such as print or electronic transmission, statements in legal proceedings, lectures and public oral presentations, and published materials. Psychologists do not knowingly make public statements that are false, deceptive, or fraudulent concerning their research, practice, or other work activities or those of persons or organizations with which they are affiliated.

(b) Psychologists do not make false, deceptive, or fraudulent statements concerning (1) their training, experience, or competence; (2) their academic degrees; (3) their credentials; (4) their institutional or association affiliations; (5) their services; (6) the scientific or clinical basis for, or results or degree of success of, their services; (7) their fees; or (8) their publications or research findings.

(c) Psychologists claim degrees as credentials for their health services only if those degrees (1) were earned from a regionally accredited educational institution or (2) were the basis for psychology licensure by the state in which they practice.

5.02 Statements by Others

(a) Psychologists who engage others to create or place public statements that promote their professional practice, products, or activities retain professional responsibility for such statements.

(b) Psychologists do not compensate employees of press, radio, television, or other communication media in return for publicity in a news item. (See also Standard 1.01, Misuse of Psychologists' Work.)

(c) A paid advertisement relating to psychologists' activities must be identified or clearly recognizable as such.

5.03 Descriptions of Workshops and Non-Degree-Granting Educational Programs

To the degree to which they exercise control, psychologists responsible for announcements, catalogs, brochures, or advertisements describing workshops, seminars, or other non-degree-granting educational programs ensure that they accurately describe the audience for which the program is intended, the educational objectives, the presenters, and the fees involved.

5.04 Media Presentations

When psychologists provide public advice or comment via print, internet, or other electronic transmission, they take precautions to ensure that statements (1) are based on their professional knowledge, training, or experience in accord with appropriate psychological literature and practice; (2) are otherwise consistent with this Ethics Code; and (3) do not indicate that a professional relationship has been established with the recipient. (See also Standard 2.04, Bases for Scientific and Professional Judgments.)

5.05 Testimonials

Psychologists do not solicit testimonials from current therapy clients/patients or other persons who because of their particular circumstances are vulnerable to undue influence.

5.06 In-Person Solicitation

Psychologists do not engage, directly or through agents, in uninvited in-person solicitation of business from actual or potential therapy clients/patients or other persons who because of their particular circumstances are vulnerable to undue influence. However, this prohibition does not preclude (1) attempting to implement appropriate collateral contacts for the purpose of benefiting an already engaged therapy client/patient or (2) providing disaster or community outreach services.

6. Record Keeping and Fees

6.01 Documentation of Professional and Scientific Work and Maintenance of Records

Psychologists create, and to the extent the records are under their control, maintain, disseminate, store, retain, and dispose of records and data relating to their professional and scientific work in order to (1) facilitate provision of services later by them or by other professionals, (2) allow for replication of research design and analyses, (3) meet institutional requirements, (4) ensure accuracy of billing and payments, and (5) ensure compliance with law. (See also Standard 4.01, Maintaining Confidentiality.)

6.02 Maintenance, Dissemination, and Disposal of Confidential Records of Professional and Scientific Work

(a) Psychologists maintain confidentiality in creating, storing, accessing, transferring, and disposing of records under their control, whether these are written, automated, or in any other medium. (See also Standards 4.01, Maintaining Confidentiality, and 6.01, Documentation of Professional and Scientific Work and Maintenance of Records.)

(b) If confidential information concerning recipients of psychological services is entered into databases or systems of records available to persons whose access has not been consented to by the recipient, psychologists use coding or other techniques to avoid the inclusion of personal identifiers.

(c) Psychologists make plans in advance to facilitate the appropriate transfer and to protect the confidentiality of records and data in the event of psychologists' withdrawal from positions or practice. (See also Standards 3.12, Interruption of Psychological Services, and 10.09, Interruption of Therapy.)

6.03 Withholding Records for Nonpayment

Psychologists may not withhold records under their control that are requested and needed for a client's/patient's emergency treatment solely because payment has not been received.

6.04 Fees and Financial Arrangements

(a) As early as is feasible in a professional or scientific relationship, psychologists and recipients of psychological services reach an agreement specifying compensation and billing arrangements.

(b) Psychologists' fee practices are consistent with law.

(c) Psychologists do not misrepresent their fees.

(d) If limitations to services can be anticipated because of limitations in financing, this is discussed with the recipient of services as early as is feasible. (See also Standards 10.09, Interruption of Therapy, and 10.10, Terminating Therapy.)

(e) If the recipient of services does not pay for services as agreed, and if psychologists intend to use collection agencies or legal measures to collect the fees, psychologists first inform the person that such measures will be taken and provide that person an opportunity to make prompt payment. (See also Standards 4.05, Disclosures; 6.03, Withholding Records for Nonpayment; and 10.01, Informed Consent to Therapy.)

6.05 Barter With Clients/Patients

Barter is the acceptance of goods, services, or other nonmonetary remuneration from clients/patients in return for psychological services. Psychologists may barter only if (1) it is not clinically contraindicated, and (2) the resulting arrangement is not exploitative. (See also Standards 3.05, Multiple Relationships, and 6.04, Fees and Financial Arrangements.)

6.06 Accuracy in Reports to Payors and Funding Sources

In their reports to payors for services or sources of research funding, psychologists take reasonable steps to ensure the accurate reporting of the nature of the service provided or research conducted, the fees, charges, or payments, and where applicable, the identity of the provider, the findings, and the diagnosis. (See also Standards 4.01, Maintaining Confidentiality; 4.04, Minimizing Intrusions on Privacy; and 4.05, Disclosures.)

6.07 Referrals and Fees

When psychologists pay, receive payment from, or divide fees with another professional, other than in an employer-employee relationship, the payment to each is based on the services provided (clinical, consulta-tive, administrative, or other) and is not based on the referral itself. (See also Standard 3.09, Cooperation With Other Professionals.)

7. Education and Training

7.01 Design of Education and Training Programs

Psychologists responsible for education and training programs take reasonable steps to ensure that the programs are designed to provide the appropriate knowledge and proper experiences, and to meet the requirements for licensure, certification, or other goals for which claims are made by the program. (See also Standard 5.03, Descriptions of Workshops and Non-Degree-Granting Educational Programs.)

7.02 Descriptions of Education and Training Programs

Psychologists responsible for education and training programs take reasonable steps to ensure that there is a current and accurate description of the program content (including participation in required course- or program-related counseling, psychotherapy, experiential groups, consulting projects, or community service), training goals and objectives, stipends and benefits, and requirements that must be met for satisfactory completion of the program. This information must be made readily available to all interested parties.

7.03 Accuracy in Teaching

(a) Psychologists take reasonable steps to ensure that course syllabi are accurate regarding the subject matter to be covered, bases for evaluating progress, and the nature of course experiences. This standard does not preclude an instructor from modifying course content or requirements when the instructor considers it pedagogically necessary or desirable, so long as students are made aware of these modifications in a manner that enables them to fulfill course requirements. (See also Standard 5.01, Avoidance of False or Deceptive Statements.)

(b) When engaged in teaching or training, psychologists present psychological information accurately. (See also Standard 2.03, Maintaining Competence.)

7.04 Student Disclosure of Personal Information

Psychologists do not require students or supervisees to disclose personal information in course- or program-related activities, either orally or in writing, regarding sexual history, history of abuse and neglect, psychological treatment, and relationships with parents, peers, and spouses or significant others except if (1) the program or training facility has clearly identified this requirement in its admissions and program materials or (2) the information is necessary to evaluate or obtain assistance for students whose personal problems could reasonably be judged to be preventing them from performing their training- or professionally related activities in a competent manner or posing a threat to the students or others.

7.05 Mandatory Individual or Group Therapy

(a) When individual or group therapy is a program or course requirement, psychologists responsible for that program allow students in undergraduate and graduate programs the option of selecting such therapy from practitioners unaffiliated with the program. (See also Standard 7.02, Descriptions of Education and Training Programs.)

(b) Faculty who are or are likely to be responsible for evaluating students' academic performance do not themselves provide that therapy. (See also Standard 3.05, Multiple Relationships.)

7.06 Assessing Student and Supervisee Performance

(a) In academic and supervisory relationships, psychologists establish a timely and specific process for providing feedback to students and supervisees. Information regarding the process is provided to the student at the beginning of supervision.

(b) Psychologists evaluate students and supervisees on the basis of their actual performance on relevant and established program requirements.

7.07 Sexual Relationships With Students and Supervisees

Psychologists do not engage in sexual relationships with students or supervisees who are in their department, agency, or training center or over whom psychologists have or are likely to have evaluative authority. (See also Standard 3.05, Multiple Relationships.)

8. Research and Publication

8.01 Institutional Approval

When institutional approval is required, psychologists provide accurate information about their research proposals and obtain approval prior to conducting the research. They conduct the research in accordance with the approved research protocol.

8.02 Informed Consent to Research

(a) When obtaining informed consent as required in Standard 3.10, Informed Consent, psychologists inform participants about (1) the purpose of the research, expected duration, and procedures; (2) their right to decline to participate and to withdraw from the research once participation has begun; (3) the foreseeable consequences of declining or withdrawing; (4) reasonably foreseeable factors that may be expected to influence their willingness to participate such as potential risks, discomfort, or adverse effects; (5) any prospective research benefits; (6) limits of confidentiality; (7) incentives for participation; and (8) whom to contact for questions about the research and research participants' rights. They provide opportunity for the prospective participants to ask questions and receive answers. (See also Standards 8.03, Informed Consent for Recording Voices and Images in Research; 8.05, Dispensing With Informed Consent for Research; and 8.07, Deception in Research.)

(b) Psychologists conducting intervention research involving the use of experimental treatments clarify to participants at the outset of the research (1) the experimental nature of the treatment; (2) the services that will or will not be available to the control group(s) if appropriate; (3) the means by which assignment to treatment and control groups will be made; (4) available treatment alternatives if an individual does not wish to participate in the research or wishes to withdraw once a study has begun; and (5) compensation for or monetary costs of participating including, if appropriate, whether reimbursement from the participant or a third-party payor will be sought. (See also Standard 8.02a, Informed Consent to Research.)

8.03 Informed Consent for Recording Voices and Images in Research

Psychologists obtain informed consent from research participants prior to recording their voices or images for data collection unless (1) the research consists solely of naturalistic observations in public places, and it is not anticipated that the recording will be used in a manner that could cause personal identification or harm, or (2) the research design includes deception, and consent for the use of the recording is obtained during debriefing. (See also Standard 8.07, Deception in Research.)

8.04 Client/Patient, Student, and Subordinate Research Participants

(a) When psychologists conduct research with clients/patients, students, or subordinates as participants, psychologists take steps to protect the prospective participants from adverse consequences of declining or withdrawing from participation.

(b) When research participation is a course requirement or an opportunity for extra credit, the prospective participant is given the choice of equitable alternative activities.

8.05 Dispensing With Informed Consent for Research

Psychologists may dispense with informed consent only (1) where research would not reasonably be assumed to create distress or harm and involves **(a)** the study of normal educational practices, curricula, or classroom management methods conducted in educational settings; **(b)** only anonymous questionnaires, naturalistic observations, or archival research for which disclosure of responses would not place participants at risk of criminal or civil liability or damage their financial standing, employability, or reputation, and confidentiality is protected; or **(c)** the study of factors related to job or organization effectiveness conducted in organizational settings for which there is no risk to participants' employability, and confidentiality is protected or (2) where otherwise permitted by law or federal or institutional regulations.

8.06 Offering Inducements for Research Participation

(a) Psychologists make reasonable efforts to avoid offering excessive or inappropriate financial or other inducements for research participation when such inducements are likely to coerce participation.

(b) When offering professional services as an inducement for research participation, psychologists clarify the nature of the services, as well as the risks, obligations, and limitations. (See also Standard 6.05, Barter With Clients/Patients.)

8.07 Deception in Research

(a) Psychologists do not conduct a study involving deception unless they have determined that the use of deceptive techniques is justified by the study's significant prospective scientific, educational, or applied value and that effective nondeceptive alternative procedures are not feasible.

(b) Psychologists do not deceive prospective participants about research that is reasonably expected to cause physical pain or severe emotional distress.

(c) Psychologists explain any deception that is an integral feature of the design and conduct of an experiment to participants as early as is feasible, preferably at the conclusion of their participation, but no later than at the conclusion of the data collection, and permit participants to withdraw their data. (See also Standard 8.08, Debriefing.)

8.08 Debriefing

(a) Psychologists provide a prompt opportunity for participants to obtain appropriate information about the nature, results, and conclusions of the research, and they take reasonable steps to correct any misconceptions that participants may have of which the psychologists are aware.

(b) If scientific or humane values justify delaying or withholding this information, psychologists take reasonable measures to reduce the risk of harm.

(c) When psychologists become aware that research procedures have harmed a participant, they take reasonable steps to minimize the harm.

8.09 Humane Care and Use of Animals in Research

(a) Psychologists acquire, care for, use, and dispose of animals in compliance with current federal, state, and local laws and regulations, and with professional standards.

(b) Psychologists trained in research methods and experienced in the care of laboratory animals supervise all procedures involving animals and are responsible for ensuring appropriate consideration of their comfort, health, and humane treatment.

(c) Psychologists ensure that all individuals under their supervision who are using animals have received instruction in research methods and in the care, maintenance, and handling of the species being used, to the extent appropriate to their role. (See also Standard 2.05, Delegation of Work to Others.)

(d) Psychologists make reasonable efforts to minimize the discomfort, infection, illness, and pain of animal subjects.

(e) Psychologists use a procedure subjecting animals to pain, stress, or privation only when an alternative procedure is unavailable and the goal is justified by its prospective scientific, educational, or applied value.

(f) Psychologists perform surgical procedures under appropriate anesthesia and follow techniques to avoid infection and minimize pain during and after surgery.

(g) When it is appropriate that an animal's life be terminated, psychologists proceed rapidly, with an effort to minimize pain and in accordance with accepted procedures.

8.10 Reporting Research Results

(a) Psychologists do not fabricate data. (See also Standard 5.01a, Avoidance of False or Deceptive Statements.)

(b) If psychologists discover significant errors in their published data, they take reasonable steps to correct such errors in a correction, retraction, erratum, or other appropriate publication means.

8.11 Plagiarism

Psychologists do not present portions of another's work or data as their own, even if the other work or data source is cited occasionally.

8.12 Publication Credit

(a) Psychologists take responsibility and credit, including authorship credit, only for work they have actually performed or to which they have substantially contributed. (See also Standard 8.12b, Publication Credit.)

(b) Principal authorship and other publication credits accurately reflect the relative scientific or professional contributions of the individuals involved, regardless of their relative status. Mere possession of an institutional position, such as department chair, does not justify authorship credit. Minor contributions to the research or to the writing for publications are acknowledged appropriately, such as in footnotes or in an introductory statement.

(c) Except under exceptional circumstances, a student is listed as principal author on any multiple-authored article that is substantially based on the student's doctoral dissertation. Faculty advisors discuss publication credit with students as early as feasible and throughout the research and publication process as appropriate. (See also Standard 8.12b, Publication Credit.)

8.13 Duplicate Publication of Data

Psychologists do not publish, as original data, data that have been previously published. This does not preclude republishing data when they are accompanied by proper acknowledgment.

8.14 Sharing Research Data for Verification

(a) After research results are published, psychologists do not withhold the data on which their conclusions are based from other competent professionals who seek to verify the substantive claims through reanalysis and who intend to use such data only for that purpose, provided that the confidentiality of the participants can be protected and unless legal rights concerning proprietary data preclude their release. This does not preclude psychologists from requiring that such individuals or groups be responsible for costs associated with the provision of such information.

(b) Psychologists who request data from other psychologists to verify the substantive claims through reanalysis may use shared data only for the declared purpose. Requesting psychologists obtain prior written agreement for all other uses of the data.

8.15 Reviewers

Psychologists who review material submitted for presentation, publication, grant, or research proposal review respect the confidentiality of and the proprietary rights in such information of those who submitted it.

9. Assessment

9.01 Bases for Assessments

(a) Psychologists base the opinions contained in their recommendations, reports, and diagnostic or evaluative statements, including forensic testimony, on information and techniques sufficient to substantiate their findings. (See also Standard 2.04, Bases for Scientific and Professional Judgments.)

(b) Except as noted in 9.01c, psychologists provide opinions of the psychological characteristics of individuals only after they have conducted an examination of the individuals adequate to support their statements or conclusions. When, despite reasonable efforts, such an examination is not practical, psychologists document the efforts they made and the result of those efforts, clarify the probable impact of their limited information on the reliability and validity of their opinions, and appropriately limit the nature and extent of their conclusions or recommendations. (See also Standards 2.01, Boundaries of Competence, and 9.06, Interpreting Assessment Results.)

(c) When psychologists conduct a record review or provide consultation or supervision and an individual examination is not warranted or necessary for the opinion, psychologists explain this and the sources of information on which they based their conclusions and recommendations.

9.02 Use of Assessments

(a) Psychologists administer, adapt, score, interpret, or use assessment techniques, interviews, tests, or instruments in a manner and for purposes that are appropriate in light of the research on or evidence of the usefulness and proper application of the techniques.

(b) Psychologists use assessment instruments whose validity and reliability have been established for use with members of the population tested. When such validity or reliability has not been established, psychologists describe the strengths and limitations of test results and interpretation.

(c) Psychologists use assessment methods that are appropriate to an individual's language preference and competence, unless the use of an alternative language is relevant to the assessment issues.

9.03 Informed Consent in Assessments

(a) Psychologists obtain informed consent for assessments, evaluations, or diagnostic services, as described in Standard 3.10, Informed Consent, except when (1) testing is mandated by law or governmental regulations; (2) informed consent is implied because testing is conducted as a routine educational, institutional, or organizational activity (e.g., when participants voluntarily agree to assessment when applying for a job); or (3) one purpose of the testing is to evaluate decisional capacity. Informed consent includes an explanation of the nature and purpose of the assessment, fees, involvement of third parties, and limits of confidentiality and sufficient opportunity for the client/patient to ask questions and receive answers.

(b) Psychologists inform persons with questionable capacity to consent or for whom testing is mandated by law or governmental regulations about the nature and purpose of the proposed assessment services, using language that is reasonably understandable to the person being assessed.

(c) Psychologists using the services of an interpreter obtain informed consent from the client/patient to use that interpreter, ensure that confidentiality of test results and test security are maintained, and include in their recommendations, reports, and diagnostic or evaluative statements, including forensic testimony, discussion of any limitations on the data obtained. (See also Standards 2.05, Delegation of Work to Others; 4.01, Maintaining Confidentiality; 9.01, Bases for Assessments; 9.06, Interpreting Assessment Results; and 9.07, Assessment by Unqualified Persons.)

9.04 Release of Test Data

(a) The term test data refers to raw and scaled scores, client/patient responses to test questions or stimuli, and psychologists' notes and recordings concerning client/patient statements and behavior during an examination. Those portions of test materials that include client/patient responses are included in the definition of test data. Pursuant to a client/patient release, psychologists provide test data to the client/patient or other persons identified in the release. Psychologists may refrain from releasing test data to protect a client/patient or others from substantial harm or misuse or misrepresentation of the data or the test, recognizing that in many instances release of confidential information under these circumstances is regulated by law. (See also Standard 9.11, Maintaining Test Security.)

(b) In the absence of a client/patient release, psychologists provide test data only as required by law or court order.

9.05 Test Construction

Psychologists who develop tests and other assessment techniques use appropriate psychometric procedures and current scientific or professional knowledge for test design, standardization, validation, reduction or elimination of bias, and recommendations for use.

9.06 Interpreting Assessment Results

When interpreting assessment results, including automated interpretations, psychologists take into account the purpose of the assessment as well as the various test factors, test-taking abilities, and other characteristics of the person being assessed, such as situational, personal, linguistic, and cultural differences, that might affect psychologists' judgments or reduce the accuracy of their interpretations. They indicate any significant limitations of their interpretations. (See also Standards 2.01b and c, Boundaries of Competence, and 3.01, Unfair Discrimination.)

9.07 Assessment by Unqualified Persons

Psychologists do not promote the use of psychological assessment techniques by unqualified persons, except when such use is conducted for training purposes with appropriate supervision. (See also Standard 2.05, Delegation of Work to Others.)

9.08 Obsolete Tests and Outdated Test Results

(a) Psychologists do not base their assessment or intervention decisions or recommendations on data or test results that are outdated for the current purpose.

(b) Psychologists do not base such decisions or recommendations on tests and measures that are obsolete and not useful for the current purpose.

9.09 Test Scoring and Interpretation Services

(a) Psychologists who offer assessment or scoring services to other professionals accurately describe the purpose, norms, validity, reliability, and applications of the procedures and any special qualifications applicable to their use.

(b) Psychologists select scoring and interpretation services (including automated services) on the basis of evidence of the validity of the program and procedures as well as on other appropriate considerations. (See also Standard 2.01b and c, Boundaries of Competence.)

(c) Psychologists retain responsibility for the appropriate application, interpretation, and use of assessment instruments, whether they score and interpret such tests themselves or use automated or other services.

9.10 Explaining Assessment Results

Regardless of whether the scoring and interpretation are done by psychologists, by employees or assistants, or by automated or other outside services, psychologists take reasonable steps to ensure that explanations of results are given to the individual or designated representative unless the nature of the relationship precludes provision of an explanation of results (such as in some organizational consulting, preemployment or security screenings, and forensic evaluations), and this fact has been clearly explained to the person being assessed in advance.

9.11 Maintaining Test Security

The term test materials refers to manuals, instruments, protocols, and test questions or stimuli and does not include test data as defined in Standard 9.04, Release of Test Data. Psychologists make reasonable efforts to maintain the integrity and security of test materials and other assessment techniques consistent with law and contractual obligations, and in a manner that permits adherence to this Ethics Code.

10. Therapy

10.01 Informed Consent to Therapy

(a) When obtaining informed consent to therapy as required in Standard 3.10, Informed Consent, psychologists inform clients/patients as early as is feasible in the therapeutic relationship about the nature and anticipated course of therapy, fees, involvement of third parties, and limits of confidentiality and provide sufficient opportunity for the client/patient to ask questions and receive answers. (See also Standards 4.02, Discussing the Limits of Confidentiality, and 6.04, Fees and Financial Arrangements.)

(b) When obtaining informed consent for treatment for which generally recognized techniques and procedures have not been established, psychologists inform their clients/patients of the developing nature of the treatment, the potential risks involved, alternative treatments that may be available, and the voluntary nature of their participation. (See also Standards 2.01e, Boundaries of Competence, and 3.10, Informed Consent.)

(c) When the therapist is a trainee and the legal responsibility for the treatment provided resides with the supervisor, the client/patient, as part of the informed consent procedure, is informed that the therapist is in training and is being supervised and is given the name of the supervisor.

10.02 Therapy Involving Couples or Families

(a) When psychologists agree to provide services to several persons who have a relationship (such as spouses, significant others, or parents and children), they take reasonable steps to clarify at the outset (1) which of the individuals are clients/patients and (2) the relationship the psychologist will have with each person. This clarification includes the psychologist's role and the probable uses of the services provided or the information obtained. (See also Standard 4.02, Discussing the Limits of Confidentiality.)

(b) If it becomes apparent that psychologists may be called on to perform potentially conflicting roles (such as family therapist and then witness for one party in divorce proceedings), psychologists take reasonable steps to clarify and modify, or withdraw from, roles appropriately. (See also Standard 3.05c, Multiple Relationships.)

10.03 Group Therapy

When psychologists provide services to several persons in a group setting, they describe at the outset the roles and responsibilities of all parties and the limits of confidentiality.

10.04 Providing Therapy to Those Served by Others

In deciding whether to offer or provide services to those already receiving mental health services elsewhere, psychologists carefully consider the treatment issues and the potential client's/patient's welfare. Psychologists discuss these issues with the client/patient or another legally authorized person on behalf of the client/patient in order to minimize the risk of confusion and conflict, consult with the other service providers when appropriate, and proceed with caution and sensitivity to the therapeutic issues.

10.05 Sexual Intimacies With Current Therapy Clients/Patients

Psychologists do not engage in sexual intimacies with current therapy clients/patients.

10.06 Sexual Intimacies With Relatives or Significant Others of Current Therapy Clients/Patients

Psychologists do not engage in sexual intimacies with individuals they know to be close relatives, guardians, or significant others of current clients/patients. Psychologists do not terminate therapy to circumvent this standard.

10.07 Therapy With Former Sexual Partners

Psychologists do not accept as therapy clients/patients persons with whom they have engaged in sexual intimacies.

10.08 Sexual Intimacies With Former Therapy Clients/Patients

(a) Psychologists do not engage in sexual intimacies with former clients/patients for at least two years after cessation or termination of therapy.

(b) Psychologists do not engage in sexual intimacies with former clients/patients even after a two-year interval except in the most unusual circumstances. Psychologists who engage in such activity after the two years following cessation or termination of therapy and of having no sexual contact with the former client/patient bear the burden of demonstrating that there has been no exploitation, in light of all relevant factors, including (1) the amount of time that has passed since therapy terminated; (2) the nature, duration, and intensity of the therapy; (3) the circumstances of termination; (4) the client's/patient's personal history; (5) the client's/patient's current mental status; (6) the likelihood of adverse impact on the client/patient; and (7) any statements or actions made by the therapist during the course of therapy suggesting or inviting the possibility of a posttermination sexual or romantic relationship with the client/patient. (See also Standard 3.05, Multiple Relationships.)

10.09 Interruption of Therapy

When entering into employment or contractual relationships, psychologists make reasonable efforts to provide for orderly and appropriate resolution of responsibility for client/patient care in the event that the employment or contractual relationship ends, with paramount consideration given to the welfare of the client/patient. (See also Standard 3.12, Interruption of Psychological Services.)

10.10 Terminating Therapy

(a) Psychologists terminate therapy when it becomes reasonably clear that the client/patient no longer needs the service, is not likely to benefit, or is being harmed by continued service.

(b) Psychologists may terminate therapy when threatened or otherwise endangered by the client/patient or another person with whom the client/patient has a relationship.

(c) Except where precluded by the actions of clients/patients or third-party payors, prior to termination psychologists provide pretermination counseling and suggest alternative service providers as appropriate.

The Psychologist's Bookshelf

A

Aaronson, B. S. (1972). Color perception and effect. *American Journal of Clinical Hypnosis, 14,* 38–43.

Abeles, N. (1997). Memory problems in later life. *APA Monitor, 28*(6), 2.

Aber, J. L., & Allen, J. P. (1987). Effects of maltreatment of young children on young children's socioemotional development: An attachment theory perspective. *Developmental Psychology, 23,* 406–414.

Abramson, M. Y., Metalsky, G. I., & Alloy, L. B. (1989). Hopelessness-depression: A theory-based subtype of depression. *Psychological Review, 9,* 358–372.

Ackerman, G. L. (1993). A congressional view of youth suicide. *American Psychologist, 48,* 183–184.

Adams, D. M., Overholser, J. C., & Spirito, A. (1992, August). *Life stress related to adolescent suicide attempts.* Paper presented at the meeting of the American Psychological Association, Washington, DC.

Ader, D. N., & Johnson, S. B. (1994). Sample description, reporting, and analysis of sex in psychological research: A look at APA and APA division journals in 1990. *American Psychologist, 49,* 216–218.

Adler, A. (1927). *Understanding human nature.* Greenwich, CT: Fawcett.

Adler, T. (1993a). Shy, bold temperament? It's mostly in the genes. *APA Monitor, 24*(1), 7–8.

Agras, W. S., & Kirkley, B. G. (1986). Bulimia: Theories of etiology. In K. D. Brownell & J. P. Foreyt (Eds.), *Handbook of eating disorders.* New York: Basic Books.

Ainsworth, M. D. S. (1973). The development of infant-mother attachment. In B. Caldwell & H. Ricciuti (Eds.), *Review of child development research* (Vol. 3). Chicago: University of Chicago Press.

Ainsworth, M. D. S., Blehar, M. L., Waters, E., & Wall, S. (1978). *Patterns of attachment.* Hillsdale, NJ: Lawrence Erlbaum.

Akhtar, N., & Bradley, E. J. (1991). Social information processing deficits of aggressive children: Present findings and implications for social skills training. *Clinical Psychology Review, 11,* 621–644.

Alexander, C. N., et al. (1996). Trial of stress reduction for hypertension in older African Americans: II. Sex and risk subgroup analysis. *Hypertension, 28,* 228–237.

Allison, D. B., et al. (1999). Annual deaths attributable to obesity in the United States. *Journal of the American Medical Association online, 282*(16).

Allison, J., Blatt, S. J., & Zimet, C. N. (1988). *The interpretation of psychological tests.* Washington, DC: Hemisphere.

Allison, K. W., Crawford, I., Echemendia, R., Robinson, L. V., & Knepp, D. (1994). Human diversity and professional competence. *American Psychologist, 49,* 792–796.

Allport, G. (1937). *Personality: A psychological interpretation.* New York: Holt, Rinehart and Winston.

Allport, G. (1965). *Letters from Jenny.* New York: Harcourt Brace Jovanovich.

Allport, G., & Odbert, H. S. (1936). Trait names: A psycho-lexical study. *Psychological Monographs, 47*(211), 1–171.

Amato, P. R., & Keith, B. (1991). Parental divorce and the well–being of children: A meta-analysis. *Psychological Bulletin, 110,* 26–46.

American Association of University Women. (1992). *How schools shortchange women: The A.A.U.W. report.* Washington, DC: A.A.U.W. Educational Foundation.

American Heart Association online (2000a). *2000 Heart and stroke statistical update.* http://www.american-heart.org.

American Lung Association (2000). *Smoking fact sheet,* http:/www.lungusa.org.

American Polygraph Association. (1992). Cited in Bashore, T. R., & Rapp, P. E. (1993). Are there alternatives to traditional polygraph procedures? *Psychological Bulletin, 113,* 3–22.

American Psychiatric Association. (2000). *Diagnostic and statistical manual of mental disorders* (4th ed., text revision) *(DSMIV – TR).*

American Psychological Association. (1993b). Guidelines for providers of psychological services to ethnic, linguistic, and culturally diverse populations. *American Psychologist, 48,* 45–48.

American Psychological Association. (1994a). *Ethical principles of psychologists and code of conduct.* Washington, DC: APA.

American Psychological Association. (1994b). *Publication manual of the American Psychological Association* (4th ed.). Washington, DC: APA.

Anastasi, A., & Urbina, S. (1997). *Psychological testing*, (7th ed.). Englewood Cliffs, NJ: Prentice Hall. This book familiarizes the reader with the basics of test construction and prepares the reader to effectively evaluate different tests, choose tests for particular purposes and individual examinees, and interpret scores properly.

Anderson, C. A., & Dill, K. E. (2000). Video games and aggressive thoughts, feelings, and behavior in the laboratory and in life. *Journal of Personality and Social Psychology, 78*(4), 772–790.

Andersson, T., & Magnusson, D. (1990). Biological maturation in adolescence and the development of drinking habits and alcohol abuse among young males: A prospective longitudinal study. *Journal of Youth and Adolescence, 19*(1), 33–41.

Annunziata, J., & Jacobson-Kram, P. (1995). *Solving your problems together: Family therapy for the whole family*. Washington, DC: American Psychological Association.

APA Research Office (2000). First-year (full-time) students in doctoral-level departments of psychology by race/ethnicity: 1999–2000. *Graduate Study in Psychology 2000*. Washington, D.C.: American Psychological Association.

Archer, S. L. (1991). Gender differences in identity development. In J. Brooks-Gunn, R. Lerner, & A. C. Petersen (Eds.), *Encyclopedia of adolescence, II*. New York: Garland.

Arnet, J. J. (2004). *Emerging adulthood: The winding road from the late teens through the twenties*. New York: Oxford University Press.

Asch, S. E. (1955). Opinions and social pressure. *Scientific American, 193*, 31–35.

Atchley, R. C. (1991). *Social forces and aging* (6th ed.). Belmont, CA: Wadsworth.

Atkinson, R. C. (1975). Mnemotechnics in second-language learning. *American Psychologist, 30*, 821–828.

Attie, I., Brooks-Gunn, J., & Petersen, A. C. (1990). A developmental perspective on eating disorders and eating problems. In M. Lewis & S. M. Miller (Eds.), *Handbook of developmental psychopathology*. New York: Plenum Press.

Averill, J. R. (1993). Autonomic response patterns during sadness and mirth. *Psychophysiology, 5*, 399–414.

Ayllon, T., & Haughton, E. (1962). Control of the behavior of schizophrenic patients by food. *Journal of the Experimental Analysis of Behavior, 5*, 343–352.

Azar, B. (1995). Breaking through barriers to creativity. *APA Monitor, 26*(8), 1, 20.

Azar, B. (1996). Scientists examine cancer patients' fears. *APA Monitor, 27*(8), 32.

Azar, B. (1997). It may cause anxiety, but day care can benefit kids. *APA Monitor, 28*(6), 13.

B

Baddeley, A. D. (1982). *Your memory: A user's guide*. New York: Macmillan.

Baker, C. W., Whisman, M. A., & Brownell, K. D. (2000). Studying intergenerational transmission of eating attitudes and behaviors: Methodological and conceptual questions. *Health Psychology, 19*(4), 376–381.

Baldo, J. V., Delis, D. C., Wilkins, D. P., & Shimamura, A. P. (2004). Is it bigger than a breadbox? Performance of patients with prefrontal lesions on a new executive function test. *Archives of Clinical Neuropsychology, 19*(3), 407–419.

Baldry, A. C. (2003). Bullying in schools and exposure to domestic violence. *Child Abuse & Neglect, 27*(7), 713–732.

Baltes, P. B. (1997). On the incomplete architecture of human ontogeny: Selection, optimization, and compensation as foundation of developmental theory. *American Psychologist, 52*, 366–380.

Baltes, P., & Baltes, M. (1995). Cited in Margoshes, P. (1995). For many, old age is the prime of life. *APA Monitor, 26*(5), 36–37.

Banaji, M., Greenwald, A. (1995). Implicit social cognition: Attitudes, self-esteem, and stereotypes. *Psychological Review*.

Banaji, M., Greenwald, A., Rudman, L. A., & Farnham, S. D. (2002). A unified theory of implicit attitudes, stereotypes, self-esteem, and self-concept. *Psychological Review*.

Bandura, A., Taylor, C. B., Williams, S. I., Medford, I. N., & Barchas, J. D. (1985). Catecholamine secretion as a function of perceived coping self-efficacy. *Journal of Consulting and Clinical Psychology, 53*, 406–414.

Banks, S. M., et al. (1995). The effects of message framing on mammography utilization. *Health Psychology, 14*, 178–184.

Barber, T. X. (2000). A deeper understanding of hypnosis: Its secrets, its nature, its essence. *American Journal of Clinical Hypnosis, 42*(3–4), 208–272.

Barlow, D. H. (1994). Cited in Howard, K., Barlow, D., Christiensen, A., & Frank, E. (1994). *Evaluating outcomes of psychological interventions: Evaluating the effectiveness of psychotherapy.* Symposium conducted at the meeting of the American Psychological Association, Los Angeles.

Barlow, D. H. (1996). Health care policy, psychotherapy research, and the future of psychotherapy. *American Psychologist, 51,* 1050–1058.

Barlow, D. H., Adler, C. M., Craske, M. G., & Kirshenbaum, S. (1989). "Fear of Panic": An investigation of its role in panic occurrence, phobic avoidance, and treatment outcome. *Behaviour Research and Therapy, 27*(4), 391–396.

Barnes, D. (1987). Biological issues in schizophrenia. *Science, 235,* 430–433.

Baron, M., Gruen, R., Ranier, J., Kane, J., & Asnis, L. (1985). A family study of schizophrenia and normal control probands: Implications for the spectrum concept of schizophrenia. *American Journal of Psychiatry, 142,* 447–455.

Baron, R. A., & Richardson, D. R. (1994). *Human aggression* (2nd ed.). New York: Plenum Press.

Barringer, F. (1993, April 25). Polling on sexual issues has its drawbacks. *The New York Times,* p. A23.

Bartecchi, C. E., MacKenzie, T. D., & Schrier, R. W. (1994). The human cost of tobacco use. *New England Journal of Medicine, 330,* 907–912.

Bartoshuk, L. M. (2000). Psychophysical advances aid the study of genetic variation in taste. *Appetite, 34*(1), 105.

Bashore, T. R., & Rapp, P. E. (1993). Are there alternatives to traditional polygraph procedures? *Psychological Bulletin, 113,* 3–22.

Basic Behavioral Science Task Force of the National Advisory Mental Health Council. (1996). Basic behavioral science research for mental health: Vulnerability and resilience. *American Psychologist, 51,* 22–28.

Bass, E., & Davis, L. (1994). *The courage to heal: A guide for women survivors of child sexual abuse* (3rd ed.). New York: HarperCollins. Step-by-step self-help book for women who have survived childhood sexual abuse.

Bateman, D. N. (2000). Triptans and migraine. *The Lancet, 355,* 860–861.

Baumeister, R. F., Stillwell, A. M., & Heatherton, T. F. (1994). Guilt: An interpersonal approach. *Psychologial Bulletin, 115,* 243–267.

Baumrind, D. (1989). Rearing competent children. In W. Damon (Ed.), *Child development today and tomorrow.* San Francisco: Jossey-Bass.

Baumrind, D. (1991a). The influence of parenting style on adolescent competence and substance abuse. *Journal of Early Adolescence, 11,* 56–95.

Baumrind, D. (1991b). Parenting styles and adolescent development. In J. Brooks-Gunn, R. Lerner, & A. C. Petersen, (Eds.), *Encyclopedia of adolescence, II.* New York: Garland.

Beah, I. (2007). *A long way gone: Memoirs of a boy soldier.* New York: Sarah Crichton Books. First person account by a child soldier from Sierra Leone.

Beck, A. T., & Freeman, A. (1990). *Cognitive therapy of personality disorders.* New York: Guilford.

Bekoff, M. (2002). *Minding animals: Awareness, emotions, and heart.* New York: Oxford University Press.

Beller, M., & Gafni, N. (2000). Can item format (multiple choice vs. open-ended) account for gender differences in mathematics achievement? *Sex Roles, 42*(1–2), 1–21.

Belsky, J. (1990). Developmental risks associated with infant day care. I. S. Cherazi (Ed.), *Psychosocial issues in day care* (pp. 37–68). New York: American Psychiatric Press.

Belsky, J. (1993). Etiology of child maltreatment: A developmental-ecological analysis. *Psychological Bulletin, 114,* 413–434.

Bem, D. J., & Honorton, C. (1994). Does psi exist? Replicable evidence for an anomalous process of information transfer. *Psychological Bulletin, 115,* 4–18.

Bem, S. L. (1993). *The lenses of gender.* New Haven: Yale University Press.

Bennett, J. C. (1991). The irrationality of the catharsis theory of aggression as justification for educators' support of interscholastic football. *Perceptual and Motor Skills, 72,* 415–418.

Benson, H., & Klipper, M. Z. (2000). *The relaxation response.* New York: HarperCollins.

Berger, B. D. (1993). Drinking to cope with stress: The effect of self-efficacy and alcohol expectancy on alcohol consumption. *Dissertation Abstracts International, 53,* 12–B. (6539)

Berger, K. S. (1994). *The developing person through the life span* (3rd ed.). New York: Worth.

Berkowitz, L. (1993). *Aggression: Its causes, consequences, and control.* New York: McGraw-Hill. This book includes a discussion of violence-prone personalities, domestic violence, gun control, violence in media, and control of aggression as well as various policy issues.

Berkowitz, L. (1994). Is something missing? Some observations prompted by the cognitive-neoassociationist view of anger and emotional aggression. In L. R. Huesmann (Ed.), *Aggressive behavior: current perspectives.* New York: Plenum.

Berman, A. L., & Jobes, D. A. (1991). *Adolescent suicide: Assessment and intervention.* Washington, DC: American Psychological Association.

Berman, M., Gladue, B., & Taylor, S. (1993). The effects of hormones, type A behavior pattern, and provocation on aggression in men. *Motivation and Emotion, 17,* 125–138.

Bernal, M. E., & Castro, F. G. (1994). Are clinical psychologists prepared for service and research with ethnic minorities? *American Psychologist, 49,* 797–805.

Berndt, T. J., & Perry, T. B. (1990). Distinctive features and effects of early adolescent friendships. In R. Montemayor, G. R. Adams, & T. P. Gullotta (Eds.), *From childhood to adolescence: A transitional period?* Newbury Park, CA: Sage.

Bernhardt, P. C., Dabbs, J. M., Jr., Fielden, J. A., & Lutter, C. D. (1998). Testosterone changes during vicarious experiences of winning and losing among fans at sporting events. *Physiology & Behavior, 65*(1) 59–62.

Bernstein, D., et al. (2005) False memories about food can lead to food avoidance. *Social Cognition 23*(1), 11–34.

Bersoff, D. (1994). Cited in DeAngelis, T. (1994). Experts see little impact from insanity plea ruling. *APA Monitor, 25*(6), 28.

Berzonsky, M. C., Kuk, L. S., & Storer, C. J. (1993, March). *Identity development, autonomy, and personal effectiveness.* Paper presented at the meeting of the Society for Research in Child Development, New Orleans, LA.

Bettencourt, B. A., Brewer, M. B., Croak, M. R., & Miller, N. (1992). Cooperation and the reduction of intergroup bias: The role of reward structure and social orientation. *Journal of Experimental Social Psychology, 28,* 301–319.

Beutler, L. E. (1991). Have all won and must all have prizes? *Journal of Consulting and Clinical Psychology, 59,* 226–232.

Bichey, B. G., Miyamoto, R. T. (2008). Outcomes in bilateral cochlear implantation. *Otolaryngology—Head and Neck Surgery, 138*(5), 655–661.

Billings, D. W., Folkman, S., Acree, M., & Moskowitz, J. T. (2000). Coping and physical health during caregiving: The roles of positive and negative affect. *Journal of Personality and Social Psychology, 79*(1), 131–142.

Birks, Y., & Roger, D. (2000). Identifying components of type-A behaviour: "Toxic" and "non-toxic" achieving. *Personality & Individual Differences, 28*(6), 1093–1105.

Bjorkqvist, K., Lagerspetz, K. M., & Kaukiainen, A. (1992). Do girls manipulate and boys fight? Developmental trends in regard to direct and indirect aggression. *Aggressive Behavior, 18,* 117–127.

Blakeslee, S. (1992, January 7). Scientists unraveling chemistry of dreams. *The New York Times,* pp. C1, C10.

Blanchard, E. B., et al. (1990a). A controlled evaluation of thermal biofeedback and thermal feedback combined with cognitive therapy in the treatment of vascular headache. *Journal of Consulting and Clinical Psychology, 58,* 216–224.

Blass, T. (1991). Understanding behavior in the Milgram obedience experiment: The roles of personality, situations, and their interactions. *Journal of Personality and Social Psychology, 60,* 398–413.

Blum, R. W., Harmon, B., Harris, L., Bergeisen, L., & Resnick, M. D. (1992). American Indian-Alaska native youth health. *Journal of the American Medical Association, 267,* 1637–1644.

Bohon, L. M., Singer, R. D., & Santos, S. J. (1993). The effects of real-world status and manipulated status on the self-esteem and social competition of Anglo-Americans and Mexican-Americans. *Hispanic Journal of Behavioral Sciences, 15,* 63–79.

Bond, R., & Smith, P. B. (1996). Culture and conformity: A meta-analysis of studies using Asch's line judgment task. *Psychological Bulletin, 119,* 111–137.

Bonin, M. F., McCreary, D. R., & Sadava, S. W. (2000). Problem drinking behavior in two community-based samples of adults: Influence of gender, coping, loneliness, and depression. *Psychology of Addictive Behaviors, 14*(2), 151–161.

Boniwell, I. (2006). *Positive psychology in a nutshell.* London: PWBC.

Bordo, S. (1993). *Unbearable weight: Feminism, Western culture, and the body.* Berkeley: University of California Press.

Bornstein, K. (1995). *Gender outlaw: On men, women and the rest of us.* New York: Vintage Books.

Bouchard, T. J., Jr., & Loehlin, J. C. (2001). Genes, evolution, and personality. *Behavior Genetics, 31*(3), 243–273.

Bouchard, T. J., Jr., Lykken, D. T., McGue, M., Segal, N. L., & Tellegren, A. (1990). Sources of human psychological differences: The Minnesota study of twins reared apart. *Science, 250,* 223–228.

Bowers, K. S., & Woody, E. Z. (1996). Hypnotic amnesia and the paradox of intentional forgetting. *Journal of Abnormal Psychology, 105,* 381–390.

Bowman, M. L. (1989). Testing individual differences in ancient China. *American Psychologist, 44,* 576–578.

Bradley, R. H., et al. (1989). Home environment and cognitive development in the first three years of life: A collaborative study involving six sites and three ethnic groups in North America. *Developmental Psychology, 25,* 217–235.

Brain-link camera gives blind a limited view. (2000, January 18). *The New York Times online.*

Brainerd, C. J., & Reyna, V. F. (2005). *The Science of False Memory.* New York: Oxford University Press.

Brandstätter, H., & Farthofer, A. (2003). Influence of part-time work on university students' academic performance. *Zeitschrift für Arbeits-und Organisationspsychologie, 47*(3), 134–145.

Brenner, J. (1992). Cited in Williams, L. (1992, February 6). Woman's image in a mirror: Who defines what she sees? *The New Times,* pp. A1, B7.

Brannigan, G. G., & Merrens, M. R. (1993). *The undaunted psychologist: Adventures in research.* New York: McGraw-Hill. Fascinating stories from 15 research psychologists describing what psychological research is really like—how they got their ideas, how they pursued them, and the successes and failures along the way.

Broberg, A. G., Wessels, H., Lamb, M. E., & Hwang, C. P. (1997). Effects of day care on the development of cognitive abilities in 8-year-olds: A longitudinal study. *Developmental Psychology, 33*(1), 62–69.

Brody, J. E. (1995a). Cited in DeAngelis, T. (1995). Eat well, keep fit, and let go of stress. *APA Monitor, 26*(10), 20.

Brook, J. S., Whiteman, M. M., & Finch, S. (1993). Childhood aggression, adolescent delinquency, and drug use: A longitudinal study. *Journal of Genetic Psychology, 153,* 369–383.

Brown, B. B., Mounts, N., Lamborn, S. D., & Steinberg, L. (1993). Parenting practices and peer group affiliation in adolescence. *Child Development, 64,* 467–482.

Brown, D. E. (1991). *Human universals.* Philadelphia: Temple University Press.

Brownell, K. D., & Rodin, J. (1994). The dieting maelstrom: Is it possible and advisable to lose weight? *American Psychologist, 49,* 781–791.

Brownell, K. D., & Wadden, T. A. (1992). Obesity: Understanding a serious, prevalent, and refactory disorder. *Journal of Consulting and Clinical Psychology, 60,* 505–517.

Browning, C. (1992). *Ordinary men: Reserve Police Battalion 101 and the Final Solution in Poland.* New York: HarperCollins.

Buchanan, R. W., Pearlson, G., & Tamminga, C. A. (2004). Prefrontal cortex, structural analysis: Segmenting the prefrontal cortex. *American Journal of Psychiatry, 161*(11), 1978.

Budiansky, S. (1998). *If a lion could talk: Animal intelligence and the evolution of consciousness.* New York: Free Press.

Budzynski, T. H., & Stoyra, J. M. (1984). Biofeedback methods in the treatment of anxiety and stress. In R. I. Woolfolk & P. M. Lehrer (Eds.), *Principles and practice of stress management.* New York: Guilford.

Burger, J. M. (1999). The foot-in-the-door compliance procedure: A multiple-process analysis and review. *Personality & Social Psychology Review, 3*(4), 303–325.

Burish, T. G., Carey, M. P., Krozely, M. G., & Greco, F. A. (1987). Conditioned side effects induced by cancer chemotherapy: Prevention through behavioral treatment. *Journal of Consulting and Clinical Psychology, 55,* 42–48.

Burns, G. L., & Farina, A. (1987). Physical attractiveness and self-perception of mental disorder. *Journal of Abnormal Psychology, 96,* 161–163.

Burnstein, E., & Schul, Y. (1982). The informational basis of social judgments: Operations in forming an impression of another person. *Journal of Experimental Social Psychology, 18,* 217–234.

Burroughs, A. (2002). *Running with scissors: A memoir.* New York: St. Martin's. Includes characters with depression, anxiety, psychosis, OCD, and more.

Bushman, B. J., Baumeister, R. F., & Stack, A. D. (1999). Catharsis, aggression, and persuasive influence: Self-fulfilling or self-defeating prophecies? *Journal of Personality & Social Psychology, 76*(3), 367–376.

Buss, D. M. (1992). Is there a universal human nature? *Contemporary Psychology, 37,* 1262–1263.

Buss, D. M. (1994). *The evolution of desire: Strategies of human mating.* New York: Basic Books.

Buss, D. M. (1999). Adaptive individual differences revisited. *Journal of Personality, 67*(2), 259–264.

Butler, J. C. (2000). Personality and emotional correlates of right-wing authoritarianism. *Social Behavior & Personality, 28*(1), 1–14.

Butterfield, F. (1992, January 1). Studies find a family link to criminality. *The New York Times,* pp. A1, A8.

Byrnes, J., & Takahira, S. (1993). Explaining gender differences on SAT-math items. *Developmental Psychology, 29,* 805–810.

Caldwell, C. B., & Gotteman, I. I. (1990). Schizophrenics kill themselves too: A review of the risk factors for suicide. *Schizophrenia Bulletin, 16,* 571–589.

Califano, J. A. (1995). The wrong way to stay slim. *New England Journal of Medicine, 333,* 1214–1216.

Camarena, P. M. (1991). Conformity in adolescence. In R. M. Lerner, A. C. Petersen, & J. Brooks-Gunn (Eds.), *Encyclopedia of adolescence.* New York: Garland.

Campos, J. J. (2000). Cited in Azar, B. (2000). What's in a face? *Monitor on Psychology, 31*(1), 44–45.

Campos, J. J., Langer, A., & Krowitz, A. (1970). Cardiac responses on the visual cliff in prelocomotor infants. *Science, 170,* 196–197.

Cannon, W. B. (1927). The James-Lange theory of emotions: A critical examination and an alternative theory. *American Journal of Psychology, 39,* 106–124.

Carey, G. (1992). Twin imitation for antisocial behavior: Implications for genetic and family environment research. *Journal of Abnormal Psychology, 101,* 18–25.

Carlson, J. G., & Hatfield, E. (1992). *Psychology of emotion.* Fort Worth, TX: Harcourt Brace Jovanovich.

Carpenter, S. (2001). Sleep deprivation may be undermining teen health. *APA Monitor Online, 32*(9), September/October.

Carrère, S., Buehlman, K. T., Gottman, J. M., Coan, J. A., & Ruckstuhl, L. (2000). Predicting marital stability and divorce in newlywed couples. *Journal of Family Psychology, 14*(1), 42–58.

Casey, B. J., Jones, R. M., Hare, T. A. (2008). The adolescent brain. *Annals of the New York Academy of Sciences, 1124*(01): 111–126. http://Firstsearch.oclc.org.

Caspi, A., Lynam, D., Moffitt, T. E., & Silva, P. A. (1993). Unraveling girls' delinquency: Biological, dispositional, and contextual contributions to adolescent misbehavior. *Developmental Psychology, 29,* 19–30.

Cattell, R. (1965). *The scientific analysis of personality.* Baltimore: Penguin.

Cavaliere, F. (1996). Bilingual schools face big political challenges. *APA Monitor, 27*(2), 36.

Cavanaugh, J. C., & Green, E. E. (1990). I believe, therefore I can: Self-efficacy beliefs in memory aging. In E. A. Lovelace (Ed.), *Aging and cognition: Mental processes, self-awareness, and interventions.* Amsterdam: Elsevier.

Ceci, S. J., & Bruck, M. (1993). Suggestibility of the child witness. *Psychological Bulletin, 113,* 403–439.

Centers for Disease Control and Prevention. (1993). Infant mortality—United States, 1990. *Morbidity and Mortality Weekly Report, 42,* 161–165.

Centers for Disease Control and Prevention. (1993, October). *HIV/AIDS surveillance: Third quarter edition. U.S. AIDS cases reported through September 1993.* Atlanta, GA: U.S. Department of Health and Human Services.

Centers for Disease Control and Prevention. (2000, June 9). Youth risk behavior surveillance—United States, 1999. *Morbidity and Mortality Weekly Report, 49*(SS05); 1–96.

Chance, S. E., Brown, R. T., Dabbs, J. M., Jr., & Casey, R. (2000). Testosterone, intelligence and behavior disorders in young boys. *Personality & Individual Differences, 28*(3) 437–445.

Chang, E. C., & Sanna, L. J. (Eds.). (2003). *Virtue, vice, and personality: The complexity of behavior.* Washington, D. C.: American Psychological Association. Leading researchers focus on some of the most notable personality variables including self-esteem, optimism, intelligence, personal control, rumination, perfectionism, and neuroticism.

Charles, S. T., Reynolds, C. A., Gatz, M. (2001). Age-related differences and change in positive and negative affect over 23 years. *Journal of Personality and Social Psychology, 80*(1), 136–151.

Chase, T. (2002). *When rabbit howls: The troops for Truddi Chase.* New York: Berkeley. This book is an autobiographical account by Truddi Chase of her experience of multiple personality disorder.

Chassin, L., Presson, C. C., Pitts, S. C., & Sherman, S. J. (2000). The natural history of cigarette smoking from adolescence to adulthood in a Midwestern community sample: Multiple trajectories and their psychological correlates. *Health Psychology, 19,* 223–231.

Chira, S. (1992, February 12). Bias against girls found rife in schools, with lasting damage. *The New York Times,* pp. A1, A23.

Chodorow, N. (1991). *Feminism and psychoanalytic theory.* New Haven: Yale University Press.

Chomsky, N. (1991). Linguistics and cognitive science: Problems and mysteries. In A. Kasher (Ed.), *The Chomskyan turn.* Cambridge, MA: Blackwell.

Cialdini, R. B. (1993). *Influence: Science and practice* (3rd ed.). New York: HarperCollins.

Cialdini, R. B. (Ed.). (2008). *Influence: The psychology of persuasion* (5th ed.). New York: Allyn & Bacon. This is a new edition of a book on the six basic principles of influence and persuasion.

Cialdini, R. B. (2000). Cited in McKinley, J. C., Jr. (2000, August 11). It isn't just a game: Clues to avid rooting. *The New York Times online.*

Clark, K. B. (1955/1988). *Prejudice and your child.* Middletown, CT: Wesleyan University Press.

Clark, K. B., & Clark, M. P. (1947). Racial identification and preference in Negro children. In T. M. Newcomb & E. L. Hartley (Eds.), *Readings in Social Psychology.* New York: Holt, Rinehart and Winston.

Clark, R., Anderson, N. B., Clark, V. R., & Williams, D. R. (1999). Racism as a stressor for African Americans. *American Psychologist, 54*(10), 805–816.

Clarke-Stewart, K. A. (1989). Infant day care: Maligned or malignant? *American Psychologist, 44,* 266–273.

Clarke-Stewart, K. A. (1991). A home is not a school: The effects of child care on children's development. *Journal of Social Issues, 47,* 105–123.

Clarke-Stewart, K. A., Vandell, D. L., McCartney, K., Owen, M. T., & Booth, C. (2000). Effects of parental separation and divorce on very young children. *Journal of Family Psychology, 14*(2), 304–326.

Cohen, D., et al. (2000). Absence of cognitive impairment at long-term follow-up in adolescents treated with ECT for severe mood disorder. *American Journal of Psychiatry, 157,* 460–462.

Cohen, S., & Williamson, G. M. (1991). Stress and infectious disease in humans. *Psychological Bulletin, 109,* 5–24.

Coleman, L. (1990). Cited in Goleman, G. (1990, August 2). The quiet comeback of electroshock therapy. *The New York Times,* p. B5.

Collier, G. (1994). *Social origins of mental ability.* New York: John Wiley & Sons.

Collins, J. F. (2000). Biracial Japanese American identity: An evolving process. *Cultural Diversity & Ethnic Minority Psychology, 6*(2), 115–133.

Collins, W. A., & Russell, G. (1991). Mother-child and father-child relationships in middle childhood and adolescence: A developmental analysis. *Developmental Review, 11,* 99–136.

Colvin, M. K., Funnell, M. G., & Gazzaniga, M. S. (2005). Numerical processing in the two hemispheres: Studies of a split–brain patient. *Brain & Cognition, 57*(1), 43–52.

Comas-Diaz, L. (1994, February). Race and gender in psychotherapy with women of color. *Winter roundtable on cross-cultural counseling and psychotherapy: Race and gender.* New York: Teachers College, Columbia University.

Conger, J. J. (1978). Adolescence: A time for becoming. In M. Lamb (Ed.), *Social and personality development.* New York: Holt, Rinehart and Winston.

Coolidge, F. L., DenBoer, J. W., & Segal, D. L. (2004). Personality and neuropsychological correlates of bullying behavior. *Personality & Individual Differences, 36*(7), 1559–1569.

Cools, J., Schotte, D. E., & McNally, R. J. (1992). Emotional arousal and overeating in restrained eaters. *Journal of Abnormal Psychology, 101,* 348-351.

Cooper, J. R., Bloom, F. E., & Roth, R. H. (1991). *The biochemical basis of neuropharmacology.* New York: Oxford University Press.

Cooper, W. (2004). Antipsychotic drug prescriptions nearly double for children with ADHA. *Archives of Pediatric Adolescent Medicine,* August 3, 2004.

Corballis, P. M., Funnell, M. G., & Gazzaniga, M. S. (2002). Hemispheric asymmetries for simple visual judgments in the split brain. *Neuropsychologia, 40*(4), 401-410.

Cousins, N. (1979). *Anatomy of an illness as perceived by the patient: Reflections on healing and regeneration.* New York: Norton.

Covey, S. R. (1989). *The seven habits of highly effective people.* New York: Simon & Schuster.

Cox, B. J., Borger, S. C., Asmundson, G. J. G., & Taylor, S. (2000). Hypochondriasis: Dimensions of hypochondriasis and the five-factor model of personality. *Personality & Individual Differences, 29*(1), 99-108.

Cox, W. M., & Alm, R. (2005, February 28). Scientists are made, not born. *The New York Times Magazine.*

Crain, W. C. (1992). *Theories of development: Concepts and applications* (3rd ed.). Englewood Cliffs, NJ: Prentice-Hall.

Cramer, R. E., McMaster, M. R., Bartell, P. A., & Dragna, M. (1988). Subject competence and minimization of the bystander effect. *Journal of Applied Social Psychology, 18*, 1133–1148.

Crosby, F. J., & Jaskar, K. L. (1993). Women and men at home and at work: Realities and illusions. In S. Oskamp & M. Costanzo (Eds.), *Gender issues in contemporary society*. Newbury Park, CA: Sage.

Cross, W. E., Parham, T. A., & Helms, J. E. (1991). The states of Black identity development: Nigrescence models. In R. Jones (Ed.), *Black psychology* (3rd ed, pp. 319–338). Hampton, VA: Cobb & Henry.

Crowe, R. A. (1990). Astrology and the scientific method. *Psychological Reports, 67,* 163–191.

Csikszentmyhalyi, M. (1990). *Flow: The psychology of optimal experience*. New York: HarperCollins. Csik-szentmihalyi posits that endeavors that involve our whole being and use our skills to the utmost lead to long-term happiness.

Cummings, J. L. (1995, June 10). Dementia: the failing brain. *Lancet,* p. 772.

Curfman, G. D. (1993a). The health benefits of exercise: A critical reappraisal. *New England Journal of Medicine, 328*, 574–576.

Curfman, G. D. (1993b). Is exercise beneficial—or hazardous—to your heart? *New England Journal of Medicine, 329*, 1730–1731.

Curtis, L., Masselink, L., et al (2004). Use of atypical antipsychotic drugs by children and adolescents in the United States: A retrospective cohort study. *Abstr Academy Health Meeting*; abstract no. 1158.

Curtis, L., Masselink, L., et al (2005). Prevalence of atypical antipsychotic drug use among commercially insured youths in the United States. *Archives of Pediatrics and Adolescent Medicine, 159*, 362–366.

Cytowic, R. G. (1993). *The man who tasted shapes*. New York: Warner Books. Fascinating stories of synesthesia.

Dabbs, J. M., Jr., Hargrove, M. F., & Heusel, C. (1996). Testosterone differences among college fraternities: Well-behaved vs rambunctious. *Personality & Individual Differences, 20*(2), 157–161.

Dalai Lama, Gardner, H., Goleman, D., & Benson, H. (1991). *Mindscience, An East-West dialogue: The Harvard mind science symposium*. Somerville, MA: Wisdom Publications. An account of experiments by Western scientists on Tibetan meditators who were practicing tumo, or inner heat yoga.

Damasio, H., & Damasio, A. (1992, September). Brain and language. *Scientific American,* pp. 89–95.

Danner, D., Snowdon, D. & Friesen, W. (2001). Positive emotions early in life and the longevity: Findings from the nun study. *Journal of Personality and Social Psychology, 80*, 804–813.

Darwin, C. (1872). *The expression of the emotions in man and animals.* London: J. Murray.

Davidson, E. S., Yasuna, A., & Tower, A. (1979). The effects of television cartoons on sex-role stereotyping in young girls. *Child Development, 50,* 597–600.

Davidson, J. E. (1986). The role of insight in giftedness. In R. J. Sternberg & J. E. Davidson (Eds.), *Conceptions of giftedness*. New York: Cambridge University Press.

Davies, P. T., & Cummings, E. M. (1994). Marital conflict and child adjustment. *Psychological Bulletin, 116*, 387–411.

Davis, J. H. (1975). The design processes of 6– and 12–person mock juries assigned unanimous and two-thirds majority rules. *Journal of Personality and Social Psychology, 32*, 1–14.

Davison, G., & Neale, J. (1990). *Abnormal psychology* (5th ed.). New York: John Wiley & Sons.

Dawes, R. M. (1999). Two methods for studying the incremental validity of a Rorschach variable. *Psychological Assessment, 11*(3), 297–302.

De Houwer, J., Thomas, S., & Baeyens, F. (2001). Associative learning of likes and dislikes: A review of 25 years of research on human evaluative conditioning. *Psychological Bulletin, 127*(6), 853–869.

DeAngelis, T. (1993a). It's baaack: TV violence, concern for kid viewers. *APA Monitor, 24*(8), 16.

DeAngelis, T. (1993b). Law helps American Indians enter field. *APA Monitor, 24*(3), 26–27.

DeAngelis, T. (1994). Public's view of insanity plea quite inaccurate, study finds. *APA Monitor, 25*(6), 28.

DeAngelis, T. (1995). Mental health care is elusive for Hispanic. *APA Monitor, 26*(7), 49.

DeAngelis, T. (1997). Abused children have more conflicts with friends. *APA Monitor, 28*(6), 32.

DeGree, C. E., & Snyder, C. R. (1995). Adler's psychology (of use) today: Personal history of traumatic life events as a self-handicapping strategy. *Journal of Personality and Social Psychology, 48,* 1512–1519.

DeKovic, M., & Janssens, J. (1992). Parents' child-rearing style and child's sociometric status. *Developmental Psychology, 28,* 925–932.

Dement, W. C., with Vaughan, C. (1999). *The promise of sleep: A pioneer in sleep medicine explains the vital connection between health, happiness and a good night's sleep.* New York: Delacorte.

Denmark, F. L. (1998). Women and psychology: An international perspective. *American Psychologist, 53*(4), 465–473.

DePaulo, B. M. (1992). Nonverbal behavior and self-presentation. *Psychological Bulletin, 111,* 203–243.

Desmond, A. M. (1994). Adolescent pregnancy in the United States: Not a minority issue. *Health Care for Women International, 15*(4), 325–331.

Deutsch, M., & Collins, M. (1951). *Interracial housing: A psychological evaluation of a social experiment.* Minneapolis: University of Minnesota Press.

DeWit, D. J., et al. (2000). Age at first alcohol use: A risk factor for the development of alcohol disorders. *American Journal of Psychiatry, 157,* 745–750.

Digman, J. M., & Inouye, J. (1986). Specification of the five robust factors of personality. *Journal of Personality and Social Psychology, 50,* 116–123.

DiLalla, D. L., Carey, G., Gottesman, I. I., & Bouchard, T. J., Jr. (1996). Heritability of MMPI personality indicators of psychopathology in twins reared apart. *Journal of Abnormal Psychology, 105,* 491–499.

DiLalla, L. F., & Gottesman, I. I. (1991). Biological and genetic contributors to violence: Widom's untold tale. *Psychological Bulletin, 109,* 125–129.

Dix, T. (1991). The affective organization of parenting: Adaptive and maladaptive processes. *Psychological Bulletin, 110,* 3–25.

Doctors tie male mentality to shorter life span. (1995, June 14). *The New York Times,* p. C14.

Doob, A. N., & Wood, L. (1972). Catharsis and aggression: The effects of annoyance and retaliation on aggressive behavior. *Journal of Personality and Social Psychology, 22,* 236–245.

Dovidio, J. H., Evans, N., & Tyler, R. B. (1986). Racial stereotypes: The contents of their cognitive representations. *Journal of Experimental Social Psychology, 22,* 22–37.

Draguns, J. G. (1988). Personality and culture: Are they relevant for the enhancement of quality of mental life? In P. R. Dasen, J. W. Berry, & N. Sartorius (Eds.), *Health and cross-cultural psychology: Toward applications.* Newberry Park, CA: Sage.

Du Bois, W. E. B. (1903/1990). *The souls of black folk.* New York: Random House.

Dubbert, P. M. (1992). Exercise in behavioral medicine. *Journal of Consulting and Clinical Psychology, 60,* 613–618.

DuBois, D. L., & Hirsh, B. J. (1990). School and neighborhood friendship patterns of Blacks and Whites in adolescence. *Child Development, 61,* 524–536.

Dumas, J. E., & LaFreniere, P. J. (1993). Mother-child relationships as a support of support or stress: A comparison of competent, average, aggressive, and anxious dyads. *Child Development, 64.*

Duncan, J., et al. (2000). A neural basis for general intelligence. *Science, 289*(5478), 457–460.

Duncker, K. (1945). On problem solving. *Psychological Monographs,* 58. (Whole No. 270).

Dunphy, D. C. (1963). The social structure of urban adolescent peer groups. *Sociometry, 26,* 230–246.

E

Eagly, A. (2007). *Through the labyrinth: The truth about how women become leaders.* Boston: Harvard Business School Press.

Eagly, A. H., & Chaiken, S. (1993). *The psychology of attitudes.* Fort Worth, TX: Harcourt Brace Jovanovich.

Eagly, A. H., Ashmore, R. D., Makhijani, M. G., & Longo, L. C. (1991). What is beautiful is good, but . . . : A meta-analytic review of research on the physical attractiveness stereotype. *Psychological Bulletin, 110,* 109–128.

Egeland, B., Jacobvitz, D., & Sroufe, L. A. (1988). Breaking the cycle of abuse. *Child Development, 59,* 1080–1088.

Egeth, H. E. (1993). What do we *not* know about eyewitness identification? *American Psychologist, 48,* 577–580.

Ekman, P. (1980). *The face of man.* New York: Garland.

Ekman, P. (1993). Facial expression and emotion. *American Psychologist, 48,* 384–392.

Ekvall, S. W. (Ed.). (1993). *Pediatric nutrition in chronic diseases and developmental disorders: Prevention, assessment, and treatment.* New York: Oxford University Press.

Elegant, S. (2008, June 2). Roused by disaster. *Time,* pp. 30–33.

Elias, M. J., & Zins, J. E. (2003). Bullying, other forms of peer harassment, and victimization in the schools: Issues for school psychology research and practice. *Journal of Applied School Psychology, 19*(2), 1–5.

Ellenbogen, G. (Ed.) (1993). *Oral sadism and the vegetarian personality: Readings from the Journal of Polymorphous Perversity.* New York: Brunner/Mazel. Pokes fun at all theories and big-name theorists.

Ellis, A. (1977). The basic clinical theory of rational-emotive therapy. In A. Ellis & R. Grieger (Eds.), *Handbook of rational-emotive therapy.* New York: Springer.

Ellis, A., & Dryden, W. (1987). *The practice of rational emotional therapy.* New York: Springer.

Ellis, E. M. (2000). *Divorce wars: Interventions with families in conflict.* Washington, D.C.: American Psychological Association.

Ellsworth, P. C., Carlsmith, J. M., & Henson, A. (1972). The stare as a stimulus to flight in human subjects. *Journal of Personality and Social Psychology, 21,* 302–311.

Emde, R. (1993). Cited in Adler, T. (1993). Shy, bold temperament? It's mostly in the genes. *APA Monitor, 24*(1), 7, 8.

Engels, G. I., Garnefski, N., & Diekstra, R. F. W. (1993). Efficacy of rational-emotive therapy: A quantitative analysis. *Journal of Consulting and Clinical Psychology, 61,* 1083–1090.

Erel, O., Oberman, Y., & Yirmiya, N. (2000). Maternal versus nonmaternal care and seven domains of children's development. *Psychological Bulletin, 126*(5), 727–747.

Erikson, E. H. (1950). *Childhood and society.* New York: Norton.

Erikson, E. H. (1963). *Childhood and society* (2nd ed.). New York: Norton.

Erikson, E. H. (1968). *Identity: Youth and crisis.* New York: Norton.

Erikson, E. H. (1975). *Life history and the historical moment.* New York: Norton.

Erikson, E. H. (1982). *The life cycle completed.* New York: Norton.

Etaugh, C., & Rathus, S. A. (1995). *The world of children.* Fort Worth, TX: Harcourt Brace Jovanovich.

Etcoff, N. L. (1994). Cited in Brody, J. E. (1994, March 21). Notions of beauty transcend culture, new study suggests. *The New York Times,* p. A14.

Eysenck, H. J. (1953). *The structure of human personality.* London: Methuen.

F

Fagot, B. I., Hagan, R., Leinbach, M. D., & Kronsberg, S. (1985). Differential reactions to assertive and communicative acts of toddler boys and girls. *Child Development, 56,* 1499–1505.

Fallon, A. E., & Rozin, P. (1985). Sex differences in perceptions of desirable body shape. *Journal of Abnormal Psychology, 94,* 102–105.

Feingold, A. (1988). Matching for attractiveness in romantic partners and same-sex friends: A meta-analysis and theoretical critique. *Psychological Bulletin, 104,* 226–235.

Feingold, A. (1992a). Gender differences in mate selection preferences: A test of the parental investment model. *Psychological Bulletin, 112,* 125–139.

Feingold, A. (1992b). Good-looking people are not what we think. *Psychological Bulletin, 111,* 304–341.

Feiring, C. (1993, March). *Developing concepts of romance from 15 to 18 years.* Paper presented at the meeting of the Society for Research in Child Development, New Orleans, LA.

Fernández-Aráoz, C. (2007). *Great people decisions.* Hoboken, NJ: Wiley.

Feshbach, S. (1994). Nationalism, patriotism, and aggression: A clarification of functional differences. In L. R. Huesmann (Ed.), *Aggressive behavior: Current perspectives.* New York: Plenum Press.

Festinger, L. (1957). *A theory of cognitive dissonance.* Stanford, CA: Stanford University Press.

Field, T. M. (1991). Young children's adaptations to repeated separations from their mothers. *Child Development, 62,* 539–547.

Finkelhor, D., & Dziuba-Leatherman, J. (1994). Victimization of children. *American Psychologist, 49,* 173–183.

Finn, P. R., Sharkansky, E. J., Brandt, K. M., & Turcotte, N. (2000). The effects of familial risk, personality, and expectancies on alcohol use and abuse. *Journal of Abnormal Psychology, 109*(1), 122–133.

Fischer, K. W., Shavber, P. R., & Carochan, P. (1990). How emotions develop and how they organize development. *Cognition and Emotion, 4,* 81–127.

Fisher, C. B., & Fyrberg, D. (1994). Participant partners: College students weigh the costs and benefits of deceptive research. *American Psychologist, 49,* 417–427.

Fisher, H. E. (1992). *Anatomy of love: The natural history of monogamy, adultery and divorce.* New York: Norton.

Fiske, S. T. (1989). *Interdependence and stereotyping: From the laboratory to the Supreme Court (and back).* Paper presented to the meeting of the American Psychological Association, New Orleans, LA.

Fiske, S. T. (1993). Controlling other people: The impact of power on stereotyping. *American Psychologist, 48,* 621–628.

Fiske, S. T., & Taylor, S. E. (1984). *Social cognition.* Reading, MA: Addison-Wesley.

Fitzgibbon, M. L., Stolley, M. R., & Kirschenbaum, D. S. (1993). Obese people who seek treatment have different characteristics than those who do not seek treatment. *Health Psychology, 12,* 342–345.

Flack, W. F., Jr., Laird, J. D., & Cavallaro, L. A. (1999). Separate and combined effects of facial expressions and bodily postures on emotional feelings. *European Journal of Social Psychology, 29*(2–3), 203–217.

Flavell, J. H., Miller, P. H., & Miller, S. A. (1993). *Cognitive development* (3rd ed.). Englewood Cliffs, NJ: Prentice-Hall.

Flegal, K. M., Carroll, M. D., Ogden, C. L., & Johnson, C. L. (2002). Prevalence and trends in obesity among U.S. adults, 1999–2000. *Journal of the American Medical Association, 288*(14), 1723–1727.

Fling, S., Smith, L., Rodriguez, T., Thornton, D., et al. (1992). Video games, aggression, and self-esteem: A survey. *Social Behavior & Personality, 20,* 39–45.

Foster-Clark, F. S., & Blyth, D. A. (1991). Peer relations and influences. In R. M. Lerner, A. C. Petersen, & J. Brooks-Gunn (Eds.), *Encyclopedia of adolescence.* New York: Garland.

Fowler, W., Ogston, K., Roberts–Fiati, G., & Swenson, A. (1993, February). *The long term development of giftedness and high competencies in children enriched in language during infancy.* Paper presented at the Esther Katz Rosen Symposium on the Psychological Development of Gifted Children, University of Kansas, Lawrence.

Franklin, E. & Wright, W. (1991). *Sins of the father: The landmark Franklin case, a daughter, a memory, and a murder.* New York: Ballantine.

Frangione, B. (2000, July). Amyloid and dementia: To be or not to be. Paper presented to the World Alzheimer Congress 2000, Washington, DC.

Frankl, V. E. (1984). *Man's search for meaning.* New York: Pocket Books. In this book, first published in 1946, Frankl discusses his experiences as a concentration camp prisoner and describes his psychotherapeutic method of finding a reason to live.

Franzoi, S. L., & Herzog, M. E. (1987). Judging physical attractiveness: What body aspects do we use? *Personality and Social Psychology Bulletin, 13,* 19–33.

Freud, S. (1933/1964). New introductory lectures. In J. Strachey (Ed. and Trans.), *The standard edition of the complete psychological works of Sigmund Freud* (Vol. 22). London: Hogarth.

Freud, S. (1936). *The problem of anxiety.* New York: Norton.

Freud, S. (1952). *A general introduction to psychoanalysis.* New York: Washington Square Press. (Original work published 1920).

Freud, S. (1997) *The interpretation of dreams* (rev. ed.). Hertfordshire, England: Wordsworth Editions. (Original work published 1900) Classic introduction to the unconscious and the structure of the id, ego, and superego.

Friedman, M., & Ulmer, D. (1984). *Treating type A behavior and your heart.* New York: Fawcett Crest.

Frodi, A. M., Macauley, J., & Thome, P. R. (1977). Are women always less aggressive than men? A review of the experimental literature. *Psychological Bulletin, 84,* 634–660.

Fromm-Reichmann, F. (1948). Notes on the development of treatment of schizophrenics by psychoanalytic psychotherapy. *Psychiatry, 11,* 263–273.

Galambos, N. L. (1992). Parent-adolescent relations. *Current Directions in Psychological Science, 1,* 146–149.

Galambos, N. L., & Almeida, D. M. (1992). Does parent-adolescent conflict increase in early adolescence? *Journal of Marriage and the Family, 54,* 737–747.

Gallagher, A. M., et al.(2000). Gender differences in advanced mathematical problem solving. *Journal of Experimental Child Psychology, 75*(3), 165–190.

Gardner, H. (1983). *Frames of mind: The theory of multiple intelligences.* New York: Basic Books.

Gardner, H. (1993). *Creating minds: An anatomy of creativity seen through the lives of Freud, Einstein, Picasso, Stravinsky, Eliot, Graham and Gandhi.* New York: Basic Books.

Gardner, H. (1995, November). Reflections on multiple intelligences: Myths and messages. *Phi Delta Kappan, 77,* 200–208.

Gardner, H. (2006). *Five minds for the future.* Cambridge: Harvard Business Press. Gardner describes five cognitive abilities he believes will be required for leaders to successfully meet the needs of our global future.

Garland, A. F., & Zigler, E. (1993). Adolescent suicide prevention. *American Psychologist, 48,* 169–182.

Gauthier, J., Côte, G., & French, D. (1994). The role of home practice in the thermal biofeedback treatment of migraine headache. *Journal of Consulting and Clinical Psychology, 62,* 180–184.

Geen, R. G., Stonner, D., & Shope, G. L. (1975). The facilitation of aggression by aggression: Evidence against the catharsis hypothesis. *Journal of Personality and Social Psychology, 31,* 721–726.

Geschwind, N. (1979, September). Specializations of the human brain. *Scientific American,* pp. 180–199.

Gibbs, J. T. (1992). Negotiating ethnic identity: Issues for Black-White biracial adolescents. In M. P. P. Root (Ed.), *Racially mixed people in America.* Newbury Park, CA: Sage.

Gibson, M., & Ogbu, J. (Eds.). (1991). *Minority status and schooling: A comparative study of immigrant and involuntary minorities.* New York: Garland.

Giedd, J. N. (2008). The teen brain: insights from neuroimaging. *The Journal of Adolescent Health, 42*(4), 335-43.

Gifford, Robert (2007). *Environmental psychology: principles and practice* (4th ed.). Colville, WA: Optimal Books.

Gilbert, S. J. (1981). Another look at the Milgram obedience studies: The role of the gradated series of shocks. *Personality and Social Psychology Bulletin, 7,* 690–695.

Gilligan, C., Rogers, A. G., & Tolman, D. L. (Eds.). (1991). *Women, girls, and psychotherapy.* New York: Haworth.

Gilligan, C., Ward, J. V., & Taylor, J. M. (1989). *Mapping the moral domain: A contribution of women's thinking to psychological theory and education.* Cambridge: Harvard University Press.

Gilligan, C. (1993). *In a different voice: Psychological theory and women's development.* Cambridge: Harvard University Press. Best-selling and highly influential account of the biases that influence most traditional theories of human development.

Gillin, J. C. (1991). The long and short of sleeping pills. *New England Journal of Medicine, 324,* 1735–1736.

Gleason, J. B., & Ratner, N. B. (1993). Language development in children. In J. B. Gleason & N. B. Ratner (Eds.), *Psycholinguistics.* Fort Worth, TX: Harcourt Brace Jovanovich.

Gleitman, H., Rozin, P., & Sabini, J. (1997). Solomon E. Asch (1907–1996). *American Psychologist, 52,* 984–985.

Goldberg, P. (1983). *The intuitive edge: Understanding and developing intuition.* New York: Tarcher.

Goldfried, M. R., & Padawer, W. (1982). Current status and future directions in psychotherapy. In M. R. Goldfried (Ed.), *Converging themes in psychotherapy: Trends in psychodynamic, humanistic, and behavioral practice.* New York: Springer.

Goldsmith, H. H. (1993). Cited in Adler, T. (1993a). Shy, bold temperament? It's mostly in the genes. *APA Monitor, 24*(1), 7–8.

Goldstein, M., Baker, B., & Jamison, K. (1986). *Abnormal Psychology* (2nd ed.). Boston: Little, Brown.

Goleman, D. (1995a, March 28). The brain manages happiness and sadness in different centers. *The New York Times,* pp. C1, C9.

Goleman, D. (1995b, May 2). Biologists find site of working memory. *The New York Times,* pp. C1, C9.

Goleman, D. J. (1995d). *Emotional intelligence.* New York: Bantam Books.

Goleman, D., with a foreword by the Dalai Lama. (2003). *Destructive emotions: How can we overcome them? A scientific dialogue with the Dalai Lama.* New York: Bantam.

THE PSYCHOLOGIST'S BOOKSHELF

Gollwitzer, P. M., & Bargh, J. A. (Eds.). (1996). *The psychology of action: Linking cognition and motivation to behavior*. New York: Guildford Press.

Golombok, S., & Fivesh, R. (1994). *Gender development*. New York: Cambridge University Press.

Goode, E. (2000, June 25). Thinner: The male battle with anorexia. *The New York Times*, p. MH8.

Goodnow, J. J., & Bowes, J. M. (1994). *Men, women, and household work*. Melbourne: Oxford University Press.

Goodwin, F. K., & Jamison, K. R. (1990). *Manic-depressive illness*. New York: Oxford University Press.

Gorman, J., Liebowitz, M., Fyer, A., & Stein, J. (1989). A neuroanatomical hypothesis for panic disorder. *The American Journal of Psychiatry, 146,* 148–161.

Gottesman, I., & Shileds, J. (1982). *Schizophrenia: The epigenetic puzzle*. New York: Cambridge University Press.

Gottfried, A. E., Fleming, J. S., & Gottfried, A. W. (1994). Role of parental motivational practices in children's academic intrinsic motivation and achievement. *Journal of Educational Psychology, 86,* 104–113.

Gottman, J. M., Coan, J., Carrère, S. & Swanson, C. (1998). Predicting marital happiness and stability from newlywed interactions. *Journal of Marriage and the Family, 60,* 5–22.

Green, S. K., Buchanan, D. R., & Heuer, S. K. (1984). Winners, losers, and choosers: A field investigation of dating initiation. *Personality and Social Psychology Bulletin, 10,* 502–511.

Greene, A. S., & Saxe, L. (1990). *Tall tales told to teachers*. Unpublished manuscript, Brandeis University.

Greene, B. A. (1992). Still here: A perspective on psychotherapy with African American women. In J. Chrisler & D. Howard (Eds.), *New directions in feminist psychology*. New York: Springer.

Greene, B. A. (1993). African American women. In L. Comas-Diaz & B. A. Greene (Eds.), *Women of color and mental health*. New York: Guilford.

Greeno, C. G., & Wing, R. R. (1994). Stress-induced eating. *Psychological Bulletin, 115,* 444–464.

Gregory, N. (2004). Crime and the family: Like grandfather, like father, like son? *British Journal of Forensic Practice, 6*(4), 32–36.

Grey, J., Feldon, J., Rawlins, J., Hemsley, D., & Smith, A. (1991). The neuropsychology of schizophrenia. *Behavioral and Brain Sciences, 14,* 1–84.

Griffin, R. S., & Gross, A. M. (2004). Childhood bullying: Current empirical findings and future directions for research. *Aggression & Violent Behavior, 9*(4), 379–400.

Grogger, J., & Bronars, S. (1993). The socioeconomic consequences of teenage childbearing: Findings from a natural experiment. *Family Planning Perspectives, 25,* 156–161.

Grön, G., Wunderlich, A. P., Spitzer, M., Tomczak, R. & Riepe, M. W. (2000). Brain activation during human navigation: gender-different neural networks as substrate of performance. *Nature Neuroscience, 3*(4), 404–408.

Grych, J. H., & Fincham, F. D. (1993). Children's appraisals of marital conflict. *Child Development, 64,* 215–230.

Guilford, J. P. (1967). *The nature of human intelligence*. New York: McGraw-Hill.

Gulevich, G., Dement, W., & Johnson, L. (1966). Psychiatric and EEG observations on a case of prolonged (264 hours) wakefulness. *Archives of General Psychiatry, 15,* 29–35.

H

Haaf, R. A., Smith, P. H., & Smitley, S. (1983). Infant response to facelike patterns under fixed trial and infant–control procedures. *Child Development, 54,* 172–177.

Haaland, K. Y. (1992). Introduction to the special section on the emotional concomitants of brain damage. *Journal of Consulting and Clinical Psychology, 50,* 327–328.

Haan, M. N. (2000, July). Cognitive decline is not normal in aging. Paper presented to the World Alzheimer Congress 2000, Washington, DC.

Haber, R. N. (1980). Eidetic images are not just imaginary. *Psychology Today, 14*(11), 72–82.

Halpern, D. F., & LaMay, M. L. (2000). The smarter sex: A critical review of sex differences in intelligence. *Educational Psychology Review, 12*(2), 229–246.

Hansson, R. O., Stroebe, M. S. (2006). *Bereavement in late life: Coping, adaptation, and developmental influence*. Washington, DC: American Psychological Association.

Harkins, S. (1987). Social loafing and social facilitation. *Journal of Experimental Social Psychology, 23,* 1–18.

Harlow, H. F. (1959). Love in infant monkeys. *Scientific American, 200,* 68–86.

Hartup, W. W. (1993). Adolescents and their friends. In B. Laursen (Ed.), Close friendships in adolescence. *New Directions in Child Development,* no. 60. San Francisco: Jossey-Bass.

Haselton, Martie G., & Ketelaar, Timothy (2005). Irrational emotions or emotional wisdom? The evolutionary psychology of emotions and behavior. In J. Forgas (Ed.), *Hearts and minds.* New York: Psychology Press.

Hashima, P. Y., & Finkelhor, D. (1999). Violent victimization of youth versus adults in the National Crime Victimization Survey. *Journal of Interpersonal Violence, 14*(8), 799–820.

Hassin, R., ed. (2006). *The new unconscious.* New York: Oxford University Press

Hassinger, H. J., Semenchuk, E. M., & O'Brien, W. H. (1999). Appraisal and coping responses to pain and stress in migraine headache sufferers. *Journal of Behavioral Medicine, 22*(4), 327–340.

Hawkins, J. D., Catalano, R. F., & Miller, J. Y. (1992). Risk and protective factors for alcohol and other drug problems in adolescence and early adulthood: Implications for substance abuse prevention. *Psychological Bulletin, 112,* 64–105.

Hayes, K. J., & Hayes, C. (1951). The intellectual development of a home-raised chimpanzee. *Proceedings of the American Philosophical Society, 95,* 105–109.

Hayflick, L. (1994). *How and why we age.* New York: Ballantine.

Hays, K. F. (1995). Putting sport psychology into (your) practice. *Professional Psychology: Research and Practice, 26,* 33–40.

Heatherton, T. F., Mahamedi, F., Striepe, M., Field, A. E., & Keel, P. (1997). A 10–year longitudinal study of body weight, dieting, and eating disorder symptoms. *Journal of Abnormal Psychology, 106,* 117–125.

Heckler, M. (1985). The fight against Alzheimer's disease. *American Psychologist, 40,* 1240–1244.

Helms, J. E. (1992). Why is there no study of cultural equivalence of standardized cognitive ability testing? *American Psychologist, 47,* 1083–1101.

Helson, R. (1993). In K. D. Hulbert & D. T. Schuster (Eds.), *Women's lives through time* (pp. 190–210). San Francisco: Jossey-Bass.

Helson, R., & Moane, G. (1987). Personality change in women from college to midlife. *Journal of Personality and Social Psychology, 53,* 176–186.

Helson, R., Stewart, A. J. & Ostrove, J. (1995). Identity in three cohorts of midlife women. *Journal of Personality and Social Psychology, 69,* 544–557.

Hensley, W. E. (1994). Height as a basis for interpersonal attraction. *Adolescence, 29*(114), 469–474.

Henson, H. K. (2002). Sex, drugs, and cults. *The Human Nature Review 2* (August 23), 343–355,

Herek, G. M. (1993). Sexual orientation and military service: A social science perspective. *American Psychologist, 48,* 538–549.

Hergenhahn, B. R. (2005). *An introduction to the history of psychology* (5th ed). Belmont, CA: Wadsworth.

Herrmann, D. J. (1991). *Super memory.* Emmaus, PA: Rodale.

Hershenson, R. (2000, August 6). Debating the Mozart theory. *The New York Times magazine online.*

Heston, L. L. (1966). Psychiatric disorders in foster home reared children of schizophrenic mothers. *British Journal of Psychiatry, 112,* 819–825.

Hiller, J. B., Rosenthal, R., Bornstein, R. F., Berry, D. T. R., & Brunell-Neuleib, S. (1999). A comparative meta-analysis of Rorschach and MMPI validity. *Psychological Assessment, 11*(3), 278–296.

Hirschfeld, R. M. A., & Goodwin, F. K. (1988). Mood disorders. In J. A. Talbott, R. E. Hales, & S. C. Yudofsky (Eds.), *Textbook of psychiatry.* Washington, DC: American Psychiatric Press.

Hobfoll, S. E., Ritter, C., Lavin, J., Hulsizer, M. R., & Cameron, R. P. (1995). Depression prevalence and incidence among inner-city pregnant and postpartum women. *Journal of Consulting and Clinical Psychology, 63,* 445–453.

Hock, R. (1998). *Forty studies that changed psychology: Explorations into the history of psychological research, 6th Edition.* New Jersey: Prentice Hall. Pivotal studies that shaped psychology; includes overview, history, and interpretation of each study.

Hoffman, C., & Hurst, N. (1990). Gender stereotypes: Perception or rationalization? *Journal of Personality and Social Psychology, 58,* 197–208.

Hoge, C. W., McGurk, D., Thomas, J. L., Cox, A. L., Engle, C. C., Castro, C. A. (2008). Mild traumatic brain injury in U.S. soldiers returning from Iraq. *New England Journal of Medicine, 358,* 453–463.

Holden, C. (1980). Identical twins reared apart. *Science, 207,* 1323–1325.

Holden, G. W., & Ritchie, K. L. (1991). Linking extreme marital discord, child rearing, and child behavior problems. *Child Development, 62,* 311–327.

Holland, J. J. (2000, July 25). Groups link media to child violence. *The Associated Press online.*

Hollinger, L. M., & Buschmann, M. B. (1993). Factors influencing the perception of touch by elderly nursing home residents and their health caregivers. *International Journal of Nursing Studies, 30,* 445–461.

Hollmann, F. W., & Mulder, T. J. (2000, January 13). Census Bureau projects doubling of nation's population by 2100. Washington, DC: U.S. Census Bureau Public Information Office.

Holloway, J. H. (2004). Part-time work and student achievement. Alexandria VA: Association for Supervision and Curriculum Development.

Holmes, S. A. (1996, October 5). U.S. reports drop in rate of births to unwed women. *The New York Times,* pp. A1, A9.

Honan, W. H. (1966, April 11). Male professors keep 30% lead in pay over women, study says. *The New York Times,* p. B9.

Horgan, O., & MacLachlan, M. (2004). Psychosocial adjustment to lower-limb amputation: A review. *Disability & Rehabilitation: An International Multidisciplinary Journal, 26*(14–15), 837–850.

Horn, J. M. (1983). The Texas adoption project: Adopted children and their intellectual resemblance to biological and adoptive parents. *Child Development, 54,* 268–275.

Horney, K. (1937). *The neurotic personality of our time.* New York: Norton.

Horney, K. (1993). *Feminine psychology.* New York: Norton. This book is a collection of papers based on Horney's clinical observations. With essays originally published in the '20s and '30s, Horney refuted Freud's depiction of the female psyche and argued that understanding women included more than understanding their differences from men

Hoffman, D. D. (1998). *Visual intelligence: How we create what we see.* New York: Norton.

Huesmann, L. R., & Miller, L. S. (1994). Long-term effects of repeated exposure to media violence in childhood. In L. R. Huesmann (Ed.), *Aggressive behavior: Current perspectives.* New York: Plenum Press.

Hultquist, C. M., et al. (1995). The effect of smoking and light activity on metabolism in men. *Health Psychology, 14,* 124–131.

Hunsley, J., & Bailey, J. M. (1999). The clinical utility of the Rorschach: Unfulfilled promises and an uncertain future. *Psychological Assessment, 11*(3), 266–277.

Hunter, S. C., & Boyle, J. M. E. (2004). Appraisal and coping strategy use in victims of school bullying. *British Journal of Educational Psychology, 74*(1), 83–107.

Hyde, J. S., & Plant, E. A. (1995). Magnitude of psychological gender differences: Another side to the story. *American Psychologist, 50,* 159–161.

Hyman, R. (1994). Anomaly or artifact? Comments on Bem and Honorton. *Psychological Bulletin, 115,* 19–24.

Iacono, W. G., & Lykken, D. T. (1997). The validity of the lie detector: Two surveys of scientific opinion. *Journal of Applied Psychology, 82*(3), 426–433.

Ironson, G. (1993). Cited in Adler, T. (1993). Men and women affected by stress, but differently. *APA Monitor, 24*(7), 8–9.

Izard, C. E. (1989). The structure and function of emotions: Implications for cognition, motivation, and personality. In I. S. Cohen (Ed.), *The G. Stanley Hall Lecture Series* (Vol. 9, pp. 37–73). Washington, DC: American Psychological Association.

Izard, C. E. (1990). Facial expression and the regulation of emotions. *Journal of Personality and Social Psychology, 58,* 487–498.

Izard, C. E. (1994). Basic emotions, relations among emotions, and emotion-cognition relations. *Psychological Bulletin, 115,* 561–565.

Jacklin, C. N., Maccoby, E. E., & Dick, A. E. (1973). Barrier behavior and toy preference: Sex differences (and their absence) in the year-old child. *Child Development, 44,* 196–200.

Jacks, J. Z., & Devine, P. G. (2000). Attitude importance, forewarning of message content, and resistance to persuasion. *Basic & Applied Social Psychology, 22*(1) 19–29.

Jacobson, N. S., & Addis, M. E. (1993). Research on couples and couples therapy: What do we know? Where are we going? *Journal of Consulting and Clinical Psychology, 61,* 85–93.

Jacobson, N. S., & Hollon, S. D. (1996). Cognitive-behavior therapy versus pharmacotherapy: Now that the jury's returned its verdict, it's time to present the rest of the evidence. *Journal of Consulting and Clinical Psychology, 64,* 74–80.

James, W. (1890). *The principles of psychology* (Vols. 1 and 2). New York: Henry Holt and Company.

James, W. (1902/1958). *Varieties of religious experience.* New York: Mentor Books.

Janos, P. M. (1987). A fifty-year follow-up of Terman's youngest college students and IQ-matched agemates. *Gifted Child Quarterly, 31,* 55–58.

Jeffery, R. W., et al. (2000). Long-term maintenance of weight loss: Current status. *Health Psychology, 19*(Suppl 1), 5–16.

Johnson, A. (1997). *The gender knot: Unraveling our patriarchal legacy.* Philadelphia: Temple University Press. This book describes how patriarchy works in ways that can include both men and women in the conversation and in the solution.

Johnson, B. T., & Eagly, A. H. (1989). Effects of involvement on persuasion: A meta-analysis. *Psychological Bulletin, 106,* 290–314.

Johnson, D. J. (1992). Developmental pathways: Toward an ecological theoretical formulation of race identity in Black-White biracial children. In M. P. P. Root (Ed.), *Racially mixed people in America.* Newbury Park, CA: Sage.

Johnson, S. (2004). *Mind wide open: Your brain and the neuroscience of everyday life.* New York: Scribner's. Discussion of cutting-edge brain science and how it has changed our understanding of daily events in human life.

Johnson, W., Emde, R. N., Pannabecker, B., Stenberg, C., & Davis, M. (1982). Maternal perception of infant emotion from birth to 18 months. *Infant Behavior and Development, 5,* 313–322.

Johnstone, E., Owens, D., Bydder, G., Colter, N., Crow, T., & Frith, C. (1989). The spectrum of structural brain changes in schizophrenia: Age of onset as a predictor of cognitive and clinical impairments and their cerebral correlates. *Psychological Medicine, 19,* 91–103.

Joiner, T. E., Heatherton, T. F., Rudd, M. D., & Schmidt, N. B. (1997). Perfectionism, perceived weight status, and bulimic symptoms. *Journal of Abnormal Psychology, 106,* 145–153.

Jones, E. E. (1990). *Interpersonal perception.* New York: W. H. Freeman.

Jones, M. C. (1924). Elimination of children's fears. *Journal of Experimental Psychology, 7,* 381–390.

Jones, S. R. G. (1992). Was there a Hawthorne effect? *American Journal of Sociology, 98,* 451–468.

Judd, C. M., & Park, B. (1988). Out-group homogeneity: Judgments of variability at the individual and group levels. *Journal of Personality and Social Psychology, 54,* 778–788.

Jung, C. G. (1917/1966). *The collected works of C. G. Jung No. 7: Two essays on analytical psychology.* Princeton, NJ: Princeton University Press.

Jung, C. J. (1936/1968). *The collected works of C. G. Jung No. 9, Pt. 1: The archetypes and the collective uncontious.* Princeton, NJ: Princeton University Press.

Jung, C. G. (1997). *Man and his symbols.* New York: Dell. This is a nontechnical presentation of Jung's basic ideas.

K

Kamphaus, R. W., Petoskey, M. D., & Rowe, E. W. (2000). Current trends in psychological testing of children. *Professional Psychology: Research and Practice, 31*(2), 155–164.

Kane, J. M. (1996). Schizophrenia. *New England Journal of Medicine, 334,* 34–41.

Kang, H. K. & Hyams, K. C. (2005). Mental health care needs among recent war veterans. *New England Journal of Medicine, 352*:1289.

Kanner, A. D., Coyne, J. C., Schaefer, C., & Lazarus, R. S. (1981). Comparison of two modes of stress measurement: Daily hassles and uplifts versus major life events. *Journal of Behavioral Medicine, 4,* 1–39.

Kantrowitz, B. (1992, August 3). Teenagers and AIDS. *Newsweek,* pp. 45–50.

Kaplan, S. J. (1991). Physical abuse and neglect. In M. Lewis (Ed.), *Child and adolescent psychiatry: A comprehensive textbook* (pp. 1010–1019). Baltimore, MD: Williams & Wilkins.

Karney, B. R., & Bradbury, T. N. (1995). The longitudinal course of marital quality and stability: A review of theory, method, and research. *Psychological Bulletin, 118,* 3–34.

Katzman, M., Wolchik, S., & Braver, S. (1984). The prevalence of frequent binge eating and bulimia in nonclinical sample. *International Journal of Eating Disorders, 3,* 53–62.

Katzman, R. (2000, July). Epidemiology of Alzheimer's disease. Paper presented to the World Alzheimer Congress 2000, Washington, DC.

Kaye, W. H.; Klump, K. L., Frank, G. K. W., & Strober, M. (2000). Anorexia and bulimia nervosa. *Annual Review of Medicine, 51,* 299–313.

Kaysen, S. (1993). *Girl, interrupted.* New York: Vintage. Memoir of a girl committed to a mental hospital at age 18 for two years.

Kazdin, A. E. (1993). Adolescent mental health: Prevention and treatment programs. *American Pscyhologist, 48,* 127–141.

Kellner, R. (1990). Somatization: Theories and research. *Journal of Nervous and Mental Disease, 178*, 150–160.

Kemeny, M. E. (1993). Emotions and the immune system. In B. Moyers (Ed.), *Healing and the mind.* New York: Doubleday.

Kemper, P., & Murtaugh, C. M. (1991). Lifetime use of nursing home care. *New England Journal of Medicine, 324,* 595–600.

Kershner, J. R., & Ledger, G. (1985). Effect of sex, intelligence, and style of thinking on creativity: A comparison of gifted and average IQ children. *Journal of Personality and Social Psychology, 48,* 1033–1040.

Khanna, R., & Rathee, R. (1992). Altruism, mood, and help to drug addicts. Special Series I: Alcohol and drug use. *Journal of Personality and Clinical Studies, 8,* 23–26.

Kihlstrom, J. F., Glisky, M. L., & Angiulo, M. J. (1994). Dissociative tendencies and dissociative disorders. *Journal of Abnormal Psychology, 103,* 117–124.

Kilborn, P. T. (1995, March 16). Women and minorities still face "glass ceilings." *The New York Times,* p. A22.

Kimble, D. P. (1992). *Biological psychology* (2nd ed.). Fort Worth, TX: Harcourt Brace Jovanovich.

Kinnunen, T., Zamansky, H. S., & Block, M. L. (1994). Is the hypnotized patient lying? *Journal of Abnormal Psychology, 103,* 184–191.

Kirchler, E., Pombeni, M. L., & Palmonari, A. (1991). Sweet sixteen . . . : Adolescents' problems and the peer group as a source of support. *European Journal of Psychology of Education, 6,* 393–410.

Kleinmuntz, B., & Szucko, J. J. (1984). Lie detection in ancient and modern times: A call for contemporary scientific study. *American Psychologist, 39,* 766–776.

Knafo, A., Iervolino, A. C., & Plomin, R. (2005). Masculine girls and feminine boys: Genetic and environmental contributions to atypical gender development in early childhood. *Journal of Personality & Social Psychology, 88*(2), 400–412.

Kohlberg, L. (1969). *Stages in the development of moral thought and action.* New York: Holt, Rinehart and Winston.

Kohn, A. (1990). *The brighter side of human nature: Altruism and empathy in everyday life.* New York: Basic Books. Author argues that it is natural for humans to be caring, generous, empathetic, altruistic and kind rather than selfish, self-interested and aggressive.

Kohout, J., & Williams, S. (1999). Far more psychology degrees are going to women. *APA Monitor online, 30*(10).

Kolata, G. (2000, January 18). True secret of fad diets: It's calories. *The New York Times,* p. F7.

Kooijman, C. M., et al. (2000). Phantom pain and phantom sensations in upper limb amputees: An epidemiological study. *Pain, 87*(1), 33–41.

Kopera-Frye, K., Ager, J., Saltz, E., Poindexter, J., & Lee, S. (1993, March). *Predictors of adolescent delinquency.* Paper presented at the meeting of the Society for Research in Child Development, New Orleans, LA.

Kotre, J. (1995). *White gloves: How we create ourselves through memory.* New York: Free Press. Kotre describes how personal histories and identity are influenced by changes in autobiographical memory over time.

Kreisman, J. J., & Straus, H. (1989). *I hate you - don't leave me: Understanding the borderline personality.* New York: Avon Books.

Kübler-Ross, E. (1969). *On death and dying.* New York: Macmillan.

Kuczmarski, R. J. (1992). Prevalence of overweight and weight gain in the United States. *American Journal of Clinical Nutrition, 55*(Suppl.), 495S–502S.

Kuczynski, L. (Ed.). (2003). *Handbook of dynamics in parent-child relations.* Thousand Oaks, CA: Sage.

Kunkel, D., & Roberts, D. (1991). Young minds and marketplace values: Issues in children's television advertising. *Journal of Social Issues, 47,* 57–72.

Kurzweil, R. (2000, June 19). Will my PC be smarter than I am? *Time magazine,* pp. 82–83.

Kushner, H. S. (1981). *When bad things happen to good people.* New York: Avon Books.

Kutner, L. (1993, February 4). For both boys and girls, early or late puberty can lead to social or emotional problems. *The New York Times,* p. B6.

Kyle, T. M., & Williams, S. (2000, May). Results of the 1998–1999 APA survey of graduate departments of psychology, Tables 13A & 13B. APA Research Office. Washington, DC: American Psychological Association.

L

LaFramboise, T. (1994). Cited in DeAngelis, T. (1994). History, culture affect treatment for Indians. *APA Monitor, 27*(10), 36.

Lagerspetz, K. M., Bjorkqvist, K., & Peltonen, T. (1988). Is indirect aggression typical of females? Gender differences in aggressiveness in 11– to 12-year-old children. *Aggressive Behavior, 14,* 403–414.

Lamb, M. E. (1977). Father-infant and mother-infant interaction in the first year of life. *Child Development, 48,* 167–181.

Lambert, W. E. (1990). Persistent issues in bilingualism. In B. Harley et al. (Eds.), *The development of second language proficiency.* Cambridge: Cambridge University Press.

Lambert, W. E., Genesee, F., Holobow, N., & Chartrand, L. (1991). *Bilingual education for majority English-speaking children.* Montreal: McGill University Press.

Lang, F. R., Staudinger, U. M., Carstensen, L. L. (1998). Perspectives on socioemotional selectivity in late life: How personality and social context do (and do not) make a difference. *Journals of Gerontology: Psychological Sciences and Social Sciences, 53B*(1), 21–29.

Langer, E. J. (1997). The power of mindful learning. Cambridge, MA: Da Capo. Langer explores the myths of learning (e.g., forgetting is bad, delayed gratification is good).

Langlois, J. H. (1994). Cited in Brody, J. E. (1994, March 21). Notions of beauty transcend culture, new study suggests. *The New York Times,* p. A14.

Langlois, J. H., et al. (2000). Maxims or myths of beauty? A meta-analytic and theoretical review. *Psychological Bulletin, 126*(3), 390–423.

Larson, R., & Richards, M. H. (1991). Daily companionship in late childhood and early adolescence: Changing development contexts. *Child Development, 62,* 284–300.

Laufer, A., & Harel, Y. (2003). Correlation between school perception and pupil involvement in bullying, physical fights and weapon carrying. *Megamot, 42*(3), 437–459.

Lazarus, R. S. (1991). Cognition and motivation in emotion. *American Psychologist, 46,* 352–367.

Leary, W. E. (1991, October 22). Black hypertension may reflect other ills. *The New York Times,* p. C3.

Leary, W. E. (1995, May 2). Billions suffering needlessly, study says. *The New York Times,* p. C5.

LeDoux, J. E. (1994, June). Emotion, memory, and the brain. *Scientific American,* pp. 50–57.

Lefcourt, H. M., & Martin, R. A. (1986). *Humor and life stress: Antidote to adversity.* New York: Springer.

Leff, J., & Vaughn, C. (1985). *Expressed emotion in families.* New York: Guilford.

Leippe, M. R. (1985). The influence of eye-witness non-identifications on mock-jurors' judgments of a court case. *Journal of Applied Social Psychology, 15,* 656–672.

Lenneberg, E. H. (1967). *Biological foundations of language.* New York: John Wiley & Sons.

Leon, G. R., & Dinklage, D. (1989). Obesity and anorexia nervosa. In T. H. Ollendick & M. Hersen (Eds.), *Handbook of child psychopathology* (2nd ed., pp. 247–263). New York: Plenum.

Levinson, D. J., Darrow, C. N., Klein, E. B., Levinson, M. H., & McKee, B. (1978). *The seasons of a man's life.* New York: Knopf.

Levy, S. R., & Killen, M. (2008) *Intergroup attitudes and relations in childhood through adulthood.* New York: Oxford University Press. Describes how individuals make judgments and interact with individuals from different groups or categories (e.g., gender, race, age, culture, religion, sexual orientation, and body type).

Lewin, K. (1935) *A dynamic theory of personality.* New York: McGraw-Hill.

Lewin, K. (1936) *Principles of topological psychology.* New York: McGraw-Hill.

Lewin, T. (1995, December 7). Parents poll shows higher incidence of child abuse. *The New York Times,* p. B16.

Lewin, T. (1995, September 18). Women are becoming equal providers. *The New York Times,* p. A27.

Lewin, K., LIippit, R. and White, R. K. (1939). Patterns of aggressive behavior in experimentally created social climates. *Journal of Social Psychology*, 10, 271-301. Classic research on leadership styles.

Lewinsohn, P. M., et al. (1994). Adolescent psychopathology: II. Psychosocial risk factors for depression. *Journal of Abnormal Psychology, 103,* 302–315.

Lewis, D. O. (1998). *Guilty by reason of insanity: A psychiatrist explores the minds of killers.* New York: Ballantine. A compassionate, insightful, and fascinating study of the minds of killers that concludes that almost all killers suffer from brain damage, psychotic symptoms, and/or a severely disturbed childhood.

Lewis-Fernández, R. & Kleinman, A. (1994). Culture, personality, and psychopathology. *Journal of Abnormal Psychology, 103,* 67–71.

Lichtenstein, P., et al. (2000). Environmental and heritable factors in the causation of cancer: Analyses of cohorts of twins from Sweden, Denmark, and Finland. *New England Journal of Medicine, 343*(2), 78–85.

Liebert, R. M., Sprafkin, J. N., & Davidson, E. S. (1989). *The early window: Effects of television on children and youth* (3rd ed.). New York: Pergamon.

Lillqvist, O., & Lindeman, M. (1998). Belief in astrology as a strategy for self-verification and coping with negative life-events. *European Psychologist, 3*(3), 202–208.

Lindsay, R. C. L., Lim, R., Marando, L., & Culley, D. (1986). Mock-juror evaluations of eyewitness testimony: A test of metamemory hypotheses. *Journal of Applied Social Psychology, 16,* 447–459.

Linville, P. W., Fischer, G. W., & Salovey, P. (1989). Perceived distribution of the characteristics of in-group and out-group members. *Journal of Personality and Social Psychology, 57,* 165–188.

Lips, H. (1993). *Sex and gender: An introduction* (2nd ed.). Mountain View, CA: Mayfield.

Lisanby, S. H., et al. (2000). The effects of electroconvulsive therapy on memory of autobiographical and public events. *Archives of General Psychiatry, 57*(6), 581–590.

Lochman, J. E., & Dodge, K. A. (1994). Social-cognitive processes of severely violent, moderately aggressive, and nonagressive boys. *Journal of Consulting and Clinical Psychology, 62,* 366–374.

Loehlin, J. C., Willerman, L., & Horn, J. M. (1988). Human behavior genetics. *Annual Review of Psychology, 39,* 101–133.

Loftus, E. F. (1975). Leading questions and the eyewitness report. *Cognitive Psychology, 7,* 560–572.

Loftus, E. F. (1993). Psychologists in the eyewitness world. *American Psychologist, 48,* 550–552.

Loftus, E. F. (2003). Make-Believe Memories. *American Psychologist, 58,* 864–873.

Loftus, E. F. (2004). Memories of things unseen. *Current Directions in Psychological Science, 13*(4) 145–147.

Loftus, E., & Ketcham, K. (1994). *The myth of repressed memory: False memories and allegations of sexual abuse.* New York: St. Martin's.

Loftus, E. F., & Loftus, G. R. (1980). On the permanence of stored information in the brain. *American Psychologist, 35,* 409–420.

Loftus, E. F., & Pickerell, J. E. (1995) The formation of false memories. *Psychiatric Annals 25,* 720–725.

Lore, R. K., & Schultz, L. A. (1993). Control of human aggression: A comparative perspective. *American Psychologist, 48,* 16–25.

Lown, J., & Dolan, E. (1988). Financial challenges in remarriage. *Lifestyles: Family and Economic Issues, 9,* 73–88.

Lubell, S. (2004, February 19). On the therapists's couch, a jolt of virtual reality. *The New York Times online.*

Luchins, A. S., & Luchins, E. H. (1959). *Rigidity of behavior.* Eugene, OR: University of Oregon Press.

Maccoby, E. E. (1990). Gender and relationships. *American Psychologist, 45,* 513–520.

Maccoby, E. E. (1998). *The two sexes: Growing up apart, coming together (family and public policy).* Cambridge: Harvard University Press. Eleanor Maccoby, a pioneer researcher in child development, discusses the significant effects of childhood experiences and same-sex play groups.

Maccoby, E., & Martin, J. A. (1983). Socialization in the context of the family: Parent-child interaction. In E. M. Hetherington (Ed.), *Handbook of child psychology* (Vol. 4). New York: John Wiley & Sons.

MacDonald, K. (1992). Warmth as a developmental construct: An evolutionary analysis. *Child Development, 63,* 753–773.

Mackert, B., et al. (2003). The eloquence of silent cortex: Analysis of afferent input to deafferented cortex in arm amputees. *Neuroreport, 14*(3), 409–412.

Mackie, D. M., Worth, L. T., & Asuncion, A. G. (1990). Processing of persuasive in-group messages. *Journal of Personality and Social Psychology, 58,* 812–822.

Maier, N. R. F. (1931). Reasoning in human beings: II. The solution of a problem and its appearance in consciousness. *Journal of Comparative Psychology, 12,* 181–194.

Manke, B. (1993, March). *Dimensions of intimacy during adolescence: Correlates and antecedents.* Paper presented at the meeting of the Society for Research in Child Development, New Orleans, LA.

Manson, J. E., et al. (1995). Body weight and mortality among women. *New England Journal of Medicine, 333,* 677–685.

March, J., Johnston, H., & Greist, J. (1989). Obsessive-compulsive disorder. *American Family Practice, 39,* 175–182.

Marcia, J. E. (1966). Development and validation of ego identity status. *Journal of Personality and Social Psychology, 3,* 551–558.

Marcia, J. E., Waterman, A. S., Matteson, D. R., Archer, S. L., & Orlofsky, J. L. (1993). *Ego identity: A handbook for psychosocial research.* New York: Springer.

Markel, H. (2000, July 25). Anorexia can strike boys, too. *The New York Times online.*

Markman, H. J., Renick, M. J., Floyd, F. J., Stanley, S. M., & Clements, M. (1993). Preventing marital distress through communication and conflict management training: A 4- and 5-year follow-up. *Journal of Consulting and Clinical Psychology, 61,* 70–77.

Markus, H., & Kitayama, S. (1991). Culture and the self: Implications for cognition, emotion, and motivation. *Psychological Review, 98*(2), 224–253.

Marriott, M. (1991, June 5). Beyond "yuck" for girls in science. *The New York Times,* p. A26.

Marsh, H. W., Craven, R. G., & Debus, R. (1991). Self-concepts of young children 5 to 8 years of age: Measurement and multidimensional structure. *Journal of Educational Psychology, 83,* 377–392.

Martin, R. A., & Lefcourt, H. M. (1983). Sense of humor as a moderator of the relation between stressors and moods. *Journal of Personality and Social Psychology, 45,* 1313–1324.

Maruyama, G., Fraser, S. C., & Miller, N. (1982). Personal responsibility and altruism in children. *Journal of Personality and Social Psychology, 42,* 658–664.

Maslow, A. H. (1970). *Motivation and personality* (2nd ed.). New York: Harper & Row.

Maslow, A. H. (1968). *Toward a Psychology of Being* (3rd ed.). New York: John Wiley & Sons. In this classic work, Maslow writes about values, growth, well-being, peak experiences, and self-actualization.

Matarazzo, J. D. (1990). Psychological assessment versus psychological testing. *American Psychologist, 45,* 999–1017.

Matlin, M. W. (1999). *The psychology of women* (4th ed.). Fort Worth, TX: Harcourt College Publishers.

Mayberg, H. S., et al. (2005). Deep brain stimulation for treatment-resistant depression. *Neuron, 45,* 651–660.

Maybury-Lewis, D. (1992). *Millennium: Tribal wisdom and the modern world.* New York: Viking.

McCall, R. B. (1977). Children's IQs as predictors of adult educational and occupational status. *Science, 297,* 482–483.

McCarley, R. W. (1992). Cited in Blakeslee, S. (1992, January 7). Scientists unraveling chemistry of dreams. *The New York Times,* pp. C1, C10.

McCarthy, K. (1993). Research on women's health doesn't show whole picture. *APA Monitor, 24*(7), 14–15.

McClave, E. Z. (2000). Linguistic functions of head movements in the context of speech. *Journal of Pragmatics, 32*(7), 855–878.

McClelland, D. C. (1965). Achievement and entrepreneurship: A longitudinal study. *Journal of Personality and Social Psychology, 1,* 389–392.

McCourt, K., et al. (1999). Authoritarianism revisited: Genetic and environmental influences examined in twins reared apart and together. *Personality & Individual Differences, 27*(5), 985–1014.

McCrae, R. R., Costa, P. T., Jr., et al. (2000). Nature over nurture: Temperament, personality, and life span development. *Journal of Personality & Social Psychology, 78*(1), 173–186.

McDougall, W. (1908). *An introduction to social psychology.* London: Methuen.

McIntosh, H. (1996). Solitude provides an emotional tune-up. *APA Monitor, 26*(3), 1, 10.

Mead, M. (1935). *Sex and temperament in three primitive societies.* New York: Dell.

Metalsky, G. I., Joiner, T. E., Jr., Hardin, T. S., & Abramson, L. Y. (1993). Depressive reactions to failure in naturalistic setting: A test of the hopelessness and self-esteem theories of depression. *Journal of Abnormal Psychology, 102,* 101–109.

Mevkens, F. L. (1990). Coming of age—The chemoprevention of cancer. *New England Journal of Medicine, 323,* 825–827.

Meyer, G. J. (2000). Incremental validity of the Rorschach Prognostic Rating scale over the MMPI Ego Strength Scale and IQ. *Journal of Personality Assessment, 74*(3), 356–370.

Michaelson, R. (1993). Tug-of-war is developing over defining retardation. *APA Monitor, 24*(5), 34–35.

Mikesell, R. H., Lusterman, D., & McDaniel, S. (Eds.). (1995). *Family psychology and systems therapy.* Washington, DC: American Psychological Association.

Milgram, S. (1963). Behavioral study of obedience. *Journal of Abnormal and Social Psychology, 67,* 371–378.

Milgram, S. (1974). *Obedience to authority: An experimental view.* New York: Harper Torchbooks. Highly readable account of Milgram's classic series of experiments including implications of those studies for understanding human behavior. An appendix includes a consideration of various ethical issues raised by the experiments.

Millon, T. (1981). *Disorders of personality.* New York: John Wiley & Sons.

Mills, J. C., (2003) *Gentle willow: A story for children about dying (*2nd Edition). Washington, DC: Magination Press.

Mintz, L. B., Bartels, K. M., & Rideout, C. A. (1995). Training in counseling ethnic minorities and race-based availability of graduate school resources. *Professional Psychology: Research in Practice, 26,* 316–321.

Mitchell, J. E., & Eckert, E. D. (1987). Scope and significance of eating disorders. *Journal of Consulting and Clinical Psychology, 55,* 628–634.

Mokdad, A. H., et al. (2000). The continuing epidemic of obesity in the United States. *Journal of the American Medical Association online, 284*(13).

Moldin, S. O. (1994). Indicators of liability to schizophrenia: Perspectives from genetic epidemiology. *Schizophrenia Bulletin, 20*(1), 169–184.

Moliterno, D. J., et al. (1994). Coronary-artery vasoconstriction induced by cocaine, cigarette smoking, or both. *New England Journal of Medicine, 330,* 454–459.

Mom, Dad, I want a job. (1993, May 17). *U.S. News & World Report,* pp. 68–72.

Montemayor, R., & Flannery, D. J. (1991). Parent-adolescent relations in middle and late adolescence. In R. M. Lerner, A. C. Petersen, & J. Brooks-Gunn (Eds.), *Encyclopedia of adolescence.* New York: Garland.

Moore, K. A., & Stief, T. M. (1992). Changes in marriage and fertility behavior: Behavior versus attitudes of young adults. *Youth and Society, 22,* 362–386.

Morrison, A. M., & Von Glinow, M. A. (1990). Women and minorities in management. *American Psychologist, 45,* 200–209.

Mott, M. (2005, January 4). Did animals sense tsunami was coming? *National Geographic News online.*

Mulvihill, K. (2000, March 14). Many miss out on migraine remedies. *The New York Times online.*

Munro, G. D., & Munro, J. E. (2000). Using daily horoscopes to demonstrate expectancy confirmation. *Teaching of Psychology, 27*(2), 114–116.

Murray, B. (1996). College youth haunted by increased pressures. *APA Monitor, 26*(4), 47.

Mussweiler, T., & Bodenhausen, G. V. (2002). I know you are, but what am I? Self-evaluative consequences of judging in-group and out-group members. *Journal of Personality & Social Psychology, 82*(1), 19–32.

Myers, D. G., & Bishop, G. D. (1970). Discussion effects on racial attitudes. *Science, 169,* 778–779.

Nansel, T. R., Haynie, D. L., & Simons-Morton, B. G. (2003). The association of bullying and victimization with middle school adjustment. *Journal of Applied School Psychology, 19*(2), 45–61.

Nantais, K. M., & Schellenberg, E. G. (1999). The Mozart effect: An artifact of preference. *Psychological Science, 10*(4), 370–373.

Nasar, S. (1998). *A beautiful mind: A biography of John Forbes Nash, Jr., winner of the Nobel Prize in economics.* New York: Simon & Schuster. This is a biography of John Nash, who suffered from schizophrenia.

National Center for Health Statistics, Centers for Disease Control and Prevention, Health E-Stats. (2001). Prevalence of overweight among children and adolescents: United States, 1999.

Neher, A. (1991). Maslow's theory of motivation: A critique. *Journal of Humanistic Psychology, 31,* 89–112.

Neisser, U., et al. (1996). Intelligence: Knowns and unknowns. *American Psychologist, 51*(2), 77–101.

Nevid, J. S., Rathus, S. A., & Greene, B. A. (1997). *Abnormal psychology in a changing world* (3rd ed.). Englewood Cliffs, NJ: Prentice-Hall.

Newcomb, M. D., & Bentler, P. M. (1992, August). *Substance abuse and gender: Accounting for the differences.* Paper presented at the meeting of the American Psychological Association, Washington, DC.

Nicholson, I. A. (2002). *Inventing personality: Gordon Allport and the science of selfhood.* Washington, DC: American Psychological Association.

Nigg, J. T., & Goldsmith, H. H. (1994). Genetics of personality disorders: Perspectives from personality and psychopathology research. *Psychological Bulletin, 115,* 346–380.

Noller, P., & Callan, V. J. (1990). Adolescents' perceptions of the nature of their communication with parents. *Journal of Youth and Adolescence, 19,* 349–362.

Norton, A., & Moorman, J. (1987). Current trends in marriage and divorce among American women. *Journal of Marriage and the Family, 49,* 3–14.

Nosek, B. A., Greenwald, A. G., Banaji, M. R. (2005). Understanding and using the implicit association test. *Personality and Social Psychology Bulletin, 31,* 166–180.

Novacek, J., Raskin, R., & Hogan, R. (1991). Why do adolescents use drugs? Age, sex, and user differences. *Journal of Youth and Adolescence, 20,* 475–492.

THE PSYCHOLOGIST'S BOOKSHELF

O

Oberman, L. M., Hubbard, E. M., McCleery, J. P., Altschuler, E. L., Ramachandran, V. S., Pineda, J. A. (2005). EEG evidence for mirror neuron dysfunction in autism. *Cognitive Brain Research, 24,* 190–198.

Ogbu, J. U. (1993). Differences in cultural frame of reference. *International Journal of Behavioral Development, 16,* 483–506.

Oldenburg, D. (2005, January 9). Animals' "reported sixth sense" is explored. *The Washington Post online.*

Olds, J. (1969) The central nervous system and the reinforcement of behavior. *American Psychologist, 24,* 114–132.

Osborne, C. (Ed.). (1968). *I have a dream: The story of Martin Luther King in text and pictures.* New York: Time-Life Books.

Osofsky, J. D., Osofsky, H. J., & Diamond, M. O. (1988). The transition to parenthood: Special tasks and risk factors for adolescent parents. In G. Y. Michaels & W. A. Goldberg (Eds.), *The transition to parenthood: Current theory and research.* New York: Cambridge University Press.

Otani, H., et al. (2005). Remembering a nuclear accident in Japan: Did it trigger flashbulb memories? *Memory, 13*(1), 6–20.

P

Paley, V. G. (1997). *The girl with the brown crayon.* Cambridge: Harvard University Press. This book tells a simple personal story of a teacher and a child, interweaving the themes of race, identity, gender, and the essential human needs to create and to belong.

Pantiel, M. (1995, September). Should your teenager work? *Better Homes and Gardens,* p. 226.

Pantin, H. M., & Carver, C. S. (1982). Induced competence and the bystander effect. *Journal of Applied Social Psychology, 12,* 100–111.

Papousek, M., Papousek, H., & Symmes, D. (1991). The meanings of melodies in motherese in tone and stress languages. *Infant Behavior and Development, 14,* 415–440.

Park, J., & Banaji, M. R. (2000). Mood and heuristics: The influence of happy and sad states on sensitivity and bias in stereotyping. *Journal of Personality & Social Psychology, 78*(6), 1005–1023.

Parker, J. G., & Herrera, C. (1996). Interpersonal processes in friendship: A comparison of abused and nonabused children's experience. *Developmental Psychology, 32,* 1025–1038.

Patterson, D. R. (2004). Treating pain with hypnosis. *Current Directions in Psychological Science, 13*(6), 252–255.

Pavlov, I. P. (1960). *Conditioned reflexes: An investigation of the physiological activity of the cerebral cortex.* Mineola, NY: Dover Publications. First published in 1927, this book contains 23 lectures from Pavlov describing 25 years of his work and the work of his assistants.

Pearlman, C. (1994, January). Pets can be great friends: Research shows animal owners have less stress and live longer lives. *Safety & Health,* pp. 80–81.

Pelzer, D., (1995). *A child called "it": One child's courage to survive.* Deerfield Beach, FL: Health Communications. Startling account of one of the worst cases of child abuse in history.

Penninx, B. W. et al. (1998). Chronically depressed mood and cancer risk in older persons. *Journal of the National Cancer Institute, 90,* 1888–1893.

Peppard, P. E., Young, T., Palta, M., & Skatrud, J. (2000). Prospective study of the association between sleep-disordered breathing and hypertension. *The New England Journal of Medicine online, 342*(19).

Pereira, B., Mendonça, D., Neto, C., Valente, L., & Smith, P. K. (2004). Bullying in Portuguese schools. *School Psychology International, 25*(2), 241–254.

Perils of part-time work for teens. (1991, March 30). *Science News,* p. 205.

Perry, C. L. (1991). Programs for smoking prevention with early adolescents. In R. M. Lerner, A. C. Petersen, & J. Brooks-Gunn (Eds.), *Encyclopedia of adolescence.* New York: Garland.

Peterson, C., & Seligman, M. E. P. (1985). The learned helplessness model of depression: Current status of theory and research. In E. E. Beckham & W. R. Leber (Eds.), *Handbook of depression* (pp. 914–939). Homewood, IL: Dorsey.

Peterson, C., & Seligman, E. P. (Eds.). (2004). *Character strengths and virtues: A handbook and classification*. New York: Oxford University Press. The CSV has been dubbed the "UnDSM." The book discusses 24 human strengths (e.g., curiosity, wisdom, zest, forgiveness, and gratitude).

Petty, R. E., Gleicher, F., & Baker, S. M. (1991). Multiple roles for affect in persuasion. In J. Forgas (Ed.), *Emotion and social judgments*. London: Pergamon.

Petty, R. E., Wegener, D. T., & Fabrigar, L. R. (1997). Attitudes and attitude change. *Annual Review of Psychology, 48,* 609–647.

Phinney, J. S. (2000). Identity formation across cultures: The interaction of personal, societal, and historical change. *Human Development, 43*(1), 27–31.

Phinney, J. S., & Devich-Navarro, M. (1997). Variations in bicultural identification among African American and Mexican American adolescents. *Journal of Research on Adolescence, 7*(1), 3–32.

Phinney, J. S., & Rosenthal, D. A. (1992). Ethnic identity in adolescence. In G. R. Adams, T. P. Gullotta, & R. Montemayor (Eds.), *Adolescent identity formation*. Newbury Park, CA: Sage.

Phinney, J. S., Chavira, V., & Williamson, L. (1992). Acculturation attitudes and self-esteem among high school and college students. *Youth and society, 23*(3), 299–312.

Piaget, J. (1932). *The moral judgment of the child*. New York: Harcourt Brace Jovanovich.

Pinker, S. (1990). Language acquisition. In D. N. Osherson & H. Lasnik (Eds.), *An invitation to cognitive science: Language* (Vol. 1). Cambridge: MIT Press.

Pinker, S. (1994a, June 19). Building a better brain. *The New York Times Book Review,* pp. 13–14.

Pinker, S. (1994b). *The language instinct: How the mind creates language*. New York: William Morrow.

Pinnell, C. M., & Covino, N. A. (2000). Empirical findings on the use of hypnosis in medicine: A critical review. *International Journal of Clinical & Experimental Hypnosis, 48*(2), 170–194.

Piper, M. (1994). *Reviving Ophelia: Saving the selves of adolescent girls*. New York: G. P. Putnam's Sons. This book explores the effects of U.S. culture on the lives of adolescent girls.

Plomin, R., & McGuffin, P. (2003). Psychopathology in the postgenomic era. *Annual Review of Psychology, 54,* 205–228.

Pollack, W. S. (1999). *Real boys: Rescuing our sons from the myths of boyhood*. New York: Henry Holt. This book explores the effects of U.S. culture on the lives of adolescent boys.

Pombeni, M. L., Kirchler, E., & Palmonari, A. (1990). Identification with peers as a strategy to muddle through the troubles of the adolescent years. *Journal of Adolescence, 13,* 351–369.

Pope-Davis, D. B., Reynolds, A. L., Dings, J. G., & Nielson, D. (1995). Examining multicultural counseling competencies of graduate students in psychology. *Professional Psychology: Research and Practice, 26,* 322–329.

Posner, M. I., & Raichle, M. E. (1994). *Images of mind*. New York: W. H. Freeman.

Power, Thomas G. (2000). *Play and exploration in children and animals*. Mahwah, NJ: Lawrence Erlbaum Associates.

Price, L. H., & Heninger, G. R. (1994). Lithium in the treatment of mood disorders. *New England Journal of Medicine, 331,* 591–598.

Prochaska, J. O., & Norcross, J. C. (1999). *Systems of psychotherapy* (4th ed.). Pacific Grove, CA: Brooks/Cole.

Pratkanis, A. R., & Aronson, E. (1992). *Age of propaganda: The everyday use and abuse of persuasion*. New York: Freeman. Describes how propaganda influences our behavior, how we can protect ourselves from unwanted propaganda, and how we can use persuasion wisely.

Putallaz, M., & Heflin, A. H. (1990). Parent-child interaction. In S. R. Asher & J. D. Coie (Eds.), *Peer rejection in childhood*. New York: Cambridge University Press.

Putnam, F., Guroff, J., Silberman, E., Barban, L., & Post, R. (1986). The clinical phenomenology of multiple personality disorder: Review of 100 recent cases. *Journal of Clinical Psychiatry, 47,* 285–293.

Quinn, S. (1987). *A mind of her own: The life of Karen Horney*. New York: Summit Books.

R

Rakowski, W. (1995). Cited in Margoshes, P. (1995). For many, old age is the prime of life. *APA Monitor, 26*(5), 36–37.

Rapoport, J. (1989a, March). The biology of obsessions and compulsions. *Scientific American,* pp. 83–89.

Rapoport, J. L. (1989b). *The boy who couldn't stop washing.* New York: Penguin.

Rathus, J. H., & Sanderson, W. C. (1999). *Marital distress: Cognitive behavioral interventions for couples.* Northvale, NJ: Jason Aronson.

Rathus, S. A. (2006). *Childhood and adolescence: Voyages in development* (2nd. ed.) Belmont, CA: Wadsworth.

Rathus, S. A., Nevid, J. S., & Fichner-Rathus, L. (1997). *Human sexuality in a world of diversity* (3rd ed.). Boston: Allyn & Bacon.

Rauscher, F. H. (1998). Response to Katie Overy's paper, "Can music really 'improve' the mind?" *Psychology of Music, 26*(2), 197–199.

Reis, H. T., et al. (1990). What is smiling is beautiful and good. *European Journal of Social Psychology, 20,* 259–267.

Reisman, J. M. (1990). Intimacy in same-sex friendships. *Sex Roles, 23,* 65–72.

Reivich, K., & Shatte, A. (2002). *The Resilience Factor: 7 keys to finding your inner strength and overcoming life's hurdles.* New York: Broadway Books. Reivich and Shatte integrate resilience theory and research to provide seven practical strategies to increase people's capacity to overcome adversity, negotiate daily obstacles, and bounce back from life-altering events.

Remafedi, G. (1990). Study group report on impact of television portrayals of gender roles on youth. *Journal of Adolescent Health Care, 11*(1), 59–61.

Renzulli, J. S. (1986). The three ring conception of giftedness: A developmental model for creative productivity. In R. J. Sternberg & J. E. Davidson (Eds.), *Conceptions of giftedness.* New York: Cambridge University Press.

Richter, S., & Barbara, H. (2003). Bullying behavior: Current issues, research, and interventions. *Journal of Developmental & Behavioral Pediatrics, 24*(5), 382–383.

Rickard, T. C., et al., (2000). The calculating brain: An fMRI study. *Neuropsychologia, 38*(3), 325–335.

Rinn, W. E. (1991). Neuropsychology of facial expression. In R. S. Feldman & B. Rime (Eds.), *Fundamentals of nonverbal behavior.* Cambridge: Cambridge University Press.

Ritvo, E. R., Freeman, B. J., Mason-Brothers, A., Mo, A., & Ritvo, A. M. (1985). Concordance for the syndrome of autism in 40 pairs of afflicted twins. *American Journal of Psychiatry, 142,* 74–77.

Robbins, C., & Ehri, L. C. (1994). Reading storybooks to kindergartners helps them to learn new vocabulary words. *Journal of Educational Psychology, 86,* 54–64.

Robinson, N. M. (1992, August). *Development and variation: The challenge of nurturing gifted young children.* Paper presented at the meeting of the American Psychological Association, Washington, DC.

Robinson, P. (1993). *Freud and his critics.* Berkeley: University of California Press.

Rogers, C. (1951). *Client-centered therapy.* Boston: Houghton Mifflin.

Rogers, C. (1961). *On becoming a person: A therapist's view of psychotherapy.* Boston: Houghton Mifflin. Classic introduction to the Humanist perspective and Client-Centered Therapy.

Rogers, C. (1977). *On personal power: Inner strength and its revolutionary impact.* New York: Delacorte.

Rogers, C. (1986). Client-centered therapy. In I. Kutash & A. Wolf (Eds.), *Psychotherapist's casebook.* San Francisco: Jossey-Bass.

Rose, R. J. (1995). Genes and human behavior. *Annual Review of Psychology, 46,* 625–654.

Rosenthal, E. (1993, July 20). Listening to the emotional needs of cancer patients. *The New York Times,* pp. C1, C7.

Roseth, C. J., Johnson, D. W., and Johnson, R. T. (2008). Promoting early adolescents' achievement and peer relationships: the effects of cooperative, competitive, and individualistic goal structures. *Psychological Bulletin, 134* (pp. 223-246).

Roskies, E., et al. (1986). The Montreal Type A Intervention Project: Major findings. *Health Psychology, 5,* 45–69.

Ross, A. (1987). *Personality: The scientific study of complex human behavior.* New York: Holt, Rinehart and Winston.

Rubinstein, S., & Caballero, B. (2000). Is Miss America an undernourished role model? *Journal of the American Medical Association online, 283*(12).

Ruble, D. N., & Ruble, T. L. (1982). Sex stereotypes. In A. G. Miller (Ed.), *In the eye of the beholder: Contemporary issues in stereotyping.* New York: Praeger.

Rymer, R. (1993). *Genie: An abused child's flight from silence.* New York: HarperCollins.

S

Saarni, C. (1990). Emotional competence: How emotions and relationships become integrated. In R. Thompson (Ed.), *Nebraska Symposium on Motivation: Vol. 36. Socioemotional development.* Lincoln, NE: University of Nebraska Press.

Sacks, O. (1989). *Seeing voices: A journey into the world of the deaf*. New York: HarperCollins.

Sacks, O. (1995). *An anthropologist on Mars: Seven paradoxical tales*. New York: Knopf. Sacks' sixth book on the theme of what he calls "the paradox of disease," in which neurological disorders call forth latent adaptive powers in human beings.

Sacks, O. (1998). *The man who mistook his wife for a hat: And other clinical tales*. New York: Touchstone. Oliver Sacks tells the life stories of people afflicted with neurological disorders.

Sadker, M., & Sadker, D. (1994). *How America's schools cheat girls*. New York: Scribners.

Sadock, B., & Sadock, V. (2007). *Kaplan and Sadock's synopsis of psychiatry: Behavioral sciences / Clinical psychiatry* (10th ed). Philadelphia: Lippincott, Williams & Wilkins.

Salovey, P., Rothman, A. J., Detweiler, J. B., & Steward, W. T. (2000). Emotional states and physical health. *American Psychologist, 55,* 110–121.

Sanders, G. S., & Chiu, W. (1988). Eyewitness errors in free recall of actions. *Journal of Applied Social Psychology, 18,* 1241–1259.

Sangrador, J. L., & Yela, C. (2000). "What is beautiful is loved": Physical attractiveness in love relationships in a representative sample. *Social Behavior & Personality, 28*(3) 207–218.

Sansone, R. A., & Levitt, J. L. (2005). Borderline personality and eating disorders. *Eating Disorders: The Journal of Treatment & Prevention, 13*(1), 71–83.

Santee, R. T., & Maslach, C. (1982). To agree or not to agree: Personal dissent amid social pressure to conform. *Journal of Personality and Social Psychology, 42,* 690–700.

Sattler, J. M. (1988). *Assessment of children*. San Diego: Jerome M. Sattler.

Savage-Rumbaugh, E. S., Murphy, J., Sevcik, R. A., Brakke, K. E., Williams, S. L., & Rumbaugh, D. M., with commentary by Bates, E. (1993). Language comprehension in ape and child. *Monographs of the Society for Research in Child Development, 58*(233), 1–254.

Saxe, L., & Ben-Shakhar, G. (1999). Admissibility of polygraph tests: The application of scientific standards post-Daubert. *Psychology, Public Policy, & Law, 5*(1), 203–223.

Scarr, S., & Weinberg, R. A. (1983). The Minnesota adoption studies: Genetic differences and malleability. *Child Development, 54,* 260–267.

Schachter, S. (1959). *The psychology of affiliation*. Stanford, CA: Stanford University Press.

Schacter, D. L. (1992). Understanding implicit memory: A cognitive neuroscience approach. *American Psychologist, 47*(4), 559–569.

Schaie, K. W. (1993). The Seattle longitudinal studies of adult intelligence. *Current Directions, 2,* 171–175.

Schaie, K. W. (1994). The course of adult intellectual development. *American Psychologist, 49,* 304–313.

Schenk, D. (2000, July). *A possible vaccine for Alzheimer's disease*. Paper presented to the World Alzheimer Congress 2000, Washington, DC.

Schneider, W., & Bjorklund, D. (1992). Expertise, aptitude, and strategic remembering. *Child Development, 63,* 461–473.

Schulman, P. (1995). Explanatory style and achievement in school and work. In G. Buchanan & M. E. P. Seligman (Eds.), *Explanatory style*. Hillsdale, NJ: Lawrence Erlbaum.

Schwarz, N., Bless, H., & Bohner, G. (1991). Mood and persuasion: Affective states influence the processing of persuasive communications. In M. Zanna (Ed.), *Advances in experimental social psychology* (Vol. 24). New York: Academic Press.

Schweinhart, L. J., & Weikart, D. P. (Eds.). (1993). *Significant benefits: The High / Scope Perry Preschool Study through age 27*. Ypsilanti, MI: High/Scope Press.

Seal, K. H., Bertenthal, D., Miner, C. R., et. al. (2007). Bringing the war back home: mental health disorder among 103,788 U.S. veterans returning from Iraq and Afghanistan seen at Department of Veterans Affairs facilities. *Archives of Internal Medicine, 167,* 476–482.

Segal, N. (1993). Twin, sibling, and adoption methods. *American Psychologist, 48,* 943–956.

Segall, M. H., Campbell, D. T., & Herskovits, M. J. (1966). *The influence of culture on visual perception*. New York: Bobbs-Merrill.

Seligman, M. E. P. (1975). *Helplessness: On depression, development, and death*. New York: W. H. Freeman.

Seligman, M. E. P. (1990). *Learned optimism*. New York: Pocket Books.

Seligman, M. E. P. (1996, August). *Predicting and preventing depression*. Master lecture presented to the meeting of the American Psychological Association, Toronto.

Seligman, M. E. P., (2002). *Authentic happiness: Using the new positive psychology to realize your potential for lasting happiness.* New York: Free Press. Martin Seligman describes how to focus on mental health instead of mental illness.

Seligman, M. E. P. & Csikszentmihalyi, M. (2000). Positive psychology: An introduction. *American Psychologist, 55,* 5–14.

Seligman, M. E. P., Steen, T., Park, N., Peterson, P. (2005). Positive psychology progress, empirical validation of interventions. *American Psychologist, 60*(5), 410–421.

Selkoe, D. J. (1992). Aging brain, aging mind. *Scientific American, 267*(3), 134–142.

Selye, H. (1976). *The stress of life* (rev. ed.). New York: McGraw-Hill.

Seppa, N. (1997). Children's TV remains steeped in violence. *APA Monitor, 28*(6), 36.

Shah, M., & Jeffery, R. W. (1991). Is obesity due to overeating and inactivity or to a defective metabolic rate? A review. *Annals of Behavioral Medicine, 13,* 73–81.

Shayley, A. Y., et al. (2000). Auditory startle response in trauma survivors with posttraumatic stress disorder: A prospective study. *American Journal of Psychiatry, 157,* 255–261.

Sheehy, G. (1976). *Passages: Predictable crises of adult life.* New York: Dutton.

Sheehy, G. (1995). *New passages: Mapping your life across time.* New York: Random House.

Shenal, B. V., & Harrison, D. W. (2003). Investigation of the laterality of hostility, cardiovascular regulation, and auditory recognition. *International Journal of Neuroscience, 113*(2), 205–222.

Shoda, Y., Mischel, W., & Peake, P. K. (1990). Predicting adolescent cognitive and self-regulatory competencies from preschool delay of gratification: Identifying diagnostic conditions. *Developmental Psychology, 26(6),* 978-986.

Shoham-Salomon, V. (1991). Introduction to special section on client-therapy interaction research. *Journal of Consulting and Clinical Psychology, 59,* 203–204.

Shotland, R. L., & Heinold, W. D. (1985). Bystander response to arterial bleeding: Helping skills, the decision-making process, and differentiating the helping response. *Journal of Personality and Social Psychology, 49,* 347–356.

Shusterman, G., & Saxe, L. (1990). *Deception in romantic relationships.* Unpublished manuscript.

Siegal, M. (1987). Are sons and daughters treated more differently by fathers than by mothers? *Developmental Review, 7,* 183–209.

Siegel, L. J., & Senna, J. J. (1994). *Juvenile delinquency: Theory, practice and law.* St. Paul, MN: West.

Silver, E., Cirincione, C., & Steadman, H. J. (1994, February). Cited in DeAngelis, T. (1994). Demythologizing inaccurate perceptions of the insanity defense. *Law and Human Behavior, 18*(1), 63–70.

Silver, R. C., Holman, E. A., McIntosh, D. N., Poulin, M., Gil-Rivas, V. (2002). Nationwide longitudinal study of psychological responses to September 11. *Journal of the American Medical Association, 288*(10), 1235–1244.

Simon, H. A. (1990). A mechanism for social selection and successful altruism. *Science, 250,* 1665–1668.

Simons, R. K., Whitbeck, L. B., Conger, R. D., & Chyi-In, W. (1991). Intergenerational transmission of harsh parenting. *Developmental Psychology, 27,* 159–171.

Simonton, D. (1988). Age and outstanding achievement: What do we know after a century of research? *Psychological Bulletin, 104,* 251–267.

Simonton, D. K. (2000). Creativity: Cognitive, personal, developmental, and social aspects. *American Psychologist, 55,* 151–158.

Singh, R., & Ho, S. Y. (2000). Attitudes and attraction: A new test of the attraction, repulsion and similarity-dissimilarity asymmetry hypotheses. *British Journal of Social Psychology, 39*(2), 197–211.

Skinner, B. F. (1938/1966). *The behavior of organisms.* New York: Appleton Century Crofts.

Skinner, B. F. (1971). *Beyond Freedom and Dignity.* New York: Knopf.

Skinner, B. F. (1987). Whatever happened to psychology as the science of behavior? *American Psychologist, 42,* 780–786.

Sleek, S. (1996). Side effects undermine drug compliance. *APA Monitor, 26*(3), 32.

Sleepers suffer WTC nightmares. (2001, November 22). *The Associated Press.*

Smetana, J. G., Yau, J., Restrepo, A., & Braeges, J. L. (1991). Conflict and adaptation in adolescence: Adolescent–parent conflict. In M. E. Colten & S. Gore (Eds.), *Adolescent stress: Causes and consequences.* New York: Aldine de Gruyter.

Smetana, J., & Gaines, C. (1999). Adolescent-parent conflict in middle-class African American families. *Child Development, 70*(6), 1447–1463.

Smith, E. R., & Mackie, D. M. (1995). *Social psychology.* New York: Worth.

Smith, P. K., Boulton, M. J., & Cowie, H. (1993). The impact of cooperative group work on ethnic relations in middle school. *Social Psychology International, 14,* 21–42.

Smith, S. M., Glenberg, A. M., & Bjork, R. A. (1978). Environmental context and human memory. *Memory and Cognition, 6,* 342–355.

Snow, C. E., (1993). Bilingualism and second language acquisition. In J. Berko-Gleason & N. B. Ratner (Eds.), *Psycholinguistics.* Fort Worth, TX: Harcourt Brace Jovanovich.

Snyder, M., & DeBono, G. (1989). Understanding the functions of attitudes. In A. R. Pratkanis et al. (Eds.), *Attitude structure and function.* Hillsdale, NJ: Lawrence Erlbaum.

Snyderman, M., & Rothman, S. (1990). *The I.Q. controversy.* New Brunswick, NJ: Transaction.

Sokal, M. M. (Ed.). (1990). *Psychological testing and American society: 1890-1930.* New Brunswick, NJ: Rutgers University Press. History of the testing movement and its founders.

Soldz, S., & McCullough, L. (Eds.). (2000) *Reconciling empirical knowledge and clinical experience: The art and science of psychotherapy.* Washington, DC: American Psychological Association.

Solomon, R. L. (1980). The opponent-process theory of acquired motivation: The costs of pleasure and the benefits of pain. *American Psychologist, 35,* 691–712.

Southern, T., & Jones, E. D. (1991). *The academic acceleration of gifted children.* New York: Teachers College Press.

Spano, S. (2002). Adolescent brain development. *ACT for Youth Upstate Center of Excellence Research Facts and Findings.* May 1.

Spanos, N. O. (1994). Multiple identity enactments and multiple personality disorder: A sociocultural perspective. *Psychological Bulletin, 116*(1), 143–165.

Spencer, M. B., & Markstrom-Adams, C. (1990). Identity processes among racial and ethnic minority children in America. *Child Development, 61,* 290–310.

Spencer, M. B., Dornbusch, S. M., & Mont-Reynaud, R. (1990). Challenges in studying minority youth. In S. S. Feldman & G. R. Elliott (Eds.), *At the threshold: The developing adolescent.* Cambridge, MA: Harvard University Press.

Spinks, S. (2002). Adolescent brains are works in progress: here's why. *Frontline,* January 31.

Squire, L. R. (1993). Memory and the hippocampus. *Psychological Review, 99,* 195–231.

Squire, L. R. (1996, August). Memory systems of the brain. Master lecture presented to the meeting of the American Psychological Association, Toronto.

Stacy, A. W., Bentler, P. M., & Flay, B. R. (1994). Attitudes and health behavior in diverse populations: Drunk driving, alcohol use, binge eating, marijuana use, and cigarette use. *Health Psychology, 13,* 73–85.

Steinberg, L. (1991). Parent-adolescent relations. In R. M. Lerner, A. C. Petersen, & J. Brooks-Gunn (Eds.), *Encyclopedia of adolescence.* New York: Garland.

Steinberg, L., Lamborn, S. F., Dornbusch, S. M., & Darling, N. (1992). Impact of parenting practices on adolescent achievement: Authoritative parenting, school involvement, and encouragement to succeed. *Child Development, 63,* 1266–1281.

Steinbrook, R. (1992). The polygraph test—A flawed diagnostic method. *New England Journal of Medicine, 327,* 122–123.

Steinhauer, J. (1995, July 6). No marriage, no apologies. *The New York Times,* pp. C1, C7.

Sternberg, R. J. (1990). Wisdom and its relations to intelligence and creativity. In R. J. Sternberg (Ed.), *Wisdom: Its nature, origins, and development.* New York: Cambridge University Press.

Sternberg, R. J. (1996). *Successful intelligence.* New York: Simon & Schuster.

Sternberg, R. J. (1995). *In search of the human mind.* Fort Worth, TX: Harcourt Brace Jovanovich.

Sternberg, R. J. (1997). The concept of intelligence and its role in lifelong learning and success. *American Psychologist, 52,* 1030–1037.

Sternberg, R. J. (1997). What does it mean to be smart? *Educational Leadership, 54,* 20–24.

Sternberg, R. J. (2001). What is the common thread of creativity? *American Psychologist, 56*(4), 360–362.

Sternberg, R. J., & Lubart, T. I. (1995). *Defying the crowd: Cultivating creativity in a culture of conformity.* New York: Free Press.

Sternberg, R. J., Wagner, R. K., Williams, W. M., & Horvath, J. A. (1995). Testing common sense. *American Psychologist, 50,* 912–927.

Stock, R. (1995, June 1). Wrongheaded views persist about the old. *The New York Times,* p. C8.

Stone, N. M. (1993). Parental abuse as a precursor to childhood onset depression and suicidality. *Child Psychiatry and Human Development, 24,* 13–24.

Strober, M., et al. (2000). Controlled family study of anorexia nervosa and bulimia nervosa: Evidence of shared liability and transmission of partial syndromes. *American Journal of Psychiatry, 157,* 393–401.

Strughold, H. (1924). On the density and thresholds in the areas of pain on the epidermis in the various regions of the body. *Z. Biol, 80,* (in German), 367–380.

Strupp, H. H. (1992). The future of psychodynamic psychotherapy. *Psychotherapy, 29,* 21–27.

Stunkard, A. J., & Sørensen, T. I. A. (1993). Obesity and socioeconomic status—A complex relation. *New England Journal of Medicine, 329,* 1036–1037.

Suddath, R., Casanova, M., Goldberg, T., Daniel, D., Kelsoe, J., & Weinberger, D. (1989). Temporal lobe pathology in schizophrenia: A quantitative magnetic resonance imaging study. *American Journal of Psychiatry, 146,* 464–472.

Sullivan, J. M. (2000). Cellular and molecular mechanisms underlying learning and memory impairments produced by cannabinoids. *Learning & Memory, 7*(3), 132–139.

Sundberg, N. D. (1990). *Assessment of persons* (2nd ed.). Englewood Cliffs, NJ: Prentice-Hall.

Swearer, S. M., & Cary, P. T. (2003). Perceptions and attitudes toward bullying in middle school youth: A developmental examination across the bully/victim continuum. *Journal of Applied School Psychology, 19*(2), 63–79.

T

Tannen, D. (1990). *You just don't understand.* New York: Ballantine Books.

Tanner, J. M. (1978). *Fetus into man: Physical growth from conception to maturity* (p. 118). Cambridge, MA: Harvard University Press.

Tanner, J. M. (1991). Adolescent growth spurt. In R. M. Lerner, A. C. Petersen, & J. Brooks-Gunn (Eds.), *Encyclopedia of adolescence.* New York: Garland.

Tavris, C. (1989). *Anger: The misunderstood emotion,* (rev. ed.). New York: Touchstone.

Taylor, I., & Taylor, M. M. (1990). *Psycholinguistics: Learning and using language.* Englewood Cliffs, NJ: Prentice-Hall.

Taylor, J. B. (2006). *My stroke of insight: A brain scientist's personal journey.* New York: Viking. Neuroanatomist Jill Bolte Taylor describes her recovery after a stroke.

Taylor, S. E. (1990). Health psychology: The science and the field. *American Psychologist, 45,* 40–50.

Teachout, T. (2000, April 2). For more artists, a fine old age. *The New York Times online.*

Teri, L., & Wagner, A. (1992). Alzheimer's disease and depression. *Journal of Consulting and Clinical Psychology, 60,* 379–391.

Tetlock, P. E. (1983). Accountability and complexity of thought. *Journal of Personality and Social Psychology, 45,* 74–83.

Tharp, R. G. (1991). Cultural diversity and treatment of children. *Journal of Consulting and Clinical Psychology, 59,* 799–812.

Thase, M. E., & Kupfer, D. J. (1996). Recent developments in the pharmacotherapy of mood disorders. *Journal of Consulting and Clinical Psychology, 64,* 646–659.

Thompson, R. A. (1991a). Attachment theory and research. In M. Lewis (Ed.), *Child and adolescent psychiatry: A comprehensive textbook.* Baltimore, MD: Williams & Wilkins.

Thompson, R. A. (1991b). Infant daycare: Concerns, controversies, choices. In J. V. Lerner & N. L. Galambos (Eds.), *Employed mothers and their children* (pp. 9–36). New York: Garland.

Thompson, R. A., & Limber, S. P. (1990). "Social anxiety" in infancy: Stranger and separation reaction. In H. Leitenberg (Ed.), *Handbook of social and evaluation anxiety.* New York: Plenum Press.

Tillfors, M., et al. (2001). Cerebral blood flow in subjects with social phobia during stressful speaking tasks: A PET study. *American Journal of Psychiatry, 158*(8), 1220–1226.

Tkachuk, G. A. & Martin, G. L. (1999). Exercise therapy for patients with psychiatric disorders: Research and clinical implications. *Professional Psychology: Research and Practice, 30*(3), 275–282.

Togersen, S. (1983). Genetic factors in anxiety disorders. *Archives of General Psychiatry, 40,* 1085–1089.

Triandis, H. C. (1994). *Culture and social behavior.* New York: McGraw-Hill.

Turnbull, C. (1961). Some observations regarding the experiences and behavior of the Bambuti Pygmies. *American Journal of Psychology, 74,* 301–308.

Turner, S., Beidel, D., & Nathan, R. (1985). Biological factors in obsessive-compulsive disorders. *Psychological Bulletin, 97,* 430–450.

U

United States Bureau of the Census. (2000). *Statistical abstract of the United States* (120th ed.). Washington, DC: U.S. Government Printing Office.

United States Bureau of the Census. (annual). *Current population reports.* Washington, DC: U.S. Government Printing Office.

United States National Center for Health Statistics. (annual). *Vital statistics of the United States* and *Monthly vital statistics reports.*

United States Public Health Service (1967). *Vital statistics of the United States,* 1900–1967.

The University of Chicago Medical Center, press release: Sleep loss boosts appetite: may encourage weight gain, based on finding from a study by Eve Van Cauter, M.D., December 6, 2004

V

Vaillant, G. E. (1994). Ego mechanisms of defense and personality psychopathology. *Journal of Abnormal Psychology, 103,* 44–50.

Valenstein, E. S. (1986). *Great and desperate cures: The rise and decline of psychosurgery and other radical treatments for mental illness.* New York: Basic Books.

van Hiel, A., Kossowska, M., & Mervielde, I. (2000). The relationship between Openness to Experience and political ideology. *Personality & Individual Differences, 28*(4) 741–751.

Venneman, S. S., Knowles, L. R. (2005). Sniffing Out Efficacy: Sniffy Lite, a Virtual Animal Lab. *Teaching of Psychology, 32(1),* 66–68

Vernberg, E. M., La Greca, A. M., Silverman, W. K., & Prinstein, M. J. (1996). Prediction of posttraumatic stress symptoms in children after Hurricane Andrew. *Journal of Abnormal Psychology, 105,* 237–248.

Vik, P. W., Carrello, P., Tate, S. R., & Field, C. (2000). Progression of consequences among heavy-drinking college students. *Psychology of Addictive Behaviors, 14*(2), 91–101.

Voyer, D., Voyer, S., & Bryden, M. P. (1995). Magnitude of sex differences in spatial abilities: A meta-analysis and consideration of critical variables. *Psychological Bulletin, 117,* 250– 270.

W

Wadden, T. A., et al. (1997). Exercise in the treatment of obesity. *Journal of Consulting and Clinical Psychology, 65,* 269–277.

Wade, C., & Tavris, C. (1993). *Critical and creative thinking: The case of love and war.* New York: Harper-Collins.

Wade, T. D., Bulik, C. M., Neale, M., & Kendler, K. S. (2000). Anorexia nervosa and major depression: Shared genetic and environmental risk factors. *American Journal of Psychiatry, 157*(3), 469–471.

Wagner, R. K. (1997). Intelligence, training, and employment. (1997). *American Psychologist, 52,* 1059–1069.

Wallerstein, J. S., & Blakeslee, S. (1989). *Second chances: Women and children a decade after divorce.* New York: Ticknor & Fields.

Walsh, W. B., & Betz, N. E. (1990). *Tests and assessment* (2nd ed.). Englewood Cliffs, NJ: Prentice-Hall.

Wang, X., et al. (2000). Longitudinal study of earthquake-related PTSD in a randomly selected community sample in North China. *American Journal of Psychiatry, 157,* 1260–1266.

Wann, D. L., & Waddill, P. J. (2003). Predicting sport fan motivation using anatomical sex and gender role orientation. *North American Journal of Psychology, 5*(3), 485–498.

Wann, D. L., Royalty, J., & Roberts, A. (2000). The self-presentation of sports fans: Investigating the importance of team identification and self-esteem. *Journal of Sport Behavior, 23*(2), 198–206.

Watson, J. B. (1924). *Behaviorism.* New York: Norton.

Weil, A. (2004). *The natural mind: A revolutionary approach to the drug problem.* New York: Houghton Mifflin

Weiner, R. D. (2000). Retrograde amnesia with electroconvulsive therapy. *Archives of General Psychiatry online, 57*(6).

Weiss, J. M (1982, August). *A model for the neurochemical study of depression.* Paper presented at the meeting of the American Psychological Association, Washington, DC.

Welch, K. M. A. (1993). Drug therapy of migraine. *New England Journal of Medicine, 329,* 1476–1483.

Wells, G. L. (1993). What do we know about eyewitness identification? *American Psychologist, 48,* 553–571.

Wells, G. L., et al. (2000). From the lab to the police station: A successful application of eyewitness research. *American Psychologist, 55*(6), 581–598.

Wetzler, S. E., & Sweeney, J. A. (1986). Childhood amnesia. In D. C. Rubin (Ed.), *Autobiographical memory.* New York: Cambridge University Press.

Wheeler, A., Archbold, S., Gregory, S., Skipp, A. (2007, May 28). Cochlear implants: The young people's perspective. *Journal of Deaf Studies and Deaf Education online.*

Widiger, T. A., & Costa, P. T., Jr. (1994). Personality and personality disorders. *Journal of Abnormal Psychology, 103,* 78–91.

Wiggins, J. G., Jr. (1994). Would you want your child to be a psychologist? *American Psychologist, 49,* 485–492.

Wilder, D. A. (1990). Some determinants of the persuasive power of in-groups and out-groups: Organization of information and attribution of independence. *Journal of Personality and Social Psychology, 59,* 1202–1213.

Wilgoren, J. (2000, March 15). Effort to curb binge drinking in college falls short. *The New York Times,* p. A16.

Williams, J. E., & Best, D. L. (1994). Cross-cultural views of women and men. In W. J. Lonner & R. Malpass (Eds.), *Psychology and culture.* Boston: Allyn & Bacon.

Wills, T. A., McNamara, G., Vaccaro, D., & Hirky, A. E. (1996). Escalated substance abuse: A longitudinal grouping analysis from early to middle adolescence. *Journal of Abnormal Psychology, 195,* 166–180.

Wilson, E. O. (1975). *Sociobiology: The new synthesis.* Cambridge, MA: Harvard University Press.

Winner, E. (2000). The origins and ends of giftedness. *American Psychologist, 55,* 159–169.

Wintre, M. G., & Sugar, L. A. (2000). Relationships with parents, personality, and the university transition. *Journal of College Student Development, 41*(2), 202–214.

Wolf, N. (1991). *The beauty myth: How images of beauty are used against women.* New York: William Morrow.

Wolpe, J. (1990). *The practice of behavior therapy* (4th ed.). New York: Pergamon.

Wood, J. M., Bootzin, R. R., Rosenhan, D., Nolen-Hoeksema, S., & Jourden, F. (1992). Effects of the 1989 San Francisco earthquake on frequency and content of nightmares. *Journal of Abnormal Psychology, 101,* 219–224.

Wood, W. (2000). Attitude change: Persuasion and social influence. *Annual Review of Psychology, 51,* 539–570.

Wood, W., & Eagly, A. H. (2000). Once again, the origins of sex differences. *American Psychologist, 55*(9), 1062–1063.

Wurtzel, E. (1994). *Prozac nation: Young and depressed in America.* New York: Penguin Group. What it means to be young, depressed, and medicated.

Yalom, I. D. (2000). *Love's executioner and other tales of psychotherapy.* New York: HarperCollins. This book includes ten eloquent, engaging tales of personal transformation told through the eyes of a psychotherapist.

Yalom, I. D., & Leszyz, M., (2005). *The theory and practice of group psychotherapy* (5th ed.). New York: Basic Books.

Yoder, J. D., & Kahn, A. S. (1993). Working toward an inclusive psychology of women. *American Psychologist, 48,* 846–850.

Yokota, F., & Thompson, K. M. (2000). Violence in G-rated animated films. *Journal of the American Medical Association, 283,* 2716–2720.

Youniss, J., & Haynie, D. L. (1992). Friendship in adolescence. *Developmental and Behavioral Pediatrics, 13,* 59–66.

Z

Zalloua, P. A., et al. (2008). Y-chromosomal diversity in Lebanon is structured by recent historical events. *The American Journal of Human Genetics,* doi:10.1016/ j.ajhg.2008.01.020

Zajonc, R. B. (1980). Compresence. In P. Paulus (Ed.), *The psychology of group influence.* Hillsdale, NJ: Erlbaum.

Zigler, E. (1995). *Modernizing early childhood intervention to better serve children and families in poverty.* Master lecture delivered at the meeting of the American Psychological Association, New York.

Zigler, E., Taussig, C., & Black, K. (1992). Early childhood intervention: A promising preventative for juvenile delinquency. *American Psychologist, 47,* 997–1006.

Zimbardo, Philip G. (1997). What messages are behind today's cults? *APA Monitor,* May, 1997.

Zipfel, S., et al. (2000). Long-term prognosis in anorexia nervosa: Lessons from a 21-year follow-up study. *The Lancet, 355*(9205), 721–722.

English and Spanish Glossary

MARK	AS IN	RESPELLING	EXAMPLE
a	alphabet	a	*AL-fuh-bet
ā	Asia	ay	AY-zhuh
ä	cart, top	ah	KAHRT, TAHP
e	let, ten	e	LET, TEN
ē	even, leaf	ee	EE-vuhn, LEEF
i	it, tip, British	i	IT, TIP, BRIT-ish
ī	site, buy, Ohio	y	SYT, BY, oh-HY-oh
	iris	eye	EYE-ris
k	card	k	KAHRD
ō	over, rainbow	oh	OH-vuhr, RAYN-boh
ù	book, wood	ooh	BOOHK, WOOHD
ó	all, orchid	aw	AWL, AWR-kid
ói	foil, coin	oy	FOYL, KOYN
aù	out	ow	OWT
ə	cup, butter	uh	KUHP, BUHT-uhr
ü	rule, food	oo	ROOL, FOOD
yü	few	yoo	FYOO
zh	vision	zh	VIZH-uhn

*A syllable printed in capital letters receives heavier emphasis than the other syllable(s) in a word.

Phonetic Respelling and Pronunciation Guide

Some of the vocabulary terms in this textbook have been respelled to help you pronounce them. The letter combinations used in the respelling throughout the narrative are explained in the following phonetic respelling and pronunciation guide. The guide is adapted from *Merriam-Webster's Collegiate Dictionary, 11th Edition; Merriam-Webster's Geographical Dictionary;* and *Merriam-Webster's Biographical Dictionary.*

A

absolute threshold the weakest amount of a particular stimulus that can be sensed (p. 97)
umbral absoluto menor cantidad de un estímulo en particular que puede percibirse (pág. 97)

acculturation the process of adapting to a new or different culture (p. 413)
aculturación proceso de adaptarse a una cultura nueva o diferente (pág. 413)

achievement knowledge and skills gained from experience and education (p. 249)
logro destrezas y conocimientos obtenidos a través de la experiencia y la educación (pág. 249)

achievement motivation the desire to persevere with work and to avoid distraction in order to reach personal goals (p. 375)
motivación de logro deseo de perseverar mediante el trabajo y de evitar las distracciones para alcanzar objetivos personales (pág. 375)

achievement test test that measures the amount of knowledge one has in specific academic areas (p. 427)
prueba de logro evaluación que mide el conocimiento adquirido en áreas académicas específicas (pág. 427)

active coping response to a stressor that reduces stress by changing the situation to eliminate or lessen the negative effects of the stressor (p. 488)
afrontamiento activo respuesta a un factor estresante en la que se modifica la situación para eliminar o disminuir los efectos negativos del factor y así reducir el estrés (pág. 488)

active listening empathic listening in which the listener acknowledges, restates, and clarifies the speaker's thoughts and concerns (p. 542)
escucha activa escucha empática en la que el receptor reconoce, reformula y aclara los pensamientos y las preocupaciones del emisor (pág. 542)

actor-observer bias the tendency to attribute one's own behavior to situational factors but to attribute the behavior of others to dispositional factors (p. 577)
sesgo actor-observador tendencia a atribuir la conducta propia a factores situacionales y la conducta de otros a factores disposicionales (pág. 577)

addiction a compulsive need for and use of a habit-forming substance (p. 145)
adicción necesidad y uso compulsivos de una sustancia que genera hábito (pág. 145)

adolescent growth spurt a sudden, brief burst of physical growth during which adolescents typically make great gains in height and weight (p. 307)
estirón de la adolescencia una explosión repentina y breve de crecimiento físico durante la que los adolescentes suelen crecer considerablemente en peso y estatura (pág. 307)

affiliation the desire to join with others and to be a part of something larger than oneself (p. 378)
afiliación deseo de unirse a otros y de formar parte de algo más grande que uno mismo (pág. 378)

afterimage the visual impression that remains after the original image has been removed (p. 104)
imagen persistente impresión visual que permanece después de que desaparece la imagen original (pág. 104)

agoraphobia a fear of crowded, public places (p. 506)
agorafobia miedo a los lugares públicos en los che hay mucha gente (pág. 506)

algorithm a problem-solving strategy that eventually leads to a solution; usually involves trying random solutions to a problem in a systematic way (p. 221)
algoritmo estrategia para resolver problemas que finalmente ofrece una solución; suele consistir en probar al azar una serie de soluciones para resolver un problema de manera sistemática (pág. 221)

altered state of consciousness a type of consciousness other than normal waking consciousness (p. 131)
estado alterado de conciencia cualquier estado de conciencia diferente del estado de conciencia normal de vigilia (pág. 131)

altruism unselfish regard for the welfare of others (p. 605)
altruismo preocupación desinteresada por el bienestar de los demás (pág. 605)

Alzheimer's disease an irreversible, progressive brain disorder characterized by the deterioration of memory, language, and eventually, physical functioning (p. 345)
enfermedad de Alzheimer trastorno del cerebro irreversible y progresivo caracterizado por el deterioro de la memoria, del lenguaje y, finalmente, del funcionamiento físico (pág. 345)

amphetamine a type of stimulant often used to stay awake or to reduce appetite (p. 146)
anfetamina tipo de estimulante que suele usarse para permanecer despierto o para reducir el apetito (pág. 146)

anchoring heuristic the process of making decisions based on certain ideas or standards held by the decision maker (p. 233)
heurística de anclaje el proceso de tomar decisiones a partir de ciertas ideas o normas propias de quien toma la decisión (pág. 233)

anorexia nervosa an eating disorder characterized by extreme weight loss due to self-starvation (p. 321)
anorexia nerviosa trastorno de la alimentación caracterizado por la pérdida extrema de peso que se debe a la inanición voluntaria (pág. 321)

anterograde amnesia the inability to form new memories because of brain trauma (p. 205)
amnesia anterógrada la incapacidad de formar recuerdos nuevos a causa de un trauma cerebral (pág. 205)

antianxiety drug a type of medication that relieves anxiety disorders and panic disorders by depressing the activity of the central nervous system (p. 550)
fármaco ansiolítico tipo de medicamento que alivia los trastornos de ansiedad y pánico mediante la depresión de la actividad del sistema nervioso central (pág. 550)

antidepressant drug a type of medication used to treat major depression by increasing the amount of one or both of the neurotransmitters noradrenaline and serotonin (p. 550)
fármaco antidepresivo tipo de medicamento que se usa para tratar las depresiones graves mediante el aumento de la cantidad de noradrenalina o de serotonina, o de ambos neurotransmisores a la vez (pág. 550)

antipsychotic drug a type of medication used to reduce agitation, delusions, and hallucinations by blocking the activity of dopamine in the brain; also called a major tranquilizer (p. 551)
fármaco antipsicótico tipo de medicamento que se usa para reducir la agitación, el delirio y las alucinaciones mediante el bloqueo de la actividad de la dopamina en el cerebro; también se conoce como tranquilizante mayor (pág. 551)

approach-approach conflict a type of conflict involving a choice between two positive but mutually exclusive options (p. 475)
conflicto de atracción-atracción tipo de conflicto que implica una elección entre dos opciones positivas pero excluyentes entre sí (pág. 475)

approach-avoidance conflict a type of conflict involving a single goal that has both positive and negative aspects (p. 475)
conflicto de atracción-evitación tipo de conflicto que implica un objetivo único que tiene aspectos tanto positivos como negativos (pág. 475)

aptitude test a test that is designed to predict a person's future performance or capacity to learn (p. 427)

prueba de aptitud prueba desarrollada para predecir el rendimiento o la capacidad para aprender de una persona (pág. 427)

archetypes original models from which later forms develop; in Jung's personality theory, archetypes are primitive images or concepts that reside in the collective unconscious (p. 401)

arquetipos modelos originales a partir de los que se desarrollan formas posteriores; en la teoría de la personalidad de Jung, los arquetipos son imágenes o conceptos primitivos que se encuentran en el inconsciente colectivo (pág. 401)

association areas areas of the cerebral cortex that are involved in such mental operations as thinking, memory, learning, and problem solving (p. 76)

áreas de asociación áreas de la corteza cerebral relacionadas con operaciones mentales como el pensamiento, la memoria, el aprendizaje y la resolución de problemas (pág. 76)

associationism the theory that our understanding of the world occurs through ideas associated with similar sensory experiences and perceptions (p. 17)

asociacionismo teoría que afirma que comprendemos el mundo a través de ideas asociadas a percepciones y experiencias sensoriales similares (pág. 17)

attachment an active and intense emotional relationship between two people that endures over time (p. 285)

apego relación emocional activa e intensa entre dos personas que perdura en el tiempo (pág. 285)

attitude an enduring belief about people, places, or objects that evokes certain feelings and influences behavior (p. 563)

actitud creencia duradera acerca de personas, lugares u objetos que evoca ciertos sentimientos e influye en la conducta (pág. 563)

attraction in social psychology, an attitude of liking (positive attraction) or disliking (negative attraction) (p. 581)

atracción en psicología social, una actitud de gusto (atracción positiva) o disgusto (atracción negativa) (pág. 581)

attribution theory the suggestion that there is a tendency to explain a person's behavior in terms of the situation or the person's personality (p. 577)

teoría de la atribución la propuesta de que hay una tendencia a explicar la conducta de una persona de acuerdo con la situación o la personalidad de la persona (pág. 577)

auditory nerve the cranial nerve that carries sound from the cochlea of the inner ear to the brain (p. 108)

nervio auditivo nervio craneal que lleva el sonido desde la cóclea del oído interno hacia el cerebro (pág. 108)

authoritarian a leadership or parenting style that stresses unquestioning obedience (p. 288)

autoritario tipo de liderazgo o estilo de crianza que se basa en la obediencia sin cuestionamientos (pág. 288)

authoritarian leader a leader who makes decisions for the group and tells other group members what to do (p. 593)

líder autoritario líder que toma las decisiones del grupo y ordena qué hacer a los demás miembros (pág. 593)

authoritative a leadership or parenting style based on recognized authority or knowledge and characterized by mutual respect (p. 288)

autoritativo tipo de liderazgo o estilo parental basado en la autoridad o el conocimiento admitidos que se caracteriza por el respeto mutuo (pág. 288)

autonomic nervous system the subdivision of the peripheral nervous system that regulates body functions, such as respiration and digestion (p. 71)

sistema nervioso autónomo subdivisión del sistema nervioso periférico que regula las funciones corporales, como la respiración y la digestión (pág. 71)

availability heuristic the tendency to make decisions on the basis of information that is available in one's immediate consciousness (p. 232)

heurística de la disponibilidad tendencia de una persona a tomar decisiones a partir de la información disponible en su conciencia inmediata (pág. 232)

aversive conditioning a type of counterconditioning that links an unpleasant state with an unwanted behavior in an attempt to eliminate the behavior (p. 547)

condicionamiento aversivo tipo de contracondicionamiento que une un estado desagradable con una conducta no deseada para eliminar esa conducta (pág. 547)

avoidance-avoidance conflict a type of conflict involving a choice between two negative or undesirable options (p. 475)

conflicto de evitación-evitación tipo de conflicto que implica una elección entre dos opciones negativas o indeseables (pág. 475)

axon a long tubelike structure attached to a neuron that transmits impulses away from the neuron cell body (p. 67)

axón estructura larga en forma de tubo unida a una neurona que transmite impulsos desde el cuerpo celular de la neurona (pág. 67)

axon terminals small fibers branching out from an axon (p. 68)

terminales axonales pequeñas fibras del axón que se ramifican (pág. 68)

B

balance theory the view that people have a need to organize their perceptions, opinions, and beliefs in a manner that is in harmony with those of the people around them (p. 376)

teoría del equilibrio teoría que afirma que las personas necesitan organizar sus percepciones, opiniones y creencias de una manera que esté en armonía con las de las personas que las rodean (pág. 376)

basic research research that is conducted for its own sake, that is, that has no immediate application (p. 12)

investigación básica investigación que se realiza con el único fin de investigar, es decir, que no tiene aplicación inmediata (pág. 12)

behavior any action that people can observe or measure (p. 5)

conducta toda acción que se puede observar o medir (pág. 5)

behaviorism the school of psychology, founded by John Watson, that defines psychology as the scientific study of observable behavior (p. 20)

conductismo escuela de la Psicología, fundada por John Watson, que define la psicología como el estudio científico de la conducta observable (pág. 20)

behavior-rating scales systematic means of recording the frequency with which certain behaviors occur (p. 423)

escala de evaluación de la conducta método sistemático para registrar la frecuencia de ciertas conductas (pág. 423)

bereaved mourning after the death of a loved one (p. 354)

aflicción estado de duelo después de la muerte de un ser querido (pág. 354)

bias a predisposition to a certain point of view despite the facts (p. 41)

sesgo predisposición a mantener determinado punto de vista a pesar de los hechos (pág. 41)

binocular cues visual cues for depth that require the use of both eyes (p. 119)

claves binoculares claves visuales mediante las cuales se percibe la profundidad, para las que se requiere el uso de ambos ojos (pág. 119)

biofeedback a system for monitoring and feeding back information about certain biological processes, such as blood pressure (p. 140)

biorretroalimentación sistema de monitoreo y retroalimentación de información sobre ciertos procesos biológicos, como la presión arterial (pág. 140)

biological perspective the psychological perspective that emphasizes the influence of biology on behavior (p. 23)

perspectiva biológica perspectiva psicológica que enfatiza la influencia de la biología en la conducta (pág. 23)

bipolar disorder a disorder in which a person's mood changes from depression to wild elation and back again (p. 510)

trastorno bipolar trastorno en el que los estados de ánimo de una persona se alternan una y otra vez entre la depresión y la euforia descontrolada (pág. 510)

blind spot the part of the retina that contains no photoreceptors (p. 103)

punto ciego la parte de la retina que no contiene fotorreceptores (pág. 103)

bulimia nervosa an eating disorder in which enormous quantities of food are consumed and then purged by means of laxatives or self-induced vomiting (p. 321)

bulimia nerviosa trastorno de la alimentación que se caracteriza por la ingesta de enormes cantidades de comida y su posterior purga mediante laxantes o vómitos inducidos (pág. 321)

bystander effect the tendency for a person to be less likely to give aid if other bystanders are present (p. 606)

efecto espectador tendencia por la cual es menos probable que una persona ayude a otra si hay otras personas mirando (pág. 606)

case study an in-depth study of a single person or group to reveal some universal principle (p. 45)
estudio de caso estudio exhaustivo de una sola persona o un solo grupo realizado para revelar algún principio universal (pág. 45)

catatonic stupor an immobile, expressionless, coma-like state associated with schizophrenia (p. 520)
estupor catatónico estado de inmovilidad y falta de expresión, similar a un estado de coma, asociado a la esquizofrenia (pág. 520)

catharsis in psychology, the release of aggressive energy through action or fantasy (p. 602)
catarsis en psicología, la liberación de la energía agresiva mediante la acción o la fantasía (pág. 602)

cell body the part of a neuron that produces the energy needed for the activity of the cell (p. 67)
cuerpo celular parte de la neurona que produce la energía necesaria para la actividad celular (pág. 67)

cellular damage theories the view that aging occurs because body cells lose the capacity to reproduce and maintain themselves as a result of damage (p. 344)
teorías del daño celular concepción que afirma que el envejecimiento ocurre porque las células del cuerpo pierden la capacidad de reproducirse y mantenerse sanas tras sufrir un daño (pág. 344)

central nervous system the part of the nervous system that consists of the brain and spinal cord (p. 67)
sistema nervioso central parte del sistema nervioso que comprende el encéfalo y la médula espinal (pág. 67)

central route a method of persuasion that uses evidence and logical arguments to influence people (p. 568)
vía central método de persuasión en el que se usan pruebas y argumentos lógicos para influir en las personas (pág. 568)

cerebellum the area of the brain that is responsible for voluntary movement and balance (p. 73)
cerebelo área del encéfalo que controla el movimiento voluntario y el equilibrio (pág. 73)

cerebral cortex the bumpy, convoluted surface of the brain; the body's control and information-processing center (p. 75)
corteza cerebral la superficie irregular y convoluta del encéfalo; el centro del control corporal y del procesamiento de la información (pág. 75)

cerebrum the large mass of the forebrain, consisting of two hemispheres (p. 75)
cerebro gran masa del encéfalo anterior, que consta de dos hemisferios (pág. 75)

chaining in operant conditioning, combining the steps of a sequence to progress toward a final action (p. 170)
encadenamiento en el condicionamiento operante, la combinación de los pasos de una secuencia con el objetivo de progresar hacia una acción final (pág. 170)

childhood the stage of life that follows infancy and spans the period from the second birthday to the beginning of adolescence (p. 279)
niñez etapa de la vida que sigue a la infancia y abarca el período que se extiende desde los dos años hasta el comienzo de la adolescencia (pág. 279)

chromosome a microscopic threadlike structure in the nucleus of every living cell; it contains genes, the basic units of heredity (p. 85)
cromosoma estructura microscópica filiforme que se halla en el núcleo de todas las células vivas; contiene los genes, las unidades básicas de la herencia (pág. 85)

chunking the mental process of organizing information into meaningful units, or "chunks" (p. 198)
agrupación proceso mental de organizar la información en unidades de significado o bloques de información (pág. 198)

circadian rhythm a regular sequence of biological processes, such as temperature and sleep, that occurs every 24 hours (p. 133)
ritmo circadiano secuencia regular de procesos biológicos, como la temperatura y el sueño, que ocurre cada 24 horas (pág. 133)

classical conditioning a type of learning in which a neutral stimulus comes to elicit an unconditioned response when that neutral stimulus is repeatedly paired with a stimulus that normally causes an unconditioned response (p. 159)
condicionamiento clásico tipo de aprendizaje en el que un estímulo neutro logra provocar una respuesta incondicionada cuando se asocia repetidamente a un estímulo que suele provocar una respuesta incondicionada (pág. 159)

clique a small, exclusive group of people within a larger group (p. 313)
clique grupo pequeño y exclusivo de personas dentro de un grupo más grande (pág. 313)

closure the tendency to perceive a complete or whole figure even when there are gaps in sensory information (p. 116)
cierre tendencia a percibir una figura completa o entera incluso cuando faltan elementos en la información sensorial (pág. 116)

ENGLISH AND SPANISH GLOSSARY

cochlea the fluid-filled structure of the inner ear that transmits sound impulses to the auditory nerve (p. 108)

cóclea estructura del oído interno llena de fluido que transmite impulsos sonoros al nervio auditivo (pág. 108)

cognitive activities private, unmeasurable mental processes such as dreams, perceptions, thoughts, and memories (p. 5)

actividades cognitivas procesos mentales privados que no pueden medirse, como los sueños, las percepciones, los pensamientos y los recuerdos (pág. 5)

cognitive anchor a persistent belief that develops early in life and shapes the way a person sees and interprets the world (p. 564)

anclaje cognitivo creencia persistente que se desarrolla en los primeros años de vida y determina la manera en que una persona ve e interpreta el mundo (pág. 564)

cognitive consistency the state in which a person's thoughts and behaviors match his or her beliefs and the expectations of others (p. 376)

consistencia cognitiva estado en el que los pensamientos y las conductas de una persona se corresponden con sus creencias y con las expectativas de los demás (pág. 376)

cognitive-dissonance theory the theory that suggests that people make attitudinal changes to reduce the tension that occurs when their thoughts and attitudes are inconsistent with their actions (p. 377)

teoría de la disonancia cognitiva teoría que sugiere que las personas cambian sus actitudes para reducir la tensión que surge cuando sus pensamientos y actitudes no se corresponden con sus acciones (pág. 377)

cognitive evaluation a process in which a person forms beliefs based on evidence from many sources (p. 563)

evaluación cognitiva proceso por el cual una persona fundamenta sus creencias con pruebas que provienen de muchas fuentes (pág. 563)

cognitive perspective the perspective that emphasizes the role of thought processes in determining behavior (p. 23)

perspectiva cognitiva la perspectiva que enfatiza el rol de los procesos de pensamiento en la determinación de la conducta (pág. 23)

cognitive restructuring a method of coping in which one changes the thoughts one has in a particular situation (p. 439)

reestructuración cognitiva método de afrontamiento por el que una persona cambia los pensamientos que tiene en una situación particular (pág. 439)

collective unconscious Jung's concept of a shared, inherited body of memory that all humans have (p. 401)

inconsciente colectivo concepto desarrollado por Jung que describe un conjunto heredado y compartido de recuerdos que tienen todos los seres humanos (pág. 401)

commitment a pledge or promise between two people to share a life together (p. 583)

compromiso promesa o acuerdo entre dos personas para compartir una vida en común (pág. 583)

common fate the tendency to perceive objects that are moving together as belonging together (p. 117)

destino común tendencia a percibir objetos que se mueven juntos como si formaran un grupo (pág. 117)

complementary the colors across from each other on the color wheel (p. 103)

complementarios se dice de los colores que se encuentran uno frente a otro en el círculo cromático (pág. 103)

concept a mental structure used to categorize objects, people, or events that share similar characteristics (p. 215)

concepto estructura mental que se usa para categorizar objetos, personas o sucesos que comparten características similares (pág. 215)

concrete-operational stage according to Piaget, the stage of cognitive development during which children acquire the ability to think logically (p. 297)

etapa operacional concreta según Piaget, etapa del desarrollo cognitivo durante la que los niños adquieren la capacidad de pensar lógicamente (pág. 297)

conditional positive regard the expression of love or esteem given only when an individual exhibits suitable behavior (p. 291)

estimación positiva condicional expresión de amor o estima que se da únicamente cuando un individuo exhibe una conducta adecuada (pág. 291)

conditioned response a learned response to a previously neutral stimulus (p. 160)

respuesta condicionada respuesta aprendida ante un estímulo que antes era neutro (pág. 160)

ENGLISH AND SPANISH GLOSSARY

conditioned stimulus a previously neutral stimulus that, because of pairing with an unconditioned stimulus, now causes a conditioned response (p. 160)

estímulo condicionado estímulo neutro que, debido a la asociación con un estímulo incondicionado, provoca una respuesta condicionada (pág. 160)

conditioning a type of learning that involves stimulus-response connections, in which the response is conditional on the stimulus (p. 159)

condicionamiento tipo de aprendizaje basado en relaciones de estímulo-respuesta, en el que el estímulo condiciona la respuesta (pág. 159)

conductive deafness hearing loss caused by damage to the middle ear, thus interfering with the transmission of sound waves to the cochlea (p. 108)

sordera conductiva pérdida de la audición provocada por una lesión en el oído medio que dificulta la transmisión de las ondas sonoras hacia la cóclea (pág. 108)

conform to change one's attitudes or behavior in accordance with generally accepted standards (p. 595)

conformar cambiar las actitudes o conductas personales de acuerdo con normas aceptadas por todos (pág. 595)

congruence agreement; in psychology, consistency between one's self-concept and one's experience (p. 411)

congruencia acuerdo; en psicología, coherencia entre el concepto que una persona tiene de sí misma y su experiencia (pág. 411)

consciousness awareness of oneself and one's environment (p. 129)

conciencia reconocimiento de uno mismo y de su entorno (pág.129)

construct idea that cannot be seen or measured directly (p. 35)

constructo idea que no se puede ver ni medir directamente (pág. 35)

contact comfort the instinctual need to touch and be touched by something soft, such as skin or fur (p. 286)

comodidad de contacto necesidad instintiva de tocar y sentir algo suave, como la piel o el pelaje (pág. 286)

context-dependent memories information that is more easily retrieved in the context or situation in which it was encoded and stored (p. 193)

recuerdos contextuales información que se recuerda más fácilmente en el contexto o la situación donde se codificó y almacenó (pág. 193)

continuity the perceptual tendency to group stimuli into continuous patterns (p. 117)

continuidad tendencia perceptiva a agrupar estímulos en patrones continuos (pág.117)

continuous reinforcement the reinforcement of a desired response every time it occurs (p. 168)

refuerzo continuo refuerzo de una respuesta deseada cada vez que ocurre (pág. 168)

control group in an experiment, the group that does not receive the treatment (p. 52)

grupo de control en un experimento, el grupo que no recibe el tratamiento (pág. 52)

conventional moral reasoning the level of moral development at which a person makes judgments based on conventional standards of right and wrong (p. 298)

razonamiento moral convencional nivel de desarrollo moral en el que una persona hace juicios basándose en normas convencionales sobre el bien y el mal (pág. 298)

convergent thinking directed thinking; thinking that is limited to available facts (p. 217)

pensamiento convergente pensamiento dirigido; pensamiento limitado a los datos disponibles (pág. 217)

corpus callosum the nerve fibers that connect the left and right hemispheres of the cerebral cortex (p. 75)

cuerpo calloso conjunto de fibras nerviosas que conectan los hemisferios izquierdo y derecho de la corteza cerebral (pág. 75)

correlation the relationship between variables (p. 48)

correlación relación entre variables (pág. 48)

counterconditioning a therapy procedure based on classical conditioning that replaces a negative response to a stimulus with a positive response (p. 162)

contracondicionamiento procedimiento terapéutico basado en el condicionamiento clásico que reemplaza una respuesta negativa a un estímulo con una respuesta positiva (pág. 162)

cramming preparing hastily for an exam (p. 439)

memorización intensiva preparación breve y acelerada para un examen (pág. 439)

creativity the ability to invent new solutions to problems or to create original or ingenious materials (p. 260)

creatividad capacidad de inventar nuevas soluciones a problemas o crear materiales originales o ingeniosos (pág. 260)

critical period a stage or point in development during which a person or animal is best suited to learn a particular skill or behavior pattern (p. 276)

período crítico etapa o momento del desarrollo en que una persona o un animal está más preparado para aprender una destreza o un patrón de conducta específicos (pág. 276)

cross-linking a possible cause of aging in which proteins within a cell bind together, toughening body tissues and eventually leading to the breakdown of various bodily processes (p. 345)

entrecruzamiento posible causa del envejecimiento; enlace de proteínas dentro de una célula responsable de que se endurezcan los tejidos del cuerpo y, con el tiempo, fallen diversos procesos fisiológicos (pág. 345)

cross-sectional method a method of research that looks at different age groups at the same time in order to understand changes that occur during the life span (p. 46)

método transversal método de investigación por el que se observan grupos de distintas edades al mismo tiempo para comprender los cambios que ocurren durante el ciclo vital (pág. 46)

crowd large groups of people who share attitudes and a group identity (p. 313)

multitud grupo grande de personas que comparten actitudes y una identidad grupal (pág. 313)

crystallized intelligence accumulated skills, knowledge, and experience (p. 264)

inteligencia cristalizada destrezas, experiencias y conocimientos acumulados (pág. 264)

culture-bound syndrome a cluster of symptoms that is considered a recognizable disease only within a specific culture or society (p. 500)

síndrome limitado a una cultura conjunto de síntomas que se consideran una enfermedad reconocible solo dentro de una cultura o sociedad específicas (pág. 500)

decay disintegration; in psychology, the fading away of memory over time (p. 204)

deterioro desintegración; en psicología, la desaparición gradual de la memoria con el paso del tiempo (pág. 204)

deductive reasoning a form of thinking in which conclusions are inferred from premises; the conclusions are true if the premises are true (p. 230)

razonamiento deductivo forma de pensamiento en la que se infieren conclusiones a partir de premisas; las conclusiones son verdaderas si las premisas son verdaderas (pág. 230)

defense mechanisms psychological distortions used to remain psychologically stable or in balance (p. 398)

mecanismos de defensa distorsiones psicológicas que se usan para permanecer estable o equilibrado desde el punto de vista psicológico (pág. 398)

defensive coping a response to a stressor that temporarily reduces stress but may be harmful in the long run because it neither changes the situation nor removes the stressor (p. 488)

afrontamiento defensivo respuesta a un factor estresante que reduce temporalmente el estrés pero puede ser perjudicial a largo plazo porque no modifica la situación ni elimina el factor estresante (pág. 488)

delusion an erroneous belief, as of persecution or grandeur, that may accompany certain psychotic disorders (p. 147)

delirio creencia errónea, por ejemplo, de persecución o de grandeza, que puede acompañar ciertos trastornos psicóticos (pág. 147)

dementia a serious loss of cognitive function (p. 345)

demencia pérdida grave de las funciones cognitivas (pág. 345)

democratic leader a leader who encourages group members to express and discuss their ideas and to make their own decisions (p. 593)

líder democrático líder que anima a los miembros del grupo a expresar y debatir sus ideas, y a tomar sus propias decisiones (pág. 593)

dendrites the branchlike extensions of a neuron that receive impulses and conduct them toward the cell body (p. 67)

dendritas extensiones ramificadas de una neurona que reciben impulsos y los conducen hacia el cuerpo de la célula (pág. 67)

dependent variable in an experiment, the factor that is being measured and that may change in response to manipulations of the independent variable (p. 52)

variable dependiente en un experimento, el factor que se mide y que puede variar de acuerdo con las manipulaciones de la variable independiente (pág. 52)

depersonalization a dissociative disorder characterized by persistent or recurrent feelings of detachment from one's mental processes or body (p. 516)

despersonalización trastorno disociativo caracterizado por sentimientos persistentes o recurrentes de desapego de los propios procesos mentales o corporales (pág. 516)

depressant a drug that reduces neural activity and slows body functions (p. 145)

depresivo fármaco que reduce la actividad neuronal y lentifica las funciones fisiológicas (pág. 145)

depression a psychological disorder characterized by extreme sadness, an inability to concentrate, and feelings of helplessness and great sadness (p. 510)

depresión trastorno psicológico caracterizado por una tristeza extrema, la incapacidad de concentrarse y sentimientos de impotencia y gran tristeza (pág. 510)

detoxification the removal of a poisonous or otherwise harmful substance, such as alcohol or other drugs, from the body (p. 149)

desintoxicación eliminación del cuerpo de una sustancia venenosa o dañina, como el alcohol u otras drogas (pág. 149)

developmental psychology the branch of psychology that studies the physical, cognitive, and social changes that occur throughout the life cycle (p. 275)

psicología del desarrollo rama de la psicología que estudia los cambios físicos, cognitivos y sociales que ocurren durante el ciclo vital (pág. 275)

difference reduction a problem-solving method that involves reducing the difference between the present situation and the desired one (p. 223)

reducción de la diferencia método de resolución de problemas que consiste en reducir la diferencia entre la situación presente y la deseada (pág. 223)

difference threshold the minimum amount of difference that can be detected between two stimuli (p. 98)

umbral de diferencia menor diferencia que se puede detectar entre dos estímulos (pág. 98)

diffusion of responsibility the sharing of responsibility for a decision or behavior among the members of a group (p. 591)

difusión de la responsabilidad fenómeno por el que todos los miembros de un grupo comparten la responsabilidad por una decisión o una conducta (pág. 591)

discrimination (1) in classical conditioning, the ability to distinguish the conditioned stimulus from other stimuli that are similar (p. 161); (2) unfair treatment of a person or group based on prejudice (p. 573)

discriminación (1) en el condicionamiento clásico, la capacidad de distinguir el estímulo condicionado de otros estímulos similares (pág. 161); (2) tratamiento injusto de una persona o grupo basado en prejuicios (pág. 573)

dissociation the separation of certain personality components or mental processes from conscious thought (p. 516)

disociación separación de ciertos componentes de la personalidad o procesos mentales del pensamiento consciente (pág. 516)

distress stress that is damaging or negative (p. 473)

angustia estrés que resulta perjudicial o negativo (pág. 473)

distributed learning learning that occurs regularly and is distributed over time (p. 181)

aprendizaje distribuido aprendizaje que ocurre regularmente y se distribuye en el tiempo (pág. 181)

divergent thinking a thought process that attempts to generate multiple solutions to a problem; nondirected thinking (p. 217)

pensamiento divergente proceso de pensamiento que intenta generar múltiples soluciones a un problema; pensamiento no dirigido (pág. 217)

double-blind study an experiment in which neither the participant nor the researcher knows whether the participant has received the treatment or the placebo (p. 54)

estudio doble ciego experimento en el que ni los participantes ni el investigador saben quiénes recibieron el tratamiento y quiénes, el placebo (pág. 54)

dream analysis a technique used by psychoanalysts to interpret the content of patients' dreams (p. 540)

análisis de los sueños técnica que usan los psicoanalistas para interpretar el contenido de los sueños de los pacientes (pág. 540)

drives conditions of arousal or tension within an organism that motivate the organism; usually associated with a need (p. 365)

impulsos condiciones de excitación o tensión dentro de un organismo que lo motivan; suelen estar asociados a una necesidad (pág. 365)

echoic memory the sensory register that briefly holds traces of aural stimuli (p. 197)
memoria ecoica registro sensorial que retiene brevemente los restos de los estímulos aditivos (pág. 197)

ego in psychoanalytic theory, the personality component that is conscious and that controls behavior (p. 397)
el Yo (ego) en la teoría psicoanalítica, el componente de la personalidad que es consciente y controla la conducta (pág. 397)

ego integrity according to Erikson, the belief in late adulthood that life is still meaningful and worthwhile; also the wisdom to accept one's approaching death (p. 347)
integridad del Yo según Erikson, la creencia en la adultez tardía de que la vida aún tiene significado y de que vale la pena vivirla; también la sabiduría para aceptar la propia muerte que se acerca (pág. 347)

eidetic imagery the maintenance of a very detailed visual memory over long periods of time (p. 197)
imaginería eidética permanencia de un recuerdo visual muy detallado durante un período de tiempo extendido (pág. 197)

elaborative rehearsal methods for remembering new information by creating meaningful links to information already known (p. 191)
repaso de elaboración métodos para recordar información nueva mediante la creación de vínculos significativos con información ya conocida (pág. 191)

electroconvulsive therapy a radical treatment for psychological disorders that involves passing an electric current through the brain of an anesthetized patient (p. 551)
terapia electroconvulsiva tratamiento radical para trastornos psicológicos que consiste en aplicar una corriente eléctrica al cerebro de un paciente anestesiado (pág. 551)

emotional appeal a type of persuasive communication that influences behavior on the basis of feelings rather than on an analysis of the issues (p. 569)
apelación a las emociones tipo de comunicación persuasiva que influye en la conducta basándose en los sentimientos en lugar de basarse en un análisis del tema (pág. 569)

emotions states of feeling that involve physical arousal, expressive behaviors, and conscious experience (p. 380)
emociones sentimientos que provocan reacción física, conductas expresivas y experiencia consciente (pág. 380)

empty-nest syndrome a sense of depression and a loss of purpose that some parents experience when the youngest child leaves home (p. 341)
síndrome del nido vacío sentimiento de depresión y pérdida de los objetivos que sienten algunos padres cuando el hijo o la hija más joven se va de la casa (pág. 341)

encoding the translation of information into a form that can be stored in memory (p. 190)
codificación traducción de la información a una forma que se puede almacenar en la memoria (pág. 190)

endocrine system the glands that secrete hormones into the bloodstream (p. 81)
sistema endocrino conjunto de glándulas que secretan hormonas que llegan al flujo sanguíneo (pág. 81)

episodic memory memory of specific experienced events (p. 189)
memoria episódica memoria específica de sucesos vividos (pág. 189)

ethics rules and standards for proper and responsible behavior (p. 55)
ética conjunto de reglas y normas para una conducta apropiada y responsable (pág. 55)

ethnography the study of human cultures (p. 461)
etnografía estudio de las culturas humanas (pág. 461)

eustress stress that is positive or motivating (p. 473)
eustrés estrés que es positivo y que motiva (pág. 473)

euthanasia the act of killing or enabling the death of a hopelessly sick or injured individual in a relatively painless way; also called mercy killing (p. 353)
eutanasia acto de matar o posibilitar la muerte de una manera relativamente indolora de un individuo enfermo o herido que no tiene esperanzas de recuperación; también se conoce como "muerte por compasión" (pág. 353)

evaluation apprehension concern that others are judging one's performance (p. 591)
temor a la evaluación preocupación de que los demás evalúen el rendimiento propio (pág. 591)

evolutionary perspective the theory that focuses on the evolution of behavior and mental processes (p. 23)
perspectiva evolutiva teoría que se centra en la evolución de la conducta y los procesos mentales (pág. 23)

experimental group in a study, the participants who receive the treatment (p. 52)
grupo experimental en un estudio, los participantes que reciben el tratamiento (pág. 52)

ENGLISH AND SPANISH GLOSSARY

explicit memory memory of specific information (p. 189)

memoria explícita memoria de información específica (pág. 189)

explicit norms spoken or written rules of social behavior, such as traffic rules (p. 595)

normas explícitas reglas de conducta social orales o escritas, como las normas del tráfico (pág. 595)

extinction in classical conditioning, the disappearance of a conditioned response when an unconditioned stimulus no longer follows a conditioned stimulus (p. 161)

extinción en el condicionamiento clásico, la desaparición de una respuesta condicionada cuando un estímulo incondicionado deja de seguir a un estímulo condicionado (pág. 161)

extrinsic rewards something external given in response to the attainment of a goal, such as good grades (p. 376)

recompensa extrínseca algo externo que se da como respuesta por el cumplimiento de un objetivo, por ejemplo, una buena calificación (pág. 376)

extrovert a person who tends to be active and self-expressive, and who gains energy from interaction with others (p. 394)

extrovertido/a persona que suele ser activa y expresar sus emociones, y que obtiene energía de la interacción con los demás (pág. 394)

F

flooding a fear-reduction technique based on the principles of classical conditioning that involves exposing the individual to a harmless stimulus until fear responses to that stimulus are extinguished (p. 162)

técnica de inmersión técnica de reducción del miedo, basada en los principios del condicionamiento clásico, que consiste en exponer al individuo a un estímulo inofensivo hasta que las respuestas de miedo frente a ese estímulo se extinguen (pág. 162)

fluid intelligence the ability to respond quickly to novel situations (p. 264)

inteligencia fluida capacidad de responder rápidamente ante situaciones nuevas (pág. 264)

foot-in-the-door effect the tendency for people to comply with a large request after they have agreed to smaller requests (p. 599)

efecto del pie en la puerta tendencia de las personas a cumplir un pedido más importante después de haber aceptado pedidos menores (pág. 599)

forced-choice format a method of presenting test questions that requires a respondent to select one of several possible answers (p. 428)

formato de elección forzada método de presentar preguntas en una prueba donde el participante debe elegir una de varias respuestas posibles (pág. 428)

formal-operational stage according to Piaget, the stage of cognitive development during which people begin to think logically about abstract concepts (p. 297)

etapa operacional formal según Piaget, etapa del desarrollo cognitivo durante la que las personas comienzan a pensar lógicamente sobre conceptos abstractos (pág. 297)

free association in psychoanalysis, the uncensored uttering of all thoughts that come to mind (p. 540)

asociación libre en psicoanálisis, la expresión sin censura de todos los pensamientos que vienen a la mente (pág. 540)

free radical an unstable molecule present in the human body that is thought by some scientists to be a cause of aging (p. 344)

radical libre molécula inestable presente en el cuerpo humano que, según algunos científicos, es una de las causas del envejecimiento (pág. 344)

functional fixedness a barrier to problem solving that involves the tendency to think of objects only in terms of their common uses (p. 226)

firmeza funcional obstáculo a la resolución de problemas que supone una tendencia a pensar en los objetos solo en términos de su uso corriente (pág. 226)

functionalism the school of psychology, founded by William James, that emphasizes the purposes of behavior and mental processes and what they accomplish for the individual (p. 19)

funcionalismo escuela de la Psicología, fundada por William James, que enfatiza los propósitos de la conducta y de los procesos mentales y lo que aportan al individuo (pág. 19)

fundamental attribution error a bias in social perception characterized by the tendency to assume that others generally act on the basis of their dispositions, even when there is evidence suggesting the importance of their situations (p. 577)

error fundamental de atribución sesgo en la percepción social caracterizado por la tendencia a suponer que otras personas actúan generalmente a partir de su forma de ser, aun cuando hay pruebas que sugieren la importancia de la situación en la que se encuentran (pág. 577)

gate theory the suggestion that only a certain amount of information can be processed by the nervous system at a given time (p. 113)
　teoría de la puerta la propuesta de que el sistema nervioso solamente puede procesar cierta cantidad de información en un momento determinado (pág. 113)

gender classifications of sex, based on mostly nonbiological traits such as physical structure and appearance (p. 447)
　género clasificaciones de sexo basadas principalmente en rasgos que no son biológicos, como la estructura y la apariencia físicas (pág. 447)

gender roles the differing sets of behaviors that a culture considers appropriate for males or females (p. 447)
　roles de género distintos patrones de conducta que una cultura considera apropiados para el hombre y la mujer (pág. 447)

gender schema the set of traits and behaviors by which a child learns to classify male and female gender roles and by which the child models and measures his or her own relation to those roles (p. 457)
　esquema de género conjunto de rasgos y conductas con los que un niño aprende a clasificar los roles masculinos y femeninos, y que toma como referencia para compararse y establecer su relación con esos roles (pág. 457)

gender stereotypes oversimplified generalizations about the characteristics of males and females (p. 447)
　estereotipos de género generalizaciones simplificadas en exceso sobre las características masculinas y femeninas (pág. 447)

gender typing the process by which people learn to conform to gender roles (p. 454)
　tipificación de género proceso por el que las personas aprenden a adaptarse a los roles de género (pág. 454)

general adaptation syndrome (GAS) the three-stage sequence of behavior in response to stress, consisting of an alarm reaction, a resistance stage, and an exhaustion stage (p. 480)
　síndrome general de adaptación (SGA) la secuencia de conducta en tres etapas de respuesta al estrés; consiste en una reacción de alarma, una etapa de resistencia y una etapa de agotamiento (pág. 480)

generalization the tendency to respond in the same way to stimuli that have similar characteristics (p. 161)
　generalización tendencia a responder de la misma manera ante estímulos con características similares (pág. 161)

generativity according to Erikson, the ability to create, originate, and produce throughout adulthood (p. 339)
　generatividad según Erikson, capacidad de crear, originar y producir durante la adultez (pág. 339)

genes the basic building blocks of heredity (p. 85)
　genes unidades básicas que constituyen la herencia (pág. 85)

Gestalt psychology the school of psychology that emphasizes the tendency to organize perceptions of individual parts into meaningful wholes (p. 21)
　psicología de la Gestalt escuela de la Psicología que enfatiza la tendencia a organizar percepciones de partes individuales en unidades significativas (pág. 21)

gifted a term used to describe children with IQ scores above 130 or children with outstanding talent for performing at much higher levels than others of the same age and background (p. 259)
　superdotado/a término que se usa para describir a un niño o una niña que tiene un coeficiente intelectual superior a 130 o un talento excepcional que le permite alcanzar un rendimiento muy superior al de otros niños de su misma edad y su mismo entorno (pág. 259)

group polarization the strengthening of a group's shared attitudes over time (p. 592)
　polarización grupal consolidación en el tiempo de las actitudes que comparte un grupo (pág. 592)

hallucination a false sensory perception that occurs in the absence of any actual stimulus (p. 146)
　alucinación percepción sensorial falsa que ocurre en ausencia de un estímulo real (pág. 146)

hallucinogen a psychedelic drug, such as LSD, that distorts perceptions and evokes sensory images in the absence of actual sensory input (p. 148)
　alucinógeno droga psicodélica, como el LSD, que distorsiona la percepción y provoca imágenes sensoriales en ausencia de un estímulo sensorial real (pág. 148)

health psychology the school of psychology concerned with the relationship between psychological factors and the prevention and treatment of physical illness (p. 483)
　psicología de la salud escuela de la Psicología que estudia la relación entre los factores psicológicos y la prevención y el tratamiento de las enfermedades físicas (pág. 483)

heredity the genetic transmission of traits from one generation to the next (p. 85)
　herencia transmisión genética de rasgos de una generación a la siguiente (pág. 85)

ENGLISH AND SPANISH GLOSSARY

ENGLISH AND SPANISH GLOSSARY

heritability the proportion of variation among individuals that can be attributed to genes (p. 262)
heredabilidad proporción de variación entre individuos que puede atribuirse a los genes (pág. 262)

heuristic a strategy for making judgments and solving problems; rules of thumb (p. 221)
heurística estrategia para hacer juicios de valor y resolver problemas; regla general (pág. 221)

homeostasis an internal balance or equilibrium that is achieved through adjustments of the nervous system (p. 366)
homeostasis equilibrio interno que se logra mediante ajustes del sistema nervioso (pág. 366)

hormones chemicals produced by the endocrine glands that regulate specific body functions (p. 81)
hormonas sustancias químicas producidas por las glándulas endocrinas que regulan funciones fisiológicas específicas (pág. 81)

hospice a type of care for terminally ill patients; an organization that provides such care (p. 353)
hospicio tipo de atención para enfermos terminales; una organización que brinda esa atención (pág. 353)

humanistic perspective the psychological view that stresses the human capacity for self-fulfillment and the importance of consciousness, self-awareness, and the freedom to make choices (p. 24)
perspectiva humanista perspectiva psicológica que enfatiza la capacidad humana de autorrealización y la importancia de la conciencia propia y la libertad para tomar decisiones (pág. 24)

humanistic therapy a treatment method based on the assumption that most people are basically good and have a natural tendency to strive for self-actualization (p. 542)
terapia humanista método de tratamiento basado en la suposición de que todas las personas son básicamente buenas y tienen una tendencia natural a luchar por la actualización propia (pág. 542)

hypnosis a condition in which people appear to be highly suggestible and to behave as if they are in a trance (p. 140)
hipnosis condición en la que las personas parecen muy sugestionables y parecen comportarse como si estuvieran en trance (pág. 140)

hypothalamus the neural structure located below the thalamus that controls temperature, hunger, thirst, and various aspects of emotion (p. 74)
hipotálamo estructura neuronal ubicada debajo del tálamo que controla la temperatura, el hambre, la sed y varios aspectos de las emociones (pág. 74)

hypothesis a prediction or assumption about behavior that is tested through scientific research (p. 35)
hipótesis predicción o suposición sobre la conducta que se evalúa mediante la investigación científica (pág. 35)

iconic memory the sensory register that briefly holds mental images of visual stimuli (p. 197)
memoria icónica registro sensorial que mantiene brevemente imágenes mentales de estímulos visuales (pág. 197)

id in psychoanalytic theory, the reservoir of unconscious psychic energy that strives to satisfy basic sexual and aggressive drives (p. 397)
el Ello (id) en la teoría psicoanalítica, el depósito de energía psíquica inconsciente que busca satisfacer impulsos básicos sexuales y agresivos (pág. 397)

identity who you are and what you stand for (your values) (p. 334)
identidad quiénes somos y qué defendemos (nuestros valores) (pág. 334)

identity achievement a stage in identity development in which a person has committed to an occupational direction and made decisions about important life questions (p. 317)
logro de identidad etapa del desarrollo de la identidad en la que una persona se compromete con una dirección ocupacional y toma decisiones sobre cuestiones importantes de la vida (pág. 317)

identity crisis a period of inner conflict during which one examines one's values and makes decisions about one's life direction (p. 316)
crisis de identidad período de conflicto interior en el que una persona examina sus valores y toma decisiones sobre el rumbo de su vida (pág. 316)

identity diffusion the constant search for meaning and identity without committing oneself to a set of personal beliefs or an occupational path (p. 317)
difusión de identidad búsqueda constante de sentido e identidad sin comprometerse con un conjunto de creencias personales o un camino ocupacional (pág. 317)

identity foreclosure the act of making a commitment based on other's values in order to avoid an identity crisis (p. 317)
hipoteca de identidad aceptación de un compromiso basado en los valores de otros para evitar una crisis de identidad (pág. 317)

identity moratorium a period of time in the development of identity in which a person delays making a decision about important issues but actively explores various alternatives (p. 316)
moratoria de identidad período del desarrollo de la identidad en el que una persona se demora en tomar una decisión sobre cuestiones importantes pero explora activamente alternativas diversas (pág. 316)

identity status according to Marcia, one of four reaction patterns or processes in the development of identity during adolescence (p. 316)

　estatus de identidad según Marcia, uno de los cuatro patrones o procesos de reacción en el desarrollo de la identidad durante la adolescencia (pág. 316)

implicit memory memory of which you are not consciously aware; generally includes skills and procedures one has learned (p. 189)

　memoria implícita memoria de la que uno no es consciente; suele incluir destrezas y procedimientos aprendidos (pág. 189)

implicit norms unspoken, unwritten standards of behavior for a group of people (p. 595)

　normas implícitas normas de conducta para un grupo de personas que no se especifican de manera oral ni escrita (pág. 595)

imprinting the process by which animals form strong attachments during a critical period very early in life (p. 286)

　impronta proceso por el que los animales forman fuertes lazos de apego durante un período crítico en los primeros momentos de la vida (pág. 286)

incubation effect the tendency to arrive at a solution after a period of time away from the problem (p. 228)

　efecto de incubación tendencia a hallar una solución después de pasar un tiempo sin pensar en el problema (pág. 228)

independent variable the factor that is manipulated by the researcher to determine its effect on another variable (p. 52)

　variable independiente factor que manipula el investigador para determinar su efecto sobre otra variable (pág. 52)

inductive reasoning a form of thinking that involves using individual cases or particular facts to reach a general conclusion (p. 230)

　razonamiento inductivo modalidad de pensamiento que consiste en usar casos individuales o hechos particulares para llegar a una conclusión general (pág. 230)

infancy in humans, the stage of life from birth to age two (p. 279)

　infancia en los seres humanos, etapa de la vida que comprende desde el nacimiento hasta los dos años de edad (pág. 279)

infantile amnesia the inability to remember events that occurred during one's early years (before age three) (p. 205)

　amnesia infantil incapacidad de recordar sucesos que ocurrieron durante los primeros años de vida (antes de los tres años de edad) (pág. 205)

inferiority complex according to Adler, feelings of inadequacy and insecurity that serve as a central source of motivation (p. 401)

　complejo de inferioridad según Adler, sentimientos de inadecuación e inseguridad que sirven como fuente central de motivación (pág. 401)

insomnia a sleep disorder characterized by recurring problems in falling asleep or staying asleep (p. 136)

　insomnio trastorno del sueño caracterizado por problemas recurrentes para contraer el sueño o permanecer dormido (pág. 136)

instincts complex, unlearned behaviors that are present throughout a species (p. 365)

　instintos conductas complejas no aprendidas que están presentes en todos los miembros de una especie (pág. 365)

intelligence the capacity to learn from experience, solve problems, and adapt to a changing environment (p. 249)

　inteligencia capacidad de aprender de la experiencia, resolver problemas y adaptarse a un entorno cambiante (pág. 249)

intelligence quotient the ratio of mental age to chronological age multiplied by 100; the average performance for a given age is assigned a score of 100 (p. 253)

　coeficiente intelectual razón de la edad mental a la edad cronológica, multiplicada por 100; el rendimiento promedio para una edad determinada se representa con un puntaje de 100 (pág. 253)

interference the process that occurs when new information in short-term memory pushes or crowds out and replaces what was already there (p. 198)

　interferencia proceso que ocurre cuando la información nueva que ingresa en la memoria de corto plazo empuja la información que se encontraba allí o se acumula y la reemplaza (pág. 198)

intimacy feelings of closeness and concern for another person (p. 583)

　intimidad sentimientos de cercanía y preocupación por otra persona (pág. 583)

intoxication a state of drunkenness characterized by impaired coordination and judgment (p. 145)

　intoxicación estado de ebriedad caracterizado por una reducción en la coordinación y el juicio (pág. 145)

intrinsic rewards internal rewards, such as self-satisfaction, that are given in response to the attainment of a goal (p. 376)

　recompensas intrínsecas recompensas internas, como la autosatisfacción, que se obtienen al alcanzar un objetivo (pág. 376)

ENGLISH AND SPANISH GLOSSARY

introspection an examination of one's own thoughts and feelings (p. 17)

introspección examen de los pensamientos y sentimientos propios (pág. 17)

introvert a person who tends to be interested in his or her own thoughts and feelings, and who turns inward rather than to other people for ideas and energy (p. 394)

introvertido/a persona que suele interesarse por sus propios pensamientos y sentimientos, y se repliega en sí mismo en busca de ideas y energía en lugar de interactuar con otros (pág. 394)

juvenile delinquency a violation of the law committed by a child or adolescent (p. 324)

delincuencia juvenil violación de la ley cometida por un niño o un adolescente (pág. 324)

K

kinesthesis the sense that provides information about the position and movement of individual body parts (p. 114)

cenestesia sentido que brinda información sobre la posición y el movimiento de cada una de las partes del cuerpo (pág. 114)

laboratory observation the study of behavior in a controlled situation (p. 48)

observación de laboratorio estudio de la conducta en una situación controlada (pág. 48)

laissez-faire leader a leader who stands back from decision-making and allows group members to explore and express their own ideas (p. 593)

líder laissez-faire líder que no toma decisiones, sino que permite que los miembros del grupo exploren sus propias ideas y las expresen (pág. 593)

language the communication of ideas through sounds and symbols that are arranged according to the rules of grammar (p. 235)

lenguaje comunicación de ideas mediante sonidos y símbolos que se ordenan según las reglas de la gramática (pág. 235)

language acquisition device the inborn ability of humans to acquire language (p. 235)

dispositivo de adquisición del lenguaje capacidad innata de los seres humanos de adquirir el lenguaje (pág. 235)

latent content according to Freud, the hidden meaning of a dream (p. 540)

contenido latente según Freud, el significado oculto de un sueño (pág. 540)

latent learning learning that occurs but remains hidden until there is a need to use it (p. 173)

aprendizaje latente aprendizaje que permanece oculto hasta que surge la necesidad de usarlo (pág. 173)

lateralization the development, prior to birth, of the tendencies of the brain's left and right hemispheres to specialize in certain functions (p. 455)

lateralización desarrollo, previo al nacimiento, de las tendencias de los hemisferios izquierdo y derecho del cerebro a especializarse en ciertas funciones (pág. 455)

learning perspective the psychological perspective that emphasizes the effects of experience on behavior (p. 25)

perspectiva del aprendizaje perspectiva psicológica que enfatiza los efectos de la experiencia en la conducta (pág. 25)

lens the transparent structure of the eye that focuses light on the retina (p. 102)

cristalino estructura transparente del ojo que refracta la luz en dirección a la retina (pág. 102)

limbic system a group of neural structures at the base of the cerebral hemispheres that is associated with emotion and motivation (p. 74)

sistema límbico grupo de estructuras neuronales que se halla en la base de los hemisferios cerebrales; se asocia con la emoción y la motivación (pág. 74)

lithium a chemical used to treat the mood swings of bipolar disorder (p. 550)

litio sustancia química que se usa para tratar los cambios anímicos abruptos del trastorno bipolar (pág. 550)

living will legal document in which the signer requests to be allowed to die rather than be kept alive by artificial means if disabled beyond a reasonable expectation of recovery (p. 353)

testamento vital documento legal en el que el firmante solicita que lo dejen morir en lugar de que lo mantengan vivo por medios artificiales en caso de quedar incapacitado sin esperanza razonable de recuperación (pág. 353)

longitudinal method a type of research in which the same people are studied over a long time period (p. 46)

método longitudinal tipo de investigación en el que se estudia a las mismas personas durante un período de tiempo extendido (pág. 46)

long-term memory the type or stage of memory capable of large and relatively permanent storage (p. 199)

memoria a largo plazo tipo o etapa de memoria que tiene una capacidad de almacenamiento grande y relativamente permanente (pág. 199)

M

maintenance rehearsal the repetition of new information in an attempt to remember it (p. 191)

repaso de mantenimiento repetición de información nueva con el fin de recordarla (pág. 191)

mania a mood characterized by extreme excitement, elation, hyperactivity, and chaotic behavior (p. 511)

manía estado anímico caracterizado por excitación extrema, euforia, hiperactividad y conducta caótica (pág. 511)

manifest content according to Freud, the apparent and remembered content of a dream (p. 540)

contenido manifiesto según Freud, el contenido recordado y aparente de un sueño (pág. 540)

massed learning learning that does not occur regularly but occurs all at one time (p. 181)

aprendizaje masivo aprendizaje que no ocurre regularmente sino que ocurre todo de una sola vez (pág. 181)

matching hypothesis the view that people tend to choose other people similar to themselves in attractiveness and attitudes in the formation of interpersonal relationships (p. 582)

hipótesis del emparejamiento la idea de que, al momento de formar relaciones interpersonales, las personas suelen elegir a otros que se les parecen en cuanto a atractivo y actitudes (pág. 582)

maturation developmental changes that occur as a result of automatic, genetically determined signals (p. 275)

maduración cambios que forman parte del desarrollo y que ocurren como resultado de señales automáticas y determinadas genéticamente (pág. 275)

means-end analysis a heuristic device in which a solution to a problem is found by evaluating the difference between the current situation and the goal (p. 224)

análisis medios-fin dispositivo heurístico por el que se evalúa la diferencia entre la situación actual y el objetivo para hallar una solución a un problema (pág. 224)

meditation a systematic narrowing of attention that slows the metabolism and helps produce feelings of relaxation (p. 140)

meditación reducción sistemática de la atención que lentifica el metabolismo y ayuda a producir sentimientos de relajación (pág. 140)

medulla a structure at the base of the brain stem that controls vital functions such as heartbeat and breathing (p. 73)

médula estructura situada en la base del tronco encefálico que controla funciones vitales como el ritmo cardíaco y la respiración (pág. 73)

memory the mental functions and processes by which information is encoded, stored, and retrieved; information stored in the mind (p. 189)

memoria funciones y procesos mentales por los que se codifica, se almacena y se recuerda la información; la información se almacena en la mente (pág. 189)

menarche a female's first menstrual period (p. 309)

menarca primer período menstrual de la mujer (pág. 309)

menopause the cessation of menstruation; also, the biological changes that a woman experiences during the years of her declining ability to reproduce (p. 341)

menopausia cese de la menstruación; también, los cambios biológicos que experimenta una mujer durante los años en que disminuye su capacidad reproductora (pág. 341)

mental age the level of intellectual functioning, which is compared to chronological age to give an IQ (p. 253)

edad mental nivel de funcionamiento intelectual que se compara con la edad cronológica para obtener el coeficiente intelectual o CI (pág. 253)

mental retardation intellectual functioning that is below average, as indicated by an intelligence score at or below 70 (p. 258)

retraso mental funcionamiento intelectual por debajo del promedio, señalado por un puntaje de inteligencia igual o inferior a 70 (pág. 258)

mental set the tendency to approach a new problem in a way that has been successful in the past (p. 225)

disposición mental tendencia a abordar un problema nuevo de una manera que ha sido exitosa en el pasado (pág. 225)

metacognition planning, evaluating, and monitoring mental activities; thinking about thinking (p. 217)
metacognición capacidad de planear, evaluar y monitorear actividades mentales; pensamiento sobre el pensamiento (pág. 217)

midlife crisis a turning point experienced by many people between ages 45 to 65, when they realize that life may be half over and they reassess the next phase of their lives (p. 340)
crisis de la mediana edad momento decisivo que experimentan muchas personas entre los 45 y 65 años de edad, cuando se dan cuenta de que ya ha pasado la mitad de la vida y vuelven a evaluar la siguiente etapa (pág. 340)

midlife transition a period in middle adulthood when a person's perspective on his or her life may change significantly (p. 339)
transición de la mediana edad período de la adultez intermedia en el que la perspectiva de una persona sobre su vida puede cambiar de manera significativa (pág. 339)

migraine headache a headache characterized by sudden onset and severe throbbing pain on one side of the head (p. 483)
migraña dolor de cabeza caracterizado por un comienzo súbito y un dolor severo y punzante en un lado de la cabeza (pág. 483)

modeling the process of learning behavior through the observation and imitation of others (p. 457)
modelado proceso de aprender una conducta mediante la observación y la imitación de otros (pág. 457)

monocular cues cues for distance that need only one eye to be perceived (p. 118)
claves monoculares claves para percibir la distancia que se ven con un solo ojo (pág. 118)

morpheme the smallest unit of meaning in a language (p. 236)
morfema unidad mínima de significado en un lenguaje (pág. 236)

motive a need or desire that energizes and directs behavior (p. 365)
motivo necesidad o deseo que da energía a la conducta y la dirige (pág. 365)

multiple approach-avoidance conflict a conflict involving a choice between two or more options, each of which has both positive and negative aspects (p. 476)
conflicto múltiple de atracción-evitación conflicto que implica una elección entre dos o más opciones que tienen aspectos tanto positivos como negativos (pág. 476)

myelin a white, fatty substance that insulates axons and enables rapid transmission of neural impulses (p. 68)
mielina sustancia blanca y grasa que aísla los axones y propicia la transmisión rápida de impulsos neuronales (pág. 68)

narcolepsy an uncommon sleep disorder characterized by brief attacks of REM sleep, often at inopportune moments (p. 137)
narcolepsia trastorno del sueño poco común caracterizado por breves ataques de sueño REM, a menudo en momentos inoportunos (pág. 137)

narcotic a type of drug that dulls the senses, relieves pain, and induces sleep; the term is usually reserved for those drugs derived from the opium poppy plant (p. 145)
narcótico tipo de droga que embota los sentidos, alivia el dolor e induce el sueño; el término se suele reservar para las drogas derivadas de la amapola, la planta del opio (pág. 145)

naturalistic observation the study of behavior in naturally occurring situations without manipulation or control on the part of the observer (p. 47)
observación naturalista estudio de la conducta en situaciones que ocurren naturalmente, sin manipulación ni control por parte del observador (pág. 47)

need the biological or psychological requirements for the well-being of an organism (p. 365)
necesidad cada uno de los requisitos biológicos o psicológicos necesarios para el bienestar de un organismo (pág. 365)

negative correlation the relationship between two variables in which one variable increases as the other variable decreases (p. 49)
correlación negativa relación entre dos variables en la que una variable aumenta a medida que la otra disminuye (pág. 49)

negative reinforcers unpleasant stimuli that increase the frequency of behavior when they are removed (p. 166)
refuerzos negativos estímulos desagradables que aumentan la frecuencia de una conducta cuando se eliminan (pág. 166)

neuron a nerve cell; the basic building block of the nervous system (p. 67)
neurona célula nerviosa; la unidad básica del sistema nervioso (pág. 67)

neurotransmitter a chemical messenger that carries impulses across the synaptic gaps between neurons (p. 68)
neurotransmisor mensajero químico que transmite impulsos a través de los espacios sinápticos de las neuronas (pág. 68)

night terror a sleep disorder characterized by high arousal and apparent terror; unlike nightmares, night terrors are seldom remembered (p. 136)
terror nocturno trastorno del sueño caracterizado por un despertar brusco y un sentimiento de terror evidente; a diferencia de las pesadillas, los terrores nocturnos no suelen recordarse (pág. 136)

nonconscious descriptive of bodily processes, such as the growing of hair, of which we are not aware (p. 131)
inconsciente se dice de los procesos fisiológicos, como el crecimiento del pelo, de los cuales no somos conscientes (pág. 131)

nondirective therapy a type of therapy in which the client rather than the therapist is encouraged to take the lead (p. 542)
terapia no directiva tipo de terapia en la que se anima al paciente, en lugar de al terapeuta, a tomar la iniciativa (pág. 542)

norm an established standard of performance or behavior (p. 424)
norma regla establecida de comportamiento o conducta (pág. 424)

norm group a group of test takers whose scores establish the norm for a particular test (p. 425)
grupo de norma grupo de participantes en una prueba cuyos puntajes establecen la norma para esa prueba en particular (pág. 425)

nurturance loving care and attention (p. 449)
crianza atención y cuidado brindados con afecto (pág. 449)

obese a condition characterized by excessive body fat (p. 371)
obeso/a se dice de quien sufre una afección caracterizada por una cantidad excesiva de grasa corporal (pág. 371)

objective test a test that has a group of standardized test items and specific answers that are considered to be correct (p. 431)
prueba objetiva prueba compuesta por un grupo de preguntas de evaluación estandarizadas y respuestas específicas que se consideran correctas (pág. 431)

object permanence the awareness that people and objects continue to exist even when they cannot be perceived (p. 295)
permanencia del objeto comprensión de que las personas y los objetos siguen existiendo aun cuando no pueden percibirse (pág. 295)

observational learning learning by observing and imitating the behavior of others (p. 173)
aprendizaje observacional aprendizaje que ocurre a partir de la observación y la imitación de la conducta ajena (pág. 173)

obsessive-compulsive disorder (OCD) a type of anxiety disorder characterized by obsessions—unwanted thoughts, ideas, or mental images that occur over and over again (p. 507)
trastorno obsesivo-compulsivo (TOC) tipo de trastorno de ansiedad caracterizado por obsesiones (pensamientos, ideas o imágenes mentales no deseados que aparecen una y otra vez) (pág. 507)

olfactory nerve the nerve that transmits information about odors from receptor neurons to the brain (p. 112)
nervio olfativo nervio que transmite la información de los olores desde las neuronas receptoras hasta el cerebro (pág. 112)

open-ended format test format in which there are no right or wrong, clearly specified answers (p. 433)
formato abierto formato de prueba en el que no hay respuestas correctas o erróneas claramente especificadas (pág. 433)

operant conditioning learning that is strengthened when behavior is followed by positive reinforcement (p. 165)
condicionamiento operante aprendizaje que se refuerza cuando después de una conducta se obtiene un refuerzo positivo (pág. 165)

opponent-process theory according to Solomon, the idea that an intense emotion often is followed by its opposite (p. 382)

teoría de los procesos opuestos según Solomon, la idea de que después de una emoción intensa suele darse la emoción opuesta (pág. 382)

overregularization the formation of plurals and the past tense of irregular nouns and verbs according to rules of grammar that apply to regular nouns and verbs; characteristic of the speech of young children (p. 239)

sobrerregularización la formación de plurales y formas verbales irregulares según reglas gramaticales que se aplican a sustantivos, adjetivos y verbos regulares; es característico del discurso de los niños pequeños (pág. 239)

P

panic attack a relatively short period of intense fear or discomfort, characterized by terror and other frightening sensations such as shortness of breath, rapid heart rate, or other distressing physical symptoms (p. 506)

ataque de pánico período relativamente corto de miedo o incomodidad intensos, caracterizado por el terror y otras sensaciones alarmantes, como falta de aire, pulso cardíaco acelerado y otros síntomas físicos de angustia (pág. 506)

partial reinforcement a type of conditioned learning in which only some of the responses are reinforced (p. 168)

refuerzo parcial tipo de aprendizaje condicionado en el que solo se refuerzan algunas de las respuestas (pág. 168)

passion an aroused state of intense desire for another person (p. 583)

pasión estado emocional de deseo intenso por otra persona (pág. 583)

patriarchy a social organization marked by the supremacy of males in the clan, family, or society (p. 334)

patriarcado organización social que se distingue por la supremacía de los hombres en el clan, la familia o la sociedad (pág. 334)

peer pressure pressure from friends to conform to their goals, attitudes, and behavior (p. 314)

presión paritaria presión de los amigos para que una persona actúe conforme a los objetivos, actitudes y conducta de ellos (pág. 314)

perception the psychological process of organizing and interpreting sensory stimulation (p. 97)

percepción el proceso psicológico de organizar e interpretar estímulos sensoriales (pág. 97)

peripheral nervous system the neurons that connect the central nervous system to the rest of the body, including the muscles and glands (p. 67)

sistema nervioso periférico conjunto de neuronas que conectan el sistema nervioso central con el resto del cuerpo, incluidos los músculos y las glándulas (pág. 67)

peripheral route a method of persuasion characterized by an emphasis on factors other than the message itself (p. 568)

vía periférica método de persuasión caracterizado por poner el énfasis en factores distintos del mensaje en sí (pág. 568)

personality the patterns of feelings, thoughts, and behavior that set people apart from one another (p. 393)

personalidad los patrones de sentimientos, pensamientos y conducta que distinguen a una persona de otra (pág. 393)

personality disorder a pattern of inflexible traits that disrupts social life or work and causes distress (p. 525)

trastorno de personalidad patrón de rasgos inflexibles que afecta la vida social o el trabajo y provoca angustia (pág. 525)

person-centered therapy a humanistic therapy, developed by Carl Rogers, in which the therapist creates an accepting, empathic environment to facilitate the client's growth (p. 542)

terapia centrada en la persona terapia humanista, desarrollada por Carl Rogers, en la que el terapeuta crea un entorno de empatía y aceptación para favorecer el crecimiento del paciente (pág. 542)

persuasion the attempt to influence people's attitudes and choices through argument, entreaty, or explanation (p. 568)

persuasión intento de influir en las actitudes y elecciones de los demás mediante argumentos, ruegos o explicaciones (pág. 568)

phobia an excessive, irrational fear out of proportion to the actual danger (p. 505)

fobia miedo excesivo e irracional, desproporcionado con respecto al peligro real (pág. 505)

phoneme the basic sound unit in a spoken language (p. 236)

fonema unidad básica de sonido de un lenguaje hablado (pág. 236)

photoreceptors neurons that are sensitive to light (p. 102)

fotorreceptores neuronas sensibles a la luz (pág. 102)

placebo an inert substance used in controlled experiments to test the effectiveness of another substance (p. 53)

placebo sustancia inerte que se usa en experimentos controlados para probar la efectividad de otra sustancia (pág. 53)

pons a brain structure located at the top of the brain stem that is involved in respiration, movement, and sleep (p. 73)

protuberancia anular estructura cerebral situada en la parte superior del tronco cerebral que interviene en la respiración, el movimiento y el sueño (pág. 73)

positive correlation a relationship between variables in which one variable increases as the other variable also increases (p. 48)

correlación positiva relación entre variables en la que una variable aumenta a medida que la otra también aumenta (pág. 48)

positive reinforcers encouraging stimuli that increase the frequency of a behavior when they are presented (p. 166)

refuerzos positivos estímulos alentadores que aumentan la frecuencia de una conducta cuando se presentan (pág. 166)

postconventional moral reasoning according to Kohlberg, a level of moral development during which moral judgments are derived from a person's own moral standards (p. 298)

razonamiento moral posconvencional según Kohlberg, nivel de desarrollo moral en el que los juicios morales se derivan de las normas morales propias de una persona (pág. 298)

posthypnotic suggestion instructions given to a person under hypnosis that are supposed to be carried out after the hypnosis session has ended (p. 142)

sugestión poshipnótica instrucciones que se dan a una persona bajo hipnosis que, se supone, se ejecutan cuando termina la sesión de hipnosis (pág. 142)

post-traumatic stress disorder (PTSD) a disorder caused by a distressing event outside the range of normal human experience and characterized by intense, persistent feelings of anxiety and avoidance of stimuli associated with the event (p. 508)

trastorno de estrés postraumático (TEPT) trastorno causado por un acontecimiento angustiante que se halla fuera del rango de la experiencia humana normal y se caracteriza por sentimientos intensos y persistentes de ansiedad, y por el intento de evitar los estímulos asociados con el acontecimiento (pág. 508)

preconscious descriptive of information that is not conscious but is retrievable into conscious awareness (p. 130)

preconsciente se dice de la información que no es consciente pero que puede hallarse y hacerse consciente (pág. 130)

preconventional moral reasoning according to Kohlberg, a level of moral development in which moral judgments are based on fear of punishment or desire for pleasure (p. 298)

razonamiento moral preconvencional según Kohlberg, nivel de desarrollo moral en el que los juicios morales se basan en el miedo al castigo o el deseo de placer (pág. 298)

prefrontal lobotomy a radical form of psychosurgery in which a section of the frontal lobe of the brain is severed or destroyed (p. 552)

lobotomía prefrontal forma radical de psicocirugía en la que se extirpa o se destruye una sección del lóbulo frontal del cerebro (pág. 552)

prejudice an unjustifiable, and usually negative, attitude toward a person or group (p. 572)

prejuicio actitud injustificada, y generalmente negativa, hacia una persona o un grupo (pág. 572)

premise a statement or assertion that serves as the basis for an argument (p. 230)

premisa afirmación o enunciado que sirve de base a un argumento (pág. 230)

preoperational stage in Piaget's theory, the stage during which a child learns to use language but does not yet think logically (p. 296)

etapa preoperacional en la teoría de Piaget, etapa durante la que un niño aprende a usar el lenguaje pero todavía no piensa lógicamente (pág. 296)

primacy effect (1) the tendency to recall the initial item or items in a series (p. 197); (2) the tendency to form opinions of others based on first impressions (p. 577)

efecto de primacía (1) tendencia a recordar el elemento inicial o los elementos iniciales de una serie (pág. 197); (2) tendencia a formar opiniones acerca de otras personas a partir de la primera impresión (pág. 577)

primary reinforcers stimuli, such as food or warmth, that have reinforcement value without learning (p. 166)

refuerzos primarios estímulos, como la comida o el calor, que tienen valor de refuerzo sin aprendizaje (pág. 166)

primary sex characteristics the organs that make sexual reproduction possible, such as the ovaries and testes (p. 308)

características sexuales primarias los órganos responsables de la reproducción sexual, como los ovarios y los testículos (pág. 308)

principle a basic truth or law (p. 7)
principio una verdad o ley básicas (pág. 7)

prodigy a child who develops a special skill or talent to an adult level (p. 259)

prodigio un niño o una niña que desarrolla una destreza o un talento especial al nivel de un adulto (pág. 259)

programmed theories the view that aging is the result of genetics (p. 344)

teorías programadas concepción que afirma que el envejecimiento es el resultado de la genética (pág. 344)

ENGLISH AND SPANISH GLOSSARY

projection in psychoanalytic theory, the defense mechanism by which people attribute their own unacceptable impulses to others (p. 399)
proyección en la teoría psicoanalítica, mecanismo de defensa por el que las personas atribuyen sus propios impulsos inaceptables a otras personas (pág. 399)

projective test a psychological test that presents ambiguous stimuli designed to elicit a response that reflects the test taker's feelings, interests, and biases (p. 433)
test proyectivo prueba psicológica que presenta estímulos ambiguos para suscitar una respuesta que refleja los sentimientos, intereses y sesgos de la persona (pág. 433)

prototype an original model on which others in the same category are patterned (p. 215)
prototipo modelo original que sirve para crear otros de la misma categoría (pág. 215)

proximity the perceptual tendency to group together visual and auditory events that are near each other (p. 116)
proximidad tendencia perceptiva a agrupar los sucesos visuales o auditivos que están cerca (pág. 116)

psychiatrist a medical doctor who specializes in the treatment of psychological problems and who can prescribe medication for clients (p. 10)
psiquiatra médico especializado en el tratamiento de problemas psicológicos que puede prescribir medicamentos a los pacientes (pág. 10)

psychoanalysis the school of psychology, founded by Sigmund Freud, that emphasizes the importance of unconscious motives and internal conflicts as determinants of human behavior (p. 19)
psicoanálisis escuela de la Psicología, fundada por Sigmund Freud, que enfatiza la importancia de los motivos inconscientes y los conflictos internos como determinantes de la conducta humana (pág. 19)

psychoanalytic perspective the perspective that stresses the influences of unconscious forces on human behavior (p. 24)
perspectiva psicoanalítica perspectiva que enfatiza la influencia de las fuerzas inconscientes en la conducta humana (pág. 24)

psychodynamic thinking the theory that most of what exists in an individual's mind is unconscious and consists of conflicting impulses, urges, and wishes (p. 20)
pensamiento psicodinámico teoría que afirma que la mayor parte de lo que existe en la mente de un individuo es inconsciente y consiste en impulsos y deseos que entran en conflicto (pág. 20)

psycholinguistics the psychology of language (p. 235)
psicolingüística psicología del lenguaje (pág. 235)

psychological constructs theoretical entities, or concepts, that enable one to discuss something that cannot be seen, touched, or measured directly (p. 5)
constructos psicológicos entidades teóricas, o conceptos, que permiten hablar de algo que no se puede ver, tocar ni medir directamente (pág. 5)

psychological disorder a behavior pattern or mental process that causes serious personal suffering or interferes with a person's ability to cope with everyday life (p. 499)
trastorno psicológico patrón de conducta o proceso mental que provoca un sufrimiento personal grave en una persona o que interfiere con su capacidad de actuar en la vida cotidiana (pág. 499)

psychology the scientific study of behavior and mental processes (p. 5)
Psicología estudio científico de la conducta y los procesos mentales (pág. 5)

psychosurgery biological treatments in which specific areas or structures of the brain are removed or destroyed to change behavior (p. 552)
psicocirugía tratamientos biológicos en los que se eliminan o se destruyen áreas o estructuras específicas del cerebro para modificar la conducta (pág. 552)

psychotherapy the application of psychological principles and techniques to influence a person's thoughts, feelings, or behaviors in an attempt to help that person overcome psychological disorders or adjust to problems in living (p. 535)
psicoterapia aplicación de técnicas y principios psicológicos para influir en los pensamientos, los sentimientos o la conducta de una persona, con el fin de ayudarla a superar trastornos psicológicos o a afrontar problemas de la vida (pág. 535)

puberty the period of sexual maturation; the onset of one's ability to reproduce (p. 308)
pubertad período de maduración sexual; el comienzo de la capacidad reproductora (pág. 308)

pupil the opening in the center of the eye that adjusts to the amount of light entering (p. 102)
pupila apertura del centro del ojo que se ajusta a la cantidad de luz que llega al ojo (pág. 102)

random sample a survey population, selected by chance, which fairly represents the general population (p. 40)
muestra aleatoria población elegida al azar para realizar una encuesta y que representa aproximadamente a la población general (pág. 40)

rapid-eye-movement sleep a stage of sleep characterized by rapid eye movements and linked to dreaming; also called REM sleep (p. 134)
fase de movimiento ocular rápido del sueño etapa del sueño caracterizada por movimientos oculares rápidos y relacionada con la actividad de soñar; también llamada fase REM (por su sigla en inglés) (pág. 134)

rational-emotive behavior therapy a confrontational cognitive therapy, developed by Albert Ellis, that encourages people to challenge illogical, self-defeating thoughts and attitudes (p. 545)
terapia racional-emotiva terapia cognitiva de confrontación, desarrollada por Albert Ellis, que anima a la persona a desafiar las actitudes y los pensamientos ilógicos y contraproducentes (pág. 545)

rationalization in psychoanalytic theory, the defense mechanism by which an individual finds justifications for unacceptable thoughts, impulses, or behaviors (p. 398)
racionalización en la teoría psicoanalítica, el mecanismo de defensa por el que un individuo encuentra justificaciones para pensamientos, impulsos o conductas inaceptables (pág. 398)

reasoning the process of drawing logical conclusions from facts and arguments (p. 230)
razonamiento proceso de sacar conclusiones lógicas a partir de hechos y argumentos (pág. 230)

recall nonimmediate retrieval of learned information (p. 203)
recuerdo recuperación posterior de información aprendida (pág. 203)

recency effect (1) the tendency to recall the last item in a series (p. 197); (2) the tendency for people to change their opinions of others based on recent interactions (p. 577)
efecto de recencia (1) tendencia a recordar el último elemento de una serie (pág. 197); (2) tendencia humana a cambiar la opinión de otra persona a partir de interacciones recientes (pág. 577)

reciprocity in interpersonal relationships, the tendency to return feelings and attitudes that are expressed about us (p. 582)
reciprocidad en las relaciones interpersonales, tendencia de una persona a responder con sentimientos y actitudes similares a los que recibe (pág. 582)

recognition a memory process in which one identifies objects or events that have previously been encountered (p. 202)
reconocimiento proceso de la memoria por el que se identifican objetos o sucesos hallados previamente (pág. 202)

recombination the mental rearrangement of elements of a problem (p. 227)
recombinación reorganización mental de los elementos de un problema (pág. 227)

reflex an automatic, unlearned response to a sensory stimulus (p. 279)
reflejo respuesta automática y no aprendida a un estímulo sensorial (pág. 279)

regression in psychoanalytic theory, a defense mechanism by which an individual retreats to an earlier stage of development when faced with anxiety (p. 398)
regresión en la teoría psicoanalítica, mecanismo de defensa por el que un individuo vuelve a una etapa de desarrollo anterior como reacción ante la ansiedad (pág. 398)

reinforcement a stimulus or event that follows a response and increases the frequency of that response (p. 165)
refuerzo estímulo o suceso que sigue a una respuesta y aumenta su frecuencia (pág. 165)

relearning learning something a second time, usually in less time than it was originally learned (p. 204)
reaprendizaje aprendizaje de algo por segunda vez, generalmente en menos tiempo que la primera vez (pág. 204)

reliability the extent to which a test yields consistent results (p. 254)
confiabilidad grado en que una prueba ofrece resultados coherentes (pág. 254)

replicate to repeat a research study, usually with different participants and in different situations, to confirm the results of the original study (p. 36)
replicar repetir un estudio de investigación, generalmente con otros participantes y en situaciones diferentes, para confirmar los resultados de la investigación original (pág. 36)

representativeness heuristic the process of making decisions about a sample according to the population that the sample appears to represent (p. 233)
heurística de la representatividad proceso de tomar decisiones acerca de una muestra de acuerdo con la población que la muestra parece representar (pág. 233)

ENGLISH AND SPANISH GLOSSARY

repression in psychoanalytic theory, the defense mechanism that removes anxiety-arousing thoughts, feelings, and memories from one's consciousness (p. 398)
represión en la teoría psicoanalítica, mecanismo de defensa que elimina de la conciencia los pensamientos, sentimientos y recuerdos que provocan ansiedad (pág. 398)

resistance in psychoanalysis, a blocking from consciousness of issues that might cause anxiety (p. 540)
resistencia en psicoanálisis, el acto de bloquear de la conciencia las ideas que pueden provocar ansiedad (pág. 540)

reticular activating system the part of the brain that is involved in attention, sleep, and arousal (p. 73)
sistema de activación reticular parte del cerebro que interviene en la atención, el sueño y la excitación (pág. 73)

retina the light-sensitive inner surface of the eye that contains the rods, cones, and neurons that process visual stimuli (p. 102)
retina superficie interior del ojo sensible a la luz que contiene los bastones, los conos y las neuronas que procesan los estímulos visuales (pág. 102)

retinal disparity a binocular cue for perceiving depth based on the difference between the two images of an object that the retina receives as the object moves closer (p. 119)
disparidad retiniana clave binocular que permite percibir la profundidad a partir de la diferencia entre las dos imágenes de un objeto que registra la retina a medida que el objeto se acerca (pág. 119)

retrieval the process of recalling information from memory storage (p. 192)
recuperación proceso de recordar información almacenada en la memoria (pág. 192)

retrograde amnesia the failure to remember events that occurred prior to physical trauma because of the effects of the trauma (p. 204)
amnesia retrógrada incapacidad de recordar acontecimientos ocurridos antes de un trauma físico, a causa de los efectos del trauma (pág. 204)

risky shift the tendency to make riskier decisions as a member of a group than as an individual acting alone (p. 591)
cambio hacia el riesgo tendencia a tomar decisiones más riesgosas como miembro de un grupo que como individuo (pág. 591)

sales resistance the ability to refuse a request or sales pitch (p. 570)
resistencia a la venta capacidad de rechazar discursos de pedidos o de ventas (pág. 570)

sample a representative segment of a target population (p. 40)
muestra segmento representativo de una población objetivo (pág. 40)

scapegoat a person or group unfairly blamed for the problems of others (p. 574)
chivo expiatorio persona o grupo al que se acusa injustamente de ser responsable de los problemas de otros (pág. 574)

schedule of reinforcement a timetable for when and how often reinforcement for a particular behavior occurs (p. 168)
programa de refuerzo tabla horaria que especifica cuándo y cómo se reforzará una conducta determinada (pág. 168)

schema an idea or mental framework that helps one organize and interpret information (p. 200)
esquema idea o marco mental que permite organizar e interpretar información (pág. 200)

schizophrenia a serious psychological disorder characterized by loss of contact with reality and distortions in thinking, perception, emotion, and behavior (p. 519)
esquizofrenia trastorno psicológico grave caracterizado por la pérdida de contacto con la realidad y distorsiones en el pensamiento, la percepción, la emoción y la conducta (pág. 519)

secondary reinforcers stimuli that increase the probability of a response because of their association with a primary reinforcer (p. 166)
refuerzos secundarios estímulos que aumentan la probabilidad de una respuesta debido a su asociación con un refuerzo primario (pág. 166)

secondary sex characteristics sexual characteristics that are not involved in reproduction, such as the growth of facial hair in males and the rounding of hips and breasts in females (p. 308)
características sexuales secundarias características sexuales que no están asociadas con la reproducción, como el crecimiento del vello facial en los hombres y la redondez de la cadera y el busto en las mujeres (pág. 308)

selective attention the focusing of attention on a particular stimulus (p. 129)
atención selectiva enfoque de la atención en un estímulo particular (pág. 129)

self-actualization according to Abraham Maslow, the self-motivated striving to reach one's potential (p. 366)

actualización propia según Abraham Maslow, el esfuerzo motivado por uno mismo para desarrollar el potencial propio (pág. 366)

self-concept one's view of oneself as an individual (p. 410)

autoconcepto opinión que tiene una persona sobre sí misma como individuo (pág. 410)

self-efficacy expectation a person's beliefs that he or she can bring about desired changes or goals through his or her own efforts (p. 478)

expectativa de autoeficacia confianza que tiene una persona de que puede provocar los cambios u objetivos deseados con su propio esfuerzo (pág. 478)

self-esteem the value or worth that people attach to themselves (p. 291)

autoestima valor o estima que una persona siente por sí misma (pág. 291)

self-help group a type of therapy group in which members share a common problem, such as alcoholism (p. 538)

grupo de autoayuda tipo de terapia grupal en el que los miembros tienen un problema en común, por ejemplo, el alcoholismo (pág. 538)

self-report an interview or questionnaire in which a person reports his or her attitudes, feelings, and behaviors (p. 423)

autoinforme entrevista o cuestionario en el que una persona informa sobre sus actitudes, sentimientos y conductas (pág. 423)

self-serving bias the tendency to view one's successes as stemming from internal factors and one's failures as stemming from external factors (p. 577)

sesgo de beneficio propio tendencia a ver los éxitos propios como consecuencia de factores internos y los fracasos como consecuencia de factores externos (pág. 577)

semantic memory memory of general knowledge and information (p. 189)

memoria semántica memoria de conocimiento e información generales (pág. 189)

semantics the study of meaning in language; the relationship between language and the objects depicted by the language (p. 237)

semántica estudio del significado en el lenguaje; la relación entre el lenguaje y los objetos que describe (pág. 237)

senile dementia a decrease in mental ability that sometimes occurs after the age of 65 (p. 345)

demencia senil disminución de la capacidad mental que, a veces, ocurre a partir de los 65 años de edad (pág. 345)

sensation the stimulation of sensory receptors and the transmission of sensory information to the central nervous system (p. 97)

sensación estimulación de los receptores sensoriales y la transmisión de la información sensorial al sistema nervioso central (pág. 97)

sensorimotor stage according to Piaget, the stage during which infants know the world mostly in terms of their sensory impressions and motor activities (p. 295)

etapa sensoriomotriz según Piaget, etapa en la que el infante conoce el mundo principalmente a partir de sus impresiones sensoriales y actividades motoras (pág. 295)

sensorineural deafness deafness that usually results from damage to the inner ear or to the auditory nerve (p. 109)

sordera neurosensorial sordera que suele producirse a partir de una lesión en el oído interno o el nervio auditivo (pág. 109)

sensory adaptation the process by which people become more sensitive to weak stimuli and less sensitive to unchanging stimuli (p. 98)

adaptación sensorial proceso por el que las personas se vuelven más sensibles a estímulos débiles y menos sensibles a los estímulos que no cambian (pág. 98)

sensory deprivation a state in which there is little or no sensory stimulation (p. 374)

privación sensorial estado en el que la estimulación sensorial es escasa o nula (pág. 374)

sensory memory the immediate, initial recording of sensory information in the memory system (p. 197)

memoria sensorial registro inmediato e inicial de información sensorial en el sistema de la memoria (pág. 197)

separation anxiety beginning at about eight months, distress that is sometimes experienced by infants when they are separated from their primary caregivers (p. 285)

ansiedad por separación angustia que, a veces, experimentan los infantes a partir de los ocho meses de edad cuando deben separarse de quienes los cuidan (pág. 285)

shaping in operant conditioning, a procedure in which reinforcement guides behavior toward closer approximations of the desired goal (p. 170)

aproximación en el condicionamiento operante, procedimiento en el que el refuerzo guía la conducta hacia aproximaciones cada vez más cercanas al objetivo deseado (pág. 170)

ENGLISH AND SPANISH GLOSSARY

short-term memory also called working memory, memory that holds information briefly before it is either stored in long-term memory or forgotten (p. 197)

memoria a corto plazo tipo o etapa de memoria que guarda la información brevemente antes de que se almacene en la memoria a largo plazo o bien se olvide; también llamada memoria de trabajo (pág. 197)

signal-detection theory a method of distinguishing sensory stimuli that takes into account not only the strength of the stimuli but also such elements as setting and one's physical state, mood, and attitudes (p. 99)

teoría de detección de señales método para distinguir los estímulos sensoriales en el que no solo se tiene en cuenta la fuerza de los estímulos, sino también otros elementos, como el ambiente y el estado físico de la persona, su estado de ánimo y sus actitudes (pág. 99)

similarity the perceptual tendency to group together elements that seem alike (p. 117)

similitud tendencia perceptiva a agrupar los elementos que parecen similares (pág. 117)

single-blind study a study in which the participants are unaware of whether they are in the control group or the experimental group (p. 53)

estudio simple ciego estudio en el que los participantes no saben si están en el grupo de control o en el grupo experimental (pág. 53)

sleep apnea a sleep disorder in which breathing is interrupted (p. 137)

apnea del sueño trastorno del sueño en el que se interrumpe la respiración (pág. 137)

social cognitive theory the theory that personality is shaped and learning is acquired by the interaction of personal, behavioral, and environmental factors (p. 407)

teoría social cognitiva teoría que afirma que la personalidad se forma y el aprendizaje se adquiere mediante la interacción de factores personales, conductuales y ambientales (pág. 407)

social decision scheme rules for predicting the final outcome of group decision-making (p. 591)

esquema de decisión social reglas para predecir el resultado final de la toma de decisiones de un grupo (pág. 591)

social facilitation improved performance of tasks because of the presence of others (p. 591)

facilitación social mejora en el rendimiento propio ante la presencia de otras personas (pág. 591)

socialization the process by which people, especially children, learn socially desirable behavior by means of verbal messages; the systematic use of rewards and punishments, and other teaching methods (p. 406)

socialización proceso por el que las personas, especialmente en la niñez, aprenden las conductas deseables desde el punto de vista social mediante mensajes verbales, el uso sistemático de recompensas y castigos, y otros métodos de enseñanza (pág. 406)

social-learning theory the theory that suggests that people can change their environments or create new ones (p. 25)

teoría del aprendizaje social teoría que sugiere que las personas pueden modificar su entorno o crear uno nuevo (pág. 25)

social loafing the tendency for people to exert less effort toward completing a task when they are part of a group than when they are performing the task alone (p. 591)

haraganería social tendencia de las personas a esforzarse menos para terminar una tarea cuando forman parte de un grupo que cuando trabajan individualmente (pág. 591)

social norm explicit and implicit rules that reflect social expectations and influence the ways in which people behave in social situations (p. 595)

norma social reglas explícitas e implícitas que reflejan expectativas sociales e influyen en la forma en que las personas se comportan en situaciones sociales (pág. 595)

social perception the ways in which people form and modify their impressions of others (p. 577)

percepción social maneras en que las personas forman y modifican sus impresiones de los demás (pág. 577)

social phobia an irrational fear of social situations in which one might be exposed to the close scrutiny of others (p. 506)

fobia social miedo irracional a situaciones sociales en las que una persona puede quedar expuesta al escrutinio riguroso de otros (pág. 506)

sociocultural perspective in psychology, the perspective that focuses on the influences of ethnicity, gender, culture, and socio-economic status on behavior and mental processes (p. 26)

perspectiva sociocultural en psicología, perspectiva que se centra en las influencias de la etnia, el género, la cultura y el nivel socioeconómico en la conducta y los procesos mentales (pág. 26)

somatic nervous system the division of the peripheral nervous system that connects the central nervous system with sensory receptors, muscles, and the skin (p. 70)

sistema nervioso somático división del sistema nervioso periférico que conecta el sistema nervioso central con los receptores sensoriales, los músculos y la piel (pág. 70)

somatization the expression of psychological distress through physical symptoms; it comes from the Greek word for "body" (p. 517)

somatización expresión de un conflicto psicológico mediante síntomas físicos; viene de la palabra griega que significa "cuerpo" (pág. 517)

spinal cord a column of nerves within the spine that transmits messages to and from the brain (p. 69)

médula espinal columna de nervios dentro de la columna vertebral que transmite mensajes hasta el cerebro y desde él (pág. 69)

spontaneous recovery the reappearance of an extinguished conditioned response after some time has passed (p. 161)

recuperación espontánea reaparición de una respuesta condicionada extinguida después de que ha pasado cierto tiempo (pág. 161)

standard deviation a measure of the distance of every score to the mean (p. 54)

desviación estándar medida de la distancia entre cada puntaje y la media (pág. 54)

standardized tests tests for which norms are based on the performance of a range of individuals (p. 424)

pruebas estandarizadas pruebas cuyas normas se basan en el rendimiento de un rango de individuos (pág. 424)

state-dependent memories information that is more easily retrieved when one is in the same physiological or emotional state as when the memory was originally encoded or learned (p. 194)

memoria dependiente del estado información que se recuerda más fácilmente cuando se está en el mismo estado fisiológico o emocional que cuando se codificó o aprendió esa información (pág. 194)

status offenses actions that are illegal when committed by a minor, such as consuming alcohol (p. 324)

infracciones de menores acciones que son ilegales cuando las realiza un menor, por ejemplo, el consumo de alcohol (pág. 324)

stimulant a drug that increases neural activity and speeds up body functions (p. 146)

estimulante droga que aumenta la actividad neuronal y acelera las funciones fisiológicas (pág. 146)

stimulus motives desires for increased stimulation (p. 374)

motivos de estímulo deseos de un aumento de estimulación (pág. 374)

storage the maintenance of encoded information over time (p. 191)

almacenamiento mantenimiento de información codificada durante un tiempo (pág. 191)

stranger anxiety beginning at about eight months, the fear of strangers that infants commonly display (p. 285)

ansiedad ante extraños miedo a los extraños que suelen mostrar los infantes y que comienza aproximadamente a los ocho meses de edad (pág. 285)

stratified sample a sample drawn in such a way that known subgroups within a population are represented in proportion to their numbers in the general population (p. 40)

muestra estratificada muestra tomada de modo que los subgrupos conocidos de una población queden representados según su proporción numérica dentro de la población general (pág. 40)

stress the physical and mental strain a person experiences in association with demands to adapt to a challenging situation (p. 473)

estrés tensión física y mental que siente una persona ante la exigencia de adaptarse a una situación que supone un desafío (pág. 473)

stressor an event or circumstance that produces stress (p. 473)

factor estresante acontecimiento o circunstancia que produce estrés (pág. 473)

stroboscopic motion a visual illusion in which the perception of motion is generated by the rapid progression of images or objects that are not actually moving at all (p. 118)

movimiento estroboscópico ilusión óptica que consiste en percibir movimiento ante una progresión rápida de imágenes u objetos que en realidad no se mueven (pág. 118)

structuralism the school of psychology, founded by Wilhelm Wundt, that maintains that conscious experience breaks down into objective sensations and subjective feelings (p. 18)

estructuralismo escuela de la Psicología, fundada por Wilhelm Wundt, que afirma que la experiencia consciente se divide en sensaciones objetivas y sentimientos subjetivos (pág. 18)

successive approximations in operant conditioning, a series of behaviors that gradually become more similar to a desired behavior (p. 548)

aproximaciones sucesivas en el condicionamiento operante, serie de conductas que gradualmente se vuelven más similares a una conducta deseada (pág. 548)

superego according to Freud, the part of personality that represents the individual's internalized ideals and provides standards for judgment (p. 398)
el Superyó (Superego) según Freud, la parte de la personalidad que representa los ideales interiorizados del individuo y brinda normas para el juicio (pág. 398)

survey a research technique for acquiring data about the attitudes or behaviors of a group of people, usually by asking questions of a representative, random sample (p. 39)
encuesta técnica de investigación para adquirir datos sobre las actitudes y conductas de un grupo de personas; generalmente consiste en hacer preguntas a una muestra representativa y aleatoria (pág. 39)

symbol an object or an act that stands for something else (p. 215)
símbolo objeto o acto que representa otra cosa (pág. 215)

synapse the junction between the axon terminals of the sending neuron and the dendrites of the receiving neuron (p. 68)
sinapsis unión entre las terminales axonales de la neurona emisora y las dendritas de la neurona receptora (pág. 68)

syntax the ways in which words and phrases are arranged into grammatical sentences (p. 236)
sintaxis formas en que las palabras y frases se ordenan para formar oraciones gramaticales (pág. 236)

systematic desensitization a type of counterconditioning, used to treat phobias, in which a pleasant, relaxed state is associated with gradually increasing anxiety-triggering stimuli (p. 162)
desensibilización sistemática tipo de contracondicionamiento, usado para tratar fobias, en el que se asocia un estado relajado y agradable con una exposición cada vez mayor al estímulo que provoca ansiedad (pág. 162)

target population the total group to be studied or described and from whom samples may be drawn (p. 39)
población objetivo grupo total que se desea estudiar o describir, del que se toman muestras (pág. 39)

taste aversion a type of classical conditioning in which a previously desirable or neutral food comes to be perceived as repugnant because it is associated with negative stimulation (p. 160)
aversión al gusto tipo de condicionamiento clásico en el que un alimento previamente deseable o neutro pasa a percibirse como repugnante porque se lo relaciona con un estímulo negativo (pág. 160)

test-retest reliability a method for determining the reliability of a test by comparing a test taker's scores on the same test taken on separate occasions (p. 254)
confiabilidad prueba-reprueba método para determinar la confiabilidad de una prueba; consiste en comparar los puntajes que obtiene una persona al realizar la prueba en dos ocasiones distintas (pág. 254)

thalamus the structure of the brain that relays messages from the sense organs to the cerebral cortex (p. 73)
tálamo estructura del cerebro que transmite mensajes desde los órganos sensoriales hacia la corteza cerebral (pág. 73)

theory a statement that attempts to explain why something is the way it is and happens the way it does (p. 7)
teoría enunciado que intenta explicar por qué algo es como es y sucede de la manera en que sucede (pág. 7)

thinking mental activity that involves understanding, manipulating, and communicating information (p. 215)
pensamiento actividad mental que implica comprensión, manipulación y comunicación (pág. 215)

trait an aspect of personality that is considered to be reasonably consistent (p. 393)
rasgo aspecto de la personalidad que se considera coherente dentro de los términos razonables (pág. 393)

transference in psychoanalysis, the patient's transfer of emotions associated with other relationships to the therapist (p. 540)
transferencia en psicoanálisis, tendencia del paciente a asociar con el terapeuta emociones que en realidad siente por otras personas (pág. 540)

transformed score a score that has been changed from a raw score in a systematic way (p. 254)

puntaje transformado puntaje que se ha modificado a partir de un puntaje bruto de manera sistemática (pág. 254)

triangular model of love according to the psychologist Robert J. Sternberg, the components of love, which include passion, intimacy, and commitment (p. 583)

modelo triangular del amor según el psicólogo Robert J. Sternberg, los componentes del amor, que son la pasión, la intimidad y el compromiso (pág. 583)

two-sided argument a method of discrediting an opponent by presenting his or her argument and then refuting it (p. 568)

argumento de dos puntos de vista método para desacreditar a un oponente que consiste en presentar su argumento y luego refutarlo (pág. 568)

unconditional positive regard a consistent expression of love and acceptance shown regardless of changing situations or behaviors (p. 291)

estimación positiva incondicional expresión coherente de amor y aceptación que se muestra independientemente de los cambios de situación o conducta (pág. 291)

unconditioned response in classical conditioning, an unlearned, automatic response (p. 160)

respuesta incondicionada en el condicionamiento clásico, respuesta no aprendida y automática (pág. 160)

unconditioned stimulus in classical conditioning, a stimulus that elicits an unlearned, automatic response (p. 160)

estímulo incondicionado en el condicionamiento clásico, estímulo que provoca una respuesta no aprendida y automática (pág. 160)

unconscious according to Freud, a reservoir of mostly unacceptable thoughts, wishes, feelings, and memories of which we are unaware but which influences our behavior (p. 130)

inconsciente según Freud, un depósito de pensamientos, deseos, sentimientos y recuerdos, en su mayoría inaceptables, que la persona no conoce pero que influyen en su conducta (pág. 130)

validity the extent to which a test measures what it is supposed to measure (p. 254)

validez grado en que una prueba mide lo que se supone que debe medir (pág. 254)

validity scale a group of test items that suggest whether or not the test taker is answering honestly (p. 424)

escala de validez grupo de preguntas de una prueba que sugieren si el participante está respondiendo de manera honesta o no (pág. 424)

variables factors that are measured or controlled in a scientific study (p. 52)

variables factores que se miden o se controlan en un estudio científico (pág. 52)

vestibular sense the sense that provides information about the position of the body (p. 114)

sentido vestibular sentido que brinda información sobre la posición del cuerpo (pág. 114)

visual acuity keenness or sharpness of vision (p. 103)

acuidad visual agudeza o nitidez del sentido de la vista (pág. 103)

vocational interest inventories tests that are used to help people make decisions about career options (p. 428)

tests de interés vocacional pruebas que ayudan a las personas a tomar decisiones sobre sus opciones profesionales (pág. 428)

volunteer bias the concept that people who volunteer to participate in research studies often differ from those who do not volunteer (p. 42)

sesgo del voluntario el concepto de que las personas que participan en una investigación de manera voluntaria suelen actuar de modo diferente de los que no son voluntarios (pág. 42)

Index

INDEX

S

Credits and Acknowledgments

CREDITS AND ACKNOWLEDGMENTS

UNIT 7 CHAPTER 20: 560 © Bettmann/CORBIS; 561 © Suzanne DeChillo/The New York Times/Redux; 562 © AP Photo/Bullit Marquez; 564 © AP Photo/Don Ryan; 566 © AP Photo/Rick Bowmer; 569 Courtesy of The Montana Meth Project; 571 © Monica Almeida/The New York Times/Redux Pictures; 573 © Ozier Muhammad/The New York Times/Redux Pictures; 575 (t) © AP Photo/Robert F. Bukaty, (b) © AP Photo/Shawn Patrick Ouellette; 576 © Scot Frei/Corbis; 578 © JUPITERIMAGES/PIXLAND/Alamy; 580 © Frans Lemmens/Getty Images; 582 (t) © Sven Torfinn/Panos, (cl) © Asian Art & Archaeology, Inc./CORBIS, (cr) The Art Archive/Archaeological and Ethnological Museum Guatemala City/Gianni Dagli Orti, (b) © Patrik Giardino/CORBIS. **CHAPTER 21:** 588 (b) © AP Photo/MTI, Szilard Koszticsak; 589 © Nadia Borowski Scott/San Diego Union-Tribune/Zuma Press; 594 © USHMM. The views or opinions expressed in this book, and the context in which the images are used, do not necessarily reflect the views or policy of, nor imply approval or endorsement by, the United States Holocaust Memorial Museum, (bkgd) Marie-france Bélanger/iStockphoto.com; 596 Cultura/drr.net; 600 (t) © Brooks Kraft/Sygma/Corbis, (b) © Ezio Petersen/Bettmann/CORBIS; 603 © Chris Thomaidis/Stone/Getty Images; 604 © AP Photo/The Plain Dealer, Chris Stephens; 605 © AP Photo/Michael Conroy; 607 (t) © Eros Hoagland/Redux Pictures, (b) © Jean Chung/The New York Times/Redux Pictures; 609 (all) **Source:** ©1965 by Stanley Milgram. From the film OBEDIENCE, copyright 1965 by Stanley Milgram, and distributed by Penn State Media Sales. Permission granted by Alexandra Milgram. **Careers in Psychology:** 612 © Nice One Productions/Corbis

Reference: R2 © Peter Augustin/Digital Vision/Getty Images; R4 © Mike Wilkes/drr.net; R5 © CORBIS; R6 © Sam Falk/Photo Researchers, Inc.; R8 © Corbis; R10 © Photo by Nina Leen/Time Life Pictures/Getty Images; R11 © PunchStock; R12 © Jon Brenneis/Life Magazine/Time & Life Pictures/Getty Images; R13 © 1965 by Stanley Milgram. From the film OBEDIENCE, copyright 1965 by Stanley Milgram, and distributed by Penn State Media Sales. Permission granted by Alexandra Milgram; R14 © Gregor Schuster/zefa/Corbis; R15 © PunchStock; R16 © Frans Lemmens/zefa/Corbis; R17 © John Zich/Corbis; R18 © Eros Hoagland/Redux; R19 © Gjon Mili /Time Life Pictures/Getty Images; R20 © Mariano Constanzo/epa/Corbis; R21 © Elena Seibert

For permission to reprint copyrighted material, grateful acknowledgment is made to the following sources:

American Psychiatric Association: "Some Culture-Bound Syndromes," "Categories of Psychological Disorders in the DSM-IV," "Two Examples of Somatoform Disorders," "Types of Mood Disorders and Their Characteristics," "Characteristics of Schizophrenia and Other Psychotic Disorders," and "Personality Disorders and Their Characteristics," adapted from the *Diagnostic and Statistical Manual of Mental Disorders, Fourth Edition, Text Revision.* Copyright © 2000 by the American Psychiatric Association.

American Psychological Association: "Ethical Principles of Psychologists and Code of Conduct," from *American Psychologist,* vol. 47, pp. 1597-1611, 1992. Copyright © 1992 by the American Psychological Association. Revised Fall 2002. For current standards, see www.apa.org/ethics. From "Ethical Principles," from *Ethics for Psychologists: A Commentary on the APA Ethics Code* by Mathilda B. Canter, Bruce E. Bennett, Stanley E. Jones, and Thomas F. Nagy. Copyright © 1994 by the American Psychological Association.

The Free Press, a division of Simon & Schuster, Inc.: From "Adolescence and Stress" by Anne C. Petersen and Ralph Spiga, from *Handbook of Stress: Theoretical and Clinical Aspects,* edited by Leo Goldberger and Shlomo Brenitz. Copyright © 1982 by The Free Press.

Pearson Education, Inc.: From "Self-Actualizing People: A Study of Psychological Health," from *Motivation and Personality* by Abraham H. Maslow. Copyright © 1954 by Harper and Row Publishers, Inc.; copyright © 1970 by Abraham H. Maslow.

Routledge: From Introduction: "Through the Looking Glass," from *Worlds of Sense: Exploring the Senses in History and Across Cultures* by Constance Classen. Copyright © 1993 by Constance Classen.

Simon & Schuster, Inc.: From "Third Stage: Bargaining," from *On Death and Dying* by Elizabeth Kübler-Ross, M.D. Copyright © 1969 by Elizabeth Kübler-Ross.

SOURCES CITED:

Bar graph from "Autobiographical Memory" by Martin A. Conway from *Memory,* edited by Elizabeth Ligon Bjork and Robert A. Bjork. Published by Academic Press, Inc., San Diego, CA, 1996.

From "Individual Psychology" by Alfred Adler from *Psychologies of 1930,* edited by Carl Murchison. Published by Clark University Press, Worchester, MA, 1930.

Bar graph (Identical and fraternal twins as best friends) from *Entwined Lives: Twins and What They Tell Us About Human Behavior* by Nancy L. Segal, Ph.D. Published by Dutton, New York, 1999.

STAFF CREDITS:

Lissa B. Anderson, Joseph M. Barron, Julie Beckman–Key, Julie Berggren, Scott H. Bilow, Paul Blankman, Lisa Brennan, Andy Christiansen, Chris Clark, Christine Devall, Michelle Dike, Christina Fiore, Jean Fujita, Bob Fullilove, Lisa Goodrich, Betsy Harris, Jericho Hernandez, Tim Hovde, Bill Hurd, Kristina Jernt, Jane A. Kirschman, Kathy Klein, Liann Lech, Annemarie Leonard, Joe Melomo, Richard Metzger, Andrew Miles, Mercedes Newman, Janice Noske, Nathan O'Neal, Jay W. Powers, Jarred Prejean, Shelly Ramos, Michelle Rimsa, Gene Rumann, Chris Smith, Greg Sorenson, Rich Sparks, Jeannie Taylor, Alesia Tyree, Sherri Whitmarsh, Kyle Van Horn